Do you see a man diligent
and skillful in his business?
He shall stand before kings:

Proverbs
Chapter 22
Verse 29

TAX SHELTERS
and
TAX-FREE INCOME
for
EVERYONE

To Wilma Rose

TAX SHELTERS
and
TAX-FREE INCOME
for
EVERYONE

VOLUME II
Fourth Edition

by

William C. Drollinger
and
William C. Drollinger, Jr.

Epic Publications, Inc.
Orchard Lake, Michigan
1981

Library of Congress Card Number: 81-125456

ISBN 0-914244-06-X

Composition by Detroit Offset Printing, Inc.

PREFACE

Tax shelters have grown from a stimulant for passive investments to a hero of operating businesses. Tax shelter investors can now become entrepreneurs of operating companies by first using the tax shelter concept of deducting business start-up costs as limited partners and later having their interest converted to common stock in the enterprise if it prospers.

Every area of business can benefit from tax shelters. This along with other areas of interest means an increasingly expanding role for the financial planner who became a professional just a few years ago. The financial planner must work with the general concepts of inflation, taxes, leverage, safety, liquidity, diversification, professional management, income now, income later, self completion, etc., and the specifics of annuities, autographs, banks, bonds, borrowing, budgeting, business planning, call options, car buying, certificates of deposit, collectibles, commodity trading, company matching savings plans, consolidating loans, corporate bonds, diamonds, estate planning, foreign stocks, foreign currencies, gold, gold shares, government bonds, insurance, investment portfolios, loans, money market funds, municipal bonds, mutual funds, rare books, rare coins, real estate, real estate investment trusts, retirement plans, second mortgages, silver, stamps, stock markets, Swiss banks, Swiss francs, tax shelters, time sharing, trusts, wine, etc. The areas of study are so numerous and broad that in depth knowledge of all areas is difficult. What happened in the medical and legal professions is helping to form the financial planning profession. General practitioner doctors refer to medical specialists who in turn refer to other specialists. General counsel attorneys refer to legal specialists who in turn refer to other specialists. General coordinating advisor financial planners will refer to financial specialists who in turn will refer to other specialists.

Like doctors and lawyers, financial planners should have professional schools requiring three to four years of basic financial study with the further opportunity for graduate specialization.

PREFACE

As the role of the financial planner has expanded so have his products. Investments to help against inflation and reduce taxes are now available for low budget citizens. Even gold interests can be purchased for very little money. Life insurance, still the most widely purchased tax shelter because of the tax free build-up of cash values, income tax-free and possibly estate tax-free death proceeds, has been stretched to include money market cash values and adjustable death protection. Financial planners are proving that whatever the mind can conceive and believe, man can achieve.

ACKNOWLEDGEMENTS

The assistance of Merrill Lynch, Pierce, Fenner & Smith, Inc., E. F. Hutton & Company, Inc., Bache Halsey Stuart Shields Incorporated, Arthur Andersen & Co. and many other fine people in the preparation of this book is gratefully acknowledged.

TABLE OF CONTENTS

INTRODUCTION

This Book is designed and published solely for general information purposes regarding certain types of investment vehicles and should not be deemed to constitute the rendering of tax advice. This Book is in no respect an offer to sell or a solicitation of interest as to any particular security, nor is it written or disseminated to generate interest in any specific offering of securities. In addition, in considering any tax shelter investment, a prospective investor should consult with his tax advisor as to probable tax consequences and the suitability of a tax investment.

We are all in a race against inflation as we reach toward our personal financial goals—and high taxes are one of the worst hurdles we have to overcome along the way.

In order to stay even with inflation, you needed to double your income between 1969 and 1979. But after paying higher taxes in the considerably higher bracket that income would place you in, you would end up way behind. A recent study by a major accounting firm found that between 1972 and 1979, executives whose compensation rose by as much as 104% suffered "real" after-tax decreases in income.

As it stands now, most of us pay everything we earn in the first four months of each year to the Government. That's what the average bite for local, state and federal taxes comes to, according to The Tax Foundation.

Tax shelters are one of the vehicles that many investors may consider using to reach their personal financial goals. Put simply, a good tax shelter lets you use dollars that would otherwise be paid in taxes, along with some out of your own pocket, to acquire assets that will help increase your net worth. To understand how that works, you have to look at how a tax shelter is set up, as well as what it does.

It may be helpful to contrast a tax shelter with an investment in the stock of a company. A tax shelter is a business that's set up in a way that lets you, as an investor, participate in the economic and tax benefits that any business enjoys. Because it's a direct investment, the profits and the tax benefits flow through directly to you. On the other hand, when you purchase a stock, you own a share of the company and the company owns the assets. Only a portion of its after-tax income will be distributed to you as a dividend—and that will be taxed a second time when you pay your individual taxes. Any tax benefits are accounted for at the corporate level and have no direct impact on your tax return.

A tax shelter usually involves the purchase of assets such as real estate, capital equipment or, in the case of oil and gas, drilling rights. Under existing tax legislation, these areas of the economy have the benefit of certain tax incentives. These incentives, together with the economic potential of the underlying assets, can provide investors in sound tax investments in these areas with a return in the form of cash flow, plus the opportunity to make a profit when the underlying assets are sold. For example, real estate values have been rising in line with, and in some cases exceeding, the cost of construction—which has been going up at an annual rate of around 10%. The price of oil has risen some 600% since 1973, while the cost of drilling has only gone up by some 125% in that same period of time.

Investment in real estate provides the country with housing and commercial facilities. Oil and gas investments help to develop our own natural resources and ease the nation's increasing dependence on foreign oil. Investments in equipment provide businesses with the tools they need to increase productivity. For these reasons, the Government has created tax incentives for such investments.

CAN YOU BENEFIT FROM A TAX SHELTER

Tax shelters are not suitable for all investors. We suggest that you consider investing in one only if it fits in with your personal financial needs and goals. Some tax shelters are appropriate for the risk portion of an investor's portfolio. Some tax shelters represent sound diversification into assets that can benefit from inflation, but because there is risk involved, you must be prepared for the possibility of losses. Moreover, tax shelters are generally not freely and easily transferable. Thus, investors may not be able to liquidate their investment at their own pleasure or in the event of an emergency.

The higher your tax bracket, the more benefit you can derive from most tax shelters because part of your investment return comes from tax benefits. The tax bracket at which any extra income you receive is taxed is your marginal tax bracket.

An appropriate tax shelter should only be made after a careful review of the individual's financial condition.

In effect, a substantial part of the investment you make is money you would otherwise have paid to the IRS. Nevertheless, you should not choose a tax shelter on that basis alone. You should also consider your desire for tax-sheltered income and long-term capital gains and choose an investment that is structured to meet your personal objectives. There are tax shelters to suit almost any need or goal, as you can see from the following description of tax shelters.

QUALITY IS THE KEY

The economic viability of a tax shelter is the foundation on which all of the other benefits rest. Only a well-structured and well-managed program that's based on a sound business venture can deliver maximum benefits to investors. Since a good tax shelter is usually a way of deferring or postponing taxes, the money you invest should be put into an asset that should appreciate in value and/or generate substantial cash flow over its economic life. A tax shelter that makes economic sense probably can deliver both tax-sheltered income and long-term capital gains. Economically weak programs are by their very nature prone to failure and an investment that fails does the opposite of what you are trying to accomplish—the preservation of capital and, even more important, the preservation of purchasing power.

It is important to choose tax shelters that are economically sound for another reason. Investments designed solely for tax losses, not economic profits, face serious challenge by the IRS. According to the tax code, "if such activity is not engaged in for profit, no deduction attributable to such activity shall be allowed." So, an underlying motive of tax losses alone would seriously weaken the very possibility of obtaining the desirable tax losses.

WHAT TO LOOK FOR IN A TAX SHELTER

Since individual investment and tax considerations are crucial to the success of a tax investment, any prospective investments should be carefully examined from these two viewpoints. We strongly recommend that you retain an accountant or an attorney who is familiar with tax investments to help you evaluate programs you are considering. If you are thinking of investing a large sum of money, have an expert in the type of program you are considering examine its investment fundamentals for you. This type of advice is well worth the fees. What's more, the fees are tax deductible. Here are some specifics to keep in mind.

Management

Since each tax shelter is in essence a new venture, the search for quality really comes down to looking for a program that will be run by people who know what they are doing. One of the best ways to determine quality is to review the prospectus or offering memorandum to see how well the general partner's previous programs have worked out. If the previous programs have been successful, make sure that the program you are being offered is similar to ones that were successful in the past. You want to capitalize on proven skill and experience. We cannot stress too strongly that a tax shelter should make economic as well as tax sense. Investment quality is the foundation on which all the benefits of a tax shelter rest. And the quality of that foundation is a function of the people who are responsible for it—the general partner, or manager, and his staff.

Placement Agent

We think that you would be wise to concentrate on programs offered by sound financial intermediaries with reputations for quality and integrity. Large, well-established firms have enough experts on hand to screen hundreds of potential tax investments to find and structure the relative few that meet their investment standards. In effect, they do much of the analytical and due diligence work for you.

Size of Program

One of the major benefits of a large tax shelter program is that it can afford to diversify its investments. The greater the diversity, the more its risks are spread. In addition, larger partnerships can spread front-end costs such as commissions, management fees, legal expenses, and other start-up expenses over a greater number of investors to reduce your proportional share of these costs.

The Sharing Arrangements

Profits and losses should be shared fairly by the general and limited partners and there are established standards in each investment area. Generally speaking, the limited partners (the investors) should get most of the economic and tax benefits until they recoup their investment. Only then should the general partner receive an equitable share of the profits as an incentive to good management.

The Tax Posture

Your advisor should examine the tax posture of a potential tax investment to make sure that the program's tax aspects meet the intent as well as the letter of the law. You can get a good handle on a program's tax aspects by reading the offering memorandum. You may also deduce a program's tax risks by whether those selling it stress tax savings or investment potential. If they stress tax savings rather than investment potential, be wary of it.

Now that we've explained what to look for in a good tax investment, let's talk about how a tax shelter works.

HOW TAX SHELTERS WORK

A tax shelter is usually set up either as a limited partnership or a sole proprietorship. Both types of business organization allow the profits and losses generated by the investment to flow directly down to your tax return because both provide for direct investment in tangible assets such as real estate, equipment, or oil and gas.

Form of Organization

Most of the tax shelters offered are set up as limited partnerships. A general partner manages the business and you and other limited partners put up the capital. This form of ownership benefits the limited partners in a number of ways.

By pooling resources with other investors you can acquire a direct participation in a portfolio large enough to be diversified and made up of high-quality assets.

You can invest a limited amount of money—often as little as $5,000. And, your liability is usually limited to the amount of cash investment. You are not responsible beyond your investment for any of the partnership debts or other liabilities. These obligations are the responsibility of the general partner.

Unlike a corporation, which can go on forever, a partnership's life is limited. The date the partnership is scheduled to end will be specified in the prospectus. When the assets are sold, the partnership ends, and your share of any proceeds will be distributed to you. If the partnership terminates after you retire, the proceeds distributed to you and the income realized by you will probably be taxed at a lower rate.

As a limited partner, your role is that of a passive investor. The general partner manages the program and relieves you of any managerial responsibility.

When you buy a tax shelter that's set up as a sole proprietorship you become the sole owner of the investment assets. Some equipment leasing tax investments are set up as sole proprietorships. They normally require substantially greater net worth and a larger cash investment than would an investment in a limited partnership. However, you have greater flexibility as a sole proprietor. For example, you can select the way the equipment will be financed, depreciated, and even how it will be sold. Generally speaking, a management company takes care of all the day-to-day operations just as the general partner does in a limited partnership. The difference is that usually you can cancel the management contract, whereas it may be difficult for limited partners to fire the partnership's general partner, without possible adverse income tax consequences.

Form of Offering

Limited partnerships and sole proprietorships are either publicly or privately offered. The sponsors of a publicly offered tax shelter must file a registration statement and offering documents (including a prospectus) with the Securities and Exchange Commission (SEC). The SEC reviews the registration statement and prospectus to determine whether they meet the disclosure requirements of the Securities Act of 1933. Such review does not mean that the SEC has judged or approved the merits of the investment.

A tax shelter program that is not publicly offered is called a private offering. It differs from a public program in a couple of ways. For example, a private offering can be sold only to a limited number of qualified investors and it is not registered with the SEC; however, private offerings are sold by means of an offering memorandum which may be reviewed by some of the regulatory authorities of the states in which it will be offered. Private offerings can generally be made more quickly and at a lower cost than public offerings because SEC registration is often both time consuming and costly. Private offerings are for sophisticated investors and usually have higher minimum investment requirements.

TAX BENEFITS AND TAX SAVINGS

As an investor in a tax shelter that's set up as a limited partnership or a sole proprietorship, you can enjoy the tax benefits of depreciation, the depletion allowance, and the investment tax credit. Here's how these tax benefits work.

Deductions

The tax deductions from a tax shelter program lower your taxable income—and therefore the taxes you'll have to pay. The reduction in taxes is called tax savings.

What's more, the tax savings start at your highest marginal tax rate—the rate at which each additional dollar of income is taxed. The higher your tax bracket is, the greater the tax benefits will be.

Depreciation

Depreciation deductions allow you, in effect, to recover the capital cost of equipment or a building tax free over the asset's "useful life." The "useful life" is a period for accounting purposes only and can be shorter than the asset's actual life. For example, consider a building that has a "useful life" of 30 years. Each year you can deduct 3.3% of the cost as straight line depreciation. You fully recover the cost in 30 years but the building may have an economic life of 50 years or more.

In some cases where the Government deems it appropriate, you can use accelerated depreciation. It is called accelerated because you deduct a greater percentage of the building's cost in the early years. These depreciation deductions are higher than straight line deductions in the early years and then start to taper off and become lower than straight line deductions in later years. For example, with a useful life of 30 years, under the 200% double-declining method you could deduct 6.6% of an asset's cost in the first year while straight line depreciation would allow you to deduct only 3.3% of its cost.

Depletion

The depletion allowance allows you to recover the cost of assets such as oil or gas, coal, and other minerals that are extracted from the ground. In a sense, depletion is similar to depreciation. Each barrel of oil pumped from the ground depletes the remaining supply of oil by one barrel. By giving you a tax deduction to recover your costs of acquiring that oil or gas, the Government encourages further exploration and development.

There are two types of depletion allowance for oil and gas. Percentage depletion presently allows you to shelter as much as 22% of each property's gross income–up to a maximum of 50% of net income–from taxes. Cost depletion lets you deduct a fixed amount from every barrel of oil sold. The amount per barrel that you can deduct is based on the cost of acquiring the oil. For example, if it costs $1,000,000 to acquire an oil well that is expected to produce 100,000 barrels of oil, $10 of the revenues from each barrel of oil sold will be sheltered from taxes. Of the two types of depletion, percentage depletion usually can give a greater tax saving because you may be able to recover an amount that's greater than your actual costs. The amount of percentage depletion allowed is scheduled to decline in the future.

The Investment Tax Credit

The investment tax credit (ITC), a dollar for dollar reduction of taxes due, has been designed to foster capital investments that boost productivity. The ITC can amount to as much as 10% of the cost of equipment or other tangible personal property that is: (1) used in business to produce income, (2) has a useful life of at least three years, and (3) can be depreciated. To retain the full ITC, the asset must be held for at least seven years. The effect of the ITC is an even bigger tax break than depreciation or the depletion allowance because an investment tax credit is a direct reduction of your tax liability.

Deferral of Taxes

That's not to say that tax shelters eliminate taxes. They don't. *As a general rule, they simply defer the taxes to a later time.* Deferring taxes makes a lot of sense because a dollar today may be worth more than a dollar tomorrow. For one thing, the dollars that escape being taxed today can be invested to earn even more money for you. For another, you will be able to use those dollars now before they lose any more of their purchasing power. And when you do pay the taxes that you have deferred, you will be paying them with dollars that have lost some of their value. Moreover, you can choose a tax shelter that provides that the taxes you have deferred will be payable when you have retired and are in a lower tax bracket. You should be aware, however, that the income tax payable by a limited partner by reason of taxable income of the partnership may exceed the cash distributed to such limited partner from the partnership.

Long-Term Capital Gains

Tax shelters can change income that might otherwise be taxed at up to a 70% rate into capital gains that will be taxed at a maximum 28% rate. So, a good tax shelter can also be a good hedge against inflation and can increase your net worth in real terms.

Tax-Sheltered Income

Immediate tax benefits are only part of the story. Some investment programs will also generate some tax-sheltered income. For example, the cash flow to the investors in the early years of some tax investment programs in real estate and equipment leasing is almost totally sheltered from income taxes by depreciation deductions. And a good part of the cash pumped out by an oil and gas program is sheltered from taxes by the depletion allowance.

Leverage

Archimedes, the ancient Greek who discovered the physical principle of leverage, once said: "Give me where to stand and I will move the earth." Financial leverage works the same way. It lets you control a lot of assets with a comparatively small investment. For example, if you own your own house, chances are that you used a mortgage to buy it. Consider, for a moment, how that works. Let's say that you bought a $100,000 house with a $25,000 down payment and financed the rest with a mortgage. Assume further that the value of the house climbs to $150,000 in the next five years. That boosts your equity in the house by $50,000. Your equity in the house is its total value less the mortgage still outstanding. As you pay off your mortgage, your equity increases. Since you used only $25,000 of your own money to buy the house, that $50,000 gain in value works out to a 200% return on investment versus a return of only 50% if you paid cash.

And to top it all off, you've been getting some handsome interest deductions which effectively lower the cost of carrying your investment in the house. For example, if the mortgage carries a 10% interest rate and you are in the 50% tax bracket, you are actually paying a 5% after-tax interest rate. And that is far lower than the rate the house has appreciated in value.

It works the same way with a leveraged tax shelter. You increase the economic and tax benefits in relation to your cash investment. In most cases, you have to be "at risk" or personally liable for any loan in order to be able to deduct an amount greater than your investment. Real estate is the only exception. You don't have to assume any personal liability for the loan in a real estate investment as long as the loan is a non-recourse obligation, that is, no individual or entity is liable to repay the loan.

SPECIAL TAX CONSIDERATIONS

In an effort to prevent some investors from sheltering all of their income from taxes, Congress has passed some laws that increase your tax on some of the very items that give you tax savings. Once again we would like to stress the importance of consulting with your tax advisor prior to participating in any tax investment. In addition to the items discussed below, there are certain "recapture taxes" which are discussed below in connection with the description of specific types of investments.

Investment Indebtedness

If you leverage your investments with borrowed funds, the amount of annual interest you can deduct on those loans is limited to the net income from your investment plus $10,000. Example: Assume that you borrow $100,000 at 12% to buy various investments. Assume further that after all expenses, the net income from these investments works out to just $1,000. Although the annual interest on the loan amounts to $12,000, you would be able to deduct only $11,000 of that interest. That's the sum of your net income from investments ($1,000) plus $10,000. If your investments paid an income of $2,000 or more, you could deduct $12,000, or all the interest on your loan. Any interest that cannot be deducted because of this limitation may be carried forward.

Investment indebtedness covers any investment-related loan, including stocks bought on margin, as well as your pro rata share of loans made by a tax investment in which you have invested. However, your home mortgage or mortgages taken out by a partnership can be important exceptions; they are not usually considered investment indebtedness.

Maximum Tax

Personal service income—salary, consulting fees, and other types of compensation for your personal services—is subject to no more than a 50% tax rate. Passive income such as dividends and interest can be taxed at up to a 70% tax rate.

Preference Items

Every dollar of so-called tax preference items that you deduct will convert a dollar of personal service income to passive income for tax purposes. For example, if you are a married individual, filing a joint return, with earned taxable income of $150,000 and you have $40,000 of tax preference items, $40,000 of your earned income will be treated as passive income, which can be taxed at a higher rate than personal service income. In this example, the $40,000 that is converted to passive income will be taxed at a 64% rate instead of a 50% rate. While tax preferences may reduce some of the tax savings from a tax shelter, they don't eliminate them. In this case, for example, the tax preferences save you $20,000 ($40,000 x 50%) but at a cost of $5,600 in additional taxes for a net savings of $14,000. The cost is the difference between what you would have paid at a 50% maximum tax rate and what you now have to pay at a passive-income tax rate. The tax on $40,000 of passive income in your effective tax bracket (64%) works out to $25,600, which is just $5,600 more than the $20,000 you would have paid at a 50% rate. Note that preference items are also subject to the 15% add-on minimum tax.

Tax preference items include: (1) the amount of accelerated depreciation taken on real property and on leased personal property that is in excess of what you could have deducted under a straight line method of depreciation, (2) intangible drilling costs on productive wells, and (3) the amount that percentage depletion exceeds cost depletion.

Add-On Minimum Tax

The add-on minimum tax imposes an extra 15% tax on certain tax preference items that are in excess of one-half of your regular income taxes or $10,000–whichever is greater. Since it takes at least $10,000 of preference items to trigger the add-on minimum tax, only those investors who invest a substantial amount in a tax shelter will face the tax. And chances are that one-half of their regular income taxes will more than match the amount of preference items needed to trigger the add-on minimum tax.

Alternative Minimum Tax

The alternative minimum tax may affect relatively few individuals because only those with a substantial amount of long-term capital gains and "excess itemized deductions" are subject to it. (Excess itemized deductions include those for interest expenses and charitable contributions where such deductions exceed 60% of adjusted gross income. Deductions for casualty losses, medical bills, and state and local taxes are excluded from this "excess itemized" category.)

The alternative minimum tax is computed separately from the regular income tax computation and if it results in a greater amount supersedes the regular tax.

The income base subject to the alternative minimum tax is computed by adding back to regular taxable income the excluded portion (60%) of long-term capital gains and the "excess itemized deductions." This amount, reduced by a $20,000 exemption, is subject to the following alternative minimum tax rates:

Amount	Rate
Less than $40,000	10%
$40,000 to $80,000	20%
Over $80,000	25%

All of the foregoing special tax considerations may limit the effectiveness of a tax investment in lowering an individual taxpayer's income tax liability. Investors should consult their own tax advisors.

Any investment can be affected by changes in the tax law. For example, the Tax Reform Act of 1976 changed the rules for many types of investments. For instance, the 1976 law lengthened the holding period used to determine a long-term capital gain to one year from six months. Other provisions limited the tax benefits of several types of tax shelters. On the other hand, sometimes changes are made in the tax law in order to favor tax shelters. For example, the Revenue Act of 1978 reduced the effective long-term capital gain rate to a maximum of 28%.

REAL ESTATE

The Economic Foundation

While there's no guarantee that real estate values will, in general, continue to climb, the purchase of good commercial properties in growth areas has in the past proved to be a prudent investment. The demand for good commercial and residential properties is generally greater than the existing supply. Real estate values tend to rise in relation to construction costs—which have been rising at around a 10% annual rate since 1973. It is important to keep in mind that property values depend, in great part, on how the properties are managed as well as where they are located. How the properties are financed, rented up, operated, and refinanced or sold will in large part determine your return on the tax shelter. For example, an apartment building in an economically depressed area won't fare as well as an apartment building in a thriving area. And keep in mind the old axiom: the three most important things to look for in a real estate investment are location, location, and location.

Investing in New vs. Old Buildings

The amount of immediate tax benefits you will be able to enjoy and your return on investment from a real estate tax investment both depend in great part on whether the program is engaged in constructing new buildings or buying existing ones. That's because of the trade-off between risk and return that is inherent in any kind of investment.

As a rule, a tax shelter program that constructs new buildings is somewhat riskier but potentially more rewarding than one which buys existing buildings. First, let's look at some of the risks. Any delay in construction can be expensive because the interest payment clock keeps ticking. The cost of supplies and labor may also be rising. And once the building is completed, there's always the risk that it won't rent up as fast as you would like.

Offsetting these risks are tax benefits that enhance the potential economic gains. In terms of tax benefits, new buildings can be depreciated at a faster rate than existing buildings. That gives you larger immediate tax savings and also helps shelter more of the income from the property from taxes in the early years. Moreover, the financing leverage that's possible on new construction is usually greater than that for existing buildings. As we previously mentioned, leverage can dramatically boost the tax savings as well as the economic return from a real estate investment.

By contrast, investing in existing property is safer but provides fewer tax benefits. An existing property is a safer investment because of the very fact that it is a seasoned operation.

You know what you are getting in terms of revenues and also what the operating costs will be like.

For another, the mortgage on an existing property can often be assumed by the purchaser and older mortgages generally have lower interest rates. However, because the property may have appreciated and some portion of the debt been paid, the assumption of an older mortgage usually results in less leverage and a greater equity investment.

Commercial Real Estate

Commercial properties such as shopping centers, office buildings, and industrial properties, which are leased to tenants who are financially sound, tend to be an attractive real estate investment.

Moreover, many commercial properties are rented out on long-term leases that give you some protection against inflation. For example, some leases have escalator clauses that allow the building's owner to "pass through" increases in taxes and operating costs to the tenants by raising the rent annually. Certain leases carry that concept one step further by providing that the tenant pay for the building's maintenance and energy costs. The owners of shopping centers may also ask for an overage rent in addition to a long-term lease. Thus, a shopping center's tenant may have to pay an additional rent that's based on a percentage of its sales.

All or part of the income you get from an investment in commercial real estate may be sheltered from income taxes by depreciation, particularly in the early years.

What's more, you have a chance of making a long-term capital gain when the commercial real estate is sold. Income producing properties are in great demand and hence can often be sold at substantial profit. In addition, when the building is sold, the gain will normally be a long-term capital gain, except for depreciation recapture, and you will have converted income that was taxable at rates of 50% to 70% into a gain that is taxable at no more than a 28% rate.

Apartment Complexes

Apartment properties are generally privately owned and financed as opposed to Government-assisted. Usually, they are rented to middle and upper income tenants. The rental periods are much shorter than those of commercial properties. The increased frequency of tenant turnover means that there could be more of a problem with vacancies. Demand for apartments in most areas, however, is running far ahead of the supply. The supply of apartments may become tighter because older units are being torn down and a growing number of apartments are being converted to condominiums or cooperatives.

The economic benefits of an apartment complex are three: (1) potential for capital appreciation, (2) equity buildup resulting from paying down the mortgage, and (3) cash flow.

The tax benefits of an apartment complex are normally greater than those of a commercial real estate investment. Conventional residential properties, especially newly constructed ones, can be depreciated at a more accelerated rate than commercial properties. The faster you can depreciate a building, the larger your tax deductions in the early years will be. The Government presently allows faster depreciation on new residential construction than on commercial properties as an incentive to build more housing.

Government-Assisted Housing

Government-assisted housing offers generous tax-shelter advantages because it can be leveraged to a far greater extent than other types of real estate investments. Some Government programs will guarantee mortgages of up to 90% of the property's completion cost. By contrast, in a private, conventionally financed apartment complex, the maximum mortgage is generally not in excess of 75% of the property's cost. And the terms of a Government-assisted mortgage are also more favorable. You are allowed up to 40 years to repay the mortgage–longer than most private lenders would agree to.

The increased leverage available from these programs can offer you much greater tax savings per dollar of investment than you can get with other types of real estate investment. The best way to demonstrate that is by looking at the impact of leverage on a building that costs $1,000,000. In case A you can borrow 75% of the purchase price–$750,000. In case B you can finance 90% of the purchase price–$900,000. Now let's assume that the building has a useful life of 30 years and you take the maximum accelerated depreciation. That would give you a first year depreciation deduction of $66,700. However, in case A (75% leverage), the depreciation in the first year amounts to 27% of your down payment. In case B (90% leverage), depreciation amounts to 67% of your down payment—more than twice as much as in case A.

The primary objective of Government-assisted programs is to provide housing for low and moderate income families. While Government-assisted housing programs offer some generous tax benefits, the cash flow and appreciation potential on your investment may be somewhat limited because of high debt service and limits on rent increases. Depreciation recapture regulations favor this type of investment and you can also take certain deductions incurred during the construction period, which are limited in other types of real estate investments. Some Government-assisted programs also offer investors some other special tax incentives which are not available in non-Government programs.

In summary, the ownership of high quality real estate should prove to be an attractive investment over the foreseeable future. In addition, as previously mentioned, each type of real estate investment offers different types of tax benefits.

EQUIPMENT LEASING TAX SHELTERS

Equipment leasing tax investments are booming because they offer investors the potential for high annual returns, as well as greater tax savings than most other kinds of tax investment. As a general rule, you can figure that the annual gross rental rate on equipment will work out to between 12% and 16% of its cost. And inflation tends to work in your favor by helping to raise leasing rates as well as the value of the equipment you own. Since the rates can be computed as a percentage of the equipment's cost, the rising cost of new equipment will raise leasing rates in dollar terms. And as the cost of new equipment rises, it tends to raise the value of well-maintained existing equipment. For their part, the businesses leasing the equipment get to enjoy all the benefits of the equipment without having to tie up the capital necessary to buy the equipment.

Types of Equipment

Equipment leasing is now a multibillion dollar field. It involves a number of different types of equipment including computers, medical diagnostic equipment, automobiles, farm machinery, aircraft, cable TV, dry cargo containers, railroad cars, and river barges. In short, any equipment that can be leased for business purposes probably could be used in an equipment leasing tax investment.

Transportation equipment, such as railroad cars and river barges offers an attractive combination of solid economic potential and desirable tax benefits. Transportation equipment enjoys a large market because the transportation industry is so vital to the economic well-being of the country; in addition, transporting goods by rail and water is energy efficient, an important factor in this era of tight fuel supplies. And because the equipment is standardized, it can be used by any number of different users. By contrast, equipment for which the market is very limited faces a big risk if the industry it serves runs into rough times. And unlike equipment that involves rapidly changing technology, as computers do, there's little danger of obsolescence. Railroad cars and river barges haven't changed very much over the years, so older equipment can be just as useful as newer equipment. Consequently, it tends to hold value well and to continue earning high rates. Because the value of existing transportation equipment tends to be pulled higher by the increasing cost of new equipment, an investor who has owned a railroad car for years can often sell it for the original cost, or more.

On the risk side, an investor should be aware that precisely because equipment leasing investments operate as businesses (which is one of the major reasons they are eligible for substantial tax benefits), such investments are, to some degree, subject to fluctuating economic conditions and to changes in the supply/demand relationship applying to a given asset at a particular point in time. In fact, it is generally accepted that the primary risk in such investments is the classic "businessman's risk"—that an economic downturn will adversely affect the value of the equipment and the owner's ability to re-lease it at favorable rates for some temporary period of time.

That's why these investments are viewed as long-term propositions. The rationale includes two basic premises: (1) that the trend of the economy is inflationary, and (2) that, over the long term, the economy will prove, on the average, to be healthy, despite fluctuations upward and downward.

A Unique Form of Ownership

One of the attractive features of some equipment leasing tax investments, such as railcars, is the fact that you are the sole proprietor. You own the cars directly and hire a manager to supervise their day-to-day operation. As a sole proprietor you can tailor the investment to your specific financial needs and goals. You can choose the amount of financing you want to use, make the tax elections which work best for you, and decide when the equipment will be refinanced, and even when it will be sold. However, equipment leasing tax investments can also be structured as limited partnerships, depending on the nature and cost of the equipment.

In most leasing tax investments that are sole proprietorships, you arrange for an experienced equipment management company to manage the equipment for you. The company plays a role similar to that of the general partner in a limited partnership. The major difference is that you pay a fixed management fee—not a percentage share—and that you make the significant decisions concerning disposition of the assets.

It should be kept in mind that the "at risk" rules generally apply to this type of investment so that you may not claim deductions in excess of the actual amount you risk.

Types of Leases

There are basically two types of leasing arrangements: long-term full-payout leases and short-term operating leases. Long-term full-payout leases offer individual investors fewer tax benefits than operating leases and thus are better suited for corporations. (Under the Tax Reform Act of 1976, individual investors cannot claim the investment tax credit (ITC) for equipment if it is leased on a long-term full-payout basis.) As its name implies, a long-term full-payout lease: (1) often runs for most of the useful life of the equipment being leased, (2) provides for lease payments that generally return the cost of the equipment to the owner, and (3) is a net lease, that is, the lessee, the user of the equipment, pays all the operating costs including maintenance and insurance.

In contrast, an operating lease is for a shorter term than a full-payout lease and probably has a higher risk/reward profile, but it can provide you with greater tax benefits than a long-term full-payout lease.

For one thing, if the following two tests are met, you will be entitled to an investment tax credit of 10% of the purchase piece of new equipment: (1) the length of an operating lease must be less than 50% of the period chosen to depreciate the equipment, and (2) during the first twelve months of operation, operating costs (*not* counting interest or depreciation expense) must amount to more than 15% of the income generated from the lease. An additional benefit is the opportunity to renegotiate the lease during your period of ownership and possibly raise rents to increase your income.

Tax Benefits

Individual investors in an equipment leasing tax investment can get substantial tax benefits from the investment tax credit and accelerated depreciation. A typical tax investment in new equipment would give you a one-time, first year investment tax credit amounting to 10% of the equipment's purchase price. As we noted before, the ITC cuts your tax liability dollar for dollar and therefore is worth far more than a tax deduction–which only lowers your taxable income.

Now, let's look at the tax savings from depreciation. Under certain conditions, equipment may be depreciated over a period that is significantly shorter than its actual economic life. This is accomplished by electing to use "class life" which is called the "Asset Depreciation Range" (ADR). For example, although a well-maintained railcar has a 20-year plus economic life, it may be depreciated in as little as 12 years. In addition, double-declining balance (200%) accelerated depreciation may be used. Assume that you purchase three railcars having a depreciable life of 12 years at a cost of $150,000. Since you can take double the usual depreciation on the cars, this accelerated form of depreciation allows you to deduct $25,000 in the first year, instead of only $12,500.

Leverage Enhances the Benefits

The use of leverage boosts the impact of both the economic and tax benefits from an equipment leasing tax investment. For instance, let's assume that you pay 25%, or $37,500, down and finance the remaining $112,500 of the $150,000 purchase price through a recourse loan, one for which you assume personal liability. Your $37,500 down payment earns you an investment tax credit of approximately $15,000, which, in effect, reduces your investment to $22,500. All of the income from the lease will be tax sheltered in the early years because of the depreciation and interest deductions.

The amount of cash flow you get from an equipment leasing tax shelter depends on the amount of leverage you use. Equipment leasing tax investments that involve a lot of leverage will give you substantial tax benefits, but little cash flow during the investment's early years. That's because most of the cash from the investment will have to be used to repay the loan, especially at current, high interest rates. By the same token, equipment leasing tax investments that use little leverage provide you less in tax savings, but more in income.

In this same example of a highly leveraged equipment leasing tax investment, the ITC of $15,000 amounts to 40% of the money you invested. In addition, the first year's depreciation comes to $25,000 or 66% of the amount you invested. As you can see, your tax savings from the ITC and the depreciation deduction in the first year add up to a substantial portion of your entire cash investment, if you use leverage.

Generally, you should count on owning the equipment for at least seven years. If you sell it before then, you will have to repay part or all of the investment tax credit. Barring that, as sole proprietor, you can sell the equipment at any time, but, if the equipment is subject to a lease, the new owner will have to honor this lease.

Tax Consequences of Equipment Sales

However, when you do sell the equipment, a substantial part of the proceeds is taxed as ordinary income even if you have owned it for longer than a year. The amount of this ordinary income portion will equal the depreciation deductions that you took previously. This is called depreciation recapture. Thus, if you have taken $100,000 of depreciation deductions over the years of ownership, and you sell the equipment for a gain of $100,000, the full amount of the gain is subject to the depreciation recapture rules and taxed as ordinary income at rates of up to 70%. Depreciation recapture means that you will have ordinary income equal to the difference between your depreciated basis and your selling price, unless the selling price is greater than original cost. In that case, the amount over original cost will be taxed as a long-term capital gain.

For instance, let's go back to our example of the three railroad cars that you bought for $150,000. Let's assume that you have taken $135,000 depreciation. Now, let's assume that the rising cost of steel and labor has driven the price of new cars so high that your cars are worth $180,000. In that case, $135,000 would be taxed as ordinary income (at rates of up to 70%) as a recapture of depreciation and $30,000 would be taxed as long-term capital gains (at rates of up to 28%). Of course, it may be possible to offset some or all of this tax liability by making new tax investments during the year the cars are sold.

In a sense, you could look at depreciation recapture as a long-term interest-free loan. The tax savings you received from the depreciation deductions you have taken gave you the use of money that would otherwise have been lost to taxes. Moreover, you get to repay the loan in dollars that will have been cheapened by inflation. In addition, you may delay recapture by refinancing rather than selling the cars.

As you can see, equipment leasing is in many ways like a real estate tax shelter. You can write down your cost with depreciation deductions, keep the investment's income or use it to carry borrowings which give you leveraged tax benefits. Both investments can be prime beneficiaries of inflation. The principal difference is that the "at risk" rules do not apply to real estate investments but do apply to equipment leasing.

OIL AND GAS TAX SHELTERS

The soaring price of oil and gas has dramatically improved the economic fundamentals of an oil and gas tax investment. That can clearly be seen in the incredible earnings gains that the major oil companies report each quarter. To put it simply, the world is dependent on oil as an energy source. In fact, rising demand has pushed oil prices higher than the cost of finding and developing it. Since 1973, the price of crude oil has leaped by over 600%, while drilling costs have risen by only approximately 125%, according to industry data. Natural gas prices have risen approximately 550% compared to drilling cost increases of about 132%.

The improved economic fundamentals for oil and gas investment benefit investors in several major ways. First, the reserves needed to make a find worthwhile don't have to be as large as they had to be when oil was selling for $4.25 a barrel. Thus, more wells will provide an economic return. Second, the potential profits from a significant strike are much better than before. And third, a direct investment in oil and gas appears to be a good hedge against inflation because the price of oil and gas is expected to continue to rise. Oil or gas reserves provide investors with a stream of income as the oil or gas is produced, and as the price of oil and gas moves steadily higher, the income stream also increases.

That's not to say that oil and gas tax shelters have become a sure thing. They haven't. Risks are still great because less than one-half of all wells drilled find oil or gas in economically commercial quantities. Prices are subject to government control. The general trend does seem to lean toward increases in prices to encourage exploration and lessen our dependence on foreign imports. But part of the gain may be taxed away by the new excise tax on oil, the windfall profits tax.

Types of Programs

There are three basic types of oil and gas tax shelters: exploration programs, development programs, and balanced programs.

Exploration programs, as their name implies, try to find oil and gas in new areas or in geological formations that have not been productive in the past, consequently drilling risks are highest for this type of program. One way to reduce the risk in unexplored areas is to acquire a large number of drilling sites to provide diversification.

There are some advantages in exploration programs. The prices of acquiring drilling leases can be the least expensive. By the same token, royalties to property owners and others are also lower than those on properties with proven reserves. (A royalty is a percentage of the revenues produced by a well, which is paid to someone other than the operator. The lower the royalties, the higher the percentage of income from the well that will be available to the investors.) Because of lower costs for leases and royalties, a successful exploration program can be a rewarding investment.

Development programs are those that drill in areas or geological formations where previous exploration has found oil or gas. Consequently, the risks are much lower than those of an exploratory program and the return on investment probably won't be as high. As a result, the program has to pay more for leases and royalties. Because the support and transportation facilities may already be in place, income from production may begin sooner than for an exploratory program.

Balanced programs combine exploratory drilling with development drilling. The exploratory drilling gives the program a chance to make some large profits, while the development drilling reduces the degree of risk. For all oil and gas tax investments the best advice is simply this: you should diversify your investments to spread your risk—by either investing in two or three different programs or in the same program over two or three years.

In an effort to encourage greater oil and gas exploration and development, Congress has given investors some very generous tax incentives. Investors in oil and gas programs can usually deduct between 50% and 90% of the amount invested in the first year, with smaller deductions in later years. The tax savings from these deductions reduce the out-of-pocket cost for the investment. And that, in turn, means that only a portion of your money is actually at risk in the investment.

An oil and gas tax investment provides investors with three basic tax benefits—immediate tax deductions, tax-sheltered income, and conversion of income to long-term capital gains. All of these benefits are of course subject to possible revisions of the present tax laws.

Immediate Tax Deductions

Intangible drilling costs—which include expenses such as labor, chemicals, and other materials that have no salvage value—can be deducted in the year they are paid. Most of these costs, which normally amount to most of the cost of drilling a well to its total depth, are paid in the program's first year.

Tax-Sheltered Income

Depletion allowances are a method by which the investor can shelter part of each property's gross income from taxes. There are two basic methods for applying the depletion allowance: (1) percentage depletion and (2) cost depletion. The investor will use the method that produces the greatest tax advantage, which will usually be the percentage depletion allowance. This currently allows the investor to shelter up to 22% of oil and gas gross income, which could total more than the original cost. Depletion allowances are scheduled to decline in the future as follows: 1981 20%, 1982 18%, 1983 16%, 1984 and thereafter 15%.

Here's an example that shows how the numbers might work out with percentage depletion. Assume a property has gross revenues of $1,000,000 and operating expenses of $150,000. That would leave a net income of $850,000, of which $220,000 (22% x $1,000,000) would be distributed to investors tax-free. As you can see, the depletion allowance shelters almost 26% of the net income from the property. The balance of the income, $630,000 in this example, is taxed as ordinary income. The overall impact could lower the effective tax rate you pay on oil and gas income.

Finally, the depletion allowance, unlike depreciation, is never recaptured. That's why some tax shelter advisors think that oil and gas tax investments are the only true tax shelters around.

Conversion of Income to Long-Term Capital Gains

Most programs have a provision that allows the limited partners to sell their interest back to the program's sponsor. If you decide to sell your partnership interest back to the sponsor, most of the proceeds will be taxed as long-term capital gains. Thus, you will have converted unearned income that might have been subject to as much as a 70% rate into a capital gain taxable at no more than a 28% rate. The amount of cash you will be offered is usually based on an independent appraisal of the partnership's future revenues from its oil and gas reserves. The amount will be minus a discount from the partnership income stream so it probably won't match the total return you could get by staying in the program. If you sell your interest in the early years, some of the intangible drilling deductions that you have taken would be recaptured and taxed as ordinary income. This is one reason why oil and gas investments should be regarded as long-term commitments.

OTHER TYPES OF TAX SHELTERS

In addition to the three types of tax shelters described above—real estate, equipment leasing, and oil and gas ventures—there are other types of tax shelters. As we pointed out before, almost any kind of business, including agriculture, mining, and entertainment, can be set up as a partnership that allows investors to benefit directly from owning assets. The following are descriptions of some other types of tax shelter programs:

Agricultural tax shelters include cattle feeding or breeding programs, crop partnerships, and timber operations.

Cattle feeding tax shelters are basically a way of deferring taxes from one year to another. The programs buy young steers, called feeder cattle, in the summer or fall. The cost of fattening them for slaughter, which takes between six and nine months, is deductible as the cattle are fed. Recourse financing, loans for which you assume personal liability, adds leverage to boost those deductions to between 100% and 150% of your investment. When the cattle are fattened and sold, the income is taxed at up to a 70% rate. You can get the cost deductions in one year and record the income in the following year. Cattle feeding programs carry substantial risks because of fluctuations in feed as well as cattle prices.

Cattle breeding programs are longer term ventures. Such programs buy small herds of cattle for breeding purposes. Besides deducting operating costs, investors can also depreciate the cattle, which are considered a productive asset. And because they have a relatively short life span, depreciation is fairly rapid. As the herd builds up, some of the cattle are sold. The profits on cattle held for breeding for over two years are treated as long-term capital gains.

Crops

Almost anything that can be grown in an orchard, vineyard, or field can be used as the basis of a tax shelter. Irrigation ditches, barns and other types of structures, as well as farm equipment, can be depreciated at accelerated rates. Some types of farm equipment can also qualify for the 10% investment tax credit.

Income from the sale of crops is taxed as ordinary income. Losses due to bad weather, disease, or poor market conditions are deductible as ordinary losses. Most of these ventures engage in farming as a land-holding technique. If any of the crop land is sold at a profit, it will be taxed at long-term capital gains rates, assuming it has been held for more than one year.

Timber

Such a partnership will own stands of timber, part of which it cuts periodically for sale to saw mills or paper mills. Operating costs and depreciation on equipment give the investors tax deductions. Some of the equipment used in the timber operations may also qualify for the 10% investment tax credit. Because timber is considered a wasting asset, investors can shelter some of the proceeds from the timber sales from taxes through non-cost deductions such as depletion. Moreover, income from timber sales will be taxed as long-term capital gains. And land that's sold at a profit will also be taxed as long-term capital gains, if it has been held for more than one year. The major risks are fire, diseases that can damage the trees, and fluctuations in the price of timber.

Mining

Extractive industry tax shelters include any business that is involved in mining, especially coal mining.

A coal tax investment is in some ways like an oil and gas tax shelter. Coal, like oil and gas, is rising in value. And investors can use the depletion allowance to shelter part of their earnings from taxes. The major difference is that investors in a coal investment have no intangible drilling costs to deduct. Some mine development expenses are deductible as incurred. The mining equipment purchased for the operations can give investors a substantial investment tax credit as well as significant deductions for accelerated depreciation. In addition, investors can deduct certain prepaid royalties for the coal mined.

The Arts

Entertainment tax shelters are in businesses such as movies, plays, master recordings, books, and even lithographs. Recent tax legislation has not been favorable to these types of investments.

Whether or not you make a profit in a movie tax shelter depends on how the public reacts to your film. And that's impossible to predict, even for films that have stars with box-office appeal. The tax savings are easier to predict. The cost of making or buying a film can be depreciated fairly quickly under what is called the income forecast method, which is an attempt to estimate the box-office life of a film. In addition, investors can also take an investment tax credit for the entire cost of producing a film if 80% or more of that cost is incurred in the United States. If less than 80% of the cost is incurred here, investors can only get a tax credit for those production expenses directly attributable to the United States, excluding overhead and screen rights.

In a master recording or lithograph tax shelter, investors own a master litho plate or a recording disk from which copies can be made. If the copies sell, the profits will be taxed as ordinary income. In the meantime, investors can get tax savings from the 10% investment tax credit and accelerated depreciation on the fair-market value of the master litho or recording disk.

FEATURES AND BENEFITS OF DIFFERENT TYPES OF TAX SHELTERS

Investment	Potential Economic Features	Potential Tax Benefits
Real Estate		
Existing Commercial	Appreciation potential Immediate income Equity build-up Low leverage	Shelter of cash flow from straight line depreciation Capital gains
New Construction	Appreciation potential Possible income in later years Moderate to high leverage	Accelerated depreciation gives sizeable deductions in early years Capital gains
Government Subsidized Housing	Residual value Mortgage guarantees Rental assistance High leverage	High leverage magnifies deductions in early years (multiple write-off) Capital gains

FEATURES AND BENEFITS OF DIFFERENT TYPES OF TAX SHELTERS (Continued)

Investment	Potential Economic Features	Potential Tax Benefits
Oil and Gas		
Developmental	Lower risk with commensurate reward potential Potential for cash flow to begin near-term	Full deduction of intangible drilling costs in first two years Partial shelter of income from depletion allowance
Exploratory	Higher risk with commensurate reward potential Potential for cash flow to begin longer term	Full deduction of intangible drilling costs in first two years Partial shelter of income from depletion allowance
Balanced	Exploratory segment offers upside potential Development segment limits risk Initial cash flow may be diverted for subsequent drilling	Full deduction of intangible drilling costs in first two years Partial shelter of income from depletion allowance
Leasing		
Equipment	Cash flow from rental Residual value of equipment plus possible appreciation Leverage	Tax savings through investment tax credit Deferral of taxes through accelerated depreciation

The assistance of Merrill Lynch, Pierce, Fenner & Smith, Inc. in the preparation of this material is gratefully acknowledged.

GLOSSARY

Note: terms in *italics* are defined elsewhere in the glossary.

Accelerated Depreciation–Any method of *depreciation* which permits *deduction* of a greater percentage of the cost of an asset in early years of the asset's useful life with smaller deductions in later years. Two methods are widely used: (1) the "sum-of-the-years-digits" method and (2) the more popular "declining balance" method. Under the declining balance, annual deductions are calculated as a percentage of the *straight line depreciation* rate, i.e., 200% declining balance (also called "double declining balance") available for new residential construction; 150% declining balance, available for new commercial construction; 125% declining balance for existing improved real estate. Note that accelerated depreciation is usually a *tax preference item.*

Assessment–Additional amounts of money which a *limited partner* in a *tax sheltered partnership* may be required to furnish beyond his original *subscription.* A given program, depending on the terms, may be either "assessable" or "non-assessable." An assessable program may have limited or unlimited assessments. Assessments may be optional or mandatory.

"At-Risk" Limitations–This limitation is designed to prevent non-corporate taxpayers from deducting losses in excess of their economic investment in the activity involved. These rules now apply to all activities except real estate and certain companies leasing equipment. In addition, where your amount of investment deemed to be "at risk" is reduced below zero (by distributions or change of status of liabilities from recourse to non-recourse), income recognition may be required of deductions previously taken.

Blind Pool Program–A *tax sheltered partnership* which, at the time sale of *subscriptions* begins, does not have the *proceeds* of the offering allocated to specific projects or properties. (Contrast with *specified property program.*)

Capital Asset–Any asset (property, equipment, livestock, etc.) which is: (1) used in a trade or business (except inventories or items held for sale to customers), (2) held for production of income, or (3) given the effect of a capital asset by a tax law provision. With certain exceptions, capital assets–including interests in *tax shelter partnerships*–are subject to *capital gains* treatment on any profit (or loss) arising from sale or exchange.

Capital Gains–Usually gain (or loss) from sale or exchange of any property is included in income and taxed at ordinary income tax rates. However, if the gain is from the sale or exchange of a *capital asset* owned for more than 12 months, the tax is calculated at the lower long term capital gains rate, generally no more than 28%. Almost all types of *tax sheltered investments* except cattle feeding and equipment leasing offer some capital gains opportunities. Certain types of real estate, and oil and gas offer the most potential. It has been said that capital gains offer the major source of tax relief. Note however that capital gains benefits may be reduced by *recapture*. Note also that 60% of long-term capital gains may be taxed under the alternative minimum tax.

Cash Liquidating Value–The amount, generally based on an evaluation of a qualified independent appraiser, which will be paid by the *general partner* for an interest in a *tax sheltered partnership* upon exercise by a *limited partner* of his right to receive such value. Programs that offer cash liquidation can be described as offering "liquidity," as opposed to illiquid programs which do not have cash liquidating features.

Conversion–Obtaining current tax *deductions* against ordinary income while turning future revenues into income taxable at more favorable *capital gains rates* or lower rates derived from favorable tax features such as *depletion* or *depreciation.*

Deductions–In this context, the interest, taxes, *depreciation, depletion* and other expenses incurred in the trade or business of a *tax sheltered partnership* which are passed on to the *limited partners* thereby reducing their taxable income and, ultimately, their tax liability. The "ordinary and necessary" expenses of any business are allowable as deductions; however, certain forms of *tax sheltered intangible drilling costs* associated oil and gas,

(2) depreciation and interest costs associated with real estate, equipment leasing and certain agricultural tax shelters, particularly when *leverage* is employed, and (3) the feed and maintenance costs associated with cattle feeding. Ideally, a *tax sheltered partnership* will generate deductions in excess of income for the first year or first few years thereby permitting program *limited partners* to recover part or all of their investments out of *tax losses.*

Deferral–In this context, a form of tax shelter that results from an investment timed so that *deductions* take place during the investor's high income years and taxable income is realized after retirement, in some other period of reduced income, or at a time when the tax will be more convenient to pay. Equipment leasing and certain types of real estate offer the best deferral opportunities.

Depletion–A form of *deduction* that applies to "wasting asset" interest. The purpose is to encourage exploration for new deposits by permitting recovery of exploration and development costs out of tax savings. The annual depletion deduction for any mineral property is the greater of "cost depletion" (based on the ratio of annual production to remaining reserves) and "percentage depletion" (a fixed annual percent). The major advantage of percentage depletion is that benefits are available each year a property produces income and do not cease when the cost of the property has been recovered. Oil and gas, timber and minerals all offer some depletion. Percentage depletion on oil and gas is 22% of gross income from each property limited to the lesser of 65% of the individual's taxable income or 50% of the taxable income from the property. However, beginning in 1981, this percentage decreases down to 15% ratably from 1981-1984. Percentage depletion on other minerals ranges from 22% for sulphur down to 5% for clay and shale. Note that percentage depletion is a *tax preference item.*

Depreciation–A form of *deduction* to permit recovery of the cost (less any salvage value) of an asset in the form of tax savings. This cost recovery is spread over the asset's "useful life" as an annual deduction from taxable income. Depreciation is most attractive in real estate, equipment leasing and some types of cattle breeding, especially if *leverage* is employed. Tax laws permit choosing a constant annual depreciation amount over useful life (called straight-line depreciation) or, in some cases, one of several *accelerated depreciation* methods.

Double Declining Balance—See: *accelerated depreciation.*

Front End Load—A slang term for the total of *organizational and offering expenses plus management fees*; i.e., the total deductions from the *offering amount* to arrive at the *proceeds* of a *tax sheltered partnership.* (See also: *management fees.*)

General Partner—In this context, the manager or sponsor of a *tax sheltered investment* which has been organized as a *limited partnership.* (See *limited partnership* for details.)

Intangible Drilling Costs—A tax *deduction* for certain expenditures incurred in drilling and completing oil and gas wells. "Intangibles" are the items which have no salvage value (commonly non-material costs such as labor, chemicals, drill-site preparation, etc.). Intangibles frequently account for 50% to 80% of the cost of drilling and completing a given well. Note that intangible drilling costs on producing wells in excess of oil and gas net income is a *tax preference item.*

Joint Venture—A form of business organization. In this context, a *tax sheltered investment* in which the manager and the investors share jointly in the ownership, management authority and liability. (Contrast with *limited partnership.*)

Leverage—In this context, a method of increasing a tax shelter through borrowing (see *non-recourse loans* and *recourse loans*) as a part of a *tax sheltered investment.* The investor (in certain circumstances) is permitted *deductions* for interest, *management fees, depreciation,* etc., on the amount he invests plus his pro-rata share of the amount the partnership borrows on a non-recourse basis or any amounts for which he is personally liable on a recourse basis. Any properly-structured loans, therefore, serve to increase total deductions from income for tax purposes. Real estate offers excellent leverage possibilities, as do cattle breeding and equipment leasing.

Limited Partner—In this context, the purchaser of a *subscription* in a *tax sheltered investment* which has been organized as a *limited partnership*; i.e., an investor.

Limited Partnership–A form of business organization in which some partners exchange their right to participate in management for a limitation on their liability for partnership losses. Commonly, *limited partners* have liability only to the extent of their investment in the business plus their share of any undistributed profits. To establish limited liability, there must be at least one *general partner* who is fully liable for all claims against the business. Limited partnerships are a popular organizational form for *tax sheltered investments* because of the ease with which tax benefits flow through the partnership to the individual partners. (Contrast with *joint venture.*)

Liquidity–See: *cash liquidating value.*

Management Fee–An amount paid to the *general partner* of a *tax sheltered partnership* to cover *organization* and *offering expenses* and/or to repay costs of operating and administrating the partnership, commonly expressed as a percentage of the total *offering amount.* Prior to the Tax Reform Act of 1976, the management fee was claimed as a *deduction* by many limited partnerships. Under present law, only the general partner's reimbursements to cover costs of operating and administrating the partnership are considered fully deductible. (See also: *front-end load.*)

Maximum Tax–Individuals are taxed at a maximum rate of 50% on that portion of their taxable income attributable to personal service income. However, the amount of income eligible for the maximum rate is offset by the amount the year's *tax preference items.* The amount offset is taxable as unearned income at rates of up to 70%.

Minimum Subscription–The smallest dollar amount which an investor must initially commit in order to become a limited partner in a *tax sheltered partnership,* usually one or more *units.* In a *public program* the minimum subscription is generally almost always \$5,000. (See also: *subscription.*)

Minimum Tax–15% of total tax preference items which exceed

the greater of $10,000 or one-half the taxpayer's regular Federal income tax liability. (See also: *tax preference items.*)

Alternative Minimum Tax–A tax on regular taxable income plus the long-term capital gain preference (60% untaxed portion) plus adjusted itemized deductions in excess of 50% of adjusted gross income. The resulting "alternative minimum taxable income," after a specific exemption of $20,000, is subject to the following rates of tax: 10% on the first $40,000; 20% on the next $40,000 and 25% of any excess. This tax replaces the regular tax (including the 15% minimum tax) if it exceeds that tax.

Non-Cash Charges–*Deductions* for *depreciation and depletion* which aren't actually paid to anyone, yet are subtracted from taxable income before calculating tax due. *Tax sheltered partnerships* such as real estate and equipment leasing which employ *leverage* may be able to pyramid non-cash charges to the point that limited partners receive *tax sheltered cash flow* in the early years against which there is limited or no tax liability.

Non-Recourse Loan–In this context, any borrowing by a *tax sheltered partnership,* structured in such a way that lenders can look only to specific assets pledged for repayment and not to the individual assets of the various partners. However, in the event of a foreclosure, if partnership cash and assets aren't sufficient to repay the loan balance, the limited partners may be left with a substantial tax bill because of "forgiveness of debt." Real estate is the only tax shelter area where non-recourse financing is permitted. (Contrast with *recourse loan*; see also: *leverage.*)

Offering Amount–The total dollar amount sought by a *general partner* from prospective *limited partners in a particular tax sheltered partnership.*

Organization and Offering Expenses–Those expenses incurred in connection with preparing a *tax sheltered partnership* for registration with Federal and/or state securities agencies and subsequently selling subscriptions to *limited partners.* Organizational and offering expenses typically include legal fees, printing costs, registration fees, sales commissions and selling costs. (See also: *Management fee; front-end load.*)

Private Program—A *tax sheltered partnership* which is offered and sold pursuant to the private offering exemption available under the Securities Act of 1933 and/or some registration exemption allowed under the securities laws of one or more states; i.e., a program which is not registered with the Securities and Exchange Commission. (Contrast with *public program.*)

Proceeds—The dollar amount remaining for the general partner to conduct partnership operations after deduction of *organization and operating expenses* or other items of *front-end load* from the total amount committed.

Public Program—A *tax sheltered partnership* which is registered with the Securities and Exchange Commission (SEC) and distributed in a public offering by broker dealers and/or employees of the *general partner.* The principal differences between a public program and a *private program* relate to: (1) the number of *investors,* which may be several hundred in a public program, but which is limited, with certain exceptions, to 35 in a private program; (2) *minimum subscription: $5,000 in a public program, $50,000 or more in a private program;* and (3) *the fact that "private" investors are subject to stricter suitability standards.*

Recapture—Upon profitable sales of certain assets, *capital gains* may be severely restricted when previously claimed *deductions* for *depreciation, farming losses, intangible drilling costs* or *investment credit* are taken back into ordinary income (i.e., "recaptured"). Since ordinary income tax rates can run as high as 70%—versus 28% for capital gains—recapture can severely reduce or eliminate capital gains benefits. The amount of recapture depends on the type of asset, holding period, type of depreciation (straight-line or accelerated) as well as dollar amount of "recaptured" deductions.

Recourse Loan—In this context, any borrowing by a *tax shelter* investor for which he is personally liable. (Contrast with *nonrecourse loan.*)

Specified Property Program—A *tax sheltered partnership* which, at the time of sale of *subscriptions* begins, has the proceeds of the offering allocated to definite projects or properties which are described in detail in the prospectus of offering circular. (Contrast with *blind pool program.*)

Straight Line Depreciation–See: *depreciation.*

Subchapter S Corporation–A form of corporation with a limited number of qualified stockholders who elect to utilize a specific tax law provision which permits them to be taxed so the corporation pays no taxes and each stockholder reports his share of the corporate income (or loss) on his own tax return. (Also called a "Tax Option Corporation.")

Subscription–The total dollar amount for which a *limited partner* in a *tax sheltered partnership* initially commits. Legally it represents the amount he is obligated to pay, exclusive of any *assessment* amount which he has the option to reject. (See also: *unit.*)

Tax Loss–A situation that occurs when the *deductions* generated by a *tax sheltered partnership* exceed program revenues. Thus, the *limited partner's* taxable income is lower, resulting in a tax saving. Ideally, a *tax sheltered partnership* will generate enough tax losses the first year or first few years to permit the limited partners to recover their investment from "tax savings." However, *recapture* may ultimately limit these benefits.

Tax Preference Items–Items of tax preference subject to the 15% *minimum tax* include: *accelerated depreciation* in excess of *straight line depreciation* on real property and leased personal property, appreciation on certain stock options, excess intangible drilling costs on productive wells and excess percentage depletion.

Tax Savings–See: *tax losses.*

Tax Sheltered Cash Flow–The situation that arises when *noncash charges* and other *deductions* exceed gross income from a tax shelter partnership so that the program has cash to distribute to *limited partners* even though the cash they may receive involves no current tax liability or is taxed at a lower rate. Real estate and equipment leasing programs employing *accelerated depreciation* and *leverage* are the best sources of the tax sheltered cash flow.

Tax Sheltered Investment—An investment that has an expectation of economic profit, made even more attractive because of the timing of the profit or the way it is taxed, generally having some or all of the following characteristics:

(a) *Deferral* of taxes,
(b) *Conversion* of *deductions* to possible future *capital gains,*
(c) *Leverage.*

The flow-through of tax benefits is a material factor whether the entity is organized as a *limited partnership, joint venture* or *Subchapter S Corporation* and whether it is offered to investors as a *private program* or a *public program.* Common forms of tax sheltered investments include: real estate, oil and gas, equipment leasing and agriculture.

Tax Sheltered Partnership—A *tax sheltered investment* organized as a *limited partnership.* Commonly, a tax sheltered program is created to mutually benefit a *general partner* and a group of *limited partners.* It may be organized as a *public program* or a *private program.*

Unit—The smallest dollar amount into which *subscriptions* in a *tax shelter partnership* may be divided, usually $1,000 or $5,000. For example, a $1 million *public program* might consist of 200 units of $5,000 each. Alternately, it might consist of 1,000 units of $1,000 each. Each type would normally have a *minimum subscription* of $5,000.

Chapter One

REAL ESTATE

U.S. Population is projected to increase by roughly 50% by the year 2000. Other factors pointing to a continuing healthy climate for real estate investment include: the spread of cities, increased leisure and retirement time, urban renewal and the shrinking supply of available land.

Because of widespread home ownership, most people understand real estate. Many investors, therefore, choose real estate when first diversifying their investments beyond stocks and bonds.

The field is vast; any real estate investment could involve several cycles of development, operation, demolition and redevelopment. You'll find investments that involve holding land, or constructing and operating apartments, office buildings, warehouses, shopping centers, mobile home parks and recreational facilities—to name a few.

The sponsors of most real estate programs are generally real estate developers or real estate brokers. Some sponsors also have subsidiaries which manage properties, place mortgages, rent furniture, and so forth.

Sponsors usually invest very little cash in their programs. They contribute the expertise to invest in properties which meet partnership objectives. The sponsors and their affiliates usually receive compensation from some combination of markup on sale of properties, brokerage commissions on purchases and sales, property management fees, reimbursement of specified expenses and/or a share of revenues or profits from partnership properties.

Although programs vary greatly, all have common characteristics. The differences relate to the types of properties they purchase or develop. You may select among single-property programs or those which invest in multiple properties. A program prospectus may describe the exact properties selected for investment. Or, it may involve an unspecified "blind pool," granting the sponsor authority to select any properties meeting partnership objectives. Some programs—generally larger ones—invest in both specified and unspecified properties.

You'll find public and private real estate programs concentrate in four areas: new improved real estate, existing improved real estate, government assisted housing and raw land.

You should note that the "at risk" rules do not, at this time apply to real estate investments. Therefore, you should be able to invest in a real estate program without assuming personal liability on borrowings obtained to finance the program.

New improved real estate may appeal to you if you're risk and deduction oriented. These partnerships build on raw land, replace existing buildings or purchase newly constructed "first owner" properties. They generally use leverage, management fees, interest and maximum depreciation to generate deductions. The goal is investment recovery through tax savings within 5 to 7 years and, because of leverage, there is usually little or no cash flow for the first several years.

Most new-property programs concentrate on residential development, principally apartments, because more favorable 200% "double-declining balance" depreciation is available (versus at 150% rate for new commercial properties such as office buildings and shopping centers). High deductions, high leverage and new (hence untried) properties create a high risk investment offering potential for rapid investment recovery and capital gain. However, you may be required to "recapture" (at ordinary income tax rates) depreciation taken on the property in excess of amounts allowable under straight line depreciation.

Existing improved real estate may suit you if you need tax sheltered income at lower risk. These lower leveraged partnerships generally purchase used (Hence more predictable) apartment properties with depreciation generally limited to 125% of the straight line rate; used commercial properties (straight line depreciation) and sometimes included for diversification.

These programs offer lower first year write-offs, usually less than 50%. However, some do provide tax sheltered cash flow. Lower risk, lower deductions, tax sheltered cash flow, moderate capital gain possibilities . . . these are the characteristics of existing real estate.

Federal and State assisted housing programs offer a variety of investment opportunities, including large first year deductions.

Most offer annual deductions continuing for ten to twenty years. Federal and State assisted housing typically involves construction or rehabilitation of properties for low-income, middle-income or elderly tenants. Each involves some form of government assistance, such as rent subsidies or loan guarantees.

Raw land programs try to buy unimproved or underdeveloped property (forest, farm land, marsh, etc.) near urban centers and hold it (often several years) for sale to a developer or land speculator at a profit that may well be taxed at favored capital gain rates. Most of the annual expenses of carrying land are deductible but these are usually small relative to total investment; land is not depreciable. Since this investment stresses very long term capital gain and minimal tax shelter, few public programs invest exclusively in raw land.

Real estate tax objectives vary greatly with the type of program chosen; each type offers different deductions, income shelter and capital gains. First year deductions are usually greatest in government assisted housing programs.

Income shelter is leverage sensitive; cash flow in highly leveraged programs normally goes to retiring debt rather than into your pocket as tax-free cash. Income shelter is usually highest from partnerships which purchase existing residential or commercial real estate on a low-leverage or unleveraged basis.

Capital gain treatment is available in all types of real estate programs. However, recapture seriously affects profitability of projects which utilize accelerated depreciation and are sold after only a few years.

As a real estate investor, you have a wide range of possibilities. You may hold on to a partnership interest, collecting the available tax benefits and income, for several years. Or, in some partnerships, you may wait for two to three years (or possibly longer) until a value for your interest is established, then sell, hoping for capital gain.

Although real estate investments may be less risky than some other shelters, definite risk is involved. Profitability depends on leverage, interest rates, percentage occupancy, operating costs, location, competition, and a host of other factors. The key factor, however, is management: the sponsor must have the ability to conduct successful operations before your partnership can succeed.

Some real estate investors through continuous investing year after year create heavy writeoffs from current year investments and residual writeoffs from prior year investments. This combination of current and residual writeoffs can produce enormous cash flow and result in very little tax.

Certain specialized real estate programs have developed such as motels and mini-warehouses. One major mini-warehouse program has a four phase investment cycle designed to produce positive cash flow promptly rather than generating negative earnings:

PHASE I

Capital Contribution

Partnership capital is used to acquire land and construct mini-warehouse facilities on a cash only basis. (Loans for construction or long-term financing will not be employed during Phase I or II.)

PHASE II

Cash Distribution from Operations

After completion of construction and the ensuing rent-up period, operating income may become available for distribution to Investors. Past experience has resulted in most public partnership facilities operating profitably within 3 to 4 months of completion. (There is no assurance that the Partnership's projects will attain these results.)

PHASE III

Special Distribution from Financing

After approximately 7 years, financing of the properties will be considered. Cash proceeds from financing will be distributed to Investors. Cash distributions from operations may continue to be made to Investors with any funds available after debt service.

PHASE IV

Sale Distribution

From 7 to 10 years after completion of construction, it is expected that the Partnership will sell its properties. Sale proceeds will be used to repay outstanding mortgage loan balances, if any, and any remaining proceeds will be distributed to the Partners.

Four real estate illustrations are set forth below. First one shows the main benefits of real estate investments. Second example depicts a private placement of an existing, commercial office building. Third is a mobile home park program. Fourth offering represents a public program for new subsidized housing.

Certain questions arise concerning subsidized housing:

What types of amenities can a subsidized housing project provide?

Many subsidized housing projects offer swimming pools, saunas, and recreational facilities. The building standards set forth by the various governmental agencies are, in most cases, at least as stringent as many local building codes, and may often be more stringent, especially in the areas of sound control and fire detection.

What are the effects of a foreclosure?

In the event of a foreclosure, the investor would be required to pay income taxes on his share of the gain realized by the Partnership, which includes the outstanding principal balance of mortgage debt. If the depreciation deductions resulted from use of accelerated methods of depreciation, all or a portion of such tax liability may be taxed at ordinary income rates (generally referred to as a "recapture"). An investor in subsidized housing is given total forgiveness of recapture after 200 months. After 100 months, the portion of the gain taxable as ordinary income diminishes, at the rate of 1% per month, to zero at 200 months. Depreciation in excess of straight line depreciation always remains subject to recapture in the case of conventional real estate.

How are subsidized projects financed?

Subsidized housing projects are generally financed by the following methods:

(1) State housing finance agencies sell tax-exempt bonds and then lend the proceeds to developers in the form of mortgages to encourage the development of low and middle-income housing.
(2) Federal agencies may guarantee mortgages, which are then sold to banks, pension funds, and other investors.
(3) Some subsidized housing projects are financed by conventional mortgages given by banks and savings and loan associations.

The interest rates in the first two categories are generally significantly lower than those available in the conventional mortgage market.

What is Section 8?

Section 8 of the United States Housing Act of 1937, as amended, is the primary federal housing rent subsidy program. This program provides for payments to be made directly to project owners on behalf of qualified low-income tenants. Among its other features, Section 8 provides that:

(1) Qualified tenants will pay no more than 25% of their gross income in rent, with the government funding the difference. The rent subsidy, payable by the federal government, shall be adjusted annually by an adjustment factor designed to absorb inflationary increases and expenses. There can be no assurance that the automatic annual adjustment factor will allow an increase in contract rents sufficient to cover the increased costs of operating the project or, if such factor is not sufficient, that the project will be qualified for the special annual adjustment.
(2) If the tenant moves out of the project, the government will continue to pay 80% of the subsidy for a 60-day period.
(3) Should the project apartment remain vacant after that period, HUD could agree to pay the mortgage payments, pro-rated to that vacant apartment, for an additional 12-month period.

What is the potential for appreciation of the property?

HUD's minimum property standards demand quality of construction. Those projects which are well-located and attractive could possibly therefore, appreciate, over the long term, as much as similar conventional projects in the same area.

Who qualifies as a tenant for Section 8?

HUD has determined an economic standard for "lower income" and "very low income" persons. "Very low income" persons are defined as persons whose income does not exceed 50% of the median in the locality. "Lower income" persons are defined as persons whose income does not exceed 80% of the median in the locality.

Much space was devoted to subsidized housing because of the Congressional interest in it.

REAL ESTATE

I. REAL ESTATE AND TOTAL ASSET MANAGEMENT

A) *Establishment of a measure of investment performance*

1. The change in the absolute dollar value is no longer an appropriate or sufficient measure because of the impact of taxes and inflation.

– The two-way squeeze: While inflation has the effect of shifting someone's income into a higher tax bracket, it also makes it harder for that same person to maintain his or her standard of living.

– The demise of the dollar: If 1967 = $1.00, then the purchasing power in 1970 = $.86, in 1973 = $.75 and it is estimated that it will equal $.58 in 1976.

– Impact of taxes and inflation on the income of a family of four: In order to maintain the same standard of living that it had enjoyed in 1970 on an income of $20,000, the family would have required an income of $29,000 (or 45% more) in 1976.

– Impact of taxes and inflation on a 6% Savings Account: After paying taxes at 40% and assuming a 5% rate of inflation, the net value of $10,000 investment after one year would be $9,845.

Analysis:	Investment	$10,000
	Plus: Interest	600
	Less: Taxes	(240)
	Inflation	(515)
	Net Value	$ 9,845

The investor has had a loss in purchasing power of 1.55%

– Rate of return required to keep pace with specific tax rates and inflation rates.

Tax Bracket	Rate of Inflation 3%	5%	10%
40%	5.2%	8.8%	18.5%
50%	6.2%	10.5%	22.2%
60%	7.7%	13.2%	27.8%

– If an investor were in the 50% tax bracket, he would need to achieve a 22% pre-tax rate of return in a period with 10% inflation needed to maintain the purchasing power of the funds he invested.

2. *Definition of a measure of performance: Effective Return*

Investment
Plus: Yield
Minus: Taxes
Inflation

Effective Return

Question: How can an investment in Real Estate help maximize the effective return?

II. THE TOTAL RETURN FROM A REAL ESTATE INVESTMENT

A) *Cash Flow:* The net cash remaining after all expenses (including debt service) have been paid from the revenues (rental income) generated by a property.

B) *Tax Shelter:* The excess of reported expenses over income from a property which may be used as an offset against income on what taxes would otherwise have been paid.

Net Income–Statement for the operations of a property that is used for (tax) reporting purposes.

B) 1. *Partially sheltered cash flow.*

Net Income		*Cash Flow*	
Rental Income	$100	Rental Income	$100
Less: Oper. Exp.	(40)	Less: Oper. Exp.	(40)
Net Oper. Income	$ 60	Net Oper. Income	$ 60
Less: Interest	(35)	Less: Debt Service	(45)
Depreciation	(22)	(Int. & Prin.)	
Net Income or (Loss)	$3	Net Cash Flow	$ 15

Analysis: Because of the depreciation deduction taken in the calculation of reported income, part ($12) of the $15 cash flow is sheltered from taxes.

2. *Fully sheltered cash flow with excess losses.*

Net Income		*Cash Flow*	
Rental Income	$100	Rental Income	$100
Less: Oper. Exp.	(40)	Less: Oper. Exp.	(40)
Net Oper. Income	$ 60	Net Oper. Income	$ 60
Less: Interest	(35)	Less: Debt Service	(45)
Depreciation	(43)	(Int. & Prin.)	
Net Income or (Loss)	$(18)	Net Cash Flow	$ 15

Analysis: With accelerated depreciation in the early years of the operation of a property not only is the cash flow usually fully sheltered from taxes, but in many cases there will be an excess loss that may be used to shelter income from other sources. In this case, not only is the $15 cash flow sheltered from taxes, but there is an excess loss of $18.

Note: Under the provisions of the Tax Reform Act of 1976, the use of accelerated depreciation may have further tax implications in the calculation of an individual's maximum and minimum taxes.

C) *Mortgage amortization:* The reduction of the amount of the mortgage on a property through the periodic mortgage payments is often referred to as equity build-up.

1. Mortgage payments consist of two parts–interest and principal repayment.

2. Example of mortgage amortization: Assume a property is bought and sold for the *same* price, and that between the time of purchase and sale, the owner has made mortgage payments such that the outstanding balance has been reduced by $10,000.

	Purchase	Sale
Price	$100,000	$100,000
Mortgage	75,000	65,000
Cash	$ 25,000	$ 35,000

Mortgage Amortization: $10,000 or 40% on investment of $25,000.

D) *Appreciation*: Through careful selection and management, the value of real property may increase in value over time.

1. Valuation of real estate: There are several methods including replacement cost, gross income multiple and cash flow multiple or "cap" (capitalization) rate.

   – Example of a "cap" rate: If a property has a $60,000 cash flow and the market supports a 10% "cap" rate, its price would be $600,000.

2. The appreciation potential for real estate is one of the key factors in the long-term inflation hedge which can be provided by such an investment.

   – Example of inflation hedge: Assume one uses the "cap" rate to price a property. If you buy a building today and inflation drives the cost of similar buildings up over a period of time, future buildings would need to change higher rents in order to be economical. This will, assuming adequate demand for space, permit rental increases in existing buildings which would result in increased cash flows and increased market values.

– Example of leverage: With the use of borrowed funds (leverage), the amount of gain on a property can be affected. If one purchases a $600,000 property for cash and it appreciates 20%, he has realized $120,000 or a 20% gain (before taxes) on his investment. However, if he were to have used only $150,000 cash (plus a $450,000 mortgage) to purchase the property, that $120,000 gain would be equal to an 80% gain (before taxes) on his cash investment.

Note: Assuming that there had been mortgage amortization of 10% or $45,000, the gain on his investment would have been $165,000 or 137% on his cash investment.

E) *Analysis of the EFFECTIVE RETURN* from a real estate investment.

Investment
Plus: yield ..... cash flow
Less: taxes ..... shelter for the cash flow and in some instances excess losses to shelter other incomes
inflation ... with mortgage amortization potential, real estate can offer a long-term inflation hedge

Effective Return

III. REAL ESTATE INVESTMENT ALTERNATIVES

A) *Private placement:*

1. Rule 146
2. Characteristics
   – single property
   – large minimum investment per investor
   – investment often paid in installments
   – risks/reward considerations

B) *Public Offering:*

1. Securities Act of 1933

2. Characteristics
   - several properties
   - small minimum investment per investor
   - investments made in single payment
   - risks/reward considerations
3. Types
   - FHA, "shelter," income, triple-net lease

C) *Types of Offerings:*

	Return Components		
	Tax Benefits	Cash Flow	Appreciation Potential
subsidized-FHA	yes	limited	limited
conventional-"shelter"	yes	yes	yes
conventional-"income"	limited	yes	yes
triple-net lease	limited	yes	limited

D) *Tax benefits:* single versus installment investments.

	Installment			Single Payment		
	Amount Invested	Loss as % of Amount Invested	Amount of Tax Benefits	Amount Invested	Loss as % of Amount Invested	Amount of Tax Benefits
Year 1	$ 60	100%	$ 60	$100	55%	$ 55
Year 2	30	80	24		20	20
Year 3	10	80	8		17	17
	$100		$ 92	$100		$ 92

Note: the total dollar amount of tax benefits are the same at the end of three years.

E) *Other important investment consideration:*

1. Real estate cycle
   - developmental phase
   - rent-up phase
   - operational phase

2. Type of Property
   - residential
   - commercial
   - industrial
   - special purpose

IV. RETURN ANALYSIS TECHNIQUES

A) *Total return and average return*

Year	Reported Loss		Tax Savings*		"Sheltered" Cash Flow
1	40%		20%		2%
2	20		10		4
3	18		9		6
4	16		8		6
		Total	47%	plus	18% = 65%
		Average	65%	divided by	4 = 16%

*assuming 50% tax bracket

B) *Payback period:*

Year	Reported Loss	Tax Savings*	"Sheltered" Cash Flow	Cumulative Benefits
1	40%	20%	2%	22%
2	20	10	4	36
3	18	9	6	51
4	16	8	6	65
5	14	7	6	78
6	12	6	6	90
7	10	5	6	101

*assuming a 50% tax bracket

C) *Effective yield:* In comparing real estate investments to other alternatives, one of the ways in which you can make an allowance for the tax benefits is to treat them as a return of principal. Thus, you can calculate the yield in much the same way you would if you bought a bond at a discount.

Year	Tax Savings	Net Investment*	"Sheltered" Cash Flow	Effective Yield
1	$20	$80	$2	2%
2	10	70	5	6
3	9	61	6	9
4	8	53	6	10

*assuming initial investment of $100.

D) *Discounted return on investment (internal rate of return).*

In making a discounted ROI analysis one uses a discount rate to equate future payments to a "present value." Having established this common reference one can compare two or more investments with income streams that differ in both their timing and absolute amounts of return.

EXAMPLE A
"shelter"

Property—"first user" property that is conventionally financed.

Characteristics

a) Property has no previous operating history which can be used in assessing the value or risks.
b) Cash flow that is substantially "sheltered" from taxes over life of property.
c) Excess tax losses, which can be used to "shelter" income from other sources, during the early years of the operation of the property.

Assumptions

Purchase price	$350,000
Mortgage	250,000
Cash	$100,000

Appreciation	2% per year on the total value of the property
Mortgage amortization	1% per year on the mortgage or 2½% per year on the cash
Tax Bracket of owner	50%

Calculation of Return (numbers in $000's)

Year	Reported Losses	Tax Savings*	Cash Flow	Total Benefits	Cumulative Benefits
1	$40	$20	$2	$ 22	$ 22
2	20	10	4	14	36
3	18	9	6	15	51
4	16	8	6	14	65
5	14	7	6	13	78
6	12	6	6	12	90
7	10	5	6	11	101
8	8	4	6	10	111
9	6	3	6	9	120
10	4	2	6	8	128
10	After-tax proceeds on sale			$109	$237

Total Return: $237,000 or 237%

Average Annual Return: $13,700 or 13.7%

Payback Period: 7 years

Discounted Rate of Return: 16%

NOTE: All of the above are *after-tax* returns.

*No consideration has been given to the tax consequences resulting from the fact that excess depreciation (the amount by which accelerated depreciation exceeds straight line depreciation) will be treated as a tax preference under the Tax Reform Act of 1976.

EXAMPLE B
"income"

Property—"existing" property that is conventionally financed.

Characteristics

a) Property has previous operating history which can be used in assessing value or risks.
b) Cash flow that is substantially "sheltered" from taxes over life of property.
c) Little or no excess tax losses to "shelter" income from other sources.

Assumptions

Purchase price	$300,000
Mortgage	200,000
Cash	$100,000
Appreciation	2% per year on the total value of the property
Mortgage amortization	1.5% per year on the mortgage or 3% per year on the cash
Tax Bracket of owner	30%

Calculation of Return (numbers in $000's)

Year	Reported Losses	Tax Savings	Cash Flow	Total Benefits	Cumulative Benefits
1	$6	$1.8	$0	$ 1.8	$ 1.8
2	5	1.5	7	8.5	10.3
3	4	1.2	7	8.2	18.5
4	3	.9	7	7.9	26.4
5	2	.6	7	7.6	34.0
6	1	.3	7	7.3	41.3
7	0	0	7	7.0	48.3
8	(1)	(.3)	7	6.7	55.0
9	(2)	(.6)	7	6.4	61.4
10	(3)	(.9)	7	6.1	67.5
10	After-tax proceeds on sale			$142.0	$209.5

Total Return: $209,500 or 209%

Average Annual Return: $10,950 or 10.9%

Payback Period: 10 years (if property is sold)

Discounted Rate of Return: 10%

NOTE: All of the above are *after-tax* returns.

COMMERCIAL REAL ESTATE

INTRODUCTION

COMMERCIAL, LTD. is a limited partnership formed to acquire, own and operate a suburban office park.

The Partnership will purchase the Project from an unaffiliated Seller. The purchase price of $3,975,000, is payable as follows: $3,000,000 by executing and delivering to Seller at Closing the Purchase Money Note and by paying the $975,000 balance of the purchase price in cash at Closing.

The Partnership shall finance the initial purchase of the Project with a portion of the subscriptions made by the Partners. The Purchase Money Note executed and delivered at Closing will have a full prepayment privilege, shall be payable interest only on a monthly basis at the rate of twelve (12%) percent per annum for the first twenty-four (24) months inclusive, and at the rate of eleven and seventy-five one hundred (11.75%) percent per annum through maturity. Commencing on the first day of June, Year 3, and continuing on the first day of each and every month thereafter through and including the first day of April, Year 10, principal and interest shall be due and payable in equal, consecutive monthly installments in the amount of $30,282 each. The entire outstanding principal balance, together with accrued but unpaid interest, shall be due and payable in full on the first day of May, Year 10. Provided, however, the entire outstanding principal balance, together with accrued but unpaid interest, shall at the option of Seller upon at least ninety (90) days written notice to the Partnership, be due and payable in full on the first day of May, Year 8, in the event that the term of the Public Utility Leases are extended in writing by the Partnership or its successor in title thereto for a minimum of three years at least the market rate prevailing at the time of extension.

The Limited Partners will invest an aggregate of $1,505,000 in the Partnership which amount is divided into 35 Units or $43,000 per Unit. The Units will be sold to no more than 35 purchasers as defined in the Rule, and each Limited Partner will be required to purchase at least one Unit. However, the General Partners reserve the right to accept subscriptions for less than one Unit.

The $43,000 will be payable in two installments, as follows: $38,000 at the time of executing the Subscription Agreement and $5,000 on April 30, Year 2. In the event that any portion of the Public Utility Leases are terminated at any time after February Year 2, the Limited Partners may be required to contribute up to an additional $8,500 per Unit during the period after February 28, Year 2 to the termination of the Partnership. Upon signing the Subscription Agreement, each investor will be required to give the Partnership his or her promissory notes evidencing his or her obligation to pay the second installment and the conditional installment.

THE PROJECT

Property Description

It is a suburban office park containing 98,696 square feet in 2 2-story buildings on an 8.7 acre site. The buildings are masonry and glass with flat built-up roofs on metal decks. The Project was built in seven years, is landscaped, and provides free parking for 522 cars or 5.3 spaces for each 1,000 square feet of net rentable space.

The Project is 86.2% occupied, and the tenants of the Project pay rents ranging from $6.56 to $9.50 per square foot. Vacant space is being offered at $9.00 to $9.50 per square foot.

Public Utility leases approximately 49% of the office space available within the Project. The leases with Public Utility will expire in February Year 9; however, Public Utility has the option of terminating these leases at any time after February Year 2. In the event that any such lease is cancelled at any time after February Year 2, the Partnership can require an additional capital contribution of $8,500 per Unit to fund short term rent loss for tenant improvements. There can be no assurance that new tenants could be found to occupy any space vacated by Public Utility.

The General Partners have been informed that an existing tenant intends to vacate the 5,672 square feet it occupies when its lease expires on April 30, Year 1. This will reduce occupancy to 80.5% if no new tenants are found before the Closing.

The architectural design of the buildings permits all of the tenants to have a private entrance directly from the outside. The interior walls and partitions are painted of vinyl clad 1/2″ gypsum board over metal studs; standard floor covering is wall-to-wall carpeting with vinyl tile flooring in some areas. The ceilings are suspended acoustical tile with recessed florescent lighting and heating/air conditioning vents. The Project is served by underground electrical and telephone cables.

The exteriors of the buildings are brick with field stone accent on concrete block, on structural steel framing with some aluminum facia. Floors are concrete on slab, on grade level, and lightweight concrete on metal deck on the second floor. Fenestration is single pane glass with one inch slat horizontal blinds. Lavatories are within the suites. They have simulated marble vanities, painted or vinyl walls and tile floors. The central heating ventilation and air conditioning system is electric with four units on each building. They are multi-zone systems with fan powered mixing boxes and individual thermostats. The system is equipped with timers and economizers.

Generally, the Partnership pays for electricity, water, sewerage, refuse removal, and janitorial service, which is typical in the leasing of office space in the area.

CAPITALIZATION

The following is a description of the funds that are anticipated to be available for the acquisition of the Project and related expenses:

Purchase Money Note	$3,000,000
Limited Partner's Initial Capital Contribution	$1,330,000
TOTAL	$4,330,000

ESTIMATED USE OF PROCEEDS

The following is an outline of the estimated use of the contributions by the Limited Partners and the General Partners showing the use of the proceeds.

From Proceeds Received at Closing:	Amount	Percentage of Total Proceeds
Down Payment on Property	$ 975,000	65.0%
Capital Reserve	83,000	5.5%
Operating Reserve	55,600	3.5%
Closing, Syndication and Escrow Expense	35,000	2.5%
Due Diligence Expense	5,000	.5%
Broker-dealer Commission	106,400	7.0%
Initial Management Fee	70,000	4.5%
Subtotal:	$1,330,000	88.5%
From Proceeds Received on April 30, Year 2:		
Additional Capital and Operating Reserve	$ 101,000	6.5%
General Partners Fee	$ 60,000	4.0%
Broker-dealer Commission	$ 14,000	1.0%
Subtotal:	$ 175,000	11.5%
TOTAL	$1,505,000	100.0%

Proceeds Received From Conditional Contributions after February 28, Year 2	Amount	Percentage of Proceeds Received after February Year 2
Capital and Rent Loss Reserve	$273,700	92.0%
Broker-dealer Commission	23,800	8.0%
TOTAL	$297,500	100.0%

COMPENSATION TO THE GENERAL PARTNERS AND AFFILIATES

The following is a summary of the compensation to be paid to the General Partners and certain of their affiliates in connection with the transactions contemplated herein.

Investment Stage

1. Management Fee at Closing
   - Marketing Analysis
   - Marketing Administration
   - Financial Analysis
   - Financial Administration
   - Development of New Rent and Marketing Structure — $70,000
2. Fee on April 30, Year 2
   - Marketing Analysis
   - Marketing Administration
   - Financial Analysis
   - Financial Administration
   - Development of New Rent and Marketing Structure — $60,000
3. All costs incurred by the General Partners or their affiliates in organizing the Partnership and purchasing the Project, including the $25,000 earnest money deposit, shall be borne by the Partnership.

Operational Stage

1. Tax Loss Accrual to General Partners individually.
2. Cash Flow Participation—Cash Flow will be distributed 99% to the Limited Partners and 1% to the General Partners until the Limited Partners have received a 7% cumulative, non-compounding preferred return on their capital contributions. Thereafter, Cash Flow will be distributed 95% to the Limited Partners and 5% to the General Partners. No distributions of Cash Flow of the Partnership are anticipated during the first thirty-two (32) months of operation.

3. Management Fee–The Partnership shall enter into a management agreement with Properties, Inc., providing for the operation and management by Properties, Inc., of the Project for a fee equal to 5% of the Gross Revenues derived from the Project. A portion of the management fee equal to 1% of the Gross Revenues derived from the Project will be paid only if Budgeted Cash Flow of the Project is achieved on an annual basis. The General Partners have a controlling equity interest in Properties, Inc.

Liquidation Stage

1. Subordinated Incentive Fee–After the Limited Partners have received a cumulative, non-compounding return of 7% on their investment from Cash Flow or Sales Proceeds, the General Partners shall receive 28% of the Sales Proceeds resulting from a sale of the Project.

2. Sales of Refinancing Commission–The General Partners shall receive a sales commission of 1% of the proceeds from the sale of the Project. The General Partners shall also be entitled to 1% of the excess of the new debt incurred pursuant to a refinancing over the amount of existing debt cancelled.

3. Service fees payable if the Project is sold and the Partnership retains a mortgage. Such fees will be payable monthly in accordance with the payment schedule of the mortgage, and shall be based on the face amount of the mortgage as determined at the beginning of each year. No other fees will be earned during this period.

(a) Wraparound Mortgage	0.25% of the face amount of the mortgage.
(b) Second Mortgage	0.50% of the face amount of the mortgage.

BENEFITS OF A COMMERCIAL REAL ESTATE FUND

Cash Flow and Taxable Income Projections:

	Year 1 8 Mo.		Year 2		Year 3		Year 4		Year 5		Year 6	
	Cash	Tax	Cash	Tax	Cash	Tax	Cash	Tax	Cash	Tax	Cash	Tax
Gross Income (1)												
Cent. Tenants	207,500	207,500	445,500	445,500	490,000	490,000	527,000	527,000	569,000	569,000	614,500	614,500
Public Utility	223,500	223,500	349,000	349,000	363,000	363,000	377,500	377,500	392,500	392,500	408,000	408,000
	431,000	431,000	794,500	794,500	853,000	853,000	904,500	904,500	961,500	961,500	1,022,500	1,022,500
Operating Expenses (2) $3.75/sq. ft.	(246,500)	(246,500)	(399,500)	(399,500)	(431,500)	(431,500)	(466,000)	(466,000)	(503,500)	(503,500)	(544,000)	(544,000)
Net Income	184,500	184,500	395,000	395,000	421,500	421,500	438,500	438,500	458,000	458,000	478,500	478,500
Debt Service	(239,760)		(360,000)		(362,000)		(363,600)		(363,600)		(363,600)	
Interest		(239,760)		(360,000)		(354,500)		(351,500)		(350,000)		(348,500)
Cash Flow	(55,260)		35,000		59,500		74,900		94,400		114,900	
General Partners Fee	(70,000)	(50,000)	(60,000)	(50,000)								
Depreciation (3)		(465,183)		(668,608)		(582,669)		(299,682)		(174,857)		(170,190)
Extraordinary 1st & 2nd Year Expense (4)		(50,000)		(25,000)								
Taxable Loss		(620,443)		(708,600)		(515,669)		(212,682)		(66,857)		(40,190)
Estimated Taxable Income (Loss) per 1/35 Partnership Interest		(16,841)		(19,234)		(13,997)		(5,773)		(1,815)		(1,091)

(1) Gross In come - Year 1 based on current rent roll at current 85% occupancy. Anticipated leasing activity during this year offset by the planned move out of one tenant having 5,672 sq. ft. (5½%) of the project's space. Year 2 and Year 3 based on 95% occupancy with Public Utility lease escalated at 4% per year based on recent increases in operating expenses and using the current schedule for general office space increase at 10% per year to reflect current escalation clauses in all multi-year leases and market rates on vacant space. Year 4 to Year 8 based on the Public Utility lease continuing to escalate at 4% and general office space (total 50,443 sq. ft.) leasing at $11.000 per square foot increased at 8% as all but 17% of the existing general office leases expire before Year 4. Year 9 (Public Utility lease expires 2/Year 9) based on the entire park being leased at $15 per sq. ft. at an occupancy rate of 80% to compensate for the two months Public Utility occupies its space and the lease up of this space. Year 10 based on previous years rate increased 8% at 95% occupancy.

(2) Operating Expenses increased at 8% per year.

(3) Includes most organization expenses and fees.

(4) Includes fees for tax advice, plus items listed under capital items, which can be expensed.

Cash Flow and Taxable Income Projections:

	Year 7		Year 8		Year 9		Year 10	
	Cash	Tax	Cash	Tax	Cash	Tax	Cash	Tax
Gross Income (1) Cen. Tenants	663,500	663,500	716,500	716,500	1,184,500	1,184,500	1,519,000	1,519,000
Public Utility	424,500	424,500	441,500	441,500				
	1,088,000	1,088,000	1,158,000	1,158,000	1,184,500	1,184,500	1,519,000	1,519,000
Operating Expenses (2) $3.75/sq. ft.	(587,500)	(587,500)	(634,500)	(634,500)	(685,500)	(685,500)	(740,500)	(740,500)
Net Income	500,500	500,500	523,500	523,500	499,000	499,000	778,500	778,500
Debt Service	(363,600)		(363,600)		(363,600)		Matures 5/Year 10	
Interest		(347,000)		(345,000)		(341,000)		
Cash Flow	136,900		159,900		135,400			
General Partners Fee								
Depreciation (3)		(167,857)		(122,619)		(100,000)		(100,000)
Extraordinary 1st & 2nd Year Expense (4)								
Taxable Loss		(14,357)		55,881		58,000		
Estimated Taxable Income (Loss) per 1/35 Partnership Interest		(390)		1,517		1,574		

Potential in 8 2/3 years:

Gross Potential Income	$ 1,519,000
Gross Rent Multiplier	x 7.5
Sales Price	$11,392,500
Rehabilitation of Public Utility Space	(450,000)
Sales Expense	(230,000)
Mortgage Balance	(2,870,000)
Net Proceeds	$ 7,842,500
Original Investment	1,505,000
Limited Partners Share of Gain	4,563,000
Total Returned	$ 6,068,000
1/35 Unit	173,371
Cash Flow During Holding Period	22,300
Cash Tax Savings @ 50% Bracket	29,365
Sub Total	$ 225,036
Capital Gain Tax @ 28%	
Distribution at Sale	173,371
Original Investment	(43,000)
	$ 130,371
Tax Sheltered Distributions During Holding Period	16,292
	$ 146,663
	x .28%
	$ 41,065

Recap of Total Benefit After Taxes - On $43,000 Investment

Sub Total from Above	$ 225,036
Capital Gains Tax	41,065
After Tax Return	$ 183,971

NOTE: Computations assume an average distribution of 7% per year - if not received annually, limited partners would receive same from sale or refinancing proceeds.

Investors Position at End of 6 2/3 Years - 50% Bracket

Original Cash Invested	\$ 43,000
Cash Tax Savings = 50% Bracket	
(\$58,731 x 50%)	(29,365)
Tax Sheltered Cash Flow	(14,376)
Cash Basis in Investment	(\$ 741)

Investors Position at End of 6 2/3 Years - 70% Bracket

Original Cash Invested	\$ 43,000
Cash Tax Savings - 70% Bracket	
(\$58,731 x 70%)	(41,112)
Tax Sheltered Cash Flow	(14,376)
Cash Basis in Investment	(\$ 12,488)

Investors Position at End of 4 2/3 Years - 50% Bracket

Original Cash Invested	\$ 43,000
Cash Tax Savings - 50% Bracket	
(\$57,346 x 50%)	(28,673)
Tax Sheltered Cash Flow	(7,360)
Cash Basis in Investment	\$ 6,967

Investors Position at End of 4 2/3 Years - 70% Bracket

Original Cash Invested	\$ 43,000
Cash Tax Savings - 70% Bracket	
(\$57,346 x 70%)	(40,142)
Tax Sheltered Cash Flow	(7,360)
Cash Basis in Investment	(\$ 4,502)

Investors Position at End of 8 2/3 Years - 50% Bracket

Original Cash Invested	\$ 43,000
Cash Tax Savings - 50% Bracket	(29,365)
Tax Sheltered Cash Flow	(16,292)
Non-Sheltered Cash Flow	(6,008)
Cash Basis in Investment	(\$ 8,665)

Investors Position at End of 8 2/3 Years - 70% Bracket

Original Cash Invested	$ 43,000
Cash Tax Savings - 70% Bracket	(41,112)
Tax Sheltered Cash Flow	(16,292)
Non-Sheltered Cash Flow	(6,008)
Cash Basis in Investment	($ 20,412)

FINANCIAL BENEFITS TO A LIMITED PARTNERSHIP ASSUMING THE ACHIEVEMENT OF PRO FORMA RESULTS

Year	Capital Contribution	Federal Income Tax Deduction	Tax Free Cash Flow
1 (8 mos)	$38,000	$16,841	$ -0-
2	5,000	19,084	933
3	-0-	13,915	1,638
4	-0-	5,732	2,119
5	-0-	1,774	2,670
6	-0-	1,050	3,225
7	-0-	355	3,791
Total	$43,000	$58,731	$14,376

PERCENTAGE RETURNS TO AN INVESTOR IN THE 50% TAX BRACKET INCLUDING THE DOLLAR VALUE OF TAX WRITE-OFFS*

Year	Amount at Risk	Tax Saving	Tax Free Cash Flow	Total Return	% Return on Amount at Risk	% Return Full Sub. ($43,000)
1	$38,000	$8,420	$ -0-	$ 8,420	22%	19.5%
2	34,980	9,542	933	10,475	30%	24.3%
3	24,505	6,958	1,638	8,596	35%	20.0%
4	15,909	2,866	2,119	4,985	31%	11.6%
5	10,924	887	2,670	3,557	32%	8.3%
6	7,367	525	3,225	3,750	51%	8.7%
7	3,617	168	3,791	3,959	109%	9.2%

*Do not include the potential for capital gains.

FINANCIAL BENEFITS TO A LIMITED PARTNERSHIP ASSUMING THE ACHIVEMENT OF PRO FORMA RESULTS

Year	Capital Contribution	Federal Income Tax Deduction	Tax Free Cash Flow
1 (8 mos)	$38,000	$16,841	$ -0-
2	5,000	19,084	933
3	-0-	13,915	1,638
4	-0-	5,732	2,119
5	-0-	1,774	2,670
6	-0-	1,050	3,225
7	-0-	355	3,791
Total	$43,000	$58,731	$14,376

PERCENTAGE RETURNS TO AN INVESTOR IN THE 60% TAX BRACKET INCLUDING THE DOLLAR VALUE OF TAX WRITE-OFFS*

Year	Amount at Risk	Tax Saving	Tax Free Cash Flow	Total Return	% Return on Amount at Risk	% Return Full Sub. ($43,000)
1	$38,000	$10,105	$ -0-	$10,105	27%	23.5%
2	32,895	11,450	933	12,383	38%	28.6%
3	20,512	8,349	1,638	9,987	49%	23.2%
4	10,525	3,439	2,119	5,558	53%	12.9%
5	4,967	1,064	2,670	3,734	75%	8.7%
6	1,233	630	3,225	3,855	312%	9.0%

*Do not include the potential for capital gains.

FINANCIAL BENEFITS TO A LIMITED PARTNERSHIP ASSUMING THE ACHIEVEMENT OF PRO FORMA RESULTS

Year	Capital Contribution	Federal Income Tax Deduction	Tax Free Cash Flow
1 (8 mos)	$38,000	$16,841	$ -0-
2	5,000	19,084	933
3	-0-	13,915	1,638
4	-0-	5,732	2,119
5	-0-	1,774	2,670
6	-0-	1,050	3,225
7	-0-	355	3,791
	$43,000	$58,731	$14,376

PERCENTAGE RETURNS TO AN INVESTOR IN THE 70% TAX BRACKET INCLUDING THE DOLLAR VALUE OF TAX WRITE-OFFS*

Year	Amount at Risk	Tax Saving	Tax Free Cash Flow	Total Return	% Return on Amount at Risk	% Return on Full Sub. ($43,000)
1	$38,000	$11,789	$ -0-	$11,789	31%	27.4%
2	31,211	13,358	933	14,291	46%	33.2%
3	16,920	9,740	1,638	11,378	67%	26.5%
4	5,542	4,012	2,119	6,131	110%	14.3%

*Do not include the potential for capital gains.

RISKS OF A COMMERCIAL REAL ESTATE FUND

Decline in Tax Losses. One of the important aspects of this investment is its tax consequences. In the early years, a Partner should realize a substantial tax loss, due primarily to the Partnership's use of depreciation and the interest costs of the Purchase Money Note. As is illustrated in the attached Projections, the tax loss from this investment is expected to be realized beginning in Year 1. It is anticipated that the tax losses from the Project will decline to the point at which the taxable income from the Project will exceed its Cash Flow. This situation, known as the "crossover point," will arise sometime after the maturity of the Purchase Money Note and the refinancing of the Project, although it is presently impossible to predict the precise year in which this will occur. At such time, a Partner will be taxed on more money than he or she receives from his or her investment. The tax due in such later years could exceed the monies distributable from the Partnership. See "Federal Tax Consequences" and also the Projections attached to this Memorandum.

Balloon Payment. The Purchase Money Note is due nine years from Closing, at which time a balloon payment of approximately $2,870,000 will be due. Under certain circumstances, the Purchase Money Note will be due seven years from Closing, at which time a balloon payment of approximately $2,911,200 will be due. Prior to the date when the Purchase Money Note becomes due, the Partnership will be required to sell, refinance or otherwise to make provision for the payment of the $2,870,000 or $2,911,200, respectively, due at maturity. There can be no assurance that a sale, refinancing or other arrangements will be possible at the time of maturity of the Purchase Money Note or at such earlier time as may be satisfactory to the Partnership given all of the facts and circumstances surrounding the Project at any one point in time.

TAX ASPECTS OF A COMMERCIAL REAL ESTATE FUND

Tax Losses Resulting from the Ownership of Real Property Decline from Year to Year

It is anticipated that the Partnership's losses recognized for tax purposes from the ownership and operation of the Project will decline over time, and ultimately result in taxable income in excess of Cash Flow from normal operations. This is due to two principal reasons. First, the amount of depreciation deductions available annually under an accelerated depreciation method, and certain nonrecurrent fees, are larger or occur only in the early years. Second, the debt service on a level payment mortgage is such that each year the amount of amortization of debt principal (which is non-deductible in computing taxable income or loss) increases and the amount of deductible interest decreases. The non-cash deduction for depreciation permits the Partnership to use an equal amount of operating income, without tax thereon, to pay the non-deductible mortgage principal payments. As a result of the decline in deductions for interest, depreciation and other nonrecurrent items, and the increase in non-deductible amortization payments, it is expected that the tax losses from the project will decline to the point at which the taxable income from the project will exceed its cash flow. This crossover point will occur some time after the maturity of the purchase money note and the refinancing of the project, although it is presently impossible to predict the precise year in which this will occur.

Sale and Deduction Recapture

If the Partnership sells the Project or if a Limited Partner sells or gives away his or her interest in the Partnership, the transferor will realize a taxable gain to the extent that the total of cash plus the fair market value of the property received on the transfer, plus the outstanding principal amount of and accrued interest on the Partnership's indebtedness (or in the case of a transfer of a Partnership interest by a Partner, the transferor's pro rata share of such amount) at the time of such sale exceeds the seller's tax basis for the property sold. Gain realized by the Partnership on sale or other disposition of the Project (or by a Partner on the sale of an interest) will generally be treated as long-term capital gain (if the Project, or the interest, has been held longer than 12 months) except for the portion thereof which is taxable as ordinary income due to depreciation recapture existing with respect to the Project.

Depreciation recapture is that portion of gain realized or deemed realized on a sale or other disposition which is attributable to depreciation of personal property and to the excess accelerated depreciation over straight-line depreciation on real property. In the case of a sale by a Partner of an interest in the Partnership, depreciation recapture is the Partner's pro rata share of the depreciation recapture which would result from the disposition by the Partnership of its property at the time of the Partner's disposition of the interest in question. Depreciation recapture can also occur with respect to a gift or other disposition of either Partnership property or a Partnership interest.

In such instances, the fair market value of the depreciable property or pro rata share thereof is considerated to be sales consideration. The Partnership will acquire property with respect to which accelerated depreciation deductions will be taken. It is not presently possible to estimate the potential gain attributable to depreciable property and therefor the amount of any ordinary gain.

It should be noted that the amount of taxable gain realized on a sale and, possibly, the income taxes attributable thereto, may exceed any proceeds therefrom if the depreciation deductions have reduced the tax basis of the Project to less than the amount of the outstanding mortgage balances. Other circumstances involving a sale of the Project which might result in the Partners not receiving sufficient cash with which to pay any tax liability generated by the sale include: (i) the sale or transfer of the Project pursuant to foreclosure of a mortgage, or other financing instrument, as described below; (ii) the sale of the Project at a time when all or part of the net proceeds thereof may have to be retained by the Partnership to support its remaining operations; or (iii) the sale of the Project for proceeds which include non-liquid assets, such as promissory notes of the purchaser.

Foreclosure, Condemnation, Etc.

Investors should be aware that future tax benefits to the Partnership may be eliminated by the early disposition of the Project, resulting from, for example, foreclosure of a mortgage or any other involuntary act, i.e., condemnation, resulting in such disposition.

If a default occurs under the Purchase Money Note and the mortgagee forecloses or accepts a deed in lieu of foreclosure, the Partnership will realize a taxable gain or loss equal to the excess or deficiency, as the case may be, of the amount of the outstanding mortgages over the then depreciated basis of that portion of the Project conveyed. A portion of any gain realized may be treated as ordinary income.

To the extent that such income is not offset by other losses of the Partnership during the year in which foreclosure takes place, each Partner will be taxable on his or her distributive share of such income even though the investor may receive no cash distribution from the Partnership and will thus have a tax liability without a distribution of cash for use in paying such liability.

If upon foreclosure there is any reportable loss, each Partner would treat his or her share thereof under section 1231 of the Code.

Refinancing of Partnership Property

No gain or loss will be recognized on the refinancing of Partnership obligations as long as the new mortgage is non-recourse and equals or exceeds the unpaid balance of the old obligation. Any refinancing proceeds distributed to the Partners would reduce the tax basis of the distributee's interest in the Partnership but not be taxable income to the Partner if at the time of distribution the distributee's tax basis in his or her Partnership interest equals or exceeds the amount distributed. Each Limited Partner will increase the tax basis in his or her Partnership interest by such Partner's pro rata share of the portion of such refinancing which constituted "non-recourse liabilities" but the total basis of the Partners attributable to the debt to which the Project is subject may not exceed the fair market value of the property. Any increase in indebtedness will not produce an asset with respect to which additional depreciation deductions can be taken unless the proceeds are used to acquire depreciable property.

MOBILE HOME PARK INDUSTRY

Because of the high cost of traditional housing, a mobile home program is shown below.

A mobile home park is designed to accommodate detached single-family dwellings which are manufactured offsite and not of a permanent nature. Such dwellings, commonly referred to as mobile homes or "coaches" (which should be distinguished from travel trailers) are manufactured in a variety of styles and sizes. In substantially occupied and better equipped parks, coaches, once located, are rarely transported to another site and are typically sold by owners to subsequent occupants.

The modern mobile home park is limited, as is the case with any other real property development providing housing, by factors such as geography, topography, size and funds available for development. Generally, modern mobile home park developments contain streets, buildings for recreation, gutters, green areas, various utility facilities and other common facilities, which, as distinguished from the mobile homes, are the property of the park owner. In addition to such general improvements, certain mobile home parks include luxury improvements, such as water recreational facilities (swimming pools and boating), restaurants, golf courses, and other items. Some mobile home parks also provide supervised and professionally planned leisure time activities.

Each owner of a mobile home leases the site on which it is located from the owner of the park, typically under some form of lease agreement. The mobile home is placed on the site by its owner-occupant (usually on top of concrete blocks) and landscaping is generally undertaken by the coach owner.

Management of a mobile home park typically includes maintenance of common areas, such as street repair and landscaping, and also may include grass cutting and utility maintenance. Trash removal may also be provided. Utility service to occupants is conducted in a variety of ways: in some parks, mobile home occupants are charged directly by the utility companies; in others (such as the Park) the park owner is metered for the utility charges and subcharges the mobile home occupant; in still other cases, the mobile home park owner pays the amount charged for the utility services, and the rentals paid by the occupants of the coaches include utility charges.

SUMMARY OF THE OFFERING

Securities Offered

The securities being offered are investments in a limited partnership which has agreed to acquire a mobile home park community. Two separate securities, $450,000 of limited partnership units ("Partnership Units") and $450,000 of partnership nonrecourse promissory notes bearing interest at the rate of 16% per annum ("Promissory Notes") and being offered by the Partnership. For each Partnership Unit purchased by an investor, an investor will also be required to purchase Promissory Notes in the aggregate principal amount of $18,000.

Amount of Offering

The Partnership is offering an aggregate of 25 Partnership Units in the amount of $18,000 each in the aggregate amount of $450,000 and Promissory Notes in the aggregate principal amount of $450,000. Each investor shall agree to subscribe for at least one combined share which is composed of one (1) Partnership Unit ($18,000) and a Promissory Note in the principal amount of $18,000 aggregating $36,000. The investor's minimum investment of $36,000 is payable in three installments. The first installment of $12,000 is paid upon the signing of the Subscription Agreement. The second installment of $12,000 is payable on or before June 30, Year Two; and the third installment of $12,000 is payable on or before June 30, Year Three. At the Closing Date, the Partnership shall issue to the investors Promissory Notes in the face amount of $6,000 per Combined Share subscribed and shall thereafter issue two additional Promissory Notes to such purchasers in the amount of $6,000 per Combined Share subscribed upon receipt by the Partnership of the purchasers installment payments on June 30, Year Two, and June 30, Year Three. The obligation of the subscriber to pay the second and third installments is evidenced by a Subscription Note.

Partnership Business

The Partnership intends to purchase, own and operate a 191-site mobile home park community. The Partnership will enter into a Management Contract with Development, Ltd., an affiliate of the General Partners, pursuant to which Development, Ltd. will manage and supervise the daily operations of the Park.

Partnership Investment Objectives and Policies

The Partnership will purchase the Park with a view towards: (1) generating distributions of Disbursable Cash expected to commence in Year Five; (2) obtaining capital appreciation of the Park; (3) meeting payments of Debt Service, including payments of principal and interest on the Promissory Notes; (4) certain tax benefits; (5) potential for gain from appreciation in value of the Park and build up of equity through reduction of indebtedness, which gain, if any, would be realized upon the Sale or Refinancing of the Park; and (6) to obtain financing which would permit early redemption of the Promissory Notes.

Compensation to General Partners and Affiliates

The General Partners and their Affiliates will receive substantial fees and distributions in connection with the purchase, management, sale or refinancing of the Park.

Limited Partners' Share of Cash Distributions

Through the Partnership fiscal year, Year Five, the Limited Partners will receive 99% of all Disbursable Cash. Beginning in Partnership fiscal year, Year Six, the Limited Partners will receive Disbursable Cash, if available, in the greater amount of 10% of their Adjusted Capital Contribution or 50% of all Disbursable Cash, but in no event greater than 99% of Disbursable Cash. It is not anticipated that there will be any distribution of Disbursable Cash prior to Year Five.

Limited Partners' Share of Sale or Refinancing Proceeds

Upon a Sale or Refinancing of the Park (or a liquidation of the Partnership which is treated as a Sale or Refinancing), to the extent of available funds each Limited Partner shall have returned to him his Capital Contribution and his pro rata share (based on the ratio of his Capital Contribution to the Capital Contribution of all Limited Partners) of 50% of any Partnership funds then remaining from such Sale or Refinancing (or liquidation).

Obligations of Partnership to Promissory Note Holders

Promissory Notes bear interest at the rate of 16 percent (16%) per annum of the principal amount outstanding. The obligation of the investor to purchase Promissory Notes is payable in three installments. Interest will accrue from the Closing Date and will be paid quarterly commencing September 30, Year One. Interest only on the Promissory Notes will be paid through December 31, Year Three. After that date the principal amount of the Promissory Notes will be amortized over a twenty-five year amortization schedule providing for level payments of principal and interest. The Promissory Notes may be redeemed by the Partnership without penalty, in whole or in part, prior to their maturity dates. Until payment in full of the principal and interest of the Promissory Notes, the holders thereof have a preferential right over Limited Partner Unit Holders to Sale or Refinancing Proceeds. Promissory Notes are not secured by any specified Partnership property nor by any sinking fund. Neither the General Partners nor any of the Limited Partners are personally liable for payment of the Promissory Notes. The Promissory Note Holders shall have recourse as general creditors to assets of the Partnership or proceeds of Sale or Refinancing of the Park after satisfaction of the claims of secured creditors thereon. The Promissory Notes will be issued pursuant to the terms of a Trust Indenture between the Partnership and co-trustees.

Leverage

The Partnership will purchase the Park from an Affiliate pursuant to the terms of a land contract for a purchase price of $1,360,000 (which includes certain estimated prepaid items such as prepaid rent, general taxes, security deposits, insurance premiums and utility bills). Total Partnership indebtedness, including the aggregate principal amount of Promissory Notes on June 30, Year Three, will be approximately 77% of the total purchase price of the Park.

Termination of the Partnership

The Partnership will terminate on December 31, Year 30, unless sooner terminated as provided in the Partnership Agreement.

Depreciation Method

The Partnership intends to depreciate the Park using straight-line methods of depreciation.

PRO FORMA BALANCE SHEET (1)
AT JULY 1, YEAR 1

ASSETS		
Property and improvements:		
Land		$ 90,000
Roads		280,000
Mobile home park improvements		935,000
Community buildings		40,000
Equipment		15,000
		$1,360,000
Organization costs		10,000
General Partners' Guarantee Obligation		25,000
Working Capital Reserve		505
		$1,395,505
LIABILITIES		
Land Contract Indebtedness		$1,175,505
Promissory Notes		150,000
		$1,325,505
PARTNERS' CAPITAL		
General Partners		0
Limited Partners:		
Capital contributions	$450,000	
Less syndication expenses	80,000	
	$370,000	
Less subscriptions receivable	300,000	
		$ 70,000
		$1,395,505

FIFTY-FOUR (54) MONTH PRO FORMA STATEMENT OF PROFITS AND LOSSES FOR TAX PURPOSES AND DISBURSABLE CASH

	6 Months Year 1	Year 2	Year 3	Year 4	Year 5
Rental Income (1)	$ 98,900	$ 215,600	$233,400	$251,200	$269,000
Operating Expenses @ 38%	37,600	81,900	88,700	95,500	102,200
Operating Income exclusive of Interest, Depreciation and Management Fees	$ 61,300	$ 133,700	$144,700	$155,700	$166,800
Interest-Existing (2)	(20,200)	(40,200)	(39,800)	(39,400)	(39,000)
Down Payment Interest @ 12%	(34,500)	(52,500)	(18,000)	0	0
Interest-Promissory Notes @ 16%	(12,000)	(36,000)	(60,000)	(71,900)	(71,600)
Guarantee Fee	(25,000)	(25,000)	0	0	0
Organization Fee	(1,000)	(2,000)	(2,000)	(2,000)	(2,000)
Management Fee @ 7% (3)	(7,000)	(15,100)	(16,300)	(17,600)	(18,800)
Depreciation (4)	(41,000)	(82,000)	(82,000)	(82,000)	(82,000)
Tax (Loss)	$(79,400)	$(119,100)	$ (73,400)	$ (57,200)	$ (46,600)
Add:					
Depreciation	41,000	82,000	82,000	82,000	82,000
Guarantee Fee	25,000	25,000	0	0	0
Organization Fee	1,000	2,000	2,000	2,000	2,000
Accrued Management Fee	7,000	15,100	0	0	0
Less:					
Principal Payments-Existing	(2,600)	(5,400)	(5,800)	(6,200)	(6,600)
Principal Payments-Partner's Notes	0	0	0	(1,500)	(1,800)
Repayment of Accrued Management Fee and Year 1 Negative Cash Flow	0	0	(4,800)	(19,100)	(6,200)
Cash Flow (5)	$ (8,000)	$ 0	$ 0	$ 0	$ 22,800

Notes

(1) Current rentals are:

191 sites @ 89 x 12 months =	$203,988
Less vacancy factor of 3%	6,120
Total net rental income for Year 1	$197,868
½ year	98,934

Projections assume annual $8 per month per site rent increases during Year 2 through Year 5.

(2) The Partnership will purchase the Park for $1,360,000 pursuant to the terms of a land contract. The land contract provides that the Partnership will make a total down payment of $759,495 to the Seller in three installments. The first installment of $184,495 will be paid on or before June 30, Year 1; the second installment of $275,000 will be paid on or before June 30, Year 2; and the third installment of $300,000 will be paid on or before June 30, Year 3. Unpaid down payment installments will bear interest at twelve percent (12%) per annum. The remaining amount of the purchase price will bear interest at the rate of six and three-quarters percent (6¾%) per annum and requires monthly payments of principal and interest in the amount of $3,800.

(3) Development, Ltd. will receive a management fee of 7% of gross income per year.

(4) The purchase price of the Partnership's assets are allocated as follows:

Item	Amount	Useful Life	Annual Depreciation
Land	$ 90,000	-	$ -
Roads	280,000	10	28,000
Buildings	40,000	20	2,000
Improvements	935,000	20	47,000
Equipment	15,000	5	3,000
Organization Fees (amortizable)	10,000	5	2,000
Organization Fees (non-amortizable)	5,000	-	-
Syndication Fees	75,000	-	-
	$1,450,000		$82,000/year

(5) The General Partners have agreed to fund all negative cash flow through interest-free loans to the Partnership. It is anticipated that the Year 1 and Year 2 negative cash flow amount will be repaid to the Partnership during Year 4 and Year 5.

MOBILE HOME PARK INDUSTRY

PROJECTED LIMITED PARTNER'S RETURN ON INVESTMENT RESULTING FROM SALE OF PARK AT JUNE 30, YEAR 6 ASSUMING VARIOUS RATES OF APPRECIATION

(Unaudited)

ASSUMED ANNUAL RATE OF APPRECIATION (1)	0%	5%	10%
ESTIMATES PROCEEDS FROM SALE OF PARK	1,500,000	1,914,422	2,415,765
Less: Land Contract Balance	570,475	570,475	570,475
Partnership Note Balance	445,792	445,792	445,792
Limited Partner Capital Contribution	450,000	450,000	450,000
NET SALE PROCEEDS	33,733	448,155	949,498
BALANCE TO BE DISTRIBUTED	33,733	448,155	949,498
50% to Limited Partners	16,867	224,078	474,949
50% to General Partners	16,866	224,077	474,949
TOTAL PROCEEDS TO LIMITED PARTNERS	466,867	674,078	924,949
PROCEEDS PER UNIT (1/25)	18,675	26,963	36,998
TOTAL TAX BASIS	51,000	51,000	51,000
TAX BASIS PER UNIT (1/25)	2,040	2,040	2,040
TOTAL GAIN (Net Sales Proceeds Less Tax Basis)			
Capital Gain	415,867	623,078	873,949
Ordinary Income	0	0	0
TOTAL GAIN PER UNIT (1/25)	16,635	24,923	34,958

MOBILE HOME PARK INDUSTRY

PROJECTED RETURN ON INVESTMENT
0% APPRECIATION
(per Unit)

	Investor Tax Bracket		
PARTNERSHIP UNIT	30%	50%	70%
Tax Savings (2)	4,596	7,661	10,725
Cash Distributions (Cash Flow) (3)	1,368	1,368	1,368
Cash Returned at Sale	18,675	18,675	18,675
Tax on Sale			
Capital Gain	1,996	3,327	4,658
Ordinary Income	0	0	0
After-tax Proceeds	22,463	24,377	30,768
Less Capital Contributions	18,000	18,000	18,000
Net Gain	4,463	6,377	12,768
Average annual after-tax return on paid-in-cash portion of Capital Contribution (4)	6.20%	8.86%	17.73%
PARTNERSHIP NOTES			
Interest Distribution	11,330	11,330	11,330
Tax on Interest - ordinary income	3,399	5,665	7,931
Net Interest Income - after-tax	7,931	5,665	3,399

MOBILE HOME PARK INDUSTRY

PROJECTED RETURN ON INVESTMENT
5% APPRECIATION
(per Unit)

	Investor Tax Bracket		
PARTNERSHIP UNIT	30%	50%	70%
Tax Savings	4,596	7,661	10,725
Cash Distribution (Cash Flow)	1,368	1,368	1,368
Cash Returned at Sale	26,963	26,963	26,963
Tax on Sale			
Capital Gain	3,236	5,393	7,550
Ordinary Income	0	0	0
After-tax Proceeds	29,691	30,599	31,506
Less Capital Contributions	18,000	18,000	18,000
Net Gain	11,691	12,599	13,506
Average annual after-tax return on paid-in-cash portion of Capital Contribution	16.24%	17.50%	18.75%
PARTNERSHIP NOTES			
Interest Distribution	11,330	11,330	11,330
Tax on Interest - ordinary income	3,399	5,665	7,931
Net Interest Income - after-tax	7,931	5,665	3,399

MOBILE HOME PARK INDUSTRY

PROJECTED RETURN ON INVESTMENT
10% APPRECIATION
(per Unit)

	Investor Tax Bracket		
PARTNERSHIP UNIT	30%	50%	70%
Tax Savings	4,596	7,661	10.725
Cash Distribution (Cash Flow)	1,368	1,368	1,368
Cash Returned on Sale	36,998	36,998	36,998
Tax on Sale:			
Capital Gain	4,440	7,400	10,359
Ordinary Income	0	0	0
After-tax Proceeds	38,522	38,627	38,732
Less Capital Contributions	18,000	18,000	18,000
Net Gain	20,522	20,627	20,732
Average annual after-tax return on paid-in-cash portion of Capital Contribution	28.50%	28.65%	28.79%
PARTNERSHIP NOTES			
Interest Distribution	11,330	11,330	11,330
Tax on Interest - ordinary income	3,399	5,665	7,931
Net Interest Income - after-tax	7,931	5,665	3,399

Notes

(1) The assumed annual rate of appreciation is compounded annually and is based on the total amount of capital raised plus the land contract indebtedness.

(2) Tax Savings is the total projected Losses for Tax Purposes per Partnership Unit through calendar Year Five multiplied by the applicable investor tax bracket.

(3) Cash Distributions is the total projected distributions of Disbursable Cash per Unit through Year Five.

(4) The Average Annual Return on the paid-in-cash portion of Capital Contribution is determined by dividing the five-year average Net Gain by the average of the investor's paid-in cash portion of his Capital Contribution. Specifically, it is Net Gain divided by five (5) years divided by $14,000.

ANATOMY OF A TURNAROUND

The following is an article by Craig Hall that appeared in the Real Estate Review, May 1977:

A conservative route to good investment returns.

Turnaround Opportunities in Residential Properties

Craig Hall

A TURNAROUND OF an unsuccessful property is one of the avenues to profit in real estate. Turnaround opportunities exist even in prosperous times, and they are particularly available after recessions or periods of overbuilding. Converting a property into a successful turnaround requires many skills, including those of negotiation, management, marketing, and financing. But the first essential is a correct analysis of the opportunity. A candidate for successful turnaround usually exhibits the following characteristics:

☐ The property is producing substantially less income than one would expect, given its cost, size, or other characteristics.

☐ The property's location is fundamentally good. The property may have been developed prematurely for the area or the area may be temporarily overdeveloped.

☐ The basic physical plant is solid and structurally sound. Cosmetic improvements may be required, and some structural changes may be necessary, but all such defects are of a type which can be corrected.

☐ Finally, the owner is ready to admit, at least to himself, that the property has financial problems. He must inwardly welcome the chance to sell.

HOW TURNAROUND OPPORTUNITIES ARE MADE

Turnaround opportunities are created by various conditions. Each calls for a different kind of analysis. Each requires different action capacity and skills on the part of the purchaser.

The Overbuilt Market

Overbuilding is rarely the sole cause of underperforming property. More often, it is the final straw which sinks a property already vulnerable because of errors in planning or management. Nevertheless, a recession, a sharp change in an area's growth pattern, or simply too much follow-the-leader building in a limited area may cause otherwise sound projects to slide into trouble. If the overbuilding was simply cyclical, either the result of a temporary drop in the growth of demand due to a generalized recession or the result of too many projects coming onstream at one time, and if population in the area continues to grow at the old rate, eventually the vacancies will be absorbed. Possible scarcities may emerge. But financially pressed owners may not have sufficient staying power for the turnaround. Often, the recovery is beginning just when existing owners are finally ready to throw in the towel.

Craig Hall is President of the Standard Realty Group and Sports Illustrated Court Clubs, Southfield, Michigan. This article is condensed from his forthcoming book, *The Real Estate Turnaround*, to be published by Prentice-Hall, Inc.

"Monument" Properties

Sometimes a builder is driven by ego or other motivations to put more quality into a project than renters are willing to pay for. This may create a turnaround situation with the greatest potential for new owner profit. The price paid by a new owner will reflect the property's current performance, possibly the present value of its expected income stream. The new owner should not pay for the extra quality and therefore should not have to recover its cost in the rent structure. Nevertheless, the special touches such as marble windowsills and steel construction will increase the property's rentability and enhance its value over time. A variation of the monument is occasionally created when amenities are provided before the market is ready for them—for example, the installation of whirlpool baths in apartments in the Midwest in 1973.

Marketing Difficulties

A property may be in the wrong location for its market, or it may not be offering the services appropriate to its market. Identifying and correcting these problems may provide an unusually rapid turnaround.

Consider the following example:

A good fifty-unit apartment complex had operated for five years with a vacancy of fifteen to twenty units under several able managements. Each manager had attributed the vacancy problem to excessive competition in the area. Some had tried to solve it by cutting rents.

After interviewing residents, as well as some prospects who decided not to rent, a new purchaser discovered that the property was not delivering the service and snob appeal which tenants expected, given the rent levels in the building. Rents were too high for a low-income market, but services were inadequate for a high-income market. The new owner raised rents and upgraded both services and maintenance. In less than a year, the property had 100 percent occupancy and a waiting list.

Undercapitalization

Builders most commonly face this problem in periods of steeply rising construction costs and interest rates. Because they are unable to get adequate financing, they may skimp on the final construction stages, or they may be short of cash to carry them through the rent-up phase. Faced with a negative or marginal cash flow, an owner may try to get into the black by reducing maintenance and stretching out payments to suppliers. This nurtures tenant resentment and creates an unattractive property and a poor reputation in the community. Eventually, it leads to still lower rental income and a downward spiral in the viability of the troubled property.

After a property has been through the downward cycle, tenants (and even local government officials) may develop an emotional investment in the success of the turnaround owner. The new owner who starts to correct problems may be regarded as a "white knight." The community, the lender, and the tenants are eager to help him make money from his investment because he is providing a needed service in conserving and improving distressed property.

ANALYZING FOR LONG-TERM POTENTIAL

Determining that a residential property is indeed a turnaround opportunity requires substantial analytical effort and skills. The prospective owner must proceed with due deliberation, making full use of the myriad sources of information available to him.

Will the Market Get Better?

It is important to determine if the overbuilding in a given market is cyclical in nature, and therefore offers good prospects of early recovery, or if it is the result of long-term causes. There are many long-term causes of area decline. There are changes in demand patterns: Businesses leave an area for many reasons; populations migrate both for economic and noneconomic reasons; locations become unattractive. Similarly, many other factors affect the supply of residential facilities in an area. Behind the visible inventory, there may be projects in the pipeline; there may be many projects left partially complete or temporarily converted to other uses, as is the case now in South Florida. A reliable judgment as to whether overbuilding is temporary or whether it is the result of basic trends requires an analysis of data for at least the last ten years and planning indicators for the next ten years. The investor must study population trends, economic indicators, housing demand for both multiple- and single-family, rent scales, and land values.

Is the Location Favorable?

Poorly located property, such as property in low-income inner-city areas, are best avoided by non-specialist investors. However, some properties may flounder even though there is nothing adverse in the location if they have been built for the wrong market in that location. Or a property may be well-located but ahead of its time. The area may potentially be desirable but may not yet have all the desired attributes. On the other hand, a location with an excellent reputation may be on the decline. When analyzing both market and location, investors should either use the services of reliable professionals or follow detailed checklists to make sure nothing is overlooked. Such lists are concerned with the following factors:

- Proximity to major arteries and transportation facilities;
- Neighborhood characteristics;
- Community facilities;
- Public utilities and improvements;
- Local ordinances and zoning; and
- Long-range governmental plans affecting the area.

USING PEOPLE AS AN INFORMATION RESOURCE

Statistics and physical inspections are valuable, but the real experts on a property and its area are the people who live there. Wise investors make it a point to interview tenants and employees. If the owner will not permit in-depth interviews, investors should attempt to strike up casual conversations. They should also interview employers and chambers of commerce or similar organizations in the area. In some cases, it will be useful to undertake opinion surveys of other projects in the area in order to provide comparisons with the project in which the investor is interested.

It is surprising how frank and helpful people tend to be when interviewed. When tenants or employees in a project that has many operating problems learn that a resale may be in the offing, they hope for relief from their problems and frustrations and are eager to offer facts and advice.

Impressions gained from "people research," supplementing or overriding the statistical findings, have saved many investors from potential disasters or have alerted them to profitable opportunities.

One case example makes the point. The investor had already placed an option at an extremely low square-foot price on a downtown office building in a small city. The building dated from the 1890s and retained the charm of the century, but it was also sound and well-maintained. The city was engaged in extensive downtown development. Plans included the construction of a new parking structure nearby. The investor was excited and impressed by the location.

However, when he interviewed the managers and secretaries in the other office buildings in the area, he found that most people who lived in the area were interested in moving out of downtown and into the new growth areas at the edge of the city. Many of the secretaries said that they would not use the new parking structure because they would be afraid of riding its elevators.

FOCUS ON OPERATING PROBLEMS

Once the investor determines that he has a suitable turnaround candidate, he must find out why the project is not reaching its potential. What are its operating problems? He must study the project's operating records and the competitive market. Things to watch for include:

- Major changes in occupancy rate;
- Tenant turnover rate;
- Rent schedules and their comparison with competitive rents;
- Excessive (or inadequate) management or maintenance costs;
- Deferred maintenance;
- Local real estate taxes and their level of assessment (relating to the possibility of appeal after acquisition);
- Significant changes in advertising costs, which may signal a specific rental difficulty or an artificial cutback to increase net income.

CONCLUSION

With proper analysis, the acquisition of properties for turnaround is a conservative investment which may yield returns better than most speculative ventures.

SPECIAL ILLUSTRATION OF SUBSIDIZED HOUSING

G ASSOCIATES
(A Limited Partnership)

$800,000
Limited Partnership Interests

20 Units at $40,000 per Unit

Payable in Six Installments and Subject to Increase or Decrease in Certain Circumstances.

Purpose

To acquire, develop, construct, own and operate in a Federally subsidized "Section 8" 100-unit rental apartment project for families. Construction mortgage financing is being provided by M, with Federal Housing Administration ("FHA") mortgage insurance under Section 221(d)(4) of the National Housing Act; permanent financing will be provided by the Government National Mortgage Association ("GNMA"), with such FHA mortgage insurance.

Project Description

The Project will consist of twelve two-story buildings containing 28 one-bedroom units, 48 two-bedroom units, 22 three-bedroom units and 2 four-bedroom units, all to be constructed on a 14,40-acre parcel of land. In addition, there will be one superintendent's apartment located in a service building.

Partnership Termination

The Partnership Agreement provides that the existence of the Partnership shall continue until December 15, Year 50, unless sooner terminated.

Sources of Funds

Mortgage Loan	$3,124,800
Capital Contributions of Limited Limited Partners	$ 800,000
Estimated Rental Income through Final Endorsement	$ 56,500
Total:	$3,981,300

Construction and Permanent Financing

M has provided a construction mortgage loan (the "Construction Loan") to the Partnership in the amount of $3,124,800. The Construction Loan will bear interest at the rate of 13% per annum. At or shortly after Final Endorsement, the Government National Mortgage Association will acquire the Construction loan for the Project (the "Permanent Loan"). The Permanent Loan will bear interest at a rate of 7½% per annum over a 40-year period.

Government Subsidies

The Mortgage Loan will be insured by FHA under the provisions of Section 221(d)(4) of the National Housing Act. In addition, Housing Assistance Payments have been conditionally committed by the Federal government for 100 apartments in the initial maximum amount of $51,760 per annum under Section 8 of the United States Housing Act of 1937, as amended.

Due Dates and Prior Conditions to Payment of Capital Contributions of Limited Partners

(a)	First Installment on admission of Limited Partners.	$ 45,000 ($ 2,250/Unit)
(b)	Second Installment on February 15, Year 2	$270,000 ($ 13,500/Unit)

(c)	Third Installment on the latest of February 15, Year 3, (ii) issuance of temporary certificates of occupancy for 100% of the apartment units and (iii) execution of the HAP Contract for not less than 34 apartment units.	$145,000 ($ 7,250/Unit)
(d)	Fourth Installment on the latest of (i) 6 months after the due date for payment of the Third Installment, (ii) February 15, Year 4, (iii) Project achievement of an occupancy rate for any three consecutive months of not less than 95% of the apartment units under signed leases by tenants who qualify under the Section 8 Contract, (iv) execution of the HAP Contract for 100 apartment units and (v) Final Endorsement	$130,000 ($ 6,500/Unit)
(e)	Fifth Installment on the latest of (i) 6 months after the due date for payment of the Fourth Installment and (ii) February 15, Year 5	$115,000 ($ 5,750/Unit)
(f)	Sixth Installment on the latest of (i) 6 months after the due date of payment of the Fifth Installment and (ii) February 15, Year 6	$ 95,000 ($ 4,750/Unit)
		$800,000 ($ 40,000/Unit)

Payment of the Second and each subsequent Installment of the Investors' Capital Contributions is also conditional upon receipt of a certification from the General Partner that (i) no material default by the Partnership under any of the Project Documents has been declared, (ii) the General Partner has no knowledge of the existence of any material default by the

Partnership under any of the Project Documents and (iii) the conditions precedent for payment of the Installment have been met.

Adjustment of Amount of Capital Contribution of Investor Limited Partners

If the principal amount of the Mortgage at Final Endorsement is greater or less than $3,124,800, the amount of Capital Contributions per Unit will be increased or decreased respectively by the same percentage as the percentage by which the principal amount of the Mortgage is increased or decreased (subject to a maximum increase or decrease of $5,000 per Unit).

Allocation of Cash Flow

(a) Cash Flow from normal operations and available for distribution to the Partners will be distributed 98.999% to the Investor Limited Partners (until Final Endorsement, then 99%), .001% to the Special Limited Partner (until Final Endorsement) and 1% to the General Partner.

(b) Any net proceeds from Capital Transactions (such as a sale or refinancing of the Project) after giving effect to certain priorities including repayment of certain loans which may be made by the General Partner and certain other priorities including repayment of the Partners' Capital Contributions (less distributions), will be distributed 50% to the Investor Limited Partners and 50% to the General Partner.

Allocation of Taxable Income

(a) Taxable income and losses from normal operations are determined in the same manner as profits and losses as follows: 98.999% of such profits and losses will be allocated to the Investor Limited Partners (until Final Endorsement, then 99%), .001% to the Special Limited Partner (until Final Endorsement) and 1% to the General Partner.

(b) Upon the sale of the Project or other similar event (after giving effect in the allocation of profits to adjustments among Partners for previous capital payments, prior allocations of profit and loss and distributions of Cash Flow and to certain other priorities) taxable income and losses will be a located 50% to the Investor Limited Partners and 50% to the General Partner.

Certain Obligations General Partners

(a) *Purchase Obligation:* If by June 30, Year 4, (i) Final Endorsement has not occurred, and (ii) the Section 8 Contract has not been executed for all the apartment units to receive subsidies, the General Partner will be required to purchase the Interests of all Investor Limited Partners desiring to sell the same. If the holders of 50% or more the Investor Limited Partners' Interest in the Partnership accept the General Partner's offer to purchase their Interests, then the General Partner may require that the non-accepting Investor Limited Partners tender their Interests. If prior to Final Endorsement (i) the Lender has commenced foreclosure proceedings or irrevocably refused to make any further advances under the Mortgage Loan, or (ii) the General Partner has withdrawn voluntarily from the Partnership without the Consent of the Investor Limited Partners, the General Partner will be required to purchase the Interests of all Investor Limited Partners desiring to sell the same.

(b) *Operating Loss Guarantee:* The General Partner is obligated to lend funds to the Partnership or to defer receipt of certain of its fees payable or to be paid by the Partnership to cover Operating Deficits incurred during the first three years following Final Endorsement (up to $125,000 in the aggregate).

(c) *Development Guarantee:* To cover development deficits, the General Partner is obligated to defer receipt of its Development Fee (in the amount of $305,604) and interest thereon as well as any Additional Development Fee.

(d) *Letters of Credit:* The General Partner, on behalf of the Partnership, has provided the Lender with letters of credit aggregating $97,696 to secure certain of the Partnership's obligations under the Mortgage Loan Documents. Any sums drawn down on such letters of credit, any expenses of the General Partner in connection with the issuance and maintenance of any such letters of credit will be repaid out of the earliest subsequent Capital Contributions after such sums are drawn or expense incurred.

Construction Contract

The Construction Contract with the Contractor provides for the completion of construction of the Project for a price not to exceed $2,519,261, plus the amount by which $220,038 (the estimated amount of mortgage interest for 13 months) exceeds the actual cost for mortgage interest, provided that construction is completed not later than 13 months from Initial Endorsement. In addition, under certain circumstances, the Partnership will pay interest on any construction retentions at a rate equal to the Bank prime rate. The Contractor has provided performance and payment bonds in the amount of $2,519,261.

Limited Liability

No Limited Partner (other than a General Partner who is also a Limited Partner) shall be liable for any of the debts of the Partnership or be required to contribute any capital to the Partnership other than his agreed Capital Contribution (as the amount thereof may be increased or decreased, if the amount of the Mortgage is increased or decreased) and except that in certain circumstances a Limited Partner may be required to repay to the Partnership with interest any portion of his Capital Contribution which has been returned to him through distribution, to the extent such repayment is necessary to discharge the Partnership's liabilities to creditors. In addition, Limited Partners may be obligated to pay interest on any portion of their Capital Contributions as to which payment is in default under the terms of the Partnership Agreement and may, under certain circumstances, be obligated to pay the costs of Partnership tax audits and appeals.

Depreciation and Accounting

The Partnership intends to depreciate its property using the sum-of-the-years digits method of accelerated depreciation, subject to a possible conversion to the straight-line method in such year as it becomes advantageous to the Partnership. The Partnership will elect initially to be on the accrual method of accounting.

USE OF PROCEEDS

The anticipated sources of funds of the Partnership for development of the Project and the uses thereof are expected to be as set forth below. The Capital Contributions of the Investor Limited Partners will be held in trust by the Partnership to be used only for the purposes set forth below (although the exact amounts may vary from such estimates) and for such other purposes as specifically provided in the Partnership Agreement.

Sources of Funds

Mortgage Loan	$3,124,800
Capital Contributions of Limited Partners	800,000 (1)
Estimated Rental Income Through Final Endorsement	56,500
	$3,981,300

Uses of Funds:

These Proceeds have been or are expected to be disbursed for the following items:

Cost of land	$ 115,428
Construction cost	2,519,261 (3)
Architect's fee	45,000
Survey and other fees	3,000
Real estate taxes	7,333
Insurance	10,000
Title and recording fees	35,000
Construction period interest	264,318
Legal, organizational and accounting	29,500
Investor services fee	6,000 (4)
Lease-up fees	48,172 (2)
FHA mortgage insurance premium	19,530
Loan financing fees	212,486
Deferral and guarantee fee	15,000(4)
Purchase fee	25,000(4)
Development fee	305,604(4)(5)
Interest on development fee	97,168(4)
Supervisory salaries	65,000(4)
Estimated operating espenses	45,000
Selling commissions	76,000(4)
Interest on Note	37,500(4)(6)
	$3,981,300

(1) The General Partner has made only a nominal cash contribution to the capital of the Partnership, which amount is not included in these sums.
(2) $38,172 of this amount is payable out of Capital Contributions.
(3) $134,556 of this amount is payable out of Capital Contributions.
(4) Payable out of Capital Contributions.
(5) The General Partner has agreed to pay Promoters, the aggregate sum of $80,000 for discontinuing their involvement with the Project and for assigning all of their right, title and interest in the Project to the General Partner. The General Partner has also agreed to reimburse Promoters the aggregate sum of $24,189.28 for sums expended in connection with the development of the Project. The General Partner will not seek reimbursement from the Partnership for these payments.
(6) The Partnership is obligated to pay $300,000 to the Venture payable at the rate of 10% per annum over 41.25 years.

PROJECTED PER UNIT RESULTS(1)

Year(s)	Capital Contributions	Income or (Loss)	Write-off Ratio	Cash Flow	Total Ratio	Tax Preference Items(4)
1	$ 2,250	$(3,579)	1.59	$ -	1.59	-
2	13,500	(27,366)	2.03	-	2.03	1,548
3	7,250	(14,232)	1.96	790	2.07	6,465
4	6,500	(12,601)	1.94	790	2.06	5,322
5	5,750	(10,907)	1.90	790	2.03	4,302
6	4,750	(9,051)	1.91	790	2.07	3,692
7-20	-	(53,995)	-	11,060	-	15,689
Totals(3) 1-20	$40,000	$131,731	3.29	$14,220	3.65	37,018

(1) The per unit annual results represent a prediction of future events and assumptions which may or may not occur. These results should

not be relied upon to indicate actual results which might be obtained. These results do not take into account gain from sale or foreclosure. Year 21 is the year in which the projections assume that a limited partner will sell his partnership interest for $1.00.

(2) The projected Year 1 taxable losses for investors who are admitted in December is projected to be $2,431 ($1,148 less than for investors who are admitted in November, Year 1).

(3) Year 20 is the last year in which the tax deductible losses from the Project are projected to exceed the taxable income from the Project.

(4) The effect of tax preference items on the minimum and maximum taxes has not been considered.

Exhibit 1

G ASSOCIATES
A Limited Partnership
Projection of Tax Losses (Income) and Potential Benefits
for a $40,000 (5.0% of Offering) Investor in the 50%
Federal Income Tax Bracket (Unaudited)

Year	Cash Contrib	Cumulative Cash Contrib	Tax (Loss) Gain	Tax Savings (Cost)	Cash Flow	Cash + Net Tax Savings	Cumulative Cash + Net Tax Savings	Net Benefits
1	$ 2250	$ 2250	$(3579)	$ 1789	$ -	$ 1789	$ 1789	$ (461)
2	13500	15750	(27366)	13683	-	13683	15472	(278)
3	7250	23000	(14232)	7116	790	7906	23378	378
4	6500	29500	(12601)	6301	790	7091	30469	969
5	5750	35250	(10907)	5454	790	6244	36713	1463
6	4750	40000	(9051)	4526	790	5316	42029	2029
7	-	40000	(7759)	3880	790	4670	46699	6699
8	-	40000	(7283)	3642	790	4432	51131	11131
9	-	40000	(6601)	3300	790	4090	55221	15221
10	-	40000	(5913)	2957	790	3747	58968	18968
11	-	40000	(5219)	2609	790	3399	62367	22367
12	-	40000	(4519)	2260	790	3050	65417	25417
13	-	40000	(3861)	1931	790	2721	68138	28138
14	-	40000	(3375)	1687	790	2477	70615	30615
15	-	40000	(2879)	1440	790	2230	72845	32845
16	-	40000	(2361)	1180	790	1970	74815	34815
17	-	40000	(1859)	929	790	1719	76534	36534
18	-	40000	(1332)	666	790	1456	77990	37990
19	-	40000	(793)	396	790	1186	79176	39176
20	-	40000	(241)	120	790	910	80086	40086
TOTALS			$(131731)	$65866	$14220	$80086		

SPECIAL ILLUSTRATION OF SUBSIDIZED HOUSING

G ASSOCIATES

Exhibit 2

A Limited Partnership
Projection of Tax Losses (Income) and Potential Benefits for a $40,000 (5.0% of Offering) Investor in the 60% Federal Income Tax Bracket (Unaudited)

Year	Cash Contrib	Cumulative Cash Contrib	Tax (Loss) Gain	Tax Savings (Cost)	Cash Flow	Cash + Net Tax Savings	Cumulative Cash + Net Tax Savings	Net Benefits
1	$ 2250	$ 2250	$ (3579)	$ 2147	$ -	$ 2147	$ 2147	$ (103)
2	13500	1570	(27366)	16420	-	16420	18567	2817
3	7250	23000	(14232)	8539	790	9329	27896	4896
4	6500	29500	(12601)	7561	790	8351	36247	6747
5	5750	35250	(10907)	6544	790	7334	43581	8331
6	4750	40000	(9051)	5431	790	6221	49802	9802
7	-	40000	(7759)	4656	790	5446	55248	15248
8	-	40000	(7283)	4370	790	5160	60408	20408
9	-	40000	(6601)	3961	790	4751	65159	25159
10	-	40000	(5913)	3548	790	4338	69497	29497
11	-	40000	(5219)	3131	790	3921	73418	33418
12	-	40000	(4519)	2712	790	3502	76920	36920
13	-	40000	(3861)	2317	790	3107	80027	40027
14	-	40000	(3375)	2025	790	2815	82842	42842
15	-	40000	(2879)	1727	790	2517	85359	45359
16	-	40000	(2361)	1416	790	2206	87565	47565
17	-	40000	(1859)	1115	790	1905	89470	49470
18	-	40000	(1332)	799	790	1589	91059	51059
19	-	40000	(793)	476	790	1266	92325	52325
20	-	40000	(241)	144	790	934	93259	53259
TOTALS			$(131731)	$79039	$14220	$93259		

SPECIAL ILLUSTRATION OF SUBSIDIZED HOUSING

G ASSOCIATES

Exhibit 3

A Limited Partnership
Projection of Tax Losses (Income) and Potential Benefits for a $40,000 (5.0% of Offering) Investor in the 70% Federal Income Tax Bracket (Unaudited)

Year	Cash Contrib	Cumulative Cash Contrib	Tax (Loss) Gain	Tax Savings (Cost)	Cash Flow	Cash + Net Tax Savings	Cumulative Cash + Net Tax Savings	Net Benefits
1	$ 2250	$ 2250	$ (3579)	$ 2505	$ -	$ 2505	$ 2505	$ 255
2	13500	15750	(27366)	19156	-	19156	21661	5911
3	7250	23000	(14232)	9963	790	10753	32414	9414
4	6500	29500	(12601)	8821	790	9611	42025	12525
5	5750	35250	(10907)	7635	790	8425	50450	15200
6	4750	40000	(9051)	6336	790	7126	57576	17576
7	-	40000	(7759)	5431	790	6221	63797	23797
8	-	40000	(7283)	5098	790	5888	69685	29685
9	-	40000	(6601)	4621	790	5411	75096	35096
10	-	40000	(5913)	4139	790	4929	80025	40025
11	-	40000	(5219)	3653	790	4443	84468	44468
12	-	40000	(4519)	3163	790	3953	88421	48421
13	-	40000	(3861)	2703	790	3493	91914	51914
14	-	40000	(3375)	2362	790	3152	95066	55066
15	-	40000	(2879)	2015	790	2805	97871	57871
16	-	40000	(2361)	1653	790	2443	100314	60314
17	-	40000	(1859)	1301	790	2091	102405	62405
18	-	40000	(1332)	932	790	1722	104127	64127
19	-	40000	(793)	555	790	1345	105472	65472
20	-	40000	(241)	168	790	958	106430	66430
TOTALS			$(131731)	$92210	$14220	$106430		

GOVERNMENT ASSISTANCE PROGRAMS

The Department of Housing and Urban Development ("HUD"), through the Federal Housing Administration ("FHA"), administers a variety of federal programs for low and moderate income housing in which the Partnership may participate. The Department of Agriculture, through the Farmers Home Administration ("FmHA"), administers similar housing programs for nonurban areas. These programs generally provide for three forms of assistance: subsidies of rents; mortgage interest payments; and mortgage loan insurance. The Partnership may also invest in projects in which certain states provide low and moderate income housing assistance under programs eligible for federal assistance under Section 236(b) of the National Housing Act of 1964, as amended, and Section 8 of the United States Housing Act of 1937, as amended. The term "Agency" as used herein shall refer to HUD, FHA, FmHA, or an appropriate state regulatory and financing agency.

The federal subsidies for any fiscal year are set forth in the enabling legislation. Except for the Section 8 program discussed below, once the FHA has contracted to furnish assistance to a project, the federal government is generally obligated to continue subsidy payments and mortgage insurance for the term of the mortgage (generally 40 years). There are no legal limitations on the total outstanding amounts of mortgage insurance that the FHA can issue on multi-family projects. Financing of housing projects under state housing programs is limited to the total amount of tax-exempt bonding authority established by the respective legislatures.

The discussion which follows describes various federal and state government assistance programs which the Partnership may consider in determining investments to be made by it. The list is not intended to be all-inclusive, nor can there be any assurance that the terms of such programs, or the regulations governing them, will not change. The Partnership is unable to predict which of the government-assistance programs described below will be utilized by the local limited partnerships in which the Partnership will invest, and the discussion of such programs is intended to give prospective investors an understanding of various types of programs which may be available for the Partnership's investments.

Section 8 Housing Assistance Payments Program

General Terms. The Section 8 Program provides for rent subsidies to enable lower-income families to afford safe, decent and sanitary housing. Under this program, HUD, either directly or through an agency of a local Public Housing Agency ("PHA"), makes payments to project owners on behalf of qualified lower-income tenants in the amount of the difference between what the household can afford and the HUD-approved rent for an adequate housing unit. Such payments are made under a Housing Assistance Payments Contract ("HAP Contract"). The typical HAP Contract requires that there be established for each unit receiving Section 8 assistance a "Contract Rent," which generally cannot exceed the HUD-established fair market rent for comparable housing in the project's market area. The Contract Rent must be reasonable in relation to quality, location, amenities, and mortgage payments of the project.

Initial Amount of Subsidy. Section 8 subsidies are based upon the Contract Rent applicable to specified dwelling units. The amount of the subsidy actually payable to a local limited partnership by HUD is the difference between the Contract Rent and the payment made to the local limited partnership by the tenant (as determined by HUD). The HUD determination of the amount of the rental assistance subsidy payment is based on an established economic standard for "lower-income" and "very low income" families. "Very low income" families are defined as families whose income does not exceed 50% of the median in the locality; "lower-income" families are defined as families whose income does not exceed 80% of the median in the locality.

In the case of "lower-income" families, the tenant housing cost (rent plus utility allowance, if any) is limited to no more than 30% of family income; in the case of "very low income" families, such housing cost is limited to no more than 25% of family income; and in the case of "very low income" families, and in certain other situations, the housing cost may be as low as 15% of family income. The owner is specifically required to lease at least 30% of the assisted units to such very low income families, during the initial rent-up period, and to use his best efforts to maintain that level of occupancy by such families thereafter. The owner is also required, however, to use his best efforts to lease units to families with a range of income so that the *average* of incomes for all tenant families is *at or above* 40% of the median income of the area. The owner is responsible for the collection of the tenants' rental payments. Thus, the total rental income from subsidized housing units payable to the local limited partnership is equal to the Contract Rent, with part of the contract rent being met by direct tenant payments, and the remainder being paid by HUD. The proportion of the Contract Rent actually paid by HUD and that actually paid by tenants will vary according to tenants' certified income.

Limitations on Subsidy. Generally, the Section 8 subsidy is payable in respect to the dwelling unit only when it is occupied by a "very low income" or "lower-income" family. The law and HUD regulations, however, provide for payment of the subsidy under certain limited circumstances even when the dwelling unit is not occupied; projects will receive Section 8 payments with respect to units not rented at the time the HAP Contract becomes effective and with respect to units which are rented to eligible families and subsequently vacated, at not more than 80% of the Contract Rent rate for leased units for a period of up to 60 days. Thereafter, payments will resume at the time vacated units are leased to eligible tenants. In addition to the 60-day coverage at 80% of Contract Rent, projects may be entitled to further payments for up to one year beyond the 60 days, in the amount of debt service attributable to the vacant units, if a good faith effort is made to rent the vacant units and the units in question are maintained in a decent, safe, and sanitary condition. Should a vacancy occur after any such unit is re-rented to a tenant qualified to receive Section 8 assistance, subsidy payments as described above would again be payable with respect to the unit. Under recent regulations, HAP Contracts between the owner and HUD are to be executed for a single term of 20, 30, or 40 years depending on, among other things, the type of financing to be used for the project.

If at any time after six months from the effective date of the HAP Contract, the project fails for a continuous period of six months to have at least 90% (80% in the case of substantially rehabilitated projects) of the Section 8 units leased or available for lease by qualified tenants, the number of units receiving payments may be reduced to a number equal to not less than 110% of the number then being leased or available for lease by qualified tenants. Such units may, upon satisfaction of certain HUD requirements, be restored at a later date.

Limitation on Distributions. Under recently issued HUD regulations, the distributions of project funds to profit-motivated owners of certain newly constructed projects, may be limited to a ten percent return on equity (defined by HUD as replacement cost of the project) during the first year of operation and ten percent return on the revalued replacement cost in subsequent years. In the case of projects limited to occupancy by senior citizens, the owner's return on equity is limited to six percent of replacement cost. Funds in excess of those which may be distributed to owners are to be placed in a residual receipts account. These distributions do not apply to small (50 units or less) projects or partially assisted projects.

Compliance with Subsidy Contracts. The HAP Contract and related agreements contain numerous undertakings on the part of the local limited partnership, including maintenance of the project as decent, safe, and sanitary housing and compliance with a number of requirements typical of federal contracts (such as those relating to nondiscrimination, equal employment opportunity, relocation, pollution control, and labor standards). Noncompliance by the local limited partnership might endanger the payment of the federal subsidy.

Adjustments of Subsidy Amounts. The statute and applicable regulations contain various provisions for review and readjustment of the amount of the Contract Rent upward or downward, subject to the limitation that in no case shall the adjustment lower the Contract Rent below that effective on the date of the HAP Contract.

Provision is made in the regulations for HUD to determine an Annual Adjustment Factor at least annually and to publish such Factors in the Federal Register. On each anniversary date of the HAP Contract, Contract Rents are automatically adjusted in accordance with the Factor, so long as HUD has determined that there is no material difference between such government-assisted and nonassisted rent levels in the project's market area. In the case of federally insured projects, in which less than the full number of rental units is covered by Section 8, however, the Annual Adjustment Factor may be limited in its effect to the formula rent maximum established by HUD. In addition, provision is made in the regulations for special additional adjustments to reflect increases in actual and necessary expenses of owning and maintaining the subsidized units which have resulted from substantial general increases in real property taxes, utility rate or similar costs, to the extent that such general increases are not adequately compensated for by the Annual Adjustments. The regulations provide that adjustments in the Contract Rent shall not result in material differences between the rents charged in the project and rents for comparable unassisted apartments, as determined by HUD.

There can be no assurance that the Annual Adjustment Factor will allow an increase in Contract Rents sufficient to cover the increased costs of operating the project or that, if such Factor is not sufficient, the project will be qualified for a special additional adjustment.

Funding of Increases in Subsidy. The initial source of funds for payment of increased subsidies which may result from the adjustment described above is a special reserve account to be established for the project. This account is to be funded by payments from HUD in the amount by which the Contract Rents exceed the actual subsidy paid by HUD. (This reserve amount is, in effect, the amount of rent payable by the tenants.) In addition, the regulations provide that when the HUD-approved estimate of required rent subsidy exceeds the maximum payable under the HAP Contract then in effect, and would cause the amount in the reserve fund to be less than 40% of the amounts payable under the HAP Contract, HUD shall take additional steps (as authorized by Section 8(c)(6) of the Housing and Community Development Act of 1974) to obtain funds to bring the amount in the account to the 40% level. Such steps include execution of contracts for assistance payments in excess of the amounts required at the time of initial rental of dwelling units, the allocation of new authorizations for the purpose of amending existing housing assistance contracts, and other measures, as stated in the Housing and Community Development Act of 1974, "to assure that assistance payments are increased on a timely basis to cover increases in maximum monthly rents or decreases in family incomes."

Section 221(d)(4) Program

Section 221(d)(4) provides for federal insurance of private mortgages to finance new or rehabilitated rental housing projects containing five or more units designed to provide housing for families of moderate income who have been displaced as a result of urban renewal, government action, or disaster. This program is designed to provide housing for families or moderate income, and does not contain income requirements for project tenants; however, a project which is eligible for assistance under this program may include as tenants, families receiving assistance under the Section 8 Program. Private entities owning such projects can receive insurance under this program for up to 90% of the FHA approved replacement cost of the project. The replacement term of the mortgage loan is limited to the lesser of 40 years or three-fourths of the remaining economic life of the project. FHA regulations place limits on the principal amount of the mortgage loan, which may vary depending upon the size of the units and the type of project.

Elderly (62 years or older), handicapped, or displaced single persons are deemed to constitute "families" for the purpose of satisfying eligible tenant requirements. There are no income requirements for occupants.

Mortgages insured under Section 221(d)(4) may be repaid in full, at any time after 30 days' notice to the mortgagee of the mortgagor's intention to do so, and the mortgages may contain a provision for a prepayment charge. No prepayment charge is required, however, if 15% or less of the original principal amount of the loan is prepaid in any calendar year.

Section 236 Program

Section 236 provides for federal insurance of private mortgages with terms of up to 40 years for up to 90% of the FHA-approved replacement cost of projects. Private entities owning such projects must be organized exclusively for the purpose of providing housing. The project rents, after mortgage interest, principal payments, reserves, and expenses, may not provide them in excess of a 6% return on their FHA-determined equity investment in a project.

The program also provides interest subsidies, the benefits of which the owner must pass on to the eligible tenants in the form of lower rents. The subsidy amount is equal to the difference between the payment that would be required for principal, interest, and mortgage insurance on a market interest rate mortgage and the amount that would be required on a mortgage with an interest rate of 1%. A basic rental charge is determined assuming a 1% interest rate mortgage and each tenant must pay the larger of the basic rental charge or 25% of his monthly income. Section 236 projects will benefit primarily families whose incomes are between $5,000 and $6,500 per year in average cost areas, and substantially more in the case of large families living in high cost areas. Up to 20% of the apartment units in a Section 236 project (or up to 40% with FHA approval) may receive additional subsidies under the Rent Supplement Program described below, thus reaching residents with lower incomes.

Mortgages insured under Section 236 may be repaid in full, at any time, to permit a sale to qualified tenant cooperatives or non-profit groups approved by the FHA and financed by a mortgage insured under Section 236. Twenty years after Final Endorsement (which occurs upon completion of the project, certification of its actual cost, and insurance by FHA of the permanent mortgage), such mortgage may be repaid in full, without FHA consent, for any reason, provided the mortgage is not then receiving payments under a rent supplement contract. FHA consent is required for any other prepayment in full.

In order to assist qualified tenant cooperatives or non-profit groups in the purchase of such projects, the FHA may insure a new mortgage in an amount intended to enable the seller to recover his original investment in the project, provided the project's operations will support the new mortgage.

Section 221(d)(3) Program

Rent Supplement Programs provide for federal payments to be made directly to project owners on behalf of qualified low income tenants. The tenants receive benefits through lower rents. Most projects receiving such assistance are financed under Section 221(d)(3), with federally-insured but unsubsidized, market interest rate mortgage loans in amounts up to 90% of the project's replacement cost. The Section 221(d)(3) market interest rate program is designed to assist private industry in providing rental and cooperative housing for low and moderate income families. Preference or priority of occupancy is given to families who have been displaced because of urban renewal, other governmental action, or a major disaster.

Section 515 Program

Loans for the provision of rental housing in non-urban areas are provided by the Farmers Home Administration ("FmHA"), the rural credit agency of the United States Department of Agriculture, under Section 515 of the Housing Act of 1949, as amended. Under this program, direct loans are made available to provide rental units for persons of low and moderate income and for those aged 62 and older. Loans are made to developers demonstrating ability and experience in the successful operation of rental housing, for projects in open country and communities having a population of up to 20,000 persons for a maximum of 60 years. Each project financed by FmHA is required to establish reserve funds from rental income to meet long-term capital replacement needs. Return on initial investment in a project is limited to a maximum of 8% per year.

Occupancy of apartments for rentals ranging from "basic rent" to "market rent" is restricted to families having incomes (as adjusted by deductions for dependent children and other factors) under $15,600. "Basic rent" is a rental charge determined on the basis of operating a rental housing project with payments of principal and interest on the mortgage loan to be repaid over the term of the loan at 1% per annum. "Market rent" is a rental charge determined on the basis of operating a rental project with payments of principal and interest on the mortgage loan to be repaid at a market rate of interest as established by FmHA from time to time.

FmHA can for certain Section 515 projects commit to provide assistance under an interest Credit and Rental Assistance Agreement. Under this Agreement, a project may receive an interest subsidy from FmHA equal to the difference between the payment required for principal and interest on the mortgage at the market rate established by FmHA and the payment which would be required for principal and interest on the mortgage at an interest rate of 1%. The benefits of these assistance payments are passed on to the tenants in the form of reduced rentals; the subsidy is reduced, however, to the extent that rentals exceed "basic rent." In a project assisted under an Interest Credit and Rental Assistance Agreement, families with incomes of $11,200 or less pay the "basic rent," which increases, with income, on a sliding scale to a maximum of "market rent" of 25% of adjusted income.

Other Section 515 projects may receive subsidy under the Section 8 Program described above. Under the terms of an agreement with HUD, FmHA can provide additional assistance to a project receiving Section 8 assistance by reducing the interest rate of the project, pursuant to an interest Credit and Rental Assistance Agreement, by as much as 2% below the market rate of interest as established by FmHA. In projects assisted by Section 8, the HUD regulations regarding family income govern occupancy and assistance standards.

Rehabilitation Projects; Certified Historic Structures

The Partnership may invest in local limited partnerships owning or leasing existing projects which are being partially or totally rehabilitated. Section 167(k) of the Code provides that a taxpayer may elect to compute depreciation on capital expenditures incurred in rehabilitating low-income rental housing under the straight-line method, using a useful life of 60 months. Only those rehabilitation expenses incurred either before January 1, 1982 or pursuant to a binding contract entered into before January 1, 1982 are eligible for such depreciation method. The expense must be for the rehabilitation of existing low-cost rental housing (except for properties which will be used as hotels, motels, and other transient facilities) to be defined in regulations consistent with the policies of the Leased Housing Program under Section 8 of the United States Housing Act of 1937, as amended. The improvement must have a useful life of more than five years, and the cost over any consecutive two-year period must exceed $3,000 per dwelling unit. Not more than $20,000 per dwelling unit may be taken into account under present law.

The Partnership may also invest in local limited partnerships owning or leasing existing projects which are certified historic structures and are being substantially or totally rehabilitated. Section 191 of the Code permits a taxpayer to elect to amortize over five years any capital expenditures attributable to the rehabilitation of a certified historic structure incurred before

June 15, 1981. This election under Section 191 of the Code is restricted to properties subject to depreciation under Section 167; depreciation for that portion of adjusted basis which is not amortized under Section 191 may be taken in accordance with Section 167 of the Code. In order to qualify, not only must the building be a certified historic structure, but the rehabilitation work must be certified by the Secretary of the Interior as being consistent with the historic character of the property or its environs. Alternatively, Section 167 of the Code permits a taxpayer to depreciate the adjusted basis of substantially rehabilitated historic structures as though the taxpayer were the first user of the property. This enables the taxpayer to use accelerated depreciation methods for rehabilitated historic property. In order to qualify for Section 167 accelerated depreciation, the value of certified rehabilitation must be in excess of the greater of the adjusted basis of the property or $5,000, and the expenditures must occur before July 1, 1981. There are no maximum dollar limitations on the amount of rehabilitation expenses for each dwelling unit.

Government Regulations

All federally-insured projects are subject to a standard regulatory agreement between the FHA and the owner of the project, which may be a limited distribution entity, i.e., a partnership or a corporation in which the investment return (cash flow) is limited. After providing for FHA prescribed or allowable reserves, mortgage principal and interest payments and operating and other costs, the owners of limited distribution entities may be permitted a maximum 6% cash return per annum on their stated equity under Section 236 programs. Federal subsidies for eligible tenants reduce their rents to levels significantly below those for comparable accommodations. To remain eligible for subsidies, their incomes may not exceed HUD established levels. HUD does not guarantee occupancy. If apartments are available, after giving priority to families of low and moderate income, they may be rented to the public at large at market rates and the applicable rent subsidy may remain unused. (The specific restrictions regarding the use of such subsidy allocations and rebates of rental amounts vary according to the specific program. Certain programs have FHA interest subsidies which extend to the project and are firm contractual commitments of the Federal Government for the 40-year life of the mortgage.)

When a project has failed to produce sufficient cash to cover its debt service, HUD has, when warranted by the circumstances, approved deferment of replacement reserve and/or mortgage principal payments for specified periods. However, HUD does not insure the profitability of projects, and there can be no assurance that projects in which the Partnership invests will be profitable or that any such adjustments will be granted in the future.

State and Local Assisted Programs

A number of states, including Illinois, Massachusetts, Michigan, New Jersey, New York, Pennsylvania, and West Virginia, as well as a number of local governmental bodies such as New York City, have established programs in which a state or local housing agency makes direct mortgage loans to developers to finance the construction of new multi-family housing. Subject to stringent project feasibility standards which vary from state to state, certain states self-insure mortgages on qualifying projects. Such mortgage loans are typically available for both the construction and the permanent financing of the project. Certain state and local programs require the establishment of contingency reserve funds for unanticipated or extraordinary costs. Such reserve funds may be provided out of mortgage proceeds or by letters of credit from the developers. The funds may be held in reserve for substantial periods of time after a project achieves rent-up. Funds to finance such projects are obtained through the sale of tax-exempt notes and bonds. The documentation relating to such notes or bonds may prohibit extensions of payments of mortgage interest or principal, or both, by the borrower. The market interest rate obtainable on such notes and bonds is generally lower than that for FHA-insured mortgage loans, and permits the state housing agency to make its construction and permanent mortgage loans for projects at generally lower interest rates. This enables the rent schedule for the dwelling units in the projects to be somewhat lower than in comparable FHA-insured projects. The repayment schedule for such loans may provide for 40 to 50 year terms. In addition, Section 236(b) permits the FHA to apply interest reduction subsidies to such state-assisted projects even though the state housing agency's mortgage loans may not be FHA-insured. The basic rents in such projects may be established as if the interest on the mortgage loan for the project were 1% through this combination of state assistance and FHA Section 236(b) interest reduction subsidies.

In the case of state-assisted housing programs, the local limited partnership must be approved by the state housing agency. The regulations of the state housing agencies regarding cash return to the project owners and the operation of the project are in general similar to the FHA regulations for federal projects.

Tax Abatement Programs

Various state and local governments provide for exemptions from and reduction of real property taxes for certain projects. Although the Partnership will consider or may consider investing in local limited partnerships which are eligible for such tax reductions, the Partnership is unable to predict whether its investments will include projects which are eligible for such tax reductions.

One of New York State's programs provides that new or rehabilitated multiple dwellings (defined as a dwelling occupied or to be occupied by three or more independent families) the construction or rehabilitation of which commenced after January 1, 1975 and before January 1, 1982 and which is to be completed before December 31, 1983, shall be exempt from local taxes (other than assessments for local improvements) during the construction period and thereafter for a period of ten years. For the first two years of such ten-year period the tax exemption is complete and declines by 20% in each of the next four two-year periods. The maximum rents which may be charged in the exempt multiple dwelling and the total project costs and expenses are determined by the Department of Housing Preservation and Development, which must certify and approve such amounts. Tax exemptions for projects containing more than 20 dwelling units must also be approved by the local community planning board.

Another form of tax abatement program is that provided by New York City. Under that program, increases in the assessed valuation of certain property resulting from conversions of or improvements to existing buildings or alterations made to reduce unhealthy or dangerous conditions are exempt from local taxes for a period of twelve years if the construction is completed within three years from the commencement thereof. In addition, taxes on such property may be reduced by an amount equalling up to 100% of reasonable construction costs, depending upon the type of work and location. A limit of 8-1/3% of the reasonable cost of such conversions or alterations may be deducted each year for a period which is presently up to a maximum of 20 years; the amount of tax abatement in any consecutive period may not exceed the amount of taxes payable in such period. The types of properties eligible for such benefits are limited to various types of multiple dwellings, including buildings receiving local or HUD loan assistance, or, with certain exceptions, buildings on which rents charged after the conversions or alterations must be certified by the Department of Housing Preservation and Development. Property receiving other state or local tax abatement assistance is not eligible for the benefits described above.

INVESTMENT OBJECTIVES AND POLICIES

Investment Objectives

The Partnership's primary investment objective is to invest, as a limited partner, in local limited partnerships which own or lease a newly-constructed or rehabilitated government-assisted housing project. Such housing projects are typically begun by private developers who select the sites and apply for government mortgage insurance and/or subsidies.

Investors should note that development of the Partnership's investment policies includes consideration of certain aspects of government-assisted housing which differ from similar aspects of conventional housing, including (1) greater financing leverage than usual in conventional projects, which provides for greater depreciation and certain provisions regarding "recapture", (2) a measure of protection, in those projects with rental assistance payments, against increased costs and difficulties in raising tenant rental payments to meet such costs, (3) review of projects by various agencies, such as HUD, for compliance with construction and other standards, and (4) the availability of various contingency reserves required in connection with HUD or other agency programs.

Government-assisted housing is, however, subject to special conditions and risks including, but not limited to, (1) general surveillance by HUD or other agencies, which includes the application of rental and other guidelines affecting tenant eligibility and rent levels, (2) limitations on return on investment (cash flow), which have the effect of limiting return to an effective level of 2.4% on stated equity, varying with the governmental agency involved and the amount of the Partnership's investment, (3) limitations on salability, as contained in regulatory agreements with various government agencies, (4) requirements for justifying rental increases and operational changes to applicable agencies which must approve them, with possible attendant delays in their implementation, and (5) the uncertain effects of changes in complex rules and regulations governing such government assistance programs, or changes in the manner in which those regulations are interpreted. HUD has taken the position that buildings which participate in HUD programs are exempt from local rent control or stabilization legislation which would otherwise be applicable and that HUD rental policies and guidelines apply. During the process of application for, or implementation of, HUD-approved rental increases, the applicability of local rent stabilization programs could be asserted with the result that the implementation of any such rental increases could be delayed.

The Partnership may also invest up to 10% of the amount available for investment in local limited partnerships owning non-government-assisted housing projects.

The Partnership will not develop projects, but will acquire interests in the local limited partnerships formed or to be formed by the developers. Normally, the developer becomes the managing general partner of such local limited partnership and thereby assumes responsibility for the day-to-day operations of developing, constructing or rehabilitating, maintaining, and managing the project. In some cases, the developer may not continue as a general partner of the local limited partnership after completion of construction or rehabilitation of the project. In such event, a qualified person or entity will be substituted as managing general partner with the consent of the Partnership. Affiliates of the developer may become general partners of the local limited partnership and may also enter into management agreements with such partnership.

Investment Policies

The criteria for selecting particular projects for investment by the Partnership include capability of the development group, including the history and performance of the sponsor, general contractor, architect, management agent, and others associated with the development; financial strength of the local general partners; analysis of all data supplied by the developer to HUD, the Federal Housing Administration ("FHA"), or local agency to obtain cost commitments, with special attention to the cost of construction (including provisions for completion of the project), proposed rents, and costs of property operations; general rental market conditions in the area of the proposed development (including vacancy rates) and the expenses of comparable projects; and in the case of existing projects, the history and performance of the project.

In general, sale of the Partnership's interest in a local limited partnership will be subject to various restrictions. It is anticipated that these considerations could lead to a holding period of approximately 20 years or longer. The General Partners may, however, hold limited partnership interests longer or sell them sooner consistent with the terms of local limited partnership agreements, the Partnership Agreement, and the best interests of the Partnership.

Except for interim commitments discussed below, the Partnership will invest in other local limited partnerships owning federal, state, or local government-assisted or other housing projects. The following is a summary of certain policies and restrictions of the Partnership Agreement.

The following investment policies may not be changed without approval by Limited Partners owning a majority of the outstanding Limited Partnership interests:

1. Except for interim commitments in short-term government obligations, commercial paper (investment grade), and tax-exempt notes and bonds or registered investment companies holding such securities, not less than 90% of the amount available for investment will be invested initially in local limited partnerships which will own or lease federal, state, and local government-assisted housing projects. Such projects may subsequently be refinanced or converted to other uses with a view to realizing greater cash flow or capital gains. Reinvestment of cash

flow (excluding proceeds resulting from a disposition or refinancing of property) shall not be permitted. The Partnership will have the right to invest up to 10% of the aggregate amount available for investment at any time in local limited partnerships or joint ventures (providing that the Partnership will not be generally liable for any such venture's debts) which will own or lease housing projects which are not government-assisted.

2. Interests in such local limited partnerships will be acquired with a view toward maximizing tax deductions to a degree consistent with the Partnership's other investment objectives, and with cash income and long-term appreciation as considerations, but not with a view to early resale. The Partnership will not acquire or lease properties or interests therein from, or sell or lease properties or interests therein to, the General Partners or their affiliates. Limited partnership interests may, however, be acquired in the name of the General Partners or their affiliates on behalf of the Partnership.

3. The Partnership will seek to avoid depreciation recapture and defer taxes by not selling any interests in projects for a period of ten years except under exempted sales to qualified tenant groups or in transactions which, in the option of the tax advisers of the Partnership, will qualify for long-term capital gains. There is no assurance, however, that the Partnership will be able to avoid depreciation recapture.

4. The Partnership will not voluntarily sell and project, or cause a project to be sold, except under exempted sales to qualified tenant groups, if the cash proceeds would be less than the taxes due on such sale at the then maximum state and federal capital gains tax rates. Reinvestment of proceeds resulting from a disposition (or refinancing) will not take place unless cash will be distributed to the Partners from the proceeds of such sales sufficient to pay the state and federal taxes at the then maximum rates, and in no event can such proceeds be reinvested after five years. Until such date, the balance of the proceeds may also be distributed to the Partners.

5. The Partnership may borrow against its interest in individual projects only to defray expenses or preserve its interest in such individual projects. It may not pledge or encumber other projects for this purpose. Such borrowings are limited to that amount for which the Partnership can reasonably expect to meet debt service requirements from aggregate, anticipated net cash flow.

6. The Partnership will not issue senior securities (except as stated in paragraph 5 above), invest in other issuers for the purpose of exercising control (other than housing partnerships), or underwrite the securities of other issuers or offer Units or Limited Partnership interests in exchange for property.

7. Except in a case in which a single project exceeds this limitation, not more than 25% of the Partnership's portfolio may be sold and reinvested within any single year, except in exempted sales to qualified tenant groups.

8. No loans will be made by the Partnership other than (a) to local project developers in connection with the acquisition of a project by the Partnership, or (b) to local limited partnerships in which the Partnership has an equity interest. No loans will be made to the General Partners or to their affiliates.

9. Investment commitments regarding government-assisted housing projects will be based on HUD/FHA or state agency approval of feasibility. No significant contributions to local limited partnerships owning or leasing such projects will be made prior to Initial Endorsement by HUD/FHA or its equivalent for non-FHA projects.

10. Some of the projects in which the Partnership may acquire an interest may receive financing arranged by affiliates of the General Partners and compensation for services in arranging such financing may be paid to such affiliates at usual and customary rates.

11. The Partnership will not sell all or substantially all of its assets in any single transaction or related series of transactions, without obtaining the consent of the Limited Partners owning a majority of the Limited Partnership Interests.

As a limited partner of the local limited partnership, the Partnership will not have the right to manage the operations of such partnership, except under limited circumstances. The General Partners will endeavor to negotiate with the general partner of the local limited partnership for the right to approve or disapprove the sale of a project, the right to demand a dissolution of the local limited partnership, and the right to demand, upon the occurrence of certain events, the resignation of such local general partner. With a view to maintaining the continuity of a local limited partnership in such a case, the General Partners may also endeavor to provide for a substitute corporate general partner, the capital stock of which may be owned by the

General Partners. No assurance can be given, however, that the foregoing rights will be present in each local limited partnership agreement or that, if present, their exercise will not cause the Partnership to be deemed a general partner of such local limited partnership. Unless it is deemed that the Partnership is taking part in the control of the local limited partnership's business, the Partnership will not have any liability beyond its investment for obligations of the local limited partnership.

The Partnership will normally acquire at least a 95% interest in the profits and losses of the local limited partnership, with the balance remaining with the general partner/developer. The Partnership will always acquire at least a 50% interest in such items. The interest of the Partnership in the proceeds of the refinancing or sale of a project, depending on the amount of appreciation realized, may range from 50% to 95%.

The Partnership will normally make its capital contributions to the local limited partnership in stages and the aggregate of such contributions may exceed the amount available for investment received from the initial sale of Units. The Partnership will usually be obligated to make one contribution each year, over a period of two to five years, with each contribution due on a specified date, provided that certain conditions regarding construction or operation of the project have been fulfilled. For example, the Partnership's contribution could be made on specific dates over a four-year period subject to satisfaction of some or all of the following requirements: (1) admission of the Partnership as a limited partner to the local limited partnership; (2) funding of the construction loan, and/or completion or rehabilitation of a substantial portion of the project prior to payment of the second contribution; (3) completion of the project, commencement of subsidy payments, if any, and operation of the project at breakeven level for 90 consecutive days immediately preceding such third contribution; and (4) funding of the project's permanent loan and operation of the project at a breakeven level for 90 consecutive days immediately preceding such final contribution.

The Local General Partners

Under the terms of the local limited partnership agreement, general partners of the local limited partnership will ordinarily be required to (1) guarantee completion of construction or rehabilitation of the project, which completion will also normally be secured by a payment and performance bond in the amount required by the governmental housing authority subsidizing the project; (2) provide certain funds needed by the local limited partnership to defray any operating deficits for a specific period following construction (usually from one to three years); and (3) provide all funds in excess of the Partnership's capital contributions, rental income from the project, and the proceeds of the mortgage loan needed for completion of the project. The general partners of the local limited partnership will also generally undertake to complete the project in accordance with the plans and specifications, satisfy all requirements for a certificate of occupancy, and generally exercise reasonable care and diligence in connection with the construction, operation, and maintenance of the project, including obtaining adequate insurance coverage. In addition, the general partners will normally warrant that (1) the local limited partnership has or will obtain good title to the land, or, if the project is being leased by the local limited partnership, that such leave is valid and enforceable in accordance with its terms; (2) the land is properly zoned for the intended use; and (3) all subsidy agreements and endorsements, if applicable, are in full force and effect.

The local general partners will ordinarily deliver to the Partnership financial statements satisfactory to the General Partners and agree to maintain at all times a stated net worth. Counsel for such general partners, as a condition to payment by the Partnership of its initial capital contribution, will deliver to the Partnership an opinion that the local limited partnership will be treated as a partnership for federal income tax purposes. The Partnership will also obtain opinions from such counsel that the local limited partnership is duly organized and validly existing under local laws and that, upon admission, the Partnership will become a limited partner thereof.

The local general partners will receive fees from the local limited partnership in consideration for management of such partnership and the project, their agreement to fund certain deficits discussed above, the initial rent-up of the project, and for other services rendered to such partnership.

Investment Limitations

The Partnership intends that not less than 90% of its investments will be in local limited partnerships which own or lease government-assisted housing projects. The number and availability of projects eligible to receive government subsidies depends upon many factors beyond the Partnership's control, such as the amount of money made available by federal and state governments for such projects.

The Partnership may also have up to 10% of its investments in local limited partnerships owning conventional housing projects which are not government-assisted. The Partnership will not, however, acquire an interest in another partnership which does not constitute at least 50% of all limited partnership interests therein.

Pending expenditures of funds, or to provide a source from which to meet contingencies, the proceeds of the offering may be temporarily invested in short-term highly liquid investments where there is appropriate safety of principal, such as U.S. Treasury Bonds or Bills, bank certificates of deposit, other short-term government obligations, commercial paper (investment grade), and tax-exempt notes and bonds, or registered investment companies holding such securities. Any proceeds of the offering of the Units not invested within 18 months from the date of the Prospectus (except for necessary operating reserves) shall be distributed pro rata to the Limited Partners as a return of capital.

THE OFFERING

Units are being offered at $5,000 per Unit, minimum purchase 1 Unit ($5,000). No Units will be sold unless a minimum 240 Units have been subscribed for.

The Units are composed of (i) two Limited Partnership Interests and (ii) a warrant to purchase two additional Limited Partnership Interests (the "Additional Limited Partnership interests"). The Warrants will entitle the limited partners of the Partnership (the "Limited Partners") to purchase the Additional Limited Partnership Interests for $2,500 each. In the event that any Warrant is not exercised, the Additional Limited Partnership Interests to which such unexercised Warrant relates may be sold by the Partnership to other qualifying offerees. In such event the minimum purchase will bc two Additional Limited Partnership Interests for an aggregate purchase price of $5,000. Under certain circumstances upon the non-exercise of the Warrants, the Additional Limited Partnership Interests may be sold for less than $2,500 each. The Warrants will not be transferable except upon the transfer of a Unit.

The Partnership will invest, as a limited partner, in other limited partnerships ("local limited partnerships"), each of which will own or lease and will operate a newly-constructed, to-be-constructed, or rehabilitated housing project. The Partnership will invest at least 90% of the amount available for investment in local limited partnerships owning or leasing housing projects which will receive various forms of federal, state, or local assistance and which may or may not be classified as "low-income housing" under the Internal Revenue Code. The balance may be invested in such partnerships or other partnerships owning conventional housing projects.

It is not expected that any of the local limited partnerships in which the Partnership invests will generate cash flow sufficient to provide for distributions to the Limited Partners in any material amount. Such cash flow, if any, would first be used to meet operating expenses of the Partnership. Of the cash flow that may be distributed by the Partnership, the Limited Partners shall receive 99% of such distributions and the General Partners shall receive 1%, *provided* that such amount received by the General Partners shall be *reduced* by the amount paid to them as an annual management fee for such year. The General Partner will contribute to the Partnership less than 1% of its capital. The Limited Partners as a group shall generally be allocated 99% of the Partnership's profits and losses and the General Partners shall be allocated 1% of such items, except on dissolution.

Profits or losses incurred by the Partnership in Year One will be allocated 99% to the Limited Partners as a group and 1% to the General Partners as a group. The Limited Partners' portion of the Partnership's Year One profits or losses will be allocated among them in proportion to the number of Limited Partnership Interests held by each Limited Partner and the date of each Limited Partner's admission into the Partnership.

Profits and Losses Subsequent to Year One. Commencing in Year Two and thereafter, 62.5% of the Partnership's profits, losses, and cash distributions, if any, ("Tax Items") will be allocated to the Additional Limited Partnership Interests, whether purchased pursuant to the exercise of the Warrants or otherwise, and 37.5% of such Tax Items will be allocated to the Limited Partnership Interests purchased in Year One. This allocation will continue until each Tax Item allocated to each Additional Limited Partnership interest equals the total amount of each Tax Item allocated to each Limited Partnership Interest acquired upon purchase of the Units. Thereafter, all Limited Partnership Interests will be allocated Partnership Tax Items on an identical basis.

The result of the foregoing allocations will be that in the Partnership's early years any Limited Partner who does not exercise his Warrants will have in proportion to his capital contribution, a smaller interest in Partnership Tax Items compared to the Limited Partners who exercise their Warrants or to investors who purchase Additional Limited Partnership Interests. Because the proportion of losses allocated to the Limited Partners in Year One will vary depending upon the respective Monthly Closing Dates, the weighted average of the Tax Items allocated per Limited Partnership Interest purchased in Year One will be used for measuring against the Tax Items allocated to each Additional Limited Partnership Interest purchased in Year Two.

The housing projects owned or leased by the local limited partnerships in which the Partnership will invest will be subject to mortgage obligations. The aggregate ratio of the invested assets of the Partnership compared to its equity in the local limited partnerships is expected to be approximately 7 to 1. This financing ratio could vary depending upon the amount of capital raised in this offering and the amount of Additional Limited Partnership Interests sold pursuant to Warrants or otherwise.

BENEFITS OF GOVERNMENT ASSISTANCE PROGRAMS

(1) tax benefits to an investor on a current basis including deductions for interest, depreciation, and taxes to the extent permitted by law;

(2) reasonable protection for the Partnership's capital investments;

(3) potential for appreciation, subject to consideration of capital preservation; and

(4) potential for future cash distributions from operations (on a limited basis), refinancing, or sale of a project.

RISK FACTORS OF GOVERNMENT ASSISTANCE PROGRAMS

1. *No assurance can be given that the Partnership will be successful in obtaining suitable investments, or that, if investments are made, the objectives of the Partnership will be achieved.* Such objectives may be adversely effected by a number of factors such as government budgeting, which may result in reducing or eliminating certain federal, state, or local government subsidy programs, and high interest rates which may adversely impact construction and the development of subsidized housing for which financing has not been obtained.

2. *Risks of Real Estate Ownership.* The Partnership, as a limited partner in the local limited partnerships in which it will invest, will be subject to the risks incident to the construction, management, and ownership of improved real estate. Neither the Partnership's investments nor the projects will be readily marketable. The Partnership investments will be subject to adverse general economic conditions, and, accordingly, the status of the national economy, including substantial unemployment and concurrent inflation, could increase vacancy levels, rental payment defaults, and operating expenses, which, in turn, could substantially increase the risk of operating losses for the projects. The local limited partnerships' equity in the projects will be subject to loss through foreclosure which might occur because of a number of factors. Operating expenses may increase beyond the rent levels permitted by appropriate regulatory agencies, or rental income may decline due to vacancies.

These problems may result from a number of factors, many of which cannot be controlled by the General Partners and are, due to limited cash flow and other factors, more likely to occur in subsidized housing, including adverse changes in the financial condition of local general partners, improper management, changes in the housing patterns in the area, increased real estate taxes, vandalism (with attendant extra repair, replacement, and security costs), rent strikes, and other collection difficulties, vacancies, rent controls, and operating and maintenance costs which may be higher than in conventional housing. Further, the amount of the mortgage on each project is high in relation to the Partnership's equity, with consequent higher debt service than if less leverage were utilized. Increases in construction costs, real estate taxes, utilities, and other costs will adversely affect project viability. If federal, state, or local regulatory bodies do not approve adequate rent increases to offset increased costs, cash returns, if any, to the Partnership may be precluded, or if rental receipts, net of other operating expense, are insufficient to service a project's debt, the loss through foreclosure of the local limited partnerships' equity in the projects may result.

3. *Need for Management Experience; Lack of Partnership Control.* The success of the Partnership will, to a large extent, depend on the quality of the management by the local limited partnerships who have the authority to make all management decisions relating to the operation of the projects by the management organizations they may employ, and the supervision furnished by the General Partners. The General Partners have not had extensive experience in the management of government-assisted projects or long-term experience in the supervision of such management operations. The identity and management experience of the local limited partnerships and their general partners are not known. Low and moderate income housing requires management to be particularly responsive to tenants' social and economic needs and may require special attention to the protection of the physical property. Further, the Limited Partners have, under the terms and conditions of the Partnership Agreement and the Limited Partnership Act, limited rights with respect to management of the Partnership and, accordingly, will not be able to exercise any control with respect to its business decisions and operations.

4. *Shortage of Energy Sources.* Present and anticipated shortages of natural gas, crude oil, refined petroleum products, and other sources of energy may have adverse effects on owners of real estate in general and the Partnership in particular. Operating expenses may be higher than anticipated due to the increase in costs, including taxes imposed on imported oil, and the decrease in availability of heating oil, natural gas, and other fuels. The local limited partnerships' ability to pass such increased costs on

to tenants may be limited. Furthermore, the demand for apartment units may be affected by the proximity of such properties to public transportation, the availability of gasoline, the possibility of mandatory gasoline rationing, and similar factors. The Partnership can give no assurance as to the impact, if any, of these problems upon the Partnership and the projects.

5. *Limited Transferability of Units.* Prospective investors should be fully aware of the long-term nature of their investment in the Partnership. Accordingly, purchasers of the Units and Additional Limited Partnership Interests will need to bear the economic risk of their investment for an indefinite period of time. Warrants cannot be transferred except as part of a Unit, and Limited Partnership Interests shall not be transferable until after twenty years.

TAX ASPECTS OF GOVERNMENT ASSISTANCE PROGRAMS

1. Tax Consequences of Warrants

Because each Unit initially offered consists of two Limited Partnership Interests and one Warrant to purchase two Additional Limited Partnership Interests at $2,500 each, a Limited Partner will be required to allocate the $5,000 purchase price of each Unit between the two Limited Partnership Interests and the Warrant.

Because the Warrant and the initial Limited Partnership Interests will be treated as separate assets, the basis (cost) of the Warrant held by a Limited Partner will not be included in computing the basis of a Limited Partner's initial Limited Partnership Interests, which will therefore be less than the $5,000 paid for each Unit. As is the case with the cost of Limited Partnership Interests, the portion of the $5,000 cost of a Unit allocable to the Warrant will be a non-deductible capital expenditure.

Each Additional Limited Partnership Interest acquired upon exercise of a Warrant entities a Limited Partner to 62.5/37.5 of the profits, losses, and cash distributions, if any, ("Tax Items") allocable to an initial Limited Partnership Interest until each Tax Item allocated to each Additional Limited Partnership Interest equals the total amount of each Tax Item allocated to each initial Limited Partnership Interest. This allocation feature arguably makes the Additional Limited Partnership Interests more valuable to investors than the initial Limited Partnership Interests and, to that extent, gives the Warrants a present value. However, because the only difference between an initial Limited Partnership Interest and an Additional Limited Partnership Interest is the greater share of Partnership Tax Items allocable to the latter for a limited period, the Partnership intends to value the Warrants based only upon the net savings to the Partnership in underwriting commissions on the issuance of Additional Limited Partnership Interests pursuant to the exercise of Warrants. Thus, the Partnership will assign a value of $12.50 to each Warrant and a value of $2,493.75 to each of the two initial Limited Partnership Interests, all of which comprise a $5,000 Unit. There can be no assurance, however, that the Service will accept the Partnership's allocation or that the allocation, if challenged by the Service, will be sustained in court. Any other allocation, such as one which increases the amount allocated to the Warrants and reduces the amount allocated to the Initial Limited Partnership Interests, will affect the magnitude of the following tax consequences to Limited Partners.

In the event that a Limited Partner exercises his Warrants and acquires Additional Limited Partnership Interests, the basis of those Additional Limited Partnership Interests will be the sum of the additional cash investment by the Limited Partner and the basis of his Warrants. Therefore, a Limited Partner who exercises his Warrants will have a higher basis in his Additional Limited Partnership Interests than in his initial Limited Partnership Interests. In the event that a Limited Partner fails to exercise his Warrants, he will recognize a short-term capital loss in an amount equal to the basis of his Warrants. In addition, upon the lapse of Warrants, the Partnership will recognize an identical amount of income. It is unclear under present law whether such income will be short-term capital gain or ordinary income, but it is probable that the Service will take the position, as it has in a series of Revenue Rulings, that the income will constitute ordinary income. See e.g., Rev. Rul. 72-198, 1972-1 C.B. 223; Rev. Rul. 78-181, 1978-1 C.B. 261; Rev. Rul. 58-234, 1958-1 C.B. 279; Rev. Rul. 63-183, 1963-1 C.B. 285; and Treas. Reg. §1.1234-1(b). The Partnership Agreement allocates all income recognized by the Partnership upon the expiration of Warrants to non-exercising Limited Partners. Assuming that such income constitutes ordinary income, it may not be fully offset by the short-term loss recognized by a non-exercising Limited Partner because of the statutory limitation on the deductibility of capital losses. Furthermore, failure to exercise the Warrants will reduce a Limited Partner's proportionate interest in Partnership income and losses and, to that extent, tax shelter benefits to be derived from the Partnership.

2. "At Risk" Provisions of the Code

Section 704(d) of the Code, as amended by the 1976 Act, provided that the tax basis of a partner's interest in a partnership *for the purpose of determining the extent to which partnership losses allocable to him can be claimed* did not include any portion of partnership liabilities with respect to which he had no personal liability, i.e., was not "at risk." This limitation, however, was made specifically inapplicable to any partnership "the principal activity of which is investing in real property (other than mineral property)."

3. Depreciation, Allocation of Purchase Price, and Useful Lives

Allocation of a unitary purchase price between depreciable and non-depreciable assets and the determination of useful lives of depreciable assets are factual questions, and the Partnership can give no assurance that the allocations made by or the useful lives assigned to depreciable assets by the local limited partnership will be accepted by the Service. If amounts allocated to depreciable assets are decreased and the amounts allocated to non-depreciable assets are increased. Partnership losses will be decreased or Partnership profits will be increased. Similarly, if the useful lives assigned to depreciable assets are increased, Partnership losses will be decreased or Partnership profits will be increased in the Partnership's early years.

It is anticipated that the local limited partnerships will utilize, wherever possible, the so-called "double-declining balance" or the sum of the years-digits methods of depreciation described in section 167(b)(2) and (3) of the Code with respect to capital expenditures incurred in acquiring, constructing, or improving real estate to the extent that such expenditures are not depreciated under Section 167(k)(1) of the Code. Real property owned by the Partnership or any local limited partnership may be depreciated under this method only if all of the following requirements are satisfied: (1) the Partnership or local limited partnership possesses a depreciable interest for federal income tax purposes (i.e., an economic investment) in the assets to be depreciated; (2) the real property constitutes "residential property located within the United States" within the meaning of Section 167(j)(2)(A)(i) of the Code; (3) the original use of the property commences with the Partnership or local limited partnership within the meaning of Section 167(j)(2)(A)(ii) of the Code; and (4) the useful life of the property is at least three years. Use of these accelerated methods of depreciation may subject the Partnership or a local limited partnership to recapture of depreciation.

4. Expenditures Incurred to Rehabilitate Low-Income Housing and Certified Historic Structures

Section 167(k) of the Code, as amended by the 1978 Act, provides that a taxpayer may elect to compute depreciation on capital expenditures incurred in rehabilitating low-income rental housing under the straightline method using a useful life of 60 months. Only those rehabilitation expenditures incurred pursuant to a binding contract entered into before January 1, 1982, or those expenditures incurred as part of rehabilitation which is begun before January 1, 1982, are eligible for depreciation under this method. The aggregate amount of rehabilitation expenditures which may be so depreciated may not exceed $20,000 per low-income rental housing dwelling unit, and such expenditures will not qualify at all for this rapid method of depreciation unless over a period of two consecutive years the aggregate amount of rehabilitation expenditures with respect to each unit exceeds $3,000. Upon the disposition, by whatever means, of real property which has been depreciated under the foregoing method, all or a portion of the excess of the amounts depreciated under Section 167(k) over the straight-line depreciation computed using the asset's actual useful life may be taxable as ordinary income, depending upon the length of time the property was held by the taxpayer. It is anticipated that, where appropriate, one or more of the local limited partnerships will elect Section 167(k) amortization.

Section 191 of the Code, as adopted by the 1976 Act and amended by the 1978 Act, permits taxpayers to amortize over five years the expenses incurred in rehabilitating certified historic structures or, alternatively, to depreciate substantially rehabilitated historic structures using accelerated depreciation methods. It is anticipated that the Partnership may invest in local limited partnerships which acquire and rehabilitate such certified historic structures. Upon the disposition, by whatever means, of such a certified historic structure, a local limited partnership would be required to recapture, as ordinary income, the excess of the accelerated depreciation or rapid amortization (depending on which of the two alternative methods were chosen) over the otherwise allowable straight-line depreciation computed using the asset's actual useful life.

5. Depreciation Recapture

Upon the sale or other disposition of real estate depreciated under an accelerated method, such as the double-declining balance method, the sum of the years-digits method, or 60-month straight-line depreciation under Section 167(k) or Section 191, all or a portion of the excess of accelerated depreciation over normal straight-line depreciation ("excess depreciation") may be subject to recapture, i.e., will be taxed as ordinary income to the extent of gain realized (or deemed realized). In the case of "low-income" housing, however, excess depreciation is subject to full recapture for the first eight years and four months, declining 1% per month thereafter to zero at the end of sixteen years and eight months. Government-assisted housing which qualifies as "low-income" housing is defined as:

(a) Residential real estate with respect to which a mortgage is insured under Section 221(d)(3) or 236 of the National Housing Act, or housing financed or assisted by direct loan or tax abatement under similar provisions of state or local laws and with respect to which the owner is subject to the restrictions described in Section 1039(b)(1)(B) of the Code.

(b) Dwelling units which, on the average, are held for occupancy by families or individuals eligible to receive subsidies under Section 8 of the United States Housing Act of 1937, as amended, or under the provisions of state or local law authorizing similar levels of subsidy for lower-income families.

(c) Residential real estate with respect to which a depreciation deduction for rehabilitation expenditures is allowed under Section 167(k) of the Code; and

(d) Residential real estate with respect to which a loan is made or insured under Title V of the Housing Act of 1949.

Excess depreciation taken on all residential real estate except that described above and on all non-residential real estate is always subject to recapture in full, as is all depreciation of personal and certain other property. The Partnership's policy is to avoid depreciation recapture whenever feasible by preventing the local limited partnerships from selling any projects, except under exempted sales to qualified tenant groups, if recapture would result. Particularly in the case of involuntary dispositions, however, it could be impossible to avoid recapture.

6. Sale to Tenant Groups

Section 1039 of the Code generally provides that if the Partnership or a local limited partnership makes an approved sale of a qualified low-income housing project to the tenants (or a cooperative or other non-profit organization formed on their behalf) resulting in gain for tax purposes, and if the net amount realized is reinvested in full in another qualified project within one year, the Partnership and, therefore, the Limited Partners will not be required to recognize any gain on the sale. In such event, for depreciation recapture purposes, the holding period of the newly acquired project would include the holding period of the property sold, and the potential depreciation recapture of the newly acquired project will include the potential depreciation recapture of the property sold. However, the tax basis of the newly acquired project will be reduced by the gain not recognized on the sale and, as a consequence, depreciation deductions on such project will be significantly less than deductions available on newly acquired projects. If, however, any sale of a project results in the local limited partnership realizing a *loss,* such loss will be recognized and passed through the Partnership and, therefore, to the Limited Partners.

Real estate programs, on balance, offer low to medium first year deductions, leverage-sensitive cash flow, medium comparative risk and possible capital gain treatment, subject in most instances, to recapture adjustment.

REAL ESTATE GLOSSARY

ACQUISITION FEES

The total of all fees and commissions paid to *affiliates* or non-affiliates in connection with the purchase of a property for a real estate investment program. Acquisition fees include real estate commissions, development fees, *selection fees,* and non-recurring management fees, but do not include loan fees *(points)* paid for mortgage brokerage services.

AFFILIATE

A person or entity directly or indirectly controlled by another person or entity, including any officer, director or partner of the entity. If such person is an officer, director or partner, the company for which the person acts in such capacity is also considered an affiliate.

ALL-INCLUSIVE PROMISSORY NOTE/ALL-INCLUSIVE DEED

(See "Wrap-Around Financing")

ALTERNATIVE MINIMUM TAX

Created under the *Revenue Act of 1978,* this federal income tax is calculated on the total of taxable income plus the excluded portion of *capital gains* and excess itemized deductions. The alternative minimum tax is applicable only to taxable years ending after December 31, 1978, and is on a graduated scale (after an exclusion of $20,000), from 10% to a maximum of 25% on alternative minimum taxable income. Not an add-on tax, this is only paid to the extent that it exceeds the sum of the regular federal income tax and the add-on minimum tax. The alternative minimum tax does not apply to corporations.

AMORTIZATION OF DEBT

(See "Equity Build")

AMORTIZING LOAN

A loan payable in equal monthly or other periodic installments to retire the original principal without requiring a special payment or baloon payment prior to maturity.

APPRAISED VALUE

An expert opinion of the value of a property or other asset; valuation. The methods which appraisers use to arrive at an appraised value are:

Appraisal by Comparison

Comparing a piece of property with other similar properties to arrive at an estimate. Sometimes referred to as Market Approach.

Appraisal by Income

Primarily concerned with the net return that a property will bring.

Appraisal by Summation

An estimation based upon the replacement value of a property. Sometimes known as Cost Approach.

(See "M.A.I. Appraisal")

ASK

When quoted by a securities broker, an "ask" or "asked price" is the lowest price anyone has offered to accept for a given security (see "Bid").

AT-RISK PROVISIONS

Provisions in the *Tax Reform Act of 1976* which drastically limited deductions from *tax shelters* by limiting the deductions to amounts "at risk," and defining that phrase to exclude borrowed amounts (i) with respect to which an investor has no personal liability; (ii) from related persons and those with an interest in the activity; and (iii) protected against loss by guarantees, stop loss agreements and similar arrangements. However, real estate investors continue to realize tax and economic advantages of non-recourse financing because real estate is exempt from the at-risk provisions.

BALLOON PAYMENT

A special payment or full payment on the principal amount of a mortgage prior to the date of normal *amortization,* as provided in the note.

BEST-EFFORTS BASIS

Regarding the sale of real estate program interests, an offering of securities whereby a *broker dealer* firm uses best efforts to sell interests and receives commissions on those sales, with the understanding that the firm might not sell the entire issue and that others, including the issuer, may sell the interests.

BID

When quoted by a securities broker, a bid is the highest price anyone has offered to pay for a given security and may be refused by the seller, who can quote an "asked" price, the lowest the seller will take for the security.

A "bid and asked" price from a broker is a firm quote to buy from the seller at the bid price or to sell to the buyer at the asked price (see "Ask").

BLANKET MORTGAGE LOAN

A *mortgage loan* which covers more than one property.

BLUE-SKY LAWS

Regulations of states and territories concerning the registration, solicitation and sale of securities. A security offering "blue-skyed" in a particular state can be offered for sale there, subject to the state's applicable securities laws.

BOOK VALUE

The historical cost of a real estate asset reduced by accumulated *depreciation*. A real estate asset's book value usually varies from actual market value (see "Net Asset Value").

BOTTOM LINE

Investor benefits from equity ownership of income property are not readily apparent from financial statements prepared in accordance with generally accepted accounting principles *(GAAP)*. The bottom line for a real estate investor is the sum of his or her share of the cash flow from the property, amounts received from the sale or refinancing of the property, plus tax benefits during the period of ownership of the property and from the sale of the property (capital gains, except to the extent that the property was depreciated under an accelerated method, rather than ordinary income). In addition to the cash flow and appreciation realized upon sale, some benefits result from the conversion of ordinary income (during the holding period) to capital gains on sale (again, except to the extent that the property was depreciated under an accelerated method) (see "Capital Gains" and "Depreciation").

BROKEN DEALER

A firm registered with the *SEC* and the securities or corporate commissions department of the state in which it sells investment securities and who may employ licensed agents for that purpose.

CAPITAL CONTRIBUTIONS

The total of all investors' contributed capital in a real estate investment program without the deduction of selling expenses or outlay for the operation or organization of the program (see "Invested Capital").

CAPITAL GAINS (Long-Term Gains)

Income (equal to the excess of sales price over *tax basis*) from the sale of a capital asset (such as real property held by someone other than a "dealer") held by the seller for more than one year. Long-term capital gains are subject to lower federal income tax rates than is ordinary income because, under the *Revenue Act of 1978,* only 40% of an individual's net capital gains received after October 31, 1978 is subject to regular federal income tax (50% was recognized before the Revenue Act of 1978) (see "Alternative Minimum Tax").

CAPITAL IMPROVEMENT

Improvement or replacement of a capital asset which is expected to produce benefits beyond one year.

CAPITALIZATION OF INCOME

An approach to evaluate income property based on its *net income.*

CASH FLOW

The cash funds provided from operations, including lease payments on *net leases* from sellers and interest on cash and short-term investments, without deductions for non-cash expenses (such as *depreciation* and *amortization* of imputed interest), after deducting cash funds used to pay all other expenses, debt payments, *capital improvements* and replacements. Cash flow figures may give a good indication of earning power, but are in a constant state of flux because of varied periods of replacement or improvement activity.

CASH-ON-CASH RETURN

The percentage of return for an investment in a property, measured by dividing spendable cash by the total cash investment. From an investor's standpoint in large real estate investment programs, the percentage is figured by dividing the distributed cash by the investor's contributed capital.

CERTIFICATES OF DEPOSIT (CDs)

Certificates issued by financial institutions for cash deposits. If left on deposit for a specified length of time, a CD usually earns a higher rate of interest than a savings account. If a CD is cashed in before its maturity date, the selling rate is discounted from the face value by the amount of the pro-rated interest to maturity date.

CHATTEL BONUS DEPRECIATION
Chattel bonus depreciation is allowed one time only in the taxable year in which new or used personal property (such as equipment or furnishings) acquired for business or investment purposes, is first placed into service, provided that the useful life of the property acquired is not less than six years. In any one taxable year, a single taxpayer, corporation (or controlled group of corporations), or partnership may not claim more than $2,000 of chattel bonus depreciation. (A married taxpayer filing a joint return may not claim more than $4,000 of annual chattel bonus depreciation.)

CLOSED MORTGAGE
A mortgage that cannot be paid off until maturity.

COLLATERAL
Property or securities pledged to a creditor by a borrower as security for a loan.

COLLECTED RENTS
Amounts actually collected for the use or occupancy of improved property.

COMMISSIONER OF CORPORATIONS
The state official who has regulatory authority over the sale of securities in California, including real estate *syndications*. In other states, the title and jurisdiction over real estate syndications may vary.

COMPARABLE SALES (Comparables)
The selling price of property similarly situated in a similar market in the recent past.

DEBT SERVICE
The regular payments of principal and/or interest required by terms of a note or contract.

DEFERRED GAIN
The amount of profit realized upon the sale of properties but not recognized as taxable income because of the installment recognition technique (see "Installment Sale").

DEFERRED INCOME

For accounting purposes, "unearned income" carried as a liability because it was received before carned and, absent an agreement to the contrary, must be returned to the payor if not ultimately earned; for example, rent collected in advance of a tenant's occupancy of an income property.

DEMOGRAPHICS

An area's vital statistics (population, income, density, growth, economic trends, distribution, occupations, lifestyles) which have a potential effect on real estate.

DEPRECIATION

The allowable tax and accounting deduction for the *amortization* of the actual cost of improved property over its useful life. No direct cash outlay is required. Depreciation is assumed, for tax and accounting purposes, to represent the utilization of assets expected to exist beyond one year, even though the assets may be appreciating in value. Land is considered to have a perpetual life and, therefore, only the improvements are considered depreciable.

Straight-Line Depreciation

The recognition of depreciation in equal annual amounts over the estimated useful life of an asset.

Accelerated Depreciation

Methods of depreciation which recognize amounts in excess of straight-line depreciation during the initial years of the asset's useful life. Various methods of accelerated depreciation are allowable for federal tax purposes, but result in the *recapture* of ordinary taxable income equal to amounts depreciated in excess of that allowable for straight-line depreciation upon the sale or other disposition of the asset. The excess of accelerated depreciation over straight-line depreciation is considered an item of a tax preference with respect to leased property (see "Tax Preference").

Accumulated Depreciation

Sum of depreciation taken using either of the above depreciation methods.

DISCOUNTED NOTE (Discounted Paper)

A note secured by *real property* and purchased for less than face amount to increase the effect of *yield* on the note to the lender.

DISTRIBUTIONS
Cash or other property paid to investors in a real estate investment program. Distributions generally arise from the *cash flow* produced during the ownership of property and amounts realized from sales or refinancings.

DIVIDEND
Distribution to its shareholders by a corporation or a *real estate investment trust.*

DIVIDEND REINVESTMENT PLAN
A system for automatically investing cash distributions in shares or fractional shares which are then credited to an investor's account and on which additional *dividends* are earned.

DUE DILIGENCE EXAMINATION
Investigation of an issuer of securities which is conducted by a broker dealer in order to verify claims and representations made by the issuer or *sponsor.*

DUE-ON-SALE CLAUSE
A provision in a note secured by a mortgage or a deed of trust allowing the holder of the note the option to demand full payment upon transfer of title.

ECONOMIC BENEFITS
The benefits resulting from *cash flow,* mortgage *amortization,* and appreciation of a property, not including tax benefits.

ECONOMIC CONSIDERATION
Includes all fees, commissions and *expenses of acquisition* for a property.

ECONOMIC GAIN
The difference between the total *economic consideration* and the net proceeds from sale, after deducting closing costs and sales commissions. Any accumulated *depreciation* previously deducted for financial purposes is not considered.

EQUITY (Property)
The difference between the current market value and the existing debt.

EQUITY BUILD
An increase in the equity of a real estate investment due to reduction *(amortization)* of existing loans by payments of principal. Equity build is not realized in cash until the sale and collection of sales proceeds of a property for a price of at

least its original cost or until the refinancing of a property for an amount at least equal to the original mortgage.

EQUITY DOLLARS

The actual cash outlay to the seller at the time of purchase, including cash deposits which are paid to the seller prior to close of escrow and are attributable to the *purchase price* of the property.

EQUITY KICKER

Provision for a lender's equity participation in a *real property* as an inducement to lend funds.

EQUITY TRUST

A real estate investment trust (REIT) which acquires income-producing properties, as contrasted with a *mortgage REIT,* which makes or purchases loans on real estate (see also "Real Estate Investment Trust").

ESCALATION CLAUSE

A provision in a lease that allows increases in rent when the landlord's actual costs rise.

EXCULPATORY CLAUSE

A provision in a mortgage or deed of trust which limits the rights of the *mortgagee* to a simple foreclosure and recovery of the building, and prohibits the mortgagee from claiming a deficiency or personal judgment against the former owner.

EXPENSES OF ACQUISITION

An economic measure of acquisition cost which includes the down payment, mortgage, *prepaid interest,* loan *points,* real estate brokerage commissions, investment advisory fees, and closing costs.

EXPOSURE COST

In connection with a purchase/*leaseback* transaction, the cost of the building less the amount of equity pledged by the *lessee.* Example: Purchaser pays $10,000 down and gives the seller a $90,000 all-inclusive note. The underlying note is $70,000. The all-inclusive note refers to a lease agreement, and gives the purchaser/*lessor* a right to off-set against the $20,000 equity of the seller/lessee. Thus, the exposure cost is only $80,000, although the total cost was $100,000.

EXTRAORDINARY ITEM

Pertaining to income statements, an event or transaction unusual in nature and adjudged unlikely to occur in the foreseeable future in the environment in which the entity functions, an item not directly related to ongoing operations with impact on net income/net loss; for example, a major casualty loss or a prohibition under a newly enacted law or regulation. More specifically related to equity real estate investments, the result of foreclosure, debt restructuring or involuntary termination of *leaseback* agreement. Useful in helping investors determine amounts representative of income or losses in order to project future income potential.

FAIR, JUST AND EQUITABLE STANDARD

The standard a *sponsor*'s compensation must meet before the *Commission of Corporations* will allow a security to be offered in the commissioner's jurisdiction.

FEASIBILITY STUDY

A report, which is not an appraisal, on a particular *real property* analyzing the attractiveness of the property as a proposed investment based on such factors as anticipated *cash flow* and potential appreciation.

FIDUCIARY

An agent acting on behalf of a limited partner or a shareholder, for example, in a financial transaction.

FINANCIAL ACCOUNTING STANDARDS BOARD (FASB)

Seven-person national board, including four CPAs, which establishes standards of, and issues policies on, financial accounting and reporting.

FIRST MORTGAGE

A mortgage which takes priority over all other liens upon the same *real property* and which must be satisfied before any other claims on the proceeds of a property sale.

FIRST MORTGAGE LOAN

A loan for which a *first mortgage* is used as security or *collateral.*

FISCAL YEAR

A 12-month period used for accounting and tax purposes; does not necessarily coincide with the calendar year.

FUNDS FROM OPERATIONS (FFO)

The excess of operating revenues and recognized *(GAAP gains)* on sales of property realized from real estate investments over the costs of operations. Occasionally identified on a *statement of changes in financial position* as an indicator of earnings on real estate investments. FFO identifies, better than *net income,* the earnings realized from equity investments in real estate.

GAAP (Financial Reporting)

Method of finance using generally accepted accounting principles (GAAP), as determined by standards set forth by the *Financial Accounting Standards Board.* Results in standardization of accounting methods and the process used to compare financial results in various kinds of statements.

GAAP GAIN

The profit recognized upon the sale of property in accordance with generally accepted accounting principles (GAAP). Unlike gains reported for tax purposes, GAAP gain is dependent upon many economic considerations, including the buyer's initial and continuing cash investment, and upon the ability of the property to provide *cash flow* to service debt provided by the seller at the time of sale.

GENERAL PARTNER

(see "Limited Partnership")

GOVERNMENT NATIONAL MORTGAGE ASSOCIATION MODIFIED PASS-THROUGH PARTICIPATION CERTIFICATES (GNMAs)

A collection of mortgages secured by *real property* and the credit of the federal government and sold to investors at going market rates. GNMA, a quasi-governmental entity, services the mortgages and passes the principal and interest amounts collected on to the investors. GNMAs are also known as "Ginnie Maes."

GROSS MULTIPLIER

A method (only one of many items to be considered in a valuation estimate) used to roughly approximate the value of income property based on its potential rental income. Example: The gross rental income from an apartment building is $100,000 per annum. If an appraiser adopts a gross multiplier of 6.7, it is said that, based on the gross multiplier, the value of the building is $670,000.

HYPOTHECATION LOAN

A loan secured or collateralized by an existing *mortgage loan,* but without the retirement, reconveyance or sale of the existing loan.

IMPOUND ACCOUNT

In a securities offering, a fund set up in a financial institution to hold the subscription monies of investors, at a prescribed interest rate, until such time as the entity in which they invest receives a specified amount of money from subscribers. When the "impound" amount is reached, the funds are released to the entity for use as described in the *prospectus* of the program.

INDIVIDUAL RETIREMENT ACCOUNT (IRA)

A tax-deductible investment which allows deferral of tax on the income it produces. IRAs are for employed persons not participating in company- or union-sponsored retirement or pension plans. Maximum annual tax-deductible deposit is $1,500, or 15% of gross salary, whichever is less. The non-employed spouse of an IRA participant also may have an account. The combined total yearly contribution for both accounts cannot exceed 15% of the working spouse's compensation or $1,750, whichever is less. Provisions of the *Revenue Act of 1978* permit additional employer contributions under specific circumstances up to the difference between $7,500 and the amount contributed by the employee.

INFLATION

A decrease in purchasing power of the dollar. The inflationary spiral illustrates inflated dollars: increased wages force up costs of goods and services, which, in turn, raise prices. Higher prices increase the demand for higher wages, and the cycle continues. Inflation is also identified by an increase in the money supply, independent of any actual growth in productivity.

INFLATION HEDGE

The protection against *inflation* that may be afforded by an investment because of appreciation at a rate equivalent to or greater than the rate of inflation.

INSTALLMENT SALE

The sale of a property in which a portion of the selling price (including liabilities assumed or taken subject to) is paid other than in the taxable year of the sale, the obligation to make such subsequent payment often being evidenced by notes receivable payable by the buyer in regular installments. Installment sales are particularly suitable for real estate *limited partnerships* because: (1) increased sales price generally results from a more flexible structuring of the sale from the buyer's standpoint; (2) limited partners (on the cash basis method of accounting) are able to spread the payment of their personal income taxes on the gain realized on a qualifying installment sale over a longer period; (3) *alternative minimum tax* effects from *capital gains* can be diluted or possibly eliminated due to the spread of tax recognition over many years; and (4) the partnership earns interest income (taxable) during the collection period of the installment notes.

INTERSTATE OFFERING
An offering of securities in more than one state. Such offering is regulated both by federal securities laws and by the securities laws of each state where offered.

INTRASTATE OFFERING
An offering of securities within only one state, restricted to residents of that state, and regulated by the securities laws of that state.

INVESTED CAPITAL
Capital contributions of investors in a real estate investment program, less the sum of cumulative *surplus funds* distributed to investors.

INVESTMENT INTEREST
Interest paid or accrued on indebtedness incurred or continued to purchase or carry property held for investment, rather than in a trade or business or for personal use (such as one's principal residence). In real estate, investment interest typically applies to *leaseback* transactions under triple net leases. The amount of such interest which can be deducted for income tax purposes is limited.

INVESTOR BENEFITS
The total benefits to the investor in *real property,* including *cash flow, equity build,* appreciation, and various tax benefits.

JUNIOR MORTGAGE
A mortgage which is subject to the priority of one or more senior mortgages.

JUNIOR MORTGAGE LOAN
A loan for which a *junior mortgage* is used as security or *collateral.* A junior mortgage loan takes priority after first *mortgage loan* (see "Wrap-around Mortgage Loan").

KEOGH PLAN

A retirement plan for self-employed individuals which allows an annual tax deductible contribution of up to $7,500 or 15% of business taxable income, whichever is less.

LEASEBACK

Upon purchase of a *real property,* the practice of leasing the property back to the seller for a definite time period, requiring the payment of *cash-on-cash returns.* When extended over long periods of time, a leaseback is similar to providing a loan to the seller, with the property as *collateral.* When utilized over short periods of time, a leaseback is an often-used method of obtaining a seller's guarantee of *cash flow* during the start-up operations of a newly developed property.

LESSEE

A person or entity who enters into a contractual relationship to use property owned by another. (In real estate, commonly referred to as a tenant.)

LESSOR

An owner of a property who allows another person or entity to make use of that property under a contractual relationship. (In real estate, commonly referred to as a landlord.)

LEVERAGING

The act of acquiring ownership utilizing borrowed funds. To the extent the amount paid for borrowed funds is less than that earned from ownership, the leverage improves the *bottom line.* (The reverse is also true.)

LIMITED PARTNER

(see "Limited Partnership")

LIMITED PARTNERSHIP

An association of two or more persons (persons includes corporation), at least one of whom is a limited partner and at least one of whom is a general partner. The general partner manages the partnership business; limited partners are passive investors and do not have the right to manage, although they may be given substantial powers in the limited partnership agreement with respect to certain partnership transactions. A limited partnership usually has from a few limited partners to hundreds or even thousands. One of the characteristics distinguishing a limited partnership from other forms such as a corporation is its limited life. A self-liquidating limited partnership would liquidate itself by distributing to the limited partners the net sales or refinancing proceeds other than those needed for operating contingencies or cash reserves.

LIQUIDATION

Conversion of securities, real estate, or other assets into cash.

LOAN CONSTANT

A rate which refers to the annual periodic payments on an *amortizing loan* (i.e., principal and interest). If the interest rate is lower and/or the loan term is longer, the loan constant is lower. Conversely, the loan constant increases with a higher interest rate and/or a shorter term.

LOCK-IN CLAUSE

A provision in a note prohibiting *prepayment.*

M.A.I. APPRAISAL

An appraisal by a Member of the American Institute of Appraisers.

MARKET MAKER

Brokerage firm (generally involved in the *over-the-counter market*) which stands willing to transact orders for the purchase or sale of the securities of a publicly traded company at any time.

MASTER LESSEE

A *lessee* of a property primarily responsible to the *lessor* and who, in turn, subleases the property to others.

MORTGAGE LOAN

A note, debenture, bond or other evidence of debt or obligation which may or may not be negotiable but is secured (or collateralized) by one or more mortgages.

MORTGAGE REDUCTION

(see "Equity Build")

MORTGAGE REIT

A mortgage REIT is one which specializes in either making or buying permanent *mortgage loans* or in providing short-term (interim) financing on large construction and development projects. (see "Real Estate Investment Trust").

MORTGAGEE

One who holds a note secured by a mortgage on property.

MORTGAGOR

One who owes a note secured by a mortgage on property.

NASDAQ (NASD Automated Quotation System)
A computerized communications network which provides video terminal readings of current stock quotations for more than 2,600 *over-the-counter* (OTC) stocks. NASDAQ furnishes price ranges, price earnings ratios, and *dividend* information, with a variety of indices. NASDAQ quotations are also carried in major metropolitan and financial newspapers with coded names for stocks listed.

NATIONAL ASSOCIATION OF SECURITIES DEALERS, INC. (NASD)
Self-regulating body which licenses brokers and dealers handling securities offerings, reviews the terms of an offering's underwriting arrangements and advertising literature, and, while not a governmental agency, acts as a watchdog to see that its regulations and those of the *SEC* are followed for the investors protection in offerings of securities.

NET ASSET VALUE
In a *real estate investment trust,* the *book value* of the trust's total assets minus the trust's liabilities.

NET CONTRIBUTED CAPITAL
Total contributed capital of an investor less *surplus funds* distributed from the sales or refinancings of investment properties.

NET GAIN
(see "Economic Gain")

NET INCOME/NET LOSS (Pre-Tax)
The excess (income) or deficit (loss) of gross revenues (from rents, interest, gains from sale, etc.) over expenses (from operations, property taxes, interest, depreciation, etc.).

NET LEASE
A lease in which the tenant *(lessee)* pays the *real property* taxes and operating expenses, and the landlord pays for major repairs and *debt service.*

NET, NET LEASE
A lease in which the tenant *(lessee)* pays the *real property* taxes, operating expenses, and insurance, and the landlord pays for major maintenance and for *debt service.*

NET, NET, NET LEASE (Triple Net Lease)
A lease in which the tenant *(lessee)* pays all of the costs of

ownership, including *debt service,* and the landlord's responsibilities are limited to major improvements to the property.

NON-RECOURSE DEBT

A loan which, in the event of default, limits the remedies of the creditor to recovery of stated *collateral* (i.e., land and improvements) and prohibits a personal judgment or other recourse against the owner for any deficiency caused when the property is liquidated to satisfy the loan balance. The repayment of a non-recourse debt is secured only by the *real property* involved (see "At-Risk Provisions").

OCCUPANCY RATE

The percentage of occupancy of an income property, calculated, in multi-family housing, as the number of rent-paying units divided by the number of rentable units as of a given date. In commercial/industrial complexes, calculated as the number of square feet leased divided by the number of leasable square feet as of a given date.

OFFERING CIRCULAR

(see "Prospectus")

OFFSET PROVISION

In a note, a stipulation referring to performance of the note holder in some other manner, such as under a lease agreement, or which may refer to performance of the building which secures the note, and gives the borrower, if certain items occur, the right to subtract amounts due without disbursing cash.

OVER-THE-COUNTER (OTC) MARKET

Network of securities dealers who trade among themselves, acting as principals or as brokers for customers. As the largest such securities market in the world, the OTC trades corporate bonds, municipal, state and federal government obligations, stocks, mutual fund shares, and *real estate investment trusts* (see "NASDAQ").

PARTICIPATION LOAN

One in which the "lead" lender arranges for other lenders to furnish part of the funds required.

PARTNERSHIP

(see "Limited Partnership")

PERCENTAGE LEASE

A lease in which the rental includes a percentage of the

volume of sales, usually in addition to a guaranteed minimum.

POINTS

Amounts paid to a lender as a loan fee. In effect, points are interest on interest. For federal income tax purposes, points must be amortized over the term of the loan (except in the purchase of homes, in which case points are deducted when actually paid, so long as such payment of points is an established business practice in the area in which the indebtedness is incurred and the amount of the payment does not exceed the amount generally charged in such area).

PREPAID INTEREST

The payment of advance interest on a loan. Such prepayments are deductible for federal income tax purposes only in the taxable years for which the interest expense accrues (i.e., on an accrual basis).

PREPAYMENT PRIVILEGE

A provision in a note, resulting from the use of the words "or more," or other similar language, giving to the *mortgagor* the privilege of paying all or part of the unpaid balance of the note at any time without penalty.

PRINCIPAL OR PRIME TENANT

A corporation, a person, or group of related persons, who is the largest single occupant of a piece of *real property* and who generally occupies more than 25% of the aggregate square footage.

PRO FORMA

For form only; in financial statements, figures prepared on an "as if" basis, the "as if" assumptions stated clearly and the figures calculated as they would have pertained had certain facts or items been present at a particular time.

PRO FORMA PROJECTIONS

Statements of the anticipated operating income and expense of property based on assumptions about various financial factors.

PRO FORMA RENTS

Figures on rental income at an income property; based on an "as if" basis; for instance, estimated gross income at an apartment complex, figured as if rental prices were increased to uniform, projected market levels are actually collected as of a given date on a given type of unit.

PROPERTY MANAGEMENT FEE

The fee paid for day-to-day professional management services.

PROSPECTUS

A disclosure document required by the *Securities Act of 1933* which details pertinent facts about an issuer offering an interstate security for public sale and which must be presented to all prospective buyers of the security. A prospectus must disclose, for example, possible *risk factors* to potential investors, details about the *sponsor* of the investment, its history *(track record),* its products, its officers, and such information as financial reports, investor qualifications, competition, market conditions, lawsuits, the intended use of the proceeds of the offering, and commissions and expenses of the underwriter. When distributed prior to the effectiveness by the *SEC* of a registration statement, a prospectus is called a *"red herring"* or a "preliminary prospectus."

A prospectus is sometimes referred to as an "offering circular," a term which describes only a disclosure document for an *intrastate offering.*

Prospectuses and offering circulars are updated, as required by the SEC, with sticker supplements.

PROXY

Written authorization from an investor to authorize voting of his or her interest; issued by the management of a corporation or investment program concurrently with a proxy statement which discloses information which the investors need in order to vote their proxies. Such proxies are required for entities registered under the *Securities Exchange Act of 1934.*

PURCHASE-LEASEBACK

(see "Leaseback")

PURCHASE MONEY LOAN

A loan used for the purchase of *real property.* The lender can be either the seller or a third party. The real property acts as the sole *collateral* for the loan so in the event of a default, there is no personal liability to the purchaser/borrower.

PURCHASE PRICE

The total price paid for a property (including all acquisition fees and liens and mortgages on the properties).

REAL ESTATE INVESTMENT TRUST (REIT)

A corporation, trust, or association which satisfies the various detailed requirements under federal tax laws (one of which is that it be managed by one or more trustees or directors), a REIT usually invests in real estate mortgages or equities for the benefit of its investors. Under the Real Estate Investment Act of 1961, a qualified REIT does not pay taxes at the trust level, so long as it meets certain criteria (including distributing out as *dividends* at least 90% of its annual real estate investment trust taxable income [95% for taxable years beginning after December 31, 1979]) and to the extent that its real estate investment trust taxable income is distributed to investors.

An *equity trust* is essentially a landlord, investing in equities in income-producing real estate. Income is derived primarily from rents off the properties. The *mortgage REIT,* on the other hand, either provides short-term (interim) financing on large construction and development projects or makes or buys permanent *mortgage loans.*

REAL PROPERTY

Includes buildings, land, improvements, fixtures, and equipment and interests therein, but does not include mortgages, *mortgage loans* or interests therein.

RECAPTURE OF DEPRECIATION

The inclusion as ordinary income of certain excess accelerated depreciation deductions previously taken, upon the occurrence of a sale or certain other dispositions of a property (see "Depreciation").

RED HERRING

A preliminary prospectus or offering circular which outlines information required by the *SEC* about a new offering or securities issue, its *sponsor,* directors, officers, and details of operations (see "Prospectus").

REGISTERED REPRESENTATIVE

An employee of a brokerage house who has met stock exchange qualifications as to knowledge of the securities business, acts as a customer's broker, and is compensated on a commission basis. (see "Broker Dealer").

REGULAR PRINCIPAL PAYMENTS

Monthly and/or annual payments required to amortize a note

or contract payable, exclusive of special or *balloon payments.*

REPLACEMENT COST

A figure which indicates the estimated cost of replacing the *capital improvements* on an operating *real property,* together with estimates of depreciation and accumulated *depreciation* based on such cost. It is based on the lowest amount that would have to be paid in the normal course of business to construct a new asset of equivalent operating or productive capability. Replacement cost estimates generally do not reflect a property's current market value and are sometimes figured on a square-footage basis in regards to constructing a comparable new building in the same geographical area, with reference to published indices.

REPRODUCTION COST

One of the three approaches to value used in connection with *appraised value,* which also allows for deferred maintenance and *depreciation.*

RESERVES

A percentage of the original *capital contributions* of investors; funds from the proceeds of an offering that are not invested in property but are set aside to provide for contingencies, deferred maintenance, and expenses for major repairs and replacements.

RETURN OF CAPITAL

A *distribution* to an investor from a source other than *net income* as determined for tax or accounting purposes. For tax purposes, a return of capital is not taxable.

RETURN ON INVESTMENT

Rate of pre-tax profit earned in relation to the value of a shareholder's original *invested capital*; stated as a percentage of the original *purchase price* and referred to as *"yield"* when a shareholder owns a small portion of the equity of a particular, usually large, investment.

REVENUE ACT OF 1978

Generally favorable to individual real estate investors, this federal income tax act provides, among other things: (1) reduction from 50% to 40% the amount of an individual's net *capital gains* which are subject to ordinary income tax rates; and (2) elimination of the excluded portion of net capital gains as an item which is subject to the minimum tax on *tax preference* items and which reduces the amount of personal service income eligible for the 50% maximum tax. The change described in "(1)" relates to gains from sales occurring after October 31, 1978; those in "(2)" relate to gains derived in taxable years ending after December 31, 1978. Under the Act, capital gains received after October 31, 1978 are subject to an *alternative minimum tax,* usually more favorable to investors than taxes under the pre-Revenue Act of 1978 minimum tax provisions as they related to the excluded portion of net capital gains as an item of tax preference.

RISK FACTORS

In real estate investment programs, factors affecting real estate values are considered unpredictable risks, about which potential investors should be warned. Examples of risks: changes in, or rulings on, federal or state tax laws; governmental regulations affecting rents, fuel, energy, environmental factors; changes in interest rates and in the availability of long-term mortgage funds; changes in the neighborhood of the properties acquired or in the area's competition; and possible default by *lessees* in purchase/*leaseback* transactions.

SCHEDULED RENTS

The amounts of rental income due from income properties, based on rental schedules, taking into account the occupied and rent-paying units as of a given date, plus the rents which would be due (at any new rental rates) on vacant units if they were rented as of that same date.

SECONDARY MORTGAGE MARKET

The process of lenders selling their mortgages in bulk, with continually fluctuating interest rates, comprises the secondary mortgage market.

SECURITIES ACT OF 1933

A federal act regulated and enforced by the *SEC* which requires, among other things, the registration and use of a *prospectus* whenever a security is sold publicly (unless the security or the manner of the offering is expressly exempt from such registration process).

SECURITIES EXCHANGE ACT OF 1934

A federal act regulated and enforced by the *SEC* which supplements the *Securities Act of 1933* and contains requirements which were designed to protect investors and to regulate the trading of securities in open market trading (secondary market). Such regulations require, among other items, the use of prescribed *proxy* statements when investors: votes are solicited, the disclosure of management's and large shareholders' holdings of securities; controls on the resale of such securities; and periodic (monthly, quarterly, annual) filing with the SEC of financial and disclosure reports of the issuer.

SECURITIES & EXCHANGE COMMISSION (SEC)

An independent U.S. government regulatory and enforcement agency which supervises investment trading activities and registers companies and those securities which fall under its jurisdiction. The SEC also administers statutes to enforce disclosure requirements which were designed to protect investors in securities offerings.

SECURITY BROKERAGE FEES

Commissions for the sale of units of interest or shares in a real estate investment program.

SELECTION FEE

Non-recurring, non-refundable, and non-cancellable compensation to the *sponsor*(s) of a real estate investment program for providing professional research, analysis, advice, and consultation.

SHARES

The beneficial interests of the shareholders of a *real estate investment trust.* Each share represents a *capital contribution* to the trust and entitles the shareholder to rights and interests as defined in the declaration of the trust.

SOFT DOLLARS

That portion of the funds advanced by an investor which result in immediate federal income tax deductions rather than in the creation of an asset which is subject to amortization or *depreciation.*

SOFT REAL ESTATE (OR RENTAL) MARKET

A condition under which there is a substantial vacancy factor in the market area.

SPONSOR

Any person directly or indirectly instrumental in organizing, wholly or in part, or any person who will manage or participate in the management of a real estate investment program.

STATEMENT OF CHANGES IN FINANCIAL POSITION
A financial statement designed to show, for a specified period of time, the sources of funds acquired by a business or a real estate investment program and the distribution and general effect of such funds upon the various groups of assets, liabilities and capital of that business or program.

STEP-UP INTEREST PAYMENTS (Variable Interest Rates)
Variations in interest rates prescribed to occur at specified times, as opposed to fixed-term interest rates or those which vary with independent economic indicators.

SUBJECT-TO PROVISION
A provision in a property's purchase agreement which conditions the close of escrow, such as one giving the purchaser the right to verify, for instance, rental income and expenses, structural soundness, or a waiver of *due-on-sale clause* before the transaction is finally consummated.

SUBORDINATED INCENTIVE FEE
Compensation to the *sponsor*(s) of a real estate investment program representing potential economic benefits from the operations, sales, or refinancings of the program's properties dependent upon first achieving stated returns to investors. This fee is considered an added incentive for the profitable operations and sales of properties in the program.

SUNBELT
Parts of the Southwest, Southeast, South with moderate climates and currently positive economic and *demographic* trends; includes Southern California and the states of Arizona, New Mexico, Oklahoma, Texas, Arkansas, Louisiana, Tennessee, Mississippi, Alabama, Georgia, North and South Carolina, Virginia, and Florida. Sunbelt regions have recently attracted industry as well as major purchasers of income property for any of several reasons: (1) low or no state income taxes; (2) relatively low property taxes and lower costs of living; and (3) population growth and good employment opportunities.

SURPLUS FUNDS
The net cash funds or proceeds (including lump sum prepayments by buyers) resulting from the financing, refinancing, or sale of the assets of a real estate investment program after deduction of all expenses incurred in connection therewith,

including any real estate commissions and brokerage fees paid; plus all net cash proceeds subsequently received on any installment payment on promissory notes and/or installment contracts held in connection with the sale of assets; less such amounts for working capital reserves as deemed reasonably necessary for future operations.

SYNDICATION (Real Estate)

Formal group of investors who pool their funds for investments in *real property* to gain the advantages of: (1) a larger and more diversified property portfolio than they could purchase individually; (2) research and analysis ability of the *sponsor*(s); (3) professional management; (4) limited liability; (5) greater potential for capital appreciation upon the sale of the property; (6) economies of scale since the administrative costs, including legal, accounting and investment management, are spread among many investors and among many types and sizes of properties (see "Limited Partnership" and "Real Estate Investment Trust").

SYNDICATOR (Real Estate)

The sponsor of a real estate *syndication.*

TAKEOUT COMMITMENT

A commitment by a lending institution to assume or liquidate a short-term construction loan and issue a permanent mortgage.

TAX BASIS–ADJUSTED (Investment in a real estate investment trust or limited partnership)

(a) *Real estate investment trust*–For federal income tax purposes, the amount of money plus the adjusted tax basis of other property* contributed, reduced (but not below zero) by those real estate investment trust distributions which are non-taxable. (To the extent that an investor receives distributions which would otherwise reduce his adjusted tax basis below zero, he must recognize *capital gains*). (b) *Limited partnership*–For federal income tax purposes, the amount of money, plus the adjusted tax basis of other property* contributed, plus the limited partner's share (in accordance with the extent of his share of partnership profits) of non-recourse

*Normally, only money and no "other property" is contributed to a real estate investment trust or a syndicated limited partnership. The table in the text assumes that no such "other property" has, in fact, been contributed.

partnership liabilities, reduced (but not below zero) by the amount of money and the adjusted tax basis of other property distributed to the partner and by the partner's allocable share of partnership losses, and increased by the partner's allocable share of partnership income (both taxable and tax-exempt). (To the extent that a partner receives distributions which would otherwise reduce his adjusted tax basis below zero, he must recognize taxable income, which, depending upon the facts and circumstances, may be ordinary income or capital gain.)

	Partnership	Trust
Money contributed	$1,000	$1,000
Allocable share of non-recourse debt	3,000	–
Cumulative cash distributions (assumed fully taxable to REIT investors)	(600)	
Cumulative tax loss	(1,200)	–
Adjusted tax basis	$2,200	$1,000

TAX BASIS–ADJUSTED (Property Ownership)

The original tax basis of *real property* is the cost of that property if purchased, the fair market value of that property if inherited prior to 1980* or if received as compensation, and the basis of the donor if received by gift, and is increased by any gift taxes paid by the donor. The adjusted tax basis of real property is increased by the cost of any *capital improvements* and reduced by the amount of any accumulated *depreciation.* Accumulated depreciation is the total of all depreciation deductions taken with respect to that property.

TAX DEFERRED INCOME

Cash flow on which no tax is presently payable, generally because the depreciation deduction is at least as large as the

*Under current law, the adjusted tax basis of property inherited after 1979 will instead be determined under the complex carryover basis rules of Section 1023 of the Internal Revenue Code, as amended. However, carryover basis rules were recently eliminated.

cash flow. The tax is thus deferred until the property is subsequently sold.

TAX LOSS CARRY-FORWARD

In the filing of corporate or individual tax reports, the deduction of the operating losses of prior years' operations from the profits of the current year before calculating tax liability. If losses exceed the profits of the current year and designated prior years, the balance is carried forward for a designated number of years.

TAX LOSS PASS-THROUGH

In a real estate *limited partnership,* the tax loss in excess of that which is allocated to shelter cash *distributions* to limited partners and which may be utilized by a limited partner to offset other income.

TAX PREFERENCE

For federal income tax purposes, investors are subject to a tax over and above normal taxes which is equal to the excess of 15% of tax preferences over the greater of $10,000 ($5,000 in the case of married taxpayers filing separate returns) or one-half of the regular federal income tax liability (less certain credits). Tax preferences include, among others, adjusted itemized deductions, depletion allowances, intangible drilling costs and the excess of accelerated *depreciation* over straight-line depreciation on *real property*. For non-corporate taxpayers, in taxable years ending prior to January 1, 1979, the excluded portion of net *capital gains* was also a tax preference item which was subject to this 15% "minimum tax." (For corporate taxpayers, the excluded portion of net capital gains remains an item of tax preference which is subject to the minimum tax.)

Items of tax preference (other than the excluded portion of net capital gains) also reduce (on a dollar-for-dollar basis) the amount of an individual's personal service income which is eligible for the 50% maximum tax. (For taxable years ending prior to January 1, 1979, the items of tax preference which reduced such personal service income included the excluded portion of net capital gains.)

Two tax preference items, adjusted itemized deductions and the excluded portion of net capital gains, constitute part of the tax base (together with a taxpayer's regular taxable income, less certain deductions) of the alternative minimum tax. (See "Alternative Minimum Tax.")

TAX REFORM ACT OF 1976 (TRA)

Federal tax legislation signed October 4, 1976, which was designed to reduce tax loopholes. One of the purposes of the TRA, as it pertains to real estate, was to stem the so-called artificial losses taken on interest and taxes paid during construction projects; on accelerated *depreciation*; and on *prepaid interest* and *points* used to reduce tax liabilities created from other income.

Although the Act had a major negative impact on many *tax shelters* because of *at-risk provisions,* real estate investments are exempted from those provisions.

TAX SHELTER

The use of tax losses to offset or "shelter" taxable income of the taxpayer from other sources. Investment programs are referred to as "tax shelters" when they "shelter" at least a portion of this outside taxable income from taxation.

TAX-SHELTERED PROGRAM

A tax-sheltered investment program is one which has provisions allowed by the federal government to reduce tax liability to its investors by using special credits or allowances and which acts as a device for reinvesting earnings on capital without paying income tax on those earnings.

TOTAL COST OF ACQUISITION

Represents the total cash down payment, real estate commission, closing costs, escrow and/or appraisal fees, and the amount due on the contract of sale, all-inclusive promissory note, promissory note and/or existing debt on the property (see "Purchase Price").

TRACK HISTORY (Track Record)

The previous operating results of prior *syndications* of the *syndicator* or *sponsor* of a real estate program.

TRUST

(see "Real Estate Investment Trust")

UNAMORTIZED DISCOUNT

An accounting treatment required by GAAP which results from the stated interest rate on a note or contract payable being less than the prevailing interest rate at the time the related property was acquired. The discount is amortized using the effective interest method over the terms of the note or contract.

UNAMORTIZED PREMIUM

An accounting treatment required by *GAAP* which results from the stated interest rate on a note or contract payable being in excess of the prevailing interest rate at the time the related property was acquired. The premium is amortized using the effective interest method over the terms of the note or contract.

WRAP-AROUND FINANCING

A debt instrument which results from the creation of an all-inclusive promissory note (AIPN) or a contract of sale. It leaves intact existing debt on *real property* (i.e., underlying loan) and may be utilized in the sale or purchase of property. Example: Seller's building is encumbered by a $70,000 mortgage at 7% interest. Seller sells building for $100,000, $15,000 down, and carries back an $85,000 all-inclusive note at 8% interest. From the payments on the $85,000 note, the seller will discharge the payments required on the $70,000 note, and therefore his equity in his all-inclusive note is $15,000.

An investor/seller tends to benefit from this type of financing because recognition of full *capital gains* is delayed until the wrap-around note is paid off, thereby deferring the investor's tax liability (see "Installment Sale").

WRAP-AROUND MORTGAGE LOAN

A loan in an amount equal to the balance due under an existing mortgage loan, which is not retired, plus an additional amount advanced by the lender holding the wrap-around loan. The wrap-around provides for a total payment that includes the payment on the underlying loan.

YIELD

The total return on an investment.

The assistance of Consolidated Capital Equities Corporation in the preparation of this Glossary is gratefully acknowledged.

Suite 701, Wells Fargo Building
333 Hegenberger Road
Oakland, CA 94621
(415) 638-3000
Toll free
In California: (800) 772-2443
Out of State: (800) 227-1870

Chapter Two

ENERGY

Demand for oil and gas is growing; available supplies are dwindling; prices, which remained relatively stable for almost twenty years, have risen and continue to rise sharply. Generally favorable tax treatment, coupled with the growing energy crisis, makes oil and gas one of the more attractive all-around tax sheltered investments.

Industry statistics indicate only about one of nine "wildcat wells" drilled to explore for a new oil or gas "field" is successful; only about one out of about 40 to 50 is a significant commercial success. Once a field is discovered, risk drops and returns become more predictable. About 80% of all "development wells," those drilled adjacent to existing producing wells, are successful.

For many years, very wealthy investors have utilized oil and gas joint ventures and private limited partnerships as key tax shelter tools. In the late 1960's, publicly registered programs appeared in significant numbers. Minimum investments of $5,000 and $10,000 brought oil and gas within reach of approximately one million qualified investors.

In most oil and gas limited partnerships, the sponsor is an operating company that explores for and produces oil and gas. Except in the case of "tangible-intangible" sharing arrangements, the sponsor seldom makes a significant direct investment in partnership wells. He supplies oil-and-gas-finding expertise and is compensated by some combination of expense reimbursement, management fees, partnership gross income (an "overriding royalty"), net income (a "working interest" or "net profits interest" depending on details), or a share of net income after investors recover certain costs (a "reversionary interest" or "working interest after payout").

Your investment in a tangible-intangible sharing arrangement goes for non-salvagable "intangible drilling costs," thus generating deductions equal to your cost investment (versus 70% to 90% for the other formulas). In a tangible-intangible sharing arrangement, the sponsor pays all costs which are not deductible for tax purposes—for example, the equipment used to lift the oil and gas. Understandably, tangible-intangible deals are most popular with investors. Although it is probably the best-all-around approach, a tangible-intangible sharing arrangement is not superior in all cases. Operating costs in the drilling area, the sharing arrangement, percentage of wildcats versus development wells and a myriad of other factors influence attractiveness.

Although you'll find a variety of oil and gas partnerships, the field is not nearly as diverse as real estate. Most oil and gas programs today are "multiple property—blind pools." That is, sponsors attempt to invest in as many attractive wells as possible that meet the program's investment and risk criteria, but specific drilling sites aren't predetermined.

There are three basic approaches to drilling risk in oil and gas programs: high risk, potentially high return "wildcat programs," which only drill wells exploring for new fields; lower risk, low return "development programs," which only drill adjacent to existing producing wells; and "balanced programs," which drill a mixture of wildcat wells and development wells.

Most oil and gas programs offer first year deductions equal to 70% to 100% of the amount invested. Assuming drilling success, income from your program is partially sheltered by the depletion allowance. Depletion with respect to oil or gas property may, in many cases, be deductible to the extent of as much as 50% of net income from the property. This means—since your share comes from partnership net income—as much as 50 cents of every dollar you receive may be tax free, as long as your partnership's properties produce. Oil and gas capital gain potential is somewhat greater than that of other tax shelters in that the only "recaptured" deduction is the amount claimed as an intangible drilling expense.

Depending on drilling success, the type of wells leverage and other factors, you may begin collecting depletion-sheltered income within a year but you may have to wait—up to five years if pipeline construction is necessary. Generally, the higher the risk, the longer the wait and greater the return. Once cash flow begins, you can collect it until the wells deplete . . . up to 20 years or longer in some cases. Alternatively, your partnership may allow you to "cash in" as soon as a value has been established, but usually not before two years. Sometimes the sponsor will offer to exchange your partnership interest for cash or stock.

The major risk in oil and gas is that "dry holes" will be drilled. The risk that a single wildcat will be dry is tremendous; even development wells involve risk. However, partnership diversification among many wells softens the overall risk factor.

Oil and gas is a good all around tax shelter. It offers high first year deductions and partially tax sheltered cash flow. Although all oil and gas programs are risky, the risk/reward ratio varies considerably between wildcat, balanced and development programs.

With the substantial increase in oil prices, development drilling and investments in producing wells have become more interesting to investors. Producing wells attract investors looking for a return higher than that generally available in other investments.

The sponsor of a producing well program has the following to say about its opportunity:

OIL INCOME OBJECTIVES

1. An Income-Oriented Investment—where management's objective is to acquire producing oil and gas properties that will generate regular income to Limited Partners.

2. No Drilling—the Program concentrates solely on the acquisition of existing producing oil and gas properties.

3. Regularity of Distributions—available funds are paid each calendar quarter with monthly options offered.

4. Maintenance of Investment Capital—possible through reinvestment of capital distributions into future partnerships.

5. Repurchase Options—through a "Right of Presentment" obligating the General Partner to buy back interests for the established "Purchase Price."

6. Modest Tax Benefits—on initial investment plus operating expenses, depletion, depreciation and interest deductions in the future.

IF INCOME IS YOUR OBJECTIVE . . .

Investments that have income as their objective have multiplied in recent years and grown in popularity. Among the many popular income investments are various types of bonds, income-oriented real estate investment trusts, mutual funds, certificates of deposit, and, of course, savings and loan accounts and dividend-paying stocks.

Let's look at another income investment. Although this Program is relatively recent in origin, it is based on a concept that is a hundred years old. Direct ownership of the natural resources that provide 75% of America's energy needs has appealed to investors for years but has generally been limited to oil companies, wealthy individuals and institutional investors.

With the introduction of our Oil Income Program, we made ownership of this asset available to a wide variety of investors through the Program's limited partnership format.

By pooling your funds with those of other investors, known as Limited Partners, an Oil Income Program limited partnership can buy interest in a number of existing oil and natural gas properties, thereby diversifying its investment capital. The oil and gas production from each well is sold, and the income flows back to the partnership to be distributed quarterly to the Limited Partner investors and to the General Partner. Attractive property purchases are difficult, however, as explained more fully later.

We buy existing income-producing oil and gas properties from a variety of sources, including oil companies and individuals who discovered and developed the properties.

People use income from investments to fulfill various goals. When searching for a suitable investment to achieve these goals, many people look for these features:

Attractive Yield
Immediate Income
Sound Asset Base
Liquidity

Let's discuss how the Oil Income Program seeks to achieve these objectives.

Yield

What can you expect from this investment?

The Oil Income Program is designed to attract those investors seeking income. No precise percentage yield can be set forth. The return you may realize from this investment will be influenced by many factors that cannot be predicted with certainty. Of particular importance to partnership performance will be future oil and gas prices which, in turn, are largely affected by the forces of supply and demand and, of course, by governmental regulation.

Purchasing producing properties for attractive yield is a difficult task as our experience has shown.

You, as a Limited Partner, and we, as General Partner, mutually benefit when good producing properties are acquired. This is because aside from recovering the nonrecurring first year start-up expenses, our principal compensation is a 15% interest in the oil and gas reserves acquired. We pay 15% of the partnership operating expenses too, so it's also in our interest to keep costs down.

Receipt of Income

How soon can you expect your first distribution?

Approximate Partnership Formation Date	First Scheduled Partnership Distribution	Months Included in Distribution
February 10	May 15	February March
April 8	August 15	April May June
September 9	November 15	September
November 7	February 15	November December

As you can see from this table, your first distribution payment covers activities from the date your partnership is formed. Upon partnership formation, we begin to evaluate and purchase properties that are expected to meet the Program's objectives. This important acquisition phase may take up to 12 months or more.

Until a partnership's capital funds are used for property purchase, they are generally placed in time deposits, short-term governmental obligations and commercial paper. During the acquisition phase, the General Partner has a contractual obligation to make quarterly distributions at an annual rate of at least 4%, although economic conditions have made possible higher returns in recent years.

Your distributions are expected to gradually increase as properties are acquired and the partnership enters its operations phase. Distributions reach higher levels during this phase which for any one partnership may last 10-15 years or more until the wells are depleted.

You should recognize, however, that delays in making purchases or unsatisfactory performance may reduce the distributions you receive.

At the time of your investment or at any time thereafter, you may elect one of three ways to receive your quarterly distributions:

Option I. You reinvest all distributions in future partnerships to be formed in this Program. In this way, you may build your asset base.

Option II. You specify the amount of your distribution you would like to receive in cash, and the balance is reinvested in future partnerships to be formed in this Program.

Option III. You receive all your distributions in cash, knowing full well that at some point the asset base will be depleted entirely.

Asset Base

What factors affect its value?

No income investment is stronger than its underlying assets. As we have noted, the Oil Income Program involves direct ownership of a natural resource—petroleum. In a free market environment, the value of oil and natural gas, like other commodities, is determined according to the forces of supply and demand. Of course, government controls such as those now in effect and proposed for the future will affect the market for oil and natural gas.

Liquidity

Can you withdraw?

The Oil Income Program is structured as a long-term investment; however, if you find it necessary to withdraw from the Program, you have the right to do so at any time. If you withdraw after the partnership has invested its capital in properties, you are entitled to receive a purchase price for your interest based primarily on independent engineering. If you withdraw before a purchase price can be set, the payment is to be 80% of your original investment less 30% of any prior oil and gas revenues distributed to you. While there is no ready market for partnership interests, the General Partner is contractually obligated to purchase any such interests tendered, subject to its financial ability to do so and certain limitations as described in the prospectus. The General Partner intends to purchase all interests tendered, although it is not obligated to accept for purchase more than 3.5% of the Limited Partners' interests in any partnership of this offering in any month.

Risk Factors to Consider

Competition for attractive producing properties is intense. Purchases of these properties are based on available geologic and engineering data, the quality of which will vary in each case. Obviously we cannot guarantee that we can purchase properties that will meet the Program's objective.

Under the terms of our prospectus, we make no commitments for the purchase of properties until a partnership is formed. Further, at the time of your investment, there may be previously formed partnerships with significant amounts of unexpected funds. This may delay property purchases by future partnerships.

The sale of oil and gas is highly regulated, and no one can predict with certainty what the consequences of future governmental regulations may be on oil and gas prices.

Decisions regarding property acquisitions, operation of the properties and financing may pose potential conflicts of interest between the General Partner, the various partnerships it manages or its affiliates. Every effort is made to avoid or resolve such conflicts, but there can be no assurance of success in all instances.

The General Partner is placing greater emphasis on the possibility of future oil and gas price increases when determining the amount to pay for some producing properties. If price increases do not occur for those properties, revenues will be less than anticipated.

Borrowed funds allow a partnership to purchase more properties than it could using partnership capital alone and increase a partnership's exposure to possible future price increases. There is always a degree of risk associated with borrowing funds, including the possibility that revenues may not be sufficient to pay the principal and interest or that debt repayment may cause taxable income to partners to exceed the net cash proceeds available to them. However, the General Partner will continue to use borrowed funds until, in its judgment, it becomes uneconomic to do so.

Separate records and accounts must be maintained for each monthly Oil Income Program partnership, which can be costly and time-consuming as well as increasing the possibility for clerical and administrative error. Also, there is no assurance of liquidity if you choose to withdraw from the Program, as previously discussed.

Tax Considerations

Tax considerations usually associated with a drilling investment are not a material factor in the Oil Income Program. This is because we buy only existing, producing oil and natural gas properties for this Program and does not engage in any drilling operations.

In the opinion of counsel, Oil Income Program partnerships should be treated as partnerships for income tax purposes, rather than corporations. Thus, there should be only one level of income tax payable with respect to partnership operations. As a Limited Partner, you will pay taxes on your allocable share of any partnership taxable income. You will not be subject to the two levels of taxation found in the corporate form of business operations—that is, a tax at corporate rates on the corporate taxable income, followed by a second tax on dividends paid to shareholders.

Deductions during the property purchasing phase of a partnership's operations should include a part of the 15% guaranteed payment to the General Partner and that portion (if any) of the reimbursement to the General Partner for non-capital general and administrative expenses. However, the Internal Revenue Service has indicated it may contest the current deductability of the payment to the General Partner. During the partnership's operations and production phase, Limited Partners will be entitled to deductions for depletion, operating expenses and interest payments, as well as depreciation on equipment.

Petroleum Demand—Our View

The demand for petroleum products is increasing faster than are additions to supply. Today, oil and natural gas provide about 75% of our total energy needs. We're convinced that petroleum will continue to be our primary source of energy, at least until the end of this century.

Therefore, your direct ownership of oil and natural gas properties through the Oil Income Program represents attractive income potential in a high demand industry and has made sense to a great many investors.

In most states, investment in Oil Income Program can be made in any amount of $2,500 or more (e.g., $2,506.46). After your initial investment, most states permit you to invest $50 or more in new partnerships at any time.

With oil and gas prices rising, it is interesting to survey the following Industry Finding Costs:

Risks and Returns

The following discussion requires the development of assumptions. These assumptions, if not carefully considered, can take on the aura of fact, thus giving the impression that the examples used are firm projections of returns. They are not. While the *potential* for returns does exist, the *risk* of realizing lower returns or no returns is very real.

The objective of any business venture is to sell goods or services at a price that will cover both the initial cost of the goods as well as thc additional fixed and variable expenses involved in doing business. Hopefully, the price will more than cover these costs, thus resulting in a profit. Also, hopefully, this profit will be sufficient to provide a reasonable return on investment to the venturer. For instance, the shirt retailer may buy an inventory of shirts at $5 per shirt and price the shirts at $10. If the merchandise is priced correctly and if the public buys the merchandise at that price, both a profit and a reasonable return on the investment should be realized. There are a number of variable factors at work, however, which lend an element of risk to the whole situation.

In many respects, the oil and gas business is exactly the same. The risks involved are of a somewhat different nature. The cost of finding a barrel of oil (or oil equivalent) is analogous to the acquisition cost of each shirt in the retailer's inventory. Unfortunately, because of the uncertainty involved in estimating reserves, the oil company does not know what a barrel of oil will cost to find until well after the exploration dollars have been spent. Early in the productive life of most oil and gas wells, and periodically thereafter, most oil companies engaged a petroleum engineer to prepare reserve estimates. Such an engineering review may result in an increase or decrease in the estimate of proven reserves. If the engineer's estimate of proven reserves increases, then the cost of finding each barrel of reserves is decreased (and vice-versa).

What Are Finding Costs?

Simply stated, finding costs are the total dollars spent in the effort to discover reserves of oil and gas. Finding costs are generally expressed in per-unit terms. Therefore, if a total of $100,000 is expended in geological and geophysical, leasehold acquisition, drilling, and completion costs to find 10,000 barrels of oil, the resulting finding cost is expressed as $10 per barrel. Note that none of the costs involved in producing that oil, such as lifting costs, taxes, and royalties are included in the finding cost computation. While the dollars expended to find the reserves can be fixed precisely very early in the life of a well, the exact amount of reserves discovered will only be known when the last oil or gas is produced. Reserve changes obviously affect finding costs. For example, if further evaluations result in the reserve estimate being revised to 5,000 barrels, the resulting finding cost would escalate to $20 per barrel. While reserve estimates will probably change for a particular well during its productive life, the oil and gas industry periodically reports average finding costs for both the industry as a whole and for particular firms.

Where Are Finding Costs in the Oil and Gas Industry?

As shown below, in 1978 the domestic oil and gas industry found a barrel of oil or oil equivalent[1] for $5.70.[2]

Estimated Petroleum Finding Costs
United States[2]

Year	Cost Per Gross Barrel[3]
1968	.78
1969	1.20
1970	.33
1971	1.15
1972	1.53
1973	1.43
1974	2.43
1975	3.35
1976	5.60
1977	4.37
1978	5.70
1979	8.35

[1] 6 mcf gas = 1 bbl oil.
[2] Source: *Petroleum Outlook,* May, 1979 and May, 1980, John S. Herold, Inc.
[3] Before consideration of royalty interests.

To understand this aspect of oil and gas economics, let's compare the 1978 finding costs of $5.70 per barrel to the then prevailing price of crude oil.

Example 1

$13.00	Approximate Wellhead Price
1.62	12.5% Royalties
.57	5% Severance Tax (Net of Royalties' Share)
1.30	10% Lifting Cost
$ 9.51	Pre-Tax Cash Flow

In 1978, therefore, domestic industry-wide averages for oil and gas exploration generated pre-tax cash flow of $9.51 for each $5.70 invested.

What Is the Potential for Limited Partner Investors?

Using (a) an oil price of $20 per barrel, a conservative figure used in late 1979 for prospect evaluation purposes, (b) the 1979 industry-wide average finding cost of $8.35,[1] and (c) a typical General Partner/Limited Partner sharing arrangement,[2] the following results are reflected.

Example 2

$20.00	Wellhead Price
4.80	24% Royalties[3]
.76	5% Severance Tax (Net of Royalties' Share)
2.00	10% Lifting Cost
$12.44	
1.87	General Partner's Net Revenue Share
.62	5% Program Costs
$ 9.95	Limited Partner's Pre-Tax Cash Flow[4]

Using this price example and the industry finding cost, the limited partners would realize $9.95 forreach $8.35 invested.[5]

[1] Actual finding costs for any well or group of wells may, of course, be substantially greater.

[2] The sharing arrangement for Programs, used in these hypotheticals, provides for the allocation of net revenues 15% to the General Partner and 85% to Limited Partners.

[3] The combination of landowner and overriding royalties. The percentage is greater than Example 1 to reflect actual experience. Higher landowner royalties plus overriding royalties to originating geologists have resulted in net revenue leases of approximately 76%.

[4] No consideration is given to any windfall profits tax.

[5] Of course, if no oil is found a limited partner would receive no return on the investment.

A limited partner could realize an even higher return on an investment if a lower finding cost or a higher price for production can be achieved. For instance, the following results occur when a barrel of oil is sold for $40 at the wellhead. This was the prevailing price in the spring of 1980.[1]

Example 3

$40.00	Wellhead Price
9.60	24% Royalties
1.52	5% Severance Tax (Net of Royalties' Share)
4.87	30% Windfall Profits Tax[2]
4.00	10% Lifting Cost
$20.01	
3.00	General Partner's Net Revenue Share
1.00	5% Program Costs
$16.01	Limited Partner's Pre-Tax Cash Flow

Clearly, as the price per barrel increases without corresponding increases in the finding cost, the return on investment becomes more and more attractive. Even assuming a continued 15% rate of inflation in finding costs during 1980, using this hypothetical example, limited partners would realize $16.01 for each $9.60 invested.[3]

The Current Environment

What we are experiencing now is a change in the market due to phased decontrol of oil and decontrol of some oil and gas. Consequently, prices have risen at a rate disproportionate to the increases in finding costs. This creates an unusual opportunity for the investor, but it is an opportunity of uncertain duration. Regardless of the permanency of the situation, the critical question at this point is whether a general partner offers the passive

[1] Source: *Oil & Gas Journal,* May 19, 1980. Oil found by 1980 and subsequent Programs will be deemed newly discovered oil, and is thus no longer subject to government price controls.

[2] Net of Royalties' Share and assumes a base of $18.63 per barrel, adjusted for severance taxes.

[3] Of course, if no oil is found, a limited partner would receive no return on the investment.

investor a realistic opportunity to take advantage of this disparity between finding costs and selling price. This, of course, is the risk inherent in any oil and gas investment.

In evaluating oil and gas offerings, it is well to be familiar with the average daily crude oil production per well for the major oil producing states and crude oil production by state as follows:

Average Daily Crude Oil Production per Well, Calendar 1979*

State	Barrels Per Well/Day	Number of Oil Wells
1. Utah	59.0	1,346
2. Louisiana	54.5	24,767
3. North Dakota	40.5	1,908
4. Mississippi	37.4	2,556
5. Wyoming	35.6	10,059
6. Colorado	26.8	3,402
7. Michigan	24.6	3,890
8. Montana	22.5	3,573
9. California	21.6	44,674
10. Texas	16.6	168,123
11. New Mexico	14.2	15,045
12. Nebraska	10.8	1,535
13. Arkansas	6.8	7,698
14. Oklahoma	5.2	76,505
15. Kansas	3.3	47,379
16. Illinois	2.6	24,067
17. Indiana	2.3	5,296
18. Ohio	1.7	19,177
19. Kentucky	1.1	14,097
20. West Virginia	0.5	14,225
21. New York	0.4	4,800
22. Pennsylvania	0.3	27,768

*Table excludes those states with less than 1,000 oil wells.

Source: Independent Petroleum Association of America.

Crude Oil Production by State, Calendar 1979

State	Barrels of Crude Oil Produced	Number of Wells Producing Oil at 12-31-79
1. Texas	980,839,000	168,123
2. Alaska	511,327,000	400
3. Louisiana	413,230,000	24,767
4. California	351,926,000	44,674
5. Oklahoma	128,441,000	76,505
6. Wyoming	124,062,000	10,059
7. New Mexico	74,420,000	15,045
8. Kansas	53,253,000	47,379
9. Florida	47,967,000	115
10. Michigan	34,589,000	3,890
11. Mississippi	35,582,000	2,556
12. Colorado	31,652,000	3,402
13. North Dakota	29,389,000	1,908
14. Montana	29,116,000	3,573
15. Utah	26,882,000	1,346
16. Illinois	20,254,000	24,067
17. Arkansas	18,414,000	7,698
18. Ohio	11,953,000	19,177
19. Alabama	10,322,000	514
20. Nebraska	5,891,000	1,535
21. Kentucky	5,533,000	14,097
22. Indiana	4,733,000	5,296
23. Pennsylvania	2,816,000	27,768
24. West Virginia	2,465,000	14,225
25. Nevada	1,274,000	28
26. New York	855,000	4,800
27. South Dakota	801,000	88
28. Tennessee	614,000	338
29. Arizona	490,000	35
30. Missouri	54,000	188

Source: Independent Petroleum Association of America

Because of the enormous interest in locating energy supplies, illustrations are set forth below showing an energy leasing satellite program and material for oil and gas programs achieving varied financial objectives.

ENERGY

ENERGY LEASING COMPANY

Business and Scope of Activities—The business scope of activities and purposes of this Company shall be to utilize technical and scientific studies derived from satellites and siesmics to locate geographic areas wherein previously undetected structures favorable to the accumulation of oil and/or gas is likely to occur; to acquire potentially valuable leases covering tract of land wherein such structures exist; to sell to reputable oil companies the sights to develop such tracts of land; and to retain for the benefit of the general and limited partners such sale proceeds and overrides as are in the best interest of the partnership.

EXAMPLE OF AN ENERGY LEASING COMPANY PROGRAM

Introduction

This introduction is to explain in detail the securing and disbursing of original capital, the return of capital to the investors, and the distribution of profit by the Partnership, plus transactions with Earthview Corporation and the oil companies.

1) The original capital necessary is $135,000 contributed as follows:

a) Limited Partners will pay $15,000 for each 10% interest in the Partnership. The Limited Partners will own no more than 90% of the Partnership.

b) The General Partner, Energy Leasing Company, will own a 10% interest. The General Partner will manage and operate the Partnership. There may be a reasonable monthly or annual fee charged by the General Partner for these services and expenses. This should not exceed 2% of the gross income of the Partnership.

c) There will be no more than 25 Limited Partners and two General Partners.

2) Partnership Expenses:

a) This is the amount of money the Partnership must raise before Earthview will finish the land study, assign an area to the Partnership and go after leases on the area. We guarantee a minimum of 4,000 acres leased for this amount.

b) Some of the items are fixed (F) and others are variable (V) as the situation changes. This seismic confirmation of the area is conducted to back up Landsat data because oil company personnel will understand it better.

3) The figures and data presented and the Limited Partnership Agreement are based on the best information, facts and knowledge we can obtain from experts in the oil industry and allied technical people or from articles and estimates written by these experts. We assume no responsibility if the profits and percentages do not turn out exactly as indicated.

4) The General Partners believe that there is less risk when an investment is made in this venture than buying part of the working interest in one or more wells. There is an excellent prospect of getting all your original investment plus a small profit back. There is also a good prospect of earning royalties yielding a larger income quickly for many years, more than any investment we know about.

There Is, However, Some Risk Involved—A similar risk as a person investing in company stocks, fast food stores and restaurant franchises, your own business, wholesale, retail or industrial or other types of business. We advise anyone to study this disclosure statement along with the Limited Partnership Agreement at least 48 hours before investing. Then invest only if you can afford to lose all or part of that investment without personal financial hardship.

ENERGY LEASING COMPANY

Partnership Expenses and Cash Disbursements

1. Partnership Expenses and Sale of Leases	
A. Advance sales expense (Earthview)	$ 5,000.00 (F)
B. Money for leasing (Earthview)	$ 60,000.00 (F)
C. Landsat (satellite) Topographic image study (Earthview)	$ 40,000.00 (F)
D. Seismic confirmation (Earthview)	$ 20,000.00 (F)
E. Fund for contingencies and future lease	$ 5,000.00 (V)
F. Accounting and miscellaneous costs	$ 5,000.00 (F)
TOTAL	$135,000.00 (F)

Hypothetical Example of Sales of Leases for $200,000.00

2. A 10% Limited Partners interest cost	$ 15,000.00 (F)
Maximum Limited Partner interest 90%	$135,000.00 (F)
3. Package Sale	$200,000.00 (V)
4. Cash left after return of original capital	$ 65,000.00 (V)
5. Know's fee	$ 9,000.00 (F)
	$ 56,000.00
6. Earthview 25% commission	$ 14,000.00 (V)
7. Balance to Partnership	$ 42,000.00 (V)

8. If leases are sold for lower or higher price, the above figures will change.
9. Note (F) is fixed, (V) is variable.

PURPOSE

The basic purposes of Energy Leasing Company is to obtain investment capital to pay Earthview Corporation and to help locate prospective land areas where oil and/or gas may be found. We do this by computerized Landsat photography backed up by seismic tests.

After we have found this area, we lease the mineral rights on a minimum of 4,000 acres, maximum 10,000 acres. We then prepare a package including photographs and all the test data, plus the lease contracts, which we sell to any oil company who will buy.

This sale usually occurs within one year for a cash price above the cost of the Partnership capital yielding a profit. The contract also calls for an overriding royalty of 10% minimum and 12½% maximum on all oil and gas produced on this land. This overriding royalty is similar to the royalty paid the land owner.

We sign the leases over to Energy Leasing Company with a copy of the contract. When the oil company pays for the contract, the investment dollars provided by the Limited Partners is paid back. The remaining cash from the sale of the leases is then paid first to Dr. Know's expenses and commission, then Earthview commission. The remaining money profit is divided among all the Partners in accordance with the instructions in the Limited Partnership Agreement.

The General Partner raises the original capital, keeps the records, pays all the bills, manages the funds, the profits and royalties and is paid no fees until all the investing partners have their investment capital paid back.

The General Partner distributes the royalties to all Partners every six months on a calendar year basis. All functions of the Limited Partnership are performed in accordance with the Limited Partnership laws in the State and any S.E.C. regulations covering same.

The General Partner, except in a case where the General Partner is a Corporation, will promptly call an information meeting upon request by 25% in interest or more of the investors in any class of securities who are unaffiliated with a promoter or affiliate of the promoter.

For management services, the General Partners collectively, shall secure a sum of 2% of the gross revenues of the Partnership provided that such sum shall not be computed nor paid until the entire capital contribution of each Partner shall have been returned in full—thereafter the 2% shall be computed and paid monthly.

LEASING PARTNERSHIP PARTICIPATION WITH EARTHVIEW

1. The leases are obtained by a staff of leasing experts who are paid about $3 per acre for each acre leased. The General Partner attempts to get the lease rights for $3 per acre, but will

pay up to a maximum of $7 per acre for a good lease. Cost per acre thus runs from $6 to $10 for the Partnership.

2. When we have obtained, under an assumed name, all the lease land that can be obtained for $60,000.00, all the leases are turned over to the Partnership who owns them.

3. We then put the whole package together with Landsat photographs, computer calculations, seismic readings, soil analysis, fault analysis, geophysicist analysis, and lease agreements and our representatives call on the oil companies to sell the product.

4. From the time the Partnership has raised the full $135,000.00 to the sale of the package, should take from 8 months to 1 year. One completion was made in 4 months. It is also possible to hold out longer than a year in order to get a higher price.

5. Lease parcels of 4,000 acres or less have sold for over $1,000,000.00.

6. The contract signed with the purchaser will be in the name of the Partnership. The contract spells out in some detail, the number of wells the purchaser must drill in a time span and the depth to which wells must be drilled. The purchaser is also required to renew the leases. If any of these requirements are not met, the leases revert back to the Partnership, and may be resold.

EARTHVIEW CORPORATION

The Earthview Corporation was founded by Eye Know, President, in 1973 for the purpose of applied satellite remote sensing for petroleum and mineral explorations. He is President, and a leading expert in this field.

An impressive resume of Dr. Know's educational and background experience is included on attached sheets. In addition, Dr. Know has on his staff: Vice President, Master Geophysicist, Mathematician Geology Geophysicist, Doctor Geologist, Computer Scientist, Master Computer Scientist, Tech. Optronics Operator, Master, Geology and Remote Sensing.

Earthview Corporation is located in Ann Arbor, Michigan because of the tremendous computer technology and soft ware, and other high technology help and research that is available through the University of Michigan. They have purchased computer equipment themselves that only five other companies in the U.S.A. own.

Earthview purchases computer compatible Landsat tapes and processes them to enhance features of special interest to clients. The tapes are produced through U.S.A. owned Landsat satellite orbiting over 500 miles above the earth. Earthview owns unique soft ware programs, supplies and interprets high quality Landsat images while providing a wide range of remote sensing services.

They have done or are doing work for such major companies and governments at Brazil, Australia, Jordan, Dominican Republic, U.S.A. and five major oil companies and two of the largest international mining companies (Anglo-American) and others.

LEASING AND OIL ROYALTIES

When land is leased for mineral rights through our joint efforts:

1. We guarantee no less than 4,000 acres leased, averages at least 6,000 acres and we try to get 10,000 acres for each Partnership.
2. The land owner gets $4 to $7 per acre for leasing mineral rights on his property plus 1/8 or 12.5% overriding interest on all oil taken from wells drilled on his property.
3. When we sell leases for the Partnership, we retain 12.5% override for the Partnership. Sometimes in a fast transaction, we retain only 10% override.
4. The purchaser that buys the leases owns the remaining 75% or 77½% which is called the working interest. All drilling, pumping, piping, maintenance, and other expenses are paid by the 75% or 77½% working interest. Their net profit comes only after all these expenses are paid.
5. The landowner and the Partnership interest own clear royalties (12.5%) or (10%) of the selling price of the oil as it comes from the well. If the working interest drills 1 or 100 wells, neither the landowner nor the Partnership have any more well costs to pay. Their cash flow is clear.

DIVISION OIL ROYALTIES TO PARTNERSHIP

1. Average of all successful oil and gas wells drilled in Michigan in 1980, including wildcats, is 46.2%. About 1½ wells per day are completed in Michigan. Wells on proved and tested land average a much higher success rate (67%). This average initial output of completed wells is 150 barrels per day.

2. Crude oil sales today are about $40 per barrel.

3. One well total output before costs: 100%

4. Division royalty from a well or wells:

A. Landowner				12.5%
B. Working group	(Min)	75%	(Max)	77.5%
C. Partnership	(Max)	12.5%	(Min)	10%

5. Division of royalty between partners and Earthview
   A. Earthview (not negotiable) 3.5% of well production
   B. Limited Partnership (Max) 9% of well production
   C. Limited Partnership (Min) 6.5% of well production

6. Standard well density allowed 1 per 40 acres.

7. Maximum wells allowed on 4,000-acre block–100. The Partnership makes no representation as to how many wells may in fact be drilled by the oil company. It would be very rare to complete 100 wells per 4,000 acres.

FOOTNOTE:

According to A.P.I. (American Petroleum Institute) Publication for U.S.A. (all states)

Wells completed through April, 1979		15,235	
Found	Oil	5,497	
Found	Gas	4,583	
		10,080	64%

Wells completed through April, 1980		17,739	
Found	Oil	7,291	
Found	Gas	4,747	
		11,938	67%

General Information

Pitts Energy Group, Dallas, Texas published report says:

U.S.A. Reserves, oil equivalent by year 2000	210,000,000,000 BBOE
U.S.A. Reserves 1980 oil equivalent	50,000,000,000 BBOE

Oil and Gas Journal, August 4, 1980

Completed in 1979 as Producers

Wild Cat	28.8%
Wild Cat (record 1977)	26.9%
All wells 1979	66.4%
All wells 1978	63.6%
Wild Cat wells 1979	10,488
All wells	51,000
New fields opened	1,162

New Reserves Oil 1979 (U.S.A.)	454,620,000 BLS
Gas 1979	4,100,000,000 BLS
Total Oil Produced 1979	3,110,000,000 BLS

Note: BBOE - total of oil, gas and natural gas liquids.

BENEFITS OF AN ENERGY LEASING COMPANY

The advantage of mineral acquisition tied in with a competent land study from satellites backed by seismic studies and eventual sales to an oil company is the minimum risk, assurance of income from every well on the property without further investment, a high probability that all of the original investment plus some profit will be returned within twelve months and favorable tax consideration once the developing company produces oil.

Most block lease projects are being sold in excess of \$30-\$50 per acre and some areas upwards of \$100 per acre. Investment in oil and gas minerals during the 1980s will probably yield the highest return on investment, provided they are competently selected.

Assumption Projection

A 6,000 acre field with 40-acre spacing and 150 barrels per day allowable has a potential of $30,000,000.00 for a 9% overriding interest. This is not considered a large field and this is an annual return if all wells are good.

The original investment of $135,000 will be returned to the Partnership upon sale of the lease to the oil company in addition to a split of profits agreed to by the Partnership. There is no other cost involvement in drilling, completing, pumping or maintaining any of the wells, except a remote possibility of a renewal fee if the project is not sold within 12 months. This fee should not exceed $20,000.00 and most likely would be about $10,000.00. It is very unlikely that the project would not be sold before renewal fees on the acreage are due.

Drilling and finding oil or gas on every 40-acre plot is only a very remote possibility. It seldom ever happens.

RISK FACTORS

A) The General Partners hire and depend on Earthview Corporation, Dr. Know, President, and his staff of experts through Landsat Photos, computer technology to find earth structure faults where the rock and sand structure is right for the possible accumulation of gas, oil and other minerals.

B) The General Partners also hire Earthview to back up these findings with seismic tests of the area around any faults they find. Siesmic testing has been used by companies looking for minerals for years.

C) The General Partners have no control over these tests and must depend on the experience, reputation and honesty of Earthview.

D) The General Partners, in conjunction with Earthview hire independent men or companies who are experts in mineral rights leasing to obtain the number of good lease acres, specified in the Partnership. We also must depend on the reputation, experience, and honesty of these men.

E) The General Partners and Earthview then must sell these leased mineral rights to a company interested, paying an amount equal to or more than the Partnership costs, plus a royalty on the oil or gas produced from wells on the property.

F) We then must depend on the purchasing company to pay Energy Leasing Company the sale price and the royalties on time.

G) *If any or all of items A, B, C, D, E, F do not happen as planned, the partnership may not be able to reach the goals outlined in the partnership disclosure statement. There is always the possibility that this limited partnership could lose money.*

This booklet was prepared by Arthur Andersen & Co. for McCormick Oil & Gas Company to illustrate various aspects of the federal income tax treatment of an investment in an oil and gas drilling program and the federal tax effects on an investor should he decide to keep the investment or dispose of his investment by one of several methods.

The following points should be considered when reviewing this booklet:

Investments in an oil and gas drilling program involve a very high degree of risk. It is partially because of this degree of risk in exploring for oil and gas that investments in such activities receive relatively favorable federal tax treatment. No attempt is made herein to discuss the risk of an investment in an oil and gas drilling program. The examples used in this booklet were selected solely to demonstrate the tax benefits of such an investment and should not be taken as an indication of the results to be expected from such an investment. Some of the examples assume a return on investment which is highly improbable. Because the primary purpose of this booklet is to demonstrate the tax treatment of an investment in an oil and gas program, no consideration was given in any of the examples used to the time value of the money invested. If the time value of the money invested had been reflected in the examples, then depending upon the period of time involved, many of the benefits described in the following pages of this booklet would be less significant.

In a booklet of this type, it is not feasible to comment on all of the federal income tax consequences of an investment in an oil and gas drilling program. While this booklet discusses some of the principal federal income tax consequences of such an investment, the effect upon a particular investor or group of investors depends largely upon the particular income tax position of such investors and no assurance can be given that any deductions, credits or any other federal income tax advantage which is described herein will be available to a particular investor or group of investors.

The federal income tax consequences described in this booklet are not intended as a substitute for careful tax planning, and persons contemplating an investment in an oil and gas drilling program should consult their tax advisors relating to their own tax matters.

This booklet is not an offer to sell nor a solicitation of an offer to buy an interest in any McCormick Oil & Gas Program. The offer is made only by a prospectus, a copy of which is being distributed with this booklet, and the contents hereof are qualified in their entirety by the detailed information appearing in such prospectus.

Houston, Texas

Tax Benefits of an Oil and Gas Investment

This booklet will illustrate that the tax and economic characteristics of an oil and gas investment can often work in concert to produce a multifaceted tool for personal and family financial planning. A word of caution should be noted at the outset of this discussion:

> An oil and gas investment should not be considered solely or primarily for the tax benefits to be derived therefrom.

However, an oil and gas investment cannot be properly evaluated without understanding its inherent tax implications.

An oil and gas investment receives favorable tax treatment in that most of the cost is "deducted" going in, and a significant amount of the income from the investment is "improved" coming out. This booklet will discuss the economic significance of an investment's immediate deductibility, the tax characteristics of income flowing from the investment and the effect of a disposition of the investment by gift to a relative or to a charity or by a sale of the investment.

The Deduction for Intangible Drilling Costs

An investor in an oil and gas exploration program should expect to receive tax deductions equal to approximately 100% of his investment by the end of the second year of operation. This rapid "writeoff" of one's investment is made possible, in part, because of the deduction available for intangible drilling costs. In most businesses, the cost of acquiring an income-producing asset must be recovered over its useful life and is not currently deductible. However, the tax laws allow the deduction of intangible drilling costs not only on dry holes but also on successful wells. While certain other costs in drilling successful wells are not currently deductible, many drilling programs are structured to ensure full deductibility of the investment, either by special allocation of such costs to the program sponsor or through the use of "nonrecourse" loans to the program to finance such costs. Nonrecourse debt is secured only by the underlying oil and gas property and not by the credit or guarantee of the investor. This financing technique is discussed further on page 19.

Comparison of Income Required to Make Alternative Investments

Assumptions:

— 70% tax bracket investor
— $10,000 investment

Question:

How much current income must be available to an investor to make a $10,000 investment in XYZ Company stock, as contrasted to ABC Oil and Gas Drilling Program?

	Stock Investment	Oil and Gas Investment*
Income Required	$33,333	$10,000
Deductions	—	(10,000)
Taxable Income	$33,333	$ —
Taxes Payable at 70%	(23,333)	—
Income Available for Investment	$10,000	$10,000

*Does not consider minimum and maximum tax effects discussed later in this booklet.

Answer:

It will cost the investor $23,333 more, after taxes, to invest $10,000 in the stock than to invest the same amount in the oil and gas drilling program. An investor in the 50% tax bracket would require $10,000 more, after taxes, to invest $10,000 in stock than to invest the same amount in the oil and gas drilling program. In evaluating this example an investor should remember that generally there will be a significantly greater risk involved in a drilling program investment than in a stock investment.

The critical concept to understand from this example is:

> An investor with $33,333 of income available for investment purposes does not have $33,333 to invest unless his investment is immediately deductible for tax purposes. What he does have available for investment is that which remains after taxes have been paid. In the case of an investor in the 70% tax bracket only $10,000 of the $33,333 remains available for investment after taxes. Conversely, all of the income is available for investment in an oil and gas investment because generally 100% of the investment is deductible.

Stated another way, a 70% tax bracket investor in oil and gas will have recovered 70% of his original investment over a two-year period through a reduction of his income tax, even if the investor has not received any cash distribution from the investment. Thus, at that point, the net cash outlay for the investment is $3,000 versus $10,000 for the stock.

This example reflects 100% deductibility of the investment in an oil and gas program. Such percentage will generally not be available until at least the end of the second year. Additionally, the above example, and most of the other examples used, do not consider any adverse tax effects the oil and gas investment might cause such as increasing minimum tax liability, decreasing maximum tax benefits and other matters discussed later in this booklet. The impact of these adverse tax effects depends primarily on the nature and extent of the investor's other income and deductions, and, as a result, are discussed separately later in this booklet under "Other Tax Considerations Relating to an Investment in Oil and Gas Exploration."

Return On Investment

Having explained that an investor used "pretax income dollars" to acquire an investment in oil and gas exploration activities, this discussion will focus on an equally important concept.

> When an investor acquires an interest in a successful oil and gas exploration activity, he is not merely buying a future income stream that is similar in nature to the type of income which he invested. He is also converting "normal taxable income" into one of several types of income or capital gain that is accorded tax treatment which is distinctly more favorable.

This favorable tax treatment manifests itself over a wide spectrum of personal and family financial planning alternatives. Four alternative courses of action are as follows:

1. Keep the investment
2. Sell the investment
3. Give the investment to minor children
4. Give the investment to charity

The Depletion Deduction

In the first of the four alternatives mentioned above and to a lesser degree in the third alternative, the depletion deduction is the key to favorable tax treatment.

The depletion deduction enables an investor to deduct from income the cost of an oil and gas lease over the productive life of the property. However, unlike other capital recovery mechanisms, the percentage depletion allowance is available to certain investors even after the cost of the oil and gas lease has been completely recouped because it is based upon a percentage of the gross income from the property. The percentage depletion rate was reduced effective in 1981 to 20% of income before operating costs and taxes, subject to certain limitations which are discussed later in this booklet. Further reductions are scheduled through 1984. Starting in 1984, the percentage depletion deduction will be 15%. In the examples used in this booklet, percentage depletion is calculated at an average rate over the life of the property of 18% of gross oil and gas revenue.

It should be emphasized that the percentage depletion deduction often excludes more than 20% of net oil and gas income from taxation. This occurs because the depletion percentage is applied to gross rather than net income. Thus, production taxes, operating costs and overhead generally will not reduce the amount of depletion available. The true tax benefit derived from the depletion deduction is illustrated by an aftertax comparison of oil and gas income, with an alternative type of investment income.

Comparison of Alternative Income Streams

Assumptions:

- 70% tax bracket investor
- Net income from each investment equals $10,000 per year
- Lease operating expense equals 20% of gross oil and gas revenue
- Depletion is calculated at an average rate over the life of the property of 18% of gross oil and gas revenue, and both the investor and the property qualify for percentage depletion.

Question:

What is the cash remaining, after taxes, from dividend income, and alternatively, oil and gas income, assuming an investor starts with a like amount of net income in each case?

Answer:

The investor receives 53% more cash, after taxes, from the oil and gas income than from dividend income. The illustration assumes that the amounts not sheltered through the depletion deduction ($7,750 in this example) are taxable at a 70% rate. An investor in the 50% tax bracket receives 23% more cash after taxes. Many oil and gas professionals continue to shelter their oil and gas income into lower tax brackets by additional investments in the oil and gas industry or by investing in other types of tax shelters. Because of the tax benefits derived by the depletion deduction, significant savings sometimes result. However, an investor's tax counsel should be consulted before deciding on such a program.

In evaluating the above example, an investor should keep in mind that generally there will be a significantly greater risk involved in acquiring the oil and gas property which produces the depletable income than in acquiring the stock which produces the dividend income. Oil and gas income receives more favorable tax treatment than dividend income because the property generating the oil and gas income is a wasting asset which eventually will be exhausted, and thus, a portion of oil and gas income is really a return of capital. Dividend income on the other hand theoretically can continue for so long as the payor company generates profit.

	Dividend Income	Oil & Gas Income*	Difference
Gross Income	$10,000	$12,500	
Expenses	—	2,500	
Net Income	$10,000	$10,000	
Depletion ($12,500 x 18%)	—	2,250	
Taxable Income	$10,000	$ 7,750	
Tax	7,000	5,425	
Net Aftertax Income	$ 3,000	$ 2,325	
Add back depletion (a noncash deduction)	—	2,250	
Aftertax Cash Available	$ 3,000	$ 4,575	$1,575
Percentage Difference			53%

*Does not consider minimum and maximum tax effects discussed later in this booklet.

Analysis of Financial Planning Alternatives

1. Continued Ownership of an Oil and Gas Investment

As illustrated above, the primary tax advantage relating to the receipt of oil and gas income is that a portion of this income is received tax free through the depletion deduction.

Together, the depletion deduction and the intangible drilling cost deduction make the aftertax cash return on even a "one for one" oil and gas investment economically successful for the investor. The following illustration demonstrates this principle.

After-Tax Cash Return Analysis

Assumptions:

- 70% tax bracket investor
- $10,000 investment
- Depletion rate is 18% over the life of the property, and both the investor and the property qualify for percentage depletion
- Lease operating expense equals 20% of gross revenue
- In Case 1, investor recovers $10,000 over life of investment; $20,000 in Case 2
- No compounding or discount analysis is considered

	Case 1* One for One		Case 2* Two for One	
Investment	$10,000		$10,000	
Taxes Saved at 70%	(7,000)		(7,000)	
Net Investment	$	$3,000	$	$3,000
Gross Income Received	12,500		25,000	
Expenses	(2,500)		(5,000)	
Net Income	$10,000		$20,000	
Depletion ($12,500 and $25,000 x 18%)	(2,250)		(4,500)	
Taxable Income	$ 7,750		$15,500	
Tax at 70%	(5,425)		(10,850)	
Net Aftertax Income	$ 2,325		$ 4,650	
Add Back Depletion (a noncash deduction)	2,250		4,500	
Aftertax Cash Return		$4,575		$9,150
Aftertax Return Over Aftertax Investment		1.525		3.05

*Does not consider minimum and maximum tax effects discussed later in this booklet.

Question:

What aftertax cash return can an investor expect to achieve if he ultimately receives $10,000 or, alternatively, $20,000 over the life of his interest in an oil and gas investment?

Answer:

On a "break even" oil and gas investment (Case 1), the investor still is able to recover over one and one-half times his aftertax investment. Should the investor receive twice his original investment back over the life of the property (Case 2), he will recover over three times his aftertax investment. For a taxpayer in the 50% tax bracket, recovery of cash would be 1.225 and 2.45 times his aftertax investment. This example assumes the taxpayer does not shelter the income remaining after the depletion deduction. As mentioned earlier, many experienced oil and gas investors continually shelter "after-depletion" income to achieve even greater "aftertax" cash returns.

2. Sale of Oil and Gas Investment

The Revenue Act of 1978 created a significantly more favorable atmosphere for the sale of property qualifying for long-term capital gain treatment because it:

1. Reduced the maximum overall capital gain taxation rate from a possible high of 49% (including 15% minimum tax for tax preference) to 28%, subject to certain limitations.
2. Excluded the tax preference portion of long-term capital gain from the list of tax preference items which reduce personal service income qualifying for the maximum tax on personal service income.

As noted above, capital gains are no longer an item of tax preference potentially taxable at a rate of 15%. Substituted for "regular minimum tax" treatment of capital gains was an "alternative minimum tax" computation for capital gains and excess itemized deductions. The "alternative minimum tax" has limited application, but its effects should be discussed with a tax advisor prior to the sale of an oil and gas property.

The concept of "intangible drilling cost recapture" was introduced by the Tax Reduction Act of 1975. Recapture causes gain from the sale of oil and gas properties to be treated as ordinary income to the extent of the excess of the intangible cost deductions which are allocable to such properties over the deductions that would have been allowed had such expenses with respect to successful wells been capitalized and recovered through cost depletion.

Intangible costs on successful wells generally represent only a minor portion of total costs actually deducted by an oil and gas "exploratory" program; therefore, the negative impact of the recapture of successful IDC may not be particularly harsh. Further, the majority of deductible costs on "exploratory" programs come from costs on dry holes which are not affected by the recapture provisions.

The interaction of these law changes are shown in the following illustration:

	Case 1*		Case 2*	
	One to One		Two to One	
Investment	$10,000		$10,000	
Tax Savings at 70%	(7,000)		(7,000)	
Aftertax Cost of Investment		$ 3,000		$ 3,000
Sales Price	$10,000	$10,000	$20,000	$20,000
Less Tax Basis	—		—	
Gain on Sale	$10,000		$20,000	
Intangible Drilling Cost Recapture	(3,000)		(3,000)	
Gain Eligible for Long-Term Capital Gain Treatment	$ 7,000		$17,000	
Capital Gain Exclusion	(4,200)		(10,200)	
Taxable Gain	$ 2,800		$ 6,800	
Add Intangible Drilling Cost Recapture	$ 3,000		$ 3,000	
Taxable Income From Sale	$ 5,800		$ 9,800	
Tax at 70%	$ 4,060	(4,060)	$ 6,860	(6,860)
Aftertax Cash Return From Sale		$ 5,940		$13,140
Aftertax Cash Return Over Aftertax Cost of Investment		1.98		4.38

*Does not consider minimum and maximum tax effects discussed later in this booklet.

Assumptions:

— 70% tax bracket investor
— In Case 1, a sales price equal to the pretax cost of the investment is assumed; in Case 2, a sales price equal to twice the pretax cost of the investment is assumed
— Investor is not subject to alternative minimum tax
— Intangible drilling cost recapture is assumed to equal 30% of original investment
— No compounding or discount analysis is considered

Question:

What overall aftertax cash return over original aftertax cost can be expected from the sale of an oil and gas investment?

Answer:

In a "one to one" deal (Case 1), the investor recovers cash equal to 1.98 times his original investment after taxes. For a sale where twice the original investment is recovered, the investor receives cash equal to 4.38 times original investment after taxes. For an investor in the 50% tax bracket the cash received is equal to 1.42 and 3.02 times his original investment after taxes in the "one-for-one" and the "two-for-one" cases, respectively.

3. Transfer of Oil and Gas Properties to Minor Children

One longstanding method of transferring appreciating or income-producing assets from one's estate is through lifetime gifts. These gifts enable the donor to eliminate the appreciation from his estate, transfer the income to a "lower-bracket" taxpayer and at the same time observe the manner in which the donee handles the accumulation of additional wealth.

One of the most attractive possibilities for fully maximizing the tax benefits of an oil and gas investment is the transfer of the investment to minor children. The tax laws provide planning opportunities in family situations which might work as follows:

1. The investor acquires the investment with high tax bracket dollars.
2. He makes the gift at a time when no further cash contribution is required and at a time when he has utilized virtually all of the investment's front-end tax deductions, but before significant amounts of income are generated.
3. The transfer is made before the properties are fully evaluated, and in many programs additional drilling will prove the properties to be more valuable than at the time of transfer. As a result, gift taxes are minimized, or if the gift is not too large, eliminated entirely.
4. Cash flow from the investment goes into the child's tax bracket, which in most cases is minimal or at least substantially lower than the parents'.
5. Even in the case of wealthy families, where the child might already be in a reasonably high tax bracket, it may be attractive to transfer the property before its value is fully established, in order to avoid estate taxes on the expected appreciation in value.

An illustration of this planning technique is to show the effect such a transfer can have on the cost of providing a child with a $40,000 cash fund over a four-year period. In order for a parent in the 70% tax bracket to finance a $40,000 fund out of aftertax income, he must generate approximately $133,500 of income over four years. The illustration below suggests a far less costly funding mechanism.

Assumptions:

— 70% tax bracket investor
— Availability of unified estate and gift tax credit, if applicable
— Child does not have significant income from other sources
— In Case 1, investment generates income equal to original investment. Twice the original investment is assumed to be generated by the investment in Case 2.
— Depletion rate is 18% and child and property qualify for percentage depletion
— Lease operating expense equals 20% of gross revenue
— No compounding or discount analysis is considered

Question:

What is the aftertax cost of accumulating the $40,000 fund over a four-year period through the gift of an oil and gas investment?

	Case 1*		Case 2*
	One to One		Two to One
Investment Required	$48,000		$24,000
Tax Saved at 70%	(33,600)		(16,800)
Aftertax Cost of Investment	$14,400		$ 7,200
Transfer Cost (assuming utilization of unified gift and estate tax credit)	—		—
Total Aftertax Cost of Transfer	$14,400		$ 7,200
Income Flow to Child			
Gross Income		$60,000	
Expenses		(12,000)	
Net Income		$48,000	
Depletion ($60,000 x 18%)		(10,800)	
Taxable Income		$37,200	
Tax (top bracket of 21%)		(6,052)	
Net Income Aftertax		$31,148	
Add Back Depletion (a noncash deduction)		10,800	
Aftertax Cash Flow		$41,948	

*Does not consider minimum and maximum tax effects discussed later in this booklet.

Answer:

The aftertax cost of providing a $40,000 fund to a 70% bracket taxpayer is $14,400 if the oil and gas investment given away returns cash equal to the original purchase price in four years. The aftertax cost of such fund drops to $7,200 if the investment returns twice the original purchase price. This appears "too good to be true" when compared with the cost of accumulating such a fund with what the investor has left over after taxes, earlier stated to approximate $133,500. However, this result can be achieved if the investment produces the pretax returns used in these examples.

For an investor in the 50% tax bracket, the aftertax cost of providing a $40,000 fund through the gift of an oil and gas property would be $24,000 and $12,000, respectively.

For many practical as well as legal reasons, it is not prudent to transfer property outright to minor children. Consequently, most gifts to minor children are to trusts created for the minor child's benefit. In gifts to a conventional trust, the applicable gift tax, if any, is computed with reference to the value of the property donated, determined at the time of donation. However, where property is transferred in trust for at least 10 years with the donor (parent) retaining a remainder interest, there are two advantages.

1. The donor receives his property back at the end of the 10-year term, and
2. The gift tax is based on a maximum of 44% of the value of the property donated, determined at the time of donation.

Where oil and gas properties are donated to such a term trust, the potential gift tax savings could be substantial. This is so because the Internal Revenue Service has prescribed rules which arbitrarily establish the value of a term gift without regard to the expected yield during the term of the trust. In the case of a 10-year trust, the present value of 10 years' income is deemed to be about 44% of the total value of the property for gift tax purposes. Thus, even though a much larger percentage of an oil and gas property's value may be recovered during the existence of the 10-year trust, the value of the gift is nevertheless based on 44% of the property's value at the time the gift is made.

The potential gift tax savings will, of course, depend on the donated property; however, many oil and gas properties produce a significant percentage of their total recoverable oil and gas reserves within 10 years of the time production is established.

Many alternatives exist; however, the economic effect of losing depletion through the transfer of a producing property must be considered in weighing alternatives. Possible uses are:

1. Providing a daughter with resources to make her and her future family less dependent on her husband's business fortunes.
2. Assisting a child to accumulate resources to provide a down payment for a home or, alternatively, eliminate a costly mortgage.
3. Providing funds to a widowed mother.
4. Providing funds to begin an insurance program for a child which the child can subsequently take over when his earning power permits.
5. Providing a child with funds to pay for such child's college or graduate school.

The tax advantage of such gifts to 10-year trusts is found in the ability of the donor to transfer "pretax" rather than "aftertax" dollars to a donee of his choice. Thus, more dollars are transferred to a donee generally in a lower tax bracket, resulting in more of the income from the asset remaining in the family.

4. Gift of Oil and Gas Investment to Charity

There are many worthwhile charities hard at work in this country. Their operations can require large sums of money, and fundraising is becoming an increasingly important function in their overall operation.

Many investors ask the question: How can I provide the greatest benefit to my favorite charity at the least economic cost to myself? The gift of an oil and gas investment is one good answer to this question as the following illustration will demonstrate.

Assumptions:

- —70% tax bracket investor
- —$10,000 original investment
- —In Case 1, the donated property is assumed to have a value equal to the amount of the original investment. In Case 2, the donated property is assumed to have a value equal to twice the amount of the original investment. In both cases, it is assumed that the donated property will produce income over its life equal to twice its present value.
- —Intangible drilling cost recapture is assumed to equal 30% of the original investment.
- —Holding period of donated property is longer than one year.

Question:

What is the aftertax cost of transferring an oil and gas investment to charity?

Answer:

In Case 1, the investor has been able to transfer a future income stream having a present worth of $10,000 to charity at no aftertax cost to himself. In fact, he is $1,900 better off after taxes than if he had never invested or made the charitable contribution. Where the donated property

	Case 1* One to One		Case 2* Two to One	
Investment	$10,000		$10,000	
Tax Savings at 70%	(7,000)		(7,000)	
Aftertax Cost of Investment	$ 3,000	$3,000	$ 3,000	$ 3,000
Charitable Contribution	$10,000		$20,000	
Less Intangible Drilling Cost Recapture	(3,000)		(3,000)	
Deductible Contribution	$ 7,000		$17,000	
Tax Savings at 70%	$ 4,900	$4,900	$11,900	$11,900
Overall Aftertax (Cost) Benefit		$1,900		$ 8,900

*Does not consider minimum and maximum tax effects discussed later in this booklet.

	Case 1*	Case 2*
Oil and gas income	$20,000	$40,000
Depletion (18%)	3,600	7,200
Net taxable income	$16,400	$32,800
Tax (70%)	11,480	22,960
Net income after tax	$ 4,920	$ 9,840
Add back—Depletion	3,600	7,200
Aftertax cash retained	$ 8,520	$17,040

*Does not consider minimum and maximum tax effects discussed later in this booklet.

is more valuable (Case 2), the investor is actually $8,900 better off, and his favorite charity is the recipient of a future income stream having a present worth of $20,000. For an investor in the 50% tax bracket, the overall cost in initial Case 1 is $1,500, while in Case 2 that investor is $3,500 better off after making the gift.

Thus, the 70% investor retains $8,500 and $17,040 should he keep the properties with $20,000 and $40,000 of future net income. However, by giving the property to a qualified charity, the charity would keep the entire $20,000 or $40,000 at an after-tax savings as reflected in the earlier example. An investor in the 50% tax bracket would retain $11,800 in Case 1 and $23,600 in Case 2.

Charitable contributions of appreciated property are subject to certain limitations under the tax law. In addition, there are limitations imposed by the Internal Revenue Service which may preclude ownership of the property by certain charities. Investors should consult with their tax advisors before completing gifts of oil and gas properties to charity.

Other Tax Considerations Relating to an Investment in Oil and Gas Exploration

Introduction

Because legislation intended to encourage exploration for oil and gas creates so many opportunities for an investor to substantially reduce or even eliminate his income tax liability, Congress has enacted other legislation which ensures that most investors in oil and gas exploration will pay some tax. Additionally, intangible drilling cost recapture causes a later sale of an oil and gas property to be less attractive taxwise than the sale of other investment assets. Oil and gas exploration may also cause increased taxation of personal service income earned by an investor. These unfavorable tax aspects are discussed in general terms below. Certainly, each investor should discuss these provisions with his own tax advisor to determine their effect on his personal income tax planning.

The Minimum Tax

The minimum tax on items of tax preference was enacted by Congress in 1969 as a result of its concern with the increasing trend toward tax deferral through investment in activities which yielded large current tax benefits in relation to the amount invested. In its present form its basic principles of operation for individual taxpayers are as follows:

1. A taxpayer totals all of his items of tax preference.
2. This sum is then reduced by $10,000 or one-half of the taxpayer's income tax liability, whichever is larger.
3. A tax rate of 15% is then applied to any remaining items of tax preference.

Two items of tax preference typically arise from oil and gas exploration activity: "excess intangible drilling costs" (excess IDC) and "percentage depletion in excess of leasehold cost" (excess percentage depletion). Basically, excess IDC occurs when IDC for any given year exceed a taxpayer's "net income from oil and gas properties." Excess percentage depletion occurs when the aggregate of depletion deductions arising from any given property exceeds the cost of that property.

The effect of the minimum tax on the economics of an oil and gas investment is dependent upon the size of any investor's income stream from other sources and whether the investor is generating items of tax preference from other investment activities.

Alternative Minimum Tax

In considering changes in the minimum tax provisions of the Code, the Senate Finance Committee decided that the present tax structure has resulted in imposing a large minimum tax on individuals who already are paying substantial regular taxes, particularly where large capital gains are involved. Conversely, taxpayers paying little or no regular tax are taxed only at 15% rate on their preference items. To correct these perceived inequities, the 1978 Act created a new alternative minimum tax, applicable only to the capital gains and excess itemized deduction preference items. The new minimum tax will apply only to the extent it exceeds an individual's regular tax liability plus his regular minimum tax which continues for preference items other than capital gains and excess itemized deductions.

The tax base for the alternative minimum tax is the taxpayer's taxable income (with adjustments for certain net operating losses) plus the capital gain and excess itemized deduction tax preferences reduced by a $20,000 exemption. This amount is then taxed as follows:

Amount Subject to Alternative Minimum Tax	Tax Rate
First $40,000	10%
$40,000-$80,000	20%
Over $80,000	25%

The tax is payable only if it exceeds the taxpayer's regular tax liability plus the regular minimum tax.

The effect of this change in the tax laws is felt primarily by taxpayers who have large amounts of income which qualify as long-term capital gain. Those taxpayers find that a point is reached where even though income may be taxed as high as 70%, the tax benefit of each dollar of deduction is only 25%. Therefore, investors are cautioned to consult with their tax advisors to determine the impact of the alternative minimum tax on their personal tax planning objectives.

Maximum Tax On Personal Service Income

Items of tax preference other than capital gains and excess itemized deductions also affect the computation of the maximum tax on personal service income (50% top tax bracket). For an investor to be affected by this interaction, he must earn personal service income in excess of $60,000 per year although the effect does not usually begin to be a material factor until personal service income approaches $100,000.

When a taxpayer is so affected, each dollar of tax preference converts one dollar of income eligible for taxation at a maximum of 50% into ordinary income subject to taxation at a rate as high as 70%. It is impossible to compute the effect of this interaction except on a case-by-case basis. Therefore, each investor should discuss the applicability of this interaction with his personal tax advisor.

Intangible Drilling Cost Recapture

IDC incurred and deducted incident to drilling an oil or gas well on a property after December 31, 1975, must be recaptured as ordinary income upon the sale of other disposition of the property at a gain, under provisions similar to those for depreciation recapture. The recapture amount is limited to the lesser of the gain on sale or disposition or the excess of the intangible cost deductions which are allocated to such properties over the deductions that would have been allowed had such expenses with respect to successful wells been capitalized and recovered through cost depletion. The recapture rule applies only to the IDC incurred on the property sold, and the amount of recapture is the lesser of the IDC incurred or the gain or sale or disposition. For example, if a producing property having a tax basis of $1,000 is sold for $10,000, a $9,000 gain results. If the taxpayer incurred $6,000 of IDC in developing the well, then $6,000 of the $9,000 gain is subject to ordinary income treatment, and the remaining $3,000 of gain would be subject to capital gains treatment. Recapture of IDC will reduce the economic gain to a seller by increasing the tax payable on his gain.

Debt Financed Oil and Gas Exploration Activities

Nonrecourse debt at one time was a very popular financing technique used in investments to generate tax deductions in excess of actual cash invested. Nonrecourse debt is secured solely by assets, with no personal liability being assumed by any individual, corporation or other entity. In order to prevent taxpayer abuse of this financing technique, deductions claimed by all taxpayers other than "regular" corporations now cannot exceed the actual amount a taxpayer has "at risk" (except in the case of real property investments). To an investor in an oil and gas drilling venture, his amount at risk would generally be his original cash investment and undistributed profits plus any indebtedness of the venture for which the investor is personally liable. It is still possible for the investor to benefit from "nonrecourse" financing to pay for any costs that are not "tax" deductible. For example, assume an investor makes a $10,000 investment in and oil and gas drilling program and 30% or $3,000 of the investor's capital contribution is for nondeductible items such as syndication fees. Further exploration in the second year of the program will result in additional expenses. By borrowing amounts on a "nonrecourse" basis up to the amount of the nondeductible cost ($3,000) the investor is assured deductions equal to 100% of his "at-risk" basis, $10,000.

Limitations on the Deduction of Percentage Depletion

The most frequently encountered limitations imposed on the percentage depletion deduction are as follows:

1. Percentage depletion on any given property may not exceed 50% of net income from that property. This usually occurs only during the first year when heavy exploration exists on the property or in the case of a marginal property.
2. No percentage depletion is allowed on certain properties, the principal value of which has been proved before ownership is acquired.
3. An investor's percentage depletion deduction, in total, may not exceed 65% of his taxable income as adjusted pursuant to the tax regulations. This limitation is generally only applicable to taxpayers heavily involved in the oil and gas business, sheltering most of their "other" income through IDC.

There are several other, more complicated, limitations affecting the availability of percentage depletion for some taxpayers, including a maximum depletable quantity for each taxpayer of 1,000 barrels (or 6,000 MCF of gas) for 1981 and future years. Each investor should discuss these matters with his personal tax advisor.

It should also be noted that the percentage depletion deduction will be:

Years	Percentage Depletion Rate
1981	20%
1982	18%
1983	16%
1984 and thereafter	15%

In this booklet, an 18% rate has been used which is in keeping with industry averages.

Who Should Invest in an Oil and Gas Drilling Program?

To take best advantage of the tax attributes from an oil and gas investment, the investor should be in at least the 50% tax bracket. His net worth and cash flow from other sources should be substantial enough that his lifestyle would not be interrupted if his investment became worthless.

An investor who meets the above requisites does not automatically become a good candidate for an oil and gas investment. Since 1969, the way ordinary income such as wages, salary, interest and dividends have been taxed has changed drastically. The effective rate of tax savings from an oil and gas investment varies significantly depending on the character of the investor's income. These are (1) personal service income, such as wages and salary, subject to the 50% maximum tax, (2) other ordinary income, such as interest and dividends, subject to tax at the highest tax bracket corresponding to the investor's taxable income, and (3) long-term capital gain from the sale or exchange of a capital asset held for more than one year.

The effective rate of tax savings from an oil

and gas investment to an investor in the following situations will be illustrated:

Case 1: The investor is self-employed with substantial passive income. He has no personal service income subject to the maximum tax.

Case 2: The investor is a professional person with substantial personal service income subject to the maximum tax. He has no passive income, such as interest and dividends.

Case 3: The investor is a professional person with substantial personal service income subject to the maximum tax. He also has substantial passive income.

Case 4: The investor has a moderate amount of both personal service income and passive income. He also has a substantial long-term capital gain.

Case 5: The investor has substantial tax preference items from sources other than the long-term capital gains deduction and adjusted itemized deduction.

Each graph below shows the relationship that exists between the effective rate of tax savings and a specific variable for the facts given and assumptions made. As the facts and assumptions vary, that relationship may vary. The general form of the curves will not change. The effective rate of tax savings for a specific variable may change. The investor should be able to fit his individual tax situation into one of these cases and determine his approximate tax savings from an oil and gas investment.

Assumptions: (Cases 1 and 2)

1. The investor is married and files a joint return.
2. The investor puts $10,000 into an oil and gas drilling program that produces an $8,000 first year IDC deduction and $3,000 of tax preference items.
3. The investor is assumed to have no other tax preference items. There is no minimum tax liability because the $3,000 tax preference is more than offset by the $10,000 exemption.
4. Personal exemptions and the zero bracket amount are assumed to be immaterial and have been ignored.

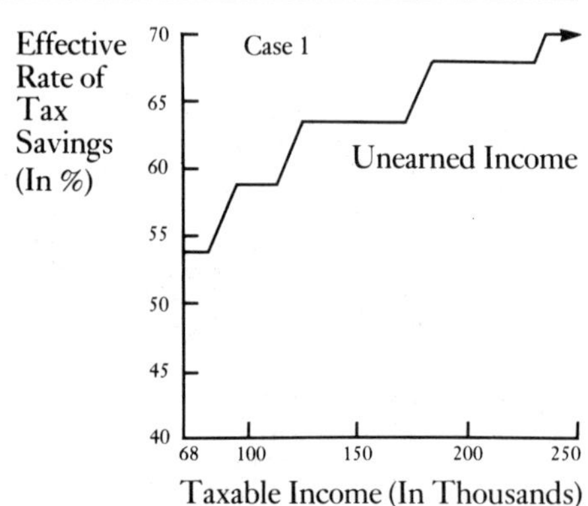

As illustrated above, the investor with substantial passive income (Case 1) obtains significant benefits from an oil and gas investment. The drilling deduction reduces taxable income that would otherwise be taxed at the investor's highest tax bracket. Therefore, the effective rate of tax savings to this investor is the greatest per dollar invested, an effective way to shelter income.

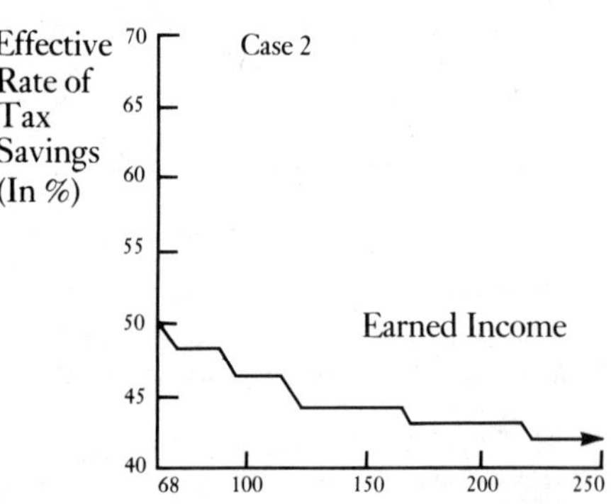

By contrast, the investor with substantial personal service income (Case 2) has a decreasing effective rate of tax savings as his personal service income increases. A portion of his earnings that would otherwise be taxed at a maximum 50% rate is converted to ordinary income and taxed at the investor's highest tax rate based upon his taxable income. The portion converted to ordinary income in the illustration is equal to the tax preference amount. Tax preference items other than the long-term capital gains deduction reduces personal service income eligible for the 50% maximum rate on earned income dollar for dollar. The drilling deductions reduce taxable income that is already being taxed at the more preferable maximum tax rate. The result is an effective rate of tax savings of less than 50%.

Assumptions: (Case 3)

1. The same as in Case 1 and Case 2.
2. The investor has personal service income of $103,200.

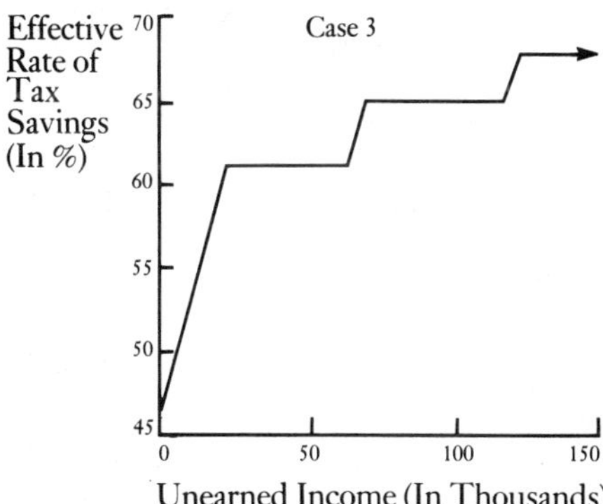

As illustrated above, the more passive income an investor receives during the year, the greater his effective rate of tax saving from his oil and gas investment. With very little passive income the investor in Case 3 approaches the effective rate of tax savings obtained by the investor in Case 1. As passive income increases, the investor's effective rate of tax savings approaches that obtained by the investor in Case 2. We have already seen that when passive income is less than the tax preference items (in this case $3,000), the effective rate of tax savings is less than 50%.

When the drilling deduction (in this case $8,000) is greater than the passive income, a part of the deduction is offsetting income at the maximum rate of 50%. The investor starts to benefit more significantly when his passive income is equal to or greater than the drilling deduction. At this point, the entire deduction is reducing income that would otherwise be taxed at the investor's highest tax bracket corresponding to his taxable income. The investor's effective rate of tax savings can approach 65%-70% when his taxable income is in the highest tax bracket, an effective way to shelter income.

Assumptions: (Case 4)

1. The investor is married and files a joint return.
2. The investor puts $30,000 into an oil and gas program that produces a $24,000 first year IDC deduction and $7,200 of tax preference items.
3. The investor has personal service income of $59,400 and passive income of $50,000.
4. The investor is assumed to have no tax preference items other than the long-term capital gains deduction.
5. Personal exemptions and the zero bracket amount are assumed to be immaterial and have been ignored.

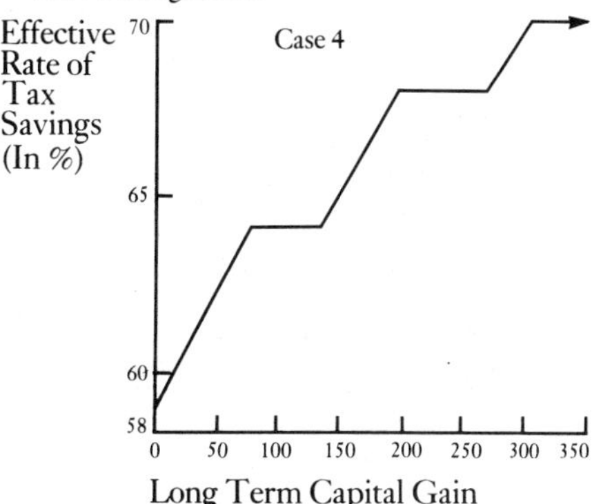

As illustrated the investor with substantial long-term capital gains obtains significant benefits from an oil and gas investment. Starting November 1, 1978, 60% of a long-term capital gain is not taxed because of the increase from 50% to 60% in the long-term capital gains deduction. The remaining 40% is subject to tax at the highest tax bracket corresponding to the investor's taxable income. The drilling deduction reduces taxable income that would otherwise be taxed at the investor's highest tax bracket. Therefore, the effective rate of tax savings per dollar invested to this investor can be as great as that recognized by the investor in Case 1 above, an effective way to shelter income.

The restructuring of the tax on capital gains by the Tax Reform Act of 1978 could increase the appeal of investing in an oil and gas program for the purpose of sheltering long-term capital gain; however, the effect of the "alternative minimum tax" must be considered. Prior law contained, in part, the following detrimental provisions:

1. The long-term capital gains deduction was an item of tax preference subject to the 15% add-on minimum tax.
2. The long-term capital gains deduction reduced personal service income eligible for the 50% maximum rate dollar for dollar.

Below is a comparison of the effective rate of tax savings due to this change in the law.

Assumptions: (Case 5)

1. The investor is married and files a joint return.
2. The investor puts $50,000 into an oil and gas drilling program that produces a $40,000 first year IDC deduction and $14,000 of tax preference items.
3. The other tax preference items do not include the long-term capital gains deduction or the adjusted itemized deduction.
4. Personal exemptions and the zero bracket amount are assumed to be immaterial and have been ignored.

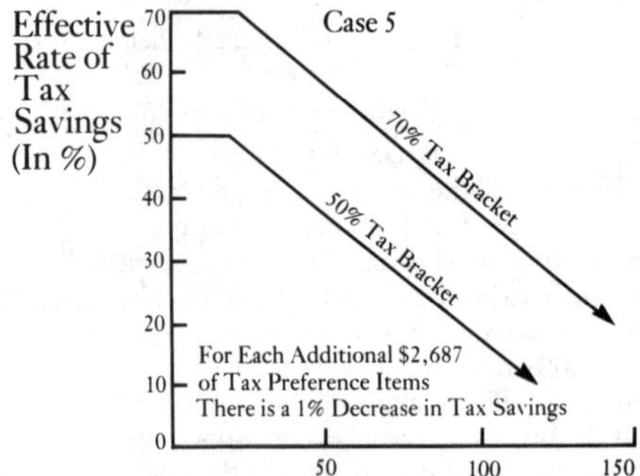

As illustrated above, an investor with substantial tax preference items from other sources reduces the effective rate of tax savings from his oil and gas investment because of the additional add-on minimum tax liability. An investor in this situation should carefully weigh the expected return on investment against the risk incurred. A successful drilling program would incur additional tax preference items (i.e., IDC and depletion) that would further reduce the overall tax savings. Any investor in this situation should consult with his tax advisor before investing. The effective rate of tax savings illustrated in Cases 1, 2, 3 and 4 will be reduced to the extent Case 5 applies. Therefore, Case 5 should be considered in conjunction with the other cases.

OIL AND GAS TAXATION AND REGULATION

The following material summarizes the special features of oil and gas taxation, general tax provisions and competition, markets and regulation.

Special Features of Oil and Gas Taxation

The following is a summary of some of the principal features of federal income taxation of oil and gas operations.

Lease Acquisition Costs. The cost of acquiring oil and gas leasehold interests, or other similar oil and gas property interests, is a capital expenditure and must be recovered through depletion deductions if the Lease is productive. If a Lease is proved worthless and is abandoned, the cost of acquisition less any depletion claimed may be deducted in full in the year it becomes worthless as an ordinary loss.

Geophysical Costs. The cost of geophysical exploration must be capitalized as part of the Leasehold Acquisition Costs if a property is acquired or retained on the basis of data from such exploration. Otherwise, such costs may be deducted as ordinary losses.

Intangible Drilling and Development Costs. The Partnership Agreement provides that an election will be made under §263(c) of the Internal Revenue Code to deduct as an expense all "intangible drilling and development costs." Such costs generally include costs for drilling and labor, fuel, supplies, and other costs for items without salvage value which are incurred in preparing wells for production. Assuming a proper election by each Partnership, each Limited Partner will be entitled to deduct his distributive share of the intangible drilling and development costs incurred by the Partnership. Such deducted costs may be subject to recapture as ordinary income under certain circumstances, and a portion of such deducted costs may be taxed as an item of tax preference.

Depreciation. The cost of equipment such as casing, tubing, tanks, pumping units and several other types of tangible properties cannot be deducted currently but must be capitalized and recovered through deductions for depreciation. Each Limited Partner is entitled to deduct his distributive share of a Partnership's deductions for depreciation with respect to such cost items. These costs may also be eligible for accelerated depreciation and for the investment tax credit.

Depletion. The owner of an economic interest in an oil or gas property is entitled to a depletion deduction for the production and sale of oil and gas from the property. The availability of depletion deductions is computed separately by each partner and not at the partnership level. The amount of this deduction is the greater of cost depletion or percentage depletion, if percentage depletion is available to the taxpayer under the Tax Reduction of 1975, as discussed below. In the event that percentage depletion is not available to the taxpayer, only cost depletion may be deducted.

Under the cost depletion method, the capitalized costs of an oil or gas property are deductible over the life of the property through annual depletion deductions. Thus, the cost depletion deduction is limited to the capitalized cost of the property. The cost depletion deduction for each year is calculated by dividing the cost of a property by the estimated recoverable reserves, and multiplying the resulting quotient by the number of units of production sold during that year.

Under the percentage depletion method, the owner of an economic interest in an oil or gas property may deduct an amount equal to a percentage (discussed below) of his gross income from the depletable property for the taxable year. The percentage depletion deduction is limited, however, to 50% of the taxable income to the owner from the property for each taxable year, computed without allowance for depletion.

The Tax Reduction Act of 1975 eliminated percentage depletion with respect to oil and gas produced on and after January 1, 1975, subject to four exceptions. The four exceptions apply in the following situations: (i) a taxpayer who is not involved, either directly or through a corporation, partnership, estate or trust in which the taxpayer owns an interest of 5% or more, in the retail sale of oil or natural gas, or any product derived therefrom, or in the operation of a refinery which refines more than

50,000 barrels of crude oil on any day during the taxable year ("Small Producer Allowance"); (ii) domestic natural gas produced and sold by the producer, before July 1, 1976, which was then subject to Federal Power Commission regulations, the price for which was not adjusted to reflect to any extent the increase in tax resulting from the repeal of percentage depletion ("Regulated Natural Gas"); (iii) domestic natural gas sold by the producer under a contract, in effect on February 1, 1975, under which the price of such gas cannot be adjusted to reflect to any extent the increase in taxes resulting from the repeal of percentage depletion ("Fixed Contract Gas"); and (iv) any geothermal deposit in the United States or its possessions which is determined to be a gas well ("Geothermal Gas"). A person is not considered a retailer, for purposes of the Small Producer Allowance, (i) with respect to bulk oil and gas sales to industrial or commercial users, (ii) with respect to sales made outside the United States if none of the seller's domestic production is exported during the taxable year or the immediately preceding taxable year, and (iii) if retail gross sales of oil or gas products do not exceed $5,000,000 for the taxable year.

The percentage depletion rate for Regulated Natural Gas, Fixed Contract Gas and Geothermal Gas is 22%, but the depletion rate for the Small Producer Allowance, except for secondary or tertiary production, will be 20% in 1981, 18% in 1982, 16% in 1983, and 15% thereafter. The 22% rate will apply to secondary and tertiary production that qualifies under the Small Producer Allowance through 1983, and thereafter will be reduced to 15%.

The Small Producer Allowance is the exception most likely to be available to a holder of an interest in a Partnership. Under the Small Producer Allowance, a taxpayer is allowed to deduct percentage depletion only to the extent that his average daily production of domestic crude oil does not exceed 1,000 barrels per day.

If a taxpayer has both oil and natural gas production, the amount depletable by a Small Producer may be allocated between the two types of production. For this purpose, each 6,000 cubic feet of domestic natural gas production is regarded as equivalent to one barrel of oil. In determining whether a taxpayer's average daily production of oil or gas exceeds his depletable quantity, his aggregate production for the taxable year is divided by the number of days in the taxable year to arrive at the average daily production. Production of crude oil or natural gas resulting from secondary or tertiary processes is not taken into account in calculating a taxpayer's average daily production, but the specified number of barrels of average daily production upon which a taxpayer may claim depletion is reduced by the taxpayer's average daily secondary or tertiary production for the taxable year.

The amount of production of oil and gas depletable under the Small Producer Allowance must be allocated among the taxpayer and certain controlled or related persons and family members in proportion to the respective production by such persons during the period in question.

The depletion deduction allowed under the Small Producer Allowance is limited to 65% of the taxpayer's total taxable income for the year, computed without regard to percentage depletion under the Small Producer Allowance and any net operating loss or capital loss carryback, and reduced, in the case of an individual, by the zero bracket amount. If deduction of an amount is disallowed because of the 65% limitation, the deduction may be carried over to the following taxable year and deducted, if the percentage depletion for the year plus the deduction carryover does not exceed 65% of the taxpayer's total taxable income for the year.

Percentage depletion is not available under most circumstances to a transferee of a "proven" oil or gas property transferred after December 31, 1974, unless the property was transferred at death, or the transfer was made in certain situations where the amount of depletable production is allocated between the transferor and transferee. An oil or gas property is considered to be "proven" if the principal value of the property has been demonstrated by prospecting or exploration or discovery work. The foregoing rule also applies to the transfer of an interest in a partnership and certain trusts which own an interest in a proven oil or gas property. Proven property is not considered to be transferred because of changes in beneficiaries under a trust due to births, adoptions and deaths of any beneficiary if the transferee was a beneficiary of the trust prior to the transfer or is a lineal descendant of the grantor or any other beneficiary.

The availability of depletion, both cost and percentage, will be determined separately by each partner and not at the partnership level. The Tax Reform Act of 1976 specifically provides that a partnership shall allocate to each partner his proportionate share of the adjusted basis of each partnership oil or gas property and that each partner shall separately keep records of his share of the adjusted basis in such property, adjust such share of the adjusted basis for any depletion taken on such property, and use such adjusted basis each year in the computation of his cost depletion or in the computation of his gain or loss on the disposition of such property by the Partnerships.

Each prospective Limited Partner should consult his personal tax advisor to determine whether percentage depletion would be available to him under the Tax Reduction Act of 1975 and the Tax Reform Act of 1976.

Sale of Oil and Gas Properties. Gains and losses from sales of oil and gas properties held for more than one year and not held primarily for sale to customers, except to the extent of recapture of intangible drilling and development costs and of depreciation on equipment, will be gains and losses described in Section 1231 of the Code. In general, a Section 1231 gain or loss includes sales or exchanges of real or depreciable property used in a trade or business. A Limited Partner's net Section 1231 gain will be treated as a long-term capital gain while a net Section 1231 loss will be an ordinary deduction from gross income. If oil or gas property is sold, expenditures allocable to the property which have been deducted as intangible drilling and development costs (reduced by the amount that would have been deductible as cost depletion had such costs been capitalized) will be recaptured as ordinary income to the extent of the gain realized. If a portion of an oil or gas property (other than an undivided interest) is sold, the entire amount of such costs are allocated to that portion and recaptured as ordinary income to the extent of the gain.

Sale of Limited Partnership Interests. The gain or loss realized upon the sale by a Limited Partner of his interest in a Partnership, assuming that the interest has been held by him for more than one year and that he is not a "dealer" for purposes of the Code, will be a long-term capital gain or loss, except for that portion which is attributable to the Limited Partner's share of the Partnership's unrealized receivables and inventory items which have substantially appreciated in value, which will be taxed to the Limited Partner as ordinary income. Unrealized receivables for this purpose include intangible drilling and development costs and depreciation on equipment subject to recapture. If a non-recourse loan is outstanding at the time of the sale, the selling Limited Partner may be treated as realizing an amount equal to his proportionate share of the loss in addition to other proceeds actually realized. Under the Revenue Act of 1978, 40% of the taxpayer's net capital gain is generally taxed at ordinary rates.

Farm-Out Transactions. A type of Farm-out transaction whereby a Partnership might acquire a leasehold interest would be a transaction in which, for the drilling of a well on a particular drill site, a Partnership would become entitled to an assignment of 100% of the leasehold interest in the drill site acreage (until such time as its drilling, completing and production costs had been recovered out of production therefrom) and a lesser fractional interest in the portion of the tract exclusive of the drill site acreage. Until recently, it was understood that the party farming out the acreage incurred no gain or loss upon the assignment of such acreage, and that such party receiving the acreage realized no income in connection with the receipt thereof. In Revenue Ruling 77-176, 1977-1 C.B. 77, the Internal Revenue Service ruled that the transfer of rights in property other than the drill site acreage in this type of transaction would be deemed (by the party transferring the property) to be a sale of such other property on which gain or loss is to be realized. It further ruled that while the party receiving the acreage and incurring the cost of drilling the well on the drill site could elect to deduct such costs as intangible drilling and development costs, such party realized ordinary income to the extent of the value of the acreage earned exclusive of the drill site acreage. Each Partnership, in acquiring acreage in a Farm-out or similar transaction, will attempt to structure the transaction in a way which will either eliminate or minimize to the fullest extent possible the tax consequences set forth in this ruling. Nonetheless, this ruling may have adverse tax implications for a Partnership if and when it enters into such Farm-out agreements, since it may be required to recognize ordinary income in connection with the acquisition of Prospects under such arrangements. Further, in the case of Prospects which it farms-out to other parties, it may be required to recognize gain or loss upon the transfer of an interest in the transferred property.

Deductions in Excess of Capital Contributions. Deductions of losses incurred by a Partnership and allocated to a Limited Partner in a particular year are limited to his adjusted basis for his Units at the end of that taxable year and further limited by the "at risk" provisions of Code Section 465. Adjusted basis is determined by the amount of the Limited Partner's contribution of money to a Partnership plus his share of the profits and gains of the Partnership less distributions to him, his share of the losses allocated to him and any cost depletion claimed by him on Partnership oil and gas properties. Such adjusted basis may also be increased by a Limited Partner's share of Partnership liabilities or by the increase in his individual liabilities by reason of his assumption of Partnership liabilities. A Limited Partner will not be able to deduct a loss allocated to him for any year to the extent that loss exceeds the amount with respect to which he is "at risk" for a Partnership at the close of the year within the meaning of Section 465. A Limited Partner will be considered to be "at risk" only to the extent of the sum of (i) his contribution of money to the Partnership and (ii) his share of undistributed income of the Partnership, less any losses claimed in earlier years.

General Tax Provisions

Except for the special rules which apply to the taxation of oil and gas properties, each Limited Partner will determine his tax deductions and income under the rules normally applicable to all taxpayers. The following is a brief summary of some of the major federal income tax laws which may affect a Limited Partner. This summary is not intended to be a complete statement of the federal income tax provisions which would apply to each Limited Partner.

Minimum Tax-Tax Preference Items. A taxpayer is subject to a minimum tax (the "add-on minimum tax," which is in addition to his regular income tax) equal to 15% of the amount by which certain tax preference items exceed the greater of $10,000 or one-half of the taxpayer's regular federal income tax. The following are among the tax preference items taken into account for this purpose:

(a) The excess of intangible drilling costs (other than those incurred in drilling a non-productive well) over the sum of

(1) the amount that would be deductible if such costs were capitalized and either amortized over 10 years or deducted over the life of the well as cost depletion and (2) the taxpayer's "net income from oil and gas properties" (as determined without regard to deductions attributable to properties with no gross income);

(b) the excess of accelerated depreciation deductions taken on certain types of property over straight-line depreciation; and

(c) the excess of the depletion deduction for the current year over the adjusted basis of the property to which the deduction relates.

The Revenue Act of 1978 established an alternative minimum tax, which is payable only to the extent it exceeds the sum of the taxpayer's regular federal income tax and such "add-on minimum tax." The alternative minimum tax is imposed upon a figure obtained by taking the taxpayer's gross income, reduced by (1) the deductions allowed for the taxable year and (2) any amounts included in income under Section 86 or 667 of the Internal Revenue Code, and increased by the sum of the tax preference items for adjusted itemized deductions and capital gains. To the extent this alternative minimum taxable income exceeds $20,000, the following tax rates are imposed:

$0 – $ 20,000	0%
$20,000 – $ 60,000	10%
$60,000 – $100,000	20%
over $100,000	25%

Maximum Tax on Personal Service Income. A maximum tax rate of 50% exists for an individual's personal service income (applicable to married taxpayers only if they file a joint return). Personal service income must be reduced on a dollar-for-dollar basis, without exemption, by items of tax preference in determining the personal service income subject to the 50% rate.

The Crude Oil Windfall Profit Tax Act of 1980. The windfall tax is a new tax on a portion of the sales price received for domestically produced crude oil according to classification of the oil in one of three tiers. Tier one oil includes oil which would have been lower or upper tier oil had previous federal price controls remained in effect. Tier two oil includes production from stripper well properties and from a National Petroleum Reserve in which the United States has an economic interest. Tier three oil includes newly discovered oil, certain heavy oil, and incremental tertiary oil. The windfall profit tax rates are: 70% on tier one oil, 60% on tier two oil, and 30% on tier three oil. The windfall profit tax rates are applied to the incremental difference between the removal or sales price of domestic crude oil and an artificially determined price at which the crude oil could have been sold under federal price controls previously in effect. Independent producers are allowed reduced tax rates—50% for tier one oil and 30% for tier two oil, on their combined production of tier one and tier two oil up to 1,000 barrels per day. In the case of a partnership, the reduced rates are computed on the partner level.

State Taxes. The Partnerships may operate in states which impose a tax on each Limited Partner on his share of the income derived from a Partnership's activities in such states. In addition, to the extent that a Partnership operates in certain jurisdictions, estate or inheritance taxes may be payable therein after the death of a Limited Partner. Accordingly, a Limited Partner may be subject to income taxes or estate taxes, or both, in states in which a Partnership does business, as well as in his own state of domicile. Depending on the location of Partnership leases and on applicable state and local laws, deductions which are available to Limited Partners for federal income tax purposes may not be available for state and local tax purposes.

COMPETITION, MARKETS AND REGULATION

Competition

There are a large number of companies and individuals engaged in the exploration for oil and gas. Accordingly, there is a high degree of competition for desirable Leases, drilling rigs, tubular goods, and other equipment. Many of the companies so engaged possess larger staffs and financial resources sufficient to pay far greater sums for the purchase of leases and equipment than the Partnerships. There are likewise numerous companies and individuals engaged in the organization and conduct of oil and gas drilling programs, and there is a high degree of competition among such companies in the offering of their programs.

Markets

The marketing of any oil and gas found and produced by the Partnerships will be affected by a number of factors which are beyond the Partnerships' control and whose exact effect cannot be accurately predicted. These factors include crude oil imports, the availability of adequate pipeline and other transportation facilities, the marketing of competitive fuels, and other matters affecting the availability of a ready market, such as fluctuating supply and demand. It should be noted that the supply of natural gas in the intrastate market of Oklahoma has exceeded demand for the last several years. To the extent that this continues, and if the Partnerships are unable to obtain adequate access to the interstate market because of limited gas transmission facilities, this may adversely affect the Partnership's results of operations.

In addition, marketing of oil and gas is restricted by certain existing price regulations.

Regulation

Federal Natural Gas Regulations. Natural gas is typically sold under long-term contracts to either intrastate or interstate pipeline companies and, on occasion, directly to industrial users. In the fall of 1978, Congress passed and the President signed into law the "Natural Gas Policy Act of 1978" (the "Gas Policy Act"). The Gas Policy Act and the Natural Gas Act of 1954 regulate the sale of natural gas.

The Partnerships do not plan to acquire any producing wells; therefore substantially all natural gas which would be sold by the Partnership would be classified as either new natural gas, high cost natural gas or natural gas produced from new onshore wells, as those terms are used in the Gas Policy Act.

New natural gas is generally defined to include gas produced from (1) new onshore wells which are 2.5 miles or more from a "marker well," generally defined as a well which produced natural gas in commercial quantities at any time between January 1, 1970 and April 20, 1977, (2) any new well which is completed at a depth of at least 1,000 feet deeper than the deepest completion location of each market well within 2.5 miles of such new well or (3) a reservoir from which natural gas was not produced in commercial quantities prior to April 20, 1977. The definition includes natural gas shipped in intrastate pipelines. The Gas Policy Act sets a price ceiling for new natural gas sold by the Partnerships, as adjusted for inflation and after the application of a growth factor, equal to $2.640 per million Btu's ("MMBtu") for December 1980.

High cost natural gas is defined to include gas which is produced from a well (a) upon which drilling began on or after February 19, 1977 and where production is from a completion level below 15,000 feet or (b) the drilling of which has been determined to involve the use of difficult or costly processes. Price controls on high cost natural gas were removed as of November 1979.

A new onshore production well is defined to include a well the drilling of which began on or after February 19, 1977, which satisfies certain well-spacing requirements and which is not within certain specified proration units applicable to the producing natural gas reservoir. The price ceiling under the Gas Policy Act and the regulations thereunder for sales made by the Partnerships of any natural gas produced from new, onshore production wells, as adjusted for inflation, is $2,346 per MMBtu for December 1980.

In addition, the rate ceilings allow for adjustments for state severance taxes and costs of compressing, gathering, and transporting natural gas, and other similar costs, as those costs are allowed by order or rule of the Federal Energy Regulatory Commission.

Price controls on new natural gas and gas produced from new, onshore production wells with completion locations deeper than 5,000 feet will be removed on January 1, 1985. Price controls will be removed from gas produced from new, onshore production wells with gas completion locations located at a depth of 5,000 feet or less, beginning July 1, 1987. However, the President is given the power to impose price controls on deregulated gas which could remain in effect until December 31, 1988.

Federal Crude Oil Regulations Prior to January 28, 1981, sales of crude oil and certain petroleum products were regulated by the Department of Energy (the "DOE") by authority of the Emergency Petroleum Allocation Act of 1973, as amended by the Energy Policy and Conservation Act of 1975, as amended (the "EPCA"). Although mandatory price controls on domestic crude oil expired on May 31, 1979, the President on April 5, 1979 pursuant to discretionary authority to reimpose price controls until October 1, 1981, continued price controls in effect and directed the DOE to phase out such controls on domestic crude oil by September 30, 1981, when statutory authority under the EPCA expires. The DOE thereafter promulgated regulations implementing a program for the phased decontrol of oil.

On January 28, 1981, the President ordered an immediate and orderly decontrol of crude oil and refined petroleum products previously subject to the price and allocation controls, which order supersedes the April 5, 1979 order providing for phased decontrol. In order to provide an orderly termination of controls, the January 28, 1981 order provides that all reporting and record-keeping requirements shall be continued in effect until eliminated or modified by the Secretary of Energy and that certain provisions of the controls relating to the state set-aside program for middle distillates, the "buy-sell" program for refiners, the Canadian Allocation Program and the special allocation of middle distillates for surface passenger mass transportation shall be continued in effect until March 31, 1981. Such order also directs the Secretary of Energy to take such action as may be necessary to implement the order.

There can be no assurance that the President or the Secretary of Energy will not modify the program of decontrol or that Congress will not reinstate mandatory controls. The President retains, until September 30, 1981, the authority to adjust price controls in any way the administration deems necessary.

Other Federal Regulation. Other bills passed by Congress and signed into law by the President in the fall of 1978 as part of a comprehensive national energy plan prohibit the use of oil and natural gas in new fuel-burning installations and electric power plants, subject to certain exceptions, and restrict the use of such fuels in certain existing installations. It is impossible to predict the effect that these provisions will have upon future demand for oil and gas.

The Partnerships' drilling and producing operations will also be subject to environmental protection regulations established by Federal agencies.

State Regulation. Each of the states in which the Partnerships may operate has statutory provisions regulating the production and sale of oil and gas. These regulations typically require permits for the drilling and spacing of wells, encourage the prevention of waste of petroleum resources, set allowable rates of production, seek to prevent and require clean-up of pollution and often require oil companies to take exceptional measures to prevent ecological and environmental damage.

WINDFALL PROFITS TAX

President Carter, on April 2, 1980 signed into law the Crude Oil Windfall Profit Tax Act of 1980 (the "Act"). The "windfall profits" tax applies to domestic crude oil produced after February 29, 1980 and will be phased out over a 33-month period starting in January 1988 or when $227.3 billion has been raised by the tax. The windfall profit tax is an excise, or severance, tax applying to crude oil produced in the United States according to its classification in one of three tiers. For each tier the taxable "windfall profit" is the difference between the selling price of the oil and the base price (adjusted for inflation occurring after the second quarter of 1979), minus an adjustment for the State severance tax on the windfall profit. However, the "windfall profit" that is subject to tax cannot exceed 90 percent of the "net income" from a property (as defined in Section 4988(b)(3) of the Internal Revenue Code). The windfall profit tax is a deductible business expense under the income tax. For purposes of computing percentage depletion, gross income from the property is not reduced by the windfall profit.

Tier One Tax

For oil in tier one the tax is 70 percent of the windfall profit. The windfall profit for tier one oil is the difference between the actual selling price of the oil and its May 1979 upper tier ceiling price (which averaged $13.02 per barrel) less $0.21, adjusted for inflation. The tier one tax applies to all oil that would have been controlled as lower or upper tier oil if the pre-June 1979 price controls had remained in effect (generally, oil discovered prior to 1979), including production from the Sadlerochit reservoir on the Alaskan North Slope. Tier one does *not* include (1) oil from stripper well properties (2) oil in which the U.S. has an economic interest and which is produced from a National Petroleum Reserve, (3) most oil deregulated as front-end financing for tertiary recovery projects, (4) newly discovered oil, (5) certain heavy oil or (6) incremental tertiary oil. Generally, these categories of oil are taxed in other tiers.

Tier Two Tax

For oil in tier two the tax is 60 percent of the difference between the actual selling price of the oil and $15.20, adjusted for inflation and for differences in quality and location. Tier two oil includes only oil produced from stripper well properties (i.e. those properties where the average daily production per well has been 10 barrels or less per day during any consecutive 12-month period after 1972) and oil produced from a National Petroleum Reserve in which the U.S. has an economic interest.

Tier Three Tax

For oil in tier three the tax is 30 percent of the difference between the actual selling price of the oil and $16.55, adjusted for inflation, plus 2 percent and for differences in quality and location. Tier three oil consists only of taxable production which is (1) newly discovered oil, (2) certain heavy oil, or (3) incremental tertiary oil. "Newly discovered oil" has the same definition for tax purposes as it has for price control purposes and is defined as (i) crude oil from an outer continental shelf area for which the lease was entered into on or after January 1, 1979, or (ii) an onshore property from which no oil was produced in calendar year 1978. For tax purposes "heavy oil" is defined as, (1) oil with an API specific gravity of 16 degrees or less for the last month of production prior to July 1979 for which the property had production, or (2) oil which has such a specific gravity for the taxable period. For tax purposes "incremental tertiary oil" is that amount of production from a property on which the producer uses a qualified tertiary method in excess of a statutory base level.

Reduced Rates for Independent Producers

The Act provides for reduced windfall profit tax rates on oil produced by "independent producers." Independent producers are allowed reduced tax rates on so much of their combined production of tier one and tier two oil as does not exceed 1,000 barrels a day. If an independent producer's daily production of tier one and tier two oil exceeds 1,000 barrels, the reduced rates apply ratably to each of these categories of oil (but not in excess of a total of 1,000 barrels a day). For tier one oil the special rate is 50, rather than 70, percent; for tier two oil the rate is 30, rather than 60, percent. These reduced rates apply only with respect to working interests which were held on January 1, 1980, and do not apply to integrated oil companies or to owners of royalty or similar interests. A producer and a controlled corporation must share one 1,000 barrel quantity. In the case of partnerships, the reduced rates are computed on the partner level.

STATEMENT BY

CHARLES W. DUNCAN, SECRETARY

DEPARTMENT OF ENERGY

BEFORE THE

JOINT ECONOMIC COMMITTEE

U.S. SENATE

JANUARY 30, 1980

Mr. Chairman, I appreciate this opportunity to appear before you today to discuss a broad range of energy and economic issues.

IMPACT OF 1979

The past year has been dominated by turmoil in the world oil market. First, the Iranian revolution curtailed one-fifth of OPEC's production capacity, and dramatically tightened the world oil market overnight. During the summer months we faced gasoline lines, as the full effects of the Iranian oil cutoff reached this country. While the lines receded in August, the oil market remained tight through the fall as importing nations stocked up on supplies. By the end of the year, world oil prices were about 50 percent higher compared to summer prices. U.S. refiners have been paying almost $30 per barrel for imported oil, double the price paid the same time last year and about ten times the price paid in 1970. Spot prices of about $38 per barrel are even higher.

As in 1973, the impact of the energy events of 1979 will be felt for many years to come. High prices and limited supplies will permanently change the way we utilize energy. I would like to outline for you today the legacy of 1979–the impacts of the past year on our energy future.

Before the Iranian revolution, the Department of Energy believed that forces were at work to cause sharp price increases and perhaps even shortages by the mid to late 1980's. Supply was expected to peak sometime in this decade, whereas world demand for oil would continue to rise. The Iranian revolution has accelerated these trends. Continued large price increases, as well as shortages, are a distinct possibility for the next several years. It is quite possible that the political impact of the Iranian revolution on other Middle East countries will be in the form of reduced investment in new oil production capacity.

Free world oil consumption is expected to drop by about 1 million barrels per day (MMBD) in 1980 because of higher prices, the effects of conservation, and the expected economic slowdown in the U.S. and other Organization for Economic

Cooperation and Development (OECD) countries. However, considerable uncertainties on the supply side could make for a tight market. In part the uncertainties themselves, by raising the demand for inventories, have enabled higher prices to prevail. In addition OPEC production is likely to fall by 1-2 MMBD while non-OPEC production should increase by about 1 MMBD. If the OPEC cutbacks are limited, supplies should be adequate, though possibly at higher prices. If OPEC production falls by several MMBD, shortages could return in 1980, and would undoubtedly be accompanied by further major price increases.

For the longer term, we now anticipate that even by 1985 OPEC oil production will not exceed significantly the current production level of about 31 MMBD. Since OPEC's internal consumption is expected to rise by about 1 MMBD during this period, less oil will be available for export. Other non-OPEC producers are in the aggregate expected at best to make up this loss. However, increased competition for scarce oil may come from the Soviet Union and Eastern Europe, which might cease oil exports and become a net importer by the middle of the decade. Thus, the U.S. will have to be prepared to import no more, and likely much less, oil during this period.

The impacts on the U.S. economy from the oil price shocks of 1979 have been and will be considerable. Consumer prices for energy will continue to rise much faster than the over-all Consumer Price Index although by somewhat less than in 1979. Real GNP is projected to be as much as 2 percent lower in 1980 than would have occurred otherwise with a correspondingly higher unemployment rate of between 0.5 and 1 percentage points. The U.S. oil import bill will increase to about 80 billion dollars, about 22 billion dollars of which is attributable to price increases associated with the Caracas OPEC meeting.

Two additional points regarding the 1979 world oil price increases are worth noting. First only a negligible amount of the projected 1980 and 1981 increases in the Consumer Price Index is attributable to the Administration's phased decontrol program. Secondly, though painful, especially for low income households, higher prices have had, and will continue to have the beneficial effect of reducing demand for these fuels, and thus lessening our dependence on insecure imports.

ENERGY STRATEGY

The Administration's strategy for dealing with these problems is conditioned by the nature of the transition from an oil-dependent economy to an energy-diversified economy. For the next 5 years—the short term—the world will continue to rely heavily on oil, which supplied 60 percent of the world's energy in 1979. The most readily available and economical source of energy for this period is conservation. In the mid-term—between 1985 and 2000—the world will move away from an energy system dependent on oil towards one relying on coal and coal-derived synthetics, solar technologies, oil shale, unconventional gas supplies and nuclear power. Beyond the year 2000—the long term—the world will move further in the direction of renewable energy sources and advanced nuclear technologies.

We intend to rely as much as possible on market forces to bring about this transition. Large-scale commercial utilization of new energy technologies will and should be largely the responsibility of private enterprise. Accordingly, a critical component of this Administration's energy policy is to provide a stable commercial and regulatory climate to enable it to accomplish this mission at minimum cost to the economy. We have underway a careful review of the Department's existing regulations to eliminate those that have outgrown their usefulness. We expect to publish shortly a list of regulations that we intend to eliminate. We are also going to publish a schedule for deregulation so that the September, 1981 expiration of existing regulatory authority will be met smoothly and on schedule.

Markets alone cannot reduce our dependence on foreign sources of oil quickly enough. There are public benefits to import reductions such as restraint on increases in oil prices that result from lower U.S. demand and reduced vulnerability to supply disruptions. Therefore, the government must act to reduce the quantities imported below what market forces are likely to accomplish. The Department seeks to rely on regulation only as a last resort and as required by current statutes. There are a number of ways to stimulate conservation and increased domestic energy supply without imposing additional regulatory burdens on the economy. Voluntary initiatives, buttressed by appropriate economic incentives and information, are preferred methods for reducing oil imports and changing our energy balance. In order to ensure that regulations issued by the Department are soundly conceived and consistent with this policy, approval must be granted by the Deputy Secretary or me before any significant regulation is developed.

Our highest priority programs are aimed at cutting energy demand during the next several years. The policy of oil decontrol is introducing more realistic prices into the marketplace, and thus making an important contribution to reducing demand. At the same time the Administration's proposed Windfall Profits Tax is designed to ameliorate certain hardships related to increasing prices.

The Department's contingency planning efforts include setting gasoline consumption targets for each State. We are also developing a nationwide gasoline rationing plan to enforce compliance with the targets, to be used in the event of a severe supply disruption. The President has stated that U.S. imports will never exceed 8.5 MMBD in any year. In his State of the Union address for 1980, the President announced that the U.S. import ceiling for 1980 would again be set at 8.2 MMBD. While we currently expect to achieve even lower levels of imports, the President has made clear his intention to enforce this ceiling through the use of an import fee if imports threaten to exceed the 8.2 MMBD level.

These efforts are only one part of the spectrum of Departmental programs intended to reduce demand. The Administration requests almost 1 billion dollars in budget authority in fiscal year 1981 to encourage as well as provide the means for more efficient use of energy. Some of these funds will be spent on research and development. However, the bulk of Federal expenditures will be used for retrofits of schools and hospitals, weatherization assistance for low-income, elderly, and handicapped persons who live in old, less energy-efficient housing, and grants for other State and local conservation activities. Private households and businesses will continue to benefit from tax credits designed to encourage investments in conservation and renewable resource use. Low- and moderate-income persons will have access to subsidized loans for this purpose through the Conservation and Solar Bank to be created through pending legislation proposed by the President.

One other important part of the Administration's plans to reduce vulnerability to imports is the Strategic Petroleum Reserve. Funds are available in the budget for resumption of oil acquisition in 1980. The budget plan calls for about 250 million barrels in storage by 1983; up to 750 million barrels are planned by 1989. An additional 250 million barrels of storage may be established later. A billion barrel reserve would provide adequate protection against lost imports.

Since we will still, in spite of these efforts, be quite vulnerable to supply disruptions during the next decade, we intend to encourage as much as possible imports of both oil and natural gas from a number of countries, in particular Canada and Mexico. Net future oil imports from Canada are expected to decline from their current small level of about 100,000 barrels per day. U.S. oil imports from Mexico, however, are projected to increase to around 1 MMBD compared with the current level of over 600,000 barrels per day. Canadian exports of natural gas are currently about one trillion cubic feet. Imports around this level are expected to be maintained until Canadian domestic demand reaches its production capacity level in the mid 1990's. Mexico has just commenced exporting gas, at a level of around 100 billion cubic feet this year. There is potential for increased exports, but no precise figures are currently available.

The suddenness of the rise in energy prices has cuased substantial hardships for many low-income families. It will also, now that oil is being decontrolled, provide substantial windfalls to a small group of individuals and companies. This situation must be remedied via the Windfall Profits Tax. This tax will, among other things, provide $2.4 billion annually to assist the poor in paying higher energy bills. For the current winter, the Administration has already acted quickly to ensure that low-income persons were and are given relief. This means of aiding the poor, which does not offset the stimulus of higher prices to conserve, is far superior to controlling prices, which not only yields benefits to rich and poor alike, but also impedes energy conservation efforts.

The bulk of the funds from this tax will assist our mid term and long term policy of increasing the supply of domestic substitutes for oil which are economically and environmentally acceptable. Conservation programs must and will be pursued vigorously, but are not by themselves sufficient; new domestic sources of energy must be developed or expanded. Private enterprises are working to move new energy technologies to the stage at which they are ready for large-scale commercial use. However, alternative technologies are in various stages of development and incentives are necessary to expedite this process for the public benefit. Therefore, the Department supports research, development, demonstration, and commercialization activities in many areas of energy technology.

PROJECTED SUPPLIES

Total U.S. production of oil, including natural gas liquids, is expected at best to remain near current levels of 10 MMBD through 1985. Even with decontrol and high world oil prices, production in the lower forty-eight States is expected to decline during the decade, offset somewhat by increased production from new sources of oil such as Alaska, offshore oil, and enhanced oil recovery. U.S. net demand for oil is forecast at 16-18 MMBD in 1985, slightly below the 1979 level of 18.4 MMBD.

U.S. natural gas consumption in 1979 remained about the same as in recent years at around 19 trillion cubic feet. By 1985, natural gas consumption should increase slightly to 20-21 trillion cubic feet, despite continued declines in conventional lower-48 production. Most of the increase will be due to increased use of gas imports, Alaskan production and some gas from unconventional sources. The substantial rise in drilling activities already apparent due to recent natural gas legislation will increase reserves in the next few years, forestalling somewhat the projected decline in gas reserves and production.

Total consumption of electricity increased by about 3 percent in 1979 to about 2.1 billion kilowatt-hours. Nuclear power supplied a little less than 12 percent of this total. At the end of 1979, there were 71 nuclear reactors with a combined capacity of 52 gigawatts (GWe) in operation. Our estimate for the future growth in the nuclear-generated share of electricity has been reduced in the aftermath of the accident at Three Mile Island. The erosion of nuclear growth forecasts has numerous causes. Along with the rapidly growing financial burden of building and operating nuclear plants, two major factors are heightened concerns about reactor safety and radioactive waste management. The Department, at the direction of the President, is increasing its efforts with regard to both of these concerns. Nuclear capacity in the United States now appears likely to increase to 150-200 GWe by 2000. The range of future nuclear capacity depends on completion of the 100 GWe of capacity currently under construction or with their construction permit granted, and on the outcome of management and regulatory decision on another 50 GWe awaiting construction authorization or in the planning stages.

Coal consumption grew in 1979 by more than 50 million tons, to a level of about 700 million tons. Coal consumption will increase to about 900 million tons by 1985. A substantial portion of this increase can be achieved through effective coal conversion efforts. Of this projected total, about 25 percent will be consumed in the industrial sector, and the rest by utilities to produce electricity.

Solar and renewable energy sources contributed about 5 quads to our energy supply in 1979, about the same as in 1978. Renewable supplies in the United States are projected to increase by about 20 percent by 1985. One area which shows promise in the near term is alcohol fuels. On January 11, 1980, the President announced a national target for alcohol production capacity of 500 million gallons per year in 1981, more than 6 times the 80 million gallons produced in 1979.

The proposed Energy Security Corporation will help the private sector make investments in the production of synthetic fuels from coal, biomass, peat, oil shale, and tar sands. In December the Joint House-Senate conference on the Energy Security Bill, S.932, adopted a goal of 2 MMBD of synfuels production by 1992. These efforts will be assisted by the proposed Energy Mobilization Board. The Board will be authorized to designate certain non-nuclear facilities as critical to achieving the nation's import reduction goals and to establish binding schedules for Federal, State, and local decision-making with respect to these projects.

CONCLUSION

In conclusion I would like to stress that the transition from an oil-dependent to an energy-diversified economy represents a joining of national resources and resolution on a scale never before attempted in peacetime. It is, however, no more insurmountable a challenge than many we have faced successfully in the past. But it requires a close partnership between the public and private sectors. It requires the long-term integration of different energy approaches in the face of factors sometimes beyond our control. And it requires a recognition that there are no short cuts, no technological miracles, and no quick solutions dictated in Washington that by themselves will make this necessary transition significantly shorter or less demanding.

Mr. Chairman, I would be pleased to answer any questions you and the Committee might have.

POSTURE STATEMENT

Introduction

The Department of Energy sees its mission as assuring the Nation's orderly transition from an economy dependent upon oil to an economy relying upon diversified energy sources. This report summarizes the Department's efforts to accomplish its mission during fiscal year 1979, its programs for fiscal year 1980, and its plans for fiscal year 1981.

This report can be evaluated only in the context of the Department's assessment of the energy outlook for the Nation and the world. The Department anticipates that the transition in energy use will occur in roughly three phases. For the next 5 years the world will continue to rely heavily on oil, which supplied about half of the world's energy in 1979. During the forthcoming 5-year period, the most readily available, economic source of additional energy is conservation, or the more efficient use of the energy now being consumed. In addition, the use of natural gas, coal, uranium, and renewable resources can help reduce growth in the demand for oil. Some non-OPEC nations, notably Mexico and the United Kingdom, are expected to increase their oil and gas production. In the medium term, from 1985 to 2000, the world will begin to make a significant move away from oil dependence. During this period, the world has several attractive options for reducing demand for oil and diversifying its energy supply. These include more coal and coal-derived synthetic fuels, solar technologies, oil shale, unconventional gas supplies and nuclear power, as well as continued improvements in the efficiency of energy use. Beyond the year 2000, the world will move further toward renewable energy sources and advanced nuclear technologies. These technologies will displace both traditional fuels and non-renewable unconventional sources of energy, but improvements in cost and technical performance must be achieved before they can be adopted widely.

This posture statement gives an overview of the Department's policies, programs and strategies. It first describes current conditions of energy supply and demand. It then sets out our current view of the progress we will make in the coming years to limit demand and maintain supply. Finally, it outlines the Department's strategy and programs for fiscal year 1981. Succeeding chapters of the annual report detail each of the Department's major programs.

The Department's assessment of the world energy outlook demonstrates that, for many decades ahead, we must pursue efforts to limit demand and to expand and diversify supply with equal diligence. No single energy source, no single restraint on demand and no single technological innovation can resolve our current energy problems. Their resolution can come only by the pursuit of many distinct and sometimes complicated programs, unified primarily by their common need for full cooperation of all branches of government and for the long term support of sectors of the American public and economy.

Current Conditions

During 1979, the energy demand situation improved while the energy supply outlook deteriorated, particularly for sources outside the United States. Oil price increases throughout 1979 by the Organization of Petroleum Exporting Countries (OPEC) limited demand not only for crude oil and petroleum products, but also for fuels whose prices tend to track the price of oil. In this period, world oil prices doubled. The landed cost of imported oil to United States refiners rose from an average of $15 per barrel at the beginning of 1979 to an average of $29 per barrel in December. This section sets out the Department's assessment of current conditions, first with respect to demand for energy, then with respect to supplies of energy for both the United States and the industrialized countries outside the United States.

Current Energy Demand

A very substantial proportion of the world's demand for energy is for oil. This demand occurs in sectors of the economy such as transportation where large-scale substitution of other energy sources are not now possible. There has been relatively little shift, worldwide, to other forms of energy—natural gas, coal and solar—although demand for these sources did increase in 1979 over 1978 levels.

United States Energy Demand: In 1979, total energy demand in the United States increased only slightly above 1978 levels. This was caused primarily by the combined effects of a slowdown in economic growth and significantly higher energy prices. Limits on supply caused by the Iranian revolution and other factors depressed consumption at the beginning of the peak driving season. These limits and substantially higher prices helped keep gasoline consumption over the year at about 400,000 barrels per day, roughly 5 percent, below 1978 levels. In the fourth quarter, after physical shortages had disappeared, gasoline demand was 700,000 barrels per day lower than in the same period of 1978 as a result of higher prices and conservation. Consumption of other petroleum products–home heating oil, diesel fuel, jet fuel, and residual oil–remained near 1978 levels of about 11.4 millions barrels per day. Overall, consumption of petroleum in 1979 was slightly lower than in 1978.

Natural gas consumption in 1979 remained about the same as in recent years at 19.5 trillion cubic feet (tcf). Industrial demand for gas decreased slightly in 1979 to about 7.8 tcf from 8.3 tcf in the prior year. Use of gas by electric utilities increased slightly to 3.4 tcf from 3.1 tcf in 1978. Some of the net decrease in consumption in these sectors was absorbed by the residential and commercial sectors, which increased their use of natural gas from 7.5 tcf in 1978 to about 7.8 tcf.

Coal consumption grew in 1979 by more than 50 million tons largely due to increases in coal use by electric utilities. The 1979 consumption level–about 700 million tons–reflects the return of growth trends exhibited before the coal strike and low production levels in 1978. A faster rate of increase in coal use can only be achieved by resolving such issues as stringent environmental controls and the high cost of handling, transporting, and using coal. These barriers and the problems they represent may be overcome through technological advances in conversion of coal to synthetic gas and liquids, through the development of systems that will burn coal in a more efficient and environmentally acceptable manner, and through financial incentives to utilities to encourage substituting coal for petroleum-based fuels.

Total consumption of electricity grew by 3 percent in 1979, to a total of 2.1 trillion kilowatt hours from a total of 2 trillion kilowatt hours in 1978. About 40 percent of this electricity was used in the industrial sector, 23 percent was used in the commercial sector and 33 percent was used in the residential sector. This pattern of use reflected little change from 1978.

Demand for energy produced by solar devices and renewable energy sources (hydroelectric power and energy from plant materials) remained about the same as in 1978. More than 3 primary quads[1] of low- and high-head hydroelectric power were used to generate electricity and about 2 quads of forest products were consumed as fuel by the pulp and paper industry. The use of wood for home heating also gave indications of an increase.

World Energy Demand: The availability and price of oil dominates world energy use. The world has not appreciably substituted other fuels for oil and world oil consumption increased between 1973 and 1979. The United States is less dependent on oil than the rest of the Free World, using oil for only 46 percent of its primary energy needs compared to 58 percent for the remainder of the Free World as shown in Table 1.

Table 1. – Shares of primary consumption (1979)

Energy Type	United States (percent)	Non-U.S.–Free World (percent)
Oil	46	58
Gas	25	13
Coal	19	17
Nuclear	4	2
Renewables	6	10
Total	100	100

Free World natural gas consumption outside the U.S. has remained stable in recent years at about 14 quads consumed. Demand for electricity increased and caused a substantial derivative demand for nuclear power, which accounted for about 3 quads of primary energy in those countries in 1979–three times the 1973 level. In 1979, the Free World outside the U.S. used

1. One quad equals one quadrillion, or 10^{15}, British thermal units (Btu's).

about 10 quads of energy from renewable sources, slightly higher than the amount used in 1978.

Current Energy Supply

In 1979, petroleum constituted about 53 percent of the Free World's energy supply. Throughout the Free World, however, substantial amounts of energy are supplied by coal (18 percent), gas (18 percent), renewable resources (8 percent), and nuclear power (3 percent). Diversification of supply away from oil is proceeding throughout the world, but slowly.

United States Energy Supply: The United States is not energy poor, but we have not made sufficient use of our abundant domestic resources. Table 2 shows that the United States produces approximately 78 percent of its energy needs. We produce more domestic energy per capita than Europe or Japan consume per capita. Although imports of oil represent only 21 percent of our energy consumption, our continued reliance on imports for nearly half of our current petroleum requirements remains a very substantial problem. Each of the domestic

Table 2. – Sources of primary energy consumption

Domestic Production	1979
	(percent)
Oil	25
Gas	24
Coal	19
Nuclear	4
Renewables	6
Subtotal	78
Imports	
Oil	21
Gas	1
Subtotal	22
Total	100

sources is discussed below. Foreign sources are discussed in the succeeding section on world supplies.

Domestic production of crude oil and natural gas liquids remained about the same as in 1978 at 10.3 million barrels a day (MMBD) compared to 10.2 MMBD in 1979. With net domestic petroleum demand at 18.5 MMBD, the level of net oil imports, excluding imports for the Strategic Petroleum Reserve, was 7.7 MMBD. Imports for the Strategic Petroleum Reserve were negligible after August 1979, but averaged 60,000 barrels a day for this year. Substantial quantities of imported oil were used to build private inventories throughout the year.

The amounts of oil imported from specific foreign sources change frequently. The breakdown of imports by country of origin for 1979 is given in Table 3. Imports from Saudi Arabia, Nigeria, Libya and Venezuela increased in 1979 to offset reductions from other countries, including Iran.

In 1979, domestic production of natural gas did not increase above 1978 levels of 19.1 trillion cubic feet, although drilling activity was substantially higher than last year. Through the third quarter of 1979, the number of exploratory wells increased by 25 percent, while the number of developmental wells increased by 12 percent.

Coal production in 1979 reached a record level of 760 million tons, including about 60 million tons that were exported, an increase of 8 percent over record 1977 production levels. Over 100 million tons of excess coal production capacity still existed.

Nuclear energy continues to be an essential element of the Nation's electric supply system. In 1978, nuclear energy generated approximately 13 percent of the domestic electricity. This figure was slightly lower in 1979 due to the shutdown of nuclear capacity in response to safety and other concerns, that were highlighted by the Three Mile Island accident. There were 71 nuclear reactors with a combined capacity of 52 million watts (gigawatts) in operation or start-up testing at the end of 1979. Construction of another four nuclear generating stations with a combined capacity of 4 gigawatts had been completed by the end of 1979. These stations are currently awaiting licensing and are likely to begin commercial operation in 1980. After the Three Mile Island accident, the President endorsed the Nuclear Regulatory Commission's approach which called for a short pause in licensing activities so that the Commission could focus on safety improvements. He urged the Commission to expedite

Table 3. – Gross U.S. imports of crude oil and petroleum products

(millions of barrels per day)

	1979[1]
OPEC	
Saudi Arabia	1.3
Iran	0.3
Nigeria	1.0
Libya	0.7
Venezuela	0.7
Algeria	0.6
Indonesia	0.4
United Arab Emirates	0.3
Other	0.2
Total OPEC	5.5
Non-OPEC	
Bahamas	0.1
Canada	0.5
Mexico	0.4
Netherlands Antilles	0.2
Puerto Rico	0.1
Trinidad/Tobago	0.2
Virgin Islands	0.4
Other	0.7
Total non-OPEC	2.7
Total imports	8.2

1. These figures are gross imports based on data from the first eleven months of the year. Imports from Iran were suspended by the President on November 12, 1979. No imports for the Strategic Petroleum Reserve are included. Imported petroleum products are counted on a par with crude oil. The sources of the crude refined into products overseas and then imported into the United States are not known. To get net oil imports, subtract U.S. petroleum exports of about 450,000 barrels per day.

Note: Totals may not add due to rounding.

this process so that it could resume licensing not later than June 1980.

Solar energy and renewable energy sources, which include biomass, hydroelectricity, geothermal power, and wind, now contribute 5 quads to national energy supply, primarily from biomass (including an estimated 2 quads of forest by-products) and hydroelectricity. Recent oil price increases, coupled with Federal and state financial or regulatory inventives, have begun to accelerate the rate at which solar power technologies are readied for the market. The primary technologies that showed increases in the market place in 1979 include active and passive space heating and solar hot water heating for residential and commercial buildings. A major effort to advance alcohol fuels, which began in 1977, yielded significant results in 1979. This program emphasizes the production of gasohol, which is a mixture of 10 percent ethanol and 90 percent unleaded gasoline. As a result of the 4 cents per gallon excise tax exemption that the President signed into law in November 1978 and the substantial increases in the price of gasoline, ethanol for fuel production capacity increased to about 80 million gallons per year at the end of 1979 from a negligible level in 1977.

Current Energy Supply Outside the United States: Oil dominated the energy supply situation outside the United States, as it did domestically. The major developments on the supply side were substantial OPEC price increases announced at the April, June and December meetings; the oil price increases announced independently by members of OPEC throughout the year; the increasing volume of oil traded on the spot market at prices significantly higher than posted OPEC prices; the announcements by some OPEC member countries of plans to hold down future production; and the Iranian revolution and subsequent production shutdown in January. The increase in world oil prices throughout the year can be seen in Table 4.

Disorder in the world oil market was reflected in the increase in sales on the spot market and a reversal in the traditional relationship between spot market prices and long-term contract prices. With the exception of a brief flurry of activity during 1973-74, the fraction of oil traded in the spot market in recent years has averaged less than 5 percent of oil traded. In the last months of 1979, however, industry sources believe that at least 15 percent of internationally traded oil was sold on the spot

Table 4. – World price of internationally-traded oil

(dollars per barrel)

Beginning of:	Price
January 1979	13.77
February	14.14
March	14.59
April	16.22
May	16.34
June	17.44
July	20.55
August	20.62
September	20.77
October	20.90
November	24.01
December	24.01
January 1980	27.28

market. In the past, the spot market has been a place where excess oil was traded at prices near or even below contract levels. In 1979, however, spot market prices soared to over $45 per barrel, in some cases reaching levels more than 200 percent above contract prices. In turn, these high prices encouraged increases in the price of contract oil.

In 1979, the Free World's supply of oil produced outside the United States remained near 1978 levels at about 40 million barrels per day, about 31 MMBD of which was produced by OPEC nations. Despite curtailments of Iranian production, supplies remained stable primarily because Saudi Arabia and Kuwait raised production above expected levels.

During 1979, total supplies of energy produced in the Free World outside the United States from sources other than oil also remained generally at about 1978 levels. Foreign Free World natural gas production remained stable at about 7 MMBD oil equivalent after a decline in 1974-75. Except in Australia and Canada, foreign coal production in industrialized countries has not grown for the past two decades. Increases in Australian and Canadian production has helped offset declines in Western Europe and Japan. Coal production in 1979 remained at about 109 MMBD of oil equivalent. Nuclear power production has continued its rapid growth. In 1979, Free World generation of nuclear power outside the United States increased by 10 percent and is now approximately equal to United States levels of about 3 quads or the equivalent of 1.5 MMBD of oil. Renewable energy production in 1979 consisted primarily of hydroelectric power and remained at a level equivalent to nearly 5 MMBD of oil.

Energy Outlook

The future holds some encouragement relative to the delicate balance that currently characterizes the energy demand and supply relationship with respect to the major sources of energy. In the United States, we expect continued progress in restraining the growth in energy demand, particularly with respect to oil. This seems likely to be coupled with continued progress in developing technologies for domestic energy production from all sources and with accelerated energy diversification. The Administration's replacement cost pricing policy, particularly for oil and natural gas, has resulted in a substantial reduction in projected energy consumption. The Administration's decision to allow domestic crude oil prices to rise to world levels in October 1981, in concert with deregulation of natural gas prices at the wellhead under the National Gas Policy Act, have already begun to improve the Nation's capacity to satisfy future energy needs, while encouraging energy conservation.

Worldwide, oil production will dominate international energy supply in the near term. A reduction in OPEC production is possible in 1980. Increases in non-OPEC production, particularly from the North Sea and Mexico, could partially offset this decline. Gains in world non-oil energy production, especially from coal and nuclear sources, are expected to continue during the next five years as the world continues the transition to non-oil energy supplies.

This section summarizes the Department's current assessment of future conditions through 1985 with respect to both demand for energy and expected supplies of energy to meet that demand. These forecasts, though inherently uncertain, represent the Department's best estimates.

Future Energy Demand

Energy demand worldwide will continue to be influenced heavily by oil prices through 1990. Future plans by OPEC to hold production down will drive prices up and force the oil consuming nations to constrain demand for oil and switch to other fuels. By 1985, the United States will make some progress in reducing demand for oil, and greater progress thereafter as visible domestic substitutes become available. Through 1985, other industrialized nations are expected to continue improving the efficiency with which they use energy. Their consumption of oil will remain about the same as in 1979. Demand for natural gas and electricity, particularly for electricity produced by coal-fired and nuclear plants, will continue to rise, but worldwide direct coal consumption will not grow significantly until after 1985.

Future United States Energy Demand: Energy consumption will be held near current levels over the next 5 years. A resumption in economic growth will not increase end-use energy consumption as much as in the past because it will occur in the context of higher prices and improvements in efficiency. But consumers will be shifting to the use of energy in converted forms, such as electricity and synthetic fuels, rather than in the primary forms of oil and gas. Because of the conversion losses, primary energy consumption may grow even as end-use consumption remains constant. However, this shift in energy use will help move the Nation away from dependence on petroleum.

United States petroleum consumption in 1985 will likely be lower than current levels. Consumption of natural gas, coal, and electricity will increase. The 3 to 8 percent reduction in petroleum consumption from current levels expected by 1985—a savings of as much as 1.5 MMBD—will be due primarily to the increasing efficiency of automobiles, utility and industry boiler conversions from oil to coal, and fuel shifting and conservation in the residential and commercial sectors. As much as one-third of this reduction would result directly from the effects of the Administration's initiatives to remove controls from oil prices. By 1985, total natural gas consumption will increase slightly from 20 to 21 trillion cubic feet. Most of the increase will be attributable to gas hookups for new and converting residential customers. Use by industry of 50 to 60 million more tons of coal will be stimulated by the coal conversion provisions of the Powerplant and Industrial Fuel Use Act of 1978.

The demand for electricity is expected to grow at about 4 percent per year between now and 1985. The major share of the primary energy inputs to generating plants will be provided by coal and nuclear energy. Coal consumption by utilities will rise from about 500 million tons in 1979 to nearly 700 million tons by 1985. Oil and gas use by utilities will decrease by 1985, but the level of savings will depend largely on measures taken to replace oil-fired utility plants. Renewable sources hold great potential for the future, but demand cannot be expected to increase significantly by 1985 because of the time required to develop cost-effective and efficient technologies.

Future Energy Demand Outside the United States: Petroleum consumption in the Free World outside the United States will increase slightly by 1985, but will retain its share of total energy demand. The overwhelming dependence on oil for transportation uses will not change significantly by the mid-1980s. By 1985, natural gas consumption will have increased by about 20 percent over current levels and will constitute an expanding share of end-use demand. This increase in natural gas will occur primarily in the industrial sector, which is more readily equipped to shift from dependence on petroleum than other economic sectors. Direct coal consumption by industry is expected to remain near current levels between now and 1985, but its share of total Free World energy consumption outside the U.S. will increase in subsequent years. Demand for electricity will increase by about 3 percent per year through 1985, as it captures a slightly higher share of total energy consumption. Demand for energy from renewable sources is not expected to expand significantly by 1985, although rapid growth in demand for decentralized solar space and water heating will occur in the 1990s.

Future Energy Supply

Between now and 1985, decreases in United States oil and gas production will be exceeded by increased production from coal, nuclear and renewable sources. Likewise, outside the United States, declining overall production of oil will be accompanied by increasing gas, coal and nuclear energy production. Steady progress will be made in the use of solar and renewable energy sources.

Future Energy Supply in the United States: Oil production in the United States is expected to remain near current levels of 9 to 10 million barrels per day through the year 2000. Declines in conventional production, resulting from depletion of resources on shore in the lower forty-eight states, will be offset by new production from Alaska, shale and enhanced oil recovery. But if total oil resources in the United States, particularly those offshore, are less than previously estimated, even higher world oil prices may not offset the continued decline in conventional production.

Conventional gas supplies in the United States will continue to decline in the lower forty-eight states from 9 MMBD oil equivalent in 1979 to 8 MMBD in 1985 and to 7 MMBD in 1990. The Alaskan natural gas pipeline will compensate for some of this decline. Gas from Alaska's North Slope can replace the equivalent of approximately 425,000 barrels of oil per day by 1985. After 1985, exploration of the large gas resources that exist in unconventional formations and production of synthetic gas will further offset production declines.

As the price of oil rises, United States coal will capture an increasing share of industrial energy and electric utility markets and, eventually, will become a feedstock for the production of synthetic fuels. Abundant domestic resources of coal ensure that there will be sufficient supply for all our energy requirements that coal can meet. With the deployment of technologies currently under development, synthetic liquids produced from coal will grow markedly after 1985.

Nuclear power may provide a substantial substitute for oil use in the future. Almost 10 percent of the oil used in the United States, approximately 1.5 million barrels per day in 1979, is burned in utility generating plants. Nuclear energy could displace much of this oil. Our estimates suggest that the nuclear units scheduled to enter commercial operations between now and the end of 1982 could displace about 250,000 barrels of oil per day, if their production reflects historical trends. Licensing of new nuclear power plants for operation has been suspended temporarily by the Nuclear Regulatory Commission but, as the Commission implements the recommendations of the Kemeny Commission and those of its own internal review groups, we anticipate a renewal of licensing by mid-1980.

Our estimate of the future growth in the nuclear-generated share of electricity was reduced in the aftermath of the accident at Three Mile Island. This continues the trend of reduced forecasts that began in the early 1970s. The erosion of nuclear growth forecasts has numerous causes. Along with the rapidly growing financial burden of building and operating nuclear plants, two major factors were heightened concerns about reactor safety and radioactive waste management. The President has directed increased efforts on both of these concerns. Nuclear capacity in the United States now appears likely to increase from current levels of about 50 gigawatts to 150 to 200 gigawatts by 2000. The range of future nuclear capacity depends on completion of the 100 gigawatts of capacity currently under construction or with their construction permit granted, and on the outcome of management and regulatory decisions on another 50 gigawatts awaiting construction authorization or in the planning stages.

Renewable supplies in the United States are projected to increase from 5 quads in 1979 to 6 quads in 1985 and 7 quads in 1990. One area of increase in the near-term will be alcohol fuels. On January 11, 1980, the President announced a national target for alcohol production capacity of 500 million gallons per year. In addition to use in gasohol, some of the alcohol produced will probably be burned directly, particularly in farm vehicles. Further research, experimentation and development of liquid or gaseous fuels from biomass is now being carried out. These technologies are in varying stages of development and will not make significant contributions without further cost reductions and subsequent market development. During the 1990's the contribution of renewables to total energy demand is expected to increase rapidly toward the goal of serving 20 percent of the Nation's requirement in 2000.

Future Energy Supply Outside the United States: Worldwide oil production (excluding the United States and Communist countries) should increase about 1 million barrels per day above 1979 levels to equal 41 MMBD in 1980. It is expected to range between 41 and 55 MMBD in 1985 and from 41 to 60 MMBD in 1990. These estimates will depend primarily on the oil production policies of OPEC countries. A number of oil producing countries with reserves that are large relative to current production levels are increasing their production capacities slowly if at all. These cautious policies reflect a strong preference for production rates that stretch reserves over longer periods and an aversion to even a slight risk of limiting the amount of oil ultimately recoverable. Conventional oil production will decline steadily in the 1990s.

In the next few years, OPEC countries are unlikely to increase their collective oil production significantly above the current level of 31 MMBD. Although by 1985 OPEC production capacity may increase to 36 MMBD, actual output is likely to be constrained by non-technical considerations. Indeed, the Persian Gulf producers—Saudi Arabia, the United Arab Emirates, Kuwait, Iraq, and Iran—have ample reserves to support increased production.

Extensive exploration worldwide will cause a continued increase in non-OPEC oil production. Output will rise sharply in North Sea fields. By 1982, North Sea production should be at or near its peak level of about 3.5 MMBD, 2.8 MMBD of which will be produced from the British sector and 0.7 MMBD from Norway. Unless new large fields are found, however, production from the North Sea will begin to decline in 1983 or 1984. Substantial increases in oil production are expected from Mexico, Egypt, India, and Malaysia in the next several years, but most of these gains will either support increased oil use in the producing countries themselves or offset increased consumption in other developing nations.

Eastern European nations, when the Soviet Union is included, have been net suppliers to the world market. They export about 1 MMBD, mainly to Western Europe. As a group, these nations may become net importers within 3 to 4 years if East European imports more than offset Soviet exports. Oil production in the Soviet Union is expected to peak in the next year or two, as the amount of discovered reserves has fallen sharply in recent years.

China should be able to produce more oil than it consumes in the 1980s. To export more than 500,000 barrels per day, however, China will need to make considerable headway in locating and developing exploitable reserves or the enforcement of strict controls on domestic oil consumption.

Free World natural gas production outside the U.S. should be equivalent to about 7 MMBD of oil in 1980. It is expected to range between 6 to 12 MMBD of oil in 1985 and 6 to 15 MMBD in 1990. Eastern European nations, including the Soviet Union, will produce an additional 7 MMBD and, in 1980, China will add about 1 MMBD to the world supply of natural gas. Following a decline in 1975, production of natural gas in the industrialized world has been stable for the past four years at about 16 MMBD oil equivalent. In the immediate future, production in these industrial countries will decline once again, but worldwide natural gas supplies should increase during the 1980s as production expands in OPEC and in other countries with promising resources such as Mexico.

Foreign Free World coal supply is now expected to increase from about 10 MMBD oil equivalent in 1979 to about 14 MMBD in 1985 and 15 MMBD in 1990. Coal consumption will reverse its decline and start to increase in Western Europe and Japan. Canada and Australia will continue to expand their production and use of coal.

Free World nuclear energy supply outside the U.S. is expected to increase from about 3 quads in 1979 to between 6 and 15 quads in 1985 and between 15 and 22 quads in 1990. During the next few years, nuclear power will prove the largest single potential source of additional energy production in the industrialized world. It will be the only additional source for some Western European countries and for Japan.

In the mid-term, energy supplies from renewable sources will remain only a small part of Free World energy supply Outside the U.S., renewable supplies are projected to increase from about 10 quads in 1979 to 13 to 19 quads in 1985 and to 14 to 22 quads in 1990. An additional amount of energy from forest and agriculture products is not currently counted in energy statistics.

Departmental Strategy and Programs

The Nation's objective is clear: in 10 years—by 1990—we must cut out dependence on foreign oil by 50 percent, while maintaining a strong and growing economy. Current Department of Energy programs, together with Administration proposals under consideration by the Congress and the efforts of other Federal agencies, provide the Nation's first comprehensive energy strategy. This effort includes a balanced emphasis on both reduction of demand and increase in supply. If successful, our energy strategy will maintain our national security, strengthen the domestic economy and assure an adequate energy supply.

This section first describes the Department's fiscal year 1981 program to limit demand for energy. It next examines the programs to increase the availability of supplies from major energy sources. A third subsection explains the Department's energy-related programs for regulation, information and international affairs. The fourth subsection describes other Departmental programs for general science, defense and administration

Demand Reduction

The Department has four major efforts under way to constrain demand: (1) conservation programs to improve energy efficiency; (2) phased decontrol of energy prices to ensure that the market price of energy reflects its replacement cost; (3) import limitations on oil; and (4) contingency planning, including various forms of voluntary and mandatory rationing of scarce energy supplies. DOE and the Department of State are also engaged in a vigorous effort to promote international agreement on a planned reduction of demand for energy, particularly oil, in the twenty member countries of the International Energy Agency.

Conservation: The Department's conservation programs are designed to reduce the growth of energy demand by encouraging and providing the means for more efficient use of energy. These programs encompass a wide range of efforts, including public information, financial assistance, research and development, and energy conservation standards. Because conservation depends on the actions of tens of millions of individuals, businesses and institutions, the conservation programs are tailored to the specific characteristics and needs of each energy using sector of the economy.

The Department's fiscal year 1981 budget provides direct funding of $1,067 billion to pursue the objective of energy conservation, as shown in the following table. Additional funds are located elsewhere in the Federal budget, particularly through the Solar Energy and Conservation Bank, which, if established by Congress, is budgeted to receive $2.3 billion for construction subsidies from 1980 through 1984. These programs will be complemented by an estimated $739 million in conservation tax credits and supporting programs being implemented by other Federal agencies.

The Energy Information Campaign is a national advertising campaign using television, radio, newspapers and magazines. The advertising campaign will emphasize the efficient use of energy in homes and for personal transportation. A test program in fiscal year 1980, requested in the $7 million budget supplemental, will provide the data needed to launch full-scale campaign in fiscal year 1981. The Department is requesting budget authority of $50 million for fiscal year 1981.

Table 5. – Department of Energy budget authorities for conservation programs

	FY 1980	FY 1981
	(millions of dollars)	
Public Education		
Energy information campaign	$ 7	$ 50
Research and Development		
Buildings and community systems	$106[1]	$ 97
Industrial	60	59
Transportation	118	113
Conservation multi-sector	17	29
Subtotal	$301	$ 298
Grant Programs		
State and local	$457	$ 569
Energy Impact Assistance[2]	50	150
Total conservation	$815	$1,067

1. This includes $4 million for implementing the Emergency Building Temperature Control program which is not authorized beyond 1980.

2. Although Energy Impact Assistance funding is requested as part of the Department's conservation appropriation, it is passed through to the Farmers Home Administration for administration. These funds assist communities in meeting needs associated with efforts to increase energy supply.

Conservation research and development activities are designed to maximize conservation efforts undertaken by all sectors of the American economy and to accelerate the development of innovative equipment and processes. Substantial energy savings are possible over the net 20 years, but this high potential is often accompanied by significant technical risk and long-lead times for implementation. The fiscal year 1981 budget includes $298 million for conservation research and development activities in buildings and community systems, industrial and transportation sectors. Budget authority for these programs remains roughly equal to fiscal year 1980 levels because of the increased incentives that now exist for private investment in improved technologies.

The Department's conservation grant programs provide Federal funds to the State and local governments to facilitate energy conservation. These programs are funded at $569 million in fiscal year 1981, an increase of 25 percent over the previous year. Major fiscal year 1981 grant activities include:

1. The Energy Management Partnership Act, now before Congress, which will broaden state and local energy management capabilities and consolidate several existing grant programs and the Energy Extension Service;
2. Energy audits and energy conservation measures for schools and hospitals throughout the Nation; and
3. Weatherization assistance for low-income persons, particularly those who are elderly or handicapped.

In addition, the President has proposed that legislation be enacted to establish the Solar Energy and Conservation Bank and to authorize subsidized long term loans to residential conservation investments by lower income households. Legislation now pending in Congress would authorize more than $2 billion over four years for such loans. Energy investments under these subsidized loans would reduce family energy budgets by more than the amounts needed to repay the loans.

Conservation regulatory programs include the establishment of energy efficiency standards for buildings and appliances, implementation of Residential Conservation Service programs and further evaluation of the feasibility of establishing efficiency standards for industrial equipment. The Department's proposed Building Energy Performance Standards will be completed in fiscal year 1980 and efficiency standards for certain categories of appliances will be proposed. State plans for implementing the Residential Conservation Service, which requires utilities to provide conservation services to their residential customers, will be received and reviewed. These and other regulatory efforts will help ensure that new automobiles, buildings, and appliances are designed and built to minimize energy use.

Decontrol: On April 5, 1979, President Carter directed the Department of Energy to phase out controls on all domestically produced crude oil by September 30, 1979. This phased decontrol program began on June 1, 1979, with new incentives for those categories of oil where the maximum amount of new exploration and production will result. Beginning on January 1, 1980, prices are being allowed to increase gradually for upper and lower-tier oil that does not qualify for one of the special incentive categories. Increases in the prices of oil as a result of decontrol prices will cause substantial reductions in overall oil demand and stimulate domestic oil production. Coupled with the decontrol of oil prices, the President proposed the Windfall Profits Tax to recoup much of the income the producers would receive as a result of decontrol and oil price increases.

Import Limitations: On July 15, 1979, President Carter announced that United States net imports on foreign oil will never again exceed an annual average of 8.6 million barrels per day. He announced his intention to establish specific import ceilings each year, and set this overall limitation at 8.2 million barrels per day for 1979. Other nations made similar commitments to limit their imports at a December 1979 meeting of the 20-nation International Energy Agency.

In his State of the Union address for 1980, the President announced that the U.S. import ceiling for 1980 would again be set at 8.2 million barrels per day. While we currently expect to achieve even lower levels of imports, the President made clear his intention to enforce this ceiling through the use of an import fee if imports threaten to exceed the 8.2 MMBD level.

Contingency Planning: Contingency planning is a key element for managing energy demand in periods of shortage. The Department has two principal planning efforts under way, pursuant to authority granted by the Emergency Energy Conservation Act of 1979. First, a national gasoline consumption target will be set. This national target will be allocated among the States through voluntary state targets for gasoline consumption developed in consultation with the States. The targets will be published in early 1980. In the event of serious petroleum supply interruptions, these voluntary targets could be made mandatory. Second, the Department is developing a gasoline rationing plan that will be sent to the Congress early in 1980. The Department is exploring simplified rationing plans based on license plates, coupons, or credit cards as alternatives to full-scale gasoline rationing.

International Actions Taken to Reduce Demand: The United States has contributed a renewed and vigorous leadership to the international effort to coordinate reductions in the demand for energy, particularly oil. In June 1979, the seven major western industrialized countries—the United States, Canada, the United Kingdom, France, West Germany, Italy and Japan—held their annual economic summit in Tokyo. Those countries agreed to take several energy-related actions. Most important were their decisions to freeze 1985 imports for each country to 1977-78 levels and to restrict their oil imports in 1980. A follow-up meeting of the energy ministers of the seven summit nations in September reinforced these commitments.

This initiative was followed by a December ministerial-level meeting of the International Energy Agency (IEA), called at the request of the United States. At that meeting the twenty member countries agreed on binding oil import ceilings for 1980 and 1985 for each member. The ceilings chosen will limit the collective demand of the members to 23.1 million barrels per day, plus bunker fuel, in 1980 and 24.6 MMBD in 1985. More importantly, the members agreed to meet quarterly to review the world oil supply situation and, if necessary, to revise downward the previously determined national ceilings. The members also established within the IEA a mechanism to review each IEA country's performance to assure compliance with the ceilings.

Supply Expansion

The Nation must develop economically and environmentally acceptable substitutes for oil. The prime responsibility for the development of alternate energy sources lies with the private sector. The Federal Government, however, has a role to play in meeting that responsibility. The techniques available to the Federal Government in this effort include:

1. Direct Federal expenditures for research and development and for efforts to remove barriers to the commercial use of existing technologies;
2. Financial incentives such as tax credits, loan guarantees and grants to encourage private expenditures for energy producing capacity;
3. Direct production of energy, such as development of the Naval Petroleum Reserves, the enrichment of uranium for use in light water reactors and the distribution and marketing of power from Federal hydroelectric dams; and

4. Maintenance of a substantial reserve of petroleum to protect the nation from its vulnerability to disruption in oil supplies.

The Department's fiscal year 1981 budget provides for the use of each of these means for increasing supply.

Research, Development and Applications: The Department's fiscal year 1981 budget provides $4,092 billion to pursue energy research and development programs to facilitate the entry of technologies into the private sector. The development of our fossil, nuclear and renewable resources in an environmentally acceptable manner is critical to changing the nation's long-term energy supply profile. Maintaining the research base necessary to assure continued technical achievements is of equal importance.

Table 6. – Budget authority for research, development, and applications

	1980	1981
	(millions of dollars)	
Fossil energy	$ 897	$1,165
Solar and other renewables	771	868
Electric energy systems and storage	104	112
Magnetic fusion	356	404
Nuclear Fission	1,186	925
Environment	235	261
Supporting research	252	297
General purpose facilities	0	60
General reduction	-71	0
Total research, development and applications	$3,730	$4,092

Fossil Energy: Table 6 shows that in fiscal year 1981 the resources devoted to fossil energy research and development have increased substantially over fiscal year 1980 to a level of $1.165 billion. This level of support is indicative of the expanded role that domestic fossil resources are expected to play between 1985 and 2000. Coal will play a central role in the Nation's fossil energy programs. Administration plans to accelerate the production and utilization of coal include $673 million of funding for research and development of advanced technologies for the conversion of coal synthetic liquids, gases and solids. Construction will begin on two solvent-refined coal demonstration plants and a large-scale facility to produce synthetic high Btu gas. The two liquefaction pilot plants, known as Exxon Donor Solvent and H-coal, will be in operation, generating valuable data to support future commercial size facilities. The remaining $374 million provided for coal research and development is focused on:

1. Improving direct combustion technologies;
2. Developing new technologies to increase energy conversion efficiency through means such as fuel cells and magnetohydrodynamics;
3. Developing advanced pollution control technology to support required conversions of utility and industrial boilers coal; and
4. A major new initiative to demonstrate the acceptability of coal-oil mixtures in utility and industrial boilers.

The Department's petroleum program will develop new and improved technologies for recovering oil from existing and potential oil reservoirs, as well as from unconventional sources such as oil shale or tar sands. Work will continue to define and to improve methods to exploit the Nation's unconventional gas resources, including Eastern gas shales and Western gas sands. Total funds provided for petroleum and gas programs, including commercialization activities, are $118 million.

Solar and Other Renewables: The goal of obtaining as much as 20 percent of the Nation's energy needs from solar energy, including hydropower, by the turn of the century is reflected in the increased level of resources allocated to these research and development activities in fiscal year 1981. In addition to $868 million in direct expenditures, solar tax credits of $355 million and tax credits for geothermal development totalling $52 million will also be available. Solar technology development activities in fiscal year 1981 include:

1. Continued photovoltaic research and development in thin films, novel concentrators and advanced materials;
2. Completion of the 10 megawatt central receiver power plant;
3. Expanded development of small-scale wind energy systems and fabrication of advanced intermediate and large-scale experimental systems; and
4. Establishment of the Solar Energy Information Data Bank to collect, analyze and disseminate data on solar technologies.

Solar applications programs complement these technology developments. They are intended to eliminate the economic and institutional barriers to early use of solar energy technologies and systems in housing, commerce, industry and agriculture.

Geothermal activities in fiscal year 1981 are directed toward the following activities:

1. The use of hydrothermal energy for commercial electricity generation and direct heat applications;
2. Evaluation of the economic recoverability of methane, thermal and hydraulic energy from geopressured resources;
3. Development of the technologies to reduce the cost of energy recovery from all geothermal resources; and
4. Effort to extract energy economically from hot dry rock.

The program is being carried out through a combination of hardware developments demonstration plants, technical support to prospective users and loan guarantees. Budget authority totalling $197 million will be requested for geothermal activities in fiscal year 1981.

The fiscal year 1981 budget requests $19 million for further commercial development of low-head hydroelectric power resources at existing dam sites and for new initiatives involving power production from river current.

Electric Energy Systems and Storage: Better methods of transmitting and storing electric energy are critical to the development of new and improved energy technologies. The fiscal year 1981 budget includes a total of $112 million for this purpose. The $40 million requested for electric energy systems in fiscal year 1981 will be used to continue development of the means to integrate new electric energy technologies into existing electric utility systems and to provide new options for increased power transmission and storage. The $72 million requested for an energy storage systems program in fiscal year 1981 will be used to develop reliable, low cost, safe and environmentally acceptable energy storage systems and components for use in transportation systems, systems for heating and cooling buildings, industrial processes, solar power systems and utilities.

Nuclear Energy: The Department's nuclear energy programs are aimed both at nuclear fission and at magnetic fusion. Nuclear fission programs are undertaken by the Department to develop the nuclear technology base and to provide the underpinning for the nation's nonproliferation policy. Fiscal year 1981 funding for nuclear fission activities totals $925 million in seven programs, representing a significant decrease from previous years. Funding for the Liquid Metal Fast Breeder Reactor has been reduced in light of current projections that breeder reactors will not be needed until after the year 2020. The level of funding for fiscal 1981 will maintain the technological base needed to keep the breeder option open and is consistent with United States nonproliferation goals. Activities will be focused on the operation of the Fast Flux Test Facility at Richland, Washington, its supporting facilities and associated test programs. Development will also continue on the water cooled breeder reactor at the Shippingport Atomic Power Station. Also, the naval reactors research and development programs, contained in the Department's defense programs, help support the nuclear fission energy option.

In response to the accident at the Three Mile Island generating station, the President appointed the Kemey Commission to investigate nuclear power and recommended ways to assure its safety. The report of this group revealed serious shortcomings in the system that regulates and manages nuclear power. The Department of Energy, which has no regulatory or managerial mission in the operation of commercial nuclear power plants, is working with the private sector in matters of nuclear safety. The Department is assisting industry with numerous activities including:

1. Dissemination and interpretation of data on nuclear plant operating experience gained by the Nuclear Regulatory Commission, DOE and the industry itself;

2. Identification of appropriate technologies that could improve the safety and reliability of nuclear plants; and
3. Collection and dissemination of the maximum amount of relevant technical data from analysis of the Three Mile Island accident.

A major activity in fiscal year 1981 is continued and expanded research and development to increase the safety and efficiency of light water reactors. A total of $55 million is provided for this important program, compared to $41 million in fiscal year 1980.

The Department is proceeding with a broad-based technical program for the interim management and permanent disposal of radioactive wastes. The fiscal year 1981 commercial waste management budget of $299 million provides for further expansion of an investigation launched in fiscal year 1980 into the use of geological formations other than salt for isolation of nuclear waste. Investigations also continue in salt formations. The spent nuclear fuel program, funded at $20 million in fiscal year 1981, continues to provide technical and operational support for the President's commitment to provide interim storage for commercially generated spent nuclear fuel. Separate legislation was proposed in 1979 to provide borrowing authority of $300 million, necessary for the acquisition of storage capacity which will be required by 1983. The Administration continues to support that legislative proposal. This program is based on plans presented by the Interagency Review Group for Nuclear Waste Management, appointed last year by the President to create a unified Federal policy for the management of radioactive waste. Of particular concern to the review group was the role of the States in nuclear waste management and the development of effective relationship between Federal and State governments. The findings and recommendations of this group will be the subject of a Presidential policy announcement during 1980.

Funding for the Advanced Isotope Separation Technology program will be increased to $87 million. This will permit the continued development of uranium separation processes that offer potential for the production of enriched uranium at a substantially reduced cost.

Magnetic fusion is expected to be a long-term source of electric energy. Funding of $404 million is provided in fiscal 1981 to continue development of magnetic fusion technology.

The program will develop the sound technical and engineering foundation necessary to design, construct and operate complex experiments and facilities. Progress, measured by improvements in plasma density, temperature and confinement time, has been encouraging. Activities in fiscal year 1981 include continued construction of the Tokamak Fusion Test Reactor and the Mirror Fusion Test Facility. Both are scheduled for completion in 1982. The Fusion Materials Irradiation Test Facility, which will provide the necessary testing capability for materials development and engineering generation, will be completed two years later. In addition, other tokamak and mirror experimental devices will be operated to continue development of a strong scientific base for the eventual design of a fusion engineering test facility.

Environment: The Department's environmental programs associated with energy supply are designed to ensure that the evaluation of environmental impacts is incorporated in energy technology development and deployment activities. The budget request for these environmental programs for fiscal year 1981 is $261 million. Major activities will include efforts to predict the effects of increased levels of carbon dioxide in the atmosphere; determine the long-term effects of low-level radiation exposure; and conduct research on selected energy projects, such as the solvent-refined coal and geothermal demonstration projects. The Department's Project Environmental Planning System is designed to ensure that environmental considerations are considered at every step of the decision-making process, from the earliest design activities through completion.

Support for Energy Research: The Department's supporting research programs provide the scientific base for energy technology development. The fiscal year 1981 budget includes $297 million for basic energy research programs that seek fundamental knowledge of the physical and biological sciences, engineering and mathematics as they affect the production of energy and its conversion into other forms. In fiscal year 1981, the Department will move forward with its investigations into the chemistry of coal, the processes of combustion, and new approaches to the use of solar energy and the isolation of nuclear waste. The Chemical and Materials Sciences Laboratory at Lawrence Berkeley Laboratory will be completed. Cooperative research in universities, industry and national laboratories will be supported in order to speed the transfer of technology.

Direct Energy Production: In addition to the research, development and application of energy technologies, the Department is also responsible for producing energy. These activities include:

1. The production and sale of enriched uranium for use in domestic and foreign nuclear-powered electrical generating plants;
2. The development, production, and sale of oil from the Naval Petroleum Reserves; and
3. The distribution and sale of electric power in five power marketing areas.

These services and products are sold to the private sector at prices that are sufficient to recover the full costs of their production and distribution over a reasonable period of time. Revenues obtained from the sale of enriched uranium offset the costs incurred by the Department in providing enriching services. Revenues generated from the sale of oil from the Naval Petroleum Reserves and the marketing of power produced by four of the five power marketing administrations revert directly to the United States Treasury. In fiscal year 1981, productions and distribution costs will be $1.7 billion, while anticipated revenues will total over $3.7 billion.

The Department presently enriches uranium for domestic and foreign nuclear power reactor customers and to meet government needs at three gaseous diffusion plants located in Oak Ridge, Tennessee; Portsmouth, Ohio; and Paducah, Kentucky. The fiscal year 1981 budget authority request of $88 million is based on production of 9.5 million separative work units (SWU). Sales of 10.8 million SWU are anticipated in fiscal year 1981, some of which will come from inventory. Construction of the Portsmouth Gas Centrifuge Enrichment Plant is a major project in the Department's efforts to reduce the amount of paper needed for enrichment purposes. The Plant is scheduled to provide 2.2 million SWU of capacity by the end of 1988 and is funded at $319 million in fiscal year 1981.

The three Naval Petroleum Reserves comprise the ninth largest known domestic petroleum resource. The fiscal year 1981 budget request provides for continued operation and development of the reserve and the resumption of exploratory drilling at Naval Petroleum Reserve Number 1 after a temporary halt in fiscal year 1980. The request anticipates that the federal share of production from the Naval Production Reserves will be 160,000 barrels per day.

The five Power Marketing Administrations operate high voltage transmission systems to distribute electric power produced at Federal hydroelectric generating projects. The Power Marketing Administrations are the Alaska Power Administration; Bonneville Power Administration, which serves the Pacific Northwest; and the Southeastern, Southwestern and Western Area Power Administration.

Strategic Petroleum Reserve: The largest element of DOE's contingency planning for supply interruptions is the Strategic Petroleum Reserve. In December 1975, legislation was enacted to establish a reserve of up to 1 billion barrels of oil to reduce the nation's vulnerability to a severe petroleum supply interruption. Preparation of storage facilities is proceeding and funds are available in the budget for resumption of oil acquisition in 1980. The revised schedule calls for expansion of the current 92 million barrel supply to 248 million barrels by 1983, with 750 million barrels in storage by 1989. The latter figure includes 24 million barrels in storage regional petroleum storage. No decision has yet been made on the final 250 million barrels of the reserve capacity.

Energy Security Corporation: In July 1979, the President asked Congress to enact legislation creating an independent Energy Security Corporation that would assist the private sector in making investments in the production of synthetic fuels (both liquids and gases) from coal, biomass, peat and oil shale and in the development of unconventional natural gas reserves. As proposed, the Corporation's objective will be the development of domestic production capacity; it would not engage in research and development activities. The President has also asked that it be given the authority to provide support for gasohol production.

The Corporation will be an independent, government-sponsored enterprise with a Congressional charter. It will be located outside the Executive Branch, independent of any Government agency. The Corporation will be managed by a seven-person board of directors: a chairman and three other outside directors would be appointed by the President and confirmed by the Senate. In addition, the Secretaries of Energy, Treasury and one other department will sit on the board. The Administration has set a goal that synthetic fuels developed through the Energy Security Corporation will replace 1.75 million barrels of imported oil per day by 1990.

Alternative Fuel Development and Production: On November 27, 1979, Public Law 96-126 was signed appropriating $2.208 billion to the Department to stimulate alternative fuel production in anticipation of the formation of the Energy Security Corporation. The Department will implement this program during 1980 through feasibility study grants, cooperative agreements, loan guarantees, and price guarantees or purchase commitments.

The Energy Mobilization Board: The Administration has acted under existing authority to reduce delays in granting permits to critical energy facilities. Two actions already have been taken. Procedures for setting decision schedules for critical energy facilities were established in April 1979 under the direction of the Office of Management and Budget and the Council on Environmental Quality issued regulations reforming and streamlining the requirements of the National Environmental Policy Act in November 1979.

To meet 1990 targets for oil import reduction, however, substantial additional authority is needed to accelerate the development of domestic energy production capacity. The Energy Mobilization Board proposed by the President will have three members and will be located within the Executive Office of the President. Board members will serve at the pleasure of the President and will be confirmed by the Senate. As proposed, the Board will be authorized to designate certain non-nuclear facilities as priority energy projects critical to achieving the Nation's import reduction goals. For each designated project, the Board will establish binding schedules for federal, state and local decision-making. Judicial review of decisions by the Board will take place on an expedited basis in the United States Courts of Appeals.

Other Energy-related Programs

The Department of Energy performs several other energy-related roles for the nation that affect generally both demand and supply. These include regulatory measures, energy information processing and international affairs.

Regulation: The regulatory activities assigned to the Department are the responsibility of the Federal Energy Regulatory Commission, the Economic Regulatory Administration and the Office of Hearings and Appeals. In fiscal year 1981, funding for regulatory activities total $239 million.

Energy Information Administration: The Department's energy information collection, analysis and dissemination responsibilities are carried out by the Energy Information Administration (EIA) which will receive funding in fiscal year 1981 of $116 million. EIA gathers and publishes basic energy statistics on the reserves, production, processing, distribution, consumption and price of the various energy sources. Energy information activities are being expanded in several areas. Better information will be sought concerning the financial conditions of energy firms; oil and gas reserves, production and storage; end-use consumption; emerging sources of energy; and possible energy emergencies. These and other programs will reduce the government's dependence on private organizations for basic energy statistics. In addition, EIA also supports the regulatory and program energy information requirements of the Department. Another mission of EIA is to produce forecasts of future trends in the supply, demand and price of energy as well as analysis of the impacts of those trends. A wide range of economic, statistical and structural models are developed and used to produce the forecasts and analyses. Finally, to improve the credibility and usefulness of energy information, a multi-year program of information validation is being constructed to enhance its quality, timeliness and organization.

International Affairs: Solutions to energy problems can no longer be confined to the initiatives undertaken by individual countries. The distinction between world and domestic energy problems has become blurred as domestic energy policy is increasingly influenced by world events. Responsibility for the conduct of the nation's international affairs rests primarily with the Department of State, but the Department of Energy has an important role in analyzing international energy problems and promoting cooperation with other countries to provide solutions to these problems. Five million dollars has been requested for the Department's Office of International Affairs in fiscal year 1981.

Other Programs

There are three other functions in the Department—general science programs, defense programs and administration.

General Sciences: The purpose of the Department's General Sciences program is to gain deeper understanding of the structure and behavior of matter by pursuing fundamental knowledge in physical and life sciences. General Sciences programs are not specific to any particular technology. Rather, investigations into areas beyond existing frontiers of knowledge are expected to yield long-term scientific and technological breakthroughs. The fiscal year 1981 request for General Science programs totals $523 million.

Defense Programs: The Department of Energy provides the requirements of the Department of Defense for nuclear weapons, nuclear materials and management of nuclear waste. The Department is also charged with the responsibility of improving the technology for verification of nuclear test treaty compliance and of the development of nuclear materials safeguards and security procedures, including classification of sensitive information. Inertial Confinement Fusion technology is part of the Defense Programs mission because of its relevance to nuclear weapons development. The Naval Reactor Development program, managed as a part of the Nuclear Fission Program, designs, develops and tests improved naval nuclear propulsion plants and reactor cores needed for naval ship propulsion. Total fiscal year 1981 funding for DOE Defense Programs is $3,443 million, up from $3,008 million in fiscal year 1980.

Departmental Administration: Activities in this category include general management and administration of the Department. Fiscal year 1981 funding requested for these activities totals

$362 million, an increase of $87 million over the fiscal year 1980 level. This request includes $292 million to provide for the management support costs associated with headquarters staff functions and multiprogram field offices (this includes executive management, legal assistance and counsel, financial management, audit and investigative activities, external communications, engineering and construction management, administrative activities, minority economic impact, and equal employment opportunity). In addition, funds are provided for policy analyses and systems studies; efforts directed toward the Department's communications with State, local and tribal government; in-house energy management for retrofit and fuels conversion projects; and security investigations. These costs are partially offset by miscellaneous revenues.

Management Initiatives

Recent changes, implemented in October 1979, streamlined the organization and better defined responsibilities for accomplishing Department objectives. These changes were designed to provide better services to the public and to improve cooperation with the Congress.

The principal components of the Department are divided into three groups. The first group includes offices that report directly to the Secretary and Deputy Secretary. These include Legislative Affairs, Public Affairs, Consumer Affairs, and Intergovernmental Affairs which work directly with the public; state, local and tribal governments; and other entities of the Federal Government. The Policy and Evaluation Office, the General Counsel, the Economic Regulatory Administration, the Energy Information Administration, the International Affairs Office, the Inspector General, the Office of Hearings and Appeals, and the Board of Contract Appeals also report directly to the Secretary and Deputy Secretary.

The second group includes the Department's research, development, resource applications, and revenue-producing activities. These offices–Conservation and Solar Energy, Fossil Energy, Nuclear Energy, Resource Applications, Energy Research, Defense Programs and Environment–report to the Secretary and Deputy Secretary through the Under Secretary. The Fossil Energy and Nuclear Energy offices were created from the former Energy Technology organization which was dissolved to better align technology developments with other program activities.

The third group reports to the Secretary and the Deputy Secretary through the Chief Financial Officer. It comprises those offices with day-to-day responsibility for the management of the Department's financial, procurement and personnel resources. These offices include the Controller, Administration, Procurement and Contract Management, and Equal Opportunity. The Office of Minority Economic Impact reports to the Secretary but coordinates its activities with the Chief Financial Officer.

Four primary objectives have now been met: *First,* we have improved lines of control from top management to ensure that policies and procedures are better defined and that there is a mechanism to ensure they are consistently followed. Better lines of demarcation have been established between activities so that responsibilities for the success or failure of DOE undertakings are firmly assigned and, finally, improved control systems have been put in place to monitor the Department's performance.

Second, we have improved our service to the public and our cooperation with State, local and tribal governments. Our public information systems are critical to the accomplishment of the Department's mission. Many of our program objectives, such as conservation, can be achieved only through the decisions made on a daily basis by each American. Communications with citizens groups are important in fostering public understanding of our energy problems and solutions. Our mechanisms for cooperation with State, local and tribal governments must function smoothly because they bear an increasingly important role with respect to the Nation's energy transition from oil to other sources of supply.

Third, we have improved our capability to supply the Congress with the information it needs to formulate legislative policy and to maintain close liaison between the Administration and Congress in dealing with energy matters.

Fourth, the operational management of the Department has improved significantly. New management systems have been established for planning, programming and budgeting; project management and control; and project acquisition approval. The Department has initiated a comprehensive financial management improvement program, established new guidelines and procedures for the use of consultants and has taken steps to improve the responsiveness of its procurement system. Finally, most of the critical personnel shortages have been corrected, including the addition of manpower resources for Conservation and Solar activities and the Inspector General.

In pursuing these objectives, the Department is aware that organizational change can have a disruptive effect in the short run. For that reason, emphasis was placed on efficient lines of control while most organizational components below the Assistant Secretary level was left intact. Now that the organization is in place, the Department is in a better position to fulfill the mandate with which it has been charged by the President and the Congress to develop and carry out an effective energy policy that will allow the Nation to move smoothly toward a healthy economy drawing on diverse energy sources.

Conclusion

The transition we face has far-reaching implications. It represents a joining of national resources and resolution, and international collaboration on a scale never before attempted in peacetime. It represents a new stage in the continuing evolution of America. From the beginning, our country has been a nation in transition. Much of our history has been built on creative change. We have refused to be static socially, economically or technologically. As a Nation and a people, we are not strangers to the challenges and opportunities of new circumstances. The transition from an oil-dependent economy to an energy-diversified society is, we believe, no more insurmountable a challenge than many we have faced successfully in the past. But it requires a close partnership between the public and private sectors; it requires the long-term intergration of different energy approaches in the face of factors sometimes beyond our control and it requires a recognition that there are no short cuts, no technological miracles, and no quick solutions dictated in Washington that by themselves will make the transition significantly shorter or less demanding. The days of cheap, accessible energy are over. Every American must participate in bringing America forward; no one should be left behind. The national energy program outlined here enlists the cooperation of all segments of our society to free our National from excessive foreign dependence and to ensure that America enters the next century secure in her own resources.

THE PRESIDENT'S
COMMISSION ON COAL

Recommendations and Summary Findings

Washington, D.C. March 1980

The President's Commission on Coal

600 E Street, N.W., Suite 500
Washington, D. C. 20004
(202) 376-2001

March 3, 1980

The President
The White House
Washington, D. C.

Dear Mr. President:

When you appointed this Commission in the spring of 1978, there was national concern about the consequences of a strike in the coal industry that had lasted 111 days. Labor-management issues, in the broadest sense, were the focus of the Commission's assignment.

Since that time, domestic and world events have broadened and heightened the significance of the Commission's mandate:

- Repeated OPEC price increases have more than doubled the price of imported oil, which now stands at approximately ten times its 1973 level. The cost of oil is a central element in domestic inflation.

- The accident at the nuclear powerplant at Three Mile Island raised new doubts about public acceptance of nuclear power as an alternative to oil.

- The revolution in Iran and the recent Soviet invasion of Afghanistan have placed the security of world oil supplies in a new and more dangerous context.

For sale by the Superintendent of Documents, U.S. Government Printing Office
Washington, D.C. 20402

Stock Number 052-003-00740-1

The President
Page two

Consequently, we report to you at a time of perilous world conditions.

There are no instant solutions to the Nation's energy problem. Even under the best of circumstances, it will take many years to overcome the constant threat that is posed to national security and to economic stability by continued reliance on foreign oil. It is, therefore, imperative that the Nation continue to pursue aggressively those courses of action designed to reduce dependence on imported oil.

It is the view of the Commission that coal can make a significant contribution toward this objective. The Nation has coal in abundance beneath its own soil, and it has an industry in place and the resource of people needed and ready to mine that coal.

This coal can be burned in compliance with the Clean Air Act at less cost than imported oil.

In this setting, we have the honor to transmit to you the final report of The President's Commission on Coal.

John D. Rockefeller IV
Chairman

Jesse F. Core

Marvin Friedman

W. Dewey Presley

Willard Wirtz

INTRODUCTION

Survival of America as a free and powerful Nation demands strong measures to reduce the foreign oil dependence that threatens the Nation's security and is having a devastating effect on the domestic economy.

We now send nearly $95 billion annually to foreign nations to buy more than 2.9 billion barrels of their oil per year. A growing population and economy will increase dependence on foreign oil unless firm steps are taken immediately to reduce the need for it.

Energy conservation is vital, but it will not do the job alone. The future of nuclear energy is clouded. Solar energy and synthetic fuels promise help in future decades, but will not provide the entire solution. Nor can coal do it alone.

But coal is America's most abundant energy resource, with about one-third of the world's reserves lying beneath our soil.

There are legitimate concerns associated with the use of coal. These relate to environmental protection and public health, the safety of coal miners, stability in labor-management relations, and coalfield living conditions.

The Commission concludes that the problems associated with coal use can be overcome, and that this Nation must begin to rely more heavily on its vast coal deposits to reduce much of our intolerable dependence on imported oil.

This will require rearrangement of current fuel uses.

- o Coal must replace oil and natural gas now used in generating electricity and in large industrial boilers.
- o Natural gas must be directed toward replacing oil in home and commercial heating and in industrial uses where coal is impractical.
- o Oil must be directed primarily toward petrochemical products and transportation uses.

Since the Commission began its deliberations, there has been increasing awareness that the 1980s will be a decade of dangerous energy vulnerability. A proven energy production strategy for these years is essential. Stepped-up coal use is the practical solution. Strong legislation, including mandatory reductions of utility and industrial oil and natural gas use, is already overdue.

Greater reliance on coal requires insuring environmental integrity, safety in the mines, stability in labor-management relations, and adequate living conditions in mining communities.

The Commission's recommendations for increased coal use recognize these needs. Summarized with the recommendations are the Commission's principal findings and conclusions.

REPLACING FOREIGN OIL WITH COAL

The United States must rapidly reduce its dependence on foreign oil. Vast reserves of domestic coal are readily available to assist in this effort. Synthetic fuels from coal can contribute significantly to oil replacement in the mid-1990s. In the nearer term, the most practical and the cheapest measures are the accelerated construction of new coal-fired utility and industrial boilers, the reconversion of coal-capable boilers to coal where practical, and the use of coal-oil mixtures. Recommendations to save more than 2 million barrels of imported oil per day by 1990 are outlined below. Further reductions may be necessary.

Recommendations:

1. That increases in utility oil and natural gas use beyond present levels be prohibited.

2. That utility oil and natural gas use be reduced to 40 percent of present levels by 1990.

3. That oil and natural gas use be prohibited in coal-capable utility boilers operating more than 1,500 hours per year after 1985.

4. That oil and natural gas use be prohibited in "non-peaking" utility units constructed after 1980.

5. That oil and natural gas use be prohibited in coal-capable industrial boilers over 5 megawatts equivalent after 1985.

6. That oil and natural gas use be prohibited in new large industrial boilers over 5 megawatts equivalent constructed after 1980.

7. That the additional cost of the reconversion and new construction of coal-fired units necessary to meet the reduction target be shared nationally, in order to ease the burden on electricity consumers. To keep electricity rates from rising above what would occur with continued oil and natural gas use, Federal grant assistance of up to $15 billion should be provided.

8. That the State Regulatory Utility Commissions cooperate fully in setting rates sufficient but no higher than those reasonably required to attract the private capital necessary to meet the oil and natural gas reduction target.

9. That oil and natural gas replacement authority under existing laws, specifically the Energy Supply and Environmental Coordination Act and the Powerplant and Industrial Fuel Use Act, be vigorously enforced.

10. That the Interstate Commerce Commission stop its practice of imposing disproportionate rates on railroad coal-hauling.

11. That the Congress enact legislation to develop an industry capable of producing significant quantities of synthetic fuels from coal in the 1990s.

Findings:

1. Coal accounts for more than 80 percent of our domestic fossil fuel reserves but supplies only 18 percent of U. S. energy needs, principally as a boiler fuel in the generation of electricity.

2. The use of 5.5 million barrels of oil and natural gas per day in utility and industrial boilers is a significant element in the Nation's dependence on imported oil.

3. Coal readily available can be used to fire a substantial number of boilers now fired by oil and natural gas, replacing more than 2 million barrels of imported oil per day by 1990.

4. Ample coal is available to meet the requirements of a major oil and natural gas replacement program. The United States has more mineable coal reserves than any other country, a supply that will last hundreds of years. Current annual excess production capacity in the industry stands at nearly 200 million tons.

5. Capital is available to finance expansions and openings of mines as necessary and a sufficient work force is available to produce coal as needed.

6. An oil and natural gas replacement program will require substantial capital investment. However, these investments will pay for themselves in the long run from the substantially lower costs of coal as a fuel. Saving more than 2 million barrels of oil per day will ease inflationary pressures and strengthen the dollar as approximately $25 billion will be trimmed from the nearly $95 billion now expended annually for foreign oil.

7. The Interstate Commerce Commission (ICC) has a policy of permitting higher railroad rates for hauling coal; the result is that coal haulage subsidizes other freight traffic on the Nation's railroads. Railroad rates for coal have increased rapidly in recent years, most rapidly in the West. The undue burden placed on coal haulage by the ICC is slowing the rate of voluntary coal conversion and raising the delivered price of domestic coal to the point where imported coal -- principally from Australia, Poland, and South Africa -- is cheaper to some users.

ENVIRONMENT

Increased use of coal must be achieved without compromising the environment. The combustion of coal sufficient to replace more than 2 million barrels of oil per day need not increase air pollution above what would otherwise occur. Surface mine laws require the reclamation of the land to at least its condition prior to mining. Coal mined responsibly and burned cleanly remains cheaper than oil as a boiler fuel.

Recommendations:

1. That the accelerated construction of new coal-fired utility and industrial boilers, the reconversion of coal-capable boilers, and the use of coal-oil mixtures -- necessary to meet the oil and natural gas reduction targets -- meet the provisions of the Clean Air Act.

   - That the scheduled reviews of the national health standards on which the Clean Air Act is based be conducted in accordance with the best available data and analyses, to assure that the cost of meeting the current standards does not place an excessive burden on consumers.

   - That the Environmental Protection Agency fully exercise the flexibility within the Clean Air Act to hasten the replacement of oil and natural gas with coal; and that the successful use of more sophisticated air emissions modeling in coal reconversion in New England be undertaken with all coal reconversions.

2. That the surface mining required for current and recommended expanded coal use meet the provisions of the Surface Mining Control and Reclamation Act.

Findings:

1. The Commission shares the concerns that have been expressed publicly about the environmental and health consequences of increased use of fossil fuels. The burning of any fossil fuel has potential environmental and health consequences that demand close and constant public attention and the highest degree of private-user responsibility.

2. The Commission's careful conclusion is that a program of replacing oil with coal in compliance with the Clean Air Act will not increase emissions of environmental and health-related pollutants and will cause, at most, minimal increases in atmospheric concentrations of carbon dioxide.

3. New coal-burning powerplants built under the Clean Air Act New Source Performance Standards will cause in most instances, no more, and generally fewer, sulfur dioxide, nitrogen oxide, and particulate emissions than most existing oil units. The replacement of older oil units with new, relatively clean coal units allows increased reliance on coal with no net increase in environmental and health-related emissions.

4. The best available information indicates that the maximum possible effect of the proposed oil and natural gas replacement program will be a cumulative increase by 1990 of about one-hundredth of one-percent in world atmospheric concentrations of carbon dioxide, compared with using more oil instead.

5. The Commission believes that the clean burning of coal is essential because emissions from coal -- like emissions from other fossil fuels, both mobile and stationary, and from natural processes -- contain nitrogen oxides, sulfur oxides, and particulates that have been linked to respiratory disease and to the increased acidity of rainfall and of lakes.

There is concern among scientists that increasing atmospheric concentrations of carbon dioxide -- resulting, in part, from the burning of fossil fuels -- could result in warming of the Earth's atmosphere toward the middle of the next century.

6. The Surface Mining Control and Reclamation Act of 1977 brought all States under the same standards for protection of land and water. Under the Act, surface-mined lands must be reclaimed to support pre-existing or higher uses, approximate original contours must be restored, and the disturbance to ground and surface waters must be kept to a minimum.

7. The Surface Mining Act is in the process of being implemented and is the focus of controversy that needs to be resolved. The principal issues are its impact on the operators, the effectiveness of some of its provisions, its enforcement, its cost to the consumer, and its potential for eliminating the small operator from the industry.

COAL MINE SAFETY

Underground coal mining can and must be made safer. It is the most hazardous major occupation because a substantial number of mines, large and small, operate far more dangerously than can be justified, given existing technology, practice, and experience.

Recommendations:

1. That shared responsibility by management and labor for improving the safety of underground mining include acceptance of the principle that coal companies not prepared to operate safe mines and miners not prepared to observe safe mining practices have no place in the industry.

2. That the Mine Safety and Health Administration (MSHA) increase its inspection and enforcement activities in those mines identified in Commission studies as having accident and fatality rates consistently and substantially above national averages.

3. That a thorough investigation of the factors that distinguish the safest from the most dangerous mines be undertaken immediately by the National Academy of Sciences, cooperating with labor, management, and MSHA; that this investigation start from the Commission's findings that unacceptably wide variation exists in the safety experience among larger underground mines and that fatalities are disproportionately high in smaller underground mines; and that specific recommendations be made to management, labor, and MSHA for the exercise of continued joint responsibility for improving underground mine safety.

4. That the Bituminous Coal Operators' Association (BCOA), the United Mine Workers of America (UMWA), and MSHA continue the joint task force on safety established in cooperation with the Commission.

Findings:

1. In 1979, there were 144 fatalities and more than 18,000 disabling injuries resulting from the mining of more than 750 million tons of coal. Continuation of current accident rates in surface and underground mining would result in an expected 200 fatalities and and more than 25,000 disabling injuries in 1985, when production is estimated to rise above 1 billion tons per year.

2. Underground coal mining is the most hazardous occupation in the United States. It is twice as dangerous as manufacturing and three times more dangerous than surface mining.

3. Major improvements in coal mine safety have occurred since implementation of the Coal Mine Health and Safety Act of 1969. However, the safety of the miner continues to require attention and always will.

4. The greatest improvement in mine safety since the 1969 Act had already occurred by mid-decade. By 1974, 80 percent of the reduction in fatality incidence had been achieved. The incidence of disabling injuries has been increasing since 1975. In 1979, the fatality rate increased for the first time in a decade.

5. Three-fourths of the 115 fatal injuries in underground mines in 1979 resulted from collapse of mine roofs and walls and from haulage accidents.

6. Fatalities are disproportionately clustered in mines employing 50 or fewer persons. These mines account for 15 percent of underground work hours, but for more than 40 percent of all underground mine fatalities.

7. Among major underground coal producers, overall disabling injury rates vary sevenfold. This wide variation strongly suggests that in some mines, operators, miners and Federal inspectors are working together to insure safety, and in others they are not.

LABOR-MANAGEMENT RELATIONS

Increased reliance by the Nation on the use of coal will require greater stability in labor-management relations. The past record is one of suspicion, hostility, and costly controversy. Only as the coal operators and the miners' union show necessary regard for guaranteeing an adequate supply of coal can the public be expected to accept increased coal use as a sound national policy.

Recommendations:

1. That the UMWA and the BCOA begin discussion immediately of the issues and problems relevant to the 1981 negotiations.

2. That the union leadership continue its efforts to stop wildcat strikes and "stranger" picketing, and that the developing pattern of arbitration awards regarding these activities be respected.

3. That labor and management continue efforts to improve productivity in mining and that they expand training programs in the areas of job safety, increased productivity, grievance handling, and labor-management relations.

4. That the parties establish a labor-management committee with a neutral chairperson selected by the two sides for continuing action on the broad range of issues of mutual concern.

Findings:

1. Unstable labor-management relations in the coal industry are unfortunately part of its history.

    o Since 1966, the coal industry has been unable to reach contract agreement without a strike on five consecutive occasions, culminating in the 111-day strike in 1977-1978.

- Wildcat strike activity increased sharply during the late 1960s, reaching unprecedented levels during the 1974-1977 period. By 1977, lost time due to unauthorized strikes reached 2.3 million workdays. This compares with the period 1958-1967, when annual workdays lost to wildcat strikes averaged 117,000.

- Work stoppages in response to stranger picketing, although diminishing, represent a continuing problem.

- Strained labor-management relations during the 1970s were the result of substantial internal and external changes confronting the BCOA and the UMWA.

- The resurgence of the industry under changed circumstances after 20 years of decline and stagnation is the principal external fact confronting the BCOA and the UMWA. This resurgence has been accompanied by a transition toward surface mining, increased western operations, increased non-union production, and the entry of oil companies into the coal industry.

- In the decade preceding the 111-day strike, the UMWA had experienced substantial internal turmoil accompanied by disruption and dissension at top leadership levels, a massive influx of young, inexperienced workers to its ranks, and major changes in its structure.

- The BCOA, the principal negotiating arm of the coal industry since 1950, has been severely strained by the changes within the industry and the diverse interests of its membership. The interests of surface operators differ from those of underground operators, those in the East differ from those in the West, and the approach to labor relations and collective bargaining of the traditional operators differs from that favored by many of the newer producers.

- The $1.9 billion of unfunded liability for pension benefits to retired miners under the 1950 Pension Plan is a legacy of the years of stagnation and decline in the industry. Annual payments of approximately $2,800 per underground miner and $6,500 per surface miner are required under the Bituminous Coal Wage Agreement to meet current payments for pensions and to provide full funding for past service by the end of 1986. The pension of a miner under the 1950 Plan is a flat $275 per month. The responsibility of member companies of the BCOA for that liability will be a continuing source of concern to the parties.

2. There are signs of improvement in labor-management relations in the coal industry.

   - Young miners and supervisors are maturing and gaining experience in mining.

   - Wildcat strikes have declined 90 percent since commencement of the current contract.

   - Following a decade of decline, labor productivity shows signs of improving. The greatest percentage gains appear to be in eastern underground mines.

   - There is a growing appreciation by both management and labor of the link between good labor-management relations and productivity. Intensive mine site studies by the Commission indicate that absenteeism, equipment maintenance practices, management commitment to safety, willingness to settle grievances at the earliest stage, and respect -- or lack of it -- between management and labor are the principal factors separating the productive from the unproductive mines.

- The joint task force, established by the BCOA, the UMWA, and MSHA, under the auspices of the Commission, has demonstrated the value of continuing communication among labor, management, and government on the vital issues of mine safety.

- With assistance from MSHA and the Commission, the UMWA and the BCOA have expanded and improved their training of mine safety committee members on the proper handling of safety grievances at the mine site.

3. The activities of the Commission, in separate and joint meetings held with officials of the UMWA and the BCOA, helped to underscore the public concern over the instability in labor relations between the parties. The meetings appear to have played a major role in the significant progress in labor relations stability that has taken place in the industry since the strike of 1977-1978. Despite this progress, it must be noted that the issues confronting both the UMWA and the BCOA during the period of transition contain the seeds for continued controversy and conflict.

COAL MINERS' LIVING CONDITIONS

If the Nation is to expand coal production during the 1980s, considerations of equity, stable labor-management relations, and improved productivity demand that attention be given to the living conditions of miners and their families.

Existing private and governmental institutions and resources can address many social problems over time, but the failure of traditional means of providing housing for miners stands as the central problem that must be resolved.

Recommendations:

1. That coal companies and other large landholders operating in areas lacking sufficient, adequate housing for miners make available at fair market value parcels of suitable land to be used for construction of new housing.

2. That coal companies retain sufficient amounts of necessary local working capital in regional lending institutions committed to using these funds to support a much expanded home construction and mortgage lending base in the area.

3. That the appropriate regional commissions or other governmental subdivisions, in cooperation with miners and operators, identify and secure public sector funding and other available resources required to spur coalfield housing and meet necessary utility, road, and site preparation requirements; and that serious consideration be given to selective use of the powers of eminent domain to acquire lands otherwise unavailable for housing development.

Findings:

1. Miners' living conditions have improved significantly over the past generation. Increased wages, higher educational levels, improved health care, the demise of company towns and stores, and an end to extreme isolation of coal mining areas place the coal-mining family more closely in line with mainstream America.

2. Expanded coal production will, however, bring a new set of problems or exacerbate old ones in the rural and semi-rural areas of central Appalachia and the West.

   - In Appalachia, which contains 80 percent of the coal-mining labor force, lack of available and suitable land, an inadequate construction industry, insufficient mortgage-lending capacity, difficult terrain, and contradictory Federal programs have combined to create a substantial housing shortage.

   - In the West, the "boomtown" phenomenon caused by rapid population growth will strain the resources of small communities to provide basic public services. Inflation caused by intense demand for limited housing will put decent housing out of reach for many mining families.

   - Roads in many coal-producing communities are heavily used for the truck transportation of coal. Often these roads are not built to the standards necessary for coal haulage, and the traffic flow of trucks and personal vehicles creates dangerous conditions.

CONCLUSION

Throughout its term, the Commission has been keenly aware of the linkage between national security, the condition of the economy, and the Nation's dependence on imported oil. The security of the United States and the ability to control inflation will remain compromised as long as the dangerous dependence on foreign oil continues. This is the sober reality on which the Commission's recommendation for strong governmental action to increase utility and industrial coal use is based.

The Commission recognizes, as well, that acceptance of increased coal use is linked with concern over the environment, the safety of miners, stability in labor-management relations, and living conditions of miners and their families. The Commission's recommendations in these areas are interdependent. The validity of some depends on responsiveness to others. The central proposal for large-scale expansion of coal use and the expenditure of billions of dollars of public funds requires a high degree of public and private responsibility and cooperation to assure that the highest practicable environmental protection standards will be implemented, that effective mining safety measures will be taken, that stable labor-management relations will be established in the coal industry, and that adequate housing and living conditions for miners and their families will be provided.

There are two areas of special concern. With respect to increased coal use and protection of the environment, the differences that now exist must give way to accommodation. In labor-management relations, the distrust within and between the two sides must be put behind them. The Commission considers it essential that a process or forum be established for continued constructive accommodation of these potentially, though needlessly, competing interests.

The Commission, therefore, strongly urges establishment, through the Office of the President, after consultation with representatives of all interests involved, of a White House Coal Advisory Council. The Council should consist of representatives of labor, management, and the public, to assist in and to assure implementation of the recommendations contained in this report.

The Council will provide an opportunity for management, labor, and the public to work cooperatively with government officials on matters of mutual concern that affect the ability of the Nation to strengthen its security and its economy by relying on domestic coal for a greater share of the Nation's energy requirements. Toward this end, the Council will permit a continued effort to reconcile constructively whatever differences develop, either between various private interests or between private and public interests, respecting at the same time, so far as labor-management relations are concerned, the necessity of maintaining the values of private collective bargaining. It will involve the participation and therefore enlist the responsibility of those upon whose efforts and actions the effectiveness of the proposed coal-use expansion policy and programs depends. It will permit continuing advice to the parties, and to the President and the Congress and the public, regarding progress -- or lack of it -- toward the interrelated goals identified in the Commission's report.

COAL-CAPABLE UTILITY PLANTS BURNING OIL OR GAS

AS OF JANUARY 1980

State	Utility	Plant	Unit
Arkansas	Arkansas Power & Light	Ritchie	1 2
		Moses	1 2
Colorado	Central Telephone & Utility	Pueblo	4 5 6
	Public Service of Colorado	Zuni	1 2
		Alamosa	4 5 6
		Valmont	1 2 3 4
Connecticut	Connecticut Light & Power	Devon	1 3 4 5 6 7 8
		Montville	1 2 3 4 5
		Norwalk Harbor	1 2
	Hartford Electric	Middletown	1 2 3
	United Illuminating	Bridgeport Harbor	1 2 3
		English	7 8
		Steel Pt.	9 11
Delaware	Delmarva Power & Light	Edgemoor	1 2 3 4
	Dover Electric Co.	McKee Run	1 2
District of Columbia	Potomac Electric Power	Benning	10 11 12 13 14
		Buzzard Pt.	2 3 4 5 6
Florida	Tampa Electric Power	Gannon	1 2 3 4
Georgia	Georgia Power Co.	McManus	1 2
	Savannah Electric Power	Effingham	1

State	Utility	Plant	Unit
Illinois	Central Illinois Public Service	Hutsonville	1 2
	Commonwealth Edison	Collins	4 5
		Ridgeland	1 2 3 4
	Illinois Power Co.	Wood River	1 2 3
		Havana	1 2 3 4 5
	Iowa Illinois Gas & Electric	Moline	5 6 7
	Union Electric	Venice #2	1 2 3 4 5 6
	University of Illinois	Abbott	1 2 3 4 5 6 7
Indiana	Indianapolis Light & Power	Stout	3 4
		Pritchard	1 2
Kansas	Kansas City Bd. of Public Utilities	Quindaro 3	7 8 9
	Kansas Power & Light	Lawrence	2 3
		Techumseh	3 4
Maine	Central Maine Power	Mason	1 2 3 4 5
Maryland	Baltimore Gas & Electric	Gould St.	3
		Riverside	1 2 3 4 5
		Brandon Shores	1 2
		Westport	1 3 4
		Crane	1 2
		Wagner	1 2
	Delmarva Power & Light	Vienna	5 6 7

State	Utility	Plant	Unit
Massachusetts	Boston Edison	Mystic	4 5 6
		New Boston	1 2
	Cambridge Electric	Kendall Square	1 2 3
	Canal Electric	Canal	1
	Holyoke Water Power	Mt. Tom	1
	Montaupt Electric	Somerset	5 6
	New Bedford G & E	Cannon Street	1 2
	New England Electric	Brayton Point	3
		Salem Harbor	1 2 3
	West Massachusetts Electric	West Springfield	1 2 3
Michigan	Consumers Power Co.	Weadock	4 5 6
		Karn	3 4
		Morrow	1 2 3 4
	Detroit Edison	Delray	11 12 13 14 15 16
		St. Clair	5
		River Rouge	1
		Conners Creek	8 9 10 12 13 14
	Wyandotte Dept. of Municipal Service	Wyandotte	4
Minnesota	Austin Utilities	Austin	1 2 3 4 5
	Interstate Power	Fox Lake	1 2 3
Missouri	Union Electric	Ashley	1 7 8 9
	St. Joseph Power & Light	Edmond St.	4 5 7
		Lake Rd.	3

State	Utility	Plant	Unit
Nebraska	City of Lincoln	K. Street	2 3
	Omaha Public Power Dist.	Jones Street	11 12
New Hampshire	Public Service of New Hampshire	Schiller	3 4 5 6
New Jersey	Deepwater Operating Co.	Deepwater	1 3 4 5 6 7
	Public Service Electric & Gas	Bergen	1 2
		Burlington	6 7
		Hudson	1
		Kearney	7 8
		Sewaren	1 2 3 4
	Jersey Central Power	Werner	4
		Sayreville	1 2 3 4 5
		Gilbert	1 2 3
	Vineland Electric	Down	4 5 6 7 8 9
New York	Central Hudson Gas & Electric	Danskammer	1 2 3 4
	Consolidated Edison	Waterside	4 5 6 7 8 9 14 15
		East River	5 6 7
		59th Street	13 14 15
		74th Street	3 9 10 11
		Hudson Avenue	5 6 7 8 10
		Arthur Kill	2 3
		Astoria	1 2 3 4 5
		Ravenswood	1 2 3
	Long Island Lighting Company	Barrett	1 2
		Far Rockaway	4
		Glenwood	4 5
		Northport	1 2 3 4
		Port Jefferson	1 2 3 4

State	Utility	Plant	Unit
	Niagara Mohawk Power	Albany	1 2 3 4
		Oswego	1 2 3 4
	Orange & Rockland Utilities	Lovett	1 2 3 4 5
Ohio	Dayton Power & Light	Tait	1 2 3 7 8
Oklahoma	Oklahoma Gas & Electric	Mustang	1 2 3 4
		Muskogee	3
		Osage	1 2
		Horseshoe Lake	4 6
	Grand River Dam Authority	Chouteau	1 2 3 4 5 6
Pennsylvania	Philadelphia Electric	Cromby	2
		Delaware	7 8
		Chester	5 6
		Richmond	9 12
		Schuykill	1 3 9
		Southwark	1 2
	West Penn Power	Springdale	7 8
Rhode Island	Narragansett Electric	Manchester	9 10 11
		South Street	12 1HP 1LP
Virginia	Virginia Electric Power Co.	Chesterfield	1 2 3 4
		Portsmouth	1 2 3
		Possum Point	1 2 3 4
		Yorktown	1 2
	APS, Potomac Edison	Riverton	1

DISABLING INJURY INCIDENCE RATES OF THE TWENTY LARGEST UNDERGROUND COAL COMPANIES JANUARY, 1978 - JUNE, 1979

Company	Incidence Rate 1/	1978 Underground Production	Ranking by Production	Number of Under-ground Mines
1. United States Steel Corporation	3.02	10,379,000	4th	28
2. Mapco, Inc.	4.91	2,882,431	17th	7
3. Island Creek Coal Company	5.44	13,589,589	3rd	47
4. Old Ben Coal Company	5.96	3,825,734	14th	5
5. Bethlehem Steel Corporation	5.96	8,201,342	6th	31
6. Alabama By-Products Corporation	6.17	2,914,601	16th	6
7. Consolidation Coal Company	6.92	25,729,000	1st	57
8. Freeman United Coal Mining Company	8.14	4,111,399	13th	5
9. Pittston Company	8.21	8,935,030	5th	72
10. Peabody Coal Company	9.17	15,849,912	2nd	26
ALL UNDERGROUND COAL MINES	10.04	243,500,000	--	2,494
11. Valley Camp Coal Company	11.72	2,695,700	18th	13
12. Rochester & Pittsburgh Coal Company	11.77	4,163,858	12th	11
13. American Electric Power	12.35	4,735,777	10th	24
14. Republic Steel Corporation	13.43	2,566,534	19th	6
15. North American Coal Company	13.60	6,552,355	7th	15
16. American Coal Company	13.81	2,544,789	20th	5
17. Jones & Laughlin Steel Corporation	14.49	3,639,637	15th	12
18. Zeigler Coal Company	16.38	4,324,971	11th	6
19. Eastern Associated Coal Corporation	17.63	5,716,776	9th	26
20. Westmoreland Coal Company	21.01	6,041,052	8th	29

1/ Lost workday cases per 200,000 work hours.

Sources: Keystone Coal Industry Manual and the United States Department of Labor, Mine Safety and Health Administration.

☆ U.S. GOVERNMENT PRINTING OFFICE : 1980 O—315-330

The President's Commission on Coal

John D. Rockefeller IV
Governor of West Virginia
Chairman

Jesse F. Core
Adjunct Professor of Mining Engineering
Pennsylvania State University
University Park, Pennsylvania

Marvin Friedman
Vice President
Ruttenberg, Friedman, Kilgallon, Gutchess and Associates, Inc.
Washington, D.C.

W. Dewey Presley
Director and Chairman of the Executive Committee
First International Bancshares
Dallas, Texas

Willard Wirtz
Wirtz and Lapointe
Washington, D.C.

Ex Officio

Walter D. Huddleston
United States Senator from Kentucky

Charles H. Percy
United States Senator from Illinois

Jennings Randolph
United States Senator from West Virginia

Charles W. Duncan Jr.*
United States Secretary of Energy

John Buchanan
United States Representative from Alabama

Austin J. Murphy
United States Representative from Pennsylvania

Carl D. Perkins
United States Representative from Kentucky

Ray Marshall
United States Secretary of Labor

Staff

Michael S. Koleda
Executive Director

James M. Childress
Nancy Creason
Elizabeth S. Fitzsimmons
William P. Hobgood**
L. Erick Kanter
Nada Samuels
J. Allen Wampler
Melissa A. Wolford
Bette Zabell

*Succeeded James R. Schlesinger on August 24, 1979.
**Advisor on labor-management relations.

Chapter Three

EQUIPMENT LEASING

Leasing, as a method of financing capital assets for industry, has grown tremendously in recent years. Capital assets frequently financed by leasing include computers, airplanes, railroad rolling stock, ships, pollution control equipment and industrial machinery. Tax shelter in equipment leasing results from accelerated depreciation (200% declining balance on new equipment, 150% declining balance on used equipment) coupled with interest deductions from borrowings.

Leasing of equipment came into existence in the late 1940's and by the mid-1960's was in full bloom. The rebirth of the Investment Tax Credit in 1971 gave further stimulus to equipment leasing so that today there are a number of leasing companies in existence as well as many banks that have entered the marketplace as lessors.

In most equipment leasing limited partnerships, the sponsor is a company that specializes in financing equipment lease transactions–ranging from large, national lessors to small, local equipment brokers that own little, if any, equipment.

Sponsors usually invest very little cash in their programs. They contribute their expertise in locating and arranging equipment lease transactions and maintaining an ongoing relationship with the lessees. Their compensation is derived from a combination of initial fees, continuing management fees, and a share of the residual value of the equipment (value after the expiration of the original lease).

Most equipment leasing programs invest in a number of leases with several lessees. The partnership purchases the equipment and then "net leases" it under a "hell or highwater" lease which obligates the lessee to pay the rent, maintenance and other costs related to the equipment in all instances.

The required investment in an equipment lease program is usually a percentage (10% to 25%) of the cost of the equipment. The balance of the purchase price is provided by lending institutions. Prior to the Tax Reform Act of 1976, these borrowings were without recourse to the partnership or to any partner. However, under the new rules it may be necessary for investors to assume personal liability for a portion of the borrowing. Therefore, it is important that the lessee have a top credit rating and be unconditionally obligated to pay the rent with respect to equipment.

Equipment leasing tax objectives are summarized in one word: "deferral." Deferral is a means of postponing a tax liability until a later–more convenient–time. Here's how the deferral works: In years when your tax liability is high, you invest in an equipment leasing program. You deduct a large amount of depreciation in the first year along with miscellaneous front-end expenses and interest on the borrowings. After the first few years the lease will begin generating taxable income, because depreciation and interest will be less, although there may not be any cash income to the investor because of debt service payments due on the borrowings. However, you should note that by the time this happens, the investor has had the use of the considerable tax savings for a significant period of time.

Equipment leases usually run from 5 to 10 years. When the lease comes to an end, the partnership will own the equipment, typically free of all debts. Depending on the value of the equipment at the end of the lease, profit could be generated, all or virtually all of which will be "recaptured" and taxed as ordinary income.

The major risk is that the lessee of the equipment will default, so a good equipment leasing program will contain leases involving major corporations with superior credit ratings.

Equipment leasing is involved in many vital industries. This involvement for a particular partnership is detailed as follows:

1. *Transportation Equipment.*

(a) *Railroad Rolling Stock.* Railroad rolling stock includes boxcars, tank cars, hoppers cars, flatcars, locomotives and various other equipment used by railroads in the maintenance of their railroad track. Boxcars and flatcars can come in a variety of designs, some of which are general purpose and some of which are special purpose. Special purpose boxcars and flatcars are used for the shipment of specific products whereas a general purpose can be used for the shipment of a wide variety of products. Boxcars may be refrigerated for the shipment of perishable goods. Boxcars generally are furnished by the railroad for the shipment of goods, through a manufacturer, in order to assure that cars will be available when needed, although the shipper may furnish its own. Tank cars are used for the shipment of liquids over long distances and hopper cars are used for the shipment of various commodities, including coal and grains, from its point of origin to the user. Many electric utilities lease hopper cars for the shipment of coal from the mine to the generating plant. When a number of such hopper cars are put together in a single train and dedicated to a particular service, the train is called a "unit train" and will make round trips between the mine and the generating plant. Railcars are manufactured by companies such as AMF, Pullman, Union Tank Car, General American Transportation and a variety of other companies. Locomotives are the power unit to pull railcars and come in a variety of designs depending on the geographic terrain they are to be used on, the length of the train to be pulled and the distance over which the train is to be pulled. Locomotives vary in size by the amount of horsepower which they can produce. Locomotives are manufactured in the United States by either General Motors or General Electric.

(b) *Tractors, Trailers and Heavy Duty Trucks.* Tractors, trailers and trucks are used for the shipment of various products and goods from one location to another. Tractor-trailer rigs are often used for longer shipments and delivery of larger pieces; whereas heavy-duty trucks are generally used for the more local delivery of large products. A "tractor" refers to the power unit of a tractor-trailer combination. The tractor cab is generally manufactured by one company and the engine and drive train by another. Common manufacturers of the cab of a tractor include Ford, White, Peterbuilt, GMC and Kenworth. Engines may be manufactured by the same company as the cab, such as Ford and GMC, or by another source such as Cummins or Caterpillar. The engine may use gasoline or diesel fuel. A variety of configurations of tractors are available, including one design in which the driver has a berth behind the steering compartment where an alternative driver may sleep. Trailers are the container portion of a tractor-trailer rig and come in a variety of sizes and designs depending on the product to be shipped. Trailers may be up to 45 feet long in most states and most commonly have a set of twin axles (eight wheels) to carry the load. A trailer may be enclosed on a flat bed for the shipment of large or oversized products, and may be refrigerated for the shipment of perishable products. Trailers are manufactured by a number of companies including, Freuhauf, Gindy, Trailmobile, and Strick. The Partnership intends to invest in trailers that can be used for the shipment of a wide variety of goods and are not limited to specific applications. Heavy-duty trucks are large trucks in which the engine and load carrying part are mounted on a single frame. These trucks can be used for the local delivery of large products or for the hauling of construction materials. Heavy-duty trucks are manufactured by GMC, Ford and various other manufacturers.

(c) *Aircraft.* Aircraft includes a wide variety of airplanes from small single-engine aircraft to airline-type jets. The Partnership may invest in commercial and corporate aircraft, although it presently intends to invest principally in corporate aircraft which range in cost from a minimum of approximately $250,000 to a maximum of $9,000,000. Corporate aircraft are used by many corporations to move employees from city to city more quickly than could be done using normal commercial aviation. Corporate aircraft are also used for locations that do not have scheduled air service and for the delivery of components and products, needed on a rush basis, at various manufacturing and service facilities. Corporate aircraft are manufactured by Beech, Cessna, Lockheed, Piper, North American Rockwell, Gates Learjet, as well as a number of foreign manufacturers who export their aircraft into the United States. All corporate aircraft are registered with the FAA.

(d) *Intermodel Containers and Chassis.* They include general dry cargo containers and special purpose containers such as refrigerator containers, tank containers, half-height containers and open-top containers. The containers acquired by the Partnership will probably be 20 foot or 40 foot containers made of steel or aluminum.

(e) *Barges.* Barges include tank barges and hopper barges. Tank barges transport primarily liquid commodities, whereas hopper barges are used to transport most solid commodities.

(f) *Material Handling Equipment.* Material handling equipment includes many varieties of fork lift trucks. They can either be battery-powered or gas-powered, and are often used in warehouses and factories for the movement of products from one work station to another, or from a warehouse to a truck for shipment, or for the storing of products. The equipment comes in a variety of styles depending on the design of the product to be moved and the design of the shipping and warehouse facility. The majority of this type of equipment is standard and can be used by a variety of industries.

2. *Office Equipment.* The Partnership may also acquire and lease the following types of Office Equipment.

(a) *Photocopying Equipment.* The Partnership intends to acquire and lease photocopying equipment which will most probably be manufactured by IBN, Kodak or Xerox. The Partnership may also acquire data processing equipment.

(b) *Computer Equipment.* The Partnership intends to acquire and lease computer equipment, which may include the following types:

(i) *Computer Peripheral Equipment.* Computer peripheral equipment consists of numerous devices which are used in connection with a computer system's central processing unit (the so-called "brain" of a computer system). Some such devices are tape drives, disc drives, tape controllers, disc controllers, printers, card readers, card punches, and their related control units, all of which, in some way, are related to the processing, storing, and retrieving of information by the computer.

(ii) *Computer Terminal Systems.* Generally, terminals are devices which produce and display information which the user of a computer desires. In some cases terminals are located great distances from the computer itself and may be linked to the central processing unit by telephone lines, radio signals, and other electronic methods. Terminals may be classified by the nature of their output (hard copy or display, alphanumeric or graphic information) or according to their interactive capability, i.e., their ability to send as well as to receive information. Terminals may also be classified according to their level of intelligence (their ability to perform complex functions). Some terminals have the capability of transmitting and receiving large volumes of information over a short period of time; some such terminals are often referred to as "batch" terminals in that batchers of information are typically transmitted and received by such devices. Other types of terminals include character type terminals which transmit or receive information character by character.

(iii) *Small Computer Systems.* A small computer system will typically consist of a central processing unit, disc and/or tape drives, card and/or paper tape readers and punches, printers and interactive typewriters or video display type terminals. Small computer systems will oftentimes also possess data communications capabilities of a limited nature. A computer system of this type is generally used by businesses in their accounting, inventory control, and sales management operations.

(c) *Graphic Processing Equipment.* Graphic processing equipment includes print setters, printing presses, automatic drafting machines and all equipment which is used for the visual display of designs, drawing and printed matter. Printing presses come in a wide variety of sizes depending upon the application in which they are used. Some printing presses are of a single color, whereas others can apply up to eight colors in a single pass of the paper through the press. Photo typesetters are used for the setting of type for publications such as newspapers and magazines. Computerized type setters have become very common in recent years and simplify the type setting job and allow for simple correction of mistakes and simplified lay-out of printed pages. Automatic drafting machines enable designers to make changes in engineering drawings without the time required to make a completely new drawing by hand. Automatic drafting machines are computer controlled visual displays of drawings.

3. *Miscellaneous Equipment*

(a) *Machine Tools.* These include a wide variety of metalworking machinery, including lathes, drilling presses, turning mills, grinders, metal bending equipment, metal slitting equipment, and other metal forming equipment used in the production of a wide variety of machinery and equipment. Some form of machine tool is used in virtually every production process of a metal product or component. While some machine tools and metalworking equipment are built for a particular end product, the majority of machine tools can be used in a wide variety of industries.

(b) *Miscellaneous.* These include, among others, store fixtures, display cases, and freezers.

Another partnership was designed to purchase and lease the following equipment:

(1) Office equipment, including typewriters, dictating machines, specialized telephone systems, photocopiers, office furniture and word processing equipment.

(2) Retail and wholesale merchandising equipment, including such retail store equipment as electronic cash registers, credit and check verification systems, electronic pricing systems and weight scales, as well as store fixtures, store display equipment and point-of-sale data processing terminals.

(3) Medical and dental equipment, including diagnostic equipment, X-ray equipment and related film processing equipment, emergency medical equipment, specialized treatment equipment and office and billing equipment for medical and dental offices.

Some of the industries and partnerships involved in equipment leasing are of special interest.

THE MARINE CONTAINER INDUSTRY

General

A marine container is a large reusable box designed for the efficient carriage of cargo with a minimum of exposure to loss through damage or theft. The introduction of containerization has made it possible to transport goods from origin to final destination without the repetitious handling required by the traditional "break-bulk" method of shipment. After goods are loaded at the origin, the container is sealed until unloaded at final destination. Moreover, containers are designed to be compatible with equipment used in the shipment of goods by rail, sea, or highway. (Shipment by container is often referred to as "intermodal" transportation.) The advantages of containerization are:

1. *Reduction of handling costs.* Since goods are typically transported by a combination of modes between origin and final destination, substantial savings in the labor costs of handling are realized each time there is a transfer from one mode to another.

2. *Reduction of theft and damage.* Pilferage of and damage to break-bulk cargo during the loading and unloading process have been serious problems in the transportation industry. Containerization eliminates direct access to goods in transit, and therefore has minimized the exposure of goods to both theft and damage. The cost of insurance to cover these risks has presumably been reduced as well.

3. *Reduction of transit times.* The time required to transfer a container from one mode of transport to another is a fraction of the time required to unload and reload break-bulk goods. The reduction of transit times promotes the growth of international trade and enhances the competitive advantages of surface transportation. But, more importantly, it means better utilization of the large investment in transportation equipment, particularly ocean-going vessels, by the industry. The amount of port time of vessels has a significant impact on a shipping company's profits.

Most containers have wooden floors and are otherwise constructed of steel, although fiberglass-reinforced plywood ("FRP") and aluminum are also in common usage. The key standard applicable to containers is their size. Today most containers are constructed in 20 or 40 foot lengths, are 8 feet wide, and are 8½ feet high. For purposes of data collection and statistics, the industry standard of 20-foot equivalent units or "TEU's" is often cited, where a 40-foot container is equivalent to two

20-foot containers. Standardization of the construction characteristics of marine containers has been developed through the efforts of several national and international organizations, primarily the International Organization for Standardization (the "ISO"), a body composed of national standards associations from some 55 countries, located in Geneva, Switzerland.

While there are several types of containers in use, they primarily fall into two general categories. The first is the general dry cargo container, which is by far the most prevalent container in use today. The second category is the special purpose container, designed to carry particular types of cargo. Examples of this latter category are refrigerated containers, tank containers, half-height containers, and open-top containers. The Containers to be acquired by the Fund are new, ISO general dry cargo containers. IEA anticipates that the majority of these will be 20-foot Containers constructed of steel. The Fund may also purchase aluminum and FRP Containers if attractive term leases are committed to by lessees prior to purchase of these more expensive Containers by the Fund.

The Container Market

At the end of 1980, there were an estimated 3 million TEU's in the worldwide fleet, compared to approximately 270 thousand in 1969, representing a compounded annual rate of growth of 24%. Through the end of 1980 over $20 billion had been invested in containers and related handling equipment, of which over $10 billion had been invested since 1974. The rapid growth of containerization began with the standardization of equipment sizes by international agreement in the early 1960's. Initially confined to the highly competitive trade routes among the industrialized nations, containerization expanded into substantially all free-world trade routes by the early 1970s.

With the growth in containerization has come the introduction of the containership, which has rapidly increased the container carrying capacity of the world's vessels. This capacity can be measured in terms of "cells," where a cell represents the space for one TEU on a vessel. The table on the following page shows the growth in cells and the container fleet since 1969.

GROWTH IN CONTAINERIZATION*

	1969	1971	1973	1975	1977	1979	1980
World Cell Capacity of Vessels (1000 TEU's)	94	160	430	600	720	1072	1244
World Container Fleet (1000 TEU's)	270	480	1092	1279	1736	2650	3000
Number of Containers per available cell	2.9	3.0	2.5	2.1	2.4	2.5	2.4

*The figures presented are estimates taken from industry magazines and research reports.

In concept three containers are needed to support each vessel cell, so that at any given time, one container is positioned at the origin, a second container at the destination, and a third container is in transit on the vessel. The above table suggests that this relationship existed during the early 1970s. Then the container-to-cell ratio declined as the industry entered a period of extremely rapid growth in vessel cell capacity. Since 1975 the ratio has again been increasing.

Sources of Supply of Containers

Marine containers are manufactured throughout the world, primarily in the industrialized nations of the free world, but also to a lesser extent in the developing nations and in Eastern Europe. Over time, Japan has been the leading producer, primarily because of the country's high net outbound flow of containers in world trade. Other major producers have been the United States, the United Kingdom, Italy, and France. Because of rising demand for containerized exports and the availability of relatively inexpensive labor, recent growth in production has been significant in Korea, Taiwan, Hong Kong, and most recently, China.

The Fund intends to purchase Containers wherever the factors of quality, price and lease demand are favorable, but expects that initial purchases will be made from among the countries of Korea, Japan, and Taiwan.

Future Growth

IEA anticipates that a number of factors will contribute to the continued growth of the container market. Among these factors are the following:

1. *Growth in inland container movements.* The "port-to-port" movement of containers is rapidly giving way to "door-to-door" and "landbridge" movements which require the transport of containers beyond port areas. This, in turn, increases in transit times and the number of containers required to support a vessel cell.

2. *Expansion of world trade.* Basic foreign trade volumes are expected to expand as industrialized countries seek exports in order to earn the hard currency required to pay for their energy requirements. The World Bank, in its "World Development Report, 1980," projects the growth of world trade at 5.2% per year between 1980 and 1985, and 5.7% per year between 1985 and 1990. In addition, as world trade expands, containerization is likely to expand to new trade routes, particularly to the developing nations and the few industrialized nations which have not yet participated in containerization.

3. *Economies of containerization.* The economies of containerization are expected to further stimulate the movement of cargoes which would not otherwise move in international trade, or which presently move in international trade but not in containers. For example, containerization has facilitated the movement of hundreds of tons of waste paper annually from the United States to the Far East.

4. *Demand for new production.* The demand for new production of containers is expected to be further favorably influenced by the need to begin replacement of containers approaching the end of their economic useful lives.

5. *Conversion to container vessels and container port facilities.* At the end of 1977, the gross tonnage of container vessels comprised only 10% of the gross tonnage of all general cargo vessels. As the older vessels are scrapped, the world fleet is likely to become more containerized. In addition, lack of port

facilities for handling containers, particularly in the developing nations, has constrained the growth in containerization of cargo moving to and from those locations. As port facilities are converted to manage container vessels, there will be further capacity to handle containerized cargo.

There can, of course, be no assurance that the foregoing factors will materialize and thus stimulate the growth of the container market. In particular, the future expansion of world trade is subject to a number of risk factors, including the instability of foreign governments, the continued absence of major wars, and the possibility of restrictions imposed on foreign trade by governments concerned with their balance of payments and currency values.

Container Leasing

Container leasing originated during the 1960s as the shipping industry was testing the new technology of containerization. At that time, ocean carriers were not yet prepared to commit to purchasing containers or were unable to supply all of their needs during the period of rapid transition to containerization. Container leasing companies still serve the primary function of providing containers to supplement carriers' own fleets. However, the role of container leasing companies has broadened substantially over time. The types of leases available today are an indication of this development.

The four basic types of leasing programs are as follows:

1. *Short-term leases: one-way or round-trip leases.* A one-way or "trip" lease is designed to assist carriers to deal with trade imbalances (more containerized cargo moving in one direction than another) through one-way rental programs that allow a carrier to pick up a container in one port and drop it off in another after one leg of a voyage. In addition to saving the carrier the cost of owning the containers that would not be fully utilized, this short-term, per-diem leasing program enables carriers to avoid the operating costs associated with back-hauling empty containers. Short-term or round-trip leases permit carriers to meet peak or seasonal requirements, thus allowing them to supply temporary needs without having to make a substantial investment in containers that sit idle for the remainder of the

year. Lease rates are highest in this category of leases, and often include a drop-off charge for the privilege of returning the equipment to a location other than the points of origin.

2. *Term Leases.* Under the term lease the carrier leases a specified number of containers for a period of time ranging from one to five years. Term leases are attractive to ocean carriers who are expanding their fleets or who are initiating new services. They may also be used by carriers to provide equipment in untested markets. These leases usually contain an escape clause allowing the lessee to redeliver equipment prior to expiration of the lease, providing that a termination payment is made.

In addition, the large investment made by ocean carriers in vessels has often created financial structures heavily burdened with debt. As a consequence, many ocean carriers simply do not have the funds to acquire the level of containers their operations require. Term leases also can fulfill this market need, permitting leasing companies using these types of leases to maintain relatively high lease rates.

3. *Operating Service or Master Leases.* The operating service or master lease is a sophisticated extension of the trip lease and is designed to provide a greater degree of flexibility to the carriers. The aim of these programs is to meet the customer's overall leasing requirements by making containers available where and when needed. These lease programs vary widely since they typically are tailored to the carrier's specific needs. The lessee may be required to maintain a minimum quantity of containers on lease in return for a guaranteed supply of containers and redelivery privileges to accommodate the carrier's trade imbalances. Other master leases consist only of a pricing plan covering all trip leases of a lessee. The growing use of operating service or master leases reflects the trend among container leasing companies to assume increased responsibility for controlling and repositioning carriers' containers on a worldwide basis. However, as a consequence of this service, the leasing companies that concentrate on this market must maintain large worldwide organizations to properly service their lessees, thus giving rise to high operating and maintenance costs.

The primary types of leases to be utilized by the Fund will be short-term and term leases, as well as operating service or master leases if such leases are available on attractive terms to the Fund.

4. *Financial Leverage Leases.* The financial leverage lease is essentially an alternative form of financing containers. It is most often offered to carriers that use containers to and from the United States but who are unable to utilize certain tax benefits of ownership under the United States tax laws. These leases vary in term from 8 to 10 years and provide the carrier with a low effective implicit rate of interest. The Fund will not engage in any such leasing of its Containers.

The growth rate of container leasing companies has greatly exceeded the growth rate of containerization. The following table illustrates the growth since 1969.

GROWTH IN LEASING COMPANY FLEET OF CONTAINERS*

	1969	1971	1973	1975	1977	1979	1980
Total Fleet (1000 TEU's)	270	480	1092	1279	1736	2650	3000
Leasing Company Fleet (1000 TEU's)	50	125	368	537	792	1415	1700
Leasing Company Share	19%	26%	34%	42%	46%	53%	56%

*The figures presented are estimates taken from "Containerization International" and other industry magazines and research reports.

FREIGHT TRANSPORTATION ON THE INLAND WATERWAYS

General

Most freight moving on the more than 25,000 miles of United States inland waterways is carried in unmanned, nonself-propelled river barges concentrated in groups or strings propelled by towing vessels. Such groups or strings of barges, whether pushed by a towboat or pulled by a tugboat, are commonly referred to as a "tow." Increasing economic demand for water transportation service over the last three decades has stimulated improvement in domestic water channels as well as improvements in equipment and the technology of operations. River barge service offers the lowest cost mode of transportation for certain commodities whose source and destination of movement are contiguous to navigable routes. River barge service is also the most energy efficient mode of transportation.

Virtually any commodity can be shipped by water. The inland waterways industry has developed a variety of types and sizes of barges for the handling of products ranging from coal in open hopper barges to chemicals in insulated barges, and from dredge rock in dump scows to railroad cars on car floats.

Tank barges and hopper barges are the two principal types of barges in use in the U.S. domestic waterways. While tank barges transport primarily liquid commodities, such as oil and liquid chemicals, hopper barges are used to transport most solid commodities in bulk or package. Typical cargo for carriage by dry cargo barges might include any of the following: grain and grain by-products, coffee, soy beans, paper and paper products, dry chemicals, bauxite, aluminum and aluminum products, machinery and parts, rubber and rubber products, soda ash, sugar, containers and, in some cases, packaged goods. The two types of hopper barges (open and covered) comprise the most versatile and most numerous of all river barges in the U.S. inland fleet.

By providing transportation for bulk-loading commodities that need protection from the elements, the covered dry cargo barge serves a wide variety of shippers in domestic inland waters, Such barges differ from the open hopper variety in that they are equipped with raintight covers over the entire cargo hold. Hopper barges are also designated by hull configuration as a "rake" or "box" barge. A properly formed tow requires that the front and back row of barges be rakes to efficiently move through the water, although rakes may be used in any position in a tow. The Barges, which will be owned by the Partnership, are jumbo covered hopper barges with a rake hull configuration.

Description of Inland Waterways System

There are more than 25,000 miles of navigable inland waterway channels in the continental United States, exclusive of the

Great Lakes. With the exception of the New York State Barge Canal, all of these waterways are federal projects, and nearly 62% of the total usable riverways have a depth of nine feet or more. The Partnership's Barges will be operated at a nine-foot draft and, therefore will be able to transport freight on approximately 16,000 of the 25,000 navigable miles of domestic inland waterways. With the exception of the Upper Mississippi Waterway, the Missouri River and the New York State Barge Canal (each of which is closed by icing for an average of three or four months–December to March–each year), all of the inland channels are open to navigation twelve months of the year.

The fluctuations in climate, such as winter cold, spring flooding, summer heat and drought periods, produce wide variations in water depths of a natural river. A series of dams which create pools of water in an improved river to a large extent overcomes this problem and provides a stable channel for navigation.

Navigation locks are the means by which river traffic is passed from one level to another created by the dams. The size of lock chambers that pass vessels from one level of water to the other in canalized streams have tended to dictate standardization of the dimensions of vessels using the inland channels. Thus, lock chambers of adequate size to accommodate the type of tows that operate on a waterway are essential to the efficient movement of waterborne freight and also important to the economics of barge transportation.

Operations

In waterways, such as the Lower Mississippi River, where there are open stretches of water without dams and locks, larger towboats can handle tows comprising as many as 48 barges, greatly increasing the amount of freight that may be moved without significantly increased cost other than fuel. In the Missouri River the size of the two can vary between three to nine barges depending on the distance from the confluence of the Missouri Tiver with the Mississippi River. For example, between Omaha and Sioux City, the tow is normally comprised of three barges, while between St. Louis and Kansas City, eight to nine barges are generally moved in a tow.

Generally, the type of water (e.g., combined effect of currents, tide, wind and surface conditions) determine which of the two methods of towing (push-towing or pull-towing) is used and therefore, the type of power unit, either towboat or tugboat. On most inland systems where the water routes are protected by surrounding land masses and where the waters are relatively calm, or where a system of locks and dams creates relative calmness, the towboat is used for push-towing operations. For push-towing, the barges are tied rigidly together with steel cables to form a single unit, and this unit is then lashed solidly against the boat's towing knees. The power unit working at the rear of the two can handle a greater number of barges with greater speed under more absolute control than can be handled in pull-towing operations. This is primarily due to the rigidity of the tow, use of Kort nozzles, distance between propellers and flanking rudders. The relatively flat-bottomed towboat with appropriate power to its propellers also has two sets of rudders which afford maximum control for forward and backing, and flanking movements such as are required to navigate the restricted river channels and canals.

Because the Missouri River is a free-flowing shallow draft type of river with no locks and dams, operation of it requires shallow draft towboats and a specialized type of operation. The General Partner believes that the Barges are suited for such service.

The Offshore Contract Drilling Industry

The offshore contract drilling industry provides offshore drilling equipment, and the management and personnel to operate the equipment, to oil and gas companies on a contract basis. The term of a contract may be for one well, multiple wells, or a fixed term ranging generally from six months to three years. Those companies providing the offshore drilling equipment and services generally have no economic interest in or risk from the results of the drilling or production programs.

The industry has grown rapidly since 1960 because of the potential for oil and gas discoveries offshore and the improved technology for offshore drilling and production. The Arab oil embargo in 1973 and the subsequent escalation in world oil prices increased oil and gas exploration activities both onshore and offshore. Oil and gas discoveries in the Gulf of Mexico and the North Sea have caused a considerable portion of this growth, although discoveries in many other regions have also contributed. Currently, there are increased pressures for many countries to explore for oil and gas on their continental shelves because of uncertainty regarding the availability and price of petroleum products from the Middle East and the increasing balance of payments deficits caused by high levels of imports of such products.

In the Gulf of Mexico offshore the United States, demand for offshore rigs has increased because of the significant past and projected future increases in oil and gas prices. In addition, significant blocks of leased offshore acreage in the Gulf of Mexico require defined amounts of drilling to prevent forfeiture of such leases.

As the offshore drilling industry has evolved, various types of drilling units have been developed to serve the requirements of drilling offshore. The type of equipment needed depends in part upon water depth, typical weather conditions and wave heights, strength of current, bottom conditions, and depth of drill hole required. Drilling units can generally be classed as exploratory, development, or workover rigs. Exploratory rigs are typically used to drill one or a small number of wells in each of a number of locations in order to determine whether hydrocarbons are present. Development rigs are generally used in conjunction with a fixed drilling platform put in place by an oil company to drill many wells in one are to exploit fully a field. Workover rigs are used to work in previously drilled wells to perforate new zones of oil or gas, perform various remedial services, or to set new or additional production tubing. The most commonly used offshore drilling rigs are described below.

Exploratory Rigs

Slot Type Jack-Up—A slot type jack-up is a self-elevating platform equipped with legs (and, in some cases a mat attached to the bottom of the legs) which can be lowered to the sealed and support the main section of the drilling platform. During drilling operations, the platform is elevated to a position above the surface of the water. Jack-up drilling units are generally subject to a maximum water depth of 300 feet. These units are used for both exploratory and limited development drilling. The size of the slot dictates to a great degree the maximum size of wellhead platform over which the rig can operate.

Cantilever Type Jack-Up—A cantilever type jack-up, such as the Rig, is essentially the same as a slot type jack-up, except the drilling machinery can be cantilevered out over the stern of the unit. In this configuration, the cantilever type jack-up may be utilized for exploratory drilling or development drilling over existing platforms. This type of rig is particularly useful over fixed platforms too light-weight or small to support drilling machinery loads and for complex well workover service.

Drillship and Drill Barge—These drilling units are ship-shaped and are equipped for drilling while floating on the water in calm weather areas. The units are positioned over the well either through the use of an anchoring system or by the use of computer-controlled thruster systems located in the vessel. Drillships and drill barges have operated in deeper water than other types of offshore units and usually work in deeper water than jack-up rigs.

Semi-Submersible Drilling Unit—These drilling units are floating drilling platforms which by means of a water ballasting system can be submerged to a pre-determined draft so that a substantial portion of the drilling unit (primarily the lower hulls) supporting the columns or other stabilizing devices is below the water surface during the drilling operations. These units are positioned over the well in a manner similar to drillships and are customarily used in exploratory drilling in rougher and deeper water (for example, the North Sea) than most other types of offshore units.

Submersible Drilling Unit—This unit is similar to a semi-submersible drilling unit, but the lower platform rests on the seabed during drilling operations. The maximum water depth limitation for a submersible drilling unit is approximately 175 feet of water, but most units are limited to water depths of significantly less than 100 feet.

Development Rigs

Tender/Platform—This type of rig is used for development drilling on a fixed platform. A floating hull (the tender) is used as crew quarters and holds supplies and machinery, while drilling equipment is placed on the platform itself. Use of a tender allows the platform to be smaller by eliminating the space required for crew quarters and certain types of supplies and machinery.

Self-Contained Platform—This type of rig is used for development drilling on fixed platforms large enough to accommodate all machinery, supplies, and crew quarters. Such rigs are advantageous in deep water, where a larger platform is required, and in rough water, where a floating tender would be impractical. Generally, production platforms are built by the oil companies owning the production and the platform rigs are provided by a contract drilling company.

A company engaged in onshore contract drilling describes its operation as follows:

CONTRACT DRILLING

The Company operates 29 rotary drilling rigs, three workover rigs and one inland drilling barge, which are employed in onshore contract drilling of oil and gas wells for various oil and gas producers. In addition to its rigs, the Company provides the crews and most of the ancillary equipment used in conjunction with the rigs. Of the Company's 33 rigs, 15 drilling rigs operate in South and South-Central Texas, four drilling rigs and three workover rigs operate in northwestern Peru, 10 drilling rigs operate in western Canada and the drilling barge operates in Louisiana inland waters. The Company's drilling activities in the United States and in Peru are conducted by wholly owned subsidiaries and its Canadian operations are conducted by a subsidiary owned 80% by the Company and 20% by key employees of the subsidiary. In addition, the Company has interests in drilling joint ventures in Brazil and Argentina.

The Company has contracts for construction of four additional onshore drilling rigs (two for use in Venezuela and two for use in Venezuela or Texas) and two barge rigs (for use in Texas and Louisiana).

Description of Rigs

Each of the drilling rigs consists of engines, drawworks, mast, pumps to circulate the drilling fluid, blowout preventers, the drillstring and related equipment. The engines power a rotary table that turns a bit consisting of rotating cones covered with sharp teeth, so that the hole is drilled by grinding the rock, which is then carried to the surface by the drilling fluid. The intended well depth and the drilling site conditions are the principal factors that determine the size and type of rig most suitable for a particular drilling job.

The Company's workover rigs are equipped with engines, drawworks, mast, pumps and blowout preventers (on a smaller scale than the drilling rigs). They are used to complete new wells after the hole has been drilled by a drilling rig, and to repair various downhole problems that occur in older producing wells.

The Company's drilling barge is used primarily in inland waters. The rig machinery, storage facilities and living quarters for the crew are built onto the barge. The barge is towered by tugs from one location to another. At location, the internal portion of the hull is flooded with water to sink the barge into working position. After the job is completed, the water inside the hull is pumped out to put the barge in a floating position for tow to another location.

Organizations have developed to service equipment leasing for shippers, corporate owner/users and investors. One such organization specializes in the transportation industry and describes its services as follows:

We deal in railroad cars, such as coal, tank, and covered hopper cars, and in river barges.

For shippers, we provide
- Railcars and barges for leasing and brokering
- Periodic railcar maintenance service
- Wreck repair service
- Railcar replacement insurance
- Railcar cleaning service

For corporate owner/users, we offer
- Full railcar fleet management
- Railcar maintenance and wreck repair service
- Maintenance-management insurance

For investors, we
- Negotiate the purchase of equipment
- Provide investment opportunities in transportation equipment
- Establish limited partnerships to purchase equipment

Pool revenue and expenses of individually owned equipment
Provide complete fleet management services
Manage equipment owned by limited partnerships
Negotiate leases
Collect monthly rental fees on behalf of investors

In all of the equipment leasing programs mentioned in this section, the investment tax credit is an important investor benefit and care should be exercised to qualify for it.

Noncorporate Lessors—Individuals and other noncorporate lessors (including Subchapter S corporations) may be precluded from using investment credit generated by a leasing transaction from offsetting their regular tax liability. The investment credit is not available to these lessors unless (i) the term of the initial lease, including options to renew or extend, is less than 50% of the useful life of the leased property, and (ii) for the first 12 months after the property is transferred to the first lessee, the sum of certain deductions with respect to the leased property exceeds 15% of the rental income produced by that property.

The term of a lease, in addition to including options to renew or extend, includes the aggregate terms of "successive leases." However, if a second lease of the same item of property is not interrelated or tied in some manner to the first lease, with the result that the second lease is subject to independent negotiation between the lessor and the lessee, the two leases do not constitute "successive leases" that will be treated as one lease for purposes of the investment credit.

To illustrate the advantages of equipment leasing, a jet aircraft program and a railroad car program are shown.

AEROSPACE

INDUSTRY STATUS AND FORECAST

World economic and political conditions are adversely affecting the aerospace industry. Of great concern is the deteriorating financial condition of the world's airlines. The slowing of passenger and freight traffic growth in 1980 pushed the 103 members of the International Air Transport Association (IATA) into "the bleakest year in international aviation history." For 1981, IATA projected scheduled passenger increases of only 3 percent to 10 percent, depending on the route, compared to an average annual increase of almost 9 percent in 1975-80.

The U.S. airline industry, with an operating deficit expected to exceed $850 million in 1980, may not be able to continue all its needed modernization programs. Wheat First Securities, industry analysts, has predicted that the 1981 deficit may exceed $400 million.

On the more optimistic side, major aircraft manufacturers generally agree that the worldwide jetliner market should be 5,000 transports valued at more than $100 billion (1979 dollars) in the next 15 years. Other forecasts of worldwide requirements for transports in 1978-90 range from more than 6,800 units predicted in May 1980 by Merrill Lynch Pierce Fenner & Smith and 6,450 units predicted in July 1980 by Oppenheimer & Company. The steady decline in air traffic should be reversed around 1982, according to Value Line, an investment advisory service.

In constant dollars, manufacturers of aircraft can expect a 9 percent decline in the value of shipments in 1981. Engine manufacturers can expect 7 percent real growth; aircraft equipment manufacturers, 4 percent real growth, and missile and space vehicle manufacturers, a 21 percent real growth.

The compound annual real rate of growth in the value of shipments by the entire aerospace industry in 1980-85 is forecast at .4 percent. During this period, the projected rates of change by sector are: a decline of 3 percent in aircraft shipments and expansions of 2 percent and 1 percent, respectively, in the aerospace engine industry and the aircraft equipment industry.

The guided missile and the space vehicle industries, treated together, are expected to achieve an 8 percent compound annual rate of growth in the 5-year period ending in 1985. Of the two, the missile industry holds the greater growth potential.

Aerospace Outlook Cloudy

World production of petroleum has risen approximately 13 percent since 1973. During the same period, proven petroleum reserves increased by only 2 percent. The free world and China have 89 percent of the proven world petroleum reserves, 31 years of product at current pumping rates. Russia and satellite countries have 11 percent of proven reserves, 16 years.

The aerospace industry's dependence on petroleum is enormous. Each day, more than 12.8 million gallons of fuel are consumed by more than 400 Boeing 747's, comprising only 7 percent of the world's airline transports. Most 747's can carry 44,000 gallons of fuel, fly an average of 10 hours a day, and consume 3,200 gallons an hour.

U.S. aviation of all types consume 10.7 percent of all transportation fuel used in the United States. U.S. airlines consume 69 percent of the aviation fuel and account for 7.3 percent of all petroleum used in the United States; the military, 23 percent; and general aviation, .8 percent.

Alternate energy for aviation, primarily synthesis fuel derived from oil shale, will not be available in sufficient quantities for 15 years.

Foreign shares of the world aerospace market will increase in the 1980's. Europe's A300 widebodied Airbus in June 1980 had an order backlog of 169 units compared to 51 units in June 1978. Boeing still led the widebodied backlog in June 1980 with 260 units. However, the Airbus backlog of 169 exceeds the combined total of McDonnell Douglas (29 DC-10's) and Lockheed (48 L-1011's). The Airbus aircraft, with considerable European government-subsidized support, will continue to expand its market share at the expense of the U.S. industry. In addition, Japan has targeted its aerospace industry for financial assistance, as it has done in the past with electronics and autos. Competition will increase not only from Europe and Japan but also from strengthened aircraft industries in Canada, Brazil, Israel, Indonesia, the Philippines, Australia, and Poland.

Reported values of U.S. aerospace shipments and exports mask a rapidly increasing foreign content. Large transports shipped during 1980–428 units valued at $11.1 billion–had an estimated 7.5 percent foreign content. In 1980 shipments of many smaller turboprop executive and commuter aircraft–800 units valued at $560 million–had an estimated 25 percent foreign content. Foreign content of U.S. aerospace shipments will soon show substantial increases as military and civil shared production programs reach higher levels. U.S. commitments to foreign buyers in negotiating sales of military products involve, on occasion, high "offset" values, some, reportedly, as high as 125 percent such as on the long range patrol aircraft sale to Canada.

In terms of both units and value, over 60 percent of the large transports manufactured in the United States during the past 7 years were for export. U.S. manufacturers have new transports in storage valued at $350 million–with another $150 million under construction–for which builders do not hold export licenses. When these aircraft were ordered and progress payments initiated (2 years ago) there was a reasonable assurance that export licenses would be granted. Foreign competitors, citing the uncertainties of U.S. export licensing policy in their marketing strategies, are achieving growing success in those nations where buyers of military and civil aviation producers seek to assure continuity of supply.

EQUIPMENT LEASING

JET AIRCRAFT

JETS, LTD.

$8,370,000

(A Limited Partnership)

PURPOSE

To acquire a Wide Body Jet from Smooth Flight Airlines to be leased to Soft Landing Airways, an Aircraft Charter Company.

EQUIPMENT COST

Total $22,000,000 which includes parts and two additional Rolls Royce engines.

GENERAL PARTNER

Twenty-two thousand ($22,000) per Unit. In order to utilize the full tax benefits each investor will assume his pro-rata portion of the partnership debt. For each unit, a $217,143 recourse promissory note.

The $22,000 investment unit will be payable as follows:

Year 1 - $7,000
Year 2 - $8,000 plus 10% simple interest
Year 3 - $7,000 plus 10% simple interest

TAX & CASH FLOW CONSIDERATIONS—PER UNIT INVESTMENT

		Write-Off	%	Cash Flow
A.	Year 1	$44,898	641	$ 0
	Year 2	77,677	858	1,626
	Year 3	50,859	727	1,954
	Year 4	29,141	-	1,954
	Year 5	24,509	-	1,954
	Year 6	18,938	-	1,954

followed by taxable gain beginning in Year 9.

B. The possibility of realizing gain in future years from sale of aircraft.

LESSEE

Soft Landing Airways is a new charter airline created by a former Smooth Flight Executive, with 36 years airline experience. Soft Landing has obtained charter contracts with several charter travel companies to fly between U.S. and Canada to Ireland, England and Israel. The projections indicate a healthy profit in the first year of operation.

FINANCING

Loans totaling $22,000,000 are being provided by Financial Group of Vancouver, Canada at 18.66% interest for 10 years, with a $7,000,000 balloon payment. Smooth Flight is committed to $14,400,000 (65%) of the loan. The Limited Partners of the Partnership are committed to the balance of $7,600,000 (35%) of the loan.

ACCOUNTING AND TAX CONVENTIONS

The projections shown in the exhibits assume that the Partnership is on a cash basis for income tax purposes.

The Depreciation schedule will be over 10 full years using 150% Declining Balance for 3 years, then straight line for the remaining life.

COMPENSATION AND SERVICES

All Limited Partnership Units will be sold without marketing expenses or selling commissions payable by the Partnership.

The Partnership has contracted with Jetlease to find, acquire, and lease the aircraft. Further, Jetlease will structure and document the transactions. Jetlease will be paid a fee of 3.5% of the purchase price or $770,000.

Jetlease may pay referral fees for the placement of Units in the Partnership.

Jetlease will also provide the ongoing accounting, monitoring of the lease and communication between the Partnership and the lessee. Jetlease will receive .75% (3/4 of 1%) of the total revenue of the lease.

REMARKETING FEE

The General Partner will enter into an agreement with Jetlease to remarket the aircraft at the end of the lease term.

The General Partner will share in the residual proceeds on a subordinated basis. After the Limited Partners have received 100% of their original investment plus 10% cumulative, the excess, if any, will be distributed as follows:

50% to the Limited Partners
50% to the General Partners

OTHER CONSIDERATIONS

In considering most equipment, the effect of "wear and tear" will affect the residual value of the property. Obsolescence will also effect the value. So long as the lease is in effect, these factors will not affect the lessor.

While there can be no guarantee of the residual value, there is strong evidence that a Wide Body Jet will maintain its value.

By Federal regulation, aircraft carrying passengers must rigidly comply to a schedule of check-ups and overhauls. Thus, a ten year old airplane will be "like new."

Jetlease will use its best efforts to maximize the lessor's income from sale or re-lease of the equipment. However, it must be recognized that the equipment is subject to technological and economic obsolescence and that no representation is made as to the collateral or residual value of the Wide Body Jet.

SCHEDULE I

PURCHASE AND LEASE OF WIDE BODY JET AIRCRAFT ($22,000,000) WITH 100% FINANCING AT 18.6% FOR 10 YEARS WITH A $7,000,000 BALLOON PAYMENT FOR THE 50% TAXPAYER

NOTES	Year 1 0 Revenue 6 Mo. Depr.	Year 2 10 Mo. Rev.	Year 3	Year 4	Year 5	Year 6	Year 7	Year 8	Year 9	Year 10	Year 11	Year 12 0 Depr. 2 Mo. Rev.
1 Lease Revenue	0	4634560	5561481	5561481	5561481	5561481	5561481	5561481	5561481	5561481	5561481	926914
2 Less: Debt Service	0	3835650	4602720	4602720	4602720	4602720	4602720	4602720	4602720	4602720	4602720	767120
3 Insurance/Maintenance	0	706960	848352	848352	848352	848352	848352	848352	848352	848352	848352	141392
4 Jetlease Management Fee	0	35000	42000	42000	42000	42000	42000	42000	42000	42000	42000	7000
NET CASH FLOW	0	56950	68409	68409	68409	68409	48402	68409	68409	68409	68409	11401
TAX DEDUCTIONS												
5 Depreciation	1571429	2918367	2501458	1876093	1876093	1876093	1876093	1876093	1876093	1876093	1876093	0
6 Interest Expense	0	3377901	2949734	3814943	3652832	3457864	3223382	2941371	2602208	2194301	1703719	229551
Insurance/Maint.	0	706960	848352	848352	848352	848352	848352	848352	848352	848352	848352	141392
Jetlease Mgt. Fee	0	35000	42000	42000	42000	42000	42000	42000	42000	42000	42000	7000
Total Deductions	1571429	7038228	7341544	6581388	6419277	6224309	5989827	5707816	5368653	4960746	4480164	377943
Gain (Loss)	(1547429)	(2403668)	(1780063)	(1019907)	(857796)	(662828)	(428346)	(146335)	192828	600735	1091317	548971
Gain (Loss) Cum.	(1547429)	(3951097)	(5731160)	(6751067)	(7608863)	(8271691)	(8700037)	(8846372)	(8653544)	(8052809)	(6961492)	(6412521)
7 Taxes Saved (Paid)	773714	1201834	890031	509953	428898	331414	214173	73167	(96414)	(300367)	(545158)	(274485)
Taxes Saved (Cum.)	773714	1978548	2865579	3375533	3804431	4135845	4350018	4423185	4326771	4026404	3482245	3206760
8 INVESTMENT	24500	280000	245000									
% Write-Off	641%	858%	727%									
% Write-Off Cum.	641%	817%	788%	921%	1032%	1118%	1174%	1195%	1168%	1090%	950%	878%
Yield-Tax Only	320%	409%	363%									
Yield-Tax Only Cum.	320%	409%	394%	460%	516%	559%	586%	596%	583%	544%	474%	438%
Yield-Cash on Cash	0	11%	9%	9%	9%	9%	9%	9%	9%	9%	9%	2%
9 Cash Flow & Taxes Saved (Paid and Invested at 10%		740714	1524984	2646334	3505026	4372579	5233493	6067314	6847441	7539677	8100446	8556013

SCHEDULE I - PER UNIT ($22,000) BREAKDOWN

PURCHASE AND LEASE OF WIDE BODY JET AIRCRAFT ($22,000,000) WITH
100% FINANCING AT 18.6% FOR 10 YEARS WITH A $7,000,000 BALLOON PAYMENT FOR THE 50% TAXPAYER

	Year 1 0 Revenue 6 Mo. Dep.	Year 2 10 Mo.	Year 3	Year 4	Year 5	Year 6	Year 7	Year 8	Year 9	Year 10	Year 11	Year 12 0 Dep. 2 Mo.
1 Lease Revenue	0	132415	158899	158899	158899	158899	158899	158899	158899	158899	158899	26483
2 Less: Debt Service	0	109590	131506	131506	131506	131506	131506	131506	131506	131506	131506	21917
3 Insurance/Maint.	0	20199	24239	24239	24239	24239	24239	24239	24239	24239	24239	4040
4 Jetlease Mangt. Fee	0	1000	1200	1200	1200	1200	1200	1200	1200	1200	1200	200
NET CASH FLOW	0	1626	1954	1954	1954	1954	1954	1954	1954	1954	1954	326
TAX DEDUCTIONS												
5 Depreciation	44898	83382	71470	53603	53603	53603	53603	53603	53603	53603	53603	0
6 Interest Expense	0	96511	112849	108998	104367	98796	92097	84039	74349	62694	48678	6559
Insurance/Maint.	0	20199	24239	24239	24239	24239	24239	24239	24239	24329	24239	4040
Jetlease Mangt. Fee	0	1200	1200	1200	1200	1200	1200	1200	1200	1200	1200	200
Total Deductions	44898	201092	209758	188040	183408	177837	171138	163080	153390	141736	128045	10798
Gain (Loss)	(44898)	(77677)	(50859)	(29141)	(24509)	(18938)	(12239)	(4181)	5509	17163	30854	15685
Gain (Loss) Cum.	(44898)	(122575)	(173434)	(202575)	(227084)	(246022)	(258261)	(262442)	(256933)	(239770)	(208916)	(193231)
7 Taxes Saved (Paid)	22449	38838	25430	14571	12255	9469	6120	2091	(1102)	(8582)	(15427)	(7843)
Taxes Saved (Cum.)	22449	61287	86714	101288	113543	123012	129132	131223	130121	121539	106112	98269
8 INVESTMENT	7000	8000	7000									
% Write-Off	641%	858%	727%									
% Write-Off-Cum.	641%	817%	788%	921%	1032%	1118%	1174%	1195%	1168%	1090%	950%	878%
Yield-Tax Only	320%	429%	363%									
Yield-Tax Only-Cum.	320%	409%	394%	460%	516%	559%	586%	596%	583%	544%	474%	438%
Yield-Cash on Cash	0	11%	9%	9%	9%	9%	9%	9%	9%	9%	9%	2%
9 Cash Flow & Taxes Saved (Paid) and		21164	47832	80317	105344	130676	155875	180363	203315	225548	242630	254656

NOTES TO PROJECTIONS

1. 2.1066% of aircraft cost per month.
2. $22,000,000 for 10 years at 18.6% with a $700,000 balloon payment.
3. Expenses fixed at $70,696.00 per month.
4. Jetlease management fee of .755% of gross revenue.
5. 150% declining balance through 1982, converting to straight line in 1983. 10.5 year useful life, "half year" convention for 1980 under ADR.
6. Rule of 78's.
7. Assumes 50% tax bracket.
8. Cash investment of $245,000 ($7,000.00 per Unit) upon subscription $280,000 ($8,000.00 per Unit) January 15, Year 2 and $245,000 (7,000 per Unit) January 15, Year 3, for total cash investment of $770,000 ($22,000 per Unit).
9. Assumes investor invested tax dollars saved (after deduction of cash investment) and net cash flow at 10% APR compounded monthly and pays taxes due in later years from that source–taxes due from interest income not considered.
10. Assumes a fair market value of $12,000,000 (55%).
11. Balloon payment on financing.
12. Jetlease sales commission of 10%.
13. Limited partners to receive initial investment, plus 10% prior to General Partner participation.
14. Limited Partners net proceeds of sale, plus 10 above.

    The information and material contained herein were obtained from sources believed to be reliable, however, all projections contained herein are estimates. No guarantees can or are being given as to the accuracy or completeness, or as to the actual economic benefits which will flow from the ownership of the equipment since each situation will vary due to type and cost of equipment, prevailing interest rates, terms and conditions of financing and leases, and, generally, other economic, financial and legal matters which cannot be predicted at this time.

SALE OF AIRCRAFT AT END OF TERM - YEAR 2

Notes		
10	Sale Proceeds	12,000,000
11	Less Balloon Payment	7,000,000
12	Less Sales Commission	1,200,000
	Net Proceeds of Sale	3,800,000
13	To Make up for Cumulative 10%	162,968
	Net to Partnership	3,637,032
	50% to Limited Partners	1,818,516
14	Plus 9 Above - Cumulative Tax Savings and Cash Flow Invested at 10%	8,436,172
	Total Return	10,254,688

FOR A SINGLE UNIT

Notes		
10	Sale Proceeds	342,857
11	Less: Balloon Payment	200,000
12	Sales Commission	34,285
	Net Proceeds from Sale	108,572
13	To Make up for Cumulative 10%	4,660
	Net to Partnership	103,912
	Limited Partner's Share	51,956
14	Plus 9 Above - Cumulative Tax Savings and Cash Flow Invested at 10%	251,402
	Total Return	303,358

RAILROAD FREIGHT CARS

INDUSTRY STATUS AND FORECAST

The estimated 70,000 new railroad freight car deliveries in 1981 are about 7 percent below the level of 1980 deliveries. Freight car production and orders in 1980 were below the very high levels of 1979, and they are expected to continue at these lower levels into 1981. At the beginning of 1980, the backlog of new cars on order and undelivered was 119,000, or more than a year's deliveries. New orders fell drastically in 1980, to about half the 119,281 new orders placed in 1979. Production was sustained by the large backlog, however.

Prospects are that orders will increase moderately during 1981. Factors influencing this estimate include an expected resumption of real growth in GNP, continued growth in domestic and export demand for coal, high liquid fuel prices, and Government regulation and legislation designed to allow greater freedom to railroad management. A negative factor in new car orders in the near term is the decision by the Interstate Commerce Commission in August 1980 to eliminate "incentive per diem" payments for types of freight cars deemed in short supply. "Incentive per diem" is an extra daily rental charge railroads pay on freight cars that do not belong to them. The "incentive per diem" program, designed to encourage outside investment for the purchase of railroad cars, has been in effect about 10 years. Under the program, the practice by outside companies of buying freight cars and leasing them to the railroads and shippers had grown considerably. This, together with a decline in the economy, has led to a surplus of freight cars. It is expected that a resumption of real growth in the economy will eliminate the 1980 car surplus and halt the decline in orders for new cars.

Final delivery figures for new freight cars were a record 90,000 units in 1979, which indicates that industry capacity was about 12 percent more than had been estimated. New foundry capacity in the United States, together with an increase in parts imported, have reduced the capacity constraint resulting from shortages of components. Presently, the value of industry shipments is growing faster than unit deliveries, as carbuilders' labor and material costs rise. The year-to-year percent increases in the Producers Price Index for railroad equipment averaged about 9 percent from 1975 through 1980. This trend is expected to continue. The value of industry shipments should reach $3.3 billion in 1981, an increase of 2 percent over 1980, despite the decline in unit deliveries between 1980 and 1981.

In recent years, box cars have been a relatively large proportion of all cars built. The product mix of new orders is shifting, however, toward an increased proportion of gondolas and covered and uncovered hoppers, reflecting the need for cars to haul coal and grain. Increases in the use of intermodal rail-truck service are expected as fuel prices rise, because trains are more fuel efficient than trucks for certain long-distance freight movements. Several new freight car designs are being introduced to increase the efficiency of intermodal services. At least six different new designs are under construction or undergoing testing by suppliers and the railroads.

Foreign Trade

The recent boom in freight car building produced an increase in imports as some capacity limitations developed in U.S. components supply. Imports rose from $30 million in 1976 to $350 million in 1980. The decline in new car orders is expected to reduce imports, and in 1981 the value of imports of railroad freight cars and parts is expected to drop to about $300 million. Canada remains the largest source of imports, accounting for about half of the total value, and is the major supplier of cars. Japan and France supply most of the wheels and axles, but no single supplier is dominant in the supply of other parts.

Exports of parts for 1981 are forecast at $120 million, up 8 percent over 1980. Canada and Mexico are our major export markets for railroad freight cars and parts, receiving about half of the total of these exports.

Outlook for 1985

Deliveries of freight cars are expected to average about 75,000 cars annually through 1985. This forecast is based on the expectation of growing shipments of coal and grain, the relative fuel efficiency of the railroads, and continued real growth of the economy.

SPECIAL ILLUSTRATION OF LEVERAGED LEASE FINANCING

B CORPORATION
LEVERAGED LEASE FINANCING
COVERED HOPPER CARS

G Corporation has been asked by B Corporation to finance the lease of 100 covered hopper cars to a subsidiary of B Corporation. This letter describes the transaction and the economic impact to an investor (the "Owner-Lessor") of an investment in the transaction.

I. *Description of Transaction*

1.1 *Parties*

It is contemplated that the following parties will be participating in this lease transaction in the respective capacities indicated below:

a. *Lessee:* Bcar, a wholly-owned subsidiary of B Corporation. Bcar will sublease the covered hopper cars to major corporations who will use the hopper cars for shipping products primarily in the plastics industry.

b. *Lenders:* Institution Lenders to be arranged by G.

c. *Owner-Lessor:* Equity Investors arranged by Broker-Dealer.

d. *Insurance Underwriters:* A Leased Property Depreciation Insurance Policy will be arranged by G.

1.2 *Equipment*

a. One hundred covered hopper cars, 5750 cubic feet, manufactured by North American Car.

b. *Equipment Cost:* $4,150,000.00 (100 cars at $41,500 per car).

c. *Equipment Delivery:* On or about October 15, Year One.

1.3 *Proposed Legal Structure*

The Lessee will assign his on-order position with the Manufacturer to the Owner-Lessor. The Owner-Lessor will then purchase the equipment from the Manufacturer and will lease the equipment to the Lessee pursuant to the Lease Agreement. Approximately 82.45% of the total purchase price of the equipment will be supplied by the Lenders, who will receive a security interest and chattel mortgage in the equipment, as well as a direct assignment of the Lease and Lease payments.

1.4 *Funding*

It is proposed that the Owner-Lessor will supply, as equity, 30% of the total cost of the equipment, or approximately $1,245,000 including fees. The Lenders will supply the remaining 82.4% of the total cost of the equipment, or approximately $3,421,675. Over the 10-year lease term, 14.47% or $600,505 will amortized, and the remaining 67.98% or $2,821,170 will be an interest only balloon note due at the end of the lease term. The funds advanced by the Lenders will be non-recourse to the Owner-Lessor, will be subject to prepayment only in the event of a destruction of the equipment (or voluntary termination of the lease by the Lessee as hereinafter described), and will be secured in the manner described in Section 1.3 above. The Lease rental payments have been calculated so as to be sufficient to fully pay the principal and interest on the amortized note and the interest on the balloon note. The Lessee will make all rental payments directly to the Lenders, who will apply all payments so received, first to payment of principal and accrued interest then due, and second, to payment of the balance of such funds, if any, to the Owner-Lessor.

1.5 *Insurance*

The Lender and Lessor will be named loss payee under a Leased Property Depreciation Insurance Policy in amounts sufficient to cover any unamortized principal balances or balloon payments due upon expiration of the firm lease term. The insurance will also cover a position of the Lessor's equity investment.

1.6 *Lease Information*

a. *Term:* 10 years from October, Year One.

b. *Rentals*

1. *Basic Rent:* There will be 40 quarterly rental payments, each payable in arrears. Payments on the long-term debt will be coincident with the rental payments.

2. *Lease Rate Factor:* The Lease Rate Factor expressed as a percentage of total cost of the equipment is as follows:

Basic Rent Payment Numbers	Lease Rate Factor
1-40	2.519%

c. *Other Lease Provisions*

1. *Renewal Option:* The Lessee will have the right to renew the Lease at the expiration of the Basic Lease Term for an additional 13 years at the following quarterly in arreas lease rates.

Lease Rate Factor	Debt Rate
2.3952	10.25%
2.5190	11.25%
2.6458	12.25%

These rates and terms are sufficient to fully amortize the remaining debt.

2. *Purchase Right of First Refusal:* The Lessee will have a right of first refusal, exercisable for an agreed-upon period of time following the expiration of the Basic Lease Term, to purchase the equipment at the price equal to its then fair market value.

3. *Termination:* The Lease will terminate only under the following conditions:

(i) In the event the equipment is destroyed or otherwise rendered permanently unfit for service, the Lessee would pay the Stipulated Loss Value (as more fully described below) plus all other sums payable in such an event.

(ii) Occurrence of an Event of Default as such term will be defined in the Lease.

(iii) At the time following the first anniversary of the commencement of the Lease. if the Lessee makes a good faith determination that the equipment has become economically absolete or surplus to the Lessee's requirements the Lessee will pay the Termination Value (as more fully described below) plus all other sums payable in such an event.

4. *"Net" Lease:* The Lease will be "net" to the Owner-Lessor with the Lessee responsible for such things as maintenance, insurance, compliance with applicable laws and taxes.

II. *Calculations*

2.1 G's calculations of the effects of the Owner-Lessor's participation in this transaction are set forth in Schedules A and B enclosed. Such calculations are based on the assumptions described in the Schedules, and are expressed as a percentage of the total cost of the equipment.

2.2 *Source of Benefits*

Investment recovery and yield to the Owner-Lessor, as indicated on the investment analysis, are composed of the following:

a. *Investment Tax Credit:* An investment tax credit equal to 10% of the total cost of the equipment, or $415,000.

b. *Accelerated Depreciation:* The tax effects of 200% declining balance switching to sum of the years-digits depreciation over 12 years on 100% of the total cost of the equipment. Depreciation is based on 100% of equipment cost to a 0% salvage value under the Class Life System of depreciation for equipment.

c. *Interest Deduction:* The tax deductibility of interest payments on the non-recourse debt supplied by the Lenders.

d. *Fee Deduction:* The tax deduction of the front end fees on a straight line basis over the term of the lease.

e. *Cash Flow:* The excess of rental payments over debt service payments.

f. *Residual Value:* Realization at the conclusion of the basic lease term of assumed residual values of the equipment.

g. *Opportunity Interest Rate (OIR):* A time value of money analysis of the positive and negative after-tax cash flows of the transaction.

III. *Services of G*

3.1 *Additional Calculations and Evaluations*

G will employ its facilities to assist the Owner-Lessor in any additional calculations or evaluations in connection with the Owner-Lessor's analysis of this transaction.

3.2 *Preparation of Stipulated Loss Schedule*

G will calculate this schedule for the transaction. Stipulated Loss Values are designed to preserve Owner-Lessor's investment and yield, provide for payment of taxes (based on the assumptions set forth in the investment analysis) due as a result of casualty, pay the balance due on the non-recourse debt, and recognize loss of the residual value of the equipment.

3.3 *Preparation of Lease Documentation*

G will be responsible for the preparation of all Lease documentation connected with this transaction. This will include working with the Owner-Lessor, the Lessee, the Lenders, and counsel for the respective parties. All documentation will be subject to the approval of the Owner-Lessor.

3.4 *Sale or Lease of the Equipment*

Upon the expiration or termination of the Lease, G shall be responsible for and shall, as exclusive agent for the Owner-Lessor, arrange for the sale or re-lease of the equipment, depending upon the profitability or economic feasibility of each alternative.

3.5 *Expenses*

G shall be responsible for the expenses of the preparation of Lease documentation, closing and filing fees, and legal fees for obtaining an opinion of clear title to the equipment. The Owner-Lessor will be responsible for only those expenses incurred in its own review of the documentation (e.g., its own accounting or legal fees).

IV. *Compensation*

4.1 *Front End Fee*

For performance of the above described and related services, G will receive a fee from the Owner-Lessor, calculated and payable in the following manner: On the date the equipment is purchased from the Manufacturer, the Owner-Lessor will pay to G a cash amount equal to 12.45% of the total cost of the equipment paid for on such closing date. Out of this amount G will pay the cost of the Depreciation Insurance Policy, the debt placement fee, the equity placement fee, and the documentation and closing costs outlined above.

5750 Cubic Foot Covered Hopper Designed for Commodities Weighing Between 23 and 34 Pounds Per Cubic Foot

Cubic Capacity	5750 cu. ft.	Center of Gravity	
Each End Compartment	1575 cu. ft.	Loaded Car	98"
Center Compartment	(2) 1300 cu. ft	Trucks	100 ton
Roof Hatches	Ten 20" inside diameter	Gross Rail Load	263,000 lbs.
Discharge System Vacuum-Pneumatic		Lightweight	67,000 lbs.
Outlets	4 Double Groove 6¼" O.D.	Payload Weight	Up to 196,000 lbs.
Height–Top of Rail To Discharge Outlet	8 7/16"	Bearings	Roller
Gravity		Minimum Horizontal Curve Negotiability	
Outlets	4 (13" x 42") Rack & Pinion)		
Height–Top of Rail To Discharge Outlet	11"	Coupled to AAR Base Car	231 ft.
Hopper Slope	45°	Coupled to Similar Car	234 ft.

SCHEDULE A

COVERED HOPPER CAR ANALYSIS
As a Percent of Equipment Cost

Year	Lease Revenues	Depreciation	Interest Expense Amortized Debt	Interest Expense Ballon Debt	Fees	Net Income (Loss)	Cash Flow	Total Cash & Tax Benefits (50% Bracket) Annual	Cumulative	% of Equity 0% OIR	% of Equity 5% OIR
1	-	8.333	-	-	-	(8.333)	10.000*	14.167	14.167	47%	47%
2	10.076	15.278	1.592	7.648	1.245	(15.687)	-	7.843	22.010	73	71
3	10.076	13.258	1.494	7.648	1.245	(13.569)	-	6.785	28.795	96	92
4	10.076	11.995	1.386	7.648	1.245	(12.198)	-	6.099	34.894	116	112
5	10.076	10.732	1.262	7.648	1.245	(10.811)	-	5.405	40.299	134	130
6	10.076	9.470	1.127	7.648	1.245	(9.414)	-	4.707	45.006	150	148
7	10.076	8.207	.974	7.648	1.245	(7.998)	-	3.999	49.005	163	163
8	10.076	6.944	.802	7.648	1.245	(6.563)	-	3.282	52.287	174	177
9	10.076	5.682	.613	7.648	1.245	(5.112)	-	2.556	54.843	183	190
10	10.076	4.419	.399	7.648	1.245	(3.635)	-	1.817	56.660	189	200
11	10.076	3.157	.161	7.648	1.245	(2.135)	-	1.068	57.728	192	209

RESIDUAL VALUES

0-67.98%	Year 12
85.00%	Year 12
100.00%	Year 12
120.00%	Year 12

TRANSACTION PARAMETERS:

LRF = 2.519 Quarterly in Arrears
Lease Term = 10 Years
Depreciation = DDB Switching to SYD over 12 Years
6 Months in Year One
Fees = Straight/Lined over 10 Years
*ITC = 10%
OIR = Opportunity Interest Rate

Equipment Cost	= 100.000
Front End Fees	= 12.450
TOTAL	= 112.450
Amortized Debt at 11¼%	= 14.470
Balloon Debt at 11¼%	= 67.980
Equity Investment	= 30.000
TOTAL	= 112.450

SCHEDULE B

COVERED HOPPER CAR ANALYSIS
As a Percent of Equipment Cost

Year	Lease Revenues	Depre-ciation	Interest Expense Amortized Debt	Interest Expense Balloon Debt	Fees	Net Income (Loss)	Cash Flow	Total Cash & Tax Benefits (50% Bracket) Annual	Cumu-lative	% of Equity 0% OIR	% of Equity 5% OIR
1	-	8.333	-	-	-	(8.333)	10.000*	14.167	14.167	47%	47%
2	10.076	15.278	1.592	7.648	1.245	(15.687)	-	7.843	22.010	73	71
3	10.076	13.258	1.494	7.648	1.245	(13.569)	-	6.785	28.795	96	92
4	10.076	11.995	1.386	7.648	1.245	(12.198)	-	6.099	34.894	116	112
5	10.076	10.732	1.262	7.648	1.245	(10.811)	-	5.405	40.299	134	130
6	10.076	9.470	1.127	7.648	1.245	(9.414)	-	4.707	45.006	150	148
7	10.076	8.207	.974	7.648	1.245	(7.998)	-	3.999	49.005	163	163
8	10.076	6.944	.802	7.648	1.245	(6.563)	-	3.282	52.287	174	177
9	10.076	5.682	.613	7.648	1.245	(5.112)	-	2.556	54.843	183	190
10	10.076	4.419	.399	7.648	1.245	(3.635)	-	1.817	56.660	189	200
11	10.076	3.157	.161	7.648	1.245	(2.135)	-	1.068	57.728	192	209
12	10.076	1.894	7.547	-	-	.635	.060	(.258	57.470	192	214
13	10.076	.631	7.257	-	-	2.188	.061	(1.033)	56.437	188	216
14	10.076	-	6.933	-	-	3.143	.060	(1.511)	54.926	183	217
15	10.076	-	6.571	-	-	3.505	.061	(1.692)	53.234	177	217
16	10.076	-	6.167	-	-	3.909	.060	(1.894)	51.340	171	216
17	10.076	-	5.716	-	-	4.360	.061	(2.119)	49.221	164	215
18	10.076	-	5.212	-	-	4.864	.060	(2.372)	46.849	156	213
19	10.076	-	4.647	-	-	5.429	.061	(2.654)	44.195	147	210
20	10.076	-	4.017	-	-	6.059	.060	(2.969)	41.226	137	205
21	10.076	-	3.313	-	-	6.763	.061	(3.321)	37.905	126	199
22	10.076	-	2.527	-	-	7.549	.060	(3.714)	34.191	114	192
23	10.076	-	1.648	-	-	8.428	.061	(4.153)	30.038	100	183
24	10.076	-	.667	-	-	9.409	.060	(4.645)	25.393	85	171

RESIDUAL VALUE

15%	Year 25
30%	Year 25
45%	Year 25
60%	Year 25

TRANSACTION PARAMETERS:

Year 1 - Year 11: Same as Schedule A

Year 12 - Year 25: Same Lease Revenues
Amortized Baloon Debt (67.98%) Over 13 Years at 11¼%

EQUIPMENT LEASING

THE PRIVATE RAILROAD CAR INDUSTRY

General Considerations

At the end of 1978, there were approximately 1,652,800 railroad freight cars in service in the United States. Of these, approximately 1,295,400 cars were owned or held under long-term financial lease by the railroads and 357,400 cars were owned by individuals, firms, corporations and car leasing companies, including cars owned and/or operated by railroad-controlled private car lines. The practice of U.S. railroads using privately-owned cars grew from the fact that the varied nature of commodity shipments were best handled in specialized cars which the railroads did not or were not in a position to supply to shippers. "Private car lines" (railroad car leasing companies) gradually came into existence as a direct result of this practice. Some companies leased cars to shippers, who in turn made them available to railroads, and in some cases leased cars to the railroad themselves.

Federal law and regulations provide that it is the duty of common carrier railroads to furnish such cars other than tank cars as may be reasonably necessary to the transportation of all commodities they hold themselves out to carry. Railroads also have the exclusive right to furnish cars. Use of privately-owned freight cars, then, is optional with the railroads and they are not required to use them if they are able to furnish cars of their own. The approval of the railroad on which privately-owned covered hopper cars are to be used is required before such cars can be placed in service or assigned to handle traffic.

In recent years, the demand for covered hopper cars has been expanding and most railroads approve and in many cases encourage the use of such privately-owned cars. Some major railroads have published tariffs involving unit train movements of grain or fertilizer which require shippers to furnish privately-owned cars. However, see "OT-5 Series," below. As a result, the number of privately-owned covered hopper cars have been growing rapidly, and now is approximately 33% of the combined railroad and privately-owned fleets. About 63% of the privately-owned cars are less than 10 years old. The privately-owned cars are owned by various types of companies, including grain growers, milling companies, and a few leasing companies, and by individuals. The non-shipper-owned cars are usually leased to shippers and are used in railroad service by such shipper-lessees.

At the end of 1978, approximately 246,100 U.S. covered hopper cars were in service. Approximately 165,300 of these cars were railroad-owned and 80,800 were privately-owned. Of the privately-owned cars, approximately 72% were owned by four owner-lessors: GATX, Inc.; ACF Industries, Inc. (Shippers Car Line Division); The Flying Tiger Corporation (North American Car Corporation); and Pullman Incorporated (Pullman Transport Leasing Co.). The other privately-owned covered hopper cars were owned by various types of companies and individuals, some of whom are lessors and some of whom use their cars to ship commodities which they use or produce or in which they trade. Covered hopper cars managed by the Manager under other investment programs are included in this latter group of cars.

The total number of covered hopper cars in service has increased 162% from 153,500 to 246,100 in the past decade, while ownership of general service plain box cars declined from about 412,000 to 262,000, a decrease of nearly 36%. For the handling of many bulk commodities, the 100-ton covered hopper car is becoming a new standard car due to inherent efficiencies in loading and unloading, as contrasted with the plain box car. This is especially true in the grain industry, where, prompted by unit train and other type incentive rates which encourage or require the use of covered hopper cars, the shift from plain box cars to covered hopper cars has been accelerating.

Government Regulations

Railroad car leasing companies (private car lines) are not common carriers and are not subject to Federal and state regulation as are common carriers. Basically, they operate as any other unregulated business and are free to set their own lease terms and rates and make their own business decisions in accordance with the competition in their marketplace. However, there are certain areas in which their operations are or can be affected by governmental regulation and by rules adopted as standards by the railroad industry.

To be eligible for operation on United States railroads, all railroad freight cars must be built to meet Association of American Railroads ("AAR") construction specifications and standards. In addition, all such cars must meet certain federal regulations with respect to safety appliances and features which are promulgated and administered by the U.S. Department of Transportation ("DOT"). The manufacturer is required to deliver the cars in a condition which satisfies the above requirements.

Operation of freight cars in railroad interchange service is subject to the AAR Mechanical Interchange Rules. The Rules prescribe mechanical, maintenance and related standards and provide an orderly method for placing responsibility for maintenance and repair on all cars operated in interchange between railroads and car owners and for the payment of the cost of such repairs. ABC, sponsor of the management program, is a subscriber to these Rules.

Operation and maintenance of freight cars are also subject to federal regulation under the Federal Railroad Safety Act, which is administered by DOT. Certain "minimum standards" under that Act were adopted during 1977. These "minimum standards" relate to maintenance and inspection of railroad freight cars and are similar to many of those contained in the AAR Mechanical Interchange Rules.

In order to be operated on the railroads, all private cars must be assigned "reporting marks" by the AAR. These are identifying initials which are placed on each car together with a number which identifies the car as one authorized by the railroads for use in their service. These reporting marks and numbers and certain descriptive data for each car are registered in the Official Railway Equipment Register for the purposes of identification, payment of mileage allowances and billing of repair costs. The reporting mark "WXYZ" has been reserved for ABC and will be used for those Cars which are managed in the Program.

Reporting marks and numbers of all cars, together with data on car specifications, are also registered in the AAR Universal Machine Language Equipment Register ("UMLER"). This is a computerized data file which maintains in machine language form most of the information contained in the Official Railway Equipment Register, together with certain information which is used by AAR and most individual railroads in their computerized car distribution, accounting and statistical systems.

Leasing

The majority of shippers furnishing covered hopper cars for railroad use, and occasionally the railroads themselves, have found it desirable to lease rather than to own such cars for one or more of the following reasons:

1. The lessee desires to avoid tying up working capital, thereby keeping it free for other operating uses;
2. The lessee desires to avoid maintenance and repair responsibilities, operating problems and details of administration;
3. The lessee desires to maintain borrowing capacity for other purposes;
4. The lessee's demand for cars may be cyclical or seasonal;
5. The lessee seeks protection from obsolescence or inefficiency due to change of technology, products or markets; and/or
6. The lessee is not in a tax position to benefit directly from the federal tax consequences arising from car ownership.

There are two basic forms of leases for cars of private ownership. The first is the net finance lease, which is normally written for a substantial portion of the foreseeable useful life of the leased cars. Under net finance leases the lessee undertakes the responsibility of operating the cars as if the lessee owned them and pays all the costs of their maintenance and operation. This form of lease is not generally used by ABC in its current car management programs since use of a net finance lease will not permit the Owner to claim an investment tax credit with respect to purchase of a Car. Although a few of ABC's leases may provide for the lessee to pay a small portion of the costs of maintenance, such leases will be structured in a manner which will assure the Owner the availability of an investment tax credit.

The second basic form of lease is the service lease, in which the lessor undertakes to provide and pay for the operation and maintenance of the leased cars. This is the form of lease most common for cars of private ownership and is the kind generally offered by ABC. Service leases are either short- or long-term. Short-term leases cover periods which range from a single trip (spot leases) to up to about three years. Long-term leases cover periods which range from three to fifteen years or more, with five to twelve years being the most common.

There are two ways in which an owner of a railroad car is compensated for the use of such equipment. The first is the "mileage allowance," whereby the railroads pay the "owner of the marks" a "rate per mile." The term "owner of the marks" refers to the reporting marks placed on the railroad car identifying the owner of the car and who is to receive mileage allowances from railroads. Although the participants in the Program are the owners of the Cars and would normally be the "owner of the marks," ABC will register the Cars as WXYZ cars for administrative convenience.

The current mileage allowance on covered hopper cars is described in the Mileage Tariff 7-F authorized by the Interstate Commerce Commission ("ICC"). These mileage allowances are established by the ICC and continue in force until further order of the ICC, and are used by the railroads in determining the mileage payable to the "owner of the marks." ABC cannot predict what future actions, if any, the ICC or the railroad may take with respect to mileage allowances or other tariff rules which might affect the operation of the Cars.

The current mileage allowances paid by railroads for use of private covered hopper cars are as follows:

Age or Depreciated Value	Allowance (Cents per car mile)
Cars 30 years of age or over	5.5
Cars less than 30 years of age:	
Nil to $4,999	7.3
$5,000 to $9,999	8.2
$10,000 to $14,999	9.5
$15,000 to $19,999	10.5
$20,000 and over	12.0

The allowance for private covered hopper cars is usually paid on both loaded and empty miles of actual travel of cars. However, by special exception to the tariff, many railroads have chosen to pay double the mileage allowance on loaded car miles computed on the shortest distance between stations shown in published freight mileage tariffs rather than the mileage allowance per car mile loaded or empty.

Mileage allowances are paid by each of the railroads over whose lines the Cars run as compensation to the owner for use of the owner's car rather than railroad owned equipment, while the lease rental payments are made by the lessee or user of the car on some fixed rental basis. Almost all leases for covered hopper cars contain a provision whereby the lessee receives mileage allowances up to the rental amount, either from the owner after receipt by the owner, or as a reduction in rent. Since mileage allowances are paid by the railroad several months after they have accrued and it takes a period of time to isolate the allowances attributable to a particular car, rental is usually collected from the lessee when due and mileage allowances paid to lessees after receipt. ABC will place any funds received as mileage allowances with respect to Cars managed under the Management Program in a segregated bank account commingled with mileage allowances received for cars managed by ABC in its other investor programs and will use these funds to make payments of mileage allowance due to lessees with respect to cars managed under such programs.

The second method of compensation involves a fixed minimum rental, which is agreed to in advance on the basis of, among other things, the length of time the car will be used and the commodities which will be carried. In addition, some service leases provide for a rental in addition to the fixed rate in the form of a charge per car mile for all miles run above a stated maximum per car per year. This charge may vary from $.01 to $.02 per car mile above the stated maximum, which generally varies from 20,000 to 40,000 car miles per car year, and is made to offset the cost of accelerated wear on moving parts which occurs in such high mileage service.

Many railroad car leases involve a combination of both methods described above. Generally, a fixed rental is agreed upon in advance with the lessee, subject to credits for mileage allowances paid by the railroads. If the mileage allowance paid by the railroad to the lessor is less than the fixed rate, the lessee must pay the difference. However, if the mileage allowance is greater than the fixed rental, the lessor credits the lessee's account up to the amount of the fixed rental rate and upon termination of a lease will receive the excess mileage allowance.

When private cars are leased directly to a railroad, in some cases the lessee railroad pays a negotiated lease rental to the lessor and operates the leased cars as if they were owned by the railroad and, in other cases, such cars are operated as private cars under railroad control. In the latter case, the railroads using the cars pay the tariff mileage allowance to the lessor, who in turn may credit such revenues against the lease rental payments of the lessee railroad or may retain them as the sole lease rental.

OT-5 Series

Before an owner of private railroad cars may load cars at a point on a railroad line, the owner must obtain the consent of the railroad line to the use of the cars on that line under AAR Circular OT-5 Series. The OT-5 Series sets out the rules provided by the AAR for the assignment of reporting marks and mechanical designations to railroad cars. When the owner of a railroad car applies for the mark he must obtain the consent of the originating line haul carrier on which the car will be loaded. There is no cost associated with the obtaining of consents. A form is filed with the Secretary, Operating–Transportation Division of the AAR. The proposed originating carrier is notified and the Secretary approves or disapproves the application in accordance with the directions of the carrier. Since 1972, when ABC and its affiliates began managing investor owned railcars they have had no instance where an originating carrier has refused consent. Generally in the past, owners of railroad equipment have been able to obtain consent to use the cars for the entire term of the lease, but recently some railroads have shortened the effective period of such consents. Difficulties in obtaining consents may somewhat restrict ABC's ability to lease the Cars to other lessees subsequent to the termination of some or all of the Leases.

Competition

Service lease rental rates are highly competitive and are not subject to regulation by the ICC as are the mileage allowances paid by the railroads for use of private cars. Lease rental rates are principally affected by the demand for and the supply of cars as between different owner-lessors. In times of high demand relative to supply, lessees tend to bid up lease rental rates to get the cars they need. In times of low demand relative to supply, owner-lessors tend to quote lower rates in order to keep their cars on lease and earning rental. Secondarily, lease rental rates reflect the cost of cars, interest costs on the investment, maintenance and operating costs, property taxes, other direct operating costs and the level of railroad mileage allowances. The major competitors for lease of privately owned covered hopper cars are GATX, Inc., ACF Industries, Inc. (Shippers Car Line Division), The Flying Tiger Corporation (North American Car Corporation) and Pullman Incorporated (Pullman Transport Leasing Co.). ABC, which presently manages approximately 1,100 covered hopper cars, has only a small percentage of the available fleet.

Residual Value of Cars

Railroad covered hopper cars are relatively simple and sturdily-built units of capital equipment, and are physically capable of a substantial useful life assuming proper maintenance. However, the value of such cars for continued employment in leased service or for resale cannot be forecast with certainty. There are factors which could tend to limit those values. Current practices and past trends give an indication of what those values might be in the future, but an investor must evaluate independently the risks of this aspect of freight car ownership.

The value of a car for continued employment in leased service depends more on the factors of supply and demand than on the physical age of the car. Some decrease in lease rental rates for older cars may be expected to occur, but current lease rental rates for well-maintained older cars are nearly the same as for new cars of the same type and size.

The market value of a used car depends on its physical condition, the demand for cars of its type and its remaining useful life in relation to the cost of new cars at that time. Covered hopper car construction cost factors established and maintained by the AAR reflect increases in the unit cost of new cars.

The following table sets forth with respect to covered hopper cars and for the period from 1959 through 1978 the following information:

Column I: The unit cost of new cars, which is generally the price charged by the manufacturer of the cars;

such price, therefore, will not include the commencement fee payable to CARCO, Seller of covered hopper cars.

Column II: The Settlement Value Factor. This figure is a function of two factors, the inflation factor (which is based on the estimated reproduction cost prescribed by the AAR) and the depreciation factor (also set by AAR, which is presently equal to 3.6% per year). For example, if a car is destroyed in the year of purchase, the percentage is equal to 100%. For any year subsequent to the year of purchase, this percentage is first increased for the inflation factor and then reduced 3.6% per year for each year from the date of purchase to the date of destruction.

Column III: The Settlement Value is the amount payable by railroads under AAR Rule 107 for a totally destroyed car. Column III indicates Settlement Value for a car that was destroyed in 1978. This figure is the product of Columns I and II, and is termed depreciated reproduction cost or "Settlement Value."

Year Built and Sold	Column I Unit Cost of New Cars	Column II Settlement Value Factor (%)	Column III AAR Rule 107 "Settlement Value"
1959	$11,532	78.86	$ 9,094
1960	13,892	82.54	11,466
1961	11,615	92.58	10,753
1962	15,263	98.57	15,045
1963	14,455	104.27	15,072
1964	14,673	104.58	15,345
1965	14,582	106.40	15,515
1966	15,487	112.77	17,465
1967	15,074	123.52	18,619
1968	14,728	130.89	19,277
1969	15,201	134.21	20,401
1970	16,221	127.41	20,667
1971	15,930	134.74	21,464
1972	18,079	125.44	22,678

Year Built and Sold	Column I Unit Cost of New Cars	Column II Settlement Value Factor (%)	Column III AAR Rule 107 "Settlement Value"
1973	$18,000	128.92	$23,206
1974	20,000	119.40	23,880
1975	26,480*	95.00	25,156
1976	27,497*	95.25	26,191
1977	28,545*	96.40	27,517
1978	31,086*	100.00	31,086

*Preliminary.

There is no reliable way of forecasting whether or not the increase in the price of new cars will continue in the future. It is important to note that during the past 20 years the price of railroad equipment has risen at a more rapid rate than the average of all industrial or other commodities. However, the price of new covered hopper cars is not the only factor relevant to the selling price of used covered hopper cars. If the demand for cars were to decrease, it might not be possible to sell used cars at an advantageous price despite the fact that inflation had driven up the cost of new cars.

There are many other factors which could affect the value of the Cars. Among these factors are cost and availability of raw materials for railcar construction, inflation, wear and tear on the car, technological advances in railcar construction and in the transportation industry, financial strength of the railroads, available supply of new railcars, and demand for the use of these cars. Since a railcar's component parts are primarily made up of different types of steel, changes in the price of steel and its supply could have significant effect on railcar construction. While there currently is no shortage of steel, there is a shortage in some railcar components (due to casting process). During 1978, the shortage of side frames and bolsters (trucks) was a matter of continuing concern in the industry. A number of foreign suppliers began to market trucks actively in the domestic market and these imports are expected to influence 1979 delivery patterns.

Future technological advances in railcar construction and in the transportation industry are almost impossible to predict.

One significant change that has occurred recently in the covered hopper fleet is the gradual replacement of 70 ton cars with 100 ton cars.

The financing of equipment is a major railroad problem. Many railroads find paying mileage allowances more advantageous than owning railcars themselves. The ability to increase car supply is directly related to earnings. Many railroads in grain producing regions are no longer financially viable and cannot afford the larger capital investments necessary for the purchase or leasing of numerous covered hopper cars (4,000 cu.ft. capacity and over), which are most often used for hauling grains. Over 55,000 cars or 58 percent of the total U.S. fleet of covered hopper cars suitable for hauling grain were privately owned, as of April 1, 1978.

The available supply and demand for covered hopper cars will also substantially affect a car's residual value. Currently the equipment industry is faced with increasing backlogs. The backlog for covered hopper railroad cars increased from 2,918 at the end of 1976 to 3,993 at the end of 1977 or an increase of 37% and by October, 1978, the backlog was 19,618 or an increase of 491% over the end of 1977. The U.S. covered hopper fleet totaled 246,100 cars as of January 1, 1979. During the calendar year 1978, nearly 10,300 cars were added to the covered hopper fleet. From January 1, 1972, through the same date in 1979, about 66,200 cars (a 26.9 percent increase) were added to this fleet.

Along with an increasing supply of covered hopper cars has come an increasing demand. Not only is grain transportation demanding more covered hoppers, but fertilizers, minerals, chemicals and plastic are also strongly competing for these cars. Rail, however, is not the only mode of transportation used to move grain. Grain movements by barge have substantially increased in recent years and trucks are also used to move grain. Higher fuel costs could restrict long-haul grain movements by trucks and emphasize the fuel efficiency of rail, but this advantage could be offset by higher freight rates.

If railroads maintain their present share of off-farm movements, the estimated grain transportation demand for 1985 indicates that approximately 17,000 additional covered hopper cars will be required over the number now dedicated to grain transportation in the 1977-78 marketing year. The required total will be approximately 88,000 cars by 1985. This projection is based on an average of 15 car trips per year. If the railroad can increase the utilization rate to 16 car trips per year it has been estimated that only an additional 12,000 cars will be needed in 1985.

The factor of mechanical or economic obsolescence may also affect the future value of covered hopper cars, particularly of cars more than 20 years old. Under present rules, any freight car over 20 years of age cannot be sold (or its reporting marks changed) and continued in use in interchange service unless it meets or is modified to meet certain currently-prescribed mechanical standards. All freight cars up to 25 years old with structural weakness or damage cannot be sold for use in interchange service without being brought up to current standards. The costs of such modifications must, under presently-applicable rules, amount to at least 50% of the AAR reproduction value at the time. All cars 25 years or older cannot be given the rebuilt status but must be brought up to the currently prescribed mechanical standards before they are sold. There is no assurance that, in the future, the age limits will not be reduced or the prescribed mechanical standards (or the amounts required to be expended in meeting them) will not be increased.

EXAMPLE OF A PRIVATE RAILROAD CAR PROGRAM

The Management Program. Covered Hopper Railcar Management Program.

Sponsor and Manager. Railcar Management, Inc., ("ABC," the "Sponsor" or the "Manager").

Seller of Covered Hopper Cars. CARCO, a California corporation ("CARCO").

The Offering. Opportunity to purchase 1,250 Covered Hopper Railroad Cars (the "Cars") from CARCO, as Seller, together with option of entering into 10-year Management Agreements with the Manager for the management of the Cars as agent for the investor-car owner.

Description of Covered Hopper Cars. 100-ton triple hopper, 4,750 cubic foot railroad cars with center pockets, gravity discharge and trough hatch roof.

Minimum Investment. One (1) Car (with optional Management Agreement) for an estimated maximum purchase price of $50,351 including Initial Storage and Transit Costs of approximately $200. The amount of the Manufacturer's Invoice Price and of the Initial Storage and Transit Costs are estimates based on current purchase orders and estimated delivery dates and such estimates are subject to adjustment upon delivery of the Car. In addition, each investor who elects to enter into the Management Program, must pay a $50 ICC filing fee for the filing of the Management Agreement. The actual price paid by an investor will depend on the Manufacturer's Invoice Price for that investor's particular Car at the time of closing. Not all investors will pay the same price for a Car.

Terms of Purchase and Financing. The Sponsor and CARCO require (a) that each investor make a deposit of at least 30% of the Subscription Price with their subscription for a Car or Unit and (b) that payment in full for the Car or Unit be made at the time of delivery of the Car. Should an investor need to borrow any portion of the purcahse price of the Car or Unit, the Sponsor is advised and believes, depending upon the creditworthiness of the investor, that several sources of capital exist, including borrowing from banks and other financial institutions. The nature of any borrowing (e.g. whether on a recourse or nonrecourse basis) will restrict the ability of individuals and certain other taxpayers to take advantage of some of the tax benefits otherwise available.

The Management Program. Generally, gross revenues and expenses of all Cars owned by participants in the Management Program will be pooled and any net operating income distributed (or net losses charged) to the participants, pro rata, (regardless of any variance in the actual cost of the Units on Closing). For its management services, ABC will receive a monthly management fee of $55 per Car during the first five years of the Management Contract; thereafter, the Management Fee will be increased (or decreased) by a percentage based upon the Indexes of Railroad Material Prices and Wage Rates published by the Association of American Railroads.

ABC will, at the option of an investor who finances Car purchases from borrowings, make monthly distributions out of earnings in order to assist such investor to pay debt service thereon, so long as such debt service is due on the first or last day of each month, commencing at the end of the first fiscal quarter following delivery of the Car. ABC will charge a $7 per Car per month fee for such services. In addition, ABC will, if the investor so elects, use its best efforts to obtain refinancing of any such loans which become due within the fifth year of the term of the Management Agreement (and at such other times as ABC may agree) and ABC will receive such fee as the investor and ABC may agree upon with respect to refinancing which is arranged by ABC for such borrower. In addition, during the term of the Management Agreement (which will be for 10 years) and for four months thereafter, ABC will have an exclusive right of sale and will receive as a sales commission, upon any sale to a third party (other than upon foreclosure), the sum of (i) 4% of gross sale proceeds and (ii) 25% of the amount by which gross sale proceeds exceed 100% of the original purchase price. Thus, if an investor's Car is sold for 100% of the original purchase price ABC would receive 4% of the gross sales proceeds. If, for example, a Car is sold for 110% of the original purchase price ABC would receive 4% of the amount up to the original price plus 29% of any amount in excess thereof.

ABC, AS MANAGER, HAS OBTAINED 12 LEASES FOR A TOTAL OF 840 CARS AND HAS NOT OBTAINED TO DATE ANY CONTRACTUAL ARRANGEMENTS FOR LEASES OF THE BALANCE OF THE CARS. However, the Manager has submitted lease proposals with respect to an additional 225 of the Cars and expects that such proposals will, in due course, become binding leases. IF AN INVESTOR ELECTS TO ENTER INTO A MANAGEMENT AGREEMENT, IT IS A CONDITION OF THE CLOSING OF A SALE AND DELIVERY OF A CAR THAT EACH SUCH CAR BE SUBJECT TO A BINDING LEASE.

An investor is not required to participate in the Management Program as a condition to purchase of the Cars. However, without the express consent of ABC (which consent is expected to be withheld), the Leases will cover only Cars managed under the Management Program. INVESTORS WHO ELECT TO PARTICIPATE IN THE MANAGEMENT PROGRAM MAY RECEIVE A PREFERENCE IN THE ALLOCATION OF CARS AS THEY BECOME AVAILABLE FOR DELIVERY. THE

SELLER RESERVES THE RIGHT IN ITS SOLE DISCRETION TO REJECT ANY SUBSCRIPTION. CARS WILL NOT NECESSARILY BE ASSIGNED TO INVESTORS IN THE ORDER IN WHICH THE SUBSCRIPTIONS ARE RECEIVED.

Management Program–Investment Objectives. The Management Program's objectives are to provide participants in the Management Program with (i) the benefits of continuing income, a portion of which will be "sheltered" from federal income taxes (however, purchasers of Cars who have borrowed to finance a substantial portion of the purchase price of their Cars should note that not operating income from their Cars may not be sufficient to pay the monthly debt service on such borrowings); (ii) an investment tax credit (in 1979 or 1980, depending on the date of delivery of the Car), in an amount varying between 9% and 10% of their total investment, depending upon each investor's determination of the amount to be used as a basis for calculation of total equipment cost; and (iii) maintenance of substantial residual value (for continued operation or sale) upon expiration of the Management Program.

Analytic models of the cash flow and taxable income or loss which may result from purchase, management and sale of a Car, and the assumptions on the basis on which such model has been prepared, are set forth under "Analytic Models of Car Operation." The model is based solely on the prior experience of the Manager. No assurance can be given as to the actual amount or certainty of any present or future cash benefits or tax consequences which may flow from investment in this Management Program.

There is no assurance that any or all of such objectives or the results under such Analytic Model will actually be obtained.

ESTIMATED USE OF PROCEEDS

The following table sets forth information concerning the use of proceeds of the offering of Units.

	Per Unit/Car		Total	
	Amount	Percent	Amount	Percent
Payable to Covered Hopper Car Manufacturers[1]	$45,592	90.55%	$56,806,162	90.55%
Commencement Fee paid to CARCO[2]	4,559	9.05%	5,680,616	9.05%
Initial Storage and Transit Costs[1]	200	0.40[5]	250,000	0.40[5]
Total	$50,351	100.00%	$62,736,778	100.00%

1. Estimate based on present quoted Manufacturers' Invoice Prices and current information available to Sponsor which includes estimated escalation in the price of Cars.
2. From which CARCO will pay (a) Lease Negotiation Fees to ABC of 1% of the Manufacturer's Invoice Price (estimated at $455.92) per Car; (b) Placement Fees to the Managing Placement Agent of 5% of the Manufacturer's Invoice Price for each Car (estimated at up to $2,279.60 per Unit or Car); and (c) retain the balance as a Car Acquisition Fee on sale of the Cars (from which CARCO will pay the expenses of this offering, estimated at $275,000).

COMPENSATION AND FEES TO THE MANAGER AND ITS AFFILIATES

The following table summarizes the type, estimated maximum amounts and recipients of compensation to be paid to the Manager and its affiliates. Such fees or other compensation will be paid regardless of the success or profitability of the Management Program's operations. Such compensation and fees were established by the Manager and are not based on arm's length negotiations. Except for those fees specifically listed herein no other compensation or fees will be paid to the Manager and its affiliates.

Entity Receiving Compensation	Type of Compensation	Estimated Maximum Amounts
	Offering, Organizational and Car Acquisition Stage	
CARCO . . (the Seller of Cars)	*Commencement Fee* equal to 10% of Manufacturer's Invoice Price for Cars (estimated at $4,599.20 per Car), which may be reduced, as described below, under certain circumstances. From this Commencement Fee, CARCO will pay (a) a Placement Fee to the Managing Placement Agent equal to 5% of Manufacturer's Invoice Price of each Car sold (estimated at $2,279.60 per Car or Unit) and (b) the Lease Negotiation Fee described herein to ABC. The balance of the fee will be retained by CARCO as a Car Acquisition Fee from which CARCO will pay all expenses of this offering.	Actual amount depends on the number of Cars sold, the Manufacturer's Invoice Price of the Cars sold, and the number of cars leased under the leases, but is not expected to exceed $5,680,616, of which CARCO is expected to retain not in excess of $2,001,247. (Assumes all 1,250 Cars are sold and participate in the Management Program.)
ABC. . . . (the Manaager)	*Lease Negotiation Fee* equal to 1% of the Manufacturer's Invoice Price of each Car sold and leased under the Leases (estimated at $455.92) per Car sold. CARCO's commencement fee will be reduced by the amount of the Lease Negotiation Fee payable with respect to any Car not leased under the leases, which eventuality is not anticipated.	Actual amount depends on the number of Cars sold, the Manufacturer's Invoice Price of the Cars sold and the number of Cars leased under the Leases, but is not expected to exceed $568,062. (Assumes all 1,250 Cars are sold and participate in the Management Program.)
AB . . . . Securities . . . (the Managing Placement Agency)	*Placement Agent's Fee* equal to 5% of the Manufacturer's Invoice Price of each Car sold. A portion (up to 4% of the Manufacturer's Invoice Price of each Car) of such fees may be reallowed to nonaffiliated securities broker-dealers to the extent they participate in the offering.	Actual amount depends on number of Cars sold, the amount of the Manufacturer's Invoice Price, and the amount reallowed to nonaffiliated broker-dealers, but is not expected to exceed $1,476,644. (Assumes all 1,250 Cars are sold, and that 500 Cars are sold by AB Securities itself and 750 Cars are sold by nonaffiliated broker-dealers.)

Entity Receiving Compensation	Type of Compensation	Estimated Maximum Amounts
	Operational Stage	
ABC . . . (the	*Base Management Fee* equal to $55 per month per Car which will be subject to adjustment after the initial five years of the term of the Management Agreement.	$825,000 annually. (Assumes all 1,250 Cars are sold and participate in the Management Program.)
	Re-leasing Fee equal to 2% of gross rentals received per month under each lease of a Car entered into after the initial lease applicable to such Car.	Indeterminate
	Servicing Fee of $7 per Car per month for participants who finance Car purchases and request special monthly distributions.	Indeterminate
	Refinancing Fee (in an amount to be negotiated) for assisting borrower in refinancing a loan made to finance a Car purchase if Manager's services are utilized.	Indeterminate
GHI	*Subleasing Fee*	Indeterminate
JKL	Repair of wrecked Cars and wheel replacement and Car maintenance costs. Sale of wheel and axle sets to original manufacturers of Cars.	Indeterminate
	Liquidation (Sale) Stage	
ABC . . . (the Manager)	*Sales commissions* (if Car is sold during term of a Management Agreement or within 4 months thereafter, other than as a result of foreclosure, total destruction or sale to ABC or its affiliates) equal to (i) 4% of the gross sales proceeds plus (ii) 25% of the amount by which gross sale proceeds exceed the original Price to the Public of the Car.	Indeterminate

THE CARS

General

Each of the Cars will be a new 4,750 cubic foot capacity, gravity discharge covered hopper car to be used in the transportation and shipping of agricultural products and certain other dry bulk commodities. The Cars will have three compartments and will be equipped with a 24″ x 47′8″ trough hatch and 24″ x 30″ discharge gates in each compartment and will be manufactured in accordance with the specifications required by the American Association of Railroads for railroad freight cars to be used in interchange service.

Each Car is equipped with 100-ton capacity trucks of Grade B cast steel. The Car itself is basically a long covered box that can accommodate dry bulk commodities. The trough hatch is particularly well suited for loading of grain. The hatch is covered to protect the cargo from moisture and the elements. Cars manufactured by Trinity Industries, Inc., will have four roof hatch covers per car, whereas the cars manufactured by Portec, Inc., will have three such covers. The Manager does not believe that this variance in the number of covers affects either the operation or value of the Cars.

Covered hopper cars are generally used for hauling grain (wheat, barley, corn, soy beans, etc.). The Cars may also be used to haul other dry bulk commodities, such as chemicals, fertilizers, dolomite, borax and sugar.

CARCO has received acceptances of purchase orders for 450 of the Cars to be manufactured by Trinity Industries, Inc. ("Trinity") and for an additional 800 of the Cars, which will be included in this offering, to be manufactured by Portec, Inc. ("Portec").

Warranties. Trinity will warrant, for a period of one year, that each of the Cars manufactured by it will be free from defects in material and workmanship. This warranty does not cover or apply to any product, accessory, part or attachment which is not manufactured by Trinity. Each purchaser making a claim under this warranty must give written notice to Trinity prior to expiration of the warranty period. If Trinity determines that the alleged defect is the result of faulty material or one hundred twenty (120) days after receipt of the defective part or car.

Portec will warrant that its equipment will be free from defects in material or workmanship under normal use and service. The warranty excludes specialties incorporated in the equipment specified by the Purchaser and not manufactured by Portec. Portec's obligation under the warranty will be limited to making good at any of its three manufacturing facilities any part or parts of such equipment which shall, within one year after the delivery of the equipment to the Purchaser, be returned to Portec with transportation charges prepaid and which Portec's examination discloses to its satisfaction to have been defective. This warranty does not apply to (i) any components which have been repaired or altered unless repaired or altered by Portec or its authorized service representatives, if, in Portec's judgment, such repairs or alterations affect the stability of the equipment or (ii) any equipment which has been subject to misuse, negligence or accident.

The only warranties made with respect to the cars will be those made by Trinity and Portec as specified above. CARCO OR ABC MAKE NO WARRANTIES OR REPRESENTATIONS WITH RESPECT TO THE FITNESS OR MERCHANTABILITY OF THE CARS.

LEASES

Leases

ABC has entered into 12 leases for 840 of the Cars to be included in the Program. The leases will commence with the delivery of the Cars. The rental for these Cars is to be equal to 1.1% (1.15% in the case of the one lease for 50 of the Cars) of the manufacturer's actual invoice price of a particular Car per month (e.g., $501.51 per car per month based upon a manufacturer's Invoice Price of $45,592 and a rate of 1.1%), subject to escalation. In addition, the leases provide with slight variations for payment of 2¢ per mile for every mile in excess of 30,000 miles per Car per year travelled by the Cars covered by the leases. In case of some leases, three companies will use the Cars on a "split lease" basis with one of the lessees using all of the Cars for several months during each year and additional lessees each using a portion of the Cars for specified periods during the balance of the year.

IT IS A CONDITION OF THE SALE AND DELIVERY OF EACH CAR TO AN INVESTOR WHO PARTICIPATES IN THE MANAGEMENT PROGRAM THAT SUCH CAR BE SUBJECT TO A BINDING LEASE. INVESTORS WHO ELECT TO PARTICIPATE IN THE MANAGEMENT PROGRAM MAY RECEIVE A PREFERENCE IN THE ALLOCATION OF CARS AS SUCH CARS BECOME AVAILABLE FOR DELIVERY. ADDITIONALLY, IN DETERMINING ORDER OF DELIVERY OF CARS, ABC WILL USE ITS DISCRETION TO ASSIGN CARS TO LEASES IN A MANNER WHICH WILL INSURE PRESERVATION OF THE INVESTMENT TAX CREDIT FOR EACH INVESTOR.

It is anticipated that all leases to be entered into will provide that ABC is acting as agent for certain undisclosed principals as lessors and that ABC has the right from time to time to identify the principals as lessors under the leases. The Cars of purchasers who elect to have their Cars managed under the Management Program will be leased under the leases to be entered into prior to delivery of the Cars (and it is expected that purchasers of Cars who elect not to participate in the Management Program will make their own arrangements for the lease or other commercial use of their Cars). At the time of the purchase of Cars by an investor who elects to participate in the Program, and before such Cars are delivered to a lessee under a lease, ABC will identify such investor as a principal/lessor to the lessees under such lease. The purchaser will, upon purchase of the Cars, be the lessor under the lease with respect to the Cars purchased. Such Cars will be delivered to the lessee by ABC on behalf of the purchaser.

Under the existing leases as well as leases to be negotiated, the lessor ordinarily will be obligated to pay any property taxes and to maintain the Cars in good running condition (including repairs needed because of a defect in the manufacture of the Cars). If a car needs repairs, rent will normally abate after 7 days and will continue to abate until the cars have been returned to the lessee. The lessees will be obligated to pay all other operating expenses and may have the right to make ordinary running repairs on the Cars and to receive reimbursement for such repairs from the participants.

Generally, the lessee is responsible for the loss, damage or destruction to the cars provided such loss, damage or destruction was not the result of negligence, recklessness or wilful misconduct of the participant or ABC. Although any alterations, changes or additions to the cars are the responsibility of the participant, the leases will normally provide for an increase in the rental rate which will be based on the same method under which the original rental rate was computed. However, rent will normally abate after 7 to 10 days after the car is removed from service for the purpose of making such changes, alterations and additions, and will cease to abate after the car is returned to the lessee. Under the Management Agreement, ABC will act as agent for the participants in administering the above provisions of the leases and the other provisions of any leases entered into on behalf of the participants.

In the event that CARCO is unable to sell a sufficient number of Cars which become subject to the Management Program, and that ABC is, therefore, unable to provide sufficient Cars to meet any lease requirement, a lessee may take the position that it has a right to terminate the particular lease with respect to all Cars, including Cars already subject to the Management Program. Although it is unclear whether a lessee would have such a right, ABC believes that, regardless of whether or not such a right exists, the risk that the Cars would be off lease for any substantial period is not significant in light of the following considerations:

(a) Although no assurance in this regard can be given, ABC believes that it should be able to lease substitute Cars in the short-term market to the extent it is necessary to fulfill the requirements of a lease. ABC has also agreed under the Management Agreement to bear any expenses in obtaining such substitute cars, and the income and expenses of such substitute cars will not be pooled with the income and expense of the Cars of the investors.

(b) Even if the lessees rightfully terminated any then existing leases, although the Cars may be off lease for a relatively short period, ABC feels that, in light of the present short supply of covered hopper cars relative to the demand for such cars, and the current level of rental rates to be negotiated under the proposed leases, it would be able to re-lease the Cars to other lessees at rental rates which would approximate the rental rates under the proposed leases.

ABC will attempt to lease Cars on behalf of participants only to lessees who have substantial assets or who, in the opinion of

ABC, will be in a position to bear the obligations under the lease.

ABC has agreed that it will enforce the obligations of the lessees, on behalf of participants, under any leases regarding the location of the use of the Cars so that the Cars will not be used outside the United States for any periods longer than those specified in the respective leases. ABC will also require that any leases entered into (or any other arrangements made for the use of the Cars) will contain provisions regarding the identity of the lessees or sublessees of the Cars and the location of the use of the Cars so as to avoid recapture of any allowable investment tax credit claimed with respect to the Cars. If such provisions were not then obtainable from any lessees acceptable to ABC, subsequent leases would not be entered into without the prior written consent of each participant whose Cars would be subject to such leases.

THE MANAGER

ABC will act as Manager under the Program. ABC, a wholly-owned subsidiary of DEF, Inc.

ABC is one of the six main subsidiaries of DEF, Inc., which presently functions as a holding company, through its subsidiaries is primarily engaged in providing a complete range of maintenance, leasing and marketing services for railroad rolling stock and has expanded its services to meet the needs of individual and corporate investors and of lessees and other users of specialized types of railroad cars.

The subsidiaries of DEF are for (1) equipment purchases, (2) investment and management services, (3) railcar leasing services, (4) railcar maintenance, (5) economic, transportation, and engineering consulting services, and (6) sale of securities. Their specific activities are described below:

(1) CARCO is newly formed in 1979 to arrange for and handle the purchase and delivery of all railroad car and other transportation equipment for sale to investors and for the account of the DEF companies.

(2) ABC, the Manager and Sponsor of the Management Program, provides a full-range of management and investment services to investors in railroad equipment. ABC now manages

through the 13 investor pools previously sponosred by it or its affiliates, a fleet of railroad cars—totalling 1,365 cars, which ABC believes to be one of the largest fleets of investor-owned railroad cars in the United States.

(3) GHI provides a wide range of flexible railroad car leasing contracts to shippers of bulk materials, as well as maintenance management contracts to railroad car lessees or owners. GHI utilizes three types of leases: (1) Short Term (from one month to two years); (2) Medium Term (from three years to seven years); and (3) Long Term (from eight years to 15 years). For covered hopper cars, GHI utilizes all three types of leases. GHI has developed a number of leasing programs, including a three-year, "three-corner" program whereby hopper cars are leased for the peak demand periods of three or more different shippers. As an example, a fertilizer company may use the cars for four months each year, a grain company for five months each year, and finally a railroad for the remaining three months.

Tank cars are generally leased for shippers to the petroleum, liquid fertilizer, and vegetable product industries.

GHI also handles a maintenance management contract for lessees or car owners which includes handling payments of running repairs, verification of mileage credit, auditing and payment of property taxes, and scheduling heavy repairs.

(4) JKL began operating the first production-line maintenance facility in the United States primarily for privately owned and leased coal cars in unit-train service. JKL's principal maintenance facility, which cost approximately $8 million for land, building and equipment, is located at Ajax, Nebraska, adjacent to the main line of Burlington Northern Railroad, which carries the bulk of the coal from mines in the Powder River Basin of Wyoming to utilities in the Midwest and the Southwest. The Ajax facility is geared to a rapid car turnaround time, and can provide service to as many as 8,000 coal cars under long-term contract, with approximately 4,000 cars currently going through the periodic maintenance shop each year. The Ajax facility also has wreck repair and car rebuilding capabilities, as well as a $3 million automated wheel shop operating as its subsidiary. JKL Wheels, Inc. estimates that approximately 40 to 50 percent of the cost for unit-train maintenance is directly wheel-oriented.

While the Ajax facility is primarily involved in the repair of unit-coal train railcars, it is not operating at capacity and has recently undertaken the repair of wrecked covered hopper cars. It is not anticipated that routine maintenance of hopper cars will be performed at the Ajax facility. There has been no specific agreement with JKL with respect to a grant of preference for repair of wrecked cars from the Program at the Ajax facility.

JKL maintains a second but smaller maintenance and repair facility at Mork, Montana, located on both the Chicago, Milwaukee, St. Paul & Pacific Railroad and the Burlington Northern Railroad lines. This facility can handle investor-owned covered hopper cars and unit-train coal cars moving grain and coal primarily eastward in the northern portion of the United States. The shop has facilities for making light repairs and handling wrecked cars, but transfers worn wheel and axle sets to Ajax. A third maintenance facility for coal, covered hoppers, and other types of cars is planned for the Fiesty, Texas, area to become operational in 1980, although its specific location and the financing of its construction have not yet been determined. There is no assurance that the Fiesty facility will be built.

The capability of the Ajax and Mork facilities to undertake repairs of wrecked hopper cars provides to the Management Program a controlled maintenance facility for the repair of wrecked hopper cars at a time when, on an industry-wide basis, ABC believes there is a shortage of such facilities. Even though there may be adequate plant capacity, due to plant location and the probable dispersement of cars geographically, there can be no assurance that in the future JKL will be able to provide wreck repair services for all cars in programs managed by JKL.

(5) MNO is primarily engaged in offering economic and engineering consulting services to utilities, mining companies, and other users of specialized railcars. Its service include systems design, tariff analysis, car specifications, cost evaluation, market analysis, and expert witness testimony.

MNO has developed a series of computer programs that predict the wear-life of car components, determine when maintenance should take place, and provide complete reports of maintenance costs on a car-by-car basis, item by item for coal cars in unit-train service. These computer programs have provided DEF's maintenance subsidiary, JKL with an effective system which will be used to control and evaluate repairs made to cars in this Management Program.

(6) PQR Securities, the Managing Placement Agent, is a newly-formed subsidiary of DEF, Inc., which will act as a broker-dealer of securities and which has been accepted as a member of the National Association of Securities Dealers, Inc.

ABC and its affiliates will make the day-to-day decisions with respect to management, leasing and maintenance of the Cars. ABC anticipates that the Management Program will benefit from the experience and capabilities of the officers and employees of ABC who have substantial experience in railroad car leasing and maintenance.

DESCRIPTION OF THE MANAGEMENT PROGRAM

General

Each investor who desires to have ABC manage his Cars and participate in the ABC Covered Hopper Railcar Management Program will be required to enter into a Management Agreement with ABC. The term of the Management Agreement is ten years, but it may be terminated earlier upon loss, destruction or sale of a Car or withdrawal of a Car on account of the owner's refusal to make a required improvement or alteration.

The Management Agreement provides that ABC, on behalf of a participant, will, among other things, use its best efforts to arrange for the leasing of such participant's Cars to shippers, railroads or others on long or short-term leases or on such other terms and conditions as may be satisfactory to ABC. ABC will place reporting marks on the Cars and perform all managerial and administrative functions necessary for the operation of the Cars, including repairing and maintaining the Cars, and keeping adequate records of their operation. In addition, ABC will act as agent for the participant in collecting revenues (including per diem earnings, indemnity payments and insurance awards), investing excess funds pending distribution and in disbursing the participant's funds to pay, among other things, operating expenses.

The revenue from the Cars during the term of the Management Agreement may vary depending on the use of, and demand for, the Cars by lessees. In addition, expenses (such as maintenance and repair costs) may vary from time to time from one Car to another. In order to equalize the income to each participant, income and operating expenses for all Cars owned by participants in the Program and interest earned on excess funds pending distribution will, in general, be pooled and distributed on a pro rata basis during the term of the Management Agreement, based upon the number of Cars participating and the date on which such Cars are delivered to a lessee. Revenue and expenses for up to 1,250 Cars will be pooled, depending upon the number of Cars purchased and the number of investors who elect to participate in the Management Program. The revenues and expenses of Cars purchased under this Program will not be pooled with revenues and expenses of any other cars purchased or managed by ABC.

At the expiration of the Management Agreement, a Car owner could personally manage his Cars, enter into another management agreement with ABC on such terms and conditions as they might then agree or negotiate a management agreement with another railcar management firm. Alternatively, the owner might seek to enter into a new lease for the Cars (under which the owner would have little, if any, responsibility for management or maintenance of the Cars) or could seek to sell the Cars. (It should be noted that a Car may be subject to a lease at the termination of the Management Agreement.)

Pooling of Revenue and Expenses

The Management Agreement provides that, with certain exceptions, ABC will pool all income and expenses (other than the Management Fee paid to ABC) in connection with the operation of the Cars purchased by investors who elect to enter into the Management Agreement, including interest earned on excess funds pending distribution. All expenses incurred in connection with the management, use and operation of the Cars, including, but not limited to, repairs, maintenance, improvements, taxes, adjustments or refunds payable to railroads or others, registration fees, insurance premiums, tariff charges, legal and auditing expenses of reporting to investors and the Securities and Exchange Commission, and certain losses from liabilities (including attorney's fees in connection therewith) not covered by insurance (up to the lesser of $2,500 per occurrence for liability to third parties for both personal injury and property damage and the deductible under any third-party liability insurance policies) will be deducted from the gross income and the remaining amount will be credited (or charged) to participants on a pro rata basis (in proportion to the number of Cars participating and the number of days of each Car in the Management Program). However, the Management Fee payable to ABC with respect to each Car and income, costs and expenses associated with ownership of Cars such as expenses or losses resulting from damage to a Car, amounts recovered under any insurance or from any other party in connection with destruction or loss of a Car, the costs of certain special improvements, and commissions payable on the sale of a Car will be borne solely by or payable solely to the owner of that Car and will not be pooled expenses or revenue. Moreover, any additional storage or transit costs payable by a participant in the Program will be payable out of the gross revenue allocable to such participant.

In addition, if (a) any participant who has financed the purchase of Cars from borrowings shall so request and (b) the debt service on such borrowing is payable on the first or last day of each month. ABC will forward to the lender (as a distribution for the benefit of such participant) the lesser of (i) such participant's share of net earnings for the preceding month in the case of debt service due on the last day of each month and for the second month prior to the month in which debt service is payable in the case of debt service payable on the first of each month and (ii) such participant's debt service then due. Such transfer will be made not less than three days prior to the date such debt service is payable and, if the net earnings so transferred to the lender are less than the debt service then due, ABC will, not later than five days prior to the date such debt service is payable, send the participant written notice of such deficiency and the amount thereof. (The payment of such deficiency is the sole responsibility of the borrowing participant and failure to make such payment *promptly* will normally constitute a default on such participant's loan.) Depending upon the due dates for the first few installments of debt service, an investor may have to pay such installments from funds other than his or her share of net earnings, if any. ABC will charge each participant an additional fee of $7 per car per month for such services in connection with debt service payments.

Within seventy-five (75) days after the end of each quarter, ABC will distribute to each participant such participant's pro rata share of any net earnings for such quarter (reduced by (i) such participant's pro rata share of any reserves that ABC deems to be necessary and (ii) any net earnings of such participant for such quarter transferred by ABC to the lender to permit such participant to pay debt service). If such participant's share of net earnings, as reduced by net earnings applied to payment of debt service, is less than zero, the amount of the deficiency must be paid by such participant to ABC within ten days of notification from ABC of the amount of such deficiency.

If any earnings for a calendar quarter are received or expenses paid either before or after the end of such quarter, they will be included in the quarterly settlement for the quarter in which such earnings were either received or such expenses paid and accounted for as if they related to such preceding or subsequent quarter; however, if such earnings are received or expenses paid within one year of the quarter to which they relate and the amount involved exceeds $500 per Car, they will be accounted for with the earnings and expenses for such quarter. In addition, until the second quarter following the quarter in which the last car to be managed by ABC under the Management Program is delivered to a lessee, all such earnings and expenses will be accounted for with the earnings and expenses for the quarter to which they relate.

Sublease of Cars

In the event a lessee of a participant's Cars is unable to utilize such Cars for all or a part of a specified lease period, the lessee may sublease the Cars with or without the consent of ABC or the participant, depending upon the terms of the lease. An affiliate of ABC may either assist the lessee in subleasing the Cars or itself sublease the Cars from such lessee. In the event that an affiliate of ABC assists a leassee of the Cars in obtaining a sublease or subleases Cars from a lessee and in turn subleases to a third party, such affiliate will retain any compensation realized as a result of such transaction. No affiliate of ABC has at the date of this writing any understanding with any lessee or prospective lessee to sublease, or arrange for the sublease of, Cars.

Initial Inspection; Repairs and Maintenance; and Modifications and Improvements

Railroad cars undergo extensive inspection and testing by the manufacturer prior to delivery. Also representatives or agents of CARCO and ABC will visit the manufacturer to inspect the railroad cars before acceptance from the manufacturer. The railroad equipment carries a warranty for parts and labor from the manufacturer for one year. If mechanized or structural modifications or improvements are required in the future, they will be chargeable to the Car owner. It is not possible to predict the nature or cost of any such required modifications, if any.

Repairs or new covered hopper cars have typically been minor, generally confined to replacement of brake shoes and similar repairs. However, the frequency and expense of repair and maintenance expenses may be expected to increase as the Cars age. For example, it may be anticipated that, after approximately 8 to 12 years of normal use (depending on the condition of the roadbed and track, the number of miles traveled, the weight of loads transported and other factors), the wheels on the Cars would have to be replaced. The cost of a wheel change would depend upon whether the existing wheels were replaced with new or with second-hand, re-turned wheels, but, at presently-prevailing rates, if all the wheels on a Car were replaced with new wheels, the cost of such repair could be approximately $3,100. Such wheels may be purchased from JKL Wheels, Inc., an affiliate of ABC, at prices to be negotiated, which may be deemed not to be at arm's length.

Although participants in the Management Program will be purchasing new Cars, no assurance can be given that the Cars will not, in fact, require extensive maintenance during the term of the Management Program. In addition, although, for analytic purposes, maintenance expenses are thought of as occurring at regular intervals, based on statistical averages, it may be anticipated that maintenance expenses actually will be incurred at irregular and unpredictable intervals. No assurance can be given as to when maintenance, extensive or otherwise, might be required or the amount thereof. It should also be noted that due either to the location of a Car at the time repair is required or to the inadequate capacity of existing repair facilities, a Car may be off lease and remain unproductive for a period in excess of the period of coverage of available business interruption insurance, if any, which might apply with respect to such repair.

If a Car is damaged, the cost of repair of such damage will not be a pooled expense but will be the sole responsibility of the owner of such Car. Such owner, however, would be entitled to receive any insurance benefits or railroad or lessee indemnity payments payable in connection with such damage. Although no precise distinction can be drawn between damage, which is the responsibility of the owner, and maintenance repairs, which are a pooled expense, the former will normally result from a casualty occurrence such as an accident, while the latter will cover those expenses necessitated as a result of the use and age of a car.

If modifications to any Car are required, ABC will arrange for the modification, but the costs will not be pooled and will be the responsibility of the individual participant. However, no modifications or alterations will be made without the consent of the owner of the Car affected (which consent will be deemed given if the owner does not object within 30 days after notice of the modification and the cost thereof). If such owner will not consent to the making of such improvement or alteration, such owner may withdraw from the Management Program (but it should be noted that, since such modifications are usually those required by the AAR, ICC, DOT or other regulatory agency, it is unlikely that a Car could be operated without such improvements or alterations having been made).

If a Car is lost or destroyed, the Management Agreement will terminate with respect to that Car. The owner of that Car will thereafter not participate in the Management Program with respect to that Car and any insurance payment received as a result of the loss or total destruction will not be pooled and will be the property of the participant whose Car is involved.

Insurance and Fidelity Bond

ABC will, on behalf of the participants in the Program, purchase and maintain as an expense of the Management Program on an apportioned basis the following insurance, when available at rates that ABC considers reasonable:

(i) Comprehensive General Liability insurance with limits of $25,000,000 Combined Single Limits per occurrence for bodily injury and property damage arising out of ownership and operation of the Cars. With respect to claims for Products and Completed Operations, Contractual Liability and Independent Contractors Liability, there is an annual aggregate limit of $25,000,000 Combined Single Limits. The coverage has a $2,500 deductible per occurrence and this deductible (which includes attorneys' fees) will be a pooled expense. Liabilities, however, in excess of the above insurance limits, if any, will be the sole responsibility of the participant who owns the Cars which created the liability. The policy is subject to an exclusion of liability arising out of workers' compensation and unemployment laws (including disability benefits and FELA).

(ii) "All Risk" Physical Damage insurance for each Car up to a $60,000 maximum replacement cost subject to a $1,000 deductible and a $1,000,000 policy limit, both applicable on an occurrence basis. This $1,000,000 aggregate limit per occurrence includes both Physical Damage and the Business Interruption Insurance discussed in (iii) below. Coverage will insure most casualty risks; exclusions eliminate insurance for loss caused by faulty material or workmanship, inherent vice, gradual deterioration, mechanical breakdown, employee dishonesty, war, rebellion or insurrection and nuclear fission. The $1,000 deductible and any uninsured or excluded risks are the responsibility of the individual Car owner.

(iii) Business Interruption insurance for up to $600 per Car per month subject to an aggregate of $6,000 maximum per Car. This insurance covers loss of income caused by the perils insured against in subparagraph (ii) above. Payments under Business Interruption policies commence only after a specified minimum waiting period (currently 10 days).

The foregoing is only a general description and does not purport to be an exhaustive analysis of the terms and conditions of the insurance afforded. Prospective investors are invited to inspect the proposed policies on file with the Securities and Exchange Commission as an Exhibit to the Registration Statement herein and in the ABC offices.

If ABC believes that any such insurance is unobtainable or is available and maintainable only at rates which ABC considers unreasonably high, ABC will advise the participants in the Management Program. The participants may then individually elect whether to self-insure or to seek or purchase insurance to the extent such insurance is available. Participants are also free at any time (at their own expense) to seek such other or additional insurance as they deem desirable.

Additionally, DEF, the parent of ABC, will provide at its expense a fidelity bonds in the amount of $500,000 per occurrence which will bond its employees and all operations of DEF and its subsidiaries, including CARCO and ABC, against defalcations or other misappropriation of funds.

Tort Liability

A Car owner may be exposed to tort liability as a result of Car ownership. To the extent that any liability for torts resulting from Car ownership is not covered by or exceeds insurance the personal assets of an owner may be reached by an injured party. ABC and its affiliates have experienced no instance of personal liability of an owner in any of its prior railcar programs.

ABC will use its best efforts to minimize the tort liability exposure of a Car owner. The efforts will include the operation of the Cars under the Code of Rules of the AAR to the extent reasonably possible, the negotiation of lease terms providing reasonable indemnification to the Car owner, and the purchase of liability insurance on behalf of the owner.

Pursuant to the Interchange Rules of the AAR and related Interchange Agreements, while any railcar is in the cars and custody of a railroad, the carrier normally assumes liability for personal injury or property damage arising from the use or possession of the Cars.

Furthermore, ABC, on behalf of the participants in the Management Program, intends to negotiate and enter into leases which will provide that the lessor will be indemnified by the lessee against all losses or claims for injury to or death of persons, loss of or damage to property and economic loss due to nonavailability of Cars, unless such loss is caused by the lessor's neglect or willful act. However, ABC cannot give any assurance that all future leases will provide such terms.

Subject to a $2,500 deductible, the $25,000,000 Comprehensive General Liability policy will provide Contingent Railcar Leasing Liability insurance which protects the Car owners and ABC if any claim occurs where neither the lessee nor the carrier is responsible. This insurance provides a limit of $25,000,000 each and every occurrence for claims against the Car owner and/or ABC, should any occur; however, the policy contains a separate $25,000,000 annual aggregate limit for Products/Completed Operations, Contractual Liability and Independent Contractors Liability. If any claims are paid in a particular policy year under these three coverages, the aggregate limit is reduced by the amount of such paid claim. The $25,000,000 aggregate limits apply separately to and are fully reinstated for each policy year.

Compensation

ABC is entitled to receive, quarterly, a management fee equal to $55 per month per Car managed by ABC. Effective September 1, 1984, the monthly management fee will be increased (or decreased) by the percentage increase (or decrease) in the Wage Rate and Supplement Indexes (Western District), published by the Association of American Railroads, for the period January 1, 1979, through December 31, 1983.

ABC will also be entitled to a lease negotiation fee of 2% of all rentals received with respect to each Car, payable monthly, for the re-leasing of that Car subsequent to the termination of the original lease for such Car. In addition, if a participant financed the purchase of his Car and requests ABC to make monthly distributions of net revenues to facilitate the servicing of such loan, ABC will be entitled to a fee of $7 per month for each Car with respect to which such distributions are made.

A participant also will agree in the Management Agreement to indemnify and hold harmless and release ABC against all claims, liabilities and losses arising from use, operation, control, possession, maintenance, repair or storage of the Cars except for claims, liabilities or losses arising from ABC's negligence, gross negligence, bad faith, recklessness, gross misconduct or willful misconduct.

During the term of the Management Agreement and for the period of four months after the expiration thereof, a participant may not sell or dispose of the Cars managed under the Management Agreement without first offering ABC the right to purchase such Cars for the same consideration being offered in writing by a bona fide purchaser. This limitation, however, will be effective only if the participant has actively initiated the sales negotiation or if the potential purchaser is a competitor of

ABC. If ABC exercises its right of first refusal and resells the Car to a third party (other than an affiliate) within 90 days thereof, the participant who owned that Car will be entitled to the excess, if any, of the gross sales price of the Car over the sum of (i) the purchase price paid to ABC to such participant, (ii) ABC's commission as described below, and (iii) any expense incurred in connection with the resale, including commissions paid to brokers or broker-dealers.

ABC will also have the exclusive right to sell a participant's Cars and ABC will be entitled to a commission on the sale of a Car to a third party, which commission will be equal to the sum of (i) 4% of the gross sales proceeds and (ii) 25% of the amount by which gross sale proceeds exceed the participant's total original purchase price for the Car (including DEF's Commencement Fee and Initial Transit and Storage Costs). No commission will be payable in connection with a loss or destruction of a Car, a sale or other disposition of a Car to ABC or its affiliates, or a sale upon foreclosure.

ABC's Expenses; Other Programs

ABC, except as noted below, will pay for all of its expenses of managerial and administrative services rendered in connection with the accounting for collection of rental payments and per diem mileage allowances, the keeping of all books and records, supervision of covered hopper car operations, and all overhead items, which include legal and accounting fees, salaries, rent, travel and telephone expenses. Expenses of auditing and reporting the results of the Management Program (including legal and auditing expenses) pursuant to the requirements of the Securities and Exchange Act of 1934 and various state securities administrators will be charged to and pooled with other expenses of the Management Program allocable to investors and owners of Cars. Income and expenses attributable to covered hopper cars or other cars which are not owned by participants in this Management Program will not be pooled with that from any Cars owned by participants in this Management Program.

Reports

Statements of earnings, if any, for each participant's Cars will be provided quarterly within 75 days after the end of each of the first three calendar quarters and a report will be provided annually within 75 days of the close of each calendar year. Within such period of time annually, ABC will also supply each participant with a statement for use in the preparation of such participant's federal income tax returns. In addition, the independent accountants who act as auditors to ABC will make a review of the operations (which review will not constitute and is not intended to be an audit) and ABC will deliver such report to participant within 90 days after the end of each calendar year. The fees of the independent accountants and other legal and accounting expenses incurred in connection with the preparation of the above-described reports will be a pooled expense borne by the participants in the Management Program.

To the extent that quarterly and annual reports are filed pursuant to the provisions of the Securities and Exchange Act of 1934, as amended, or as a result of undertakings in connection with this offering, such reports may be substituted by the Manager in lieu of those otherwise provided for herein.

OFFERING AND SALE OF AND PAYMENT FOR CARS

Offering of Cars

PQR, an affiliate of CARCO and ABC has entered into a Managing Placement Agent Agreement with CARCO and PQR pursuant to which ABC Securities has agreed to act as Managing Placement Agent for CARCO and ABC to assist in the offering to qualified investors of Cars and the opportunity to participate in the Management Program. PQR Securities has advised CARCO and ABC that PQR Securities may offer Cars and the opportunity to participate in the Management Program through other dealers ("Selected Agents") chosen by PQR Securities, who will enter into a Selected Agent Agreement with PQR Securities. The offering is being made on a "best efforts" basis, which means that neither PQR Securities nor any of the Selected Agents have any obligation to purchase any Cars, but are only required to use their best efforts in offering the Cars and the opportunity to participate in the Management Program.

In the Managing Placement Agent Agreement, CARCO has agreed to pay PQR Securities a placement fee equal in amount to 5% of the Manufacturer's Invoice Price of each Car sold, and

PQR Securities has advised CARCO and ABC that PQR Securities will allow to the Selected Agents a selling commission equal to an amount up to 4% of the Manufacturer's Invoice Price of Cars sold by them.

The offering will continue until all 1,250 Cars are sold (unless the Sponsor elects to extend the period of the offering and amends the Program appropriately).

PQR Securities and its affiliates will not receive, directly or indirectly, any payments or compensation in connection with the offering and sale of Cars or the offering of the opportunity to participate in the Management Program, except as described above.

The Managing Placement Agent Agreement contains cross-indemnity provisions with respect to certain liabilities, including liabilities under the Securities Act of 1933. The indemnities of ABC and CARCO will inure to the benefit of the Selected Agents participating in the offering. Since such indemnity agreements are made by CARCO and ABC, successful assertion by PQR Securities or any Selected Agent of a claim for indemnification would not affect any Car owner's investment or the operations of the Management Program. PQR Securities and the Selected Agents may be deemed to be "underwriters," as that term is defined in the Securities Act of 1933, in connection with this offering.

INVESTORS WHO ELECT TO PARTICIPATE IN THE MANAGEMENT PROGRAM MAY RECEIVE A PREFERENCE IN THE ALLOCATION OF CARS AS SUCH CARS BECOME AVAILABLE FOR DELIVERY. IN ADDITION, IN DETERMINING DELIVERY OF CARS AND ASSIGNMENT OF CARS TO PARTICULAR LEASES, ABC WILL USE ITS DISCRETION TO ASSIGN CARS TO LEASES IN A MANNER WHICH WILL BEST INSURE PRESERVATION OF THE INVESTMENT TAX CREDIT FOR EACH INVESTOR. AS A RESULT, CARS MAY NOT, IN ALL CASES, BE DELIVERED IN THE ORDER IN WHICH SUBSCRIPTIONS ARE RECEIVED.

Each prospective investor must agree to purchase at least one Car and CARCO will not, under any circumstances, accept subscriptions for fractional interests in a Car.

Payment for Cars

Each investor who subscribes to purchase Cars will, by execution of the Subscription Agreement and the Purchase Contract, agree to pay a Purchase Price per Car equal to the sum of (i) the actual Manufacturer's Invoice Price for the Car or Cars purchased by such investor, plus (ii) a Commencement Fee equal in amount to 10% of such actual Manufacturer's Invoice Price, plus (iii) Initial Storage and Transit Costs attributable to such Car or Cars (subject to certain limits, in the case of Cars to be managed by ABC under the Management Program), plus (iv) in the case of any investor entering into a Management Agreement the $50 fee of the ICC for filing such Agreement with the ICC pursuant to 49 U.S.C., Section 11303 (Section 20c of the Interstate Commerce Act of 1920, as amended). The actual amount of such Purchase Price will only be finally determined after the actual purchase and sale of such investor's Cars and the delivery of such Cars to the initial lessee thereof.

ASSUMPTIONS UNDERLYING THE ANALYTIC MODELS

The attached models of the results of ownership and operation of one Car under the Management Program have been prepared on the cash basis using actual calendar years and on the basis of the assumptions listed below. In the models, numbers have been rounded, which may produce small arithmetic inconsistencies. Analytic Model I represents purchase of a Car which is first placed in service in Year One. Analytic Model II represents purchase of a Car which is first placed in service in Year Two. In each case throughout these assumptions the figures for Model I Cars appear in text whereas the figures for Model II Cars appear in brackets immediately following the Model I figures.

A. Assumptions Relating Generally to the Purchase of One Car and the Structure of the Management Program:

1. *Car Purchase; Management Agreement.* In Year One [for Model II Cars, Year Two], the investor purchases one Car and enters into a Management Agreement with ABC.

2. *Leases.* Beginning at the time of purchase and extending without interruption through Year Four [for Model II Cars], the Cars are subject to one or more leases containing similar provisions.

3. *Initial Storage and Transit Expenses.* No storage or transportation costs are incurred by the Car owner upon the purchase of the Cars.

4. *Car Acquisition Cost.* The total acquisition cost of the Car is $40,151, which is the sum of:

(i) the $45,592 purchase price paid to the manufacturer thereof; and
(ii) the $4,559 Commencement Fee paid to CARCO.

5. *Loan Amortization.* To evaluate the effects of borrowing, Supplement One to Model I and Supplement One to Model II present the following alternative loan amortization schedules relating to a loan to the Car owner advanced in Year One [for Model II Cars, Year Two], with repayment monthly in arrears in level payments combining principal and interest: (a) borrowing equal to 50% or 70% of the Car acquisition cost described in paragraph 4 above, (b) simple interest at the rate of 11%, 13% or 15%, and (c) amortization over a term of either 12 or 15 years. The applicable amortization schedule may be inserted by the prospective investor in the analytic models to determine the effect of financing with respect to the purchase of a Car.

If an owner elects to have ABC service any debt, such owner will be required to pay ABC a fee of $7 per month per Car. In such event, such fee (multiplied by the number of months in the applicable period) should be inserted by such owner in the analytic model.

B. Assumptions Relating to Revenues and Expenses of Car Operation:

6. *Timing of Receipt/Payment.* All amounts receivable or payable will be received or paid in full on the due dates thereof.

7. *Rental Receipts.* Monthly rentals under the Leases are equal to 1.1% of the manufacturer's invoice price of the Cars, or $501.51 per month per Car, based on the cost stated in paragraph 4 above. No mileage allowances in excess of monthly rentals are received.

8. *Operating Expenses.* Annual operating expenses are as follows: [Note that the initial figures for Model II Cars take into account the assumed rates of escalation]

year. The schedules in Supplement Two to Model II assume that the Car owner will elect to use the modified half-year convention, pursuant to which the depreciation allowance for a Car purchased during the first half of 1980 will be determined by treating the Car as placed in service in Year One, the first day of the first half of the owner's taxable year.

14. *First-Year Depreciation.* The schedules in Supplement Two to Model I and Supplement Two to Model II assume, for his Year One [for Model II Cars, Year Two] tax year, that the Car owner claims "bonus depreciation" with respect to the Car in the amount of $4,000 (20% of the cost of the Car up to $20,000) *or* that the Car owner claims no bonus depreciation on the Car. The amount of bonus depreciation on all eligible property (railcars and other) placed in service during the year by such Car owner is limited to $4,000, regardless of the number of Cars purchased or the amount of other eligible property owned by such Car owner. The maximum amount of bonus depreciation which may be claimed by a Car owner other than a trust or a married person filing a joint return is $2,000; and a trust is not entitled to any bonus depreciation.

15. *Depreciation Methods and Useful Lives.* The schedules in Supplement Two to Model I and Supplement Two to Model II make two alternative assumptions in determining each year's depreciation allowance for the Car:

(i) The owner uses a depreciable life for the Car of 12 years, the minimum useful life permitted under the ADR System, and takes accelerated depreciation deductions as follows: The owner will initially utilize the 200% declining balance method and will change to the sum-of-the-years'-digits method when the latter method results in greater depreciation deductions than the former.

(ii) The owner uses a 15-year depreciable life for the Car, the designated class life under the ADR System, and utilizes the straight-line method.

16. *Salvage Value.* In determining depreciation in the schedules in Supplement Two to Model I and Supplement Two to Model II, the salvage value of the Car is no greater than 10% of cost (as described in paragraph 11, above), which is reduced by up to 10% of cost pursuant to Section 167(f) of the Code. This

10. *Owner's Filing Status.* The Car owner is an individual taxpayer who prepares his income tax return on the cash basis and has a calendar taxable year.

11. *Basis of Cars for Investment Tax Credit and Depreciation.* The cost of the Car for federal income tax purposes will be $49,695.10, if each of the following is included:

(i) The purchase price paid to the manufacturer thereof ($45,592);
(ii) The portion of the Commencement Fee paid to and retained by CARCO which is attributed to the acquisition of the Car ($1,823.60); and
(iii) The portion of the Commencement Fee paid to CARCO and paid to a placement agent ($2,279.50).

The schedules of depreciation shown in Supplement Two to Model I and Supplement Two to Model II assumes three alternative situations: First, that the basis for depreciation includes the price paid to the manufacturer of the Car the fee paid to CARCO and paid by CARCO to a placement agent; second, that it includes the purchase price and the fee paid to and retained by CARCO for Car acquisition; and third that it includes only the price paid to the manufacturer of the Car. However, the Supplements do not incorporate schedules showing the amortization of items (ii) and (iii) to the extent either of such items is not capitalized to the cost of the Cars. If an owner determines to exclude items (ii) and (iii) from his computation of the basis of the Car for federal income tax purposes, such owner should consult with his tax advisor to determine the proper treatment of such items.

12. *Class Life Asset Depreciation Range System.* The schedules in Supplement Two to Model I and Supplement Two to Model II assume that the Car owner will elect to use the Class Life Asset Depreciation Range ("ADR") System for the determination of the depreciation allowance for the Car.

13. *First-Year Depreciation Convention.* The schedule in Supplement Two to Model I assume that the Car owner will elect to use the half-year convention, pursuant to which the depreciation allowance for a Car purchased during Year One will be determined by treating the Car as placed in service in Year One, the first day of the second half of the owner's taxable

(i) ABC's fixed management fee in the amount of $165 per quarter.

(ii) State property taxes in the amount of $48 per quarter per Car [for Model II Cars, $53] escalated to reflect an assumed 10% per annum rate of inflation.

(iii) Insurance premiums in the amount of $28 per quarter per Car [for Model II Cars, $31] escalated to reflect an assumed 10% per annum rate of inflation.

(iv) Maintenance expenses in the amount of $53 per quarter per Car [for Model II Cars, $61] escalated to reflect both an assumed 10% per annum rate of inflation and an assumed 5% per annum increase in expense as a function of increased age.

(v) Expenses for accountants' annual review of the operations of the Management Program and legal and accounting expenses for the preparation of reports filed with the Securities and Exchange Commission of $15 per quarter per Car.

The analytic models do not take into account the Lease Renegotiation Fee of 2% of gross rentals which will be payable to ABC with respect to any lease which ABC negotiates upon termination of the initial lease. This amount has not been included since the average initial lease term is in excess of the period covered by the analytic model.

The operating expenses described above may fluctuate significantly over the short term and will be affected by the actual inflation rates (which have been assumed to be equal to 10% per annum), the age of the Cars and the number of Cars in the Management Program. While operating expenses are given in periodic amounts, such expenses will not actually be incurred on a uniform periodic basis.

C. Assumptions Relating Primarily to Federal In come Taxes:

9. *Governing In come Tax Law.* The federal income tax treatment of the Car owner during the entire period covered by the analytic models will be governed by the Code, as presently amended, and the Regulations thereunder, current Internal Revenue Service published rulings and existing court decisions.

assumption is based upon the expectation that the Car owner intends to hold the Car for its entire economic useful life.

17. *Lease Negotiation Fee.* The portion of the Commencement Fee paid to CARCO which is paid to ABC as a fee for its lease negotiation services ($455.92 per Car) is amortized proportionately over five years, as shown in Supplement Three to Model I and Supplement Three to Model II.

18. *Minimum Tax on Excess Accelerated Depreciation.* The excess of the amount of depreciation deducted over the amount of depreciation deductible under the straight-line method utilizing a 15-year useful life is an item of tax preference that (i) will reduce any "personal service income" of the Car owner on a dollar-for-dollar basis and give rise to "unearned" income in the same amount, which may be subject to taxation at rates in excess of 50%, and (ii) may subject the Car owner, depending upon the owner's particular tax situation, to the tax on the tax preference items. The column entitled "Excess" Depreciation Deducted in the schedules in Supplement Two to Model I and Supplement Two to Model II set forth the amount of tax preference items which will be present if an owner elects to depreciate a Car under the method of depreciation described in paragraph 15(i) above.

19. *Maximum Tax on Personal Service Income.* No provision has been made in any of the depreciation schedules in Supplement Two to Model I and Supplement Two to Model II to reflect any effect upon a Car owner of either (i) the recharacterization of personal service income as "unearned" income taxable at rates in excess of 50%, as described in paragraph 18, above, or (ii) the fact that income from operation of the Cars would not constitute personal service income.

20. *Destruction; Other Loss of ITC.* None of the Cars are assumed to be (i) lost, stolen, destroyed or sold, prior to end of Year Four [for Model II Cars, Year Five], (ii) used predominantly outside the United States or (iii) leased to a tax-exempt or governmental entity, prior to end of Year Four [for Model II Cars, Year Five].

21. *Pooling of Income and Expense.* The sharing of expenses and division of income among participants in the Management Program are as provided for in the Management Agreement and are recognized for tax purposes.

22. *Miscellaneous Tax Issues.* For federal income tax purposes:

(i) The owner of the Car (and no other person, including a partnership comprised of all participants in the Management Program and/or ABC or such owner and ABC) will be considered the owner of the Car.

(ii) The Leases will be considered "operating leases" in that they satisfy the requirements of Section 46(e) (3) (B) of the Code.

(iii) Neither the participants in the Management Program nor ABC will be considered lessees of the Car.

(iv) Interest on any debt financing applied to the purchase of the Car will not be subject to any limitation on the deductibility of interest because (a) the Cars will not be considered property held for investment pursuant to Section 163(d) (4) (A) of the Code, and (b) no Car owner will be deemed to have incurred such financing to purchase or carry tax-exempt obligations.

(v) The management fees payable under the Management Agreement are ordinary and necessary expenses in carrying on the business of operating the Car and, therefore, are deductible under Section 162 of the Code.

(vi) The original use of the Car commences with the Car owner.

D. Assumptions Relating to Risks of Additional or Unanticipated Expenses or Losses:

23. *Tort Liability.* The Car owner does not incur any tort liability with respect to the operation of the Car prior to end of Year Four [for Model II Cars, Year Five].

24. *Alterations.* No capital improvements, structural changes or major repairs are required for the Car prior to end of Year Four [for Model II Cars, Year Five].

25. *State Law.* No provision has been made for any state or local taxes (such as sales, franchise or income taxes) other than the state property taxes referred to in paragraph 8(ii).

MODEL I

ANALYTIC MODEL OF CAR OPERATION

Total Car Cost: $50,151

Placed in Service: 11/1/of Year One

	Year One (2 Mos.)	Year Two	Year Three	Year Four
Section I:				
CASH FLOW FROM OPERATIONS				
Cash Income				
Rental Income	$1,003	$6,018	$6,018	$6,018
Cash Expenses				
Maintenance	35	244	280	322
Property Taxes	32	212	232	256
Insurance	19	124	136	150
Management Fee	110	660	660	660
Reporting Expenses . . .	10	60	60	60
Total Cash Expenses .	206	1,300	1,368	1,448
Net Cash Flow from Operations	$ 797	$4,718	$4,650	$4,570
Section II:				
PRE-TAX CASH FLOW COMPUTATION				
Net Cash Flow from Operations	$ 797	$4,718	$4,650	$4,570
Less:				
Debt-Related Cash Flow:				
Principal Payments . . .	—	—	—	—
Interest Expense	—	—	—	—
Debt Service Fee	—	—	—	—
Total Debt Payments	—	—	—	—
Equals Pre-Tax Cash Flow .	$ —	$ —	$ —	$ —

Section III: TAXABLE INCOME COMPUTATION				
Net Cash Flow from Operations	$ 797	$4,718	$4,650	$4,570
Less:				
Interest Expense	—	—	—	—
Debt Service Fee	—	—	—	—
Depreciation Expense .	—	—	—	—
Lease Fee Amortization (5 yr. SL) . . .	15	91	91	91
Total Non-operational Expenses	—	—	—	—
Equals Taxable Income	$ —	$ —	$ —	$ —

Note Regarding Method

Pre-Tax Cash Flow (i.e., cash flow exclusive of tax liability or benefit) is computed in Section II, above, by deducting debt payments and, if applicable, a debt service fee from Net Cash Flow from Operations.

Taxable income (or loss) is computed in Section III, above, by deducting non-operational expenses (non-cash expenses and debt related expenses) from Net Cash Flow from Operations.

An investment tax credit in an amount varying between 9% and 10% of an owner's basis in the Car, may be available.

Supplement One to Model I:
LOAN AMORTIZATION SCHEDULES

Initial Principal: (See paragraph 4 of assumptions.)

Columns (a): $25,075.50 or 50% of total acquisition cost
Columns (b): $35,105.70 or 70% of total acquisition cost

Date of Loan: November 1, of Year One

Repayment: Level periodic payment of combined principal and interest, monthly in arrears.

Part I of this Supplement relates to a loan bearing interest at a simple annual interest rate of 11%, amortized over 12 or 15 years. Part II of this Supplement relates to a loan bearing interest at a simple annual interest rate of 13%, amortized over 12 or 15 years. Part III of this Supplement relates to a loan bearng interest at a simple annual interest rate of 15%, amortized over 12 or 15 years.

Part I

(a) Interest Rate: 11%
Amortization: 12 years

	(a)	(b)
Initial Principal:	$25,075.50	$35,105.70
Monthly Payment Amount:	314.34	440.07

	(a) Interest Expense	(a) Principal Repay-ment	(a) Principal Balance	(b) Interest Expense	(b) Principal Repay-ment	(b) Principal Balance
Initial	$ 0	$ 0	$25,076	$ 0	$ 0	$35,106
Year 1 (2 pmts) ..	459	170	24,906	643	238	34,868
Year 2	2,686	1,086	23,820	3,760	1,520	33,348
Year 3	2,560	1,212	22,608	3,584	1,696	31,651
Year 4	2,520	1,352	21,256	3,388	1,893	29,758
Year 5	2,264	1,508	19,748	3,169	2,112	27,647
Year 6	2,089	1,683	18,065	2,925	2,356	25,291
Year 7	1,894	1,878	16,187	2,652	2,629	22,662
Year 8	1,677	2,095	14,092	2,348	2,933	19,729
Year 9	1,435	2,337	11,755	2,008	3,272	16,456
Year 10	1,164	2,608	9,147	1,630	3,651	12,805
Year 11	862	2,910	6,237	1,207	4,074	8,732
Year 12	526	3,246	2,991	736	4,545	4,187
Year 13 (10 pmts) .	153	2,991	0	214	4,187	0

(b) Interest Rate: 11%
Amortization: 15 years

	(a)	(b)
Initial Principal:	$25,075.50	$35,105.70
Monthly Payment Amount	285.01	399.01

	(a) Interest Expense	(a) Principal Repay-ment	(a) Principal Balance	(b) Interest Expense	(b) Principal Repay-ment	(b) Principal Balance
Initial	$ 0	$ 0	$25,076	$ 0	$ 0	$35,106
Year 1 (2 pmts) ..	459	111	24,965	643	155	34,951
Tear 2	2,711	709	24,256	3,796	993	33,958
Year 3	2,629	791	23,465	3,681	1,107	32,850
Year 4	2,537	883	22,582	3,552	1,236	31,615
Year 5	2,435	985	21,597	3,410	1,379	30,236
Year 6	2,321	1,099	20,499	3,250	1,538	28,698
Year 7	2,194	1,226	19,273	3,072	1,716	26,982
Year 8	2,052	1,368	17,905	2,873	1,915	25,067
Year 9	1,894	1,526	16,379	2,652	2,136	22,931
Year 10 ,,,,,,,,	1,718	1,703	14,677	2,405	2,384	20,547
Year 11	1,521	1,900	12,777	2,129	2,659	17,888
Year 12	1,301	2,119	10,658	1,821	2,967	14,921
Year 13	1,056	2,365	8,293	1,478	3,310	11,611
Year 14	782	2,638	5,655	1,095	3,694	7,917
Year 15	477	2,944	2,712	667	4,121	3,796
Year 16 (10 pmts) .	139	2,712	0	194	3,796	0

Part II

(a) Interest Rate: 13%
Amortization: 12 years

	(a)	(b)
Initial Principal:	$25,075.50	$35,105.70
Monthly Payment Amount:	344.69	482.57

	(a) Interest Expense	(a) Principal Repayment	(a) Principal Balance	(b) Interest Expense	(b) Principal Repayment	(b) Principal Balance
Initial	$ 0	$ 0	$25,076	$ 0	$ 0	$35,106
Year 1 (2 pmts) . .	543	147	24,929	760	206	34,900
Year 2	3,185	951	23,978	4,460	1,331	33,569
Year 3	3,054	1,082	22,895	4,276	1,515	32,054
Year 4	2,905	1,232	21,664	4,067	1,724	30,329
Year 5	2,735	1,402	20,262	3,829	1,962	28,367
Year 6	2,541	1,595	18,667	3,558	2,233	26,134
Year 7	2,321	1,815	16,852	3,250	2,541	23,593
Year 8	2,071	2,066	14,786	2,899	2,892	20,701
Year 9	1,785	2,351	12,435	2,500	3,291	17,409
Year 10	1,461	2,675	9,760	2,045	3,746	13,664
Year 11	1,092	3,045	6,715	1,528	4,263	9,401
Year 12	671	3,465	3,250	940	4,851	4,550
Year 13 (10 pmts) .	197	3,250	0	276	4,550	0

(b) Interest Rate: 13%
Amortization: 15 years

	(a)	(b)
Initial Principal:	$25,075.50	$35,105.70
Monthly Payment Amount:	317.27	444.17

	(a) Interest Expense	(a) Principal Repayment	(a) Principal Balance	(b) Interest Expense	(b) Principal Repayment	(b) Principal Balance
Initial	$ 0	$ 0	$25,076	$ 0	$ 0	$35,106
Year 1 (2 pmts) . .	543	92	24,984	760	128	34,977
Year 2	3,213	594	24,390	4,499	831	34,146
Year 3	3,131	676	23,714	4,384	946	33,200
Year 4	3,038	769	22,945	4,253	1,077	32,123
Year 5	2,932	875	22,070	4,105	1,225	30,898
Year 6	2,811	996	21,074	3,936	1,395	29,503
Year 7	2,674	1,134	19,940	3,743	1,587	27,916
Year 8	2,517	1,290	18,650	3,524	1,806	26,110
Year 9	2,339	1,468	17,182	3,275	2,055	24,055
Year 10	2,136	1,671	15,511	2,991	2,339	21,715
Year 11	1,906	1,901	13,610	2,668	2,662	19,054
Year 12	1,643	2,164	11,446	2,301	3,029	16,024
Year 13	1,345	2,463	8,983	1,883	3,448	12,577
Year 14	1,005	2,802	6,181	1,407	3,923	8,653
Year 15	618	3,189	2,992	865	4,465	4,188
Year 16	181	2,992	0	254	4,188	0

Part III

(a) Interest Rate: 15%
Amortization: 12 years

	(a)	(b)
Initial Principal:	$25,075.50	$35,105.70
Monthly Payment Amount:	376.35	526.89

	(a) Interest Expense	(a) Principal Repay-ment	(a) Principal Balance	(b) Interest Expense	(b) Principal Repay-ment	(b) Principal Balance
Initial	$ 0	$ 0	$25,076	$ 0	$ 0	$35,106
Year 1 (2 pmts) . . .	626	127	24,949	877	177	34,928
Year 2	3,687	829	24,120	5,162	1,161	33,767
Year 3	3,554	963	23,157	4,975	1,348	32,420
Year 4	3,399	1,117	22,039	4,758	1,564	30,855
Year 5	3,219	1,297	20,742	4,507	1,816	29,039
Year 6	3,011	1,506	19,237	4,215	2,108	26,931
Year 7	2,769	1,748	17,489	3,876	2,447	24,485
Year 8	2,488	2,029	15,460	3,483	2,840	21,645
Year 9	2,162	2,355	13,106	3,026	3,297	18,348
Year1 0	1,783	2,733	10,372	2,496	3,827	14,521
Year 11	1,344	3,173	7,200	1,881	4,442	10,080
Year 12	834	3,683	3,517	1,167	5,156	4,924
Year 13 (10 pmts) . .	246	3,517	0	345	4,924	0

(b) Interest Rate: 15%
Amortization: 15 years

	(a)	(b)
Initial Principal:	$25,075.50	$35,105.70
Monthly Payment Amount:	350.95	491.33

	(a) Interest Expense	(a) Principal Repay-ment	(a) Principal Balance	(b) Interest Expense	(b) Principal Repay-ment	(b) Principal Balance
Initial	$ 0	$ 0	$25,076	$ 0	$ 0	$35,106
Year 1 (2 pmts)	626	75	25,000	877	106	35,000
Year 2	3,717	495	24,505	5,204	692	34,308
Year 3	3,637	574	23,931	5,092	804	33,504
Year 4	3,545	666	23,265	4,963	933	32,571
Year 5	3,438	773	22,492	4,813	1,083	31,488
Year 6	3,314	898	21,594	4,639	1,257	30,232
Year 7	3,169	1,042	20,552	4,437	1,459	28,773
Year 8	3,002	1,210	19,342	4,203	1,693	27,079
Year 9	2,807	1,404	17,938	3,930	1,966	25,114
Year 10	2,582	1,630	16,309	3,614	2,282	22,832
Year 11	2,320	1,892	14,417	3,248	2,648	20,184
Year 12	2,016	2,196	12,221	2,822	3,074	17,110
Year 13	1,663	2,549	9,672	2,328	3,568	13,541
Year 14	1,253	2,959	6,714	1,754	4,142	9,400
Year 15	777	3,434	3,280	1,088	4,808	4,592
Year 16 (10 pmts) . .	230	3,280	0	322	4,592	0

Supplement Two to Model I:

DEPRECIATION SCHEDULES

Shared Assumptions

The Schedules below utilize alternatives described primarily in paragraphs 9 through 16 of the assumptions. All Schedules assume an election of the ADR System, the half-year convention, and a salvage value no greater than 10% of the initial basis of the Car.

Different Assumptions

Part I below assumes that the Car owner files a joint return and elects to deduct $4,000 "bonus" depreciation. Part II assumes that the Car owner does not elect to deduct "bonus" depreciation. Each Part presents a separate Schedule for three alternative initial basis amounts (see paragraph 11 of the assumptions). Each Schedule also shows deductions on both a 12-year accelerated basis and a 15-year straight-line basis (see paragraph 15 of the assumptions) and the amount of "excess" depreciation, equal to the difference between the accelerated (over 12 years) and the straight-line (over 15 years) amounts (see paragraph 18 of the assumptions).

Part I: Bonus Depreciation: $4,000

(a) Depreciable Basis: $49,695.10
(Bonus Depreciation: 4,000.00)

Depreciation Schedule

	12-year Accelerated Depreciation	15-year Straight-Line Depreciation	"Excess" Depreciation Deducted
Year 1 (½ year)	$7,808	$5,523	$2,285
Year 2	6,981	3,046	3,935
Year 3	6,058	3,046	3,012
Year 4	5,481	3,046	2,435
Year 5	4,904	3,046	1,858
Year 6	4,327	3,046	1,281
Year 7	3,750	3,046	704
Year 8	3,173	3,046	127
Year 9	2,596	3,046	0
Year 10	2,019	3,046	0
Year 11	1,442	3,046	0
Year 12	865	3,046	0
Year 13	288	3,046	0
Year 14	0	3,046	0
Year 15	0	3,046	0
Year 16	0	1,523	0

(b) Depreciable Basis: $47,415.60
(Bonus Depreciation: 4,000.00)

Depreciation Schedule

	12-year Accelerated Depreciation	15-year Straight-Line Depreciation	"Excess" Depreciation Deducted
Year 1 (½ year)	$7,618	$5,447	$2,171
Year 2	6,633	2,894	3,739
Year 3	5,756	2,894	2,862
Year 4	5,208	2,894	2,314
Year 5	4,660	2,894	1,766
Year 6	4,111	2,894	1,217
Year 7	3,563	2,894	669
Year 8	3,015	2,894	121
Year 9	2,467	2,894	0
Year 10	1,919	2,894	0
Year 11	1,370	2,894	0
Year 12	822	2,894	0
Year 13	274	2,894	0
Year 14	0	2,894	0
Year 15	0	2,894	0
Year 16	0	1,447	0

(c) Depreciable Basis: $45,592.00
(Bonus Depreciation: 4,000.00)

Depreciation Schedule

	12-year Accelerated Depreciation	15-year Straight-Line Depreciation	"Excess" Depreciation Deducted
Year 1 (½ year)	$7,466	$5,386	$2,080
Year 2	6,354	2,773	3,581
Year 3	5,514	2,773	2,741
Year 4	4,989	2,773	2,216
Year 5	4,464	2,773	1,691
Year 6	3,939	2,773	1,166
Year 7	3,413	2,773	640
Year 8	2,888	2,773	115
Year 9	2,363	2,773	0
Year 10	1,838	2,773	0
Year 11	1,313	2,773	0
Year 12	788	2,773	0
Year 13	262	2,773	0
Year 14	0	2,773	0
Year 15	0	2,773	0
Year 16	0	1,386	0

Part II: No Bonus Depreciation

(a) Depreciable Basis: $49,695.10
(No Bonus Depreciation)

Depreciation Schedule

	12-year Accelerated Depreciation	15-year Straight-Line Depreciation	"Excess" Depreciation Deducted
Year 1 (½ year)	$4,141	$1,657	$2,484
Year 2	7,592	3,313	4,279
Year 3	6,588	3,313	3,275
Year 4	5,961	3,313	2,648
Year 5	5,333	3,313	2,020
Year 6	4,706	3,313	1,393
Year 7	4,079	3,313	766
Year 8	3,451	3,313	138
Year 9	2,824	3,313	0
Year 10	2,196	3,313	0
Year 11	1,569	3,313	0
Year 12	941	3,313	0
Year 13	314	3,313	0
Year 14	0	3,313	0
Year 15	0	3,313	0
Year 16	0	1,657	0

(b) Depreciable Basis: $47,415.60
(No Bonus Depreciation)

Depreciation Schedule

	12-year Accelerated Depreciation	15-year Straight-Line Depreciation	"Excess" Depreciation Deducted
Year 1 (½ year)	$3,951	$1,581	$2,370
Year 2	7,244	3,161	4,083
Year 3	6,286	3,161	3,125
Year 4	5,687	3,161	2,526
Year 5	5,089	3,161	1,928
Year 6	4,490	3,161	1,329
Year 7	3,891	3,161	730
Year 8	3,293	3,161	132
Year 9	2,694	3,161	0
Year 10	2,095	3,161	0
Year 11	1,497	3,161	0
Year 12	898	3,161	0
Year 13	300	3,161	0
Year 14	0	3,161	0
Year 15	0	3,161	0
Year 16	0	1,581	0

(c) Depreciable Basis: $45,592.00
(No Bonus Depreciation)

	Depreciation Schedule		
	12-year Accelerated Depreciation	15-year Straight-Line Depreciation	"Excess" Depreciation Deducted
Year 1 (½ year)	$3,799	$1,520	$2,279
Year 2	6,965	3,039	3,926
Year 3	6,044	3,039	3,005
Year 4	5,469	3,039	2,430
Year 5	4,893	3,039	1,854
Year 6	4,317	3,039	1,278
Year 7	3,742	3,039	703
Year 8	3,166	3,039	127
Year 9	2,590	3,039	0
Year 10	2,015	3,039	0
Year 11	1,439	3,039	0
Year 12	863	3,039	0
Year 13	288	3,039	0
Year 14	0	3,039	0
Year 15	0	3,039	0
Year 16	0	1,520	0

Supplement Three to Model I:

LEASE NEGOTIATION FEE AMORTIZATION

(See Paragraph 17)

Fee Amount: $455.92 per Car
Amortization Term: 60 months
Amortization Method: straight-line

Tax Year	Number of Months	Deductible Amount	Adjusted Basis
Year 1	2	$15.20	$440.72
Year 2	12	91.18	349.54
Year 3	12	91.19	258.36
Year 4	12	91.18	167.18
Year 5	12	91.18	76.00
Year 6	10	76.00	0

MODEL II

ANALYTIC MODEL OF CAR OPERATION

Total Car Cost: $50,151

Placed in Service: 4/1/of Year Two

	Year Two (9 Mos.)	Year Three	Year Four	Year Five
Section I:				
CASH FLOW FROM OPERATIONS				
Cash In come				
Rental Income	$4,514	$6,018	$6,018	$6,018
Cash Expenses				
Maintenance	183	280	322	371
Property Taxes.	159	232	256	280
Insurance	93	136	150	165
Management Fee	495	660	660	660
Reporting Expenses . . .	45	60	60	60
Total Cash Expenses .	975	1,368	1,448	1,536
Net Cash Flow from Operations	$3,539	$4,650	$4,570	$4,482
Section II:				
PRE-TAX CASH FLOW COMPUTATION				
Net Cash Flow from Operations	$3,539	$4,650	$4,570	$4,482
Less:				
Debt-Related Cash Flow:				
Principal Payments . . .	—	—	—	—
Interest Expense	—	—	—	—
Debt Service Fee	—	—	—	—
Total Debt Payments	—	—	—	—
Equals Pre-Tax Cash Flow .	$ —	$ —	$ —	$ —

	Year Two (9 Mos.)	Year Three	Year Four	Year Five
Section III: TAXABLE INCOME COMPUTATION				
Net Cash Flow from Operations	$3,539	$4,650	$4,570	$4,482
Less:				
Interest Expense	—	—	—	—
Debt Service Fee	—	—	—	—
Depreciation Expense . .	—	—	—	—
Lease Fee Amortization (5 yr. SL)	68	91	91	91
Total Non-operational Expenses	—	—	—	—
Equals Taxable Income . .	$ —	$ —	$ —	$ —

Note Regarding Method

Pre-Tax Cash Flow (i.e., cash flow exclusive of tax liability or benefit) is computed in Section II, above, by deducting debt payments and, if applicable, a debt service fee from Net Cash Flow from Operations.

Taxable income (or loss) is computed in Section III, above, by deducting non-operational expenses (non-cash expenses and debt related expenses) from Net Cash Flow from Operations.

An investment tax credit in an amount varying between 9% and 10% of an owner's basis in the Car, may be available.

Supplement One to Model I:

LOAN AMORTIZATION SCHEDULES

Initial Principal: (See paragraph 4 of assumptions.)

Columns (a): $25,075.50 or 50% of total acquisition cost
Columns (b): $35,105.70 or 70% of total acquisition cost

Date of Loan: April 1, Year Two

Repayment: Level periodic payment of combined principal and interest, monthly in arrears.

Part I of this Supplement relates to a loan bearing interest at a simple annual interest rate of 11%, amortized over 12 or 15 years. Part II of this Supplement relates to a loan bearing interest at a simple annual interest rate of 13%, amortized over 12 or 15 years. Part III of this Supplement relates to a loan bearing interest at a simple annual interest rate of 15%, amortized over 12 or 15 years.

Part I

(a) Interest Rate: 11%
Amortization: 12 years

	(a)	(b)
Initial Principal:	$25,075.50	$35,105.70
Monthly Payment Amount:	314.34	440.07

	(a) Interest Expense	(a) Principal Repayment	(a) Principal Balance	(b) Interest Expense	(b) Principal Repayment	(b) Principal Balance
Initial	$ 0	$ 0	$25,076	$ 0	$ 0	$35,106
Year Two (9 pmts)	2,040	789	24,287	2,856	1,104	34,001
Year Three	2,614	1,158	23,129	3,660	1,621	32,381
Year Four	2,480	1,292	21,837	3,473	1,808	30,572
Year Five	2,331	1,441	20,396	3,263	2,018	28,555
Year Six	2,164	1,608	18,788	3,030	2,251	26,304
Year Seven	1,978	1,794	16,994	2,769	2,512	23,792
Year Eight	1,770	2,002	14,993	2,479	2,802	20,990
Year Nine	1,539	2,233	12,760	2,154	3,126	17,863
Year Ten	1,280	2,492	10,268	1,793	3,488	14,375
Year Eleven	992	2,780	7,488	1,389	3,892	10,483
Year Twelve	670	3,102	4,387	939	4,342	6,141
Year Thirteen	312	3,461	926	436	4,845	1,296
Year Fourteen (3 pmts)	17	926	0	24	1,296	0

(b) Interest Rate: 11%
Amortization: 15 years

	(a)	(b)
Initial Principal:	$25,075.50	$35,105.70
Monthly Payment Amount:	285.01	399.01

	(a) Interest Expense	(a) Principal Repayment	(a) Principal Balance	(b) Interest Expense	(b) Principal Repayment	(b) Principal Balance
Initial	$ 0	$ 0	$25,076	$ 0	$ 0	$35,106
Year Two (9 pmts)	2,050	515	24,561	2,870	721	34,385
Year Three	2,664	756	23,805	3,730	1,058	33,327
Year Four	2,577	843	22,962	3,608	1,181	32,146
Year Five	2,479	941	22,021	3,471	1,317	30,829
Year Six	2,370	1,050	20,971	3,319	1,470	29,359
Year Seven	2,249	1,171	19,800	3,149	1,640	27,720
Year Eight	2,113	1,307	18,493	2,959	1,829	25,891
Year Nine	1,962	1,458	17,035	2,747	2,041	23,850
Year Ten	1,794	1,627	15,409	2,511	2,277	21,572
Year Eleven	1,605	1,815	13,594	2,247	2,541	19,032
Year Twelve	1,395	2,025	11,569	1,953	2,835	16,197
Year Thirteen	1,161	2,259	9,310	1,625	3,163	13,034
Year Fourteen	900	2,521	6,789	1,259	3,529	9,505
Year Fifteen	608	2,812	3,977	851	3,937	5,568
Year Sixteen	282	3,138	840	395	4,393	1,175
Year Seventeen (3 pmts)	15	840	0	22	1,175	0

Part II

(a) Interest Rate: 13%
Amortization: 12 years

	(a)	(b)
Initial Principal:	$25,075.50	$35,105.70
Monthly Payment Amount:	344.69	482.57

	(a) Interest Expense	(a) Principal Repay-ment	(a) Principal Balance	(b) Interest Expense	(b) Principal Repay-ment	(b) Principal Balance
Initial	$ 0	$ 0	$25,076	$ 0	$ 0	$35,106
Year Two (9 pmts)	2,416	687	24,389	3,382	961	34,144
Year Three	3,111	1,025	23,363	4,355	1,436	32,709
Year Four	2,969	1,167	22,196	4,157	1,634	31,075
Year Five	2,808	1,328	20,868	3,932	1,859	29,216
Year Six	2,625	1,511	19,357	3,675	2,116	27,100
Year Seven	2,416	1,720	17,637	3,383	2,408	24,692
Year Eight	2,179	1,957	15,680	3,050	2,740	21,951
Year Nine	1,909	2,228	13,452	2,672	3,119	18,833
Year Ten	1,601	2,535	10,917	2,242	3,549	15,284
Year Eleven	1,251	2,885	8,032	1,752	4,039	11,245
Year Twelve	853	3,283	4,749	1,194	4,597	6,648
Year Thirteen	400	3,736	1,012	560	5,231	1,417
Year Fourteen (3 pmts)	22	1,012	0	31	1,417	0

(b) Interest Rate: 13%
Amortization: 15 years

	(a)	(b)
Initial Principal:	$25,075.50	$35,105.70
Monthly Payment Amount:	317.27	444.17

	(a) Interest Expense	(a) Principal Repay-ment	(a) Principal Balance	(b) Interest Expense	(b) Principal Repay-ment	(b) Principal Balance
Initial	$ 0	$ 0	$25,076	$ 0	$ 0	$35,106
Year Two (9 pmts)	2,427	429	24,647	3,397	600	34,505
Year Three	3,167	640	24,006	4,434	897	33,609
Year Four	3,078	729	23,278	4,310	1,020	32,589
Year Five	2,978	829	22,448	4,169	1,161	31,427
Year Six	2,863	944	21,504	4,009	1,321	30,106
Year Seven	2,733	1,074	20,430	3,826	1,504	28,602
Year Eight	2,585	1,222	19,208	3,619	1,711	26,891
Year Nine	2,416	1,391	17,817	3,382	1,948	24,943
Year Ten	2,224	1,583	16,234	3,114	2,216	22,727
Year Eleven	2,006	1,802	14,432	2,808	2,522	20,205
Year Twelve	1,757	2,050	12,382	2,460	2,871	17,334
Year Thirteen	1,474	2,333	10,048	2,063	3,267	14,067
Year Fourteen	1,152	2,655	7,393	1,612	2,718	10,350
Year Fifteen	785	3,022	4,371	1,099	4,230	6,119
Year Sixteen	368	3,439	932	515	4,815	1,304
Year Seventeen (3 pmts)	20	932	0	28	1,304	0

Part III

(a) Interest Rate: 15%
Amortization: 12 years

	(a)	(b)
Initial Principal:	$25,075.50	$35,105.70
Monthly Payment Amount:	376.35	526.89

	Interest Expense	Principal Repay-ment	Principal Balance	Interest Expense	Principal Repay-ment	Principal Balance
Initial.	$ 0	$ 0	$25,076	$ 0	$ 0	$35,106
Year Two (9 pmts) . .	2,792	595	24,480	3,909	833	34,272
Year Three	3,612	905	23,575	5,056	1,267	33,006
Year Four	3,466	1,050	22,525	4,852	1,470	31,535
Year Five	3,297	1,219	21,306	4,616	1,707	29,829
Year Six	3,101	1,415	19,891	4,342	1,981	27,848
Year Seven	2,874	1,642	18,249	4,023	2,299	25,549
Year Eight	2,610	1,906	16,343	3,654	2,669	22,880
Year Nine	2,303	2,213	14,130	3,225	3,098	19,781
Year Ten	1,948	2,569	11,561	2,727	3,596	16,185
Year Eleven	1,535	2,982	8,579	2,149	4,174	12,011
Year Twelve	1,055	3,461	5,119	1,478	4.845	7,166
Year Thirteen	499	4,017	1,101	699	5,624	1,542
Year Fourteen (3 pmts).	28	1,101	0	39	1,542	0

(b) Interest Rate: 15%
Amortization: 15 years

	(a)	(b)
Initial Principal:	$25,075.50	$35,105.70
Monthly Payment Amount:	350.95	491.33

	Interest Expense	Principal Repay-ment	Principal Balance	Interest Expense	Principal Repay-ment	Principal Balance
Initial.	$ 0	$ 0	$25,076	$ 0	$ 0	$35,106
Year Two (9 pmts) .	2,804	355	24,721	3,925	497	34,609
Year Three , ...	3,672	539	24,181	5,141	755	33,854
Year Four	3,585	626	23,555	5,019	877	32,977
Year Five	3,485	727	22,828	4,878	1,018	31,959
Year Six	3,368	844	21,984	4,715	1,181	30,778
Year Seven	3,232	979	21,005	4,525	1,371	29,407
Year Eight	3,075	1,137	19,868	4,305	1,591	27,816
Year Nine	2,892	1,319	18,549	4,049	1,847	25,969
Year Ten	2,680	1,532	17,017	3.752	2,144	23,824
Year Eleven.	2,434	1,778	15,240	3,407	2,489	21,335
Year Twelve	2,148	2,064	13,176	3,007	2,889	18,446
Year Thirteen	1,816	2,395	10,781	2,543	3,353	15,093
Year Fourteen	1,431	2,780	8,000	2,004	3,892	11,201
Year Fifteen	984	3,227	4,773	1,378	4,518	6,682
Year Sixteen	465	3,746	1,027	652	5,245	1,438
Year Seventeen (3 pmts).	26	1,027	0	36	1,438	0

Supplement Two to Model I:

DEPRECIATION SCHEDULES

Shared Assumptions

The Schedules below utilize alternatives described primarily in paragraphs 9 through 16 of the assumptions. All Schedules assume an election of the ADR System, the half-year convention, and a salvage value no greater than 10% of the initial basis of the Car.

Different Assumptions

Part I below assumes that the Car owner files a joint return and elects to deduct $4,000 "bonus" depreciation. Part II assumes that the Car owner does not elect to deduct "bonus" depreciation. Each Part presents a separate Schedule for three alternative initial basis amounts (see paragraph 11 of the assumptions). Each Schedule also shows deductions on both a 12-year accelerated basis and a 15-year straight-line basis (see paragraph 15 of the assumptions) and the amount of "excess" depreciation, equal to the difference between the accelerated (over 12 years) and the straight-line (over 15 years) amounts (see paragraph 18 of the assumptions).

Part I: Bonus Depreciation: $4,000

(a) Depreciable Basis: $49,695.10
(Bonus Depreciation: 4,000.00)

Depreciation Schedule

	12-Year Accelerated Depreciation	15-Year Straight-Line Depreciation	"Excess" Depreciation Deducted
Year One	$11,616	$7,046	$4,570
Year Two	6,347	3,046	3,301
Year Three	5,507	3,046	2,461
Year Four	4,983	3,046	1,937
Year Five	4,458	3,046	1,412
Year Six	3,934	3,046	888
Year Seven	3,409	3,046	363
Year Eight	2,885	3,046	0
Year Nine	2,360	3,046	0
Year Ten	1,836	3,046	0
Year Eleven	1,311	3,046	0
Year Twelve	787	3,046	0
Year Thirteen	262	3,046	0
Year Fourteen	0	3,046	0
Year Fifteen	0	3,046	0

(b) Depreciable Basis: $47,415.60
(Bonus Depreciation: 4,000.00

Depreciation Schedule

	12-year Accelerated Depreciation	15-year Straight-Line Depreciation	"Excess" Depreciation Deducted
Year One	$11,236	$6,894	$4,342
Year Two	6,030	2,894	3,136
Year Three	5,233	2,894	2,339
Year Four	4,734	2,894	1,840
Year Five	4,236	2,894	1,342
Year Six	3,738	2,894	844
Year Seven	3,239	2,894	345
Year Eight	2,741	2,894	0
Year Nine	2,243	2,894	0
Year Ten	1,744	2,894	0
Year Eleven	1,246	2,894	0
Year Twelve	748	2,894	0
Year Thirteen	250	2,894	0
Year Fourteen	0	2,894	0
Year Fifteen	0	2,894	0

(c) Depreciable Basis: $45,592.00
(Bonus Depreciation: 4,000.00)

Depreciation Schedule

	12-year Accelerated Depreciation	15-year Straight-Line Depreciation	"Excess" Depreciation Deducted
Year One	$10,932	$6,773	$4,159
Year Two	5,777	2,773	3,004
Year Three	5,013	2,773	2,240
Year Four	4,535	2,773	1,762
Year Five	4,058	2,773	1,285
Year Six	3,581	2,773	808
Year Seven	3,103	2,773	330
Year Eight	2,626	2,773	0
Year Nine	2,148	2,773	0
Year Ten	1,671	2,773	0
Year Eleven	1,194	2,773	0
Year Twelve	716	2,773	0
Year Thirteen	238	2,773	0
Year Fourteen	0	2,773	0
Year Fifteen	0	2,773	0

Part II: No Bonus Depreciation

(a) Depreciable Basis: $49,695.10
(No Bonus Depreciation)

	Depreciation Schedule		
	12-year Accelerated Depreciation	15-year Straight-Line Depreciation	"Excess" Depreciation Deducted
Year One	$8,283	$3,313	$4,970
Year Two	6,902	3,313	3,589
Year Three	5,989	3,313	2,676
Year Four	5,419	3,313	2,106
Year Five	4,849	3,313	1,536
Year Six	4,278	3,313	965
Year Seven	3,708	3,313	395
Year Eight	3,137	3,313	0
Year Nine	2,567	3,313	0
Year Ten	1,996	3,313	0
Year Eleven	1,426	3,313	0
Year Twelve	856	3,313	0
Year Thirteen	286	3,313	0
Year Fourteen	0	3,313	0
Year Fifteen	0	3,313	0

(b) Depreciable Basis: $47,415.60
(No Bonus Depreciation)

	Depreciation Schedule		
	12-year Accelerated Depreciation	15-year Straight-Line Depreciation	"Excess" Depreciation Deducted
Year One	$7,903	$3,161	$4,742
Year Two	6,585	3,161	3,424
Year Three	5,715	3,161	2,554
Year Four	5,170	3,161	2,009
Year Five	4,626	3,161	1,465
Year Six	4,082	3,161	921
Year Seven	3,538	3,161	377
Year Eight	2,993	3,161	0
Year Nine	2,449	3,161	0
Year Ten	1,905	3,161	0
Year Eleven	1,361	3,161	0
Year Twelve	816	3,161	0
Year Thirteen	272	3,161	0
Year Fourteen	0	3,161	0
Year Fifteen	0	3,161	0

(c) Depreciable Basis: $45,592.00
(No Bonus Depreciation)

	Depreciation Schedule		
	12-year Accelerated Depreciation	15-year Straight-Line Depreciation	"Excess" Depreciation Deducted
Year One	$7,599	$3,039	$4,560
Year Two	6,332	3,039	3,293
Year Three	5,495	3,039	2,456
Year Four	4,972	3,039	1,933
Year Five	4,448	3,039	1,409
Year Six	3,925	3,039	886
Year Seven	3,402	3,039	363
Year Eight	2,878	3,039	0
Year Nine	2,355	3,039	0
Year Ten	1,832	3,039	0
Year Eleven	1,308	3,039	0
Year Twelve	785	3,039	0
Year Thirteen	262	3,039	0
Year Fourteen	0	3,039	0
Year Fifteen	0	3,039	0

Supplement Three to Model II

LEASE NEGOTIATION FEE AMORTIZATION

(See Paragraph 17)

Fee Amount: $455.92 per Car
Amortization Term: 60 months
Amortization Method: straight-line

Tax Year	Number of Months	Deductible Amount	Adjusted Basis
Year One	9	$68.40	$387.52
Year Two	12	91.18	296.34
Year Three	12	91.18	205.16
Year Four	12	91.18	113.98
Year Five	12	91.18	22.80
Year Six	3	22.80	0

BENEFITS OF HOPPER RAILCAR LEASING PROGRAM

The Management Program's objectives are to provide investors who purchase Cars and participate in the Management Program (i) the right to share earnings, if any, generated by Cars owned by participants in the Program (regardless of the revenues and expenses from each particular participant's car) distributions from which will be made quarterly (to commence the first quarter following delivery of the Car), a portion or all (depending upon the tax elections made by a participant with respect to his Car) of which initially will be "tax sheltered" (except that investors who finance a substantial portion of the purchase price of their Car may not receive distributions sufficient to pay the monthly debt service on such borrowings); (ii) an investment tax credit in Year One or Year Two (depending on the delivery date of the investor's Car); and (iii) the maintenance of a substantial residual value (for continued operation and sale) in the Cars upon expiration of the Management Program.

INITIALLY, IT IS ANTICIPATED THAT, IF CERTAIN ELECTIONS ARE MADE BY AN INVESTOR, CAR OWNERSHIP WILL RESULT IN TAX LOSSES IN EXCESS OF ANY RENTAL INCOME TO OFFSET AN INVESTOR'S OTHER SOURCES OF INCOME. HOWEVER, AN INVESTOR MAY THEREAFTER REALIZE SUBSTANTIAL TAXABLE INCOME AND THE ECONOMIC BENEFIT OF THE INITIAL TAX LOSSES MAY BE REDUCED OR COMPLETELY OFFSET BY LOSS OF THE BENEFIT OF THE MAXIMUM TAX ON PERSONAL SERVICE INCOME OR THE IMPOSITION OF TAX ON ITEMS OF TAX PREFERENCE. THE "TAX SHELTER" OR TAX DEFERRAL AFFORDED BY SUCH INITIAL TAX LOSSES WILL ONLY DEFER TO LATER YEARS AN INVESTOR'S OVERALL TAX LIABILITY AND THE BENEFIT OF SUCH TAX DEFERRAL WILL DEPEND IN PART ON AN INVESTOR'S ABILITY TO PROFITABLY UTILIZE (BY INVESTMENT OR OTHERWISE) THE TAX SAVING ARISING FROM SUCH DEFERRAL. THERE IS NO ASSURANCE, HOWEVER, THAT ANY OR ALL OF THESE OBJECTIVES WILL ACTUALLY BE ATTAINED.

RISKS OF A HOPPER RAILCAR LEASING PROGRAM

1. *Business Risks of Car Operations.* Car ownership and operation is a business and, like any business, is dependent upon the maintenance of acceptable levels of income and operating expense. The principal business risk associated with Car ownership and operation is the possible inability to keep all the Cars fully leased at rentals which, after payment of operating expenses, provide, together with any anticipated sale proceeds or salvage value, a return acceptable to the Car owner. The ability to so lease the Cars may be adversely affected by the economic and business factors to which railroads and railroad freight transportation generally and the railroad car leasing industry in particular are subject, most of which are beyond the control of the Car owner, ABC and the users of Cars. Such factors include:

(a) general economic conditions, such as inflation and fluctuations in general business conditions;

(b) conditions particularly affecting transportation of freight by covered hopper railcar, such as the supply and demand at any particular location for commodities normally transported by covered hopper railcar;

(c) the supply of railcars generally or at any particular place or at any particular time;

(d) increases in the maintenance expenses, taxes, insurance costs and management fees attributable to the Cars which cannot be offset by increased rental revenues from the Cars;

(e) the possible unavailability on practicable terms of insurance on the Cars in the amounts and against the risks that the Car owner and/or ABC consider advisable;

(f) bankruptcies, contract disputes or defaults in payment by users of Cars resulting in uncollectible amounts and loss of revenues during periods when Cars are off lease;

(g) changes in the governmental regulations, safety standards, tariff rate structures and mileage allowances collectible from railroads applicable to the operations of privately-owned railroad equipment, which may result in additional expenses or reduced revenues for Car operations; and

(h) deterioration of the U.S. railroad system (or failure to make necessary improvements or additions thereto) or changes in the methods or economies of freight transportation which tend to reduce demand for (or limit growth in demand for) covered hopper railcars as a means of freight transportation.

An investor should also be aware that AAR Interchange Rules require that, if an investor sells his car or the AAR reporting marks on the car are changed after the car is 20 years old, he or the purchaser will be required to rehabilitate the car prior to further use in interchange service. Such rehabilitation would require an expenditure to bring the car up to the currently-prescribed mechanical standards for a rebuilt car. If a car is less than 25 years old and the cost of rehabilitation is at least 50% of the AAR reproduction value at that time, the car will be given rebuilt status. It should be noted that reporting marks would be required to be changed if ABC were removed as manager or if the Management Agreement were terminated after having been in effect for a period of 20 years.

2. *Leasing of Cars.* The principal risk associated with Car ownership and operation is, as indicated above, the possible inability to keep the Cars fully leased on acceptable rental and other terms. Moreover, owners must hold their Cars at least seven years in order to avoid any recapture of investment tax credit claimed with respect to the Cars. However, it is anticipated that the leases will not have terms beyond three to five years and that they will not provide for any renewals and, therefore, must be replaced by new leases at their expiration dates in order that the Car owners may continue to receive rental income. However, there can be no assurance that, at the expiration of any particular lease there would be demand for covered hopper railcars such as the Cars from commercially acceptable lessees on commercially acceptable terms. Moreover, in the case of Cars leased under "split leases" (that is, an agreement of separate, but interdependent, lessees pursuant to which the same Cars are used by several lessees, each lessee using the Cars during a designated portion of each year of the lease term), upon the expiration of any particular such Lease, even if there were substantial demand generally for covered hopper railcars such as the Cars it might not be possible to negotiate commercially acceptable replacement leases covering the Cars which had been subject to such lease during the period of each year during which such Cars would be available.

3. *Real Abatements.* There may be circumstances under which, even though the Cars are then leased, the payment of rentals will be suspended or postponed. It is anticipated that any leases of the Cars will provide that rentals will abate after some brief period (normally seven days under the form of lease ABC now uses) after the Cars are reported as unfit for service as a result of either a casualty (less than complete destruction) or the failure of the lessor to properly maintain and repair the Cars, and such abatement will continue until the Cars have been repaired and returned to service. If the abatement of rental charges is due to such a casualty, a Car owner would usually receive payments under business interruption insurance, commencing some period (now, 10 days) after such casualty.

4. *Residual Value of Cars.* The ultimate cash return from investments in Cars (without giving effect to any tax savings) will depend in part upon the continuing value (either for sale or continued operation) of the Cars. The residual value of Cars will depend upon many factors beyond the control of the Car owner or ABC. Since the Cars do not experience rapid physical deterioration and have not historically experienced substantial technological obsolescence, the principal factors affecting such value are supply and demand, the condition of the Cars (which may be affected by age, use and maintenance of the Cars) and the cost of new covered hopper cars (which is affected by the availability and cost of raw materials used in railcar construction, inflation, general economic conditions, regulatory standards applicable to railcar construction and technological advances in railcar construction). In addition, the residual value of Cars may be affected by other factors, including regulatory standards applicable to railcar operation, changes in or deterioration of the U.S. railroad system, developments in transportation technology, the availability and cost of energy resources for competing methods of freight transportation and developments in domestic trade patterns.

5. *Personal Liability.* Car owners will be personally liable for all expenses and obligations of ownership and operation of their Cars. As a result, Car owners may be required to pay:

(a) any operating expenses and management fees with respect to their Cars and, in the case of Car owners who finance part of the purchase of their Cars from borrowings, debt service which cannot be paid from rent revenues from such Cars;

(b) any claims (subject to certain limited exceptions, in the case of participants in the Management Program) for uninsured property damage or personal injury caused by or arising out of their Cars;

(c) the cost of additions, improvements or modifications to their Cars; and

(d) any amounts necessary to indemnify and hold harmless ABC against any claims arising from management, operation or use of the Cars, but not including claims based on ABC's negligence, gross negligence, bad faith, gross misconduct, willful misconduct or recklessness.

(e) any mileage allowances due lessees under the leases which ABC fails or is unable to pay. If ABC fails to make timely payments of the mileage allowance to the lessees, the obligation to make these payments would be a personal obligation of the owner. The owner would then have a claim against ABC for reimbursement of any such amount and if ABC were insolvent would share with general creditors of ABC in any claim for reimbursement.

6. *Leverage.* Some Car owners may elect to finance their purchase of Cars with borrowed funds. While such leverage permits the acquisition of Cars with a smaller out-of-pocket investment than would otherwise be possible, it increases the sensitivity of the investment to adverse developments. For example,

(a) since it may be assumed that debt service (principal plus interest) on such borrowings will not fluctuate with increases or decreases in Car revenues or utilization, relatively small fluctuations in gross revenues may result in marked fluctuations in the rate of return;

(b) if cash income from operations is insufficient to pay debt service on such borrowings, the Car owner must either pay any deficiency or risk default and foreclosure on such Cars and, if the loans are with recourse to the borrower (and it may be assumed, both for tax and credit reasons, that loans generally will be made with recourse to the borrower), any deficiency will be a personal obligation of the borrower, enforceable against the borrower's personal assets;

(c) if the loans will not be fully amortized prior to maturity and a "balloon" payment cannot be refinanced at maturity on acceptable terms, the borrower may be required to sell his investment in the Cars in order to repay such loans (and the borrower may have personal liability for any deficiency); and

(d) if the interest rate on the loans fluctuates (for example, with the prime lending rate or commercial paper rates), or the loans have very short maturities or are payable on demand, the borrower will bear the risk of variations in interest rates (and comparatively small variations in interest rates may result in marked fluctuations in the rate of return).

(e) if the term of any loan extends beyond the term of the Management Agreement and such investor does not thereafter enter into a program similar to this Program, fluctuations in revenue derived from his Cars will have a substantially greater impact since he will not be sharing in revenues from Cars owned by other investors and, therefore, the possibility of reduced funds available to amortize any debt service.

In addition, the financing documents for any loan may impose upon a borrower burdensome restrictions or grant to a lender additional security or rights with respect to the Cars which will affect the borrower's ability to deal with his, her or its Cars or protect his interest therein.

7. *Competition.* In managing the Cars, ABC (and, through ABC, the Car owners) will be in competition with other equipment leasing managers, leasing companies and institutions engaged in leasing or otherwise marketing or re-marketing railcars or railroad freight transportation. Many of these competitors are larger in terms of fleets of cars and financial resources and have considerably more experience in equipment leasing than ABC or its affiliates.

8. *Challenge of Investment Tax Credit and Tax Deductions.* Any one or more of the following might be challenged or disallowed by the Internal Revenue Service (the "IRS"):

(a) There can be no assurance that the IRS would not challenge the claim by Car owners of an investment tax credit on account of their investments in the Cars, assessing either that the Car owners, or some of them, are disqualified from claiming such tax credit under Section 46(e) (3) of the Internal Revenue Code of 1954, as amended (the "Code"), or that a portion of such tax credit was properly allocable to ABC.

(b) Some Car owners may elect to include in the cost of the Cars (i) the portion of CARCO's Commencement Fee allocated by CARCO to the Car acquisition services and (ii) the portion of CARCO's Commencement Fee payable to the Managing Placement Agent or the Selected Agents as a placement agent's fee and to compute the amounts of investment tax credit and depreciation deductions claimed with respect to the Cars on the basis of such cost. However, there can be no assurance that the IRS would not challenge the amount of investment tax credit or depreciation deductions so claimed, asserting that part or all of one or both of such portions of such Commencement Fee may not properly be included in the basis of qualified investment property (asserting, instead that part or all of one or both of such portions of such fee are attributable to an asset other than the Cars and, therefore, are not depreciable or amortizable or are properly depreciated or amortized only over some other, longer period).

(c) The IRS might challenge the amount or timing of depreciation deductions claimed by a Car owner, asserting that the salvage value claimed in computing depreciation should have been higher.

(d) Some Car owners may elect to amortize over the period of the Leases the portion of CARCO's Commencement Fee paid to ABC for lease negotiation services. However, there can be no assurance that the IRS would not challenge such deductions, claiming that part or all of such portion of such Commencement Fee is properly amortized only over some other, longer period or periods or that part or all of such fee is a non-amortizable capital asset of the Car owner.

(e) The IRS might challenge the deductibility of all or some portions of the management fees paid to ABC, claiming that one or more of such payments are a partnership distribution, rather than a business expense, or that one or more of such payments are in excess of the "fair market" fee and, therefore, are not deductible as a necessary business expense.

(f) The IRS might challenge, in whole or in part, the deductibility by Car owners of interest expenses on borrowings to finance their Car purchases, asserting that such interest is on indebteness incurred for investment purposes and, therefore, under Section 163(d) of the Code, is deductible by individuals and certain other taxpayers only subject to certain limitations.

(g) Depending upon the structure and terms of any borrowings by Car owners to finance Car purchases, the IRS might challenge the deductibility by individuals and certain other taxpayers of some losses from Car ownership and operation, asserting that under Section 465 of the Code the borrower is not "at risk" with respect to all or a portion of the amount borrowed.

The challenge or disallowance by the IRS of any such credits or deductions could cause Car owners to pay additional taxes plus interest and, under certain circumstances, a penalty for the year for which such credits or deductions had been claimed.

9. *Taxable Gain on Sale of Cars.* All, or a substantial part, of any taxable gain upon the sale or other disposition of Cars will be treated as ordinary income as a result of "depreciation recapture." Moreover, if such Cars were disposed of within seven years after first being placed in service, all or a part of the investment tax credit would be recaptured.

10. *Additional Taxes.* A Car owner may be subject to other taxes in connection with ownership, holding or sale of Cars.

(a) In the case of individuals, the excess of accelerated depreciation over straight-line depreciation on leased property is an item of tax preference. In the case of corporations, a portion of any net capital gain is a tax preference. Tax preferences in excess of specified amounts are subject to an additional tax of 15%, which may reduce the after-tax return to certain prospective investors from Car ownership.

(b) The Revenue Act of 1978 imposed a new tax on noncorporate taxpayers entitled the "alternative minimum tax." Prospective Car purchasers with substantial long-term capital gains and/or substantial tax credits may be subject to the "alternative minimum tax" and, because such tax is not reduced by tax credits, may be denied the benefits of any investment tax credit for Car purchases. Moreover, any long-term capital gains which Car owners realize upon sale or other disposition of their Cars may, in certain circumstances, subject such Car owners in the future to the "alternative minimum tax."

(c) Personal service income (generally, wages, salary, pensions and the like) of individuals is not taxed at a rate in excess of 50%. However, the amount of income subject to such "maximum tax" is reduced, and the amount of income subject to taxation at regular rates is increased, by the amount of any tax preferences. Such recharacterization of income could reduce the after-tax return to certain prospective investors from Car ownership. In addition, income earned from the Cars will not be personal service income and, therefore, may be subject to rates in excess of the maximum tax, notwithstanding that losses in early years of Car ownership may have offset only personal service income.

(d) Car owners may now or in the future be subject to additional taxes, such as state or local income, franchise, personal property or intangible taxes, as a result of ownership or operation of the Cars. In addition, any use of the Cars in Canada or Mexico may subject Car owners to income taxation in Canada or Mexico. Taxable income or loss attributable to such use will be foreign source income or loss for U.S. tax purposes and may affect the foreign tax credit to which a Car owner with other foreign source income would otherwise be entitled.

11. *Loss of Investment Tax Credit on Use of Cars Outside United States.* If, in any taxable year, a Car is used outside the United States for more than 50% of such taxable year, the investment tax credit otherwise allowable in such taxable year with respect to such Car will not be allowed, or, if such investment tax credit had been claimed in a previous year (within seven years after such Car had been placed in service), will be recaptured, in whole or in part, in such taxable year. In order to prevent any such disallowance or recapture of the investment tax credit, it will be the policy of ABC to incorporate in any lease of Cars provisions requiring that such Cars will not be used in any calendar year outside the continental United States for more than 50% of such year or a pro rata portion thereof for any period consisting of less than a calendar year. However, no assurance can be given that lessees will observe such lease provisions or that, for reasons beyond the control of such lessees, such Cars will not otherwise be detained outside the United States long enough to cause loss or recapture of the investment tax credit. Further, fiscal year taxpayers should be aware that,

although ABC will attempt to assign Cars of fiscal year taxpayers to leases in a manner which will not result in disallowance or recapture of the investment tax credit, the limitation on use in the leases will be imposed on the lessees with reference to calendar years while the 50% test prescribed by the Code is imposed with reference to the tax year of the taxpayer.

12. *Deferred Tax Liability.* The benefit which any particular Car owner may derive from investment in the Cars will depend in part on the ability of such owner to utilize profitably (by investment or otherwise) the tax deferral arising from the tax losses in the early years of the Car ownership.

13. *Effect of Bankruptcy of Manager or Its Affiliates.* In the event of the bankruptcy of or the filing of a petition for reorganization or for an arrangement of ABC or its affiliates under the Bankruptcy Act, the disbursement of revenues from the operation of an investor's Car may be suspended or postponed for a period of time which would require the owner to pay from the owner's personal assets any payments due for debt service, or possibly even operating expenses, with respect to such Car and could require the obtaining of a new manager for the Management Program. Since the funds of the Management Program will be segregated in clearly identifiable trust bank accounts for the benefit of Car owners and since other entities are in the business of managing railcars similar to the Cars, it is not anticipated that such suspension or postponement of revenues would be for a substantial period of time. However, in the event of such insolvency proceedings relating to ABC, an investor could incur personal liability for the payment of mileage allowances to lessees and would be relegated to having a claim against ABC in the event segregated funds for the payment of mileage allowances were not sufficient for such purpose.

14. *Possible Joint Liability.* Although the relationship between any participant in the Management Program and ABC under the Management Agreement is intended to be one of principal and agent, the possible legal consequences under state law of the pooling arrangement upon, and the possible legal classification of, the relationships among such participant, ABC and other participants in the Management Program are not clear. The possible treatment of relations among the participants in

the Management Program and/or ABC under state law is made more complex by the possible treatment of the Car owners as partners (for the purpose of operation, but not ownership, of the Cars) for federal income tax purposes. If the relationship among the participants in the Management Program or between such participants and ABC is viewed as a general partnership or joint venture, participants could be held personally liable for liabilities of, and claims against, the pool to the extent not satisfied by the pool (including liabilities or claims incurred by any other participants on behalf of or with respect to the pool, even though, under the Management Agreement, such participants would not be entitled to incur any liabilities or claims on behalf of the pool).

15. *Illiquidity of Investment.* Although new and used covered hopper railcars are regularly purchased and sold, there is not expected to be a ready market for Cars and there are significant restrictions on the transferability of Cars. Moreover, lenders providing debt financing for Car purchasers may impose conditions on the sale of such Cars or the application of the sale proceeds. Finally, transferability of Cars (or interests therein) managed under a Management Agreement may be limited by state securities laws.

TAX ASPECTS OF HOPPER RAILCAR LEASING PROGRAM

1. Investment Tax Credit.

General. Section 38 of the Code provides a tax credit against ordinary federal income taxes for investment in certain depreciable property. This tax credit, referred to as the investment tax credit, is applied directly against a taxpayer's liability for tax. The Code, however, imposes a limitation on the amount of the credit that can be taken in any taxable year. These limitations are as follows: For taxable years ending after December 31, 1978 and on or before December 31, 1979, the credit cannot exceed $25,000 plus 60% of the taxpayer's liability in excess of $25,000 for the taxable year. For taxable years ending after December 31, 1979, the foregoing limitation is gradually increased over a three-year period to $25,000 plus 90% of the taxpayer's liability in excess of $25,000 for the year in question. The investment tax credit does not reduce the depreciable basis of qualifying property and, except in the case of certain dispositions discussed below, is a permanent reduction in tax liability to the extent of the credit rather than a mere deferral of tax liability. To the extent that a taxpayer is eligible for investment tax credits from multiple sources, all such credits must be accumulated in determining the ceiling for available credits in any one taxable year. If the amount of the investment tax credits exceeds the limitation provided for any taxable year, the unused tax credits may be carried back to each of the three taxable years preceding the unused credit year and carried forward to each of the seven taxable years following the unused credit year. In the event of a carry-back or carry-forward of an investment tax credit, the same limitations as to the amount of credit in a taxable year will previal. The Tax Reform Act of 1976 provides a "first-in-first-out" rule with respect to carryovers. Thus, credits carried over from a previous year are used first and, to the extent that the applicable limitations are not exceeded, investment credits earned currently are used.

Amount of Credit. Under existing law, an investment tax credit in the amount of 10% of the qualified investment of new qualifying property with a useful life of seven years or more is available. (Corporations with employee stock ownership plans may be eligible for an extra 1% credit for a total credit of 11% if the extra 1% is contributed to an employee stock ownership plan, funded by transfers of employer securities.) Qualified investment is a specified percentage of the basis of new qualifying property placed in service by a taxpayer during the taxable year. The applicable percentage for property with a useful life of three years or more, but less than five years is 33-1/3%; the applicable percentage for property with a useful life of five years or more, but less than seven years, is 66-2/3%; and the applicable percentage for property with a useful life of seven years or more is 100%. Qualifying property is, in general, tangible personal property, such as the Cars, and certain other tangible property (expressly designated or excluded in Section 48(a) of the Code) which is depreciable, has a useful life of at least three years, and, except as specified in Section 48(a) (2) (B) of the Code, is not used predominantly outside the United

Qualified Investment. The qualified investment in new property, such as the Cars, with respect to which an investment tax credit may be claimed is the basis of such property for tax purposes. As a general rule, in addition to the cost of such property, costs incident to the acquisition of such property may be included in the basis thereof, while costs which represent separate identifiable assets, such as lease acquisition costs, may not be included in basis. As indicated above, CARCO has allocated a portion of its commencement fee among the various services that it or ABC has performed in connection with the acquisition of the Cars and the arranging of the lease. In order to preserve the right to claim the maximum investment tax credit which may be available, a Car owner may desire to include in the basis of the Cars the portion of CARCO's commencement fee which CARCO has attributed to the acquisition of the Cars and the portion of such commencement fee paid to PQR Securities. However, there can be no assurance that, if a Car owner did so include such portions of such fee in basis, the IRS would not challenge the amount of investment tax credit claimed by such Car owner, asserting that all or a part of either the portion of CARCO's commencement fee attributed to the acquisition of the Cars or the portion of such commencement fee paid to PQR Securities is in fact attributable to items other than acquisition of the Cars. The IRS might assert that the portion of CARCO's commencement fee attributable to the Cars is attributable to other items such as the leases. Moreover, the IRS might assert that part or all of the portion of CARCO's commencement fee payable to PQR Securities is attributable to the Management Program or other items rather than the Cars, and, if the Management Program is treated as a partnership for federal income tax purposes and any part of the fee paid to PQR Securities is attributed to the Management Program, a non-amortizable capital asset. In the event the IRS successfully challenged the inclusion of all or a part of CARCO's commencement fee in the basis of the Cars, a ratable portion of the investment tax credit may be lost. ABC believes, however, that, since the commencement fee is payable to CARCO by any purchaser of Cars, without regard to whether such purchaser participates in the Management Program, such fee is properly attributable to the Cars.

Circumstances when Credit Is Unavailable. Under Section 46(e) (3) (B) of the Code, an investment tax credit will not be available to non-corporate taxpayers and corporations which are Subchapter S corporations with respect to Cars which are subject to a lease, unless (i) the term of the lease (including options to renew) is less than 50% of the Car's depreciable life selected for tax purposes and (ii) for the first 12 months after the date on which the Cars are transferred to the lessee, the sum of the deductions with respect to such Cars which are allowed solely by reason of Section 162 of the Code (other than rents and reimbursed amounts) exceeds 15% of the gross rental income produced by the Cars. Section 46(e) (3) (B) does not apply to corporate Car owners (other than Subchapter S corporations) and, therefore, neither the terms of the leases in relation to the useful lives of their Cars nor the amount of expenses deductible solely under Section 162 will affect their ability to claim investment tax credit. The following discussion is not applicable to such Car owners.

(a) *The Leases as Net Leases*

(i) *Terms of Leases.* It is anticipated that the lease terms will be less than six years. Therefore, provided an owner of Cars elects to depreciate such Cars over a life of not less than 12 years, the "less than 50% requirement" referred to in clause (i), above, will be satisfied.

(ii) *Section 162 Expenses.* Section 162 provides in part that a taxpayer is allowed a deduction for all ordinary and necessary expenses paid or incurred during a taxable year in carrying on a trade or business. In general, costs such as insurance and ordinary maintenance and repairs of the Cars are deductible by reason of Section 162, while taxes, interest and depreciation are deductible by reason of Sections 163, 164 and 167 of the Code, respectively, and not solely by reason of Section 162.

The IRS has treated the rental of personal property as the conduct of a trade or business, and thus ABC's management fee, being an expense paid by Car owners in carrying on that trade or business, should be deductible. ABC believes that its fee is reasonable compensation for the management services to be rendered by it under the Management Agreement. Thus, the expense test referred to above will be satisfied so long as the management fee, insurance premiums and maintenance expenses exceed 15% of gross rentals.

No assurance can be given, however, that the IRS will not challenge the deductibility of all or a portion of ABC's management fee, asserting that such fee, or the challenged portion thereof, is in excess of the "fair market" fee for such services and, therefore, not a "necessary" business expense.

The IRS might also assert that ABC and a participant in the Management Program are partners; the amount payable to ABC as a management fee is, in fact, a partnership distribution; the management fee, as a partnership distribution, is not deductible under Section 162; and, as a result, the leases would not satisfy the "15% test" of Section 46(e) (3) (B) of the Code.

ABC does not intend to be in partnership with, and, as an economic matter, does not view itself as being in a partnership with, any or all of the participants in the Program. In any event, even if a participant and ABC were held to constitute a partnership, ABC believes that the $55 per month per Car payable to ABC as a management fee would constitute a so-called "guaranteed payment" under Section 707(c) of the Code, rather than a partnership distribution. That Section provides that "to the extent determined without regard to the income of the partnership, payment to a partner for services . . . shall be considered as made to one who is not a member of the partnership . . . for purposes of Section 162." Thus, since the management fee payable to ABC is determined without regard to the net income or loss from Cars, it would be treated as if it were not a payment to a partner, and, for the reasons set forth above, ABC believes it would be deductible under Section 162 as an ordinary and necessary business expense. However, a "guaranteed payment" is deductible only to the extent that the amount paid would be deductible if paid to a third party. Thus, no assurance can be given that the IRS could not challenge the deductibility of at least a portion of a "guaranteed payment," asserting that such payment was in excess of a "necessity" business expense. In addition, ABC believes that, if it were held to be a partner, the IRS might be able to successfully challenge the deductibility of the 2% re-lease fee, asserting that such payment was a partnership distribution and not a guaranteed payment under Section 707(c) of the Code. The re-lease fee is different from the management fee in that the amount is computed as a percentage of gross rentals. However, since it is anticipated that the term of the initial leases will exceed one year, the re-lease fee will not be payable during the 12-month period during which the 15%

test must be met. Therefore, whether or not the re-lease fee is deductible under Section 707(c) will not affect an owner's entitlement to the investment tax credit.

(b) *The Management Agreement as a Net Lease.*

In *Meagher v. Commissioner,* the IRS took the position that a management agreement similar in many respects to the Management Agreement with ABC in a program similar in many respects to the Program constituted a lease and argued that the management agreement being for a term more than 50% of the useful life of the managed cars, the taxpayer-owners (who were individuals) should be denied the benefit of the investment tax credit as a result of the application of Section 46(e) (3) (B) of the Code (the IRS did not in that case address the issue of whether the management agreement asserted to be a lease was a "net" lease). The Tax Court in *Meagher* held that the management agreement in question was not a lease, but instead was a contract for the management of personal property as it purported to be. Accordingly, the taxpayer-owners were not denied the investment tax credit. And, the IRS has now determined, in a recent private letter (Ltr. 7845010), that a management agreement similar to the one in *Meagher* ist not a lease.

Partnership. ABC does not intend to be in partnership with, and, as an economic matter, does not view itself as being in partnership with, any or all of the participants in the Management Program. Even if ABC were treated as a partner in a partnership with any or all of such participants, the Cars would still be treated as being owned by the participants. However, if the IRS successfully asserted that such Cars were owned by the asserted partnership, then ABC would be entitled to its "partnership share" of the investment tax credit and the investor would receive only a portion of the investment tax credit otherwise available. Since the Management Agreement does not, and is not intended to, provide for any sharing between ABC and any other person of profits or losses from Car operations, no prediction can be made as to what the IRS might assert to be ABC's "interest" in the asserted partnership or ABC's "partnership share" of such investment tax credit.

Recapture. If Cars are sold or otherwise disposed of by an owner before the close of the seventh year from the date such

Cars were first placed in service, then all or a portion of the investment tax credit claimed by the owner with respect to such Cars would be recaptured, resulting in a retroactive decrease in the amount of the allowable investment tax credit. If the disposition of the Cars occurs prior to the expiration of three years after such Cars were first placed in service, 100% of the investment tax credit will be recaptured; if such disposition occurs after three years, but within five years, 66-2/3% of the investment tax credit will be recaptured; and if the disposition occurs after five years, but before seven years, 33-1/3% of the investment tax credit will be recaptured. In such an event, the owner's tax liability for the taxable year during which the sale or disposition of the Cars occurred would be increased to the extent of the retroactive decrease in the amount of allowable investment tax credit. For such purpose, any sale or destruction of the Cars, sublease or re-lease of the Cars to certain organizations (including most tax-exempt organizations or any government entities), or use of the Cars predominantly outside the United States will be treated as a disposition of the Cars.

Section 48(a) (2) (A) provides that the tax credit provided by Section 38 may not be claimed with respect to property which is used predominantly outside the United States and Section 47(a) (1) of the Code provides, as indicated above, that if, in any year, property ceases to be property with respect to which investment tax credit may be claimed (e.g., if such property is used predominantly outside the United States), it will be deemed to have been disposed of and, depending upon the year in which disposition takes place, investment tax credit theretofore claimed with respect to such property may be recaptured. The Regulations under Section 48(a) (2) (A) of the Code state that the determination of whether property is used predominantly outside the United States is made by comparing the period of time in a taxable year during which the property is physically located outside the United States with the period of time in such year during which the property is physically located within the United States. If the property is physically located outside the United States for more than 50% of such year, the property will be considered used predominantly outside the United States during that year. If property is placed in service after the first day of a taxable year, such determination is made with respect to the period beginning on the date on which the property is placed in service and ending on the last day of such taxable year.

It is anticipated all of the leases to be negotiated with respect to the Cars owned by investors who elect to participate in Management Program will provide that the Cars must be used predominantly within the continental United States. Consequently, if the lessees observe the covenants in the leases relating to use of the Cars outside the United States, the investment tax credit will be available with respect to the Cars and will not be recaptured during the terms of the leases. However, no assurance can be given that the lessees will perform their covenants regarding the location of the use of the Cars or that the Cars will not otherwise be detained outside the United States. ABC has agreed in the Management Agreement to enforce the terms of the leases so that the Cars will not be used predominantly outside of the United States during the remainder of Year One and each calendar year thereafter for the remaining terms of the leases and has further agreed that any leases (including short-term "spot" leases) which it arranges for the Cars upon termination of the leases will contain provision regarding the identity of the lessees or sublessees of the Cars and the location of use of the Cars and will use its best efforts to allocate Cars of non-calendar year investors so as to avoid recapture of any allowable investment tax credit claimed with respect to the Cars. Fiscal year taxpayers, however, should be aware that the limitation on use in the leases will be imposed with reference to calendar years while the predominant use test prescribed by the Code is imposed with reference to the taxable year of the taxpayer. Furthermore, ABC's obligation as set forth above with respect to the initial leases will only relate to calendar year taxpayers since the leases will generally be entered into prior to the sale of a Car. ABC, however will use its best efforts in the initial delivery of Cars and in subsequent assignment of Cars to leases so as to assign any fiscal year taxpayers to leases which will best assure that the use of the Car under the leases will not result in recapture of any allowable investment tax credit.

2. Depreciation and Other Deductions

General. Section 167 of the Code permits a taxpayer to claim a depreciation deduction in determining taxable income from property which, like the Cars, is used in a trade or business or for the production of income. That deduction is an offset to current cash receipts from such Cars even though depreciation is not a current out-of-pocket cash expense. Depreciation deductions are allowed based on the entire cost of the Cars, even though such Cars may be financed in part with borrowed money.

Methods of Computing Depreciation. Section 167 provides as a depreciation deduction for property a "reasonable allowance for the exhaustion, wear and tear" of the property. The Regulations under Section 167 and various Revenue Rulings and Revenue Procedures set forth detailed methods for the calculation of the annual allowance, rules for determining the amounts of depreciation to be taken in any particular year, guides as to the useful lives of property and standards for determining or ignoring salvage values of property.

One set of such regulations establishes a comprehensive system for computing depreciation referred to as the Asset Depreciation Range "Class Life" ("ADR") system. The ADR system provides specific allowable methods of depreciation, useful lives for specific classes of property, conventions for determining the amounts of depreciation to be taken in the year property is placed in service, rules for determining when property is placed in service and specific rules relating to the treatment of salvage values.

Any Car owner may elect to utilize the ADR system for the purpose of computing depreciation deductions for his Cars. Under that system, the useful life of such Cars is 15 years, and a taxpayer may use a depreciation range which varies up to 20% from the class life. Thus, any useful life from a minimum of 12 years to a maximum of 18 years may be elected by the owner.

A taxpayer who elects to use the ADR system must also use a so-called "averaging convention" in determining when depreciation commences. Under one such convention, the "modified half-year convention," any property placed in service during the first half of a taxpayer's tax year is treated as if it had been placed in service on the first day of such tax year and any property placed in service during the second half of such tax year is treated as if it had been placed in service on the first day of the next tax year. Under a second averaging convention, the "half-year convention," any property placed in service during a taxpayer's tax year is treated as if it had been placed in service on the first day of the second half of that year. An investor, other than an individual, should note that, under the existing

ADR Regulation, if it were formed on a day other than the first day of such taxpayer's fiscal year, the tax year for purposes of applying the first year averaging conventions commences on the date of formation and ends on the last day of such year, thus resulting in a taxable year of less than 12 months.

The IRS has recently proposed an amendment to the Regulations with respect to the application of the first year conventions under ADR. If this amendment were adopted as proposed, ABC believes that the amount of the depreciation deduction otherwise available to certain investors who elect ADR would be reduced for the year in which the Cars are placed in service. The proposed amendment provides that a taxable year for purposes of applying the ADR conventions would not include any period before a Car owner begins engaging in a trade or business or holding depreciable property for the production of income. In other words, if a Car purchaser is not already engaging in a trade or business or holding depreciable property for income at the time of purchase of his Car, his tax year for purposes of the half-year or modified half-year conventions would commence at the time of purchase of such Car. For example, the depreciation deduction under the half-year convention would be equal to one-half of this short year and not six months. Similarly, under the modified half-year convention, the depreciation deduction would be for the number of months in such short year and not 12 months. However, the depreciation which such Car owner was unable to deduct during the first year of operations would not be lost since the basis would be greater for purposes of computing depreciation deductions for subsequent years.

The proposed amendment is unclear as to whether an individual who is an employee would be considered to be engaged in a trade or business as used in this proposed Regulation, or additionally, whether a taxpayer who is holding other depreciable property for production of income which is not subject to the ADR system, such as real estate, would be affected by the proposed Regulation. It is currently proposed by the IRS that this amendment to the Regulation, if adopted, become effective as of November 14, 1979. However, comments will be received until January 14, 1980, and ABC is unable to predict whether the Regulation will in fact be adopted, what the substance of any final Regulation would be, when a final decision would be made with respect to adoption, or what effective date will ultimately be chosen.

In lieu of using ADR, a Car owner may claim depreciation based on the actual useful life of the Cars as determined on the basis of the taxpayer's own facts and circumstances. However, use of the facts and circumstances method of depreciation will normally produce a longer depreciation period than use of the depreciation period permitted by ADR. In any event, a participant should not select a useful life of less than 12 years in order to satisfy the statutory requirement regarding eligibility for the investment tax credit. A Car owner who determines Car life on the basis of facts or circumstances would not generally be entitled to utilize an averaging convention in determining the first year's depreciation. Rather, the first year's depreciation would be computed from the date on which such owner's Cars are first placed in service.

In determining the treatment of their Cars for depreciation purposes, Car owners should note that if the ADR system is to be applied to any eligible property acquired in a given year, it must be applied with respect to all property subject to the ADR system and acquired in that year. Thus, a Car owner who acquired or plans to acquire any property subject to the ADR system (and not just other railroad cars or locomotives) during any particular taxable year must either elect to utilize the ADR system for that year for all such property or must determine useful lives for all such property on the basis of the facts and circumstances method. Moreover, Car owners who elect to utilize the ADR system and which have acquired or plan to acquire other property subject to the ADR system in the same taxable year in which owner's Cars are placed in service should note that the same averaging convention must be applied with respect to all property which is acquired in a given year and is subject to the ADR system—a taxpayer may not apply the modified half-year convention with respect to property acquisitions in the first half of the year and the half-year convention with respect to property acquisitions in the second half of the year.

The Code and the Regulations thereunder provide various methods for the computation of the annual depreciation allowance with respect to new depreciable property. Such methods include the 200% declining balance, sum-of-the-years'-digits, 150% declining balance, sinking fund and straight-line methods. Although taxpayers who have elected to employ one method of computing depreciation normally may not switch to a different method without the consent of the Commissioner of Internal

Revenue, any taxpayer may switch without the consent of the Commissioner from any declining balance method to the straight-line method and any taxpayer who has elected to utilize the ADR system may switch without consent from the method then being employed to any less accelerated method of computing depreciation. In addition, by filing an application on Form 3115 and complying with the provisions of Revenue Procedure 74-11, any taxpayer may be reasonably assured of being permitted to make certain other changes in methods of depreciation, including changing from any declining balance method to any other declining balance method or from any declining balance method to the sum-of-the-years'-digits or sinking fund methods.

Basis. As described in greater detail under "Investment Tax Credit," an owner may desire to include in the depreciable basis of the Cars, on which the owner would calculate the depreciation allowance for such Cars, the portion of CARCO's commencement fee allocated by CARCO to services rendered in connection with the acquisition of such Cars and the portion of such fee payable to PQR Securities as a Placement Fee. There can be no assurance that the IRS would not challenge the amount of depreciation claimed by a Car owner computing depreciation on such method, claiming that all or part of either or both such portions of such commencement fee may not properly be included in the basis of such Cars. The IRS might assert that the portion of CARCO's commencement fee attributed to the Cars is attributable to other items such as the leases. Moreover, the IRS might assert that part or all of the portion of CARCO's commencement fee payable to PQR Securities is attributable to the Program or other items, rather than the Cars. If the IRS successfully challenged such inclusion in the basis of any Car, the depreciation deductions available to the Car owner would be reduced accordingly.

Salvage Value. Property may be depreciated to its salvage value; that is, the value of such property which reasonably may be expected to remain at the end of the useful life of the property in the taxpayer's business. Such determination must be made on the basis of the actual facts and circumstances of the taxpayer's business. Thus, a Car owner who anticipated owning and operating the Cars for their entire useful life could determine the salvage value on the basis of the anticipated value of the Car at the end of such time, even though such Car owner might, utilizing the ADR system, have depreciated such Cars over 12 years. However, a Car owner who had determined depreciation on the basis of facts and circumstances would determine the salvage value on the basis of the anticipated value of the Car at the end of the useful life adopted by the Car owner for purposes of depreciation.

Using any declining balance method of computing depreciation, the annual depreciation allowance for an asset is determined without adjustment for the salvage value of the asset being depreciated, except that no asset may be depreciated below the reasonable salvage value of such asset. Using the straight-line method, the annual depreciation allowance for an asset is determined on the basis of the difference between the original basis for the property and the salvage value thereof.

An amount of salvage value not exceeding 10% of basis may be disregarded, and, within limits provided in the Regulations under the Code, the IRS will not readjust assumed salvage values. Thus, if a Car owner expects to hold the Cars for their entire useful life and expects that the salvage value of the Cars will not be in excess of 10%, salvage value can be ignored for purposes of determining depreciation. No assurance can be given, however, that the IRS would not challenge such salvage value (or any other salvage value assigned to Cars by the owner thereof) and assert that the salvage value thereof should have been higher. Any such successful challenge by the IRS would, in the case of Cars depreciated under a declining balance method, result in the disallowance of depreciation deductions after the Cars had been depreciated to such salvage value as the IRS had asserted was reasonable, and, in the case of Cars depreciated under the straight-line method, result in a decrease in the amount of the annual depreciation deductions during the entire life of the Cars. However, while any successful challenge of the assumed salvage value of the Cars will be likely to reduce the overall depreciation deduction, the remaining basis of the Cars would be higher by the amount of such adjustment and, as a result, any taxable gain on sale or disposition of the Cars would be correspondingly reduced.

Bonus Depreciation. In addition to any other depreciation deductions which a taxpayer may be entitled to claim in any tax year, Section 179 of the Code permits the claim of an additional allowance, so-called "bonus depreciation," equal to 20% of the cost of depreciable tangible personal property with a useful life of six years or more which is acquired by the taxpayer during such tax year. However, in any tax year the cost of eligible property with respect to which bonus depreciation may be claimed is limited to $10,000 for a single person, $20,000 for a husband and wife filing a joint return, or $10,000 for a corporation (together with all other members of the control group of which such corporation is a part). As a result, the maximum amount of bonus depreciation which an individual may claim in any one tax year is $2,000 ($4,000 in the case of a husband and wife filing a joint return) or $2,000 in the case of a corporation and the members of its control group. In addition, the amount of bonus depreciation which can be claimed with respect to qualifying property owned by a partnership is limited to $2,000 (as if the partnership were a taxpayer). A trust is not entitled to any bonus depreciation. If a purchaser of Cars had already elected to claim bonus depreciation with respect to other property qualifying under Section 179, the amount of bonus depreciation which could be claimed with respect to such Cars would be reduced (and, conversely, the claim of bonus depreciation with respect to such Cars would limit the amount of bonus depreciation which could be claimed with respect to other qualifying property).

Amortization of Various Fees. From its commencement fee, CARCO will pay PQR Securities a Placement Agent's Fee and will pay ABC a Lease Negotiation Fee. CARCO has attributed the balance with respect to each Car to compensation for services in connection with the acquisition of such Cars.

CARCO believes that the Lease Negotiation Fee payable to ABC is properly amortized over the lives of the leases. In the event that the inclusion of all or a portion of the Placement Fee in the cost of the Cars were successfully challenged by the IRS, such Fee or portion thereof might be treated as a non-amortizable capital asset of the participants in the Management Program.

Although the amounts of ABC's Lease Negotiation Fee and the portion of CARCO's fee allocable to Car acquisition services have not been determined in arm's length negotiation, ABC believes that such allocations are reasonable and consistent with the fees that would be paid and accepted for similar services in transactions between unrelated parties. Such allocations reflect the allocation in fact made by CARCO for profit center accounting purposes and, in the case of ABC's Lease Negotiation Fee, is the amount by which the commencement fee will be reduced to all Car purchasers electing not to participate in the Management Program or to lease their Cars under the leases. However, no assurance can be given that the IRS will not challenge the amortization of any or all of the foregoing fees, claiming either that all or a portion of any of such fees are in fact attributable to some other services or assets or claiming that some or all of such fees should be amortized over some other, longer period or that some or all of such fees are nonamortizable capital assets of the Car owners.

3. Limitations on Deduction of Losses

In General. Section 465 of the Code (added by the Tax Reform Act of 1976 and amended by the Revenue Act of 1978) provides that, with respect to an activity, the amount of any losses (otherwise allowable for the year in question) which may be deducted by individuals, Subchapter S corporations, or "closely held corporations" (i.e., one in which five or fewer individuals own, with the application of constructive ownership rules, more than 50% of the outstanding stock) cannot exceed the aggregate amount with respect to which such taxpayer is "at risk" in such activity at the close of the tax year. Certain corporations, however, which are "actively engaged in equipment leasing" are exempt from the provisions of Section 465.

Under Section 465, a taxpayer is generally to be considered "at risk" with respect to an activity to the extent of cash, and the adjusted basis of other property, contributed to the activity, as well as any amounts borrowed for use in the activity with respect to which the taxpayer has personal liability for payment from his personal assets. However, if the taxpayer borrows money to contribute to the activity and the lender's only recourse is to either the taxpayer's interest in the activity of property used in the activity, the amount of the proceeds of the borrowing are to be considered amounts financed on a nonrecourse basis and do not increase the taxpayer's amount at risk. In addition, a taxpayer will not be considered "at risk" with respect to amounts borrowed for use in an activity (or which are contributed to the activity) where the amounts are borrowed from any person who has an interest in the activity (other than as a creditor) or from certain relatives or affiliates of the taxpayer.

Also, a taxpayer will not be considered to be "at risk," even as to the equity capital which such taxpayer has contributed to the activity, to the extent that the taxpayer is protected against economic loss of all or part of such capital by reason of an agreement or arrangement for compensation or reimbursement of any loss which the taxpayer may suffer. The insurance proposed to be carried on or with respect to the Cars for damage, destruction, third-party liability and business interruption, and the obligation of Car users to pay a stated amount in settlement of claims for loss of Cars, are not agreements of the type which would result in a Car owner not being "at risk" with respect to the Cars. And, while ABC believes that the residual value of the Cars will be substantial, neither such residual value nor any belief therein is protection against economic loss of the type which would result in a Car owner not being "at risk."

In any event, Car owners which are individuals, Subchapter S corporations, or "closely held corporations" should consider the effect of the "at risk" provisions in seeking to arrange debt financing for Car purchases. Other corporate Car owners are not subject to the provisions of Section 465.

Recapture. In addition to extending Section 465 to closely held corporations (as well as to all activities other than real estate), the Revenue Act of 1978 amended Section 465 of the Code to require the recapture of previously allowed losses where the amount at risk is reduced below zero (by distributions to the taxpayer, changes in the status of indebtedness from recourse to nonrecourse, the commencement of a guarantee or other similar arrangement which affects the taxpayer's risk of loss). Under that Act, the taxpayer will be required to recognize income to the extent that his at risk basis is so reduced below zero. This amendment, however, requires a taxpayer to recapture only those losses occurring in taxable years beginning after December 31, 1978. Losses incurred in prior taxable years will not be considered when reducing a taxpayer's at risk basis. In addition, if a taxpayer's at risk basis is a negative amount as of the close of the taxpayer's last taxable year beginning before January 1, 1979, such negative amount, rather than zero, will be the taxpayer's at risk for subsequent taxable years.

4. Limitations on the Deductibility of Interest

Excess Investment Interest. Section 163(d) of the Code limits the amount of "investment interest" which non-corporate taxpayers and corporations which are Subchapter S corporations may deduct for federal income tax purposes. However, investment interest the deduction of which is disallowed in any year may be carried over to subsequent years. Under Section 163(d), a taxpayer may deduct investment interest from all sources to the extent of: (a) $10,000 ($5,000 for a married taxpayer filing a separate return and zero for a trust), (b) the taxpayer's "net investment income" and (c) the amount by which the interest deductions allowable under Section 163 (determined without regard to Section 163(d)) and certain other out-of-pocket expenses attributable to the taxpayer's property which is subject to a net lease exceed the rental income produced by such property.

Investment interest is defined as "interest paid or accrued on indebtedness incurred or continued to purchase or carry property held for investment." Property, such as the Cars, which is used in a trade or business (as described under "Investment Tax Credit above) normally would not be considered an "investment" and, thus, the deductibility of interest on indebtedness to purchase or carry such property would not be limited by Section 163(d). However, leased property, such as the Cars, will be treated as property held for investment unless *both* (i) the deductions with respect to the property (during each taxable year) which are allowable solely by reason of Section 162 equal or exceed 15% of the rental income produced by such property and (ii) the lessor is neither guaranteed a specified return nor guaranteed in whole or in part against loss of income.

ABC believes that the expenses with respect to operation of the Cars deductible solely by reason of Section 162 will equal or exceed 15% of gross rentals each year (although no assurance can be given that actual expenses in any year will equal or exceed 15% of actual income in such year). And, based upon the terms and conditions of the Management Agreement and the anticipated leases, a participant in the Management Program is neither guaranteed a specified return nor guaranteed in whole or in part against loss of income.

In considering whether a lessor is guaranteed a return or protected against loss, proposed Treasury Regulations provide as follows:

"A net lease of the type described in this paragraph will result, for instance, if the lessee is obligated to pay all the expenses attributable to the property which the lessor will incur or accrue for a period covered by the lease and, in the event of complete or partial destruction of the property, the lessee is obligated either to continue to pay the full rent for such period or a lump-sum amount equivalent to the present value of such rental payments. Further, the lease will be a net lease if the lessor's liability for expenses is fixed by contracts with parties related to the lessee. On the other hand, a third party's guarantee that the lessor will receive a fixed or determined rental payment shall not, in and of itself, result in the arrangement being a net lease."

It is not anticipated that the lessees under the leases will indemnify the Car owner against any loss, destruction or damage resulting from an owner's negligent or willful act (or the negligent or willful act of any of an owner's agents, including ABC). Furthermore, it is anticipated that the Car owner and not the lessee will be required, among other things, to purchase any insurance on the Cars with respect to either casualty or liability and to pay all maintenance expenses, to pay any management fee payable to ABC, and to pay for all alterations or improvements which may be made to the Cars. Therefore, based on the above, ABC believes that a Car owner is neither guaranteed a specified return nor guaranteed in whole or in part against loss of income in connection with the lease of the Cars.

For the foregoing reasons, ABC believes that a Car is not an "investment" and, accordingly, that Section 163(d) should not be applicable to the deductibility of interest paid on debt financing for Car purchases. However, as heretofore indicated, there can be no assurance that the IRS could not successfully assert that all or a portion of the management fee payable to ABC is not properly deductible by a Car owner and there can be no assurance that, in any given year, the sum of all Section 162 expenses will actually exceed 15% of gross rentals. If the "15% test" were not satisfied for any reason, the deductibility of interest on Car financing might be limited by Section 163(d). However, because the amount of any Car owner's investment interest which would be subject to disallowance in any year would depend upon the income and expenses of such owner, the extent, if any, to which interest incurred to purchase or carry a Car would be subject to disallowance would depend upon the facts of such owner's particular tax situation. In any event, Section 163(d) would not offset the deductibility of interest by corporate Car owners (other than Subchapter S corporations).

Interest Related to Tax-exempt Obligations. Section 265(2) of the Code provides that interest on indebtedness incurred or continued to "purchase or carry" tax-exempt bonds is not deductible. It has been held that if indebtedness is incurred to avoid liquidating tax-exempt bonds, Section 265(2) will operate to preclude the deduction of interest on such indebtedness. However, whether the indebtedness is incurred for that purpose must be decided on the basis of the individual circumstances of any particular case.

In the case of an investor who holds tax-exempt securities and who plans to finance the purchase of Cars from borrowed funds, it is possible that the IRS will seek to disallow the deductibility of all or a portion of the interest expenses incurred by such investor on such Car financing, claiming that the indebtedness was incurred to "purchase or carry" tax-exempt bonds.

5. Sale or Other Disposition of Cars

Upon a sale or other disposition of a Car (inlcuding a sale or other disposition resulting from destruction of such Car or from foreclosure or other enforcement of a security interest in such Car given to secure debt financing for the purchase price thereof), the owner of such Car will realize gain or loss equal to the difference between (a) the basis of such Car at the time of sale or disposition and (b) the amount realized upon sale or disposition. Since, historically, covered hopper cars have maintained a substantial residual value, it may be anticipated that the depreciated basis of any Car at the time of sale will be appreciably less than the amount realized upon sale or disposition (especially if the owner has claimed accelerated depreciation).

Upon the sale or other disposition of personal property, all of the depreciation theretofore deducted will, to the extent of any gains, be subject to "recapture" under Section 1245 of the Code—that is, taxed as ordinary income. Depreciation recapture under Section 1245 of the Code cannot be avoided by holding the Cars for any specified period of time.

Under Section 1231 of the Code, if the sum of the gains on sale or exchange of certain assets (generally, depreciable property, other than inventory and literary properties, used in a trade or business and held for more than one year) and the gains from certain compulsory or involuntary conversions exceed the losses on such sales, exchanges and conversions, all such gains and losses will be treated as capital gains and losses (hereinafter referred to as a "Section 1231 gain or loss"). However, if such losses exceed such gains, all such losses and gains will be treated as ordinary gains and losses.

There is a special rule under Section 1231 for casualty and theft losses on depreciable business property and capital assets held for more than twelve months. Such gains and losses must be separately grouped together and, if casualty gains equal or exceed casualty losses, then the gains and losses are further grouped with other Section 1231 transactions to determine whether there is an overall Section 1231 gain or loss. If the casualty or theft losses exceed gains, the resulting net loss is not further grouped with other Section 1231 transactions, but is, instead, excluded from Section 1231 and treated as an ordinary loss.

If a Car has been held for less than one year or the seller of the Car is a "dealer" in property like the Cars, any gain or loss will be treated as short-term capital gain (loss) or ordinary income (loss), as the case may be. Except under those circumstances, any Section 1231 gain recognized with respect to the Cars in excess of the amount of depreciation theretofore claimed on such Car (which depreciation is subject to recapture, as described above)—that is, gain attributable to proceeds in excess of the original purchase price of such Cars—will be capital gains, provided the sum of all Section 1231 gains exceeds the sum of all Section 1231 losses, as discussed above.

The taxation of capital gains is specifically provided for under the Code. Although the Revenue Act of 1978 repealed the alternative 25% rate on the first $50,000 of such gains effective as of January 1, 1979, the effective rate for both individuals and corporations was otherwise reduced. In the case of individuals, only 40% of the excess of net long-term capital gains over net short-term capital losses is included in gross income. In the case of corporations, the excess of net long-term capital gains over net short-term capital losses is taxed at the rate of 28% (if such rate results in a lower tax than the regular corporate income tax rates).

Upon the sale or other disposition of a Car before the close of the seventh year from the date such Car was first placed in service, all or a portion of the investment tax credit previously allowed on such Car will be recaptured. In addition, if Cars are subject to a lease at the time at which they are sold by the owner to a new purchaser, such purchaser will not be entitled to claim the investment tax credit with respect to such Cars. Property which is leased to the same person or entity both before and after a purchase does not qualify as the type of used property which is eligible for the investment tax credit. Treas. Regs. § 1.48-3(a) (2) (i).

6. Transfer of Cars by Gift or Death

Since the tax consequences of any gift or transfer of Cars will depend upon the particular circumstances of the individuals or organizations involved in the transaction, a participant should consult tax counsel before making any gift of his Cars.

A gift of Cars may result in income tax liability to the donor if the liabilities on the Cars exceed the donor's adjusted tax basis in such Cars at the time of the gift and the donee agrees to pay the liabilities. In such a case, the IRS will take the position that the amount treated as a true gift would be limited to the amount by which the fair market value of the Cars exceeds the liabilities thereon and that the donor would realize income to the extent the liabilities exceed his adjusted tax basis in the Cars. In addition, the fair market value of the Cars, reduced by the amount of liabilities to which the Cars are subject if the donee agrees to pay such liabilities, will constitute a gift for Federal gift tax purposes and may be subject to state gift taxes as well. In the event that a gift of the Cars is made before the end of seven years from the date any Car is deemed to have been placed in service, investment tax credits previously allowed will be recaptured.

It is likely that a participant would realize income on a gift to a charitable organization to the extent that the liabilities on the Cars exceeded the portion of his adjusted basis for such Cars which bears the same ratio to his total adjusted basis as such liabilities bear to the fair market value of the Cars. This special rule as to allocation of basis results from the bargain sale to charity rules contained in Code Section 1011(b). Furthermore, if a Car is donated before the end of seven years from the date any Car is deemed to have been placed in service, all or a portion of the investment tax credit previously allowed will be recaptured.

If a participant dies while owning Cars, the fair market value of such Cars at death (or, if elected, at the alternate valuation date), reduced by the amount of liabilities to which the property is subject, will be subject to federal estate taxation. Neither the transfer at death to a successor owner nor a distribution by the deceased owner's estate to a successor owner will be considered a sale or exchange giving rise to a capital gains tax nor will such a disposition give rise to recapture of the investment tax credit. While such transfer or distribution would not generally constitute events giving rise to depreciation recapture, in certain circumstances depreciation recapture will result upon the distribution of a Car by the deceased owner's estate to a successor owner. Generally, the successor owner will take the same adjusted basis in the Cars as the deceased had (increased by a portion of the federal and state estate taxes paid thereon), if the deceased dies subsequent to December 31, 1979, except that, in certain circumstances, a successor owner who takes the Cars from the deceased's estate will take a basis in the Cars equal to their fair market value. Upon a future sale or disposition of the Cars, the successor owner may be subject to depreciation recapture, and the amount of such recapture may include depreciation taken by the deceased. If the deceased dies during 1979, the successor owner will take a "step-up" basis in the Cars equal to the fair market value at date of death, with certain adjustments.

7. Other Taxes

In addition to federal income taxes, Car owners may be subject to other taxes, such as state and local franchise, personal property or income taxes, and estate or inheritance taxes, which may be imposed by various jurisdictions. Although a detailed analysis of these various taxes cannot be presented here, prospective investors should consider possible state or local tax consequences of Car ownership and operation. For example, the leasing of the Cars may represent, under the laws of a particular state, sufficient activity to be deemed to be doing business in that jurisdiction. And an owner's items of income, gain, loss, deduction or credit may be subject to income taxation in jurisdictions in which the owner is doing business (including as a result of Car leasing operations) as well as in the jurisdiction in which such Car owner is resident. Furthermore, some states do not recognize the ADR system for purposes of determining state income taxes. Thus, it is possible that some participants may have to calculate depreciation deductions by two different methods: One way for Federal income tax purposes and another way for state tax purposes.

Without limiting the generality of the foregoing, an owner may be subject to income taxation in Canada or Mexico. Moreover, rental revenues, if any, from use of the Cars in Canada or in Mexico may become subject to the Canadian or Mexican withholding tax.

8. Foreign Source Income

Use of the Cars in Canada or Mexico would give rise to rentals and related deductions deemed to have a foreign source for federal income tax purposes. In general, the Code permits a taxpayer with foreign source taxable income to credit against such taxpayer's United States income tax on such foreign source taxable income all or a portion of foreign income taxes paid with respect to such income. However, Section 904 of the Code imposes limitations on the foreign tax credit available to a taxpayer in any taxable year, depending on the amounts of such taxpayer's foreign source taxable income and such taxpayer's entire taxable income for such year. Thus, losses attributable to the Cars while used in Canada or Mexico may affect the ability of a Car owner to credit against such owner's U.S. income tax either taxes paid on other foreign source taxable income or the Canadian or Mexican income tax referred to above (to the extent payable by the owner). That is, a Car owner who has foreign source taxable income may receive reduced benefits from foreign tax credits resulting from foreign taxes paid with respect to such income because losses attributable to the Cars while used in Canada or Mexico (together with other foreign source losses) must be applied to reduce such taxpayer's foreign source taxable income. This may reduce the overall benefit to such a Car owner of purchase of the Cars and participation in the Management Program. However, as indicated above, although ABC cannot predict how many Cars will be used in Canada or Mexico or how long any Cars may be in Canada or

Mexico, it believes that the lessees of the Cars will adhere to any limitations on use of the Cars in Canada or Mexico contained in the leases of such Cars.

GLOSSARY

AAR: Association of American Railroads is a self-regulating body with the responsibility of coordinating the movements of railroad cars.

Impound Account: A separate account in which the Managing Placement Agent will deposit the payment(s) contributed by the investor to be held in trust until certain conditions are satisfied.

Excess Mileage Allowance: Monies paid by a railroad to the owners of private railcars which are in excess of the basic monthly lease rate and result from increased usage of the cars.

ICC: Interstate Commerce Commission, a federal agency which is responsible for economic regulation of railroads, motor carriers and domestic water carriers.

Mileage Allowance: An allowance per car-mile paid by railroads for the use of privately owned railcars as specified by railroads' Mileage Tariff 7-F issued by the Interstate Commerce Commission.

Official Railway Equipment Register: A tariff publication showing by reporting marks and car numbers the capacity, length and dimensions of railcars operated by the railroads and private car companies of North America.

UMLER: Universal Machine Language Equipment Register is a computerized master car data file containing the reporting marks and numbers of all cars together with data on car specifications.

Equipment leasing is a medium risk investment which, if properly handled, can offer significant deductions in early years and some income tax shelter. This is a medium term investment of from 5 to 10 years and can be used to defer tax liability.

Chapter Four

INDUSTRIAL DESIGN

When John DeLorean reached out for venture capital for his automobile, he offered a limited partnership tax shelter for his investors to give them writeoffs for start up losses and then ownership in his operating company.

The programs of this chapter show the tremendous, positive force of tax shelters in industry. Custom automobiles and designer accessories, satellite communications, computers and computer graphics software are outstanding examples of tax shelters at work for industrial progress.

CUSTOM AUTOMOBILES AND DESIGNER ACCESSORIES

INTRODUCTION

STERLING MOTORS, INC. ("Sterling") has granted to International Designer Corporation ("IDC") a subdistributorship for the Henry Designer Collection of Automobiles and Fashion Boutiques in certain territories in the United States. IDC proposes to grant to certain individuals or corporations the distribution rights to the Henry Designer Collection of Automobiles and Fashion Boutiques of designer softgoods for the general automotive market (the "Distributorship") for the territory (the "Territory") described in the Distribution Agreement.

DESIGNER COLLECTION

List of Basic Automobile Products for Fashion Line

A. Limited Production Custom Henry I
   1. Interior options
   2. Paint options
   3. Performance options

B. Dealer Installed Henry Designer Conversion Kits
   1. Logos and metal trim components
   2. Interior trim components
   3. Accessories
   4. Software gift accessories

C. Fashion Henry Boutiques
   1. Basic display unit
   2. Software Personal Driving Accessories
      i) Driving Shoes–Fashion licensee
      ii) Driving Gloves–Fashion licensee
      iii) Driving Glasses–Fashion licensee
      vi) Racing Watch–Fashion licensee
      v) Racing Jacket–Fashion licensee

- vi) Driving Cape–Fashion licensee
- vii) Coordinated fashion accessories, belts, ties, scarves, handbags, sweaters, umbrellas
- viii) Coordinated fashion jewelry with corporate logo
- ix) Calculators, travel radios and clocks

3. Hardware automotive accessories
   - i) Designer wheels–submanufacturing agent
   - ii) Floor mats–submanufacturing agent
   - iii) Car Covers–submanufacturing agent
   - iv) Seat Covers–submanufacturing agent
   - v) Chrome Grills–submanufacturing agent
   - vi) Chrome trim–submanufacturing agent
   - vii) Specialty lights–submanufacturing agent
   - viii) Radios and Speakers–submanufacturing agent
   - ix) Tires–submanufacturing agent
   - x) Various travel containers, such as picnic baskets, safety kits, tool carriers, etc.
   - xi) Auto Blankets–Fashion licensee
   - xii) Designer Graphics and metal castings

D. Direct Mail and Mass Media Sales

1. In most areas we will be using the same basic product grouping listed above for these marketing efforts.
2. From time to time we will introduce new products based on market experience and response.
3. Each year new Fashion licenses are being created providing new products and market opportunities which we may choose to work with.

The distribution rights will be sold only to Purchasers with substantial assets who have the ability (or access to reliable advice) to prudently weigh the economic risks against the potential financial gains of this Offering and who are in the business of either selling automobiles or automobile products, or operating licenses similar to the Distributorship, or are in some other active business similar to these that would make them qualified to distribute the Products.

The distribution rights for a Territory will be sold for a distribution fee as set forth in the Distribution Agreement, the first year's payment consisting of a cash payment and the delivery of a recourse promissory note for the balance. The cash portion of the initial payment is due upon the execution and delivery of the Distribution Agreement. A Purchaser will pay the balance of the first year's distribution fee by delivering a recourse promissory note (the "Note") to IDC, which will bear interest at the rate of six percent (6%) per annum, be due and payable approximately ten (10) years after execution prepayable at any time without penalty and shall impose personal liability on the Purchaser. A copy of the Note is attached to the Distribution Agreement. The nonpayment of the Note will result in a forfeiture of the distribution rights and will result in personal liability to a Purchaser.

A Purchaser desiring to avail himself of this investment will enter into a Distribution Agreement with IDC to acquire the distribution rights. This investment is offered on a first come basis subject to the absolute right of IDC to reject any Purchaser's offer for any reason. The Purchaser will acquire the distribution rights in the Territory only.

THE BUSINESS

Past Performance of Sterling Motors, Inc.

The Henry Designer Program was initially established by Sterling as an "after-market" dealer installed conversion package suitable for the complete Henry line with approximately 10 adjusted color variations. The package consisted of the Fashion nameplate, special two-tone point design, decals, a unique safety seat, trunk rugs, luggage, safety kit and Auto Club membership. These items not directly relating to styling, were intended to add value to the package without necessitating additional labor costs. A final dealer cost of $1,395 was established. The cost of installation was estimated to be $450, and the suggested retail price installed was $2,995.

Sterling Motors, Inc. and Design Sales Group, Inc., its marketing agent, initiated a sales team with national and regional sales managers. A sales package was made available to salesmen and dealers, which included two or four kits plus point-of-sale material such as brochures, taped edited commercials, television commercials and sales incentive programs. All products were designed to be shipped to the dealer F.O.B. Detroit through a fulfillment subcontractor in Detroit.

A comprehensive program of promotion was implemented which utilized a bi-level approach:

(1) A series of trade paper advertisements announcing the program to Henry dealers and inviting them to Florida for a sales presentation. This effort was coordinated with a telephone sales campaign. Moreover, a follow-up system was employed wherein each dealer was contacted regularly.

(2) A national promotional tour was instituted in major marketing cities. Mr. Frank Fashion held a press conference in New York in February of 1979 and there introduced his new automotive designs. As a result, Management believes that the public relational efforts were beneficial as a result of television coverage, magazine commentary and newspaper articles which followed Mr. Fashion's press conference. A prototype Henry I by Frank Fashion was presented to distributors, dealers and tradespeople at a private party in New York City's Studio 54. These events were augmented by the New York Auto Show, the NADA Show in Las Vegas and the Fashion Show at F.I.T. in New York City. At each of these presentations Management believes that Henry I was favorably received by the trade.

The following conclusions reflect Sterling's evaluation of (a) its products, (b) its modus operandi and (c) its marketing approach although the following represents Management's conclusions and is not a guaranty of future performance.

1. There is wide acceptance on both the wholesale and retail level for the "Frank Fashion" label.

2. In order to achieve a rate of growth consistent with original projections, a more diversified product line based on what has been learned from Henry dealers over the past twelve months is required.

3. Further, it has been necessary to scale down the base price of the Frank Fashion package to create a more acceptable price structure for Henry dealers.

4. The $2,995 retail cost of the installed kit was beyond the range of many buyers. Therefore, a package has been structured to create a broader market and a basic price of $1,695 with sufficient options to bring the maximum cost to $3,000.

5. The Fashion Boutique has been developed whereby all automobile dealers, not just Henry dealers, may offer additional accessory Fashion designed items for sale.

6. On the negative side, original sales projections failed to provide adequate lead time for development of product sales and distribution. The experience of Management is that a period of ten to twelve months was necessary to fully develop product and provide for distribution with several more months of concentrated promotion and sales effort to achieve the initial sales goals. Due to the current slump in automobile sales in general and Henry in particular sales performance of the Henry Designer Collection has been disappointing.

Management believes that certain prior situations initially hampered Sterling's earlier marketing efforts including the following sequence of events:

1. Inadequate programs of product development and distribution.
2. Mr. Fashion's decision in 1978 not to appear at three major promotional and sales functions sponosred by Sterling.
3. General management and operational problems of Sterling.

Management believes that most of the major product and distribution problems have been resolved and that Mr. Fashion will now make every effort to support and cooperate in the design and related program promotion of the Henry Designer Program and Fashion Boutiques, although there are no assurance that this will be the case.

Notwithstanding earlier obstacles, Management is more confident of its ability to achieve the goals set forth herein. Management's confidence is predicated upon the following experiences over the past eighteen months, although there is no assurance that these factors will make the Distributorship profitable or that the forecasts described below will prove to be accurate.

1. Wide acceptance on both the wholesale and retail levels for the Frank Fashion label.
2. Market testing in New York City resulting in a test market dealer, achieving a favorable sales volume for the past twelve months.
3. Management's belief that Henry buyers are the most likely to spend additional money for after-market status products such as the Henry Designer Collection.

4. Extensive discussions with manufacturers of after-market automotive products indicating the possibility on their part of entering into submanufacturing agreements involving sales guarantees and royalty arrangements.

5. Competitive and regulatory market conditions which have begun to erode the Henry dealers high profit margin position requiring them to sell imaginative aftermarket products to attract customers and increase profits. The foregoing is also applicable to automobile dealers in general which would appear to make Fashion Boutiques an attractive medium for increasing their profits, however, there can be no assurance that this will be the case.

6. Consistent growth in the exclusive limited automobile market both in this country and internationally.

The financial statement indicates that Sterling received approximately $873,741 in Distribution Fees in 1979/80 fiscal year and that these fees were applied as follows:

Selling Expenses	– $442,243
Design Costs	– $ 93,450
License Costs	– $ 30,000
General Office Administration Expenses	– $315,000

Based on the above expenditures and its current operating deficit and outstanding liabilities, unless Sterling receives additional proceeds from the sale, either directly or indirectly, of distributorships, or is able to obtain financing in lieu of granting distributorships or is able to increase its gross revenues, there is a serious question of whether it will be able to remain in operation and keep the license in good standing.

Sterling intends to engage regional and state distributors for the products including distributors in the northeast United States, covering New York, New Jersey, Delaware and eastern Pennsylvania. Generally a sales distributor agrees to purchase an agreed upon amount of products and guaranties a 5% sales penetration over a given period of time. The northeast distributor is Designer Henry International, Ltd. It is owned by a Henry dealer and financed by Henry Holding Corporation. To date, this distributor has taken delivery on approximately $105,000 worth of inventory and currently has a full time salesman covering the Territory and dealerships handling the Fashion products.

Contracts with two agents have been signed in the Washington, D.C. area and in California. The Washington agreement includes the territories of Maryland, North Carolina and Virginia and the California agreement covers California, New Mexico, Arizona and Utah. New sales agreements are under consideration for the southeastern United States, Texas and Illinois. The purpose of the sales agreement concept is to enable Sterling to develop a sales and service network of highly qualified people with low investment on the part of Sterling. The sales distributors profit is based upon an approximate 25% markup over the manufacturer's cost. The startup capital requirements are approximately $100,000. A territory to be purchased by a Purchaser will not be affected by any of the above-described agreements unless the Purchaser independently agrees to engage subagents to assist it in its promotion and sales efforts.

Current Operations

Management of Sterling is currently reviewing its product line and has made a trip to Paris to meet with Frank Fashion. Sterling has also developed the Fashion automotive softgoods display unit (the Fashion Boutique) relating to the sale of Fashion designed softgoods for the general automotive market. In addition, Standard has developed products for sale by Henry dealers such as floor mats, wheels and the like. Sterling estimates that approximately 30 dealers have the products on consignment or are selling inventory as of this date. Due to Sterling's lack of working capital, it executed a line of credit from an unrelated Lender to finance its inventory up to an amount of $500,000 with interest payable at 4% over prime rate. The Lender has been secured by a security interest on all such inventory and an assignment of Sterling's accounts receivables.

Management is concerned with the trend toward smaller American and European cars which has seriously adversely affected sales of standard size and large size cars. However, it is Management's opinion that there is a significant market for exotic limited production automobiles such as the Frank Fashion custom designed Henry I. Mr. Fashion created this design, and the prototypes were built in New York City under the direction of Fashion's assistant and Jack Race of Sterling. Final revisions were completed in Paris and versions of the limited edition Henry I are being built in Detroit by a custom-built auto manufacturer under the supervision of Frank Fashion's design staff and Jack Race.

Products

Management intends that the following products will be included in the Products available to Purchasers for distribution:

1. Henry I which Management believes will have an approximate retail price of $55,000.
2. Component car kits to be wholesaled to Henry dealers which will cost from $400 to $1,500.
3. Automobile accessories to be wholesaled to Henry dealers.
4. Gift accessories to be wholesaled to automobile dealers in general.

In connection with some of the above-described activities, to the extent that Sterling directly makes sales of automobile accessories not through Henry dealers such as direct mail sales to consumers or Henry factory installed products, then a distributor for a Territory will receive an agreed upon payment for sales made to users in his Territory. A Purchaser of a distributorship in Year One will not participate in Year One sales of the Henry One.

As described above, Sterling plans to engage local distributors such as a potential Purchaser to help market the products. Advertising materials will be mailed to automobile dealers prior to actual distribution in the Territories. In addition, heavy telephone canvassing to dealers will be made by Sterling which will indicate what products are being offered. An additional step will be to either sell or lease to dealers a Fashion Boutique display rack at a cost of approximately $440 which will be used to display merchandise bearing the label "Fashion." Another method of promotion will be through national and regional magazines. Also, brochures and other point-of-sale material will be supplied to Henry users and automobile dealers in general.

Sterling has displayed the Henry Designer Collection, Fashion Boutique, and the custom designed Henry I in the World Trade Center in New York and Century City in California and has completed negotiations to display the Collection and the Henry I in other key locations.

AGREEMENTS

License Agreement with Frank Fashion

Sterling has entered into a License Agreement with Frank Fashion, a French corporation, which has been modified, granting to Sterling the exclusive rights to use the "Frank Fashion" trademark in the continental United States of America, including the States of Alaska and Hawaii and Canada, on, and in connection with the design and outfitting of automobile interiors and exteriors, the sale and distribution of the Fashion Boutique and designer softgoods for the automobile market. The License Agreement, as modified, provides for Fashion to retain control over advertising and the development and distribution of products bearing its trade name and these restrictions shall apply to any Purchaser of a Distributorship.

The term of the modified License Agreement is for ten years. In the event that net sales during the fifth annual period do not equal or exceed $2,000,000 (which amount is subject to increases based upon a cost-of-living formula provided for in the modified License Agreement), then the Licensor ("Fashion") shall have the right to terminate the License.

The License Agreement provides for annual royalty payments as follows:

1. $25,000 for the annual period to and including June 30, Year Two.
2. $30,000 for the annual period ending June 30, Year Three.
3. $35,000 for the annual period ending June 30, Year Four.
4. $40,000 for the annual period ending June 30, Year Five.
5. A $10,000 increase for each year thereafter with $100,000 for each annual period ending June 30, Year Ten and thereafter.

The License Agreement also provides for minimum royalty payments equal to 3% of net sales, which amount shall be reduced by the amount of any minimum annual royalty payments as provided above, which royalty payments are payable quarterly.

Distributorship Agreement

Sterling has entered into a Distributorship Agreement with International Designer Corporation ("IDC") providing for the subfranchise by Sterling of certain rights with respect to the Henry Designer Collection and Fashion Boutiques to IDC in certain territories in the United States. IDC will be paying to Sterling in consideration of this Distributorship 75% of all cash and approximately 100% of the recourse note proceeds received in connection with Distributorship fee payments. In addition, a royalty payment schedule has been established by Sterling in connection with sales in specific territories over and above the fixed amount of gross revenues. The term of the Distribution Agreement is equal to the term of the modified License Agreement with Fashion including any renewals thereof.

IDC will be granting subdistributorships to Purchasers which will correspond to the rights received from Sterling except that purchasers of a Distributorship in Year One will not participate in the sales of the Henry I made during Year One.

BENEFITS OF A CUSTOM AUTOMOBILE AND DESIGNER ACCESSORY FUND

FRANK FASHION DESIGNER COLLECTION

BRIEF SUMMARY OF BENEFITS: FRANK FASHION HENRY DESIGNER COLLECTION OF AUTOMOBILE ACCESSORIES FOR HENRYS AND FASHION BOUTIQUES OF DESIGNER SOFTGOODS FOR THE GENERAL AUTOMOTIVE MARKET

This transaction enables the Purchaser to acquire for his own account the exclusive right to distribute the Frank Fashion Designer Collection for Henry in his exclusive territory. Each territory will comprise itself of a specific number of Henry Sales and will be entitled to receive all profits from any and all sales of the Designers Collection Package in his territory.

Total Purchase Price:	$530,000
Cash:	$ 30,000
Recourse Promissory Note:	$ 75,000
Paid from Profit of Territory:	$425,000

Purchase Schedule—Potential Tax Benefits:

Year	Cash Purchase	Taxable Profit or (Loss)	Tax on Taxable Profit or (Loss)	Cumulative Return	Cumulative Return Less Investment	Ratio
One	$30,000	($105,000)	($52,000)	$52,000	$22,500	3.5

ASSUMPTIONS USED

The following projected statements are predicated on a territory selling approximately 2,000 automobiles annually (using "HENRY NEW CAR REGISTRATIONS" schedule attached). Purchaser pays $530,000 for a distributorship, $105,000 initially, payable $30,000 in cash, the balance in recourse notes payable over a period of ten (10) years with interest at six per cent (6%). The remaining balance of $425,000 is payable from the net profit of the territory, without interest and without recourse to the purchaser.

Sales—Based on five marketing concepts presently in use or to be implemented shortly, as follows:

1. Direct Mail
2. Designer Styling Kits
3. Henry Series of Automobiles
4. Sub Manufacturing
5. In-Dealer Boutiques

It is assumed that the distributorship purchaser will have no sales in their territory until Year Two.

1. *Direct Mail*—A direct mail campaign of driver related gift products to new Henry buyers during the last three years will begin in Year Two. It is assumed that a .6% response will be obtained with an average purchase of $50.000. A 20% annual growth factor is assumed.

2. *Designer Styling Kits*—Assumes in Year One that 2% of all Henry buyers will select this option. The percentage market

saturation increases to 2½% in Year Two; 3% in Year Three; 4% in Year Four; 5% in Year Five; 6% in Year Six; 8% in Year Seven; and 10% thereafter.

3. *Henry Series of Automobile*—Assumes nationwide sales of 150 Units in Year One*; 225 in Year Two; 250 in Year Three; 275 in Year Four; 300 in Year Five; 325 in Year Six; 350 in Year Seven; 375 in Year Eight and 400 annually thereafter.

*Purchasers of Distributorships in Year One will not participate in sales of Henry Automobiles made in Year One.

4. *Sub Manufacturing*—A 10% royalty fee will be charged to manufacturers licensed to manufacture and sell Frank Fashion automotive products, in addition to initial $10,000 per manufacture fee. This program should begin in Year Two. Sub-manufacturers would reasonably have minimum sales of $1,000,000 annually. Royalty income and initial fees are assumed to be $550,000 in Year Two; $500,000 in Year Three; $610,000 in Year Four; $600,000 in Year Five; $710,000 in Year Six; $700,000 in Year Seven; $810,000 in Year Eight; $800,000 in Year Nine; $910,000 in Year Ten; and $900,000 in Year Eleven.

5. *In-Dealer Boutiques*—Assumes that 20% of Henry dealers and 20% additional thereafter will install Boutiques on their premises. The Year One is projected to be a test-year with dealers achieving an average of $3,000 of merchandise. For the Year Two, it is projected that dealers will average $12,000 of sales annually, and that per dealer sales will increase 15% annually thereafter.

Cost of Sales—Cost of Sales for the various marketing projections outlined above, are as follows:

1. Direct Mail—50% of selling price.
2. Designer Styling Kits—54% of selling price.
3. Henry Series of Automobiles—77/78% of selling price.
4. Sub-Manufacturing—30% of royalties received (exclusive of initial fees) paid to Frank Fashion.
5. In-Dealer Boutiques—77.27% of selling price.

Marketing Fee—The marketing agreement, if elected, provides for the payment of a 5% of sales marketing fee.

For Taxpayer in 50% Tax Bracket
Tax Consequences on Purchase of Typical/Distribution Area

$30,000 Initial Payment

Year	Investment	Taxable Profit or (Loss)	Ratio	Tax on Taxable Profit or Loss	Cash Flow	Annual Return	Cumulative Return	Cumulative Return Less Investment
1	30,000	(105,000)	3.5	(52,500)		52,500	52,500	22,500
2		15,645		7,823	8,145	322	52,822	22,822
3		16,788		8,394	9,288	894	53,716	23,716
4		17,897		8,949	10,397	1,448	55,164	25,164
5		19,702		9,851	12,202	2,351	57,515	27,515
6		21,610		10,805	14,110	3,305	60,820	30,820
7		24,311		12,156	16,811	4,655	65,475	35,475
8		27,465		13,733	19,965	6,232	71,707	41,707
9		31,883		15,942	24,383	8,441	80,148	50,148
10		37,410		18,705	29,910	11,205	91,353	61,353
11		44,475		22,238	36,975	14,737	106,090	76,090

Projected Statement of Cash Flow
Typical Distribution Area

	1	2	3	4	5	6	7	8	9	10	11
Cash Provided By:											
Purchaser	30,000										
Gross Sales		120,032	139,627	164,699	194,933	233,929	283,558	349,030	433,861	544,413	691,057
Less: Cost of Sales		83,885	98,808	116,967	139,334	167,923	204,819	253,313	316,935	398,882	509,579
Gross Profit on Sales		36,147	40,819	47,732	55,599	66,006	78,739	95,717	116,926	145,531	181,478
Total Cash Sources	30,000	36,147	40,819	47,732	55,599	66,006	78,739	95,717	116,926	145,531	181,478
Cash Needed For:											
Initial Distributorship Fee	30,000										
Note Payment—Initial Distributorship Fee		7,500	7,500	7,500	7,500	7,500	7,500	7,500	7,500	7,500	7,500
On-Going Distributorship Fee		10,000	13,000	18,000	23,000	30,000	38,000	49,000	62,000	80,000	102,000
Marketing Fee		6,002	6,981	8,235	9,747	11,696	14,178	17,452	21,693	27,221	34,553
Interest		4,500	4,050	3,600	3,150	2,700	2,250	1,800	1,350	900	450
Total Use of Funds	30,000	28,002	31,531	37,335	43,397	51,896	61,928	75,752	92,543	115,621	114,503
Excess of Sources Over Uses of Funds		8,145	9,288	6,397	12,202	14,110	16,811	19,965	24,383	29,910	36,975

Projected Statement of Income
Profit or (Loss)
Typical Distribution Area

$30,000 Initial Payment

	1	2	3	4	5	6	7	8	9	10	11
Income:											
Gross Sales		120,032	139,627	164,699	194,933	233,929	263,558	349,030	433,861	544,413	691,057
Less: Cost of Sales		83,885	98,808	116,967	139,334	167,923	204,819	253,313	316,935	398,882	509,579
Gross Profit on Sales		36,147	40,819	47,732	55,599	66,006	78,739	95,717	116,926	145,531	181,478
Expenses:											
Initial Distributorship Fee	105,000										
On-Going Distributorship Fee		10,000	13,000	18,000	23,000	30,000	38,000	49,000	62,000	80,000	102,000
Marketing Fee		6,002	6,981	8,235	9,747	11,696	14,178	17,452	21,693	27,221	34,553
Interest		4,500	4,050	3,600	3,150	2,700	2,250	1,800	1,350	900	450
Total Expenses	105,000	20,502	24,031	29,835	35,897	44,396	54,428	68,252	85,043	108,121	137,003
Net Profit or (Loss)	(105,000)	15,645	16,788	17,897	19,702	21,610	24,311	27,465	31,883	37,410	44,475

Projected Sales for Sterling Motors, Inc.
For All Distributorships

	1	2	3	4	5	6
Sales						
Henry Automobiles*	6,750,000	10,125,000	11,250,000	12,375,000	13,500,000	14,625,000
Styling Packages	3,240,000	3,487,500	3,678,750	3,901,500	4,135,500	4,383,000
In Dealer Boutiques	1,280,000	4,608,000	6,348,000	8,760,240	12,081,831	16,664,536
Direct Mail		1,575,000	1,890,000	2,269,800	2,723,760	3,268,500
Submanufacturing License Income in Dealer Boutiques		550,000	500,000	610,000	600,000	710,000
Gross Sales of Company	11,270,000	20,345,500	23,666,750	27,916,540	33,041,091	39,651,036
Gross Sales for Distribution Area of $30,000 Purchase		120,032	139,627	164,699	194,933	233,929
Cost of Sales						
Henry Automobiles*	5,250,000	7,875,000	8,750,000	9,625,000	10,500,000	11,375,000
Styling Packages	1,749,600	1,833,250	1,986,525	2,106,810	2,233,170	2,366,820
In Dealer Boutiques	1,125,415	3,572,775	4,916,515	6,799,126	9,342,116	12,876,954
Direct Mail		787,500	94,500	1,134,900	1,361,880	1,634,250
Submanufacturing License Agreements in Dealer Boutiques		150,000	150,000	180,000	180,000	210,000
Gross Sales of Company	8,125,015	14,218,525	16,748,040	19,825,836	23,617,166	28,463,024
Gross Profit	3,144,985	6,126,975	6,918,710	8,090,704	9,423,925	11,188.012
Cost of Sales for Distribution Area of $30,000 Purchase		83,885	98,808	116,967	139,334	167,923

*Purchasers of Distributorships in Year One will not participate in sales of the Henry I Automobiles made in Year One.

Projected Sales for Sterling Motors, Inc.
For All Distributorships

	7	8	9	10	11
Sales					
Henry Automobiles*	15,750,000	16,875,000	18,000,000	18,000,000	18,000,000
Styling Packages	4,689,000	5,015,250	5,265,000	6,095,250	6,095,250
In Dealer Boutiques	23,001,884	31,753,699	43,826,490	60,495,245	84,005,860
Direct Mail	3,922,214	4,706,654	5,647,982	6,777,576	8,133,091
Submanufacturing License Income in Dealer Boutiques	700,000	810,000	800,000	910,000	900,000
Gross Sales of Company	48,063,098	59,160,603	73,539,472	92,278,071	117,134,201
Gross Sales for Distribution Area of $30,000 Purchase	283,558	349,030	433,861	544,413	691,057
Cost of Sales					
Henry Automobiles*	12,250,000	13,125,000	14,000,000	14,000,000	14,000,000
Styling Packages	2,532,060	2,708,235	2,843,100	3,291,435	3,291,435
In Dealer Boutiques	17,763,717	24,509,962	33,813,445	46,660,204	64,745,706
Direct Mail	1,961,107	2,353,327	2,823,991	3,388,788	4,066,545
Submanufacturing License Agreements in Dealer Boutiques	210,000	240,000	240,000	270,000	270,000
Gross Sales of Company	34,716,884	42,936,524	53,720,536	67,610,427	86,373,686
Gross Profit	13,346,214	16,224,079	19,818,936	24,667,644	30,760,515
Cost of Sales for Distribution Area of $30,000 Purchase	204,819	253,313	316,935	398,882	509,579

*Purchasers of Distributorships in Year One will not participate in sales of the Henry Automobiles made in Year One.

RISK ASPECTS OF A CUSTOM AUTOMOBILE AND DESIGNER ACCESSORY FUND

RISK FACTORS

A prospective Purchaser should carefully consider the following Risk Factors in addition to other possible risk factors prior to the purchase of the Distributorship.

A. Competition in the Industry

Due to the highly competitive nature of the automobile accessory industry, the profit potential of the Distributorship is subject to a high degree of risk. The Distributorship will be competing with accessories developed by other companies, most of which possess substantially greater financial resources than IDC, Sterling and the Purchaser. Sterling has no way of measuring the probable success or failure of the sale of the Distributorship. It is possible that other designer packages for automobiles or for automotive boutiques may be developed which directly or indirectly are competitive.

B. Pricing of Henry Designer Collection

There is no assurance that the price for the Frank Fashion Designer Collection of automotive accessories will be competitive. The American automobile industry is subject to the fluctuations of the American and worldwide economy and numerous other factors and the price structure established herein for the Henry Designer Collection may be too expensive. The items in the collection are non-essential, luxury items, there may be times when consumers, although willing to purchase higher priced automobiles, may not desire to pay for the luxury extras such as the Henry Designer Collection described herein. Further, the current recession and higher fuel costs have severely adversely affected the sale of full-sized automobiles and the sale of small cars both domestic and foreign has substantially eroded the market for larger luxury automobiles.

Furthermore, although presence on the market of designer automobiles such as the Blass, Pucci, Cartier and Givenchy Lincoln Continentals may indicate a demand for designer inspired luxury automobiles, there is a risk that these products will present a competitive position which the Frank Fashion Henry Designer Collection may not be able to meet.

C. Marketing and Promotion

1. General

Commercial use of the Distributorship is mainly dependent on the ability of the Purchaser to compete actively and to expand the time, money and energy necessary to maximize the product's potential. There is no assurance that a Purchaser will be successful in marketing or distributing the Distributorship. Each Purchaser will be responsible for making his or its own marketing arrangements.

2. Style–Obsolescence

Automobile accessories such as those included in the Henry Designer Collection are in a highly competitive field in which style changes have occurred at a rapid pace. The risk of change in the desirability and marketability of the Henry Designer Collection is very high.

3. Unauthorized Use

Each Distribution Agreement for a Territory will restrict the unauthorized use of the Distributorship outside of a Purchaser's Territory. There can be no assurance that such restrictions will be effective. It may be difficult and expensive to detect unauthorized use of the Distributorships and such unauthorized actions may adversely affect the competitive position of the Distributorship in the Territory.

4. Market Analysis

A detailed market study relating to the Henry Designer Collection has not been made. Attached to the Memorandum as an exhibit are statistics concerning sales of Henrys in the United States. The Lincoln Continental has introduced the factory installed designer color coordinated package of the following designers: Cartier, Pucci, Givenchy and Blass. It is noteworthy that the Lincoln Continental process is different than that contemplated by the Henry Designer Collection package since the Lincoln concept involves factory installation of color-coordinated items without the addition of the accessories included in the Designer Collection package. In addition, a competitive Gucci designer Henry automobile was introduced in the market. This car, like the Lincoln Continental, involves factory installation, unlike the Henry Designer Collection. The Henry Designer Collection provides for installation at the dealer level rather than factory installation, thus leading to the possibility of greater revenues to the dealer. The success of the Gucci Henry is unpredictable at this time.

Sterling is of the opinion that the Henry Designer Collection package is competitive with the Lincoln Designer automobile since the Henry Designer Collection package offers the consumer, in addition to a color-coordination, many items not included in the Lincoln automobile. HOWEVER, NO ASSURANCES CAN BE GIVEN AS TO THE ACCURACY OF SUCH OPINION, NOR ARE ANY ASSURANCES GIVEN THAT THE OPINION IS A REFLECTIVE ANALYSIS OF POTENTIAL MARKETING SUCCESS OF THE HENRY DESIGNER COLLECTION.

C. Foreclosure of Distributorship Rights

If income generated by such Distributorship is insufficient to pay the Note in full, the holder of the Note may foreclose on the Distributorship and seek a deficiency judgment against the Purchaser. The Purchaser would thereby lose all of his or its interest in and to the Distributorship and would realize income measured by the difference between the unpaid debt and Purchaser's then current basis in the Distributorship. In such event, the Purchaser would likely incur certain income tax liabilities.

D. Possible Personal Liability

In connection with the purchase of the Distributorship, a Purchaser may personally incur certain unforeseen liabilities to third parties. For example, the Distributorship or its components may infringe upon the proprietary rights of others. The Purchaser will be secondarily liable in such event. Although IDC will agree to indemnify the Purchaser against such liabilities, IDC may refuse or be unable to perform its indemnity obligations to the Purchaser. In addition, a Purchaser will be personally liable for the payment of the Note.

E. Economic Conditions and Fuel Shortage

Management of Standard believes that the demand for the Henry Designer Collection will in large part be dependent upon the general conditions of the economy, and in particular, the status and developments concerning the price of gasoline. The economic recession has caused consumers to be more reluctant to purchase luxury items. In addition to the recession there is a continuing fuel shortage which has caused Henry car sales to drastically decline together with a corresponding increase in fuel prices.

F. Default in License Agreement

In the event that Sterling does not receive sufficient distribution fees to pay the royalties due under the License Agreement, then the Licensor, Fashion, may cancel the License Agreement and a Purchaser may lose his right in the Distributorship. In addition, Fashion has the option of terminating the License Agreement as modified in the event that gross sales for the year ending on Fifth Annual Period do not equal or exceed $2,000,000, which amount will be increased by a cost-of-living index specified in the License Agreement. There are no assurances that these gross sales figures will be reached and if not reached, whether Fashion will exercise its option to terminate the License Agreement. The sales figures for the first two years of the License Agreement prior to its modification were only a fraction of the amount necessary to insure a renewal of the License Agreement for the second 5 year term. In addition, Fashion may attempt to declare a default under the License Agreement based upon other terms and conditions contained therein such as the right of Fashion to approve products and advertising. The management of Sterling believes that its relationship with Fashion is now favorable and the management has been working closely with Fashion's organization in developing new products for the Henry Designer Collection, Fashion Boutiques and the Henry I.

G. Dependence Upon Frank Fashion

The value and possible success of the Distributorship will be dependent upon the continued notoriety of the trade name "Frank Fashion" as well as the cooperation of Fashion's organization in helping to design products and promote their distribution in the United States. There is no assurance that Fashion will cooperate with Sterling, although he is obligated to do so under the License Agreement.

H. Deductibility of First Installment of Distributorship Fee

Section 1253(d) of the Code governs the deductibility of amounts paid by a transferee in connection with a transfer or disposition of a franchise. In general, amounts paid by the transferee which are contingent upon the productivity use or disposition of the franchise are deductible under Section 162 of the Code (as an ordinary and necessary business expense) for the taxable year in which such amounts are paid or incurred. On the other hand, if the parties to the transfer agree upon the payment of a principal sum and if the transferor is deemed to retain a significant power, right or continuing interest in the franchise, then the timing of the deduction for the payment of such principal sum will depend upon the manner in which such principal sum is discharged. Under proposed regulations, if the principal sum is payable in a series of unequal installments, then each such installment will be deductible in the year in which payment is made provided that the following requirements are satisfied:

a) The payout period extends over the life of the transfer agreement or for a period of more than 10 taxable years;

b) No such payment exceeds 20% of the principal sum; and

c) No more than 75% of the principal sum is paid in the first half of the period of the transfer agreement or in the period of 10 consecutive taxable years which begins with the taxable year in which the first such payment is made, whichever such period is shorter.

The Distribution Agreement contains a fixed distribution fee payable by the Distributor in a series of unequal annual installments over the period of the Agreement. None of the installments payable under the Agreement exceed 20% of the total fixed fee and an amount less than 75% of such fixed fee is payable during the first half of the term of the Distribution Agreement.

The opinion of Tax Counsel will indicate that the Distributorship should constitute a "franchise" and that IDC should be deemed to have retained a significant power, right or continuing interest with respect to the Distributorship—both within the meaning and for the purposes of Section 1253(d)(2) of the Code. As such, a Distributor should have a basis to claim a deduction with respect to the payment of the first installment of the fixed distribution fee in the taxable year in which such installment is paid, such deduction being an amount equal to the cash paid. It should be noted, however, that, according to Tax Counsel, the IRS could claim, among other things, that the deferred portion of the distribution fee fixed in the Distribution Agreement should not be considered part of the "principal sum" payable under that Agreement for purposes of Section 1253(d)(2). In addition, or alternatively, Tax Counsel is of the opinion that the IRS could successfully contend that, even as to a Distributor who uses the accrual method of accounting with respect to his activities relating to the Distributorship, delivery of the recourse note in partial satisfaction of the first installment of the fixed distribution fee does not constitute payment for purposes of that Section. The IRS could also claim that the Distributor cannot properly use the accrual method of accounting with respect to the Distributorship because, among other reasons, such method would not clearly reflect income.

If the IRS successfully contends that the deferred portion of the fixed distribution fee is not considered part of the "principal sum" for purposes of Section 1253(d)(2), and/or that delivery of the Distributor's recourse note in partial satisfaction of the first installment of the fixed distribution fee does not constitute payment for purposes of that Section, and/or that the Distributor may not properly use the accrual method of accounting with respect to the Distributorship, then, at best, only a portion of the first installment would be deductible in Year One—which portion would not exceed the amount of cash paid by the Distributor in partial satisfaction of the first installment. Prospective Distributors should consult their tax advisors with respect to the magnitude of the adverse consequences which could result in the event that the IRS is sustained in a challenge of the deductibility of the first installment. It should be noted that the opinion of Tax Counsel does not and will not relate to the deductibility of subsequent installments, and prospective Distributors should consult their own tax advisors with respect to the same.

CABLE TELEVISION

INDUSTRY STATUS AND FORECAST

Basic cable television subscribers numbered an estimated 17.3 million at the end of 1980. This was an increase of 11 percent, or 1.7 million subscribers, from 1979. A further increase of 10 percent, to 19 million, is projected for 1981.

Basic subscriber revenues are estimated to have reached $1.72 billion in 1980, an increase of 17 percent from 1979. A further rise of 17 percent to $2 billion is projected for 1981.

Basic cable subscribers who also subscribe to a premium pay cable service reached an estimated 6.5 million at the end of 1980—an estimated penetration of 38 percent of all cable homes. Pay cable revenues for 1980 were an estimated $600 million. The number of pay cable subscribers is expected to increase about 30 percent in 1981 to 8.5 million, with revenues rising 33 percent to an estimated $800 million. Pay cable revenues are shared by the cable systems, program syndicators, program producers, and organized sports.

Upsurge in Cable Activity

Prospects for the cable television industry during the 1980's are very good because of the recent availability of satellite channels for the economical distribution of programs and because of the growing popularity of premium pay cable.

Prior to the availability of domestic communications satellites, cable systems were largely dependent for their programming on local television stations, plus one or two so-called distant stations. With the advent of satellites and low-cost earth stations, cable systems have ready access to premium programing provided by such cable program services as Home Box Office (Time, Inc.), Showtime (Viacom-Teleprompter), The Movie Channel (Warner-Amex), Home Theater Network, and others.

Consumer demand for premium cable programing is now the moving force for growth and profitability in the cable TV industry. Basic cable service began in smaller communities where television reception was limited or nonexistent. It then moved into suburban areas and a few cities, but the higher cost of wiring large cities kept cable systems out of many urban markets. With the addition of one or more levels of premium pay cable to a basic system, the economic viability of cable TV in city areas is greatly improved. The competitive process for the award of a cable franchise is now under way in a number of large cities, and other cities have terms for the introduction of cable under study. The processes of making a study of requirements and terms for a particular municipal cable TV franchise and of evaluating competing offers from aspiring cable system operators can take many months, particularly in larger communities.

Cable television is now recognized as a well established and successful industry. The availability of financing for the construction or expansion of cable systems has not been a problem for several years, although financing costs have been high. Cable systems are capital intensive, and many systems are highly leveraged.

Motion pictures, supplemented by sports, have been the mainstay of pay cable, primarily in response to subscriber demand. The supply of existing movies is not inexhaustible, however. Cable program suppliers are, therefore, looking for new sources of entertainment programing and other video fare. Producers of motion pictures and other entertainment forms are benefiting from the added demand and competition for their products. With the numerous channels cable can provide, cable program suppliers expect to increase the variety of special interest programing appealing to individual demographic groups, something mass-audience-oriented network broadcasters cannot do.

Cable systems have not yet become a significant medium for advertising. Until domestic satellites made de facto cable networking possible, individual cable systems could not deliver audiences large enough to compete with television stations and other media. Advertising experts believe that when cable reaches 30 percent of all television homes it will become a viable advertising medium. Based on present trends, this should occur in 1984.

The nonentertainment uses of cable systems, such as for two-way communications, data bank access, and alarm systems, have not yet been significantly exploited. The best known exception to this is the Warner-Amex Qube system, the first significant two-way interactive cable communications system. This subscriber response system is in operation in Columbus, Ohio, and is being included in a new system to be built in Houston, Texas. The cable industry will undoubtedly respond to any adequate markets demand for these ancilliary services. At present, the industry is concentrating its resources on the development of existing systems and on the construction of new systems to meet the public demand for a greater diversity of entertainment and sports programing.

Growth to Continue

The number of basic cable television subscribers is expected to increase at a compound annual rate of about 10 percent to 27.8 million in 1985. Basic subscriber revenues are projected to rise at a compound annual rate of 16.6 percent to about $3.7 billion in current dollars in 1985.

Subscribers to premium pay cable service are expected to number about 16 million in 1985, reflecting a compound annual growth rate of 19.7 percent. Pay cable revenues are expected to climb at a compound annual rate of 29.7 percent to $2.2 billion in current dollars in 1985.

THE SATELLITE COMMUNICATIONS BUSINESS

Satellite technology has produced one of the most important advances in today's telecommunication. Satellites, orbiting approximately 23,500 miles above the earth over the equator circle the earth every twenty-four hours, thereby appearing to be in a stationary orbit above the equator. This permits the use of fixed antennas at various earth sites which are pointed toward the satellite. Depending upon the orbit, one satellite can serve the entire continental U.S., Hawaii and most of Alaska.

Communication satellites are relay stations in space. Signals are transmitted from a ground station and received by the satellite which, in turn, retransmits these signals back to earth stations. The retransmission essentially is a broadcast which can be received by any earth station in the U.S. which has appropriate compatible equipment, including a receiver and antenna.

Because of antenna limitations aboard a satellite, and the great distances involved, a transmission power of about 3,000 watts is employed. To minimize interference with other satellites and terrestrial facilities, highly directional earth station antennas are used. The current minimum requirement calls for a 10-meter "antenna" for video uplink transmission.

Communications satellites incorporate a number of transponders or communications channels. Each transponder is capable of carring one standard television transmission, or various multiple audio channels. Data can also be transmitted at extremely high rates. It is possible to mix data and audio transmissions and to partition transponders for such use. While it is possible to transmit video, audio and data signals simultaneously, the addition of data to a video transmission produces practical operational problems because transmission of video signals generally is on a continuous basis, while data transmission is usually sporadic, random and two-way by its nature.

The cost of satellite communications is distance insensitive while the cost of terrestrial microwave communications is very much a function of distance. Depending upon the precise application, the break-even point between terrestrial and satellite communications is about 700 miles. Terrestrial communications is also inherently point-to-point. Point-to-multipoint communications can be accomplished only by extending lines from the origination point to each point of termination. In contrast, the communications satellite transponder broadcasts signals received from the earth station. These signals can be received at any point in the U.S. where there exists an earth station, with appropriate equipment, having its antenna oriented toward the satellite.

A major disadvantage of satellite transmission is the time delay between transmission to the satellite and retransmission to the earth. The delay of approximately 270 milliseconds is problematic for two-way communications such as telephone conversations and data transmission. The General Partner in the example hereinafter described is Satellite Contact Network, Inc. ("SCN"). SCN does not propose to use the Station to transmit telephone conversations, except possibly as a private package for special institutional users. The problem of delay applicable to data communications may be solved by using a device called a satellite delay compensation unit.

Western Union presently has three and RCA two satellites in orbit, and each offer to sell full time and occasional use time on these satellites. On December 10, 1979, RCA Corp. lost contact with the satellite it had launched on December 7, 1979. WESTAR I, which is the first Western Union satellite, is expected to reach the end of its useful life within about two years. Other domestic communications satellites are operated by AT&T/GTE and COMSAT.

RCA satellites primarily serve the cable television industry which have in place approximately 1,400 "receive only" earth stations. In contrast, Western Union satellites primarily transmit broadcast quality signals. To a limited extent, the satellites of RCA and Western Union have been used for data and audio transmission. They have also been employed for video transmission by companies such as Hughes Television Network. The major networks, especially NBC, are also said to be seriously evaluating the use of satellites to partially replace or augment their terrestrial system, currently operated by AT&T Long Lines.

A primary limitation on the use of satellites for video transmission has been the lack of transmit and receive ground stations. RCA has stations in about 6 locations. These stations have limited capability and virtually their entire capacity is now reserved. Western Union has approximately 8 stations with uplink and downlink time available in some locations. Other organizations have built receive and transmit stations—primarily for their own use. A few stations are available on a common carrier basis for public use. These stations, however, are not built to a common standard and do not form a network. Furthermore, some of these station owners do not have access to full-time transponders.

The essence of this project is to build an earth station which will use a full-time transponder, with the capability to fill needs for video, broadcast audio and data communications not adequately addressed by presently available facilities.

EXAMPLE OF A SATELLITE COMMUNICATION FUND

It is proposed that a group of limited partners acquire an initial interest of 99% in the profits and losses of Space Link Associates, (the "Partnership") a limited partnership to be organized with Satellite Contact Network, Inc., as the General Partner. The Limited Partners will subscribe $2,275,000 to the capital of the Partnership and may be subject to full recourse liabilities at the discretion of the General Partner of approximately $3,780,000. The Partnership will acquire, construct and operate an earth station (the "Station").

The General Partner will have an interest of 1% of the Partnership's profit and losses for which it will subscribe $1,000.00 to the capital of the Partnership.

THE PARTNERSHIP

The Partnership Organization

The Partnership will be organized promptly upon the successful sale of the Units offered hereby. In connection with the construction of the Station and the acquisition of its related Equipment, Satellite Contact Network, Inc. ("SCN"), the General Partner, will execute a construction agreement with Aries wherein, Aries will agree to turn over to the Partnership, on a turn-key basis, the Earth Station and its related Equipment. Aries in turn proposes to enter into a subcontract construction agreement with Airwave Associates, Inc., ("AA"), wherein AA would furnish to the Partnership the Station and its related Equipment on a turn-key basis.

Compensation to the General Partner (SCN)

The General Partner will receive an initial sublicense fee of $240,000 relating to the sublicense of SCN's transponder time to the Partnership. Further, SCN will be entitled to a sublicense fee of $70,000 in each subsequent calendar year of the Partnership for such transponder sublicense.

Responsibility of the General Partner

The General Partner, subject to the Management Agreement, shall have the responsibility for the management and control of all aspects of the business of the Partnership. In the course of such management the General Partner may lease, license, mortgage or otherwise dispose of or deal with the Station and its equipment and may employ such persons and agents, either affiliated or unaffiliated, as it deems appropriate for the operations and management of the Partnership.

Allocation of Profits and Losses

All profits and losses of the Partnership for any fiscal year shall be allocated among the Partners in proportion to their respective interests in profits and losses of the Partnership on an annual basis.

Distribution of Cash Flow

The General Partner has discretion as to the amounts and timing of distributions, subject to the maintenance of reserves against possible losses and proper operation of Partnership business and payment of other Partnership obligations, including, but not limited to the payment of management, license and administrative expenses.

As soon as practicable after the end of each calendar quarter, subject to the foregoing discretion of the General Partner, the General Partner shall distribute the Cash Flow, if any, realized during such calendar quarter.

Sale of Station

In the event the Station is sold at the discretion of the General Partner, the gross proceeds of such sale shall be distributed to the Limited Partners after deduction for payment of the outstanding loan from Alpha and after return to the Limited Partners of 100% of their investment in the Partnership the excess proceeds shall be distributed to the Limited Partners in accordance with their P&L Percentages and to the General Partner, as follows:

Excess Proceeds	Limited Partners	General Partner
$1 million	70%	30%
Next $1 million	60%	40%
Next $1 million and Any Additional Proceeds	50%	50%

Term and Dissolution

The Partnership will continue for a maximum period of forty years but may be dissolved at an earlier date, if any of the following contingencies occur:

A. The Partnership sells the Station.
B. The filing of a petition in bankruptcy with respect to the General Partner which is not discharged or vacated within ninety (90) days from the date thereof; however, the Partnership may be reconstituted upon the occurrence of such events.

Assumption of Liabilities

The Partnership Agreement provides that each Partner shall assume at the discretion of SCN, personal liability for a portion of the Partnership's construction Loan and that each Partner execute an Assumption Agreement. While Partnership revenues will be applied to the payment of the Loan, a Partner's liability under his Assumption Agreement will be a direct personal liability of each Partner to the Lender.

The amount of a Partner's obligation under the Assumption Agreement, is generally determined at any time as the Partner's P&L percentage multiplied by the outstanding balance of the Loan, plus any accrued but unpaid interest thereon. The Assumption Agreement provides that should the Lender seek to enforce any liabilities under an Assumption Agreement, it shall seek to do so with respect to all Partners at the same time in proportion to their respective P&L Percentages. The potential maximum liability of a Limited Partner owning one unit will be approximately $108,000 plus the interest on the Loan at the rate of 6% per annum from the commencement of the Loan to the payment thereof. The Assumption Agreement shall provide that the total per Unit liability assumed shall in no event exceed approximately $108,000 plus interest.

In the event of a default under the Loan, the Partners may be required to discharge their assumed liabilities in full. The assumption of personal liability for a share of the Partnership's Loan materially increases a Limited Partner's investment risk.

SUBSCRIPTIONS TO PARTNERSHIP INTERESTS

The total number of Units in the Partnership to be sold will be thirty-five. Full Units will be sold at a price of $65,000 per Unit although larger units may be subscribed to and accepted at the sole discretion of the General Partner. Subscription for Units shall be payable as follows:

A. $65,000 representing the initial subscription capital contribution payable in cash at the time the Subscription Agreement is executed.

B. (i) $27,000 in cash, representing the initial subscription capital contribution under the Agreement, simultaneously with the execution of the Subscription Agreement.

(ii) $38,000 per unit representing the additional subscription capital contribution under the Agreement which obligation is to be evidenced by the investor's execution and delivery of an unconditional personal liability promissory note (the "Note") in the amount of $38,000 with interest at the rate of 14¾% per annum, together with an irrevocable letter of credit payable to the order of the Partnership with interest at the rate of 14¾% per annum.

In addition, each Limited Partner will be required, at the discretion of SCN, to assume personal liability for a portion of the Partnership's Loan in an amount equal to approximately $108,000 per unit, plus interest and to execute an Assumption Agreement.

Sale of Partnership Units

The Partnership will pay a fee of up to $5,200 per Unit to qualified broker-dealers who effect sales of the Units. Any funds allocated for these fees and not paid will remain in the Partnership as working capital.

Use of Partnership Funds

The Partnership intends to use the $6,056,000 of the gross proceeds (which include the $3,780,000 Loan obtained by the Partnership to construct and equip the Station) invested by the Partners in connection with the Partnership interests in the following manner:

A. The sum of $4,250,000 which includes the Loan for construction of the Station and acquisition of related equipment.
B. Syndication costs $182,000.
C. Organization costs $30,000.
D. Initial management fee to Manager $340,000.
E. Initial sublicense fee to General Partner $240,000.
F. Additional fee to Manager for advertising, marketing, promotional costs, rental of transponder time and professional fees relating to the operations of the Partnership after the Station is operational $614,000.
G. Warranty fee to Aries $400,000.

SUMMARY OF EXAMPLE

1. General

Satellite Contact Network, Inc. ("SCN") has obtained use of an unprotected full time transponder (channel) on one of Western Union's existing satellites for a three year term.

SCN has also obtained from RCA AMERICOM ("RCA") full-time preemptible transponder service for a one year term with a month-to-month extension thereafter, predicated upon mutual agreement between AT&T and RCA.

The rights to the unprotected full time transponder from Western Union and the rights to the preemptible full-time transponder from RCA form the bases for the Partnership's Plan to construct, maintain and operate an earth station ("Station") with uplink-downlink services for video, audio and data signal transmission via microwave to and from the satellite to the various users of the Station.

Although a site for the erection of the Station has not been finalized as yet, the final site choice will be made from among those sites enumerated in the application of SCN, the general partner of the Partnership, pursuant to Section 214 of the Communications Act of 1934, for authority to provide video, audio and data signals via satellite which application has received conditional approval from the FCC. The proposed sites in question are Washington/Baltimore, Philadelphia, Boston, Miami/Orlando, Cleveland, Los Angeles, Tampa, Houston, Kansas City, Denver, Pittsburgh, Las Vegas, Chicago, Dallas, Minneapolis, St. Louis, Nashville and Cincinnati.

2. Business of SCN, the General Partner

SCN, a corporation wholly owned by Principal Network, Inc. ("PNI"), will be the General Partner of the Partnership, with full authority to oversee site selection, building, maintenance and staffing the Station as well as full discretion with regard to licensing, obtaining business, establishing rates for the use of transponder time and all other functions associated with managing the Station. SCN's award of an unprotected full time transponder for a three year term on an existing in orbit Western Union satellite and RCA's furnishing SCN a preemptible fulltime transponder on AT&T's COMSTAR D-2 existing in orbit satellite will form the major bases for advertising the availability of high quality video, and audio transmissions via satellite.

It is intended that SCN will, in the future, act as General Partner to other earth stations built and operated in the continental United States, which stations, it is proposed, will eventually form an integrated satellite communications network, however there can be no assurance that such network will be established.

As General Partner of the Partnership, SCN will acquire a 1% interest in the Partnership and will have sole discretion to make all business decisions involving the Partnership and its financial and technical operations, including the right to determine, on an ongoing basis, whether the Partnership's promissory note, delivered to the builder of the Station shall be "recourse" or "non-recourse" in nature.

In consideration for providing unlimited usage of transponder time, if available, pursuant to its Licenses to the Partnership, SCN will receive an initial License fee of $240,000 this year and $70,000 annually thereafter.

3. Transponder Time

SCN will have available to it an unprotected full-time transponder on an existing, operational Western Union satellite for a three year term. SCN will also have available to it a preemptible full-time transponder on the existing operational AT&T COMSTAR D-2. This transponder is available for a one year term with month-to-month extension thereafter by mutual agreement of RCA and AT&T. In addition to the satellites referred to above, there are three other commercial satellites on which transponder time may be made available to the Partnership.

4. The Construction

The Partnership intends to contract with Aries Technology Construction Corporation, ("Aries"), 60% of the stock of which is owned by John Doe and 40% is owned by Principal Network, Inc. for the construction of the Station. The site for the construction will be chosen from among those candidate locations for earth station construction contained in SCN's license application before the FCC.

It is anticipated that Aries will, in turn, sub-contract with Airwave Associates ("AA"), for the delivery of a "turn key" fully operative earth station.

The construction will be financed by Aries which, as Lender, will take back a promissory note in the amount of $3,780,000, executed by SCN as General Partner, on behalf of the Partnership, plus a $470,000 cash down payment which includes $50,000 for the construction of the building to house the Station's equipment. Aries will be receiving a substantial profit in connection with such construction. Aries shall warrant under its warranty agreement that it shall repair all structural and operational defects of the Station for a warranty fee under the proposed construction contract of $400,000.

As part of the obligation incurred by each Limited Partner in connection with acquiring an interest in the Partnership, each subscribing Limited Partner will be required, simultaneously with the execution of the Limited Partnership Agreement (the "Agreement"), to execute an Assumption Agreement whereby the Limited Partner agrees to be bound by the decision of the General Partner, made on an annual basis, as to whether the Partnership's note to Aries is to be recourse or non-recourse and, the extent thereof. Such determination will be solely at the option of the General Partner.

5. SCN Management Corporation "Manager," a recently formed corporation that is a wholly-owned subsidiary of SCN shall perform services for the Partnership pursuant to a management contract to assist the Partnership in managing the operation of the Station.

6. Earth Station Revenue

A. Marketing and Development of Customers

The General Partner shall have the obligation and authority to contract for advertising, marketing and promotional costs and to develop any information reasonably designed to determine the nature and extent of the market within the general area of the Station site to be serviced by the Local Loop for regular full time as well as occasional users of satellite communications services. To that end, SCN has already undertaken to obtain written commitments or letters of intent from several potential substantial customers such as the Public Service Satellite Consortium; Midwest TeleProductions, the Hughes Television Network and Robert Wold & Company. There can be no assurance that commitments will be received from such substantial customers for full-time satellite use and if no such customers are obtained the projected revenues of the Station will be materially adversely affected. Other full time and occasional users have been solicited by SCN and this process is due to continue and intensify as the Station nears completion.

B. Charges for Services (Tariffs)

At present, the General Partner has come to no final decision concerning rates to be charged potential customers for use of the Station. The tariff structure will be fully developed by SCN following final FCC approval of its application for grant of authority. It is also anticipated that SCN will file a tariff for resale of transponder time. Although there have been no tariffs filed to date by the General Partner, such tariffs generally depend upon the band width, quality and nature of services to customers, security of the transmission, services packaged and time of use.

In addition, different rates will be established for repeated service, full time service, and special uses as opposed to occasional use rates.

7. Compensation

A. Compensation to the General Partner

Pursuant to the proposed Limited Partnership Agreement, the General Partner, Satellite Contact Network, Inc. ("SCN") as such will be authorized to administer and manage the operations of the Station, including without limiting, the generality thereof, the following matters:

1. Collection of financial data concerning the Station's operations; and
2. The accounting for and distribution of revenue earned by the Station.

Pursuant to the terms of the Limited Partnership Agreement, SCN will be entitled to receive the following fee:

An initial license fee of $240,000 relating to its sublicense of transponder time to the Partnership and subsequent calendar years, a $70,000 per annum license fee.

B. Compensation to the Manager

Pursuant to the terms of the Management Agreement with the Partnership, the Manager will be entitled to receive the following fees:

A. An initial fee of $340,000 in consideration of management services rendered by it and to cover the anticipated costs of the initial substantial operating expenses of the Partnership which will be payable out of the proceeds of the offering to the Manager.

B. An annual Management fee equal to 25% of the Partnership's gross revenues in Year One and for subsequent calendar years with a minimum fee of $35,000 per year. It intends to reimburse itself for expenses incurred by it in operating the Station from such management fees and any excess of such fees over such expenses shall be retained by the Manager as profit.

C. In addition, the manager will be entitled to receive in Year One the following additional amounts in order to help to defray the costs of:

Initial advertising, marketing and promotional costs	$304,000
Rental of transponder time	210,000
Professional fees	100,000
	$614,000

These expenses shall relate to the operations of the Partnership after the Station is in operation.

9. Subscription to the Partnership Interest

The total number of units to be sold will be thirty-five. The units will be sold at a price of $65,000 per Unit. Subscriptions are payable as follows at the option of the Investor:

A. $65,000 in cash on subscription.

B. (i) $27,000 in cash on execution of the subscription agreement.

(ii) $38,000 as a further contribution due in Year Two, evidenced by the investor's execution and delivery upon subscription of an unconditional promissory note (Note) bearing interest at the rate of 14¾% per annum, together with an irrevocable letter of credit in that amount.

At the sole discretion of the General Partner, each Limited Partner may be required to assume a portion of the Partnership's construction loan in an aggregate maximum amount for a full Unit equal to approximately $108,000.

10. Depreciation

The Station's equipment will be depreciated over an eight-year life. Initially, the Partnership intends to use the double-declining balance method of depreciation to depreciate the Station's equipment and to change to the straight-line method of depreciation when such a change would be advantageous. The Station's building shall be depreciated over a 50 year life using the straight-line method of depreciation.

11. Investment Credit

It is anticipated that the Limited Partners will claim investment tax credit with respect to their allocable shares of the Partnership's cost of the Station's equipment ("Equipment").

12. Source and Uses of Proceeds

The following table summarizes the expected source and uses of the proceeds in the aggregate amount of $2,276,000 contributed or to be contributed to the capital of the Partnership by the General Partner and/or the Limited Partners and borrowed by the Partnership.

Gross Proceeds	Source of Proceeds	Percentage of Gross Proceeds
Limited Partners' Contributions	$2,275,000	37.56%
Construction Loan Proceeds	$3,780,000	62.41%
General Partner's Contribution	$ 1,000	.03%
Total Gross Proceeds	$6,056,000	100.0 %

	Use of Proceeds	Percentage of Gross Proceeds
Cash Payment and amounts borrowed for construction of Station and acquisition of related Equipment	$4,250,000	70.08%
Syndication Costs	$ 182,000	3.01%
Organization Expenses	$ 30,000	.50%
Management Fee	$ 340,000	5.62%
Initial License Fee	$ 240,000	3.96%
Rental of Transponder Time	$ 210,000	3.46%
Advertising, Marketing and Promotional Costs	$ 304,000	5.02%
Professional Fees	$ 100,000	1.65%
Warranty Fee	$ 400,000	6.60%
Total Application of Gross Proceeds	$6,056,000	100.00%

PLAN OF OPERATION

This proposal calls for the construction of a receive/transmit ("uplink-downlink") earth station at a cost of approximately $4,250,000 to the Partnership which includes purchase of all equipment and physical facilities. This earth station should be capable of transmitting and receiving video, broadcast quality audio and digital communication signals and could be capable of interphase with various other uplink and downlink systems as well as alternate terrestrial forms of communication.

SCN has obtained use of an unprotected full-time transponder on one of Western Union's existing satellites for a period of three years. SCN has also made arrangements with RCA to furnish it with a preemptible full-time transponder on COMSTAR D-2 for a one year term with month-to-month extension thereafter predicated upon mutual agreement between AT&T and RCA. A long-term lease agreement between Western Union and SCN awarding SCN an unprotected full-time transponder or a similar long-term lease agreement between RCA and SCN awarding SCN a preemptible full-time transponder should be viewed as a condition precedent to the Station's capability and the marketability of the Station for those potential customers who may require the availability of a transponder full-time.

It should be recognized that the construction time-table contains a number of long-lead times including raising of funds, ordering equipment, confirming FCC approvals, obtaining a suitable site, designing various components of the system and signing a number of agreements with, among others, Airwave Associates and Digital Contact Corporation and obtaining letters of intent or commitment from potential customers such as Hughes Television Network, Public Service Satellite Consortium and Robert Wold & Company.

It is contemplated that, with the building, development and eventual on-line operation of other earth stations that the Station will be compatible and may become part of a satellite communications network.

THE EQUIPMENT

Equipment Capabilities

The Earth Station has been designed for high reliability standards similar to those used by AT&T. The transmitter and receiver will be fully backed-up with "hot stand-by" units operating in parallel available for immediate, uninterrupted switch-over in the event of a failure. The video transmit aspect of the Station also will have diesel back-up generators.

Once the Station is constructed and becomes operational, the transponder becomes an integral part of the Station's operation. While the Station can be used to provide uplink and downlink services to customers over their own occasional-use or full-time transponders, projection of revenues from these sources is extremely difficult to predict.

The ability of the Station to serve full-time customers will depend upon its success in negotiating long-term agreements and development of mutually agreeable sites. Certain users, such as Hughes Television Network and Robert Wold & Company have purchased blocks of occasional-use time from

Western Union. The Station could be used to meet some of their needs and discussions with these companies are under way, however, there can be no assurance that any agreements with Hughes Television and Robert Wold & Company will be consummated.

An individual earth station can transmit and receive multiple signals simultaneously. Assuming a fixed hourly rate for transmit and receive services, the revenue potential of the station is dramatically enhanced by transmitting and receiving as many signals simultaneously as the market permits.

Synopsis of Technical Data

Earth station transmitting equipment consists of arrangements to modify television signals received at the station via interconnect facilities from the customer, combine the TV signal with the audio portion of the program, and turn the combined signal into an electronic form that can be transmitted as a microwave up to a satellite transponder. The Station will also be equipped with a receiving arrangement to pick up the signals sent down from the satellite and reconvert it to a form that can be sent on to the customer.

Transmitting

Picture and voice information of a television signal arrive separately at the earth station. These two signals are combined into one complex signal and changed in form in a frequency modulated transmitter (FMT). The output of this device is a signal suitable for conversion to microwave which will be employed to radiate the signal up to the satellite. This signal is then fed into a device referred to as an up converter which performs the function just described. The output from the up converter then goes into a high power amplifier (HPA) which raises it to a power level sufficient to reach the satellite antenna (about three kilowatts).

The high powered signal is next sent through a waveguide system to the 12 meter dish antenna which focuses the signal into a narrow beam and radiates it up to the satellite transponder.

Those portions of the Station's Equipment which are subject to failure will have hot standby units to provide service if such primary equipment fails.

Receiving

Signals sent down from the satellite are received on the antenna, separated from the signals being transmitted by a wave-guide separation system, and fed through a switch into a low power amplifier (LNA). Two of these are provided with an automatic system to replace the working LNA with the stand-by, should it fail. The output of the LNA, now raised to a power level where it can be further processed, is fed through a splitting arrangement which splits the signal into two portions of equal magnitude and provides the input for two video receivers. In the receivers the signal is reconverted to a form suitable for transmission over interconnect facilities to the customer. Finally, the output from each receiver is fed into a demodulation unit which separates the audio portion of the program from the picture.

A switching arrangement selects the output of one of the receiving systems for transmission to the customer, automatically switching to the other, should the working system fail.

An emergency power system will be provided that senses power failures and activates the engine driven generation arrangement when needed.

All equipment and systems in the Station are to be monitored and controlled by an alarm and status panel which can be accessed via telephone company land lines for remote operation.

Description of Proposed Equipment

The Partnership's construction effort will consist of an earth station capable of simultaneously transmitting to and receiving from transponders on any one satellite at one time. The transponder will relay a video signal with its associated voice channel transmitted to it from the Station down to other currently operative stations or vice versa. In addition to providing video service the Station will be designed to accommodate two-way digital data transmission and broadcast quality audio channels which are planned to be offered as a service at a later time. If the initial revenues from the Station are insufficient, the Partnership might not be able to provide such digital transmission and/or audio channels.

The Building

The building will be designed to accommodate two way video and two way data equipment. The building will include an automatic emergency power generating system to obviate commercial failures. The arrangement used will be a battery backed, engine driven alternator system which will provide interruption free power transfer.

The Antennas

One twelve meter satellite antenna will be provided with the Station. A foundation for a second antenna will also be installed at time of original construction, to increase future capability and to also lower future construction cost.

It is anticipated that a tower equipped with dish type microwave antennas may be provided, in anticipation of the necessity to interconnect the Station with a distant distribution terminal or customer location. The necessity for such microwave antennas is dependent upon the actual site chosen and utilized by the Partnership for the Station itself.

Radio

In general, all transmit and receive radio equipment with the exception of passive elements such as waveguide runs and the antenna, will be designed and installed with a hot running spare arranged to automatically take over should the working unit fail.

Air conditioning and heating equipment will be provided to maintain the equipment environment at optimum.

Control

The Station will be equipped with an alarm and control unit which can be remotely assessed from points other than at the actual station site using the telephone company's Direct Distance Dialing message network. This arrangement will automatically notify the control center of station alarm conditions such as equipment or power failure, open door, etc. It will also provide control office capability to switch equipment into and cut off service, start the emergency power generation system, and determine the operating status of all critical items in the Station.

BENEFITS OF A SATELLITE COMMUNICATIONS FUND

Year One $27,000 Cash
Year Two $38,000 Promissory Note & Letter of Credit

Space Link Associates ($65,000 Per Limited Partnership Partnership Unit Investment)
Illustration of Contemplated Tax Consequences for Taxpayer in 50% Tax Bracket

Year	Investment	Taxable Profit (Loss)	Investment Tax Credit	Annual Ratio	Cumulative Ratio	Tax Savings Resulting from Taxable Profit & Loss & ITC	Cash Flow	Annual Return	Cumulative Return	Cumulative Return Less Investment
1	$27,000	($57,636)	$11,880	3.01	3.01	$40,698	--	$40,698	$40,698	$13,698
2	$38,000	($36,516	--	.96	1.81	$18,258	--	$18,258	$58,956	($6,044)
3	--	($20,743)	--	--	2.13	$10,372	--	$10,372	$69,328	$ 4,328
4	--	($15,379)	--	--	2.37	$ 7,689	--	$ 7,689	$77,017	$12,017
5	--	($ 8,973	--	--	2.51	$ 4,487	--	$ 4,487	$81,504	$16,504
6	--	($ 5,920)	--	--	2.60	$ 2,960	--	$ 2,960	$84,464	$19,464
7	--	($ 2,121)	--	--	2.63	$ 1,060	--	$ 1,060	$85,524	$20,524
8	--	($ 303)	--	--	2.64	$ 151	--	$ 151	$85,675	$20,675
9	--	$ 9,413	--	--	--	($ 4,707)	$ 4,776	$ 69	$85,744	$20,744
10	--	$16,005	--	--	--	($ 8,003)	$ 8,254	$ 251	$85,995	$20,995
11	--	$20,839	--	--	--	($10,419	$10,967	$ 548	$86,543	$21,543
12	--	$22,176	--	--	--	($11,088)	$11,597	$ 509	$87,052	$22,052
13	--	$26,297	--	--	--	($13,149)	$13,597	$ 448	$87,500	$27,500
14	--	$27,061	--	--	--	($13,530)	$13,653	$ 123	$87,623	$27,623
15	--	$31,351	--	--	--	($15,676)	$15,822	$ 146	$87,769	$27,769
16	--	$32,285	--	--	--	($16,143)	$23,120	$ 6,977	$94,746	$29,746

Notes to Illustration

(1) This illustration assumes that the General Partner will elect to convert a sufficient amount of the Limited Recourse Note to Recourse, annually in order to pass through to the limited partners, all of the losses anticipated.

(2) No effect is shown in this illustration for any interest that may be paid by a limited partner in connection with promissory notes and letters of credit.

SPACE LINK ASSOCIATES

Effect on Limited Partners Using Various Modifications to Projections
for the 13 Year Period Fourth Through Sixteenth Years

The following summary reflects the effects to a limited partners investment, using gross revenue figures that vary from the illustrations of contemplated results of operations and contemplated cash flow appearing in the Private Placement Memo. As previously stated, the forecasts are conservative and were prepared using only simple "up link" and "down link" revenue sources. The combinations of other sources of revenue are so diverse, and since there are no published industry statistics to relate to, it is impossible to forecast the gross income potential of the earth station. The following summary gives an indication of such results at various other levels of gross income.

	As Presently Reflected	10% Additional Revenue	25% Additional Revenue	50% Additional Revenue	100% Additional Revenue
Earth Station Revenue	$13,945,920	$15,340,512	$17,432,400	$20,918,880	$27,391,840
Expenses					
License Fees	910,000	910,000	910,000	910,000	910,000
Management Fees and Costs	3,486,481	3,835,128	4,358,100	5,229,720	6,972,960
Interest	2,055,696	2,055,696	2,055,696	2,055,696	2,055,696
Depreciation–Earth Station	2,066,203	2,066,203	2,066,203	2,066,203	2,066,203
Depreciation–Building and Land Improvements	13,000	13,000	13,000	13,000	13,000
Total Expenses	8,531,380	8,880,027	9,402,999	10,274,619	12,017,859
Net Profit Before Taxes	5,414,540	6,460,485	8,029,401	10,644,261	15,873,981
Federal and State Taxes at 50%	2,707,270	3,230,243	4,014,701	5,322,131	7,936,991
Net Profit	2,707,270	3,230,242	4,014,700	5,322,130	7,936,990
Add: Depreciation	2,079,203	2,079,203	2,079,203	2,079,203	2,079,203
	4,786,473	5,309,445	6,093,903	7,401,333	10,016,193
Less: Repayment of Limited Recourse Note	3,780,000	3,780,000	3,780,000	3,780,000	3,780,000
Net Cash Flow	$ 1,006,473	$ 1,529,445	$ 2,313,903	$ 3,621,333	$ 6,236,193
99% Applicable to Limited Partners	$ 996,408	$ 1,514,151	$ 2,290,764	$ 3,585,120	$ 6,173,831
Per Limited Partner Unit	$ 28,469	$ 43,261	$ 65,450	$ 102,432	$ 176,395

SPACE LINK ASSOCIATES

Illustration of Potential Selling Price of Earth Station in Year Sixteen

The following illustration reflects the potential selling price of the Earth Station in Year Sixteen, after all of the Limited Recourse Notes have been paid. The potential selling price is shown using various net income levels and various multiples of net income. The communications industry has traditionally used net cash flow earnings in the year of sale as the basis for valuing a business for sale, with a minimum multiple of eight.

The assumptions merely reflect the allocation of selling price to the limited partners, in accordance with the Limited Partnership Agreement. No effect is given to the tax consequences on any possible sale transaction including capital gains tax, and depreciation and investment credit recapture.

	As Presently Reflected	10% Additional Revenue	25% Additional Revenue	50% Additional Revenue	100% Additional Revenue
Net Profit before taxes—Year Sixteen	$ 1,141,375	$ 1,264,562	$ 1,449,344	$ 1,757,312	$ 2,373,250
Federal and State Taxes at 50%	$ 570,688	$ 632,281	$ 724,672	$ 878,656	$ 1,186,625
Net Profit	$ 570,687	$ 632,281	$ 724,672	$ 878,656	$ 1,186,625
Selling Price Using 8 Times Multiple	$ 4,565,496	$ 5,058,248	$ 5,797,376	$ 7,029,248	$ 9,493,000
Portion Allocable to Lim. Part.	$ 3,720,248	$ 3,966,624	$ 4,336,188	$ 4,952,124	$ 6,184,000
Per Limited Partner Unit	$ 106,293	$ 113,332	$ 123,891	$ 141,489	$ 176,686
Selling Price Using 10 Times Multiple	$ 5,706,870	$ 6,322,810	$ 7,246,720	$ 8,786,560	$11,866,250
Portion Allocable to Lim. Part.	$ 4,290,935	$ 4,598,905	$ 5,060,860	$ 5,830,780	$ 7,370,625
Per Limited Partner Unit	$ 122,598	$ 131,397	$ 144,596	$ 166,594	$ 210,589
Selling Price Using 15 Times Multiple	$ 8,560,305	$ 9,484,215	$10,870,080	$13,179,840	$17,799,375
Portion Allocable to Lim. Part.	$ 5,717,653	$ 6,179,608	$ 6,872,540	$ 8,027,420	$10,337,188
Per Limited Partner Unit	$ 163,362	$ 176,560	$ 196,358	$ 229,355	$ 295,348
Selling Price Using 20 Times Multiple	$11,413,740	$12,645,620	$14,493,440	$17,573,120	$23,732,500
Portion Allocable to Lim. Part.	$ 7,144,370	$ 7,760,310	$ 8,684,220	$10,224,060	$13,303,750
Per Limited Partner Unit	$ 204,125	$ 221,723	$ 248,121	$ 292,116	$ 380,107

RISK ASPECTS OF A SATELLITE COMMUNICATIONS FUND

The purchase, construction and operation of the Station involves a high degree of risk, the suitability of which is only for persons of substantial financial means who have no need of liquidity and who can bear the economic risks of his or her investment for an indefinite period. In evaluating this offering, a prospective investor should carefully consider the risks associated herewith, including, but not limited to the following:

1) FCC Approval & Regulation

It is anticipated that the FCC will, grant approval of authority to operate the Station, as requested in SCN's "Section 214 application" made in 1979 as amended in January, 1980, but there can be no assurance that approval will be granted or, if it is granted, that it will be granted in time to begin operations as scheduled. In order to operate the Station as contemplated herein, three approvals from the FCC are required; one to SCN would allow it to resell transponder time as a common carrier, one to the Station to allow it to provide uplink services and approval of the Station as a common carrier of satellite signals. The latter two approvals require that the Station be operational before the granting thereof.

Additionally, there can be no assurance that prospective changes in FCC Rules and Regulations will not adversely affect the operations of the Station.

2) Construction of the Station

In addition to the general risks inherent in construction of any kind, the investor should be aware of several special risks connected with construction of the Station.

First, there can be no assurance that station site selection, with all proceedings necessary to acquire or lease the real estate, will be consummated on schedule. Moreover, there can be no assurance that engineering and actual construction will be completed in substantial conformance with the plans and specifications or that such construction will be completed on schedule.

If the necessary related equipment for the operation of the Station is not installed on schedule or mobile equipment proposed to be delivered as part of the "turn key" operation is not delivered on time and operations do not commence on time, Partners will have significant adverse tax consequences.

3) Preemptibility of Transponder Time

SCN has been awarded by Western Union for a three year term an unprotected full-time transponder on one of Western Union's existing satellites. "Unprotected service on a transponder" means that while the Partnership is actually utilizing the transponder, i.e., broadcasting and the like, the transponder may not be preempted. As such, the Station's Western Union transponder may be preempted when not in actual use and the Station's revenues may be diminished by preemption of its transponder time by Western Union. "Preemption" may be defined as the function by which Western Union reassigns transponder time in the event of malfunction, disturbance or other loss of service temporary or otherwise, on Westar's I, II or III "protected" transponders on to non-protected transponders such as the Partnership's. Since the Partnership's prospective transponder time is classified as "unprotected," its transponder time could be preempted when not in actual use in the event of any problem with protected service. Such occurrences, although not frequent, have occurred in the past. SCN has made arrangements with RCA to secure a full-time preemptible transponder for a one year term with month-to-month extensions thereafter by mutual agreement of RCA and AT&T on COMSTAR D-2, an existing operational satellite. Since the Partnership's transponder accessibility will be preemptible on COMSTAR D-2 there can be no guarantee or protection of the Partnership's transponder if RCA exercises its right to preemption. The unprotected and/or preemptible nature of the Partnership's transponders sublicense could have a deleterious affect on sales of transponder time since many potential users desire protected time.

4) Technology

The offering is based upon construction, installation and operation of the Station through use of presently recognized and acceptable technological systems, to wit, the use of "analog" technology. Equipment suppliers and contractors have proposed to SCN the implementation of a far more advanced and transponder efficient technological system known as time division multiple access ("TDMA"). This system, which makes use of advanced digital technology, would greatly enhance the Station's capability to provide services, especially teleconferencing. At present the cost of this system would be prohibitive to the Partnership. Since the Partnership will not have financial capabilities of most of the companies in the communications business who have expressed substantial interest in microwave and satellite communications, it may be impossible to effectively compete with such companies in the event of significant technological advances.

5) Competition

One of the most important risks inherent in the success of a highly speculative business operation such as that proposed is the degree of competition that currently or prospectively exists for the services proposed to be rendered by the Station. Assuming completion of construction and installation, and the initiation of on-line operations on or near schedule (subject, of course, to the other risks previously enumerated), the Station will have gained a valuable lead in obtaining business for analog video, audio transmissions and data transmission.

As previously stated, the Station could not compete with any operation which would offer TDMA services, which could, effectively, foreclose the Partnership from attempting to obtain business where sophisticated scrambling aimed at prevention of unauthorized use of video and audio television transmissions on a point to multi point basis would be required by the customer. Competition for all manner of satellite communications is extensive and proceeding at an accelerated pace as both users and carriers come to realize the advantages that can flow from satellite communications. It seems highly unlikely that the Partnership can successfully compete with telecommunications companies such as RCA, Western Union, AT&T/GTE, Fairchild Industry (American Satellite Corp.) and the like, whose financial, operational, managerial and technical capabilities are far greater than those which are possessed or can be obtained by the Partnership or SCN, its General Partner, at this time or in the foreseeable future.

Therefore, the Partnership must continue to obtain a market for regular full time and occasional users that will be totally compatible with the Station's projected system, its transponder accessibility and the time frame under which the system is proposed to commence operations.

There can be no assurance, however, that as the companies in the industry invest more capital and resources into the development of satellite communications, the Station's own customer base and marketability will not be adversely affected.

TAX ASPECTS OF A SATELLITE COMMUNICATIONS FUND

Deduction of Losses

Each Limited Partner has agreed to assume personal liability with respect to the Loan at the discretion of the General Partner which liability shall be a direct obligation of the Limited Partner to the Lender under the Assumption Agreement. Counsel to the Partnership is of the opinion that a Limited Partner's initial amount of risk should include (A) the amount of such Limited Partner's Initial Subscription Capital Contribution and (B) the amount of personal liability assumed by the Limited Partner with respect to the Loan to the Partnership.

Depreciation

The Partnership intends to elect depreciation of the Station's equipment using a useful life of eight years pursuant to the Asset Depreciation Range Class Life system (Rev. Pro. 77-10, Asset Guideline Class 48.42). This depreciation period cannot be changed by either the Partnership or the Service during the remaining period of use of the asset. This election further provides that it is to cover all property first placed into service in the year of the election by the Partnership.

The Partnership also intends to elect the "Half Year" averaging convention taking one-half year's depreciation for any asset placed in service during Year One. In the event the Station is not operational during Year One, the amount of claimed depreciation would be substantially reduced.

AMORTIZATION OF CERTAIN FEES AND EXPENSES

Section 709 of the Internal Revenue Code provides that no deduction is allowable to a partnership or to any partner for any amounts paid or incurred to organize a partnership or to promote the sale (or to sell an interest in the partnership). Treasury Regulations proposed on January 10, 1980 provide that syndication costs include brokerage fees, registration fees, legal fees of the placement agent for tax and securities advice pertaining to the adequacy of tax disclosures in a private placement memo, accounting fees for preparation of representations included in the offering materials and printing of a private placement memorandum and other selling and promotional material. Thus, the $182,000 syndication costs paid will not be deductible.

Section 709 further provides that a Partnership may elect to deduct ratably over a period of not less than sixty (60) months the amounts paid or incurred in organizing the Partnership. Organizational expenses are defined as those incidental to the creation of the Partnership chargeable to the capital account and of a character expended in connection with the creation of a partnership having a determinable useful life would be amortized over that period of time.

The Partnership has allocated $30,000 of legal and accounting costs to organizational costs and intends to amortize such costs over a sixty (60) month period taking six (6) months amortization in Year One. The Partnership has allocated $182,000 to syndication costs which are not deductible or amortizable and such costs will be capitalized and will only be written off if and when the Partnership ceases operations.

Investment Tax Credit

A credit against Federal income tax for a taxable year is available, in general, in an amount equal to 10% of the qualified investment in "new Section 38 property" acquired by the taxpayer after January 21, 1975 and before January 1, 1981 and placed in service in such year by the taxpayer Section 38 property, as defined by Code Section 48, includes tangible personal property such as the Station's equipment (excluding the building and land), with respect to which depreciation or amortization is allowable and which has a useful life of three years or more.

In general, each partner takes into account separately, for his taxable year with or within which the partnership taxable year ends, his distributive share of the basis of a partnership's new Section 38 property placed in service by the partnership during the partnership's taxable year. The estimated useful life of the property for each partner is deemed to be the estimated useful life of the property in the hands of the partnership.

Investment Credit Recapture

If the Station's equipment is sold or otherwise disposed of by the Partnership, or is destroyed, before the close of the seventh year from the date the Station's equipment is first placed in service, all or a portion of the investment tax credit claimed with respect to the Station's equipment would be "recaptured," resulting in an increase in tax for the taxable year of such sale or disposition (or destruction) in the amount of the credit previously claimed but as yet unearned. If such event occurs prior to the expiration of a period of service of three years after the Station's equipment was first placed in service, 100% of the previously claimed investment credit would be recaptured; if such disposition occurs after three or more years, but prior to five years of service, 66-2/3% of the investment credit would be recaptured; if the disposition occurs after five or more years, but before seven years of service, 33-1/3% of the investment credit would be recaptured. In such event, a Partner's tax liability for the taxable year during which the sale or disposition of the Station's equipment occurs would be increased to the extent of his distributive share of the amount of claimed but unearned (i.e., "recaptured") credit.

The amount of investment tax credit for a taxable year may not exceed tax liability and if tax liability exceeds $25,000 ($12,500 in the case of a married individual filing a separate return, unless the spouse has no qualified investment or unused credit with respect to the taxable year), the tax credit is limited to $25,000 plus 70% (for taxable years ending in 1980) of the tax liability over that amount. Unused portions of the investment credit may be carried over or carried back and amounts carried over are to be applied against the current year's income tax before credits arising in the current year are used.

Sale, Foreclosure and Other Disposition of Partnership Property; Recapture

Limited Partners must report on their tax returns their allocable shares of the gain or loss realized by the Partnership in the event of a sale, foreclosure or other disposition of the Station or its equipment. The foregoing may result in taxable income to the Limited Partners even though the proceeds, if any, are not distributed to them or are less than the gain recognized.

Should the Partnership sell or otherwise dispose of the Station or its equipment prior to payment in full of any indebtedness encumbering such property and if the purchaser or transferee assumes such indebtedness or takes subject thereto, the Partnership would realize a taxable gain to the extent that the consideration received on such sale or disposition, together with the amount of the outstanding balance of such indebtedness, exceeds the adjusted basis for the Station or its equipment.

In the case of a foreclosure of the Station or its equipment subject to an indebtedness, or of a conveyance to the secured party in discharge of any debt, the Partnership would be treated as if it had made a sale or disposition of the subject property and would realize gain to the extent of the excess of the outstanding balance of such indebtedness over its adjusted basis for the Station or its equipment.

A disposition of the Earth Station's equipment will result in ordinary income ("depreciation recapture") to the extent of the lesser of (a) the gain realized on such disposition, or (b) the aggregate amount of the depreciation that was allowable with respect to the Earth Station's equipment.

Under Code Section 1231, if the sum of the gains on sales or exchanges of certain depreciable assets used in a trade or business and held for more than one year and the gains from certain compulsory or involuntary conversions, exceed the losses on such sales, exchanges and conversions, then all such gains ("Section 1231 gains") and losses ("Section 1231 losses") will be treated as capital gains and losses. However, if Section 1231 losses exceed Section 1231 gains, all such gains and losses will be treated as ordinary gains and losses.

Each Partner reports his allocable share of the combined net amounts of the Partnership's Section 1231 gains and losses for the taxable year. A partner's allocable share of any Section 1231 gain recognized with respect to the Station's equipment in excess of the amount of depreciation previously allowable with respect to the Station's equipment (which depreciation is subject to recapture, as described above) will be treated as a capital gain, provided that the sum of the Partner's Section 1231 gains exceeds the sum of his Section 1231 losses, as discussed above.

Upon the sale or other disposition of the Station's equipment before the close of the seventh year from the date the Station's equipment was first placed in service, all or a portion of the investment tax credit previously claimed with respect to the Station's equipment will be recaptured.

Deductibility of First Installment of Sublicense Fee

Section 1253(d) of the Code governs the deductibility of amounts paid by a transferee in connection with a transfer or disposition of a franchise. In general, amounts paid by the transferee which are contingent upon the productivity use or disposition of the franchise are deductible under Section 162 of the Code (as an ordinary and necessary business expense) for the taxable year in which such amounts are paid or incurred. On the other hand, if the parties to the transfer agree upon the payment of a principal sum and if the transferor is deemed to retain a significant power, right or continuing interest in the franchise, then the timing of the deduction for the payment of such principal sum will depend upon the manner in which such principal sum is discharged.

Under proposed regulations if the principal sum is payable in a series of approximately equal installments made over a period of the Sublicense agreement then each such installment is deductible when paid.

The Sublicense Agreement between SCN and the Partnership contains a fixed sublicense fee payable by the Partnership after the initial fee in a series of equal annual installments over the period of the Agreement.

The sublicense should constitute a "franchise" and SCN should be deemed to have retained a significant power, right or continuing interest with respect to the sublicense—both within the meaning and for the purposes of Section 1253(d)(2) of the Code. As such the Partnership should have a basis to claim a deduction with respect to the payment of the first installment of the fixed sublicense fee in the taxable year in which such installment is paid. It should be noted, however, that the IRS could claim, among other things, that the deferred portion of the sublicense fee fixed in the Sublicense Agreement should not be considered part of the "principal sum" payable under that Agreement for purposes of Section 1253(d)(2). The IRS could also claim that the Partnership cannot properly use the accrual method of accounting with respect to the sublicense because, among other reasons, such method would not clearly reflect income.

If the IRS successfully contends that the deferred portion of the fixed sublicense fees in years subsequent to Year One are not considered part of the principal sum for the purposes of Section 1253(d)(2) and/or that the Partnership may not properly use the accrual method of accounting with respect to the sublicense then at best, only a portion of the first installment would be deductible in Year One—which portion may be less than the amount of cash paid by the Partnership in satisfaction of the first installment. Investors should consult their tax advisors with respect to the magnitude of the adverse consequences which could result in the event that the IRS is sustained in a challenge of the deductibility of the initial sublicense installment in Year One.

Deductibility of Advertising, Marketing, Promotional, Rental of Transponder Time and Certain Professional Fees

The Partnership should be entitled to deduct the expenses paid to the Manager in Year One relating to defraying the costs of advertising, marketing, promotion, rental of transponder time and professional fees concerning the operations of the Partnership after the Station is in operation. The IRS may contend that certain of such expenses are "pre-opening expenses" incurred before operations began thus requiring such expenses to be capitalized. The Partnership will receive an opinion of counsel to the effect that such expenses are not of the pre-opening type and therefore should be deductible to the Partnership. The question of when a business begins is one of fact and may vary according to the circumstances. Accordingly, there can be no assurance that an adverse determination of the foregoing issue will not result. The Partnership intends to pay to Aries $400,000 ($200,000 applicable to Year One and $200,000 applicable to Year Two) as a warranty fee for repairing structural defects of the Station after the 30 day initial warranty period contained in the construction agreement and continuing until end of Year Two which expenses the Partnership intends to deduct as ordinary and necessary expenses of conducting the Partnership business.

Under the actual method of accounting, "an expense is deductible for the taxable year in which all events have occurred which determine the fact of liability and the amount thereof can be determined with reasonable accuracy." Payment of the initial management fee and the subsequent guaranteed portion thereof of $35,000 minimum amount annually is a condition of the transaction and further the payment of the annual management fee of 25% of the Station's revenue is also a condition of the transaction and as such amount is fixed and payable in all events based on revenue, the Partnership's liability in regard to the management fees should be considered fixed upon execution of the management agreement and receipt of the revenues referred to therein. *U.S.* v. *Anderson* 269 U.S. 422 (1926); *Guardian Investment Corp.* v. *Phinney,* 253 F.2d 326 (5th Cir. 1958); *Lawyers Title Guaranty Fund* v. *U.S.,* 492 F.2d 1182 (6th Cir. 1974). See, however, *Mooney Aircraft, Inc.* v. *U.S.,* 420 F.2d 400 (5th Cir. 1969), in which the 5th Circuit indicated that although a taxpayer had unconditionally obligated himself to pay a liability and the amount of the liability is determinable, all events may not have occurred to fix the taxpayer's liability if the point at which the obligation must be satisfied is so far in the future (15 to 30 years in that case) that payment is improbable. Cf. *Washington Post Co.* v. *U.S.,* 405 R.2d 1279 (Ct. Cl. 1969); *Kershaw Mfg. Co., Inc.* v. *Comm.,* 313 F.2d 942 (5th Cir. 1963) which hold that the date upon which the obligation must be satisfied is irrelevant if the liability is fixed and the amount of liability is determinable.

In view of the foregoing, it must be established that the management fee is reasonable in amount, is structured in accordance with commercial business practice and reflects a commercially reasonable fee structure. If it is not, the management fee may be recharacterized as a nondeductible bonus, loan or brokerage commission. If the management fee was characterized as a bonus, it would have to be capitalized instead of being currently deductible. This would result in adverse tax consequences with respect to both the timing and the amount of tax benefits associated with the investment in the Partnership, since the Partnership would lose its current deduction for the management fees.

The General Partner's wholly-owned subsidiary will be paid a minimum guaranteed fee of at least $35,000 per year for all services to be rendered in managing the operations of the Partnership. This fee shall be supplemented by a fee to the Manager of 25% of the Station's revenues in each year to be applied toward the operating costs of the Station.

For purposes of determining the deductibility of guaranteed payments to partners, the payments due to the Manager, being a wholly-owned subsidiary of SCN, may be deemed to have been made to SCN. Section 707(c) of the Code provides that such payments shall be deemed made to a non-partner and if such payments, as thus considered, constitute deductible business expenses not subject to the capitalization requirements of Section 263 of the Code, they are properly deductible by the Partnership for purposes of determining its profit and loss. Thus, if the guaranteed payments to the Manager are in payment for items appropriately chargeable to capital account (for example, organizational or syndication expenses), then such payments to the Manager are not deductible in the year paid but rather amortizable (if at all) over certain prescribed periods of time.

It should be noted that if the guaranteed fee payable to the Manager is in excess of the normal costs of securing the service to which such fee relates, the Service may contend that such excess represents a share of the profits attributable to the General Partner through its relationship with the Manager in its capacity as such and are not deductible by the Partnership. In general, see *Edward t. Pratt,* 64 T.C. 203 (1975), *aff'd in part, rev'd and rem'd in part* 550 F.2d 1023 (5th Cir. 1977) and *Jackson E. Cagle, Jr.,* 63 T.C. 86 (1974), aff'd 539 F.2d 409 (5th Cir. 1976).

Whether the guaranteed fee to the Manager is reasonable compensation for services performed and deductible is essentially a factual determination, and accordingly, no opinion can be rendered thereon.

To the extent that the Service were to be successful in recharacterizing the guaranteed fee to the Manager, (x) a part of the deduction for such payment may be denied if it is characterized as a sharing of profits or (y) the deductions for the Manager's guaranteed fee will be amortizable over several calendar years or (z) a combination of the foregoing will result.

COMPUTING EQUIPMENT

INDUSTRY STATUS AND FORECAST

Computer industry shipments for 1981 are expected to reach $32.8 billion, a 26.2 percent increase over the 1980 level. Cost pressures from material and labor inputs are likely to continue during 1981, forcing computer markets to make selected upward adjustments to prices. Nevertheless, new products with improved performance should be introduced at the same or lower prices than those of preceding models. The net effect should be that equipment performance improvements continue to offset most price increases, ensuring that constant dollar shipments are roughly equal to current dollar values. The high level of demand for most types of computer products is expected to continue through 1985, with strong growth in the auxiliary storage and terminals sectors. This growth is supported by such trends as the increasing interconnection of computers via communications links, whether by land-based systems such as cable and microwave, or by satellite. Real growth in shipments should average about 15 percent annually through 1985, reaching about $52 billion that year.

Product shipments of computers and related equipment for 1980 increased more than 24 percent above the 1979 level to $25.5 billion in current dollars, or about 20 percent in real terms. Shipments continued at a high level through mid-1980, assisted by strong overseas demand.

Labor turnover figures indicate the computer industry was better able than other manufacturing industries to weather the slow growth of the domestic economy during the first quarter of 1980, and the substantial downturn of the second quarter. For example, the new hire rate for June 1980 stood at 2.7 per 100 workers for the computer industry and 2.4 for all manufacturing. The layoff rate for the computer industry was only 0.1, versus 2.2 for all manufacturing. While order rates softened during this period for some computer makers, a generally large order backlog in the industry helped to maintain production and employment. Therefore, the industry should emerge largely unscathed from the relatively short, but sharp domestic downturn.

High interest rates in U.S. money markets caused some manufacturers difficulty during 1979 and 1980 by squeezing profit margins. Many manufacturers were forced to bear increased financing costs as users chose lease and rental arrangements over purchase of equipment. Some manufacturers' price increases during 1980 tried to offset this trend, with rate increases for leases and rentals higher than for purchase.

Cost Pressures Strong

Although equipment price increases have occurred periodically in the past, most price increases have been largely offset over time by performance improvement. However, the price increases since about mid-1979 have been uncharacteristic in their frequency and breadth. Not only have manufacturers of a wide variety of equipment, from mainframe computers to magnetic disks, raised purchase, lease, and rental rates times over this period, but the increases have affected both newly introduced as well as older products.

Manufacturers have blamed these increases on pressures from rising costs for labor and materials. Total labor costs as a percent of value added in the industry are roughly the same, 50 percent, as in all manufacturing. In the production area, average hourly earnings for all manufacturing were 8.1 percent higher in the first half of 1980 than the same period in 1979, compared to a rise of 9.6 percent for the computer industry.

However, the computer industry faced other, unique pressures. There were—and continue to be—shortages of experienced labor in such areas as software programming and systems analysis, which have tended to bid up salaries and wages. For example, one survey showed that programmers with 3 years' experience could expect to be earning about $22,000, a 16 percent increase over 1979. Such cost pressures are not likely to end soon. While there are various efforts within the industry and educational institutions to train more people in computer-related skills, it is generally conceded that shortages of certain key skills will continue for some time.

The cost of materials as a percent of shipments in the computer industry has been well below that of all manufacturing, 45 percent and 57 percent, respectively. This suggests that the computer industry is relatively less dependent on inputs than other industries. Nevertheless, key material prices rose substantially. There was a relatively large increase in the Producer Price Index between July 1979 and July 1980 for selected inputs: fractional horsepower motors and electronic connectors, 11.6 percent each; resistors, 8.6 percent; and magnet wire, 10.2 percent. Even the price index for integrated circuits (ICs) which has shown a long-term decline, rose by 11.1 percent in this period. Part of this was due to shortages in 16K RAMs (16,000 bits of data per random access memory IC) in 1979, which continued through mid-1980. The shortages led not only to higher prices, but also, for some firms, decreased production. The situation improved in the fourth quarter of 1980, which stabilized prices of this important input.

Investment Healthy

The top seven U.S. computer firms spent $2.7 billion on plant and equipment in 1979, a 27.6 percent increase over the previous year. By mid-1980, most were expanding semiconductor capacity to include production of very large-scale integrated circuits (VLSI). They also were adding to existing or building new plants throughout the world, including Ireland, Scotland, West Germany, Italy, France, Singapore, and Japan. One company alone planned to complete 3.5-million square feet of plant and laboratory space and to have an additional 7-million square feet under construction in the United States and abroad by the end of 1980.

The total 1979 research and development (R&D) expenditures of a sample of 25 computer equipment manufacturers increased 17.7 percent above the previous year's level, to nearly $3 billion. This was only slightly less than the 18.9 percent of all manufacturing in *Business Week*'s annual survey of corporate R&D expenditures. This survey contained the R&D spending of other high technology industries, such as aerospace (38.4 percent); electronics (21.4 percent), and semiconductors (33.2 percent). The computer industry did exceed the composite for all manufacturing in two other R&D measures. Expenditures per employee were more than twice as large as the composite ($3,691 vs. $1,553). Expenditures as a percent of sales were more than three and one-half times greater for the computer industry (6.8 percent vs. 1.9 percent).

Many of these computer firms are integrated manufacturers; therefore, these figures reflect R&D on a broad range of products besides computer equipment, including semiconductors and software.

Trade Continues Strong

Exports continued their strong upward growth for the fourth consecutive year with a 36.4 percent increase over 1979 to an estimated $7.5 billion, more than 29 percent of the value of 1980 product shipments. Nearly two-thirds of exports went to Western Europe, Canada, and Japan. However, expected downturns in these key economies should reduce the growth of U.S. exports to 20 percent in 1981.

Imports of computing equipment and parts rose more than 12 percent during 1980 to $1.1 billion, or approximately 6 percent of the U.S. market. With the softening in U.S. domestic demand, imports from Japan and France, two major exporters, fell by more than 20 percent below their 1979 level while those from Canada, traditionally the leading supplier, grew at about the same rate as total imports. Part of the decline in imports from Japan was due to withdrawal from the market of a U.S. distributor of a line of Japanese-made mainframe computers. The expected recovery in the U.S. economy and several new joint ventures between Japanese and U.S. firms should lead to an increase of more than 19 percent in imports during 1981.

International Comparisons

The 1979 computer production of six principal nations is shown in Table I on the next page. The United States led the next largest producer, Japan, by a factor of 4, and accounted for 55 percent of the production total of the six nations. The U.S. growth rate for 1979 was exceeded only by Italy.

Chart I compares the computer exports of these six nations and several others for 1975 and 1979. The United States was the principal exporter in both of these years, with more than 40 percent of the total. But these comparisons mask the fact that subsidiaries of U.S. computer companies are important contributors to the production and trade of most of these countries. For example, in the case of computer exports from the United Kingdom as much as 70 to 80 percent are estimated

1979 Computer Production of Principal Nations

Nation	Production (millions of) current dollars)	Percent increase 1978-79	1979 production index (U.S. = 100)
United States (E)	21,000	28.4	100
Japan	5,185*	24.8	25
France (E)	4,341	15.0	21
West Germany	3,232	8.8	15
United Kingdom	2,281	22.7	11
Italy	2,107	41.9	10
	38,146	24.7	

Sources: Official government statistical publications of each nation. Estimates (E) by the Bureau of Industrial Economics.

*Excludes parts.

to come from U.S.-owned operations there. An estimate of the "U.S.-owned" share of the $12.8 billion in exports in 1979 would be 60 to 70 percent, or about $8 billion.

This strong U.S. position is also reflected in company level comparisons. The 1979 computer-related revenues of the top seven U.S. firms increased 12 percent above the 1978 level to $31 billion. This was nearly four times the combined computer revenues of the top seven foreign firms, which rose by 16 percent to $8 billion during this same period. The relative commitment of these U.S. and foreign firms to computer products can be seen in the fact that the computer-related revenues as a percent of total revenues represent 73 percent and 21 percent for the U.S. and foreign firms, respectively.

The leadership of the United States in computers, coupled with the realization that this industry is an increasingly critical sector of a nation's economy, has motivated developed and developing countries alike to create or strengthen their own industries. In several cases, governments have encouraged joint ventures, licensing and acquisitions, to acquire rapidly the necessary technology.

Recently, as the technical proficiency of Japanese firms has advanced, they have become alternative sources to U.S. computer

Computing Equipment and Parts Exports of Principal Nations

Total Exports: $5.5 billion[1] 1975		Total Exports: $12.8 billion[1] 1979	
United States	40%	United States	43%
West Germany	22%	West Germany	14%
U.K.	13%	U.K.	14%
France	11%	France	12%
Italy	3%	Italy	5%
Japan	3%	Japan	5%
Canada	3%	Canada	3%
Sweden	3%	Sweden	3%
Netherlands	2%	Netherlands	1%

firms for new technology. Japanese companies, for example, are principal participants in joint ventures with indigenous firms in the Brazilian government's efforts to create a local minicomputer industry.

Japanese computer companies are also forming alliances with several European computer and business equipment firms for the marketing of their large to very large-scale computer processors. These cooperative efforts are mutually beneficial, giving the Japanese companies market access without the expense of establishing distribution and maintenance networks, and allowing the European firms to avoid the high costs of developing production capability in this important market sector.

Personal Computers

Personal computer sales continued to show strong growth in 1979. It is estimated that 300,000 to 350,000 desktop units in the $500 to $10,000 range were purchased worldwide, with total value exceeding $500 million. Small business, professional and educational users accounted for nearly 90 percent of this value and 70 percent of the units sold, with the remainder going to the home and hobbyist sectors. Stimulated by new product introductions–second-generation desktop systems with expanded main memory and improved graphics and software capabilities–sales were expected to double in value to almost $1 billion and reach 500,000 units in 1980.

Sales of the two leading U.S. manufacturers were estimated to have grown 170 percent in 1979, reaching a combined total of more than $200 million. However, during 1980, some manufacturers could not ship new equipment for periods as long as 4 to 6 months due to semiconductor shortages and production problems.

Small businesses and professionals increasingly are demanding high quality software. One company official predicted that 1980 sales to these users would exceed $100 million at wholesale prices, or nearly double the previous year's level. Intense competition between computer stores and discount mail-order firms in certain major metropolitan areas lowered the manufacturer's suggested retail price of some equipment by as much as 25 percent.

The direction that personal computer prices will take in the future is less clear. A number of companies hope to keep prices and profits at relatively stable levels by adding enhanced capabilities to their existing systems. Others feel that the eventual introduction of very large-scale integrated circuits at a lower cost per function and increased foreign competition will combine to reduce system prices substantially over the next few years.

The first signs of potentially strong foreign competition emerged during mid-1980. European and Japanese firms introduced hand-held models that can do some data processing and storage and act as terminals to connect to remote databases via telecommunications links. According to some forecasts, the Japanese are expected to move aggressively into the desktop computer market and by 1982 they could capture approximately 30 to 40 percent of the U.S. market for all types of personal computers.

As the home information market evolves, it will encourage the entrance of other than personal computer firms. Not only ease of use but also the ability to perform a wide range of functions will determine consumer acceptance of home information systems. Security, environmental management, home entertainment and education, and access to remote information services are examples of functions which could be offered individually or integrated in future systems. Thus, competitors could come from such diverse industries as consumer electronics, telephone equipment and services, and cable television.

Retail Distribution Grows

Personal computer manufacturers began marketing through company-owned stores and independent retail outlets as early as 1975. Their initial efforts were directed toward hobbyists. When this demand slackened and the home market evolved more slowly than expected, many of these firms turned their attention to selling complete systems and software to users in the small business, professional and education sectors. In 1978, the first entrants from the mainframe and minicomputer sectors appeared, establishing retail oriented operations directed toward this small business market, It is estimated to have a potential of 2-million customers. Other computer and business equipment firms soon followed and by mid-1980 several retail stores were marketing calculators, low-end photocopiers and word processing systems along with computing equipment and software. Both company-owned and independent retail outlets, such as consumer electronics stores and department store chains, now sell nearly 75 percent of all small business computer units priced under $15,000.

While currently emphasizing the small business user, those firms that have begun to establish distributions channels are positioning themselves for the future growth of the home information market.

Semiconductor Logic and Memory

The improvement in the price and performance of computer equipment over the years owes much to developments in semiconductors. Since the early 1970's, when integrated circuits began to replace magnetic cores in processor main memory, computer makers have used them as rapidly as they have become available in volume.

Most computers shipped during 1980 incorporated 16K RAMs in main memory. However, one computer manufacturer with advanced semiconductor production capability shipped several models with memory ICs at the next level of data capacity, 64K RAMs. Random access memory ICs of this capacity were generally available only on a sample basis for testing purposes from semiconductor manufacturers.

Laboratory prototypes of 256K and 512K RAMs were announced, and one forecast claimed that 256K ROM (read only memory) IC's would be available in sample quantities in 1981.

These developments in the memory area had their analogs in logic. There were several examples of manufacturers reducing the central processing units of mini- and mainframe computers to a single IC during 1980. In one case almost 5,000 logic circuits were placed on a chip of silicon measuring about three-tenths of an inch on a side.

These developments illustrate the increasing complexity of logic and memory functions on integrated circuits. This development has been extremely significant because it has allowed computer makers to increase the processing power of their equipment while reducing such characteristics as size and energy usage.

Magnetic Disk Storage Advances

Another active technology area during 1980 was magnetic disk storage. These units, which act as slower, auxiliary storage to high-speed semiconductor main memory, have substantially increased in performance and decreased in price for several decades. For example, since the mid-1950's when disk storage units began to appear, storage capacity, as measured by the number of megabytes per spindle (multiples of 8 million bits of data per unit of stacked disks), has increased by an average of about 25 percent per year. In contrast, prices, as measured by monthly lease charges per megabyte, have declined by almost 20 percent per year.

During 1980, large capacity magnetic disk units were introduced that could store 2.5-gigabytes of data (one gigabyte equals 8-billion bits) per storage unit. The improvement was based on the amount of data that could be stored per unit of disk surface area, which was increased to over 10 million bits per square inch from about 5 million bits per square inch. These disks were designed to be attached to large-scale processors, and included innovations such as new read and write mechanisms (so-called thin film heads) manufactured through a semiconductor process. The new heads ride closer to the surface of the disk and thus are able to sense more densely packed bits of data.

But the demand for and introduction of new disk storage products were not confined to the large-scale computer market. Small disk storage units for mini- and microcomputers were particularly active sectors. Many new products utilized technology from the large storage sector (disk diameters of 14 inches). For example, the so-called "Winchester" technology, in which read and write mechanisms and disks are sealed in a unit, protects them from contaminants that can cause malfunctions. Winchester disks of 8-inch and 5.25-inch diameters were developed for use in small business and word processing. These rigid disk systems are expected to become competitive with the flexible or "floppy" disk units currently in widespread use in these types of systems. The larger storage capacities and faster data handling of these Winchester units (20 to 80 megabytes, with average data access times of 27 milliseconds) will allow the use of more complex software programs, which in turn will result in more sophisticated uses of these smaller computer systems.

Unit shipments in 1979 of all magnetic disk storage increased 30 percent over 1978. Growth should continue near this rate during the next few years as new products announced during 1979 and 1980 reach volume shipment levels.

Computer Software

Software programs, or the instructions which guide equipment through its tasks, are the necessary partners in any computer system. Because of the increasing complexity and cost of creating software, many manufacturers have gradually separated the price of software from that of equipment, so-called unbundling. This unbundling has spread from applications programs, written for particular user-oriented tasks such as payroll accounting, to systems software, the programs governing the management to the computer system.

During the 1980's, software is expected to receive greater emphasis both from the user and from computer firms. Users will be seeking ever more sophisticated applications, exemplified by such trends as computer networking and distributed processing. In responding to these market forces, computer firms will direct more of their internal resources into software development. Some firms already have more than half of their development staffs working on software.

The growing emphasis on software can also be seen abroad. For example, a joint government private sector software development program has been inaugurated in Japan, concentrating on those types of software where they feel Japanese firms are behind competitors. Although U.S. firms currently are world leaders in many software areas, it is clear that competition will stiffen in the 1980's as it did for equipment.

Trends and Issues

The seemingly promising convergence of computers and communications technologies and markets is not occurring without considerable debate in the government and the private sectors. During 1980, the Federal Communications Commission, as a result of its Computer Inquiry II begun in 1976, ruled how major telecommunications common carriers will be allowed to compete in computer equipment and services markets. This decision will be affected by related developments in the courts and in Congress, but there is little doubt that the move toward greater deregulation in the telephone industry will profoundly influence the computer industry.

The regulation of the transmission of information across national boundaries, the issue of transborder data flows, began as early as 1973 with the passage of the Data Act in Sweden. This law governed personal data, but subsequent actions by various foreign governments have created regulations which also govern the international flow of corporate data. Although their effect on U.S. computer firms is not yet clear, the laws would seem to affect most U.S. computer companies that sell time-sharing and remote data base services in these countries. However, more generally, the laws can also have substantial adverse effects on U.S. computer firms that require a continuing flow of information among offices scattered throughout the world.

COMPUTERS

U.S. companies dominate the $100 billion-a-year world market in electronic goods. Within 10 years, according to the Washington-based Worldwatch Institute, it may rival the automobile industry as the largest in the world with a market of $400 billion annually. U.S. companies account for fully 70 percent of the sales of integrated circuits, or chips. Comprising thousands of tiny transistors, these devices are to computers what the brain is to the body. They were first made in America.

And the chips and the computers built from them became a critical part of everyday life because of the space race in the 1960s. Indeed, today's computers are the handsome children of the technology scramble that propelled this country into the world of speedy machines and intricate electronic systems.

Although the race really began before the Soviet Union launched Sputnik in 1957—in fact, when Bell Telephone Laboratories first demonstrated the transistor about 30 years ago—it took the furious development of space technology to fully launch the electronics revolution.

It is one that "promises to surpass the Industrial Revolution in its impact on human affairs," declared John S. Mayo, executive vice-president for network systems at Bell Laboratories in Murray Hill, N.J.

Behind the revolution, he believes, is the technology that permits "ever-greater increases in the complexity of integrated circuitry fabricated on a single semiconductor crystal."

The evolution of computer making can be traced from vacuum tubes to transistors to integrated circuits. Machines resembling today's digital computers were introduced in 1944 and 1946. The first, developed by IBM, was called an Automatic Sequence Controlled Calculator, the Mark I. It was a cumbersome mechanical device of gears, cams and shafts. The second, an electronic machine made up of 18,000 vacuum tubes, was called the Electronic Numerical Integrator and Calculator. It, too, was an awkward device that took weeks to rewire when snafus developed, which was often.

The breakthrough that led to the development of computers you can buy in a computer store came in 1969 when M. E. Hoff, an Intel Corp. engineer, created the microprocessor—the most important discovery in making computers smaller.

"By attaching a few additional chips to supply other basic functions such as memory, he had, in effect, created a tiny programmable computer (the microprocessor). This seemingly simple development launched a virtual revolution in machine ingelligence," according to Robert T. Lund, an assistant director and senior research associate at the Massachusetts Institute of Technology's Center for Policy Alternatives, writing in "Technology Review."

"Standard chips could be mass-produced and then tailored to specific uses by adding the appropriate programmed instructions, making 'intelligence' available at low cost for virtually any application, however unique. And unlike other programmable devices—computers and mini-computers—microprocessors were not limited in their application by size, complexity, or power consumption."

In short, "the microprocessor is as revolutionary as the wheel, the combustion engine and the light bulb, because it has the potential to effect major changes in our quality of life," Lund said.

This type of small computer-on-a-chip is found in appliances, automobiles, word processors, electronic scales, medical equipment, in fact in any device where storing information, timing actions, sensing conditions, making calculations, even communicating with a machine's operator is desired to improve its performance. In autos, microprocessors are being used to regulate engine performance, reduce emissions, control safety features and improve fuel economy.

The assistance of the Detroit Free Press in the preparation of the above material is gratefully acknowledged.

GENERAL DESCRIPTION OF THE COMPUTER INDUSTRY

Recently, mini and micro computers costing from less than $10,000 up to approximately $250,000 have been developed to serve a broad range of requirements. These computers have enabled small and medium size businesses to obtain computer capability at a comparatively reasonable cost. An additional cost (which will vary depending upon the type of computer) the Software Systems can be used on many mini computers.

All software programs are written in computer language. The Software Systems in this program utilize the DATA/BASIC language. A number of other languages have been developed and attempts are constantly being made to simplify them and make them more efficient. Computer operators using languages such as DATA/BASIC require extensive training. The value of the Systems may be adversely affected by future development and acceptance of other computer languages that require less training, and are therefore less costly to use.

The commercial success of each Software System depends, in significant part, on the quality and price of the Software Systems, compared to competitive Software systems, the ability of the Partnership, either directly or through a distributor, to obtain access to the relevant market, the receptivity of the market to the particular technology which the Software System was designed to furnish, and the ability of the Partnership, either directly or through a distributor, to provide customers with suitable service and maintenance. The Partnership has no prior experience whatsoever in the distribution, service and/or maintenance of a computer system.

The Software Systems embody a type of computer program known as application software, which is intended to provide generalized programming instruction for definable purposes. There are many other companies of larger size which have significantly greater financial resources and experience than Special, which are developing application software. *Such companies may have the expertise and market penetration to compete effectively with the program contained in the Software Systems or to totally dominate the markets to which any Software System is directed.*

BUSINESS OF THE PARTNERSHIP

The Partnership will enter into a Purchase Agreement with Hardware-Software Systems Corporation and the Partnership shall acquire certain items of computer hardware (the "Hardware"), as well as certain computer software systems (the "Systems"), for use in certain defined territories.

Under the Purchase Agreement, the Partnership will pay an aggregate price of $8,100,000, which will be paid as follows:

Cash Payment in Year One	$ 137,500
Assigment of Limited Partners' Promissory Notes Payable to the Partnership	$ 180,000
Execution of Non-Recourse Promissory Note	$7,782,500
TOTAL	$8,100,000

Although the Partnership's non-recourse promissory note matures on December 31, Year Ten, the Partnership will be required to make monthly payments to the holder thereof to the extent of 60% of any net revenues generated from the sale or commercial exploitation of the Software Systems or the Hardware during the term of the Note.

Any such payments shall be applied first against unpaid accrued interest to date and thereafter to reduce the principal balance of the Note.

The payment of the principal of and the accrued interest on the Note, and the performance of the Partnership's obligations under the Purchase Agreement shall be secured by a security interest in the Hardware and the Software Systems. In the event that the Note shall be in default for a period of one (1) year after it is due and payable, then, after ninety (90) days' written notice, the holder of the Note shall have all of the rights available pursuant to the Uniform Commercial Code, including the right to foreclose upon the Hardware and the Software Systems; provided, however, that under no circumstances shall any of the Partners be personally liable for the payment of the Note. In the even the Partnership fails both to:

(a) Expend an amount of not less than $20,000 in connection with the commercial exploitation of the Software Systems; and

(b) Reduce the outstanding principal balance of the Note by at least $400,000 during the 18-month period following the receipt by the Partnership, or its designee, of the Hardware and the Software Systems, such failure shall be deemed to be an event of default pursuant to the terms of the Note.

Set forth below are certain material terms of the Purchase Agreement. Under the Purchase Agreement, the Partnership shall acquire the Hardware and the Software Systems, which shall include among other things:

(a) All right, title and interest to the Software Systems in the designated territory, including the exclusive right to use, manufacture, promote, advertise, distribute, license, package, repackage, edit, change or vary the Software Systems in any and all fields of use;

(b) The exclusive right to enhance and revise the Software Systems in order to accommodate requirements of users thereof or to upgrade the Software Systems for use in connection with additional or new computers or advanced models of existing computers; and

(c) The exclusive right to use and permit others, under license, to use in the designated territory all available materials describing the Software Systems.

The Partnership intends to commercially exploit the Software Systems. As is customary in the industry, the Partnership will promote its Software Systems through the use of advertising and direct mail programs. Special has agreed to furnish the Partnership with advertising copy, which it has utilized or will utilize with respect to similar Software systems. The General Partner will determine whether or not to utilize such copy on behalf of the Partnership and will further determine which advertising media will be employed. The Partnership intends to use the Hardware to demonstrate its Software Systems to potential customers.

The Partnership intends to enroll the General Partner or another representative of the Partnership in the training program given by Special. The Partnership believes that subsequent to the successful completion of the training program, the General Partner or other representative of the Partnership will be qualified to demonstrate and promote the Systems.

Special has agreed to turn over any leads for potential customers that it may obtain to the Partnership with respect to the Software Systems owned by the Partnership which will be exploited in territories from which the leads arise. Special has also agreed to provide any technical data to the Partnership which is necessary in order for the Partnership to commercially exploit the Software Systems and will provide a representative, if necessary, to explain any technical aspects of the Hardware and the Software Systems. All negotiations with customers will be conducted by the Partnership.

The Partnership may also retain the services of one or more software distributors or service agencies for the purposes of commercially exploiting the Software Systems. Any such retention will be at the sole discretion of the General Partner who will also determine the terms and conditions thereof.

THE SPECIAL TRAINING PROGRAM

The Special Training Program, one of the services available to the distributors and end-users of Special, provides both a general and an in-depth view of the minicomputer industry today. Courses are directed towards laymen as well as technical people.

The course and its contents are geared to assist in the marketing of Special's Systems. In this highly competitive industry, it is essential for the General Partner to understand many of the features of the Software Systems.

This training program is also suitable for those end-users that wish to provide their own data processing services.

Special encourages all end-users, distributors and others to take advantage of its training course. Whatever the objective, Special believes that the classes will prove informative and valuable.

ACCESS TO INFORMATION

Prior to the purchase of a unit, each prospective purchaser and/or his representative will be granted access to all information concerning the Partnership or the Software Systems to be purchased thereby which the Partnership has or which it can obtain without unreasonable expense. Each prospective purchaser is encouraged to ask questions and seek additional information such as he deems material.

THE COMPUTER HARDWARE

The Reasonable 1000 is manufactured by the Mini Corporation. The Partnership will purchase the following components:

A. *Central Processing Unit ("CPU")*

The Reasonable CPU incorporates Mini's proprietary micro-programmed firmware that provides a data base management operating system. Included in the firmware are a true virtual memory manager, multi-user operating capability, dynamic file and memory management, and processors for all input and output devices. The main features of the CPU to be purchased include:

- 16K MOS Main Memory with 800 nanosecond/byte cycle time
- 16 bit micro-instruction length
- 32 hardware registers
- Realtine Clock
- Disc Controller
- Printer Controller
- Communications Controller with 2 active ports
- Power Failure Protection and Automatic Power Re-Start.

B. *Tape Drive*

The Mini tape drive is an integral part of the Reasonable system used for mass storage of archival data files, interchange of data between computers and dynamic disc file back-up. The main features are:

- 800 bpi data density
- NRZI data format
- 45 ips tape speed
- 32K byte/second data transfer rate
- 9 track IBM compatible
- Up to 10½ inch reel size

C. *Disc Drive*

Mini's 10 million character disc drive is used for on-line, random access data storage. The drive's main features include:

- 2400 RPM rotation speed
- 200K characters/second transfer rate
- 35 millisecond average access time

- 12.5 millisecond average rotation delay
- 400 cylinders per disc
- 0.3 micron positive air filtration

D. *Matrix Printer*

The Mini Matrix printer is a modularly-designed, bi-directional printer used to print reports and other documents. Within the Reasonable computer system, it can be utilized either as a remote data output station or as the main system printer. Its main features include:

- 165 character per second, bi-directional print speed
- 132 character length line
- 6 lines per inch spacing
- 96 characters ASCII subset
- 7x9 dot matrix (10 point size) character format
- Special double width character format
- 320 character data buffer

E. *Cathode Ray Tube Terminal ("CRT")*

Mini's Prism CRT is a microprocessor based high-speed interactive communications terminal that is also used as the system console. It transmits and displays information in a conversational mode. Special features include:

- Standard alphanumerics teletypewriter layout, plus screen erase, backspace, repeat and control keys
- 12 inch diagonal display
- 24 lines of data
- 80 characters per line
- 64 ASCII character set formed by 5x7 dot matrix
- 50 frames/second refresh rate synchronized to power line
- 110 to 9600 baud rates communications interface
- Standard EIA RS-232c printer interface

THE SYSTEMS

The computer software systems to be purchased by the Partnership (the "Systems") were designed, developed and manufactured by Special, Inc. ("Special"), which is a privately owned and operated corporation.

The Software Systems to be purchased by the Partnership are as follows:

Duplicating Machines and Parts Distributor
Auto Parts Distributor
Hobby Distributor
Machine Parts Distributor
Employment Agency Billing System
Metal Distributor
Liquor Distributor
Marine Parts Distributor
Route Accounting System
Dress Manufacturer
Film Processing System
Real Estate Management
Textile Converter
Business Forms Manufacturer
Meat Distributor
Wire and Cable Distributor
Industrial Chemical Distributor
Metal Forging System
Financial Management Information
Paper Manufacturer
Plumbing Supply Distributor
Medical Systems
Job Shop Manufacturing System
Electronics Parts Distribution System
Commodity Distribution System
Picture Frame and Molding Manufacturer/Distributor
Commercial Work Uniform Rental System
Mortgage, Title and Escrow System
Home and Commercial Heating Contractor

There is an appraisal of each of the Software Systems. These appraisals are rendered to the General Partner and the appraiser will be compensated from the funds derived from the purchase of the units offered hereby.

Special specializes in the development and marketing of comprehensive mini-computer systems for selected industries. By concentrating on specific markets, Special has attempted to develop effective programs that meet the needs of particular industries. Included among the Software systems Special has developed are packages for industries as diverse as apparel manufacturing, textile mills, electrical and electronic parts distribution.

The Software systems developed by Special are primarily designed for the first-time user; those without prior computer experience. Although this market has the greatest potential for software sales, it requires special design and programming techniques to make the Software systems self-explanatory and simple to maintain. This is accomplished by using data base management concepts combined with an easily used report generator for information retrieval and display. Special has developed Software systems for a variety of hardware including Mini.

The Partnership will acquire the following with respect to each Software System it purchases:

1. Operator Instructions;
2. File Layouts;
3. Flow Charts;
4. Narrative-type Descriptions of each Sub-Program Function;
5. Detail Coding (Extensive Basic); and
6. Operating System Manuals.

The Partnership will be required to represent that each Software System will be used only in the designated territory. Special will not sell to others any Software System for use in such territory which has previously been sold without the written consent of the owner thereof. There can be no assurance, however, that other parties have not developed or will not develop a system for a similar purpose which does or will compete with the Software System. Each Software System contains one or more programs and applications that are utilized by other Software Systems although no two (2) Software Systems are the same.

The Software Systems have been developed to be used in conjunction with a Mini Reasonable Computer. In the event that the Partnership desires to adapt the Software Systems to a different configuration, it will have to expend an additional substantial sum. To the extent that the foregoing computers become obsolete, outmoded, uneconomical or unavailable, the value of the Software Systems will be adversely affected unless they can be adapted to new computer hardware.

A prospective purchaser is advised to carefully examine the market potential of the territory in which the Software Systems can be commercially exploited, as well as the Software Systems themselves. Upon request, Special will provide computer facilities in the New York City Metropolitan area to a prospective purchaser, or his advisor, to operate the Software Systems through a computer and carefully examine the contents.

The Partnership will not share in any revenues received, or expenses incurred, by any other purchasers of any Systems, or purchase price paid by the Partnership to Systems Corporation will be expended or utilized for the benefit of the Partnership.

SUMMARY OF PROGRAM

Each unit of investment will consist of a limited partnership interest. There will be 15 units at *$32,000 per unit.* The purchase price of a unit is payable $20,000 upon the purchase of a unit and the remaining $12,000 will be represented by the Purchaser's twelve (12%) percent promissory note, payable in four (4) equal installments on the 1st days of February, May, August and November, Year Two. Interest on the note will not accrue prior to the purchase by the Partnership of the computer hardware and software described herein. The payment of such note shall be secured by the unit.

Units to be offered hereby will be offered in reliance upon Section 4(2) private offering exemption from the registration requirements of the Securities Act of 1933, as amended, and/or Rule 146 and the filing requirements thereunder as promulgated by the "SEC" pursuant to said act and upon the appropriate state offering registration exemption.

The General Partner of the Partnership may pay commissions not exceeding ten (10%) percent of the offering price of the Units.

The Service has indicated an intention to scrutinize leveraged transactions and it is expected that the Service will challenge the tax treatment adopted by the Partnership and/or the valuation of the systems as determined by the appraisals. Should such challenge be made, and should the Service be successful, the Partnership, as a result, will be adversely affected and will lose the tax benefits associated with the purchase of the Systems. Any such disallowance by the Service would most likely arise in connection with the audit of a tax return. The cost of any litigation regarding the challenge or disallowance will be borne by the Partnership.

Among the provisions of the Revenue Act of 1978 (the "Act") which apply to taxable years after December 31, 1978, is the extension of the "At Risk" rules to corporations that meet the stock ownership requirements of Code Section 542(a)(2); i.e., generally, corporations with respect to which more than fifty (50%) percent of the stock is owned by or for five (5) or fewer individuals.

Any income allocated to an investor, whether or not represented by distributions from the Partnership, will be subject to taxation at the highest federal tax rates. An individual who invests with funds that constitute personal service income available for the fifty (50%) percent maximum tax rate would therefore experience adverse tax effects attributable to such differential, which may eliminate the anticipated tax benefits of the investment.

Tax Factors

The Partnership intends to use the Class Life Asset Depreciation Range method of depreciation, and to depreciate its Systems on a straight line basis over seven (7) years in accordance with the regulation under Section 167 of the Internal Revenue Code. The Partnership anticipates that an investment tax credit of approximately $800,000 in Year One, based upon the value set forth in the appraisal, will be available to the Partners. The Partnership's special tax counsel has agreed to represent the Partnership at all levels of examination and appeal within the Internal Revenue Service and through the Tax Court. All of such counsel's professional fees for such representation shall be paid from the proceeds of this offering.

The General Partner

The General Partner will receive a fee in the amount of $48,000. In addition, the General Partner will receive the sum of $48,000 which will be available to be paid for organizational expenses and to others as commissions for their efforts in assisting him in the sale of Units. To the extent that such commissions are less than that amount, and the organizational expenses incurred are less, the General Partner shall be entitled to retain the balance as additional compensation. The General Partner will also receive a fee of 20% of any net proceeds received by the Partnership from the commercial exploitation of the Systems.

The Partnership

The General Partner will contribute $100. Deductions, losses and revenues will be allocated to each Partner in accordance with the ratio of his respective contribution to the capital of the Partnership.

Application of Proceeds

The proceeds from the sale of the units will be $480,000. It is intended that such proceeds will be expended substantially as follows during Year One:

Purchase of the following:	$317,500 (1) (2)

1. Central Processing Unit ("CPU")
2. Tape Drive
3. Disc Drive
4. Matrix Printer
5. Cathode Ray Tube Terminal ("CRT")
6. Computer Software Systems.

Sales Commissions	$ 48,000
Compensation of General Partner	$ 48,000
Appraisal Fee	$ 5,000
Professional Fees	$ 20,000
Printing, Filing and Miscellaneous	$ 2,800
Advertising and Promotion	$ 20,000
Working Capital	$ 18,700
TOTAL:	$480,000

(1) Includes assignment of promissory notes of limited partners in the aggregate amount of $180,000 to Hardware-Software Systems Corporation, which are due in four (4) equal installments in Year Two.

(2) Does not include the execution by the Partnership of a non-recourse note of $7,782,500, which is part of the purchase price which includes $100,000 for an exclusive license.

BENEFITS OF A HARDWARE-SOFTWARE COMPUTER PROGRAM

Deductions and losses of the Partnership, as well as revenues, profits and distributions, will be allocated to the Partners in accordance with the ratios of their respective contributions to the Partnership capital. Thus, the Limited Partners who are subscribing to the units in the aggregate amount of $480,000, will be allocated substantially all of such amounts, and the General Partner, who is contributing $100 to Partnership capital, will be allocated less than of 3/100ths of 196 thereof. All profits and losses will be determined in accordance with the accounting methods followed by the Partnership for federal income tax purposes.

RISKS OF A HARDWARE-SOFTWARE COMPUTER PROGRAM

A. *Competition in the Computer Program Industry*

Due to the highly competitive nature of the computer industry, in both the hardware and software categories, the profit potential of a System is subject to a high degree of risk. The Software Systems will be competing with programs developed by other companies, many of which possess substantially greater financial resources and experience than Special. As noted above, the programs embodied in the Software Systems are designed exclusively for use in conjunction with specified computer hardware and the commercial success of the Software Systems will depend, in part, on the availability, price and quality of the Hardware in the industries for which the Software Systems were designed. The Partnership has no way of measuring the probable success or failure of the Hardware and the Software Systems in competing with other computers and programs now or hereafter available. It is possible that other computer languages may be developed which are directly or indirectly competitive and which could render present language obsolete.

B. *Marketing and Promotion*

1. *General*

Commercial use of any of the Software Systems is dependent, among other things, on the ability of the Partnership or its distributor to compete actively and to expend the time, money and energy necessary to maximize the product's potential. There is no assurance that the Partnership will be successful in marketing or distributing the Software Systems.

Each System is designed exclusively for a specialized use in conjunction with a certain type of computer, utilizing the extended DATA/BASIC language. Since each Software System can be utilized in only the designated territory, a prospective purchaser should satisfy himself of the availability of such type of computer in that territory.

2. *Technological Changes - Obsolescence*

Computer technology (both hardware and software) is highly competitive, and technological changes occur at a rapid rate. The risk of obsolescence of any program included in the Systems or the Hardware with respect to which it was intended to function is very high. Further, the cost of entry into competition with any given computer program is relatively low. Thus, an individual or company with substantially few assets could effectively compete with the Software Systems.

3. *Unauthorized Use*

It is difficult and expensive to detect unauthorized "pirating" of programs within the Software Systems, and such unauthorized actions may adversely affect the competitive position of the Software Systems.

C. *Foreclosure*

Payment of the Note will be secured by all of the Partnership's right, title and interest in the Hardware and the Software Systems. If income generated by the Software Systems is insufficient to pay the Note in full, the holder of the Note may foreclose on the Hardware and the Software Systems under the

Security Agreement. The Partnership would thereby lose all of its interest in and to the Hardware and the Software Systems and would realize income measured by the difference between the unpaid debt and its then current basis in the Hardware and the Systems. In such event, the Partnership would likely incur certain income tax liabilities. Furthermore, a part of the depreciation taken on the Hardware and the Software Systems would be "recaptured" and taxed as ordinary income upon the sale or disposition of the Systems by the Partnership, including foreclosure. In the event a Limited Partner defaults on the payment of his Promissory Note, his interest in the Limited Partnership which has been pledged to secure such payment will be forfeited. In that event, such Limited Partner will realize adverse tax consequences through recapture of depreciation and investment tax credit.

D. *Tax Factors*

1. The Service has indicated an intention to scrutinize leveraged transactions and it is expected that the Service will challenge the tax treatment adopted by the Partnership and/or the valuation of the Systems as determined by the appraisals. Should such challenge be made, and should the Service be successful, the Partnership, as a result, will be adversely affected and will lose the tax benefits associated with the purchase of the Systems. Any such disallowance by the Service would most likely arise in connection with the audit of a tax return. The cost of any litigation regarding the challenge or disallowance will be borne by the Partnership.

2. Any Partnership revenues which may be retained in anticipation of future expenses are taken into account at the end of each tax year for income tax purposes. Consequently, a Limited Partner may have to report and pay tax on income not distributed to him.

3. There is a substantial risk that the Service will contend that the fair market value of the Systems is less than the total purchase price (comprised of cash payments, recourse and nonrecourse notes). There is no guarantee that the Service will not be successful in this contention. If the Service is successful, then the basis for depreciation and investment tax credit would be

decreased, and in turn, the depreciation and investment tax credit allowed would also be decreased. Interest payments on that portion of the Note in excess of the fair market value would also be disallowed. The appraiser of the Systems was chosen by the seller of the Systems and there has been no confirmation of the appraiser's credentials or accuracy of the appraisal.

E. *Transferability of Units*

There will be no public market for the units. In addition, units may only be transferred with the consent of the General Partner.

F. *Dissolution of the Partnership*

In the event of the death or ineligibility of a sole General Partner, the Partnership will thereupon be dissolved. In such event, the Partnership may be deemed to have disposed of the Systems and may be subject to a recapture of the investment credit. In order to prevent the foregoing, the General Partner intends to recommend the appointment of one or more corporate general partners. Any such additional general partners cannot hold such position until the Agreement of Limited Partnership is amended in accordance with its terms.

TAX ASPECTS OF A HARDWARE-SOFTWARE COMPUTER PROGRAM

a. *Methods of Depreciation*

As is generally the case with property: (i) used in a trade or business; or (ii) held for the production of income, a depreciation deduction should be allowed over the useful lives of the Hardware and the Systems. If the Systems constitute new, tangible personal property, the cost (less estimated salvage value where appropriate) of each such asset may be depreciated by using an accelerated method of depreciation as set forth in Code Section 167(b), including, but not limited to, the "declining balance" or "sum-of-the-years-digits" methods. In addition, the Partnership may, under certain circumstances, claim additional first year depreciation if the useful life of the Systems exceeds the requisite number of years.

The Partnership's allowable depreciation deductions with respect to the Hardware and the Systems are determined by its "basis" (i.e., cost) in such assets. Both the Service and the courts have recognized that non-recourse indebtedness may be included in the basis of property although the Service has recently indicated that non-recourse indebtedness may not be includible for depreciation purposes. However, the Service and some courts have stated that a taxpayer's basis will not include a non-recourse debt if the purchase price exceeds the fair market value of the asset purchased. If such excess does exist in the case of the Hardware and the Systems, part or all of the non-recourse debt might be excluded in determining the Partnership's depreciable basis for the assets, and the anticipated depreciation deductions would be reduced. The Service may challenge depreciation deductions, investment tax credits or other items by attacking the appraised value of the Hardware and the Systems by trying to show that there was no valid basis for such valuation. It is also noted that the Service may challenge the useful life and salvage value utilized by the Partnership in computing depreciation deductions, though, under certain circumstances, it is possible to reduce or entirely eliminate salvage value as a consideration.

The declining balance and sum-of-the-years-digits methods may be employed where the assets have a useful life of three (3) years or more. The Partnership may elect to change from such methods to the straight line method.

b. *Investment Tax Credit*

With certain limitations, a taxpayer is entitled to a 10% investment tax credit based on the cost of depreciable tangible personal property placed in service during the tax year.

The useful life and cost of property for investment tax credit purposes must be the same as that used in computing the allowance for depreciation. If the qualified assets have a useful life of less than three (3) years, no credit will be available; if the useful life is at least three (3) years but less than five (5) years, one-third (1/3rd) of the full credit will be allowed; between five (5) and seven (7) years, two-thirds (2/3rds) of the full credit will be allowed; and if the assets have a useful life of at least seven (7) years, a full credit will be allowed. There can be no assurance that the Service will not challenge the useful life and cost (including the inclusion of the non-recourse note as basis) utilized by the Partnership. Such a challenge, if successful, could result in a disallowance of all or a portion of the investment tax credit.

c. *License*

It may be argued by the Service that a greater portion of the purchase price is allocable to the license fee. Under such a theory, the cash downpayment and recourse note, or a portion thereof, could be characterized as a minimum license fee, and subsequent payments on the note would be characterized as additional license fees.

The economic interests and rights of the parties appear to conform to a theory of a license arrangement. The seller will have no right to any additional payments after the mortgage debt has been paid and if the Systems should develop into a success, the seller will not share in that success. However, it might be asserted that after the debt has been paid in full, the purchaser is granted a perpetual license without any further consideration. The rights and duties of the parties under the Purchase Agreement support the inference of a license since a portion of the non-recourse note has been allocated to a license fee. Normally, when a license is granted, even if it is perpetual, the licensor retains valuable rights in that which is licensed, and, therefore, imposes certain performance requirements on the licensee to protect such rights. These performance conditions may relate to the manner of exploitation of licensed matter, minimum performance standards, etc. These rights exist both while there remains an unpaid balance on the note and after the note is paid in full.

In view of the transfer of all of the seller's rights to the Systems but its right to direct or control the manner of exploitation of the Systems through the territorial limitation, the transaction between the seller and the purchaser does constitute a license. If the Service takes the position that a greater amount should be allocated to the license and prevails in its view, then to the extent of the additional value placed on the license, the purchaser will be unable to avail himself of the investment tax credit or depreciation on this additional amount. He will, however, be able to amortize the value of the license over the term of the license.

d. *Sale, Exchange or Foreclosure*

1. *Recapture of Depreciation*

All depreciation taken with respect to personal property is subject to recapture under Section 1245. The amount of recapture is equal to the gain realized upon the sale or other disposition of the property up to the amount of depreciation deductions previously taken with respect to the property. Gain that is subject to recapture is treated as ordinary income in the year recognized. That portion of the gain not subject to recapture will be treated as Section 1231 gain.

(a) *Sale of Exchange*

Upon a sale or exchange of the Hardware or the Systems, the purchaser would realize gain to the extent that the amount realized exceeds his basis. Such amount realized will include any unpaid balance on the Note.

(b) *Foreclosure*

If the holder of any lien encumbering the Hardware and the Systems accepts those assets in lieu of foreclosure or in satisfaction of a judgment for the balance of the Note, plus interest, the Partnership will realize a gain equal to the excess of any balance due on the purchase price over the then depreciated cost or basis of the assets. The portion of gain realized upon foreclosure equal to the amount of previously claimed depreciation deductions would be treated as ordinary income. The Partnership, upon foreclosure, will be deemed in receipt of gross income even though it receives no cash with respect to the transaction. However, if there are losses that were suspended by the "at risk" rules, those losses should be allowed at such time as income is realized. Such suspended losses, which would include depreciation and other operating expenses, should generally be at least equal to the gross income realized on such a foreclosure.

The Service may claim a constructive foreclosure has occurred in the event no payments of principal or interest are made for a period of time, or in the absence of actual foreclosure after maturity of the Note. In the event of a constructive foreclosure, the tax consequences attributable to the Partnership would be similar to those occurring upon an actual foreclosure.

2. *Recapture of Investment Tax Credit*

In the event of sale, disposition or foreclosure prior to expiration of the useful life of the Hardware and the Systems, there may be a recapture, in whole or in part, of the investment tax credit previously taken. The amount of such recapture will depend upon the useful life of the assets and the date of sale or disposition. Further, if the assets are used predominantly outside the United States at any time, this may result in recapture or disallowance of the investment tax credit, in whole or in part, depending upon when foreign use occurs.

3. *Economic Consequences*

In the event of foreclosure or constructive foreclosure, it is likely that the net cash proceeds, if any, received by the Partnership upon a sale or other disposition would be significantly less than the income recognized for that year with respect to the transactions. While certain losses that may have been "suspended" by the "at risk" rules should be available to offset income of this nature, it is likely that cash contributions by the Partners would not be recovered.

COMPUTER GRAPHICS SOFTWARE

PLAN OF BUSINESS

General

The Partnership is newly organized and has no substantial business history, assets or staff of employees. Computer was incorporated in 1975 and has been developing and marketing computer graphics software packages on a small scale since that time. The primary business of the Partnership will be to market computer graphics software and to undertake research and development in connection therewith. As its capital contribution, Computer will license on an exclusive basis to the Partnership all of Computer's knowledge and technology related to its computer graphics software packages, and will make available to the partnership its production facilities, equipment and personnel for the development and production of its software packages.

Computer believes that it has designed the Drafting Package to be a computer graphics software package that possesses technological advantages that make it innovative in the market it is directed to, as well as being offered at a price lower than that charged by the manufacturers of computer graphics software offering dissimilar, but technologically comparable, packages. Computer believes that a significant market exists for the Drafting Package and the software packages intended to be developed in the future. The computer graphics software industry is as yet still in its infancy and there is no assurance that the Partnership's development and marketing effort will enable it to capture its intended share of the software market.

Since its inception, Computer has been engaged principally in the development and organizational phase of its business. The marketing of the packages have been carried on only on a small scale since their development. Computer has only recently begun to market the Drafting Package commercially after its having been in the development stage for the last two years. Prior to the development of the software package, the inventor wrote computer graphics software on a custom basis for various companies using different systems of hardware.

Description and Operation of the Drafting and Graphic Post-Processors Packages

The graphics software packages currently offered by Computer are of two types: (i) the first and the initial focus of the Partnership's marketing effort is called the Drafting Package, recently developed by the inventor and in the initial stages of marketing by Computer. The Drafting Package provides a comparatively low-cost, computer aided, two-dimensional drafting system for use with the Terrific 2000 Series Graphics Computing System, which is referred to throughout this material as the "hardware." The Drafting Package is designed for general use by draftsmen, designers and engineers; and (ii) Computer has, for the last three years, offered highly sophisticated and specialized software packages called graphic post-processors ("G.P.P.'s") which also function on equipment manufactured only by Terrific. Graphic Post-Processors read all of the punched holes on the paper or aluminized tape that is used to direct the operation of a numerically controlled machine tool and causes a display or a map of the machine tools drill path to be displayed on a screen. Its value to a user is that it quickly shows precisely all of the operations that the machine tool will perform when the tape is fed into the tool without a time-consuming and therefore expensive trial run cut on a test block of material.

The Drafting Package was designed to allow the operator sitting at the hardware keyboard to perform all of the common graphics operations that are encountered by today's draftsmen. Every line, dimension, notation and line style in common use today is incorporated in the performance of the Drafting Package. It has the potential for increasing the speed, accuracy and uniformity of the draftsman's performance and work product. The microprocessor and plotter supplied by Terrific accomplish all the drawing of pictures, symbols, lettering and notation. The Drafting Package does not require any knowledge of a computer program language. The user works only in the nomenclature of standard drafting symbols. It has been Computer's experience that after an initial orientation period, user operation of training on the Drafting Package has been extremely rapid.

The Terrific hardware used in conjunction with the software packages consists of a desk-top size microprocessor, an 19-inch screen and a variety of peripheral accessories, including plotters and printers. The hardware requires no special environment (no air conditioning, no special humidifier, no special power requirements). The hardware is a standard microprocessor system without modifications. Terrific is a 35 year-old Oregon based company that is currently the world's largest manufacturer of oscilloscopes and precision measurement equipment. They have been manufacturing products in the computer graphics market since 1972 and introduced the hardware used in conjunction with the Drafting Package in 1978. Terrific has sales and service representatives and conjunction facilities throughout the United States and the world.

Computer has had no warranty claims to date on the Drafting Package or various Graphic Post-Processor software packages since their introduction. Computer has incorporated a "source code" in all its software packages that will permit service personnel to transmit corrections, fixes, changes and improvements to the software program via telephone line. The General Partners believe this feature in the software may greatly reduce the cost of warranty service if required.

Marketing

The Partnership plans an aggressive media advertisement program and marketing effort for the Drafting Package and subsequent software packages developed by the Partnership designed to reach management and individuals involved with drafting and drafting operations in any size company. Among other plans in the marketing effort, the following methods are contemplated: (i) A telephone program utilizing WATTS lines and the industrial guides that are available on a state-by-state basis will be used to locate companies and specific departments that are actively seeking, investigating or interested in computer rated drafting situations; (ii) A central tracking system will be utilized to follow all active inquiries from the first reception of literature, through demonstrations to their final decisions, (iii) A follow-up system directly tied to the central tracking system wherein the Partnership will have its own direct field operations people or area managers to assist in closing any contract that may require additional support in the form of a higher level

Partnership management person to reach those higher levels of management in the customer's company to effect the final favorable decision; (iv) A lead generation program that would use either people currently working for the major computer hardware vendors or the group of people within firms who discover a need in their own areas and departments that could make use of the Partnership's software packages; and (v) Local seminars designed to educate interested companies in the ways computer aided drafting is used and how it can increase productivity. Operating hardware/software systems would be available for demonstrations to those attending a seminar. Field installers/customer representatives responsible for ongoing maintenance and servicing of various customer accounts will be provided for on an on-going basis to keep pace with the number of software packages leased.

The Drafting Package is currently being marketed by Computer on the basis of a renewable five-year license for a one time cost of $9,500 for the software package materials. Installation, training, a software support program and options for the Drafting Package are available and are supplied at an additional charge. The software support program offers 12 months of remedial service at a fixed fee per month. The actual Drafting Package contains a source code, a listing, a magnetic tape containing a disc operating program, a flexible disc, a Drafting Package Manual and menu detailing the use of the software. The package also includes a limited 90-day warranty. The Drafting Package license fee is marketed on a pre-hardware system basis; each license fee covers only one single designated hardware system. Additional software packages used by the customer would require the payment of additional license fees for each separate package.

Because the hardware components used in connection with the Drafting Package are all over-the-counter items manufactured by Terrific and require no special modification to be compatible with the Drafting Package, Drafting Package installation does not affect the warranties given by Terrific on their computing systems. It is anticipated that for customers lacking appropriate Terrific hardware the Partnership will offer an entire hardwaresoftware combination by acquiring the hardware directly from Terrific and renting or selling the hardware in turn to the customer. A complete system price covering all Terrific hardware and software would range from $40,000 for the minimum performance features to $80,000 for a complete system with all available options.

Competition

To the best of the knowledge of the General Partners, no other company in the United States currently offers a specific two-dimensional drafting package comparable to the Drafting Package that is being marketed toward the drafting-engineering environment in the Drafting Package's price range. The General Partners know of only two companies that actually merchandise, on a small scale, computer graphics software packages technologically comparable to the Drafting Package and compatible with Terrific hardware that are directed toward the printed circuit electrical schematic industries and the construction industry. The minimum software package cost from these two companies is three to six times higher than the basic Drafting Package. However, there can be no assurance that other companies with greater financial resources, national facilities and greater reputations in the marketplace will not develop and market software packages that directly compete with the Drafting Package and the future software packages marketed by the Partnership.

It is the opinion of the General Partners that because of the unique educational background, expertise and talents of the inventor, the prospect of an equivalent software package being developed by a competitor is unlikely without great financial expenditure and the effort of a large programming staff.

Research and Development

Computer has pursued a program of research, development and testing of both the Drafting Package and various Graphic Post-Processor packages preliminary to marketing the packages commercially, and the Partnership expects to carry on the same program on a much larger scale depending on the proceeds of the offering. The research and development of different software packages would include the conceptual formulation and the design and testing of prototypes and would take place almost exclusively in the Partnership's facilities. The software package development would initially start with the inventor or someone of similar competence and experience creating a list of computer instructions which causes a computer drafting system to register command inputs, process that information into displays on a screen, and in turn transfer the displays on a screen to be received and printed out to a mechanical pen and ink plotter. This stage of development in a software package could be termed the package "lay-out" stage and would normally encompass from 60% to 80% of the personnel time devoted to the development of any particular software package. Once the entire running program for a software package has been assembled with all of its operative sub-routines, it would then be turned over to the manager of software for the partnership, who will be responsible for running the program through an exhaustive series of tests. Concurrently, all routines would be examined, a derivative set of notes and operational procedures developed. These would eventually form the operation's manual and provide specific test set-up procedures and de-bug cycles for that particular package. At this point, the package would then be available for license.

It is presently contemplated that the Partnership's software development could be directed and channeled along four general lines: (i) development of other software packages offering different functions and performance, such as a facilities layout package designed to be used by any business in laying out their facilities with such things as water, electrical and air conditioning components and all incidentals relative to structures and surrounding grounds, and an electrical schematic package for electrical layout and design applications; (ii) development of existing and future software packages to be compatible with more than one manufacturer's hardware; (iii) development of existing and future software packages to function in connection with a centralized mini-computer to provide a software database management and communication system (known in the trade as "networking") involving many separate stations using a software package connected to a central mini-computer; and (iv) development of software packages more sophisticated than Computer's current Graphic Post-Processors aimed toward the numerical control machine tool market to allow a user to directly control or steer a numerically controlled machine tool whether human or robot operated. The Partnership's efforts will be directed along the foregoing lines to the extent and degree permitted by the proceeds obtained from this offering and the results of its marketing effort. All software development will either be performed by or under the direct supervision of the inventor.

Property and Equipment

Computer's present business, because of its small size, is being operated out of the inventor's personal residence. This property is a ranch-type house, the full basement of which is directed or utilized by Computer for development and demonstration purposes of Computer products. Upon sale of the minimum number of Units, the Partnership's offices, demonstration facilities and main research and development operations will be conducted at a new facility proposed to be located in Michigan. It is contemplated that the Partnership will lease space in a building that would allow for further expansion of operations as the level of Partnership business expands. The Partnership will continue to use a portion of the inventor's residence as a small research and development facility and will pay its proportionate share of the inventor's utilities for the use thereof.

The Partnership also plans to reimburse Computer for the lease of various computer hardware systems, the number of which will be determined by the amount of proceeds of this offering, but at the minimum, will include two complete Terrific hardware systems. One system would be used for both demonstration and research and development work and the other solely for research and development.

Copyrights and Trademarks

United States Copyright protection has been filed for the Drafting Package manual given to licensees of the Drafting Package. The Partnership also plans to copyright the Drafting Package program as well. To prevent unauthorized duplication and/or marketing of the Partnership's software packages, a special concealed coding system has been developed by Computer to specifically identify each software package licensed by the Partnership. The code will be known and identifiable only to Partnership's personnel. If any program package is duplicated by either an authorized customer or in the possession of a non authorized person, the Partnership's personnel will be able to determine the identity of the original licensee of the package.

Computer holds no registered trademarks. Computer claims a common law trademark on its name.

THE OFFERING

The offerors, Computer Corporation, and the Partnership offer securities of both the Corporation and the Partnership in units ("Units"), each Unit consisting of 20 shares of common stock, par value \$.01 per share (each share being hereinafter referred to as a "Share") and a \$9,500 limited partnership interest ("Interest"). The offering price is \$10,000 per Unit. The offering is made on either of two bases: (i) fifteen (15) Unit Combinations, each Unit Combination consisting of fifteen (15) Units for a purchase price of \$150,000 with the purchase price payable on a partially deferred basis as hereinafter described, and (ii) thirty-five (35) individual Units offered for a cash purchase price of \$10,000.

Each Unit Combination will be sold on a deferred payment basis, with \$25,001 of the purchase price payable in cash or check at the date of subscription with the balance being payable at such time by delivery of four promissory notes for \$25,000 each and one promissory note for \$24,999, the first falling due on March 29, Year Two and the remaining four in one year intervals thereafter, the last note to come due being the note for \$24,999. The promissory notes must be secured by a \$124,999 letter of credit from a bank acceptable to the Offerors. Aside from the fifteen (15) Unit Combinations, each individual Unit will be sold for \$10,000 payable in cash or check on the date of subscription.

USE OF PROCEEDS

The maximum and minimum net proceeds of this offering to the Offerors, after deduction of maximum broker-dealer sales commissions, finder's fees and estimated expenses, are as follows:

	Maximum	Minimum
Proceeds of Offering	\$2,600,000	\$350,000
Less: Assumed Selling Broker's Commissions and Finder's Fees for all Units	260,000	35,000
Net Proceeds to Corporation	117,000	15,750
Capital Contribution to Partnership	2,223,000	299,250
Organizational Expenses	43,000	43,000
Net Proceeds to Partnership	\$2,180,000	\$256,250

The Corporation

The following table sets forth the Corporation's capitalization at March 30, Year 1 and as adjusted to reflect the sale of the maximum and minimum number of Units offered hereunder, after deduction of the maximum brokerage commissions and finder's fees:

	March 30, Year One	As Adjusted Maximum Proceeds	As Adjusted Minimum Proceeds
Common Stock, .01 par value, 4 million authorized, 39,000 issued and outstanding as of March 30, Year One; 39,300 shares will be issued and outstanding if the mininum number of Units are sold, and 44,200 shares will be issued and outstanding if the maximum number of Units are sold.	$ 390	$ 442	$ 393
Preferred Stock $.01 par value, 1 million shares authorized, 0 shares issued	-0-	-0-	-0-
Additional paid in capital	1,310	118,258	17,057
Retained Earnings	12,734	12,734	12,734
Total Shareholder Equity	$14,434	$131,434	$30,184
Equity per Share	$ 0.37	$ 2.97	$ 0.77

The General Partners have agreed to provide for the right to incorporate the Limited Partnership into Computer Corporation at any time in the event that: (i) Computer Corporation secures a tentative firm commitment underwriting agreement for the public offering of its common stock; and (ii) immediately after such incorporation, all present Limited Partners hold the maximum percentage of the common stock of Computer Corporation provided for in the Limited Partnership Agreement.

General Partners' Right to Incorporate and Reorganize. The General Partners have the exclusive right to incorporate the Partnership if they determine it to be in the best interest of the Partnership's business. No such incorporation may have the effect of issuing shares of stock with dividend rights at the time of the issuance that would alter the then rights of the Partners inter se under the Agreement regarding their relative profit-sharing percentages. The Agreement provides for a fixed equity interest in the Corporation, or in any successor or transferee corporation, which must be received by the Limited Partners.

The following chart indicates the minimum percentages of stock ownership which the Limited Partners must receive on any such incorporation or reorganization. Any other variation of the rights of Partners inter se that is deemed reasonably appropriate by the General Partners, in their sole discretion, may be affected by such incorporation, but such incorporation shall be tax free to the Partners to the maximum extent possible and the aggregate book value of the shares of stock issued to Partners shall equal the aggregate of all Partners' Equity Accounts at the time of incorporation. Any other form of incorporation of all or a portion of the Partnership business or reorganization on any terms and conditions with any tax results may be effected pursuant to both the majority vote of the General Partners and consent of at least a majority in Partnership interest of the then holders of all the then Limited Partners Interests, consenting as one aggregate class.

Amounts paid in cash to the Limited Partners	Required to have this percentage of common stock in Computer Corporation after any such incorporation (said percentage to include amounts of stock already owned by the Limited Partners before such incorporation).
Paid an amount equal to at least one (1) time their Capital Contributions but less than two (2) times their Capital Contributions	Not less than 40%

Paid an amount greater than two (2) times their Capital Contributions, but less than three (3) times that amount	Not less than 36%
Paid an amount greater than three (3) times their Capital Contributions, but less than four (4) times that amount	Not less than 32%
Paid an amount greater than four (4) times their Capital Contributions, but less than five (5) times that amount	Not less than 28%
Paid an amount greater than five (5) times their Capital Contributions, but less than six (6) times that amount	Not less than 24%
Paid an amount greater than six (6) times their Capital Contributions.	Not less than 20%

No such incorporation may take place until the Limited Partners have received aggregate cash distributions equal to the aggregate capital contributions of all present Limited Partners, including those made by promissory notes, even though such notes may not have become due or been paid. Should less than the maximum amount of Units offered be sold, the guaranteed percentage amounts shall be reduced by multiplying each of the aforesaid percentage amounts by the fraction obtained by dividing the maximum number of Units offered into the actual number of Units sold thereunder.

Retirement of Interests. The General Partners may, from time to time, in their sole discretion, retire a Limited Partner for any good faith reason, either voluntarily or involuntarily on the part of the retired Limited Partner, but such involuntary retirement shall only be effected if the General Partners determine that the best business interests of the Partnership shall be be served by the retirement of a Limited Partner. In the case of a voluntary retirement, such Limited Partner must request the same by notice to the General Partners, who, in their sole discretion, may grant such request if such voluntary retirement is not deemed to have an adverse effect upon the present or reasonably foreseeable debt service expenses and requirements of the Partnership. The General Partners are under no obligation to grant any such request and the General Partners shall not be obligated to expend time, effort or incur expenses in order to determine whether any such retirement can or should be made. The General Partners, in their sole discretion, shall determine the amount to be received upon such redemption, as well as the terms and conditions of any pay-out. No such retirement shall give rise to rights in other Partners to a pro rata retirement of any of their Partnership Interests.

Term and Dissolution. The Partnership will continue until March 19, Year Twenty, but may be terminated at an earlier date if certain contingencies occur.

PROJECTION OF PARTNERSHIP TAXABLE INCOME OR LOSS

For the period from May 1, Year One through December 31, Year Six

	May 1, Year One through December 31, Year One	Year Ending December 21,				
		Year Two	Year Three	Year Four	Year Five	Year Six
REVENUES						
Sales	$ 130,000	$3,360,000	$7,010,000	$19,020,000	$40,770,000	$70,830,000
EXPENSES						
Marketing and administrative expenses	1,365,000	3,711,000	5,301,000	10,563,000	20,134,000	34,918,000
Interest	48,000	181,000	170,000	112,000	55,000	12,000
Management fee	100,000	150,000	150,000	3,553,000	10,085,000	17,591,000
Amortization of organizational costs	2,000	3,000	3,000	3,000	3,000	1,000
	1,515,000	4,045,000	5,624,000	14,231,000	30,277,000	52,522,000
Projected partnership taxable income or (loss)	$(1,385,000)	$ (685,000)	$1,386,000	$ 4,789,000	$10,493,000	$18,308,000

PROJECTION OF PARTNERSHIP CASH FLOW

For the period from May 1, Year One through December 31, Year Six

	May 1, Year One through December 31, Year One	Year ending December 31,				
		Year Two	Year Three	Year Four	Year Five	Year Six
CASH RECEIPTS						
Partners' Capital contributions	$ 689,000	$ 356,000	$ 356,000	$ 356,000	$ 356,000	$ 357,000
Revenues	130,000	3,360,000	7,010,000	19,020,000	40,770,000	70,830,000
Proceeds from loan financing	796,000	361,000	-	-	-	-
	1,615,000	4,077,000	7,366,000	19,376,000	41,126,000	71,187,000
CASH DISBURSEMENTS						
Marketing and administrative expenses	1,365,000	3,711,000	5,301,000	10,563,000	20,134,000	34,918,000
Interest	48,000	181,000	170,000	112,000	55,000	12,000
Management fee	100,000	150,000	150,000	3,553,000	10,085,000	17,591,000
Loan principal repayment	-	-	320,000	320,000	320,000	197,000
Organizational costs	15,000	-	-	-	-	-
Syndication costs	18,000	-	-	-	-	-
Broker's commissions	69,000	35,000	36,000	35,000	36,000	36,000
	1,615,000	4,077,000	5,977,000	14,583,000	30,630,000	52,754,000
Projected cash distributed to partners	$ -	$ -	$1,389,000	$ 4,793,000	$10,496,000	$18,433,000

PROJECTION OF CASH FLOW TO LIMITED PARTNERS

For the period from May 1, Year One through December 31, Year Six

	Taxable income (loss) allocated to limited partners	TaxTax savings (liability)	Investment tax credit (recapture)	Cash flow to limited partners	Net tax savings (liability) investment tax credit (recapture) and cash flow Period	Cumulative
50% tax bracket						
May 1, Year One through Dec. 31, Year One	$ (1,371,000)	$ 686,000	$65,000	$ -	$ 751,000	$ 751,000
Year ending December 31,						
Year Two	(678,000)	339,000	30,000	-	369,000	1,120,000
Year Three	1,372,000	(686,000)	1,000	1,375,000	690,000	1,810,000
Year Four	4,741,000	(2,317,000)	8,000	4,745,000	2,382,000	4,192,000
Year Five	6,497,000	(3,248,000)	(46,000)	6,650,000	3,356,000	7,548,000
Year Six	1,831,000	(916,000)	3,000	1,843,000	930,000	8,478,000
	$12,392,000	$(6,196,000)	$61,000	$14,613,000		
60% tax bracket						
May 1, Year One through Dec. 31, Year One	$ (1,371,000)	$ 823,000	$65,000	$ -	$ 888,000	$ 888,000
Year ending December 31,						
Year Two	(678,000)	407,000	30,000	-	437,000	1,325,000
Year Three	1,372,000	(823,000)	1,000	1,375,000	553,000	1,878,000
Year Four	4,741,000	(2,845,000)	8,000	4,745,000	1,908,000	3,786,000
Year Five	6,497,000	(3,898,000)	(46,000)	6,650,000	2,706,000	6,492,000
Year Six	1,831,000	(1,099,000)	3,000	1,843,000	747,000	7,239,000
	$12,392,000	$(7,435,000)	$61,000	$14,613,000		
70% tax bracket						
May 1, Year One through Dec. 31, Year One	$ (1,371,000)	$ 960,000	$65,000	$ -	$1,025,000	$1,025,000
Year ending December 31,						
Year Two	(678,000)	475,000	30,000	-	505,000	1,530,000
Year Three	1,372,000	(960,000)	1,000	1,375,000	416,000	1,946,000
Year Four	4,741,000	(3,319,000)	8,000	4,745,000	1,434,000	3,380,000
Year Five	6,497,000	(4,548,000)	(46,000)	6,650,000	2,056,000	5,436,000
Year Six	1,831,000	(1,282,000)	3,000	1,843,000	564,000	6,000,000
	$12,392,000	$(8,674,000)	$61,000	$14,613,000		

PROJECTION OF BENEFIT TO PURCHASER OF ONE COMBINATION UNIT
For the period from May 1, Year One through December 31, Year Six

	Contri-bution	Taxable income (loss)	Tax savings (liability)	Invest-ment tax credit (re-capture)	Cash	Net tax savings (liability) invest. tax credit (recap.) & cash flow	Annual net cash (invest-ment) benefit	Cumula-tive net cash (invest-ment) benefit
50% tax bracket								
May 1, Year One through Dec. 31, Year One	$ 25,001	$ (79,096)	$ 39,548	$3,750	$ -	$ 43,298	$ 18,297	$ 18,297
Year ending Dec. 31,								
Year Two	25,000	(39,115)	19,558	1,731	-	21,289	(3,711)	14,586
Year Three	25,000	79,154	(39,577)	58	79,327	39,808	14,808	29,394
Year Four	25,000	273,519	(136,760)	462	273,750	137,452	112,452	141,846
Year Five	25,000	374,827	(187,414)	(2,654)	383,654	193,586	168,586	310,432
Year Six	24,999	105,634	(52,817)	172	106,327	53,682	28,683	339,115
	$150,000	$714,923	$(357,462)	$3,519	$843,058	$489,115		
60% tax bracket								
May 1, Year One through Dec. 31, Year One	$ 25,001	$ (79,096)	$(47,458)	$3,750	$ -	$ 51,208	$ 26,207	$ 26,207
Year ending Dec. 31,								
Year Two	25,000	(39,115)	23,469	1,731	-	25,200	200	26,407
Year Three	25,000	79,154	47,492	58	79,327	31,893	6,893	33,300
Year Four	25,000	273,519	(164,111)	462	273,750	110,101	85,101	118,401
Year Five	25,000	374,827	(224,896)	(2,654)	383,654	156,104	131,104	249,505
Year Six	24,999	105,634	(63,380)	172	106,327	43,119	18,120	267,625
	$150,000	$714,923	$(428,952)	$3,519	$843,058	$417,625		
70% tax bracket								
May 1, Year One through Dec. 31, Year One	$ 25,001	$ (79,096)	$ 55,367	$3,750	$ -	$ 59,117	$ 34,116	$ 34,116
Year ending Dec. 31,								
Year Two	25,000	(39,115)	27,381	1,731	-	29,112	4,112	38,228
Year Three	25,000	79,154	(55,408)	58	79,327	23,977	(1,023)	37,205
Year Four	25,000	273,519	(191,463)	462	273,750	82,749	57,749	94,954
Year Five	25,000	374,827	(262,379)	(2,654)	383,654	118,621	93,621	188,575
Year Six	24,999	105,634	(73,944)	172	106,327	32,555	7,556	196,131
	$150,000	$714,923	$(500,446)	$3,519	$843,058	$346,131		

PROJECTION OF BENEFIT TO PURCHASER OF ONE INDIVIDUAL UNIT

For the period from May 1, Year One through December 31, Year Six

	Contribution	Taxable income (loss)	Tax savings (liability)	Investment tax credit (recapture)	Cash	Net tax savings (liability invest. tax credit (recap.) & cash flow	Annual net cash (investment) benefit	Cumulative net cash (investment) benefit
50% tax bracket								
May 1, Year One through Dec. 31, Year One	$10,000	$ (5,273)	$ 2,637	$250	$ -	$ 2,887	$ (7,113)	$ (7,113)
Year ending Dec. 31,								
Year Two	-	(2,608)	1,304	115	-	1,419	1,419	(5,694)
Year Three	-	5,277	(2,639)	4	5,289	2,654	2,654	(3,040)
Year Four	-	18,235	(9,118)	31	18,250	9,163	9,163	6,123
Year Five	-	24,988	(12,494)	(177)	25,577	12,906	12,906	19,029
Year Six	-	7,042	(3,521)	12	7,088	3,579	3,579	22,608
	$10,000	$47,661	$(23,831)	$235	$56,204	$32,608		
60% tax bracket								
May 1, Year One through Dec. 31, Year One	$10,000	$ (5,273)	$ 3,164	$250	$ -	$ 3,414	$ (6,586)	$ (6,586)
Year ending Dec. 31,								
Year Two	-	(2,608)	1,565	115	-	1,680	1,680	(4,906)
Year Three	-	5,277	(3,166)	4	5,289	2,127	2,127	(2,779)
Year Four	-	18,235	(10,941)	31	18,250	7,340	7,340	4,561
Year Five	-	24,988	(14,993)	(177)	25,577	10,407	10,407	14,968
Year Six	-	7,042	(4,225)	12	7,088	2,875	2,875	17,843
	$10,000	$47,661	$(28,596)	$235	$56,204	$27,843		
70% tax bracket								
May 1, Year One through Dec. 31, Year One	$10,000	$ (5,273)	$ 3,691	$250	$ -	$ 3,941	$ (6,059)	$ (6,059)
Year ending Dec. 31,								
Year Two	-	(2,608)	1,826	115	-	1,941	1,941	(4,118)
Year Three	-	5,277	(3,694)	4	5,289	1,599	1,599	(2,519)
Year Four	-	18,235	(12,765)	31	18,250	5,516	5,516	2,997
Year Five	-	24,988	(17,492)	(177)	25,577	7,908	7,908	10,905
Year Six	-	7,042	(4,929)	12	7,088	2,171	2,171	13,076
	$10,000	$47,661	$(33,363)	$235	$56,204	$23,076		

BENEFITS OF A COMPUTER GRAPHICS SOFTWARE PROGRAM

Partnership Allocations

Subject to certain deferrals of the Partners' rights in the income, profits, losses, deductions and credits of the Partnership to assure that no Partners sustain a loss in their capital accounts while other Partners earn a profit in their drawing accounts or that on dissolution of the Partnership no Partners are precluded from receiving loss allocations while they have a basis in their Partnership interests while other Partners are allocated a loss that they are precluded from using due to their lack of basis in their Partnership interests, the Limited Partners will be initially allocated, pro rata based on the number of outstanding interests then held by each of them and then outstanding in total, 99% of the Partnership's losses, deductions and credits and (until the aggregate cash distribution to the Limited Partners shall equal five times the amount of the aggregate capital contributions of all Limited Partners) will be allocated 50% of the income, profits and gains resulting from operations of the Partnership, the General Partners will each share equally in and be allocated a 1% permanent interest in all of the aforesaid items and Computer will additionally be specifically allocated 49% of the Partnership's income, profits and gains. Subsequent to the distribution of aggregate cash distributions to the Limited Partners which equal or exceed five times the amount of the aggregate capital contributions of all present Limited Partners, the aforesaid 50% interest of the Limited Partners in the income, profits and gains of the Partnership will be reduced by 45% to 5% and this 45% interest in income, profits and gains shall be transferred and specifically allocated to Computer General Partner.

The General Partners will have, in their sole and exclusive discretion, the option to pay out to Partners the Partnership's net pretax income, if any, computed on the cash as opposed to the accrual basis, which is not required for operations. The General Partners shall use their best efforts to distribute at least sufficient cash to enable the Partners to pay any federal income taxes reasonably anticipated on the Partnership's income. Sufficient cash in this regard shall be deemed to be at least 60% of the Partnership's taxable income computed on the cash basis for any taxable year.

RISKS OF A COMPUTER GRAPHICS SOFTWARE PROGRAM

High Risk Involved in Computer Graphics Software Business. Because the success of the Partnership in marketing operations will be dependent to a large extent on general economic conditions, customer acceptance and business demand for computer graphics software packages, matters over which the Partnership will not have any control, and which are affected by numerous and varied economic and other factors that are extremely difficult or impossible to predict with any degree of accuracy, the securities offered hereunder are speculative and subject to a high degree of risk. Investors should be aware that they may sustain a substantial or total loss of their investment or may receive a return that is substantially below alternate forms of investment.

Risks Inherent in Computer Graphics Software Industry. It is likely that the computer graphics software industry will become more competitive and subject to price erosion in the future as more companies enter the market place and begin offering software packages with different capabilities and over a wide range of prices. The computer hardware that must be used in conjunction with any software system is also subject to rapid technological change which can result in unpredictable hardware and/or software obsolescence. Companies in the software industry must therefore continually improve and innovate already technologically complex products. The costs of keeping abreast of rapid technological innovations may be substantial and any planning misjudgments by the Partnership either in product design or compatibility with certain manufacturers of hardware, might have a material adverse effect on its future profits.

Competition. The General Partners of the Partnership are not aware of any company in the United States offering a specific two-dimensional drafting package comparable to the Drafting Package that directs itself to the particular market place, the drafting-engineering environment, that the marketing effort of the Partnership will be aimed at. The General Partners know of only two companies that actually merchandise, on a small scale, computer graphics software packages technologically comparable with the Drafting Package and compatible with Terrific hardware that are directed toward the printed circuit-electrical schematic industries and the construction industry. The minimum software package cost from these companies is three to six times higher than the cost of the basic Drafting Package now marketed by Computer. However, there can be no assurance that other companies with greater financial resources, national facilities and greater reputations in the marketplace will not develop and market software packages that directly compete with the Drafting Package and the future software packages marketed by the Partnership. The Partnership's ability to compete may be significantly limited by its small initial size, limited resources and lack of an established sales organization.

Uncertain Results of Research and Development Activities. A substantial portion of the proceeds of the offering made hereby will be allocated to an expanded program of research and development, including the proposed development of computer graphics software packages offering performance and capabilities in areas in which Computer has not heretofore offered software. If the Partnership is not successful in its efforts to create new readily marketable software packages, substantial operating losses could be incurred which may exceed income from the Partnership's marketing operations. Furthermore, even if products or processes are developed, a substantial period of time may elapse between the development of such products and their successful commercial exploitation.

Current Dependence on Single Manufacturer of Hardware. The computer graphics software packages currently marketed by Computer are compatible only with the Terrific 2060 Graphics Computing Systems, which limited compatibility requires that prospective purchasers of the current Computer developed software packages possess or make arrangements to buy or lease the appropriate Terrific hardware. Terrific is one of the largest manufacturers of computer graphics hardware in the United States. The Partnership anticipates being able to acquire equipment directly from Terrific on an "original equipment manufacturer" basis and then renting or leasing the entire hardware-software combination to the customer requiring a complete computer graphics system. The Partnership also plans to develop compatible versions of the Drafting Package and future software packages for hardware manufactured by Huge Corporation and Dynamic Corporation to the extent and as permitted by the proceeds of this offering and the results of the marketing effort of the Partnership.

Dependence on Key Personnel. The business of the Partnership and Computer is extremely reliant upon the services of the inventor who will conduct and be in charge of software development and marketing of software packages, respectively. In the event that the inventor's services are unavailable to the Partnership or Computer for any reason, the operations of the Partnership and Computer would be severely damaged. The Partnership and Computer are likely to have a particularly difficult time in finding experienced and adequately trained personnel to replace the aforesaid individuals because of the relatively small number of replacements and the great demand for the services of such persons by other computer software firms. If available at reasonable prices, the Partnership intends to obtain approximately $1,000,000 of "Key-man" insurance on the life of the inventor as a hedge against at least a portion of the loss of their services to the Partnership, but it is not believed that this insurance would even come close to insuring against the full damage that the Partnership would sustain if either of them were to die in the near term. In addition to expanding research and development activities and marketing programs from those presently carried on by Computer prior to this offering, the Partnership will be required to recruit additional qualified research, technical and service persons, as well as marketing representatives, for whose services there is considerable competition. As a consequence, Computer may have to offer relatively high compensation and other benefits to attract such persons.

Limited Prior Experience. The Partnership is newly formed and has no substantial assets, business history or employees. Computer has been in the computer graphics software business since 1975 on a small scale and has not manufactured, leased, or serviced the number of software packages contemplated in the future marketing operations of the Partnership and there is no assurance that large numbers of the Drafting Package or other software packages can be successfully marketed. To date, since its introduction, one Drafting Package with all of its options and software support packages has been sold to the Great Corporation. Six Graphic Post-Processor packages have been sold since their introduction three years ago.

Arbitrary Offering Price of Shares of Computer. The price of the Shares of Computer has been established by its Board of Directors. The primary factors involved in establishing the price per share were the amount of funds necessary for Computer to undertake the activities referred to herein and the percentage of the total equity of Computer that its Board of Directors believed should be sold pursuant to this offering. The value that the offering price purports to place on the Shares may bear no relationship to the assets, earnings or other criteria of value applicable to Computer. The price paid by Computer's current stockholders for their shares was significantly less than the price of the Shares being sold pursuant to this offering. There will be an immediate and substantial dilution but the amount of such dilution is subject to various factors which cannot be predicted with any accuracy.

Financial Requirements. The General Partners believe that the minimum net proceeds from this offering would be sufficient to enable the Partnership to begin marketing and research and development operations and to continue them on a profitable basis. If only the minimum number of Units are sold some of the software development and marketing plans of the Partnership would have to be delayed or reduced. The Partnership was organized in the Partnership form so that it could pass through to each Partner his respective share of losses should they occur prior to attainment of any such profitability. A prospective investor should be aware that if the net proceeds of this offering prove insufficient to enable the Partnership to operate profitably, the Partnership may require additional working capital from alternative sources to maintain Partnership operations and to meet expenditures. There is no assurance that such additional financing will be available or the terms upon which such financing may be obtained. The General Partners are not required by the Agreement to contribute any additional funds necessary for the operation of the Partnership's business. In such event, the Partnership may be required to sell all of its assets and/or dissolve, which in turn could cause the Partners to suffer adverse tax consequences.

No Dividends on Shares of Computer. Anticipated financial requirements of Computer make it highly unlikely that any cash dividends will be declared on its shares in the near term. Any funds that might otherwise be available for the payment of dividends will be retained for use in Computer's business. Payment of dividends out of funds legally available therefore in the future, if such funds are available, will rest in the discretion of the Board of Directors of Computer.

No Assurance of Cash Distribution from Partnership. There is no assurance as to when or whether cash will be available for distribution to the holders of Interests from the operations of the Partnership. The Partnership will bear all expenses incurred in its operations. Any other expenses will be deducted from cash funds generated from the operations of the Partnership prior to distributing cash funds to the Partners.

Control of Computer to Remain with Management. Upon completion of this offering and the sale of the maximum number of Units offered hereunder, the present officers and directors of Computer, as a group, by virtue of their beneficial ownership of Computer's outstanding shares of common stock, will be able to control the affairs and policies of Computer.

Warranty of Products. Pursuant to the terms of the warranties covering the software packages, the Partnership may be liable to correct, at its expense, any defects in operation, performance or materials of the marketed software. Computer has had no warranty claims to date on the Drafting Package or various Graphic Post Processor software packages since their introduction. Also, the aforesaid software packages require no modifications of the Terrific computer system when placed into use, insuring that all Terrific warranties are preserved. The General Partners intend that any software packages developed by the Partnership to be compatible with other manufacturers hardware will also be usable without hardware modifications. However, there is no assurance that the Partnership will not be called upon to repair or replace defective software packages at its expense under its warranties. Computer has incorporated a "source code" in all its software packages that will permit service personnel to transmit corrections, fixes, changes and improvements to any software program via telephone line. The General Partners believe this feature in the software may greatly reduce the cost of any warranty service if required.

Investment in Computer. No significant tax benefits can be expected to inure to the investor as a result of his investment in Computer. If the investor disposes of his stock in Computer at a gain, the gain may be taxable at ordinary income rates. If an investor disposes of his stock in Computer at a loss, deductibility of the loss may be subject to the restrictions applicable to capital losses. Although counsel to the Offerors has rendered its opinion that, under certain circumstances, the Computer stock will qualify as "Section 1244 Stock," as to which an ordinary loss deduction will depend upon facts and circumstances, relating to both the investor and Computer, in existence at the time of the loss.

Limited Transferability and Absence of Market for Limited Partnership Interests and Shares of Stock. The sale of Interests in the Partnership and the Shares of Computer sold as part of the Units will not be registered under the Securities Act of 1933, as amended, the Michigan Uniform Securities Act, as amended or other applicable state securities laws, and neither the Interests nor the Shares may be transferred by an investor unless that transfer is registered under applicable federal and state securities laws or the appropriate exemptions from federal and state registration are available and an opinion to that effect of counsel acceptable to Computer or the Partnership, as the case may be, has been provided.

Although the Interests and Shares are being sold as part of a single Unit, immediately after the offering each may be transferred separately subject to the restrictions of the foregoing paragraph. There is no public trading market for the Units, Interests or Shares and none is expected to develop. Moreover, the Agreement requires that the General Partners consent to assignments before an assignee may become a substituted Limited Partner in the Partnership. Consequently, holders of Interests may not be able to liquidate their investment in the event of emergencies and Interests may not be readily accepted as collateral for a loan.

TAX ASPECTS OF A COMPUTER GRAPHICS SOFTWARE PROGRAM

Research and Experimental Expenses

Under Code Section 174(a), a taxpayer is permitted to treat research and experimental expenses paid or incurred during a taxable year in connection with the conduct of a trade or business as current expenses. Research and experimental expenses are defined by applicable Regulations as experimental or laboratory type costs which generally include all costs incident to the development of an experimental or prototype product, invention or similar property, or the improvement of an already existing property of the type mentioned. The Regulations further provide that the deductibility of research and experimental expenses will not be affected by whether the taxpayer itself actually conducts research or experimentation, or whether funds are expended for research or experimentation carried on in its behalf by another person or organization. Under legislation previously introduced in Congress, the federal income tax treatment of research and experimental expenses would be significantly altered.

Incorporation of the Partnership

The General Partners have the exclusive right to incorporate the Partnership if they determine it to be in the best interest of the Partnership's business, either by (i) an irrevocable power of attorney coupled with an interest thereon which is created over all current and future Partnership interests that shall be outstanding to cause them to be exchanged for shares of the capital stock of a corporation; (ii) sale of all or substantially all Partnership assets for shares of capital stock of a corporation followed by dissolution of the Partnership; or (iii) dissolution of the Partnership and transfer of its assets received on liquidation under a similar irrevocable power coupled with an interest therein to cause them to be exchanged for capital stock of a corporation. The Agreement provides that such incorporation shall be tax free to the Partners to the maximum extent possible.

The Service, in Revenue Ruling 70-239, 1970-1 C.B. 74, considered the tax consequences of these three methods of incorporating a partnership and stated that each of these situations would be regarded as a transfer under Section 351 of the Code, which provides, in general, that no gain or loss is recognized if property is transferred to a corporation solely in exchange for stock or securities of the transferee-corporation if, immediately after the exchange, the transferor or transferors are in "control" of the corporation. Gain will be recognized if the sum of the amount of liabilities assumed by the Partnership plus the amount of liabilities to which the property transferred to the corporation is subject exceeds the total adjusted basis of such property. The Revenue Act of 1978 amended Section 357(c) to provide that if a cash-basis taxpayer transfers the assets of a going business, including the accounts payable, to a corporation in return for stock, the accounts payable will not be considered liabilities for purposes of Section 357(c) if the transferor would have been entitled to a deduction upon the payment thereof. Accordingly, if the Partnership uses the cash method of accounting, its accounts payable will not constitute liabilities under Section 357(c) for purposes of computing gain on incorporation to the extent that the payment on such accounts would be deductible. Also, to the extent a transferor in a Section 351 transaction receives consideration other than stock or securities of the transferee-corporation ("boot"), any gain realized by the transferor is recognized under Section 351(b) to the extent of the value of such boot and is of a character determined with reference to the character of the assets transferred to the corporation. Loss is never recognized in a Section 351 transaction.

The gain, if any, which the Partnership recognizes on incorporation will be taxed as capital gain or ordinary income depending on the type of assets transferred. Also, a portion of any gain may be taxed as ordinary income if there is any depreciation recapture. Upon incorporation, the Partners would be taxed as corporate shareholders.

Gifts of Partnership Interests

Generally, no gain or loss is recognized for federal income tax purposes as a result of a gift of property. However, if a gift of a Unit is made when a Limited Partner's allocable share of Partnership non-recourse indebtedness exceeds the adjusted basis of his interest, such Limited Partner may recognize gain for federal income tax purposes to the extent of such excess. Such excess will be taxed in the same manner as a sale of a Unit.

Gifts of a Limited Partnership interest may be subject to a gift tax imposed pursuant to the rules generally applicable to all gifts of property.

Investment in Computer

An investor's investment in Computer will be treated for federal income tax purposes as a purchase of stock in a corporation. Accordingly, no significant tax benefits can be expected to inure to the investor as a result of his investment in Computer. Because Computer will be treated as a corporation for federal income tax purposes, it will be required to pay a tax on its income, the investors will not be entitled to include in their individual tax returns their pro rata share of the income, gain, loss and credit of the corporation, the payment of taxes by the corporation will reduce the amount of cash available for distribution to the investors, and distributions from the corporation will be taxable as dividends to the extent of the accumulated earnings and profits of the corporation. If an investor disposes of his stock in Computer at a gain, the Service may, depending upon the financial condition of Computer, the composition of its assets, and other factors, take the position that the investor is not entitled to capital gain treatment as to all or part of his gain on the ground that Computer is a "collapsible corporation." No assurance can be given that the Service would not prevail with this position. If it does, any such gain would be taxable to the investor as ordinary income (presently taxable to individuals at rates up to 70%).

Counsel to the Offerors has rendered its opinion to Computer that the Computer stock to be issued to investors will qualify as "Section 1244 stock" *provided that,* among other things, more than 50% of Computer's gross receipts, for certain taxable years, are derived from sources other than royalties, rents, dividends, interest, annuities, or sales or exchanges of stock or securities. Qualification of this stock as Section 1244 stock will, in certain cases, entitle an investor to an ordinary loss deduction in the event that a loss is sustained with respect to his stock in Computer. However, qualification of the stock in Computer as Section 1244 stock does not insure an investor that he will be entitled to an ordinary loss deduction in the event that a loss is sustained with respect to his Computer stock. For example, an ordinary loss deduction in respect to a loss on Section 1244 stock is not available to a corporation, a trust, an estate or a transferee of a person to whom Section 1244 stock was issued by a corporation. Moreover, the aggregate amount that may be treated by a taxpayer as an ordinary loss in any taxable year with respect to Section 1244 stock is $50,000 (or $100,000 in the case of a husband and wife filing a joint return). Because this limitation is applied in the aggregate, and not on a corporation-by-corporation basis, an investor may obtain little or no benefit from Section 1244 characterization of the Computer stock if his loss with respect to his Computer stock was sustained in a taxable year in which he sustained substantial losses on other Section 1244 stock.

Each investor should consult his own tax advisor as to the effect classification of the Computer stock as Section 1244 stock will have in light of the investor's particular circumstances.

Tax shelters have given industry a boost, a financial innovation which may very well have favorable consequences into future centuries.

Chapter Five

AGRICULTURE

Agricultural tax shelters include cattle feeding, cattle and other livestock breeding, crops and timber. With the exception of cattle feeding and breeding, none are widely available as *public programs.*

CATTLE FEEDING

Young "feeder cattle" are purchased with partnership *proceeds.* These cattle become collateral for recourse loans to purchase more cattle and grain for the feeding period. Interest and feed costs push total first year deductions to 50% to 100%. When "finished cattle" are sold after 4 to 6 months, bank loans are repaid and the general partner's share is deducted. Any balance is ordinary income to the limited partners.

Because the holding period for cattle is 24 months, there are no capital gains. Disease and price fluctuations are major risks. Risks, however, can be partially offset, but not eliminated, with hedging and insurance.

BREEDING PROGRAMS

In addition to cattle, "breeding" refers to fur-bearing animals, other farm animals and fish or shellfish. Although the "livestock" varies, program operations are similar. An initial "herd" is purchased. First year tax losses can equal up to 50% to 90%; feed costs and depreciation are the principal deductions. Depreciation and investment tax credit is available on the initial herd but not on offspring.

Sale of offspring generates income. Except for fish and shellfish programs, most females and superior males are retained to increase herd size and quality. Capital gains are available on livestock held more than 12 months (24 months for horses and cattle). Disease and price fluctuations are major risks. *Recapture* may reduce profitability.

CROPS

The list of potential crop partnerships covers virtually anything grown in an orchard, field, grove or vineyard: fruits, nuts, grains, vegetables, etc. Wine grapes, nuts and citrus are the most popular program types.

Labor costs, interest and operating expenses are deductible. By using leverage, first year tax losses may approach 50% to 90%. Crop sales generate ordinary income. Depreciation may offer partially tax sheltered cash flow. Risks depend on weather, price fluctuations and whether new or mature properties are involved. Capital gains, subject to recapture restrictions, are primary investment objectives when the land on which the crops are grown is finally sold.

To illustrate the advantages of agriculture to investors, programs are shown covering Breeder Agency Cattle services, crops and timber and flowers.

JACK BREEDER CATTLE AGENCY SERVICES

JACK INDUSTRIES, INC. AND AFFILIATES

INTRODUCTORY STATEMENT

Jack Industries, Inc., was organized in 1928. Jack has been engaged in its agency services since 1952. For 27 years, it has been principally engaged as an agent and broker for various ranch and cattle owners in the purchase, management and sale of: (a) large tracts of rural real estate developed as ranches or farms located in the agricultural area of the United States; and (b) breeder herds located on ranches and farms in such areas, as well as feeder cattle in commercial feedlots. It has also been active in the fields of agricultural consulting, agricultural financing (specializing in the purchase and sale of chattel mortgages on cattle and purchase money mortgages on ranches and farms at the request of its clients) and in the purchase, management, leasing, sale and development of urban real estate as a broker.

Owners entering into Breeder Cattle Agency Agreements with Jack and subsequently purchasing cattle will not acquire any capital stock or other interest in Jack or any of its affiliates with the exception of the National Cattlemen's Co-operative, which furnishes breeding service. Each Owner is required to buy one share of stock in National Cattlemen's Co-operative for a nominal amount (currently $35 per share).

JACK AND AFFILIATES

The following chart shows the corporations and cooperatives which are subsidiaries or affiliates involved in the Agency Services offered herein.

SUPPLEMENT

BREEDER CATTLE AGENCY SERVICES

Jack Industries, Inc., a Delaware Corporation "Agent"

1. Provides Agency Services and Breeder Financing.
2. Holding Company.
3. Real Estate Brokers.

Dynamic Data Processing Corporation

1. Wholly-owned by Agent.
2. Provides data processing services to maintain breeder records.

Allied Cattlemen's Co-operative

1. Provides breeding services for breeder herds.
2. Agent owns less than 1% of the Co-operative but holds power of attorney for most shareholders. Most shareholders are or were breeder owners.

The Alter Corporation

1. Agent owns 14.0% of common stock in Managing Agent and has three interlocking directors.
2. Alter has ranches on which Owner's breeder cattle are maintained.

A more detailed explanation of the inter-relationship and activities of each subsidiary and affiliate is set forth below.

Dynamic Data Processing Corporation

Dynamic is a Missouri corporation incorporated in 1950 and is a wholly-owned subsidiary of Agent. All of its officers and directors are officers and directors of Agent. This company provides extensive data processing services to assist Jack and affiliates and their clients with administrative work. These services help Agent maintain each Owner's books and records, ranch and cattle location, tax information, budgets, projections, endorsements to breeder maintenance contracts (lists Owners owning type and number of cattle at each location, and settlements on maintenance contracts. For this service, each breeder Owner is charged 50 cents per head owned to cover expenses incurred for software and hardware rental and overhead. Breeder Owner programs occupy 60% to 70% of the computer and personnel time on the IBM Systems III, Model 12. Also, if a breeder Owner desires an investment analysis of his program, Dynamic handles this analysis. Reports that are out of the ordinary and which require extensive work will be charged on the basis of $30 per hour.

Allied Cattlemen's Co-operative

This is a Missouri co-operative founded in 1957. The Co-operative's primary function is to provide breeding services for breeder cattle managed by Agent. Fees are $18 per cow or heifer. The directors and officers of the Co-operative are also directors and officers of Agent, although Agent owns less than 1% of the Co-operative. The Co-operative may own the bulls used for breeding purposes or it may contract with independent ranchers to provide bulls. The Co-operative employs cattle inspectors utilized by Agent for the regular inspection of breeding herds and feeder cattle. A monthly newsletter entitled "Allied Cattlemen's Co-operative Newsletter" is published at a cost of $16 per year to any Owner or the general public at their request. In the past the Co-operative has rented agricultural equipment to ranchers and has served as the agent for distribution of agricultural textbooks. The Co-operative may buy discounted Owners' cattle notes.

Membership in the Co-operative consists mainly of ranchers and commercial feeders handling Owners' cattle, plus the Owners themselves. Selected officers of Agent are also members. Each Owner is charged $35 for membership and a stock certificate is issued in his name representing his ownership. Agent holds this certificate for the Owner and continues to do so until Owner sells all of his cattle and requests the Co-operative through the Agent to repurchase his membership and distribute his percentage of the patronage account, if any. Each member is entitled to one vote on each matter presented at the Co-operative's meetings. There are presently 972 members.

The Alter Corporation

Agent is employed by The Alter Corporation, a Delaware corporation, as Managing Agent under a three year agreement or on ninety days' written notice by either corporation. The agreement authorizes Agent to act for Alter as to cattle investments on the same terms as Owner's employment of Agent; however, Alter owns no cattle now and does not intend to do so in the immediate future. Although Agent is authorized to purchase cattle mortgages on behalf of Alter. Alter does not intend to buy any of the Owner's notes at discount.

Alter is a land holding company. It owns certain ranches on which some of Owners' breeder cattle are maintained under management of the lessees. If lessees or Alter decide, as other ranches may, to change their operations, breeder Owners may have their cattle moved to another location at Owner's expense.

The Chairman of the Board of the Agent is also the Chairman of the Board of Alter. Alter's management is composed of Agents except for a few full time and part time employees. Three members of Alter's Board are on Agent's Board. Agent owned 14.0% of Alter's outstanding common stock.

Operational Alternatives

In the various livestock activities proposed to be conducted under the Agency Agreements, there are a number of decisions on which Agent will make recommendations based on technical and operational considerations. Such advice will be predicated on achieving the best results economically and on animal husbandry considerations, but the ultimate decision must be made by Owner. These decisions will necessarily be influenced by Owner's other business activities, tax objectives, and cash flow requirements of which Agent may have no knowledge. Such decisions could include, but are not limited to, the following:

(a) Payment of feed and maintenance expenses.
(b) Sale of the steer calf crop when weaned.
(c) Retention of all heifer calves suitable for replacements for herd expansions, or sale of all heifer calves.
(d) Reduction or redemption of mortgages within one or two years by liquidation of portions of Owner's cattle.
(e) Prepayment of mortgages utilizing cash from other sources.

(f) Refinancing of Owner's cattle to provide funds for herd expansion.

Normally, Agent will recommend that Owner contract for one year with a rancher-contractor. This gives Owner flexibility to cancel the contract if performance is unsatisfactory. From time to time, Agent may take recommendations to Owner to replace a rancher-contractor. In some cases, Agent might recommend retaining a marginal rancher-contractor. It is quite possible that from time to time Owner might disagree with the recommendation of Agent. In all such cases, the wishes of Owner will be followed. To avoid confusion, such supplemental instructions will be delivered to Agent in writing.

Owner at all times has the right to direct Agent to negotiate changes in the contract, to take legal action against rancher-contractors where a breach of the contract exists, or to not take such legal action even if it is recommended by Agent. Owner may ask Agent to perform services over and beyond those required by the Agency Agreement. In the event that these are of a substantial nature, additional compensation will be arrived at by mutual agreement.

Each Owner will retain ultimate responsibility and authority with respect to all operations of his cattle and it is anticipated that Owner's activities will include the following: (a) receipt and review of current reports from Agent; (b) receipt and review of annual financial information with respect to operations of Owner's cattle; (c) receipt and review of information with respect to the results of the operations of Owner's cattle at each of the ranch locations; and (d) consultation with Agent as to Owner's policies with respect to culling, sale or retention of heifer calves and disposition of portions of Owner's breeder cattle, all after consideration of variations in current market prices. Owner has the obligation to make required annual budget payments on or before August 15 and October 15.

Agent will make such decisions as are described in this section unless an Owner directs otherwise.

Contract Services Rendered by Agent

Each Owner of breeder cattle has the responsibility to manage his cattle business. Agent will supervise for Owner the maintenance and management of Owner's cattle. Agent will, among other things locate rancher-contractors who will contract to: (a) care for, supervise, and feed Owner's cattle; (b) provide adequate and proper land and water for grazing of Owner's cattle; (c) provide all necessary veterinary care for Owner's cattle; and (d) supervise breeding of Owner's breeder cattle. Agent also acts for Owner as an inspecting, auditing and negotiating agent, with these general functions: (a) procuring brands for Owner's breeder cattle; (b) planning and supervising operational procedures which include roundups, inventories, weighouts, branding, vaccination and dehorning of Owner's breeder cattle; (c) negotiating all contracts and agreements for acquisition, operation and sale of Owner's cattle; (d) negotiating and supervising, directing and controlling all culling, marketing and breeding programs; and (e) providing inspection services for Owner's cattle at periodic intervals and supplying Owner with written reports.

Registration Under the Packers & Stockyards Act

Agent is registered with the Packer & Stockyard Administration. Annually, Agent must submit its financial statements and file reports under the provisions of the Act, so that the size and scope of the activities of Agent may be monitored by the Packers & Stockyards Division of the U.S. Department of Agriculture. This Division further monitors the brokerage and the buying and selling of breeder, feeder and stocker animals as well as the administration of customer accounts. Agent is bonded under this act regarding the handling of funds transmitted in the purchase and sale of animals.

FIDUCIARY RESPONSIBILITY OF THE AGENT

The Agent acts on behalf of the Owners within the scope of the authority granted to it by the Owners. This relationship creates a fiduciary obligation on the part of the Agent to discharge its duties in a manner which is consistent with the Agency Agreement and in a manner which does not conflict with the interests of the Owners. Therefore, the trust and confidence reposed in Agent by the Owners require the Agent to exercise diligence to assure that it avoids acts which would be contrary to the authority granted by the Owners and which would be inconsistent with the Owner's interests. The Agency Agreement does not limit the fiduciary obligations of the Agent under the principles of common law.

PLAN OF DISTRIBUTION

The Agency Services offered hereunder will only be offered by Agents' employees, directors and officers. Agent will not receive any underwriting discount or commissions. No other person is authorized to give any information or make any representations in connection with this offering.

Agency may pay compensation to persons who refer competent Owners to the Agent. Such compensation is negotiated and may range from 1% to 8% of the initial cash paid by Owner upon a sale. Said compensation will be paid as the Agent receives the initial cash payment from the Owner. The recipients of such compensation may be deemed to be "underwriters" as defined under state and Federal securities laws and accordingly, their activities may be governed by such laws.

This material is an invitation by Agent to persons in the higher income tax bracket to purchase Agency Services which cover all acts necessary for the absentee-ownership of breeder cattle, except for certain decisions as to which the Agent will make recommendations, but the ultimate decisions must be made by Owner. Agent will act in the capacity as an agent for Owner in advising and recommending to Owner types of cattle to purchase, selection of rancher, and other advice needed in the ownership of breeder cattle. Agent does not own any cattle or ranches or feedyards and only acts on behalf of Owner at his direction.

The terms and conditions of each Owner's cattle investment may vary from those presented in this material because of economic trends, individually negotiated maintenance contracts, time and circumstances. Each herd purchased as a result of the employment of Agent is contractually independent of any other purchase or contract but may be grouped with other Owners' cattle for economic reasons.

Except as otherwise specified herein, all of Agent's compensation for services will be paid for by Owner. Agent will receive no compensation from a seller for the sale of his cattle, or from a rancher or any other contractor or supplier. Agent has no interest in the contract with the rancher and in no way participates in any gain or loss from the operations or marketing of the herd.

SUPPLEMENT
BREEDER CATTLE AGENCY SERVICES

Agent reserves the right to reject employment for any reason whatsoever.

The following sequence of steps is anticipated in effecting this offering:

1. This Prospectus will be delivered to a potential Owner.
2. The prospective Owner will be asked if he would like to have presented to him a program covering recommended cattle. He will also be asked his preference as to the size of expenditure, type of financing, and tax objectives in which he is interested. Agent's recommendations as to each of these items are set forth in "Investment in Cattle."
3. Such a program will be prepared and forwarded to him together with additional information as requested.
4. Agent will also send the prospective Owner two copies of the Agency Agreement.
5. If the prospective Owner desires to purchase such a program, he will indicate his approval and return signed copies of the Agency Agreement.
6. The seller of the cattle will be asked to confirm the sale through Agent.
7. As soon as the purchase is confirmed, a noninterest bearing account will be opened in Owner's name in a Kansas City or other metropolitan bank on which Agent is authorized to draw. From this account Agent will issue checks directly to the seller, lending agencies, rancher-contractor and other people involved and will execute the necessary documents pursuant to the authority granted by the Agency Agreement. The original documentation is retained at the principal office of Agent with copies transmitted at the direction of Owner.
8. When all documents have been completed, they will be placed in a brochure, photocopied and copies forwarded to Owner.
9. From the funds placed in Owner's bank account and upon authorization by Owner, the Agent will issue a check for the management fee and initial fee, as applicable.

The By-laws of the Agent provide for indemnification of officers and directors.

CAPITALIZATION

Agent does not guarantee any contracts between Owner and a rancher-contractor, nor does Agent assume any obligations whatsoever except for those associated with the Laws of Agency in the various states in which it does business; however for the purpose of description, historical information and general background, Agent has included financial information on file with the Securities and Exchange Commission. Agent's fiduciary relationship to an Owner is that of an agent who is authorized by another to act for him as provided under the Laws of Agency.

BUSINESS OF JACK AND AFFILIATES

Current Activities of Jack Industries, Inc.

As a broker in the field of urban real estate, Jack and its subsidiaries have been active in the purchase, management, leasing, sale and development of urban real estate. In the field of agricultural land, it has been active in agricultural consulting and financing and as a real estate broker. In agricultural financing, Jack has specialized in the purchase and sale of chattel mortgages on cattle for Owners. Jack is now licensed as a real estate broker in nineteen states and the District of Columbia. Agent is a member of the National Institute of Farm Brokers. Although the sale of commercial property was originally the principal real estate activity of the Company and still plays an important role, ranch and farm land sales also have become increasingly important in the Company's activities. Since 1969, Jack has been agent and manager for Alter. Responsibilities in this area include range engineering, land development, ranch and cattle operations, and commercial property management.

Special Services to Investors, Lenders and Others with Financial Interest in Feeder Cattle

Regardless of the type of financial interest possessed by an absentee individual or a corporation in a cattle feeding venture, routine inspections are an essential safety precaution, as are title searches, inquiries to suppliers, verification of prices, credit checks, and similar prudent safeguards ("Full Services"). Fees will be determined on the degree of service required. Travel expenses are normally included within fees but may be charged extra in instances where unusually high costs are encountered.

Examples:

Number of Cattle	Number of Different Locations	Full Services	Physical Inspections Only	Typical Per Head
500	1	X		$6.00
500	1		X	4.00
500	3	X		6.50
500	3		X	4.50
10,000	4	X		4.50
10,000	4		X	3.25
10,000	8	X		5.00
10,000	8		X	3.50

Other Services

Agent offers financial consulting services, appraisal service on real estate and cattle and an independent cattle and real estate inspection service. In recent years, this last service has been expanded and in connection with this, agent has been employed by banks and other lending agencies, ranch corporations and accounting firms to conduct independent physical inspections of loan collateral and various agricultural operations.

Financing and Other Operations

Through several banking institutions, extensive lines of credit are maintained by Agent. Agent uses these lines of credit to borrow money on the notes receivable from Owners, secured by Owner's cattle. The mortgage financing department generates income from the rates charged, and the ability to furnish financing to Owners is frequently a principal factor in completing a management contract. Jacks presently has total lines of credit in the amount of $4,000,000 available to purchasers of breeding cattle. At the present time, the used portion of these lines is approximately $2,595,086. In addition to the Jack lines of credit, the sellers in many instances provide all or a portion of the requested financing to the buyers. Ranchers also provide financing in some instances for breeder owners.

Additional Services Rendered by Agent

While Agent assumes the responsibility of being informed on the industry, the market, agricultural legislation and other factors affecting agricultural operations, its agency responsibility is limited to the production of facts and recommendations based thereon. From time to time Owner must make decisions based on factors unknown to Agent, such as cash inputs or outputs desired for the year, tax consequences relating to other business activities of Owner, marketing risks versus loss sharing, and other items of a similar nature.

For this reason, it is strongly recommended that Owner familiarize himself with the industry, with his own particular operation, with actual and potential legislation and with seasonal market trends. As part of the management service, Agent, unless directed otherwise, subscribes for Owner to various trade publications and agricultural services.

Agent will further distribute to Owners, but not prospective Owners, market graphs and monographs on particular agricultural subjects, some prepared by Agent and some from outside sources, and individually requested research on operational and industrial matters.

As a matter of policy, Agent will furnish to Owner statistical information from data maintained in the usual course of business at no additional cost. Requests for research and projections not falling in that category will be subject to additional fees.

It is the policy of Agent to work closely with Owner's attorney and accountant in the event of a controversy or litigation with the Treasury Department or any other agency of the government. Depending upon the time involved and the type of question presented, it may be necessary for Agent to make an extra charge for this service.

THE CATTLE MARKET

The breeder cattle managed by Agent are generally commercial stock. The prices of such cattle will vary due to age, condition, weight and market classifications. The following table taken from the United States Department of Agriculture, "Livestock and Meat Situation," shows per capita consumption of beef. The second table shows the sales prices established by Agent. There can be no assurance, however, that Owner will be able to dispose of its cattle at these prices.

PER CAPITA MEAT CONSUMPTION BY QUARTERS

	Carcass Weight by Pounds					Retail Weight by Pounds				
Year	First	Second	Third	Fourth	Total	First	Second	Third	Fourth	Total
1970	28.3	27.9	29.0	28.5	113.7	20.9	20.6	21.5	21.1	84.1
1971	27.7	28.1	29.3	27.9	113.0	20.5	20.8	21.7	20.6	83.6
1972	28.2	28.9	29.4	29.6	116.1	20.9	21.4	21.7	21.9	85.9
1973	28.0	26.2	26.8	28.6	109.6	20.7	19.4	19.8	21.2	81.1
1974	28.3	28.8	29.4	30.3	116.8	20.9	21.3	21.8	22.4	86.4
1975	30.3	28.4	30.2	31.2	120.1	22.4	21.0	22.4	23.1	88.9
1976	32.7	31.2	33.3	31.7	128.9	24.2	23.0	24.6	23.5	95.4
1977	31.6	31.0	32.0	31.3	125.9	23.4	22.9	23.7	23.2	93.2
1978	30.5	29.8	29.7	30.4	120.4	22.6	22.1	22.0	22.5	89.2
1979	28.3[1]					21.0[1]				

STOCK CATTLE PRICES[2]
(Price Per Head)

Month	1973	1974	1975	1976	1977	1978	1979
January	$325	$410	$245	$250	$270	$275	$600
February	325	410	245	250	270	275	600
March	365	410	220	275	270	300	650
April	365	410	220	275	270	350	650
May	365	400	220	290	270	350	650
June	365	350	250	290	270	375	650
July	365	315	250	290	270	390	650
August	365	315	250	290	270	390	650
September	410	265	250	290	270	425	650
October	410	255	250	270	275	425	
November	410	245	250	270	275	450	
December	410	245	250	270	275	525	

1. Preliminary Figures.
2. These are prices for stock cows if Owner pays cash. If Owner purchases his cattle on an installment basis from selling Owner, the price would be cash price plus 10% of cash price.

SUPPLEMENT
BREEDER CATTLE AGENCY SERVICES

INVESTMENT IN CATTLE

Jack offers to act as agent for those persons or entities who meet the suitability standards and who desire to invest in commercial breeder cattle. Agent will select and purchase cattle for each Owner based on the Owner's needs and authority and will simultaneously arrange for financing of the cattle, if necessary. The following represents the usual program of investment by Owner. However, if an Owner instructs Agent to arrange for financing cattle or any other phase of his investment differently than as presented in this material, Agent will follow those instructions. Since all arrangements with rancher-contractors are individually negotiated, Owner's program may vary from that of any other Owner. For example, an Owner may have cattle at five different locations with five different ranchers under five different maintenance contracts.

In addition to individual bills of sale on the originally purchased animals, each herd of breeder cattle will normally carry an Owners identifying brand or brands. Alternate identification may be provided through a numbering or lettering code or other marketing system. This individual coding will be recorded in the Agent's computer center and will be continuously employed for the individual identification of each Owner's animals. In a few special instances to take advantage of especially favorable financing and particularly secure ranch contracts, the Agent may be required in behalf of each Owner having cattle on such a ranch to lease the old established ranch brand during the tenancy of the Owner's cattle on that particular ranch, and this leased brand system will be employed to identify cattle on that particular ranch rather than the system previously described. Agent will exert its best efforts to assure that contract ranchers carry out branding instructions in a timely manner, but it should be recognized that conditions such as inclement weather, birthing of calves, and cattle movements or relocations may temporarily curtail the physical completion of the branding.

Financing

Considerations of leverage and deductibility of interest make financing an important part of cattle herd ownership. Interest rates are traditionally higher than those charged on commercial loans and generally run two points above prime, but terms are often more liberal. Management firms operating in the agricultural field have sources of capital available for their principals. This capability is provided by Agent.

Cattle purchased are generally financed for two reasons. First, to spread the initial cost of the purchase over a three year period or longer, and second, to provide cash input in a subsequent year if Owner so elects this choice. Agent charges the new Owner 1% of the face amount of the note given to the selling Owner or Rancher as a one time placement fee for arranging the financing with a selling Owner or Rancher. The maximum amount that may be borrowed at the time of purchase is 95% of the purchase price of the cattle. No funds are borrowed to maintain the cattle. Financing is usually non-recourse. This type of financing may limit an Owner's tax deductions.

Initial financing for the purchase of a breeder cattle herd is usually offered by Owners who wish to sell all or part of their herd or by a rancher who may have part of his own herd for sale. These sellers agree to accept a 5% to 10% down payment and take back a non-recourse purchase money mortgage for the balance secured by the cattle sold. Notes are paid in installments with 40% due at the end of the first annual contract period, and the remaining balance due in equal installments over the next two years. To induce the herd Owner to provide financing for the new Owner, his cattle are priced 10% higher than the cash price. Further, a new Owner will pay interest of usually 8% to 10% on his notes.

However, upon the request of an Owner, Agent will arrange for full recourse or limited recourse financing through a Bank. Owner will use his cattle as collateral for such a loan. An Owner may request his type of financing by executing a special power of attorney and by executing the request contained in the Breeder Cattle Agency Agreement. Limited recourse financing is structured to place a limited amount of personal liability directly with the Owner. If an Owner desires a full recourse loan, he will be reasonably responsible for the whole loan. This form of financing provides the purchaser with a source of an additional amount of capital at risk to reduce any limitation of loss as required in the Tax Reform Act of 1976. Agent has made arrangements with several lending institutions to provide this form of financing to those purchasers who request it. Besides the financing fee, Agent receives no additional fee for arranging recourse financing. The terms and conditions of the financing will vary based on the requirements of the lending institutions. The interest rate will be no more than the legal usury rate as set by individual states and will be dependent upon the laws of the state in which the lending institution resides, and the notes will be for six months or one year, and may be renewable.

In some cases the rancher, an independent contractor, who contracts with the Owner to maintain and manage Owner's breeder herd, may carry the financing of the herd for the Owner. He will take back a non-recourse note secured by the cattle, payable one year from the date of the note. The note held by the rancher may be renewable on an annual basis. If the rancher cannot maintain his line of credit, the note may not be renewable. The interest rate on a rancher loan is normally one to two points over the prime rate in the rancher's locale.

About 5% of the 75,000 head of cattle annually managed by Agent are not purchased from previous Owners but from outside sources. In this instance, Agent usually provides financing. This type of financing requires that Owner pay 10% down on the purchase of the cattle and give a non-recourse note and chattel mortgage for the remaining part of the purchase price to Agent or a note and chattel mortgage for the remaining part of the price to a bank.

Agent borrows money on a recourse basis through lines of credit arranged with commercial banks. These funds in turn are loaned by Agent to Owners when purchase money or rancher financing is not available on a non-recourse basis. Agent charges Owner the interest rate required plus a guarantee fee ranging from 2% to 8% of the financed amount. A service fee is charged for establishing and handling Owner's loans. This charge is 1% of the amount borrowed each time a loan is arranged or renewed. Certain banks who provide financing will require inspection of the cattle securing their loans and such inspections will be an additional charge to the Owners.

If an Owner defaults in his payment of his chattel mortgage or his cattle business expenses, Agent at the lender's direction will liquidate Owner's cattle herd through procedures prescribed by laws of the states in which the cattle are located in order to pay the rancher maintaining the cattle, any agistor who has a possessory lien on the cattle, all third parties, breeding fees, Agent's management fee, expenses, and mortgages on the cattle based on the priorities. If there are any remaining funds, they will be distributed to the Owner. Owner is personally liable for all expenses and charges, other than the non-recourse cattle financing.

Rancher

In most cases the ranchers are not affiliated with each other or with Agent. Owner's cattle will be placed on individually negotiated maintenance contracts, usually on an annual basis, with independent-contractors operating either on their own or leased property. Good faith selection by Agent of independent-contractor ranchers does not preclude the conflicts of interest set forth herein. Because of general market conditions, weather, operating costs, and other situations, a rancher may determine that it would be more profitable to maintain his own cattle and refuse to renew Owner's contract. This might necessitate considerable expense in moving Owner's cattle. In the past three years there have been various movements of cattle. In 1975-76, 29% of 95,061 head of breeder cattle owned by all existing Owners were moved; in 1976-77, 18% of 77,299 cattle were moved; and in 1977-78, 19.5% of 72,653 cattle were moved. If another rancher could not be found within the area to maintain the Owner's cattle, portions of the Owner's herd might have to be sold regardless of current market conditions. Further, any moving or transportation of Owner's cattle could cause damage to the cattle. Rancher may decide to sell his ranch or determine it is to his best interest not to renew his lease on the ranch where Owner's cattle are located and this would have the same effect as above. Rancher may or may not maintain cattle of his own on the same ranch. In the event of inclement weather, feed or labor shortgages, he might give more favorable treatment to his own cattle than to those of Owner. Rancher may, without the knowledge of the Owner, subcontract certain responsibilities and duties to a third party which would lead to disputes between the rancher and the subcontractor involved with the Owner's cattle. The maintenance contract entered into by Agent on Owner's behalf with the rancher prohibits such assignment of responsibilities to any third person without the consent of the Owner. If the Rancher assigns his contracts then this is a breach and Agent will take all necessary steps to protect the Owners and Owners' cattle. However, Agent is not responsible for such assignment. Owner may in certain instances initially purchase cattle from ranchers for retention under maintenance contracts.

SUPPLEMENT
BREEDER CATTLE AGENCY SERVICES

There are numerous types of breeder cattle management contracts currently available to Owners. Those most often used are:

(a) *Flat Rate.* In a flat rate arrangement, the contractor is paid a fixed monthly or annual fee for providing land, pasture, labor and other items connected with the maintenance of the herd. This fee would be reduced if the cattle Owner supplied any of these items. In some instances, the Owner receives a guarantee from the rancher that the rancher will account for all animals by producing either the cattle or proof of death.

(b) *Calf-Crop Sharing.* Under this arrangement, the rancher provides the various ingredients necessary to maintain the herd and in return receives a percentage of the calf-crop subsequently produced. The actual percentage received varies in accordance with the amount of feed, labor, pasturage and other items provided by the rancher. Depending upon these variables, the rancher's share of the calf-crop could be as little as 20% or as much as 80% depending on the cost of items furnished by the rancher and all other risk factors previously discussed such as weather and disease.

(c) *Cost-Plus.* Here the Owner agrees to pay for all actual costs of maintenance, plus a fixed fee per head for labor. Cost-plus contracts may or may not include a clause providing that the rancher will indemnify the Owner against missing cattle.

(d) *Weight Gain.* Weight gain contracts generally require the cattle Owner to furnish the livestock and the rancher to provide feed, labor, land, and all other ingredients necessary to maintain the cattle. The rancher's compensation is computed on an agreed rate per pound times the weight of the calf-crop produced by mature animals or the pounds gained by yearlings or calves. Such contracts do not usually include indemnification against excessive mortality or bonuses for above-average performance.

(e) *Incentive-Type.* This contract is similar to the weight gain contract but has added provisions for above-average or below-average performance. The rancher often provides indemnities against death losses which exceed industry norms. This contract is preferred by many in the industry and, when such an arrangement can be negotiated at a reasonable price, it is recommended by Agent.

SUPPLEMENT

BREEDER CATTLE AGENCY SERVICES

It has been Agent's experience that incentive-type contracts will produce better operational results and a more favorable profit opportunity than the cost-plus contracts which are normal in the industry. Incentive-type contracts pass to rancher a substantial part of the risk of weather, disease, and mortality. With respect to cows, first calf heifers and bred yearlings the bonus or penalty is based on rancher performance as evidenced by the aggregate weight gain of calves weaned from such animals. On open yearlings and heifer calves, the weight gain of the individual animal is the determining factor.

The following are the number and types of contracts which Agent entered into on behalf of Owners for the past three years:

Type of Contract	Year One	Year Two	Year Three
Flat Rate	30	8	4
Calf-Crop Sharing	none	none	none
Cost-Plus	none	none	none
Weight Gain	none	none	none
Incentive-Type	179	116	
Including Bulls			10
Excluding Bulls			111

General Maintenance Contract

The following is a summary of the incentive-type cow-calf maintenance contracts which Agent recommends and will attempt to negotiate for Owners of cows. Contracts for bulls, heifers and yearlings are variations on the cow-calf contracts because certain provisions are not applicable to other classes of cattle.

Furnishing Livestock:	Owner will furnish cattle
Acceptance of Cattle:	Rancher certifies that he has inspected cattle prior to acceptance or waives this privilege and accepts cattle in existing condition and quality.
Rancher's Obligation:	Pasture, feed, and care for cattle in manner customary to the area and to pay for leases and personal property taxes.

SUPPLEMENT
BREEDER CATTLE AGENCY SERVICES

Period:	October 15 to October 14 unless mutually changed for round up purposes.
Estimated Payment for Feed, Labor, Use of Facilities, and Veterinary:	$65 per cow.
Bonus-Penalty:	Rancher will be paid or will owe an amount based on the percentage of calf-crop obtained. Rancher will be paid a bonus if the aggregate weight of calves produced times a rate divided from the calf-crop percentage exceeds the aggregate feed and maintenance payment. However, rancher will owe a penalty if the total is less than the aggregate feed and maintenance payment.
Financing:	A rancher who will finance cattle for Owner will be paid a higher base rate as a consideration for the financing.
Minimum Weight:	Rancher will maintain cattle above minimum weights specified.
Market Sharing:	Rancher will share in the steer proceeds if they average above a set rate per pound. This provides rancher with incentive to maintain owner's cattle during periods of high cattle prices. Otherwise he would benefit more by owning the cattle himself.
Disease Certification:	Rancher certifies that no bangs disease or any other contagious disease has been on his pasture within the past five (5) years.
Dead/Missing Cows:	Rancher will indemnify Owner or replace all dead or missing cattle over 3% of herd. Rancher is allowed one animal per contract.
Feed/Acreage/Water Guarantee:	Rancher guarantees sufficient feed, and pasturage.

SUPPLEMENT
BREEDER CATTLE AGENCY SERVICES

Roundup:	Roundups are held in the fall for inventory and culling purposes.
Calf Penalty:	Rancher will pay a penalty for all calves that have not been worked three months prior to weaning. This includes vaccinations, branding, and castration of the bull calves.
Administrative Fee:	Owner will pay rancher $1 per head if he has furnished adequate records and reports.
Branding:	Owner will pay for any registration and will furnish branding irons or ear tags.
Vaccination:	All calves and cows will be vaccinated for various contagious diseases.
Culling:	Dry cows can be sent to market prior to July 1 with $2 per head credit for unused summer pasturage.
Termination:	Contract terminates if rancher (1) dies, (2) becomes bankrupt or insolvent, (3) makes any assignment for benefit of creditors, (4) attempts to sell, mortgage, pledge, remove, dispose of, improperly brand, or injures any cattle, or (5) if any distress, execution or attachment is levied upon the cattle.
Independent-Contractor:	Rancher is an independent-contractor and not the agent or employee of Owner.
Sales:	If herd has to be sold before October 15, rancher will negotiate in good faith with Owner to cancel by Owner paying a pro rata amount plus penalty.
Bulls:	Rancher is expected to provide bull service. If rancher does not, National Cattlemen's Co-operative or another Owner at Agent's discretion will furnish bulls or bull service.

SUPPLEMENT
BREEDER CATTLE AGENCY SERVICES

Assignment: Rancher can only assign with consent of Agent.

The following table outlines the minimum base rate per pound paid at the end of each maintenance year to ranchers for maintenance on incentive-type contracts during the past eleven years by those Owners who have selected this form of contractual arrangement:

Contract Year	Cow	First Calf Heifers	Bred Yearlings	Open Yearlings	Heifer Calves
1968-1969[1]......	22¾-22¢	23¾-22¢	24¾-23¢	20-17¢	17-16¢
1969-1970[1]......	22¾-21	23¾-21	24¾-23	20-19	18-17
1970-1971[1]......	22¾-21	23¾-21	24¾-23	20-19	18-17
1971-1972[1]......	22 -20	23 -21	24 -22	20-19	18-17
1972-1973[1]......	22 -20	23 -21	24 -22	20-19½	18-18
1973-1974[1]......	22 -20	23 -21	24 -22	23-20	21-18
1974-1975[1]......	26 -24	27 -25	28 -26	26-20	24-18
1975-1976[1]......	28½-24	29½-25	30½-26	26-20	24-18
1976-1977[1]......	34½-29	36½-31	36½-31	32-20	28-18
1977-1978[1]......	34½-29	36½-31	36½-31	32-20	28-18
1978-1979[1]......	34½-29	36½-31	36½-31	32-20	28-20

1. Contracts for 1960-1975 include a market bonus as adjustments to the above rate with respect to cows, first calf heifers, and bred yearlings if the net price received for steer calves is in excess of 34½% per pound; the base rate for steer calves will be increased by 50% of the price in excess of 34½%. In the event Rancher is also furnishing non-recourse financing, he is frequently given an 1¢ per pound increase over the above rates. Contracts for 1975-1978 include a market bonus if the net price is in excess of 45¢ per pound.

These figures, based upon weights produced, will vary depending upon the area of the country and the performance of ranchers and will generate annual maintenance costs on cows, first calf heifers and bred yearlings of approximately $75 to $200.

SUPPLEMENT
BREEDER CATTLE AGENCY SERVICES

1. Employment:	Jack is employed as agent to purchase, arrange maintenance, and sell absentee-Owner's cattle.
2. Authorization:	The Agency Agreement is a power of attorney and can be used to show Owner's authorization.
3. Maintenance:	Agent may join Owner's cattle to obtain lower costs, better care, improved supervision and to uphold Owner's legal rights. Agent arranges for the purchase of cattle, pasture for breeders, care, inspections, culling, and sales, upon written authority.
4. Records:	Agent keeps Owner's books and keeps accounts at banks. Breeder cattle Owner pays for data processing expense. Breeder accounts are kept on a cash basis.
5. Insurance:	Jack obtains public liability insurance for Owners.
6. Fees:	The initial fee is between 8% and 10% of the gross purchase price of the herd. The annual management fee is 10% of all funds used to pay operating expenses but not less than $500. (There are other fees and charges payable to Agent and third parties.)
7. Financing:	Agent can arrange non-recourse loans against the cattle.
8. Default:	Agent has authority to liquidate if Owner defaults in his payments for expenses or on mortgages.

Agent acts solely on behalf of the Owner and at Owner's direction. Owner is responsible for all documents signed by Agent on Owner's behalf including bills of sale, notes and chattel mortgages, financing statements, exchange agreements, bank account documents, and maintenance contracts.

Agent's Fees and Expenses

The following sets forth and explains the initial fee and management fees paid to Agent by Owners as of the date of this material. Owners will be notified of any changes.

Initial Fee. This is paid one time only at the beginning of Agent's employment and covers the creation of the business, setting up books and records, acquiring the herd, negotiating initial contracts with ranchers, obtaining the initial financing, recording legal documents and brands, and, upon Owner's instructions, and without further charge, selling the herd when the Owner elects to terminate part or all of his business. The initial fee is based on a percentage of the gross herd purchase price.

Total Number of Head	% Fee X Herd Purchase Price
Up to 300	10
301 up to 600	9
601 up to 1,000	8
Over 1,000	Quoted upon request

Example: Owner instructs Agent to organize a cattle business involving an initial inventory of 200 cows worth \$350 each. Fee would be computed at 10% x \$350 x 200, or \$7,000.

Annual Management Fee. This fee is 10% of the total expenditures of Owner's cattle business except principal payments on chattel mortgages. If a new Owner purchases a herd on October 15, the Owner will pay, on October 15, 10% of the expenditure for 2½ months. Then, the following October, the same Owner will pay 10% of the expenditures made the first 9½ months of that calendar year and for the next 2½ months.

Example: Expenses for maintaining 200 cows (feed, pasture, breeding, insurance, inspection, veterinary, interest, etc.) total \$21,900 x 10%, coming to \$2,100.

A minimum fee of \$500 per annum will be charged.

Inspection services for feeder cattle are not included in initial or annual maintenance fees.

Purchase in Subsequent Year. Special consideration will be given to existing Owners who purchase additional cattle. As an inducement for those wishing to expand their holdings, Agent will reduce its initial fee by one-fourth for purchases in subsequent calendar years not in excess of the original number of head purchased. The minimum fee available for multiple purchases of this nature is 7.5%.

Example No. 1: Owner "X" bought 200 cows in year one. In year two, he purchases an additional 100 cows. Since his original purchase made at 10% (0-300 cows, 10%), the subsequent 100 head would be purchased at a 7.5% rate.

Example No. 2: Owner "Y" bought 650 cows in year one for which he pays an initial fee of 8% (601-1,000 cows, 8%). In year two, he purchases an additional 100 head for which he pays a fee of 7.5%.

Mortgage Guarantee and Service Fee. There is a guarantee fee for financing provided by Agent from 2% to 8% of the loan balance of Owner's mortgage per annum. A fee of 1% of the loan balance is charged for financing arranged by Agent through a rancher or selling Owner. Further, a service fee of 1% of the face amount of Owner's note each time it is established or renewed is charged.

Mortgage Collections. When an Owner sells his cattle on an installment basis and accepts a purchase money mortgage, Agent charges Owner $10 per mortgage per year for the collection of these funds. For these same Owners, an annual fee of $50 is charged for preparing tax information related to the mortgage collections. If Owners desire to sell their notes and mortgage, Agent will attempt to accommodate Owner. The notes will probably be sold at a discount.

Special Reports and Projections. A charge of $30 per hour will be made for special research, projections, budgets, and similar analyses. These would be in addition to the analyses provided all Owners.

SUPPLEMENT
BREEDER CATTLE AGENCY SERVICES

Income Tax Preparation. A fee of $50 is charged for each Owner for preparing and reviewing Schedule F. Form 1040 of the federal income tax return; Partnerships will be charged $125 per annum for preparation of Federal Form 1065. Fees for tax work requested by corporations will be quoted separately and will depend upon the responsibilities assumed by the Agent.

Proposed Deficiency. The expense of contesting any proposed IRS deficiency will be borne by Owner. Any expenses incurred by Agent at Owner's request for preparing documentation to be used in the contest and for Agent's employees expenses incurred if requested to appear at the various hearings.

Electronic Data Processing. Inventory, profit and loss, budget, and tax records are maintained on computers leased by Mid-Continent Data Processing Corporation, a wholly-owned subsidiary of Agent. A fee not to exceed 50¢ per head will be charged annually for these services.

Fees Paid to Others and Affiliates

Miscellaneous Fees. A variety of minor fees and expenses not included in the initial fee are incurred in the operation of a breeder cattle business. Recipients would include trucking firms, inspectors, blacksmiths, veterinarians, cattle associations, state brand boards, insurance companies, lawyers, etc. Currently these additional expenses average $15 per head annually, but Agent has no control over fees charged by third parties for services rendered.

Brand Fee. A fee of $2 per head is charged to breeder Owners and paid to rancher for the initial branding and identification of Owner's cattle.

Breeding Fees. Fees for breeding services are $18 per cow or heifer payable to National Cattlemen's Co-operative.

Payment of Breeder Mortgages

All breeder contracts begin on October 15 of each year. At the end of each contract year a roundup is held at the rancher's locale to determine the number of death losses, the number of calves and their weight, to cull out any cattle which will not increase or benefit the breeder herd, and to sell steers and any heifer calves or other calves necessary to continue the Owner's cattle business.

The proceeds from the sale of the culled cattle are applied first to any principal and interest payments due on any financing of the cattle. Steer proceeds are primarily used to pay the rancher's settlement and other budgeted expenses. The Agent sends a budget to each Owner in July, at which time Owner decides those steps set forth in "Operational Alternatives."

If the steer and cull proceeds are not sufficient to meet all mortgage payments and operating expenses, the Owner must provide the additional cash required. However, if the Owner cannot pay or does not desire to contribute any cash to maintain his herd, then heifer calves must also be sold to meet payments and expenses. Should all these foregoing measures prove inusfficient, then cattle will be subject to possible agistor's liens and to foreclosure by the mortgage holder. If the Owner chooses to default on his non-recourse cattle mortgage, he may lose all of his cattle but will have no personal liability for any unpaid amounts on his mortgage. However, if an Owner defaults on his mortgage and loses his cattle, he is still personally responsible for all expenses incurred in the operation of his cattle business, including Agent's fees and rancher settlements on maintenance contracts and any unpaid balance of a recourse mortgage. When an Owner defaults on his mortgage, usually in a declining market, the selling Owner who holds the mortgage or his assigns will have to liquidate the collateral or take over possession and operation. This may cause a loss to the mortgage holder.

Liquidity of the Cattle Investment

When an Owner chooses to sell his herd, Agent will first offer Owner's cattle to a new or prospective client unless otherwise instructed by the Owner. Alternatively, Agent may explore the possibility of outside marketing, should conditions dictate. When cattle are sold, Agent will furnish all documentation of sale, collect down payments or cash value for the cattle, and collect all subsequent mortgage payments resulting from the sale of the cattle. If the herd sale is a complete dispersal, Agent will do all things necessary to close out Owner's cattle operation.

Agent makes no guarantee that the cattle will be sold in any year, but it will make every effort to market the cattle to the best advantage. Breeding herds are traditionally marketed in the fall of the year, and Owners who give notice sufficiently early in the summer or fall can normally anticipate having their cattle sold by the end of that year. If notice is not given until late in the fall, opportunities for selling cattle are diminished. Although Agent is not prohibited from buying Owner's cattle, Agent, itself, makes no arrangements to buy cattle and has no plans to ever take a position in the cattle of any Owner. However, National Cattlemen's Cooperative, an affiliate of Agent, has purchased selling Owners' herd in rare instances.

Prices paid for cattle are established by a committee set up by the National Cattlemen's Cooperative. This committee is made up of five individuals, two of which are not affiliated with Agent. Prices are reported by geographical areas of the country. The committee is further guided by various publications, U.S. Department of Agriculture reports, bankers, and other authorities within the cattle industry. Prices are established on a monthly basis, or more often if market conditions dictate. The objective of the pricing committee is to establish a cash value on all classes of cattle managed by the Agent that will accurately reflect the current market for commercial breeding cattle. Accordingly, there is no difference, based on past events, in prices set for herds of current Owners and prices paid to third parties if the new Owner were to pay cash. However, if the new Owner desires to buy cattle on the installment basis, he will pay 10% premium over an all cash purchase. This applies to any seller who extends credit to a new Owner. To make allowances for variations due to geographic location and quality, all cattle are categorized by ranch location, and prices are adjusted up or down accordingly. Prices quoted to both the buying Owner and the selling Owner are those currently established by the pricing committee. Both buyer and seller are notified in the event of any change in prices before sale and purchase. Almost all calf and cull sales are arms-length transactions as are some herd sales.

In offering cattle to new Owners, emphasis is placed on the performance of the ranch on which the cattle are located, on the quality of the cattle, and on animal ages. Also considered is the date of the selling Owner's notice to place his herd into the sales inventory, and an effort is made to place each sale order in chronological sequence.

Normally all purchase money mortgages or other financing, rancher-contractor expenses, management fees, and other expenses are paid before a selling Owner receives any proceeds from his herd sale or from his steer calf sale. Market net worth statements are prepared for the selling Owners which are reasonable estimates for planning purposes subject, of course, to subsequent changes in general cattle price levels.

Additional proceeds may come from rancher contract penalties or death-loss indemnities paid by the rancher. These funds are available as the cattle are sold and as the contracts are settled, normally in the fall.

As a service to the selling Owner and at no additional charge, Agent will if so directed, attempt to sell at a discount, Owner's notes taken on the sale of their cattle, upon written instructions from the Owner, but Agent does not guarantee that it can sell them. When an Owner sells his notes he receives the equivalent of the cash price for his cattle, losing the 10% premium. The 10% premium is used as the basis for the discount of the notes.

BREEDER CATTLE PRIOR PERFORMANCE[1,2,3]

When evaluating Agent's prior performance, a new Owner must consider the effects that the following variables will have on his investment. Any or all of these variables could significantly affect the profitability of the investment.

a. When cattle were purchased?

b. What was the class (e.g. heifer, cow) and age of purchased cattle?

1. All of the performance data includes heifers (representing less than 10% of the total).

2. More than 75% of data pertains to fall purchases with sale in subsequent year and figures are based on the year from October 15 to October 14.

3. Breeder cattle consist of commercial grade cattle only.

c. Were additional cattle purchased and of what class?

d. Were cattle sold and of what class?

e. How long did Owner own his specific herd?

f. Were there exchanges of cattle?

g. Were there any operational problems (diseases, drought, floods, change of rancher)?

h. When was the herd liquidated?

i. In which state (approximately 16) and on which ranch (approximately 59) were the cattle located and maintained?

j. Which method of purchase did Owner use in purchasing his herd or additional cattle–installment or cash?

k. How were the cattle sold–auction, private sale, new Owner?

l. Did Owner refinance his herd?

m. Did Owner follow the recommendations of Agent as set forth in this Prospectus and information supplied during the ownership of Owner's herd?

Owner must also recognize that when evaluating Agent's ability to perform its services that his is but one of approximately 300 individual and separate breeder cattle businesses managed by Agent and grouped together to form the following tabulations, which may or may not be applicable to a new Owner's individual business.

SUPPLEMENT
BREEDER CATTLE AGENCY SERVICES

	Year 1	Year 2	Year 3	Year 4	Year 5	Year 6
Number of breeding cattle purchased by Owners						
Cows & first calf heifers	12,307	9,678	6,681	8,332	7,116	12,605
Yearlings	2,411	2,077	1,238	1,496	1,493	2,370
Heifer calves	6,971	8,307	4,454	200	0	0
Bulls	28	0	0	0	0	0
Total	21,717	20,062	12,373	10.028	8,609	14,975
Number of Owner's breeder cattle under Jack management						
Cows & first calf heifers	45,772	55,949	64,966	63,966	54,235	45,530
Yearlings	10,140	18,405	17,342	17,709	8,109	11,571
Heifer calves	39,690	25,881	12,594	12,469	14,102	14,799
Bulls	781	854	917	917	853	753
Total	96,333	101,089	95,242	95,061	77,299	72,653
Number of breeding cattle Owners						
New Owners purchasing herds during current year	116	78	60	53	33	72
Owners retaining herds purchased in previous year	347	415	420	350	303	220
Total	463	493	480	403	336	292

Established Owners purchasing additional cattle during current year	64	51	37	21	20	19
Owners selling herds in current year	52	53	93	112	100	116
Average herd size						
Herds purchased in current year	187	177	174	133	165	165
All herds under Jack management	216	243	226	226	215	220
Total Cash Outlay by Breeding Herd Owners	$6,945,000	$7,336,021	$7,527,599	$7,775,277	$5,978,521	$6,832,795
Average Cash Outlay per Owner used directly in breeding herd activity[4]	$ 15,135	$ 14,835	$ 13,575	$ 15,098	$ 14,451	$ 16,747
Average Fees and commissions paid to Jack[5]	3,465	2,865	2,925	2,702	3,343	3,855
Total	$ 18,600	$ 17,700	$ 16,500	$ 17,800	$ 17,794	$ 20,602
Average Breeder Sale/Purchase Price Paid and/or Received by Owners (per head)						
Cows & first calf						
Heifers *4 years old)	$ 450	$ 280	$ 275	$ 300	$ 325	$ 550
Cows (8 years old)	365	195	195	225	250	375
Yearlings	320	180	210	205	210	400

	Year 1	Year 2	Year 3	Year 4	Year 5	Year 6
Heifer calves	$ 230	$ 100	$ 110	$ 125	$ 130	$ 285
Bulls	750	500	500	525	500	700
Cull cows	225	150	150	155	173	300
Steer calves (sales prices only-product of Owner herd)	$ 254	$ 100	$ 116	$ 137	$ 169	$ 274
Average Profit (Loss) on Cash Outlay[6]	30%	(20%)	(14%)	(10%)	(5%)	10%
Average Production Factors						
Calf production rate	76%	75%	82%	80%	82%	80%
Number of steer calves produced	21,791	22,537	22,383	22,774	21,243	17,127
Weaned steer weights (pounds)	372	352	358	373	381	387
Direct cost (cow maintenance and breeding fees) of calf production	$114	$ 83	$103	$117	$110	$128
Cull Rate	18.0%	19.9%	10.0%	14.6%	11.4%	15.4%
Death Loss	3.5%	3.2%	2.9%	2.8%	2.6%	3.5%

4. Includes fees for data processing and guarantees (total of $135).

5. Includes initial fees and management fees.

6. These percentages are based on Owners who sold all of their breeder cattle in the year designated and are based on cash paid in on investment compared to cash return (cash on cash return).

SUPPLEMENT

BREEDER CATTLE AGENCY SERVICES

USE OF PROCEEDS

Because each breeder cattle program is individually negotiated to meet the request of each Owner, and because of fluctuating cattle prices, interest rates, feed prices, and other conditions surrounding the ownership of breeder cattle, it is impossible to predict the actual cash requirement necessary to enter into a breeder cattle program. Based on recent prices the minimum cash investment is $99,500 payable over a variable number of years, usually five. In addition to the $99,500 expenditure, an Owner will have to obtain loans or pay additional cash in order to purchase a cattle herd. Specific annual cash flow requirements for breeder programs are influenced by decisions of the Owner. Such ownership influences involve decisions regarding whether or not to sell each year's calf product, whether to retain suitable heifer calves as herd replacements, whether to refinance, and whether to increase or decrease the size of the breeding herd by new purchases or partial sales.

The cash investment in a breeder program will be used to pay in full for breeder cattle or make down payments on breeder cattle depending upon the Owner's choice of purchase method; to pay for bull breeding services; to prepay interest on non-recourse mortgages if breeder cattle are purchased on low-equity terms; to pay other operating costs of a breeder herd such as veterinary fees, brand registrations, inspection costs, trucking expenses; and to pay Agent its initial fee and management fee.

Based on October 15 prices, the minimum investment in the initial year of a breeder cattle business purchased on a low-equity method might be a total of $25,000 cash and a $57,600 mortgage for 100 cows. There will be cash requirements over the next four years in addition to the initial year. The minimum five year cash requirement is $99,500 which includes the first year's cash of $25,000. A mortgage of $57,600 is also required which will be amortized from the sales proceeds of Owners culls and calves. There is no known maximum amount of cash that may be required. Depending on the economy: the culls, calves, and steers sold during the ownership, and other factors, an Owner may have to pay more or less than $99,500 during the five year period.

These 100 cows, beginning in year two, will generate operating income from the production of steer calves and cull sales. The money available through calf and cull sales will normally be added to the minimum five year cash investment of $99,500 to help pay annual operating expenses.

SUPPLEMENT

BREEDER CATTLE AGENCY SERVICES

If a buying Owner were to purchase 100 head of cows at a per head price of $640, he would pay $25,000 cash on that date. The $25,000 would be applied as follows and the projected cash requirements follows:

PROJECTED EXPENSES AND CASH REQUIREMENTS
CASH BUDGET

1. Equity: 10% Downpayment		$ 6,400
Expenses:		
2. 12% Interest to December 31	$ 1,300	
3. Feed and Related Maintenence to Carry Herd to December 31	6,500	
4. Breeding Fees to Service Cows	1,800	
5. Miscellaneous Expenses to December 31	1,500	
6. Jack Industries Initial Fee	6,400	
7. Jack Industries Annual Management Fee	1,100	
8. **Total Cash Expenses:**		18,600
9. **Net Cash to Carry Herd to December 31**		$25,000

ESTIMATED AND PROJECTED OPERATING BUDGET
FALL
CASH BUDGET

1. Equity Payment		$22,000
Expenses:		
2. 12% Interest from January 1 to December 31	$ 6,700	
3. Feed and Related Maintenance to Carry Herd from October 15 to December 31	6,900	
4. Breeding Fees (October 15-December 31)	1,800	
6. Rancher Production Bonus	8,500	
7. Jack Annual Management Fee	2,500	
8. **Total Cash Expenses:**		$27,600
Income:		
9. Sale of Steer Calves	15,000	
10. Sale of Culls	5,000	
11. Total Income		(20,000)
12. Net cash payable		$29,600

Annual budget will be sent to Owners in July of each year. Each succeeding year thereafter, the Owner will be required to pay cash requirements 40% in August and 60% October of each year of ownership. If an Owner were to sell his herd during the calendar year, the cash budget would be different than set forth above.

The initial fee is a one-time expense applied toward setting up the business as set forth under the section.

The miscellaneous expenses are paid to third parties. The proceeds from the sale of calves and culls are applied toward mortgage payments and operating expenses.

BENEFITS OF BREEDER CATTLE AGENCY SERVICES

Deductions Attributable to Operations

Subject to limitations discussed below in "Tax Reform Act of 1976" and "Revenue Act of 1978," certain taxpayers engaged for profit in the business of farming (including feeding, breeding and raising of livestock) are entitled to elect the cash method of accounting for Federal income tax purposes and to deduct against ordinary income the expenses of operating and maintaining the cattle, including as an expense the depreciation on the cost of purchased cattle (but not raised cattle) acquired and used for breeding purpose. The limitations on the use of the cash method of accounting set forth below include: (1) the requirement that a farming syndicate deduct expenses in the tax year when used or consumed, not when paid; (2) the requirement that certain corporations and partnerships in which a corporation is a partner that are engaged in the trade or business of farming use the accrual method of accounting and capitalize preproductive period expenses; and (3) the requirement that a cash method taxpayer may deduct interest only in the taxable year in which and to the extent that the interest represents a charge for the use or forbearance of borrowed money during such year.

Cattle Owners will ordinarily be deemed to be "engaged in the business of farming" so long as there is present a bona fide intention and a reasonable expectation of deriving economic gain from cattle feeding, breeding, and raising activities wholly apart from and without regard to the potential favorable tax features of the arrangement. The satisfaction of the foregoing standard is in large part dependent upon the intention of the taxpayer and may be affected by the precise circumstances which attend the operation of the enterprise. There is no published authority directly holding that a breeder cattle operation under a management similar to that provided for in the Agency Agreement is engaged in the business of farming. However, the general rule for Federal income tax purposes is that one may conduct a farming business, including a livestock feeding, breeding, and raising business, through agents who bear all the burdens of management.

Owners, so long as they are deemed to be "engaged in the business of farming," would be entitled to deduct (1) operating expenses proximately related to the business, including expenses for management fees, interest, taxes, bull service, materials and supplies and (2) depreciation on purchased cattle acquired and used for breeding purposes.

The annual depreciation deduction is determined with reference to the cost (or other basis) of the breeder cattle and is based upon the anticipated useful life of the animals in the Owner's cattle business and the depreciation method employed by the Owner. Counsel expresses no opinion in respect to the useful life or the salvage value of the breeder herd.

With respect to cattle purchased from others for breeding, which have previously been used for breeding purposes, the Owner will normally be permitted to employ the straight line or 150% declining balance method in computing depreciation. Whether an Owner is a "first user" or a "second user" is an issue of fact in each case. Under the accelerated depreciation methods, annual deductions are computed on the adjusted cost of purchased animals undiminished by salvage value, but total depreciation deductions over the life of the animal may not exceed such cost less salvage value. Salvage value is the amount (generally determined at the time of acquisition) that is estimated will be obtainable on the sale or other disposition of the animal when it is no longer useful in the Owner's business. In certain cases, taxpayers except trusts) may be entitled to an additional first year or bonus depreciation of 20% in the first year of use under IRC Section 179 on $10,000 ($20,000 in the case of married persons filing joint returns) of the cost of cattle purchased having a useful life of at least six years. The cost basis for purposes of regular depreciation is reduced by the amount of the first year depreciation. Owners may elect the Section 179 allowance and will advise Agent of their decision. With respect to a partnership owning a breeder herd, there is a $10,000 limitation on the total cost of qualifying animals that may be passed on to all the partners for the purpose of computing each partner's bonus depreciation deduction. Thus, the amount of additional first-year depreciation deduction that a partnership may pass through to all of its partners is limited to $2,000 per year.

Character of Income Realized by Owner

Cattle held by purchasers for breeding purposes for 24 months or more from the date of acquisition will qualify as Section 1231 property. Any gain realized on the sale of such cattle would generally be taxed as long-term capital gain, subject to depreciation recapture. In the case of a cash basis taxpayer, recapture applies only to that portion of any realized gain which constitutes allowable depreciation with respect to cattle sold. Losses incurred on the sale of Section 1231 animals are first applied as an offset against Section 1231 gains, if any, and the balance is treated as an ordinary loss. Gains realized on the sale of breeder cattle held for less than 24 months from date of acquisition are taxed as ordinary income. Whether any particular cattle will be deemed held for breeding purposes or for sale to customers depends upon the intention of Owner. The determination of intention may be affected by Owner's actual practices with regard to utilization, sale and the time of ownership of the cattle.

RISK FACTORS

INVESTMENTS IN BREEDER CATTLE INVOLVE A HIGH DEGREE OF RISK AS TO THE POSSIBLE LOSS OF OWNER'S INVESTMENT AND AS TO THE TAX CONSEQUENCES THEREFROM. The principal risks are as follows:

Cattle Business

All Owners are advised that they are exposed to all of the risks commonly known and inherent in the cattle industry. Due to the nature of the cattle industry and to the method of financing the operations generally conducted by the Owner of a breeder cattle herd, it may be expected that financial losses will be incurred in the initial years of operation. The successful operation of commercial breeder cattle is affected by a number of important variables including: (1) overall quality of the livestock purchased, (2) subsequent herd production, (3) market fluctuation, (4) general economic conditions, (5) weather conditions, (6) incidence of disease, including but not limited to brucellosis, (7) natural calamities, (8) supply and demand in the industry, and (9) Federal regulations.

Market Fluctuations

Cattle and feed prices are subject to substantial fluctuations over both long and short periods of time. A reduction in effective beef demand in the United States would adversely affect the profitability of Owner's operations.

Death Losses

Owner usually stands the first 3% death loss of his cattle each contract year which is a normal rate in the industry. For death losses in excess of 3%, Owner is indemnified by the rancher at the price specified in the individual rancher Maintenance Contract. Rancher, however, is allowed one death loss per contract. If rancher is financially incapable of paying this indemnification, the Owner may have to stand all the death losses unless recoverable from rancher through litigation.

Price of Cattle

The purchasing and selling price for client cattle inventory is determined by a five man board of Allied Cattlemen's Co-Operative, an affiliate of Agent and not through arms-length negotiations.

Additional Payments in Future Years and Agent's Fees

The ownership and maintenance of a breeder herd is an ongoing business and normally requires an annual cash flow input to maintain that business. There will be additional payments in each year for feed, labor and pasturage.

Ranchers

Problems may be experienced with independent rancher-contractors managing Owner's herd which may make desirable the removal and replacement of those rancher-contractors. In addition, the rancher-contractor may be unable to fulfill the terms of his contract with Owner including such provisions as indemnities for dead or missing cattle or penalty payments to Owner arising from rancher's poor performance. A rancher may determine that it would be more profitable to maintain his own cattle and refuse to renew Owners' contracts which could result in moving costs being incurred by the Owners.

Some cattle may be placed on land leased by rancher-contractors. Such cattle could be subjected to undisclosed pasture liens arising from nonpayment of rent. Under maintenance contracts, Owner does not assume any obligation for the rental, but such a lien could restrict the sale or movement of Owner's cattle until such rental is satisfied. A similar situation could result in undisclosed agistor's liens from nonpayment of feed or labor bills incurred. Various types of contracts with rancher-contractors are available. However, all contracts necessarily depend on the skill, integrity, and financial ability of the rancher-contractor. These risks are minimized by (1) placing Owner's cattle at several locations, (2) regular lien searches, (3) inspections of ranches, and (4) checks with local banks and feed merchants.

A portion of the acreage on which cattle managed by Agent are maintained is covered by temporary Federal or state grazing leases and permits. The rancher could be deprived of his grazing leases and permits if the land covered thereby was offered for sale or abused by rancher.

Agent does not guarantee any contracts between Owners and Rancher-Contractors. An Owner may have to satisfy an agistor's lien (possessory lien) against his cattle in order to remove his cattle if the Rancher-Contractor is financially unable to satisfy the lien.

Lack of Liquidity or Transferability of Owner's Cattle

Commercial breeding herds are normally liquid assets if sold at proper times and in accord with the customs of the industry. Most sales of breeding herds occur in the fall. Three conditions may limit the liquidity of Owner's sale of cattle: (1) market conditions, (2) availability of buyers, and (3) time when sale occurs.

Option to Terminate by Agent or Owner

Agent and all Owners under the Breeder Cattle Agency Agreement have the right to cancel such Agency Agreement by giving 90 days' notice to the other party. If Agent should terminate the Agency Agreement for any reason, the Owners would either have to manage and care for their own cattle, take possession of their own cattle, or find other agents to manage their cattle herds.

Availability and Performance of Cattle

Agent cannot guarantee (1) that increased cattle prices will offset increased feeding costs, or (2) the availability of suitable rangelands at favorable prices, or (3) the quality of Owner's cattle.

Income Tax Risks

The Agent makes no representation that any tax benefits will result from an investment in breeder cattle, although, in certain cases, tax benefits may result from such an investment. However, such benefits may be challenged by the Internal Revenue Service or adversely affected by changes in the tax laws. If an Owner chooses to contest an adverse determination by the Internal Revenue Service, he may incur substantial professional fees and related expenses.

Tax Reform Act of 1976 and Revenue Act of 1978

It is the opinion of counsel that the changes in the tax law provided by the Tax Reform Act of 1976 ("Act") and Revenue Act of 1978 ("Rev. Act"), may have a significant adverse effect on Owner's timing of deductions and that any tax benefits to an Owner may be substantially reduced or eliminated. At the present time there are very few regulations, rulings, determinations, case law or other direct authority with respect to any of the changes and, therefore, no further interpretive opinion can be expressed with respect to the Acts. It is advised that any prospective Owner consult his tax advisor regarding the effect of such provisions.

Proposed Deficiency. If an Owner receives an adverse Internal Revenue Service determination resulting in a proposed tax deficiency, he may contest the deficiency at the administrative review level within the Internal Revenue Service. If this proves unsuccessful, the Owner can seek redress by filing a petition for redetermination of the deficiency in the U.S. Tax Court or by paying the additional tax and filing a suit for refund of tax in U.S. District Court. The expense of contesting the proposed deficiency must be borne by the Owner. Under present tax laws these expenses are deductible. However, investments should be made only by those persons willing to assume the risk of loss or reduction of any tax benefits of the investment as well as the expense of contesting an adverse determination by the Internal Revenue Service.

Agent will assist Owner in any contest. More particularly, Agent, at Owner's request, will reproduce and supply to Owner any schedules, exhibits, memoranda, records, writings, statements, reports, contracts and other documents pertinent to the issues before the Service. If such documents have previously been prepared and, at the time of the request, are in Agent's files they will be reproduced and furnished at no cost to Owner. However, if such documents are not then available to Agent and it is necessary to prepare the required documents, and Agent has the necessary information to so prepare them, Owner will be charged for the actual cost of preparation including the standard per hour rate for salaries and wages of employees. In addition, Agent, at Owner's request, will provide company personnel to appear at administrative hearings and before the District and Tax Court to testify with respect to such documents and any other matters of which they have personal knowledge and which are pertinent to the case. Owner would reimburse Agent for all travel, lodging, meals, hourly rate, and other incidental expenses incurred by such personnel for administrative and Court appearances. Owner will have to pay all further costs and expenses of contesting any deficiency.

SUPPLEMENT
BREEDER CATTLE AGENCY SERVICES

INCOME TAX CONSIDERATIONS

General

The material in this section contains a summary of the laws, rules and regulations and discusses various tax considerations relating to ownership of breeder cattle. It is anticipated that the agency services will be purchased by individuals. However, in the event an Owner is either a partnership or corporation, the income tax consequences of the purchase in such event are also discussed below. No opinion is offered as to any particular Owner.

It should be stated at the outset that there are no tax benefits inherent in the Agency contracts covered by this material. Because of the lack of direct authority in many of the areas of the tax law here involved, there is an inherent risk that the Internal Revenue Service might challenge one or more of the possible tax benefits discussed below, such as the tax status of the breeder cattle Owner and the availability, amount, and timing of deductions. If the Service were successful, tax advantages would be substantially reduced or eliminated. For this reason and others, prospective Owners should satisfy themselves independently of the tax consequences of breeder cattle ownership by obtaining the advice of their own tax counsel.

It is the Agent's policy that a taxpayer not subject to a combined Federal and State income tax rate of at least 50%, should not invest in livestock operations as an Owner. This policy is based on the experience of the Agent and takes into consideration the volatile nature of livestock prices, the many hazards of disease, weather, drought, blizzards, casualties, and problems of labor and management. An income tax bracket of 50% or higher is believed by the Agent to be necessary to utilize the possible tax advantages available to a purchaser of breeder cattle.

Tax Reform Act of 1969 and Revenue Act of 1971

The Tax Reform Act of 1969 added provisions to the Code which, in certain cases, had the effect of recapturing excess deductions incurred in connection with farm losses. Generally, under the 1969 Act, each cattle Owner was required to maintain an "Excess Deductions Account" (EDA). The effect of the EDA provisions has been eliminated for taxable years beginning after December 31, 1975, by the Tax Reform Act of 1976. The 1976 Act provides that no additions shall be made to the EDA for taxable years beginning after December 31, 1975. However, if property which is "farm recapture property" is disposed of during a taxable year beginning after December 31, 1975, the recapture rules of previous law will continue to apply, but only with respect to EDA accounts required to be maintained for one or more years beginning before December 31, 1975.

The Tax Reform Act of 1969 introduced Section 183 of the Code which deals with activities of an individual or a Subchapter S corporation, that are not engaged in for profit. In such case, the following expenses incurred by the activity are deductible: (1) those which are deductible without regard to profit motive, e.g., interest, certain taxes, etc.; and (2) other expenses only to the extent that gross income from the activity exceeds expenses deductible without regard to profit motive. This Section also creates a rebuttable presumption that the activity, e.g. farming, is engaged in for profit if it produces gross income in excess of related deductions in any two of five consecutive years of operation. The Service may overcome this presumption by evidence establishing a lack of profit motive. The test is whether the activity is begun or continued with the objective of making a profit. However, the mere fact the activity did not make a profit during two of five consecutive years does not necessarily mean certain expenses are nondeductible if the taxpayer can establish by objective facts that the losses were due to factors other than lack of profit motive. The Revenue Act of 1971 amended Section 183 to provide an election by the taxpayer to avoid a determination of whether the favorable presumption exists until the end of the fourth taxable year of the activity. If taxpayer so elects, the statutory period for assessing deficiencies attributable to such an activity is extended to the expiration of two years after the date for filing the activity's tax return (not including extensions) for the last taxable year in the period to which the election relates.

The investment credit is applicable to depreciable livestock, except horses, with useful lives of at least three years. The investment tax credit is 10% for property acquired and placed in service during the period beginning January 22, 1975 through December 31, 1980. It is unclear under existing amendments to the present statute whether the investment credit will remain permanently at 10% or will be reduced to 7% for property purchased on or after January 1, 1981. The full tax credit can be taken if cattle purchased have useful lives of seven years or more. The credit is reduced for cattle with useful lives of less than seven years. The law provides that if substantially identical cattle are sold or otherwise disposed of by a taxpayer during a one-year period of beginning six months before he acquires other cattle, the investment credit will be available only to the extent that the purchase price of such other cattle exceeds the sales price of the cattle sold. This rule does not apply if investment credit was recaptured on the sale or if the replacement is due to an involuntary conversion. Age of the cattle and the use to which they are put are important factors in determining whether disposed cattle are substantially identical to acquired cattle.

Purchases of used cattle in excess of $100,000 (or $50,000 in the case of a married person filing a separate return unless the spouse of the taxpayer has no used property which may be taken into account as qualified investment for such taxable year) do not qualify for investment credit. For the purpose of the limitation, the cost of cattle which have been used for breeding by a prior owner would have to be aggregated with the cost of other used property eligible for the investment credit that was acquired during the same taxable year, and thus, some or all of the credit may be unavailable to the purchaser. Whether an animal qualifies as "new" or "used" depends upon whether the taxpayer first used the animal for its intended purpose. Finally, disposition of the cattle prior to the end of their useful lives may result in recapture of investment credit previously taken on those cattle.

Tax Reform Act of 1976 and Revenue Act of 1978

The Tax Reform Act of 1976 ("Act") and Revenue Act of 1978 ("Rev. Act") will or may have an effect on an Owner's benefits to be derived from his cattle investment. Those provisions which the Agent believes have or will have an effect on a prospective Owner are discussed below.

Limitations on Farm Losses: IRC Section 465 establishes a limitation of loss with respect to farms or farming. Basically, the section provides that the amount of any loss (otherwise allowable in the tax year) which may be deducted in connection with a farm operation cannot exceed the aggregate amount with respect to which the taxpayer is at risk at the close of the taxable year. This limitation applies to all taxpayers other than corporations which are not Subchapter S corporations, personal holding companies, or closely held corporations. A corporation will be considered closely held if five or fewer individuals own (directly or through the application of IRC Section 318 attribution rules) 50% or more of the stock of the corporation. A taxpayer is generally to be considered "at risk" with respect to an activity to the extent of (i) his cash and the adjusted basis of other property contributed to the activity, (ii) any amounts borrowed for use in the activity with respect to which the taxpayer has personal liability for payment from his personal assets, and (iii) the net fair market value of personal assets, other than property used in the activity, which secure non-recourse borrowing. However, a taxpayer is not considered at risk with respect to amounts protected against loss through stop loss agreements, guarantees, certain non-recourse financing or similar arrangements. The term "loss" is defined as the excess of allowable deductions for the taxable year over the amount of income received or acquired by the taxpayer during the taxable year from farming operations. The amount of any loss that is not deductible by reason of the limitation may be carried over and deducted in succeeding taxable years subject to application of the at-risk rules in each such year. However, a taxpayer whose at risk amount has been reduced to zero may not deduct future losses until such times as he places additional amounts at risk. In addition, the Rev. Act provides for the recapture of previously allowed losses when the amount at risk is reduced below zero. If the amount at risk is reduced below zero (by distribution to the taxpayer, by changes in the status of the indebtedness from recourse to non-recourse, by the commencement of a guarantee or other similar arrangement which affects the taxpayers risk of loss, or otherwise), the taxpayer will recognize income to the extent that his risk basis is reduced below zero. However, the amount recaptured is limited to the excess of the losses previously allowed and which reduced the taxpayer's at risk basis in that activity for taxable years beginning after December 31, 1978, over any amounts previously recaptured.

Farming Syndicates. IRC Section 464 requires farming syndicates to deduct expenses for feed, seed, fertilizer, and other farm supplies only in the tax year when used or consumed, not when paid. A farming syndicate includes (1) a partnership or any other enterprise (other than a corporation which is not a Subchapter S corporation) engaged in the trade or business of farming if at any time interests in the partnership or other enterprise have been offered for sale in an offering required to be registered with any Federal or state agency having authority to regulate the offering of securities for sale or (2) a partnership or any other enterprise (other than a corporation which has not elected to be taxed under Subchapter S) engaged in the trade or business of farming if more than 35% of the losses during any period are allocable to limited partners or limited entrepreneurs. Pursuant to (1) above, investment interests offered under this material may result in the Owner being classified as a "farming syndicate" and thereby subject to the limitations discussed herein. In general, a limited entrepreneur means a person who has an interest in an enterprise other than a partnership and who does not actively participate in the management of a farm, depending upon the facts and circumstances.

The provision specifies five cases where an individual's activity with respect to a farm will result in his not being treated as a limited partner or limited entrepreneur. These cases cover the situations where an individual:

(1) has actively participated in the management of any trade or business of farming for a period of at least five years, and whose interest in a partnership or other enterprise is attributable to such active participation;

(2) whose principal residence is on the farm where the partnership or enterprise conducts its farming trade or business;

(3) who actively participates in the management of a business involving the raising of livestock (or is so treated under (1) or (2) and the partnership or enterprise further processes the livestock raised in that business;

(4) whose principal business activity involves active participation in the management of a trade or business of farming is also treated as not being a limited partner in any other trade or business of farming; and

(5) who is a member of the family (or a spouse of any such member) of a grandparent of an individual who is not treated as a limited partner or limited entrepreneur in situations (1) through (4) above, if the family member's interest is attributable to the active participation of that individual.

Accrual Accounting. IRC Section 447 provides that corporations (other than Subchapter S corporations, family corporations and corporations with annual gross receipts of less than $1 million) and partnerships in which a corporation is a partner and that are engaged in the trade or business of farming are required to use the accrual method of accounting and must capitalize preproductive period expenses. The Rev. Act further excepted certain two and three family controlled corporations from the provisions of the Section (IRC Sec. 447 (h)). The term "preproductive period expenses" means any amount which is attributable to crops, animals, or any other property having a crop or yield during the preproductive period of such property. The preproductive period is (1) the period before the disposition of the first marketable crop or yield in those cases where the property has a useful life of more than one year and will produce more than one crop or yield, and (2) in the case of any other property, the period before such property is disposed of. A taxpayer will be treated as having disposed of the property for purposes of this rule if it utilizes any part of the crop in its trade or business. However, certain expenses attributable to the preproduction period do not have to be capitalized and may be deducted. These include taxes and interest and any amount that is incurred on account of fire, storm, flood, or other casualty or on account of disease or drought.

A corporation is considered to be a family-owned corporation if at least 50% of the total combined voting power of all classes of stock entitled to vote and at least 50% of the total number of shares of all other classes of stock in the same corporation are owned by members of the same family. The members of the same family are an individual's parents and grandparents, the ancestors and lineal descendants of any of the above, a spouse of any of the above persons, and the estate of any of the foregoing (IRC Sec. 447 (d)). Individuals related by half blood or by legal adoption are treated as if they are related by blood. Stock ownership is also attributed through partnerships, trusts, generally through one tier corporations, and, under certain circumstances, through two tiers of corporations.

To be eligible for the multi-family exception, members of two families must own (either directly or through Sec. 447 (d) attribution rules) at least 65% of the total combined voting power of all classes of voting stock, and at least 65% of all other classes of the farming corporation's stock. If members of three families own at least 50% of the total combined voting power of all classes of voting stock and at least 50% of all other classes of the corporation's stock, the exception also applies. In addition, however, if three families are involved, the remainder of the corporation stock must be owned either directly or through attribution by the corporation's employees or a trust for the benefit of such employees. The exception applicable to multi-family corporations applies only to those engaged in the business of farming as of October 4, 1976.

A corporation (including any predecessor corporation) which does not have gross receipts exceeding $1 million in each prior taxable year beginning after December 31, 1975, does not have to use the accrual method of accounting. In computing gross receipts, all corporations that are members of a controlled group of corporations (parent-subsidiary and brother-sister) are treated as being one corporation. The Conference Committee Report states that once the level of receipts is exceeded for taxable years beginning after December 31, 1975, the corporation must change to the accrual method of accounting for its next taxable year and may not change back to the cash method of accounting even though its receipts fall below $1 million.

Prepaid Interest: IRC Sec. 461 (g) added a provision relating to the treatment of prepaid interest. This rule permits a cash method taxpayer to deduct interest only in the taxable year in which and to the extent that the interest represents a charge for the use of forbearance of borrowed money during that period.

Investment Interest: Counsel believes that the cattle purchased in this transaction qualify as property owned in the business of the Owner and should not be deemed to be property held for investment under the provisions of Section 163(d) of the Code. The Internal Revenue Service may, however, contend to the contrary, in which event, if the Service's position is sustained, Section 163(d) of the Code, as amended by the Act, limits the amount of "investment interest" annually deductible by a non-corporate taxpayer. It may be used to offset the following income items in the order listed:

(1) $10,000 ($5,000 for a married person filing a separate return)

(2) net investment income (from any investment).

In the case of a trust, number one above shall be zero. In the context of this discussion, "investment interest" (as distinguished from business interest) is, in general, interest paid or accrued on indebtedness incurred or continued to purchase or carry breeder cattle held for investment, not used in a business. No offset of investment interest is permitted against long-term capital gain. An additional deduction of up to $15,000 more per year is permitted for interest paid in connection with indebtedness incurred by the taxpayer to acquire the stock in a corporation or a partnership interest where the taxpayer, his spouse, or his children have (or acquire) at least 50% of the stock or capital interest in the enterprise. Interest deductions which are disallowed under these rules are subject to an unlimited carryover and may be deducted in future years (subject to the applicable limitation). No limitation is imposed on the deductibility of personal interest. Carryovers are to retain their character. Thus carryovers of pre-1976 interest will continue to be deductible under the limitation of previous law. Carryovers of post-1975 interest will be subject to the new rules adopted under the Act.

The applicability and effect of Section 163(d) will depend upon each Owner's particular financial position. Prospective Owners are, therefore, advised to consult their tax advisors in this regard.

Minimum Tax: The Rev. Act restructured the minimum tax provisions. The previous 15% add-on minimum tax continues in force, but after 1978 the tax no longer applies to capital gains or excess itemized deductions preference items. Instead, these two items become part of the new alternate minimum tax which becomes effective in 1979. The alternate minimum tax is payable by an individual to the extent that the alternate tax exceeds the regular income tax increased by the amount of the existing minimum tax, as revised, on preference items other than capital gains and itemized deductions. The alternate minimum tax base is the sum of an individual's taxable income, adjusted itemized deductions and the capital gains deduction. However, recognized gain from the sale of a principal residence under Sec. 1034 is not to be treated as a capital gains preference for sales occurring after July 26, 1978, in tax years ending after that date. The alternate minimum tax is an amount equal to the sum of (1) 10% of the alternate minimum taxable income above

$20,000 through $60,000, (2) 20% of such income above $60,000 up through $100,000 and (3) 25% of such income over $100,000.

The alternate minimum tax does not apply to corporations. Corporations are still subject to the minimum tax rate on certain tax preferences at a rate of 15%. The exemption for corporations is the greater of $10,000 or the full amount of the regular tax.

Maximum Tax on Earned Income: The Tax Reform Act of 1969 added IRC Section 1348 which provides for a maximum tax of 50% on personal service income. However, the amount eligible for the maximum tax rate is reduced dollar-for-dollar by the individual's items of tax preference. The Rev. Act removes capital gains as a tax preference, thus increasing the amount of personal service income eligible for the maximum tax rate. This change generally is effective with respect to a taxpayer's net capital gain attributable to post-October 21, 1978 taxable transactions and installment payments. Effective for taxable years beginning after December 31, 1978, the Rev. Act eliminates the 30% limitation on the amount from a trade or business that can be treated as personal service income for maximum tax purposes where capital is a material income producing factor. Individuals will receive the benefits of the maximum tax for income that constitutes reasonable compensation for services rendered.

Capital Gains: The Rev. Act repeals the 25% alternate tax on net capital gains of non-corporate taxpayers for taxable years beginning after December 31, 1978. The Rev. Act increases the amount of any net capital gain which a noncorporate taxpayer may deduct from gross income from 50% to 60%. The remaining 40% of the net capital gain is includable in gross income and subject to tax at the regular rate. The deducted gain is classified as a tax preference item for alternate minimum tax purposes, but not for purposes of reducing the amount of personal service income which is eligible for the maximum tax. The increase in the capital gains deduction, the elimination of the maximum tax offset, and the increase in the capital gains tax preference are effective for taxable transactions occurring, and installment payments received, after October 31, 1978. The Rev. Act reduces the alternate tax rate on corporate capital gains from 30%

to 28%. The minimum tax preference of corporate long-term capital gains will be 18/46 of the gain. This change is effective with respect to taxable transactions occurring, and installment payments received, after December 31, 1978.

SUMMARY

The foregoing discussion is intended only to summarize in general terms applicable provisions of Federal income tax laws relative to ownership of breeder cattle. Any of the provisions may be changed at any time and may or may not be retroactive to transactions entered into or completed prior to the effective date thereof. In addition, the impact of any provision may have a different effect on various Owners. It is the opinion of counsel that the changes provided by the Tax Reform Act of 1976 and Revenue Act of 1978 will have a limiting effect on Agent's previously stated objective of timing of deductions and that any tax benefits to an Owner have been substantially reduced.

The foregoing discussion of "Income Tax Consequences" sets forth an explanation of the Sections of the Tax Reform Act of 1976 and Revenue Act of 1978 which the Agent believes has or will have an effect on a prospective Owner. This material summarizes the various pertinent sections of the Acts and includes information contained in the explanation of the Acts as provided in the Report of the Joint Committee on Taxation. The Letter of Transmittal from the Chief of Staff states, with respect to the Committee Report relative to the Act, dated December 29, 1976, that "No attempt is made here to carry the explanation further than is customary in the case of committee reports and therefore it does not deal with issues which are customarily explained in regulations or ruling." At the present time there are very few regulations, rulings, determinations, case law or other direct authority with respect to any of the above changes and, therefore, no further interpretive opinion can be expressed with respect to the Acts. It is advised that any prospective Owner consult his tax advisor regarding the effect of such provisions.

SUPPLEMENT

BREEDER CATTLE AGENCY SERVICES

BREEDER CATTLE AGENCY AGREEMENT

Jack Industries, Inc.

Gentlemen:

This will confirm my arrangement with you:

1. I am desirous of purchasing and maintaining a herd of breeding cattle and I hereby employ you as my agent and agricultural consultant to negotiate and make the necessary arrangements in connection with this plan.

2. You will select and purchase breeding cattle for such amounts of money as you will be directed by me to spend from time to time. Title to these cattle shall be taken in my name or as directed by me, and the animals identified as belonging to me. Where specific permission from me is necessary to establish title for brand registrations, registration with a purebred association, bank loans, filing of financing statements and security agreements, bills of sale, etc., I hereby grant you permission to use a photocopy of this document as authorization.

3. You will arrange for the pasture, feeding and care (including veterinarians) of the cattle, as well as their offspring. You will arrange for periodic and systematic inspections of the herd(s) belonging to me and eliminate such animals (when and if necessary) which are no longer suitable for continued breeding purposes. You may join my cattle with others to get the advantage of lower costs, better care, or improved supervision. Sales beyond required culling percentages will be accomplished only at my direction. Should I be dissatisfied with the independent contract rancher with whom I have placed my cattle, I retain the privilege of directing you to move the cattle to another location upon expiration of the contracts at my expense.

4. You may take any reasonable legal action necessary to uphold my rights in cattle management contracts, mortgages, feed agreements, and other situations affecting my cattle ownership or maintenance and any legal costs will be an operating expense to me. In the event legal action must be taken by you to protect my rights regarding my cattle which are under contract with a rancher, I understand that you must act in concert for all owners having cattle with the particular rancher in question. I further understand that you, pursuant to your obligations, must

negotiate, file suit, litigate, effect settlement or take other legal steps necessary to protect all owners equally against any contract breaches by the rancher. Accordingly, I authorize you to act in such a manner and to effect the maximum degree of restitution which, in your judgment and the attorneys', is possible under the circumstances. You are also empowered to act in this manner to enforce claims against truckers and trucking companies transporting owners' cattle and against all sales agents, auction markets, order buyers and others who may from time to time handle owners' cattle under oral or written agreement.

5. You are hereby directed that where it is in my best interest from the standpoint of animal husbandry and economics, you may exchange my cattle for cattle of like kind as long as the exchange is for cattle of comparable quality and equal value.

6. I understand that your standard management techniques require dispersion of my cattle to give added protection against natural hazards and rancher/contractor malfeasance. Normally, these dispersed increments are efficiently handled by each rancher. With the passage of time, however, cull sales, new births and cattle movements reduce these increments to small numbers that are difficult to manage properly. In such circumstances, you are authorized to sell such small increments at the highest price currently being paid for animals of the size, quality, and age of the cattle comprising my small increment. Alternatively, you may trade these small increments for cattle of equal worth as explained, herein. Where trades are effected it shall be with the intent of grouping my cattle in larger increments. In no case, without my written consent, shall you sell increments of more than 5 head or sell more than 10% of my total herd inventory (exclusive of current calf crop) under your management.

7. You will keep books and accounts open for my inspection at reasonable times at your offices, and you will render accounts and reports to me in reasonable detail. All accounts will be kept on a cash basis of accounting. I understand that inventory, profit and loss, budget and tax records are maintained on an electronic data processing system, and that fees paid by you for the periodic use of computers and to national accounting firms will be an operating expense to me. You will administer all funds for me through an account to be kept in my name in a Kansas City or other metropolitan bank, subject to drafts

thereon by you through your legally appointed officers. Annual cash requirements, if required by the annual budget prepared by you and mailed to me on or before July 15, will be payable in increments on August 15 and October 15. All employees of your company handling my funds and account shall be bonded by a responsible insurance company.

8. You will insure me in responsible insurance companies against public liability with minimum limits of $500,000/ $1,000,000 for injury to persons, and $500,000 for any injury to property, and you shall send me information concerning such insurance, which may be for our joint benefit as our interests may appear. The premiums for such insurance shall be an operating expense to me.

9. Under extreme conditions, it may be necessary for you as Agent to make extraordinary arrangements with a rancher-contractor for the maintenance of an increment of my cattle herd which must be moved under difficult circumstances from its present pasture location. Should this occur, rather than truck my cattle for long distances or sell them at a local auction or through some other customary sales procedures, you may go beyond the limits of the normal cattle maintenance contracts, which you arrange on my behalf, and take such measures as you may judge necessary to preserve the herd values by finding an adequate home for the cattle thus displaced. In addition to other emergency measures, you are authorized to give the new maintenance rancher-contractor an option to purchase my herd increment at the termination date of the contract for a price of at least 20% over the fair market value which existed at the start of this contract. You shall not, however, make this type of extraordinary contract for more than 15% of my total herd without my written consent.

10. For your services you shall charge me an Initial Fee, depending upon the size of the herd, between eight percent (8%) and ten percent (10%) of the gross herd purchase price. In addition you shall charge me an Annual Management Fee equal to ten percent (10%) of the funds employed to pay all annual operating expenses, excluding down payment on and payments made to amortize the principal amounts of any notes issued or assumed by me to which my herd is subject and any fees paid by me to you, as my Agent, provided however, that the minimum Annual Management Fee shall not be less than five hundred dollars ($500). I understand that the foregoing terms

are subject to the provisions of your Registration Statement registering this Agency Agreement. You shall send me any changes to these fees.

11. You will arrange for any financing in order to purchase cattle for my account. I understand that all operating expenses of my cattle business including your Initial Fee, the annual Management Fee, and the rancher-contractor settlements for maintaining my cattle are my personal responsibility except for any non-recourse financing.

12. If you arrange initial financing or subsequent refinancing with banks on my cattle herd, I agree to pay you a service fee to cover your expenses of processing and handling any such loans and a guarantee fee which is to be a percentage of the amount guaranteed by you. I understand the percentage may be increased or decreased as the amount guaranteed to the bank(s) fluctuates and my account is to be charged accordingly. In the event you arrange financing with ranchers or other owners, you may charge a service fee of 1% of the loan balance.

13. Subject to my written instructions to the contrary, you have my power of attorney to arrange for loans against a lien on my cattle, however, without any personal liability on my part. Proceeds from such loans will be deposited in my Kansas City or other metropolitan bank account and employed in the operation of my cattle business. Where you are buying cattle subject to an existing loan, you may sign whatever documents for me that the lending agency requires. Any such document may be filed with the necessary governmental agency.

14. I acknowledge receipt of your effective Prospectus in which a form of this agreement is included.

15. During such period as Jack Industries, Inc. retains its present Agency Agreement for the management of my cattle now under their jurisdiction, I hereby give them my Power of Attorney to represent me at the meetings of any agricultural association, agricultural cooperative, cattle breeder's association, or cattlemen's association to which I presently belong or join at some future date. Jack Industries, Inc. is granted the authority to sign a proxy in my name for any annual or special stockholders or membership meeting with the right to vote for or against directors, officers, or any special matters that might come up before any such association. This authority is limited only to such associations, cooperatives, and groups which I have jointed or paid membership in, from my Kansas City account.

Any proxies signed under this authority can be revoked in writing by me at any time and in the event I personally wish to attend any such meeting, this authority is automatically revoked during such period of attendance.

While not limited to the following this authority specifically extends to meetings of the following:

American Hereford Association
American Polled Hereford Association
American Angus Association
National Cattlemen's Co-operative
The American Farm Bureau (national and all local branches)
National Cattlemen's Association (and all regional cattle associations connected with it)
Consumers Cooperative Association
Texas and Southwestern Cattle Raisers Association
New Mexico Cattle Growers Association
International Brangus Breeder Association
Kansas Livestock Association
Colorado Cattlemen's Association
Montana Stockgrowers Association
Missouri Cattlemen's Association
Wyoming Stockgrowers Association
Oklahoma Cattlemen's Association
Idaho Cattlemen's Association

16. If I, by my own act, default on any mortgage payment or payment of any operating expense, I direct you as my agent to liquidate my cattle investment at your discretion. I hereby waive any notice of any such liquidation. All funds received in the liquidation shall be applied to the following obligations according to the laws of the states in which the cattle are located: (1) rancher-contractor settlements, (2) operating bills and expenses, (3) cattle notes and mortgages, and (4) Jack's fees and charges. If there is any excess after paying all my obligations then such excess hall be paid to me.

17. I will not hold you liable for acts of negligence upon the part of personnel that you select to operate my herds as long as you exercise reasonable diligence in their selection and supervision.

18. In connection with the employment of Jack Industries, Inc. as agent relating to the selection, inspection, assistance in

the negotiation of cattle purchases and cattle maintenance and the financing thereof, and the keeping of books and records pertaining to such cattle purchased by me, the undersigned represents and warrants that:

(a) I either (i) have a net worth (exclusive of the value of my home and household effects) of at least $500,000 or (ii) have a net worth (as above) of at least $100,000 and am in a Federal and state income tax bracket in excess of 50%.

(b) I have obtained my own individual financial, tax, and legal advice with respect to the advisability of purchasing cattle, conducting a cattle business and employing Jack Industries, Inc., as my agent for the purpose mentioned above.

(c) My residence address as set forth below is my true and correct legal address.

The representations are made to induce Jack Industries, Inc. to accept employment as agent for the undersigned and Jack Industries, Inc. is hereby authorized to represent to the Securities and Exchange Commission and any or all State Commissions, whose jurisdiction embraces the Securities or Blue Sky law of any state, the truth of the above representation.

19. This shall comprise the entire agreement between us, and any prior negotiations are merged herein. Your signature below shall suffice to make this a binding agreement. This agreement may be cancelled by either party on 90 days' written notice. Further, this agreement is for the term of one year and shall automatically be renewed unless either party cancels as above provided.

RECOURSE FINANCING AUTHORIZATION

I hereby authorize Jack Industries, Inc., in connection with the above Breeder Cattle Agency Agreement to act as my agent to arrange recourse financing for the purchase of breeding cattle for me, beyond the non-recourse financing set forth in the Agency Agreement, to the limit of $______________ and to execute any and all documentation to effectuate such an arrangement.

SPECIAL POWER OF ATTORNEY IN CONNECTION WITH BREEDER CATTLE AGENCY AGREEMENT

WHEREAS, the undersigned has simultaneously herewith entered into a Breeder Cattle Agency Agreement with Jack Industries, Inc., and

WHEREAS, the undersigned has authorized Jack, as Agent, to obtain and enter into the necessary financing for the undersigned's purchase of breeder cattle.

NOW, THEREFORE, the undersigned appoints Jack Industries, Inc. and its officers and representatives to execute and deliver in the undersigned's name and on his/her behalf any and all instruments required to secure the necessary financing, including but not limited to a recourse promissory note, mortgages, financing statements, and similar documents, in order to purchase breeder cattle for the undersigned and the undersigned shall be personally liable on the said recourse promissory note for no more than $______________ and said appointment shall continue until the undersigned has sold all of his/her breeder cattle and shall include any refinancing directed by the undersigned, and all instruments so executed by Jack Industries, Inc. and its officers and representatives shall be deemed conclusively to be authorized by the undersigned.

GLOSSARY

The following are definitions of some of the more important terms used in this material.

Agistor's Lien: An encumbrance upon livestock for unpaid pasture leases, feed and veterinarian bills, and the like.

Bred Yearling: A female yearling that has been bred.

Bull: A male bovine animal of any age.

Calf: A male or female animal under twelve (12) months of age.

Calf Crop: All calves produced by a herd in a twelve (12) month period.

Calving Rate: Percentage determined by dividing the calf crop by the total number of adult female animals in the herd as of the first day of a twelve (12) month period.

Cow: Adult bovine female which has already had one calf.

Cow-Calf: A cow and her nursing calf, which she usually has at her side for approximately six (6) to eight (8) months.

Cull: An animal which, while capable of breeding, is deemed to have inferior characteristics for such factors as age, size, weight, muscling, trimness, soundness and breed character.

Culling: The process by which inferior cattle are removed from the herd and disposed of for the purpose of improving the level of quality and maintaining the age average at a constant level.

First Calf Heifer: A young female animal, 2 to 3 years of age bred to have her first calf.

Heifer: A young female animal prior to giving birth to a calf.

Open 2 Year-old Hiefer: An unbred two year old female.

Open Yearling: An unbred female yearling.

Purchase Money Chattel Mortgages: A security interest in personal property, including cattle, created upon the purchase of the property.

Replacement Heifers: Those female animals that are purchased or born to the herd and used to replace culls or to increase the size of the herd.

Steer: Castrated bull.

Yearling: Animal between twelve (12) and fourteen (14) months of age.

Weaning: The removal of calves from cows; normally six (6) to eight (8) months after birth.

LUMBER

INDUSTRY STATUS AND FORECAST

The value of lumber industry shipments in 1981 is expected to reach $11.0 billion, an increase of 15.7 percent above the 1980 figure unadjusted for inflation. In terms of real growth, lumber production is estimated at 35.5 billion board feet, an increase of 11.6 percent above the 31.8 billion feet produced in 1980.

Residential construction, the largest single user of lumber, is the key determinant of lumber production and demand. The forecast production increase is based on the anticipated volume of housing construction in 1981, an estimated 1.55 million units, 1.25 million of them single family dwellings. Other types of construction are expected to show modest increases. Continuing high mortgage rates and new construction costs will stimulate the repairs and remodeling industry.

In 1981, following the uptrend of housing, other wood-using industries, such as furniture, will recover after a depressed year. The demand for treated wood will continue to grow. The materials handling industry, strengthened by the demand for pallets and crating, will also expand production.

Should the demand rise rapidly early in the year, the softwood industry may experience difficulty in meeting it immediately. Mill inventories have been reduced to a low level, and some companies have not been building log decks for the winter months because of the uncertainty of the market. A sudden increase in demand could thus strain supply, resulting in rising prices early in the year.

1980 Characterized by Uncertainty

Dampened by the depressed level of housing construction and limited demand from other wood-consuming industries, lumber production declined, at 15 percent through the first months of 1980. Total lumber production was down 15 percent compared to the same period in 1979. Lumber production for the year was estimated at 31.8 billion board feet, a decline of 14.1 percent from 1979. Softwood lumber, about 75 percent of total lumber, was expected to reach 25.0 billion feet. Hardwood lumber was estimated at 6.8 billion feet in 1980.

Most of the decline in demand came from reductions in residential construction, although demand for all types of construction was down from the 1979 level. Other wood-consuming industries, such as furniture, pallets, repairs, and remodeling, were also operating at low levels. Total domestic lumber consumption in 1980 was estimated at 39.7 billion board feet. Both lumber manufacturers and consuming industries reduced work schedules and kept inventories to the minimum.

SOFTWOOD LUMBER

Softwood lumber was more seriously affected than hardwood lumber in 1980, because of its dependence on the residential construction industry, its largest single user. Softwood production was down nearly 20 percent at the end of July 1980 as compared with the first months of 1979. However, sawmills began to operate closer to normal capacity in the third quarter. Some mills shifted production to items in strong demand. Treated lumber continued to be purchased for railroad ties, agricultural uses, and wood foundations. Softwood production for the year was expected to reach 25.0 billion board feet, about 15.3 percent below the 1979 production of 29.5 billion board feet.

Approximately 67 percent of the softwood lumber was produced in the western States; 27 percent in the South.

Foreign demand gave the industry a boost in the first three quarters of 1980. Exports moved ahead of 1979 by about 25 percent but were expected to decline in the last quarter because of depressed economic conditions in foreign markets.

HARDWOOD LUMBER

Although the monthly rate of hardwood lumber production declined in 1980, total hardwood lumber production advanced 2.7 percent in the first 7 months of 1980 compared to the same period in 1979. Total hardwood production was expected to reach 6.8 billion board feet in 1980.

All of the hardwood consuming industries suffered from the sluggish economy. Weak demand forced furniture producers to reduce production, particularly of moderate and lower period furniture. Some companies reduced work schedules and inventories to stay in business.

The pallet industry operated at about 85 percent capacity in 1980, and for the first time in 17 years, did not exceed the previous year's production. Pallet users changed buying patterns, making frequent small purchases instead of buying in volume because of a decline in the movement of goods.

The hardwood flooring industry operated at 75 percent to 80 percent of normal production.

The foreign market proved very profitable. Hardwood exports continued the upward trend of the past few years and were expected to exceed the 1979 level. Most U.S. hardwood exports traditionally go to Europe, but the oak wilt disease in the United States now poses a problem for U.S. exports. Government and industry are working to solve the problem.

Lumber Exports Surge

Foreign trade proved to be an important ingredient in sustaining the lumber industry in 1980. In a year of depressed domestic demand, the industry's persistent efforts to develop and expand foreign markets were rewarded.

Lumber exports for the first 7 months of 1980 ran about 27 percent higher than in the comparable period in 1979. Softwood lumber exports reached 1.22 billion board feet in that period, compared with 0.97 billion feet in a similar period in 1979, an increase of about 25 percent. Hardwood lumber exports increased 30 percent during the 7-month period in 1980 to 0.217 billion feet, compared with 0.167 billion feet in the 1979 period.

Exports were expected to level off in the last quarter of 1980, because of ample inventories, depressed housing construction levels, and economic uncertainty which reduced demand in some major markets, such as Japan, Australia, and Western Europe. However, total exports for the year were expected to reach or exceed the 1979 level, possibly to a peak of 2.2 billion board feet.

Exports to Japan, the leading U.S. market, were up about 13 percent in the first three quarters of 1980. Japan buys

Western hemlock, spruce, and western pines from the United States. Canada, the second largest market, purchases both softwood and hardwood lumber. Shipments to Canada ran about 10 percent higher in the first three quarters of 1980 than in 1979. Italy, third largest market, accounted for the greatest percentage increase in exports. Shipments of Douglas fir, southern pine, and hardwoods to Italy rose 80 percent in the first three quarters of 1980 over the 1979 period. Exports to Mexico grew 46 percent in 1980, and West Germany increased its purchases by 47 percent in 1980.

Lumber exports to Australia, sixth largest market for U.S. lumber, were down about 26 percent in the first three quarters of 980 compared with 1979 due primarily to excess inventories and a depressed economy.

The six major markets accounted for about 80 percent of all U.S. lumber exports, although the United States exports to more than 150 countries throughout the world. Exports to the Middle Eastern countries have increased in recent years, and Saudi Arabia and Egypt purchased significant volumes of lumber in 1980.

Lumber Imports Down

Lumber imports respond to the rise and fall in the rate of U.S. housing construction. As a result of the sharp drop in housing, total lumber imports for 1980 were expected to reach only 9.3 billion board feet, about 18.1 percent below the 1979 level.

Approximately 97 percent of U.S. lumber imports, consisting of the softwood species used in construction, come from Canada. Despite the decline in the volume of imports, the Canadian share of U.S. total consumption is expected to reach 29 percent in 1980, a figure near the top of its range in the past several years.

Prices Decline

The Industry Price Index (1971 = 100) for SIC 2421, Sawmills and Planing Mills Industry, had risen steadily since 1974. In 1980, prices reversed this trend, and the index declined during the first 5 months, from 234.8 in January to 209.3 in May. The index began to rise again in June and reached 233.9 in

August. The 1980 index for the first 8 months of 1980 was down 7.3 percent compared with the same period in 1979.

The Producer Price Index (PPI, 1967 = 100), after fluctuating considerably in the first 8 months of 1980, registered an 8.7 percent decline to 333.5 in August, compared with 365.2 in August 1979. The softwood lumber index in August 1980 was reported at 356.7, down 9.4 percent from the 394.0 of August 1979. The hardwood lumber index declined 5.2 percent, from 261.3 in August 1979 to 247.8 in August 1980.

Employment Declined

The sawmill and planing mill industry employs 28 percent of all employees in the solid wood products industry.

The decline in residential construction and its demand for lumber and related products hurt employment. In early 1980, closures and curtailment of mill production temporarily affected a substantial number of employees. Total employment, based on the mid-year average was estimated at 177,000 employees in 1980, a decrease of 7.3 percent from 1979. The number of production workers declined 7.7 percent below 1979 to an estimated 144,000 employees.

Concentration and Productivity

Forest Industries magazine conducts an annual survey of lumber producers in the United States and Canada and publishes the results in a special issue each May. While the survey does not include every producer or total production in either country, it covered 87 percent of U.S. lumber production in 1979.

The survey by *Forest Industries* indicated continued growth of the larger U.S. lumber producers in 1979. The top 5 U.S. producers accounted for 8.2 billion board feet, 22 percent of total estimated U.S. lumber production in 1979. The production of 3 of the top 5 producers exceeded 1 billion board feet. Output of the top producer was almost 3 billion feet. The top 10 producers accounted for 10.6 billion board feet, 28 percent of total production in 1979, compared with 9.1 billion feet, 24 percent of total production in 1978.

Capacity Utilization

The western lumber industry operated at 68.5 percent of practical capacity during June 1980, compared with 91.8 percent in June 1979. Figures for the first 5 months of 1980 showed the industry operating at 73.1 percent of capacity compared with 92.4 percent in the same period of 1979. The western industry defines "practical operating capacity" as the highest actual production reached in a given month during the past 5 calendar years). At the end of September, the western industry was operating at 84 percent of normal capacity; the southern lumber industry, at about 95 percent.

New Plants

Among expansions of industry capacity in the 1980's, one South Carolina lumber company is planning a $12-million sawmill to produce 60 million board feet of pine lumber annually beginning in 1981. Another, a major wood products company, started operations at its new hardwood sawmill in North Carolina. The mill, which has a rated annual production capacity of 13 million board feet of lumber, will cut primarily furniture dimension stock of oak, poplar, and gum. The same company is building a high-speed pine sawmill in Georgia and plans to begin operations by late 1981. The plant, employing the most modern proven technology in lumber manufacturing, will have an annual capacity of 75 million board feet. The first pine sawmill of its type on the East Coast, it will be equipped with two maxi-mill headrig saw systems using electronic scanners and computers to yield maximum recovery and sawing accuracy. The plant will employ 135 people on an annual payroll of $1.4 million.

Fuel Savings

A Georgia lumber manufacturer owns what is believed to be the first high-temperature direct-fired hot gas dry kiln that operates exclusively on green wet wood residues. The system utilizes the fluidized bed concept to provide hot gases from the combustion of undried green wood waste for two 80,000 board feet lumber kilns. Conversion to wood fuel is expected to eliminate the purchase of 120 million cubic feet of natural gas annually, resulting in substantial savings and improving company's competitive position in the lumber market.

Design System for Customized Pallets

The National Wooden Pallet Association and the Virginia Polytechnic Institute, with matching funds from the Federal Government, are cooperating on the development of a computer-based design system to produce custom-tailored pallets. The revolutionary system will increase the handling capability of basic wood pallets in the movement of products from raw materials through the distribution of finished goods.

The industry increasingly relies on wood pallets not only for storage and shipment but also for the movement of raw materials and products within the plant. Since the development of the unit load, wood pallets in combination with forklift trucks have saved incalculable manhours of labor and square feet of storage space.

Outlook for 1985

Domestic demand for lumber may rise to nearly 50 billion feet in 1985. Housing starts are projected to reach 2.1 million units. Of these, 1.4 million will be single family units. Stimulated by higher mortgage rates and increasing construction costs, the repairs and remodeling industry (both residential and nonresidential) should increase about 1.6 percent annually to 1985. Other wood-consuming industries will benefit from the expansion in housing construction. Furniture shipments are expected to rise 4.1 percent annually.

Stimulated by the increasing demand for pallets and crating, the materials-handling industry expects demand to increase at the annual compound rate of 12 percent. The pallet industry, the second largest single user of total lumber, expects to produce 450 million units in 1985, 50 percent above the nearly 300 million units produced in 1979.

To meet this demand, 39.5 billion board feet of domestically produced lumber and net imports of 10.5 billion feet will be required in 1985. Should lumber exports continue at or above the 2 billion annual rate of 1970-80, total imports of 12.5 billion feet or more will be needed. According to current reports, Canada will probably be able to supply that volume in 1985, but toward the end of the decade, the reportedly fast declining supply of economically accessible timber, may reduce these exports to the United States.

The supply of readily accessible raw materials and production capacity may place limits on domestic output of lumber, particularly beyond 40 billion feet. In 1973, when housing starts exceeded 2 million units, sawmills were operating at 92 percent to 96 percent of capacity. At that time, the official number of sawmills in operation was 8,071. Additional capacity came from other wood-producing industry mills and from some small sawmills that operate only at periods of strong demand. By 1977, the number of mills had declined to 7,544, and many marginal mills had ceased unproductive operations because of rising raw material and construction costs. While new plants with increased capacity are being built and modernization and expansion of other facilities is increasing, overall capacity may not be sufficient to produce more than 40 million feet. However, the assurance of an adequate timber supply and strong demand would encourage investments in new mills or capacity expansion.

More than 51 percent of the sawtimber, the type needed for the manufacture of most wood products used for construction, is located on Federal timber lands. National forest goals call for annual harvests of 11 billion to 12.5 billion board feet by 1985. The 1980 goal was placed at 12.2 billion feet, but only 11.5 billion feet for fiscal 1981. Apparently, the additional timber supply is expected to come from private and nonindustrial timber lands. The industry has indicated that, while the timber supply could meet production goals in the long term, given the 20 to 30 years needed for trees to reach maturity, enough timber may not be available by 1985.

The domestic markets for lumber will take priority over exports in times of strong domestic demand, the foreign market potential to absorb any excess production looks promising. As the timber supply increases, production capacities expand, and trade barriers are eliminated, growing lumber exports will stimulate and strengthen the domestic lumber industry.

A 1950 forecast predicted the doubling of European demand for wood and wood products, including pulpwood, by the year 2000. Exports to Europe, particularly hardwood lumber, have been rising steadily. Housing goals in Japan, the top market for U.S. softwood lumber, are expected to be 3 percent higher for 1981-85 than in 1976-80.

The Japanese industry has announced plans to increase the proportion of lumber imports from the United States.

Lumber and wood products producers are receiving a boost in their efforts to develop overseas markets and expand exports.

The USDA Foreign Agricultural Service (FAS) has a cooperative agreement with the National Forest Products Association (NFPA) to help the industry. FAS will provide funds to the forest products industry through NFPA for market development projects overseas. The program is comparable to similar programs that FAS has for other agricultural products. The Southern Forest Products Association (SEPA) and NFPA are studying the market potential to expand lumber sales in Europe. The agency's role will then become one of helping develop the market and provide matching funds. SFPA will provide marketing and technical assistance. Other projects are under consideration.

In summary, domestic lumber production is expected to reach about 39.5 billion board feet in 1985, rising at the annual compound rate of 4.2 percent. Assuming a 10.0 percent compound annual rate of increase, the value of lumber industry shipments should reach $15.3 billion by 1985.

CROPS AND TIMBER

THE TIMBER GROWING INDUSTRY

Land Usage in the United States. About one-third of all land in the United States is covered by forests.

Location of Forested Acreage. Of the roughly 500 million acres of commercial quality forests in the United States, 39% are located in the Southeastern part of the country.

Ownership of Forested Acreage. Ownership of the 500 million acres of commercial timber is broken down into 73% held by the private sector and 27% owned by governments–federal, state or local.

Timber Growing Industry in the Southeast. The Southeastern United States is in a strategic location with regard to current and future timber and fiber needs. The most significant factor is a climate that is especially favorable to rapid growth of pine trees–a warm year-round growing season, plus good rainfall.

Southern Pine, adapted to relatively warm climates with 55 to 70 inches of rainfall per year, grows physically at a rate of 6 to 15 percent per year. Southern pine can be harvested for pulpwood approximately 18 years after planting, and for sawtimber after about 25 to 30 years. Similar harvesting cycles for Western-grown species span 50 to 85 years. Genetically superior stock can speed growth as much as five years.

Environmental Factors. The timber industry has certain regulations and controls imposed on it by federal and state governments. These controls deal primarily with matters such as the prohibition of the use of certain chemicals, limitations on controlled burning, regulations affecting timbering near waterways, and, in some jurisdictions, the state takes complete control of timber cutting. Costs of compliance, therefore, vary from one jurisdiction to another.

Supply. Government studies indicate that the annual growth of trees (hardwoods and softwoods combined) exceeds removals by a factor of approximately 1.3 to 1, but that the cutting curve is increasing much faster than the regrowth curve. Some studies project that by approximately 1985, the demand and supply curves for sawtimber will cross and thereafter cutting will exceed regrowth.

The U.S. Forest Service has estimated that by the year 2000 timber removals will exceed regrowth by 500 million board feet per year.

Demand. Demand for timber products in the United States has increased by approximately 113% in the last 50 years, as compared to a 92% rise in population.

The 12.7 billion cubic feet of timber consumed annually in this country requires the cutting of about 500 million mature trees each year. This consumption rate amounts to about two trees per year for every person in the United States. It works out that at present rates of consumption each 50 years the United States is consuming a timber supply equal to all the commercial timber now growing in the United States.

Demand for Softwoods. One government forecast estimates the demand for softwood timber (i.e., pine) will rise from approximately 48 billion board feet in 1970 to around 73 billion board feet in the year 2000, an increase of 53%.

Despite many projections of increased demand, the technology of timber growing may increase faster than anticipated, and the supply of trees available for harvesting may be even greater than the supply today. The investor must weigh for himself the many interlocking supply and demand factors, some of which are set forth above, their probable influence in the future, and their effect on future timber prices.

Prices. The rising price of timber during the past 10 years has reflected not only tightening supply-demand relationships, but also the effects of inflation. Since the year 1800, lumber prices have increased faster than the all-commodity index by approximately 1.7% per year.

ELEMENTS OF FORESTRY MANAGEMENT

Uneven-Aged Stands. Uneven-aged timber stands are naturally regenerated stands of timber. They contain trees of all ages, from seedlings to mature trees of 30 years of age or more. Wild forests are always uneven-aged stands of timber. When management is applied to a typical uneven-aged stand on good land, production can usually be doubled in 12 to 15 years. The younger the average age of trees in a stand, the greater and faster their response to management. Sometimes it is more economical to clear cut a stand and replant than to undertake improvement work. With a proper management program, an uneven-aged stand will produce 80% to 90% of the volume of an even-aged stand.

Uneven-aged stands commonly grow at annual compound physical rates of 5% to 15% per year. The higher rates are achieved on land with an above average site index (85 or above) and with more intensive management.

There is one very important distinguishing economic feature of an uneven-aged stand: it can be continuously harvested by cutting trees as they mature, thereby sustaining a flow of income based on the annual physical yield of the tract times the price level current at the time the trees are harvested. If a given timber stand is put on an seven-year cutting cycle, for instance, and the trees are cut in successive 40-acre blocks per year, a stand of 280 acres is large enough to efficiently sustain annual cutting. A given 40-acre block is thus cut every seven years.

By contrast, in an even-aged plantation, all trees are usually cut at the same time, except for early thinning cuts.

Even-Aged Stands. Even-aged timber stands are usually managed tree plantations. All trees in a given plot are of the same approximate age. Planting adjoining plots in successive years can provide a staggering of ages. Controlling spacing between the trees facilitates growth of the trees as well as reducing harvesting costs. Even-aged stands tend to yield 10% to 20% more cubic feet of timber in a 30-year harvest cycle than do managed uneven-aged stands.

Most forests available for purchase in the South are uneven-aged stands to which little or no management has been applied. Most managed forest stands are owned by large timber product companies. Less than 3% of the trees harvested each year are replaced by tree plantations.

In the case of either even-aged or uneven-aged stands, there are certain basic management practices which can be observed:

Thinning. The main purpose is to remove overcrowded or defective trees. However, sometimes thinning cuts are made primarily or partly to generate cash for the timber owner.

Weed and Underbrush Control. A management practice eliminating any remaining brush and reemerging hardwoods from a thinned stand.

Controlled burning, often annually or biannually is a common method of underbrush control. It is very effective when used with thinning for reducing or eliminating loss by unplanned fires. Removal of the debris on the forest floor by frequent burning prevents any fire from getting hot enough to cause any material damage to growing stock.

Other Elements of Modern Forestry Management. Fertilization, disease and insect control and periodic inspections of the timber stand, as well as measuring the trees and identifying mature trees for the purpose of selecting harvesting.

Young stands often have substantial amounts of grass surrounding the trees. Cattle grazing income can sometimes be generated for the first eight to ten years in the life of a stand, until the trees get so large that their shade retards growth of adequate grass.

Site Index Tables. A site index table, essentially a measure of fertility, is an important tool for predicting future growth of trees on a given site.

After making basic measurements and referring to the site index tables, the forester estimates the future growth and yield of timber for a given site for the next 5, 10, 20 or 30 years or more.

His precise measurements, together with scientifically prepared and tested site index and yield tables make it possible to predict future physical potential growth of a given stand.

Cost of Management. Forest care and costs of management of existing stands may vary from $1 to $10 per acre per year, depending on the degree of intensity. In modern forestry management each stand is given the level of management economically suitable to that site—depending on the capability of the land, stocking rate and quality of the trees, its five to 25 year growth potential, and other factors.

The cost of establishing a new stand of trees generally ranges from $25 to $125 per acre, depending on the level of land preparation, the use of fertilizer and the methods of seeding employed. A cost of $75 to $100 per acre is not uncommon today.

A typical newly-planted even-aged stand of Southern Pine trees must be allowed to grow for 25 to 30 years before it will yield a major harvest of sawtimber.

The timber grower does not customarily harvest his own timber. That job is left to the sawmills who have the equipment and personnel to cut the standing timber they buy.

BUSINESS OF THE PARTNERSHIP

The business of the Partnership will involve two principal elements:

(1) The acquisition, ownership and management of southern pine timber stands.
(2) The growing of various nursery crops through contract growers.

Timber Business. The principal business of the Partnership will be the acquisition, ownership and management of southern pine timber stands. In most instances, the Partnership will purchase the land underlying the timber, although in some cases it may acquire cutting rights to timber only and obtain no ownership interest in the land. The Partnership will acquire stands of timber, manage them, and then resell the timber either by private harvesting or by an outright sale of the timber and underlying land.

The Limited Partners will provide a minimum of $250,000 of capital in Year One of which two-thirds will be applied as fully and rapidly as possible to obtain as large a base of productive timber land and timber cutting rights as is financially feasible, given the borrowing parameters for the Partnership.

The Partnership will generally utilize the services of consulting foresters (experts in timber acquisitions and sales) to appraise prospective timber purchases. Timber stands acquired may be of all ages, either even-aged plantation stands or uneven-aged natural stands, and may range in size from 40 acres to more than 500 acres in a single block. However, since the availability of large blocks of timber is limited, the average purchase will most probably consist of from 40 to several hundred acres. It is expected that the price of such acquisitions will range from a low of approximately $300 to $400 per acre to a high of $1,500 per acre, depending on the quantity and quality of the timber and the quality and location of land on which the timber is growing. Assuming an average purchase price of $1,000 per acre, the Partnership can be expected to initially acquire approximately 1,000 acres (if initial capital of $1,500,000 is contributed). The number of acres to be acquired by the Partnership will be adjusted accordingly if more or less capital is contributed.

After acquisition of timber stands or cutting rights, the Partnership will manage the properties by planting, periodic harvesting, reforestation, and the improvement and care of timber stands to maximize growth.

Location of Timber. The timber and timber cutting rights to be acquired will be predominately pine timber stands mixtures of longleaf, slash, loblolly and short leaf in the Southeastern United States from Eastern Texas to the Atlantic seaboard. Some hardwoods are found in uneven-aged pine stands. The Partnership will endeavor to acquire a balance of timber stands which are capable of sustaining an annual physical and dimensional growth averaging at least 8% per annum. There is no assurance that this objective will be met. The Partnership will also endeavor to obtain a geographical dispersion of the timber stands so that they will not all be subject to a common risk of loss by any single natural force, such as wind, fire, insects or disease. However, there will be no precise limitations on the concentration of Partnership assets in a few timber properties. Accordingly, the question of adequacy of geographical dispersion will necessarily be left to the judgment of the General Partner.

Procedures for Acquiring Timber. Prior to purchase of any timber stand, the Partnership will generally engage the services of an independent professional forester to conduct a timber cruise to corroborate estimates of merchantable timber values. Where deemed necessary, the services of independent appraisers concerning the values of the underlying land will also be utilized. A "timber cruise," in essence, is a method of inventorying timber on a particular tract in terms of volume, grade and species of trees by a sampling technique. Market prices can be applied to the cruise results to arrive at overall current market values for the area of timber cruised. Foresters can also measure the current growth rate of a stand of trees and by use of "site indexes and yield tables" project the future production of that stand.

In making investments in timber land and timber cutting rights, the General Partner will consider such factors as: quality and maturity of standing timber, quality of the underlying land as to soils, topography, species, elevation, prior cultural practices, location, proximity to other suitable tracts, proximity to lumber mills, initial and future sites preparation and planting costs, taxes, possible long-term appreciation prospects for the timber and underlying land, safety of principal and the terms of proposed acquisition, as well as the cash flow and timing thereof expected to be generated by a particular tract.

Forest Management Plan. A comprehensive forest management plan will be developed under the direction of the General Partner for each tract of timber acquired. The plan will establish the budget for stand improvement costs, and enable the General Partner to plan the quantity and timing of timber harvests from that tract. The price and per acre yields obtained for harvested timber will be the principal variables in anticipating cash flow from a particular tract.

The timber will be managed under forest management plans that take into account existing and potential stocking and growth rates, cash flow requirements, and considerations of maximizing economic returns to the Partnership after payment of stand improvement costs. Management and harvesting plans may differ for various even-aged stands. It is expected that the principal portion of the Partnership timber will be in uneven-age stands. Tracts of growing timber acquired in a wild or natural state will generally be upgraded by application of good forest management practices. Some areas may be clear cut and converted to tree farms where appropriate in the judgment of the General Partner.

A typical well stocked stand of Southern pine will have 400 to 800 stems to the acre. When the trees are 12-20 years of age, the stand will be thinned down to 300 stems per acre as the trees reach pulpwood size, and thereafter down to 100 to 150 stems per acre to permit the more valuable trees to achieve their optimum growth as sawtimber in as short a time as possible. Thinning removes competition for sunlight, water and nutrients from the soil, making the remaining trees more valuable and at the same time generating income since the trees cut for thinning can generally be sold for pulpwood and other purposes. The above stocking and thinning activities have many variations.

Harvesting of Timber. Agreements for sale of timber will be negotiated with sawmills and other forest products companies as the General Partner's judgment deems cash flow and silviculture practices indicate timber cuttings should be made. The Partnership may use consulting foresters for this purpose, who will mark, measure, tabulate and advertise timber for sale by the Partnership for a fee or sales commission. The General Partner will negotiate for, and supervise such sales work when performed by such third parties, and will approve all sales.

Reforestation. When engaged in reforestation, the General Partner will endeavor to follow the practice of planting genetically superior stock. Such reforestation will be done with seeds or seedlings from seed stock suited to the area and land on which it is being planted. Genetic gains from the first generation stock under managed conditions will average an estimated 20% higher volume growth than obtained with seed from existing stands.

Ultimate Disposition of Timber and Other Assets. It is anticipated that the timber properties will be sold commencing in Year Six and be completed upon termination of the Partnership in Year Nine. To the extent that the Partnership receives purchase money mortgages rather than cash in connection with sales of Partnership properties there could be a delay in the Partners receiving the full amount of cash from their Units.

Crop Production. The Partnership will contract with independent farmers and/or agricultural management companies, and possibly with Affiliates of the General Partner, to act as growers or as general contractors for managing the growing crops, to either plant the crops directly or subcontract the growing to other farmers.

The crops grown for the Partnership will be on land owned by either third parties or by Affiliates. While the General Partner intends to have the Partnership engage primarily in the growing of nursery crops, if an adequate amount of such crops cannot be contracted for in any year, then the Partnership may grow winter or summer grains and forages, truck crops such as bellpeppers, squash and tomatoes, as well as various nursery crops. The Year One crops will be nursery crops such as foliage plants, flowers or trees. The Partnership crops for the current year will be planted prior to December 31, Year One. The number of acres to be planted will depend on the type of crop for which the Partnership ultimately contracts. Certain of the crops may be planted on land owned by other partnerships managed by the General Partner or Affiliates. To the extent such Affiliates are contracted with as growers for the Partnership, they will be paid on the same basis as independent growers.

The amount of equity devoted to crops in the first year is expected to be leveraged on an average of 1:1. It is anticipated that the Partnership will continue its crop growing activity after the first year, but will gradually reduce the scope of this activity as funds are transferred to fund debt service on the timber property.

The price of crop growing agreements are not known at this time since those agreements are customarily negotiated with growers on an individual basis. The General Partner will endeavor, however, to utilize crop sharing arrangements where the Partnership will put up the capital, arrange the financing and share the crop net income or losses with the farmer.

In Year One the Partnership will pay the General Partner a crop management fee equal to 3% of the aggregate cost of planting and growing any crop during the Year One-Year Two growing season, payable in Year One. In years subsequent to Year One, this fee will be 1% of such planting and growing costs, payable at the time of contracting for the crops to be grown. To the extent that the Partnership experiences profits in connection with its crop growing activities in any year, this fee may be increased to up to 3% at the discretion of the General Partner. This fee is for supervising and coordinating the Partnership's crop planting activities.

As to any crop, the Partnership is susceptible to all of the risks resulting from adverse weather and production conditions and changing prices until the crop is actually harvested and sold. If the Partnership experiences any substantial crop losses, such losses may have a significant detrimental effect on its subsequent operations and could cause the General Partner to effect an early termination of the Partnership.

Other risks that could affect the Partnership's crop operations are as follows: (i) the General Partner has Affiliates that are also in the farming business, and the sales of their products may be in competition with those of the Partnership; (ii) the Partnership has no control over the availability of supplies and raw materials, a shortage of which may affect its ability to plant or harvest its crops; and (iii) there is no assurance that, even if the Partnership's crop-growing activities are successful, there will be markets with adequate prices in which the crops may be sold.

Cash Distributions. Cash Distributions from the Partnership are not contemplated during the Partnership term. Instead, Partnership Net Income will be used to purchase additional timber properties in order to increase the capital asset base of the Partners in an endeavor to provide the Limited Partners with the maximum appreciated value in its assets upon termination.

Distributions will be allocated 99% to the Limited Partners, pro rata, and 1% to the General Partner until such time as each Unit outstanding has been allocated $1,000 plus 6% per annum on the Net Invested Capital per Unit from time to time outstanding; then the Limited Partners shall receive 75% and the General Partner 25% of all remaining proceeds.

Cash Distributions to the Limited Partners will be apportioned among the holders of Units in the ratio in which the number of Units held of record by each of them bears to the number of Units held of record by all of the Limited Partners.

Upon an event of termination of the Partnership which results in a dissolution and winding up of its affairs, the General Partner will reduce the portion of the Partnership assets which are to be distributed to cash, or cash and notes. Proceeds remaining after making the payments, or provisions for payment of all Partnership liabilities will be distributed as follows:

a. After taking into consideration all Cash Distributions to date, each Unit outstanding will be allocated an amount of cash sufficient to equal the then existing Net Invested Capital Per Unit plus 6% per annum on the Net Invested Capital Per Unit from time to time outstanding; then

b. The Limited Partners will receive 75% and the General Partner 25% of all remaining proceeds.

Assets may be distributed in kind at the sole discretion of the General Partner.

The minimum investment is comprised of twenty-five (25) Partnership Units ("Units") at $1,000 per Unit for a minimum investment commitment of $25,000 per investor. No partnership in the series will be formed until the General Partner has received minimum subscriptions aggregating $250,000 (250 Units). After the first Partnership has been formed, additional partnerships may be formed with a minimum of $150,000 (150 Units).

FIRST YEAR ALLOCATION OF CAPITAL

	Minimum Capitalization Required	Percent	Expected Maximum Contribution	Percent
Gross Subscription Amount	$250,000		$3,000,000	
First-year Cash Proceeds of Offering	250,000	100	3,000,000	100
Offering Expenses Paid to Affiliate	5,000	2	60,000	2
Organizational Expense	5,000	2	60,000	2
Commissions	25,000	10	300,000	10
Net proceeds available for investment	$215,000	86	$2,580,000	86
Cash Payment for Purchase of Timber Properties	95,000	38	1,325,000	44
Crop Planting Costs	82,500	33	990,000	33
Loan Negotiation Fee	8,400	3	83,250	3
Bookkeeping	10,000	4	10,000	.3
Timber Acquisition Costs	12,000	5	120,000	4
Timber Management Fee	4,000	2	40,000	1.3
Working Capital	3,100	1	11,750	.4
Proceeds expended	$215,000	86	$2,580,000	86

PRO FORMA SOURCES AND APPLICATIONS OF CASH
Year One through Year Eight
(Assumes $1,500,000 Total Capital)
($000's)

	One	Two	Three	Four	Five	Six	Seven	Eight	Total
Sources of Cash									
Contributed Capital	$1,500	$ -	$ -	$ -	$ -	$ -	$ -	$ -	$ 1,500
Timber Property Loans	750	-	-	-	-	-	-	-	750
Timber Sales	-	-	-	-	-	200	-	-	200
Crop Loans	720	669	618	567	516	489	409	-	3,988
Crop Sales	-	1,416	1,296	1,173	1,046	915	890	767	7,503
Interest Income	-	16	13	9	5	2	7	1	53
Total Sources	$2,970	$2,101	$1,927	$1,749	$1,567	$1,606	$1,306	$ 768	$13,994
Applications of Cash									
Offering & Org. Expenses	$ 60	$ -	$ -	$ -	$ -	$ -	$ -	$ -	$ 60
Sales Commissions	150	-	-	-	-	-	-	-	150
Land Purchase	500	-	-	-	-	-	-	-	500
Timber Purchase	500	-	-	-	-	-	-	-	500
Timber Prop. Int.	-	90	90	90	90	90	90	90	630
Timber Acquisition Fee	60	-	-	-	-	-	-	-	60
Timber Operating Exp.	10	10	10	10	10	10	10	10	80
Timber Mgmt. Fee	20	20	20	20	20	20	20	20	160
Loan Negotiation Fee	41	-	-	-	-	-	-	-	41
Bookkeeping & Acct'g Fee	10	10	10	10	10	10	10	10	80
Crop Plnt'g Costs	1,375	1,283	1,161	1,036	906	881	759	-	7,401
Crop Mgmt. Fee	41	13	12	10	9	9	8	-	102
Repymt of Crop Loans	-	720	669	618	567	516	489	409	3,988
Working Capital	203	(45)	(45)	(45)	(45)	70	(80)	229	242
Total Applications	$2,970	$2,101	$1,927	$1,749	$1,567	$1,606	$1,306	$ 768	$13,994

Note: "–" indicates zero.

PRO FORMA EIGHT YEAR SUMMARY OF TAXABLE INCOME (LOSS)
For Period Ending December 31, Year One to December 31, Year Eight
(Assumes $1,500,000 Contributed Capital)
($000's)

	One	Two	Three	Four	Five	Six	Seven	Eight	Total
Revenues									
Crop Sales	$ -	$1,416	$1,296	$1,173	$1,046	$ 915	$ 890	$ 767	$7,503
Timber Sales	-	-	-	-	-	200	-	-	200
Interest Income	-	16	13	9	5	2	7	1	53
TOTAL REVENUES	$ -	$1,432	$1,309	$1,182	$1,051	$1,117	$ 897	$ 768	$7,756
Expenses									
Crop Expenses									
Planting Costs	$1,375	$1,283	$1,161	$1,036	$ 906	$ 881	$ 759	$ -	$7,401
Crop Mgmt. Fee	41	13	12	10	9	9	8	-	102
Loan Negotiation Fee	41	-	-	-	-	-	-	-	41
Timberland Purchases									
Interest	-	90	90	90	90	90	90	90	630
Timber Expenses									
Adjustment to Basis	-	-	-	-	-	94	-	-	94
Timber Mgmt. Fee	20	20	20	20	20	20	20	20	160
Operating Expenses	10	10	10	10	10	10	10	10	80
Organization Costs	3	6	6	6	6	3	-	-	30
Bookkeeping	10	10	10	10	10	10	10	10	80
TOTAL EXPENSES	$1,500	$1,432	$1,309	$1,182	$1,051	$1,117	$ 897	$ 130	$8,618
TAXABLE INCOME (LOSS)	$(1,500)	$ -	$ -	$ -	$ -	$ -	$ -	$ 638	$ (862)

Note: "–" indicates zero.

PROPERTY APPRECIATION AT 12% AND 15%
(\$000's)
(Assumes \$1,500,000 Total Capital)

	12% Land Appr'n Rate	8% Timber Growth Rate	Combined Rate	Timber Appr'n	Land Appr'n	Total Value
One	1.00	1.00	1.00	\$ 500	\$ 500	\$1,000
Two	1.12	1.08	1.21	605	560	1,165
Three	1.25	1.17	1.46	730	625	1,355
Four	1.40	1.26	1.76	880	700	1,580
Five	1.57	1.36	2.13	1,065	785	1,850
Six	1.76	1.47	2.59	1,047	880	1,927
Seven	1.97	1.59	3.13	1,267	985	2,252
Eight	2.21	1.72	3.80	1,533	1,105	2,638

Appreciation rates assumed:

Timber growth rate	8%
Price increase of timber and land	12%

	15% Land Appr'n Rate	8% Timber Growth Rate	Combined Rate	Timber Appr'n	Land Appr'n	Total Value
One	1.00	1.00	1.00	500	500	1,000
Two	1.15	1.08	1.24	620	575	1,195
Three	1.32	1.17	1.54	700	660	1,430
Four	1.52	1.26	1.92	960	760	1,720
Five	1.75	1.36	2.38	1,190	875	2,065
Six	2.01	1.47	2.95	1,227	1,005	2,232
Seven	2.31	1.59	3.67	1,521	1,155	2,676
Eight	2.66	1.72	4.58	1,885	1,330	3,216

Appreciation rates assumed:

Timber growth rate	8%
Price increase of timber and land	15%

*Assumes sale of \$200,000 worth of timber in Year Six.

TIMBER AND LAND NET GAIN
($000's)
(Assumes $1,500,000 Total Capital)

		12% Price Growth	15% Price Growth
Value at termination*		$1,533	$1,886
Plus timber sales		200	200
Subtotal		1,733	2,086
Less initial cost		500	500
Gross gain on timber		$1,233	$1,586
Less expenses			
Interest	$ 54		
Purchase fee	60		
Bookkeeping & operating	160		
Management fee	160		
Credit fee	22	(456)	(456)
Net gain on timber		$ 777	$1,130
Land value at termination		1,105	1,330
Less initial cost		500	550
Net gain on land		$ 605	$ 830
Net gain on timber		$1,382	$1,960

*Growth Rate Assumed: 8% per year.

BENEFITS OF A CROP AND TIMBER FUND

1. To acquire a substantial base in commercial timber land in the southeast United States.

2. To engage in the growing of nursery crops and other crops for a profit and as a way to employ capital until it is

needed for payment of principal and interest payments on the timber land and operating expenses relating thereto.

3. To hold and manage the Partnership timberland for the purpose of generating long-term capital appreciation. The increase in equity is expected to occur as the result of (i) the physical growth of timber, (ii) the expected increase in the prices for timber as the result of demand exceeding supply, (iii) the expected increase in the price of timber as the result of inflation, and (iv) the expected increase in prices for the underlying land.

4. To generate income in Year Six from harvesting of pulpwood as well as thinning cuts of saw timber or the clear cutting of stands in order to pay Partnership operating costs including debt service on the financial parcels. Any excess income will be reinvested in the Partnership timber business through Year Eight.

RISKS OF A CROP AND TIMBER FUND

1. *Risks Related to Crop Growing.* Due to many factors, agriculture must be deemed a high risk activity. The Partnership will enter into contracts with various general farming contractors or directly with farmers, or both, for the growing of certain nursery and other crops. Such contractors or farmers may be Affiliates of the General Partner. If a general farming contractor or a farmer with whom the Partnership contracts fails to properly tend the copy, or if the crop suffers from bad weather, pests or other adverse growing conditions, labor or equipment problems, the Partnership can lose all or part of its crop. Furthermore, since the crops will be leveraged, a loss of a small percentage of the crop planting and cultural costs can easily translate into a total loss of Partnership equity devoted to those crops.

   Even if the crop is produced as expected, a farmer could fail to deliver the crops or receipts for the sale thereof as required, either because creditors of the farmer assert claims to the crop or its sales proceeds, or for a variety of other reasons that can arise in any contractual arrangement. The General Partner will endeavor to select capable contractors and growers. However, even capable farmers suffer substantial losses from time to time. Furthermore, the crop will most probably be pledged as collateral for crop loans which pledge, in essence, will provide an element of protection to the Partnership as well. In the event of a complete crop failure, even capable farmers can fail to meet their obligations. These are risks that the Partnership faces with respect to that part of its capital that at any one time is invested in crops.

In addition to all the risks inherent in agriculture, including loss due to weather, pests and disease, the crops to be grown by the Partnership will be subject to the economic risks resulting from price fluctuations. There is also a risk that growers who commit to grow crops for the Partnership will for unexepcted reasons be unable to fulfill their expected crop planting for the Partnership, thereby causing the Partnership to have a shortfall in expected crop expenses and deductions in any year.

The farmers who will do the actual planting and growing of crops of the Partnership have not been selected, which adds an additional risk in that the Limited Partners do not have the opportunity to evaluate the farming qualifications or the financial qualifications of those persons who will be entrusted with approximately one-third of the capital contributions to the Partnership for at least the first crop year. There is no assurance that the General Partner will be able to locate suitable crops and growers under terms satisfactory for the Partnership's purposes.

2. *Market Price Fluctuation.* A principal risk to the Partnership is a net decline in timber prices during the term of the Partnership. While the long-term trend for timber prices has historically been upward, there is no assurance it will continue upward, and in any event future prices for sawtimber stumpage and pulpwood will be subject to short-term, sharp fluctuations around the trend line.

3. *Offering Unspecified Timber.* The Partnership does not own any timber land or timber cutting rights and specific properties or rights it intends to acquire have not been identified. Subscribers will have no opportunity to evaluate the specific properties for themselves prior to investing.

4. *Generic Risks Inherent to Timber.* Any stand of timber is subject to damage by fire, insects, and disease, as well as destructive losses arising out of theft or weather conditions such as hurricanes, tornadoes, and other disasters. The Partnership will rely on (i) geographic diversification and (ii) its own forestry management practices to limit these risks. As is customary in the timber industry, the Partnership does not generally intend to obtain any insurance against such risks. Damages from any such causes are usually very localized and accordingly should affect only a small percentage of the timber in any one year, even where there is only nominal geographical dispersion.

5. *Environmental Restraints.* Public concern in recent years over the environment and the use of natural resources such as forests has brought about increased regulation and control of the timber industry by Federal and state governments. Since the Partnership does not anticipate dealing with timber cutting rights on government owned lands but rather expects to be dealing exclusively with private timber lands, it is not expected that such restrictions and controls will be materially burdensome to the Partnership. However, there is no assurance that future governmental or judicial decisions would not impact the Partnership adversely.

TAX ASPECTS OF A CROP AND TIMBER FUND

1. *Tax Aspects of Farming Operations.*

The following is a brief summary of some areas of tax law which apply uniquely to a farming operation such as the crop activity that may be carried on by the Partnership.

a. *Limitation on Deductions.* Section 464 of the Code allows a deduction for amounts paid for feed, seed, fertilizer, or other similar farm supplies only for the taxable year in which such items are actually used or consumed. This provision of the Code has the effect of preventing the Partnership from obtaining current deductions for prepaid feed, seed, fertilizer, or other similar farm supplies except in situations where such supplies are on hand at the close of the taxable year solely because the consumption of such items during the taxable year was prevented on account of fire, storm, flood, or other casualty, or on account of disease or drought. No assurances can be given that Section 464 of the Code will not have an adverse effect on the federal income tax consequences of the Partnership's projected farming operations.

b. *Deduction for Crop Growing Activities.* The Partnership will contract with various general farming contractors or directly with farmers or both, to act as growers or as general contractors for managing the growing crops, and to either plant the crops directly or subcontract the growing to other farmers. The Partnership may also contract with Affiliates to perform the foregoing services. Such contracts may require the contractor or farmer to plant, maintain, harvest, store and sell specific crops in accordance with the General Partner's instructions.

As indicated above, Section 464 of the Code limits the deduction for such cultural costs to the taxable year in which such items are actually used or consumed. The farmers may not complete the growing and harvesting of crops in Year One and accordingly Section 464 will limit the deduction to crop growing expenses actually incurred in the growing process in Year One.

It is conceivable that the Partnership may enter into crop growing contracts after the subject acreage has already been planted. This is so because every crop has its own growing season and must be planted within a given timeframe; and, therefore, in some cases it may not be practicable for the farmer to wait for the execution of such contracts before planting his crop. Since the Partnership may assume all or portions of the costs associated with planting, maintaining and harvesting the subject acreage incurred by the contractor or farmer prior to the date of the contract, the Partnership intends to deduct such cultural costs as if the Partnership had secured the use of the property and paid such costs as the crop was planted.

Furthermore, the Partnership intends to deduct all planting and cultural costs in the year in which the crops are planted and the cultural costs incurred, even though the crops may be harvested and sold in a subsequent year.

No assurance can be given that the Service will not disallow the deduction for the cultural costs incurred in the manner described above and either require that such costs be capitalized and deducted in the year in which the crops are sold or require that such expenses not be deducted at all. No assurance can be given that the Service will not be successful in the event it takes such a position and, if it is, the effect would be to reduce substantially the tax losses that the Limited Partners might otherwise recognize during the first year of Partnership operations.

The cost of seeds and young plants which are purchased for further development and cultivation prior to sale in later years may be deducted as an expense by a cash-basis taxpayer in the year of payment (Treas. Regs. Section 1.162-12(a)). In addition, the cost of growing the crop is deductible. The cost of nursery plants need not be included in an inventory at the end of the year (Treas. Regs. Section 1.471-6(a)). Therefore, expenses of the nursery crop may be deducted when paid, and these deductions are not required to be reduced by recognition in a year-end inventory. Income on the sale of the nursery plants is recognized by a cash-basis taxpayer when received.

2. *Tax Aspects of Timber Operations.*

a. *Taxation of Sale of Timber.* The measure of gain or loss on the sale or disposition of timber is the difference between the amount received and the taxpayer's adjusted basis of the timber.

There are two methods in which the sale of timber by the Partnership can result in capital gain or loss treatment. First, capital gain or loss treatment will occur if the timber is a "capital asset" within the meaning of Section 1221 of the Code, or is treated as a capital asset under Section 1231. Second, Section 631(b) affords capital gain treatment in the ease of disposal of timber held for more than 12 months by the owner thereof under a cutting contract by virtue of which the owner "retains an economic interest" in the timber. If neither of these two methods apply, any gain or loss in the sale of timber will be taxed as an ordinary gain or loss.

b. *Timber as Capital Asset.* Under Sections 1221 and 1231, capital gain or loss treatment is not available for gains or losses on property held by the Partnership *primarily* for sale to customers in the ordinary course of his trade or business.

Whether property is deemed to be held primarily for sale to customers in the ordinary course of business, as opposed to being held for investment, is a question of fact to be determined from the evidence in each particular case. Some of the principal factors to be taken into consideration are:

i. The purpose for which the property was acquired, whether for sale in the ordinary course of a business, or for long-term investment;
ii. The number, continuity, and frequency of sales, as opposed to isolated transactions;
iii. The activity of the seller with reference to the sales, or whether the seller merely accepts offers from unsolicited purchasers; and
iv. The extent of substantiality of the transactions.

c. *Retention of Economic Interest under Section 631(b).* Under a typical "cutting contract," the timber owner sells timber and is paid a stated amount per unit harvested and only for the units harvested. The timber owner retains ownership of the timber until the trees are harvested by the purchaser; the purchaser will cut and remove the trees.

Section 631(b) of the Code affords capital gain treatment in the case of disposal of timber held for more than 12 months by the owner thereof under contract, such as a cutting contract, by virtue of which the owner "retains an economic interest" in such timber. The date of disposal is deemed to be the date the timber is cut, and timber is deemed cut when the quantity of felled timber is first definitely determined.

Under Code Section 631(b), the difference between the amount realized by the seller and the "adjusted basis" of the timber is considered as though it were a gain or loss on the sale of the timber. All transactions involving parcels of property falling within the definition of "property used in the trade or business" as defined in Code Section 1231, including timber disposed of under Code Section 631(b), must be considered as a group. If all the transactions in this group result in a net gain, then that gain will be a long-term capital gain. If they result in a net loss, then that loss is treated as a deduction from ordinary income.

Although it is presently intended that all cutting contracts made by the Partnership will be structured with a view toward qualification under Section 631(b), no assurance can be given that the Partnership will, in all cases, find it desirable or feasible to do so. Moreover, even in those cases where the Partnership attempts to so structure its cutting contracts, no assurance can be given that such contracts and the transactions covered thereby will be deemed by the Internal Revenue Service or the courts to satisfy all the applicable requirements of Section 631(b). In this regard, it is emphasized that the requirements of Section 631(b) are very technical in nature and that, in many cases, contracts intended to qualify under that section have been held not to so qualify.

d. *Adjusted Basis.* Cost depletion is a means for recovering investment in standing timber. It is therefore not available to a taxpayer such as the Partnership which will recover its investment by some other means. The Partnership will recover its investment by offsetting its adjusted basis in the timber against the amount received to determine the gain or loss on the transaction.

The initial adjusted basis of the timber will be its cost to the Partnership at the time of purchase. This cost does not include the cost of land on which the timber is located; an allocation must be made. The adjusted basis may then be adjusted for capital expenditures and losses.

e. *Sale of Forest Products Other than Standing Timber.* In general, proceeds generated by a timber owner from the sale of forest products other than standing timber will be treated as ordinary income. This is true, for example, with respect to the sale of fence posts, firewood, and bark. A possible exception, pursuant to which capital gains treatment may result, relates to the lump-sum sale of tree stumps from cutover land which is acquired for investment. That exception does not apply, however, to gains from the sale of tree stumps by timber operators after merchantible timber has been harvested.

f. *Casualty, Thefts, Condemnations.* If timber owned by the Partnership is destroyed by fire or other casualty, the Partnership will have deductible loss (to be passed through ultimately to the Partners) in an amount equal to the adjusted tax basis of the timber destroyed less any insurance or other compensation received in respect to the loss. In this regard, insurance recoveries on standing timber are relatively infrequent because of the slow manner in which this aspect of the insurance business has developed and the general view in the industry that casualty insurance is not economically feasible. In general, a casualty loss is deductible in the year in which the casualty occurs, provided there is no reasonable prospect for recovery of all or part of the loss (through insurance or otherwise). The amount of deductible arising from a theft of timber is determined in a manner similar to the determination of a loss arising from a casualty. A theft loss is generally deductible in the year in which the theft is discovered.

Since the cost of determining the amount of the casualty could be greater than the casualty itself, the Partnership might decide not to attempt to determine the amount of casualty loss and take a deduction. In such an event, when the area that has suffered a casualty is logged, the depletion rate may be adjusted and the loss in timber may be claimed through an adjustment of depletion.

A combination crop and timber fund is for the investor who waits for land and timber to appreciate in value.

GLOSSARY OF FORESTRY TERMS

Board Foot (BP): A length of timber 12 inches square and one inch thick. Saw timber is usually measured in board feet, and pulpwood in cords. Growth, without distinguishing between saw timber or pulpwood, is often expressed in terms of cubic feet.

Clearcut: Harvesting all trees in a stand at the same time. Usually done to prepare for planting an even-aged plantation, or else for converting the land to crop or pasture use.

Commercial Species: Tree species suitable for industrial wood products. Excludes so-called weed species of trees.

Commercial Timberland: Forest land producing or capable of producing crops of industrial wood in excess of 20 cubic feet per acre per year, and not withdrawn from timber utilization.

Controlled Burning: Setting fire to the forest floor to keep the forest free of weeds and underbrush which compete with the trees for water and nutrients. Annual burning of dead grass and underbrush prevents damaging forest fires and by eliminating competitive vegetation promotes more vigorous growth of trees.

Cord: A stack containing 128 cubic feet. The standard dimensions are 4′ x 4′ x 8′. Pulpwood is usually measured in cords. (In some areas pulpwood is sold in units of 168 cubic feet.)

Cruise: A field survey and inventory of representative plots in a stand of timber, including individually measuring, counting and classifying all trees within the plots. The average volume of the areas sampled is then extrapolated as the average volume of the entire stand. Cruises usually are based on 5 percent to 10 percent samples. Current market values can then be attached to the inventories to determine the value of a stand. Periodic cruises can help confirm or correct projected growth rates.

D.B.H.: The abbreviation means "Diameter at breast height," a frequently used term to describe a tree measurement taken 4½′ above the ground.

Desirable Tree: Growing-stock trees of a desirable species having no serious defects to limit their present or future use. These trees are of relatively high vigor, and contain no pathogens that may result in death or serious deterioration before maturity or intended time of harvesting. This is the type of tree that forest managers endeavor to grow.

Diameter Class: A size classification based upon the measurement of a tree's diameter including outside bark at breast height. Precise measurements by a trained forester are an essential tool of modern forest planning and management.

Doyle Scale: Established method of measuring timber volume, named after the man who developed the methodology. There are other measurement systems, such as the Scribner Scale and the International Scale. It is common practice to indicate by which system measurements have been made, so they can be interrelated.

Forest Land: Land at least 10 percent covered by trees of any size, or formerly having such tree cover, and not currently developed for non-forest use.

Forest Management: The application of business methods and technical principles to the operation of forest land to increase productivity, involving use of such practices as seeding superior trees, thinning out overcrowded or undesirable trees, harvesting mature trees before they decline, controlled burning, eliminating undesirable undergrowth, controlling insects and disease, and fertilizing, among others.

Hardwoods: Trees that usually have broad leaves and are deciduous (losing leaves every year).

Ingrowth: An important forester's term to describe trees that are growing large enough in diameter during a given year or period to move into the next higher size classification. For instance, seedlings become saplings at 1″, saplings become pulpwood trees when they pass 4″ in diameter; and pulpwood trees generally become sawtimber after they reach 10″ in diameter.

Natural Regeneration: Trees seeded naturally from seeds dropped by other trees in the forest. Natural regeneration reseeds average trees, whereas the forester can select genetically superior seeds from taller, straighter parent trees. Plantations seeded by hand produce trees that grow faster and straighter.

Net Annual Growth: Where sawtimber is involved, this is the annual change in net board foot volume of live sawtimber trees. The growth of pulpwood trees is more commonly expressed in cords per acre. Sometimes expressed in percentage terms or in cubic feet terms or in cubic feet terms without distinguishing between pulp or sawtimber. For example, a given stand may be said to have an average growth rate of 12 percent per year, or it may be expressed as growing at the rate of 90 cubic feet per acre per year.

Partial Cut: Removal of selected trees either for economic or silvicultural reasons.

Plantation: A man-made forest established by planting seedlings in a prepared seedbed. The most distinguishing feature of a plantation is that all trees in a given tract are of the same age, and hence tend to be harvested all at one time, then replanted.

Pole: A straight, tall tree suitable for use as telephone poles, pilings at wharves, etc. Good quality poles are usually at least

8″ in diameter at the base and at least 25 feet tall. Sometimes pole prices run 1½ to 2 times sawtimber prices.

Pulpwood or Pulp Trees: Trees from 4″ to 8″ in diameter. Such trees are processed for the manufacture of wood pulp. Pulp, in turn, is used to make paper, cartons, etc. Most Southern Pine pulpwood trees are about 12 to 40 years old.

Saplings: Live trees of commercial species 1″ to 5″ D.B.H. and of good form and vigor.

Sawlogs: Logs which are usually at least 8′ long and have a minimum diameter of 10″ D.B.H. for softwood and 12″ D.B.H. for hardwood, and which meet certain regional standards regarding defects.

Sawtimber Stands: Timber stands in which half or more of the trees are of sawlog or pole size.

Seedlings: Live trees less than 1.0 inch in diameter.

Severance Tax: A method of taxing timber applied by many states whereby a tax is imposed on trees only at the time of cutting. The buyer of the trees usually pays this tax.

Silviculture: The science of cultivating and managing trees based on the knowledge of "silvics," the study of the life history and general characteristics of forest trees.

Site Index: For practical purposes this is similar to a measure of soil fertility, although it also takes into account topography, moisture and other factors that make trees grow tall. A site index essentially is a figure indicating how tall an average tree of a given species will grow on that site in a well stocked stand in a period of 50 years. A site index of 80, for instance, would indicate an average tree should be 80 feet high in 50 years (some site index tables are based on 100 years).

A site index table will also give probable heights for a given type of site in lesser periods of time. Once the forester has measured the site index of a particular piece of property, he can use related yield tables, and, for any given site index, predict the probable future growth rate and yield of any given stand of timber on any species on the selected site.

Stand: A large or small area of trees, usually applied to forests of commercial value.

Thinning: Removal of selected trees, usually to eliminate overcrowding or to remove diseased trees.

Thousand Board Feet (MBF): The common basis for pricing standing timber. For example, \$125 MBF means \$125 per thousand board feet.

Tree Nursery: A place where seeds are germinated and grown for six months or more. The resulting seedlings are then transplanted to their permanent site. Used as a source of genetically superior stock for establishing operations.

Uneven-Aged Stand: A forest composed of trees of various ages, usually ranging from seedlings to fully mature trees. This contrasts with even-age stands in which all trees are of the same approximate age. Uneven-aged stands are usually regenerated naturally, in contrast to man-planted even-aged plantations. An uneven-aged stand can be harvested continuously, as trees mature, while in an even-aged stand all trees mature at the same time. In the Southeast the crop cycle for an even-aged stand of pine trees runs about 30 to 35 years. In the same area an uneven-aged stand is partially harvested once every five to seven years. In the long run, trees grow up to 10 to 20 percent more in even-aged stands, because man can manage an even-aged stand better, hence the ultimate yield is superior. However, uneven-aged stands are attractive because they can produce current and continuous yields.

The assistance of Triple C Brangus Ranch, Inc., Great Plains Western Ranch Company, Inc., Timber Resources, Inc. and Sierra-Vanderbilt Corporation in the preparation of this material is gratefully acknowledged.

Sierra-Vanderbilt Corporation
United California Bank Building, Suite 200
7855 Ivanhoe Avenue, La Jolla, CA 92037
714-454-9555

11148 E. Whittier Blvd., P.O. Box 4995
Whittier, CA 90607
213-699-0571
TELEX 65-7472
TELECOPIER 213/692-1330

FLOWERS

GENERAL CONSIDERATIONS

The Fund proposes to engage in Michigan in the business of growing, harvesting and marketing trees (such as Schefflera, Areca Palm, Norfolk Island Pine, Ficus Decora, Weeping Fig, Parlor Palm and Woody Perennials) and nursery items consisting of various varieties of flowers and foliage plants (collectively "Product"). The primary objective of the Fund is to generate profits from operations and to make cash distributions of certain of those profits to the Partners. To achieve this objective it will be necessary for the Fund to expend a substantial portion of the proceeds of this offering for the purchase and cultivation of Product, such as seeds, bulbs, cuttings, liners, and supplies, such as pots, fertilizer and pesticides. These expenses are expected to generate a loss for operation for Year One (and Year Two assuming all Units are not sold in Year One), and a certain portion of that loss is expected to be deductible for federal tax purposes by the Partners. There can be no assurance that such objectives will be attained or that the Fund's capital will not depreciate.

The General Partner will oversee all of the Fund's administrative and policy activigies, including: negotiation and coordination of Product purchases; development of marketing strategy with regard to inventory purchases and sales; monitoring the development of the Product to be maintained by the Partnership at contract grower nurseries; supervision of filings with various federal and state governmental entities; and communications with Limited Partners.

Acquisition of Product. The Fund intends to enter into a requirements contract with International Foliage, Inc., a Delaware corporation with worldwide horticultural operations, to provide substantially all of the Fund's horticultural and floricultural Product.

Arrangements for the purchase of specific Product, such as seeds, bulbs, and seedlings, and supplies, such as fertilizer and containers, will be made by International Foliage after consultation with the General Partner. International Foliage will purchase immature Product and supplies from contract growers, either within or without the State of Michigan, depending on the item of Product. Although title passes to International Foliage upon execution of the contract, due to the existing customary trade practice, International Foliage will not make full payment to the growers with whom it contracts for Product purchased and will extend the balance of payments of the purchase price until the Product is mature and/or delivered. Said Product will be cultivated in accordance with and grown to predetermined specifications and sizes, within a predetermined period of time, and for a predetermined price.

The Fund will use a portion of the proceeds of the offering, together with any additional borrowed funds, to purchase and acquire title to said immature Product and supplies from International Foliage, Inc., which will make a profit on the sale of Product to the Fund of approximately 1% to 3% of sales.

The General Partner will monitor the growing of Product and supervise the cultural care efforts of the contract growers. Should a given individual grower experience problems with the growing of Product, such as improper watering, feeding or fertilizing, International Foliage, may, at the request of the General Partner, resolve the problem by offering proper technical advice.

Until invested in Product, the Fund may temporarily invest all or a part of its Capital Contributions and other funds in short-term highly liquid investment with appropriate safety of principal, such as U.S. Treasury Bonds or Bills, or insured savings accounts.

Sale of Product. The Fund intends to join and use the services of Color, Inc. ("Color"), a Florida corporation which is a marketing cooperative, to assist the Fund in developing marketing strategy and programs to sell the Fund's Product. In addition to developing this marketing strategy and providing on-going marketing analysis, Color will provide bookkeeping services for the Fund, although supervision of all formal accounting of the Fund's operations will be performed by the General Partner. After receipt of physical delivery of Product from contract growers, the Fund's employees, assisted by Color's marketing experts, will commence making sales in Michigan to wholesalers, large retailers, discount chains, and other customers.

The Fund will arrange for delivery of Product to buyers from inventories on hand at the Fund's premises or from the premises of contract growers either by means of trucks owned or leased by the Fund and driven by Fund personnel or by means of such other methods, as are available. For its efforts in developing and providing on-going marketing strategy for the Fund, and performing bookkeeping services for the Fund, Color will assess the fund 20% of sales made to wholesalers and retailers to cover its expenses. If at the end of its fiscal year, Color has funds available in excess of its expenses, these funds will be distributed to its members (including the Fund) in proportion to their patronage. Conversely, if these amounts charged are insufficient to cover expenses, then the members will fund this deficit in proportion to their patronage. In the event the Fund has inventories of Product which, in the opinion of the General Partner, cannot be sold in Michigan to wholesalers, retailers, or others, this Product may be sold to affiliated parties. In the event such sales are made with the assistance of Color, Color will assess costs (ranging from 1/2% to 10% of the sales price) which reflect the effort required of it to effectuate the transaction and perform the necessary bookkeeping.

Assuming the minimum number of Units are subscribed for, the Fund, through its corporate General Partner, Flowers General, Inc. will enter into a lease (with an option to purchase for $180,300) land and buildings in Milford, Michigan, from which the Fund will conduct its business operations. Flowers General, Inc. has a commitment from a lending institution to borrow the sum of $180,300, repayable over a ten year period with interest at approximately 1½% over the prime rate as it exists from time to time.

International Foliage, Inc. has provided the General Partner with the following chart which provides a description of the immature horticultural growing crops that were purchased by International Foliage, Inc. in prior years, the location of such items and the approximate total cost (unaudited) thereof. Some of the growing crops were held by International Foliage until maturity and then sold. However, approximately 80-90% of the immature growing crops were sold to affiliates of the Fund.

LOCATION	TREE ITEMS	NURSERY ITEMS FOLIAGE	FLOWER	TOTAL PURCHASES YEAR ONE	YEAR TWO	YEAR THREE
Australia	Palm					
	Norfolk Island Pine				$ 3,393,000	$ 3,750,000
California	Areca Palm		Amaryllis	$1,297,000	2,345,000	3,073,050
	Japonica					
	Privete					
	Japanese Boxwood					
	Jade Tree					
	Pyracantha					
	Kentia Palm					
Columbia			Carnations			3,070,000
England	Neantha Bella Palm	Pertusum		250,000	1,000,000	5,000,000
	Kentia Palm	Croton				
		Hedera				
Florida	Norfolk Island Pine	Wax Plant	Gladiolus	2,142,000	6,068,000	14,597,163
	Schefflera	Dieffenbachia	Pompons			
	Ficus Benjamina	Ardesia	Gypsophilia			
	Yucca Cane	Ivy				
	Mahogany	Cactus				
	Pony Tail Palm	Ferns				
	Palm					
Hawaii	Norfolk Island Pinw				900,000	1,368,000
Holland			Flower Bulbs	$1,197,000	$ 5,597,000	5,000,000
Israel			Bulbs			5,000,000
Ohio		Woody Perennials		500,000		
Puerto Rico	Marginata	Aglaonemia		1,001,000	2,562,000	5,000,000
Tennessee	Juniper			1,502,000		500,000
	Japanese Quince					
	Silver Maple					
	Green Ash					
	Sycamore					
	Andorra Compacta					
Thailand	Palm Tree Seeds					1,000,000
		TOTALS:		$7,889,000	$21,865,000	$47,358,213

EXAMPLE OF A FLOWER FUND

The Fund is a limited partnership organized and existing under the Michigan Uniform Limited Partnership Act. The General Partner of the Fund is Green, Ltd., a general partnership. The General Partner will have complete authority in the management and control of the Fund's affairs. Investors who purchase Units of Limited Partnership interest (the "Limited Partners") will have no right to participate in the management of the Fund's affairs, other than to vote on certain matters which affect the basic structure of the Fund as permitted by the Michigan Uniform Limited Partnership Act.

The Fund has a capitalization of $31,500 at the present time which consists of cash in the amount of $10,000, and primissory notes in the aggregate principal amount of $20,000 (due in two equal annual installments with interest at 10%) from the General Partner, and cash in the amount of $1,500 from the initial Limited Partner.

COMPENSATION OF THE GENERAL PARTNER AND ITS AFFILIATES

The following table summarizes the types and estimated amounts of compensation to be paid by the Fund to the General Partner, some of which will be paid regardless of the success or profitability of the Fund's operations. None of such fees were determined by arm's length negotiations.

Type of Compensation	Method and Amount of Compensation		
1. Initial Management	Amount:	Per Unit	$ 150
		Maximum	$300,000
		Minimum	$ 30,000
2. Partnership Management Fee:	An amount equal to two percent (2%) of the net sales of the Partnership.		
	Amount: Indeterminate		

3. Subordinated Incentive Fee:

(a) *From Operation:* Fifty percent (50%) of operating profits remaining subordinated to Limited Partner's ten percent (10%) per annum cumulative return on Capital Contributions and 100% return of their agreed capital contribution.

(b) *From Capital Gains:* Thirty per cent (30%) of operating profits remaining subordinated to Limited Partner's ten percent (10%) per annum cumulative return on Capital Contributions and 100% return of their agreed capital contribution.

Note: In addition to the foregoing, the General Partner as a General Partner has purchased for $30,000 ($10,000 in cash and a $20,000 promissory note) a one percent (1%) interest in the profits, losses, credits and deductions of the Fund.

USE OF PROCEEDS

1. Capitalization

The following table shows the capitalization of the Partnership if a maximum of 2,000 or a minimum of 200 limited partnership Units offered hereby are sold and the proposed debt borrowing of an additional 10% of aggregate limited partner investments is incurred.

	2,000 Unit Maximum	200 Unit Minimum
Proposed Debt Borrowing	$ 750,000	$ 75,000
General Partner Contribution	30,000	30,000
Initial Limited Partner Contribution	1,500	1,500
Limited Partners Contributions	3,000,000	300,000
Total Capitalization	$3,781,500	$406,500

2. Use of Proceeds

The Partnership estimates that the proceeds available to the Partnership from the sale of the general partnership interest and the maximum of 2,000 Units and minimum of 200 Units of limited partnership interests, together with the proposed debt borrowing will be applied to the Partnerships's business as set forth below:

	Per Unit	2,000 Unit Maximum	200 Unit Minimum
Organization Costs[1]	$ 45	$ 90,000	$ 9,000
Commissions to Brokers[1]	150	300,000	30,000
Printing and Advertising[1]	30	60,000	6,000
Purchase of Product, Supplies Labor, Lease and/or Purchase of Land[2]	1,500	3,031,500	331,500
Initial Management Fee[1]	150	300,000	30,000
Total[3]	$1,875	$3,781,500	$406,500

1. The Fund intends to pay Organization Costs, Commissions to Brokers, Printing and Advertising, and the Initial Management Fee through the proposed debt borrowing.

2. Funds available for estimated Product, Supplies, Labor and Leased and/or Purchased Land expenditures include the Initial Limited and General Partner contributions.

3. Other than having a proportional effect on the size of business operations, no material changes are contemplated if more than the minimum but less than the maximum number of Units are sold.

ALLOCATION OF PROFITS, LOSSES, INITIAL MANAGEMENT FEES AND EXPENSES OF ACQUIRING PRODUCT AND SUPPLIES

Losses from Operations and Deduction of Initial Management Fees and Expenses of Acquiring Product and Supplies. Losses from operation, Initial Management Fees and Cost of Product paid by the Fund will be charged 1% to the General Partner and 99% to the Limited Partners, and the portion so charged to the Limited Partners will be charged as follows:

First, all Initial Management Fees and Expenses of Acquiring Product and Supplies, to the extent such expenses are not paid from operating income, will be charged to the Limited Partners making a Capital Contribution to the Fund in the calendar year in which such payments of these items are actually paid by the Fund, in proportion to the number of Units purchased by said Limited Partners in said year; and

Secondly, all remaining losses chargeable to the Limited Partners shall be charged to the Limited Partners proportionately to the number of Capital Contribution in the Fund.

Profits and Gains from Operations. Profits from operations of the Fund and gains from capital items will be credited in the ratio of 1% to the General Partner and 99% to the Limited Partners and the portion so charged to Limited Partners will be credited to the Limited Partners in proportion to the number of Units held until all Limited Partners have received (including all prior allocations of profits and gains) in the aggregate an allocation of profits and gains from capital items equal to (1) a cumulative 10% per annum return on their respective Capital Contributions, plus (2) 100% of their Capital Contribution, plus (3) losses previously charged to Limited Partners during any loss year other than their initial year of investment. All remaining profits and gains from capital items will be allocated 50% to the General Partner and 50% to the Limited Partners in proportion to the number of Units held.

Profits and Gains Upon Dissolution and Liquidation. From and after the Fund dissolves and commences liquidation and the winding-up of its affairs, the profits and gains from the sale of Fund assets will be allocated 1% to the General Partner and 99% to the Limited Partners until the Limited Partners have received [including all prior allocations of profits and gains and distributions (to the extent not attributable to profits and gains)] an allocation of profits equal to 100% of their Capital Contribution, plus a cumulative 10% per annum return on their Capital Contribution, and all remaining profits from operations and the sale of capital assets will be allocated 70% to the Limited Partners in proportion to the number of Units held without regard to capital accounts and 30% to the General Partners; provided, however, that upon dissolution and liquidation of the Fund, any profits or gains on the sale of Fund assets shall first be allocated to the Limited Partners (before the above allocation) (if any) to the extent that they have negative capital accounts proportionate to their relative negative capital accounts.

Losses Upon Dissolution and Liquidation. From and after the Fund dissolves and commences liquidation and the winding up of its affairs, all losses, credits and deductions will be allocated 1% to the General Partner and 99% to the Limited Partners.

ALLOCATION OF CASH DISTRIBUTIONS

Distributions. Funds, if any, to the extent deemed available by the General Partner for distribution or payment (other than as part of the dissolution and liquidation of the Fund), will be distributed in such amounts and at such intervals (which it is initially anticipated will be quarterly) as the General Partner shall determine, 1% to the General Partner and 99% to the Limited Partners in proportion to the number of Units held by each Limited Partner in the same manner and priority as provided for the allocation of profit and gain from operations. However, no Partner shall be entitled to receive any distribution of operating profit or gain until he has been a Partner for one full calendar year after his initial year of investment in the Fund. In any event, to the extent available, aggregate annual distributions of Funds shall be made to the Partners in an amount of least equal to 75% of the total profits recognized for federal income tax purposes by the Fund for the preceding tax year.

Distribution on Liquidation. The net proceeds from the Fund's assets on liquidation first will be distributed (giving cumulative effect to all prior distributions to the General and Limited Partners in proportion to the amount of their capital accounts until they have received one hundred percent (100%) of their Capital Contributions, together with a sum which (when added to all prior distributions) equals a ten percent (10%) per annum cumulative return on such Capital Contributions, and then will be distributed proportionately seventy percent (70%) to the Limited Partners and thirty percent (30%) to the General Partner.

General Partner's Compensation. Before any cash distributions to the Limited Partners are made, the General Partner will receive (a) an initial Management Fee; (b) a Partnership Management Fee; and (c) subordinated incentive fees based upon operations and upon capital gains; *provided,* however, that the subordinated incentive fees are subordinated to a recovery by the Limited Partners of a sum equal to the amount of their Capital Contributions plus a 10% cumulative return on their Capital Contributions.

BENEFITS OF A FLOWER FUND

Payment Plan A:

$1,500 in cash for each Unit purchased:

	1st Year	2nd Year	3rd Year
Cash	1,500	- 0 -	- 0 -
Deductions	1,500	- 0 -	- 0 -
Yield	- 0 -	- 0 -	150

Payment Plan B:

$500 in cash and $1,000 financed, assuming 7 percent simple interest is charged over two (2) years for a subscription of 1 Unit.

	1st Year	2nd Year	3rd Year
Cash to Fund	500	- 0 -	- 0 -
Deductions	1,500	- 0 -	- 0 -
Yield	- 0 -	- 0 -	150
Borrowings	1,000	- 0 -	- 0 -
Principal Paid	- 0 -	500	500
Interest Paid	- 0 -	70	35

RISKS OF A FLOWER FUND

1. *Business Risks.* Prospective investor should carefully consider the risks associated with investment in the Fund. The

following discussion of certain risks is provided for the convenience of prospective investors. Although the risks set forth below are intended to be comprehensive, there can be no assurance that financial or tax loss cannot occur as a result of unanticipated risks or that a prospective investor may not perceive other risks which he deems material in evaluation of the merits of this investment opportunity.

Any return on an investment in the Fund will depend in part upon the Fund's ability to grow, harvest and market profitably the trees, flowers and foliage plants grown by it. In this regard, it should be noted that the Fund was just recently formed and has no history of operations.

The ornamental horticultural enterprise is essentially an agricultural enterprise, and, accordingly, is subject to risks inherent in agricultural undertakings, including:

(a) Weather conditions such as rainstorms causing flooding, hail, drought, and frost or temperatures below the tolerances of specific species may have unavoidable adverse effects in spite of reasonable precautions. As may be practicable in relation to the climatic requirements of specific species, and the financial ability of the Fund, in the discretion of the General Partner, reasonable precautions will be taken to mitigate the effects of moderate weather fluctuations such as the use of irrigation systems, greenhouses, seran mesh and grove heaters to control moisture, heavy rain and hail, excessive sunlight and low temperatures.

(b) Plant diseases, insects, and soil conditions may destroy crops or retard growth. The General Partner intends to use modern horticultural techniques to prevent or minimize the effects of these conditions such as pesticides, soil analysis, fertilizers, soil sterilization and careful evaluation of species requirements and crop growth. Although the General Partner is not aware of proposed action by the U.S. Department of Agriculture, the Environmental Protection Agency or other governmental instrumentalities to prohibit or restrict use of pesticides now used by the General Partner, no assurance can be given that in the future such action will not be taken against a particular pesticide which is most effective in preventing or controlling a particular disease or insect.

(c) Market price fluctuations for products can be affected by the timing and volume of production and the availability of, popularity of, and demand for specific species. Certain of these factors are beyond the control of the General Partner or depend upon predictions of future market conditions. These factors can adversely affect the profitability of Fund operations.

(d) Production may be adversely affected by labor unrest as a result of the movement to organize farm laborers which may involve the use of boycotts and strikes. Collective bargaining agreements entered into by unions representing farm laborers and growers and legislation may reduce the unrest, but there is no assurance that labor shortages and labor problems will not confront the Fund and cause an increase in farm operation costs.

(e) The nature of cash flow in agriculture is unpredictable. Over the years the General Partner and its affiliates have developed consistent methods of projecting costs such as labor, fuel, pot soil and seedlings; however, over the years, as the General Partner's and its affiliates' ability to project expenses has become more definitive, its ability to project cash flow from sales has become less definitive. Cash flow from sales is difficult, if not impossible, to project because of weather and supply and demand.

2. *Uninsured Losses.* Because of the cost of casualty insurance for growing crops, the General Partner does not intend to obtain such insurance. Therefore, any damage or destruction of the plants may result in loss of capital invested and any profits which might be anticipated from such assets. Because the Fund intends to contract with several growers in geographically distinct locations it is unlikely that all or a significant portion of the plants would be damaged or destroyed. However, certain disasters could have a statewide effect, such as floods, drought or plight.

To the extent that it is economically practicable, the General Partner will arrange for comprehensive insurance, including fire, liability and extended coverage on all remaining assets.

TAX ASPECTS OF A FLOWER FUND

1. *Recapture.* The Revenue Act of 1978 amended Section 465 of the Code so as to require the recapture of previously allowed losses where the amount at risk is reduced below zero

(by distribution to the taxpayer, by changes in the status of indebtedness from recourse to non-recourse, by the commencement of a guarantee or other similar arrangement which affects the taxpayer's risk of loss, or otherwise). Under the Act, if the amount at risk in any activity is reduced below zero, the taxpayer will recognize income to the extent that his or her at risk basis is so reduced. However, the amount recaptured is limited to the excess of the loss amount previously allowed in that activity over the amounts previously recaptured. The new provision requires a taxpayer to recapture only those losses occurring in taxable years beginning after December 31, 1978.

2. *Deduction of Expenses Incurred in Nursery and Tree Activities.*

Section 1.162-12(a) of the Treasury Regulations provides that a cash method farmer who does not compute income upon the crop method, may deduct as an expense the cost of seeds and young plants which are purchased for further development and cultivation prior to sale in later years. The Regulations caution, however, that a consistent practice of deducting such cost must be followed from year to year. In addition, the Code allows a taxpayer engaged in the business of farming to elect to deduct certain expenses which otherwise would be treated as capital items and added to the basis of the property acquired by the Fund. Such items consist of expenditures for soil and water conservation (Section 175 of the Code), fertilizer, lime, ground limestone, marl, or other materials to enrich, neutralize or condition land used in farming, or for the application of such materials to such land (Section 180 of the Code) and clearing land for the purpose of making such land suitable for use in farming (Section 182 of the Code).

Pursuant to the applicable Code Sections, the Fund will file an election under these Sections to deduct, rather than capitalize, such expenses, as both the Fund's nursery and tree-growing activities constitute "farming" for purposes of Section 162, 175, 180 and 182. See Rev. Rul. 59-12, 1959-1 C.B. 49; *Harold M. Clark,* 28 T.C.M. 1260, 1263 n.6 (1969).

Except for expenses for fertilizer, which are taken into account in computing a Limited Partner's distributive share of Fund income or loss, the Code places limitations on the deductibility by a Limited Partner for expenditures for soil and water conservation and clearing land. As regards to soil and water conservation expenditures, the deductibility by a Limited Partner of his distributive share of such item is limited in any one year to 25% of the Limited Partner's gross income from farming for that year. To the extent that the Limited Partner's pro rata portion of such expenses exceed 25% of his gross income from farming (from the Fund or otherwise), such excess may be carried forward to future years.

Under Section 182, the deductibility by each Limited Partner of his pro rata share of expenses for clearing land is also limited to the lesser of $5,000 or 25% of his taxable income from farming during the taxable year (from the Fund or otherwise). However, to the extent such expenses exceed these limitations, the amount is not carried forward to future years, but is capitalized to the cost of the land.

The provisions of Section 464 of the Code, as amended by the Tax Reform Act of 1976, are applicable to the deductions which will be claimed in connection with the Fund's nursery activities. This section requires, in the case of "farming syndicates," that deductions for amounts paid for seed, fertilizer or other supplies be taken only in the taxable year in which they are actually "used or consumed." While this section applies to the raising and cultivation of agricultural products, it does not apply to the raising of trees (other than trees bearing fruit or nuts), and hence should not control the deductions claimed in connection with the Fund's tree-growing activities.

The General Partner represents that the seed, fertilizer and other farm supplies purchased in connection with the Fund's nursery activities will be used during the taxable year of purchase. Accordingly, Section 464 should permit the deductibility of these expenses by the Limited Partners during the taxable year in which the purchases are made. In the event that nursery items are not "used or consumed" during the year of purchase, deductibility would be deferred until "use or consumption" occurred; and would offset any corresponding amount of gross income generated by sales during that year.

The General Partner has received an opinion that the species of plant which are characterized as "trees" and which the Fund intends to purchase are classified, on a botanical basis, as "trees." Relying on this opinion, these purchases should fall within the "tree" provisions of Section 464(e)(1). It should be noted, however, that the Service may claim that some or all of the trees purchased by the Fund do not fall within the intent of

Congress in its statutory reference to "trees." In making this argument, the Service may rely on language in the legislative history which mentions "forestry" or the growing of "timber" in discussing the "tree" provisions. Thus, the Statement of the Managers for the Conference Committee, filed on September 13, 1976, in discussing the express exclusion of the growing or raising of trees from the scope of the term "farming" as used in Section 464, states (p. 415): "Thus, this provision does not apply to forestry or the growing of timber." (Similar statements appear in other portions of the legislative history. See, Summary of the Tax Reform Act of 1976, prepared by the Joint Committee on Taxation, Section 207(a)(b), Page 7; and, Conference Committee Report on H.R. 10612, Section 204(a) (b), Page 415, and Section 204(c), Page 416.).

If this argument were, in fact, raised by the Service, the Fund has compelling counterarguments. First, the Tax Court, in the case of *Harold M. Clark, supra,* held that the growing of Oregon myrtle trees for ornamental purposes is "farming," as that term is used in Section 180 of the Code. (Section 180, unlike Section 464, does not expressly exclude the growing of trees from the definition of "farming"). Thus, the Tax Court necessarily viewed such trees to be other than "timber," as Regs. Subsections 1.180-1(b) and 1.175-3 indicate that the growing of "timber" does not constitute farming for purposes of Section 180. *Harold M. Clark, supra,* also held that the growing of Oregon myrtle trees is an activity which qualifies for favored treatment under Regs. Subsection 1.162-12 (relating to the current deductibility of the cost of seeds, etc.) and, by necessary implication, that such trees are not "timber," as that term is used in Regs. Subsection 1.611-3(a) (relating to the recovery through depletion of certain capitalized costs). Second, the word "trees," rather than "forestry" or "timber," is used in Section 464. That Congress intended by using the word "trees" to convey a broader category of included species other than "forestry" or "timber" is indicated by other sections of the Code dealing with timber, wherein the word "timber" itself is used. See Sections 611(a), 631(a), and 1231(b)(2). Finally, other language in the legislative history of the Tax Reform Act of 1976 is supportive of the argument that "trees" is broader than merely "timber" or "forestry." Specifically, the Summary of the Conference Agreement, prepared by the House Committee on Ways and Means, states (P. 5) in discussing the farming syndicate rules, that:

For purposes of the farming syndicate rules, activities involving the growing or raising of trees are not considered farming unless the activities involved fruit or nut trees. Thus, this provision does not apply to forestry or to growing of timber *(or to nursery operations involving the growing of trees).*

Even if the items purchased and claimed by the Fund to be trees are not considered "trees" under Section 464, the investor should still be entitled to deductions for purchases of nursery items in the amount of the actual cash investment. Further, in the event that the items claimed by the Fund to be trees are not considered to be "trees" within the meaning of Section 464, this should, at most, only cause a deferral of the related deductions, as such items would then be subject to the "used or consumed" requirement of Section 464. Once this test were met, deductibility should be allowed (assuming that investor is "at risk" for the amount of deductions claimed).

3. *Depreciation.* As to any equipment which the Fund may purchase, the Fund intends to make use of the method or methods of depreciation available to it which, in the opinion of the General Partner, provides the greatest advantage to the Limited Partners under the Code and the regulations thereunder in effect from time to time. Under present law, the 200% declining balance method may be adopted by the Fund for new property (other than land or improvements) used in its trade or business or held for the production of income provided such property has a useful life of at least three years. The 150% declining balance method is available for such property if it is used and also has a useful life of at least three years. New improvements on real property will also qualify for the 150% declining balance. However, used improvements of real property may only be depreciated using the straight-line method of depreciation.

Prior to the Tax Reform Act of 1976, Section 179 of the Code placed the following aggregate limitation upon each partner other than a trust with respect to the deduction of "bonus" (i.e., additional first-year) depreciation from all sources: $2,000 for corporations, single individuals and married individuals filing separate returns; and $4,000 for married individuals filing joint returns. Trusts are not entitled to any deductions for such depreciation. The Tax Reform Act of 1976, however, now imposes the above limitation at both the Partner and partnership levels. Therefore, the Fund may now only claim a maximum of $2,000 of bonus depreciation, which amount must then be apportioned among all investors. Because the accounting and bookkeeping costs to the Fund associated with the taking of bonus depreciation would exceed the nominal benefits now available to it thereunder, the Fund has chosen not to claim bonus depreciation.

Depreciation deductions reduce the cost basis used to determine the amount of gain or loss realized when the property is sold.

4. *Sale or Other Disposition of Partnership Properties.* Except as otherwise provided below with respect to depreciation recapture and recapture under Section 1252 of the Code, any profit or loss which may be realized by the Fund on the sale of any of its property (other than nursery items) will be treated as capital gain or loss under the Code unless it is determined that the Fund is a "dealer" in such assets for Federal Income Tax purposes or except to the extent that the assets sold constitute "Section 1231 assets" (i.e., real property and depreciable assets used in a trade or business and held for more than twelve months). If such property constitutes "Section 1231 assets," a Limited Partner's proportionate share of gains or losses would be combined with any other Section 1231 gains or losses incurred by him in that year and his net Section 1231 gains or losses would be taxed as gains from the sale of capital assets or constitute ordinary losses, as the case may be. A taxpayer is required to hold a capital asset for more than twelve months in order to be entitled to long-term capital gains treatment.

Under Section 1231(b)(4) of the Code, the sale of both an unharvested "crop" and the related land will be treated as "Section 1231 assets" provided the land has been held for more than twelve months. There is no case law or Revenue Ruling authority which bears directly upon the issue of whether or not the Fund's nursery or tree items would be found to constitute "crops," as that term is used in Section 1231(b)(4). The legislative history of Section 117(j) of the Internal Revenue Code of 1939 (the predecessor provision of Section 1231(b)(4) of the present Code) appears to indicate that a principal motivation behind the enactment of Section 117(j) was the desire to avoid what some courts had viewed to be the necessity of apportioning a purchase price between "crops" held for sale in the ordinary course of business (taxed at ordinary income rates) and the underlying land (taxed at capital gains rates). S. Rep. No. 781, 82d Cong., 1st Sess., 2018 (1951). This problem is no less prevalent with agricultural items than it is with horticultural items, such as nursery items and trees. Accordingly, it is the Fund's belief that those, if any, of its nursery and tree items which grow on the land would be considered "crops" for purposes of Section 1231(b)(4).

Three cautionary notes should be borne in mind in this regard. First, those nursery or tree items of the Fund which are either severed from the land or grown in pots which are not attached to the land would not be considered "crops" within the meaning of Section 1231(b)(4). Gain or loss on the sale of these items will, therefore, be taxed at ordinary income rates because the Fund will be a "dealer" with respect thereto. Second, Rev. Rul. 76-242, 1976-1 C.B. 132 appears to treat "crops," "trees," and "plants" as mutually exclusive categories. Although that Ruling does not involve Section 1231(b)(4), it may presage the Service's view that they should be treated as distinct for purposes of Section 1231(b)(4). Finally, in any event, the Fund can give no assurance that any of its items will in fact be treated as Section 1231(b)(4) "crops."

If either the Fund's nursery or tree items were found to be crops, then as set forth above, a Limited Partner's proportionate share of the gain or loss attributable to the sale of such items and the related land would be combined with other Section 1231 gains or losses incurred by him in that year and his net Section 1231 gains or losses would be taxed as capital gains or constitute ordinary losses, as the case may be. In such event, however, any deductions (whether or not for the taxable year of sale and whether for expenses, depreciation or otherwise) attributable to the production of such items will be disallowed. This may entail the filing of amended returns for prior years if any such deductions attributable to the production of such horticultural items were taken in previous years.

To the extent that the Fund's nursery or tree items are not found to constitute "crops," as that term is used in Section 1231(b)(4), then gain or loss from the sale of such items would be treated as gain or loss from the sale of property held for sale in the ordinary course of a trade or business and, accordingly, would be taxed at ordinary rates.

In the event of the disposition of any depreciable real property within one year after acquisition, or of any depreciable personal property and depreciable tangible property used as an integral part of production (even if straight-line depreciation has been taken), gain, if any, will be recaptured as ordinary income to the extent that depreciation has been previously allowed on the property. In the event of the disposition of depreciable real property held for more than one year with respect to which accelerated depreciation has been taken, depreciation in excess of the amount of depreciation which would have been allowable under the straight-line method would be recaptured as ordinary income.

If and when the Fund sells any farm land, Section 1252 of the Code provides that to the extent that the Fund takes advantage of special deductions for expenditures for soil and water conservation and land clearing operations, all conservation and land clearing deductions would be recaptured; and if the land is sold more than five but less than ten years after acquisition, the percentage of deductions recaptured is decreased by 20% each year more than five that the land is held. Furthermore, as noted below, under "Gain or Loss on Sale of Partnership Units or Liquidation of the Partnership," to the extent of the accumulated balance in a Limited Partner's "excess deductions account," if any, that Limited Partner's allocable gain upon a sale of Fund Property would be treated as ordinary income rather than capital gain under Section 1251 of the Code.

If Fund property with respect to which the investment tax credit has been taken is sold within seven years and prior to the expiration of the useful life utilized in determining the amount of credit taken, a portion, or all, of such investment credit will be recaptured, increasing the amount of tax payable that year by each Limited Partner.

5. *Gain or Loss on Sale of Partnership Units or Liquidation of the Partnership.*

As a general rule, gain or loss recognized by a limited partner (who is not a "dealer" in such property) on the sale of an interest in a partnership which has been held for more than twelve months will generally be taxable as long term capital gain or loss. However, that portion of a selling partner's gain allocable to "appreciated inventory items" and "unrealized receivables" as defined in Section 751 of the Code would be treated as ordinary income. The term "appreciated inventory items" should encompass all of the Fund's harvested nursery and tree items, and may encompass such unharvested items (such unharvested items are not "appreciated inventory items" only if they constitute "crops" within the meaning of Section 1231(b)(4); see "Sale or Other Disposition of Partnership Property," above). In addition, the term "unrealized receivables" should encompass all Fund assets subject to depreciation recapture and recapture under Section 1252 relating to special deductions for soil and water conservation expenditures and land clearing operations to the extent of such recapture, determined as if a selling Partner's proportionate share of all the Fund's properties have been sold at that time. Thus, it is possible that a substantial portion of a Limited Partner's gain or loss upon the sale of his Fund Units will be taxed at ordinary rates.

Prior to January 1, 1976, a limited partner who had "farm net losses" in any year of at least $25,000 ($12,500 in the case of a married person filing a separate return if the taxpayer's spouse has non-farm adjusted gross income) and non-farm adjusted gross income (the limited partner's adjusted gross income computed without farming income and deductions) of at least $50,000 ($25,000 in the case of a married person filing a separate return if the taxpayer's spouse has non-farm adjusted gross income) was required to establish an "excess deductions account" and make additions to this account in an amount equal to all of his "farm net losses" from all farming interests which were in excess of $25,000 in any year. A corporation or trust was required to add all "farm net losses" to such account regardless of the amount of "farm net losses" or non-farm adjusted gross income. The amount was then decreased by the limited partner's share of "farm net income" from all farming interests. To the extent of a cumulative balance in a Limited Partner's "excess deductions account," if any, gain from the sale of his interest in the Fund or the allocable gain upon the sale of Fund property will be treated as ordinary income rather than capital gain. The Tax Reform Act of 1976 provides that no additions to an excess deductions account need be made for net farm losses sustained in any taxable year beginning after December 31, 1975.

Upon liquidation or termination of the Fund, gain (or loss) will be recognized to a Partner only to the extent that the sum of cash distributed to such Partner and his proportionate share of non-recourse liabilities, exceeds (or is exceeded by) his basis in his Fund interest.

If a Limited Partner sells his interest after an investment tax credit was taken by the Fund within seven years and prior to the expiration of the useful life utilized in determining the amount of the investment credit, or if the Fund terminates or dissolves within such period, a portion of all of such investment tax credit taken by each Limited Partner must be recaptured and will increase each such Limited Partner's tax liability for the year of such sale. The amount of the investment tax credit recaptured generally will depend upon the period during which the property was held by the Fund, when the interest was sold and the percentage of interest sold relative to the interest held when the investment credit property was purchased.

Fewer agricultural programs are being offered because of price and profit problems in the industry, but the programs illustrated here continue to appear on a steady basis.

Chapter Six

ENTERTAINMENT

A fickle public and a complicated distribution network make it difficult to predict success in the entertainment business. A look into the movie industry reflects this situation.

INDUSTRY OVERVIEW

Film Production

The structure of the motion picture industry has changed substantially over the last three decades. With the spinoff of the exhibition segment of the industry from the production and distribution segments in 1948 pursuant to an antitrust decree, the independent producer became a more significant factor. Today, virtually all motion pictures are made by independent production companies with financing obtained from major studios, distributors or outside parties. Each picture is a separate business venture with its own management and employees.

From concept to completion, the making of a feature film progresses through several steps and phases. First, the producer typically acquires the rights to some literary material (e.g., a novel or story outline). Then, during a phase known as "development," the producer, with his own funds or funds obtained from others, finances the first writing of the screenplay and any additions, revisions or rewrites that may be required before a final decision is made to proceed with production.

After the screenplay has been approved for production, the project enters the "pre-production" phase. During pre-production, a director (if not previously involved) will he hired, principal cast will be committed, budgets developed, special risk insurance placed, completion guarantees acquired and "shooting" schedules and locations planned. Next, in the "production phase," principal photography, the actual "shooting" of the film, is completed. Finally, during "post-production," the film is edited, director's and producer's cuts are made and the dialogue, sound track, special effects, music and motion picture are synchronized, resulting in the negative from which prints to be released to distributors are made.

Primary responsibility for the overall planning, financing and production of the film rests with the producer, including any executive producer or person or entity arranging for and financing production. The actual creative filmmaking process, involving script consultation, casting, set and costume design, direction and photography, editing and cutting, is the responsibility of the film's director.

Film Distribution

Theatrical

Arrangements for the exhibition of a film vary greatly, but there are certain fundamental economic relationships generally applicable to the theatrical distribution of motion pictures in the United States. These are illustrated as follows: First, the owner of the theater (the "Exhibitor") receives the admission paid at the box office ("gross box office receipts") and retains, in accordance with the terms of his license from the distributor, a share, usually ranging from 10% to 75%. In those cases where the Exhibitor retains a percentage of gross box office receipts in the lower range, he is also normally permitted to first recover a negotiated charge which is intended to reimburse him for his actual operating costs. In addition, the Exhibitor will be permitted to deduct the costs of any advertising he has contributed.

The balance ("gross film rentals") is then remitted to the distributor, which licenses the exhibition of the film, typically for from 7 to 20 years, and normally has the responsibility for advertising and supplying prints and other materials to the Exhibitors. From the gross film rentals, the distributor first deducts its distribution fee, which for United States rights usually averages 30%. From this balance, the distributor reimburses itself for the actual expenses incurred in distributing the film, primarily the cost of duplicating the "negative" into prints for actual exhibition and advertising the motion picture. After recovery of distribution expenses, the remainder of the gross film rentals is available to cover the cost of producing the film (the "negative cost"). When a film is financed and distributed by a major studio, the negative cost will usually include a substantial "overhead" charge to cover the cost of the studio's production facilities, investments in the development of motion picture properties which are not produced and costs of additional staff assigned to motion picture production. An additional fee is usually charged if any of these facilities are actually used in the production of the film. After the negative cost, plus interest, is recouped, any amounts remaining constitute the film's "net profits." Net profits are usually first distributed to parties who have deferred their compensation for work done on the film and are then divided between the other profit participants pursuant to their negotiated agreements.

Foreign theatrical distribution rights are licensed on a territory-by-territory basis with the owner of the negative typically receiving an advance against the owner's percentage of gross film rentals from each territory. Under these circumstances the owner usually does not receive any payment on account of its percentage share of the foreign gross film rentals until the foreign distribution fee and expenses are recovered and the advance recouped.

Foreign theatrical distribution rights can also be licensed to a distributor in a foreign territory for a fixed license fee. In such cases, the owner of the negative is not entitled to additional payments based on the gross film rentals in such territory. Consequently, if the film is successful, under a fixed fee arrangement the owner usually realizes an amount which constitutes a smaller share of foreign gross film rentals than it would under a "percentage license" arrangement; however, if the film is unsuccessful, the flat fee usually exceeds the share of foreign revenues the owner would otherwise receive. A further advantage of the fixed license fee arrangement is that no distribution fee or expenses are applicable and the owner's cost is limited to a fee which generally averages between 10% and 15%, payable to the owner's agent involved in the licensing arrangement.

Distribution agreements typically permit the distributor to substantially curtail financial support for theatrical distribution of the film at various stages depending upon performance in selected regional markets.

Television

Network, syndicated and pay television rights typically are licensed directly by the owner of the film or, for a fee, by a distributor. Such licenses are usually for periods of between one and four years. Depending upon the subject matter of the film and other factors, it is often possible to license such rights before the film is released for theatrical distribution. In a typical pre-release licensing of United States network television rights, 10% of the license fee is paid upon execution of the agreement, 10% upon delivery of the print to the network, which customarily takes place approximately two years after the film is released for theatrical exhibition, and the balance is paid normally in equal amounts with each showing of the film by the network, with the first showing taking place in the third year following the first theatrical release.

Ancillary Rights

In addition to the theatrical and television distribution of a motion picture, an owner of a film may market other rights associated with the film. It may license rights for video cassettes and discs, the publication and promotion of music, the incorporation of original songs on the sound track for subsequent use in promotion and sound track albums, and merchandising.

Library

After the initial foreign and domestic theatrical and television distribution of a motion picture, the owner of a film typically retains its ownership rights in the film. A substantial portion of the cost of the negative will have been depreciated during the initial distribution period, so that the book value of the film will be minimal. The film may have a continuing market value, however, based upon its residual theatrical or television (pay, syndicated or network) marketability.

Competition

A number of organizations which regularly finance film productions compete for a limited number of talented filmmakers. These organizations include all of the major studios and certain distributors. In addition, two major television networks have commenced production of motion pictures for theatrical exhibition. Most of these companies have substantial financial, managerial and other resources and have established tract records and entrenched positions in the motion picture industry. The major studios are also able to guarantee distribution.

The following shows how movies get around.

It has long been a major frustration for filmgoers that movies they read about and anticipate often don't get to their city at all. Sometimes the movie arrives but is gone in an eye-blink, or is paired with "Revenge of the Swinging Vampire Cheerleaders" at some remote drive-in.

How movies get to theaters throughout the country is as complicated as laser surgery, and there are no guarantees that everyone will have a chance to see every major movie.

"There are dozens of variables to the distribution pattern of movies," says Bob Rehme, the young president of Avco Embassy Pictures in Hollywood. "The only thing you can say for sure is that, if a movie is successful, it is shown everywhere."

We'll get back to that qualifier of success and how it applies to the movies above in a few paragraphs. First, a little history.

Under the old studio system, when studios made their own movies to show in their own theaters around the country, it was much easier to track the flow of a movie. MGM movies, produced by huge staffs of studio talent and craftsmen, ended up in MGM theaters, and individual theater owners had nothing to say about it. Films were often booked an entire year in advance.

Federal anti-trust action changed all that about 30 years ago, and, with the decline in theater audiences brought on by television, most of the big studios became primarily distribution companies. The majority of movies today are made by independent production companies with independent financing and released through the distributor that offers the best deal.

With the film in hand and a marketing strategy planned, the distribution company then goes out through its branch offices and tries to book the film at a certain number of theaters throughout the country.

The buyers are the individual and chain theater owners, who bid against each other for films. In some states exhibitors often have to bid without seeing the film first. They may end up committing a guaranteed fee against a huge percentage of their box office receipts for several weeks, gambling on the appeal of the movie's stars, its advance publicity or its subject matter.

Again, there are many variables in the way films are marketed. There are dozens of films that have been completed for months, if not years, that have not been picked up for distribution by anyone. The movies have been shopped around in Hollywood and rejected as "uncommercial." They've been screened for exhibitors around the country and rejected for the same reason.

On the flip side, the studios and distribution companies often feel strongly enough about a movie's box office future that they will get involved in its financing from the beginning in order to lock it up.

Opening nationally is risky business, Rehme says.

"If you open wide, you have to spend heavily and go for broke. It costs from $3.5 to $6 million to launch a film on a broad basis. If it doesn't work, it's down the tube.

"The newspaper ads and the television ads are paid for, and it doesn't make any difference how expensive the movie was to make. An ad for 'Prom Night' costs the same as an ad for 'Raise the Titanic.' "

"Prom Night" was a low-budget Avco release that has far out-grossed Associated Film Distribution's "Raise the Titanic," which cost nearly $40 million.

Rehme says distributors seldom feel as strongly about the box office potential of their films as he did about "Hopscotch." Often distributors experiment with dozens of marketing plans, trying to find one that works.

Several years ago, Avco picked up comedienne Joan Rivers' film, "Rabbit Test," a shoestring-budgeted comedy that had the technical qualities of a bad home movie. The film had two big things to offer a distributor: It was cheap, and Rivers was anxious to use her accessibility to TV's talk shows to go out and sell it.

Avco's marketing plan worked perfectly. "Rabbit Test" was booked in theaters in three waves. The first in five midsized American cities. The second in all but the major cities. The third in the major cities.

By holding out from New York and Los Angeles, Avco avoided expected bad reviews in national publications. At the same time, getting nothing but positive exposure from Rivers on the talk show circuit, the film did brisk opening business in the hinterlands. By the time it reached the critical eyes of reviewers in the big cities, "Rabbit Test" was already in the black.

"If we're concerned about reviews, obviously we would be very careful about New York," says Rehme. "There are movies, however, where reviews don't seem to matter."

The examples of that are legion. "Friday the 13th," a unanimously panned horror film distributed by Paramount, is one of the year's box office hits.

Once in a while, a distributor will be too cautious about a movie, which was the case with Orion Pictures' "The Great Santini." The movie was made early in 1979, nearly died late in 1979 and now is being touted as a candidate in several Oscar categories for 1980.

"The Great Santini," starring Robert Duvall and Blythe Danner, is a heavy domestic drama that was filmed in Beaufort, S.C. Orion executives decided to avoid opening the film in major cities where bad reviews could put an early kiss of death on this kind of small film.

Instead, they opened it in 60 theaters near Beaufort, assuming that its heavy advance publicity would establish a quick box office record that would help sell it to exhibitors elsewhere.

The strategy backfired. The film did terrible business in the South, and, as a result, Orion couldn't get it booked anywhere else. So, they changed its name and rented theaters in a couple of other cities for showings, but still no interest was generated.

Finally, it was being shown under the title "The Ace" on airplanes and on pay TV, and Orion had all but given up on it. Then, it started developing a word-of-mouth reputation among pay TV subscribers, some of whom had enough clout to generate theatrical interest in it. In a last gasp effort, "The Great Santini" opened last summer in one theater in mid-Manhattan.

It got rave reviews from the New York critics, built up block-long lines of viewers and has since been carefully released on an exclusive first-run basis to nearly 100 theaters across the country. It has grossed $4 million so far and will likely be in the black by the time it goes into wide release.

"The Stunt Man" came even closer to oblivion before finding its way into theaters and gaining a critical acclaim as great or greater than that of "The Great Santini."

Director Richard Rush started working on "The Stunt Man" nine years ago, but couldn't get financing for it until Mel Simon Productions put up the money early in 1978. Simon had second thoughts when he saw the finished product, apparently considering it too arty for a mass audience, and left it out of a distribution package with 20th Century-Fox.

The movie was shopped around in Hollywood and rejected by every major distributor, including Avco. Rehme said he turned it down for several reasons: He didn't like it; he didn't think people were interested in films focusing on the film industry; all of its ancillary rights (pay TV, foreign distribution, etc.), which would help recoup its costs, had already been sold off.

"The Stunt Man" faced the fate of Steve McQueen's 1975 "An Enemy of the People": films of high quality and low commercial appeal that languish on the shelf.

Last June, on the insistence of two men who run a chain of theaters in Seattle, "The Stunt Man" got its chance, and for two months broke local box office records. Simon then opened it in six theaters in Los Angeles, where it got enthusiastic reviews and another batch of good box office receipts.

Using the reviews and the figures, Simon ran a campaign in the Hollywood trade papers and finally, 20th Century-Fox picked it up for national distribution.

The rest is not yet show business history. But the movie still has to do well outside Los Angeles and New York, where there is a large audience for well-crafted, out-of-the-main-stream films—a category into which "The Stunt Man" falls.

In the old studio system days, exhibitors didn't play much of a role in the success or failure of a film. Today, they are the collective force. If a film turns enough of them off, they can kill it simply by ignoring it.

"Melvin and Howard," a film about Melvin Dummar and the highly publicized Morman will of Howard Hughes, is currently showing in a few major cities and is getting the kind of reviews that generate Oscars. Yet, exhibitors scorned it en masse earlier this year and nearly killed it.

A few people who had seen it in private screenings urged the New York Film Festival organizers to show it. They did, and it opened the festival to unanimous raves. If those raves can be cashed in at the box office in the major cities, exhibitors in other parts of the country will be scrambling, despite their bias, to make their bids.

The bottom line is the old bottom line.

"First and foremost, we run a business," says Avco's Rehme. "We'd love to have a quality product that's successful in the market. If you can tell us ahead of time which films will be good and successful, you have a big future in this town."

The assistance of the Detroit Free Press in the preparation of the above material is gratefully acknowledged.

MOTION PICTURES

Industry Status and Forecast

The domestic theatrical film industry enjoyed 3 solid years of growth between 1977 and 1979, following a decline in 1975 and 1976. It appeared, however, that a reversal took place during the first 6 months of 1980, when receipts and number of tickets sold dipped slightly from a year ago. Although there was reason to be concerned about total receipts for the entire year, some of the Nation's largest exhibitors felt that the reason behind this disappointing performance was the quality of the movies themselves rather than the effects of the economic downturn. Even with new releases and year-end holiday crowds, it is doubtful that receipts in 1980 will show any appreciably real increase over 1979, although there is a possibility that some box office blockbusters might develop. Taking these various factors into consideration, theater receipts might reach $3.1 billion in 1980, 8 percent over 1979. It is anticipated that a similar 8 percent rate of growth will take place in 1981 and theater receipts will total $3.3 billion.

Theater–Admissions–Ticket Prices

It is estimated that there were 12,218 theaters in the United States in 1979, of which 9,021 were indoors with 13,331 screens and 3,197 drive-ins with 3,570 screens. Compared with the prior year, there was a drop of less than 1 percent in the number of theaters, with a 4 percent increase in the number of screens. Also, there was a significant decline of 4 percent in indoor and drive-in single screen theaters while the number of multiple screen theaters increased.

Theater admissions in the United States totaled 1.12 billion in 1979, less than 1 percent below a year earlier. Despite the slight decrease, the number was one of the highest since 1961, when attendance was 1.23 billion. For the first 5 months of 1980, there was an estimated 420 million admissions, over 4 percent below the corresponding period a year earlier.

Increases in ticket prices continued unabated in 1980 as they have over the past decade. The average admission price in 1979 was estimated at $2.52, more than 7 percent above 1978. This is the largest admission price increase since an 8 percent rise in

1975. Nevertheless, the 7 percent increase was well below the rate of over 11 percent for all services in 1979. The average ticket price for the first 5 months of 1980 was $2.64 or almost 7 percent above the corresponding period a year earlier. While certain major summer releases in 1980 commanded $5.50 adult top scales in some large markets, ticket prices were actually lowered as a marketing device in certain economically depressed areas.

Film Starts

Major Hollywood producers stepped up their film production in 1979 by 24 percent over the previous year, according to the weekly film production chart of *Variety*. They started production on 99 films during 1979 compared to 80 in 1978. The 1979 figure was the highest since 1973, the last year when major studios broke the 100 picture mark with 102 films. Independent production was also up in 1979, by 21 percent, 149 film starts as opposed to 123 a year earlier. Overall production thereby rose by 22 percent, with 248 films being launched in 1979 against 203 in 1978.

There were 141 film starts by major and independent producers through July 18, 1980, down 10 percent from the same period a year earlier. Of the total, majors started production on 83 films, up 14 percent over 1979, while independents started 53 films, down 30 percent. The rest of 1980 does not look very promising due to the Screen Actors Guild strike for royalties on films produced for pay television and home-video recording devices. Whatever the outcome of the strike, moviegoers will have fewer options of feature entertainment films, while television viewers will have a steady diet of prime-time reruns.

Figures shown on *Variety*'s production chart for the major companies should be considered virtually definitive, in that these companies routinely announce films before or as they begin shooting. Many independent productions, however, may never appear on the production chart for various reasons, such as desire by producers to maintain a low profile, need to escape attention by unions, lack of access to normal publicity channels, or failure to notify the trade. Consequently, the number of independent films listed in the chart is unrealistically low.

Negative Cost on the Upswing

Negative cost refers to the charges and expenses incurred in the acquisition and production of motion pictures. These include sound stage, film labs, editing room, construction, and raw film stock. The average negative cost of new feature films financed in whole or in part by the Motion Picture Association of America member companies was $8.5 million in 1979, up 51 percent above 1978. Furthermore, the average negative cost per feature increased by an average annual rate of 23 percent between 1972 and 1979.

The outlook for 1980 has worsened because the rise in value of silver has caused a large increase in the cost of prints. During the year, it is estimated that the cost for making a 2-hour, 35 mm print will increase by $250, raising the average cost to about $1,100.

Overseas Markets

The United States is the world's leading producer and exporter of motion picture films, occupying close to 40 percent of free world screen time. Unlike many American industries for which foreign trade is a sideline, the motion picture industry relies heavily on foreign markets. In recent years, remittals of receipts for U.S. film rentals from abroad have accounted for about 50 percent of the total cost of producing films. If this source of revenue were to diminish, it would probably be financially impossible for U.S. film producers to continue producing and distributing quality pictures.

Despite a number of problems facing American film companies operating in foreign countries, there has been a steady growth of feature film rentals over the past decade. The motion picture and television industry received $889 million from overseas rentals in 1979, 14 percent over the $777 million received in 1978. Motion pictures accounted for $608 million or 68 percent of the total, while television accounted for $281 million or 32 percent.

Record Grossing Features

The number of theatrical films earning $8 million or more each in film rentals in the United States and Canada reached a record 50 in 1979, 10 more than in 1978 and 17 more than in 1977. Unlike prior years in which high-grossing feature theatrical films were dominated by member companies of the Motion Picture Association of America, five non-member producers accounted for six films or 12 percent of those earning $8 million or more in U.S. and Canadian rentals in 1979.

From a historical standpoint it is interesting to note that in 1972 only 10 motion pictures grossed $8 million or over in domestic rentals, 9 of which reached $10 million or more, while in 1979 50 feature films grossed $8 million or over, 37 of which reached $10 million or more. Based upon information for the first half of 1980, it is unlikely that the 1979 record will be matched.

Future Prospects

For some years to come, population trends and increases in leisure time will benefit the industry. Between 1980 and 1985, total households will probably increase about 11 percent with family households rising an estimated 8 percent and non-family households by 20 percent. The faster rate of growth of non-family households suggests that the outlook for theaters will be healthy through 1985 because such households tend to go to the movies more often than the rest of the population. Conversely, the expected decline in the number of teenagers and small turnabouts in the marriage and birth rates could cut into attendance.

In addition, there will be intensified competition from films shown on home video tapes and cable television. For example, the number of cable television subscribers reached about 16 million in 1980 and is expected to increase at an annual rate of 10 percent, reaching 25 million in 1985. Subscribers get many first run films at an early stage, which has a considerable effect on theater attendance, at least in the short run. It is impossible to assess the exact impact of pay cable television on movie attendance, since television viewers tend to seek a diversion outside the home after a while. Illustrative of this is the introduction of television following World War II when attendance at theaters dropped; later the novelty wore off and people returned to theaters as a change from the routine of television viewing.

Nevertheless, the future of the movie theaters looks secure considering the increase in non-family households and the tendency of individuals to seek outside entertainment. Theater receipts, therefore, should continue to grow over the next 5 years to $4.8 billion in 1985, for an average annual rate of increase of 8 percent.

The following programs featuring movies, records and electronic and computerized games show the opportunities for high income in a successful venture.

MOVIES

INTRODUCTION

General

It is proposed that a group of Limited Partners acquire 99% of the capital, profit and loss interest in the "Partnership," a Limited Partnership to be organized with Brown and Funding Ltd. as General Partners. The Partnership will enter into an agreement with Productions, Ltd. for the Production of a feature length motion picture. The General Partners will own a one percent (1%) interest in capital, and will be entitled to one percent (1%) of the profits and losses, for which they will contribute $1,000 to the capital of the Partnership.

Sole business of the Partnership will consist of participating in the production of a feature length motion picture and thereby deriving an income interest from the exploitation of the film.

Production of the Picture

The picture will be produced by Productions, Ltd. with White and Brown as co-executive producers.

Distribution of the Picture

The picture will be distributed by Distributor Ltd., a corporation with over fifteen years experience in the worldwide distribution of feature length motion pictures. For its activities as distributor of the film, Distributor Ltd. will receive distribution fees and will have the right to recoup all distribution expenses. A schedule of the distribution fees is as follows:

SCHEDULE OF DISTRIBUTION FEES

United States and Canadian Theatrical Market		35%
United States and Canadian Theatrical Market (Subdistribution)		45%
United States and Canadian Television Market		
	Network	20%
	Syndication	35%
United States and Canadian Non-Theatrical Market (Video Disk & Tape, Armed Forces, In-flight, etc.)		50%
United States and Canadian Cable Market		
	Up to $75,000	50%
	$75,001 to $350,000	30%
	Over $350,000	25%
Flat Foreign Sales		25%
Foreign Theatrical		45%
All Other		50%

Production Budget

The total projected budget of the picture is presently set at $800,000. However, Productions, Ltd. in cooperation with the General Partners shall have the right to adjust the actual budget in order to attract well known talent or otherwise enhance the marketability of the picture. Any such adjustment will have the effect of adjusting the percentage contribution to the project of the various parties. Deferrals arranged for by the producer will be the responsibility of Productions, Ltd. and will be considered a contribution to the project by Productions, Ltd. It may be necessary to award profit participations to certain key personnel associated with the project. Productions assumes responsibility for payment of any such participations out of its share of the profits.

Partial Funding

In the event the Partnership is closed with less than 35 Units so that the Partnership is unable to fund the full $300,000 contemplated herein, Productions, Ltd. will fund any monies not funded by the Partnership. For each $10,000 under the full $300,000 funded by the Partnership, the Partnership shall assign 2.5% of all monies designated as going to the Partnership to Productions, Ltd.

Marketing Fee

Media Limited has committed itself to a promotional program prior to the completion of the picture. The Partnership has agreed to pay to Media Limited $100,000 as a fee for its services. This amount is in addition to and not a substitute for the distribution fees. Media Limited will advance all expenses in connection with this campaign and the distribution of the picture and will recoup these expenses from monies available out of the proceeds from the distribution of the picture after first taking its distribution fees from gross receipts and prior to making any distribution to the Partnership or to the Producer.

Guarantee of Completion

In the event that the costs of production exceed the actual budget as amended, Media, Ltd., the distributor, has agreed to provide all funds necessary to complete the picture provided that the following conditions are met:

(a) Productions, Ltd. and the Partnership both provide all monies in accordance with their respective commitments. That is to say that 100% of the actual budgeted funds including any amendments to the actual budget have been committed and spent on the production of the picture.

(b) Media, Ltd. has the right to take over production of the picture and complete the picture in the most expeditious manner.

(c) In the event Media, Ltd., in its sole discretion shall determine that it is either not possible or practicable to finish the picture it shall have the right to terminate the production and return all monies invested by the Limited Partners. In such event, Media, Ltd. shall become the sole owner of all elements of the Picture in whatever state of completion they may be.

In the event Media, Ltd. shall be called to commit funds to the completion of the picture as provided for herein, Media,

Ltd. shall have the right to recoup any such investment together with interest equal to the rate charged Media, Ltd., by its bank, plus 1%, but in no event less than the prime rate plus 1%, before any monies are paid to either Productions, Ltd. or the Partnership.

Purchase Option

After a period of fifteen years of active distribution, Productions, Ltd. shall have a perpetual option to purchase the Partnership's interest in and to the motion picture for the sum of $25,000.00.

THE PARTNERSHIP

Organization

The Partnership will be organized by Brown and Funding Ltd., the General Partners, who may be deemed to be the organizers and "Parents" of the Partnership.

Compensation

The General Partners will receive from the Partnership receipts regardless of the level of monies raised, a total fee of $20,000 for management of the Partnership business.

The General Partners will also receive a 1% interest in the capital profits, losses and cash flow of the Partnership.

Additional Compensation

The General Partners will receive an expense reimbursement of $15,000 during the first year of operation to cover allocated office and administrative expenses of the Partnership, not including legal and accounting fees.

Funding Ltd. and Brown will receive a fee, as and for services as co-executive producer, in an amount equal to 7% of total monies raised through the sale of Partnership units. In addition, the General Partners will be entitled to 5% of all amounts available for distribution by the Partnership, after an amount equal to the total capital investment of the Partners has been recouped by the Partnership.

The General Partners, in their sole discretion, may assign all or any part of this additional compensation to third parties who have assisted in the production of the picture or in the formation or funding of the Partnership.

The General Partners

Funding, Ltd. is a corporation organized for the purpose of acting as syndicator of motion pictures.

Brown, the President and Chief Executive officer of Funding, Ltd., has long-standing experience in the motion picture industry and was responsible for acquisitions, financing and distribution of full length feature films.

Responsibilities of the General Partners

The General Partners shall have the exclusive management and control of all aspects of the business of the Partnership. In the course of such management, the General Partners may sell, assign, convey, lease, license, mortgage or otherwise dispose of or deal with all or any part of the picture and employ such persons, including, under certain circumstances, affiliates of the General Partners, as they deem necessary for the operations of the Partnership.

Profits, Losses and Cash Flow

All profits, losses, and cash flow of the Partnership shall be allocated one percent to the General Partners and ninety-nine percent to the Limited Partners in the aggregate, pro rata, based on their respective capital interests in the Partnership except as otherwise provided in the Partnership Agreement.

Financing Costs–Special Allocation

The purchase price of a Unit to a Limited Partner who elects to defer part of the capital contribution to October 31, of next year will be $18,500 per Unit, which amount includes $2,500 for financing costs estimated to be incurred to meet Partnership requirements as a result of the Limited Partner's election. Those Limited Partners electing to defer the purchase price of a Unit will receive a special allocation of such financing costs. In the event the financing costs incurred to meet Partnership requirements as a result of a Limited Partner's election are less than the estimated amount, the Partnership Agreement will be amended to provide for a return of such excess capital contribution to such Limited Partner, notwithstanding anything contained in the Partnership Agreement to the contrary. In the event the financing costs incurred to meet the Partnership requirements as a result of the Limited Partner's election exceed the estimated amount, the Partnership will advance such sums on behalf of the Limited Partner and the Partnership will be repaid such advances from distributions to the Limited Partners pursuant to the Partnership Agreement.

The deferral of part of the capital contribution will require the Limited Partner to furnish the Partnership with one (1) irrevocable and unconditional letter of credit due October 31 of next year. Each letter of credit will bear a face amount of $16,500. The General Partners intend to discount the letter of credit with the Partnership's bank, in order to secure funds necessary for the Partnership's business. Investors considering deferral of part of their investment should be aware that banks charge a fee for the issuance of such a letter of credit and all such charges will be the sole responsibility of the Limited Partner.

Distribution of Cash Flow

The General Partners are required to distribute to the Partners, as soon after the end of each fiscal quarter of the Partnership as is reasonably practicable, the amount of cash available from income of the Partnership, if any, after deduction of all charges and expenses and reasonable reserves against contingencies.

Transfer of Interests by Limited Partners

(a) The Units are to be acquired for the account of the named owner of the Unit and not on behalf of any other person. In addition, the Units are to be acquired for investment only and not with a view toward their distribution. The Units have not been registered under the Securities Act of 1933 (the "Act") and must be held indefinitely unless they are subsequently registered under the Act or an exemption from registration is available. The owner of a Unit will be required to agree to furnish the Partnership with an opinion of counsel, in form and substance satisfactory to the Partnership that such sale is permissable without registration, prior to any such sale or transfer of the Unit. The Partnership is under no obligation to register the Units or to comply with any exemption from registration.

(b) In addition to any compliance with the terms of subparagraph (a) above, Units may be disposed of and transferees of the Units may become Limited Partners only with the prior written consent of the General Partners.

(c) The Agreement contains a legend setting forth the foregoing restrictions and those imposed by the Act.

Limitation of Liability of Limited Partner

A Limited Partner is not permitted to take any part in the management or control of the business, since to do so might cause him to lose his status as a Limited Partner and subject him to unlimited liability. A Limited Partner's liability to contribute capital to the Partnership extends no further than the purcahse price of his Units. A Limited Partner may, however, incur income tax liabilities contingent upon, among other things, the amount of proceeds received by the Partnership from the distribution and sale of the "Picture."

Term and Dissolution

The Partnership will continue for a maximum period ending in 30 years, but may be dissolved at an earlier date, if any of the following contingencies occur:

(a) The Partnership fails to close the transaction for the Production of the "Picture."

(b) The Partnership sells all of its interests in the "Picture."

(c) Upon retirement, liquidation or death of both of the General Partners or the bankruptcy or insolvency of both of the General Partners, which is not discharged or vacated within 90 days from the date thereof. However, in such event, the Partnership may be reconstituted and continued as a successor Limited Partnership under certain conditions.

Reports to Limited Partners

An annual statement, prepared by the Partnership's accountants, showing the income, expenses, assets and liabilities of the Partnership at the end of the fiscal year and the partners' distributive share of net income or loss of the Partnership for the preceding fiscal year shall be furnished to each Limited Partner.

Subscription to Partnership Interests

The total cash amount of Limited Partnership Units in the Partnership to be subscribed will be $560,000. Full Units will be sold at a price of $16,000 payable upon subscription. A maximum of 35 Limited Partners will be accepted. The Limited Partners will have the option to defer part of their contributions in the following manner. On subscription the Limited Partner must make a cash payment of $2,000 per unit. The balance of $16,500 per Unit will be due and owing on October 31 of next year, and will be secured by one irrevocable, unconditional and assignable letter of credit bearing a face amount of $16,500.

The General Partners intend to discount both of the letters of credit with the Partnership's bank in order to secure funds necessary for Partnership business. Investors will be required to pay all fees and expenses necessary to secure said letters of credit.

Units will be offered on a subject to prior sale basis. All cash received from investors will be deposited in an interest bearing special account until sufficient sums are available to purchase bank certificates of deposit, short term government securities or other similar obligations. Interest earned on such funds will be held in trust for the benefit of investors until a sufficient number of Units, necessary to assure that the minimum offering will be complete, have been purchased. After this minimum number of units have been purchased, interest earned to that date will be returned to investors based as nearly as practicable on the time and amount of each investor's contribution. Interest earned after such date will be accumulated as working capital for the partnership.

If subscriptions for 27 Units have not been received by October 24 of this year, the General Partners shall have the right to cancel all Units which have been sold and return all monies which have been received with interest as provided for above.

The General Partners reserve the right in their sole discretion to accept or reject any subscription. The General Partners reserve the right to sell all unsold Units to a party of their choice whether related or unrelated to any party involved in the transaction. Such purchaser would take the position of a Limited Partner as to Units purchased by him. Additionally, the General Partners reserve the right to deem a minimum of less than 27 Units acceptable or to close the package if suitable arrangements for deferrals or co-funding can be made with the Producer.

Use of Partnership Funds

In the event the Partnership sells all 35 Units the monies raised will be disbursed as follows:

Investment in the Production	$339,200
Marketing Fees	100,000
General Partners Fees	20,000
Printing and Packaging	12,000
Legal and Accounting	30,000
Brokerage Fees	44,800
Working Capital	15,000
Total Use of Proceeds	$561,000

In the event the Partnership sells twenty-seven Units the monies will be disbursed as follows:

Investment in the Production	$230,240
Marketing Fees	100,000
General Partners Fees	20,000
Printing and Packaging	10,000
Legal and Accounting	30,000
Brokerage Fees	34,560
Working Capital	8,200
Total Use of Proceeds	$433,000

BENEFITS OF A MOVIE FUND

The net producers' share available for distribution from the Distributor to the various parties after the Distributor has deducted all proper deductions including distribution fee and expenses will be divided as follows:

a) 100% to the Partnership until such time as the Partnership has recouped an amount equal to $650,000.

b) 50% to the Partnership and 50% to Productions, Ltd. until such time as the Partnership has received a sum which when added to the sum already received will equal $1,120,000.

c) Thereafter the net producers' share will be divided between the parties with 60% going to Productions, Ltd. and 40% to the Partnership.

RISKS OF A MOVIE FUND

1. Due to the competitive nature of the motion picture industry and the subjective nature of motion pictures, the profit potential of any motion picture is subject to a high degree of risk. The ultimate profitability of any motion picture is largely a function of the cost of its production and distribution in relation to its ultimate audience appeal, which can rarely be reliably ascertained in advance. The production cost of a film is not necessarily a reliable barometer of public reaction to such a film nor of its potential for generating income or profits to the Partnership.

Only a small percentage of all motion pictures generate a profit after recoupment of the cost of a picture to the owners of such pictures. Accordingly, there is a substantial degree of risk that exploitation of the "Picture" will not yield profits to the Partnership and the partners, and that investors may not recoup all or any portion of their capital contributions to the Partnership.

2. The gross receipts of motion pictures are dependent, among other things, upon the availability of a distribution organization which is capable of arranging for appropriate advertising and promotion, selecting proper release dates, and obtaining bookings in theatres.

In general, "distributor's gross receipts" from theatrical exploitation constitute gross box office receipts less exhibitors' fees and cooperative advertising expenses. •Accordingly, "distributor's gross receipts" with respect to theatrical revenues are normally substantially less than total gross box office receipts. "Distributor's gross receipts" with respect to television and non-theatrical revenues generally represent the outright payments without deduction to the distributor from the television stations and networks, the Armed Forces, airlines, ships and the like.

3. The Picture and the distributor will be in competition with numerous other motion picture owners and distributors which have substantial financial resources, large distribution staffs and long-established histories of distribution of motion pictures. Certain of these other companies have recently encountered financial difficulties which reflect the highly competitive character of the motion picture industry as well as the unpredictability of public reaction to motion pictures.

4. As of the date of this memorandum, no arrangements have been made for any of the cast. The success of the production will be materially dependant on the ability of such persons, who at the present time are unknown, and no assurance can be given that the Partnership will be able to make satisfactory arrangements for such persons. Furthermore, contract negotiations may require the allocation of a profit participation to one or more of such persons which if given will reduce the monies available to the Partnership from the exploitation of the film.

5. It is anticipated that the projected budget will be sufficient to complete the production of the picture. However, the budget may be amended in order to provide sufficient funds to attract talent of sufficient stature to expand the profit potential of the film. Any such amendment to the budget must be agreed to by the General Partners, whose final decision will not be subject to review by the Limited Partners. Since the profit participation of the Partnership is, in part, based upon the proportion of contribution to actual budget made by the Partnership, any such amendment to the budget will result in a corresponding decrease in the profit participation of the Partnership. While it is anticipated that such an increase in the budget would result in

an increase in the profit potential of the film sufficient to equal or surpass the profit potential to the Partnership under the current budget, there can be no assurance that such will be the case.

6. While arrangements have been made to attempt to insure the ultimate completion of the motion picture, investors should be aware that there is always a risk that the motion picture will not be completed or that once completed will not be suitable for distribution. The production of this motion picture must therefore be considered to be a "high risk" venture and participation therein is not suitable for any investor who is unable to withstand the loss of his entire investment.

7. There is no assurance that the Internal Revenue Service will not successfully challenge the appropriateness of one or more of the factors used by the Partnership in calculating depreciation and other expenses. Any such attack, if successful, would adversely affect the tax posture of an investment in the Partnership and could result in the Partners paying income tax deficiences for years in which certain Partnership losses were deducted.

8. The Internal Revenue Service may attempt to categorize the Marketing Fee which will be paid to the Distributor as a capital expenditure. If they are successful, the deductions expected this year would not be available.

9. While it is not expected to do so, the distributor, in its sole discretion, may arrange a sale of certain territories prior to the release of the picture. If this should occur, some of the anticipated investment credit would be lost.

10. The General Partners anticipate a release of the motion picture during the month of December of this year. However, this release date is based on a very tight production schedule which may be impossible to meet. The production of any motion picture involves a number of variables, many of which are beyond the control of the producers or of the General Partners. Furthermore, proper distribution of the motion picture may require the distributor to delay release of the film for any number of reasons including competition of other pictures, lack

of suitable exhibitors, or a decision to re-edit the film in order to improve profit potential. The distributor has the sole discretion as to the proper exploitation of the film and, therefore, may in its sole judgment defer release to some time after December 31 of this year. In the event the picture is released after December 31 of this year, many of the tax benefits contemplated by the Partnership will not be available until the film is released.

11. In some years the Partnership derives income from exploitation of the Picture, the Limited Partners could incur income tax liabilities in excess of cash distributions to them in such years. The Federal income tax payable by a Limited Partner upon disposition of his Units may exceed the proceeds of such disposition. Further, investors should note that a Federal income tax audit of the Partnership's tax information return may result in an audit of the returns of the Limited Partners. The Partnership will not be responsible for paying any expenses incurred by a Limited Partner in connection with an audit of his individual return.

12. The General Partners will contribute $1,000.00 to the capital of the Partnership and will own one percent (1%) of the capital, profits and losses of the Partnership. Each Unit purchased by a Limited Partner will cost $16,000.00 which will entitle the Limited Partner to approximately 2.829% of the profits, losses, and capital of the Partnership. As a result of the foregoing, the General Partners will benefit in greater proportion to their investment than such Limited Partners with respect to profits realized by the Partnership and potential tax deductions resulting therefrom.

13. The Partnership may require additional working capital in connection with its business activities. The General Partners are not required by the Limited Partnership agreement to contribute any additional funds necessary for the operation of the Partnership's business. The Limited Partners are under no obligation to contribute additional capital to the Partnership. In the event that sufficient funds are not available for the operation of the Partnership business, there is no assurance that other acceptable sources of financing will be available as required. In such event, the Partnership may be required to sell all of the

assets of the Partnership and/or dissolve, in which event the Partners would likely suffer adverse tax consequences.

14. The Internal Revenue Service in recent years has attempted to upset the deductions available to taxpayers in certain situations by claiming that the substance of the transaction was a financing arrangement rather than the conveyance of a true ownership interest. If such a position were asserted and upheld, the tax advantages associated with this package would not be available. (See "TAX FACTORS.")

15. The distributor shall have the right to exploit any market in a manner which it believes, in its sole discretion, achieves the best results. In some markets, especially foreign markets, the best manner of exploitation will be an outright sale of the rights to the film. In addition, the distributor, after testing the market will also have the authority to cut short any theatrical or cable television runs and go directly to television sales. The Partnership will rely on the distributor's judgment as to all matters related to the proper distribution of the Picture.

16. The Partnership will only receive an income interest in the monies received from the distribution of the film. The Partnership has no rights in the script and will not share in any other exploitation of the propery, or in any sequels or remakes of the Picture.

TAX ASPECTS OF A MOVIE FUND

Method of Depreciation

Income tax treatment accorded ownership and distribution of motion pictures permits amortization of the cost of a picture by one of the following methods:

1. An "Income Forecast" Method, whereby cost (less estimated value) may be amortized on a weighted basis in accordance with anticipated revenue; or,
2. The "Sliding Scale" Method, whereby a percentage of cost is allocated to each showing depending on the number of showings; or,

3. The normal methods permitted by the Internal Revenue Code of 1954 (the "Code"), Section 167(b) whereby cost less estimated residual value, may be amortized over the economic life of the Picture under the Double Declining Balance, Sum of the Years Digits, or certain other "Consistent Methods" as permitted by Section 167 of the Code.

The Partnership intends to use the Income Forecast Method which will result in the greatest advantage in accordance with projected cash flow.

Investment Credit

The Tax Reform Act of 1976 recognized court decisions allowing investment credit on a motion picture film, but only if such film is a new property determined without regard to useful life, which is a qualified film, but only to the extent that the taxpayer has an ownership interest in the film.

To be qualified, the film must be primarily for use as public entertainment or for educational purposes. "Ownership interest" is defined as a person's proportionate share of any loss which may be incurred with respect to the production costs of such film. To the extent that each Partner is "at risk," he should be considered to have an ownership interest in the film.

Amount of Investment Credit

Except as provided below in our discussion of the 90% Rule, the investment credit shall be 6-2/3% of the qualified production costs and expenses. The General Partners have reviewed the budget of the picture and are of the opinion that all of the production costs consist of qualified U.S. production costs. However, there can be no assurance that an Internal Revenue Service review may not result in a different conclusion.

The 90% Rule

A Limited Partner may be entitled to a full investment credit rather than investment credit based upon 66-2/3% of qualified production costs and expenses, if the Partner elects to be covered by the 90% Rule. The 90% Rule is merely an agreement by the taxpayer that the film or tape for investment tax credit purposes will have its useful life end at the close of the first taxable year in which the aggregate amount of depreciation would equal or exceed 90% of the basis, in this case, the production costs of the film or tape. Thus, if the useful life of the film or tape exceeded seven years, the taxpayer would be entitled to claim a full investment credit of 10% of the qualified production costs and expenses. If it exceeded five years, but is less than seven years, the taxpayer could take a credit on 66-2/3% of 10% of the qualified production costs and expenses. If the useful life is less than five years, but more than three years, the taxpayer would be entitled to 33-1/3% of 10% of the qualified production costs and expenses.

The investment credit base includes direct production costs allocable to the United States such as:

1. Compensation for services performed by actors, production personnel, directors, and producers;
2. Cost of raw stock, developing, etc.;
3. Expenses for costumes, props, scenery and similar items and costs of preparing the first distribution prints. Direct production will generally be allocated between U.S. and foreign in accordance with shooting time. (Compensation paid to U.S. persons and to Subchapter "S" corporations and partnerships to the extent includable in the gross income of U.S. persons will be allocable to the U.S.)

If at least 80% of the total direct production costs of the film are allocable to the U.S., the credit base will also include indirect U.S. and foreign productions costs (excluding direct production costs allocable outside the U.S.). If less than 80% of the direct production costs are allocable to U.S. production, the investment credit base will include only U.S. direct production costs and a pro rata share of indirect production costs. An investment tax credit on participations is also available based on 25% of 66-2/3% x 10% of the qualified participations.

Each partner will have an independent right to elect the tax credit under the 90% Rule or to take the credit on 66-2/3% of the investment tax credit base.

The 66-2/3% Rule is strongly suggested as there can be no guarantee that the contemplated distribution agreement will not be considered a disposition requiring the recapture of the credit under the 90% Rule. Furthermore, it is contemplated that more than 90% of the depreciation will be taken in the first seven years of distribution. This method of depreciation would also require a recapture under the 90% Rule.

Effects of Depreciation

The Partnership's share of the gross receipts from the Picture will constitute taxable income, and its net taxable income or loss for each year will equal its share of the net proceeds less the deduction for depreciation of the "Picture" and less interest paid on debts incurred in discounting letters of credit and any and all expenses of whatever character qualifying for immediate write-off.

"At Risk" Provision and Partner's Basis

Section 465(c) limits any otherwise allowable loss incurred by a partnership engaged in the holding and distribution of motion pictures, films or videotapes to amounts for which the taxpayer is at risk at the end of each taxable year. Any losses disallowed for failure of the taxpayer to be at risk will be allowed in succeeding years subject to the further application of the "At Risk" Rule.

A taxpayer is deemed to be at risk in an activity under Section 465(b) to the extent of:

1. The amount of money and the adjusted basis of other property he contributes to the activity.
2. Any amounts borrowed for use in the activity for which he is personally liable, and,
3. The net fair market value of his personal assets (other than property used in the activity) which are pledged as security for non-recourse borrowings. Income derived from the activity increases the "at risk" amount; losses and cash received reduce it.

A Partner may not increase his "at risk" basis:

1. By pledging collateral which is itself financed (directly or indirectly) by indebtedness which is secured by any property used in the activity Section 465(b)(2)), and
2. Indebtedness owed to a person who has an interest (other than as a creditor) in such activity or to a person who is "related" to the taxpayer within the meaning of Section 267(b).

The General Partners believe that Limited Partners who elect the deferred payment method will be considered to be at risk for their full investment since they will be required to secure letters of credit to guarantee such deferrals.

Marketing Fees

In connection with its services in promoting the Picture throughout the world prior to the completion, delivery, and release of the Picture, the Distributor will receive a fee of $100,000. Additionally, the Distributor will receive its standard distribution fees. The Partnership intends to deduct the fee when paid. There is a significant risk that the Internal Revenue Service will attempt to classify these fees as a capital expenditure. If such an attempt should prove successful, the Partnership will not be able to deduct the marketing costs until next year or may be required to amortize these expenses over a period of years.

Sale of Certain Territories

The Limited Partners will receive investment tax credit on their contribution toward the production of the Picture only to the extent they are at risk on the day the picture is first released. If the Distributor decides to sell one or more markets or territories prior to the release of the Picture, the investment tax credit available to the Limited Partners will be reduced.

Sale or Other Disposition of the "Picture"

Should the Partnership sell or otherwise dispose of the "Picture" it would recognize ordinary income to the extent of the lesser of:

1. The gain realized on the sale or other disposition computed on the basis of the difference between the Partnership's adjusted basis in the "Picture" and the purchase price, or
2. Depreciation deductions previously taken with respect to the "Picture."

The balance of any gain would be considered a capital gain.

RECORDS

INDUSTRY OVERVIEW

Retail sales of records and tapes in the U.S. totaled $4.2 billion in 1978, outgrossing every other single facet of the entertainment industry including feature films and spectator sports. Approximately 350 million album units were sold in 1979 for a total of $3.7 billion. Rock music accounts for over half of these revenues annually. With the recent introduction of videodisc and videotape marketing of musical acts, recording industry revenues particularly in the rock and pop markets should increase over the next several years.

Recording companies have invested heavily to develop new acts and performers. Wholesale developmental expenditures should, in theory, produce many new successes. However, quantity is not quality and great up-front expenditures do not create mass success. In an industry governed by unpredictable and fickle market taste even quality product requires a timeliness that is often the most profound element in a recording act's initial success. In an industry with vast profit potential and few absolutes, quality product and market awareness are essential.

THE EXECUTIVE PRODUCER

Sound Studio, acting by and thru its chief executive officer, Calvin Cassini, will fulfill the function of executive producer. Sound Studio will sign the talent to the co-production team, as well as negotiate with the side men within the framework of organizing the recording sessions. Sound Studio will coordinate the jobs of musicians, arrangers and engineers well enough to direct the project to completion.

Cassini has built three sound studios himself as well as recorded and performed both live and in the studio for the past 20 years. He has worked with and recorded name artists. He has recorded and worked in over 40 different studios in Los Angeles, Chicago, Detroit and New York.

Sound Studio will be responsible for the distribution and marketing of the record and tape masters. It will attempt to market the masters to national labels for national distribution. Until a deal can be made with a national label for a particular master, Sound Studio will cause the album to be marketed on a regional basis by Ears Records, Inc., a company owned by Cassini.

THE RECORDING FACILITY

The recording facility chosen as the site for the project will be a new state of the art, 24-track studio located in Louise, Michigan. This studio owned by Sound Studio offers a complete support and duplication systems including full-time engineers. Artist accommodations are also available.

Average recording studio rates in comparable studios in major metropolitan areas range from $100 to $200 per hour plus materials. Sound Studio has agreed to offer its facilities for a reduced package rate of $6,000 per month by defering fees and accommodating musicians in Mr. Cassini's home.

THE MASTER TAPE

The primary instrument for developing and marketing a new artist is the master tape. Professional quality master recordings can be played for a major record company to interest it in a major distribution deal. Major labels have been known to commit hundreds of thousands of dollars on the basis of master tapes.

The master tape can also be manufactured and marketed on a regional basis by a small label. If successful, a "hot master" then becomes the strongest possible instrument for negotiating material distribution.

THE OFFERING

Sound Studios headed by Calvin Cassini intends to produce at least eight (8) record album masters of the tape masters with funds raised by the investors in the Limited Partnership. The record and tape masters will be co-produced by the Limited Partnership and Sound Studio in accordance with the terms and conditions of a joint venture agreement between them. The Limited Partnership will contribute capital to the joint venture and Sound Studio will contribute all other services and capital necessary to produce the record and tape masters as set forth in the joint venture agreement.

LIMITED PARTNERSHIP

The limited partnership will contribute capital to the joint venture in accordance with the joint venture agreement and Sound Studios will provide all services of producer, also in accordance with the joint venture agreement. The risk of each limited partner will be limited to his cash contribution. The limited partners shall have a first priority on any funds recovered by the joint venture and thereafter participate in the profits in accordance with the joint venture agreement.

SUBSCRIPTIONS

Offers to subscribe to limited partnership interests are subject to acceptance by the general partner. Contributions must be paid in cash at the time of signing the limited partnership agreement and will be kept in a special bank account, and may not be used until no less than $60,000 has been raised. All contributions will be returned in full if at least $60,000 has not been received by the cut-off date, except to the extent contributions have been expended by consent of individual subscribers who have also waived their right of refund.

PRODUCTION AND DISTRIBUTION

Sound Studio will serve as the producer on this project. The project intends to produce at least 8 state of the art, rock music masters over the next twelve months. Cassini will direct the post production marketing to the several record companies and radio station programming directors with whom he has established a business relationship over the last fifteen years. If a master is reasoned to be hot, the Limited Partnership will match funds with Sound Studio for regional marketing at the discretion of the general partner.

USE OF THE PROCEEDS

Typically a rock album costs more than $50,000 to record. Often costs are in excess of $100,000 by completion. These figures can be significantly reduced through a variety of means including:

(a) a reduced studio rental rate;
(b) well rehearsed performing artists;
(c) artist/producer deferral of initial expenses and fees;
(d) flat-fee contracting of studio musicians; and
(e) comprehensive project planning.

By utilizing the expertise of Cassini Sound Studio at a reduced rate, significant savings will be realized. Musicians will be paid a weekly salary instead of by-the-hour, a relationship established thru flat fee contracting. The additional expenses are outlined as follows:

BUDGET

Legal	
Establishment of Limited Partnership, Contracts, Consultation	$ 3,000.00
Accounting	
Partnership Books of Account, Consultation, Statements	2,000.00
Travel Expenses of General Partner	
To and from Sound Studio for one year	1,500.00
Studio Time per Album	
An album can be produced within 30 days of studio time–each tune takes from 10 to 15 hours and an album has usually 10 tunes. The tunes will be mixed and remixed during this time–100 hours at $120 per hour produces the budget number. Sound Studio will defer their $6000 in costs to be repaid later out of artists' royalties–Sound Studio will pay the musicians, engineers and producer out of the partners' $6,000 per album–costs of 2″ mastering tape and any other tape products will be borne by Sound Studio.	$12,000.00

DEFERRED FEES

Sound Studio will defer its recovery of its $6,000 contribution per album until royalties are available to repay such expenses. The distribution of proceeds will address repayment of deferred fees. Under no condition can Sound Studio claim a priority payment for deferred fees in excess of the per album contribution of the Limited Partnership without written permission of the general partner of the Limited Partnership. Any decision to put more cash and services into any specific album will be decided jointly by the general partner and Sound Studio.

PARTNERSHIP INCOME

The joint venture will sign an artist to a multi-year, multi-album contract. Under this contract the artist will be required to record six long-playing albums over a five-year period. In the event the artist's first album is successful, the joint venture will want to produce additional albums. All proceeds received by the joint venture for each recording by each artist will be distributed in accordance with the percentages shown on Exhibit A. An examination of this schedule shows that the Limited Partnership will receive a larger share of the proceeds on the first two masters produced by a particular artist and a lesser percentage of the proceeds of any subsequent masters by that artist. This arrangement should increase the prospects for profit to the Limited Partnership and make the investment more attractive.

On each master produced, the Limited Partnership will receive 62.5% (being all of the amounts due the Limited Partnership and the artist) of all income received by the joint venture until its cash contributions to produce and distribute that master have been recovered. Thereafter all proceeds will be distributed in accordance with Schedule A.

The actual amount of royalty percentage paid by a national label to the venture, including the artist, is negotiable—currently industry standards provide for 16% to 26% of total net sales of records and tapes (to distributors to be paid into the artist/producer royalty package). This percentage will be negotiated at the time a record contract is entered into with a national label. The following record sales analysis should serve to indicate profit possibility and explains the computation procedure.

RECORD SALES ANALYSIS—FIRST ALBUM

	Break-Even	Successful	Very Successful	Hit
# Units Sold	51,500	300,000	700,000	1,000,000
Retail Gross ($7.98/unit)	$410,970	$2,394,000	$ 5,586,000	$7,980,000
Distributor Cost ($3.55/unit)	182,825	1,065,000	2,485,000	3,550,000
*Record Company Deductions 10%—Returns, Uncollectables, Defects, etc. 12%—Packaging *(negotiable)	40,221.50	234,300	546,700	781,000
Net for Royalty Computation	142,603.50	830,700	1,938,300	2,769,000
*Artist Producer Royalty Package at 20% of net for Royalty Computation *(negotiable)	28,520.70	166,140	387,660	553,800
Deferrals (fees, costs, recoupment) - $38,500	-00-	6,000	38,500	38,500
Artist Net (30%) (after recoup)	-00-	46,242	112,698	162,540
Sound Studio Net (37½%)	-00-	57,802.50	140,872.50	203,175
Investors Net (32½%)	28,520.70	50,095.50* *plus full recoupment of $6,000	122,089.50* *plus full recoupment of $6,000	176,085* *plus full recoupment of $6,000

EXHIBIT A

DISTRIBUTION OF GROSS RECEIPTS*

FIRST ALBUM
- Artist 30%
- Investor 32.5%
- Promotion 25%
- Sound Studio 20%

SECOND ALBUM
- Artist 35%
- Investor 27.5%
- Promotion 15%
- Sound Studio 22.5%

THIRD ALBUM AND AFTER
- Artist 50%
- Investor 12.5%
- Promotion 12.5%
- Sound Studio 25%

DISTRIBUTION OF NET PROFITS

Joint venture proceeds shall be distributed to the Limited Partnership as determined by the general partner in his sole discretion. It has already been explained how revenue will come into the partnership. Because the joint venture will sign an artist to a multi album deal, the limited partners might maintain a cash reserve to be used in the production of subsequent masters. The general partner will return the original investment as rapidly as prudent. Any excess profits will be invested in a money market fund until distributed, or used for joint venture business. As long as it is reasonable to keep some money in the partnership for business purposes, it shall be done at the end of each year. However, at least half of the profits will be distributed to the Limited Partnership.

*This schedule is based on a series of albums by one artist.

THE LIMITED PARTNERSHIP

These two entities will enter into a joint venture agreement to produce record masters for sale and distribution. Please refer to the enclosed agreement for specific information. (Joint Venture Agreement)

JOINT VENTURE AGREEMENT

LIMITED PARTNERSHIP (herein referred to as LP) and SOUND STUDIOS, INC. (herein referred to as SS) hereby agree to become Joint Ventures (herein referred to as JV) for the production of musical tapes suitable for manufacture and release in the commercial market.

Under the terms of this agreement, SS will provide the following:

1. An executive producer in the person of Calvin Cassini whose specific job shall be—

  a. To acquire the talent (recording artist(s)), and negotiate a suitable artist/producer agreement with same.

  b. Oversee all aspects of the general master production process, including scheduling and accounting of studio time, assembling and contracting any other personnel necessary for the completion of each master (STUDIO PRODUCER, engineers, side men, arrangers, etc.).

  c. Negotiation for distribution of the master tapes with a record manufacturer.

2. A professional 24-tract recording facility, professionally equipped to allow production of state of the art master tapes.

3. A STUDIO PRODUCER for the execution of any project entered into, whose specific job shall be:

  a. Consulting with the artist in the acquisition, creation and selection of material suitable for recording.

  b. Supervision of arrangement and rehearsal of material with any necessary studio musicians.

  c. Co-ordination with the studio engineer of the performance and recording of this material.

  d. Supervision and mixing of the master tape until it is in a form presentable enough to be made into a master record.

Under the terms of this agreement, LP will provide the capital for ½ (one-half) of all hard costs for the production of Master tapes for artists signed to the JV. An itemization of these costs for the production of a "typical" album follows as SCHEDULE A.

SCHEDULE A

COST OF PRODUCTION

A typical album project would be budgeted as follows:

\$18,000	Recording studio time billed at list–120 hours @ \$150.00/hr.
\$ 800	2" master tape–4 reels @ \$200/reel.
\$ 500	Recording contingency, ¼" master, dubs, cassettes, sidemen, etc.
\$ 4,000	STUDIO PRODUCER @ \$400/tune times 10 tunes.
\$23,000	TOTAL

Hard costs to JV would be as follows:

\$12,000	Recording time @ \$100/hr. Balance, which would be SS profit margin deferred until recoupable from artist royalties.
\$ 800	2" master tape–4 reels @ \$200/reel.
\$ 500	Recording contingency, copies, etc.
\$ 0	STUDIO PRODUCER will work at first for deferred fees and/or a percentage of royalties.
\$13,300	TOTAL hard costs
\$ 6,650	Amount paid by LP

In many cases, album projects may be brought in under budget or paid in part by artist. Under no conditions will album budgets exceed these amounts without written approval of representative of LP.

It is understood that the above is an approximation of an album budget and that different albums will vary in their specific costs. Each project will be budgeted in advance for the aprpoval of a representative of LP.

COMPENSATION

All income to the JV will be for royalties from the actual sale to the public of material produced by the arrangements herein described between JV and various artists. In some cases, this income may take the form of an advance against projected royalties from sales.

It is understood that payment of master production costs, including but not limited to studio time, materials, side men, arrangers, etc., will be considered an advance to the recording artist from the production team (JV) and will be recoupable by the JV first from royalties due artist from record sales. Income will be divided between the various elements of the artist/production team as follows:

50% artist
12.5% LP
12.5% SS

The remaining 25% will negotiated by Calvin Cassini among the STUDIO PRODUCER, promo men, agents and various other industry elements that may become necessary to the success of the project. In no case will LP share become less than 12.5% of the entire royalty package without written approval of the representative of LP. Illustrated, this division of the royalty paid to the artist/producer team by the record company looks like this:

Likely division of artist/producer royalty

Artist 50%
LP 12.5%
SS 12.5%
Studio Producer 12.5%
Promotion 12.5%

JV, represented by Calvin Cassini, will be negotiating with record manufacturers and distributers for these royalties, which are called points. Points are explained as follows:

A point is one percent (1%) of the wholesale sale price (manufacturer to distributor) of a record. As of November 1, 1980, this price was approximately \$3.55/album. From this price is subtracted 10% for damage, defectives, returns and handling of same, and an industry standard of 12.5% for packaging (see

THIS BUSINESS OF MUSIC, Billboard Publications, Inc. 1977, p. 18). This figure is sometimes negotiable.

Using these figures one point becomes one percent (1%) of $2.760.

In today's market, a 20 point deal to a beginning artist/production team would be considered very favorable. Should a 20 point deal be secured with a record manufacturer, compensation to the artist/producer team, using the above formula, would be as follows:

20 POINT DEAL

Artist 10 pts
LP 2.5 pts
SS 2.5 pts
Studio Producer 2.5 pts
Promotion 2.5 pts

Converted to $$ for one album

Artist 27.7¢
LP 6.9¢
SS 6.9¢
Studio Producer 6.9¢
Promotion 6.9¢

On sales of 50,000 albums

Artist $13,850
LP $3,450
SS $3,450
Studio Producer $3,450
Promotion $3,450

If production costs had been $20,000 in the preceding example LP would have recouped its entire investment (approx. $6,000) from artist's royalties, plus a profit of $3,450. SS would have recouped its hard costs, but not its entire investment, in addition to its $3,450 royalty. Artist would not be receiving any royalty checks, as royalties due artist have not yet exceeded production costs.

In this agreement, production costs from artists royalties are paid first to LP, second to SS and only after these costs are recouped does the artist begin receiving royalty checks.

The above formula will also apply to any advances by record companies against royalties, and to singles as well as album royalties.

In the event that the first album released by an artist sells moderately but does not entirely recoup production costs, royalties from future albums will be paid to JV until all production costs of any albums produced under the contract between artist and JV, are recouped.

Upon the completion of a master tape, Calvin Cassini will either:

1. Negotiate for the national manufacture and distribution of the master tape with a major label. No major label deal will be accepted that does not guarantee LP the equivalent of the above specified compensation, without written permission of the representative of LP.

2. Arrange for the mid-western test marketing of the master through existing arrangements with regional distributers, under the auspices of Ears Records, a regional record label, controlled by Calvin Cassini.

In the event of the use of this test market alternative, JV will automatically sign a favorable 20 point artist/producer royalty deal with Ears Records, Inc. which will also be the basis of any future arrangements between Ears and a national record label. If regional test marketing is successful, Ears will attempt to negotiate distribution with a major, national label, guaranteeing JV the same 20 point royalty package.

If Ears records should apply to LP for capital necessary to the successful test marketing of a particular release, a separate contract shall be negotiated between Ears and LP, spelling out what the capital may be used for (manufacturing, promotion, etc.) and detailing how LP may then participate in manufacturers profits, over and above producer/artist royalties.

It is the general plan of this venture to seek two or three artists that we feel have the potential for national acceptance and develop them over a period of 2 to 3 years, building a constituency and developing and expanding markets.

Budgets will be submitted for each project, as well as completed artist/producer agreements. These arrangements will be subject to the approval of Calvin Cassini and a representative of LP.

BENEFITS OF A RECORD FUND

Distributions of cash from operations, if any, shall be made in such amounts and at such times as the General Partner may, in the exercise of his sole discretion, determine. Until the Limited Partners have received cumulative distributions of cash from operations in an amount equal to the sum of their capital contribution, all distributions from cash from operations shall be distributed 100% to the Limited Partners in proportion to their participating percentages. Thereafter, 70% of cash from operations shall be distributed among the holders of Interests in proportion to their participating percentages and 30% of cash from operations shall be distributed to the General Partner.

RISKS OF A RECORD FUN

The business of the limited partnership will be to co-produce long playing record and tape masters with Sound Studio for the production of profit. Generally no more than 16% of the long playing record and tape masters produced each year break even and the risk of loss in this venture is high. Therefore, these limited partnership interests should not be purchased by investors needing a return on their investment or who cannot assume a total loss on their investment.

TAX ASPECTS OF A RECORD FUND

This accounting for recording costs is unique to the recording industry in that the recording costs involve the producing of a master tape from which records can be manufactured and sold, rather than the records themselves. The industry has recognized that the overwhelming majority of all currently produced masters have a useful life of less than a year from the date of release. Most popular music masters do not break-even and are discontinued. The taxation of recording costs is to treat recording costs as current expenses pursuant to the Tax Reform Act of 1976 except for corporations. The "official" position of the I.R.S., however, is that the costs incurred in preparing records for sale, are required to be written off over the period that the masters are utilized. To our knowledge, the I.R.S. has not been very active in challenging this area so our policy is to follow the industry practice and treat these costs as current expenses.

ELECTRONIC AND COMPUTERIZED GAMES

Ambassador Mortgage Company offers a proven and lucrative business with a 45 year track record doing over a billion dollars a year. This is a unique and rare opportunity for you to enter this industry and own your own business, under the guidance and professionalism of an experienced company in its field.

This is a Turn Key business that contains many major advantages that, I'm sure you will agree, would be very difficult to find in any other business.

AMBASSADOR MORTGAGE COMPANY
MACHINE COST

1 – 4 EA	Machines	$3290 EA
5 – 9 EA	Machines	$3240 EA
10 – 24 EA	Machines	$3190 EA
25 +	Machines	$3100 EA

Add $200 Ea for "Stand Up" Models.

A. Ambassador will reimburse Purchaser for one round trip air line fare (coach to Shangrila with the purchase of 10 EA Games or more as per Paragraph #5 of Agreement.

B. If payment in full accompanies agreement, Company will prepay surface freight charges as per Paragraph #6 of Agreement.

C. Any arrangements for the securement of locations for equipment will be independent of Ambassador Mortgage, between Purchaser and Professional Location Company.

D. Business and Service training will be provided by Ambassador at our Training Center at no charge to Purchaser.

QUESTIONS AND ANSWERS ABOUT THE GAMES

1. WHAT ARE THE WONDERFUL MONEY MACHINES?
   The most exciting business opportunity available—coin operated VIDEO GAMES!

2. IS THIS A NEW BUSINESS OPPORTUNITY?
   Yes, it is a ground floor opportunity. However, the industry has flourished for 49 years for a select few and is only now being made available to the general public. In good times it's good—in bad times, it's better.

3. DOES THIS OPPORTUNITY REQUIRE MY LEAVING MY PRESENT EMPLOYMENT OR BUSINESS?
   No. Although most investors want to be their own boss, they choose to remain in the security of their present employment initially, until their business income surpasses their present income.

4. HOW MUCH DO I NEED TO INVEST?
   You may start as small or as large as you like, based on the amount of time and investment you have available, and on the income you desire. Your minimum investment is $3,290.00. The minimum time required is one hour per week.

5. ARE BANKS, SAVINGS AND LOANS AND C.D.'S A BETTER INVESTMENT?
   No. With inflation, the shrinking dollar, and taxes, you are actually losing money in the majority of these so-called savings programs.

6. ARE THERE ANY TAX ADVANTAGES WITH THIS OPPORTUNITY?
   Yes. Numerous tax advantages including business expense deductions, depreciation deductions, investment tax credits, capital gains and deductible retirement plans are available to you as an owner of one or more games. Deductions could exceed 90% of the total investment the first year.

7. ARE VIDEO GAMES AND THE RELATED INDUSTRIES CONTROLLED BY THE CRIMINAL ELEMENTS?

Absolutely not! In the Depression era there was considerable influence. However, today the industry is controlled by major national and international corporations from the legitimate business community.

8. HOW DO I GET LOCATIONS FOR MY EQUIPMENT?
We work directly with several major location companies that are experienced in placing our equipment. They secure all necessary agreements, physically install the equipment with you and pass on to you their basic expertise.

9. WILL I HAVE A LOT OF EXTRA BUSINESS EXPENSES?
Virtually none. There is no need for costly warehousing and real estate, expensive vehicles, paid employees or inventory. You will operate out of your residence and keep simple records. There will be some minor expenses (all deductible) such as some extra mileage, postage and incidental expense. You may also find it possible to deduct part of the cost of your residence as a business expense.

10. CAN I LOSE MY HARD EARNED MONEY?
If you ultimately decide, for whatever reason, to get out of this business, you could lose some time and effort but not your invested money. Machines on location with income records frequently sell for far more than the original purchase price.

11. WHO TYPICALLY PLAYS VIDEO GAMES?
Games are enjoyed by people of all ages, from all walks of life.

12. IS THERE ANY SELLING INVOLVED?
Your games are your "Silent Salesmen." They do the selling for you. They are on the job constantly, day and night, summer and winter, weekdays, Sundays and holidays.

13. WHO WILL SERVICE MY GAMES?
Your games are warranteed for one year. You will have routine minor adjustments and maintenance from time to time, so we provide free factory training. Normally, only one day of training is required.

14. WHO CAN RUN THIS TYPE OF BUSINESS?
Men, women, and even high school age youths have done this successfully. Even more important, no experience is necessary!

15. CAN I SECURE A PROTECTED, EXCLUSIVE AREA?
Yes, but it does require a minimum of 25 locations with reasonable ongoing options.

16. HOW LONG BEFORE I START EARNING INCOME?
Because this is a "turnkey" opportunity and a cash business (no credit problems), the first day your money machines are on location, your cash income starts.

17. DOES THE COMPANY DO ANY FINANCING?
Initially no, but to help encourage growth of your business we provide interest free financing for expansion.

18. CAN I BE AN ABSENTEE INVESTOR?
Yes, but we suggest that you be personally involved initially so that you understand the business completely. Also, because this is a cash business, it can be tempting for an employee to skim some of the profits.

Exercisable 60 Days After Purchase Date

FINANCING OPTION

Expansion and financing . . .

To encourage growth, company agrees to provide assistance as follows:

Purchaser may reorder at any time, up to the total number of games purchased and fully paid for, and company will assist in arranging 75% (seventy-five percent) financing, said financing to be interest free to the purchaser and repayable in twelve equal monthly installments starting thirty (30) days from the date of financing being completed. If interest free loan is prepaid by the purchaser, any interest rebates or charges are payable to the company. This financing program will be made available by company on a continuing cumulative basis and is dependent on purchaser's credit status. Company must notify purchaser in writing at least thirty days prior to any changes in this program.

Submitted by ______________________ Date ____________
Company Representative

Approved by ______________________ Purchaser ________
Company Officer

Date of Approval __________________ Purchaser ________

BENEFITS OF ELECTRONIC AND COMPUTERIZED GAMES INVESTMENT

1. Tremendous profit potential
2. All cash business
3. No inventory
4. No selling
5. Patented product
6. Very little time required
7. No overhead
8. Small investment to start
9. Manufacturers warranty
10. Great tax shelter benefits
11. Company in business since 1971
12. Interest free financing for expansion
13. Complete training

RISKS OF ELECTRONIC AND COMPUTERIZED GAMES INVESTMENT

WARRANTY DOES NOT COVER

1. Labor incurred repairing or replacing warranteed parts after the Ninety (90) Day Parts and Labor Warranty has expired. See Paragraph 7 for exception.

2. Damage caused by neglect, abuse, improper operation, improper repairs, accidents or damage caused by fire, flood, acts of God or other casualties beyond the control of Ambassador Mortgage Co., Inc.

3. Game components or parts thereof which have had the identifying names and/or numbers removed, altered, defaced, or rendered illegible.

4. Components or parts not manufactured, installed, sold or authorized for use by Ambassador Mortgage Co., Inc., or modifications to Game not authorized by Ambassador Mortgage Co., Inc. *Use of such components, parts or modifications voids this Warranty in its entirity.*

5. In transit damage claims, said claims, must be filed with the carrier by Purchaser (consignee).

6. Fuses, bulbs, rubber rings and exterior of game table including cabinet, glass and line cord Potomac Mortgage Co., Inc. suggests periodic cleaning and maintenance including switch adjustments and coin rejector adjustments, which are the obligation of the Purchaser.

7. Exception to Paragraph 1. Original Purchaser may purchase extended yearly warranty on PC Board upon request. Purchaser must notify Ambassador Mortgage Co., Inc. of intent to renew warranty by registered mail, at least thirty (30) days prior to expiration of each full year, warranty extension(s) must be kept in force and continuously by Purchaser to take advantage of additional extension(s).

TAX ASPECTS OF ELECTRONIC AND COMPUTERIZED GAMES INVESTMENT

The investor may depreciate the equipment on an accelerated basis over a three-year period. He may also take advantage of the Investment Tax Credit available in the year of acquisition. Finally, he may deduct expenses incurred in connection with the investment.

Over a three year period, using the Double-Declining balance method at 200 percent Straight-Line, the depreciation tax deduction would amount to 67 percent of the cost in the first year of ownership and 22 percent in the second year, or a total of 89 percent in the first two years.

Investment Tax Credit, which is available in the year of purchase, would amount to 2-1/3 percent of the amount invested.

In dollar terms, assuming a $20,000.00 investment, the depreciation deduction would amount to approximately $13,400.00 in the first year, $4,400.00 in the second year, or a total of $17,800.00 over the first two years. The Investment Tax Credit, a direct deduction in tax, would amount to $460.00. These calculations can be applied to other amounts invested, using the percentages above.

In addition, the tax investor would be allowed a deduction for expenses incurred in connection with generating income and servicing the equipment.

Some of those deductions might be: a car for servicing the machines, a room of your home from which the business is run, a telephone, insurance, pension plan, entertainment expenses, etc.

TAX-SAVINGS

These are standard business expenses that can be deducted from gross income. A percentage of:

House

Tax

Telephone

Mortgage or Rent

Electric

Gas

Automobile

Gas

Oil

Repairs

Insurance

Tags

Title

Depreciation

RETIREMENT PLAN

Generally self-employed persons may contribute to a retirement plan up to 15% of their income or $7,500.00 per year, whichever amount is less. This income is non-taxable until it is taken out of the fund.

The entertainment business is full of high risks and stinging losses for failures and huge rewards for the fortunate few.

Chapter Seven

THE COMMODITY FUTURES MARKETS

Commodity Futures

Commodity futures contracts are contracts most often made on a commodity exchange which provide for the future delivery of various agricultural commodities, industrial commodities, foreign currencies or money market instruments at a specified date, time and place. The contractual obligations may be satisfied either by taking or making physical delivery of an approved grade of the commodity or by making an offsetting sale or purchase of an equivalent commodity futures contract on the same exchange prior to the designated date of delivery. As an example of an offsetting transaction where the physical commodity is not delivered, the contractual obligations arising from the sale of one contract of May wheat on a commodity exchange may be fulfilled at any time before delivery of the commodity is required by the purchase of one contract of May wheat on the same exchange. In such instance the difference between the price at which the futures contract was sold and the price paid for the offsetting purchase, after allowance for the brokerage commission, represents the profit or loss to the trader.

Commodity futures prices are highly volatile and are influenced by, among other things, changing supply and demand relationships, governmental agricultural and trade programs and policies, national and international political and economic events, weather and climate conditions, insects, plant diseases and purchases by foreign countries.

Contracts for future delivery of certain commodities may also be made off established exchanges. For example, forward contracts may be purchased or sold for future delivery through United States or foreign banks. In such instances, the bank generally acts as principal in the transaction and includes its anticipated profit and costs of the transaction in the prices it quotes for such contract.

In market terminology, a trader who purchases a futures contract is "long" in the futures market, and a trader who sells a futures contract is "short" in the futures market. Before a trader closes out his long or short position by an offsetting sale or purchase, his outstanding contracts are known as "open trades" or "open positions."

Among the agricultural commodities for which there are futures contracts are corn, wheat, soybeans, soybean oil, soybean meal, live cattle, live hogs, pork bellies, iced broilers, sugar, cocoa and cotton. Nonagricultural commodities for which there are futures contracts include copper, silver, gold, lumber, foreign currencies, United States Treasury Bills and Notes and mortgage-backed securities.

Two broad classifications of persons who trade in commodity futures are "hedgers" and "speculators." Commercial interests, including farmers, which market or process commodities use the futures markets primarily for hedging. Hedging is a protective procedure designed to minimize losses which may occur because of price fluctuations, for example, between the time a merchandiser or processor makes a contract to sell a raw or processed commodity and the time he must perform the contract. In such cases, at the time he contracts to sell the commodity at a future date, he will simultaneously buy futures contracts for that commodity. Subsequently, he may accept delivery under his futures contracts or he may buy the actual commodity and close out his futures position by selling futures contracts. Similarly, a farmer may hedge against price fluctuations between the day he plants his crop and the day it is ready for delivery. The farmer can look at the futures price quoted for his anticipated date of delivery, and, if the price is sufficient to cover his costs and leave him a profit he deems adequate, he can sell the futures "short," locking in the quoted price. He then fulfills his obligation on his short futures position by either delivering on the delivery date the crop he has grown or by selling his crop in the local market and closing out his short futures position by making an offsetting purchase before such delivery date. Thus the commodity markets enable the hedger to shift the risk of price fluctuations to the speculator. The usual objective of the hedger is to protect the profit which he expects to earn from his farming, merchandising or processing operations, rather than to profit from his futures trading.

The speculator, like the hedger, generally expects neither to deliver nor receive the physical commodity. However, unlike the hedger, the speculator risks his capital with the hope of making profits from price fluctuations in commodity futures contracts. The speculator is, in effect, the risk bearer who assumes the risks which the hedger seeks to avoid. Speculators rarely take delivery of the cash commodity but close out their futures positions by entering into offsetting purchases or sales of futures contracts. Since the speculator may take either a long or short position in the commodity futures market it is possible for him to make profits or incur losses regardless of the direction of price trends. There are always two parties to a commodity futures contract. If one party to such contract experiences a gain on the contract, the other party to such contract experiences an equal amount of loss. Thus, at most, only fifty percent of futures contracts can experience gain at any one time, without reference to commissions and other costs of trading which may reduce or eliminate such gain.

Commodity Regulation

Commodity exchanges provide centralized market facilities for trading in futures contracts relating to specified commodities. Among the principal exchanges in the United States are the Board of Trade of the City of Chicago, the Chicago Mercantile Exchange (including the International Monetary Market) and the Commodity Exchange, Inc. In the trading of forward contracts with banks, the banks act as principals and generally cover their net long or short positions by trading with other banks on the interbank market.

Commodity exchanges in the United States are subject to regulation under the Commodity Exchange Act, as amended (the "Act"), by the Commodity Futures Trading Commission (the "CFTC"). Under the Act, the CFTC is the governmental agency having responsibility for regulation of commodity exchanges and commodity futures trading thereon. The function of the CFTC is to implement the objectives of the Act of preventing price manipulation and excessive speculation and promoting orderly and efficient commodity futures markets.

Under the Act, futures trading in all commodities traded on domestic exchanges is regulated. The CFTC also has exclusive jurisdiction to regulate the activities of "commodity trading advisors" and "commodity pool operators" and has adopted regulations with respect to certain of their activities. In accordance with the Act, the Partnership's Trading Advisor is registered as a commodity trading advisor and the General Partner is registered as a commodity pool operator, futures commission merchant, and commodity trading advisor. The Act requires a commodity pool operator to file an application to register annually with the CFTC which discloses the organization, capital structure and identity of the management and controlling persons of each of its commodity pools, to file annually with the CFTC an annual report showing, among other things, the financial condition, any major changes in ownership and a statement of income and loss for each of its commodity pools, and authorizes the CFTC to review books and records of, and to review documents prepared by, the commodity pool operator. The CFTC requires a commodity pool operator to keep accurate, current and orderly records with respect to each pool it operates. The CFTC is authorized to suspend registration of a commodity pool operator if the CFTC finds that the trading practices of any of its pools tend to disrupt orderly market conditions, that any controlling person is subject to any order of the CFTC denying such person trading privileges on any exchange and in certain other circumstances. The Act gives similar authority to the CFTC with respect to the activities of commodity trading advisors. In the event the registration of the General Partner or the Trading Advisor as a commodity pool operator and commodity trading advisor, respectively, were terminated or suspended, the General Partner would be unable to act as general partner of the Partnership and the Trading Advisor would be unable to render commodity trading advice to the Partnership. The Trading Advisor will not execute commodity futures trades or provide other brokerage services for the Partnership. The CFTC has proposed various amendments to the rules governing the conduct of commodity pool operators and commodity trading advisors. Whether these amendments will be adopted, and if adopted, the final form thereof, are uncertain.

The Act requires all futures commission merchants to meet and maintain specified fitness and financial requirements, to account separately for all customers' funds and positions and to maintain specified books and records on customer transactions open to inspection by the staff of the CFTC. The Act authorizes the CFTC to regulate trading by commodity brokerage firms and their officers and directors, permits the CFTC to require exchange action in the event of market emergencies and establishes an administrative procedure under which commodity traders may institute complaints for damages arising from alleged violations of the Act. Included among the CFTC's powers is the power to restrict or suspend trading in commodity futures contracts. The CFTC does not regulate forward contracts traded through banks, futures trading on exchanges outside of the United States or transactions in physical commodities generally. United States banks are regulated in various ways by the Federal Reserve Board, the Comptroller of the Currency and state banking officials.

Limited partners are afforded certain rights for reparations proceedings under the Act. The CFTC has adopted rules implementing the reparations provisions of the Act which provide that any person may file a complaint for a reparations award with the CFTC for violation of the Act against a floor broker, a futures commission merchant and its associated persons, a commodity trading advisor or a commodity pool operator.

Most United States exchanges (but generally not foreign exchanges, or banks in the case of forward contracts) limit by regulations the amount of fluctuation in commodity futures contract prices during a single trading day. These regulations specify what are referred to as "daily price fluctuation limits" or more commonly "daily limits." The daily limits establish the maximum amount the price of a futures contract may vary either up or down from the previous day's settlement price at the end of the trading session. Once the daily limit has been reached in a particular commodity, no trades may be made at a price beyond the limit. Positions in the commodity could then be taken or liquidated only if traders are willing to effect trades at or within the limit during the period for trading on such day. Because the "daily limit" rule only governs price movement for a particular trading day, it does not limit losses because it may prevent the liquidation of unfavorable positions. Furthermore, commodity futures prices have occasionally moved the daily limit for several consecutive trading days with little or no trading, thereby preventing prompt liquidation of futures positions and subjecting the commodity futures trader to substantial losses for those days.

The CFTC and certain exchanges have established limits, referred to as "position limits," on the maximum net long or net short position which any speculator may hold or control in particular commodities. The position limits established by the CFTC apply to grains (including soybeans), cotton, eggs and potatoes. In addition, commodity exchanges have established position limits with respect to other commodities traded on those exchanges such as live hogs, pork bellies and iced broilers. Under the Act, the CFTC has jurisdiction to establish position limits with respect to all commodities traded on exchanges located in the United States. In addition, certain New York exchanges set limits on the total net positions that may be held by a clearing broker.

The above-described regulatory scheme may be modified from time to time by rules and regulations promulgated by the CFTC.

Margins

Commodity futures contracts are customarily bought and sold on margins which may range upward from less than five percent of the value of the contract being traded. Because of these low margins, price fluctuations occurring in commodity futures markets may create profits and losses which are greater than are customary in other forms of investment or speculation. Margin is the minimum amount of funds which must be deposited by the commodity futures trader with his commodity broker in order to initiate futures trading or to maintain his open positions in futures contracts. A margin deposit is like a cash performance bond. It helps assure the commodity trader's performance of the commodity futures contract. The minimum amount of margin required in regard to a particular futures contract is set from time to time by the exchange upon which such commodity futures contract is traded and may be significantly modified from time to time by the exchange during the term of the contract.

Brokerage firms carrying accounts for traders in commodity futures contracts may increase the amount of margin required as a matter of policy in order to afford further protection for themselves.

When the market value of a particular open commodity futures position changes to a point where the margin on deposit does not satisfy maintenance margin requirements, a margin call will be made by the trader's commodity broker. If the margin call is not met within a reasonable time, the broker may close out the trader's position. Margin requirements are computed each day by the trader's commodity broker.

Commodity brokers may permit customers with accounts of a certain size to deposit Treasury Bills or other securities rather than cash as margin. This permits the customer to earn interest on a portion of the assets in his account.

The following table sets forth examples of position limits, minimum initial margins required by the relevant exchanges for an individual trader.

Exchange and Commodity	Position Limit (1)	Size of Contract	Initial Margin Each Contract (2)
Chicago Board of Trade			
Broilers	300 contracts	30,000 lbs.	$ 625
Commercial Paper	none	$1,000,000	1,875
Corn	3,000,000 bushels	5,000 bu.	750
GNMA	600 contracts	$100,000	2,500
Oats	2,000,000 bushels	5,000 bu.	500
Plywood	600 contracts	76,032 sq. ft.	875
Silver	600 contracts	5,000 troy oz.	13,750
Soybeans	3,000,000 bushels	5,000 bu.	2,810
Soybean Oil	540 contracts	60,000 lbs.	1,125
Soybean Meal	720 contracts	100 tons	1,687
Treasury Bonds	none	$100,000	2,500
Treasury Notes	none	$1,000,000	1,125
Wheat	3,000,000 bushels	5,000 bu.	1,560
Chicago Mercantile Exchange			
Live Cattle	450 contracts(3)	40,000 lbs.	1,500
Feeder Cattle	300 contracts(3)	42,000 lbs.	1,875
Hogs	750 contracts	30,000 lbs.	1,125
Lumber	1,000 contracts	125,000 bd. ft.	1,500
Pork Bellies	250 contracts	38,000 lbs.	1,250
Eggs	150 contracts	22,500 doz.	875
New York Coffe, Sugar and Cocoa			
Coffee	none	37,000 lbs.	8,125
Sugar	none	112,000 lbs.	7,500
Cocoa	none	10 metric tons	1,875

Exchange and Commodity	Position Limit (1)	Size of Contract	Initial Margin Each Contract (2)
New York Cotton Exchange			
Cotton	300 contracts	50,000 lbs.	$ 4,375
Orange Juice	none	15,000 lbs.	750
New York Mercantile Exchange			
Potatoes	150 contracts	50,000 lbs.	375
Platinum	none	50 troy oz.	3,125
Commodity Exchange, Inc.			
Gold	none	100 troy oz.	6,250
Copper	none	25,000 lbs.	1,500
Silver	600 contracts	5,000 troy oz.	13,750
International Monetary Market			
Gold	none	100 troy oz.	6,250
Treasury Bills	none	$1,000,000	750
Treasury Notes	none	$1,000,000	625
English Pound	none	£25,000	1,875
Deutsch Mark	none	DM 125,000	1,875
French Franc	none	FF 250,000	1,500
Swiss Franc	none	SF 125,000	2,500
Japanese Yen	none	¥ 12,500,000	1,875
Canadian Dollar	none	C $100,000	1,875
Mexican Peso	none	₱ 1,000,000	5,000
Kansas City Board of Trade			
Wheat	3,000,000 bushels	5,000 bu.	1,250
Minneapolis Grain Exchange			
Wheat	3,000,000 bushels	5,000 bu.	1,560
Winnipeg Commodity Exchange			
Wheat	none	5,000 bu.	625
Barley	none	20 metric tons	125
Flaxseed	none	20 metric tons	250
Rapeseed	none	20 metric tons	250
New York Futures Exchange			
Treasury Bills	none	$1,000,000	1,875
Treasury Bonds	none	$100,000	2,500
English Pound	none	£25,000	1,875
Deutsch Mark	none	DM 125,000	1,875
Swiss Franc	none	SF 125,000	2,500
Japanese Yen	none	¥ 12,500,000	1,875
Canadian Dollars	none	C $100,000	1,875
London Metal Exchange			
Lead	none	25 metric tons	3,750
Copper	none	25 metric tons	6,250

Exchange and Commodity	Position Limit (1)	Size of Contract	Initial Margin Each Contract (2)
London Metal Exchange (cont.)			
Tin	none	5 metric tons	$ 5,000
Zinc	none	25 metric tons	2,500
Silver	none	10,000 troy oz.	12,500
Aluminum	none	25 metric tons	3,750
International Commodity Clearing House			
Coffee	none	5 metric tons	3,750
Cocoa	none	10 metric tons	5,750
Rubber	none	15 metric tons	1,562
Sugar	none	50 metric tons	10,000

NOTES TO TABLE:

(1) Position limits for corn, soybeans, wheat, cotton, eggs, oats and potatoes established by the CFTC. All other position limits established by the respective exchanges. The limits set forth reflect the maximum net long or net short position on an exchange or all exchanges. Specific commodities may have additional position limits with respect to the maximum net long or net short position in any one contract month or the maximum number of purchases or sales on any one trading day on an exchange. Certain New York exchanges set limits on the total net positions that may be held by a clearing broker.

(2) Initial margin requirements established by the respective exchanges for non-spot months. Margins are periodically reviewed and modified by the exchanges based on market conditions.

(3) Per contract month.

The following programs on gold and silver exploration and strategic metals are opportunities for the investor to acquire valuable commodities for sale.

GOLD AND SILVER

Ace Gold and Silver Exploration Program—will be a limited partnership to explore for commercially minable deposits of gold and silver in the continental United States (excluding Alaska), to develop, sell or otherwise exploit any property in which a commercially minable deposit of gold or silver may be found through exploration (either through the Partnership or subsequently organized ventures in which an interest will be retained), and, to the extent practicable, to distribute in kind any gold or silver produced. Any property on which no commercially minable ore deposit is discovered will be disposed of by sale if any purchaser can be found or, if not, by surrendering the lease to the lessor or by allowing it to lapse.

The program will be managed by its sole General Partner, Ace Exploration and Development Corporation, a diversified mining company. Ace currently operates uranium and copper mines, conducts extensive exploration for uranium, has recently completed test mining of a gold prospect in Alaska and is test mining a silver prospect in Utah.

Investors may enjoy the tax benefits provided to mineral operations and the possible tax benefits of distributions in kind.

The offering consists of 5,000 Units of Limited Partnership interest, each in the aggregate amount of $1,000. The minimum subscription of each purchaser is five Units. Subscribers for Units will become Limited Partners upon the establishment of the Partnership, and may not be assessed for any additional contributions.

The General Partner will contribute an amount equal to 15% of the total initial capital of the Partnership and may contribute mineral properties which it deems suitable for exploration in partial payment of its capital contribution. Such properties will be valued for this purpose at the amount paid by Ace to the property owners to acquire the properties. Ace has acquired leasehold rights to three mineral properties and an option to purchase a fourth, which have been the subject of prior exploration by other parties. Although the presence of gold or silver mineralization is known to exist on each property, a substantial amount of work must be performed to ascertain whether any such property contains a commercially minable deposit of gold or silver. Ace will contribute these leases and will exercise the option and contribute the purchase property to the Partnership as part of its capital contribution.

The properties being contributed to the Partnership by Ace were acquired by Ace with the intent to contribute them to the Partnership and, in Ace's opinion, require substantial exploration work in order to determine whether or not a commercially minable ore body exists on any of such properties. Other gold or silver properties held by Ace which it will not be contributing to the Partnership are properties which, based upon exploration work it has performed or which has been performed by others, it does not consider to be exploration prospects but believes to contain deposits of mineralization in sufficient quantity and quality, depending upon the market prices for the minerals, to justify commercial exploitation.

Once the Partnership has been formed, none of the properties contributed by the General Partner can be withdrawn and neither Ace nor any Affiliate of Ace may acquire any mineral property in the continental United States (excluding Alaska) for purposes of gold or silver exploration if the remaining uncommitted Invested Capital of the Partnership is sufficient to cover the cost of acquisition and exploration of such property unless (i) the property is an operating mine, (ii) a property which contains, in Ace's judgment based on exploration and development conducted by others prior to acquisition, deposits of mineralization sufficient to justify commercial exploitations, or (iii) a property located within ten statute air miles from the nearest boundary of any gold or silver property held by Ace or acquired by Ace under the above circumstances. In order to avoid a conflict of interest, the Partnership will not acquire any property within ten miles of any such property held by Ace.

From time to time, the General Partner may apply a portion of the remaining capital of the Partnership which is not believed to be needed for exploration of existing Partnership properties to the acquisition of additional properties, and also will allocate to the various properties the estimated amount to be expended thereon for exploration. The General Partner intends to select only that number of properties for exploration with respect to which the sum of the net proceeds of the sale of Units and the General Partner's contribution to capital will be sufficient to finance all exploration. Because it is not possible to ascertain with certainty the actual expenses which will be incurred with respect to the exploration of all Partnership properties, the available funds may not be sufficient, and it may be necessary to raise additional exploration funds through the sale of Additional Limited Partner interests or through the transfer of the Partnership's interest in the property to another venture. Although the Partnership Agreement does not preclude borrowing such funds, Ace believes that it is unlikely that the Partnership will borrow funds for exploration purposes. Although such exploration plans could in some cases determine whether a commercially minable ore body exists, there can be no assurance that any such determination can be made following the completion of the initial phase of exploration. It is likely that substantial amounts of additional capital would be required to perform the additional work necessary to make such a determination. In the opinion of Ace, the initial capital of the Partnership would provide sufficient funds to complete any additional exploratory work which might be required with respect to the properties it is contributing to the Partnership. The need for additional financing for exploration purposes, resulting from the acquisition properties, therefore is most likely to arise with respect to the last properties as to which exploration is completed.

The net proceeds of this offering will be devoted primarily to the acquisition and exploration of properties. In the event a commercially minable deposit is discovered, Ace expects that all or substantially all funds for commercial development and production would have to be obtained through additional financing, which might be through borrowings, the sale of interests to Supplemental Limited Partners, or the transfer of the Partnership's interest in the property to another venture. The Partnership Agreement does not limit the General Partner's flexibility in arranging such financing or transferring the property to a third party pursuant to arrangements under which the third party would undertake to conduct the commercial activities, so long as the General Partner determine such arrangements to be fair and reasonable; and neither the Partnership nor its Partners are guaranteed any continuing interest except in those instances where the General Partner or its Affiliates are to continue to participate.

The funds required for any commercial development and production would in all likelihood substantially exceed exploration costs. As a result, the Limited Partners' proportionate interests in the applicable property, to the extent they are not able to subscribe for additional capital pro rata in amounts substantially in excess of their original investments, would be diluted. Such pro rata subscription rights are only available under certain circumstances. In certain other specified circumstances, the Partners will be entitled to a 40% carried interest in the applicable property (allocated 20% to the General Partner and 20% to the Limited Partners and any Additional Limited Partners entitled thereto), and may subscribe for additional interests.

The non-capitalized organizational expenses, the offering expenses and any income from uncommitted Invested Capital, will be shared 15% by the General Partner and the remaining 85% by the Limited Partners. In general, during the exploration stage with respect to each particular property, the General Partner and Limited Partners will share allocations of any profits, losses and distributions in such proportions except where Additional Limited Partners have been admitted to finance further exploration. In that latter case, the 85% will be allocated to the Limited Partners and any Additional Limited Partners combined, subject to certain specified qualifications (primarily timing differences). The General Partner will retain its 15% interest, but must contribute, as General Partner, 15% of the total additional capital raised (exclusive of any Additional Limited Partner interests purchased by the General Partner or its Affiliates). During the commercial development and production stage, profits, losses and distributions attributable to the Partnership's interest in property not held by Supplemental Limited Partners will be allocated 50% to the General Partner and 50% to the Limited and any Additional Limited Partners.

Since income and expenses will be allocated on a property-by-property basis, the General Partner could become entitled to its 50% share of income from one property even though no part of the Invested Capital allocated to other properties has been recovered.

To the extent practicable, any distributions will be in the form of refined gold and silver. Ace, as General Partner, intends to make custody arrangements with an independent custodian such as The Chase Manhattan Bank, N.A. on behalf of the Limited Partners with respect to any gold or silver distributed to Limited Partners and to cause receipts representing their respective interests to be issued to them. To the extent gold and silver produced, if any, is not distributed in kind, it will be sold and the proceeds will be applied to Partnership purposes. Such sales may result in taxable income, and the Partners will be required to report their proportionate shares of such income. The making of any distribution is in the sole discretion of the General Partner. However, the General Partner must first set aside such reserves as are required or which it deems to be advisable for working capital, to meet liabilities and obligations of the Partnership, or for additional investments in mineral properties, provided such investments relate to commercial activities on Partnership properties and not to further exploration. As a result of this provision, the General Partner may use program revenues to acquire additional properties which are contiguous, or otherwise related, to a property of the Partnership, if any, where a minable deposit is being commercially developed. The effect is to enable the Partnership to fully exploit the immediate area in which any minable deposit is discovered, but to preclude the Partnership from utilizing any revenues for acquisition and exploration of properties in new and unrelated areas.

Ace, as General Partner, will be paid an amount equal to 5% of the amount of Partnership expenditures with respect to the acquisition of, and the conduct of exploratory and commercial activities with respect to, Partnership properties. However, this payment will not be applicable to mineral properties contributed by the General Partner or the expenses incurred by the Partnership in connection with its organization and the sale of Units. This payment is designed to compensate the General Partner for expenses incurred in connection with providing certain general and administrative services to the Partnership and is not intended to result in a profit to the General Partner. However, since no attempt will be made to compute the cost of such services, there can be no assurance that this payment will not exceed such costs.

DESCRIPTION OF PROPERTIES

Upon formation of the Partnership, Ace will contribute certain mineral properties in partial payment of its capital contribution as the General Partner. These properties are described below.

In selecting the properties which are to be contributed, Ace has applied certain criteria which it believes will result in each of such properties constituting a reasonable exploration prospect. Each of the properties is already known to contain gold or silver mineralization on the basis of work previously performed by unrelated third parties. The nature of such work ranges from exploration drilling to actual mining operations. However, the existence of gold or silver mineralization on a property does not in and of itself increase the likelihood of discovering a commercially minable deposit of ore. This will depend to a large degree on the nature of the geology pertaining to the property and, in particular, the existence of a host rock formation which is favorable for the deposition of gold or silver deposits of a significant size. The geologic formations present upon each of the properties being contributed to the Partnership by Ace are such that Ace is willing (and, in fact, is committed) to spend its own funds for the acquisition and exploration of such properties if the Partnership is not ultimately formed.

As the funds available to the Partnership will be limited, Ace has endeavored to select properties on which exploration, sufficient to determine whether or not a commercially minable deposit exists, can be conducted at a cost within such limits. The use of such criteria may, however, result in higher acquisition costs than for property about which less information is available. There are many variables involved in conducting exploration, and the cost will depend upon the criteria utilized to select exploration targets. For example, if a particular property has geologic formations favorable for deposition of minerals at a depth of 2,000 feet from the surface, it will cost many times more to explore the formation than it would cost to explore other property containing the same geologic formation at a depth of 500 feet from the surface. When only a limited amount of exploration funding is available, fewer exploratory holes can be drilled in the deeper formation, thereby decreasing the chances of a discovery. Of course, most properties which have favorable geology for mineral deposition do not contain commercially minable deposits. Where more exploration can be performed with a given amount of funds, however, more prospects can be examined, thus, to some degree, increasing the chances for success.

With respect to each of the properties to be contributed to the Partnership upon its formation, it will probably be necessary to construct milling facilities in order to produce salable products in the event commercial operations were to be conducted. In this regard, the feasibility, or estimated cost, of any such mill cannot at present be determined. In addition, it cannot at present be determined whether or not smelting or refining services would be available upon reasonable terms or within a reasonable distance if such services were either necessary or desirable for commercial operations on any of the properties.

General Characteristics of Mineral Properties and Title Thereto

Deposits of gold or silver mineralization can occur in many geologic environments, some of which are more favorable than others for the existence of such minerals in significant or potentially commercial quantities. The type of rock formation favorable for deposition of gold or silver (or other minerals) may be generally referred to as a "host rock," and the existence of a host rock favorable for gold or silver deposition is quite important to a geologist in selecting properties which will be the subject of exploration. In some cases, the existence of favorable host rock can be ascertained by a geologist from inspection of surface outcroppings or other natural conditions which expose the host rock. In other instances, the existence of favorable host rock can be ascertained by examination of mine workings, drilling data obtained by others or from a study of numerous and varied published reports upon the geology of a particular area.

It can be generally stated that the geologic environment which is favorable for deposition of mineral deposits is the result of changes which have occurred in the earth's crust over millions of years. In some instances, the changes are rather violent, such as in the case of volcanic activity or prehistoric earthquake-like occurrences causing buckling and sliding of massive areas of the earth's crust, which is the case with respect to the formation of many mountain ranges. In other instances, the changes occur gradually over hundreds of thousands (or even millions) of years whereby sedimentary rock deposits are laid down by nature through phenomenon such as lakes, oceans, rivers, erosion and similar natural forces. Over long periods of time, there may also be natural changes in the chemistry of a particular geologic formation which is particularly favorable for the deposition or concentration of gold or silver mineralization. The objective of exploration is to discover areas in which such minerals are concentrated to a degree that they may have economic value.

Most of the exploration performed by the Partnership will be accomplished through drilling programs on properties selected for exploration. Actual drilling will be performed by independent contractors who own the drilling equipment and who will operate under the close supervision of geologists employed by the General Partner. Normally, the cost of drilling will be based on the amount of footage drilled, although it is common to charge on an hourly basis when difficult drilling conditions are encountered. The drilling contractor will also generally seek compensation for mobilization and demobilization, moving time, standby time and similar items. Drilling is normally performed by either of two methods: core drilling, in which the equipment actually extracts a core of mineralization from the geologic formation being explored; or rotary drilling, in which only drill cuttings are extracted from the hole at specified intervals. In both cases, the mineralization extracted from the formation of interest is usually taken to an independent assay laboratory in order to determine the quality of the mineralization, with part of the sample being retained in the event additional assaying or metallurgical work is to be performed with respect to the sample. Metallurgical work, which is essentially research work in order to determine milling characteristics of the material, will generally be performed through a combined effort between engineers and metallurgists employed by the General Partner and independent consultants specializing in metallurgy.

As stated above, deposition of mineral deposits generally occurs through changes in the earth's crust. At times, cracks have been created which are ultimately filled with molten material from below or with solutions which, because of changing chemical conditions, precipitate solid minerals into the cracks. The result of this type of occurrence is a vein or vein-like structure which has, in effect, filled the crack or gap. It is common to find mineralized zones within such vein-like structures and many underground mines have been developed and are at present producing from vein-like structures. Veins tend to be vertical structures, although further change or upheavals in the earth's crust subsequent to formation of the vein can shift a vein more towards the horizontal. The known horizontal length over which a vein or vein-like structure extends, when tending towards the vertical, is referred to as the "strike length."

A bedded deposit can be best characterized as a layer of mineralization which sometimes occurs between two layers of a different geologic formation. It is common for bedded deposits to have been formed through a sedimentary process and, when mineralization is present in significant quantities, is often the result of chemical changes causing the precipitation of minerals from solutions flowing over or through the particular formation. It is anticipated that most of the exploration activities conducted by the Partnership will be in connection with vein-like structures or bedded deposits.

In the western United States, vast areas of land are owned by the United States Government and are classified as public domain. A substantial portion of such lands have been, for many years, open to prospecting and mineral entry by the public under federal and state mining laws. A common method of mineral entry is through location of an unpatented mining claim which creates in the locator possessory rights against third persons and the right to prospect, explore and commercially develop certain types of minerals, including gold and silver. There are essentially two types of mining claims: lode mining claims, which are generally located to acquire rights to vein or bedded type mineralized formations generally referred to as rock-in-place; or placer mining claims, which are generally located to acquire rights to mineral deposits contained within loose or unconsolidated materials generally at or near the surface, such as gravel, which materials have been deposited on the location site through such natural migration processes as glacial action, alluvial action or erosion. In some cases, particularly when a commercially minable deposit of minerals has been discovered within the boundaries of a mining claim, a patent may be obtained from the United States Government, which has the effect of conveying fee title to the mineral interests to the owner of the mining claim.

Title to a mining claim can be extremely uncertain until such time as a patent is issued to the owner of a claim. More often than not, titles to unpatented mining claims are found to have numerous defects, particularly in the case of older claims having been the subject of numerous conveyances. In view of the extremely competitive nature of the mining industry with respect to acquisition of properties which are considered to be good exploration prospects, it is the general policy of the General Partner to acquire properties, including mining claims, after having performed only a limited amount of title work with respect to such properties. The objective of the preliminary title work is to establish a reasonable likelihood, on the basis of field examination and an examination of documents of record, that title to such property is owned by the person or persons with whom negotiations for acquisition are being conducted. Curative work is generally conducted, if needed, after acquisition of a leasehold or other interest has been completed. With respect to the properties to be contributed by the General Partner to the Partnership upon its formation, the General Partner has performed preliminary title investigation work and is not aware of any title defects which could have a material adverse effect on the ability of the Partnership to conduct the exploration programs hereinafter outlined.

General Terms of Acquisition of Properties

With respect to properties acquired by mining lease, it is common to pay the lessor or property owner a bonus, rental or advance royalty upon execution of the lease, and periodically thereafter. Where practicable, the General Partner will seek to have such payments credited toward production royalties which may become payable to the lessor in the event the property is placed into commercial production. A common form of production royalty to the lessor, particularly with respect to gold or silver properties, is a percentage of the "net smelter returns" or "net mint returns" derived from sale of production obtained from the property. Although the definition of such terms may vary somewhat from lease to lease, the royalty percentage will generally be computed upon the gross sales price received from the sale of production obtained from a property, less the reasonable costs of smelting, refining (if applicable) and the cost of transportation of production from the mine or mill to the point of sale.

An additional criterion with respect to the selection of such properties is the terms of the acquisition. With respect to properties which are to be subject to leases, the terms of any such lease must be reasonable, particularly with respect to advance royalty payments, the production royalty percentage to be paid in the event of operations, and any work commitments which are undertaken upon the signing of the lease. Thus, the objective of the General Partner will be to spend as much as is reasonably possible for exploration, as opposed to the costs of acquiring exploration rights, with the resultant flexibility to abandon a prospect if the results of initial drilling activities are not encouraging. In addition, production royalties must be low enough so as not to constitute an excessive economic burden on operations if a commercial deposit is discovered. In the opinion of Ace, the costs of both the acquisition of the leasehold interests in the properties to be contributed to the Partnership, and of maintaining the leases in force, are reasonable. Moreover, in the opinion of Ace, in the event of commercial production, the production royalties which would be paid to the owner-lessors of the properties being contributed are reasonable and should not be a principal factor in determining whether or not a particular property could be placed into commercial operation, assuming the discovery of what would otherwise constitute a commercially minable deposit of ore. With respect to the Como property, which is being purchased and which will be contributed by Ace to the Partnership upon its formation. Ace believes that the purchase price is reasonable based upon the nature and extent of the unverified work performed on the property by others, particularly in light of the present price of gold.

Similar criteria will be applied by the General Partner in evaluating any additional properties to be acquired for the Partnership. Ace estimates that the cost of performing the initial phase of one of its properties will be approximately as follows:

Geologic mapping	$ 5,000
Drill site preparation	5,000
Direct drilling expense	150,000
Assaying	15,000
Supervisory salaries	10,000
Travel and miscellaneous expense	5,000
Metallurgical testing	30,000
Provision for contingencies	33,000
Estimated total cost	$253,000

BENEFITS OF A GOLD AND SILVER FUND

Distribution of Gold and Silver from the Partnership. The Partnership plans to distribute gold and silver in kind to the Partners to the extent possible, which distributions will be on a pro rata basis. It is anticipated, however, that gold and silver will be sold by the Partnership to finance Partnership operations, maintain reserves and to fund capital investments. The Partners will take into account their distributive shares of the taxable income of the Partnership resulting from such sales and their distributive shares of the depletion deduction attributable to such income. In computing Partnership taxable income, it is anticipated that only those costs accrued with respect to the production and sale of the gold and silver actually sold by the Partnership will be deducted. The costs accrued with respect to the gold and silver which may be distributed in kind will not be deducted in computing Partnership taxable income and will be included in the basis of the distributed item in the hands of the distributee Partner, but only to the extent of his basis in his Partnership interest.

If a distributee Partner's basis in his Partnership interest is less than the Partnership's basis in the distributed property, the excess basis will be lost, both to the Partnership and the Partner, unless an election to adjust the basis of undistributed Partnership property is made under sections 734 and 754 of the Code. The General Partner does not presently intend to make such an election, although it is empowered to do so by the Partnership Agreement. (See also "Disposition of Partnership Interests.")

Tax counsel have advised the General Partner that, in their opinion, no income or loss will be recognized by the Partnership or by the Partners upon the pro rata distribution of gold or silver to the Partners, other than in liquidation of the Partnership. This opinion is based on the premises that (i) upon any pro rata distribution, each Partner will receive gold and silver in an amount in proportion to his interest in such gold and silver held by the Partnership and (ii) such distributions will not cause the Partner's "at risk" amount to fall below zero.

Taxation of Sales of Gold or Silver by Partner. The tax effects of sales of gold and silver by a distributee partner are somewhat uncertain. Generally, where no gain or loss is recognized by a partner upon distribution of property from a partnership, the partner's basis in the distributed property is equal to the partnership's basis in such property prior to distribution (but not in excess of the partner's basis in his partnership interest). No gain or loss is recognized by the distributee partner until he sells the property. Section 735 of the Code provides that any gain or loss on the sale of unrealized receivables by a distributee partner is ordinary income or loss, and any gain or loss on the sale of inventory items (which might include refined gold and silver), if sold within five years of the date of distribution, is considered ordinary income or loss. If inventory items are sold by the distributee partner after five years from the date of distribution, the nature of the gain or loss from such sale is determined by reference to the character of such items in the distributee partner's hands on that date.

The Partners normally would be entitled to the benefits of depletion upon income from sales of gold and silver which had been mined and sold by the Partnership. Where the gold and silver has been distributed to the Partners, however, the Partner's right to claim depletion with respect to sales of such gold and silver and the method of computing depletion on such sales is uncertain.

Tax counsel have advised Ace that they are unable to express an opinion concerning (i) the method of computing any gain or loss recognized by a distributee partner upon sales of refined gold or silver distributed by the Partnership; (ii) the nature (i.e., capital or ordinary) of any gain or loss resulting from such sales; and (iii) the availability (and method of computing) of any depletion deduction with respect to any income resulting from such sales.

Tax counsel have further advised Ace that a distributee Partner should be entitled either to claim depletion upon ordinary income arising from sales of refined gold or silver distributed by the Partnership, or to claim capital gain or loss upon gain or loss arising from sales of such gold and silver after five years from the date of distribution, assuming that the distributee Partner is not a dealer in gold or silver at that time. However, it is anticipated that the Partners would not be entitled to both depletion on sales of gold and silver within five years of the date of distribution from the Partnership and capital gain upon such sales after five years.

RISK FACTORS OF A GOLD AND SILVER FUND

The purchase of the Units offered hereby involves a number of significant risks.

Risks of Gold and Silver Exploration

Exploration for minerals is highly speculative, even when conducted on properties known to contain significant quantities of gold or silver mineralization. Most exploration projects undertaken do not result in the discovery of commercially minable deposits of ore. Moreover, even if the results of exploration are encouraging on a particular property, there may not be sufficient funds remaining in the Partnership to conduct such further exploration as may be necessary to determine whether or not a commercially minable deposit of gold or silver exists. In such instances, the General Partner may seek such funds through borrowings or sale of additional equity interests. Alternatively, the Partnership may be required to divest itself of promising exploration prospects upon terms that may not reflect the true value of the property and which may result in the inability of the Partnership to recover any significant part of its exploration expenditures incurred with respect to such property.

Unlike programs engaged in exploration for oil and gas, in exploration programs for hard minerals the amount of money expended for exploration most often is only a minor part of the total amount required in order to develop a mine and place it into commercial production, including in some cases the construction and operation of milling or refining facilities. Thus, in the event that a commercially minable deposit of gold or silver is discovered through exploration, it may be anticipated that it will be necessary for the Partnership to raise a very substantial amount of capital to bring the mining property into production. Although the General Partner would seek to obtain such funds in part through borrowing, there is no assurance that such borrowings could be obtained on reasonable terms or in the amounts sought. The General Partner under such circumstances is authorized to sell additional equity interests in the applicable property. In specified circumstances, the Limited Partners must be given an opportunity to contribute a portion of the additional capital required. However, in the event of such an offering to Limited Partners, it is likely that a Limited Partner would be required to invest substantially more than the amount of his original investment in order to maintain his pro rata interest with respect to the property to be developed and operated. Those partners not participating in such financing would suffer dilution of their proportionate interests in the property. Under certain circumstances, the aggregate interest which the Partners' previously had in the particular property will be converted to a 40% interest in such property, allocated 20% to the General Partner and 20% to the Limited Partners and any Additional Limited Partners entitled to participate with respect to the particular property.

Alternatively, it might be necessary for the General Partner to sell or transfer, in whole or in part, an interest in the property to be developed to some third party in order to either raise the required funds for development and operations or for the purpose of disposing of the property upon the best terms and conditions reasonably available, in lieu of the Partnership developing and operating the mine.

There can be no assurance that a particular Partnership property will be developed and operated by the Partnership even if it appears on the basis of the results of exploration that a commercially minable deposit of gold or silver exists. Moreover, even if financing can be obtained for commercial exploitation of a deposit, there can be no assurance that operation of a mine, when developed, will produce minerals in sufficient quantity or under conditions enabling the mine to be profitable for the Partnership. Development and operation of a mine also involve a certain degree of risk, both operationally and with respect to the marketing or distribution of the gold or silver which might ultimately be produced. The markets into which gold and silver are sold or on which gold or silver are traded have in recent times been extremely volatile. In view of the fact that several years may be required to develop a mine and place it into production, it is possible that the marketing conditions existing at the time a decision is made to develop and operate a property may no longer exist when the property is ultimately placed in production. In such cases, it could be necessary for the Partnership to sell or otherwise dispose of the property and related production facilities upon the best terms and conditions available, in the opinion of the General Partner, in order to reduce further losses. Moreover, inflationary conditions in the economy, or adverse conditions encountered in developing a property, could result in either substantial cost overruns or the Partnership having insufficient funds to complete development of the property and the achievement of commercial operations.

Mining operations and the development of new mines and production facilities are also subject to a considerable amount of regulation by federal, state and local governmental authorities. There could be instances in which exploration or development of a property is effectively prevented by laws, rules or regulations enacted or issued by such agencies. Moreover, compliance with such requirements may add considerably to the cost of conducting exploration or development and may extend significantly the time required by the Partnership to conduct its activities, either in exploration or in development and operation of a mine. In addition, there can be no assurance that such laws, rules or regulations will not change from time to time in a manner that has a material adverse effect on the operations to be conducted by the Partnership.

Mineral properties, including those which may have encouraging exploratory results, do not lend themselves to any engineering, geological or other recognized appraisal procedures. Accordingly, it may be impossible to obtain a meaningful appraisal (and therefore an independent appraisal would probably not be sought) of the fair value of any mineral property for purposes of valuing interests to be sold to investors financing commercial activities. Although the General Partner would set the terms of the transaction as fairly as possible on the basis of the best information available, because of the absence of definitive information as to value, it is possible that the additional financing might ultimately prove unfavorable to the Limited Partners who are unable to maintain their proportionate interest. However, the decision to commence commercial operations with respect to any Partnership property will only be made following consultation with a qualified independent mining engineer or other qualified independent consultant and the receipt of a comprehensive technical and economic feasibility report of such engineer or consultant verifying the General Partner's conclusion as to the existence of a commercially minable ore body.

Unverified Information

The information available to Ace concerning properties to be contributed to the Partnership upon its formation has not been verified. Accordingly, a substantial portion of the proceeds of this offering will be expended to determine the accuracy of unverified information. In the mining exploration industry it is not uncommon for the type of information available to Ace to ultimately prove to have been false, inaccurate, misleading or incomplete.

Competition for Mineral Properties

The Partnership will compete for acquisitions of mineral properties and exploration rights with many other mining companies and others, many of which have far greater financial resources than the Partnership and larger technical staffs of geologists and other personnel than Ace.

Competition for exploration rights is particularly severe on properties known to be geologically favorable for deposits of gold or silver mineralization. Companies with greater resources may have a competitive advantage over the Partnership in bidding to acquire such properties. Thus, there is no assurance that the Partnership will obtain suitable properties or rights for utilization of all the net proceeds of the offering.

Title to Properties

A portion of the mineral properties being contributed to the Partnership by the General Partner consists of unpatented mining claims. It should be understood that there is always a degree of uncertainty with respect to the validity of any unpatented mining claim. Title problems also may impair the ability to conduct exploration or negate what might otherwise constitute encouraging results from exploration.

No Market for Units

It is not anticipated that a public market will develop for the purchase and sale of Units. A Limited Partner who desires to sell Units will be required to comply with the minimum purchase requirements and investor suitability standards imposed by applicable state securities laws and the minimum Unit requirement and other conditions imposed by the Partnership or the General Partner. In addition, the Partnership Agreement imposes certain limitations on the transfer of Units and may require the deferral of a transfer if necessary to avoid a "termination" of the Partnership for tax purposes. Consequently, holders of Units may not be able to pledge their Units as collateral or to liquidate promptly their investment at a reasonable price in the event of a personal financial emergency. Thus, Units should only be considered as a long-term investment.

Reliance on Management

All decisions concerning the management of the Partnership will be made by the General Partner. Limited Partners have no right or power to take part in the management of the Partnership. Accordingly, no person should purchase Units unless he is willing to entrust all aspects of the management of the Partnership to the General Partner.

For example, a portion of the proceeds of this offering will be used for acquisition of properties or exploration rights which have not yet been selected. Persons who purchase Units will not have an opportunity to evaluate for themselves such properties or rights or the terms of their acquisition. The purchasers of Units must depend upon the ability of the General Partner with respect to the selection of such unspecified properties or rights.

None of the officers of the General Partner will devote his full time and attention to the affairs of the Partnership.

Federal Income Tax Aspects

The federal tax law currently applicable to mineral operations should be seriously considered by the prospective investor in a mineral exploration program. Investment in the program is advised only for those persons with recurring income subject to taxation in the higher federal income tax brackets.

The Partnership Agreement initially allocates 85% of the income, deductions and credits of the Partnership to the Limited Partners and 15% to the General Partner. This allocation will be recognized for tax purposes only if it has substantial economic affect. Tax counsel have advised Ace that the Partnership and the Partners may reasonably take the position that such allocation has substantial economic effect, but tax counsel have not expressed an opinion that such allocation does, in fact, have substantial economic effect. If such allocation is not recognized for tax purposes, a part of the deductions allocated to the Limited Partners would not be allowable to them.

A Limited Partner should be aware that (i) Partners will be required to report their respective shares of Partnership income or loss for any year of the Partnership in their individual federal income tax returns for the taxable year which includes the last day of the Partnership's year, without reference to any distributions received from the Partnership during such year; and that the tax payable with respect to any Partnership income for such year may exceed the value of any distributions received; (ii) there is no assurance that payments made to the General Partner by the Partnership will be deductible by the Partnership; (iii) exploration costs incurred by the Partnership are generally subject to recapture; and (iv) depletion deductions, in part, are items of tax preference which are subject to the regular minimum tax and reduce personal service taxable income which qualifies for the maximum tax.

Tax counsel have advised Ace that, in their opinion, no income or loss will be recognized by the Partnership or by the Partners upon pro rata distributions of refined gold or silver to the Partners, other than distributions in liquidation. Such opinion is subject to a number of assumptions and is not in any way binding upon the Internal Revenue Service. Further, the tax effects of sales of gold or silver by a distributee Partner are somewhat uncertain and no opinion has been received concerning the method of reporting any income, gain or loss which may result from such sales.

Ace does not now intend to cause the Partnership to make an election, as provided under sections 734, 743 and 754 of the Internal Revenue Code, to adjust the basis of Partnership property upon transfer of interests in the Partnership (by sale or exchange or at death) and distributions of property from the Partnership. In the absence of such an election, the transferee of a Limited Partner's interest would not obtain any tax benefits from his investment in the Partnership to the extent his investment exceeded his allocable share of the Partnership's basis in its assets. Further, under some circumstances, a part or all of the Partnership's basis in property distributed to a Partner may be lost, both to the Partnership and the Partner, upon distributions of such property to the Partner.

Limited Liability

The Partnership Agreement grants the Limited Partners the rights, by majority vote of each class, to amend the Partnership Agreement (with certain restrictions), to cancel certain contracts pursuant to which the General Partner or an Affiliate provides services or equipment to the Partnership, to veto the sale of substantially all the Partnership assets as an entirety, to remove the General Partner and elect a successor, and to elect a successor, and to elect a successor if the General Partner withdraws, as well as certain other voting rights. There is uncertainty as to whether the grant or exercise of these specified rights could be deemed to be taking part in the control of the Partnership's business and, as a result, cause the Limited Partners to be deemed to be general partners of the Partnership under applicable laws, with a resulting loss of limited liability. If the Limited Partners were deemed to be general partners, Partnership obligations could be satisfied out of the personal assets of the Limited Partners.

In order to minimize the risk of the Limited Partners being deemed to be general partners, the grant of these specified rights and their exercise by the Limited Partners are subject, under the Partnership Agreement, to either the receipt from counsel of an opinion or a determination by a court proceeding that neither the grant nor exercise of such rights will be in contravention of applicable law or result in a loss of limited liability, and with respect to the rights to amend the Partnership Agreement and to remove and replace the General Partner, are further subject to either the receipt from counsel or an opinion or the issuance of a ruling from the IRS that neither the grant nor exercise of such rights will adversely affect the tax status of the Limited Partners or the Partnership. It should be noted that due to present and possible future uncertainties in this area of partnership law, it may be difficult or impossible to obtain an opinion of counsel to the effect that the Limited Partners may exercise certain of their rights without jeopardizing their status as Limited Partners.

Maintenance of the limited liability of the Limited Partners also requires compliance with certain legal requirements in jurisdictions in which the Partnership will operate and, in certain jurisdictions, the limited liability of limited partners has not been clearly established under local law. It is anticipated that, prior to commencing operations in any jurisdiction, the General Partner will obtain advice from local counsel regarding the limited liability status of the Limited Partners in such jurisdiction. The Partnership will operate in such jurisdictions in such manner as the General Partner, on the advice of responsible counsel, deems appropriate to preserve to the extent possible the limited liability of the Limited Partners.

TAX ASPECTS OF A GOLD AND SILVER FUND

The following discussion is predicated on the assumption that the Partnership will be treated as a partnership for federal income tax purposes.

Partnership Taxation

General. A partnership is not treated as a taxable entity under federal income tax laws. Instead, each partner reports on his federal income tax return his distributive share of the income, gains, losses, deductions and credits of the partnership, irrespective of any actual distributions made to such partner during his taxable year. As a general rule, the partner may apply his share of partnership losses in the taxable year against his income from other sources to the extent of his tax basis for his interest in the partnership, or, if lesser, the amount such partner has "at risk."

Allocations. Allocations generally are made on a property-by-property basis. Until commercial activity commences with respect to a property or the Partner's capital account with respect to a property has been credited with income and proceeds of sale equal to the opening balance of such account, whichever occurs first, and in the absence of admission of Additional Limited Partners, taxable profits and losses for each taxable year (and all items with respect thereto) will be allocated 15% to the General Partner and 85% to the Limited Partners in proportion to their respective capital contributions, except that losses with respect to a property arising at a time when the Partners' capital accounts with respect to such property have a zero balance will be allocated solely to the General Partner. After commercial activity commences with respect to a property or the Partner's capital account with respect to such property has been credited with income and proceeds of sale equal to the opening balance of such account, whichever occurs first, and in the absence of admission of Additional Limited Partners, the General Partner's interest in each of these items with respect to the particular property will increase to 50% and the aggregate interest of the Limited Partners will be reduced to 50%.

Section 704 of the Code, as amended by the Tax Reform Act of 1976 (the "Tax Reform Act"), provides that a partner's distributive share of income, gain, loss, deduction, or credit (or item thereof) shall be determined by the partnership agreement unless the allocations provided by the agreement do not have substantial economic effect, in which case such distributive share shall be determined in accordance with the partner's interest in the partnership (such interest to be determined by taking into account all facts and circumstances). The relevant Congressional Committee Reports pertaining to the Tax Reform Act indicate that "substantial economic effect" is dependent upon whether the allocations may affect the dollar amount of the partner's share of the total partnership income or loss independently of tax consequences, and that other factors that could possibly relate to the determination of the validity of an allocation are set forth under the present regulations. The IRS has not yet issued regulations or other administrative guidelines interpreting the partnership allocation provisions of the Tax Reform Act. In Rev. Proc. 74-22, 1974-2 C.B. 476, the IRS published a "no ruling" policy with respect to provisions in partnership agreements specifically allocating items of income, deduction or credit among the partners in a ratio that is disproportionate to their interests in the partnership.

Ace has been advised that the Partnership and its Partners may reasonably take the position that the allocations provided for in the Partnership Agreement have economic substance. However, because of the amendments to section 704 of the Code, the absence of regulations or other administrative guidelines interpreting the amended provisions of the Code, and the uncertainties raised by the positions taken by the IRS in other situations, no opinion can be given to the effect that the allocation provisions of the Partnership Agreement, in fact, have substantial economic effect. If, upon audit, the IRS should contend that an allocation made lacks substantial economic effect, there is a possibility that a part of the deductions allocated to the Limited Partners would not be allowable to them.

Returns and Elections. The Partnership will be subject to all of the provisions of the Code which govern the tax treatment of partnerships, and to similar provisions of any applicable state income tax laws. Under the Tax Reform Act a penalty is imposed upon partnerships failing to file a timely or complete partnership return. The penalty is assessed for each month or fraction of a month (but not to exceed five months) that the failure continues, at the rate of $50.00 per partner. Also, the period for assessment of tax deficiencies against partners resulting from adjustments made with respect to returns filed by a "federally registered partnership," such as the Partnership, is four years rather than the normal three years.

The Partnership will adopt a calendar year as its taxable year for income tax purposes. The Partnership will elect to deduct any development costs incurred by it. Elections regarding deductions and recapture of exploration costs must be made by each partner separately. By March 15 of each year, the Limited Partners will receive a report showing their distributive shares of income, deductions and credits for the preceding year.

Organizational Expenses. Organizational expenses (as defined in Section 709(b) of the Code) may be deducted ratably over a period of not less than 60 months. Amounts paid to promote the sale of, or to sell, partnership interests must be capitalized and may not be deducted or amortized. Such amounts may be deducted, if at all, only upon liquidation of the Partnership.

Payments to General Partner. The IRS has taken the position in Rev. Rul. 75-214, 1975-1 C.B. 185, that a payment to a partner for services, determined without regard to the income of the partnership, is deductible by the partnership only if it is ordinary and necessary business expense which is reasonable in amount. Therefore, there can be no assurance that the IRS will not take the position that the amounts to be paid to the General Partner designed to effect reimbursement of general and administrative expenses are nondeductible by the Partnership, in whole or in part, or that any such claim by the IRS would not be sustained.

Distributions. Cash distributions by the Partnership to a Partner will not result in taxable gain to such Partner unless they exceed the Partner's adjusted tax basis for his partnership interest, in which case the Partner will recognize gain in the amount of such excess. Non-liquidating distributions of property other than cash to a Partner will reduce his basis in the Partnership by an amount equal to the Partnership's basis in such property; provided, however, that the adjusted basis of the Partner may not be reduced below zero. A Partner's tax basis for determining gain or loss with respect to any property distributed to him as described in the preceding sentence will be an amount equal to the amount of reduction in his basis in the Partnership occurring by reason of such distribution, regardless of the value of the property distributed. A reduction in a Partner's share of Partnership indebtedness for which no Partner is personally liable will be treated as a cash distribution to him to the extent of such reduction. A reduction in a Partner's share of profits will result in a reduction in his share of Partnership indebtedness for which no Partner is personally liable. Under some circumstances, distributions from a partnership to a partner may cause the amount "at risk" with respect to the partnership activity to fall below zero, which could result in the recapture of previously deducted losses.

Limitations on Deduction of Losses

General. A Limited Partner may not deduct from his taxable income any deductions or losses attributable to his interest in the Partnership in excess of the *lesser* of (i) the adjusted tax basis of his investment in the Partnership at the end of the Partnership's tax year in which the deductions or losses occur or (ii) the amount as to which he is considered to be "at risk" in respect of the activities of the Partnership at the end of the Partnership's tax year in which the deductions or losses occur. As a result of these limitations, a Limited Partner normally will not be able to deduct losses attributable to his interest in the Partnership in excess of his actual cash contributions to the Partnership.

Partner's Basis. The tax basis of a Limited Partner's interest in the Partnership initially will equal his cash contributions to the Partnership. It will be increased by any subsequent cash contribution he makes to the Partnership and by his distributive share of Partnership income (taxable and exempt). It will be decreased (but not below zero) by actual distributions to him from the Partnership (valued in cases of distributions of property at an amount equal to the Partnership's tax basis) and by his distributive share of Partnership losses. Further, for purposes of of computing such tax basis, any increase in a Partner's share of liabilities of the Partnership for which no Partner is personally liable shall be treated as a cash contribution and any reduction in his share of such liabilities shall be treated as a cash distribution.

Amounts at Risk. A Limited Partner's share of losses incurred by the Partnership will not be allowed as a deduction to the extent such losses exceed the amount as to which he is "at risk" with respect to each activity of the Partnership.

The amount "at risk" is limited to the amount of money and the adjusted basis of other property the Limited Partner has contributed to the activity plus any amount he has borrowed for the purposes of such activity (other than amounts borrowed from any person who is a participant in the activity or who is a related party [as defined in the Code]) and with respect to which he is either personally liable for repayment, or has pledged property (other than property used in the activity) as security for repayment, limited, in case of pledge, to the net fair market value of his interest in the pledged property. The amount a Limited Partner has "at risk" may not include the amount of any loss that he is protected against through nonrecourse financing, guarantees, stop-loss agreements or other similar arrangements.

Under proposed regulations issued by the IRS, the "at risk" amount is increased by an amount equal to the excess of the Limited Partner's share of income from the activity during the taxable year over his share of deductions allocable to the activity for such year and is decreased by the amount of allowable losses for the taxable year and by the amount of any cash distributions during the taxable year. The "at risk" amount is also decreased by the adjusted basis in the hands of the Limited Partner of any property (other than money) distributed to the Limited Partner. The adjusted "at risk" amount determines the extent to which losses sustained in future years will be deductible. Any loss disallowed as a result of the application of these provisions may be deducted in future years to the extent that the Limited Partner places additional amounts "at risk."

Losses deducted by a Limited Partner will be subject to recapture at rates applicable to ordinary income in the event, and to the extent, his adjusted amount "at risk" falls below zero. A Partner's amount "at risk" may fall below zero and result in such recapture (i) where distributions of money or property are made to a Partner and his adjusted amount "at risk" immediately prior to such distribution is less than, in the case of a distribution of money, the amount distributed, or in the case of a distribution of property, the reduction in his basis for his Partnership interest occurring as a result of such distribution; or (ii) where the Partner becomes protected against loss with respect to any liability comprising a part of his amount "at risk" by conversion of recourse financing to nonrecourse financing, by the receipt of guarantees or by other means. Losses which are recaptured under this rule may be deducted in future years to the extent the Limited Partner places additional amounts "at risk."

Disposition of Partnership Interests

The sale or exchange of all or part of a Limited Partner's interest in the Partnership held by him for more than twelve months will, under present law, generally result in recognition of capital gain or loss. A Limited Partner's pro rata share of Partnership nonrecourse liabilities, if any, as of the date of the sale or exchange must be included in the amount realized. Therefore, the gain recognized may result in a tax liability greater than the cash proceeds, if any, from such disposition.

However, any gain realized by a Partner upon the sale of his interest in the Partnership will be ordinary income to the extent of his pro rata share of Partnership section 751 assets. Partnership section 751 assets include exploration costs and depreciation deductions which are subject to recapture and may include refined gold and silver held by the Partnership if there has been a substantial appreciation in the valve thereof. Therefore, substantial amounts of income taxable at ordinary rates may be realized by a Limited Partner upon the sale of his interest in the Partnership.

Under certain circumstances, a gift or a charitable contribution of an interest in the Partnership may also result in income or gain taxable to the donor as described above.

In the event of an assignment of a Limited Partner's interest, allocations between the assignor and assignee of deductions, credits and income of the Partnership for income tax purposes, including exploration and development costs, depreciation and depletion, shall be based on the periods during which each owned the interest. At the General Partner's election, such items may be determined with respect to the entire year of transfer and allocated on the basis of the number of days during such year for which each owned the interest, provided such an allocation will be recognized for federal income tax purposes. The admission of an assignee as a Limited Partner is subject to the consent of the General Partner.

As a result of the complexities inherent in and the substantial expenses that would be incurred in making an election to adjust the tax basis of the Partnership property provided by sections 743 and 754 of the Code, the General Partner does not presently intend to make such an election on behalf of the Partnership, although it is empowered to do so by the Partnership Agreement. The absence of any such election may, in some circumstances, result in a reduction in the value of a Partner's interest to any potential assignee.

Termination of the Partnership

The actual or constructive termination of the Partnership may have important tax consequences to the Limited Partners. All partners of any partnership which is actually or constructively terminated will be taxable in the taxable year in which such termination occurs on their distributive shares of partnership income accrued prior to the date of termination (whether or not distributed). Such partners likewise will be entitled to claim their distributive shares of deductible items arising out of costs and expenditures incurred by such partnership prior to the date of termination. In addition, partners must take into account their distributive shares of gains or losses realized from the sale or other disposition of partnership assets in liquidation of the partnership.

A partner will recognize taxable gain as a result of the pro rata distribution of partnership assets incident to termination of a partnership only to the extent that such partner's pro rata share of a partnership's cash (and the reduction, if any, in his pro rata share of a partnership's debt included in the basis of his partnership interest) at the date of termination exceeds the adjusted tax basis of his partnership interest. In addition, a loss may be recognized at partnership termination if a partner receives no distributions of any property other than money or partnership section 751 assets.

Any gain or loss recognized upon dissolution will, in general, be a capital gain or loss. However, if a partner receives or is deemed to receive more or less than his pro rata share of partnership section 751 assets in a distribution, ordinary income or loss may result to a partnership or its partners. Furthermore, the IRS may claim in some cases that the actual or constructive termination of a partnership results in investment tax credit recapture regardless of whether a gain or loss is recognized in the transaction.

Special Features of Mineral Taxation

The following is a summary of some of the principal features of federal income taxation of mineral operations (other than oil and gas) as of the date hereof:

Acquisition Costs. The cost of acquiring mineral properties is a capital expenditure and must be recovered through depletion deductions if productive. If a "property" (as defined under section 614 of the Code) is abandoned, the cost of acquisition less any depletion claimed may be deducted in full as an ordinary loss in the year it is abandoned.

Exploration Costs. Exploration costs are expenditures paid or incurred for the purpose of ascertaining the existence, location, extent, or quality of any mineral deposit before the beginning of the development stage of the mine. At the taxpayer's election, exploration costs (other than expenditures for the acquisition of property subject to depreciation) are deductible in computing taxable income for federal income tax purposes. The election to deduct exploration costs is made by deducting such costs (on a "property"-by-"property" basis) on the taxpayer's income tax return for the taxable year incurred. Such election is binding for the taxable year and all subsequent taxable years and may not be revoked unless the IRS consents to such revocation.

Each Limited Partner will be entitled to take into account on his federal income tax return, his distributive share of exploration costs incurred by the Partnership. The election to deduct such costs is not a partnership election and must be made separately by each Limited Partner. Likewise, the election of the method of recapture of such deductions, as described below, must be made separately by each Limited Partner.

If a mine reaches the producing stage, each Partner must elect either (i) to recapture exploration costs by including the full amount of exploration costs deducted by such Partner with respect to the mine in ordinary income in the year the mine reaches the producing stage, or (ii) to forego depletion deductions with respect to the mine until the total amount of depletion foregone is equal to the exploration costs previously deducted. The Regulations under Section 617 of the Code state that a mine will be considered to have reached the production stage when (i) the major portion of the mineral production is obtained from workings other than those opened for the purpose of development, or (ii) the principal activity of the mine is the production of developed ores or minerals rather than the development of additional ores or minerals for mining. Exploration costs deducted with respect to a mining property owned by the Partnership will also be subject to recapture upon receipt of a bonus or royalty with respect to such property; the disposition of all or a part of such property; the sale of an interest in the Partnership; and certain distributions of the property from the Partnership. Thus, a Limited Partner should recognize that exploration costs will generally be subject to recapture except those exploration costs incurred with respect to mineral properties which are abandoned by the Partnership.

Development Costs. The development stage of a mine commences when the existence of minerals in commercially marketable quantities has been disclosed through exploratory activities. Expenditures paid for the development of a mine during the development stage (other than expenditures for the acquisition of depreciable property) are deductible in computing taxable income for federal income tax purposes. While the deduction of development expenses may be deferred at the taxpayer's election under certain circumstances, the Partnership anticipates that it will elect to deduct currently all development expenses in computing its taxable income or loss. Development expenditures are not subject to recapture.

Depletion. The owner of an economic interest in minerals in place is entitled to a depletion deduction with respect to the production and sale of depletable minerals. This deduction is computed either on the basis of extracted units, referred to as cost depletion, or percentage depletion which is computed as a fixed percentage of gross income from mining limited to 50% of the net income from mining. Gross income and net income from mining are computed separately for each "property" (as defined in section 614 of the Code) and the higher of cost or percentage depletion is allowable in any year. Cost depletion deductions are limited to the capitalized cost of the property, while percentage depletion may be obtained as long as the property is producing income. Percentage depletion rates vary from 5% to 22% depending on the mineral produced and its source, domestic or foreign. The percentage depletion rate for gold and silver, the principal objects of the Partnership's exploration program, is 15% where production is from mines in the United States. If production is sufficient, the total deductions for percentage depletion on any property may be in excess of the capitalized cost of that property. Depletion is an "item of tax preference" to the extent it exceeds a property's capitalized cost (determined without regard to the depletion allowance for the taxable year) at the end of the taxable year.

Sales of Partnership Properties. Interests in mineral properties (other than production) and equipment, if held for twelve months by other than a dealer in such interests, are classified for income tax purposes as property described in section 1231 of the Code. Accordingly, the aggregate net gain or loss recognized in any taxable year on dispositions by the Partnership of property described in section 1231 will be treated, for federal income tax purposes, as a long-term capital gain or as an ordinary loss, as the case may be, subject to the recapture of depreciation under section 1245 and section 1250 of the Code and the recapture of exploration costs under section 617 of the Code. Also, section 47 of the Code may require recapture of investment tax credit taken on items of equipment when such items are sold, transferred or exchanged.

General Tax Provisions

The following is a brief summary of some of the major federal income tax laws which may have an impact upon a Limited Partner. This summary is not intended to be a complete statement of the federal income tax provisions which would apply to each Limited Partner.

Minimum Tax–Tax Preference Items. There are now two minimum taxes which are imposed on "tax preference items." The "alternative minimum tax" is imposed upon capital gains and excess itemized deductions and the "regular minimum tax" is imposed on other tax preference items. The regular minimum tax is equal to 15% of the amount by which "tax preference items" exceed the greater of $10,000 ($5,000 in the case of a married individual who files a separate return) or one-half of the taxpayer's regular federal income tax (less various tax credits). Tax preference items for an individual taxpayer which are subject to the regular minimum tax include depletion to the extent it exceeds the capitalized cost of a property (determined without regard to the depletion allowance for the taxable year) at the end of the taxable year. The alternative minimum tax is computed separately from the regular minimum tax and is payable only if it exceeds the taxpayer's ordinary tax liability for the year (including the regular minimum tax).

Minimum Tax on Personal Service Taxable Income. A maximum tax rate of 50% exists for an individual's personal service taxable income (applicable to married taxpayers only if they file a joint return). Personal service taxable income is determined by reducing the amount which otherwise qualifies for the 50% rate by items of tax preference (other than capital gains) on a dollar-for-dollar basis. As discussed above, depletion deductions, in part, are items of tax preference which would reduce personal service income which would otherwise qualify for the maximum tax. Further, income attributable to the operations of the Partnership will not constitute personal service income in the hands of the Limited Partners and, thus will not qualify for the maximum 50% tax rate, even though prior losses may have offset only personal service income.

Limitations on Investment Interest Deductions. Section 163(d) of the Code limits the amount of "investment interest" which taxpayers may deduct for federal income tax purposes. Under section 163(d) a taxpayer generally may deduct investment interest from all sources to the extent of: (a) $10,000 ($5,000 for a married taxpayer filing a separate return and zero for a trust), and (b) the taxpayer's "net investment income." Investment interest, the deduction of which is disallowed in any year, may be carried over to subsequent years.

Investment interest is defined as "interest paid or accrued on indebtedness incurred or continued to purchase or carry property held for investment." Therefore, the limitations on deductibility of investment interest stated above will apply with respect to any interest incurred by a Limited Partner to purchase his interest in the Partnership.

Investment Tax Credit. Section 38 of the Code provides a tax credit against federal income taxes for investment in equipment and other depreciable property. This tax credit, referred to as the investment tax credit, is equal to 10% of the "qualified investment" in "section 38 property," and directly reduces a taxpayer's liability for tax. Subject to certain limitations, the Limited Partners will be entitled to claim investment tax credit on their allocable share of qualified investment in new section 38 property in the year in which such property is placed into service by the Partnership.

Investment tax credit is subject to recapture by a Limited Partner in the event of a disposition of his interest in the section 38 property with respect to which the credit was claimed before the end of the depreciable life of such property. Events of disposition which could cause recapture include (i) the Limited Partner disposes of his interest in the Partnership (or his interest is reduced by more than 33-1/3%); or (ii) the Partnership disposes of the section 38 property.

Depreciation. The actual costs of equipment and other types of tangible property cannot be deducted currently but must be capitalized and depreciated or amortized pursuant to the applicable provisions of the Code. These costs may be eligible for accelerated depreciation. However, a $2,000 limitation on the allowance of additional first-year depreciation will be applied at both the Partnership and Partner levels. Further, all or part of the depreciation claimed may be subsequently recaptured upon disposition of the property by the Partnership or of a Partnership Unit by any individual Partner.

Other Taxes

In addition to federal income taxes, Limited Partners may be subject to state and local franchise, personal property, income and estate or inheritance taxes. Such taxes may be imposed by various jurisdictions, including the Limited Partner's residence and the states and localities in which the Partnership is organized and operates. For example, the Partnership will be doing business in every jurisdiction in which it explores for minerals and, therefore, the Limited Partners may be subject to taxation by such jurisdictions. A detailed analysis of state and local tax consequences of purchase of interests in the Partnership and the operation of the Partnership is not feasible, and prospective Limited Partners should consult their personal tax advisors regarding possible state and local tax consequences.

In addition to federal income tax and state and local taxes, the fair market value of a Limited Partner's interest in the Partnership will be subject to federal estate tax upon the death of the Limited Partner. Each Limited Partner should consult his personal tax advisor with respect to federal estate and gift tax planning involving interests in the Partnership.

GLOSSARY

The following are certain important terms.

Additional Limited Partners

Those persons who make an investment in the Partnership for the purpose of further exploration (but not for commercial development, production or operation) of a particular Partnership property in exchange for a Limited Partnership interest in such property.

Affiliate

A person (i) controlling, controlled by or under common control with another person, (ii) owning or controlling 10% or more of the outstanding voting securities of such other person, (iii) any officer, director or partner of such person, and (iv) if such other person is an officer, director or partner, any company for which such person acts in any such capacity.

Invested Capital

The amount paid to the Partnership by the Partners as capital contributions.

Partnership Section 751 Assets

Unrealized receivables (including exploration cost and depreciation deductions which are subject to recapture) and substantially appreciated inventory (which might include refined gold and silver held by the Partnership).

Sharing Ratio of a Limited Partner

The percentage obtained by dividing the Units owned by a Limited Partner by the total number of Units owned by all Limited Partners; provided, however, that in the case of any particular Partnership property as to which Additional Limited Partners make an investment, that percentage will be adjusted to the fraction thereof equal to the aggregate Limited Partnership interests of all Limited Partners in such property.

Subscription Commitment

The total amount agreed to be paid to the Partnership by a Limited Partner.

Supplemental Limited Partners

Those persons who make an investment in the Partnership for the purpose of commercial development, production or operation of a particular Partnership property in exchange for a Limited Partnership interest in such property.

Nearly all commodity transactions undertaken by the investor can qualify for capital gain. The lower tax rate on capital gains represents a major tax shelter—probably second only to mortgage interest deducted by home-owners. Besides capital gains, one other area offers tax shelter potential: commodity tax straddles.

A commodity tax straddle may, if properly structured, defer short term capital gain into the next year or convert it to long term gain. Straddling involves a simultaneous purchase and short sale of two futures contracts: agreements to respectively buy and sell stated amounts of the same commodity at set prices and times in the future.

To offset short term capital gain, you straddle a very volatile commodity (copper, silver, pork bellies) near year end, hoping for significant price movement–up or down–before December 31. If prices rise, you cover your short position at a loss; if prices fall, you liquidate the long position. Either way, the short term capital loss from commodities offsets your short term capital gain from other sources. After year end you liquidate the profitable position; this moves the short term gain into the next year or, depending on how you hold the contract, converts it to a long term capital gain. If the price doesn't move, or turns around before you can liquidate the profitable position, you'll have a loss.

Straddles are tricky, so always seek advice from your tax advisor and a broker specializing in commodity straddles.

STRATEGIC METALS

There is a capital gain tax shelter opportunity for the long-term holding of strategic metals. Remember the saying "As good as gold"? Today the saying could read "As good as strategic metals." Like gold in the 1960's and oil in the 1970's. strategic metals may be the desired commodity of the 1980's. As the demand rises without an adequate supply, the U.S. risks becoming even more dangerously dependent on other countries.

The United States imports almost all of its chromium and cobalt from a limited number of foreign suppliers located primarily in central and southern Africa, an area of increasing political instability. South Africa alone provides the United States with much of its chromite, ferrochromium and platinum group metals, a large portion of its ferromanganese, and a number of other metals. Zaire and Zambia are key sources of U.S. cobalt. Should supplies from South Africa become unavailable the United States would be dependent on its second largest supplier of chrome and platinum group metals, the Soviet Union.

The Soviet Union is fortifying its military defense by purchasing growing amounts of strategic metals. Economists believe the Soviets have not developed adequate mineral production capacities, thus, are hoarding mineral supplies so the U.S. cannot get them. As the costs of U.S. defense continue to rise and America's mining capacity nears exhaustion, the reasons for concern are all too clear.

The Importance of Strategic Metals

Strategic metals are crucial to a strong military defense and a sound peacetime economy. The unique characteristics of the 40 strategic metals serve as alloys in armaments and industrial products, plus everyday things such as stainless steel flatware, kitchen appliances and surgical instruments.

The top 10 major nonferrous industrial metals comprise the Strategic Metal Index. This index represents over 80% of the

$10 billion annual production of all free market strategic metals, and has increased over 700% in the last 8 years.

The top 10 metals and their unique qualities, uses and areas of production are:

Chromium (Cr)
*Melting point 1980°C; boiling point 2480°C.
*Highest corrosion and oxidation resistance.
*Essential in making stainless and high alloy steel.
*U.S. Imports: 47% South Africa, 32% U.S.S.R. and Albania.
*U.S. dependency: 90% on imports.

Cobalt (Co)
*Melting point 1495°C; boiling point 2900°C.
*Highest "Curie Point" (ferromagnetically stable at 1100°C).
*Used as high temperature superalloys in manufacture of jet engines.
*Major use of alloys is in production of magnets and electromagnetic compounds.
*World production: 65% Zaire.
*U.S. dependency: 90% on imports.

Columbium (NB)
*Melting point 2415°C; boiling point 3300°C.
*Highest shock resistance.
*Alloys of columbium used in heavy mining equipment, gas and oil pipelines and military equipment where high shock resistance is needed and structural steels.
*World production: 75% Brazil.
*U.S. dependecy: 100% on imports.

Indium (In)
*Melting point 156.6°C; boiling point 2000°C.
*Highest "wetting point" (ability to form seals and retail oil) and limitless deformation.
*Low melting point alloys used for glass grinding and polishing. Component of transistors and long-life spark plugs. Also used in hermetic seals between glass, metal and ceramics plus low melting point solders.
*World production: 15% U.S.S.R., 12% Japan, 21% Belgium.
*U.S. dependency: 80% on imports.

Magnesium (Mg)

*Melting point 651°C; boiling point 1197°C.

*World's lightest structural metal and highest fracture resistance.

*Major use by the aluminum industry in forming magnesium alloys for use in military equipment. Also used in production of titanium and photographic flashbulbs, incendiary bombs and flares.

*World production: 28% U.S.S.R., 48% U.S.A.

Molybdenum (Mo)

*Melting point 2620°C; sublimes at 4507°C.

*Major use in submarine hulls, aircraft carriers, combat vehicles. Also, mining equipment, machine components, oil pipelines and in the electronics industry for supporting filaments, anodes, grids and heating elements.

*World production: 75% North America.

Rhodium (Rh)

*Melting point 1966°C; boiling point 2500°C.

*Most expensive of all metals. Thin coat keeps silver from tarnishing, thus, used in high technology electronic equipment to protect silver's electrical conductivity. Used in optical instruments and searchlights for its light refracting capacity.

*World production: 51% U.S.S.R., 41% South Africa.

*U.S. dependency: 93% on imports.

Silicon (Si)

*Melting point 1410°C; boiling point 2355°C.

*Major use as alloying agent in the iron and steel industry plus aluminum industry. Price is a direct function of energy cost and demand for iron and aluminum ore in the world market.

*World production: 24% U.S.A., 22% U.S.S.R.

Tantalum (Ta)

*Melting point 2966°C; boiling point 5427°C.

*Highest ability to store electrical energy.

*Major use in production of electronic circuit components. Its high density, high melting point and acid resistance are useful in production of valves, contact points, cutting tools and surgical applications.

*World production: 37% Thailand, 10% Canada.

*U.S. dependency: 96% on imports.

Tungsten (W)

*Melting point 3410°C; boiling point 5927°C.

*Highest melting point and high temperature strength; lowest coefficient of thermal expansion.

*Major uses in machine tools, mining equipment, electrical switches, electric lamp filaments. Aerospace uses in rocket engine nozzles and leading edge of re-entry surfaces.

*World production: 23% China, 21% U.S.S.R.

*U.S. dependency: 59% on imports.

The complete list of major industrial metals includes:

Aluminum	Copper	Mercury	Silicon
Antimony	Gallium	Molbydenum	Silver
Arsenic	Germanium	Nickel	Tantalum
Beryllium	Gold	Osmium	Tellurium
Bismuth	Indium	Palladium	Tin
Cadmium	Iridium	Platinum	Titanium
Cerium	Lead	Rhenium	Tungsten
Chromium	Lithium	Rhodium	Vandaium
Cobalt	Magnesium	Ruthenium	Zinc
Columbium	Manganese	Selenium	Zirconium

Not only are the metals of the Strategic Metal Index heavily imported. The following graph shows the U.S. net import reliance of over half of all strategic metals, as of 1975-1978:

Metals
Net Import Reliance As A Percent of Apparent Consumption

Columbium	100	Cadmium	66
Titanium	100	Mercury	62
Manganese	98	Zinc	62
Tantalum	96	Tungsten	59
Chromium	90	Gold	56
Cobalt	90	Titanium (Ilmente)	46
Platinum-Group Metals	89	Silver	45
Tin	81	Antimony	43
Nickel	77	Selenium	40

Source: U.S. Bureau of Mines

Net Exports

Vanadium	25
Copper	13
Aluminum	8
Lead	8

Stockpiling . . . the Solution?

The Federal Emergency Management Agency, a branch of the U.S. Government, has been established to determine the kind and quality of metals in the national strategic stockpile. Goals for antimony, chrome, manganese, titanium and chromium barely meet the 50% requirements for three years. Bad as it sounds, there are worse situations; no other NATO ally currently has a stockpile. Germany has postponed any proposals for a stockpile.

Private investing in strategic metals can be profitable both to you and the nation's welfare. With demand increasing for a limited supply, strategic metals may be the investment of the eighties.

How the Metal Market Works

The investor must place a cash deposit with Aye Metals Company to cover his intended purchase. Once the funds are on deposit, the investor may place his order by telephone, telex or by written communication. When placing his order, the buyer will be notified of the most recent prices paid on the open market. He may instruct Aye Metals Company to buy at the market, or he may place a limited "fill or kill" order; if such an order cannot be filled within the agreed amount of time at the limited price or better, the order will be cancelled and the investor's money will be promptly refunded.

The following are specifications for purchase lots of major strategic metals. The unit sizes apply to the gross amount of metal, alloy or oxide.

STRATEGIC METALS

Material	Unit Size	Form	Packing	Quality
Antimony	5 tonnes	Ingots	Wooden cases	99.6% min. purity 0.15% max. arsenic
Beryllium	2,500 kilos	Beryllium-copper alloy	Drums	Approx. 4% beryllium content
Cadmium	2 tonnes	2" dia. balls, sticks or ingots	Wooden cases or drums	99.95% min. purity
Chromium	1 tonne	Lumps	Steel drums	99.0% min. purity
Cobalt	250 kilos	Broken cathode	Steel drums	99.5% min. purity
Columbium	2 tonnes	Ferro-columbium	Drums	60-70% columbium
Gallium	30 kilos	Semi-liquid	Plastic bottles	99.9% min. purity
Germanium	20 kilos	Ingots	Wooden boxes	99.99% min. purity 50 ohm resistivity
Hafnium	100 kilos	Sponge	Poly bottles	99.99% min. purity
Indium	50 kilos	Ingots	Drums	99.99% min. purity
Lithium	500 kilos	Ingots	Watertight containers	99.9% min. purity
Magnesium	5 tonnes	Ingots	Shrink wrapped	99.8% min. purity
Electro-Manganese	10 tonnes	Flakes	Steel drums	99.95% min. purity
Mercury	50 flasks	Liquid	Flasks of 76 lb.	99.99% min. purity
Molbydenum	1.500 kilos	Molybdenum-oxide powder	Tins or drums (N.B. tins smaller than drums)	Mo 55-65%
Rhodium	20 troy ozs.	Sponge	Plastic bottles	99.90% min. purity
Selenium	1000 kilos	Powder (-200 mesh)	Wooden cases	99.5% min. purity
Silicon	10 tonnes	Irregular lumps, 10 to 100 mm.	Metal boxes or drums	98.50% min. purity
Tantalite	200 lbs.	Ta2 O5 ore	Bags/drums	60% min. Ta2O5
Tellurium	500 kilos	Small ingots	Wooden cases	99.7% min. purity
Titanium	500 kilos	Sponge (irregular granules) T. G. 100 brand or equivalent	Drums	99.6% typical purity
Tungsten	1 tonne	Concentrate ore	Drums	66-70% WO 3
Vanadium	2 tonnes	Ferro-vanadium	Drums	78%-82% Vanadium
Zirconium	10 tonnes	Powdered concentrated ore	Drums	Varies with end use

Note: 1 tonne (metric ton) 1000 kilos 2204.6 pounds.

Purchasing Procedure

To assist each client in deciding which strategic metals to purchase, Aye Metals Company will forward to the client any information it may possess that it feels would be helpful to the client. After the client decides on a purchase of metal or metals, the purchase price and a physical amount acceptable to the client, he will forward a check to Aye Metals Company. The check will cover the purchase price, plus an additional amount approximating the cost of one quarter of a year's storage, any insurance charges and the assay charge, if any.

All checks received by Aye Metals Company will be deposited in a Trust Account, established for that purpose, in the Bank. When the client's order is executed and the confirming documents are received by Aye Metals Company, payment will be made from the Trust Account. The client will be so informed, and will receive the following documentation:

1. Purchase order delineating the metal, price, weight and purity.
2. Storage receipt, known as a "warrant."
3. Insurance policy covering the purchase (if ordered).
4. Certificate of analysis as to weight and purity.

If Aye Metals Company is unable to execute an order for the client, the client shall be so informed. Immediately fund of client's payment shall be made if so requested.

Although the strategic metals market appears to offer a substantial possibility for profit in the coming years, each client should be aware that these metals are not now traded in a formal market such as the London Metal Exchange or the Chicago Board of Trade. All purchases are made on a "bid" and "ask" basis between buyer and seller. Although there are many recognized dealers in the strategic metals market and at most times the markets are well organized, at times these markets may become illiquid. At those times "bid" and "ask" prices may show great variance and sales and purchases may have to be developed until firmer prices become established.

Aye Metals Company wishes each client to be aware that the price of these strategic metals and critical materials are subject to wide price fluctuations due to, amongst other factors, industrial use and demand.

Aye Metals Company, therefore, cautions each investor that trading of strategic metals and critical materials involves a risk and that they are unsuitable for short-term trading and only the long-term investment strategy should be considered. A period of two to five years should be considered as the holding period over which the best possible gain may be made.

Storage of Metal

Upon purchase of any of the strategic metals, Aye Metals Company will have the metals stored in a Rotterdam, Holland warehouse approved by the London Metal Exchange. All metals will be stored in "free port" storage free of government duty, control or taxation.

If the client does not wish the metal stored in Rotterdam, Aye Metals Company will arrange, on behalf of the clients, to ship the metal from Rotterdam to any place the client designates. The client will assume any and all delivery charges if he should elect this option.

Storage charges will be billed annually after the first quarter payment.

As evidence of storage, a warehouse receipt known as a "warrant" will be furnished. This warrant may be issued in (1) the name of the client, (2) any other designated name or (3) as a bearer. The client may take possession of his warrant or Aye Metals Company will deposit it in a Bank Trust Account established for that purpose in London, England or Rotterdam, Holland.

The client should be aware that a bearer warrant, if lost or stolen, can be used by the possessor of said warrant as evidence of ownership. With presentation of said warrant, the metal can be sold and the funds derived will be paid to the possessor of the warrant. No further identification is needed.

Insurance of the Metal

The client may have the metal insured by the company of his choice. The policy should be written to protect against all customary risks including physical loss or damage, riots, civil commotion, fire and strikes.

If the client wishes, Aye Metals Company will insure the purchase on his behalf, through a major world company such as Lloyd's of London.

Proof of Presence

Aye Metals Company will retain a firm of auditors who will, on an annual basis, confirm the physical presence of the client's purchase in the warehouse. Copies of this report will be provided to the purchaser whenever possible.

Assay Charges

All metals are purchased by weight and purity. Although the purchase may be accompanied by a producer's assay certificate, Aye Metals Company strongly recommends that each client obtain an assay report from a recognized authority in the field. Aye Metals Company will obtain this certificate for the client at a cost of approximately $200 per lot.

Total Cost

Above the actual purchase price of the metal and assay charges, there will be charges for the following: delivery, insurance, (if purchased for client by Aye Metals Company, acceptance, and segregating charges by the warehouse. These charges, which probably will not exceed $100 per lot, will be paid by Aye Metals Company.

Although each metal will be ordered in a standard amount, such as one ton or two hundred fifty ounces, small variations may occur. The client will be credited or billed for the amount over or under the standard amount. These variations rarely exceed three percent.

The client is advised that insurance and storage charges are due quarterly and in the currency of the native country. The client may pay these himself or Aye Metals Company will pay them on behalf of the client. A maintenance fee of 0.25% per month of the original purchase price of the material will be billed to the client quarterly.

If you are interested in commodities, strategic metals deserve consideration for long-term capital gain tax shelter.

Chapter Eight

COLLECTIBLES

Erasmus Jacobs, a poor farm boy, picked up a glittering pebble and presented it as a gift to his sister as a plaything. The year was 1867. This simple event marked the first authenticated find of a diamond in South Africa. It was only the beginning. The gift of a plaything–coupled with the discovery of an eighty-three and a half carat crystal one year later–sparked the greatest diamond rush in the history of the world. Its effect has been far-reaching, indeed. For the last one hundred years, the diamond has been sought after as personal treasure; worn as a badge of wealth or rank; and–as it began–given as a gift of the purest affection. Men have fought for them, died for them; used them as collateral for wars. And now, only recently, men have begun to invest in them.

The portability and international liquidity of diamonds are without equal. Diamonds can be sold in any country for the currency of that country.

Diamonds are controlled by DeBeers Consolidated Mines Limited. Approximately eighty-five percent of the rough diamonds of the world, including those from Russian mines, pass through DeBeers. This unrivaled control is due to the marketing policy of this giant cartel to release diamonds to the world market when demand is strong–and restrict them if demand softens.

Numismatics . . . sometimes described as "The Hobby of Kings"! Throughout history an impressive list of prominent people such as King Maxamilian I, Mayer Rothschild, The Hapsburg Emperor Charles VI, the de Medicis, John Quincy Adams, Pope Paul II and King Farouk have collected Numismatics.

The U.S. Mint began coinage in the late 1700's and until the mid-1930's mintage figures with respect to individual coins were sufficiently low so as to cause most coins minted during the pre-1933 period to be considered as scarce, if not rare. An example is the initial U.S. silver dollar minted in 1794 with a total of only 1758 coins as compared to the 1971 Eisenhower dollar which was minted for a total of more than 127 million coins. Original mintage volume is no real measure of the potential value of a coin as other conditions, such as available supply and demand can have even greater weight.

In acquiring rare coins evaluating grade or condition of the coins is of paramount importance, because a variance in grade can cause extraordinary difference in value.

Traditionally, coin collecting has been a fascinating source of historical, aesthetic and financial value. In the face of current monetary instability and worldwide inflation, people are turning to tangible assets as a potential inflation hedge and an alternative to conventional investment vehicles. This concept is not new. Throughout history, persons have held their assets in coins, precious metals and gems, especially in times of monetary deterioration.

The following programs of diamonds, colored gemstones and rare coins and currency show the opportunities available in collectibles.

DIAMONDS

Throughout history, the diamond has been recognized as the most long lasting of the world's precious possessions. Diamonds are formed by centuries of pressure and heat deep beneath the earth's crust. Diamonds are the hardest objects occurring in nature. Because of their realizable value and portability, they have represented an attractive medium for those who wish to protect their assets from economic fluctuations.

A diamond is 100% carbon and is formed by the crystallization of that carbon by heat and pressure into cubic isometric or crystal systems that are particularly high in refractive properties. The refractive properties and the hardness of diamonds set them apart from all other precious gemstones. Diamonds may range in color from colorless to yellow, brown, orange, green, blue, violet or red, with the colorless or transparent form being the most highly desirable for investment.

Diamonds were first mined in India approximately 2,500 years ago and later in the region around Brazil. In the 16th century, diamonds were found in Brazil, and in 1866, the discovery of diamonds in Africa created a "gold rush" type interest in that area. Most of the diamonds on the market today originate in Africa, but they are also mined in Russia, South America, India, Brazil and Australia. A relatively few are found in the United States.

Diamonds are customarily mined from deep within the earth or deposited by volcanic or water activity onto the beds of streams and rivers. Generally, only 20% of the diamonds discovered are suitable for cutting into polished gemstones. The remaining 80% are used for industrial purposes, principally in cutting tools. Of the diamonds selected for polishing, approximately 1% yield a final gemstone of at least one carat in weight. It is important to recognize that a substantial portion of the weight of a raw discovered stone is eliminated when the stone is polished into the customary shapes used in jewelry. Statistically speaking, approximately .2% of the raw diamonds discovered are ultimately converted to gemstones of one carat or larger. Within that relatively small number of gemstone quality diamonds, further characteristics for grading establish the uniqueness and value of each stone. These characteristics are commonly called the "four C's" and form the factors upon which a gemologist, or dealer in diamonds, places a value upon the stone. The higher the quality of the diamond, the more subtle the distinctions become and the greater the technical expertise required to establish them. The four generally recognized components (the "4C's") affecting the value of a given stone are carat weight, clarity, cut and color.

Carat Weight

The international standard for the weight of diamonds is the carat, equalling .2 grams. Each carat is subdivided into 100 points. For example, a 3/4 carat stone would weigh exactly 75 points, or 75% of the weight of 1.0 carat, or .15 grams.

As the carat weight of an individual stone increases, the price increases by more than a straight line relationship. In other words, a stone of 2.0 carats commonly costs 50% more per carat than a stone weighing only 1.0 carat. Sharp increases in per carat value commonly occur at .48, .68, .80, 1.0, 1.25, 1.5, 2.0 and 3.0 carats. This geometric progression in values is due to the smaller number of stones existing in the higher carat sizes. With respect to possible resales, larger stones, although they show higher price increases, are generally more difficult to trade. As a general rule, diamonds between 1.0 and 2.0 carats have shown both considerable appreciation in value and ready marketability.

In determining carat weight, laboratories presently use extremely accurate caratonal electronic scales which can weigh to 1/1000th part of a carat. This sophisticated equipment is believed essential to proper evaluation, since the carat weight is a prime factor in assessing the value of a diamond.

Clarity

Clarity is that characteristic of the diamond concerned with its ability to permit the passage of light through the stone, uninterrupted by inclusions, flaws or foreign matter contained therein. The number of irregularities (inclusions), their sizes and positions in the stone determines the clarity grade. Thus, clarity is defined as the degree to which the stone possesses inclusions which may diffuse or scatter the light entering the stone from the direction in which it would travel if uninterrupted. Undesirable reflections of light may be caused by the presence of foreign matter within the stone, surface defects, minute cracks, natural strains or growth planes in the crystals, and certain other imperfections. The presence of those irregularities cause a stone to be less valuable than a stone which does not possess such irregularities.

Until recently the clarity of the stone was assessed largely by simple methods which relied upon the judgment and opinion of gemologists expert in diamonds. Very little testing equipment was used, other than a good hand lens of ten power magnification or a standard microscope. By these methods the trained observer could form an opinion of the clarity of the stone.

Currently, stereo microscopes are used in modern gemological laboratories. These precision optical instruments, even a ten power magnification, are able to give higher resolution and wider fields of view than the standard jewelers microscope previously in common usage. In addition, stereo microscopes provide an ability for dark field illumination, which further enhances the experts ability to evaluate the interior of the stone. The method of quantifying clarity is a point system generally based on the size of the inclusion, its position and the extent to which it interrupts the optimum passage of light. External flaws in the diamond are evaluated with a similar system. Although there are several existing systems of terminology used to quantify clarity grades, the following terminology is utilized by a nationally recognized independent gemological laboratory: (1) Flawless: Free from internal or external blemishes when examined by a certified expert in a natural or artificial light under ten power magnification (even though the category is defined as flawless, the stone may in fact possess some modest irregularities which cannot be considered to materially affect the brilliancy of the diamond); (2) VVS_1 and VVS_2: These grades contain inclusions or surface blemishes so small that they are insignificant and difficult to locate under ten power magnification; carbon pinpoints, clouds, nicks, scratches and other minor descrepancies characterize these grades; (3) VS_1, VS_2, SI_1 and SI_2: Inclusions and blemishes of a size, number and position between those difficult to locate under ten power magnification, and those visible to the naked eye are placed in these categories. In the upper end of this range inclusions are difficult to locate, and at the lower end they are only slightly above the imperfect rating; (4) I_1 and I_2 : These stones are commonly called imperfect and contain inclusions visible to the unaided but trained eye; they may also include fractures or cleavages in the stone which may extend during ordinary wear; flaws in these categories are commonly referred to as very very slightly imperfect, very slightly imperfect, and imperfect.

CLARITY–GRADING SCALE
Investment Grade Clarities

Flawless	FL.
Internally Flawless	I.F.
VVS (Very, Very Small Inclusions)	VVS_1
	VVS_2
VS (Very Small Inclusions)	VS_1
	VS_2

Cut

The cut of a diamond refers to the proportions and dimensions of the stone with respect to certain measurements shown in the figure below.

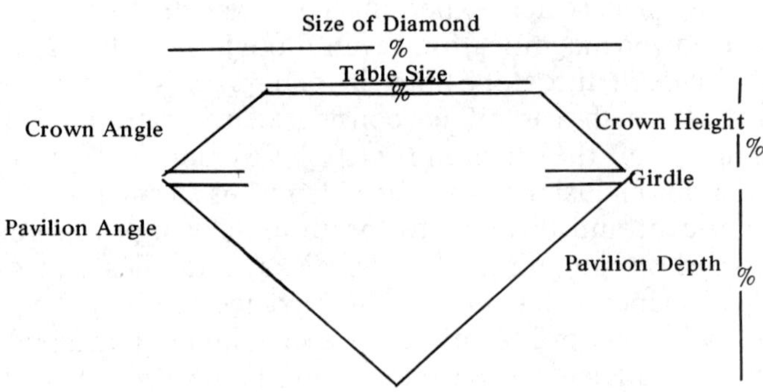

An ideally cut diamond maximizes the amount of light returned to the viewer, hence, the more finely proportioned the stone the higher the value.

The word "cut" is also sometimes used synonymously with the term "shape." The shape of the diamond refers to its design in finished form. Although occasionally stones are fashioned in a relatively unknown shape, six popular shapes or cuts commonly occur. Typically, a diamond cutter will select the shape into which to cut the raw stone in order to maximize the available carat weight of the finished stone. The six popular shapes or cuts are:

1. *Brilliant.* The round diamond that is a favorite in engagement rings. In tiny sizes, and with only 16 facets, this shape is called a single cut and is used as a side stone in rings.

2. *Emerald Cut.* So called because emeralds are often cut this way, rectangular or square, with facets polished diagonally across the corners.

3. *Marquise.* A pointed boat shape, usually long and narrow. In a ring, it tends to make the fingers look slim. This shape costs slightly more than a brilliant of the same size and quality because of additional labor in cutting.

4. *Pear Shape.* Popular in rings and often used in pendants. The world's largest cut diamond, Cullinan I, mounted in the British Royal Sceptre, is a pear shape.

5. *Oval.* An adaption of the brilliant shape. The marquise, pear shape and oval all appear to be larger than a brilliant of the same carat weight.

6. *Baguette.* Meaning "little stick," a small diamond used as a side stone in rings.

Color

Techniques and systems for color grading of polished diamonds vary to a significant extent among diamond exchanges and dealers throughout the world. Although they all have as their goal the separation of color ranges into categories, the most widely used method derives from a comparison with master sets of stones ranging in color from white to yellow. A master set is typically placed in grade order and the stone being tested is moved until it is observed to fit into a color category. Since there are many different systems of grading, each based upon its own set of master stones, the need has arisen for a method of comparison between the varied systems.

The spectrophotometer is an instrument commonly used in research in industry for measuring absorption and directional reflectance over a wide range from visible to infrared or ultraviolet. Especially modified for diamond color grading, the spectrophotometers are used in the diamond trade to measure specific wave lengths of reflectance of the diamond relative to pure barium sulphate powder, which is used as a standard of whiteness.

COLOR-GRADING SCALE
Investment Grade Colors

Colorless	D E F
Near Colorless	G H I J
Slightly Tinted	K L M N

The Diamond Market

The international diamond market is characterized by intense activity and competition in a number of established diamond exchanges in the world's major cities. These diamond exchanges function in a manner similar to our national stock exchanges in that they maintain a very active daily market giving diamonds substantial liquidity. The exchanges are open to members of the trade only.

The Diamond Market operates on several different levels. The first level of the Diamond Market involves the offering of raw stones commonly offered in parcels called "sights" through the DeBeers organization in London. These offerings are made ten times a year in stated prices to a selective list of approximately 230 buyers throughout the world who, in turn, are cutters and polishers of the stones, or may resell the raw diamonds to other manufacturers. Although a selected buyer may refuse to purchase his allocation on sight, he seldom declines the privilege as numerous other buyers are typically anxious to replace him in the offering.

WORLD FEDERATION OF DIAMOND BOURSES
List of Affiliated Organizations

ANTWERP	Antwerpsche Diamantkring S.V. Beurs Voor Den Diamanthandel Diamantclub Van Antwerpen Vrije Diamanthandel N.V.
NEW YORK	Diamond Dealers Club, Inc. Diamond Trade Association of America, Inc.
LONDON	London Diamond Bourse London Diamond Club
ISRAEL	Israel Diamond Exchange Etgar, The New Israel Club for Commerce in Diamonds Ltd.
SOUTH AFRICA	Diamond Club of South Africa

AUSTRIA	Diamant-Klub
PARIS	Club Diamantaire de Paris
MILAN	Borsa Diamanti
AMSTERDAM	Beurs Voor Den Diamanthandel

Diamonds are specifically bought and sold on these exchanges by dealers, distributors to the national wholesale markets, or speculators.

The national wholesale market is an off-the-exchange informal market by which regional distributors of cut and polished diamonds maintain inventories for sale to retail jewelers.

The retail market is, of course, the common dispensary of gemstones from which the typical individual customer would purchase his needs. Common insurance appraisals are given in estimates with reference to this market and are usually stated in terms of estimated replacement value. For example, when an individual takes a stone to a retail jeweler for an appraisal for insurance purposes, the jeweler typically will render an opinion as to the estimated replacement value of the gem at retail.

The process through which a cut and polished diamond reaches a retail customer is multi-staged, much as a manufactured item moves from the raw material to the finished inventory phase of development, taking shape and having value added at each progressive step.

To begin, a cutter will travel to London or Brussesl at an appointed time to pick up his allotment of uncut stones (his "sight," as it is termed) from the DeBeers Cartel. The "sight" is filled by a grouping of stones assigned to that particular cutter by the DeBeers Cartel for a fixed price, in a range of sizes known by the DeBeers Cartel to be that cutter's specialty, and in a spectrum of colors and clarity grades.

The cutter must either accept in total, or reject in total, the "sight" and the price. Having accepted and paid for the "sight," the cutter will then return to his facility with the raw diamonds, there to apply his skills in cutting, shaping, etc. Typically, this delicate and all important operation will cause the loss of approximately 50% of the raw weight of the stones. At this point, the original group of stones (the "sight") . . . now in a cut and polished form . . . would be sold.

PROPOSED ACTIVITIES

General

The objective of the Partnerships is to acquire Investment Grade Diamonds for investment purposes. The General Partners believe this will provide investors a convenient method for participating in an investment medium which has historically demonstrated long-term growth, conservation of capital and the possibility for profits subject to taxation at capital gains (as opposed to ordinary income) rates.

The opportunity for diversification of investment in Investment Grade Diamonds is available through participation in the Partnerships. Instead of investing in one diamond, a Limited Partner will have an interest in a portfolio of Investment Grade Diamonds of a Partnership, including larger, more expensive diamonds, which tend to appreciate more than smaller stones. During the holding period, a Partnership's diamonds will be held in a Brink's, Incorporated vault in New York, and will be inspected and appraised annually by an independent appraiser.

Investment Grade Diamonds to be purchased by the Partnerships will be held for potential appreciation and long-term capital gain. The General Partners will not trade Investment Grade Diamonds held in the portfolio of a Partnership. The General Partners believe that historical upward trends in diamond prices will continue. The General Partners intend to hold the Partnerships' Investment Grade Diamonds until such time as a sale appears to be advantageous with a view to achieving the Partnerships' investment objectives. Depending upon market conditions, the General Partners intend to hold the Partnerships' portfolios of Investment Grade Diamonds for approximately five to seven years after their acquisition. In deciding whether to sell a Partnership's diamonds, the General Partners will consider factors such as capital appreciation, anticipation of market decline based upon unprecedented occurrences in the market place, including international tensions, and Federal income tax considerations such as possible adverse Federal income tax consequences to the Limited Partners. To minimize the tax consequences of a sale, a Partnership's diamonds will not be sold until they have been held a sufficient period of time to qualify the sale for treatment as long-term capital gain or loss, as the case may be. Proceeds from the sale by a Partnership from its portfolio of Investment Grade Diamonds will not be reinvested. Such proceeds will be distributed to the Limited Partners.

Further, it should be noted that a Limited Partner should not anticipate the regular distribution of profit or loss. The nature of the business and the objective of the Partnerships is not the generation of distributable income or tax losses, but rather investment returns for long-term capital gain appreciation in the resale value of a Partnership's portfolio of Investment Grade Diamonds. There is, of course, no assurance that any diamonds will gain value in a given period of time.

Investment Objectives and Policies–Investment Grade Diamonds

Following its formation, a Partnership (represented by the General Partners and their Affiliate, Diamond Company, Incorporated) will purchase its initial grouping of Investment Grade Diamonds. These Investment Grade Diamonds will be round brilliant cut with clarities of FL. (flawless), I.F. (internally flawless), VVS_1 or VVS_2 (very very small inclusions) and the color of D, E, F (colorless) with a limitation in weight of no less than one carat. The full spectrum of finished diamonds may constitute suitable or desirable holdings for a Partnership; some to eventually satisfy needs within the jewelry industry only, and others to fill demands created by both the jewelry industry and collectors. Therefore, it is anticipated that a Partnership may buy and hold for appreciation and eventual resale finished Investment Grade Diamonds as previously described.

The General Partners intend to purchase Investment Grade Diamonds with the following specifications:

Cut–Round Brilliant
Size–One to Two Carats (larger if portfolio size warrants)
Color–D through F (not lower)
Clarity–Flawless Through VVS_2 (not lower)
Polish and Symmetry–Good
Depth Percentage–58%-62% of Girdle Diameter
Table Percentage–57%-65% of Girdle Diameter
Crown Angle–30 to 34 Degrees
Culet Size–Small or Medium
Girdle Thickness–Minimum Variation
Graining–Nil or Slight
Fluorescence–None, Faint Blue or Medium Blue

The above specifications are within the tolerances of an internationally accepted standards which produce the maximum brilliance, finest "make" and ideal finish subsequently producing the best investment value. Deviation from the above "ideal" characteristics can substantially reduce the value of the stone.

Investment in a Partnership permits a Participant to invest in a portfolio of only Investment Grade Diamonds. These select Investment Grade Diamonds have in the past tended to appreciate at a more rapid rate than diamonds toward the lower end of the color and clarity spectrum of diamonds. Thus, a Limited Partner will be able to participate in a portfolio of Investment Grade Diamonds that may otherwise be beyond his financial capability if he were purchasing individual diamonds.

Grading of Diamonds

The liquidity of Investment Grade Diamonds as an investment vehicle is directly related to the use of a certification or "diamond grading report" from an independent and recognized gemological laboratory. Investment-quality diamonds are now traded on the basis of accompanying certificates. Through the certification process or "grading," a diamond is evaluated for the criteria previously set forth herein known as the "4C's" of carat weight, clarity, cut and color. The General Partners will not purchase an Investment Grade Diamond without the seller providing a certificate as to authenticity of the diamond from the Gemological Institute of America ("GIA"), Gem Trade Laboratory, Inc., a nationally recognized independent gemological laboratory.

Unlike appraisals, certificates do not mention a dollar value—only a description of quality of the diamond—the 4C's. This allows brokers and diamond investment companies to quote prices on an Investment Grade Diamond based on a certificate's description of the diamond. However, the unique qualities of a diamond still requires human judgment. For example, to determine a diamond's color, gemologists compare it to a set of master stones. Clarity is described as "FL." (flawless), "I.F." (internally flawless) or "VVS_1" and "VVS_2," for "very very slight inclusions" in the diamond. Standard practice is to have two people check each diamond for these characteristics, and in cases where graders disagree, a third party is required. Despite these safeguards, diamond buyers and sellers are at the mercy of subtle variations in standards from laboratory to laboratory. Master stones may vary, differences in lighting may cause diamonds to be given a higher or lower grade, and even a technician's eyesight will alter gradings.

The GIA, Gem Trade Laboratory, Inc. (i) does not appraise guarantee or certify the value of diamonds; (ii) the diamond grading reports (certificates) it issues are a description of the characteristics of the diamond which is the subject of the report based upon the application of grading techniques used by it at the time of its examination; (iii) descriptions may reasonably vary as to such characteristics; and (iv) it makes no representations or warranties whatsoever regarding its diamond grading reports or diamonds described therein. A GIA, Gem Trade Laboratory, Inc. diamond grading report does not constitute a "certificate of authenticity" concerning a particular diamond nor does such report "certify" that a particular diamond is of "Investment Grade."

The General Partners have entered into an agreement with U.S. Gemological Services, Inc. ("USGS"), an independent gemological laboratory with offices in Santa Ana, California, and Chicago, Illinois, to verify the fact that Investment Grade Diamonds purchased for a Partnership's portfolio matches the certificates issued by the GIA, which certificates will be required of the sellers of the Investment Grade Diamonds. USGS will not itself issue a certification to the Partnership. USGS will seal each Investment Grade Diamond, with matching certificate in a tamper-proof case. Once sealed, a Partnership's portfolio of Investment Grade Diamonds will be placed in Brink's vaults for storage and safekeeping. The Investment Grade Diamonds will be stored there until resale, to be viewed annually only for appraisal and inventory check by each Partnership's independent certified public accountant.

Appraisal

The agreement with USGS also provides for the initial and annual appraisal of a Partnership's portfolio of Investment Grade Diamonds based upon "liquidation value."

Once a Partnership has been formed and its portfolio of Investment Grade Diamonds purchased, USGS will appraise such diamonds. USGS will thereafter annually appraise each Partnership's portfolio of Investment Grade Diamonds. The term "liquidation value" is USGS's estimate of the average price at which diamonds of the same grade, carat weight, clarity, cut and color and other qualities could be sold for within the continental United States other than at retail. Market value for diamonds at retail and at wholesale are markets where there is substantial sales data, but the sales data for any liquidation market, if there be one in fact, is less certain and has less market data availability. Accordingly, the opinions which will be expressed by USGS as to "liquidation value" of a Partnership's portfolio of Investment Grade Diamonds will be an estimate based upon data obtained from all such markets. The opinion of value to be given by USGS for any particular Investment Grade Diamond is not to be interpreted as the value of that diamond in any particular transaction, but as an appraisal of the average value of that stone within the continental United States as of the date of the appraisal. There is no assurance, however, that a Partnership could sell its portfolio of Investment Grade Diamonds in the market place for the "liquidation value" appraised, especially if the Partnership were forced to liquidate its entire portfolio at one time. There are also material expenses involved if a Partnership were forced to liquidate its portfolio; for example, through the auspices of an auction house.

USGS will appraise a Partnership's portfolio of Investment Grade Diamonds initially once the General Partners have acquired such a portfolio. Thereafter, USGS will annually appraise each Partnership's portfolio of Investment Grade Diamonds. Such appraisals will be distributed to the Limited Partners. For each Investment Grade Diamond of a Partnership verified by USGS to compare it to its GIA certificate, as well as for each such diamond appraised, the cost to the Partnership will be $25.00 per diamond. For each Investment Grade Diamond appraised by USGS on an annual basis, USGS will charge the Partnership at the rate of $15.00 per diamond. Such charges are subject to change upon 30 days notice to the General Partners by USGS. In addition to such charges, USGS will be paid for travel and subsistence expenses for its employees. USGS will conduct its initial certification verification and initial appraisal, as well as each annual appraisal at the storage location. Such appraisals are a Direct Cost of a Partnership.

The General Partners' agreement with USGS is for an initial term of one year and is automatically renewed from year to year thereafter, unless either party gives 30 days notice not to renew.

During the initial year of such agreement, either party may terminate the agreement without cause upon 30 days notice.

Transportation and Storage of Diamonds

The General Partners have entered into a contract with Brink's Incorporated, an independent contract carrier and air courier for the domestic and international transportation and storage of the Partnership's diamonds. Brink's also provides for storage of diamonds at one of its vaults. Transportation and storage charges are a Direct Cost of a Partnership.

Diamonds purchased for a Partnership will be picked up by Brink's and transported to its storage vault for permanent safekeeping. Appraisals and verifications by USGS, as well as inventory verification by a Partnership's independent certified public accountants, will take place at a secure location. A Partnership's diamonds will remain in Brink's storage vault until sold.

Insurance

Brink's Incorporated charges for transportation and storage includes comprehensive all-risk insurance. Therefore, any additional insurance necessary for a Partnership would be minimal. Any such insurance costs would be a Direct Cost of a Partnership.

Purchase of Investment Grade Diamonds

As soon as practicable after formation of a Partnership, the General Partners will acquire Investment Grade Diamonds for that Partnership's portfolio. The General Partners have no plans, agreements or understandings, written or oral, to purchase any specific Investment Grade Diamonds as of the date of this material. All Investment Grade Diamonds will be acquired by the General Partners for a Partnership through their Affiliate, Diamond Company, Incorporated, at Acquisition Cost (its cost), plus an Acquisition Fee equal to 6% of the Acquisition Cost. Diamond Company, Incorporated, although not a member of any diamond exchange, has been able to purchase Investment Grade Diamonds at "cutter price" (wholesale) through their association with members of recognized diamond exchanges. Acquisition Fees payable to Diamond Company, Incorporated by a Partnership will not, in the aggregate, exceed 5% of the Partnership's Gross Proceeds.

No General Partner or Affiliate may purchase Investment Grade Diamonds from the Partnership, nor sell any Investment Grade Diamonds to the Partnership, unless the Investment Grade Diamonds were acquired by the General Partner or Affiliate solely to facilitate their acquisition by the Partnership and only if no benefit accrues to the General Partner or Affiliate (other than Acquisition Fees as set forth above) from such transaction.

The General Partners do not anticipate engaging in trading activity with respect to a Partnership's portfolio of Investment Grade Diamonds, the principal purpose of the Partnerships being to acquire portfolios of Investment Grade Diamonds and hold such portfolios for a period of approximately five to seven years. The General Partners intend to invest a Partnership's Net Proceeds available for investment as soon as possible, depending upon the availability and quality of Investment Grade Diamonds. Five percent of a Partnership's Gross Proceeds will be retained in Reserves for Working Capital to meet ongoing Direct and General and Administrative Costs. Such Reserves will be invested in interest bearing instruments until needed. Direct and General and Administrative Costs are limited on an aggregate cumulative annual basis to 1% of Gross Proceeds of a Partnership.

Any of the Net Proceeds which have not been invested or committed to investment within 24 months from the date of this material (except for amounts utilized to pay expenses of a Partnership or amounts set aside for necessary Reserves for Working Capital) will be returned by the Partnership to the Limited Partners. All funds received by a Partnership out of the Escrow Account will be available for the general use of the Partnership from the time of such receipt until the expiration of such 24 month period. Such funds will not be segregated or held separate from other funds of a Partnership pending their use and no interest will be payable to the Limited Partners if such funds are returned to them. For the purpose of the foregoing provision, funds will be deemed to have been committed to investment and will not be returned to the Limited Partners to the extent written agreements in principle, commitment letters, letters of intent or understanding, or other agreements are in existence, regardless of whether any such investment is or is not consummated, and also to the extent that any funds have been reserved to make contingent payments, regardless of whether any such payments are or are not made.

No Borrowing for Acquisitions

The Limited Partnership Agreement prohibits borrowing by the Partnerships to acquire Investment Grade Diamonds. Therefore, there will be no "leveraging" used to finance any portion of the acquisition of Investment Grade Diamonds by a Partnership. The Partnerships are, however, permitted to borrow for future ongoing Direct and General and Administrative Costs. Direct and General and Administrative Costs of a Partnership are limited, on an aggregate cumulative annual basis, to 1% of the Gross Proceeds of a Partnership.

The General Partners or their Affiliates, may, but are not required to, loan or advance monies to a Partnership. The General Partners or their Affiliates loaning or advancing money to a Partnership may not receive interest or other financing charges or fees in excess of the amount which would be charged by unrelated lending institutions on comparable loans for the same purpose.

Resale of Partnership Diamonds

The General Partners intend to hold a Partnership's Investment Grade Diamonds until such time as a sale appears to be advantageous with a view to achieving the Partnership's investment objectives. After an anticipated holding period of approximately five to seven years, but not more than ten years, the General Partners will sell a Partnership's portfolio of Investment Grade Diamonds. In deciding whether to sell the Partnership's diamonds, the General Partners will consider factors such as capital appreciation, anticipation of market decline based upon unprecedented occurrences in the market place, including international tensions, and Federal income tax considerations such as possible adverse Federal income tax consequences to the Limited Partners. To minimize the tax consequences of a sale, a Partnership's diamonds will not be sold until they have been held a sufficient period of time to qualify the sale for treatment as long-term capital gain or loss, as the case may be. Proceeds from the sale by a Partnership from its portfolio of Investment

Grade Diamonds will not be reinvested. The General Partners intend to distribute such proceeds to the Limited Partners as Cash Distributions within thirty days after the receipt thereof.

Although multiple Partnerships may be formed by the General Partners, the entire amount of all diamond holdings by all such Partnerships would be insignificant when compared to the size of the diamond market on either the domestic or international level. Thus, the General Partners do not anticipate difficulty in selling a Partnership's diamonds at then prevailing market prices. There is no assurance, however, that a Partnership could sell its portfolio of Investment Grade Diamonds in the market place at "liquidation value," as appraised by USGS, especially if a Partnership were forced to liquidate its entire portfolio at one time. There would also be a greater expense involved, for example, if a Partnership were forced to liquidate its portfolio through the auspices of an auction house.

Conflicts could arise between Partnerships in connection with resales of diamonds in situations where a particular category of Investment Grade Diamonds is desired and a diamond meeting that specification is held in the portfolio of more than one such Partnership. In order to ameliorate any such conflicts, the General Partners have adopted a "first-in, first-out" resale policy to be applied among all such Partnerships.

No Commissions on Resale

No commissions will be paid to the General Partners or their Affiliates in connection with the sale of a Partnership's portfolio of Investment Grade Diamonds. The General Partners and their Affiliates will be reimbursed for their travel expenses, if any, in connection with such sales. However, such travel expenses will be subordinated until such time as Cash Distributions from a Partnership equal a 100% return to the Limited Partners of their aggregate Capital Contributions to a Partnership ($500 per Unit). The General Partners' determination of such travel expenses will be reviewed by the Partnerships' independent certified public accountants as part of their annual examination of each Partnership's financial statements. The actual amount of such travel expenses, if any, will depend on several factors such as the size of a Partnership's portfolio of Investment Grade Diamonds and the requirement for travel of the General Partners in order to sell and/or liquidate such diamonds.

Competition

There are numerous small and moderate size dealers of diamonds, as well as thousands of individual investors. The General Partners believe that the anticipated size of a Partnership as well as the experience of the General Partners in the acquisition of diamonds will enable the Partnerships to compete successfully with other entities in the market place.

Other Policies

It is the intention of the General Partners to conduct the business of a Partnership in such a manner as not to be deemed a "dealer" in diamonds for Federal income tax purposes. The General Partners also intend to operate the Partnerships in such a manner as not to be required to register as an investment company under the Investment Company Act of 1940.

TERMS OF THE OFFERING

Subscriptions

The General Partners propose to form up to four Limited Partnerships to be organized under the Uniform Limited Partnership Act for the purpose of acquiring Investment Grade Diamonds. The General Partners are offering to eligible persons $10,000,000 in preformation units of limited partnership interests (the "Units"), consisting of 20,000 Units at $500 per Unit, in the Partnerships. Each Participant must purchase at least five Units ($2,500) and may purchase greater amounts in multiples of one Unit ($500). A Partnership will not be formed until subscriptions for not less than 2,250 Units, aggregating $1,125,000, have been received. The General Partners or their Affiliates may purchase Units in order to satisfy a Partnership's minimum subscription requirement. Such Units will be purchased for investment and not with the intent to resell. A Participant will become a Limited Partner in only the Partnership to which his Units relate. Subscriptions are payable in full upon execution of the Subscription Agreement.

By execution of the Subscription Agreement, the subscriber agrees to become a Limited Partner in a Partnership, if that

Partnership is formed, and he further agrees to contribute to its capital the amount of his subscription. Until formation of a Partnership, all Participants' funds paid in respect to subscriptions for Units will be held in an Escrow Account with The First National Bank. Such amounts will be invested in interest bearing instruments by the Bank upon the request of the General Partners and will not be subject to the debts or obligations of the General Partners. If the required minimum in subscriptions is not obtained within the 90 day Offering period of a Partnership (unless such Offering period is extended for a period not to exceed 60 days), all amounts subscribed will be promptly refunded to subscribers in full at the conclusion of the Offering period, and each subscriber will receive his pro rata share of the net interest earned on the escrowed funds. If the required minimum in subscriptions is obtained within the Offering period and a Partnership formed, each subscriber will receive his pro rata share of the net interest earned on the escrowed funds upon formation of the Partnership within the Offering period, but in no event, later than the conclusion of the Offering period.

If a subscription is accepted by the General Partners, the Participant thereupon acquires a preformation interest in the related Partnership, which interest will be converted, Unit for Unit, into a Partnership interest upon formation of the Partnership. Under the Limited Partnership Agreement, each Participant's subscription is binding upon the Partnership after its formation, and the General Partners are required to apply subscription funds in payment of the specified Capital Contributions.

The subscription period for each Partnership will terminate 90 days from the date of commencement, unless extended by the General Partners for an additional period not to exceed 60 days. Such subscription period may be terminated at the option of the General Partners at any time during that period if subscriptions for not less than 2,250 Units aggregating $1,125,000, have been received. The subscription period for the second Partnership shall commence, if at all, after termination of the subscription period for the initial Partnership; the subscription period for the third Partnership shall commence, if at all, after termination of the subscription period for the second Partnership; and the subscription period for the fourth Partnership shall commence, if at all, after termination of the subscription period for the third Partnership. The Prospectus will be amended prior to the commencement of the subscription periods for each of the second, third and fourth Partnerships. In no event will the Partnerships' offerings extend beyond December 17, Year Two. The General Partners may, but shall not be required to, undertake the second, third and fourth Partnership offerings.

The interest of a Limited Partner in costs to be borne and Revenues to be shared by all Limited Partners, as a class, will be based on the ratio that his Capital Contributions to a Partnership bear to the total Capital Contributions of all Limited Partners in such Partnership.

Separate Funds

Funds raised in connection with each Partnership will not be commingled with the funds of any other partnership, person or entity. Following formation of a Partnership and the release of its funds from the Escrow Account at The First National Bank, a separate bank account will be established for each Partnership in which its Partnership Capital will be deposited and from which expenditures will be made.

Offering Expenses

Offering Expenses, not to exceed 1% of Gross Proceeds will be reimbursed to the General Partners. Offering Expenses in excess of 1% of Gross Proceeds will be paid by the General Partners.

Contributions of the General Partners

The General Partners will contribute, as the General Partners, 1% of a Partnership's Gross Proceeds. In return for such contribution, the General Partners shall be entitled to share 1% of a Partnership's Cash Distributions allocated to the Participants before Payout and 25% after Payout. The General Partners may also make Capital Contributions to a Partnership by purchasing Units (net of any sales commissions). The General Partners have agreed to contribute a minimum of $100,000 to the Partnerships. In the event the Gross Proceeds from the Partnerships' Offerings are less than $10,000,000, the General Partners will contribute, as the General Partners, 1% of the Partnerships' Gross Proceeds and the balance of their investment in the

Partnerships to equal $100,000 will be represented by purchases of Units.

Transferability of Units

Units may be sold, assigned, exchanged or otherwise transferred only in compliance with the terms of the Limited Partnership Agreement. However, no transferor or transferee may hold less than five $500 Units ($2,500) in a Partnership except by gift or operation of law. In the event a Limited Partner transfers all of his Units, he will cease to be a Limited Partner.

No purchaser, assignee or other transferee may become a Substitute Limited Partner without obtaining the prior written consent of the General Partners (which consent may not be unreasonably withheld) and the assigning Limited Partners. In addition, transferees must consent to be bound by the Limited Partnership Agreement and pay all expenses in connection with the transfer, and the assignment must be effected in compliance with all applicable laws.

There will be no ready market for the Units offered hereby, and Limited Partners should therefore expect to bear the economic risk of investing in a Partnership for a period not to exceed ten years.

Distribution Policy

The Partnerships' principal objective is to acquire a portfolio of Investment Grade Diamonds and to hold such diamonds for a period of approximately five to seven years in anticipation of realizing capital appreciation and resulting profits upon sale of the portfolio at the end of such period. There can be no assurance that the partnerships will be able to attain their objectives. Moreover, investors needing cash distributions as a result of their investments should consider other investments designed to produce cash distributions.

Life of the Partnership

The Partnerships' terms will be ten years unless sooner terminated upon the liquidation of a Partnership's entire portfolio of Investment Grade Diamonds. However, the Partnerships will be dissolved and terminated prior thereto (a) in the event of the bankruptcy of the General Partners, (b) if, in the opinion of the General Partners, the purposes of the Partnerships cannot be fulfilled, (c) in the event of the removal of the General Partners unless a majority in interest of all Limited Partners elects a substitute General Partner, or (d) in the event that more than 50% in interest (Units) of the Limited Partners vote to do so.

BENEFITS OF A DIAMOND FUND

The General Partners do not intend to engage in trading activity with respect to a Partnership's portfolio of Investment Grade Diamonds, the principal purpose of the Partnerships being to acquire such portfolios and holding the Investment Grade Diamonds for a period of approximately five to seven years. Investors needing an annual return on their investments should consider other investments designed to produce annual income. The Limited Partners are entitled to receive 99% of a Partnership's Cash Distributions until such time as the Limited Partners have received Cash Distributions from the Partnership, if any, equal to their initial Capital Contributions ($500 per Unit of Preformation Limited Partnership Interest) plus a cumulative annual return of 10% on their Capital Contributions of $500 per Unit. Cash Distributions will only be made upon the liquidation of all or part of a Partnership's portfolio of Investment Grade Diamonds. (The 10% cumulative annual return is intended to represent a 10% return to the Limited Partners on invested Capital Contributions, less Cash Distributions, if any, which will reduce the basis of the Capital Contributions, from time to time, upon which the 10% cumulative annual return is thereafter calculated.) At such time as the Limited Partners have received Cash Distributions from a Partnership equal to Payout, the General Partners' share will increase from 1% to 25%. There can be no assurance of Cash Distributions for Limited Partners.

RISKS OF A DIAMOND FUND

1. *Risks Involved in Investing in Diamonds*. While the prices of Investment Grade Diamonds have trended upward for many years, there can be no assurance that such trend will continue in the future. The prices of such diamonds and all rare commodities

are functions of supply and demand, and while these elements have heretofore been kept in the proper balance to yield increasing prices, there can be no assurance that demand will continue or that supplies will not be expanded or substitutes therefor discovered or developed, or that for some other reason the commodity may be devalued on the world market. In addition, while the Partnerships will take physical possession of a specified portfolio of Investment Grade Diamonds under strict security safeguards, there is always the possibility of loss or theft of the physical item; this is a risk which can be mitigated by safekeeping storage and insurance.

It is estimated the DeBeers Consolidated Mines, Ltd., a foreign cartel, controls the mining and marketing of more than 85% of the world's diamonds, thereby currently maintaining a degree of stability. Diamond prices could be depressed by the breaking of the DeBeers monopoly. Diamonds are currently being mined all over the world. The major countries are Africa, Russia, South America, India, Brazil and Australia. Political pressures in these countries could be brought upon DeBeers affecting its role of "price leadership." There is also the possibility that some synthetic diamonds might be produced for sale in the investment market.

The General Partners intend to hold the Partnership's Investment Grade Diamonds until such time as a sale appears to be advantageous with a view to achieving the Partnership's investment objectives. Depending upon market conditions, the General Partners intend to hold the Partnerships' portfolios of Investment Grade Diamonds for approximately five to seven years after their acquisition. In deciding whether to sell a Partnership's diamonds, the General Partners will consider factors such as capital appreciation, anticipation of market decline based upon unprecedented occurrences in the market place, including international tensions and Federal income tax considerations, such as possible adverse Federal income tax consequences to the Limited Partners. To minimize the tax consequences of a sale, a Partnership's diamonds will not be sold until they have been held a sufficient period of time to qualify the sale for treatment as long-term capital gain or loss, as the case may be. Proceeds form the sale by a Partnership from its portfolio of Investment Grade Diamonds will not be reinvested. The General Partners intend to distribute such proceeds to the Limited Partners within thirty days after the receipt thereof.

2. *No Government Regulation of the Industry.* The diamond industry is presently subject to no government or other type of regulation.

TAX ASPECTS OF A DIAMOND FUND

Minimum Tax for Tax Preferences

The 1976 Act imposes a minimum tax or "tax preference" in a given taxable year equal to 15% of the amount by which an individual taxpayer's aggregate "tax preferences" exceed the greater of $10,000 ($5,000 in the case of a married taxpayer filing a separate return) or one-half the regular tax liability (reduced by certain credits) for such year.

The 1978 Act modified the minimum tax provisions referred to in the foregoing paragraph by excluding the capital gains tax preference in years subsequent to 1978. The capital gains tax preference, with some modifications, will be subject to the new "alternative minimum tax" for taxable years beginning after December 31, 1978. Further, the minimum tax referred to in the foregoing paragraph will be no longer payable if the new alternative minimum tax exceeds the total of regular taxes and the minimum tax. The taxable base subject to the alternative minimum tax will be computed by adding taxable income, capital gains excluded from taxable income, and the tax preference for adjusted itemized deductions. The taxable base, reduced by a $20,000 exemption, will be subject to alternative minimum tax rates ranging from 10% to 25% on amounts ranging from less than $40,000 to over $80,000. As a result, capital gains would no longer reduce the amount of personal service income eligible for the maximum tax. The 1978 Act also repealed the 25% alternative tax on the first $50,000 of net long-term capital gain. As a result of these changes, the maximum capital gains tax rate (ignoring preference tax) for noncorporate taxpayers will be 28% (40% of the highest individual tax rate of 70% since the capital gain exclusion is now 60%).

The Partnerships themselves are not subject to tax, but the Participants will be required to take into account their respective shares of the Partnerships' tax preference items.

The effect of the minimum tax is to reduce the benefit to any Participants of intangible drilling costs on productive wells, depletion, long-term capital gains and accelerated depreciation on real property. Moreover, items of tax preference are subtracted from the amount eligible for the 50% maximum tax on earned income. The amount of minimum tax depends upon the total income tax liability of the taxpayer, and the extent, if any, to which the tax preferences may adversely affect any Partner, including the extent of benefit in respect of earned income, cannot be predicted.

It should be noted that certain states also impose a minimum tax on items of tax preference.

DIAMOND AND GOLD TRUST

DIAMOND MARKET

The price of investment grade diamonds is largely dependent upon the availability of investment grade rough diamonds, the world's known sources of which are highly concentrated. The Republic of South Africa, several republics in southern, central and Western Africa and the U.S.S.R. account for about 90% of present world rough diamond production. Some of the diamond producing areas, including the Republic of South Africa, may be subject to political instability which may have an adverse impact on the diamond production and distribution in such areas. Approximately 85% of the world diamond output is purchased for resale by the Central Selling Organization ("CSO"), a subsidiary of DeBeers Consolidated Mines Limited. As a primary world-wide marketing mechanism of the diamond industry, the CSO seeks to maintain an orderly and stable market for diamonds by regulating the quantity of diamonds which reach the market and by establishing prices. Sales for the CSO are made in London by its subsidiary, the Diamond Trading Company ("DTC"), to a select group of approximately 250 clients. In order to maintain their purchasing relationship, the DTC's clients are expected to purchase all of the diamonds offered to them by the DTC. Those not within this select group must either purchase their requirements from clients of the DTC, usually at increased cost, or seek access to that portion of the world supply not marketed by the DTC.

The DTC periodically invites its clients to submit their requirements as to the amount and type of stones they wish to purchase. Representatives of DTC's clients attend each of the 10 offerings ("sights") held by the DTC each year in London. At each sight DTC's clients purchase, at DTC's stated price, an assortment of rough stones known as a "series," the composition of which takes into account the markets in which DTC's clients operate and their quantity requirements.

The DTC has selectively increased its prices of rough diamonds on the average of once or twice a year during the last several years. Generally DTC's clients selectively adjust their selling prices upward to reflect those increases. Political events in South Africa may have an impact on diamond prices, and there is no assurance that an orderly diamond market will be maintained.

DTC sells the bulk of its diamonds in the United States to large cutters who in turn sell to diamond dealers in New York, who in turn sell to jewelry wholesalers, who in turn sell to jewelry retailers, who then sell to individual customers. With each step in the sales chain a significant mark-up is added to the resale price. Prices of diamonds may vary considerably between different sales levels and even within a given sales level.

High quality investment grade diamonds also go through a multi-level distribution chain with several mark-ups. Generally, a large direct buyer/cutter sells investment grade diamonds to: (1) a diamond dealer in New York who is a New York Diamond Dealers Club member, has access to other members for purposes of diamond trading, carries diamond inventory and bears the market risk on such inventory; or (2) a New York investment diamond wholesaler who is not a New York Diamond Dealers Club member but who carries diamond inventory and bears the market risk on that inventory. (The New York Diamond Dealers Club is a diamond trading forum for most of the major diamond cutters, dealers and brokers in New York, the center of the diamond industry in the United States.) The diamond dealer usually sells his investment grade diamonds to an investment diamond firm or a wholesaler outside New York who in turn sells to an investment firm. Finally, the investment firm, which usually has promotional and marketing emphasis, sells to the individual or institutional investor. The ultimate investor may pay mark-ups of 100% or more over the cost to the cutter.

Unlike some securities and commodities, diamond transactions are not generally regulated by governmental or self-regulatory authorities. However, such regulation may develop in the future. There is no single central marketplace or clearing house for investment grade diamonds.

In general, the diamond prices used for computing the Public Offering Price are based on average asked prices of large New York investment diamond wholesalers to substantial purchasers, and accordingly, are substantially lower than the corresponding retail price which the individual investor must normally

Investment grade diamonds are generally graded according to factors referred to as the "four C's"—carat weight, color, clarity and cut. Thc grading scale most commonly used is that of Gemological Institute of America, Inc. below.

Clarity Grading Scale

Flawless	VVS_1	VVS_2	VS_1	VS_2	SI_1	SI_2	I_1	I_2	I_3
Internally Flawless							Imperfect		

Color Grading Scale

D E F	G H I J	K L M	N O P Q R	S T U V W X Y Z	
Colorless	Near Colorless	Faint Yellow	Very Light Yellow	Light Yellow	Fancy Yellow

A carat is equal to 1/142 of an ounce. The diamonds in the Trust range from 1.0 to 5.46 carats in weight, D to H in color, and Flawless (Internally Flawless) to VS_2 in clarity. These diamonds are all round Brilliant cut of high quality.

All of the Trust diamonds were purchased by the Depositor in "arms length" transactions in which the seller was unaffiliated with the Depositor.

For purposes of evaluations pursuant hereto, the Evaluators, Trustees, Transaction Agent and Depositor shall be entitled to rely on the accuracy of the verification of the diamond grading report that the Trust has for each diamond and the diamond specifications listed below without personally inspecting the diamonds.

A. Shape and Cut:	Round Brilliant
B. Measurements:	Less than 0.20 variance in diameter
C. Weight:	As per price sheets
D. Depth %:	57.0 to 63.0%
E. Table %:	57.0 to 66.0%
F. Girdle:	Must not be extremely thin, extremely or very thick
G. Culet Size:	Must not be large

H. Polish:	"Fair to Good" or better
I. Symmetry:	"Fair to Good" or better
J. Clarity Grade:	Flawless (F)/Internally Flawless (IF) to VS_2
K. Graining:	Must not be significant or reflective
L. Color Grade	D to H
M. Fluorescence:	Must not be strong
N. Comments:	Crown angles must be no less than 30 and no greater than 35 degrees

Although the value of the Units is related to the quality of the Trust diamonds, diamond grading reports and the gemologist verifications of the Trust diamonds are not valuations, appraisals or guarantees to the Unit holders. The liability is limited to willful misconduct, gross negligence or fraud. The liability of the laboratory that issued the grading reports on the Trust diamonds is similarly limited.

GOLD MARKET

In recent years, the price of gold has been subject to dramatic downward and upward price movements over short periods of time and may be affected by international monetary and political policies, such as currency devaluations or revaluations, economic conditions within an individual country, trade imbalances, or trade or currency restrictions between countries.

The two largest national producers of gold bullion are the Republic of South Africa and the U.S.S.R. Changes in political and economic conditions affecting either country may have a direct impact on that country's sales of gold. Under South African Law, the only authorized sales agent for gold produced in South Africa is the Reserve Bank of South Africa, which through its retention policies controls the time and place of any sale of South African bullion. The South African Ministry of Mines determines gold mining policy. South Africa depends predominantly on gold sales for the foreign exchange necessary to finance its imports, and its sales policy is necessarily subject to national economic and political developments.

Since 1974 when it became legal to invest in gold, markets for gold have developed in the United States. Certain entities, including the U.S. Treasury and the International Monetary Fund, have recently conducted sales of relatively large amounts of gold bullion and may do so in the future. Any large purchases or sales of gold bullion, including sales by banks and governmental agencies, could have an effect on the price of gold bullion.

Diamond Trust is a grantor trust formed for the purposes of potential capital appreciation in a fixed collection of investment grade diamonds. The Trust assets are comprised principally of a carefully selected collection of cut and polished diamonds in the highest 25 diamond grades, namely color grades D through H and clarity grades Flawless through VS_2. The balance of the Trust assets is gold bullion that will be periodically sold and the proceeds used to pay the annual administration costs of the Trust. Each Unit represents 1/13,000 fractional undivided interest in the Trust's assets.

Trust Unit holders have no right of redemption. Prior to this offering there has been no public market for Units of the Trust, and there is no assurance that such a market will develop.

The Trust Transaction Agent will use its best efforts to sell one of the four groups of Trust diamonds listed in the Portfolio during each of the calendar years Five, Seven and Nine and the last year of the Trust. The Trustees, after paying the Transaction Agent's fee and sales expenses, will distribute the net proceeds to the Unit holders.

	Price to Public (1)	Selling Commissions (1)
Per Unit	$ 994.10	$ 79.53
Total Estimated Gross Proceeds (2)	$12,923,300	$1,033,864

(1) During the initial public offering period, the Price to Public ("Public Offering Price") will be determined daily and will be equal to the sum of (i) the value placed on the Trust diamonds by three Evaluators who will make their determinations on the basis of average asked prices of large New York investment diamond wholesalers to substantial purchasers ("Wholesalers Asked Prices") and (ii) the value of the Trust gold plus a one half percent handling fee, all divided by 13,000

units plus (iii) a sales charge of 8% of the Public Offering Price (7½% of the Public Offering Price for purchases of 100 or more Units). Depending upon the value of the diamonds and gold held by the Trust, the Price to the Public may fluctuate daily.

(2) 13,000 Units to be offered.

DEPOSITOR

Total Moxie Securities Inc., is the Depositor of the Trust.

The Depositor is engaged in the underwriting, securities and commodities brokerage business.

The Depositor has been instrumental in the organization of the Trust and may be deemed a "promoter" of the Trust within the meaning of Rule 405 under the Securities Act of 1933.

The Depositor is not an expert in diamonds and has not acted in a similar capacity in other investment entities engaged in making similar investments or otherwise made or arranged for similar investments.

Depositor's Profits

For its services, the Depositor will receive a gross sales commission equal to 8% of the Public Offering Price of the Units based on sales of less than 100 Units (7½% in the case of sales of 100 Units or more).

In addition, the Depositor realized a profit or sustained a loss, as the case may be, before the deduction of the expenses of the offering, in the amount of any difference between the cost of the Trust assets to the Trust (which is based on (1) the average asked prices of large New York investment diamond wholesalers to substantial purchasers for the underlying diamonds and (2) the cash prices of Trust gold plus a ½% handling charge on the Date of Deposit) and the price paid for the diamonds and gold at the time they were acquired by the Depositor. During the initial offering period the Depositor also may realize profits or sustain losses as a result of fluctuations after the Date of Deposit in the Wholesalers Asked Prices of the diamonds and the price of the gold and, hence, in the Public Offering received by the Depositor for Units.

RIGHTS OF UNIT HOLDERS

The Unit holders do not have any management powers over the Trust and should not be personally liable, with the exception of their investment in Trust Units, for any actions by the Trust unless they actively participate in the administration of the Trust, which is not contemplated under the Trust Agreement.

Certificates

Ownership of Units is evidenced by registered certificates executed by the Trustees and the Depositor. The Trustee is authorized to treat as the record owner of Units that person who is registered as such owner on the books of the Trustee as of the first of each month. Delivery of certificates representing Units ordered for purchase is normally made five business days following order or within a reasonable period of time thereafter. Certificates are transferable by presentation and surrender to the Trustee properly endorsed or accompanied by a written instrument or instruments of transfer. The Unit holder does not have any general rights to vote except as provided in "Amendment."

Certificates may be issued in denominations of one Unit or any multiple thereof. A Unit holder may be required to pay $2.00 per certificate reissued or transferred, and to pay any government charge that may be imposed in connection with each such transfer or interchange. For new certificates issued to replace destroyed, stolen or lost certificates, the Unit holder must furnish indemnity satisfactory to the Trustee and must pay such expenses as the Trustee may incur. Mutilated certificates must be surrendered to the Trustee for replacement.

Reports and Records

The Trustee shall furnish the Unit holders with a statement of the Unit value, based on the Diamonds Mean Value and the spot price of gold, and the expenses of the Trust for the quarter. During liquidation periods until the last diamond in the group has been sold, the Trustee will furnish the Unit holders with a statement not less than every 60 days providing the following information: (1) the diamonds sold since the last statement and the proceeds from such sale; (2) expenses associated with such sale; and (3) amount distributed per Unit. Within 90 days after the end of each calendar year beginning Year One, the Trustee will furnish to each person who at any time during the calendar year was a Unit holder of record, a statement providing the following information as of the last day of the year: (1) the amount of administrative expenses for the year, (2) the amount of gold sold during the year and the proceeds from such sales; (3) cash balance; (4) gold balance; (5) diamonds sold during the year and the gross proceeds and net proceeds after sales expenses and fees from such sales; (6) amounts distributed to Unit holders; (7) diamonds remaining in the Trust; (8) Unit value based on Diamonds Mean Value; and (9) Dealer Bid Prices of the remaining diamonds. Such statement will be prepared on an accrual basis in accordance with generally accepted accounting principles and audited by independent public accountants. To the extent the Trust is required to file a Form 10-Q under the Securities Exchange Act of 1934, the Trustee will furnish the information therein to the Unit holders within 45 days after the end of the quarterly period.

The Trustee shall keep available for inspection by Unit holders at all reasonable times during usual business hours, books of record and account of its transactions as Trustee including records of the names and addresses of Unit holders, certificates issued or held, a current list of Trust assets in the Portfolio and a copy of the Trustee Agreement.

Unit holders may obtain the Unit value figure, determined monthly on the basis of the Diamonds Mean Value, and scheduled distribution information by telephoning the Trustee after the value has been computed.

After the initial public offering period the Trust diamonds will be evaluated monthly, for purposes of rendering reports to the Trustee, on the basis of the mean (the "Diamonds Mean Value") between (1) the Wholesalers Asked Prices and (2) the average bid prices of New York diamond dealers ("Dealer Bid Prices"), which are generally lower than the Wholesale Asked Prices. The Trust diamonds will be evaluated on the basis of Dealer Bid Prices for purposes of setting minimum prices below which Trust diamonds will generally not be sold.

The Trust will pay the following fees: to the Trustee—an annual fee of 0.1% of the value of the Trust assets on the last days of the year based on the Diamonds Mean Value as defined above; to the Co-Trustee–an annual fee of 0.05% of the aforementioned value of Trust assets (but not less than $2,500 per year); to the Transaction Agent–1½% of the net proceeds of the sale of Trust diamonds after deducting extraordinary sales expenses; to each Evaluator–$200 per evaluation of the Trust diamonds. Such fees will be paid on a quarterly basis regardless of whether Trust assets have been sold for a gain, except the fees of the Transaction Agent, which will be paid upon the sale of Trust diamonds. The Trust will not pay any fees to the Depositor, which has borne all of the organizational costs of the Trust.

BENEFITS OF A DIAMOND AND GOLD TRUST

Investment in the Trust offers the following potential advantages:

Potential Capital Appreciation. While there is no assurance of capital appreciation, there is potential for the value of a Unit to appreciate substantially. Finished investment grade diamonds have generally increased in price substantially more than increases in the Consumer Price Index during the last ten years. For example, the wholesale price of a one carat "D" Flawless diamond increased from approximately $1,800 in 1970 to $53,000 in May 1980, during which period the Consumer Price Index increased from 116.3 to 245.1. Accordingly, investment grade diamonds may prove a good hedge against inflation in the future if this trend were to continue.

Professional Selection. The diamond collection deposited in the Trust has been selected with the aim of assembling a diversified collection of high quality investment grade diamonds. Such selection was made on the basis of the following criteria: possibility of future appreciation, availability of supply and ease of liquidation. The high quality of the Trust diamonds should maximize potential appreciation because of the growing scarcity of high grade diamonds, and the diversity of the collection of Trust diamonds should make the diamonds more easily liquidatable because there will be no large concentrations in any one type of diamond to be sold. The selected stones have been submitted for grading to an independent gemological laboratory,

GIA Gem Trade Laboratory, Inc. ("GTL"), a wholly owned subsidiary of Gemological Institute of America, Inc. (GIA). In the ordinary course of business that laboratory graded the Trust diamonds and furnished a report with respect to each stone as to weight, cut, clarity and color. Such gradings were subsequently verified by an independent gemologist. Thereafter, each of the diamonds was sealed. The diamond grading reports and the gemologist verification of the Trust diamonds are not guarantees, valuations or appraisals.

Protection Against Loss. The diamonds and gold in the Trust shall be insured against physical loss, except loss arising out of war, nuclear explosion, government taking and comparable causes, at all times by the Trustee. Initially, the Trustee shall have the insurance policy of the Depositor with Lloyds of London assigned to the Trust. Trust gold will be sold to pay insurance premiums, which are estimated for the first full year of the Trust to be approximately $19,500. Although the policy in effect has a three year term, there is no assurance that it can be renewed at the same premium rate.

RISKS OF A DIAMOND AND GOLD TRUST

Diamond Prices are Unpredictable. While prices of investment grade diamonds have in the last thirty-five years generally risen, there is no assurance that such prices will rise in the future and there is no guarantee that an orderly diamond market will continue to be maintained. Moreover, like other commodities, the prices of investment grade diamonds are affected by general economic conditions which might cause prices to fall in an unfavorable business environment. In addition, political instability in some diamond producing areas, including the Republic of South Africa, may have an adverse impact on diamond production and distribution in such areas.

In addition, the development of an inexpensive process for the manufacture of synthetic investment grade diamonds could adversely affect the prices of the Trust diamonds. A process for the manufacture of synthetic diamonds has been developed but it is still too expensive for synthetic diamonds to have any significant market impact. At this point there are gemological tests which can differentiate between natural and synthetic diamonds, and, accordingly, synthetic diamonds are worth considerably less today than their natural counterparts.

Diamond Liquidity. While a diamond may have appreciated greatly in value since the time of acquisition, the sale of that diamond to realize the maximum appreciation may be difficult during slow market times. The Transaction Agent, an expert in diamond selling, will attempt to avoid such problems during Trust liquidation periods by using as much of the twelve month period as is necessary. Moreover, the Unit holder has virtually no control over when the Trust diamonds are sold, and hence, the timing of their sale may be disadvantageous to the Unit holder.

Gold May Be a Speculative Investment. Although gold represents only a small portion of the Trust's assets, the price of gold has been subject to significant price fluctuations in the past and may be subject to price volatility in the future. Trust gold will be sold quarterly to pay the administrative costs of the Trust. To the extent that gold must be sold by the Trust in a market when prices are falling, the Trust supply of gold will be depleted more quickly and the Trust assets will be diminished in value.

Change of Diamond Grading Standards. It is possible that one or more of the Trust diamonds in one category could be downgraded or upgraded to another category, if there is a change in the diamond grading standards.

TAX ASPECTS OF A DIAMOND AND GOLD FUND

If the Trust is treated as a grantor trust, it would not be treated as a taxable entity and each Unit holder will be considered the owner of a pro rata portion of the Trust under Section 673(a) and/or 677(a) of the Internal Revenue Code of 1954. In general, the tax consequences of the Trust will flow through directly to the Unit holders. Each Unit holder will have a taxable event when the Trust disposes of a diamond or gold or when the Unit holder sells his Unit. The total tax cost of each Unit to a Unit holder is allocated among each of the diamonds and the gold held in the Trust (in accordance with the proportion of the Trust comprised by each diamond and the gold) in order to determine his per Unit tax cost for each diamond and the gold. Similarly, each Unit holder will be entitled to deduct his pro rata share of the Trust expenses, with the possible exception of the expenses of selling Trust assets which would reduce the amount realized.

COLORED GEMSTONES

As in diamonds, colored gemstones are graded for carat weight, color and clarity. However, unlike diamonds, in which the clarity grade (degree to which a stone is free of flaws) is critical, it is not as important in colored stone value. Minor natural flaws and surface characteristics are present in even the finest quality rubies, sapphires and emeralds. The most crucial grading factor for these gemstones is the color, which represents as much as 70 percent of the stone's value and is measured for color, rating and tone.

Therefore, it is imperative that the purchaser knows and understands the grading factors which affect the value of the stone.

Certificate Number and Date: The certificate number identifies the stone. If the certificate is lost it can be replaced if you know its number. The date the stone was certificated is also important because of the continuous refinement of grading standards. In general, a certificate should be no more than several years old.

Identification: This line defines the gemstone—ruby, sapphire, or emerald—and in some cases will identify the stone's origin. A Burmese ruby, for example, may sell for more than twice as much because of the extremely fine quality of rubies sometimes found in that area. The word "natural" simply means the stone was formed by nature and is not manufactured material.

Shape and Cut: The words round brilliant, oval brilliant, emeralds, cushion antique or oval mixed, refer to the stone's proportioning and faceting. "Oval" refers to the shape in which the stone is cut and "mixed" means a combination of cutting styles were used to fashion the stone.

Carat Weight: As in diamonds, colored stone weight is measured by metric carat, which is equivalent to 1/5 of a gram. The carat is subdivided into 100 units called points. A gemstone's weight would be expressed decimally. For example, 2.26 cts on the certificate means two carats plus 26 points. Stones one carat and larger are most popular for investment. These have the highest degree of liquidity, although there are exceptions for smaller or larger extremely fine stones.

Measurements: Each gemstone is measured to the nearest 1/100 of a millimeter, and its length, width and depth are reported on the certificate in that order. In addition to a means of identification, these measurements can tell you whether a stone is long and thin or short and squatty.

Color Grade: Color is the most crucial factor in the grading of rubies, sapphires and emeralds. The color grade is determined by examining the many factors affecting the color of the gemstone in a controlled lighting environment.

The first part of the sequence indicates the quality of color and the second number, the quantity of color.

Color Rating: The color rating (quality of color), which is scale from 1 to 10. It is also given a verbal grade. The color rating is determined by applying an analytical process called color scan. Investment grade colored stones generally have a color rating of 5.5 or better. (The lower the number the better the grade.)

Tone: The second portion of the overall color grade indicates the tone of the gem. The tonal judgment describes the amount of quantity of body color present in the gemstone, based on a reference scale of 0 (colorless) to 100 (darkest). Tone for rubies should fall between 75 to 90 percent, for sapphires between 70 to 95 percent and for emeralds between 65 to 90 percent. Sapphires and rubies with a tone rating of 75 to 80 or 85 usually command premium prices.

Color Scan: The color scan is the analytical process which defines the relationship of the predominant or primary color and the secondary colors present in the gem. (Red is the primary color for ruby, blue for sapphire and green for emerald). The higher the percentage of primary color the more desirable the gem. However, because of the nature of rubies, sapphires and emeralds, the primary color is always modified by additional secondary colors.

Light Source: It is important to view a colored stone in a controlled lighting environment because colored gem materials look different under various lighting conditions. DuroTest: Vita Lite is most commonly used to view colored stones because it is considered the best manufactured source of light.

Comments: You may see comments referring to "dichroic effect," "color zoning" or "texture." Such characteristics would be expressed as being faint, moderate, strong or prominent or a combination of those terms.

"Dichroic effect" means a stone shows two discernible different colors when viewed in the face up position. "Color zoning" means the stone exhibits bands of distinct color in areas of the stone. "Texture" is anything that inhibits light passage through the stone such as a series of tiny inclusions which together cause a fuzzy appearance.

The comments could also refer to an "Estimated Commercial Acceptability" (ECA) rating. Such additional ratings were instituted to reflect the preferences of the gem marketplace.

In addition, the comments section, on a sapphire certificate only, may refer to "heat-induced color alteration present" or "natural sapphire: treated color." Such a color enhancement treatment, though usually considered acceptable, is disclosed on the certificate because it can also cause the stone to exhibit changes such as increased dichroic effect or alter existing inclusions.

Clarity Grade: The clarity grade of a stone is the degree to which it is free from flaws called "inclusions." In diamond grading, clarity is one of the most significant factors affecting the value of the stone. In colored stones, however, clarity is not as important because even the finest quality gemstones usually have some natural inclusions. The clarity scale is from FI or "free of inclusions" to EI_3 or "excessively included." An investor should purchase colored stones with a clarity grade of MI_2 (moderately included) or better.

Proportion: An investment quality stone should have an even, pleasing shape, proper depth percentage, high brilliancy and good finish. The proportion rating is an overall analysis of all the factors affecting the stone's cut and is expressed both on a numerical scale and verbally. This rating should be six or lower for investment quality stones.

Depth %: The depth percentage is an analysis of the stone's proportion determined by dividing the stone's depth by its width. For rubies the depth percentage should generally be between 50 to 85 percent, for sapphires between 50 to 90 percent and emeralds from 45 percent to 85 percent.

Brilliancy %: The stone's brilliancy is the amount of colored light flashes reflected back to the eye through the top of the stone from the bottom. Brilliancy is expressed in percentage amounts, as a range and an average.

Average brilliancy for investment stones should be 40 percent or higher. Stones with average brilliancy of 80 or 100 percent usually command premium prices.

Rubies

Once described as "burning with a kind of inextinguishable fire," the "lord of gems" was thought to have the power to bless those who wore it with health, wealth, wisdom and love. The extremely fine quality ruby, awesome in its fiery splendor, is considered the most valuable of the colored gemstones.

Sapphire

Like the midnight sky, the rich blue sapphire was once revered as the symbol of truth and constancy. Kings sought the lustrous stone as protection from harm and envy, and many believed it had the power to remove impurities from the eyes. Sapphire, from the Latin word meaning blue, is one of the most desirable and precious of gemstones.

Emerald

The elegant emerald has fascinated mankind throughout the ages with its cool, refreshing color and history filled with mystery and superstition. Once dedicated by the Greeks to Venus, the goddess of love, the rich green gemstone was a symbol of immortality and faith. Today, the emerald is one of the most highly prized gems as well as one of the rarest and most valuable.

INVESTMENT GUIDE TO COLORED STONES

The following are suggested parameters for investment grade gemstones:

Rubies

Size: 1 carat or larger

Color Grade:
Color rating 5.5 or better/Tone 75 to 90

Clarity: MI_2 or better

Proportions: "Good" (6) or better
Depth % 50 to 85
Brilliancy % 40 to 100
Finish "Good" (6) or better

Comments:
Do not accept "moderate strong" or "strong" Dichroic effect/Color zoning/Fluorescence

Sapphires

Size: 1 carat or larger

Color Grade:
Color rating 5.5 or better/Tone 70 to 95

Clarity: MI_2 or better

Proportions: "Good" (6) or better
Depth % 50 to 90
Brilliancy % 40 to 100
Finish "Good" (6) or better

Comments:
Do not accept "moderate strong" or "strong" Dichroic effect/Color zoning/Fluorescence

Emeralds

Size: 1 carat or larger

Color Grade:
Color rating 5.5 or better/Tone 65 to 90

Clarity: HI_1 or better

Proportions: "Good" (6) or better
Depth % 45 to 85
Brilliancy % 40 or better
Finish "Good" (6) or better

Comments:
Do not accept "moderate strong" or "strong"
Dichroic effect/Color zoning/Fluorescence

Fine gemstones are attractive as investments because they are rare, beautiful and durable as well as portable and easily stored.

RARE COINS AND CURRENCY

Throughout history coins have been collected because of their artistic beauty and historical value. Because of their realizable value and portability, they have represented an attractive medium for those who wish to protect their assets from economic fluctuations.

Coins were first developed as a medium of exchange in the sixth century B.C. in Asia Minor. The use of coins, and later currency, gradually spread throughout the world as the most convenient and practical means of conducting business. Many forms of coinage have been used throughout history, but traditionally units of gold and silver have proved to be the most stable and lasting. The type of coinage and currency used by a country has generally paralleled its economic stability. The artistry of a country's money is usually a reflection of its culture and of popular styles at the time. Thus, coins and currency are an accurate historical documentation of past and present and are worthy of study and preservation by individuals, scholars and museums.

Valuation of Rare Coins and Currency

The value of rare coins and currency is based on three factors—supply, demand, and quality. The supply of rare coins and currency is obviously limited because no more can ever be produced. In addition, a certain number of items are lost each year through attrition, wear or destruction. The United States Mint began coinage in the late 1700's and until the mid-1930's mintage figures with respect to individual coins were sufficiently low so as to cause most coins minted during the pre-1933 period to be considered as scarce, if not rare. An example is the initial United States silver dollar minted in 1794, with a total of only 1,758 coins, as compared to the 1971 Eisenhower dollar, which was minted for a total of more than 127,000,000 coins. Original mintage volume, however, is not a true measure of the potential value of a coin, since other conditions such as available supply, demand and quality will have even greater weight.

The demand for rare coins and currency, however, has continued to increase as more people become interested in collecting or investing in numismatic material.

Quality or state of preservation is an important aspect of the value of numismatic material. Very few pieces of currency or coinage ever remain in their original state, exactly as when first manufactured. Therefore, perfect uncirculated items, especially older items, are usually extremely rare. Historically, items of higher quality have appreciated in value at a rate much faster than that for similar pieces of lower quality.

Grading of Coins and Currency

The importance of the quality of numismatic material to its value has lead to the development of a standard system of evaluating the state of preservation of an item. For example, United States coins are graded on a 70-point scale established and monitored by the American Numismatic Association, an organization chartered by act of Congress. The ANA has published the Grading Standards Guide which details standards to be used throughout the industry in evaluating the quality of coins. In addition, the ANA maintains a bureau which will render an impartial opinion on the grade of any United States coins submitted for examination and which will certify the authenticity of United States coins to protect purchasers. The ANA grading system includes eight general categories. About Good, Good, Very Good, Fine, Very Fine, Extremely Fine, About Uncirculated, and Mint State. Each of these categories has subdivisions based on degrees of quality within the class. For example, Mint State is divided into five subclasses: Perfect Uncirculated (MS-70), Pristine Uncirculated (MS-67), Choice Uncirculated (MS-65), Select Uncirculated (MS-63), and Typical Uncirculated (MS-60). A grading system for currency similar to the ANA standards for coins has been established by the International Bank Note Society and the Society of Paper Money Collectors. A grading system for foreign coins also exists. That system is similar to the ANA system but contains fewer subdivisions. Generally, United States coins and currency must be of Mint State (Uncirculated) quality (at least MS-60) to be considered of investment grade, although there are exceptions for certain old or scarce items. Foreign coins and certain United States tokens, patterns and private coins may be of investment grade although not meeting the requirements for Mint State quality.

Thc following listing, taken from the ANA Guide Book, illustrates the grading system as it applies to a $10 gold piece:

EAGLES–CORONET HEAD 1838-1907

Mint State *Absolutely no trace of wear.*

MS-70 Uncirculated *Perfect*
A flawless coin exactly as it was minted, with no trace of wear or injury. Must have full mint luster and brilliance. Any unusual die or planchet traits must be described.

MS-65 Uncirculated *Choice*
No trace of wear; nearly as perfect as MS-70 except for some small blemish. Has full mint luster and brilliance but may show slight discoloration. A few barely noticeable bag marks and surface abrasions may be present.

MS-60 Uncirculated *Typical*
A strictly Uncirculated coin with no trace of wear, but with blemishes more obvious than for MS-65. Has full mint luster but may lack brilliance. Surface may be lightly marred by minor bag marks and abrasions.

Check points for signs of wear: hair, coronet; wings.

About Uncirculated *Small trace of wear visible on highest points.*

AU-55 *Choice*
Obverse: There is a trace of wear on hair above eye and on coronet.
Reverse: Trace of wear visible on wing tips.
Three-quarters of the mint luster is still present.

AU-50 *Typical*
Obverse: There is a trace of wear on hair at ear and above eye, and on coronet.
Reverse: Trace of wear visible on wing tips, below eye and on claw. Half of the mint luster is still present.

EAGLES—CORONET HEAD 1838-1907

Extremely Fine *Light wear on only the highest points.*

EF-45 *Choice*

Obverse: There is light wear on coronet, and on hair above ear, eye, forelocks and top of head.

Reverse: Light wear shows on edges and tips of wings, on neck, below eye, and on claws.

Part of the mint luster is still present.

EF-40 *Typical*

Obverse: Light wear shows on coronet, hair, cheek and stars. All major details sharp.

Reverse: Light wear visible on wings, head, neck and claws. Shield is well defined.

Trace of mint luster will show.

Very Fine *Light to moderate even wear. All major features are sharp.*

VF-30 *Choice*

Obverse: There is light wear on coronet, hair and stars but most details are visible. There is a break on top line of coronet over two letters in LIBERTY. Cheekworn. LIBERTY bold.

Reverse: Light wear visible on wings and head but some details show. Vertical lines in shield complete but some are not separated; horizontal lines worn in center.

VF-20 *Typical*

Obverse: Hair worn but major details visible. Break on top line of coronet extends over at least three letters in LIBERTY. Cheek well worn. Stars worn but show most details. LIBERTY clear but shows wear.

Reverse: About half of wing feathers are visible. Very little detail shows in head.

In acquiring rare coins evaluating grade or condition of the coins is of paramount importance, because a variance in grade can cause a large difference in value. Based upon values contained in recent editions of The Coin Dealer's Newsletter and the Currency Market Review, this variance may be shown as follows:

1892-S Morgan Silver Dollar:

Grade	Current Value
Typical Uncirculated (MS-60)	$10,000
Select Uncirculated (MS-63)	$15,000
Choice Uncirculated (MS-65)	$30,000

1922 (Plain) Lincoln Cent:

Typical Uncirculated (MS-60)	$ 3,000
Choice Uncirculated (MS-65)	$ 8,500

1896 One Dollar Silver Certificate:

Crisp Uncirculated	$ 1,000
Choice Uncirculated	$ 1,900
Gem Uncirculated	$ 3,500

Grading may have even larger discrepancies at the lower end of the marketplace, e.g., grades of 10 to 20. Grading is, of course, a significant factor in any appraisal of coins. Grading is a subjective process and is open to dispute among experts.

THE OFFERING

This is an offering of Units of preformation limited partnership interests (the "Units"), in up to five limited partnerships, which will engage primarily in the acquisition of portfolios of United States and foreign rare coins and currency. The minimum aggregate investment in any one Partnership will be no less than $1,000,000 and no more than $5,000,000. The gross offering of $5,000,000 represented by 10,000 Units may all be invested in one Partnership or in up to five Partnerships. A participant will become a limited partner in only the Partnership to which his units relate. The Program's objective is to provide capital appreciation.

Investment Objectives and Policies

Following its formation, a Partnership will purchase its initial grouping of rare coins and currency. The Partnerships will invest primarily in pre-1933 United States coins, pre-1935 United States currency and foreign coins and currency. Only those items of sufficient quality to be considered of investment grade will be purchased by the Partnership. "United States Coins and Currency" include U.S. colonial and private coins and currency as well as tokens or patterns. The General Partners will attempt to diversify the holdings of each Partnership and do not anticipate any problem in diversifying, given the nature of coins and the marketplace.

The principal objective of the Program is to realize capital appreciation upon the sale of coins acquired for Partnership portfolios. No assurances can be given to the extent, if any, to which the Partnerships will be successful in attaining this objective.

Method of Purchase

The General Partner will purchase the coins and currency to be included in the Partnership's portfolios from unrelated parties in arms length transactions. Some of the material purchased may be purchased at auctions. The General Partner will receive from the Partnership acquisition fees equal to 7% of the acquisition cost of the material obtained. In addition, the sellers of material purchased by a Partnership at auctions conducted by the parent or the General Partner will pay a commission of 5% to that company, compared with the industry practice of a 10% commission.

Operations

The Partnership Agreement permits the General Partners to sell items from the Partnerships' portfolios prior to liquidation of the Partnerships and to distribute the proceeds to the Partners. However, the primary purpose of the Partnership is to acquire its portfolio of material and to hold the portfolio for a period of four to six years. There is, therefore, no guarantee that any sales of portfolio materials and the resulting distributions will be made.

The Partnership intends to invest at least 95% of the net proceeds of this offering within one year of the date the issue is closed and to use the balance within the following year.

Disposition of Coin Portfolio

It is presently anticipated that a Partnership's coin portfolio will be sold four to seven years after a Partnership commences operations. The actual sale of the portfolio will depend upon a variety of factors, not presently capable of prediction, including the future value of the coins contained in the portfolio, the availability of buyers, the state of the coin marketplace and the demand for particular coins in a Partnership's portfolio. Disposition may take place over a two year period or more. When all of a Partnership's portfolio coins and currency have been sold, and all sale proceeds have been received, the Partnership will be terminated and dissolved. Funds realized from sales may, pending distribution, be invested in short-term interest bearing securities or in savings accounts with commercial or savings banks. Any Cash Available for Distribution shall be allocated to the Partners in accordance with their interests. Distributions during liquidation shall be on the same basis as regular cash distributions, at least once annually. The General Partners or Affiliates can purchase coins sold by a Partnership, but solely at a public auction. The coins will be stored. Operating costs for storage will be a Partnership expense payable out of the established Reserve Fund. Partnership coins will be maintained separately from the General Partners' and Affiliates' coins.

Annual Liquidation Rights

In consideration of the Partnerships' primarily non-trading and non-income producing status, the Partnership Agreement will contain a liquidation provision allowing a Limited Partner the right to sell all of his interest in a Partnership by requesting the corporate General Partner to liquidate a share of the portfolio equal to his pro rata interest in the Partnership. This right shall not begin until the secondary anniversary of the formation of the Partnership. Formation shall occur when subscription for the minimum capitalization of $1,000,000 are accepted by the General Partners. The share to be liquidated will be based upon the previous yearend portfolio valuation calculated by the General Partners. The sale shall be effected at public auction. Since an auction sale may produce more or less than the yearend portfolio valuation, a withdrawing Limited Partner will receive less than his original investment if that occurs, but a Limited

Partner shall not receive by way of this liquidation privilege any sums in excess of his Net Investment, any excess to be retained for the benefit of the Partnership. Liquidations during any twelve month period after formation of a Partnership shall not exceed five percent (5%) of the Partnership's initial capital. Liquidations shall occur on first come-first served basis. As soon as an amount equal to 5% of initial capital has been liquidated, liquidations for that year will be stopped. Any Limited Partners requesting liquidation but refused because of the 5% limitation will be treated as first in line for the succeeding year's liquidation limits. Liquidation requests must be made in writing to the General Partners. The General Partners will select coins having an estimated value approximately equal to the liquidating Limited Partner's prorata share of the Partnership. Selection will be at the exclusive discretion of the Managing General Partners and will be based upon its determination as to which coins should be sold or held to the best advantage of the Partnership. Liquidation proceeds will be charged the same commissions as would be applicable upon disposition of the partnership's portfolio. Prospective participants should be aware that their aggregate annual liquidation privilege will be significantly less if this Partnership offering is terminated with minimum capitalization rather than maximum capitalization, the range being $50,000 to $250,000.

Competition

There are numerous small and moderate size coin dealers, as well as thousands of individual coin collectors in the United States. In addition, there is at least one limited partnership similar in size and objective to this Program in existence. In general, however, the purchase and sale of coins tends to be made in connection with individual coins or small collections, and there is ease of entry for both buyers and sellers. The General Partners believe that the anticipated size of the Program as well as the experience of the General Partners in the acquisition of coins will enable the Program to compete successfully with other entities in the marketplace. It is possible that the Program's size, if fully funded, could cause adverse price pressure on the marketplace when the Program buys and sells. The General Partners believe that the marketplace is of sufficient size as to make this problem a de minimum risk.

BENEFITS OF A RARE COIN AND CURRENCY PROGRAM

The objective of the Partnerships is to acquire United States and foreign rare coins and currency for investment purposes. The General Partners believe that this will provide investors with a convenient method for participating in an investment medium which has historically demonstrated long-term growth, conservation of capital and the possibility for profits subject to taxation at capital gains (as opposed to ordinary income) rates.

The Partnerships provide the investor with the opportunity for expert assistance in and diversification of an investment in rare coins and currency. Instead of investing in a single item of numismatic material selected by the investor, a Limited Partner will have an interest in a portfolio of rare coins and currency of a Partnership selected by experienced numismatists, including coins and currency of greater scarcity and/or better condition, which tend to appreciate more rapidly than more common or poorer quality coins and currency, than an investor may be able to purchase individually. During the holding period, a Partnership's coins and currency will be held in a safe deposit box, and will be inspected and appraised annually by an independent appraiser.

Rare coins and currency to be purchased by the Partnerships will be held for potential appreciation and long-term capital gain. The General Partners may sell items of rare coins and currency held in the portfolio of a Partnership prior to liquidation. Except in the case of the purchase of Units of withdrawing Limited Partners, in the event that the General Partners dispose of any portion of a Partnership's portfolio, the General Partners will distribute to the Partners the net proceeds of the sale. The primary objective of the Partnerships, however, is to hold the rare coins and currency for purposes of appreciation. Therefore, there can be no assurance that the General Partners will sell any portion of a Partnership's portfolio prior to the period of final liquidation of the Partnership, and consequently there is no assurance that a Partnership will make any cash distribution prior to the liquidation period. Depending upon market conditions, the General Partners intend to hold the Partnership's portfolios of rare coins and currency for approximately 4 to 7 years after their acquisition. In deciding whether to sell a Partnership's numismatic material, the General Partners will consider factors such as capital appreciation, anticipation of market declines or rises based on occurrences in the market place, and the federal income tax considerations such as possible adverse income tax consequences to the Limited Partners. To minimize the tax consequences of a sale, a Partnership's rare coins and currency normally will not be sold until they have been held a sufficient period of time to qualify the sale for treatment as long-term capital gain or loss, as the case may be.

ALLOCATION OF INCOME AND LOSSES AND CREDITS TO PARTNERS

Allocation of Income. Income shall be allocated between General Partners and Limited Partners as follows:

a. The Net Income and Net Loss for a year shall be allocated between the General and Limited Partners three (3%) percent and ninety-seven (97%) percent, respectively, until aggregate Net Income and Net Loss for all years (including such year) is allocated to the Limited Partners in an amount equal to their aggregate Net Investment plus twelve (12%) percent per annum (computed on the basis of simple and not compound interest) of the Net Investment of the Limited Partners outstanding from time to time.

b. Following the allocation to General and Limited Partners of Net Income and Net Loss as set forth in subparagraph a, Net Income and Net Loss shall be allocated as follows: Thirty (30%) percent to General Partners and seventy (70%) percent to the Limited Partners.

Allocation of Credits. All credits shall be allocated between the General and Limited Partners three (3%) percent and ninety-seven (97%) percent, respectively.

CASH AVAILABLE FOR DISTRIBUTION

Time and Manner of Distributions. Cash Available for Distribution shall be distributed to the Partners as cash payments annually or at such more frequent intervals as the General Partners, at their sole discretion, may determine.

Allocation Among Partners. Distributions of Cash Available for Distribution shall be allocated between and paid to the General Partners and Limited Partners as follows:

a. The Cash Available for Distribution shall be allocated between the General and Limited Partners three (3%) percent and ninety-seven (97%) percent, respectively, until total Cash Distributions have been made to the Limited Partners equal to twelve (12%) percent per annum (computed on the basis of simple and not compound interest) of the Net Investment of the Limited Partners outstanding from time to time.

b. Following receipt by the General and Limited Partners of Cash Distributions set forth in subparagraph a, all of the Cash Available for Distribution shall be paid to the Limited Partners until they have received an amount equal to one hundred (100%) percent of their Net Investment.

c. Following receipt by the General and Limited Partners of Cash Distributions set forth in subparagraphs a and b, all of the Cash Available for Distribution shall be allocated as follows: thirty (30%) percent to General Partners and seventy (70%) percent to the Limited Partners.

RISKS OF A RARE COIN AND CURRENCY PROGRAM

1. The Partnerships may concentrate their holdings in a limited number of coins or series. There is no absolute or percentage requirement for diversification. Such limited diversity may produce adverse results for the Partnerships, although the General Partners do not believe this to be a significant risk.

2. *Risks Involved in Rare Coin Business or Collections.* While the prices of numismatic material have trended upward for many years, there can be no assurance that such trend will continue in the future. A major risk is that collector demand for coins acquired by the Partnerships could diminish or disappear and, therefore, the value of the Partnerships' coins would decrease substantially. Liquidity is another major risk, since the Partnerships' ability to sell their portfolios is governed by supply and demand criteria beyond its control. A further risk is involved in the grading of coins and currency, both on purchase and sale. Overgrading on purchase may cause too high a price to be paid and vice-versa on sale. Grading is a subjective process;

experts may differ in their opinions as to the grading of an item.

The Managing General Partners and their Affiliates in their normal operations purchase numismatic material at wholesale and sell numismatic material at retail, with a mark-up of approximately eighteen percent. On behalf of the Partnerships, the Managing General Partners will buy at wholesale and charge a seven percent acquisition fee. Thus, it is probable that the portfolios of the Partnerships will have an immediate retail value significantly higher than the actual cost to the Partnerships, although such higher value cannot be guaranteed and may not be maintained over a period of time.

There is some modest risk of counterfeits. Coins will be examined and evaluated by experienced numismatists prior to purchase, which, in the normal circumstance, will eliminate counterfeits. In addition, General Partner will replace any counterfeit with genuine material, which is consistent with existing policy of Parent or General Partner.

The coin industry is generally characterized by numerous small dealers, although there is at least one other partnership similar in size and objective to this Program in existence. It is possible that, due to their size, the Partnerships, if fully funded, could adversely affect the market for coins when the Partnerships are buying or selling large quantities of coins and currency. Determination of the actual market for coins is difficult due to lack of regulation or required reporting. There may be as many as 20 firms transacting $5-25 million in sales per annum, including auctions, 50-200 firms doing $1-3 million in sales per annum and numerous small dealers transacting $100,000 to $500,000 in sales per annum. Estimates of the overall annual market are between $750 million and $1.5 billion, with trades at the American Numismatic Association's annual convention accounting for $20-40 million alone. The General Partners believe the market is sufficiently broad to allow the Partnerships to purchase or sell their portfolios over a reasonable period of time without a material adverse effect on the market.

3. *Competition.* The buying and selling of rare coins is a highly competitive business. There are numerous collectors and dealers seeking to buy and sell coins at all times. Competition may be at its greatest in connection with the Partnerships'

attempts to acquire rare and valuable coins, as such coins rarely come onto the marketplace and are much sought after. The General Partners believe that the Partnerships, whether funded at minimum or maximum levels, will constitute buyers with substantial financial resources in the marketplace.

4. *Involuntary Liquidation of Portfolio.* The Partnership Agreement permits the withdrawal, commencing two years after a Partnership's formation, of Limited Partners holding up to an aggregate of 5% of the total number of Units from the Partnership in any fiscal year on a first-come, first-served basis. The Partnership Agreement provides that such withdrawing Limited Partners will have their Units repurchased by the Partnership, and that the funds used to repurchase the Units will come from the sale of items in the Partnership portfolio selected by the managing General Partners. Thus, the Partnership could be forced to liquidate a portion of its portfolio at a time which may not be advantageous to the Partnership. In addition, a withdrawing Limited Partner will not receive more than his Net Investment upon withdrawal.

TAX ASPECTS OF A RARE COIN AND CURRENCY PROGRAM

1. *Sale or Other Disposition of Partnership Properties.* Based on the representations of the General Partners that a Partnership will not be engaged in the trade or business of dealing in coins or currency, that Partnership assets will be held for investment and not for resale, that Partnership assets will not be held primarily for sale to customers in the ordinary course of a trade or business, and that the Partnership will not sell coins and reinvest the proceeds in other coins, Partnership investments will be capital assets as defined in Section 1221, rather than inventory. Therefore, gains or losses from the sale of the properties will be capital gains or losses. If the capital asset disposed of had been held by a Partnership for more than twelve months, the result is a long-term capital gain or loss. If the asset was held less than twelve months, short-term capital gain or loss would result.

As a result of the Tax Reform Act of 1978, beginning January 1, 1979, taxation of long-term capital gains have received increased benefits, as follows: (1) Only 40% of an individual's long-term capital gain is taken into ordinary income to be taxed at regular rated instead of 50% prior to the Act, (2) the 60% of long-term capital gain which is excluded from income is no longer a preference subject to the 15% add-on minimum tax on preference income, but instead is a preference subject to a newly enacted alternative minimum tax with graduated rates, and (3) personal service (earned) income eligible for the 50% maximum tax is no longer reduced by any capital gains tax preference. Effectively, the maximum tax on capital gains (ignoring the preference tax) is 28%.

2. *Sale of Units by Limited Partners.* Gain or loss recognized by a Limited Partner who is not a "dealer" in Units on the sale of a Unit that has been held for more than one year will generally be taxable as long-term capital gain or loss.

3. *Minimum Tax for Tax Preferences.* The Tax Reform Act of 1976 imposes a minimum tax or "tax preference" in a given taxable year equal to 15% of the amount by which an individual taxpayer's aggregate "tax preferences" exceed the greater of $10,000 ($5,000 in the case of a married taxpayer filing a separate return) or one-half the regular tax liability (reduced by certain credits) for such year.

The Revenue Act of 1978 modified the minimum tax provisions referred to in the foregoing paragraph by excluding the capital gains tax preference in years subsequent to 1978. For non-corporate taxpayers, the capital gains tax preference, with some modifications, will be subject to the new "alternative minimum tax" for taxable years beginning after December 31, 1978. Further, the minimum tax referred to in the foregoing paragraph will be no longer payable if the new alternative minimum tax exceeds the total of regular taxes and the minimum tax. The taxable base subject to the alternative minimum tax will be computed by adding taxable income, capital gains excluded from taxable income, and the tax preference for adjusted itemized deductions. The taxable base, reduced by a $20,000 exemption, will be subject to alternative minimum tax rates ranging from 10% to 25% on amounts ranging from less than $40,000 to over $80,000. As a result, capital gains would no longer reduce the amount of personal service income eligible for the maximum tax. The 1978 Act also repealed the 25% alternative tax on the first $50,000 of net long-term capital gain. As a result of these changes, the maximum capital gains tax rate (ignoring preference tax) for noncorporate taxpayers will be 28% (40% of the highest individual tax rate of 70% since the capital gain exclusion is now 60%).

A Partnership itself is not subject to tax, but the Partners will be required to take into account their respective shares of the Partnership's tax preference items.

4. *Taxable Income in Excess of Cash Distributions.* It is possible that in a given year the taxable net income allocated to the Limited Partners by a Partnership will be in excess of the Cash Distributions actually made. This situation is particularly likely to occur in the event of an involuntary liquidation of Partnership assets to satisfy the withdrawal rights of Limited Partners. In such an event, it is possible that a Limited Partner's tax liability for the year would be greater than the cash distributed by the Partnership.

5. *Tax Exempt Organizations.* Certain entities, including trusts formed as part of pension or profitsharing plans, including Individual Retirement Accounts, which are qualified under Section 401(a) of the Code, and certain charitable and other organizations described in Section 501(c), are subject to tax upon their "unrelated business taxable income" even though they are otherwise tax exempt. Income from a Partnership allocable to a qualified pension or profit-sharing plan from a Partnership will not, under current statutes, regulations and judicial interpretations, be subject to the unrelated business income tax. Such plans will not be required to pay federal income taxes on income allocable from the Partnerships, but such plans also will not be allowed to deduct any losses allocated from the Partnerships. It is possible, although considered doubtful, that if a 501(c) organization becomes a Limited Partner in the Partnership, the income allocable to it will be unrelated business taxable income and, thus, subject to tax. Such tax-exempt organizations are advised to consult with tax counsel regarding these issues.

A successful investment in precious gems and rare coins and currency can yield substantial capital gains.

Chapter Nine

INVESTMENT BANKING

This is an interesting opportunity to make money in the securities business. Investment banking plays an essential role in the financial movement of the economy and is described as follows.

The current mood of the investor coupled with recent and proposed federal tax legislation offers the prospective raiser of equity capital the greatest opportunities in many years. All aspects of equity financing, new issues and secondary stock offerings, partnership and tax shelter formations, are expected to benefit from this current mood.

Because even the finest equity financing can be forestalled without the retailing capability of an investment banking firm, it is important when planning an equity financing to be aware of what an investment banker generally requires and what type of investment banker fills the need of the borrower. The following comments should be helpful in making those decisions.

I. Regional or National Firm

1. Before showing an equity package to an investment banker one should first determine what one expects of that firm and what type of firm is best suited for him. Some investment bankers are better suited for tax shelters than they are for cash flow investments. Others may be great in bringing a company public but not so great at placing a secondary stock offering of a seasoned company. Another obvious concern is the amount of equity capital being raised. Investment bankers are regulated as to the amount of their capital they can commit at any one time to underwriting functions, therefore, very large securities offerings can only be handled by very large investment bankers. Another consideration is what market penetration is expected. In a limited partnership, it is important to note that unit size (minimum investment) of many 242 and 146 offerings will preclude firms with a small account base because of the large

minimum investment. In a secondary stock offering, it may be important to an issuer to geographically expand its ownership base, consequently that issuer would not want a localized firm with local distribution capabilities underwriting its issue.

It is very important when selecting an investment banker for an equity offering to first review the capabilities of various firms and select one or two that fit your needs. Nothing can be more damaging to a new issuer than to have "shopped" the offering. Immediately an investment banker looks for problems when he discovers the equity package he is reviewing has been shopped to several other underwriters. The best approach to a prospective underwriter is to tell the underwriter that he was carefully selected and the reasons why he was selected. Immediately you have put him into a position of reviewing your package with assurance that his firm was selected on a qualitative basis, not as a last resort.

2. Given this background, the following is suggested as a guide in choosing an investment banker:

a) Tax Shelter Investment. Typically, the tax sheltered investments have high minimum purchase requirements and high suitability standards. Therefore, underwriters should be chosen who have a minimum of seventy-five salesmen and at least a moderate ($1½-$3 million) capital base. Regional or national firm is acceptable.

A typical salesman covers between 150 and 200 customers. A firm with 75 salesmen is exposed to between 11,250 and 15,000 retail customers of which a minimum of 10% generally will meet high suitability requirements. The capital base is important because a firm of this size can accept the risk of marketing these types of investments.

b) Limited Partnerships Non-Sheltered. If filing is 146 or 242 with large minimum investments, the same selection criterial as (a) apply. If filing is a Regulation A or 147, a smaller specialized firm may be selected.

c) New Issue Full Registration. Regional or national is not as important as the kind of continuing relationship that is expected of the issuer. Typically a national firm will not maintain as close a continuing relationship with a new public company as a regional will. More is expected of an investment banker in a new issue than just underwriting the stock. A secondary market must be maintained after the issuance, therefore, the underwriter should have a strong over-the-counter trading capability. To support the secondary trading in the new stock, it is helpful for the underwriter to also have a good respected research department that will follow and report on the company, therefore, the underwriter should have such a capability. To insure a wide distribution of the stock, the underwriter should have strong syndicate ties so that he can bring many other underwriters into the offering. If an investment banker fits these criteria and has the capital base to underwrite the size expected, a successful financing can take place.

d) Secondary Stock Offerings. Most such companies have strong investment banking ties by the time they require additional equity capital. If not, however, it is the time to be most selective. All the criterial in (c) apply, but obviously the investment banker who originally brought the company public either was not selected properly the first time or he is now out of business. In either case the criteria laid out in (c) should be followed.

II. Structure Requirements of Limited Partnerships from the Investment Bankers Prospective

An underwriter's primary interest in any limited partnership is to protect and enhance the investment of the limited partners. Certain standard structures for limited partnerships have evolved in the brokerage business.

1. Allocation of Cash Flow and Capital Gains. The rule of thumb is 99% to the limited partners and 1% to the general partner until the limited partners are made whole on their investment. In many cases a rate of return is applied to the limited partners' cash flow before they are considered whole, for example, 100% of investment plus 7% annual return before the general partner's split increases. After the pay back period, the split becomes less defined. However, it is generally 65%-75% limited to 35%-25% general. In some cases the limited partners are given an even greater percentage but rarely will an investment

banker consider a program with less. Capital gains on the sale or refinancing of the partnership's property are generally allocated just as post pay back cash flow.

2. Allocation of Taxable Income or Loss. 99% to the limited partner, generally over the life of the partnership.

3. General Partner's Role. General Partners are evaluated against three basic criteria; financial substance, management skill and general reputation and character. A General Partner should provide stability and continuity for the partnership, which is a passive investment for the limited partners.

The General Partner is generally required to have a financial stake in the Partnership. Schemes which attempt to leverage "sweat equity" and development expenses are not as attractive as those which show the General Partner making a reasonable financial commitment to the project.

The General Partner must have adequate net worth to support the project. This consideration goes beyond the equity contribution of the General Partner and looks to the ability of the General Partner to provide or obtain interim or additional financing as required by the Partnership.

The General Partner also provides the basic management skill and continuity to support the Partnership. The General Partner should be able to provide the project with a unique skill; continuity of management and prior experience are closely evaluated. The General Partner manages the Partnership investment and must be able to account for the Limited Partnership interests, report the results of operations, and provide tax information to the Limited Partners.

The General Partner often receives a fee for services rendered in the management of the Partnership. These fees should be reasonable and approximate those charged in an arms-length transaction. There are often transactions between the Partnership and affiliates of the General Partner. Again these transactions are scrutinized to make certain that any charges to the Partnership are fair and do not pervert the form of the transaction to pass monies to the General Partner which are substantially a pay-back of the General Partner equity.

General Partners are also expected to have sound reputations. The most obvious problems such as bankruptcy or failed projects pose substantial disclosure problems. But, a more subtle evaluation is made of the reputation of the General Partner in general.

III. Timing in Selecting an Investment Banker

Selection timing in retaining the services of an investment banker is dependent upon the securities to be offered. The lead time necessary for a secondary offering of equity for a reporting company is much shorter than for an initial issuance of stock for a non-reporting company. Generally the following guidelines should apply:

1. Limited Partnerships. After discussing with counsel the program and general structural ideas for a partnership, it is advisable to immediately seek out an underwriter. All underwriters want some input into the structural aspects of a limited partnership. Their involvement early will save re-writes later. Nothing is worse for a general partner than to find out major changes are required in a registrational statement already filed.

2. Initial Issues of Equity. A company desiring to "go public" should begin its investment banking ties many months before the targeted date of sale. If chosen early an investment banker is invaluable in aiding the company's planning. A good widget manufacturer may have a trusted general counsel who has served him well in the conduct of his everyday business, but has never dealt with the intricacies of filing with the S.E.C. He may have a great C.P.A. who performed textbook annual audits, but have they heard of the firm in Peoria? An investment banker can aid in the proper selection of a finance term and is indispensable when discussions of market timing and price earnings multiples are considered.

3. Secondary Offerings of Reporting Companies. The key here is whether the company has a long standing relationship with an underwriter and is pleased with that relationship. If the answer is yes, that underwriter should be brought in a few months before the expected target date. It is important to note that if the investment banker has a relationship with you and has a good research department, he is probably issuing reports on your stock from time to time. Don't put him in the embarassing position of perceived conflict when issuing a research

report the day before he is retained and announced as the underwriter for a secondary issue.

If the choice is to seek a new banker, it is best for the company to wait until it is near filing with the S.E.C. If a company is actively talking to the "street," the plans for an offering are not a secret for long and could have a damaging effect on the price of its stock.

IV. Potential for Equity Offering in the 80's

The investment banking community views the 80's as offering an exciting opportunity for equity financing. To put their reasoning in better light, one must have an overview of why the 70's was such a bad period for equities.

1. The need by corporations in the early 70's to leverage their capital.

2. Adverse tax laws affecting both corporations and investors.

3. ERISA and its implication on equity holdings in pension plan portfolios.

4. Dow Jones average at all time lows relative to price earnings ratio's of its components (exception 1930-34).

5. Double digit inflation and double digit interest rates.

6. Adversary relationship of the federal government.

What does the 80's offer that the 70's did not?

1. Corporations cannot afford to leverage their capital at interest rates for long term debt at 14%-16%.

2. Recent tax code revisions with proposed changes make equity investment very attractive.

3. ERISA managers are more comfortable along with equity positions in their portfolio's.

4. Dow Jones average at eight year high with universal expectations of all time high in the near future. Components are trading at higher multiples than in the last ten years.

5. The prospect for increased inflationary pressure bringing investors to equities as an inflation hedge.

6. A cooperative federal government.

In summary, if a corporation is seeking to raise capital through the issuance of equity, whether for recapitalization or expansion, the time is now. It may not be a repeat of the roaring go-go 60's, but certainly portends to be the solid 80's. Once again long range capital planning can occur to replace the short term crisis planning of recent years.

The assistance of James P. Lovay of Manley, Bennett, McDonald & Co. in the preparation of this material is gratefully acknowledged.

An investment banking offering is set forth in the following example.

INVESTMENT BANKING

PLAN OF BUSINESS

The Partnership was formed to engage in general investment banking activities at the wholesale and private syndication level, as opposed to the retail securities business. The Partnership plans to conduct its general investment banking and securities underwriting and syndication business, which will include consulting, real estate, national resources, financial and venture capital activities. The Partnership may also engage in the future in, among other things, real estate brokerage, mortgage banking and brokerage, insurance brokerage, investment and advisory activities, business, financial, real estate, retail, economic and governmental consulting, insurance brokerage, equipment leasing and other types of lending and financial business in related areas, as well as oil and gas, mining, and real estate development, operation and management. The Partnership will buy and sell securities as a broker for clients in private transactions outside of the public trading markets and will do so in the public trading markets on a limited basis, primarily at the wholesale or block trading, as opposed to the retail, level. Occasionally the Partnership may act as a dealer for its own account and risk with its own capital resources but any activity in this area will be limited due to its small capitalization. The Partnership reserves the right to expand its fields of business into any other area, including without limitation, the general retail securities business. The Partnership intends to expand and establish contacts with the various financial centers throughout the United States and Europe as rapidly as its limited resources will reasonably permit.

For the foreseeable future, the Partnership will operate on a "fully disclosed" basis, and therefore will not hold customers' securities and will not have any discretionary accounts. Its limited clearing or "back-room" functions and operations will be performed under an omnibus account agreement with the office of another registered broker-dealer yet to be identified.

The Partnership may also act as a market-maker in certain issues of securities, but initially contemplates no significant activities in this regard. Performance of a "market-making" function is accomplished by making bids for and offerings of the security in question on a continuous and competitive basis in response to inquiries from retail and wholesale customers. Purchases in this process are primarily made for the purpose of reselling as soon as possible. The Partnership will sell for its own account and at times will sell securities it does not own (selling short) with the intent of purchasing securities to deliver against these "short" contracts as soon as possible in the open market.

The Partnership plans to function as a securities underwriter in various issues from time to time, both as an originator and as a participant in nationwide and statewide syndicates, as either the sole or co-underwriter in these issues. The Partnership will also assist in the private placement of securities, as well as act as a dealer in selling groups organized by other underwriters.

In all of these transactions, there can be no assurance that the Partnership can purchase or sell securities at a profit and losses may in the future be incurred as a result of a change in the market price of a particular security that is adverse to the Partnership's position in that security.

The Partnership plans to deal in all media of the investment banking business, including, without limitation, stocks, bonds, notes, securities options, mortgages, debentures, warrants, obligations, contracts, investment contracts, commodities, evidences of indebtedness or securities of all types as defined under the Securities Act of 1933 of any private or public corporation, government or subdivision thereof or municipality, trusts, syndicates, partnerships, associations, joint ventures or individuals for its own account or for the account of others.

The Partnership will be regulated by and must comply with various federal, state and quasi-governmental agencies and applicable rules, regulations and statutes. The Securities and Exchange Commission will have jurisdiction over the business of the Partnership under the Securities Exchange Act of 1934 and its rules, which generally prescribe the sales methods, record keeping, capital and reporting requirements for securities dealers, and the Partnership will be registered as a broker-dealer thereunder prior to the start of its operations. The Partnership will be required to comply with the "net capital" rule promulgated by the Securities and Exchange Commission under the

Securities Exchange Act of 1934. The Partnership will have minimum net capital of at least the $25,000 necessary for its preliminary activities. It is possible that future activities may give rise to increases in the amount of the net capital it requires to do business. The Securities Act of 1933 regulates the registration of securities sold to the public, and the Partnership will be most directly affected by that Act when it acts as an underwriter of such securities.

The Partnership will also, before beginning operations, become registered as a broker-dealer in the State of Michigan, whose Uniform Securities Act requires that employees and General Partners conduct the Partnership's business in accordance with certain laws, rules and regulations. The Partnership may become licensed as a broker-dealer in other states as the General Partners deem advisable in their sole and exclusive discretion and upon such registration it will become subject to regulation by those states.

Prior to beginning broker-dealer operations, the Partnership will become a member in the National Association of Securities Dealers, Inc., ("NASD"), which exercises supervision over member firms and has the power to expel from the NASD or otherwise discipline members who fail to observe the rules, regulations and other standards of the NASD. In its application to the NASD for membership, the Partnership has requested both an exemption from the financial and operations principal requirement and a waiver of the NASD's normal requirement that broker-dealers employ two registered NASD qualified principals. Since the Partnership's clearing or "back-room" operations and services will be performed for the Partnership on a "fully disclosed" basis, under an omnibus account agreement with the office of another registered broker-dealer yet to be identified or engaged, the need for a financial and operations principal in the Partnership's operation is obviated. The Managing General Partner will be the general securities principal required by NASD rules and will manage the day-to-day business operations of the Partnership.

Membership in the NASD, as well as registration as a securities broker-dealer with the Securities and Exchange Commission and the State of Michigan is contingent upon sale of the minimum number (20) of Units hereunder in order to meet the minimum net capital and bonding requirements of the NASD, the Securities and Exchange Commission and the State of Michigan.

In addition to the foregoing, the Partnership is considering whether and when to organize two wholly-owned corporations, one of which would become licensed in Michigan as a real estate broker (primarily to entitle the Partnership to receive commissions on the sales of business) and the other of which would become licensed in Michigan as a finder.

TERMS OF THE OFFERING

The offer is made to investors to become limited partners in a limited partnership called Hopkins Lynch Smith & Co. Units will be sold for a purchase price of $12,500, and each Unit is subject to an additional Assessment of $6,500. (See "Assessments.") $7,000 of the purchase price per Unit is due upon execution of the Agreement or a Subscription Agreement, along with a Promissory Note for $5,500 which becomes due four months after the date on which a minimum of 20 of the initial 30 Units offered have been sold, or four months after the date on which such note is issued, whichever is later.

Default in any portion of the Purchase Price or Assessment for any Units purchased shall constitute a default in payment and cause an acceleration of the purchase price of all Units being purchased by a Partner, unless such default is cured within thirty days thereafter.

While the purchaser of all or a fractional interest in the Units of any defaulting Limited Partner must agree to make payment of any unpaid purchase price or Assessments due or coming due in the future with respect thereto, the defaulting Limited Partner will remain primarily liable at all times for all such payments until they are made and will continue at all times to be primarily liable for any deficiency if his Units cannot be sold or can only be sold for an amount less than his unpaid purchase price and/or Assessments. All such unpaid items shall be accelerated to become due and payable as of the date of default unless cured within thirty days thereafter. The Partnership shall have a lien upon the defaulted Units to secure all such defaulted payments. The Partnership has no duty to undertake to sell any of the defaulted Units or to obtain any particular price or terms of sale thereof, and the Partnership or any one or more General or Limited Partners may compete in the foreclosure sale of defaulted Units and may purchase from the defaulting Limited

Partner as aforesaid on the same terms as are contained hereunder without further authorization from other Limited or General Partners. If more than one General Partner wish to bid in the foreclosure sale, they must first designate a partner of a national firm of certified public accountants with offices in at least 25 states to determine whether or not to bid for the Partnership and, if so, to manage the Partnership's bidding procedures and decisions in such a sale. Any such accounting partner in this regard shall be immune from any suit, claim or action with regard to his activities in this matter by or in the right of any Partner, so long as they were in good faith and did not involve intentional wrongdoing on the part of the accounting partner.

A Limited Partner, in the event of a default for over thirty days on his deferred Purchase Price or any Assessment, shall be liable for the unpaid portion of the Purchase Price or Assessment for Units that were to be purchased hereunder, provided that the defaulting Limited Partner shall have no right to any income, profit, gain, losses, deductions or credits on the defaulted Units during the period of such default. The number of Units that are subject to the default provisions shall be reduced to the extent that any deferred purchase price or Assessment is recovered, net of any use of the proceeds of such recovery to cover the costs, expenses and legal fees to recover such proceeds. The Units previously purchased by the defaulting Limited Partner shall secure payment of the defaulted purchase price and/or defaulted Assessments, plus interest at 17% per annum, compounded monthly, or the highest legal rate of interest, whichever is lower, with all rights to enforce such security interest as are provided in the Michigan Uniform Commercial Code. The Partnership shall be entitled to cancel any subscription agreement for defaulted Units and to foreclose said security interest, claiming the full amount of the defaulted purchase price and Assessment plus the aforesaid interest as liquidated damages or to affirm the subscription agreement and to sue for such amounts as the measure of liquidated damages under the Agreement. By pursuing either remedy, the Partnership shall not be deemed to have elected one remedy or the other until full recovery or relief is accorded to the Partnership pursuant to a final judgment by a court of competent jurisdiction.

Investors purchasing Units hereunder may be required to make additional capital contributions to the Partnership from time to time up to a maximum of $6,500. (See "Assessments.")

Until the minimum number (20) of Units are sold, and the Partnership receives approximately simultaneous clearance to become a member of the NASD, and become registered as a securities broker-dealer with the Securities and Exchange Commission and the State of Michigan, the proceeds of sales of the Units will be held in a special interest bearing account for the sole benefit of subscribers with Bank of Detroit and will bear interest from the date of deposit in the account at the annual rate of 5¼% interest compounded daily. Unless at least the minimum number (20) of Units are sold and the aforesaid clearance and registrations are obtained within 180 days from the date hereof, the offering will terminate, none of the shares will be deemed to have been sold and all monies received will be returned in full with the aforesaid interest to subscribers. If the minimum number (20) Units are sold, such interest will be payable to the Partnership.

The Units offered hereunder will not be registered under the Securities Act of 1933, as amended (the "Act") or the Michigan Uniform Securities Act, as amended (the "Michigan Act"). The offering is made pursuant to a claim of exemption from registration under Section 4(2) and Rule 146 of the Act and Section 402(b)(9) and Rule 803.2 of the Michigan Act. The investors bear a risk insofar as there are restrictions on resale. There is no warranty or guarantee that any portion of any investor's contribution will be returned in full. In conjunction with the sale of Units, each investor will be required to represent that the Units being acquired are for the investor's own account for investment and not with a view for distribution.

Except under the limited circumstances and terms provided in the Agreement that require the consent of the General Partners, the Units may not be sold, transferred or otherwise disposed of by an investor and must therefore be held indefinitely, unless they are hereafter registered under the Act and the applicable state securities laws, or an exemption from registration under the Act and the applicable state securities law is available. The investors have no right to require registration under the Act, the Michigan Act, or any state securities law, and registration is neither contemplated nor likely.

USE OF PROCEEDS

The maximum and minimum net proceeds of this offering to the Partnership, after deduction of broker-dealer sales commissions, finder's fees and estimated expenses, are as follows:

	Maximum		Minimum	
Proceeds of Offering (1)		$375,000		$250,000
Less: Commissions and Fees	$37,500		$25,000	
Total offering expenses (including legal, accounting and printing)	$23,000	$ 60,500	$23,000	$ 48,000
Net Proceeds		$314,500		$202,000

(1) In accordance with the Agreement, Limited Partners may be required to make additional capital contributions to the Partnership from time to time up to a maximum of $6,500. (See "Assessments.") If the maximum Assessment is made, the net proceeds to the Partnership will be $509,500 if 30 Units are sold and $332,000 if the minimum number of 20 Units are sold.

The Partnership intends to use the net proceeds of this offering for working capital purposes to meet salaries and the operating expenses of the Partnership's business. The Partnership has no present intention to own any substantial physical assets to be used in its day-to-day operations.

CAPITALIZATION

The capitalization of the Partnership as of the date of this material and as adjusted to reflect the sale of Units offered hereunder is as follows, immediately after the sale of Units hereunder and prior to any use of proceeds (except for estimated maximum brokers, commissions and finder's fees and offering expenses) or any additional Assessments:

	As of the Date hereof	As Adjusted 20 Units (1)	As Adjusted 30 Units
Class I General Partnership Interests (2)	–	–	–
Class II General Partnership Interests (2)	–	–	–
Class I Units of Limited Partnership Interests	–	$202,000	$314,000
Class II Units of Limited Partnership Interests (2)	–	–	–
Class III Units of Limited Partnership Interests	–	–	–

(1) No portion of the capital contribution of any Limited Partner purchasing Units hereunder may be diluted by transfer to the capital account of any other Partner as a result of this offering. From time to time, in the event deemed advisable by the General Partners in their sole and exclusive discretion, the General Partners may sell additional Units or may create additional classes of Limited Partnership Interests at any price and on any terms and conditions that they may determine to be fair and reasonable in light of the then existing circumstances, without limitations as to the amount of such sales, provided that the terms of such sales are reasonable in light of the circumstances then prevailing.

(2) Although not paid-in, the general personal credit of the General Partners (estimated without audit to be at least $900,000 in aggregate net worth) is available to the Partnership, except to the event limited by agreement of particular Partnership creditors with respect to particular Partnership liabilities, by virtue of their agreements to act as General Partners.

ASSESSMENTS

Limited Partners (except for Messrs. Lynch, Harmon and Nathan and the trusts established by Messrs. Hopkins and Smith) may be required to make additional capital contributions to the Partnership ("Assessments") from time to time up to a maximum of $6,500 during the fifteen-month period commencing eight months after sale of the first 20 of the initial 30 Units offered hereunder, if and only if the Partnership's capital is reduced below $100,000 at any time during the fifteen-month period, commencing on the date of sale of a minimum of 20 of the initial 30 Units offered and computed in accordance with generally accepted accounting principles as in effect on the date hereof, applied on a consistent basis. The General Partners may make such Assessments up to the maximum amount in a single request or in a series of requests. The cash "down payment" portion of the purchase price of any of the initial 30 Units sold after any Assessment shall be increased by the aggregate amount of all Assessments levied per Unit through the date any such Unit is sold.

In order to make any Assessment, the General Partners shall include with the written call for such Assessment a statement of the purpose and intended use of the proceeds from such Assessment. The Limited Partners shall be liable for the Assessment during the aforesaid fifteen-month period. Thereafter, the Limited Partners shall not be liable for an Assessment.

If payment of any Assessment is not received within 30 days following mailing of the written request therefor from the General Partners, the General Partners may at their option request some or all non-defaulting Limited Partners or any third parties to make up such Assessments or may do so themselves. No other Limited or General Partners shall be required to make payment upon any such defaulted Assessment, and no Partner shall have a right to make up such Assessment, despite the fact that other Partners are doing so.

Default in any portion of the purchase price or Assessment for any Units purchased shall constitute a default in payment and an acceleration of the purchase price of all Units being purchased by a Partner, unless such default is cured within thirty days thereafter.

While the purchaser of all or a fractional interest in the Units of any defaulting Limited Partner must agree to make payment of any unpaid purchase price or Assessments due or coming due in the future with respect thereto, the defaulting Limited Partner will remain primarily liable at all times for all such payments until they are made and will continue at all times to be primarily liable for any deficiency if his Units cannot be sold or can only be sold for an amount less than his unpaid purchase price and/or Assessments. All such unpaid items shall be accelerated to become due and payable as of the date of default unless cured within thirty days thereafter. The Partnership shall have a lien to secure all such defaulted payments upon the defaulted Units. The Partnership has no duty to undertake to sell any of the defaulted Units or to obtain any particular price or terms of sale thereof and the Partnership or any one or more General or Limited Partners may compete in the foreclosure sale of defaulted Units and may purchase from the defaulting Limited Partner as aforesaid on the same terms and contained hereunder without further authorization from other Limited or General Partners. If more than one General Partner wishes to bid in the foreclosure sale, they must first designate a partner of a national firm of certified public accountants with offices in at least 25 states to determine whether or not to bid for the Partnership and, if so, to manage the Partnership's bidding procedures and decisions in such a sale. Any such accounting partner in this regard shall be immune from any suit, claim or action with regard to his activities in this matter by or in the right of any Partner, so long as they were in good faith and did not involve intentional wrongdoing on the part of the accounting partner.

THE PARTNERSHIP

Partnership Allocations

Subject to certain deferrals of the General Partners' rights in the profits, losses, deductions and credits of the Partnership to assure that no Partners sustain a loss in their capital accounts while other Partners earn a profit in their profit accounts, the income, profit, gain, losses, deductions and credits resulting from operations of the Partnership after the date on which the minimum number (20) of Units has been sold hereunder will be allocated pursuant to the following percentages:

The purchasers of the Units offered hereunder will be known as "Class I Limited Partners" and will be allocated income, profit, gain, losses, deductions and credits of the Partnership in accordance with the following provisions, containing three distinct stages:

(i) During the period from the date when the minimum number (20) of Units have been sold hereunder to the end of the Partnership tax year ending on December 31, Year Two, unless such period is sooner terminated in accordance with the provisions of (iii)(b) below, the Partners shall be allocated the income, profit, gain, losses, deductions and credits as follows (hereinafter referred to as "Original P & L Ratios"):

Limited Partners

Allocated 99% of the income, profit, gain, losses, deductions and credits according to the following percentages:

Class I Limited Partners (allocated pro rata based on the number of Units then held)	99%
Class II Limited Partners	0%
Class III Limited Partners	0%

General Partners

Allocated 1% of the income, profit, gain, losses, deductions and credits according to the following percentages:

Class I General Partners	1%
Class II General Partners	0%

If the Class I Limited Partners are required to contribute any Assessments, the above percentages shall apply as well during the Partnership tax year ending on December 31, Year Three, unless such period is sooner terminated in accordance with the provisions of (iii)(b) below, provided that if the Class I Limited Partners have been allocated losses equal to their capital contributions (including all Assessments, if any) as of Year Two, then the Intermediate P & L Ratios (see below) shall be the basis for allocating the income, profit, gain, losses, deductions and credits of the Partnership. Notwithstanding the foregoing, the Class I Limited Partners shall not be entitled to any portion of the income, profit, gain, losses, deductions and credits which accrue to the Partnership prior to the date upon which the minimum number (20) of Units have been sold in the Partnership's initial offering.

(ii) From and after the date on which the allocations set forth in (i) shall terminate and until the earlier occurrence of either event set forth in (iii), the income, profit, and gain, losses, deductions and credits of the Partnership shall be reallocated among the Partners according to the following percentages (hereinafter referred to as "Intermediate P & L Ratios"):

Limited Partners

Allocated 85 2/3% of the income, profit, gain, losses, deductions and credits according to the following percentages:

Class I Limited Partners (allocated pro rata based on the number of Units then held)	75%
Class II Limited Partners	6 2/3%
Class III Limited Partners	4%

General Partners

Allocated 14 1/3% of the income, profit, gain, losses, deductions and credits according to the following percentages:

Class I General Partners	1%
Class II General Partners	13 1/3%

(iii) The Class II and Class III Limited Partnership Interests shall increase and the Class I Limited Partnership Interests shall correspondingly decrease from the Initial or Intermediate P & L Ratio levels at any time in any taxable year in the manner outlined below upon the earlier of the following events:

(a) The Partnership has pre-tax earnings in excess of $100,000 after payment of any bonuses to General Partners and other employees, computed on an audited basis according to generally accepted accounting principles as in effect on the date hereof, applied on a consistent basis, for two (2) consecutive Partnership tax years, or

(b) Each Limited Partner has received cash distributions equal to his capital contributions(including all Assessments, if any), plus a 10% return per-year compounded annually on the declining balance of his capital contribution (including all Assessments, if any) at any time in any taxable year.

Upon the occurrence of either such event, the income, profit, gain, losses, deductions and credits of the Partnership shall be reallocated among the Partners according to the following percentages (hereinafter referred to as "Normal P & L Ratios"):

Limited Partners

Allocated 65 2/3% of the income, profit, gain, losses, deductions and credits according to the following percentages:

Class I Limited Partners (allocated pro rata based on the number of Units then held)	45%
Class II Limited Partners	16 2/3%
Class III Limited Partners	4%

General Partners

Allocated 34 1/3% of the income, profit, gains, losses, deductions and credits according to the following percentages:

Class I General Partners	1%
Class II General Partners	33 1/3%

(iv) The Partnership has already commenced operations on a minimal basis and all income, profit, gain, losses, deductions and credits resulting from these initial operations that are realized and recognized for tax purposes prior to the sale of the minimum number (20) of Units offered hereunder will be allocated in the following manner:

General Partners

Class I General Partners (1/3% each to Hopkins, Lynch and Smith	1%
Glass II General Partners Lynch 31 2/3%, Hopkins 15 5/6% and Smith 15 5/6%)	63 1/3%

Limited Partners

Class II Limited Partners (15 5/6% each to the Hopkins Irrevocable Trust and the Smith Irrevocable Trust)	31 2/3%
Class III General Partners (2% each to Harmon and Nathan)	4%

The General Partners will have, in their sole and exclusive discretion, the option to pay out to Partners net pretax income, if any, computed on the cash as opposed to the accrual basis, which is not required for operations. The General Partners shall use their best efforts to distribute at least sufficient cash to enable the Partners to pay any federal or Michigan income taxes reasonably anticipated on the Partnership's income. Sufficient cash in this regard shall be deemed to be at least 60% of the Partnership's taxable income for any taxable year. Aside from this discretionary distribution possibility, there shall be no distributions of cash or other properties of the Partnership until termination of the Partnership which shall occur not later than a date forty years from now.

PLAN OF DISTRIBUTION

The Partnership intends to offer the Units on a "best efforts" basis directly for its own account and may offer and sell the Units through broker-dealers who are members in good standing of the National Association of Securities Dealers, Inc. ("NASD") and registered as broker-dealers in the State of Michigan. A commission of 10% of the purchase price will be paid to broker-dealers for each Unit sold by them. The Partnership may also employ the services of registered investment advisors licensed to do business as a finder in the State of Michigan. On Units not sold by NASD broker-dealers, investment advisers registered as finders will receive a finder's fee (consideration) equal to 10% of the purchase price for Units sold to investors located, introduced or referred by them to the Partnership. No more than 10% of the purchase price will be paid in finder's fees or broker's commissions on any particular Unit sold and no portion of a broker's commission shall be paid to or shared with such an investment adviser. Investment advisers receiving finder's fees may reallow all or a portion of their finder's fees to other investment advisors registered in the State of Michigan. No commissions or finder's fees shall be paid on additional Assessments, if any. There is no firm commitment to purchase or sell any of the Units. The General Partners may offer some Units for sale. There will be no commissions or finder's fees paid on Units sold directly to investors by the General Partners without the services of a finder or investment adviser-finder.

BENEFITS OF AN INVESTMENT BANKING FUND

1. Possible write-offs from initial expenses.

2. Potential profits from the investment banking business.

RISK ASPECTS OF AN INVESTMENT BANKING FUND

High Risk Involved in Securities Business. Because the success of Partnership operations is dependent to a large extent on the activity of the stock market and the various national and regional stock exchanges, matters over which the Partnership will not have any control, and which are affected by numerous and varied economic and political factors that are extremely difficult and often impossible to predict with any degree of accuracy, the securities offered hereunder are speculative and subject to a high degree of risk. Investors should be aware that they may sustain a substantial or total loss of their investment or may receive a return, if any, that is substantially below alternate forms of investment. The term "securities" as used herein generally refers to traditional forms of investment securities such as common and preferred stock, mutual fund and variable annuity shares, debentures, bonds, and notes as well as to interests in business trusts, limited partnership interests (including most tax shelters) and other interests or investment contracts in business entities where the investor is looking solely to the efforts of others for his profits, and to all forms of investment termed "securities" under the various federal and state securities laws. Such securities may or may not be sold on national or local stock exchanges or on the over-the-counter market.

Risks Inherent in Investment Banking Business. The nature of the investment banking business imposes many risks to investors purchasing Units hereunder. The preponderance of fees earned by investment bankers are usually of a contingent nature for services that are often highly complex, protracted and very costly to perform. The nature of such a business focuses great importance on the Partnership's ability and/or likelihood in collecting the outstanding fees it has earned from its clients in a reasonably timely manner. As a result, the Partnership will have to invest substantial time and assets in certain projects that may never result in earnings to the Partnership and any earnings that are realized may be generated only after long delays and high costs of collection. Also, payment for the services of an investment banker may commonly take the form of restricted securities or minority positions with limited trading value or no liquidity at all. When this form of payment is contemplated, the Partnership will seek agreements from its clients to permit the Partnership to resell or transfer such securities in accordance with the federal and applicable state securities laws through the use of registration rights or redemption obligations on the part of the client, but any such assurances from clients, even if available, are no guarantee of the ability to liquidate such positions at reasonable prices, times and places. Compensation in the form of warrants creates its own distinctive risks because their value is dependent upon the Partnership having sufficient funds with which to exercise the warrants and obtain the underlying securities.

Risks Peculiar to Initial Start-Up Phase. Because of the long "lead time" involved in investment banking activities, which are typically not structured and have no specific procedure or method with which they are performed in the investment banking business, there may be a substantial period of time between the beginning of operations of the Partnership and the receipt of significant revenues, if ever, on the initial projects the Partnership may undertake. The present financing of the Partnership is heavily dependent upon the limited funds to be raised in this offering. If the Partnership fails to realize reasonably prompt earnings on its efforts, the high cost of its business operations could exhaust the funds raised hereunder, leaving the Partnership in a difficult position regarding any additional financing due to the adverse financial history it would then have. This could result in a cessation of operations and a total loss of the investors investment hereunder.

Significant Start-Up Expenses. A large portion of the proceeds of this offering will be used in meeting the initial start-up expenses of the Partnership and will not be invested in tangible assets. Investors in the Partnership will be at risk to this extent, but they may be entitled to tax deductions which could effectively reduce the net exposure of investors to these initial expenses depending upon their particular tax situations.

Capital Base Limited. Because of the limitations imposed on the size of any "firm commitment" underwriting that the Partnership could undertake as a result of the relatively small amount of the proceeds of this offering, compared to the large capitalizations of most investment banking firms, it is likely that the majority of underwriting projects that the Partnership will initially engage in will be "best efforts" private placements instead of investments for the purpose of resale. Also, the limitations of the Partnership's capital base will prevent the Partnership from employing or engaging any full-time investment and securities analysts, but the Partnership will endeavor to obtain expense payments from its clients to provide for analysts, "due diligence" reviews and other related expenses.

A "firm commitment" is an agreement whereby the Partnership would agree to purchase all of the securities in an offering for the purpose of resale by the Partnership. The fees are relatively high in this type of an agreement due to the high risks of resalability assumed by the Partnership. This is to be contrasted to a "best efforts" agreement where the Partnership does not agree to buy any of the securities being offered, but merely agrees to use its "best efforts" to sell them. The fees are normally substantial, but relatively lower in this type of an agreement compared to the "firm commitment" type, due to the relatively low risks of resale that are being assumed by the Partnership. "Firm Commitment" and "Best Efforts" agreements are the only significant types of securities underwritings employed in the investment banking community. "Due diligence" reviews consists of the careful review and investigation of all business, financial and legal aspects of the Partnership's clients to meet substantial legal requirements and practical business quality control requirements in connection with any securities underwriting.

Regulatory Compliance. The Partnership will be regulated in its activities by federal, state and quasi-governmental agencies (such as the NASD), and the costs of compliance with such regulations are high. The Securities and Exchange Commission will have jurisdiction over the Partnership under the Securities Exchange Act of 1934 and rules promulgated thereunder, which generally prescribe the sales methods, record keeping, capital and reporting requirements for securities broker-dealers. The Securities Act of 1933 and the various state "blue-sky" laws regulate the registration of securities sold to the public, as well as the private sale of securities, and the Partnership will be most directly affected by that federal act when it does business as an underwriter or distributor of such securities. Applicable federal and state securities laws also impose substantial potential liabilities for money damages, among other things, for violations thereof, both to persons who have acquired securities in underwritings as well as to the federal and state securities regulatory authorities. The Partnership is required to comply with the "net capital" rule promulgated by the Securities and Exchange Commission under the Securities Exchange Act of 1934. This rule, among other things, limits the aggregate indebtedness which may be carried by a broker-dealer, thereby restricting the volume of business which may be conducted. Prior to commencing broker-dealer operations, the Partnership will be licensed as a broker-dealer in Michigan, and the State of Michigan requires that employees, as well as officers and/or general partners of a broker-dealer, comply with certain requirements under the Michigan Uniform Securities Act and that the Partnership conduct its business within the State of Michigan according to said Act. The Partnership may become licensed in such other states as the General Partners deem advisable, and upon such licensing it will become subject to regulation by those states. The expenses of qualification in such other states may preclude the Partnership from doing business therein in the near future. Infraction of the laws, rules or regulations of any of the aforementioned statutes or agencies could subject the General Partners and the employees of the Partnership concerned and the Partnership to disciplinary proceedings, which, of course, could have an adverse effect on the Partnership. Limited Partners, such as the investors in Units, who are not employees or managers of the Partnership would not ordinarily be subject to any such sanctions. Any such disciplinary proceeding could result in the Partnership being temporarily or permanently suspended from acting as a broker-dealer.

Prior to commencing broker-dealer operations, the Partnership will be a member of the National Association of Securities Dealers, Inc., ("NASD") which exercises some supervision over member firms and has the power to expel from the NASD or otherwise discipline members who fail to observe the rules, regulations and other standards of the NASD.

Competition. The General Partners are of the opinion that many investment banking services in the State of Michigan, primarily in the field of small and medium sized financings and securities issues, other than municipal financings, are not being adequately met by the Michigan and National securities brokerage community or any other source. Based upon their several years of experience in this field in Michigan, it is the belief of Messrs. Hopkins and Lynch that this market segment can be serviced on a profitable basis, despite the existence of the competition hereinafter discussed. No assurances of any such profitability can of course be given at this early stage of the Partnership's business.

It is also the opinion of the General Partners that there is a limited amount of consulting and management talent nationally in the field of large and medium scale real estate projects, especially in the field of shopping center development, financing and management. Based on his several years of experience in this area, Mr. Smith is of the belief that this market segment can be serviced on a profitable basis, despite the existence of numerous well financed and staffed competitors with strong reputations in the real estate industry. Again, no assurance of any such profitability can be given at this early stage of the Partnership's business.

The buying, selling, trading and/or underwriting and syndicating of securities is highly competitive. The market is composed of numerous licensed and registered broker-dealers located in Michigan and throughout the United States. To some extent other broker-dealer firms, banks, insurance companies and other financiers, many with substantial capital and long-standing experience and reputation are seeking to provide the same services to the public and to the investment banking community as the Partnership hopes to offer. Competition may, therefore, be great in connection with the Partnership's attempts to acquire clients requiring the services an investment banking firm could provide.

The Partnership has not conducted any independent research to verify the size of the emerging equity issues market, and there can be no guarantee that established investment banking firms will not reorient their practices to meet new developments in the market place. The Partnership's competitionals has established Michigan and interstate contacts. The Partnership intends to seek business in all parts of the United States and the world, with primary emphasis in the State of Michigan.

No Firm Underwriting. Because there is no firm commitment for the purchase of Units, there can be no assurance that the Partnership will sell the required minimum of 20 Units, Investors' funds may thus be retained in escrow for up to six months following the date hereof.

Sale or Disposition of Property or Interest–Tax Liability. A sale of other disposition of the Partnership's property or disposition of a Limited Partner's interest in the Partnership may result in a substantial tax liability to such Limited Partner. A Limited Partner should also be aware that an investment in a partnership which provides tax shelter in large part operates to defer rather than reduce federal income taxes otherwise payable by the Limited Partner because of anticipated taxable ordinary income or capital gains in later years of the partnership. Furthermore, an investor may be sheltering income which would otherwise qualify for the maximum tax provided by Section 1348 of the Internal Revenue Code of 1954, as amended; income realized by the Partnership in later years, which will not qualify for the maximum tax, may be taxed to a Limited Partner at a rate higher than would be allowed by the maximum tax.

Under certain circumstances, the taxes payable by a Limited Partner on account of (a) the sale of Partnership property or (b) the disposition by a Limited Partner of his or her interest in the Partnership, could exceed cash distributions or the proceeds of disposition.

Limited Transferability and Absence of Market for Units. Transferability of the Units is severely restricted. The Units are being offered and (unless this restriction is waived in writing by the Partnership) sold in Michigan only, without registration under the Securities Act of 1933, as amended, based upon Section 4(2) thereof as well as Rule 146 thereunder. They are being offered and sold without registration under the Michigan Uniform Securities Act, as amended, pursuant to Section 402(b)(9) thereof and Rule 803.2, relating to transactions not involving a public offering. The Units are being sold for investment and not for distribution or resale. As a result they may have to be held indefinitely. No transfer or resale may be effected unless counsel to the Partnership furnishes an opinion to the effect that registration under both of said Acts is not required. Resale of Units and the right to substitute a transferee thereof as a Limited Partner is also restricted and requires the consent of all General Partners. Furthermore, it is not anticipated that there will be any market for resale of the Units. As a result, an investor is very likely to be unable to sell or otherwise dispose of his Units unless they are redeemed by the Partnership. The General Partners may, at any time, retire a Limited Partner for any good faith reason on a non pro rata basis with other Limited Partners, either voluntarily or involuntarily on the part of the retired Limited Partner, but a Limited Partner may not be involuntarily retired unless the best business interests of the Partnership shall be served by such retirement. Limited Partners have no right to require the Partnershp to retire their interests.

No Assurance of Cash Distribution. There is no assurance as to when or whether cash will be available for distribution to the holders of Units from the operations of the Partnership. The General Partners are reimbursed by the Partnership for certain services performed for the Partnership and expenses paid on behalf of the Partnership. The General Partners may retain other firms to perform other services. The Partnership bears all expenses incurred in its operations. All of these fees and expenses are deducted from cash funds generated from the operations of the Partnership prior to distributing cash funds to the Partners. The General Partners in their sole and exclusive discretion may make distributions to the Partners of any remaining net pretax income, computed on the cash as opposed to the accrual method of accounting. Under the Agreement, the General Partners are obligated to use their best efforts to distribute at least sufficient cash to enable the Partners to pay any federal and Michigan income taxes reasonably anticipated on the Partnership's income. Sufficient cash, in this regard, shall be deemed to be at least 60% of the Partnership's taxable income for any taxable year determined whenever possible on the cash basis.

Loss on Dissolution and Termination. In the event of a dissolution or termination of the Partnership, the proceeds realized from the liquidation of assets, if any, will be distributed to the holders of Units, but only after the satisfaction of claims of creditors. Accordingly, the ability of a Limited Partner to recover all or any portion of his or her investment under such circumstances will depend on the amount of funds so realized and claims to be satisfied therefrom.

Interests of General Partners and Affiliates. The General Partners will not contribute any capital to the Partnership as General Partners and will have a permanent 1% interest to be shared by all General Partners in office from time to time in all income, profit, loss, deductions, credits and distributions from Partnership operations. In addition, the General Partners and/or their trusts will own either additional General or Limited Partnership interests, or both which, in the aggregate, after certain conditions have been met, will entitle them to 20 or 50 percent, as the case may be, of the income, profits, losses, deductions and credits of the Partnership. Harmon and Nathan, affiliates of the General Partners, will hold Class III Limited Partnership interests entitling them each to 2% of the income, profits, losses, deductions, credits and distributions of the Partnership upon the happening of certain conditions. Messrs. Lynch and Smith will have five-year employment contracts entitling them to annual salaries of $60,000 each, adjusted for cost of living increases, plus a bonus of 10% of the Partnership's pre-tax profits and Mr. Hopkins will have a similar consulting contract, except that his annual salary is $12,000, which he is waiving through December 31, Year Two.

Successive Owners of Units. The income, profit, loss, deduction and credit distributions of the Partnership will be divided among and charged against the holders of Units, during the offering period, on a daily basis during each fiscal year according to the date their investment is accepted by the General Partners, and thereafter will be divided and charged on an annual basis. Between successive owners of any Unit, distributions will be allocated based upon the number of days that each was the owner of the Unit without regard to the results of Partnership operations during the period in which each was the owner thereof and regardless of the date upon which distributions of cash were made to each of them or the amount of such distributions. Accordingly, the holder who sells a Unit during the taxable year may be required to report a share of the Partnership income on his or her personal income tax return even though he or she received no distribution during the period of his or her ownership or the amount distributed to him or her bears no relationship to the amount which he or she is required to report, unless he provides for this contingency in connection with the transfer of his Unit(s).

General Partners–Non-Liability. Under the Agreement, the General Partners are not liable to the Partnership nor to the Limited Partners for any mistakes or errors in judgment, nor for any act or omission believed in good faith to be within the scope of authority conferred by the Agreement or for any action or omission as to which there would be no such liability if done or omitted by directors of a corporation incorporated under the then Michigan business corporation act under the business judgment rule, except for acts of gross negligence and misconduct as well as for acts or omissions involving intentional wrongdoing. Under certain circumstances and similar standards the General Partners will be entitled to indemnification from the Partnership.

Possible Requirement of Additional Financing. The General Partners believe that the net proceeds from this offering would be sufficient to enable the Partnership to begin operations and to continue them on a profitable basis. The Partnership was organized in the partnership form so that it could pass through to each Partner his respective share of Partnership losses should they occur prior to the attainment of any such profitability. A potential investor should be aware that if the net proceeds of this offering and the additional Assessments provided for under the Agreement prove insufficient, the Partnership may require additional working capital from alternative sources to maintain the Partnership operations and to meet its expenditures. There is no assurance that such additional financing will be available or the terms upon which such financing may be obtained. The General Partners are not required by the Agreement to contribute any additional funds necessary for the operation of the Partnership's business. In such event, the Partnership may be required to sell all of its assets and/or dissolve, which in turn could cause the Partners to suffer adverse tax consequences.

Assessments. In the event that some or all of the Assessments are not timely paid the ability of the Partnership to meet its goals, as well as the Partnership interest of a nonpaying Partner, will be impaired.

Liability of Limited Partners. Limited Partners' liabilities may not exceed the purchase price for their Units (including Assessments, if any) plus undistributed profits allocated to their account, pursuant to the Michigan Uniform Limited Partnership Act. However, to the extent that cash distributed to the Limited Partners by the Partnership constitutes a payment of profits or a return of all or a part of their capital contributions, the Limited Partners may be liable to repay any sum, not in excess of such return of profits and capital, plus interest, necessary to discharge the Partnership's obligations to creditors who extended credit or whose claims arose before such return, to the extent that any such distribution resulted in any insufficiency of Partnership assets to meet claims of Partnership creditors immediately after the distribution has been made.

If any Limited Partner participates in the management of the Partnership's business, he may jeopardize the limitation of liability afforded him and become liable as a general partner to Partnership creditors. Consequently, the Agreement provides that no Limited Partner shall participate in the management or control of the Partnership's business.

Limited Partners' Voting and Consent Rights. Under the Agreement, Limited Partners will have no right unilaterally to amend the Agreement, dissolve the Partnership or remove the General Partners from office. Limited Partners will, however, have the right to elect a new General Partner(s) by a majority vote, with each Limited Partner having one vote, should all the current General Partners resign or become unavailable to serve under the Agreement. The General Partners may, in their sole and exclusive discretion, incorporate the Partnership and no consent to such action by the Limited Partners is required. Amendments to the Agreement must be approved by at least a majority in Partnership Interest of Limited Partners then holding Units and in certain cases by 75% in Partnership Interests of the Limited Partners. Certain actions taken by the General Partners require the vote or consent of at least a majority in Partnership Interest of Limited Partners or a vote of higher percentages of the Partnership Interests of Limited Partners. All voting and consent provisions require a vote of all Limited Partners voting as one aggregate class, voting or consenting based upon their Partnership Interests.

Any of such vote or consent by the Limited Partners could have an adverse financial and tax effect upon certain of the Limited Partners taking such actions. In a recent opinion, Frank Kelly, the Michigan Attorney General, has stated that "Michigan law does not permit a limited partnership agreement which contains a provision allowing limited partners to take action without concurrence by the general partner." The Partnership's Limited Partnership Agreement provides that in certain limited instances the Limited Partners may act unilaterally to vote or consent to, among other things, certain actions taken by the General Partners or the election of a General Partner. Section 7 of the Uniform Limited Partnership Act, which has been adopted in the State of Michigan, states that "a limited partner shall not become liable as a general partner unless, in addition to the exercise of his rights and powers as a limited partner, he takes part in the control of the business." It is the opinion of counsel to the Partnership that the mere *inclusion* of the unilaterally exercisable limited partner voting rights described above will not subject the Limited Partners to unlimited liability to creditors under Michigan law. However, the *exercise* of these voting rights by the Limited Partners may result in their becoming liable as general partners to partnership creditors at the time of the exercise of the rights or subsequently.

State and Local Taxes. The Partnership or the Partners, or both, may be subject to state and local taxes in jurisdictions in which the Partnership may be deemed to be doing business, or in which they reside or own property or other interests. Such taxes may include personal property and intangible taxes, income taxes, sales and use taxes, estate or inheritance taxes, single business taxes, or other types of taxes. A Partner's share of the gains or losses of the Partnership may or may not be taken into consideration for state or local income tax purposes, depending upon applicable state laws, local ordinances and regulations. To the extent the Partnership does business in certain jurisdictions, estate or inheritance taxes may be payable to such jurisdictions upon the non-sale transfer of Units of a deceased Partner.

TAX ASPECTS OF AN INVESTMENT BANKING FUND

It should be noted that a Limited Partner's distributive share of Partnership taxable income will not qualify as "personal service income" under the Code and accordingly may be taxed at regular ordinary income rates which, for federal income tax purposes, may be as high as 70%. The exact tax rates applicable to any one Partner's share of the Partnership's ordinary income will vary with his own tax brackets, which could be less than the aforesaid rate. The Partnership will seek to have as much of its income realized in the form of capital gains, wherever practical, which would result in a maximum tax of 28%, but no assurances as to the amount of any such capital gain versus ordinary income treatment can be given. Due to the potential for taxation in higher brackets, the General Partners are obligated to use their best efforts to distribute at least sufficient cash to enable the Partners to pay any federal or Michigan income taxes reasonably anticipated on the Partnership's income. Sufficient cash in this regard shall be deemed to be at least 60% of the Partnership's taxable income for any taxable year. The Partnership intends to report income on the "cash" as opposed to the "accrual" basis, whenever possible. Furthermore, under the Agreement, the General Partners will review and take whatever action they deem to be appropriate to "shelter" the earnings of the Partnership from taxes, including the use of Partnership income to cover expenses of new Partnership ventures, but the General Partners will have complete discretion in this regard and are under no obligation to shelter any income of the Partnership.

Allocation of Profits and Losses

The Code provides that the distributive share of each partner shall be determined by the provisions of the partnership agreement if the partner receiving the allocation can demonstrate that the allocation has "substantial economic effect," which the Code and Regulations leave undefined. The Tax Reform Act of 1976 provides that income, losses, or items of income, gain, loss, deduction or credit must be allocated among the partners in accordance with each partner's interest in the partnership if there is no provision with respect thereto in the partnership agreement or the allocation does not have substantial economic effect. In particular, the incentive bonus provisions in the Partnership's agreements with its General Partners may be not treated as deductible expenses but as profit allocations. While the General Partners believe that the allocations set forth in the Agreement have substantial economic effect, no assurance can be given that the allocation provisions of the Agreement will not be challenged by the Service or that such a challenge, if made, would not be sustained by the courts. The net effect of any such successful challenge on the part of the Service might be to allocate profits, losses, gains and similar items to the partners on a basis less favorable than that set out in the Agreement.

Retroactive Allocations

Retroactive allocations of a full year's partnership income or loss are no longer permitted as a result of the Tax Reform Act of 1976. A Partner acquiring an interest late in the year is allocated a share of items attributable to that portion of the year during which his interest is held. This will be determined under the Agreement on a daily basis by prorating the income or loss for that tax year.

At Risk Limitation

Section 465 of the Code provides that losses attributable to many activities, including the operation of a securities broker-dealer, will be allowed to offset income derived from other sources only to the extent of the aggregate amount of an investor's "at risk" investment in the activity as of the close of the taxable year. This provision applies to any partner who is a non-corporate taxpayer, an electing small business corporation or a corporation in which 5 or fewer individuals own, actually or constructively, more than 50% of the outstanding stock. Such a partner is considered to be "at risk" with respect to the amount of money and adjusted basis of other property contributed to the Partnership, any amounts borrowed for use in the Partnership to the extent the partner is personally liable for repayment and the net fair market value of his personal assets (other than assets used in the Partnership) that secure non-recourse borrowings, the proceeds of which are used in the Partnership. A Partner is not at risk for the unauthorized portion of any non-recourse borrowing secured by his Units which has been used to finance the acquisition of such Units. Borrowing from other partners, parties with an interest (other than an interest as creditor) in the business of the Partnership or certain relatives or affiliates of a taxpayer do not qualify as amounts at risk. Further, a partner is not considered at risk with respect to any amount protected against loss through guarantee, stop-loss agreements or other similar arrangements. Only deductions in excess of income from an activity are disallowed; deductions up to the amount of gross income from the activity for the year are not affected by the at risk rules. Losses from the activities of the Partnership that are allowed or cash distributed reduce the amount at which a taxpayer is at risk. Income derived from the operations of the Partnership increase the at risk amounts. Losses disallowed as a deduction because of Section 465 become a deduction allowable to Partnership activities in the first succeeding taxable year to the extent that the investor is then at risk. The at risk limitation does not apply for the purpose of determining the basis of a partner's partnership interest and does not affect the amount of investment tax credit allowable to a taxpayer. The amount of investment tax credit does not reduce or otherwise affect the amount the taxpayer has at risk. The amount of Assessments the Limited Partners will be subject to will not increase the amount to which they will be considered to be at risk until and to the extent such Assessments are called.

Sale or Other Disposition of Partnership Properties

Except as otherwise provided below with respect to depreciation recapture, any profit or loss which may be realized by the Partnership on the sale or other disposition of any of the Partnership's property will be treated as capital gain or loss under the Code unless it is determined that the Partnership is a "dealer" in such assets for federal income tax purposes, or except to the extent that the assets sold constitute "Section 1231 assets" (i.e., real property and depreciable assets used in a trade or business held for more than twelve months). If such property constitutes "Section 1231 assets," a Limited Partner's proportionate share of gains or losses would be combined with any other Section 1231 gains or losses incurred by him or her in that year and his or her net Section 1231 gains or losses would be taxable as capital gains or constitute ordinary losses, as the case may be. It is anticipated that any property acquired by the Partnership will constitute a "Section 1231 asset."

In the event of the sale or disposition of any depreciable real property within one year after acquisition or of any depreciable personal property or depreciable tangible property used as an integral part of the production of income (even if straight-line depreciation has been taken), gain, if any, will be recaptured as ordinary income to the extent that depreciation has been previously allowed on the property. In the event of the disposition (including a sale as a result of foreclosure) of depreciable real property held for more than one year with respect to which accelerated depreciation has been taken, depreciation in excess of the amount of depreciation which would have been allowable under the straight-line method would be recaptured as ordinary income.

If Partnership property with respect to which the investment tax credit has been taken is sold within seven years and prior to the expiration of the useful life utilized in determining the amount of credit taken, a portion, or all, of such investment credit will be recaptured, increasing the amount of tax payable that year by each Limited Partner.

Any gain or loss on the sale or other disposition of (a) property which is held by the Partnership as a "dealer" or (b) property which is neither a capital asset nor a Section 1231 asset will be treated as ordinary income or loss, as the case may be. An investor should note that a taxpayer is required to hold a capital asset for more than twelve months (six months in the case of commodities) in order to be entitled to long-term capital gain treatment.

Sale of Partnership Interests

Gain or loss realized by a Limited Partner (who is not a "dealer" in such property) on sale of a Unit in the Partnership which has been held for more than twelve months will generally be taxable as long-term capital gain or loss. However, that portion of a selling Partner's gain allocable to "appreciated inventory items" and "unrealized receivables" as defined in Section 751 of the Code would be treated as ordinary income. The term "unrealized receivables" includes depreciation recapture as if a selling Partner's proportionate share of all the Partnership's properties had been sold at that time.

The amount of any gain or loss realized on a sale by a Limited Partner of his or her Unit(s) in the Partnership will be based upon the difference between the amount realized and the tax basis for his or her interest in the Partnership. Thus, for example, a Limited Partner's gain on the sale of his or her interest may substantially exceed the cash proceeds of such sale, and in some cases, the income taxes payable with respect to such gain may exceed the cash proceeds.

If a Limited Partner sells his or her interest within seven years after an investment tax credit is taken by the Partnership and prior to the expiration of the useful life utilized in determining the amount of the investment credit, a portion or all of such investment tax credit taken by the selling Limited Partner must be recaptured and will increase the Limited Partner's tax liability for the year of such sale. The amount of the investment tax credit recaptured generally will depend upon the period during which the property was held by the Partnership when the interest was sold, and the percentage of interest sold relative to the interest held when the investment credit property was purchased.

Incorporation of the Partnership

The General Partners have the exclusive right to incorporate the Partnership if they determine it to be in the best interest of the Partnership's business, either by (i) an irrevocable power of attorney coupled with an interest thereon which is created over all current and future Partnership interests that shall be outstanding to cause them to be exchanged for shares of the capital stock of a corporation; (ii) sale of all or substantially all Partnership assets for shares of capital stock of a corporation followed by dissolution of the Partnership; or (iii) dissolution of the Partnership and transfer of its assets received on liquidation under a similar irrevocable power coupled with an interest therein to cause them to be exchanged for capital stock of a corporation. The Agreement provides that such incorporation shall be tax free to the Partners to the maximum extent possible.

The Service, in Revenue Ruling 70-239, 1970-1 C.B. 74, considered the tax consequences of these three methods of incorporating a partnership and stated that each of these situations would be regarded as a transfer under Section 351 of the Code, which provides, in general, that no gain or loss is recognized if property is transferred to a corporation solely in exchange for stock or securities of the transferee–corporation if, immediately after the exchange, the transferor or transferors are in "control" of the corporation. Gain will be recognized if the sum of the amount of liabilities assumed by the Partnership plus the amount of liabilities to which the property transferred to the corporation is subject exceeds the total adjusted basis of such property. The Revenue Act of 1978 amended Section 357(c) to provide that if a cash-basis taxpayer transfers the assets of a going business, including the accounts payable, to a corporation in return for stock, the accounts payable will not be considered liabilities for purposes of Section 357(c) if the transferor would have been entitled to a deduction upon the payment thereof. Accordingly, if the Partnership uses the cash method of accounting, its accounts payable will not constitute liabilities under Section 357(c) for purposes of computing gain or incorporation to the extent that the payment on such accounts would be deductible. Also, to the extent a transferor in a Section 351 transaction receives consideration other than stock or securities of the transferee corporation ("boot"), any gain realized by the transferor is recognized under Section 351(b) to the extent of the value of such boot and is of a character determined with reference to the character of the assets transferred to the corporation. Loss is never recognized in a Section 351 transaction.

The gain, if any, which the Partnership recognizes on incorporation will be taxed as capital gain or ordinary income depending on the type of assets transferred. Also, a portion of any gain may be taxed as ordinary income if there is any depreciation recapture. Upon incorporation, the Partners would be taxed as corporate shareholders.

Gifts of Partnership Interests

Generally, no gain or loss is recognized for income tax purposes as a result of a gift of property. Gifts of a Limited Partnership interest may also be subject to a gift tax imposed pursuant to the rules generally applicable to all gifts of property.

Investment banking is a high risk enterprise but if successful could be a big winner for the investor.

Chapter Ten

ECONOMIC DEVELOPMENT CORPORATION

The use of tax-exempt bonds to stimulate the economy has reached out in many different directions as revealed in the following material.

Historically, tax-exempt municipal bonds have been a financing tool used solely by political subdivision in the United States. However, in recent years, due to legislative actions by most states, tax-exempts can now be utilized by many corporations and individuals as a financing mechanism for industrial and commercial expansion. It is timely, therefore, in any discussion of securities law to consider the alternatives that tax-exempts provide.

MUNICIPAL REVENUE BONDS

I. Growth in Revenue Bond Financings

The debt of state and local governments has grown rapidly for more than a century and a half. Municipal bonds can be traced at least back to the 1820's when America's young and vigorous cities required outside capital to develop their municipal systems. At the turn of the century some $2 billion in municipal debt was outstanding.

By 1913, this debt outstanding had reached $5 billion. In that year the 16th amendment (establishing a federal income tax) to the constitution was ratified. Interest on state and local borrowings was exempted from the new tax, and as a result, yields fell markedly on existing borrowings to reflect their equivalence to taxable corporate and U.S. government debt. In the 47 years between 1913 and 1960, the outstanding debt of state and local governments grew to $65 billion. In the last two decades the outstanding debt has increased to a phenomenal $315 billion. In fact, in 1979 more debt, $65 billion, was issued than all the debt outstanding in 1960. (See Tables 1 & 2)

Why this incredible growth in municipal bonds? Primarily it is because of two reasons. One, more investors exist today with incomes that are taxed at sufficient rates to make municipal bonds a sensible investment and two, the rise and domination of revenue bonds in the marketplace.

The first reason is obvious. As inflation has pushed tax payers into higher tax brackets the use of municipal bonds in their investment portfolios has made more sense. An individual in the 30% tax bracket investing in a municipal bond yielding 7½% is equivalent to that same individual using a taxable investment yielding 10¾%. As the tax brackets of an individual increases, this equivalency becomes even more attractive.

Table 1

STATE AND LOCAL DEBT OUSTANDING, 1945-1979

(in millions of dollars)

1979	312,793	1961	75,851
1978	291,438	1960	70,766
1977	263,160	1959	65,486
1976	239,507	1958	59,206
1975	223,843	1957	53,708
1974	207,695	1956	49,461
1973	191,215	1955	45,870
1972	176,507	1954	40,594
1971	161,798	1953	34,512
1970	144,376	1952	30,243
1969	133,145	1951	26,559
1968	123,219	1950	24,381
1967	113,703	1949	21,049
1966	105,925	1948	18,467
1965	100,278	1947	16,298
1964	92,933	1946	14,886
1963	86,932	1945	14,818
1962	81,209		

SOURCE: Federal Reserve Board.

Table 2

STATE AND LOCAL BORROWING, 1960-1979

Volume of New Issues of Long and Short Term Securities

(in millions of dollars)

Year	Long-Term	Short-Term	Total	Total Number
1979	$43,309	$21,709	$65,018	7,453
1978	48,349	21,384	69,733	8,066
1977	46,706	24,751	71,457	8,333
1976	35,314	20,079	55,392	6,932
1975	29,326	28,973	58,299	8,107
1974	22,824	29,041	51,865	7,701
1973	22,953	24,667	47,620	8,147
1972	22,941	25,222	49,163	8,420
1971	24,370	26,281	50,651	8,811
1970	17,762	17,880	35,642	7,604
1969	11,460	11,783	23,243	6,395
1968	16,374	8,659	25,033	7,887
1967	14,288	8,025	22,313	7,964
1966	11,089	6,524	17,612	7,430
1965	11,084	6,537	17,622	7,977
1964	10,544	5,423	15,967	8,138
1963	10,107	5,481	15,587	8,574
1962	8,558	4,763	13,322	8,689
1961	8,360	4,514	12,874	8,490
1960	7,230	4,006	11,236	8,397

SOURCE: Public Securities Association Municipal Securities Data Base; The Bond Buyer's Municipal Finance Statistics, 1960-1975.

The second reason for this growth is a little more subtle. Traditional municipal debt had been issued over the years primarily as general obligation bonds backed by the "full faith and credit" (taxing power) of the issuer. Revenue bonds, on the other hand, usually have no claim on other revenues of the issuer beyond revenues of the project to be financed. By 1979, revenue bond financing exceeded general obligation financing by a 2 to 1 margin (see Table 3). Just ten years ago the opposite was the norm.

Table 3

NEW ISSUES OF MUNICIPAL SECURITIES

Selected Years 1950 to 1979, by Type of Instrument

Dollar Volume (in Billions)

	General Obligation	Revenue	Total
1950	$ 3.1	$ .6	$ 3.7
1960	5.0	2.2	7.2
1970	11.9	6.2	18.1
1975	16.0	14.7	30.7
1979	12.1	31.2	43.3

SOURCE: The Daily Bond Buyer.

With the ready market of individuals looking for tax-exempt investments and with revenue bonding, municipalities have been able to expand their uses of municipal borrowings. Indeed, municipal debt has increasingly been used to support various public purpose projects once only financed by the private sector. The following are the significant uses developed in just the last decade and a half: Housing (both public and private, for rich or poor), private non-profit hospitals, private industrial pollution control projects, massive joint municipal power ventures, student loan programs, job development programs, sports stadiums, municipal leasing programs, industrial development projects and most recently economic or commercial development projects. Through these last two public purpose areas the greatest amount of potential borrowing now exists.

It is difficult to determine the outstanding debt of municipal IDRB's. In Michigan it is believed to be in excess of $500 million. The lion share of this debt has been placed privately with banking institutions and insurance companies and is very difficult to determine. In recent years, as institutional appetites for tax-exempt income has diminished, many issues have been marketed to the public by investment bankers through negotiated public offerings. Because this trend is expected to continue and increase, it is timely that potential borrowers become conscious of why an investment banker is utilized and the type of credit analysis he makes in determining the merits of these bonds.

II. Why an Investment Banker

An Investment Banker is utilized in an Industrial Development Revenue Bond project in one of two ways. The firm may be retained to act as an agent in arranging a private placement of the debt with an institutional investor. This involvement is limited to packaging a financing proposal and obtaining a commitment from an institutional investor for a take-out on the loan. The largest private source of capital available to IDRB borrowers is casualty insurance companies. Because of client relationships developed over many years, an investment banker can more readily tap this source than the borrower by himself.

The second way an investment banker can be utilized is as a principal, through a public offering of securities. When acting as a principal, the investment banker is actually committing to take down the loan and market it to its retail clients. Because of the risk the investment banker is taking and the nature of offering securities to the public, both the costs and complexities of the financing increase. However, despite the increased costs and complexity of involving an investment banker as a principal, it is becoming more and more the primary source of IDRB capital.

The reasons are twofold, 1) institutional capital in periods of high interest rates and high inflation tend to dry up and 2) the retail or individual investor is not as rate sensitive as an institutional investor. An investment banker is able to justify higher costs and more complex financings because of its ability to market bonds in all markets and at rates of interest below those demanded by institutional investors.

There are several important features and practices that distinguish municipal securities from other kinds of securities. An investment banker will usually incorporate these features in securities which they offer to the public. Unlike most other types of fixed-income securities, municipal bonds are generally issued in serial maturities. A typical offering is made up of as many as 20 or more different maturities—the serial bonds. This helps the borrower spread out debt service and stay within budget requirements. A certain number of bonds will usually come due in each year from, say, one to twenty-five years out. Generally, the longer the maturity, the higher will be the interest rate offered. Term bonds, bonds which come due at only one maturity, have become increasingly popular. They usually have a sinking fund requirement to provide for their retirement. Except for the tax exemption, term bonds are much like traditional corporate debt. Like corporate bonds, they are usually quoted by price rather than yield, and are therefore called dollar bonds. By utilizing a number of serial or term maturities, each at ascending interest rates, an investment banker can lower the overall interest cost of the borrower.

III. Structure Features Required by an Investment Banker

IDRB's are issued directly by a municipality, non-profit authority, or other governmental units in order to build a facility for a private corporation or partnership. The facility is leased to the private corporation or partnership at a rate that is sufficient to pay off the bonds. The credit of the issuing political subdivision is never at stake. The advantage to the private corporation or partnership is that the lease payments are low because the funds were raised at tax-exempt rates. These issues are generally limited in size to $10 million by federal tax legislation.

In Michigan today, most IDRB's are issued by local EDC's. An EDC is a non-profit corporation set up by a political subdivision; city, village, county, etc., for the purpose of expanding that local unit of governments' economic or tax base, and provide jobs for its citizens. Their primary clout is their ability to issue bonds at tax-exempt rates to build, renovate and in some cases acquire or preserve existing industrial and commercial facilities. They are empowered to act only at the pleasure of the governing unit and all actions that they take must be approved by the governing unit.

The transaction that typically is used in Michigan to effect these loans is a lease purchase agreement. The issuing body will borrow funds from a lender, which can be the public, and use these funds to construct or renovate a facility. The private corporation or partnership will lease the facility from the EDC under the lease purchase agreement in an amount sufficient to cover the issuers debt service on the borrowed funds. When the bonds are fully retired, the private corporation or partnership will purchase the facility from the issuer for a nominal sum, usually $10. Theoretically, the issuing body has used its tax-exempt status to raise funds which increased its local tax base and provided or retained jobs for its citizens. The lessee, being the private corporation or partnership, has built or expanded a facility at an economical rate which it may not have been able to do without the local assistance, and the investor, private or public, has received a fair tax-exempt return on his investment of capital in the project.

Pretty simple, everyone wins. Well, everyone wins, that is if the lessee pays back the debt. Because the major rating agencies, Moody's and Standard & Poor's, as a matter of policy do not issue ratings on most IDRB's, credit analysis becomes a necessity to the potential investor in an IDRB project.

First and foremost all publically offered IDRB's must be offered through an official statement that has been registered with the State Securities Bureau in any state where an offering to an individual is to be made. An official statement is the offering circular used to offer municipal bonds and is equivalent to a prospectus in a stock offering. This document must contain full disclosure of all facts relative to the investment that any prudent investor requires to make an investment decision. There are basically two types of IDRB financings: Project Financings and Corporate Financings. In some cases there is a hybrid form that has the characteristics of both types.

A project financing is one in which the principal source of repayment of the debt is the revenues generated by the project to be financed. Some examples of these are shopping centers, housing complexes and nursing homes. These projects are generally owned by partnerships or Subchapter S Corporations which can take advantage of the tax aspects of ownership, namely, depreciation. Because the principal source of repayment of the debt is the revenues generated from the project, it is imperative that those revenues be adequately defined prior to an investment decision. Typically, this is done through pro forma projections compiled by an independent source. I stress the word independent. No developer or owner will ever admit to projected revenues as being less than required to repay the debt on his project. An investment banker will generally require a feasibility report compiled by a Big 8 accounting firm or other recognized authority in the field relating to the project. This feasibility report must contain two sections. The first, or numbers section, will deal with projected revenues and balance sheets of the project and show a forecast of debt service coverage. A minimum coverage of 1.20 is required, meaning cash available for debt service in any year exceeds debt service in that year by 120%. The second section will contain a market study which shows that there is, in fact, a market for the project and will have in it displayed the demographics that were used in reaching that decision. This feasibility report must contain a cover letter of the accounting firm giving that firm "positive assurance" as to the reasonableness of its projections.

A bond offering for a project financing must contain a feasibility report compiled by an independent source of national reputation. Without it the potential investor cannot perform an adequate credit analysis.

In a corporate financing, the principal source of repayment is not the revenues of the project financed but the credit worthiness of the owner corporation. An offering circular for a corporate financing must contain a section showing the historical financing results of the owner company. Those financial statements should be audited on an annual basis for at least the five years preceding the offering. The borrowing company should show a potential investor a minimum of five years of earnings statements and two years of balance sheets including footnotes from their most recent audit. Additionally, a capitalization chart reflecting the status of the company after its current borrowing should be presented. Along with these financial statements should be presented a narrative describing the company, its history and its business. Given this information, an investor should be capable of making an intelligent determination of the company's ability to repay the debt.

The typical Indenture of Trust for a publicly offered municipal bond will contain the following security provisions:

1. The bondholders must be granted a first mortgage on the property to be financed. Title will usually remain with the issuing body until the bonds are repaid,

2. The bondholders should have a security interest in all furnishings and equipment placed within the facility and financed out of bond proceeds. Provisions should be made to allow for replacement equipment and furnishings over the life of the debt.

3. The bondholders should receive a pledge of revenues generated by the facility. This will give the bondholders a first claim on revenues in the event of default,

4. All revenue bonds should have a debt service reserve fund equal to the maximum annual principal and interest on the bonds. This added protection will afford bondholders their principal and interest payments in the event of any short term problems affecting the company or the project. Under current Michigan law this fund can be funded with proceeds from the borrowing.

5. There should be provisions in the mortgage protecting the bondholders from additional indebtedness incurred by the owner relating to the facility. This typically will involve a coverage test to be accomplished by an independent accountant,

6. Most importantly, the owner corporation or partnership must guarantee the repayment of the debt under a separate agreement known as a guarantee agreement. In the case of partnership ownership this must be in the form of personal guarantees of the general partners. Bankruptcy courts have in many cases thrown out leases in a bankruptcy action. Because the legal structure of EDC's is a lease purchase agreement, it is possible that a bankruptcy court will throw out the lease liability. A guarantee agreement can abridge that action.

IV. Importance of Unqualified Legal Opinion

To assure that the interest on the debt is indeed tax-exempt, every bond must have an unqualified approving legal opinion of a nationally recognized bond counsel as to its exemption from taxation under federal and, where applicable, state laws. If you have any doubt as to the bond counsel being of national repute, you should call the bond department of your broker/dealer and ask that the counsel's name be looked up in a trade publication known as the "Bond Buyer Red Book." All nationally recognized bond counsel's appear in this publication. Beyond assuring yourself of the tax exemption of your investment it is important to note that most firms, like Manley, Bennett, McDonald & Co., will not trade in bonds that have an opinion by bond counsels not listed in the "red book." Hence, unless the bonds you own have a recognized legal opinion, there may not exist a secondary market in which to sell the bonds prior to their stated maturity. In other words, the bonds have no liquidity.

V. Uses of Tax-Exempt Financing

Housing–There are several main types of housing revenue bonds. They are issued by state or local housing finance agencies or a unit of the local government, generally to support multi-family or single-family housing for low or moderate income families. They are also used to aid in regional redevelopment, and in some states to support housing for the aged and veterans. In Michigan the greatest amount of housing related financings are multi-family, government subsidized programs. These financings are sponsored by the Michigan State Housing Development Authority at the state level and by non-profit authorities at the local level. The typical transaction involves a developer who constructs, owns and manages a housing facility, the local or state authority who borrows the money through tax-exempt bonds to fund the project, the U.S. Housing and Urban Development who subsidizes the rentals in the project, and in many cases the Federal Housing Administration who insures the mortgages on the project. These financings are extremely complex, but plentiful in view of the need that is fulfilled.

Commercial Expansion–By virtue of the Economic Development Corporation Act, this area holds the greatest diversity of uses of tax-exempt financing. Some examples of commercial enterprises financed through publicly offered municipal bonds by investment bankers are:

- Radisson Hotels
- Elias Brothers Restaurants
- McDonald's Hamburger Restaurants
- Vic Tanny Health Clubs
- Nursing Homes
- Life Care Housing for the Elderly
- Retail Shopping Centers

- Office Buildings
- Food Growing and Processing Facilities.

And these are but a few.

Industrial Expansion–The largest borrower in this category are large industrial companies, exempted from capital expenditure tests by type of use, who fund very ambitious pollution abatement programs. Most smaller industrial expansion is carried out through the EDC act rather than the IDR act due to the fact that EDC's do not have to be approved by the State Municipal Finance Commission, while IDR's do. In 1979-80, sixteen issues of industrial companies where marketed to the public in Michigan. These issues ranged in size from $2 million to $9 million each.

The assistance of James P. Lovay of Manley, Bennett, McDonald & Co. in the preparation of this material is gratefully acknowledged.

An economic development corporation offering is set forth in the following example.

THE ECONOMIC DEVELOPMENT CORPORATION AND TAX-EXEMPT BONDS

The Limited Obligation Economic Development Revenue Bonds will be issued by the Economic Development Corporation of the County of Good in the aggregate principal amount of $3,500,000, in coupon form in the denomination of $5,000 each, registrable as to principal only, with the option of convertibility at the holder's expense to fully registered bonds in any denomination being an integral multiple of $5,000. First Bank and Trust Company of South Junction, shall be Trustee and Paying Agent. The Bonds are dated December 1. Interest on the Bonds is payable semiannually on June 1 and December 1.

The Bonds are subject to redemption prior to maturity.

The Bonds are special obligations of the Economic Development Corporation of the County of Good, payable (except to the extent payable out of moneys attributable to Bond proceeds or the income from temporary investment thereof and, under certain circumstances, proceeds from insurance and condemnation awards, as provided in the Contract and Indenture) solely from and secured by a pledge of revenues derived by the Economic Development Corporation of the County of Good under a Lease Contract with Delicious Mushroom Growers, Ltd., an Indiana Limited Partnership authorized to do business in Michigan. The Bonds are not general obligations, and do not constitute a debt or a pledge against the general credit or taxing power of the State of Michigan, any political subdivision thereof or any agency of the State or such political subdivision, but are payable solely as described above.

This Project is a new venture for Delicious Growers, Ltd., the Lessee; therefore, there is no assurance that the Company's operation of the facility will generate sufficient net revenues to meet the lease obligations. Purchase of these Bonds should be considered only by investors who have adequate financial resources and are in high Federal income tax brackets. The high rate of interest on this Series of Bonds reflects the relative risk involved.

THE COMPANY

Delicious Mushroom Growers, Ltd., (the "Company") was organized under the laws of the State of Indiana. It is authorized to do business in Michigan. The Company is in the development state. Its business office is located at 3000 Town Center, Sun, Michigan.

Upon the completion of this Bond financing and a concurrent partnership financing, the Company will grow and process mushrooms, primarily for sale to the fresh produce market in the Midwest. A portion of the planned mushroom crop will be processed and sold in frozen and canned form. The Company is currently producing a mushroom-based steak sauce under contract with a major food producer.

USE OF BOND PROCEEDS

Proceeds of the offering will be used to purchase, modernize, and reequip the mushroom-producing facilities in Sun, Michigan, now owned by a major food producer.

THE OFFERING

Securities Being Offered ...	Limited Obligation Economic Development Revenue Bonds
Lessee	Delicious Mushroom Growers, Ltd.
Maturity	Serial Bonds, Term Bonds
Interest Payable	Semiannually on June 1 and December 1
Form of Bond	Coupon or Registered as to Principal Full registration available at holder's expense
Minimum Denomination ...	$5,000
Collateral	First mortgage lien on the Project as defined

This Project is a new venture for Delicious Mushroom Growers, Ltd., the Lessee. While the General Partners of the Company believe that they can profitably grow, process, and sell mushrooms and mushroom products, there is no assurance that sufficient net revenues will be generated to meet the Lease Purchase Payments.

GENERAL CONSIDERATIONS

The Bonds are to be issued pursuant to a Mortgage and Trust Indenture between the Issuer and First Bank and Trust Company of South Junction, as Trustee. Pursuant to a Lease Purchase Contract by and between the Issuer and Delicious Mushroom Growers, Ltd., the Issuer has agreed to issue and sell the Bonds to provide funds to finance the acquisition and renovation of land, buildings, and equipment, renovate existing facilities and acquire machinery and equipment. Pursuant to the Lease Contract, the Issuer will lease the Project to the Company in consideration of rental sufficient to pay the principal of and premium (if any) and interest on the Bonds issued as and when the same shall become due.

The Lease Purchase Contract provides that a Security Deposit of $350,000 be paid to the Trustee from the General Partners (not Bond proceeds). This will establish a Debt Service Reserve Account to provide moneys to pay the principal of and interest on any Series A Bonds which would not otherwise be paid due to insufficiency of funds in the Bond Fund. The Security Deposit shall be returned to the General Partners upon the first of the following to occur: (i) when the Company's net worth ratio is not less than thirty per cent (30%) of the bond debt concerning this Project, or (ii) three years after the Closing Time.

The Bonds will be limited obligations payable solely from and secured by the revenues and receipts derived pursuant to the Lease Contract (except to the extent paid out of monies attributable to Bond proceeds, the income from the temporary investment thereof, or proceeds of insurance or condemnation awards). Pursuant to the Indenture, the Issuer will pledge and assign to the Trustee all right, title, and interest in and to the revenues and receipts from the Project to be received by it under the Lease Contract and will mortgage the Project to the Trustee.

THE ISSUER

The Issuer is a public body corporate and an instrumentality of the County of Good, Michigan, duly organized and existing under the laws and Constitution of the State of Michigan. Pursuant to the "Economic Development Corporation Act," being Public Act No. 338, Public Laws of Michigan, 1974, as amended and supplemented (the "Act"), and through proceedings of the Board of Directors of the Issuer, the Issuer is authorized to acquire and lease the Project to be located within the geographical limits of the County of Good and to issue revenue bonds to defray in whole or in part the costs of acquiring, redeveloping, reconstructing, and improving the Project.

The Bonds are limited obligations of the Issuer as hereinabove described. The County of Good, Michigan, is not liable on the Bonds or on any other obligation incurred by the Issuer under the Indenture or the Lease Agreement. The Issuer is not liable on the Bonds, except from revenues and other monies derived from the Project financed by the Bonds, or on any other obligation incurred by the Issuer under the Indenture or the Lease Contract. The Bonds are not general obligations and do not constitute a debt or a pledge against the general credit of the County of Good, Michigan, or against the credit or taxing power of the County, the State of Michigan, or any political subdivision thereof, but will be payable solely from revenues and receipts derived from the Project. No holder of any Bond will have the right to demand payment of the principal of, or premium, if any, or interest on the Bonds out of the funds to be raised by taxation.

THE PROJECT

The net proceeds of the sale of Bonds will be used to finance the cost of acquiring the land, buildings, and equipment of an existing mushroom-producing facility in the Township of Better, Michigan, to renovate existing structures and to acquire additional machinery and equipment. The production plant has been at this location since the early 1900's and was originally called Luscious Mushroom Growers. In 1960, it was purchased by a major food producer which operated the production facility until it ceased growing mushrooms in May, 1978. The major food producer, the Seller, decided to withdraw from the fresh mushroom business and from May of 1978 until the present sale contract was entered into used the Sun plant only to produce and can a mushroom steak sauce, purchasing fresh mushrooms from growers in other parts of the country for use in the steak sauce.

The property to be acquired consists of two adjoining pieces of property. On the east side of the street a 4.55 acre site is the location of a 5,200 square foot office building and a processing building of approximately 16,600 square feet of floor area. The "growing" or agricultural portion of the property is located across the street from the office and processing plant. This portion of the property contains approximately 44 acres and is the location of many buildings of various types, purposes, materials, vintages, and states of repair. A substantial portion of the net proceeds will be expended to repair and equip the purchased property.

The Project will be put into operation to grow and process an estimated four million (4,000,000) pounds of fresh mushrooms per year and to provide for the canning and distribution of steak sauce and quick-frozen mushroom products. It is expected that 150 persons will be employed the first year, with 25 to 50 employees being added within two years. The Company's Project conforms to the Better Township Development Plan; it is a desirable project bringing increased employment to the area, and no zoning change is required. All requisite municipal and county approvals have been obtained.

USE OF BOND PROCEEDS

Cost of acquiring land and buildings	$1,850,000
Cost of repairs, modernization, and equipment	868,750
Capitalized interest during start-up period	350,000
Bond discount to Underwriter	210,000
Printing, legal, accounting, and other expenses	216,000
Contingencies	5,250
Total	$3,500,000

OTHER FINANCING OF THE COMPANY

In addition to the funds provided from the Bonds described herein, Delicious Mushroom Growers, Ltd., (the "Company") will make a capital contribution to the Project to provide operating working capital. Delicious Mushroom Growers, Ltd., is now in the process of selling not more than 35 limited partnership interests to fund this equity contribution. It is a condition precedent to the issuance of the $3,500,000 of Series A Limited Obligation Revenue Bonds that the Partnership financing is complete. The Limited Partners' equity contributions will be as follows:

Gross Subscription		$900,000
Less:		
Organization Costs	$50,667	
Legal and Accounting	7,667	
Syndication	97,666	
Total		156,000
Net Limited Partners Equity Contributions to Project Working Capital		$744,000

The Partnership will deposit with the Trustee cash in the amount of $675,000, along with signed negotiable Promissory Notes, in the amount of $225,000, for a total gross subscription of $900,000.

DELICIOUS MUSHROOM GROWERS, LTD.

An Indiana Limited Partnership

The following is designed to explain why growing and canning mushrooms was chosen as an agricultural investment by the partnership and why the purchase of the property in Sun, Michigan was chosen for the partnership's investment. This report uses background information on the entire mushroom business, and information concerning the area around the Michigan plant.

General Agricultural Information

Agriculture in general has been favorable for investors since it offers a tax shelter initially and has been a hedge against inflation.

Over the years, the agricultural investments that have yielded the greatest returns are those in which the product is sold directly to the consumer (i.e., apples, fresh fish, small fruits and vegetables) or those items where the producer also controls the processing (i.e., a canning factory that grows vegetables, cans them, and sells them). These are the areas where the competition is the least and the returns to the grower have been historically the best.

Market Analysis

The market for fresh mushrooms is expanding. In 1976, the per capita consumption of mushrooms in the U.S. was 1.9 pounds. In 1977-78, the consumption was 2.5 pounds. However, U.S. consumption per capita is still far under that of most European countries. The price for fresh market mushrooms has increased since 1960. Ralston Purina, Castle and Cook, and Campbell Soup have all made large inroads into the marketing of fresh mushrooms and are spending a considerable amount of money to get entrenched in the business. It is the Partnerships' expectation that the foregoing companies will probably not be able to supply the growing demand for fresh market mushrooms. There is no assurance that the Partnerships' expectation will prove correct.

The demand for canned mushrooms is growing also. The canned mushroom market, however, is supplied primarily by foreign competition from Taiwan, Korea and Puerto Rico. However, the frozen mushroom market is in the judgment of the Partnership virtually untapped, and there is a demand for frozen mushrooms in the restaurant trade—either frozen, sliced, or frozen, battered, and breaded. As this market develops, the demand for mushrooms will be increased. Frozen mushrooms may become a U.S. product.

Sun, Michigan Production Plant

The production at Sun, Michigan (the Facility) has been at that location since the early 1900's and was originally called

Luscious Mushroom Growers. In 1960, it was purchased by the Seller.

The plant is being sold in its entirety; that is, the growing building and the canning and warehousing plants. The Seller contracted with the purchaser of the Sun facility for a minimum of three years to package steak sauce.

Sun, Michigan as a Location

Sun, Michigan is believed to be a favorable location for a mushroom growing facility for the following reasons. It is centrally located in the United States. It is close to major markets. It is close to high population areas. It has excellent transportation, rail and highway, to all parts of the United States. Moreover, it has a fairly uniform climate because of the lake effect. Good County, in which Sun is located, is one of the largest fruit and vegetable growing areas in the United States. This climate is beneficial to growing mushrooms.

Mushroom growing has been carried on for a period of time in the Sun area. There exists a pool of available labor and technology associated with mushroom growing.

There is no assurance however, that this labor pool will remain in the area.

The facility requires modernization and upgrading. The basic buildings, equipment, water, boilers, etc., for growing mushrooms, canning mushrooms presently exist and may be used until modernized and upgraded. There is room for on site expansion. Boiler capacity is adequate. A packaging warehousing facility for fresh mushrooms will be required.

MUSHROOM GROWING OPERATION

Sun, Michigan

I. PRODUCT

A. Name—Off White Button Mushroom

Scientific Name—Agaricus campestris bisporus

B. Description

1. *Historical Development*—A mushroom is a primitive plant, a member of the fungi family, the first family of plants to

appear on earth. No one knows for certain just how early mushrooms became a part of man's diet. However, we do know that they were mentioned as food in the Talmud and Chaldean writings that date from the dawn of civilization. In Egypt, as early as 1,000 B.C., the Pharoahs limited the use of mushrooms to their own tables.

Ancient Greek and Roman literature makes numerous references to them. "Food of the Gods," mushrooms were called in Roman times when a passion for mushrooms was synonymous with an unseemly and undisciplined love of luxuries. This popularity of mushrooms was partly social affectation, to be sure, but it was also based on the sound fact that they were a palatable and delicious food. It is probably worthy of emphasis that no mushrooms were cultivated then or for a long time thereafter, and the widespread demand for edible fungi was necessarily satisfied by those collected in the meadows and woods. The Romans had rules of thumb by means of which they recognized the edible kinds, and these rules probably worked fairly well most of the time. They were, however, often interwoven with superstition and disregarded real distinguishing characteristics. During the reign of the Caesars, there was a law on the statutes concerning grading and selling of mushrooms.

One finds little mention of mushrooms from the time of the Romans up to the sixteenth century. The first record of the cultivation of mushrooms was during the reign of Louis XIV (1638-1715). The development of the luxurious arts flourished during this time and mushrooms were in demand to assist in the development of fine cooking. By the year 1707, the cultivation of mushrooms had developed to the extent that the Frenchman Torunefort wrote a complete description of the methods of cultivation.

In the environs of Paris, there were many caves from which building stone had been quarried for years. It was in these abandoned caves that the bulk of the mushrooms were grown during this period. The business grew until 1867 where we have a record that a cave in Mery contained 21 miles of beds producing 3,000 lbs. of mushrooms daily.

From France the mushroom industry spread to England and other countries. In England, the industry developed to a considerable extent with mushrooms grown not in caves, but in outdoor ridge beds and later in greenhouses between vegetable or flower crops. The first knowledge of mushroom cultivation in the United States probably came from an English gardener, and the first mushroom center was round New York City. Most mushrooms in the early days of mushroom culture in the United States were grown in cellars, limestone or sand caves, cisterns, and under greenhouse benches. Mushrooms were grown commercially in the United States as far back as 1864. It was quite a flourishing industry on Long Island in 1890, at which time all spawn was still imported from France.

During the 1890's, the Kennett Square area near Philadelphia became the center of the domestic mushroom industry–and remains so today. Two reasons accounted for this area becoming the mushroom capital of the United States: First, the proliferation of railroads made it possible for Kennett Square growers to get their mushrooms to the large metropolitan areas within 24 hours–required because of the perishability of the product. Second, enterprising greenhouse operators in the Kennett Square area recognized that most United States mushrooms at that time were being imported (canning had been invented) from France and England.

It was at this time that growing mushrooms moved from under greenhouse benches to special houses (sheds) for growing mushrooms. These special houses were so successful and economical in operation in contrast to greenhouse cultivation, that soon they were used almost exclusively for growing mushrooms.

Today there are few countries in the world that do not grow at least some quantity of mushrooms.

2. *Caloric and nutritional information*–Cultivated mushrooms have the following caloric and nutritional value:

Nutritional Category	Nutritional Content (4½ oz. jar)
Calories	30.0
Protein (gm.)	3.2
Ascorbic Acid (gm.)	51.0
Niacin (mg. equiv.)	1.7
Riboflavin (mg.)	.19
Thiamin (mg.)	.05
Calcium (gm.)	.009
Phosphorous (gm.)	.08
Iron (mg.)	.9

C. Mushroom Growing/Processing—The growing mushrooms today is primarily done in windowless houses or sheds. Contrary to superstition, this is not because they prefer the dark, but rather that they do not require sunlight. Mushrooms are extremely sensitive to humidity and temperature, and it is easier to control the environment without sunlight. Steam heat and air conditioning provide even more complete control over the environment and are used in many growing houses.

Mushrooms, technically called vegetables, are plants that lack chlorophyll. Green plants containing chlorophyll can use sunlight to manufacture food from water and carbon dioxide in the air. Mushrooms are saprophytic and must depend on organic matter for nutrition.

Within the house, mushrooms are grown in beds or trays about eight inches deep, four feet wide and of various lengths. These trays are stacked about a foot apart from floor to ceiling to conserve space. Before mushroom spawn can be planted, the beds must be filled with four to six inches of specifically prepared compost. This compost, the growing medium for the mushrooms, is a mixture of stable litter, alfalfa, corn cobs, chemicals, and water. During the two to three weeks the compost is being prepared, it must be turned and watered a number of times to insure proper mixing and partial decomposition of the organic matter.

After the beds have been filled with this compost, the house is closed up. With no ventilation, the temperature is allowed to rise as a result of the heat generated in the compost, assisted with live steam, until it reaches between 135 and 140 degrees. Normally, this pasteurization process takes four to six days and is not complete until all odor of ammonia has left the compost. Pasteurization is necessary to control *harmful* fungi, insects, nematodes, and also helps insure consistently high mushroom yield.

After pasteurization is completed, the mushroom house is ventilated to bring the temperature down to 75 to 80 degrees. This temperature is suitable for hand planting bits of "spawn."

About two weeks after planting, the spawn has spread like threads throughout the compost profile. At this time the compost is covered with about an inch of pasteurized casing soil. The purpose of this soil is to provide a reservoir of water for the growing mushrooms.

Approximately three weeks after casing, the first mushrooms will appear on the surface of the beds. At this time, the temperature in the growing house is lowered to between 50 and 65 degrees depending on how rapidly developing crop or long a season is desired. Mushrooms will continue to develop for two or three months, depending on the temperature and as long as they find nutrition in the soil-compost mixture.

Mushrooms appear in sudden outbreaks at intervals of about one week. These outbreaks are called "flushes" or "breaks" and are followed by periods with only a few mushrooms appearing on the bed. The primary growth is during the first 30 days after the first mushrooms appear and about one half the total yield is harvested in the first 14 days.

Harvesting of mushrooms is a continuous operation, with the picker reaching across the wide beds while standing on a catwalk. At the same time, the picker removes any dead or damaged mushrooms and fills any holes in the bed with fresh soil.

As the nutrients in the compost are used up, the mushroom yield drops off sharply and the old compost is removed and a new preparation/growing cycle is started. It is probably worthwhile at this point to describe in detail the growing of spawn.

Although mushrooms are a primitive form of plant life, they differ considerably from most forms we know. Most forms of plant life develop when the seeds of the plant germinate, roots are sent out to explore the growing medium for food, stems and leaves push their way upwards drawing nourishment from the atmosphere, and eventually seeds are formed inside the fruit or flower. In the case of mushrooms, the seed is termed a "spore." These spores, which are invisible to the naked eye, send out root-like threads in all directions within the growing medium, and produce fruit (the mushroom itself) without the stem-and-leaf state.

D. Competition—Although there are some 500 mushroom growers in the U.S., Ralston Purina, Castle Cooke, and Butler County are the largest producers and all three of these companies brand their mushrooms.

1. *Ralston Purina:* (Country Stand brand fresh mushrooms) Ralston Purina is a large food conglomerate with 1976 sales of $3.4 billion and earning after taxes of $126 million. Capital expenditures in 1976 were $122 million with $175MM planned

for 1977. In 1973 Ralston Purina got into the business of growing and marketing fresh mushrooms.

Country Stand mushrooms are based on a daily delivery system by truck within a 600-mile radius or 12 driving hours from the producing plant. Ralston is currently in 50% of the U.S. with plants in Zellwood, Florida; Madisonville, Texas; Princeton, Illinois; and Morgan Hill, California. These plants reportedly required $24 million in capital and have an annual capacity of 5-12 MM pounds each. A fifth facility was under construction in London, Tennessee and Ralston plans to build three more and be completely national.

2. *Castle Cooke:* (Dole brand fresh mushrooms) Castle Cooke is a worldwide food processor with 1976 sales and net profits after taxes of $850MM and $38MM respectively. The company has been in the produce business for years and markets Dole brand fresh bananas and pineapples as well as mushrooms. In addition to being a long-time producer of processed mushrooms they entered the fresh mushroom business in 1973. With their recent acquisition of Mountain Mushroom Company in Utah, plus other acquisitions including West Foods and Knaust Mushrooms, Castle Cooke has become the largest fresh mushroom producer on the west coast. Castle Cooke recently closed down their case operation in St. Louis.

Castle Cooke is planning to expand mushroom production at their Illinois facility and double capacity at the modern Mountain Mushroom plant. In addition, a large percentage of previously processed production is being shifted to fresh. A branded display box of Dole mushrooms was introduced in 1975 for use in retail produce departments. Castle Cooke, like Ralston Purina, ships prepackaged fresh mushrooms directly to major chains and wholesale distributors.

3. *Butler County:* (Moonlight Brand fresh mushrooms) Because Butler County is a privately owned company specific information was difficult to obtain.

Butler County is probably the largest U.S. grower of mushrooms and sells them to both the fresh and processed markets. Located in West Winfield and Worthington, Pennsylvania, Butler County farms mushrooms using a tray system in underground caves. The larger Worthington farm alone contains over 500 acres of rooms. Each year the two mines are said to produce

40MM pounds of mushrooms. Of the staff of over a thousand persons engaged in the business of growing Moonlight mushrooms, two-thirds work underground.

Like Ralston Purina's Country Stand, the marketing of Moonlight mushrooms is a fully integrated operation. Daily deliveries by refrigerated Moonlight mushroom trailers of prepackaged product are made directly to retail distribution centers and processors throughout the country. More distant markets pay FOB Pennsylvania prices and must add air freight and other expenses to their costs.

Unlike Ralston, Butler County puts a variety of sizes in the same retail package and claims that their mushrooms are of better quality because of less handling. Moonlight mushrooms are referred to as "white creme" in color.

4. *Other Current Growers:* The other current growers are planning to increase their farming area by approximately 10% (30MM lbs.) next year. Further, they expect to allocate a larger percentage of the total output to the fresh market.

II. FROZEN MUSHROOMS

Current consumption of frozen mushrooms in the U.S. is estimated at 1-2 million pounds, less than one half of one percent of total domestic mushroom consumption. Lack of supply and technological difficulties have been the main reasons the industry has been unable to expand its frozen mushroom sales. This supply situation may improve given the current dynamics of the fresh market as well as an opportunity to market frozen byproduct

There is no assurance however these technical difficulties can be remedied and that the frozen mushroom business will be profitable.

THE MARKETING OF FRESH MUSHROOMS

I. BACKGROUND

The following is based on a review of the mushroom industry conducted by a General Partner of the Partnership).

The material is not represented to be definitive or exhaustive but is believed to be accurate.

II. SUMMARY

A. Consumption–Mushroom consumption in the USA has grown during the past ten years as noted in the table below:

10 YEAR CONSUMPTION RATE OF MUSHROOMS–USA

	1966-67	1975-76
U.S. Population	197,000,000	214,000,000
Total Pounds Consumed	200,000,000	408,000,000
Per Capita All Mushrooms	1.02	1.91
Per Capita Fresh–USA Prod	.21	.66
Per Capita Processed–USA Prod	.62	.79
Per Capita Imports to USA	.17	.41

While processed mushroom consumption has increased 28%, fresh mushroom consumption has tripled during that period. Comparative per capita consumption in the European countries is shown below:

COMPARATIVE PER CAPITA CONSUMPTION IN MAJOR EUROPEAN COUNTRIES

	Lbs./Capita
U.S.A.	1.91
France	2.57
Belgium/Luxembourg	.86
Netherlands	.76
Germany	3.66
Italy	.22
Sweden	2.25
Canada	3.10

In summary, three conclusions may be reached:

1. Per capita consumption of mushrooms is increasing in the USA;

2. Although on a much lower base, fresh mushroom consumption is growing at an even faster rate than "processed";

3. USA per capita consumption is less than several European countries.

B. Fresh Mushrooms–Increased per capita consumption of fresh mushrooms in the last 10 years has provided fresh mushroom growers with increased markets. This favorable condition has encouraged companies who are experts in marketing commodities and may compete with the Partnership to aggressively pursue this opportunity in fresh mushrooms.

Major Producers:

1. *Ralston Purina* now has large plants in Florida, Texas, Illinois and California and has one under construction in Tennessee. They now cover 50% of the domestic market and have plans for three additional plants. They are expected to cover the entire nation in 1980. To supply institutional needs, Ralston is building a plant to process by-product from five growing facilities.

2. *Castle & Cooke* has merged with several mushroom producers which has made them the largest producer in the west.

3. *Butler County* sells both to the fresh market and to processors from their cave operation to all areas of the northeast and the upper midwest. They produce 40,000,000 pounds per year.

III. DISCUSSION

A. Fresh Produce–Fresh produce accounts for 6.6% of supermarket sales with average retail margins of 31%. In addition to fruits and vegetables, produce departments carry horticulture items, nuts and juices. Growth has been relatively flat in the huge fresh vegetable business (23 billion pounds) over the last few years. Because of the economics and perishability associated with fresh produce, consumption is greatest near main production areas, and eight major cities account for 50% of fresh vegetable volume.

Consumers prefer fresh produce to either canned or frozen because fresh is perceived to be better tasting, more nutritious and more appetizing. However, storage, preparation, and waste are problems often associated with fresh produce. Despite its perceived attributes, fresh produce volume remains fairly constant and is felt to be price inelastic. (Head lettuce volume is virtually identical at $.19 or $.39/head.) Fresh produce prices are very sensitive to supply and demand fluctuations with the general rule of thumb being that retail value is three times that of farm value. However, with stable consumer demand, grower's margins vary widely due to uncertain production, concentrated supply, and perishable commodities. Because of produce perishability, deliveries are made often with supermarkets over $5MM in annual volume receiving 4.3 deliveries/week while those with less than $1MM receive 2.9 deliveries/week. Produce is sold either bulk (73%) or prepackaged (27%) with consumer preferring the former by 3½ to 1 since with bulk they are able to judge quality themselves and are fearful of being "ripped off" with a prepackaged item. It was felt a couple of years ago that nutritional labeling, UPC codes and branding possibilities would indicate a long-term trend towards prepackaged produce. However, recent information indicates a surprising return to bulk packaging. This phenomenon is due to rising labor and packaging cost, as well as consumer preference.

Palletization of produce is a growing trend in the industry. In addition, week-long price specials, and unadvertised in-store specials are gaining in popularity as techniques to simulate sales.

B. Mushrooms in General—Mushrooms are marketed either fresh, dried, frozen or canned. Although there are over a hundred different species of mushrooms, only a handful are toxic. In general, mushrooms come in three grades and four colors. Grade 1 commands the highest price and is considered to have the best appearance and mildest flavor. Grade 3 has the least attractive appearance; is the most mature; is said to be the best tasting and receives the lowest price. Grade 2 falls somewhere between Grades 1 and 3 on appearance, taste, and price attributes. Grade 1 is sold mainly to the fresh market while 2 and 3 grades are generally sold to the mushroom processor.

The four major types of mushrooms in terms of color are white, off-white, creme and brown. White mushrooms are demanded by fresh market customers in the eastern two-thirds of the United States, while brown and creme mushrooms are popular in fresh western markets. Darker mushrooms have the advantage of not showing bruises as much as their lighter colored counterparts. Creme mushrooms are said to be easier to grow and less prone to disease. Off-white and brown mushrooms are the most difficult varieties to grow. Because of perishability, fresh mushrooms must be marketed within a few days of harvest. Only whole mushrooms are sold in fresh retail markets because cutting detracts from appearance and increases perishability.

Mushrooms are grown for size and the difference in yields from various strains is not greater than +/–10%. Mushrooms are not grown in caves any more, the major exception being Butler County Mushrooms Farms, but in a controlled environment. The best growing season is October-May, however air conditioning, etc. have made it possible to extend availability into the summer months.

As only the best quality mushrooms are sold to the fresh markets, most growers sell product to both fresh and processed markets. With an obvious interaction between these markets the volumes and prices of mushrooms sold by growers to processors are dependent on the price of fresh and the selling price of imported canned. In addition, some domestic canners ship part of their fresh supply (either grown or purchased by them) to fresh markets when either they have sufficient supplies or the fresh market is more profitable.

C. Mushroom Sales

MUSHROOMS
U.S. PRODUCER SALES
(MM Lbs. Fresh Weight Equivalent)

	Total	Fresh	% Total	Processed	% Total
1966/67	165	42	25%	123	75%
1967/68	181	48	26%	133	74%
1968/69	189	56	30%	133	70%
1969/70	194	62	32%	132	68%
1970/71	207	58	28%	149	72%
1971/72	231	66	29%	165	71%
1972/73	254	77	30%	177	70%
1973/74	279	102	37%	177	63%
1974/75	299	126	42%	173	58%
1975/76	310	142	46%	168	54%

SOURCE: USDA

THE BONDS

Form of Bonds

The total principal amount of Bonds presently authorized to be issued is $3,500,000. The Bonds will be issued as coupon Bonds in the denomination of $5,000 each, registrable as to principal only with the option of convertibility at the holder's expense to fully registered Bonds without coupons in denominations of $5,000 and any integral multiple thereof. The Bonds initially issued will be dated as of December 1, and will bear interest from such date at the rates, and mature on June 1 and December 1 of the years covered. Interest on the Bonds will be paid semi-annually on June 1 and December 1 of each year. Principal of and premium, if any, and interest on the coupon Bonds and principal of and premium, if any, on the fully registered Bonds are payable at the main office of the Trustee. Interest on fully registered Bonds will be paid by checks or drafts drawn upon the Trustee and mailed to the registered owners thereof. Subject to certain conditions contained in the Indenture, coupon Bonds may be exchanged for fully registered Bonds of the same maturity without coupons and fully registered Bonds may similarly be exchanged for coupon Bonds of the same maturity. In the event any Bond is mutilated, lost, stolen, or destroyed, the Issuer may execute and the Trustee may authenticate a new Bond in accordance with the provisions therefor in the Indenture. The Issuer and the Trustee may charge the holder or owner of such Bond with their reasonable fees and expenses in this connection.

The Series A Bonds shall be subject to both mandatory and optional redemption prior to maturity.

Additional Bonds

The Issuer may but shall not be required to authorize the issuance of the Additional Bonds upon the terms and conditions provided in the Indenture. Additional Bonds may be issued only to pay any one or more of the following: (i) the cost of completing the Project; (ii) the costs of making improvements to the Project; (iii) the refunding of all or any part of the Bonds; and (iv) the costs of issuance and sale of the Additional Bonds and capitalized interest for such period and other costs reasonably related to the financing as shall be agreed upon by the Company and the Issuer; provided, however, that the Issuer and the Trustee shall be furnished with an opinion of Counsel that the issuance of Additional Bonds and the expenditure of proceeds from the sale thereof is permitted by Act No. 338, Public Acts of Michigan, 1974, as amended, and will not impair the exemption of interest on the Bonds from Federal income taxation. Prior to the issuance of any Additional Bonds, (i) their terms, the purchase price to be paid therefor, and the manner in which the proceeds therefrom are to be disbursed shall be approved in writing by the Company, (ii) the Company and the Issuer shall have entered into an amendment to the Contract, if necessary, to provide for increased rentals in an amount at least sufficient to pay the principal, premium, if any, and interest on the Additional Bonds when due, and (iii) the Issuer shall have otherwise complied with the provisions of the Indenture with respect to the issuance of such Additional Bonds. Any Improvements to the Project acquired with the proceeds of the sale of Additional Bonds shall become a part of the Project and shall be included under the Lease Purchase Contract to the same extent as if originally included hereunder. Failure by the Issuer to issue Additional Bonds shall not release the Company from any provisions of the Lease Purchase Contract, regardless of the reason for such failure.

Security for the Bonds

The Bonds are limited obligations of the Issuer payable (except to the extent payable out of monies attributable to Bond proceeds or the income from the temporary investment thereof or from the proceeds of insurance or condemnation awards) solely from and secured by a pledge to the Trustee of the rents, revenues, and receipts derived by the Issuer from the Project, including those derived pursuant to the Lease Contract. Rentals under the Lease Contract are due from the Company on such dates and in such amounts as are sufficient to pay the principal of and premium, if any, and interest on the Bonds when due. The Bonds are not general obligations and do not constitute a debt or pledge against the general credit of the County of Good or against the general credit or taxing power of the County, the State of Michigan, or any political subdivision

The Bonds shall be a limited obligation of the Issuer secured by and payable solely and only from the following:

(i) all moneys in the Acquisition Fund and the Surplus Fund, including the proceeds of the Bonds pending disbursement thereof as provided in the Mortgage and Truste Indenture;

(ii) all moneys in the Bond Fund, including all revenues of the Issuer from the Project under the Contract (or any subsequent Lease or Sale of the Project) less the obligations of the Company to the Issuer, the Board of Directors of the Issuer, and its employees, agents, and representatives under the Contract for administrative costs, taxes and governmental and public service charges, indemnity payments, and liability insurance proceeds (or similar payments under a subsequent contract), collectively the "net revenues," which net revenues pursuant to the Contract and the Indenture are to be paid directly by the Company to the Trustee and deposited in the Bond Fund;

(iii) the Project, subject and subordinate to Permitted Encumbrances (as defined in the Contract);

(iv) all of the Issuer's rights and interest in, to, and under the Contract, including the obligations of the Company and its General Partners found in the Contract, and subject to reservation by the Issuer of the right to enforce in its name and for its own benefit the obligations of the Company to the Issuer under the Contract for administrative costs, taxes and governmental and public service charges, indemnity payments, and liability insurance proceeds;

(v) all of the Issuer's rights to receive net revenues from the Project;

(vi) all of the proceeds of the foregoing, in particular Investment Income.

The foregoing are collectively the "Mortgaged Property," and in consideration of the purchase of the Bonds and the obligations of the Trustee under the Indenture and to secure payment of the principal of and interest on the Bonds and the performance of the Issuer's obligations under the Bonds and the Indenture, the Issuer hereby conveys, assigns, pledges, mortgages, and grants a security interest in the Mortgaged Property to the Trustee, and its successors and assigns.

In addition, the Indenture creates a Debt Service Reserve Fund into which the General Partners will deposit, from funds other than Bond proceeds, the sum of $350,000, which amount is to be used for the payment of principal and interest should be insufficient monies available therefor in the Bond Fund created under the Indenture. The Debt Service Reserve Fund (or "Security Deposit") is intended to provide a degree of protection to Bond holders during the first three years of the life of the Lease. A Debt Service Reserve is especially important during the start-up years of the Project. The Security Deposit shall be returned to the General Partners upon the first of the following to occur: (i) when the Company's net worth ratio as defined in the Lease Purchase Contract is not less than thirty per cent (30%) of the Bond debt of this Project, or (ii) three years after the Closing Date.

REDEMPTION OF BONDS PRIOR TO MATURITY

The Bonds are callable for redemption prior to maturity in the circumstances described below.

Extraordinary Redemption

The Series A Bonds may, at the option of the Issuer, be redeemed on any interest payment date, as a whole, at 100% of the principal amount thereof plus accrued interest to the redemption date upon exercise by the Company of its option to purchase the Project following an event wherein

(i) the Project shall have been damaged or destroyed or there shall have occurred the condemnation of such portion of the Project or the taking by eminent domain of such use or control of the Project so that the Project may not be reasonably restored within a period of six consecutive months, or that the cost of restoration of the Project is reasonably deemed by the Company to be uneconomic; or

(ii) as a result of any changes in the Constitution of the State of Michigan or the Constitution of the United States of America or of legislative or administrative action (whether federal, state, or local) or by final decree, judgment, or order of any court or administrative body (whether federal state, or local) entered after the contest thereof by the Company in good faith, the Contract shall have become void or unenforceable or impossible of performance in accordance with the intent of the parties as expressed therein, or unreasonable burdens or excessive liabilities shall have been imposed on the Issuer of the Company, including without limitation federal, state, or other ad valorem property, income, or other taxes not being imposed on the date of the Contract; or

(iii) changes in the economic availability of raw materials, operating supplies, or facilities necessary for the operation of the Project for the purposes for which it has been constructed by the Company shall have occurred, or such technological or other changes shall have occurred or been required by any governmental authority which, in the Company's reasonable judgment, render the Project uneconomic for its use.

Special Mandatory Redemption

The Series A Bonds are also subject to redemption in the event of a "Determination of Taxability" which means the issuance of a statutory notice of deficiency or ruling by the Internal Revenue Service which holds in effect that the interest payable on any of the Series A Bonds is includable in the gross income of a holder thereof (other than a holder who is a "substantial user" of the Project or "related person" as such terms are defined in the Internal Revenue Code of 1954, as amended (the "Code")) as a result of the limitations prescribed in Section 103(b)(6) of the Code, having been exceeded, or the Series A Bonds being "arbitrage bonds" under Section 103(c) of the Code, or the proceeds of the Bonds being used for purposes which are not permitted under Section 103(b)(6) or the issuance of a statement by the Company to the effect that it has exceeded or intends to exceed the maximum amount of capital expenditures permitted under Section 103(b)(6)(D) of the Code. Such a Determination of Taxability shall be deemed to have occurred on the date borne by said statutory notice of deficiency or said ruling or the date borne by such statement, whichever shall be applicable. In the event there should occur a Determination of Taxability, the Series A Bonds shall be redeemed in whole on the first interest payment date following the date of closing of the purchase of the Project under the Contract for which the requisite notice of redemption can be given after the occurrence of such event, at a redemption price equal to the sum of 108% of the principal amount thereof plus 1% additional premium for each period of six (6) months, or any part thereof from the occurrence or circumstance which has occasioned the Determination of Taxability to the date of such redemption, together with accrued interest to the redemption date.

Optional Redemption

The Series A Bonds may also, at the option of the Issuer with the consent of the Company, be redeemed prior to maturity on any interest payment date, in whole or in part in inverse order of maturity at the redemption prices (expressed as percentages of principal amount) as follows, plus accrued interest to the redemption date:

Redemption Dates	Redemption Price
Year Four	103 %
Year Five	102.5%
Year Five	102 %
Year Six	101.5%
Year Six	101 %
Year Seven	100.5%
Year Seven and thereafter to maturity	100 %

If less than all the outstanding Series A Bonds shall be called for redemption, the Trustee shall select by lot, in such manner as it shall in its discretion determine, the Series A Bonds to be redeemed.

Notice of Redemption

Notice of the call for any such redemption, which shall identify the Bonds to be redeemed, shall be given by the Trustee by publication in a financial journal or newspaper of general circulation in the City of New York, New York, not less than 30 nor more than 45 days prior to the redemption date, and in the case of redemption of Bonds at the time registered as to principal (except to bearer), upon mailing by the Trustee, a copy of the redemption notice by first-class mail not less than 30 nor more than 45 days prior to the redemption date to the registered owner of each bond to be redeemed at the address shown on the registration books; provided, however, that failure to give such notice by mailing, or any defect therein, shall not affect the validity of any proceedings for the redemption of Bonds. If all of said Bonds to be redeemed are at that time registered as to principal (except to bearer), notice by first-class mail to the owner or owners thereof not less than 30 days nor more than 45 days prior to the redemption date shall be sufficient and published noitce of the call for redemption need not be given.

THE LEASE PURCHASE CONTRACT

The following, in addition to information provided elsewhere herein, summarizes certain provisions of the Lease Purchase Contract, to which document in its entirety reference is made for the detailed provisions thereof.

Acquisition and Equipment of the Project

From the net proceeds of the sale of the Bonds, there will be deposited in the Bond Fund created under the Indenture a sum equal to the accrued interest, if any, from the date thereof to the date of their delivery to the Underwriter and capitalized interest in the amount of $350,000. The balance of the net proceeds of the Bonds will be deposited in the Acquisition Fund created under the Indenture. The Trustee is authorized to use the monies in the Acquisition Fund to pay the costs incurred by the Company or the Issuer in connection with the issuance of the Bonds and with the acquisition, construction, renovation and installation of the Project, upon the receipt by the Trustee of written requisitions of the Company. Subject to certain restrictions in the Lease Purchase Contract, all monies remaining in the Acquisition Fund after the completion of the Project may, at the direction of the Company, be (i) used to purchase Bonds in the open market in accordance with the provisions of the Indenture or (ii) deposited in the Bond Fund.

In the event that monies in the Acquisition Fund available for payment of the cost of the Project should not be sufficient to pay the remaining cost of the Project, the Company will pay the cost of completing the Project. In such event, the Company will not be entitled to any reimbursement for such excess expenditures from the Issuer, the Trustee, or the holders of the Bonds, and the Company will not be entitled to any diminution of the rents payable under the Lease Purchase Contract. The Issuer may, at the request of the Company and with the consent of the Underwriter, authorize issuance of Additional Bonds for the purpose of completing the Project.

Lease Term and Rental

The Lease Purchase Contract will become effective upon the delivery of the Bonds to the Underwriter and will expire when all the Bonds issued under the Indenture have been fully paid and retired (or provision for such payment has been made as provided in the Indenture), unless the term thereof has been terminated earlier pursuant to other provisions thereof. Rental payments will be due under the Lease Purchase Contract on or before two business days prior to each interest payment date of the Bonds in an amount which, together with other monies in the Bond Fund available therefor, will be sufficient to pay the principal of and premium, if any, and interest on the Bonds then outstanding which are payable on such interest payment date. Commencing at least two business days prior to June 1, 1987 a sum sufficient to meet the amount payable on such date as interest and one-sixth (1/6) of the amount payable as principal on the next Interest Payment Date that principal is payable and as principal, if any, due on such next Interest Payment Date by way of redemption or as acceleration provided in the Indenture by declaration or otherwise less amounts previously paid, if any, for payment of principal in excess of the foregoing requirements.

Maintenance and Modification

During the lease term, the Company will at its own expense (i) maintain the Project in reasonably safe condition and (ii) maintain the Project in good repair and in good operating condition, making from time to time all necessary repairs thereto and renewals and replacements thereof. The Company may remodel the Project or make modifications or improvements thereon or thereto from time to time as it, in its discretion, may deem to be desirable for its uses and purposes, without the prior written consent of the Issuer and the Trustee, provided that such remodeling, modifications, or improvements do not materially detract from the value of the Project or impair the exemption of interest on the Bonds from Federal income taxation. Except as provided in the Lease Purchase Contract, the cost of such remodeling, modifications, or improvements shall be paid by the Company or out of the proceeds of Additional Bonds, if any, issued by the Issuer for that purpose, and the same shall become a part of the Project and be included under the terms of the Contract.

Taxes and Other Charges

The Company, subject to its right to contest such taxes or charges as provided in the Lease Purchase Contract, will promptly pay, as the same become due, (i) all taxes and governmental charges of any kind whatsoever that may at any time be lawfully assessed or levied against or with respect to the Project or any interest therein which if not paid will become a lien on the Project prior to or on a parity with the lien of the Indenture, (ii) all lawful charges for gas, sewer, water, electricity, light, heat, power, telephone service, and other utilities and services used, rendered, or supplied to the Project, and (iii) all assessments and charges lawfully made by any governmental body for public improvements that may be secured by a lien on the Project provided that, with respect to special assessments or other governmental charges that may lawfully be paid in installments over a period of years, the Company will be obligated to pay only such installments as are required to be paid during the lease term. The Company also agrees that it will pay, in addition to all rent required under the Lease Purchase Contract, every lawful cost, expense, and obligation, for the payment of which the Issuer or the Company is or shall become liable, by reason of (i) either of their respective estates or interests in all or any portion of the Project, (ii) any right or interest of the Issuer or the Company in or under the Lease Purchase Contract, or (iii) in any manner connected with or arising out of the Company's possession, operation, maintenance, alteration, repair, rebuilding, use, or occupancy of all or any portion of the Project.

Insurance

The Company will continuously insure the Project against such risks as are customarily insured against by business or like size and type, including without limitation loss from or damage by fire, with standard extended coverage, vandalism, or malicious mischief. The Company's obligation is to maintain such insurance at all times in an amount equal to or exceeding the lesser of (i) the full insurable value of the Project or (ii) the amount, exclusive of any co-insurance, necessary to pay, retire, and redeem all of the then-outstanding Bonds. The Company is also obligated continuously to carry general liability insurance in amounts not less than $3,000,000 for bodily injury or death per occurrence, and $500,000 for property damage per occurrence. During the term of construction, the Company is also obligated to carry builder's risk or similar insurance to the extent of the full insurable value of the Project.

All insurance policies will be with insurance companies qualified under the laws of the State of Michigan and may contain a deductible clause (not to exceed $50,000 in the case of liability insurance), co-insurance features, and exceptions and exclusions comparable to those in similar policies carried by other companies engaged in businesses similar in size, character, and other respects to those in which the Company is engaged. In lieu of separate insurance policies, such insurance may be provided in the form of blanket policies of the Company covering not only the Project, but other properties owned or leased by the Company as well. All proceeds of insurance against property damage shall be payable to the Issuer, the Trustee, and the Company, as their interests may appear.

Damage, Destruction, and Condemnation

If the Project or any part thereof is damaged or destroyed, or if the Project or any part thereof is taken in condemnation or by the exercise of the power of eminent domain by any person, firm, or corporation acting under governmental authority, the Company will elect either to restore the Project and continue to make rental payments under the Lease Purchase Contract or to exercise its option to purchase the Project. If the Company elects to restore the Project, the Trustee will deposit the insurance proceeds or condemnation award into the Acquisition Fund and such monies will be used to restore the Project. If the Company elects to exercise its option to purchase the Project, the Trustee will deposit the insurance proceeds or condemnation award into the Acquisition Fund and such monies will be used to restore the Project. If the Company elects to exercise its option to purchase the Project, the Trustee will deposit the insurance proceeds or condemnation award into the Bond Fund.

Assignment and Subleasing

The Company may assign the Lease Purchase Contract or sublet the whole or any part of the Project without the consent of the Issuer or the Trustee if the use of the Project by the assignee or sublessee will not affect the validity of the Bonds under Act No. 338, Public Acts of Michigan, 1974, as amended, or impair the exemption of interest on the Bonds from Federal income taxation; provided, however, that the Company shall nevertheless remain primarily liable to the Issuer for the payment of all rent and other sums payable by it under and for the full performance of all of the covenants and conditions of the Contract.

Special Covenants

The Lease Purchase Contract will provide that the Company and the Issuer will not take, authorize, or permit to be taken any action, and that they have not taken or authorized any action, which results in interest paid on the Bonds being included in gross income of the holders thereof for purposes of Federal income taxation.

The Company will also agree that during the term of the Lease Purchase Contract it will maintain its existence and its qualification to do business in Michigan.

Company's Purchase Option and Purchase Obligations

The Company may elect to purchase the Project at any time prior to the full payment of the Bonds as set forth in the Lease Purchase Contract.

In addition, the Company is obligated to purchase the Project (i) in the event that there is a Determination of Taxability as defined in the Lease Purchase Contract or (ii) at the expiration of the Lease Purchase Contract following full payment of the Bonds.

Defaults and Remedies

Each of the following is an "Event of Default" under the Lease Purchase Contract:

(i) Failure by the Company to make when due the rental payments required to be paid as specified in the Lease Purchase Contract;

(ii) Failure by the Company to observe and perform any covenant, condition, or agreement on its part to be observed or performed for a period of forty-five days after written notice specifying such failure and requesting that it be remedied, given to the Company by the Issuer or the Trustee; provided, however, that if said Default shall be such that it cannot be corrected within such period, it shall not constitute an Event of Default if corrective action is instituted by the Company within such period and diligently pursued until the Default is corrected or if adequate security is provided by the Company to the Trustee; or

(iii) Certain events of dissolution, liquidation, assignment for the benefit of creditors, bankruptcy, insolvency, or creditor's proceedings affecting the Company.

Under the Lease Purchase Contract, a "default" is defined to mean any default by the Company in the performance or observance of any covenant, agreement, or condition contained in the Lease Purchase Contract, exclusive of any period of grace required to constitute an Event of Default.

Whenever any Event of Default shall have occurred and be continuing, the Issuer, the Trustee, or the Bondholders, to the extent authorized under the Indenture, may take one or more of the following steps:

(i) Declare all installments of rent for the remainder of the term of the Lease Purchase Contract, being such amount as is necessary to pay principal of and premium, if any, and interest on all outstanding Bonds (assuming acceleration thereof as provided in the Indenture) to be immediately due and payable;

(ii) With the consent of the Trustee, re-enter and take possession of the Project without termination of the Lease Purchase Contract, and sublease the Project for the account of the Company holding the Company liable for the difference between the rent and other amounts payable by such sublessee and the rents and other amounts payable by the Company under the Lease Purchase Contract;

(iii) With the consent of the Trustee, terminate the Lease Purchase Contracts, exclude the Company from possession of the Project, and use its best effort to lease or sell the Project to another for the account of the Company, holding the Company liable for all rent and other payments due up to the effective date of such releasing;

(iv) Require the Company to furnish copies of the books and records and any and all accounts, date, and income tax or other tax returns for the Company pertaining to the Project or the Event of Default and the remedy thereof;

(v) Take whatever action at law or in equity may appear necessary or desirable to collect the rent then due and thereafter to become due or to enforce performance and observance of any obligation, agreement, or covenant of the Company under the Lease Purchase Contract;

(vi) With the consent of the Trustee, remodel, improve, and repair the Project in order to better sublease or relet the Project, and all costs and reasonable expense thereof shall become a debt of the Company to the Issuer or the Trustee, and the Issuer or the Trustee shall be entitled to reimbursement from the first revenues or rentals received thereafter from any subleasing or reletting; and

(vii) With the consent of the Trustee, declare the Lease Purchase Contract forfeited and void, and retain whatever may have been paid thereon and the Project and all improvements that may have been made upon the Project, together with any additions and accretions thereto, and consider and treat the Company as its tenant holding over without permission, and take immediate possession of the Project, and have the Company and each and every other occupant removed and put out. A notice of forfeiture, giving the Company at least 15 days to pay any monies required to be paid hereunder or to cure other material breaches of the Lease Purchase Contract, shall be served on the Company as provided by statute prior to institution of any proceedings to recover possession of the Project.

No remedy in the Lease Purchase Contract conferred upon or reserved to the Issuer, the Trustee, or any Bondholder is intended to be exclusive of any other available remedy or remedies given under the Lease Purchase Contract, the Indenture, or now or hereafter existing at law or in equity.

Amendment to Lease Purchase Contract

The Indenture provides that the Issuer and the Trustee may, without the consent of or notice to the Bondholders, consent to any amendment, change, or modification of the Lease Purchase Contract as may be required (i) by the provisions of such Lease Purchase Contract or such Indenture, (ii) in connection with the issuance of Additional Bonds under such Indenture, (iii) for the purpose of curing any ambiguity, formal defect, or omission in the Lease Purchase Contract, (iv) to grant or pledge to the Trustee for the benefit of the Bondholders any additional security, or (v) in connection with any other change in the Lease Purchase Contract which, in the judgment of the Trustee, does not prejudice the Trustee or impair the rights of the Bondholders.

Except for such amendments, neither the Issuer nor the Trustee can consent to any amendment of the Lease Purchase Contract without the written approval or consent of the holders of not less than two-thirds of the aggregate principal amount of the then-outstanding Bonds.

THE MORTGAGE AND TRUST INDENTURE

The following, in addition to information provided elsewhere herein, summarizes certain provisions of the Indenture, to which document in its entirety reference is made for the detailed provisions thereof.

Security for the Bonds

Under the Indenture, the Issuer will mortgage the Project to the Trustee as security for the Bonds issued to finance the Project.

Assignment and Pledge

Under the Indenture, the Issuer will pledge and assign to the Trustee all of its rights, title, and interest in and to the rents, revenues, and receipts derived from the Project, including those arrived from the Lease Purchase Contract, any assignment thereof, or any sublease of the Project, for the payment of the principal of and premium, if any, and interest on the Bonds.

Acquisition Fund

The Indenture provides for the establishment of an Acquisition Fund to be held by the Trustee. Concurrently with the delivery of the Bonds, the proceeds from the sale of the Bonds, less accrued interest, if any, on the Bonds from the date thereof to the date of delivery thereof to the Underwriter, which shall be deposited in the Bond Fund created under the Indenture, will be deposited by the Trustee into the Acquisition Fund. The Trustee is authorized and directed to pay or reimburse the Company for the cost of acquisition, construction, or installation of the Project, including expenses incurred in connection with the issuance of the Bonds and, to the extent not paid from the Bond Fund, interest on the Bonds until construction of the Project is completed. Upon receipt of a certificate of completion of an office of the Company, any amount remaining in the Acquisition Fund that is not required for payment of any remaining portion of the cost of the Project will be used, subject to certain limitations provided in the Indenture, for the purchase of Bonds in the open market at no more than par or transferred into the Bond Fund.

Bond Fund

The Trustee will deposit in the Bond Fund, from the proceeds of the Bonds issued under the Indenture, an amount representing accrued interest on the Bonds from the date thereof to the date of their delivery to the Underwriter. All payments to be received by the Issuer from the Company under the Lease Purchase Contract will be assigned to the Trustee by the Issuer and will be paid directly to the Trustee for deposit in the Bond Fund. The Bond Fund will be used to pay the principal of and premium, if any, and interest on the Bonds at or price to maturity. By virtue of the assignment of the rights of the Issuer under the Lease Purchase Contract to the Trustee, monies prepaid by the Company and deposited in the Bond Fund will be used to redeem the Bonds on permissible redemption dates selected by the Company.

Debt Service Reserve Fund

The Lease Purchase Contract provides for the establishment of a Debt Service Reserve Fund to be held by the Trustee into which the General Partners will deposit, from funds other than Bond Proceeds, the sum of $350,000. The Debt Service Reserve Fund is to provide monies to pay the principal of and interest on any Series A Bonds which would not otherwise be paid due to insufficiency of funds in the Bond Fund. The Debt Service Reserve, if not used to satisfy unfunded principal and interest payments, shall be returned to the General Partners upon the first of the following to occur: (i) when the Company's net worth ratio is not less than thirty per cent (30%) of the then-outstanding Bonds, or (ii) three years after the Closing Date.

Investment of Funds; Arbitrage

Any monies held as part of the Acquisition Fund, Bond Fund, or Debt Service Reserve Fund will be invested or reinvested by the Trustee, at the direction of the Company, in (i) bonds and other direct obligations of the United States or an agency or instrumentality of the United States; (ii) certificates of deposit, savings accounts, repurchase agreements, deposit accounts, or depository receipts of any bank having capital, subordinated capital notes, surplus, and undivided profits which, when taken together, aggregate at least $5,000,000 and whose deposits are insured by the Federal Deposit Insurance Corporation; or (iii) if permitted commercial paper rated at the time of purchase within the three highest classifications established by not less than two standard rating services and which matures not more than 270 days after the date of purchase. Not more than 50% of the monies in any fund established under the Indenture may be invested in commercial paper at any time. Any investments in certificates of deposit of any single bank as described in subparagraph (ii) above will be limited to an amount which, when taken together with all of the deposits of the Company in such bank, does not exceed 50% of the capital, subordinated capital notes, surplus, and undivided profits of such bank.

All such investments will be held by or under the control of the Trustee, will be deemed to be a part of the fund for which such investments were made, and, with the exception of investments in commercial paper which shall not exceed 270 days, shall have a maturity not later than the estimated time when the funds so invested will be needed for the purchase of any such fund. Any income from and profit on such investments shall be credited to the fund for which such investments were made, and any loss resulting from such investments shall be charged to the appropriate fund.

The Issuer, the Company, and the Trustee will covenant that none of the monies held under the Indenture will be used in a manner which will cause the Bonds to be "arbitrage bonds" within the meaning of Section 103(c) of the Code.

Defaults and Remedies

Each of the following is an "Event of Default" under the Indenture:

(i) Default in the due and punctual payment of interest on any Bond;

(ii) Default in the due and punctual payment of the principal of or premium, if any, on any Bond, whether at the stated maturity thereof, or upon proceedings for the redemption thereof, or upon the maturity thereof by declaration;

(iii) Default in the performance of any other obligation under the Indenture on the Bonds and the continuance thereof for the period and after the notice specified below; and

(iv) The occurrence of any Event of Default under the Lease Purchase Contract.

No default specified in (iii) above will constitute an Event of Default under the Indenture until written notice thereof is given by the Trustee to the Company, or by at least two holders with combined holdings of not less than 25% of the principal amount of outstanding Bonds and Additional Bonds issued under the Indenture to the Company and the Trustee, and the Company has had 45 days after receipt of such notice to correct the default or cause the defaults to be corrected, and has not corrected the default or caused the default to be corrected within such period; provided, however, if the default is such that it cannot be corrected within such period, it will not constitute an Event of Default if corrective action is instituted by the Company within such period and diligently pursued until the default is corrected.

Upon the occurrence of any Event of Default and failure of the Company to timely remedy the same, the Trustee may, and upon written request of at least two holders with combined holdings of not less than 25% of the principal amount of outstanding Bonds and Additional Bonds issued under the Indenture will, enforce its rights by any one or more of the following remedies:

(i) Declare the principal amount of and interest accrued on all outstanding Bonds immediately due and payable;

(ii) Bring action upon the Bonds;

(iii) Commence judicial proceedings to enforce the Indenture (including the foreclosure of the lien of the Indenture) or preserve or protect the Project and thereupon be entitled as a matter of law to the appointment of a receiver of the Project;

(iv) If the Lease Purchase Contract shall have been terminated, and while the Bonds remain unpaid, take possession of the Project in the name of and as agent for the Issuer which shall retain title to the Project and hold, operate, and manage the same, including (a) the making of repairs and improvements as the Trustee shall deem necessary, (b) the leasing of all or any part of the Project, (c) collecting all income and revenue from the Project, and (d) paying the reasonable costs and expenses of so taking, holding, and managing the Project;

(v) Foreclosure of the mortgage lien created hereby on the Project by judicial proceedings or by advertisement, pursuant to the statute in such case provided, and the Trustee or any Bondholder may become the purchaser thereof at any foreclosure sale, if the highest bidder; and

(vi) Pursue any other available remedy to enforce payment of the Bonds.

Upon the written request of at least two holders with combined holdings of not less than 25% in aggregate principal amount of outstanding Bonds and Additional Bonds issued under the Indenture and upon reasonable indemnification of the Trustee for all costs and expenses incurred in the exercise of such rights, the Trustee must pursue one or more of the foregoing remedies as the Trustee shall deem most expedient to the interest of the Bondholders.

No holder of any Bond or coupon will have the right to institute any proceeding for the enforcement of the Indenture or any remedy thereunder unless an Event of Default shall have occurred and the Trustee shall have received the requisite request by at least two holders with combined holdings of not less than 25% in aggregate principal amount of outstanding Bonds and Additional Bonds to pursue any remedy under the Indenture, shall have been given reasonable time to pursue any such remedy, shall have been given an indemnity bond, and thereafter shall have failed or refused to institute any action under the Indenture. The foregoing conditions precedent will not, however, affect or impair the right of any Bondholder to enforce the payment of the principal of and interest on any Bond after the maturity thereof.

Waiver of Events of Default

The Trustee may in its sole discretion waive any Event of Default hereunder and its consequences and rescind any declaration of maturity of principal and in case of any such waiver or rescission, the Issuer, the Company, the Trustee, and the Bondholders shall be restored to their former positions and rights hereunder respectively, but no such waiver or rescission shall extend to or affect any subsequent or other Default, or impair any right consequent thereon.

Supplemental Indentures

The Issuer and the Trustee may, without the consent of or notice to any of the Bondholders, enter into a supplemental indenture or indentures (i) to cure any ambiguity, formal defect, or omission in the Indenture; (ii) to grant to or confer upon the Trustee, with its consent, any additional rights, remedies, power, or authority that may lawfully be granted to or conferred upon the Bondholders or the Trustee, for the benefit of the Bondholders; (iii) to grant or pledge additional security to the Trustee for the benefit of the Bondholders; (iv) to provide for the issuance of Additional Bonds; (v) to modify, amend, or supplement the Indenture or any indentures supplemental thereto in such manner as to permit the qualification thereof under the Trust Indenture Act of 1939 or any similar federal statute then in effect or to permit the qualification of the Bonds for sale under the securities laws of any of the states of the United States; and (vi) to make any other change which, in the judgment of the Trustee, is not to the prejudice of the Trustee or the Bondholders.

Exclusive of supplemental indentures for the purpose set forth in the preceding paragraph, with the consent of the holders of not less than two-thirds of the principal amount of outstanding Bonds and Additional Bonds, the Trustee may join with the Issuer to approve any supplemental indenture, except that no such supplemental indenture can permit any of the following modifications:

(i) An extension of the maturity or mandatory redemption date of the principal of, or the interest on, any Bond;

(ii) A reduction in the principal amount of, or the rate of interest on, any Bond;

(iii) A privilege or priority of any Bond or Additional Bond over any other Bond or Additional Bond; or

(iv) A reduction in the aggregate principal amount of the Bonds and Additional Bonds required for consent to such supplemental indentures.

No supplemental indenture which affects the rights of the Company shall become effective without the consent of the Company, and no supplemental indenture which changes the responsibilities of the Trustee shall become effective without the consent of the Trustee.

Discharge of Indenture Lien

If the principal, interest, and premium, if any, due on the Bonds and Additional Bonds then outstanding shall have been paid on the covenants contained in the Bonds and Additional Bonds shall have been performed and all Trustee's fees paid, then the lien of the Indenture will be discharged and the Trustee will deliver to the Issuer or the Company any written instrument necessary to evidence such discharge and to the Company any monies in its possession in excess of the amounts required to provide for payment of principal and interest on the Bonds and Additional Bonds and to pay Trustee fees under the Indenture. All outstanding Bonds and Additional Bonds shall be deemed to have been paid if there shall have been deposited with the Trustee either monies or direct obligations of the United States of America, the principal of and interest on which when due will be sufficient to pay the principal and interest on the Bonds and Additional Bonds as the same becomes due through maturity or any early redemption for which proper notice shall have been given, and to pay all expenses and fees of the Trustee.

UNDERWRITING

The "Underwriter" has agreed with the Issuer (pursuant to the Company's approval), subject to certain terms and conditions, to purchase the Bonds at a price of 94% of the principal amount thereof plus accrued interest, if any, from the date thereof to the date of their delivery to the Underwriter. Subject to such terms and conditions, the Underwriter will be committed to take and pay for all of the Bonds if any of the Bonds are taken.

The Company has agreed to indemnify the Issuer and the Underwriter against certain civil liabilities, including certain liabilities under the federal securities laws.

BENEFITS OF EOCNOMIC DEVELOPMENT CORPORATION AND TAX-EXEMPT BONDS

In the opinion of Bond Counsel, Interest on the Bonds will be exempt from all present Federal and State of Michigan, including State and municipal, income taxes, except under certain conditions as explained under the caption "Tax Exemption of Fund" herein.

RISK FACTORS OF FUND

New Business

Mushroom production involves substantial expenditures for its labor requirements. There is no assurance that the Company will be able to produce sufficient income to make these expenditures and meet the required Lease Purchase Contract payments. In the event that revenues from the Company operations are insufficient, the Company will have to obtain alternative sources of financing. There is no assurance that any such financing can be arranged.

Market for Securities

It is the intention of the Underwriter to develop and maintain a market for the securities, but it is not obligated to do so. Investors may not be able to resell any securities purchased should they need or wish to do so in the future.

Competition

The Partnership will compete with many mushroom producers for sales of mushroom products and purchases of raw mushrooms. Most of these competitors are more experienced and have greater assets than the Partnership; some of these competitors are industry leaders. There is no assurance that the Partnership can compete with these companies.

Risks Inherent in Mushroom Growing

Mushroom growing is subject to various inherent risks because of the controlled conditions under which mushrooms must be grown, including the risks of improper temperature, disease, and insects. There is no assurance that the Partnership can avoid these inherent risks in its mushroom production.

General Business Risks

The business of the Lessee will be subject to many factors, including, but not limited to, changes in general economic conditions, changes in consumer preferences, the development of other facilities which would compete directly or indirectly with the Lessee's facility, and various other factors which are not practicable or within the control of the Lessee.

TAX EXEMPTION OF FUND

In the opinion of "Bond Counsel" under existing statutes, regulations, rulings, and court decisions, provided that there be no violation of the capital expenditures limitation of Section 103(b) of the Internal Revenue Code of 1954, as amended, the interest on the Bonds is exempt from all present Federal and State of Michigan income taxes, including State and municipal income taxes, except for interest on any of the Bonds held by a "substantial user" of the Project or a "related person" as defined in the Internal Revenue Code.

Economic Development Corporations carry more risk in some cases than the typical municipal bond offering, but their help in stimulating the economy can be invaluable.

Chapter Eleven

MEDICINE

An exciting use of tax shelters is in the area of scientific research. There is great interest in the power of interferon to defeat cancer, and an offering in this field is set forth in the example following the summary of the drug business.

DRUGS

Industry Status and Forecast

The drug industry manufactures biologicals, medicinals, botanicals, and pharmaceutical preparations. The value of shipments by this industry in 1981 will increase to $25.4 billion, 16 percent higher than the 1980 value of $21.9 billion. Product shipments are expected to reach $20.8 billion, a 13.7-percent increase from the 1980 value of $18.3 billion.

Industry shipments, growing at a real annual compound rate of 3.8 percent between 1980 and 1985, should reach $13.0 billion (1972 dollars) by the end of that period. The current dollar value of shipments is forecast to reach $46.6 billion in 1985, an average annual compound growth rate of 16.3 percent during the 5-year period.

Drug industry after-tax profits, as a percentage of sales, averaged 12.9 percent in 1979, and are estimated to have topped 13 percent in 1980. Expansion in preventive medicine through immunology promises to boost sales and profits. Therapeutic advances, based on biotechnology–recombinant DNA techniques, for example–should increase industry growth and reduce costs.

Government and industry are cooperating to speed up the introduction of new drugs. The reduction in average approval time should stimulate additional research and development and result in an increase in innovative productivity.

Future Trends

New developments underway at major pharmaceutical companies could mean significant improvements in the U.S. health care situation in the near future. Human insulin developed through a DNA technique should be on the market next year. Antiviral chemotherapy and vaccine research are moving along and should produce some new drugs by 1983. New treatments for arthritis, asthma, cardiovascular disease, pain, anxiety, insomnia, and senility will probably be marketed within the next 5 years.

The 1980's should prove an exciting decade because of many new discoveries in the fight against disease. How many new products will enter the market in this decade will depend partially on the extent to which the drug approval process can be expedited.

Industry forecasts a fourfold increase in health care costs by 1990, to a total of $1 trillion in current dollars. Consumers will directly pay 25 percent of this amount, as opposed to 33 percent at the present time. The drug and drug sundries portion of this is expected to amount to $70 billion.

MEDICINE

Medical operates a commercial laboratory for the production of cell cultures and other biological products and services used in medical research. The business of Medical currently includes the production of interferon and other biological substances derived from cell cultures, the production and distribution of cell and tissue cultures, cell culture media, nutrient supplements (e.g., sera) and related products for cell cultures; contract laboratory services in cell biology, biochemistry and virology; development of new products and technology for use in cell culture production and medical research; and commercial testing.

Description of Products and Services

Interferon. Medical has produced and distributed interferon. Medical has licensed to the Partnership in this program, as part of its capital contribution, all of its knowledge and technology related to interferon and will make available to the Partnership its production facilities related to interferon. Consequently, during the existence of the Partnership, the only revenues received by Medical from interferon-related business will be the General Partner's allocated percentage of the Partnership's cash distribution in accordance with the Partnership Agreement and Medical's sales of liquid growth medium to the Partnership.

Cell Cultures. Since its inception, Medical has produced and marketed living cell cultures for use in medical and biological research. Cells and tissues are isolated from human and animal organs and fetuses, tested for purity, mycoplasma and virus, and cultured in a medium. Suitability for Medical's markets requires constant testing and stringent purity controls. On special order, Medical produces virus-infected tissues for research, including tumor viruses.

Media and Sera. Both Medical and its customers require liquid growth medium, which provides the nutrients for growing cells.

Liquid growth medium is made from powdered media and calf sera. Medical purchases the bulk of its liquid growth medium and all of its powdered media and sera from other organizations, some of which it resells under its own label. Medical is presently completing the installation of equipment for the in-house production of liquid growth medium, and it expects this facility to supply the necessary quantities for the Partnership's immediate needs. As production of interferon increases, however, all that Medical can produce, as well as additional supplies from others, will be necessary. Medical also distributes balanced salt solutions, stock concentrates (amino acids and vitamins), reagents and frozen antibiotics for use in the culture of cells and tissue. In the fiscal year ended August 31, 1980, Medical's sales of media, sera and related products amounted to approximately 18% of its total sales.

Laboratory Services. Medical established separate laboratory facilities for contract research and experimentation for others. Contract services include special order cell cultures, purification of viruses and studies relating to viruses, probes and studies of cells affected by leukemia, and studies relating to carcinogens and tumors.

Commercial Testing. As an outgrowth of the in-house work of its quality control department, Medical began to accept quality control work from other organizations. In addition to performing tests on media and sera, cell cultures and related products, Medical assays materials suspected of containing interferon to determine purity and the presence of activity.

Properties and Facilities

Medical does not own any real property, but leases a total of approximately 23,200 square feet at five locations. The leased property is used for office, laboratory, production and warehouse facilities.

Medical also leases all of its automotive equipment and some of its office and laboratory equipment.

Employees

At the present time, Medical employs a total of 50 persons, of whom 44 are full-time employees. Included among the foregoing are 16 executive and administrative personnel and 24 laboratory and technical personnel.

Research and Development

Medical conducts research and development activities in connection with the production of interferon and interferon-related products. Such activities have been primarily related to Medical's efforts to produce substantial quantities of high-purity interferon at competitive costs.

BUSINESS OF THE PARTNERSHIP

Interferon

The business of the Partnership will be to produce and market interferon and to undertake research and development in connection therewith. As its capital contribution, Medical will contribute $10,000 and will license on an exclusive basis to the Partnership all of Medical's knowledge and technology related to interferon, and will make available to the Partnership its production facilities related to interferon.

Interferon is a glyco-protein which appears to inhibit virus infection, and research is currently being conducted to determine its potential as a drug for the treatment of cancer and other viral diseases. Current biomedical research indicates that cancer and diseases such as hepatitis and arteriosclerosis have similar biologic origins involving the proliferation of diseased tissue. Interferon's most important characteristic is that it appears to prevent the growth of diseased cells, leaving the healthy cells intact. Moreover, interferon is a natural substance produced by the body and early clinical trials indicate that the human fibroblast interferon produced by Medical appears to be nearly free of dangerous side effects.

Three types of human interferon have been identified, with each one possessing certain distinguishing characteristics. Medical produces human fibroblast interferon, which is induced from the cultured fibroblasts of infant foreskins.

Another type is human leukocyte interferon which is derived from the white cell buffy coat that remains when blood is separated. Most clinical studies have used this type of interferon which primarily comes from Finland. Because leukocyte interferon is made from pooled donor blood, the source of supply for this type is inherently limited and may be less than the amount ultimately needed for world consumption. Furthermore, the impurities present in leukocyte interferon can create problems in handling and purification, and adverse side effects may occur from its use in its present form.

The third type is immune interferon which is produced by the cells of the immune system and is generally used only for *in vitro* and animal interferon research.

In addition, some competitors of Medical are attempting the production of human interferon in bacteria through the technology generally referred to as "genetic cloning."

Medical is unaware of other producers in the United States which have successfully used human fibroblast interferon in clinical studies. An important attribute of Medical's product is its potency and purity, resulting from Medical's technology. Potency refers to the number of units of purified interferon obtained at the end of the production cycle. The "purity" of interferon relates to the percentage of interferon present in a given amount of protein. Although a given interferon preparation may be highly "purified," or contain a high percentage of interferon relative to other substances, if such other substances are toxic the interferon will not be as clinically valuable as preparations without such toxic elements. Scientists differ on the standards to be used in measuring the "purity" of an interferon preparation, but the interferon produced by Medical and used in clinical studies conducted to date appears to have no significant adverse side-effects, suggesting that the non-interferon elements present in Medical's interferon preparation should be non-toxic to humans, although this can only be conclusively determined after further studies and clinical trials and after Medical's interferon is used over time on a wide basis.

Medical believes that it has developed the technological competence to produce large amounts of clinically useful human fibroblast interferon at a cost which will allow sale at a price below that now being charged by producers of human leukocyte interferon.

Despite the promise interferon has shown in laboratory tests involving various viral disease and cancer cells, very few patients have been able to receive this substance due to its current high cost and relative scarce supply. These problems are due in part to the major difficulty in recovering interferon as a biologically stable, purified powder suitable for medicinal use. Accordingly, most of the interferon previously available resulted in side-effects which inhibited full realization of its clinical potential. Only with the production of large supplies for wide-scale testing, at appropriate prices, will interferon's medical properties be established.

Using Medical's technology, the Partnership expects to overcome these two major problem areas—low purity and scarcity—by procedures which Medical believes will result in both high yields (recovery of a large number of molecules of interferon produced by the cell culture) and accompanying high product purity and potency.

Medical believes it has developed valuable technology both in the production of crude interferon and its purification. At the present time, human fibroblast interferon generally is produced by inducing cell growth in "roller bottles." Cells are placed on the inner surfaces of the bottles, liquid nutrients are placed therein, and the bottles are placed on rollers which gently turn them to enable the cells to grow. Medical has developed a device which is designed to eliminate the need for such bottles and the intensive labor necessary to constantly inject new fluid into them and to examine the cell growth. The new device, if it operates as designed, would substantially reduce the production time of crude interferon of approximately 6 weeks using the roller bottles.

The crude interferon thus produced must then be purified. It appears that the higher the purity of the interferon product the greater the likelihood of elimination of any adverse side effects from treatment. Various published materials have indicated that the interferon serum described in such studies, which was imported from Finland, had a concentration of approximately 1%. Based upon presently recognized measurement standards, Medical has been informed by independent laboratory consultants that its interferon serum now being produced has a concentration of at least 10%.

Medical's purification process involves a procedure whereby the human fibroblast interferon, freshly produced by human cells, is immediately processed to preserve a maximum of its bioactivity. In contrast, current techniques require the repeated freeze-thawing of crude interferon preparations with attendant substantial losses of activity and decay in potency. Medical believes that its program should be more cost effective because the human fibroblast interferon is constantly undergoing purification, as opposed to the production process now prevalent in which the product is manually manipulated with many "starts" and "stops." Medical believes that its production process will reduce the preparation time for interferon as a final product in vial form.

Medical has been and the Partnership may also be engaged in the development of high-purity animal leukocyte interferon for use by humans. Although interferon traditionally was thought to be species specific, some favorable results have recently been obtained in studies involving bovine and porcine leukocyte interferon. To date, Medical's work with animal leukocyte interferon has not proceeded beyond the laboratory efforts necessary to obtain a high-purity product. The Projections have not assumed that any revenues will be derived from work with animal leukocyte interferon.

Based on its experience to date in the production of human fibroblast interferon Medical believes it has developed the fundamental elements of the technology necessary to produce on a large scale clinically useful interferon which can be competitive not only on a quality basis but also on a cost basis with potential interferon production by others. These techniques, however, are still being developed and perfected, and, using the proceeds of this Offering, the Partnership expects to engage in significant expansion of the existing interferon production capacity of Medical. The method of application of the technology thus far developed by Medical to large-scale production can only be determined after the financial resources supplied by the Offering are available. It is possible that the requirements of such large-scale production will require adaptation of Medical's existing techniques or the development of new processes and equipment, which will require, in addition to the scientific expertise of the General Partner's management and consultants, a large portion of the proceeds of this Offering as well as additional capital investment, and there can be no assurance that Medical's techniques could be so adapted.

Competition

In the development, production and marketing of interferon, the Partnership will face intense competition from other firms, including some of the world's major pharmaceutical manufacturers, most of which are larger and possess greater financial resources than the Partnership.

Medical believes that its competitive advantage arises from what it sees as its ability to develop its technology to a level where it can provide the Partnership with the basis for establishing sooner than other companies the ability to produce high-quality, clinically effective interferon at a lower cost than that currently charged for interferon and which cost would be comparable with other available treatment for similar illnesses.

Although Medical believes that its technology has advanced beyond that of known competitors producing interferon, this technology does not appear to be patentable, being a sophisticated combination and application of certain procedures already known, and Medical's sole protection for its technology is in keeping secret its proprietary information and know-how. It is possible, however, that other groups will, as Medical has been able to do in the past, develop similar technology or variations thereon which will enable them to also produce a purified, clinically effective product. One or more of these groups may have significantly larger financial resources than Medical and the Partnership. While Medical and the Partnership intend to aggressively pursue the immediate production of large quantities of high-quality, clinically effective interferon, and to maintain a competitive position through continued development of their techniques in an attempt to maximize efficiency, there can be no assurance that Medical or the Partnership will succeed in this endeavor in the face of competition from larger and more established firms.

Alternative approaches under development by competitors center principally on efficient production of crude human fibroblast interferon, as through the use of novel growth substrates such as glass beads. These approaches, even if successful, might not eliminate the value of Medical's technology as a means of storage and purification of the "raw materials" produced by others. Other competitive approaches under development relate to "cloning" interferon through the use of plasmid vector. While estimated to be several years away from initial clinical application, there would be very stringent requirements for purification of interferon derived from a bacterial source which itself contained many potent human toxins. Medical's technology may be suitable as a companion technology to any breakthroughs in production of crude interferon from either cell culture or other modes of "bioengineering."

Government Regulation

The production, marketing and use of interferon is subject to extensive governmental regulation by the Food and Drug Administration ("FDA"). Medical has sold, and the Partnership will sell, its interferon pursuant to the Investigational Exemption for a New Drug filed for human fibroblast interferon. This exemption enables clinicians to conduct clinical studies with human fibroblast interferon produced by Medical.

Before a drug can be commercially marketed, the FDA must grant a New Drug Application; however, there can be no assurance that the FDA will ultimately grant a New Drug Application for the Partnership's interferon, even if, as a result of the Partnership's production of interferon it has been possible to assemble the broad clinical data to support a New Drug Application, and Medical undertakes the expense of applying for New Drug approval. Medical holds no patent rights with respect to interferon, and if other firms also developed the technology to produce large amounts of interferon they could immediately sell the product without having engaged in the expense and effort Medical would have undergone in obtaining New Drug approval.

Under the Investigational New Drug exemption, distribution of interferon is only permitted to support the assembly of clinical data to provide the foundation for a determination as to whether or not interferon should be approved as a New Drug. The justification for sale of a substance as an Investigational New Drug prior to approval as a New Drug is that the cost of producing the substance requires commercial sales. Such sales, however, are restricted to sales to authorized clinicians who are assembling data on the clinical effects of interferon. Under the Investigational New Drug exemption filed, Medical is identified as the producer of the interferon used in clinical trials and those conducted by clinicians authorized to conduct clinical trials.

Medical's production facilities are subject to physical inspection requirements and Medical must file reports with the FDA concerning Medical's sales of interferon and the clinical studies conducted by the clinicians authorized to use Medical's interferon.

There can be no assurance that the FDA will permit the unlimited sale of all the interferon produced by Medical prior to approval as a New Drug, or that it will continue to permit its distribution for clinical trials.

The offering consists of 29 Units ("Units"), each Unit at a price of $150,000 consisting of (i) a $124,138 limited partnership interest in MEDICAL ASSOCIATES (the "Partnership"), and (ii) 47,742 shares of common stock of MEDICAL RESEARCH, INC., at a purchase price of $28,862. Medical is the general partner (the "General Partner") of the Partnership.

The aggregate amount of the Offering (the "Offering") is $4,350,000, consisting of $3,600,002 for limited partnership interests in the Partnership and $749,998 for an aggregate of 1,384,918 shares of common stock of Medical, constituting approximately fifteen (15%) percent of the presently outstanding shares of common stock of Medical after giving effect to the shares issued in this Offering.

The minimum subscription is one Unit; provided, however, that in the discretion of the Placement Agent and Medical, subscriptions for amounts less than $150,000 may be accepted. Subscriptions are payable 50% in cash (of which 34.5% is for all of the shares of Medical common stock included in each Unit) and 50% by a non-interest bearing promissory note, payable to the Partnership on March 1, Year Two. In the event the note is not paid when due, the General Partner may pursue various remedies, including cancellation of the Limited Partner's entire interest in the Partnership.

The major portion of Medical's business and resources will be devoted to conducting the Partnership's business as the General Partner.

TERMS OF THE OFFERING

The price of the shares of Medical's common stock has been established by negotiations between Medical and the Placement Agent. The price paid by Medical's current stockholders for their shares was significantly less than the price of the shares being sold pursuant to this Offering, and there will be an immediate and substantial dilution of book value from the price of the Shares.

There is presently no market for shares of Medical's common stock and a market for such shares is not expected to develop in the near future. Moreover, even if a public market is created hereafter for Medical's common stock, the shares purchased pursuant to this Offering will be "restricted shares," and, as such, the right to sell such shares will be restricted under the Securities Act of 1933, as amended. In the event, however, that Medical has then already had an offering of its shares of capital stock which was registered under the Securities Act of 1933, as amended, Medical has agreed to file, at its expense, one Registration Statement to permit a sale of Medical stock held by the Limited Partners upon the demand of the holders of a majority of the shares of Medical held by the Limited Partners. In addition, Medical has agreed to grant any Limited Partner holding Medical stock the right to request inclusion of all or any part of its shares of Medical stock in any Registration Statement which Medical proposes to file with the Securities and Exchange Commission subsequent to the initial Registration Statement filed by Medical. The number of shares, however, covered by any such "piggy-back" registration is subject to being cut-back by the underwriter involved on a pro-rata basis with all other shareholders of Medical requesting "piggy-back" registration in the event that the underwriter determines it is necessary to do so to meet the financial need of Medical or the shareholder upon whose behalf the Registration Statement is filed pursuant to a contractual demand registration right. Such registration rights would not extend to transferees of the Limited Partners' shares of Medical stock and would only apply to the Shares purchased in this Offering.

Medical's authorized capital stock consists of 30,000,000 shares of $.01 par value common stock. Each outstanding share of common stock is entitled to one vote, either in person or by proxy, on all matters which may be voted upon by the holders thereof at meetings of the shareholders. Holders of common stock are entitled to such dividends as may be declared by the Board of Directors and, in the event of liquidation, dissolution, or sale of Medical, are entitled to receive on a pro rata basis, all assets of Medical remaining after satisfaction of all liabilities. Holders of the common stock have no preemptive rights to purchase additional shares of any class of Medical's capital stock in subsequent offerings.

All of the issued and outstanding shares of Medical's common stock are, and the shares offered hereby, when sold, will be fully authorized and validly issued, fully paid and non-assessable. The shares of Medical's common stock have no conversion rights and are not subject to redemption. Medical will furnish shareholders an annual report including financial reports examined by independent public accountants.

Holders of Medical's common stock are not entitled to cumulative voting in the election of directors. Therefore, the holders of more than 50% of the shares voting upon the election of directors can elect all the directors. The Company's management will continue to own a majority of the Company's outstanding stock after giving effect to the Offering.

USE OF PROCEEDS

The use of the proceeds of the Offering detailed below is a present estimate prepared by Medical of Medical's and the Partnership's needs. It is subject to change depending upon the business needs of Medical and the Partnership. It does not purport to be, nor should it be read as, an exact allocation of the proceeds of the Offering.

Medical

The $749,998 received by Medical from the sale of its common stock pursuant to the Offering will be used to pay costs of the Offering (including the allocable portion of legal fees and fees payable to the Placement Agent), reduce the level of Medical's payables and provide funds for the expansion of Medical's liquid growth medium production facilities and for working capital, as set forth in the table on the following page.

Use of Proceeds by Medical

Media Production Expansion	$ 183,550
Debt Reduction–Accounts Payable	250,000
Working Capital	120,998
Allocable Portion of Offering Costs:[1]	
Sales Commission and Investment Banking Fee[2]	117,450
Miscellaneous Expenses	18,000
Legal and Accounting	60,000
	$ 749,998

The Partnership

The $3,600,002 received by the Partnership from the sale of Limited Partnership interests will be used to pay costs of the Offering (including the allocable portion of legal fees and fees payable to the Placement Agent), purchase supplies and equipment for the production of interferon, retain additional personnel by Medical for interferon production and to provide funds for research and development as set forth in the table below:

Use of Proceeds by Partnership

Interferon Production	
Equipment and Materials	$ 740,000
Leasehold Improvements	250,000
Interferon Research and Development	300,000
Working Capital	1,853,952
Allocable Portion of Offering Costs:[1]	
Sales Commission and Investment Banking Fee[2]	274,050
Miscellaneous Expenses	42,000
Legal and Accounting	140,000
	$3,600,002

1. Medical and the Partnership have agreed that Medical will pay 30% of the Offering costs and the Partnership will pay 70% of such costs.

2. The Placement Agent is entitled to a 7% sales commission ($304,500) and a 2% investment banking fee ($87,000) payable out of the proceeds of the Offering. The Placement Agent has agreed that of the total of $391,500 in commissions and fees due to it, $261,000 will be payable upon consummation of the sale of the Units and $130,500 on the due date of the Notes, March 1, Year Two.

PROJECTIONS

There is no assurance that the projections will be realized. Production of interferon by Medical is at a low level. No assurance can be given that the production levels reflected in the projections will be attained. In any event, substantial additional financing will be necessary in Year Three and Year Four to arrive at the production levels contemplated by the projections.

ASSUMPTIONS

Prototype Production Units

An initial series of prototype interferon production units is currently under construction. The prototype units produce crude interferon, which must then be purified before it can be sold. It is expected that the initial series of prototype units will have been constructed and tested and be ready for operation by January 1, Year Two. An additional series of prototype units to produce interferon is expected to be constructed during Year Two. Based on the experience gained from the use of the prototype units more advanced production units will be developed. It is believed that the more advanced units, which are expected to be in place by the end of Year Two, will be more efficient than the initial prototype units, and result in greater production and lower costs.

Virtually all prototype equipment to be used by the Partnership in the initial stages of interferon production will be expensed rather than capitalized.

Patient Dose and Sales Price

For purposes of these Projections, it is assumed that the average daily patient dose will be 3,000,000 International Reference Units ("IRU") of interferon. This is an estimate based on early clinical studies conducted to date, and would vary depending on the particular patient being treated.

The projections assume that the selling price of interferon drops from Medical's current price level of $750 per patient dose to $350 per patient dose during Year Two. The projections assume that in Year Three and Year Four the average price of a patient dose will be approximately $150 and that production will increase using the more advanced production units.

Interferon Production Figures

Interferon production is projected at

Year	Estimated Amount of Annual Production	Estimated Average Weekly Production	Estimated Average Number of Patients Who Can Be Treated Per Week
Two	33,500 patient doses	644 patient doses	92
Three	140,000 patient doses	2,692 patient doses	385
Four	280,000 patient doses	5,385 patient doses	

The projections assume that the amount of interferon produced by each production unit will increase during Year Two from 50% of a unit's minimum production level to 85% by year end. A unit's minimum production level is the least amount of interferon which the units are expected to produce based on extrapolation from experience with smaller scale laboratory production.

Costs

The projections assume that the cost of running the production units remains constant throughout Year Two. No effect has been given to inflation in any of the projections. Projections for Year Three and Year Four assume that revenues and costs double from each prior year.

Additional Financing

The Projections assume that the Partnership will be able to successfully raise $12,000,000 to finance new production facilities to be completed in Year Three and Year Four. No effect has been given in the Projections to the costs of such financing.

Government Regulation

It is assumed that the maximum amount which could be produced will be sold without restriction imposed by governmental regulations on the amount of product distributed and that adequate numbers of clinicians and researchers will purchase the amount produced.

Assumptions Governing Losses

The losses projected for Year One are based on the assumption that the initial series of prototype production units produces no saleable product, and that any production from roller bottles is used to fulfill outstanding commitments. If any substantial quantity of saleable interferon were produced during the balance of Year One, this might substantially diminish or eliminate the losses projected for Year One.

It is assumed in the Projections that the Offering is completed by November 15, Year One.

Projected Statement of Taxable Income and Cash Flow Per $124,138 Limited Partnership Interest Assuming a 50% Tax Rate for an Investor (Year One Dollars)

Year	Cash Contribution to Partnership	Taxable Income from Partnership	Potential Tax Savings (Tax Payable)	Cash Distribution from Partnership(a)	Annual After Tax Cash Generated from Partnership	Cumulative Net Cash Position(b)
One	$49,138	$ 27,310	$ 13,655	-	$ 13,655	$(35,483)
Two	75,000	54,310	(27,155)	$ 54,310	27,155	(83,328)
Three	-	112,931	(56,465)	112,931	56,465	(26,863)
Three	-	225,862	(112,931)	225,862	112,931	86,068

(a) Cash distributions from the Partnership are based on 50% of the Partnership's profits. Cash distributions will be on a quarterly basis beginning, to the extent available, with the quarter ending June 30, Year Two, and will be made within 45 days of the end of each quarter.

(b) Represents cumulative net cash position in relationship to the limited partnership interest, excluding the cost of and profit or loss on the 47,742 shares of Medical Research, Inc.

MEDICAL ASSOCIATES, a Limited Partnership

Cash Flow Statement
(000's)
(Year One Dollars)

	Year One(a)	Year Two 1st Quarter	Year Two 2nd Quarter	Year Two 3rd Quarter	Year Two 4th Quarter	Year Two Total	Year Three	Year Four
Funds Provided								
Financing	$1,425	$2,175	-	-	-	$ 2,175	$ 7,000(c)	$ 5,000(c)
Revenues	50	1,700	$3,900	$4,200	$4,200	14,000	21,000	42,000
Total	$1,475	$3,875	$3,900	$4,200	$4,200	$16,175	$28,000	$47,000
Funds Required								
Inteferon Production:								
Operating Expenses	850	1,850	2,950	3,100	2,950	10,850	14,450	28,900
Capital Expenditures	50	250	100	100	100	550	7,000(c)	5,000(c)
Organization and Offering Costs	365	91	-	-	-	91	-	-
Distribution to Partners (b)	-	-	-	800	1,100	1,900	6,160	11,460
Total	$1,265	$2,191	$3,050	$4,000	$4,150	$13,391	$27,610	$45,360
Net Cash Position	$ 210	$1,684	$ 850	$ 200	$ 50	$ 2,784	$ 390	$ 1,650
Cumulative Cash Position	$ 210	$1,894	$2,744	$2,944	$2,994	$ 2,994	$ 3,384	$ 5,024

(a) For November and December.
(b) 50% of Partnership Income to be distributed to Limited Partners and 50% to the General Partner.
(c) New financing needed to cover $12,000,000 expenditure for new facilities.

MEDICAL ASSOCIATES, a Limited Partnership

Income Statement
(000's)
(Year One Dollars)

	Year One(a)	Year Two					Year Three	Year Four
		1st Quarter	2nd Quarter	3rd Quarter	4th Quarter	Total		
Revenues	$ 50	$1,700	$3,900	$4,200	$4,200	$14,000	$21,000	$42,000
Cost of Goods Sold	195	1,625	2,725	2,875	2,725	9,950	13,150	26,700
General and Administrative (b)	655	225	225	225	225	900	1,300	2,200
Total	850	1,850	2,950	3,100	2,950	10,850	14,450	28,900
Partnership Income (Loss)	$ (800)	$ (150)	$ 950	$1,100	$1,250	$ 3,150	$ 6,550	$13,100

(a) For November and December.
(b) Excludes Offering expenses estimated at $364,700 for Year One and $91,350 for Year Two.

MEDICAL RESEARCH, INC.

Income Statement
(000's)
(Year One Dollars)

	Year Two	Year Three	Year Four
Revenues	$1,450	$1,450	$1,450
Operating Expenses (a)	750	750	750
Pre-Tax Income	700	700	700
50% of Partnership Income	950	3,080	5,730
Total Pre-Tax Income	1,650	3,780	6,430
Income Tax (46%)	529(b)	1,739	2,958
Net Income	$1,121	$2,041	$3,472
Earnings per Share (c)	$ .11	$ .21	$ .35

(a) Excludes offering expenses estimated at $195,450.
(b) Medical is projected to have a tax loss carry forward of approximately $500,000.
(c) Based on 9,898,936 shares outstanding, giving effect to all options and warrants exercisable as of the date the Offering is concluded.

BENEFITS OF A MEDICAL FUND

Partnership losses will be allocated 99% to the Limited Partners and 1% to the General Partner. Partnership profits and distributions will be allocated 50% to the Limited Partners and 50% to the General Partner until the Limited Partners have received aggregate cash distributions equal to five (5) times the total capital contributions of the Limited Partners, which maximum distribution would be $18,000,010 if all 29 Units were sold; therefore, the Limited Partners' sole interest in the Partnership will be the right to receive up to 5% of the Partnership's income and distributions, in any year, up to a maximum of $250,000 in the aggregate to all Limited Partners per year during the balance of the Partnership's life, which terminates in eleven years.

The General Partner will have a three-year option to purchase a substantial portion of the Limited Partners' interest in the Partnership, commencing one year from the consummation of the sale of the Units. For the first year after the option becomes exercisable, the option price will be twice the capital contribution of the Limited Partners to the Partnership; for the second year, it will be two and one-half times such contribution; and for the third year, it will be three times such contribution; less, in each case, 50% of all cash distributions made or owing to the Limited Partners prior to the exercise of the option. If the option is exercised, the option price will be paid in cash and the Limited Partners will continue to be limited partners with the right to receive up to 5% of income and distributions in any year, up to a maximum of $250,000 in the aggregate to all Limited Partners per year during the balance of the life of the Partnership.

The General Partner's option to purchase a substantial portion of the Limited Partners' interest in the Partnership does not entail any right of the General Partner or Medical to call or repurchase the shares of common stock of Medical purchased as part of the Units sold in the Offering.

RISKS OF A MEDICAL FUND

Risk Factors Specifically Related to Interferon Production

The future success of the Partnership, and, to a large extent, of Medical will depend on the Partnership's ability to produce substantial quantities of clinically useful interferon at competitive prices. Although Medical has been manufacturing and marketing interferon for three years, it has not yet produced the quantities of interferon which form the basis for the financial projections and—even if such quantities can be produced—there is no assurance that they can be profitably marketed or that the amount of interferon which can be sold will not be restricted by governmental regulations.

The Partnership's ability to produce and sell interferon is conditioned on its ability to (1) successfully complete development of the technology licensed to it by Medical, (2) sell all the

the interferon it can produce without restrictions on the volume of interferon sold imposed by governmental regulation prior to approval of interferon as a "New Drug" and (3) compete against other larger and more well-established companies who may also be able to produce and market large quantities of interferon.

The sales of interferon reflected in the Projections are based on the assumption that the Partnership, by further developing Medical's technology and expanding its production facilities will be able to produce the amounts of interferon reflected in the Projections, as to which no assurance can be given.

Interferon is still in an experimental stage of development for medical use, and tests have produced varying results. It is produced and sold by Medical under applicable regulations of the Food and Drug Administration ("FDA") as an "Investigational New Drug" which exempts interferon from the requirements for licensing as a "New Drug" and which limits its use to sales to qualified physicians and researchers for the purpose of assembling clinical data on the uses and effects of interferon. The exemption permitting distribution of the Investigational New Drug was sponsored and submitted to the FDA. The exemption specifies Medical as the producer of the interferon used by those authorized to conduct clinical studies.

As a result of both the limitations imposed by the FDA and the fact that interferon's properties have not been widely tested, for the foreseeable future, the use of interferon will continue to be limited to medical research and clinical tests. There is no assurance that the results of such tests will create a larger market for interferon or that the results will continue to justify further interferon research at the current level. Furthermore, there is no assurance that the FDA will not impose restrictions on the amount of interferon which can be sold prior to its approval as a New Drug, so that, although the Partnership might have fulfilled the technological requirements to produce large amounts of clinically useful interferon, it might be restricted in the amount it could sell until interferon is approved as a New Drug. There can be no assurance that such approval will be obtained. Medical and the Partnership will be subject to FDA reporting requirements, and Medical and the Partnership will be subject to FDA physical plant inspection requirements which must be fulfilled in order for the Partnership to continue to be able to produce and sell interferon under the Investigational New Drug exemption. Therefore, Medical's ability to sell all or any part of interferon which forms the basis for the Projections is subject to such government regulation.

There are several types of interferon. Most of the medical research completed to date in this area has used human leukocyte interferon whose properties differ in certain respects from human fibroblast interferon, which is the type produced by Medical and to be produced by the Partnership. It remains to be seen whether one type of interferon is generally more effective than another or whether each type has its particular uses. Moreover, a number of other companies, many larger and more established than Medical and the Partnership, are also engaged in the development of interferon production and it may be that alternative interferon products will be developed by others which would render the Partnership's interferon uncompetitive on the basis of effectiveness or price. Thus, even if the Partnership is successful in producing large quantities of interferon, its ability to sell the product may be foreclosed in whole or in part by competition from these other companies.

Lack of Ready Transferability of Limited Partnership Interests and Shares of Stock

The sale of limited partnership interests ("Interests") in the Partnership and the shares of Medical common stock ("Shares") sold as part of the Units will not be registered under the Securities Act of 1933, as amended, or under applicable state securities laws, and neither the Interests nor the Shares may be transferred by a Limited Partner unless that transfer is registered under applicable federal and state securities laws or the appropriate exemptions from federal and state registration are available. Although the Interests and Shares are being sold as part of a single Unit, immediately after the Offering each may be transferred separately subject to the restrictions described in this paragraph. In any event, there is currently no market for Interests or Shares and there can be no assurance that a market for the Interests or Shares will be developed in the reasonably foreseeable future. Moreover, the Partnership Agreement requires the consent of the General Partner to assignments before an assignee may become a substituted Limited Partner in the Partnership. Consequently, a Limited Partner may not be able to liquidate his investment in the foreseeable future, if at all.

Common Stock of Medical

The price of the Shares has been established by negotiations between Medical and the Placement Agent. The primary factors involved in establishing the Offering price were the amount of funds necessary for Medical to undertake the activities referred to herein and the percentage of the total equity of Medical that management believed should be sold pursuant to the Offering. The value that the Offering price purports to place on the Shares may bear no relationship to the assets, earnings or other criteria of value applicable to Medical. The price paid by Medical's current stockholders for their shares was significantly less than the price of the Shares being sold pursuant to the Offering. There will be an immediate and substantial dilution of approximately $.51 from the price of the Shares.

Medical has paid dividends in only one year since its formation and intends for the foreseeable future to follow a policy of retaining all of its earnings, if any, to finance the development and expansion of its business.

Dependence on Untried Products

While Medical intends to continue the production and marketing of cell cultures, its sales of such products have declined in recent years. Medical believes that its future success will depend to a large extent on its involvement through the Partnership in the production of substantial quantities of high quality, clinically useful interferon.

Medical has also embarked on the production of liquid growth medium to meet its needs and the needs of the Partnership. The liquid growth medium is a liquid nutrient essential to the growth of cell cultures, including the interferon produced by the Partnership. Medical's liquid growth medium production facility only recently began operations and a significant expansion of these facilities will be necessary in order to meet the Partnership's need for large amounts of medium to produce the interferon contemplated by the financial projections; however, no assurance can be given that such expansion will be arranged.

TAX ASPECTS OF A MEDICAL FUND

Research and Experimental Expenses

Under Code Section 174(a), a taxpayer is permitted to treat research and experimental expenses paid or incurred during a taxable year in connection with the conduct of a trade or business as current expenses. Research and experimental expenses are defined by applicable Regulations as experimental or laboratory type costs which generally include all costs incident to the development of an experimental or prototype product, invention or similar property, or the improvement of an already existing property of the type mentioned. The Regulations further provide that the deductibility of research and experimental expenses will not be affected by whether the taxpayer itself actually conducts research or experimentation, or whether funds are expended for research or experimentation carried on in its behalf by another person or organization. Under legislation presently pending before Congress, the federal income tax treatment of research and experimental expenses would be significantly altered.

Incorporation of the Partnership

In the event that the General Partner and the Limited Partners vote to incorporate the Partnership pursuant to the Partnership Agreement, the Partnership will not be required to recognize gain or loss as a result of the incorporation except to the extent that the corporation receiving the Partnership's assets assumes liabilities of the Partnership or receives assets subject to liabilities which (i) in the aggregate exceed the aggregate tax basis of the Partnership assets received, or (ii) were assumed or taken subject to by the corporation without a valid business purpose or with a tax avoidance motive. If the only liabilities assumed or taken subject to are those connected with the operations of the business of the Partnership, it is likely that a valid business purpose, rather than a tax avoidance motive, would be held to exist with respect to the assumption of the indebtedness.

If no gain is recognized upon the incorporation of the Partnership, the adjusted tax basis of the assets in the hands of the corporation will be the same as the adjusted tax basis of such assets in the hands of the Partnership. Each Partner, upon liquidation of the Partnership, would receive stock in the corporation which would have an adjusted tax basis in his hands equal to the remaining basis of his Partnership interest.

Investment in Medical

An investor's investment in Medical will be treated for federal income tax purposes, as a purchase of stock in a corporation. Accordingly, no significant tax benefits can be expected to inure to the investor as a result of his investment in Medical. Because Medical will be treated as a corporation for federal income tax purposes, it will be required to pay a tax on its income, the investors will not be entitled to include in their individual tax retursn their pro rata share of the income, gain, loss and credit of the corporation, the payment of taxes by the corporation will reduce the amount of cash available for distribution to the investors, and distributions from the corporation will be taxable as dividends to the extent of the accumulated earnings and profits of the corporation. If an investor disposes of his stock in Medical at a gain, the IRS may, depending upon the financial condition of Medical, the composition of its assets, and other factors, take the position that the investor is not entitled to capital gain treatment as to all or part of his gain on the ground that Medical is a "collapsible corporation." No assurance can be given that the IRS would not prevail with this position. If it does, any such gain would be taxable to the investor as ordinary income (presently taxable to individuals at rates up to 70%).

Counsel to the placement agent, has rendered its opinion to Medical that the Medical stock to be issued to investors will qualify as "Section 1244 stock" *provided that,* among other things, more than 50% of Medical's gross receipts, for certain taxable years, are derived from sources other than royalties, rents, dividends, interest, annuities, or sales or exchanges of stock or securities. Qualification of this stock as Section 1244 stock will, in certain cases, entitle an investor to an ordinary loss deduction in the event that a loss is sustained with respect to his stock in Medical. However, qualification of the stock in Medical as Section 1244 stock does not insure an investor that he will be entitled to an ordinary loss deduction in the event that a loss is sustained with respect to his Medical stock. For example, an ordinary loss deduction in respect of a loss on

Section 1244 stock is not available to a corporation, a trust, an estate or a transferee of a person to whom Section 1244 stock was issued by a corporation. Moreover, the aggregate amount that may be treated by a taxpayer as an ordinary loss in any taxable year with respect to Section 1244 stock is $50,000 (or $100,000 in the case of a husband and wife filing a joint return). Because this limitation is applied in the aggregate, and not on a corporation-by-corporation basis, an investor may obtain little or no benefit from Section 1244 characterization of the Medical stock if his loss with respect to his Medical stock was sustained in a taxable year in which he sustained substantial losses on other Section 1244 stock.

Special rules apply for purposes of determining the ordinary loss deduction allowable to partners in a partnership that sustains a loss on Section 1244 stock.

While very risky as an investment, there is tremendous potential profit in the development and marketing of a desirable and successful medicine.

Chapter Twelve

SOFT DRINK

With the importance of food to the future of the world's population, tax shelters can play a meaningful role in the manufacture, advertising and marketing of food products as exemplified by the offering following the summary on the bottled and canned soft drink industry.

BOTTLED AND CANNED SOFT DRINKS

Industry Status and Forecast

The value of shipments of the bottled and canned soft drink industry is expected to reach almost $17 billion in 1981, an increase of 14 percent over estimated 1980 shipments of nearly $15 billion.

Despite higher ingredient, bottling, and transportation costs, more economical packaging and new products should result in real industry growth of 3-4 percent in 1981. As the number of 12- to 25-year-old declines over the next 5 years, soft drink producers will aim some of their increased advertising at influencing this age group to continue its consumption habits as it gets older.

Consumption Continues Upward

Industry statistics indicate that 1979 consumption of soft drinks continued the steady growth of the past two decades, although at a slower rate. Per capita consumption reached 399.6 twelve-ounce containers in 1979, or more than 16 cases per person. Consumer preference for larger, more economical and easier-to-handle containers and the continued growth in bulk usage for the away-from-home market has contributed to the 65 percent per capita growth of the 1970's.

Cola Flavor Dominates

Regular (nondiet) soft drinks accounted for 86.6 percent of packaged soft drink sales in 1979, a small decline from the 88.3 percent share held in 1978. Cola dominated the market with a 60.6 percent share, slightly less than in 1978. Lemon-lime, the second most popular flavor, displayed the biggest increase in market share—from 10.7 percent in 1978 to 13.9 percent in 1979.

Despite the required warning label on diet soft drinks containing saccharin, they increased their share of the market to 13.4 percent in 1979. Cola also is the most popular diet flavor, accounting for over 58 percent of that market, and lemon-lime is second with 18 percent. Although new diet flavors have appeared, these two traditional leaders increased their total share of the market from 70.4 percent in 1978 to 76.4 percent in 1979.

Bottled Water

Bottled and canned soft drinks also includes bottled and canned mineral water and other types of processed waters. Bottled water has been one of the fastest expanding sectors of the soft drink market in the past 2 years, and this growth is expected to continue well into the 1980's.

Industry estimates indicate that consumption of domestic bottled water in 1979 was about 320 million gallons. Consumption increased ten fold between 1975 and 1979; 10 percent real growth, compounded annually, is expected through 1984.

New product introductions and aggressive marketing are creating increased consumer interest in bottled water. While retailers continue to give increased space to this beverage, however, they and manufacturers fear that too many brands could saturate the market and weaken the industry's growth rate.

Ingredient Costs Climbing

Sugar prices were relatively stable for several years but dramatically jumped in 1980—almost 60 percent in the first half of 1980. Commodity speculation and the prospect of sugar production falling short of consumption contributed to the price increase.

High fructose corn syrup, a sugar substitute used to some extent by almost all manufacturers, becomes more attractive as the price of sugar remains high. Generally, the price of this syrup runs 10-15 percent lower than that of sugar; however, with the recent jump in sugar prices, the price margin widened. Therefore, demand for high fructose syrup exceeded supply and will continue to for some time.

Producers tried to pass along higher wage, transportation and packing costs but they ran into consumer resistance. This forced producers to discount their drinks.

Saccharin Still on Market

The original 18-month moratorium on a ban of saccharin expired May 1979 but was extended by Congress until June 30, 1981. Since the Food and Drug Administration (FDA) banned the use of cyclamates in 1970, saccharin has been the only non-caloric artificial sweetener available for use in soft drinks.

Several government and industry studies are trying to determine the possible carcinogenic effects of saccharin. If the FDA again proposes restrictions on saccharin, it would take at least 15 months to implement a ban.

Plants Decline

There were about 1,850 soft drink bottling plants in 1980 and some 50 are expected to close in 1981. Some of the decline can be attributed to merger and large companies acquiring smaller ones. Also contributing is the consolidation of the operations of several less efficient bottling plants into one plant, which leads to increased productivity and economies of scale.

Franchising Decision

On July 9, 1980, President Carter signed the Soft Drink Interbrand Competition Act. This statute amends antitrust laws to permit exclusive territorial agreements when a soft drink product of one manufacturer is in "substantial and effective competition" with products made and sold by others.

At the same time in 1980, the Federal Trade Commission (FTC) vs. The Coca Cola Company case was before the U.S. Court of Appeals of the District of Columbia. The company asked the court to overrule the 1978 FTC decision to disband the exclusive franchise system, which was called "unreasonable" and "anticompetitive." After the Soft Drink Interbrand Competition Act became law, the Coca Cola Company asked the Court to dismiss its case against the FTC. The FTC replied it had no objection and stated that the new law permits reopening of the case.

Packaging Changes

Legislation in many areas of the country restricts packaging or requires deposits on soft drink containers. Six states (Oregon, Vermont, Maine, Michigan, Iowa and Connecticut) have passed laws requiring mandatory deposits.

Despite restrictions and efforts to promote conservation, non-returnable, one-way containers continue to increase in popularity. Sales of all non-returnables rose 10.1 percent in 1979 over 1978, while sales of beverages in returnable packages dropped 5.5 percent.

The plastic bottle continued its impressive gains, increasing 102 percent in usage in 1979. Cans continue to be the packaging leader, holding 42.5 percent of the market.

Metrics Gain in Popularity

Soft drinks continue to be a leader in the conversion to metric measure in the food industry. Bottles in 1- and 2-liter sizes are now popular and commonplace in many areas of the country, and the one-half liter size is gaining more acceptance. Large bottle sales in the 24 to 64 ounce size declined in 1979, but the loss was partially offset by the rapid growth of one-liter and two-liter non-returnable bottles.

After 2 full years on the market, the two-liter bottle accounted for 14.6 percent of the total packaged volume in 1979. One-liter returnables increased 10.2 in 1979 and captured 8 percent of the returnable market. The one-liter size was the only returnable container category to post an increase in 1979.

Foreign Trade Declines

Export shipments of bottled and canned soft drinks were expected to total $77 million in 1980, a decline of 13 percent from the $88 million exported in 1979. Even though exports to Saudi Arabia declined 38 percent, it remained the major customer, accounting for 43 percent of the value of exports in 1980.

The value of imports was expected to drop to $20 million in 1980, a substantial decrease from the $58 million imported in 1979. Mineral water accounts for 71 percent of the soft drink import category. Imports of mineral water declined about 75 percent in 1980, therefore total soft drink imports dropped.

Promising Outlook

The outlook for the soft drink industry looks promising through 1985. Real growth is forecast at an annual average of 3.8 percent. Aggressive marketing techniques are expected to intensify as the highly competitive companies in the industry strive to increase their market shares. However, an adverse outcome of the saccharin controversy could change the optimistic future.

SOFT DRINK

PLAN OF BUSINESS

General

The Partnership is newly organized and has no substantial business history, assets or staff of employees. The primary business of the Partnership will be to engage in the business of the manufacture, sale and distribution of Super Drink and diet Super Drink, new Super soft drink products developed by Super Drink World Corporation (the "Licensor"), in a 66-county area, which area is represented by the Licensor to account for approximately 3.95% of United States soft drink sales. The Partnership will operate under a Territory License Agreement ("License") and Bottling Agreement from the Licensor.

The founders of the Licensor were motivated by the belief that the growth of the chain and grocery store portion of the soft drink market has rendered the dominant beverage bottlers employing traditional beverage distribution systems vulnerable to a competitor emphasizing the chain and grocery segment of the soft drink market and using modern distribution techniques. Since the widespread introduction of bottled soft drinks in the 1930's, the franchises of the major national soft drink companies have been and are characterized by the grant of perpetual rights and distribution in small, exclusive territories. Significantly, the small size of the average national soft drink company's franchise territory does not usually coincide with the food wholesalers' and chain stores' large marketing areas. The use of a "to the store door" method of distribution in each franchise territory results in the employment of large numbers of route trucks by each beverage franchisee because of this divergence of franchise and marketing areas. Consequently, any new beverage franchisee using this type of distribution method is forced to make a large capital outlay for a delivery system.

The Licensor, in an effort to exploit this divergence of beverage franchise territories and marketing areas, has divided the United States in to 28 large territories based on chain store distribution networks and television ADI markets. The territories are designed to take advantage of the food wholesalers' and chain stores' warehouse delivery systems by making truckload deliveries, using the purchaser's trucks to transport the product to their own warehouse, feasible after a sale of the product is concluded by a food broker hired by the licensee. It is anticipated that the Partnership should be able to realize significant savings in distribution costs because there will be no need for the Partnership to purchase a fleet of route trucks to deliver its product to each individual store location in the license area. By employing this simplified, direct distribution system, the Partnership expects to be able to sell its soft drinks to retailers at wholesale prices which will allow retail mark-ups ranging from 25% to 35% over the wholesale price compared to the normal mark-up of approximately 16% to 20% on other soft drinks. The proposed pricing strategy of the Super Drink product is to effect a retail price advantage over the national brands of approximately 15¢ per six pack or two liter bottle which, combined with the higher gross margin, will give the retailer an incentive to sell the Partnership's product.

A national licensing system by a new independent soft drink company was not practical until the 1970's because the contract packing (bottling and canning) industry did not exist on a nationwide scale before then. Contract packing facilities are now available in most of the United States, and their use minimizes the new licensees capital investment and overhead and maximizes operating flexibility. The majority, if not all, of the licensees of the Licensors expect to or have contracted with a local custom canner for their product requirements.

For the foreseeable future, the Partnership will direct its marketing effort to the chain store and grocery trade, the segment of the market which accounts for the largest sales volume of soft drinks, and will market only Super Drink which account for the largest percentage of soft drinks consumed. In 1979, the chain store and grocery trade accounted for approximately 60% of the volume of all soft drink sales. Super Drinks dominate the soft drink industry and have maintained a 60% market share of all soft drinks sold for many years.

Bottling and Packaging. The Partnership will purchase Super Drink extract from the Licensor and will contract to have the extract mixed and packaged by an independent custom canner.

The custom canner will produce Super Drink and Diet Super Drink in two liter and one-half liter bottles and 12 oz. can sizes and will purchase the majority of product materials used in the mixing and bottling operation upon issuance of purchase orders from the Partnership. The custom canner will also be responsible for initiating and rebating to the Partnership the deposits on all bottles or cans sold. Provisions will also be made for the custom canner to maintain a minimum of 10 days inventory, seasonably adjusted. It is anticipated that in an effort to maintain continuing flexibility and control over bottling arrangements, the Partnership agreement with its custom canner will be terminable on 30 days notice. The General Partners have no present intention to construct or purchase a bottling plant for the Partnership. However, if the operations of the Partnership grow large enough to require a significant portion of the output of a bottling plant, the General Partners may consider acquiring a bottling facility for the Partnership.

Sales and Marketing. The Partnership will use the services of food brokers who have long standing relations with the local retail trade to sell the Super Drink product to grocery chains and food wholesalers in the License area. It is anticipated that this approach to sales will minimize the Partnership's fixed overhead costs and provide instant potential access to the retail grocery and chain store trade. The vast majority of food processors rely on the services of food brokers to sell their products to the retail industry. The Licensor has estimated that food brokers handle approximately 90% of all non-perishable food items sold through chain stores and food wholesalers. A food broker normally handles fifteen to twenty non-competing products of several manufacturers and calls on the major food chains in his area on a regular basis.

The food broker will handle or make suitable arrangements for the transport of the Partnership's product and will handle most day to day retail and wholesale sales functions. It is anticipated that the amount charged by the food brokers for their services will be less than the average cost to the Partnership if it were to handle these functions. The food broker's compensation will be based on the number of cases of soft drink sold. For obvious reasons, the success of the Partnership's operations will be heavily dependent upon the ability of its food brokers. In order to protect its ability to monitor the effectiveness of its food brokers and to make other arrangements on short notice if conditions require it, the Partnership intends to enter into contracts with food brokers that are terminable on 30 days notice.

Pick-Up Service for Empties. The Nonreturnable Beverage Container Act, which generally restricts the sale of certain beverages, including soft drinks, to returnable containers on which a deposit is charged by the seller and for which a refund is payable by every dealer or distributor of that beverage in beverage containers, requires that all soft drink distributors make suitable provisions to deal with the requirements of the Act. The manufacturers of affected soft drinks by necessity must provide retail outlets with convincing guarantees that empties will be picked up at the retail level. The Partnership plans to contract with Container Redemption Service, Inc., ("CRS") an affiliate of the General Partners, for this pick-up service. CRS has been operating as a returnable container service and has entered agreements with several other beverage bottlers for pick-up services. It currently makes weekly pick-ups from an average of 1400 stores in the License area. CRS will continue to operate independently of the Partnership and the Corporation and the Partnership anticipates paying the same rates to CRS as those charged to non-affiliated parties.

Production and Delivery. The normal sequence that the Partnership will follow for production and warehouse distribution is as follows: receipt of order, packing, and shipment within a seven-day period. The chain store buyer will give a purchase requisition to the food broker for the required number of cases of product, usually to be delivered seven days from the issuance of the purchase requisition. The food broker in turn will advise the Partnership's operations manager who will schedule the order into the contract canner's production run for the following week. The canner orders the necessary packaging materials from the suppliers. It is contemplated that this procedure will permit the Partnership to operate with a minimum inventory. Upon completion of the production run, the products are delivered to the wholesaler's or chain's central warehouse by the customer's own trucks which earn a backhaul allowance of approximately 15¢ to 25¢ a case, or by the canner's trucks for a similar fee.

Pricing. The Partnership will have autonomy from the Licensor in its pricing decisions. It is anticipated that the Partnership will use a pricing strategy that will give the consumer some discount from the nationally advertised brands of Super Drink. The price of the product will be set above the price of the private label brands in order to avoid competing with a chain store's own brands. Only a portion of the price differential between the Super Drink product and the leading Super soft drinks will be attributed to lower delivery costs. The balance is made up of lower gross profit per case to the Partnership. It is anticipated that the lower gross profit per case will be offset by increased sales volume, although there can be no assurance that the sales volume will be sufficient to overcome the lower per unit gross profit. The local franchises of competitors may engage in significant price cutting to reduce any competitive edge gained through this price strategy.

In addition to predictable price competition from the major Super soft drinks, the Partnership must compete with the various private label brands. The price of private brands will generally be lower than the Partnership's product and the Partnership will have to rely heavily on advertising to establish name identification and customer loyalty for its products to meet competition of the retailer's own brands. Private brands are not widely advertised, but enjoy an advantage because of lower price and because the chain and grocery stores through which they are sold usually allocate a disproportionally large share of available shelf space to their own private brands.

Advertising. The Licensor and the Partnership's advertising strategy is to position Super Drink as a quality soft drink brand. The Licensor's ads will make no mention of price, and the shopper will discover the price advantage only at the store level in point-of-purchase advertising. It is expected that a retail customer's initial purchase will be based on price and inquisitiveness, and the quality and taste of the beverages will be the primary reason for repurchase.

The Licensor has commissioned a series of television ads and radio commercials that have been developed, and will be used in the national advertising campaign. These commercials will also be available for use by the Partnership. These commercials have a primary target of women age 25 to 49. This target audience was selected because it represents the most significant segment of purchasers of soft drinks in grocery markets. A secondary target, men age 25 to 49, has been selected so that the Super Drink brand name will be familiar to other members of the family who are frequent users and sometimes purchasers of Super Drinks and other carbonated drinks. The Partnership will also use newspaper ads and point-of-purchase advertising to promote the sale of the products. In addition, the Licensor has entered into an agreement to promote Diet Super Drink as part of a diet regimen, primarily for women.

Under the terms of the Territory License Agreement, the Partnership will be obligated to expend, or reimburse the Licensor for up to, $250,000 on advertising within the License area within the first year of the License. Under the Bottling Agreement, the Partnership must contribute 20¢ per case, calculated on the amount of Super extract purchased from the Licensor, to the Licensor for the first three years (15¢/case thereafter) to help fund an ongoing national advertising program. The Licensor will grant the Partnership a credit of 3¢ per case for the first three years of the license (2¢/case thereafter) to help offset the cost of the Partnership's local advertising. Under the terms of the License, the Partnership will be permitted to use only advertising, sales and promotional materials that are approved in writing by the Licensor.

The Licensor has informed the Partnership that it expects to begin a national advertising campaign, including television, radio and print ads, to coincide with the beginning of the heavy seasonal demand for soft drinks.

THE LICENSE

The License Agreement and the Bottling Agreement will govern all aspects of the relationship between the Partnership and the Licensor.

The License Agreement. The License Agreement grants the licensee the exclusive right to manufacture, sell and distribute Super Drink products in the "Territory." The "Territory" encompasses a 66-county area which is represented by the Licensor to contain approximately 3.95% of the United States soft drink sales. The licensee may grant sublicenses subject to the approval of the Licensor. The License Agreement continues in effect for an initial period of 10 years and is automatically extended for an indefinite number of successive 10-year periods unless the licensee gives six-months' notice of termination prior to the end of any 10-year period.

The licensee will be required to make the following payments under the License Agreement:

(1) *License Fee.* The licensee must pay a $600,000 license fee to the Licensor for the grant of the license. $25,000 of this fee must be paid outright and the remainder in the form of a $.10 per case overcharge for Super extract for the first 5.75 million "Standard Cases" ordered. A "Standard Case" is the amount of extract necessary to make 24 bottles of Super Drink holding 12 ounces each.

(2) *Advertising.* The licensee must expend $250,000 on advertising within the Territory or pay this amount to the Licensor as reimbursement for advertising expenses advanced on behalf of the licensee during the first year of the license. This initial advertising contribution by licensees is designed to provide advertising to establish product identification and demand for Super Drink products. An appropriate percentage of the Licensor's total advertising effort will be directed into the Territory.

(3) *Price.* The Licensor has agreed that it will sell the licensee the extract used in manufacturing Super Drink at a price which is 10¢ above its standard terms of sale then current for the first 5.75 million Standard Cases and at its base price for all subsequent Standard Cases. Payment for each shipment of extract must be made in advance.

The licensee has the right to assign or sublicense to third parties the right to manufacture, sell and distribute the Super Drink products in all or a portion of the Territory provided that: (i) the portion of the territory sublicensed or assigned is commercially reasonable in accordance with the Licensor's written marketing policy; (ii) the licensee must comply with all statutes, ordinances, rules and regulations of Federal, state and local governments and independent governmental agencies, including those governing the sale of sub-franchises and submitted an opinion of its counsel satisfactory to counsel for the Licensor that the licensee has so complied; (iii) obtained, by written request, the Licensor's written consent to such sublicense or assignment, which approval will not be unreasonably withheld; and (iv) the Licensor and the sublicensee or assignee shall have executed the Bottling Agreement.

The license includes not only the basic Super Drink product and the Super Drink diet product, but also any other beverage Super Drink or its affiliates may market in the future. The Licensor has not indicated an intention to expand its operations to Super beverages.

The Bottling Agreement

The Bottling Agreement governs the actual conduct of manufacturing, sales and distribution operations in the Territory. The following summary briefly describes the most significant provisions of the Bottling Agreement.

Manufacturing Facilities. The facilities used in manufacturing and bottling Super Drink must be satisfactory to the Licensor. The Partnership will arrange for such manufacturing and bottling through one or more "custom canners" in the Territory. The General Partners do not anticipate any difficulty in obtaining the Licensor's approval of the canner the Partnership selects. The Licensor is obligated to assist the licensee in making arrangements with custom canners.

Standards. In manufacturing and bottling Super Drink, the licensee must observe the procedures and standards prescribed by the Licensor to assure the quality of the product. The licensee is required to use its best efforts in effecting sales of Super Drink and to secure full distribution of Super Drink in the Territory.

Exclusivity. The licensee cannot sell Super Drink outside the Territory and the Licensor cannot allow any other person to sell Super Drink within the Territory, with one exception. The Licensor may sell Super Drink extract to any "national account" which is a company which has sales outlets in two or more of the 28 Super Drink territories for use in "post-mix" products Ii.e., beverages served from a fountain, or the like, for immediate consumption). Such "national accounts" would consist primarily of restaurant chains. Sales to national accounts by the Licensor constitute a potentially significant restriction on the market available to the licensee in the Territory. The Licensor reserves the right to distribute in the Territory any form of Super Drink product covered by the License, the distribution of which the Licensor either declines to undertake or discontinues in its entirety.

Indemnity. The licensee agrees to indemnify the Licensor against any matters arising from any act or failure to act by the licensee in manufacturing and selling Super Drink. The Licensor agrees to indemnify the licensee against any matter relating to any defect in an ingredient supplied by the Licensor. The licensee must include the Licensor as a named insured on its insurance policies.

Term. The Bottling Agreement will continue for an initial period of 10 years and will be automatically extended for an indefinite number of additional 10-year periods unless the licensee gives notice of termination at least six months prior to the end of any 10-year period.

Licensor's Right to Terminate. The Licensor can terminate the Bottling Agreement if (a) the licensee fails to cure any default under the Bottling Agreement within a reasonable time, but in no event less than thirty (30) days, after notice of default, (b) any change in the effective control of the licensee which occurs without the Licensor's consent, (c) sales and distribution of Super Drink are discontinued for more than 30 days without adequate excuse, or (d) certain events relating to the licensee occurs, such as bankruptcy, insolvency, the appointment of a receiver, or the making of any failure of the licensee to cure a duly noticed failure to perform any material obligation.

Advertising. The licensee must make continuing contributions to Super Drink's advertising program at such time as each order is placed for Super extract. The payments equal 20¢ per Standard Case during the first three years of the term of the Bottling Agreement and the 15¢ per Standard Case thereafter. After the fifth year of the License term, the required payment may be increased by the Licensor, but only to the extent that the

Consumer Price Index increases. A portion of the advertising fairly reflecting the licensee's contributions will be directed into the Territory. The Partnership will receive a credit for local advertising equal to 3¢ per Standard Case during the first three years and 2¢ per Standard Case thereafter. All advertising employed by the licensee must be approved by the Licensor. The Licensor will make its advertising available to the licensee for local use.

THE OFFERING

The offerors ("Offerors"), Super Drink corporation (the "Corporation") and Super Drinks Associates, a Michigan limited partnership (the "Partnership"), offer securities of both the Corporation and the Partnership in units ("Units"), each Unit consisting of 20 shares of Common Stock of the Corporation, par value $.01 per share (each share being hereinafter referred to as a "Share") and a $9,500 limited partnership interest in the Partnership ("Interest"). The offering price is $10,000 per Unit. The offering is made on either of two bases: (i) eight Unit Combinations, each Unit Combination consisting of fifteen Units for a purchase price of $150,000 with the purchase price being payable on a partially deferred basis as hereinafter described, and (ii) fifteen individual Units offered for a cash purchase price of $10,000.

Each Unit Combination will be sold on a deferred payment basis, with $25,001 of the purchase price payable in cash or check at the date of subscription and with the balance being payable at such time by delivery of four promissory notes for $25,000 each and one promissory note for $24,999, the first falling due 364 days from the date hereof and the remaining four in one year intervals thereafter, the last note to come due being the note for $24,999. The promissory notes must be secured by a $124,999 letter of credit from a bank acceptable to the Offerors. Aside from the eight Unit Combinations, each individual Unit will be sold for $10,000 payable in cash or check on the date of subscription.

USE OF PROCEEDS

The maximum and minimum net proceeds of this offering to the Offerors, after deduction of maximum broker-dealer sales commissions, finder's fees and estimated expenses, are as follows:

	Maximum	Minimum
Proceeds of Offering	$1,350,000	$150,000
Less: Assumed Broker's Commission and Finder's Fees for All Units	135,000	15,000
Capital Contribution to the Corporation	60,750	6,750
Organization Expenses	35,000	35,000
Net Proceeds to the Partnership	$1,119,250	$ 93,250

The Corporation

The following table sets forth the Corporation's capitalization as of the date hereof and as adjusted to reflect the sale of the maximum and minimum number of Units offered hereunder after deduction of the maximum brokerage commissions and finder's fees:

	March 23, Year One	As Adjusted Maximum Proceeds	As Adjusted Minimum Proceeds
Common Stock, $.01 par value, 4 million shares authorized, 24,300 shares issued and outstanding as of 3/23/Year One; 27,000 shares will be issued if the maximum Units are sold, 24,600 shares will be issued if the minimum Units are sold.	$243.00	$ 270.00	$ 246.00
Preferred Stock, $.01 par value, 1 million shares authorized, no shares issued or outstanding.	-0-	-0-	-0-
Additional Paid in Capital	-0-	60,723.00	6,747.00
Total Shareholder's Equity	$243.00	$60,993.00	$6,993.00
Equity per Share	$ .01	$ 2.26	$ .28

General Partners' Right to Incorporate and Reorganize. The General Partners have the exclusive right, upon 30 days notice to the Limited Partners, to incorporate the Partnership if they determine it to be in the best interest of the Partnership's business. No such incorporation may have the effect of issuing shares of stock with dividend rights at the time of the issuance that would alter the then rights of the Partners inter se under the Agreement regarding their relative profit-sharing percentages. The Agreement provides for a fixed equity interest in the Corporation, or in any successor or transferee corporation, which must be received by the Limited Partners.

The following chart indicates the minimum percentages of stock ownership which the Limited Partners must receive on any such incorporation or reorganization. Any other variation of the rights of Partners inter se that is deemed reasonably appropriate by the General Partners, in their sole discretion, may be affected by such incorporation, but such incorporation shall be tax free to the Partners to the maximum extent possible and the aggregate book value of the shares of stock issued to Partners shall equal the aggregate of all Partners' Equity Accounts at the time of incorporation. Any other form of incorporation of all or a portion of the Partnership business or reorganization on any terms and conditions with any tax results may be effected pursuant to both the majority vote of the General Partners and the consent of at least a majority in Partnership interest of the holders of all the then Limited Partnership Interests, consenting as one aggregate class.

No specific time, if ever is fixed for such incorporation, however, such incorporation may not take place in any case until such time as, in the reasonable business judgment of the General Partners, the Partnership is operating at a profit and will not incur losses in the foreseeable future. All Partners shall receive at least 30 day's notice of any such decisions to incorporate. Although no such consent shall be required for any such action, in no event may a Partner bring a legal action against any of the General Partners, the Partnership or their affiliates to challenge, bar, restrain, enjoy, prevent or otherwise review the decision of the General Partners to incorporate if such incorporation is consented to before or after the fact by the holders of a majority in Partnership Interest of the then holders of all of the then Interests.

Notwithstanding the foregoing, no such incorporation shall take place until aggregate cash distributions have been made to the Limited Partners equal to the aggregate capital contributions of all present Limited Partners, including those made by promissory notes, even though such notes may not have become due or been paid. If any such incorporation results in the exchange of Limited Partners' Interests for stock in the Corporation then the Limited Partners will have, after incorporation no less than the following percentages of the outstanding Common Stock of the Corporation:

Amounts paid in cash to the Limited Partners	Guaranteed to have this percentage of common stock in Super Drink, Ltd., after incorporation
Paid an amount greater than one (1) time their capital contributions, but less than two (2) times that amount	Not less than 49% (computed after any such incorporation)
Paid an amount greater than two (2) times their capital contributions, but less than three (3) times that amount	Not less than 44% (computed after any such incorporation)
Paid an amount greater than three (3) times their capital Contributions, but less than four (4) times that amount	Not less than 38% (computed after any such incorporation)
Paid an amount greater than four (4) times their capital contributions, but less than five (5) times that amount	Not less than 22% (computed after any such incorporation)
Paid an amount greater than five (5) times their capital contributions, but less than six (6) times that amount	Not less than 26% (computed after any such incorporation)
Paid an amount greater than six (6) times their capital contributions.	Not less than 20% (computed after any such incorporation)

Should less than the maximum amount of Units offered be sold, the guaranteed percentage amounts shall be reduced by multiplying each of the aforesaid percentage amounts by the fraction obtained by dividing the maximum number of Interests offered hereunder into the actual number Interests sold.

Retirement of Interests. The General Partners may, from time to time, in their sole discretion, retire a Limited Partner for any good faith reason, either voluntarily or involuntarily on the part of the retired Limited Partner, but such involuntary retirement shall only be effected if the General Partners determine that the best business interests of the Partnership shall be served by the retirement of a Limited Partner. In the case of a voluntary retirement, such Limited Partner must request the same by notice to the General Partners, who, in their sole discretion, may grant such request if such voluntary retirement is not deemed to have an adverse effect upon the present or reasonably foreseeable debt service expenses and requirements of the Partnership. The General Partners are under no obligation to grant any such request and the General Partners shall not be obligated to expend time, effort or incur expenses in order to determine whether any such retirement can or should be made. The General Partners, in their sole discretion, shall determine the amount to be received upon such redemption, as well as the terms and conditions of any pay-out. No such retirement shall give rise to rights in other Partners to a pro rata retirement of any of their Partnership Interests.

SUPER DRINK ASSOCIATES
(a limited partnership)
PROJECTED INCOME STATEMENTS
(in thousands)

	Six Months Ended Oct. 31, Year One	Year Ended October 31				
		Year One	Year Two	Year Three	Year Four	Year Six
Cases Sold	505	1,360	1,700	2,060	2,440	2,888
Percent of Michigan Cola Market	1.0%	1.25%	1.5%	1.75%	2.0%	2.25%
Net Sales	$ 3,990	$11,765	$16,099	$21,388	$27,740	$36,042
Cost of Products Sold	2,263	6,704	9,215	12,287	16,006	20,843
Gross Profit	1,727	5,061	6,884	9,101	11,734	15,199
Operating Expenses						
Delivery	90	267	367	489	638	830
Brokerage	80	236	324	432	563	732
Trade allowance	398	1,178	1,619	2,159	2,813	3,663
Advertising and promotion:						
Local	181	534	734	978	1,276	1,661
National	123	365	500	668	870	1,133
Selling, general and administrative	149	321	437	553	683	844
Management fees	90	136	170	220	277	327
License fees	58	155	194	193	-	-
Pickup fees	208	616	846	1,129	1,469	1,914
Other operating expenses	111	243	331	444	584	736
Amortization of organization and startup costs	8	16	16	16	16	8
Interest	100	180	140	100	60	20
Total operating expenses	1,596	4,247	5,678	7,381	9,249	11,868
Operating Income - Before introductory programs and general partner management fee	131	714	1,206	1,720	2,485	3,331
Introductor Programs						
Advertis. launch program	400	-	-	-	-	-
Local introduc. program	340	-	-	-	-	-
Local promotion	35	-	-	-	-	-
Consumer contest	135	-	-	-	-	-
Coupon program	50	-	-	-	-	-
Total introductory programs	960	-	-	-	-	-
Income (Loss) Before General Partner Management Fee	(829)	814	1,206	1,720	2,485	3,331
Annual General Partner Management Fee - 49 percent	-	-	-	843	1,218	1,632
Taxable Income (Loss)	($ 829)	$ 814	$ 1,206	$ 877	$ 1,267	$ 1,699
Taxable Income (Loss) to Limited Partners - 99 percent	($ 821)	$ 806	$ 1,194	$ 868	$ 1,254	$ 1,682

SUPER DRINK ASSOCIATES
(a limited partnership)
PROJECTED STATEMENTS OF CHANGES IN CASH POSITION
(in thousands)

	Oct. 31, Year One	Year Two	Year Three	October 31 Year Four	Year Five	Year Six
Cash Balance - Beginning of period	$ -	$ 18	$ 170	$ 231	$ 314	$ 374
Additions						
Net income (loss)	(829)	814	1,206	877	1,267	1,699
Amortization of organization costs	8	16	16	16	16	8
Increase (decrease) in accounts payable and accruals	527	157	210	255	323	329
Capital contribution	333	190	190	190	190	190
Bank loan	1,000	-	-	-	-	-
Total additions	1,039	1,195	1,792	1,569	2,110	2,600
Deductions						
Increase in accounts receivable	608	161	274	348	420	545
Increase in inventory	198	64	87	107	116	160
Organization and startup costs	215	-	-	-	-	-
Bank loan repayments	-	200	200	200	200	200
Total deductions	1,021	425	561	655	736	905
Cash Balance - Available for distribution	18	770	1,231	914	1,374	1,695
Annual Cash Distributed to -						
Limited partners	-	594	990	594	990	1,287
General partners	-	6	10	6	10	13
Cash Balance - End of period	$ 18	$ 170	$ 231	$ 314	$ 374	$ 395

SUPER DRINK ASSOCIATES
(a limited partnership)
PROJECTED INVESTMENT SUMMARY OF A $10,000
LIMITED PARTNERSHIP INTEREST
ASSUMING A 60% MARGINAL TAX BRACKET INVESTOR

Year	Taxable Income (Loss)	Tax Savings (Cost)	Cash Distribution	Annual Total Benefits	Cash Investment in Corporation and Partnership	Annual Net (Investment) Benefit	Cumulative Net (Investment) Benefit
One	($ 6,080)	($ 3,648)	$ -	$ 3,648	$10,000	($ 6,352)	($ 6,352)
Two	5,967	3,580	4,400	820	-	820	(5,532)
Three	8,847	5,308	7,333	2,025	-	2,025	(3,507)
Four	6,430	3,858	4,400	542	-	544	(2,963)
Five	9,287	5,572	7,333	1,761	-	1,761	(1,202)
Six	12,460	7,476	9,533	2,057	-	2,057	855
Total	$36,911	$22,146	$32,999	$10,853	$10,000	$ 855	

SUPER DRINK ASSOCIATES
(a limited partnership)
PROJECTED INVESTMENT SUMMARY OF A UNIT COMBINATION
OF 15 $10,000 LIMITED PARTNERSHIP INTERESTS
ASSUMING A 60% MARGINAL TAX BRACKET INVESTOR

Year	Taxable Income (Loss)	Tax Savings (Cost)	Cash Distribution	Annual Total Benefits	Cash Investment in Corporation and Partnership	Annual Net (Investment) Benefit	Cumulative Net (Investment) Benefit
One	($ 91,200)	($ 54,720)	$ -	$ 54,720	$ 25,001	$ 29,719	$ 29,719
Twc	89,500	53,700	66,000	12,300	25,000	(12,700)	17,019
Three	132,700	79,620	110,000	30,380	25,000	5,380	22,399
Four	96,400	57,840	66,000	8,160	25,000	(16,840)	5,559
Five	139,300	83,580	110,000	26,420	25,000	1,420	6,979
Six	186,900	112,140	143,000	30,860	24,999	5,861	12,840
Total	$553,600	$332,160	$495,000	$162,840	$150,000	$ 12,840	

SUPER DRINK ASSOCIATES
(a limited partnership)
PROJECTED INVESTMENT SUMMARY OF A UNIT COMBINATION
OF 15 $10,000 LIMITED PARTNERSHIP INTERESTS
ASSUMING A 70% MARGINAL TAX BRACKET INVESTOR

Year	Taxable Income (Loss)	Tax Savings (Cost)	Cash Distribution	Annual Total Benefits	Cash Investment in Corporation and Partnership	Annual Net (Investment) Benefit	Cumulative Net (Investment) Benefit
One	($ 91,200)	($ 63,840)	$ -	$ 63,840	$ 25,001	$ 38,839	$ 38,839
Two	89,500	62,650	66,000	3,350	25,000	(21,650)	17,189
Three	132,700	92,890	110,000	17,110	25,000	(7,890)	9,299
Four	96,400	67,480	66,000	(1,480)	25,000	(26,480)	(17,181)
Five	139,300	97,510	110,000	12,490	25,000	(12,510)	(29,691)
Six	186,900	130,830	143,000	12,170	24,999	(12,829)	(42,520)
Total	$553,600	$387,520	$495,000	$107,480	$150,000	($ 42,520)	

SUPER DRINK ASSOCIATES
(a limited partnership)
PROJECTED COST PER CASE PRODUCED

Item	2 Liters Super Drink	2 Liters Diet Super Drink	1/2 Liter Super Drink	1/2 Liter Diet Super Drink	12 Ounce Can Super Drink	12 Ounce Can Diet Super Drink
Super Drink syrup	$ 469	$1.220	$ .333	$ .867	$ .250	$ .650
Sugar	1.514	-	1.180	-	.832	-
Container and shell	2.580	2.580	.300	.300	1.656	1.656
Paper insert	-	-	.165	.165	-	-
Freight-in	.200	.200	-	-	.038	.038
Labels	.036	.036	.108	.108	-	-
Can ends	-	-	-	-	.552	.552
Closures	.080	.080	.235	.235	-	-
Hi-cones	-	-	-	-	.054	.054
Shrink film	-	-	-	-	.025	.025
Trays	-	-	-	-	.063	.063
Carbonation	.015	.015	.015	.015	.025	.025
Loss factor	.046	.041	.022	.015	.040	.031
Packing fee	.700	.700	.950	.950	.450	.450
Total production cost	5.640	4.872	3.308	2.655	3.985	3.544
Selling price, less 2% cash discount	9.410	9.410	5.880	5.880	6.470	6.470
Gross profit	$3.770	$4.538	$2.572	$3.225	$2.485	$2.926

BENEFITS OF A SOFT DRINK PROGRAM

Partnership Allocations

Subject to certain deferrals of the Partners' rights in the income, profits, losses, deductions and credits of the Partnership to assure that no Partners sustain a loss in their capital accounts while other Partners earn a profit in their drawing accounts and that on dissolution of the Partnership, Partners that have a basis for tax purposes in their Partnership Interests are allocated losses that otherwise would have been allocated to other Partners who may not use them because they have no basis for tax purposes in their Partnership Interests, the Limited Partners will be initially allocated, pro rata based on the number of outstanding Interests then held by each of them and the outstanding in total, 99% of the Partnership's income, profits, gains, losses, deductions and credits until the aggregate cash distributions to the Limited Partners shall equal five times the amount of their aggregate capital contributions, including those made by promissory notes, even though such notes may not have become due or been paid. The income, profits and gains of the Partnership are to be determined after payment of the annual management fee, if in effect, as hereinafter described. The General Partners will each share equally in and be allocated a 1% permanent interest in all of the aforesaid items. Upon receipt by the Limited Partners of cash distributions, on a cumulative basis, that equal the capital contributions of all Limited Partners in the aggregate, including those made by promissory notes, even though such notes may not have become due or been paid, the Corporation will be allocated 49% of the Partnership's income (determined on the same method as utilized by the Partnership on its federal income tax return prior to deduction for such fuel) or $120,000, whichever is greater, as its annual management fee thereafter. Subsequent to the distribution of aggregate cash distributions to the Limited Partners which equal or exceed five times the amount of the aggregate capital contributions of all present Limited Partners, including those made by promissory notes, even though such notes may not have become due or been paid, the aforesaid 99% interest of the Limited Partners in the income, profits, gains, losses, deductions and credits of the Partnership will be reduced to 10% and the interest of the Corporation in such items shall be correspondingly increased without reduction of the management fee discussed above.

The General Partners will have, in their sole and exclusive discretion, the option to pay out to Partners the Partnership's net pretax income, if any, computed on the cash as opposed to the accrual basis, which is not required for operations. The General Partners shall use their best efforts to distribute at least sufficient cash to enable the Partners to pay any federal income taxes reasonably anticipated on the Partnership's income.

Sufficient cash in this regard shall be deemed to be at least 60% of the Partnership's taxable income computed on the cash basis for any taxable year.

RISKS OF A SOFT DRINK PROGRAM

Risks Inherent in Soft Drink Industry. The following risks are inherent in any effort to market a new soft drink product:

(a) A newly introduced soft drink has no consumer recognition or demand, which must be generated almost entirely by advertising. The cost of advertising is high, and if the introductory national advertising campaign produced by the Licensor proves unsuccessful, it may be economically impracticable to initiate a new campaign. The initial national advertising planned by the Licensor is of limited duration. The advertising budgets of the other manufacturers in the soft drink marketplace are significantly greater than the combined planned advertising budgets of the Licensor and all of its licensees. There can be no assurance that the local or national advertising for the Super Drink product will create or develop any consumer demand for the product. Under the terms of the License, the Partnership is permitted to use only advertising, sales and promotional materials that are approved in writing by the Licensor and to use such materials only in accordance with plans and programs approved by the Licensor.

(b) The soft drink industry, particularly the Super segment of the industry, is presently dominated, at the national, and local metropolitan levels, by the competitors, a factor which the Licensor and the Partnership will rely on in competing with these dominant companies is that, as a result of lower projected distribution costs and a lower gross profit margin, it should be possible to sell the Super Drink product at a lower price than competitors. There can be no assurance that the dominant soft drink companies or their local franchises will not use their market position and greater assets to meet the price competition of the Partnership.

(c) The marketing of any soft drink product depends to a certain extent on the shelf space which retail outlets are willing to make available to the product. If retailers are unwilling to display the product in reasonable quantity and in a suitably prominent manner, the marketing efforts of the food brokers selected by the Partnership to distribute the product, and ultimately the Partnership, will be adversely affected. The Partnership will be dependent upon one or more food brokers to make suitable arrangements with wholesale and retail outlets. If the performance and effectiveness of the food brokers used by the Partnership are not satisfactory, the Partnership's operations may be severely damaged.

(d) The Nonreturnable Beverage Container Act generally prevents the sale of soft drinks to consumers in nonreturnable containers, resulting in the use of returnable containers on which a deposit is charged and refunded upon return. A soft drink manufacturer must make suitable provisions with retailers that returned containers will be picked up by the beverage manufacturer at the retail location if its product is to be marketed by the retailer. The Partnership will rely on the services of Container Redemption Service, Inc. ("CRS"), for this pick-up service for the returned containers of Super Drink. CRS has been operating as a returnable container service and has entered agreements with the licensees of other beverage manufacturers for pick-up service. It currently makes pick-ups from an average of 1400 stores in the License area on a weekly basis. The success of the Partnership's operations at the retail level will be materially dependent on the performance of CRS.

(e) The sale of any product for human consumption involves significant exposure to liability to consumers who are injured by the product. The Licensor has agreed to indemnify and hold the Partnership harmless against liabilities by reason of injury of any nature to any person or entity arising from the manufacture, sale and distribution of the cola extract supplied by the Licensor. The Partnership would also be entitled to be held harmless and indemnified under the terms of the proposed Contract Packer Agreement by the custom canner for any liability arising from faulty mixing or packaging, and will agree to maintain insurance to cover such claims. No assurance can be given as to the result of the exercise of the aforesaid rights of the Partnership, which exercise may entail long periods of time and expensive legal proceedings. A substantial products liability award against the Partnership could therefore have a material adverse effect on its operations.

Arbitrary Offering Price of Shares of the Corporation and Dilution. The price of the Shares of the Corporation has been established by its Board of Directors. The primary factors involved in establishing the price per share were the amount of funds necessary for the Corporation to undertake the activities referred to herein and the percentage of the total equity of the Corporation that its Board of Directors believed should be sold pursuant to this offering. The value that the offering price purports to place on the Shares may bear no relationship to the assets, earnings or other criteria of value applicable to the Corporation. The price paid by the Corporation's current stockholders for their shares was significantly less than the price of the Shares being sold pursuant to this offering. There will be an immediate and substantial dilution in the book value per Share to approximately $.28 per Share from the offering price of the Shares if the minimum amount of proceeds is subscribed hereunder and to $2.26 per Share from the offering price if the maximum number of Units offered hereunder are sold.

Additionally, under the provisions of the Agreement, if the Partnership were to "merge" into the Corporation after an amount paid in cash by the Partnership to the Limited Partners greater than their capital contributions thereto but less than twice their capital contributions, the Corporation would be obligated to issue in the aggregate at least 1,100 shares of Common Stock the Limited Partners as a group if the minimum number of Units are subscribed hereunder. Such action would dilute the book value per Share to approximately $.28 per Share. If the maximum number of Units are subscribed hereunder, at least 20,648 shares of Common Stock would need to be issued to the Limited Partners as a group upon such merger. This would then dilute the book value per share to approximately $1.27.

Super Drink Formulae and Trademarks. The Licensor acquired the Super Drink and Diet Super Drink extract formula from International Fad Consultants, Inc. ("IFC") in exchange for approximately 17% of the Licensor's outstanding stock. IFC has warranted to the Licensor that the formulae were developed solely by IFC and is not based on the formula of any other Super Drink and that IFC has made suitable arrangements for the production of the extract. Under the terms of the Bottling Agreement, the Licensor represents to the Partnership that it is the owner of duly registered United States trademarks for "Super Drink" and "Diet Super Drink" and all designs and slogans used in connection therewith, and agrees to defend and protect the trademarks and formulae, including defending any action contesting the validity and extent of the trademarks or the ownership of the formulae. Any successful action challenging the validity of the trademark or the ownership of the formulae or the failure of IFC to supply the Licensor with sufficient quantities of the extract, could have a material adverse effect on the Partnership's operations.

Investment in the Corporation. No significant tax benefits can be expected to inure to the investor as a result of his investment in the Shares of the Corporation, aside from the fact that the Shares should in most cases constitute capital assets in the investor's hands that may potentially entitle him to long-term capital gain treatment in the sale or exchange thereof after being held for one year, unless the Corporation is found to be a "collapsible corporation" under the Internal Revenue Code. If the investor disposes of his Shares in the Corporation at a gain, the gain may be taxable at ordinary income rates if the Corporation is found to be a "collapsible corporation" or if the Shares are deemed to be inventory in the hands of the investor. If an investor disposes of his Shares in the Corporation at a loss, deductibility of the loss may be subject to the restrictions applicable to capital losses. Although counsel to the Offerors has rendered its opinion that, under certain circumstances, the Corporation's stock will qualify as "Section 1244 Stock," as to which an ordinary loss deduction may be available, the availability of an ordinary loss deduction will depend upon facts and circumstances, relating to both the investor and the Corporation, in existence at the time of the loss. Each investor is urged to consult his own tax advisor in this regard.

Future Share Offerings. The Corporation may make additional offerings of its shares of Common Stock in the foreseeable future. The availability of additional financing from this source may induce the Offerors to revise some of their current financial plans and projections as well as their current lines of business.

TAX ASPECTS OF A SOFT DRINK PROGRAM

Incorporation of the Partnership

The General Partners have the exclusive right to incorporate the Partnership if they determine it to be in the best interest of the Partnership's business, either by (i) an irrevocable power of attorney coupled with an interest thereon which is created over all current and future Partnership interests that shall be outstanding to cause them to be exchanged for shares of the capital stock of a corporation; (ii) sale of all or substantially all Partnership assets for shares of capital stock of a corporation followed by dissolution of the Partnership; or (iii) dissolution of the Partnership and transfer of its assets received on liquidation under a similar irrevocable power coupled with an interest therein to cause them to be exchanged for capital stock of a corporation. The Agreement provides that such incorporation shall be tax free to the Partners to the maximum extent possible.

The Service, in Revenue Ruling 70-239, 1970-1 C.B. 74, considered the tax consequences of these three methods of incorporating a partnership and stated that each of these situations would be regarded as a transfer under Section 351 of the Code, which provides, in general, that no gain or loss is recognized if property is transferred to a corporation solely in exchange for stock or securities of the transferee-corporation if, immediately after the exchange, the transferor or transferors are in "control" of the corporation. Gain will be recognized if the sum of the amount of liabilities assumed by the Partnership plus the amount of liabilities to which the property transferred to the corporation is subject exceeds the total adjusted basis of such property. Also, to the extent a transferor in a Section 351 transaction receives consideration other than stock or securities of the transferee-corporation ("Boot"), any gain realized by the transferor is recognized under Section 351(b) to the extent of the value of such boot and is of a character determined with reference to the character of the assets transferred to the corporation. Loss is never recognized in a Section 351 transaction.

The gain, if any, which the Partnership recognizes on incorporation will be taxed as capital gain or ordinary income depending on the type of assets transferred. Also, a portion of any gain may be taxed as ordinary income if there is any depreciation recapture. Incorporation of the Partnership may trigger a recapture of any investment tax credit which may have been allowed to Limited Partners of the Partnership. Upon incorporation, the Partners would be taxed as corporate shareholders.

Gifts of Partnership Interests

Generally, no gain or loss is recognized for federal income tax purposes as a result of a gift of property. However, if a gift of a Unit is made when a Limited Partner's allocable share of Partnership non-recourse indebtedness exceeds the adjusted basis of his interest, such Limited Partner may recognize gain for federal income tax purposes to the extent of such excess. Such excess will be taxed in the same manner as a sale of a Unit. Gifts of a Limited Partnership interest may be subject to a gift tax imposed pursuant to the rules generally applicable to all gifts of property.

Investment in the Corporation

An investor's investment in the Shares of the Corporation will be treated for federal income tax purposes as a purchase of stock in a corporation. Accordingly, no significant tax benefits can be expected to inure to the investor as a result of his investment in the Corporation, aside from the fact that Shares in most cases would constitute capital assets in the investor's hands that may potentially entitle him to long-term capital gain treatment on the sale or exchange thereof after being held for one year unless the Corporation is found to be a "collapsible corporation" by the Service, as discussed below. Because the Corporation will be treated as a corporation for federal income tax purposes, it will be required to pay a tax on its income, the investors will not be entitled to include in their individual tax returns their pro rata share of the income, gain, loss and credit of the Corporation, the payment of taxes by the Corporation will reduce the amount of cash available for distribution to the investors, and distributions from the Corporation will be taxable as dividends to the extent of the accumulated earnings and profits of the Corporation. If an investor disposes of his shares in the Corporation at a gain, the Service may, depending upon the financial condition of the Corporation, the composition of its assets, and other factors, take the position that the investor is not entitled to capital gain treatment as to all or part of his gain on the ground that the Corporation is a "collapsible corporation" or on the grounds that the Shares constituted inventory in the hands of the investor. No assurance can be given that the Service would not prevail with this position. If it does, any such gain would be taxable to the investor as ordinary income (presently taxable to individuals at rates up to 70%).

Counsel to the Offerors has rendered its opinion to the Corporation that the Shares to be issued to investors will qualify as "Section 1244 stock" *provided that,* among other things, more than 50% of the Corporation's gross receipts, for certain taxable years, are derived from sources other than royalties, rents, dividends, interest, annuities, or sales or exchanges of stock or securities. Qualification of the Shares as Section 1244 stock will, in certain cases, entitle an investor to an ordinary loss deduction in the event that a loss is sustained with respect to his Shares in the Corporation. However, qualification of the Shares in the Corporation as Section 1244 stock does not insure an investor that he will be entitled to an ordinary loss deduction in the event that a loss is sustained with respect to his Shares. For example, an ordinary loss deduction in respect to a loss on Section 1244 stock is not available to a corporation, a trust, an estate or a transferee of a person to whom Section 1244 stock was issued by a corporation. Moreover, the aggregate amount that may be treated by a taxpayer as an ordinary loss in any taxable year with respect to Section 1244 stock is $50,000 (or $100,000 in the case of a husband and wife filing a joint return). Because this limitation is applied in the aggregate, and not on a corporation-by-corporation basis, an investor may obtain little or no benefit from Section 1244 characterization of the Corporation's shares if his loss with respect to his Shares was sustained in a taxable year in which he sustained substantial losses on other Section 1244 stock.

Each investor should consult his own tax advisor as to the effect classification of the Corporation's Shares as Section 1244 stock will have in light of the investor's particular circumstances.

The introduction of a new food product attracts fierce competition and is a risky venture. However, for the food products accepted in the market place, there can be substantial reward to the investor.

Chapter Thirteen

EMPLOYEE PLANS

Although trust assets accumulate tax-free inside an exempt trust, there is still a struggle to maintain pace with inflation. Special real estate programs and various collectibles such as rare coins have been offered to help overcome the inflation problem.

Congress passed a law increasing the opportunity for plan realty investments.

Real estate offers a lucrative place to invest assets in these inflationary times. So why haven't qualified plans taken fuller advantage of real estate investment opportunities? Basically it's because plans couldn't debt finance their investments without incurring unrelated business income. Such income is taxable based on the proportion that the debt bears to the plan's adjusted basis in the property. However, Congress recently decided to remove some of the unrelated-business-income barriers.

Thanks to the addition of Sec. 514(c)(9) to the Code by the '80 Miscellaneous Revenue Act, plans can now buy land with borrowed funds. For tax years beginning in 1981, most debt incurred by qualified plans in the acquisition *or improvement* of real estate won't be considered "acquisition indebtedness." So the income or gain from the land won't be treated as income from debt-financed property. What's more, this new tax break covers the gamut of real-property ownership, including sole ownership as well as interests in joint ventures and partnerships that buy land for investment.

Example: Say Pension Plan buys rental property for $5 million, laying out $1 million in cash and taking a mortgage for the remaining $4 million. In the first year the property produces $500,000 in income and $300,000 in deductions. Under pre-Sec. 514(c)(9) law, Plan would have had $160,000 in taxable income. Why? Since Plan financed 80% of the purchase price, it had to report an equal percentage of the income ($400,000) offset by the same percentage in deductions ($240,000). But thanks to the escape hatch, Plan now owes no tax on the property's income. Even better, any gain on sale of the property will be entirely tax free.

Exceptions: A plan will still be taxed on income and gains from debt-financed property if: (1) the purchase price wasn't fixed when the land was purchased (price adjustments at closing of title will *not* cause this exception to apply); (2) the size of the debt or the time for making payments on it in any way depends upon income or profits from the property; (3) there's a "sale-leaseback" to the seller or a related party under Sec. 267(b); (4) the property's acquired from (or leased to) a plan-related party (necessary to prevent indirect, discriminatory employer contributions through bargain sales rates to the plan); or (5) a party related to the plan or seller provides non-recourse financing that's subordinate to other indebtedness or which bears interest significantly below the going rate.

J. Gregg Buckalew and Donald Demko of Coopers & Lybrand had this to say about the new law.

For various reasons, pension funds have been slow to invest their massive assets in real estate. However, a change in existing law and changed perceptions of real estate as an investment vehicle could portend the unleashing of billions in new investment.

New Law Allows Tax Free Leveraged Investment

On December 29, 1980, President Carter signed a bill which exempts qualified retirement plan trusts from the income tax which had been levied on income from investments in debt-financed real estate. Previously, the income from such investments was treated as being unrelated business income and thus fully taxable.

The impact of the new law upon the entire real estate market could be to drive up commercial property prices, because leverage will allow pension plans to combine their dollars with debt to chase larger parcels. With total assets rapidly approaching one trillion dollars, pension fund investment in U.S. real estate is expected by many in the industry to grow to $300 billion by 1990, from less than $10 billion currently. The usually well-heeled pension plans will hardly be candidates for defaulting on their mortgage payments during bad business cycles. This will add some stable underpinings to the market, if indeed the pension funds do go for leveraging in a big way. There had been published articles which purported, prior to the new legislation, that pension plans should leverage real estate purchases despite the income tax consequences. Cases have been made that the rate of return to a pension plan from leveraged real estate should be better, net of taxes, than their otherwise untaxed securities investments. Perhaps these arguments are now even stronger.

The Future of Pension Funds and U.S. Real Estate

Real estate is often ideally suited to pension funds. Funds' outflow is actuarially predictable. Thus, their cash flow needs are usually best served by long term investments which have inflation protection. Liquidity and current value accounting for appreciation are less important than for other publicly owned lenders.

To date, most funds have invested in open and closed-end co-mingled funds. This allows for diversity in their real estate portfolios in both geography and product type. They also benefit from specialized funds, experienced managers, quality projects and a good rate of return. However, their investment in real estate has typically been only about 1 to 3 percent of their assets.

As the pension funds place a greater portion of their portfolio into real estate the larger funds will develop greater internal sophistication. This may lead them to become more comfortable with participating in joint real estate investment ventures, much like their counterparts in the insurance industry and the foreign pension funds.

A partnership program and a trust program are shown as vehicles for pension investment in real estate. These examples are followed by a rare coin fund used as a hedge against inflation.

QUALIFIED PROPERTIES

INVESTMENT OBJECTIVES AND POLICIES

General

The Partnership intends to make unleveraged acquisitions of shopping centers, office and light industrial buildings, and similar commercial real estate. All such Properties will be acquired from nonaffiliated sellers; provided, however, that the General Partners may acquire Properties in their own name, or that of any Affiliate, and temporarily hold title for the purpose of facilitating acquisition by the Partnership at a cost no greater than the cost to the General Partner or Affiliate apart from the compensation specified herein. The Partnership intends to invest primarily in existing Properties. The Partnership may also commit up to 50% of its available funds to purchase certain to-be-constructed commercial Properties. In such event, the Partnership will strive to minimize construction and lease-up risks by closing the actual purchase of such Properties only upon the receipt from the seller of letters of credit or other collateral deemed satisfactory by the General Partners as security for completion of construction and by making any additional payments to such seller contingent upon the achievement of specified lease-up, cash flow or other parameters within specified time periods.

The Partnership may utilize up to 75% of its available funds to make such investments through the use of first mortgage loans, secured by Properties, convertible into direct ownership interest in such Properties or an equity interest in the entity owning such Properties ("Equity Convertible Loans"). In general, the General Partners will structure Equity Convertible Loans, in amounts not to exceed 80% of the appraised value of any Property, to be convertible into all or a portion of the early interest after periods ranging from two but not to exceed five years, at which time repayment of loans not previously converted by the Partnership would be required Such Equity Convertible Loans would also provide for escalating interest payments, based on anticipated performance of the Property, and such other terms and conditions as the General Partners believe to be in the best interests of the Partnership. The Partnership will not reinvest proceeds from sales, including the repayment of Equity Convertible Loans, of Properties.

The Partnership's principal investment objectives will be to invest the net cash proceeds of this Offering in such commercial real estate with the goals of obtaining:

1) Capital appreciation;
2) Distributions of Net Cash from Operations attributable to rental income; and
3) Preservation and protection of capital.

To increase the Partnership's prospects of receiving a steady cash flow from its investments and, upon sale of any Property, a full return of the Partnership's investment in the Property, the Partnership expects that some or all of its investments may be in joint ventures with sellers of Properties or other persons whereby the Partnership would have certain preferential interests in cash flow or in liquidation proceeds, or both.

The following applies to holders of Units other than tax-exempt organizations and to such organizations only to the extent that the Partnership may generate some unrelated business income. *The Partnership does not offer tax benefits commonly associated with tax shelter investments.* Any tax shelter referred to herein or tax benefit will thus not be comparable to such tax shelter investments. Prospective investors should understand that one of the aspects of sheltering income distributions from the Partnership is that the tax benefit will not be to eliminate taxes otherwise payable, but rather to defer taxes until a later period. Moreover, until the Partnership invests its funds in Properties, it will not be entitled to any depreciation deductions. Under the Internal Revenue Code, tax deferral results because certain items requiring no cash outlay, primarily depreciation, are allowed as deductions in calculating taxable income. Since noncash items reduce taxable income in the year the deductions are taken, the tax bases of the affected Properties are reduced commensurately, resulting in the deferral of tax liability to a later year. Thus, the tax otherwise payable in the early years will become payable in later years. However, capital gain tax rates, rather than ordinary income tax rates, may apply to all or a portion of any tax that is deferred.

Distributions of Net Cash from Operations, even though attributable to rental income from operation of the Properties, may be treated as a return of capital, and not investment income, under generally accepted accounting principles ("GAAP") and under the Internal Revenue Code. A partnership's net income as determined in accordance with GAPP is generally calculated by subtracting depreciation as well as operating expenses from gross revenues. The significance of this is that a return of capital is treated for financial statement purposes as a reduction of partners' equity and for tax purposes as a reduction of basis and a tax-deferred distribution. Accordingly, it is possible that for both GAAP and income tax purposes, investors will be treated as having received a full return of capital, in the form of Net Cash from Operations over a period of years, before the Partnership's actual assets have been sold. As an economic matter, the amount of Limited Partners' capital remaining in the Partnership can only be determined by selling the Partnership's Properties. In this connection, prospective investors should note that, under the Partnership Agreement and the policies of the Partnership, cash distributions are not expected to be made unless Net Cash from Operations sufficient therefor has been received. The Partnership does not intend to make distributions of cash from its working capital or reserves except in the event that its working capital or reserves should prove excessive after operations commence.

The attainment of the Partnership's investment objectives will depend on many factors, including the ability of the General Partners to select suitable Properties for investment and the successful management of the operations of these Properties. Future economic conditions in the United States as a whole and, in particular, in the localities in which the Partnership's Properties are located will also be important factors, especially with regard to achievement of capital appreciation. ACCORDINGLY, THERE CAN BE NO ASSURANCE THAT ANY OR ALL THE FOREGOING OBJECTIVES WILL BE ATTAINED, IN WHOLE OR IN PART.

Joint Venture Investments and Preferred Ownership Positions

The Partnership will not own Property jointly with others unless such ownership is in the form of a partnership or joint venture and the Partnership acquires a "controlling" interest in such joint venture or partnership, as explained below. There is no limitation on the percentage of Partnership capital that can be invested in such joint ventures. In negotiating the terms of joint venture investments, the Partnership expects to be able to obtain, in some cases, certain preferential rights to cash flow and Net Proceeds from Sales with a view to meeting the Partnership's objectives. In some joint venture investments, it is expected that if the seller of a Property remains as a co-venturer, he may not make any cash contribution to the venture but will retain an interest in the Property to be owned by the venture. Such joint venture arrangements may under certain circumstances involve risks not otherwise present in direct investments, including, for example, risks associated with the possibility that the co-venture may at any time have economic or business interests or goals which are inconsistent with the business interests or goals of the Partnership. In connection with such joint venture investments a proportionately greater share of depreciation or sales proceeds may be allocable to the Partnership's co-venture or co-ventures.

Such joint ventures will be established by the Partnership and the seller or developer of a Property (or another party) pursuant to a joint venture or general partnership agreement under which the Partnership will have effective control over the management of the joint venture. The seller's retention of an interest in the Property through the joint venture will be considered in determining the purchase price of the Partnership's interest, which will be established by arm's-length negotiations. It is expected that any joint venture agreement will provide that either the Partnership or the co-venturer may initiate a sale of the Property in response to a firm written offer from an unaffiliated party, subject, however, to the right of the other venture to exercise a right of first refusal to acquire the selling co-venturer's interest in the joint venture. While each such agreement may vary in form, depending on negotiations, in no case will the co-venturer have any legal right to take action which would be contrary to the Partnership's objectives or which would prevent the Partnership from carrying on its business.

The Partnership's controlling interest in any joint venture or partnership need not represent an interest in excess of 50% in its capital or profits, but may result from provisions in the governing joint venture agreement or related documents giving the Partnership certain basic rights. For example, control may take the form of the right to make (or veto) certain management decisions concerning the lease or sale of Properties, or placing certain limitations on the rights of other parties to the venture, or providing for certain predetermined benefits for the Partnership in the event that the other party or parties to the venture should make certain decisions respecting the lease or sale of Properties owned by the venture. In addition, the Partnership, in making any such joint venture investments, will not be permitted to pay directly or indirectly more than once for the same service and will not be permitted to act indirectly through any such arrangement if it would be prohibited from doing so directly by reason of restrictions in the Partnership Agreement.

Selection of Properties

The General Partners will have the responsibility to identify Properties and will be responsible for ultimate investment decisions. Each potential Partnership investment will be submitted for review to the Partnership's Investment Committee. No Property will be acquired by the Partnership without the unanimous agreement of the Investment Committee members. The Limited Partners will not be entitled to act on any proposed Partnership investment. In evaluating real property investments, the General Partners will consider such factors as: (1) potential for capital appreciation, (2) current and projected cash flow and the ability to increase cash flow through capable management and intensive asset utilization; (3) location, condition and design of the property; (4) prospects for liquidity through sale; (5) economic growth of the community; (6) geographic location and type of property in light of the Partnership's diversification objectives; (7) credit worthiness of existing or proposed tenants; (8) availability of qualified local property managers, and (9) terms of tenants' leases, including, specifically, potential for rent increases including those arising from sharing by the Partnership in the tenants' gross receipts, and the ability to pass through operating expenses to the tenants. The General Partners will obtain an appraisal by a competent, independent appraiser prior to the acquisition of each Property.

The types of Properties in which the Partnership intends to invest are shopping centers, office and light industrial buildings, and other similar commercial real estate. The Partnership does not intend to invest in undeveloped land, single or multi-family residential homes, apartments, condominiums, resort and recreation properties, nursing homes, gaming facilities or mobile home parks. The Partnership does not intend to borrow any money or incur any indebtedness in connection with the purchase of Partnership Properties. The Partnership will not reinvest Net Proceeds from Sales.

Diversification

It is intended that investments will be made in different types of Properties in various geographic locations in order to achieve portfolio diversification, thereby minimizing the effects of changes in specific industries, local economic conditions or similar risks. However, the extent of geographic diversification will depend upon the number of separate Properties which can be purchased with the net proceeds available to the Partnership from the sale of Units. The Partnership expects to invest no more than the greater of $12,750,000, or 42.5% of the gross proceeds of the Maximum Offering (38.6% in the event the Overallotment Option is exercised in full) in any single Property. In the event that the Minimum Offering is solid, it is likely that only one Property would be purchased.

Management of Properties

In general, the Partnership's Properties will be managed by MGT, or by unaffiliated, local professional management firms subcontracted by MGT where management by MGT is not feasible. In certain instances, sellers of Properties will manage for specified periods of time. The terms of such property management services between the Partnership and MGT will be embodied in a written management agreement to be executed at the initial Closing Date. The Management Agreement will provide for MGT to receive management fees which are competitive with those which could be obtained in arm's-length negotiations, with independent parties providing comparable services in the localities in which the Properties are located, which shall not exceed 6% of the gross revenues from each Property. However, the management fee payable to MGT will not exceed 5% of the gross revenues from a Property unless MGT performs commercial leasing services with respect to such Property and no other fees are paid by the Partnership for management or leasing services with respect to such Property. To the extent that MGT subcontracts such management services to third parties, the management fees paid pursuant to such subcontracts shall be borne by MGT. Consequently, MGT may make a profit or incur a loss in connection with the Management Agreement. The Management Agreement will have an initial term of five years and will be automatically renewed for additional one-year periods unless either party gives 60 days written notice of its intention not to renew. The Management Agreement may be terminated by either party without penalty upon 60 days written notice and will automatically terminate upon dissolution of the Partnership.

It will be the responsibility of MGT to select local property managers and resident managers where appropriate and to monitor their performance. MGT will be responsible for on-site operations and maintenance, generation and collection of rental income and payment of operating expenses. The difference between rental income and expenses related to operations, including items such as local taxes and assessments, state and local income taxes, utilities, insurance premiums, maintenance, repairs and improvements (and reserves therefor), bookkeeping and payroll expenses, leasing fees, legal and accounting fees, local and resident property management fees (other than those to be borne by MGT) and other expenses incurred, will constitute the Properties' operating cash flow. The Partnership's administrative expenses must be paid out of the Partnership's share of cash flow from the various Properties which it will own.

Information about Properties

At such time during negotiations for any specific Property when, in the opinion of the General Partners, a reasonable probability exists that the Property under negotiation will be acquired, they will describe the proposed investment, the agreed-upon terms and give a description of the Property. Upon termination of the Offering Period, Limited Partners will receive reports from the Partnership containing substantially equivalent information about acquisitions and proposed acquisitions. The General Partners will retain with the Partnership records for at least 5 years the appraisal obtained in connection with the acquisition of each Property, which appraisals will be available for inspection by the Limited Partners. However, Limited Partners will not have any right to vote on or otherwise approve or disapprove any particular investment to be made by the Partnership.

Investors should not rely upon initial disclosure of any proposed acquisition as an assurance that the Partnership will ultimately consummate such proposed acquisition, or that any information provided concerning a proposed acquisition, including its agreed upon terms, will not change between the date of such information and actual purchase.

Preliminary Investments

It is not possible to determine the date when the Partnership's capital will be fully invested Pending acquisition of interests in Properties, including Equity Convertible Loans, the net proceeds of the Offering may be invested in Permitted Temporary Investments. The Partnership's reserves may be invested in similar Permitted Temporary Investments and in publicly traded bonds or notes rated A or higher by Moody's Investors Services, Inc., Standard & Poor's Corporation or Fitch Investor Service, Inc. The rate of return on such investments may be less than or greater than would be obtainable from equity investments in real property.

If all of the net proceeds of the Offering are not invested by the Partnership in Properties or committed to such investment including Equity Convertible Loans, prior to the expiration of 24 months from the date of the Prospectus, the net proceeds not so invested, committed or set aside in a working capital reserve will be promptly returned to the Limited Partners on a pro rata basis. For such purpose, funds will be deemed to be committed to investment to the extent written agreements in principle, commitment letters, letters of intent or understanding, option agreements or any similar contracts or understandings shall exist, whether or not any such investment is ultimately consummated. Funds will also be deemed to be committed to the extent any funds may have been reserved to make contingent payments in connection with any Property already acquired, whether or not any such payments are ultimately made.

All funds will be available for the general use of the Partnership during such 24-month period and may be expended in managing the Partnership and operating Partnership Properties, if any. Funds will not be segregated or held separate from other funds of the Partnership pending investment in Properties. It is expected that distributions of Net Cash from Operations or income from such Permitted Temporary Investments will commence during the first quarter following formation of the Partnership.

Other Policies

The Partnership intends to use the straight-line method of depreciating its Properties.

Until substantially all of the available funds of the Partnership have been invested or committed for investment, any Properties coming to the attention of either of the General Partners or their Affiliates which meet the investment objectives and policies of the Partnership will first be presented or offered to the Partnership and only presented or offered to others by the General Partners or their Affiliates, or purchased or otherwise acquired or sold by either of the General Partners or their Affiliates, after the Investment Committee has determined that such Property would not be a suitable investment for the Partnership.

The Partnership Agreement does not permit that Partnership, among other things, to:

(i) issue any Units after the termination of the Offering Period or issue Units in exchange for property.

(ii) make loans or investments in real estate mortgages, other than Equity Convertible Loans (except in connection with the sale or other disposition of a Property);

(iii) make loans to the General Partners or their Affiliates.

(iv) invest in or underwrite the securities of other issuers, including any publicly-offered or traded limited partnership interests, except for Permitted Temporary Investments pending utilization of Partnership funds as described above (vi) operate in such a manner as to be classified as an "investment company" for purposes of the Investment Company Act of 1940; or

(vii) permit or cause the funds of the Partnership to be commingled with the funds of any other person;

(viii) purchase or lease any Property from (except in connection with facilitating the acquisition of a Property by the Partnership), or sell or lease any Property to, the General Partners or their Affiliates.

Borrowing Policies

It will be the policy of the Partnership not to obtain any portion of the purchase price of Properties by borrowing from banks, other institutional lenders or private lenders, or by purchasing Properties subject to existing loans. The Partnership's acquisition of interests in Properties will be financed entirely out of the net cash proceeds of the Offering. The Partnership Agreement prohibits borrowing secured by Partnership real property. However, the Partnership may make Equity Convertible Loans which will be first mortgage loans, secured by Properties, convertible into equity in such Properties at the option of the Partnership. Prior to receipt of the proceeds from the sale of the Minimum Offering ($2,500,000), the Partnership will not be formed or consummate the purcahse of interests in any Properties.

The Partnership Agreement permits the General Partners or Affiliates to purchase Properties in their own name, and temporarily hold title thereto, for the purpose of facilitating the acquisition of such Properties. Accordingly, it would be possible for the General Partners or Affiliates to acquire or make commitments for a Property when the purchase price of that Property exceeds all funds then available to the Partnership, with a view to transferring the Property to the Partnership at a later time when the Partnership's funds would be sufficient to make such a purchase. Any such purchase would be discretionary with the General Partners, and no liability of any kind could be imposed upon the Partnership in connection therewith; and neither the General Partners nor any of their Affiliates would be permitted to make any profit on resale of such Property to the Partnership.

Reserves

Approximately 1.5% of the gross proceeds of this Offering will initially be reserved as working capital to meet costs and expenses of the Partnership's operations. Although the General Partners believe such reserves to be reasonable due to the unleveraged nature of all proposed Property acquisitions, if such reserves and any other available income of the Partnership are insufficient to cover the Partnership's operating expenses and liabilities, it may be necessary to accumulate additional funds from cash flow or by liquidating investments in one or more

Properties. Since the Partnership's working capital reserves may increase or decrease from time to time in order to meet anticipated costs and expenses and potential losses, the amount of Net Cash from Operations actually paid to Limited Partners may be affected.

Sale Policies

From time to time the Partnership expects to sell its Properties, taking into consideration such factors as the amount of appreciation in value, if any, to be realized, the possible risks of continued ownership and the anticipated advantages to be gained for the Partners. It is expected that most sales of Properties will be made after a period of ownership of at least five years but sales may be made at an earlier date.

Proceeds from the sale of Properties will not be reinvested but will be distributed to the Partners, so that the Partnership will, in effect, be self-liquidating.

As part payment for Properties sold, the Partnership may receive purchase money obligations secured by mortgages. In such cases, the amount of such obligations will not be included in Net Proceeds from Sales (distributable to the Partners) until and to the extent the obligations are realized in cash, sold or otherwise disposed of. In the case of a sale involving deferred payments (e.g., payments spread over two or more years), the Partnership intends to elect, for tax purposes, to report any gain on such sales under the installment method of accounting, if permissible under the Federal income tax law then in effect. However, if such election is not made or is not then available under the Internal Revenue Code, a Limited Partner may receive cash distributions in the year of sale which are materially less than his distributive share of Taxable Income and Gain from Sales for such year, in such event, a Limited Partner's tax liability with respect to his distributive share of Taxable Income and Gain from Sales may exceed his cash distributions from the Partnership for such year.

TERMS OF THE OFFERING

A minimum of 5,000 and a maximum of 60,000 Units (66,000 Units in the event the Overallotment Option is exercised in full) are offered at a price of $500 per Unit, subject to certain quantity discounts. The minimum subscription is $5,000 or ten Units ($1,500 or three Units for an individual Retirement Account ("IRA") or Keogh (H.R. 10) Plan, except in certain states which have established higher minimum subscriptions). Payments will be held in trust for the benefit of subscribers and will be deposited in a special escrow account at The Bank (the "Escrow Agent"), and will be applied only for the purposes set forth herein. Pending release to the Partnership or return to the respective subscribers, such funds may be invested in United States Government securities, certificates of deposit of banks located in the United States having a net worth of at least $50 million, bank repurchase agreements covering securities of the United States Government or governmental agencies, bankers' acceptances, unaffiliated money market funds or other similar highly liquid investments ("Permitted Temporary Investments").

The Partnership will hold all proceeds of the Offering and any income thereon in trust for the benefit of its Partners until invested in Properties in accordance with the terms hereof. The Partnership may experience delays in finding suitable Properties. Pending investment of the proceeds of the Offering in Properties, the proceeds may be invested in Permitted Temporary investments. The Partnership's reserves may be invested in similar Permitted Temporary Investments, also including publicly traded bonds or notes rated A or higher by Moody's Investors Services, Inc., Standard & Poor's Corporation or Fitch Investor Service, Inc. The rate of return on such investments may be less or greater than would be obtainable from equity investments in real property.

WHO SHOULD INVEST

The purchase of Units involves certain risks and, since the Partnership's investments will only be made on an unleveraged basis (without mortgage financing) which will not provide tax benefits commonly associated with tax shelter investments, is suitable only for persons or entities of adequate means having no need for liquidity in their investment. Such persons or entities may include, subject to the provisions of their governing instruments, any limitations relating to their tax exemption and, with respect to employee pension or profit sharing plans, the limitations discussed below, employee pension or profit sharing plans, IRA's, endowment funds and foundations, and other entities exempt from Federal income taxation such as charitable, religious, scientific or educational organizations.

Employee Benefit Plans

Since the Partnership will purchase Properties on an unleveraged basis and will operate in a manner which is intended not to result in allocation of unrelated business income in material amounts to investors which are tax exempt organizations, the General Partners believe, subject to the following discussion, that the purchase of Units would be a suitable investment for employee benefit plans if otherwise permissible under their governing instruments.

A trust (hereinafter "Employee Trust") which is a part of an employee benefit plan (such as a pension or profit sharing plan) subject to the provisions of the Employee Retirement Income Security Act of 1974 ("ERISA") should be aware of proposed regulations under Section 401(b) of ERISA which have the effect of restricting certain investments. Section 403 of ERISA requires, with certain exceptions, that all assets of an employee benefit plan ("Plan Assets") be held in trust. Plan Assets are defined under Section 401(b) of ERISA. Department of Labor Proposed Regulation § 2550.401b-1(1)(1) and (e) includes within the definition of Plan Assets, not only securities (such as stock or limited partnership interests) owned by an Employee Trust, but also the underlying assets of the issuer of the securities. An exception, which would limit Plan Assets to the security itself (and would not include the underlying assets of the issuer) is provided by Proposed Regulation § 2550.401b-1(e)(2) if the security is freely transferable, widely held, and is either (1) registered under Section 12(b) or Section 12(g) of the Securities Exchange Act of 1934 or (2) sold to the Employee Trust as part of an offering of such securities to the public pursuant to an effective registration statement under the Securities Act of 1933 and the security is registered under Section 12(b) of Section 12(g) of the Securities Exchange Act of 1934 within 120 days after the end of the fiscal year of the issuer during which the offering of such securities to the public occurred. The preamble to the proposed regulation providing for the foregoing exception states (in footnote 9) that the Department of Labor would not view an interest as freely transferable if there were restrictions on transfer imposed by the issuer. In addition, the preamble (footnote 10) states that whether interests in a company are "widely held" might vary from case to case, but that the Labor Department would not normally consider interests to be widely held if they were held by fewer than 100 persons.

The Units are intended to comply with the foregoing exception in that there will be no restrictions imposed by the Partnership on the transfer of Units; the Offering will not be initially closed unless Units will be held by at least 150 persons; and the registration requirements of the foregoing exception will be satisfied.

Employee Trusts contemplating the purchase of Units are cautioned that the foregoing exception is part of proposed regulations which may not ultimately be adopted or, if adopted, might be changed materially. Moreover, there can be no assurance that if the exception in the proposed regulations is adopted in its present form that an investment in Units will be considered by the Labor Department to qualify under the terms of the exception. Accordingly, an Employee Trust is urged to consult its legal advisor before subscribing for the purchase of Units.

ESTIMATED USE OF PROCEEDS

The following table illustrates the intended use by the Partnership of the gross proceeds of the Offering (excluding only the General Partners' $2,000 aggregate capital contribution). Many of the figures set forth represent the best estimates of the General Partners and, consequently, do not purport to be a prediction of the actual use of proceeds.

QUALIFIED PROPERTIES

	Minimum Offering		Maximum Offering	
	Amount	Percent	Amount	Percent
Gross Offering Proceeds	$2,500,000	100.0%	$30,000,000	100.0%
Less Public Offering Expenses consisting of:				
Organizational and Offering Expenses ..	175,000	7.0%	500,000	1.7%
Selling Commissions or Quantity Discounts	200,000	8.0%	2,400,000	8.0%
Amount Available for Investment	$2,125,000	85.0%	$27,100,000	90.3%
Cash Payments for Property	2,087,500	83.5%	26,650,000	88.8%
Acquisition Fees Payable to the General Partners, Affiliates and Non-Affiliates				
Initial Working Capital Reserve	37,500	1.5%	450,000	1.5%
Amount Available for Investment	$2,125,000	85.0%	$27,100,000	90.3%
Public Offering Expenses	375,000	15.0%	2,900,000	9.7%
Gross Offering Proceeds	$2,500,000	100.0%	$30,000,000	100.0%

COMPENSATION AND FEES

The following table shows all of the types of compensation, fees or other distributions that may or will be paid by the Partnership or others to the General Partners or their Affiliates other than the Selling Agent in connection with the operations of the Partnership. Although the General Partners are not affiliated with each other, the following arrangements for compensation and fees to the General Partners and Affiliates were not determined by arm's length negotiations with the Partnership.

QUALIFIED PROPERTIES

Type of Compensation and Persons to Whom Paid	Method of Computation	Estimated Maximum Dollar Amount
	Acquisition Stage	
Acquisition Fees, including real estate commissions.	Up to 4% of the Gross Proceeds of the Offering, to be paid as direct or indirect interests in Properties are acquired.	$1,200,000 ($1,320,000 in the event the Overallotment Option is exercised in full).
	Operational Stage	
General Partners' distributive share of Net Cash from Operations.	2% of all Net Cash from Operations until each Limited Partner (which will include the General Partners with respect to their purchase of Units) has received an 8% return on Adjusted Capital Value for the year of distribution. Thereafter, all Net Cash from Operations until the General Partners have received cumulative distributions of Net Cash from Operations for the year equal to 10% of the aggregate Net Cash from Operations distributed to the Partners to such point. Thereafter, 10% of all Net Cash from Operations.	
Fees for property management services to be provided for Partnership Properties.	The Properties in which direct or indirect interests will be acquired by the Partnership will be managed for annual fees not to exceed those prevailing for comparable services in the localities where Properties are located, which shall in any event not exceed 6% of gross	

Type of Compensation and Persons to Whom Paid	Method of Computation	Estimated Maximum Dollar Amount
	Operational Stage	
	revenues from each Property. To the extent that MGT contracts such management services to third parties, the costs of which shall be borne by MGT, it may make a profit or incur a loss under such management agreement.	
General Partners' distributive share of Net Proceeds from Sales.	1% of Net Proceeds from Sales until each Limited Partner (which will include the General Partners with respect to their purchase of Units) has received an amount equal to his Adjusted Capital Value and cumulative distributions (including Net Cash from Operations) equal to a 9% annual return with respect to his Adjusted Capital Value and 15% of the balance of any Net Proceeds from Sales.	
General Partners' Real Estate Brokerage Commissions.	In the case of the sale of a Property, a commission not to exceed an amount equal to 2% of the gross sales price, provided that the General Partners' commission shall be subordinated to the return to each Limited Partner of an amount equal to his Adjusted Capital Value and cumulative distributions (including Net Cash from Operations) equal to a 9% annual return with respect to his Adjusted Capital Value, and shall be reduced to the extent any other real estate brokerage commission is paid, directly or indirectly, to any other real estate broker retained by the Partnership or the General Partners in connection with such sale.	

The primary investment objectives of the Partnership are: (1) to obtain capital appreciation; (2) to provide cash distributions from rental income; and (3) to preserve and protect the capital of the Partners.

RISK FACTORS

Real Estate Investments

One of the major risks of investing in real estate is the possibility that the properties will not generate income sufficient to meet operating expenses and will generate income and capital appreciation at a rate less than that anticipated or available through investment in comparable real estate partnerships or other investments. Although the General Partners will not finance the purchase of Properties through borrowing, the income from Properties may still be affected by many factors unrelated to borrowing or leveraging, including reduction in rental income due to an inability to maintain occupancy levels, adverse changes in general economic conditions, adverse local conditions, such as competitive over-building or a decrease in employment, adverse changes in real estate zoning laws, particularly "downzoning" or industrial zoning, which may reduce the desirability of real estate in the area, or acts of God, such as earthquakes and floods.

The risk inherent in the present economic environment, as reflected by, among other things, high interest rates, with prime commercial lending rates recently having reached 20%, and high rates of inflation, may impact on the Partnership despite the absence of borrowing by the Partnership Shortages of mortgage funds may render the sale of Properties to others difficult or require the Partnership to incur credit risks if it becomes necessary to extend mortgage financing to buyers. Liquidation or dissolution of the Partnership may be delayed until any mortgage loans which the Partnership extends to buyers are repaid or sold.

Certain expenses related to real estate, such as property taxes, utility costs, maintenance and other operating costs and insurance, tend to move upward but not downward, if the income from a Property is not sufficient to meet operating expenses, the Partnership may have to advance funds to protect its investment or dispose of the Property on disadvantageous terms in order to raise needed funds.

The financial failure of a retail, office or industrial tenant resulting in the termination of the tenant's lease may cause a reduction in cash flow from the Property or a decrease in the value of the Property. In the event of such a termination, there can be no assurance that the Partnership will be able to find a new tenant for the Property at the rental previously received or to sell the Property without incurring a loss. Also, to the extent that rental income is based on a percentage of the gross receipts of retail tenants, the Partnership's cash flow will be dependent upon the success achieved by such tenants.

TAX FACTORS

Unrelated Business Income

Tax-exempt organizations, including Employee Trusts, although not generally subject to Federal income tax, are subject to tax on certain income derived from a trade or business regularly carried on by the organization which is unrelated to its exempt activities. However, such unrelated business taxable income does not in general include income from real property, gain from the sale of property other than inventory, interest, dividends and certain other types of passive investment income, unless such income is derived from "debt-financed property" as defined in Section 514 of the Code. Since the Partnership will purchase Properties on an unleveraged basis, and since the Partnership will provide no services to the tenants other than those incidental to the ownership of rental property, rental income from the Properties generally should not constitute unrelated business taxable income. The Partnership's temporary investment of funds in interest bearing instruments and deposits and investment of funds in interest bearing Equity Convertible Loans also should not give rise to unrelated business taxable income.

Notwithstanding that the General Partners intend to operate the Partnership in a manner such that the Partnership will not generate income of a type which would be taxable to tax-exempt organizations, it is possible that some unrelated business taxable income may arise for limited periods or in relatively small amounts because of business necessity or convenience. For example, certain contractual arrangements which may secure the obligations of sellers of Properties could result in a portion of the income from such Properties being treated as derived from debt-financed property for limited periods of time. In addition, such income may arise if the Partnership were required to operate a parking garage associated with a Property for the benefit of tenants for a period of time until a satisfactory lessee of the parking garage were secured. Accordingly, there can be no assurance that all income of the Partnership will not be unrelated business taxable income, but any such amounts, should they arise, would likely constitute a relatively small part of the total income of the Partnership for any taxable year. A tax-exempt organization is entitled to a $1,000 annual exclusion with respect to unrelated business taxable income.

INCOME REALTY TRUST

Income Realty Trust (the "Trust") is a California business trust which intends to conduct its operations so as to enable it to qualify as a real estate investment trust under the applicable provisions of the Internal Revenue Code, and which intends to elect to be so treated as soon as practicable. The Trustees presently anticipate that the duration of the Trust will be approximately ten years. However, the Trustees have the power to extend the duration of the Trust up to an additional twenty-five years.

Minimum proceeds will be $1,200,000, and maximum proceeds will be $27,500,000, before deduction of expenses estimated to be $60,000 at the minimum level of funding and $412,500 at the maximum level of funding.

The principal investment objective of the Trust is to obtain equity ownership of investments which will produce Cash Distributions. A portion of the Cash Distributions may be sheltered from current taxation as a return of invested capital, with a corresponding reduction in tax basis. There can be no assurance, however, that the operations of the Trust will produce any cash flow. In addition, investors should note that the Trust will not provide any deductions in excess of cash distributions which investors can use to offset their income from other sources. The Trust intends to initially invest in equity ownership in completed income-producing commercial, industrial and multi-unit residential real property generating a cash flow in an amount which the Trustees determine from time to time to be a reasonable business objective.

The Trust intends to limit its leverage to long-term borrowings incurred in connection with the acquisition or refinancing of its real estate investments, and any convertible participating notes which may be placed, as described immediately below. Total indebtedness of the Trust will not exceed 500% of Net Assets. Indebtedness secured by any individual property will not exceed 80% of the fair market value of such investment. The equity interest of the Trust will be utilized to secure such borrowings. The Trust may utilize short-term lines of credit as a source of working capital. During the early stages of its operations, the Trust may elect not to immediately leverage some of the properties it acquires.

The Trust will not engage in a short sale of any security.

The Trustees intend to place convertible participating notes with institutional investors at approximately the same time as the Shares are being offered to the public.

After minimum proceeds of $1,200,000 are raised, the Trust will make monthly distributions to Shareholders during the remainder of the first six months of the offering. The aggregate amount of the distribution for each month, on an annualized basis, will be (i) 3½ points less than the prime rate of the Bank of America in effect at the beginning of the month times $10 times the average number of Shares outstanding during the month, or (ii) such greater amount as the Trustees may decide to pay with respect to one or more months. The monthly distribution will be paid on the Shares outstanding at the end of the month. These distributions will be made whether or not the Trust has earnings computed in accordance with generally accepted accounting principles. If the Trust has no such earnings, any such distributions will probably represent a return of capital.

The Trust's general policy is that after the first six months of the offering it will distribute at least quarterly to its Shareholders all Distributable Cash from Operations and Cash from Sale or Refinancing, but in no event less than 95% of its Real Estate Investment Trust Taxable Income for each year. However, during the early phases of the Trust's operations, it is possible that the Trust will purchase one or more real estate investments with little or no leverage with the intention of refinancing such investments during the thirty (30) months following the purchase. The Trust does not intend to distribute to the Shareholders any sale or refinancing proceeds received during the thirty (30) months following acquisition. Most of such sale or refinancing proceeds would probably be reinvested in additional properties.

For its services the Advisor will be paid a Subordinated Management Fee of 8% of Cash Receipts from Operations. The Subordinated Management Fee will be conditioned upon the payment of certain Noncumulative Cash Distributions to the Shareholders. An Affiliate of the Advisor may also receive Acquisition Fees of up to 4% of the Total Price or real property acquisitions, subject to certain limitations, and the Advisor will be entitled to a Disposition Fee of 15% of all Net Cash from Sale or Refinancing received by the Trust from each property, subject to certain Cash Distributions having been paid to Shareholders. An Affiliate of the Advisor may also receive a Subordinated Real Estate Commission of up to 5% of all Net Cash from Sale or Refinancing, upon the disposition of properties.

There can be no assurance that an active trading market for the Shares will develop upon completion of this offering. The Trust is intended to have a life of approximately 10 years. Proceeds of all sales and refinancing of properties (after the first 30 months following acquisition) will be distributed to Shareholders, and the Trust will be liquidated as soon as practicable after it no longer holds any real property or notes or other proceeds from the disposition of real property.

SUMMARY OF DECLARATION OF TRUST

The following is a brief summary of some of the more important provisions of the Declaration of Trust.

Trustees

The Declaration of Trust provides that there will be not less than three nor more than seven Trustees. The range in the authorized number of Trustees may be changed by the Trustees and the exact number within the range is to be specified by the Trustees, provided that the lower end of the authorized range cannot be less than three. At the present time the exact number specified by the Trustees is six. A majority of the Trustees cannot be affiliated with the Advisor or any Affiliate of the Advisor. Each Trustee holds office for a one-year term until the election and qualification of his successor at the next Annual Meeting of Shareholders, or until his earlier resignation or removal from office or death. Any Trustee may resign at any time and may be removed at any time, with or without cause by the vote of the holders of a majority of the Shares of the Trust, and may be removed for cause by all the remaining Trustees. Vacancies existing among the Trustees by reason of death, resignation, removal or increase in the authorized number of

Trustees may be filled by appointment by a majority of the Trustees in office. No bond shall be required to secure performance of a Trustee unless otherwise required by law.

Trustees are elected annually. Shareholders are not allowed to cumulate their votes in the election of the Trustees. Therefore, the holders of a majority of the Shares, if represented at a meeting at which Trustees are to be elected, have the power to elect all of the Trustees.

Trustees may own, buy and sell Shares in the Trust. Trustees are empowered to fix the compensation of all officers whom they elect and may receive reasonable compensation for their services as Trustees and as officers of the Trust and may pay a Trustee or Trustees such compensation for special services as they deem reasonable. Certain other transactions between the Trust and a Trustee or a person or entity affiliated with a Trustee are expressly prohibited.

The Trustees may appoint an Executive Committee from among their number consisting of three members. The Executive Committee will have such powers, duties and obligations as the Trustees may deem necessary and appropriate, including the power to conduct the business and affairs of the Trust during periods between meetings of the Trustees. The Executive Committee will be required to report its activities periodically to the Trustees.

Responsibilities of Trustees, Officers and Agents

No Trustee or officer of the Trust is liable to the Trust or to any Trustee or Shareholder or to any third person except for his own bad faith, willful misfeasance, gross negligence, or reckless disregard of his duties, except that a Trustee or officer may under the laws of certain jurisdictions be liable in tort to third persons for actions in which he has personally and actively participated. All third persons are required by the Declaration of Trust to look solely to the Trust property for satisfaction of claims arising in connection with affairs of the Trust. With the exceptions stated, a Trustee or officer is entitled to be indemnified against all claims and liabilities in connection with the affairs of the Trust and to be reimbursed for all judgments and similar amounts paid, whether in settlement or otherwise, and all legal and other expenses reasonably incurred by such Trustee or officer in connection with defense of such claim or liability or proceeding. The Trust may also advance expenses to a Trustee or officer during the course of litigation, upon receipt of an undertaking from such person to repay the amount advanced if it is ultimately determined he is not entitled to indemnification.

Possible Shareholder Liability

The Declaration of Trust provides that Shareholders shall not be subject to any personal liability for the acts or obligations of the Trust and that as far as practicable every written undertaking of the Trust shall contain a provision that such undertaking is not binding upon any Shareholder personality. Counsel to the Trust are of the opinion that under the laws of California no personal liability will attach to the Shareholders under any undertaking containing such provision. It is not clear, however, whether the question of Shareholder liability would be determined by the laws of California, which is the State where the Trust is organized and where its principal office is located, or by the law of some other State in which the Trust owns property or has other contacts. It is possible, therefore, that Shareholders may be held personally liable with respect to undertakings containing such provision in those jurisdictions which decline to recognize a business trust as a valid organization of any kind. With respect to tort claims, contract claims where the provision referred to is omitted from the undertaking, claims for taxes and certain statutory liabilities in other jurisdictions, a Shareholder may be held personally liable to the extent that claims are not satisfied by the Trust. However, upon payment of any such liability, the Shareholder will, in the absence of willful misconduct, gross negligence or bad faith on his part, be entitled to reimbursement from the assets of the Trust.

The Trustees do not believe that as a practical matter the Shareholders will be exposed to any significant risk. The Trust will have substantial assets to meet its obligations and all properties owned by the Trust will, to the extent practical, be covered by insurance which the Trustees consider adequate to cover foreseeable tort claims. The Trustees intend to conduct the operations of the Trust with the advice of counsel in such a way as to avoid, as far as possible, ultimate liability of the Shareholders for liabilities of the Trust.

Sales of Shares

The Trustees may, in their discretion, issue Shares for cash, property or other consideration on such terms as they may deem advisable. The Trustees may issue additional equity securities, senior securities, and debt securities convertible into Shares in addition to The Trust–Convertible Participating Notes. The Trustees are prohibited from issuing warrants, options or similar evidences of a right to buy the Trust's securities, unless issued to all of its security holders ratably or as part of a financing arrangement, or in connection with the acquisition of properties for the Trust. The Trustees are not authorized to establish any type of stock option plan for Trustees or officers or other employees of the Trust.

Voting Rights

Except as expressly set forth herein with respect to election of Trustees, removal of Trustees and amendments and termination of the Trust, the Shareholders do not have voting rights in the conduct of the affairs of the Trust.

Redemption of Shares and Restrictions on Transfer

Under the Internal Revenue Code, two of the requirements for qualification as a real estate investment trust are that (i) during the last half of each taxable year not more than 50% of the outstanding Shares may be owned by five or fewer individuals and (ii) there must be at least 100 Shareholders on 335 days of each year. In order to meet these requirements, the Trustees are given power to redeem a sufficient number of Shares or to restrict the transfer thereof to bring or maintain the ownership of the Shares of the Trust in conformity with the requirements of the Code. The redemption price to be paid will be fair market value as reflected in the average price quotations for the Shares for the last thirty (30) days, or, if no quotations are available, as determined in good faith by the Trustees. Depending on various facts and circumstances, part or all of such redemption price might not qualify for capital gains treatment.

Reports to Shareholders and Rights of Examination

The Trustees will furnish, within 120 days following the close of each fiscal year, an annual report of the affairs of the Trust to the Shareholders, including audited financial statements, accompanied by the report of an independent public accountant. In addition, the Shareholders will be furnished quarterly reports after the close of each of the first three quarters containing financial statements, which may be unaudited. At the time of each distribution to Shareholders, the Trustees will furnish the Shareholders a statement in writing advising as to the source of the funds so distributed or, if the source thereof has not then been determined, the written statement disclosing the source shall be sent to each Shareholder who received the distribution not later than 90 days after the close of the fiscal year in which the distribution was made.

A Shareholder may inspect the books and records of the Trust during normal business hours at the principal office of the Trust upon written demand, for a purpose reasonably related to his interest as a Shareholder.

Meetings of Shareholders

An annual meeting of Shareholders will be held at which Trustees will be elected and other proper business may be discussed. The annual meeting will be held after at least fifteen days written notice to the Shareholders and after delivery to them of the Annual Report and within six months after the end of the fiscal year. However, the first Annual Meeting of Shareholders will be held within six months after the end of the first full fiscal year of operations. The Trust's fiscal year ends on December 31 of each year.

Certain Prohibited Activities

The Declaration of Trust imposes certain prohibitions upon the Trust's activities.

Investments

The Trust is prohibited from knowingly purchasing property from, selling any property to, obtaining loans from, or making loans to, any Trustee, officer, or employee of the Trust or any Affiliate of any such Trustee, officer or employee, or to or from the Advisor or any director, officer or employee of the Advisor.

The Trustees are authorized to increase the Trust's funds available for investment by borrowings made from banks or through issuance of debentures, bonds or other types of debt obligations. Use of such borrowed funds to increase the Trust's investment portfolio may increase the Trust's exposure to risk of loss. The Declaration of Trust provides that the total indebtedness of the Trust shall not exceed 500% of its Net Assets.

During periods in which it wishes to qualify as a real estate investment trust under the Internal Revenue Code, the Trust is required, for its real estate acquired through purchase, exchange, foreclosure or otherwise, to enter into a property management agreement with an independent contractor for the management of such property because under the provisions of the Internal Revenue Code and regulations thereunder, qualified real estate investment trusts are not permitted to furnish services to the tenants of properties held by the Trust or manage or operate such properties, otherwise than through an independent contractor.

Limitation on Annual Expenses

The aggregate annual expenses of the Trust, as defined, shall not exceed the least of the following:

A

Two percent (2%) of the first $10,000,000 of the Trust's Base Assets plus one percent (1%) of Base Assets in excess of $10,000,000; or

B

One and one-half percent (1½%) of the average net assets of the Trust (net assets being defined for this purpose as total invested assets at cost before deducting depreciation reserves, less total liabilities, calculated at least quarterly on a basis consistently applied); or

C

Twenty-five percent (25%) of the net income of the Trust, excluding provision for depreciation and realized capital gains and losses and extraordinary items, and before deducting advisory and servicing fees and expenses, calculated at least quarterly on a basis consistently applied; or

D

One and one-half percent (1½%) of the total invested assets of the Trust.

Acquisition and Disposition Fees and Subordinated Real Estate Commission are not subject to this limitation.

Aggregate annual expenses of the Trust for this purpose may be defined generally as all expenses, including Subordinated Management Fee, but excluding selling expenses incurred in connection with the sale of Shares, depreciation, insurance, interest, taxes, expenses connected directly with acquisition, disposition, operation or ownership of Trust assets, payments to property managers, real estate commissions on disposal of Trust assets, appraisal costs, costs of shareholder communications and relations, and costs of filing reports with governmental agencies.

The Management Agreement specifically provides that to the extent expenses, including management fees, exceed the permissible limits indicated above, the Advisor will refund such excess to the Trust or, at the option of the Trust, the Advisor's management fee will be reduced in the amount of said excess.

Amendment and Termination of the Trust

The Declaration of Trust may be amended or terminated by the vote or written consent of the holders of a majority of the outstanding Shares entitled to vote thereon, except that no amendment may be made to the Declaration of Trust which would change any rights with respect to any outstanding Shares by reducing the amount payable thereon upon liquidation, diminishing or eliminating any voting rights pertaining thereto or increasing the liability of or requiring any additional contribution or assessment from the holders thereof, without the vote or consent of the holders of two-thirds of the outstanding Shares.

The Trustees may amend the Declaration of Trust without the consent of the Shareholders to the extent that Trustees deem necessary to bring it into conformity with the applicable requirements of the Internal Revenue Code, or to other applicable Federal or state laws or regulations.

Duration

The Trust will continue, unless sooner terminated as described above, until December 31, Year Ten, provided that the Trustees can extend the term for one or more additional periods up to but not beyond December 31, Year Thirty-five. In no event will the term of the Trust extend beyond twenty years after the death of the last survivor of four persons, who are named in the Declaration of Trust.

PLAN OF DISTRIBUTION

General

The 2,500,000 Shares are offered directly by Securities Corporation, which is a wholly-owned subsidiary of Properties and a member of the National Association of Securities Dealers, Inc. ("NASD"), as Principal Distributor of such Shares for the Trust under a Principal Distributor's Agreement. The Principal Distributor is also offering the Shares through other members of the NASD which enter into a Selling Agreement with Securities Corporation. The Shares are being offered on a "best efforts" basis, which means that the Principal Distributor and other broker-dealers are not obligated to purchase any Shares but are only required to use their best efforts to sell Shares to investors. The Principal Distributor has also been granted the right to sell on behalf of the Trust, on the same basis as the 2,500,000 Shares, an additional 250,000 Shares in the event the Trust receives subscriptions for more than 2,500,000 Shares.

Except as indicated below under the subcaption "–Volume Discounts," the Trust will pay the Principal Distributor 8½% as a commission on all Shares sold out of the gross proceeds of the offering (after and only if the minimum of $1,200,000 of

Shares is sold) and the Principal Distributor will pay other broker-dealers a sales commission at the rate of 8¼% of the gross proceeds of the Shares sold by them.

With respect to sales which it makes directly, Securities Corporation will receive the sales commission in addition to the ¼% principal distributor fee.

The Advisor or an Affiliate may from time to time offer incentive programs to participating broker-dealers. In no event shall the additional incentives awarded pursuant to such programs exceed an aggregate amount of $25 per annum per participating salesman. In addition, total underwriting commissions in connection with this offering, including such additional salesman incentives, reimbursement of underwriters' expenses, and any other payments which constitute underwriting compensation, shall not exceed 10% of the gross offering proceeds.

The Principal Distributor's Agreement, which is terminable by either party on sixty days' notice without penalty, contains cross-indemnity clauses with respect to certain liabilities between the Trust and the Principal Distributor, including liabilities under the Securities Act of 1933, as amended. The indemnities of the Trust inure to the benefit of all broker-dealers participating in the offering, including the Principal Distributor. Broker-dealers participating in this offering may be deemed to be "underwriters" as that term is defined in the Securities Act of 1933.

The public offering price is Ten Dollars ($10) per Share, except as indicated below. Because the Trust is newly-formed and has no operating history, the offering price was arbitrarily established by the Trust and Securities Corporation in a non-arm's length transaction.

Volume Discounts

In connection with sales of $250,000 or more, the purchaser will pay a reduced sales commission. The schedule of sales commissions which will be applied to an investor's entire purchase is as follows:

Amount of Sale	Price Per Share	Total Commission Per Share	Proceeds to the Trust Per Share
Less than $250,000	$10.00	$0.85	$9.15
$250,000 to $499,990	$ 9.90	$0.75	$9.15
$500,000 to $999.990	$ 9.80	$0.65	$9.15
$1,000,000 to $1,499,990 ...	$ 9.65	$0.50	$9.15
$1,500,000 to $1,999,990 ...	$ 9.60	$0.45	$9.15
$2,000,000 or more	$ 9.55	$0.40	$9.15

The principal distributor fee of $0.025 per Share payable to the Principal Distributor is included in each case in the amount shown under "Total Commission Per Share" in the above table.

Subscriptions may be combined for the purpose of determining the total sales commissions payable in the case of subscriptions made by any "Purchaser" as that term is defined below. Any request to combine more than one subscription must be made in writing on a form to be supplied by the Principal Distributor, and must set forth the basis for such request. Any such request will be subject to verification by the Principal Distributor that all of such subscriptions were made by a single "Purchaser" as defined below.

For the purposes of the plan of distribution, "Purchaser" includes (i) an individual, or an individual, his or her spouse and their children under the age of 21, who purchase the Shares for his or her or their own account, (ii) a corporation, partnership, association, joint-stock company, trust, fund, or any organized group of persons, whether incorporated or not, (provided that the entities described in this clause (ii) must have been in existence for at least six months before purchasing the Shares and must have a purpose other than to purchase the Shares at a discount), (iii) an employees' trust, pension, profit-sharing, or other employee benefit plan qualified under Section 401 of the Internal Revenue Code, and (iv) all commingled trust funds maintained by a given bank (provided that such commingled trust funds must have been in existence for at least six months before purchasing the Shares and must have a purpose other than to purchase the Shares at a discount).

Escrow Arrangements

Commencing on the effective date of the Prospectus, until the minimum $1,200,000 of Shares is subscribed, all funds received by the Trust in payment of subscriptions of Shares will be placed in escrow with Bank, as Escrow Holder, and may be invested in government securities, bank and savings and loan certificates of deposit, banker's acceptances, savings accounts, high-grade commercial paper and other similar investments. When and if the funds in the escrow account are released to the Trust, interest earned on such account shall be paid to the Shareholders pro rata.

If the Trust does not obtain gross proceeds from sales of Shares of at least $1,200,000 within six months after the date of the Prospectus, this offering will terminate and all subscriptions held by the Escrow Holder will be promptly refunded to purchasers, together with interest actually paid on such account. In the event that the Trust does receive at least $1,200,000 on or before such date, the Trust will immediately commence to register purchasers of Shares as Shareholders.

If the minimum subscriptions are received the offering will terminate upon the sale of all Shares offered hereby, or on April 30, Year Two, whichever first occurs, unless the Trustees shall elect to terminate the offering before either of such events, and provided that the Trustees may also elect to extend the offering to a date no later than August 10, Year Two.

Subscription

An investor is required to purchase a minimum of 250 Shares ($2,500) on an initial order and on any reorder, except that the minimum is 100 Shares ($1,000) on an initial order and on any reorder by an Individual Retirement Account ("IRA") established under Section 408 of the Internal Revenue Code of 1954, as Amended, or by a Keogh ("H.R. 10") Plan established under Section 401(c) of said Code. All orders must be of whole Shares. Each investor will also be required to comply with respective state requirements, if any, as to minimum number of Shares purchased and/or financial qualifications of the purchaser.

Any purchase of Shares must be accompanied by tender of the full price per Share. Subscriptions will be accepted or rejected by the Trust promptly after the receipt of the purchase price. Any such payment will be promptly returned to the person making it if for any reason the offering is withdrawn or the subscription is rejected.

BENEFITS OF AN INCOME REALITY TRUST

While by no means risk-free, income-producing real estate, such as shopping centers, office buildings, and apartments, offers the investor the potential for a combination of benefits which include:

Tax-Deferred Cash Dividends

As an owner of income-producing real estate, cash distributions you receive are derived from rents paid by tenants, less the operating expenses and mortgage payments.

An important benefit that magnifies the value of such cash distributions is the owner's ability, under federal tax laws, to deduct depreciation (a non-cash item). To the extent that the depreciation deductions cover the cash distributions, the owner treats the distribution as a return of capital and lowers his tax basis in the property.

Such cash distributions are, therefore, protected from taxation until the property is sold, at which time a capital gains rate, rather than ordinary income rate, is generally applied.

Under current federal tax law, the benefit of paying at capital gains versus ordinary income tax rate is dramatic; a maximum of 28% for capital gains vs. 70% on ordinary income.

Cash distributions in excess of depreciation deductions will be taxed at ordinary income rates. There is no guarantee, of course, that the investor will realize any cash distributions from the Trust or that distributions will be sheltered.

Appreciation

Income property values are largely determined by the cash flow generated for the owners. For this reason, judicious selection, careful negotiation, effective property management, and the upward pressure of inflation on rent levels may result in substantial appreciation in value.

Equity Build-Up (Mortgage Reduction)

When a mortgage payment is made, a portion of the payment is applied to interest, and the balance is applied to reduce the mortgage. As time passes, the mortgage debt is progressively reduced, resulting in increased owner's equity assuming that the property has not declined in value.

Leverage (Mortgage)

Leverage is the use of borrowed money to acquire an asset and is a generally accepted practice in real estate acquisitions.

Leverage magnifies the potential appreciation and tax benefits available to the investor. For example, if two dollars of mortgage debt were utilized for every dollar of invested equity, a 5% annual increase in the value of the real estate portfolio would result in a 15% annual increase in the investor's equity position.

Of course, leverage also magnifies the potential losses should a property decrease in value. Given the current high interest rates, there is no assurance that satisfactory financing will be available, and there are other factors that might inhibit the availability of financing.

ADVANTAGES OF BUYING EXISTING PROPERTIES

By purchasing existing properties, an investor may be able to reduce his risk and more precisely identify the potential benefits. The reasons are:

- Construction quality and market acceptance are known.
- The prior years' operating results are known.
- There are no risks of construction cost overruns.

- A property can often be purchased utilizing an existing mortgage with a favorable interest rate.
- Existing buildings often have a competitive advantage over new buildings which normally have a higher cost of land, labor and materials and must, therefore, charge higher rents to make the new building economically feasible.

ADVANTAGES OF OWNING COMMERCIAL PROPERTIES

The structure of a typical lease for commercial properties (shopping centers and office buildings) offers benefits not available in other types of real estate investments. These include:

Predictable Minimum Base Rentals

The minimum base rental payment to be made by the tenant enables the owner to predict a substantial portion of his monthly income.

Expense Reimbursements

Although the owner pays operating expenses such as property taxes, utilities, insurance, and the maintenance of common areas, he is often protected from increases in these expenses by "expense stops" which pass on a significant portion of these increases to the tenants.

Percentage Rentals and Rent Escalators

A possible hedge against inflation through a provision known as "overage" or "percentage" rentals is often found in shopping center leases. These are additional payments made by tenants at such time as their sales volume exceeds a predetermined level. Other rent escalators include cost of living adjustments to base rent, and predetermined increases in minimum base rents.

ADVANTAGES OF OWNING APARTMENTS

Although apartments normally require more intensive management than commercial properties, they have certain investment advantages including:

Short-Term Tenancies

Short-term tenancies enable the owner to raise rents as economic conditions dictate. The possibility of raising revenues quickly in response to increased expenses offers an important protection against inflation. Of course, the risk of local rent control legislation must be carefully weighed.

Housing and Population Trends

In recent years, housing price increases have generally outstripped the rate of inflation resulting in a doubling of the median price of housing since 1968. The trend of increased housing and financing costs, combined with a growing number of wage earners under the age of 35, who through circumstance or choice decide to rent their housing, has resulted in significant opportunities in apartment ownership.

Two commonly utilized forms of real estate ownership are the limited partnership and the real estate investment trust. Both provide certain benefits to the investor, while both have some disadvantages. Income Realty Trust is actually a "bybrid" form of ownership created by combining features of each.

Liquidity

A benefit of a trust is that ownership is expressed in shares of beneficial interest. These shares, like those of a corporation, are freely transferable. Therefore, a method of disposing of shares is available if necessary. There is no assurance that an active trading market will develop.

Independent Trustees

Six real estate investment experts serve as Trustees and are responsible for the overall management of the Trust and selection of the Advisor. A majority of the Trustees is independent of the sponsor of the Trust. The Trustees have a fiduciary relationship to the investors and are charged with the conduct required of a "prudent man."

Tax Benefits

Both the trust and the partnership forms of ownership are able to provide tax-deferred cash distributions through depreciation deductions. A partnership can pass through "excess" deductions to apply against other income. A trust cannot, but it can carry forward excess losses to utilize against future years' cash distributions.

A major reason for utilizing the trust form of ownership is that it is particularly well suited to the needs of tax-exempt investors without sacrifice to the taxable investor. The IRS has ruled that distributions from a real estate investment trust are not "unrelated business taxable income" to the tax-exempt investor (Revenue Ruling 66-106).

Finite Life

Income Realty Trust has the "finite life" typical of a limited partnership. The Trustees have the stated intention of liquidating the entire portfolio of properties by the tenth year. This provides the investor an opportunity to experience the full life cycle ownership of real estate—purchase, management and sale. Thus, real estate values, not stock market values, will be realized.

Annual Valuation

In order to provide a valuation mechanism, the portfolio will be appraised annually by an independent appraiser chosen by the Trusts' auditors, and an audited "current value" balance sheet will be published along with the audit financial statements.

HOW INCOME REALTY TRUST BENEFITS THE TAX-EXEMPT INVESTOR

Income Realty Trust should be considered as an investment vehicle for a variety of tax-exempt investors, including:

- Qualified corporate pension and profit sharing plans.
- State and municipal pension and retirement plans.
- Taft-Hartley pension and retirement plans.

- Other retirement plans, such as Keoghs (HR-10), Individual Retirement Accounts (IRA), and IRA "Roll-overs."
- Endowment funds.
- Other entities intended to be exempt from federal income taxation, such as certain religious, charitable, scientific, literary and educational corporations and foundations.

Tax-exempt investors have rarely taken advantage of the opportunities which may be derived from ownership of a leveraged portfolio of income-producing real estate. There have been four significant areas of concern. Income Realty Trust has been designed to eliminate or significantly reduce the tax-exempt investors' concerns in each of these four areas as follows:

CONCERN

Diversification

Their financial assets have often been too small to permit investment in real estate without violating reasonable diversification requirements.

SOLUTION

Any size investment can be made above $2,500, enabling the fiduciary to accomplish the diversification of assets. Considering the diversification guidelines of the Employee Retirement Income Security Act (ERISA), and today's inflationary environment, fiduciaries should carefully consider that *it may be imprudent not to include* real estate in the portfolio for which they are responsible.

Unrelated Business Taxable Income

The tax-exempt investor is unwilling to incur the taxes and administrative costs that occur as the leveraged real estate portfolio generates "unrelated business taxable income."

Even though the Trust will consist of a portfolio of leveraged properties neither the cash distributions nor capital gains at sale will be taxed if the investor has tax-exempt status. This benefit is peculiar to a real estate investment trust and is not available in a partnership or through direct investment. Therefore, the problem of "unrelated business taxable income" is eliminated.

CONCERN

Illiquidity

Some tax-exempt investors have been hesitant to include in their portfolio an investment that is illiquid.

SOLUTION

The ownership of the Trust is expressed in shares of beneficial interest which are freely transferable. Therefore, an improved liquidity feature is brought to the ownership of real estate. In addition, properties will be sold and/or refinanced during the life of the Trust with proceeds paid out to the investors. This "self-liquidating" characteristic brings still another liquidity feature to the tax-exempt investor concerned with the prudent man requirements of ERISA.

Fiduciary Responsibility

The tax-exempt investor is a fiduciary and may have an aversion to participating in a limited partnership where a general partner has virtually unlimited powers.

The Board of Trustees, a majority of which is independent of the sponsor, is elected annually by the shareholders and has the fiduciary responsibility for the careful investment and continuing management of Trust assets.

HOW INCOME REALTY TRUST BENEFITS THE INDIVIDUAL INVESTOR

The taxable investor, whether an individual or a corporation, may find that many of his investment objectives can be met in Income Realty Trust, including:

- DIVERSIFICATION of assets into a portfolio of real estate that is, in turn, diversified by property type and geographical location.
- CAPITAL APPRECIATION as an inflation hedge and an opportunity for the expansion of real net worth.
- FREEDOM FROM DIRECT INVOLVEMENT in the intense management of income-producing properties.
- CASH FLOW derived from property operations that is totally or substantially tax deferred.
- LIQUIDITY through freely transferable shares.
- SELF-LIQUIDATING TRUST providing periodic return of capital as properties are sold or refinanced.

RISKS OF INCOME REALTY TRUST

Book Value of Shares and Distributions to Shareholders

It is the present intention of the Trust to distribute at least quarterly to its Shareholders substantially all Distributable Cash from Operations and Cash from Sale or Refinancing, rather than to retain such funds for additional Trust investments. In general, only that amount which the Trustees may determine to be needed by the Trust for working capital will be withheld from such distributions. An effect of this policy, unless additional capital funds for investment are obtained, is that at some future date, the Trust will have liquidated all of its assets and distributed all Net Cash from Sale or Refinancing to its Shareholders, and having no assets or sources of revenue, in effect will have self-liquidated. To the extent that Cash Distributions to Shareholders represent a return of capital or such distributions exceed earnings of the Trust, the book value of the outstanding Shares will have a corresponding diminution in value.

Possible Dilution; Future Equity Financing

The Trust is authorized, without approval of the Shareholders, to issue senior securities or additional Shares of Beneficial Interest, warrants or options to purchase such Shares, and to borrow or in any other manner to raise money, subject to the limitations of the Declaration of Trust, through the issuance of notes, debentures or other forms of obligations of the Trust. Such debt instruments may be convertible into Shares of the Trust or may be accompanied by warrants or other options to purchase Shares. The Trust may not issue warrants, options, or similar evidences of a right to buy securities of the Trust, unless issued to all of its security holders ratably or as a part of a financing arrangement or in connection with the acquisition of properties for the Trust. One or more of the foregoing issuances may dilute the interests of the Shareholders in the Trust's assets and such borrowings may increase the Trust's exposure to risk of loss. The number of Shares which the Trust is authorized to issue is unlimited. The Trustees do not presently have any plans with respect to future private or public issuances of securities, other than The Trust-Convertible Participating Notes. Whether any other issuances are made will depend on a number of factors, including future operations and financial condition of the Trust, and the condition of the securities markets.

Possible Inability to Qualify, or Disqualification, as a Real Estate Investment Trust

The Trust intends to elect to be taxed as a real estate investment trust for Federal income tax purposes as soon as practicable. Under the Code, a real estate investment trust which meets certain qualifications (including distribution to shareholders of specified percentages of taxable income and satisfaction of a minimum number of shareholders requirement) generally does not pay Federal income taxes on the ordinary income and capital gains distributed to Shareholders. The Trust policy of distributing substantially all of its Distributable Cash from Operations at least quarterly may increase the risk that it will subsequently be unable to make the required distributions to Shareholders. Should the Trust fail to qualify as a real estate investment trust or fail to make the required distributions for any taxable year, it would be taxed as a corporation, so that the distributions to its Shareholders would not be deductible by the Trust for purposes of computing its taxable income, which could result in the Trust incurring substantial Federal income tax liability for such year. Difficulties which the Trust may experience in investing the proceeds of this offering may result in substantial delay before the Trust is able to qualify as a real estate investment trust for Federal income tax purposes.

In general, if an election to be treated as a real estate investment trust under the Internal Revenue Code is terminated or revoked, the Trust cannot again elect to be treated as a real estate investment trust until the fifth taxable year beginning after the year for which the termination or revocation was effective.

Independent Contractors

To maintain its qualification under the Code, a real estate investment trust must employ independent contractors to conduct the operation and improvements of the Trust's properties. In addition, a qualified real estate investment trust cannot derive more than a specified percentage of its income from sources other than real estate. Accordingly, the Trust expects that during periods in which it wishes to qualify under the Code it will enter into agreements whereby independent contractors will agree to manage Trust properties and to perform or supply all services and material in connection with every improvement or expansion of such properties and to plan, design, construct and attempt to obtain financing and tenants for such properties.

Through such arrangements, although the Trust will be relieved of many overhead expenses, such as the salaries of architects, engineers, supervisors, leasing agents and similar persons, as well as office rentals and other costs which otherwise would be incurred, it will be required to pay independent contractors to provide such services. The Trustees believe that any net cost due to such arrangements should be more than offset by the Federal income tax advantages derived from operating as a qualified real estate investment trust. However, should the Trust or the Advisor be required to perform such improvements or manage Trust investments, the income from such properties may not be qualified income to the Trust and could jeopardize the Trust's continued qualification under the Code.

Marketability of Shares

It cannot be predicted at the present time whether the Shares of the Trust being offered hereby will be widely-held by a large number of persons. Accordingly, there is no assurance that a trading market for such Shares will develop upon the completion of this offering. Because of general conditions in the industry, shares of many real estate investment trusts for which there is a trading market have for several years been trading below their book value. So long as this situation continues, shares of such trusts may appear to some potential investors to be more attractive investments than the Shares of the Trust, thus inhibiting the development of a trading market in the Shares and diminishing their liquidity. In addition, the unsatisfactory performance in the securities markets of the shares of a number of other trusts may reduce generally the demand for shares of real estate investment trusts, including those of the Trust. Should a trading market for the Shares of the Trust develop, there is no assurance as to the price at which the Shares might be traded or that they would trade at or above book value or at or above the offering price.

After the completion of this offering, the Trust may make subsequent public offerings of its Shares or securities convertible into its Shares. Dealers who might otherwise make a market in the Shares may be precluded by applicable laws and regulations from doing so for extended periods of time if they participate in one or more of such subsequent offerings.

Fiduciary Responsibility of Trustees; Rights of Shareholders; Possible Inadequacy of Remedies

Pursuant to the Declaration of Trust, none of the Trustees, officers, employees or agents of the Trust shall be liable to any person in connection with the affairs of the Trust except for their own bad faith, willful misfeasance, gross negligence, or reckless disregard of duties. Therefore, a holder of Shares may be entitled to a more limited right of action than he would have absent such provisions in the Declaration of Trust.

Nevertheless, Shareholders who may suffer losses in connection with the purchase of the Shares being offered hereby, due to a breach of fiduciary duty by a Trustee or officer of the Trust in connection with such purchase or sale of Shares, may have the right to recover such losses from such Trustee or officer in an action based on Rule 10b-5 under the Securities Exchange Act of 1934 and may, subject to procedural and jurisdictional requirements, have the right to bring class actions.

The enforceability of provisions limiting Trustee liability may be limited by future developments in the law. In the view of the Securities and Exchange Commission, any attempt to limit Trustee liability under the Securities Act of 1933 is contrary to public policy and is unenforceable.

Investment Company Act of 1940

The Trustees do not believe that the Trust is an investment company within the meaning of the Investment Company Act of 1940, and they intend to conduct the operations of the Trust so that it will not be subject to regulation under that Act. Among other things, they will monitor the proportions of the Trust's funds which are placed in various investments so that the Trust does not come within the definition of an investment company. One result of this policy may be that in order to avoid becoming an investment company the Trust may have to forego certain investment strategies which would produce a more favorable return.

Possible Shareholder Liability

It is possible that under some circumstances investors in the Trust might be subject to certain liabilities.

Tenancy-in-Common

The Trustees do not intend to terminate the Trust until all of its assets have been disposed of. However, if for any reason termination of the Trust should occur at any time before the sale of all assets owned by the Trust, title to its property might devolve to the Shareholders as tenants-in-common. Management and disposition of the property might be difficult under this form of ownership.

TAX ASPECTS OF INCOME REALTY TRUST

Federal Income Tax

Under the Code, a trust, corporation or unincorporated association meeting certain requirements may elect to be treated as a "real estate investment trust" for purposes of Federal income taxation with the result that, subject to certain conditions and one exception relating to the net income from foreclosure property which is taxable at a rate of 46%, the trust itself will not be taxed on that portion of its ordinary or capital gain income which is currently distributed to its Shareholders.

For any year in which the Trust does not both (i) meet the requirements for electing to be taxed as a real estate investment trust and (ii) elect to be so taxed, it will be taxed as a corporation.

The Trustees believe that the Trust will probably not be able to elect to be taxed as a real estate investment trust for the year ending December 31, Year One because for such period it will not meet the income tests and the number-of-shareholder tests described herein. The Trust will make an election to be taxed as a real estate investment trust as soon as practicable. In order to secure the benefits of classification as a real estate investment trust, the Trust must distribute an amount equal to the sum of at least 85% of its real estate investment trust taxable income and 95% of the excess of its net income from foreclosing property over the tax imposed on such income to its Shareholders within certain time limits.

To be considered a real estate investment trust for purposes of the Federal income tax laws, the Trust must elect to be so treated and must meet the following requirements:

(1) At the end of each fiscal quarter, at least 75% of the value of the Total Assets of the Trust must consist of real estate assets (including interests in real property, interests in mortgages on real property, and shares in other real estate investment trusts meeting the requirements for taxation in accordance with Sections 856-860 of the Code), cash, cash items (including receivables) and government securities;

(2) At the end of each fiscal quarter, not more than 25% of the value of the Total Assets of the Trust may consist of securities other than government securities or transferable certificates of beneficial interest in other qualified real estate investment trusts; and of the "25% securities," the securities of any one issuer may not represent more than 5% of the value of the Trust's Total Assets of 10% of the outstanding voting securities of any one issuer;

(3) At least 75% of the gross income of the Trust must be derived from "rents from real property" (see discussion below), interest on obligations secured by mortgages on real property; (usurious or illegal interest does not qualify and in the case of interest on mortgages governing both real and personal property, the interest must be apportioned and only that applicable to real property will qualify); abatements and refunds of real estate taxes, gains from the sale or other disposition of real property (including interests in real property and interests in mortgages on real property), dividends or other distributions on and gain from the sale or other disposition of shares of other real estate investment trusts meeting the requirements for taxation in accordance with Sections 856-860 of the Code, income and gain derived from foreclosure property as defined in Section 856(e) of the Code, and commitment fees received for agreeing to make secured loans or to purchase or lease real property. An additional 20% of the gross income of the Trust must be derived from these same sources or from dividends, or interest, or gains from the sale or other disposition of stock or securities, or any combination of the foregoing;

(4) Gross income from sales or other dispositions of
   (a) stock or securities held for less than one year,
   (b) inventory or property held primarily for sale to customers in the ordinary course of the Trust's trade or business, other than foreclosure property as defined in Section 856(e) of the Code, and,
   (c) real property (or interests in real property and interests in mortgages on real property) held for less than four years, other than foreclosure property or property involuntarily converted through destruction, condemnation or similar event,

   must be less than 30% of the Trust's gross income;

(5) Beneficial ownership of the Trust must be held by 100 or more persons during at least 335 days of a taxable year of 12 months or during a proportionate part of a taxable year of less than 12 months;

(6) The Trust must be managed by one or more Trustees or directors;

(7) Beneficial ownership of the Trust must be evidenced by transferable certificates of beneficial interest;

(8) The Trust must not be a personal holding company (that is, more than 50% of the outstanding Shares may not be owned, directly or indirectly, by or for, five or fewer individuals, at any time during the last half of the taxable year) if all of its adjusted ordinary income constituted personal holding company income;

(9) The Trust must be an entity which would be taxed as a corporation but for the REIT provisions of the Internal Revenue Code; and

(10) The Trust must not be an insurance company, Small Business Investment Company, state chartered business development corporation, or building and loan association

The term "rents from real property" referred to in Requirement (3) above excludes, among other things, amounts received with respect to property if the Trust furnishes or renders services to the tenants of such property, or manages or operates such property, other than through an "independent contractor" from whom the Trust does not derive or receive any income. Various tests are applied in determining independent contractor status, including a prohibition against certain mutual ownership and officer and employee relationships among the Trust, the Advisor and the independent contractor.

Taxation of Trust

For any fiscal year in which the Trust does not qualify as a real estate investment trust, the Trust's taxable income will be subject to Federal income tax at corporate rates. For other fiscal years, in which it does qualify as a real estate investment trust, the Trust will be subject to Federal income tax at the usual corporate rate on its Real Estate Investment Trust Taxable Income and capital gains (after deduction of qualifying distributions to shareholders) and to Federal income tax at the rate of 46% on its net income from foreclosure property. Foreclosure property is defined by Section 856(e) of the Code to mean, if the Trust so elects, any real property (including interests in real property) and any personal property incident to such real property, acquired by a real estate investment trust as a result of the Trust having bid in such property at foreclosure or having otherwise reduced such property to ownership or possession by agreement or process of law, after there has been a default (or default was imminent) on a lease of such property or on indebtedness which such property secured. In computing its Real Estate Investment Trust Taxable Income, the Trust may deduct dividends paid to its Shareholders, provided that the deduction for dividends paid (computed without regard to capital gains dividends) for the taxable year equals or exceeds the sum of 95% of its Real Estate Investment Trust Taxable Income for such year determined without regard to the deduction for dividends paid and by excluding capital gains, and 95% of the excess of its net income from foreclosure property over the tax imposed on such income and provided the Trust complies with certain record keeping requirements. The computation of Real Estate Investment Trust Taxable Income includes income which can result from depreciation recapture upon disposition of property.

A real estate investment trust may declare and distribute a dividend after the close of its taxable year and such dividend will be considered, insofar as the Trust is concerned, as having been paid during such taxable year. Such amounts will be treated, however, as having been received by the shareholders in the taxable year in which the distribution is actually made. In order for the foregoing rules to apply, the Trust must declare the dividend before the time prescribed for filing its return with respect to the taxable year in question, including any extensions of such time, and it must actually distribute the amount of such dividends within twelve months following the close of the taxable year in question and not later than the payment date of the first regular dividend after such declaration. Notwithstanding the foregoing rules, a non-deductible excise tax will be imposed on the Trust if less than seventy-five percent (75%) of its Real Estate Investment Trust Taxable Income (as reported on the Trust's return) has been distributed by the end of the year. The excise tax is three percent (3%) of the difference between seventy-five percent (75%) of Real Estate Investment Trust Taxable Income and the amount distributed.

In the event of determination as a result of a decision by the Tax Court or a court of competent jurisdiction, a closing agreement with the Internal Revenue Service or regulations by, or an Agreement with, the Secretary of the Treasury, an adjustment (as hereinafter defined) is made for any tax year, the Trust may pay a deficiency dividend in order to comply with the 95% requirement. An "adjustment" means, (i) any increase in the sum of (A) the Trust's Real Estate Investment Trust Taxable Income determined without regard to a deduction for dividends paid and by excluding capital gain, and (B) the excess of the net income from foreclosure property over the tax imposed on such income, (ii) any increase in the excess of net capital gain over the deduction for capital gain dividends paid, or (iii) any decrease in the deduction for dividends paid determined without regard to capital gains dividends. In order to qualify for a deduction for a deficiency dividend, the Trust must file a claim therefor, within 120 days of determination. Subject to the filing of the claim, and distribution of the proper amount within 90 days after determination, the Trust will not be disqualified or be subject to tax on the amount distributed as a result of failing to meet the 95% test. The Trust would, however, be subject to interest on the amount of the deficiency dividend from the last day (without extension of time) for the Trust to file its tax return until the date the claim for the deficiency dividend is filed in addition, a non-deductible penalty equal to the amount of interest is imposed, the total penalty not to exceed 50% of the deficiency dividend deduction. If for any reason the Trust at any time fails to qualify as a real estate investment trust, it would not be entitled to the deduction for dividends paid to its Shareholders. The Trust will not be disqualified as a real estate investment trust if it fails to meet the 75% gross income test or the 95% gross income test if the following conditions are met:

(i) The Trust attaches a schedule to its income tax return for each taxable year describing the nature and amount of each item of its gross income;
(ii) The inclusion of any incorrect information in such schedule is not due to fraud with intent to evade tax; and
(iii) The failure to meet the 75% or 95% tests is due to reasonable cause and not due to willful neglect.

However, if the above conditions are met, the Trust will be subjected to a 100% tax on the Real Estate Investment Trust Taxable Income attributable to the greater amount by which the Trust failed either the 95% or the 75% tests.

The sale or disposition of property held primarily for sale in the ordinary course of the Trust's trade or business, except for foreclosure property, is a prohibited transaction. The net income derived from a prohibited transaction is subject to a tax equal to 100% of the net income derived from prohibited transactions. In determining the net income from a prohibited transaction, only expenses directly connected with a prohibited transaction are taken into account in computing the net income. Accordingly, if the Trust sells or otherwise disposes of property held primarily for sale in the ordinary course of its business, it will be subject to the 100% tax on any gains over expenses directly allocated to the transaction, and the Trust will not be entitled to allocate general administrative and overhead expenses to reduce the gain. The Revenue Act of 1978 contains certain "safe harbor" rules which establish that certain properties are not held primarily for sale in the ordinary course of a trust's trade or business.

The Trust is not allowed a deduction for dividends received by it in years for which it qualifies as a real estate investment trust under the Code.

The Trust is entitled to claim a net operating loss carryover with respect to losses incurred in a year in which it qualifies as a real estate investment trust. The net operating loss may be carried forward in computing Real Estate Investment Trust Taxable Income for eight (8) years after the year in which the loss occurred. A net operating loss cannot be carried back to any year in which the Trust qualified as a real estate investment trust under the Code, nor may it be carried back from a year in which the Trust qualified as a real estate investment trust under the Code.

The Trust may receive a deduction for capital gains dividends. The Trust will be taxed on its undistributed Real Estate Investment Trust Taxable Income. In the case of capital gains, the alternative tax may apply. The alternative tax will apply if the sum of the regular tax on the undistributed Real Estate Investment Trust Taxable Income (excluding the excess of any net long-term capital gains over the net short-term capital loss) and 28 percent of the long-term capital gain over the net short-term capital loss, less qualified capital gain dividends, is less than the regular tax on the undistributed Real Estate Investment Trust Taxable Income.

The Trust will also be subject to the minimum tax on items of tax preference. However, except for depreciation on real property in excess of straight-line depreciation, items of tax preference although determined at the Trust level, are treated as items of tax preference to its Shareholders to the extent the Trust distributes its taxable income.

Because of timing differences that may arise between the realization of taxable income and the realization of net cash flow, it is possible the Trust may not have sufficient cash flow or other liquid resources at a particular time to distribute 95% of its Real Estate Investment Trust Taxable Income and 95% of its net income from foreclosure property over the tax imposed on such income to Shareholders. If such distribution is not made with respect to any taxable year, the Trust will become taxable on all of its taxable income for such year without reduction for any distributions to Shareholders. Such taxable income, reduced by the actual amount of tax paid by the Trust, will be includable in the current or accumulated earnings and profits of the Trust and will again be taxable to Shareholders upon distribution. Additionally, because of timing differences that may arise between the realization of taxable income and the realization of net cash flow, the Trust may not have sufficient cash or other liquid resources at a particular time to satisfy its tax liabilities without resorting to borrowing.

A trust's election to be treated as a real estate investment trust under the Internal Revenue Code will automatically terminate if it does not meet the tests to be so treated. Additionally, a trust may within the first ninety days of any taxable year revoke its election. In general, if an election is thus terminated or revoked, the trust cannot again elect to be treated as a real estate investment trust until the fifth taxable year beginning after the year for which the termination or revocation was effective.

Taxation of Shareholders

In any taxable year in which the Trust qualifies as a real estate investment trust, and distributes an amount equal to the sum of 95% of its Real Estate Investment Trust Taxable Income for the year (determined without regard to the deduction for dividends paid) and 95% of the excess of its net income from foreclosure property over the tax imposed on such income, distributions from the Trust will be taxable as long-term capital gains to the extent so designated by the Trust (but not in excess of the Trust's net long-term capital gains for the taxable year), and the balance will be taxable as ordinary income to the extent of the earnings and profits of the Trust. None of such distributions will qualify for the $100 dividend exclusion for individuals or the 85% dividend received deduction for corporations. Shareholders will not be entitled to deduct any net losses of the Trust.

In Revenue Ruling 66-106 the Internal Revenue Service held that amounts distributed by a real estate investment trust to an exempt employees' pension trust do not constitute "unrelated business taxable income." Revenue rulings are interpretive in nature and are subject to potential revocation or modification by the Internal Revenue Service.

For any taxable year that the Trust fails to qualify as a real estate investment trust or distribute an amount equal to the sum of 95% of its Real Estate Investment Trust Taxable Income for the year (determined without regard to the deduction for dividends paid) and 95% of the excess of its net income from foreclosure property over the tax imposed on such income, it would not be entitled to the deduction for dividends paid to its Shareholders. Distributions from the Trust at such time would be taxable to Shareholders as dividends to the extent of the current and accumulated earnings and profits of the Trust and would be eligible for the $100 dividend exclusion for individuals or the 85% dividend received deduction for corporation.

Cash may be generated in excess of the net earnings of the Trust by reason of an excess of tax-deductible depreciation over payments required to amortize the principal of mortgages on the Trust's equity investments, or on disposition or refinancing of properties. This excess of cash will not be taxed to the Trust and upon distribution by the Trust to Shareholders, assuming that all of the Trust's current and accumulated earnings and profits have been distributed, will be deemed to be a return of capital to each Shareholder to the extent of the adjusted tax basis of his Shares; distributions in excess of such adjusted tax basis will be treated as gain from the sale or exchange of property. A Shareholder who has received a distribution in excess of current and accumulated earnings and profits of the Trust may, upon the sale of his Shares, realize a higher taxable gain or a smaller loss because the basis of his Shares as reduced will be used for purposes of computing the amount of such gain or loss.

For purposes of computing the current or accumulated earnings and profits of the Trust which, if distributed, will be taxable to the Shareholders, the Trust will be deemed to be using only the straight-line method of depreciation. However, for purposes of the computation of Real Estate Investment Trust Taxable Income, accelerated depreciation methods may be used to the extent such methods have been adopted. It is anticipated that the Trust will adopt such depreciation methods, including accelerated depreciation methods, as are consistent with the Trust's investment objective of providing partially tax sheltered cash flow to Shareholders.

Long-term capital gains distributed by the Trust must be taken into account by the Shareholders for the purpose of determining the alternative minimum tax as provided by the Revenue Act of 1978. Additionally, Shareholders must also take into account other items of tax preference of the Trust, except for excess depreciation of real property which is taxable only to the Trust, to the extent such items are attributable to the amount of distributions taken into account as income by the Shareholder. The minimum tax imposed on items of tax preference is equal to 15% of the amount by which items of tax preference exceed the greater of (1) $10,000 ($5,000 in the case of a married individual filing a separate return) or (2) one-half (all for a corporate taxpayer) the taxpayer's regular Federal income tax. In addition, items of tax preference (other than capital gains) reduce the tax base eligible for the maximum tax on personal service income.

The Trust will notify each of its Shareholders of the proportions, if any, of the distributions made during the year which constitute long-term capital gain or a return of invested capital and of the amount of any items of tax preference.

In the event a deficiency dividend is paid by the Trust as a result of an adjustment, such dividend is taxable to a Shareholder in the year in which it is made, irrespective of the Trust year for which it is made. If, as a result of a deficiency dividend, a prior ordinary income distribution is recharacterized as a capital gains distribution, a Shareholder may make a similar recharacterization by filing an amended return for the year in question, provided the statute of limitations for that year has not expired.

Each year the Trust must demand written statements from the recordholders of designated percentages of its Shares disclosing the actual owners of the Shares and must maintain within the Internal Revenue District in which it is required to file its Federal income tax return permanent records showing the information it has thus received as to the actual ownership of such Shares and a list of those persons failing or refusing to comply with such demand.

RARE COINS FOR QUALIFIED PLANS

PLAN OF BUSINESS

The primary objective of the Partnership will be to realize capital appreciation through reasonably long-term investments in United States and European coins, through the use of capital funds and retained earnings invested by limited partners, as opposed to borrowings by the Partnership. Ten percent of the Partnership's capital, up to an initial $1,000,000 (and such percentage of capital as determined by the general partner thereafter) will be retained as a liquid investment reserve, which will include holdings of cash as well as short-term highly liquid investments with a view toward appropriate safety of principal, such as bank accounts, bank certificates of deposit and/or United States government obligations. The general partner will instruct its agent to invest the balance of the Partnership's funds from time to time in the rare coin market, and to manage these investments by trading and reinvesting in the rare coin market and liquidating these investments when he deems such action to be advisable, with temporary holdings of cash, bank accounts and/or United States government obligations. The rare coin market involved shall be in both pre- and post-1933 United States and European coins, principally those United States coins which are graded as choice uncirculated (graded MS-65) or proof condition coins (graded MS-65) on the standard grading system and European coins of the highest grades obtainable, with the aim of diversifying the portfolio among a number of different series of issues whenever the portfolio manager deems it to be reasonably advisable and feasible. In the case of extremely scarce or very old pre-1933 United States coins, the purchase of uncirculated or proof condition coins may be impractical and the Partnership may purchase lesser grade coins of this type.

The Agent will have discretion in the selection of coins to be acquired by the Partnership, from whom the coins are purchased and the price to be paid by the Partnership. He will have the discretion to hold, buy, trade or sell coins in and for the portfolio whenever he feels it to be in the best interest of the Partnership. He will use his best efforts to obtain the best prices available in these actions but makes no guarantees in this regard. The general partner will be kept closely informed of the Agent's plans and purchases. The Agreement provides that the Partnership shall not regularly sell or trade coins from its portfolio, but should market circumstances require sales of portions of the portfolio, the Agent will have the discretion to sell coins should he feel it to be in the best interest of the Partnership. There shall be no distributions of cash of the Partnership to the Partners other than pursuant to the redemption provisions or as the general partner deems it advisable in his sole and exclusive discretion. Any net proceeds from coin sales not distributed to Partners will be re-invested in new coin purchases.

The general partner has arranged that all coins purchased from whatever source either will be hand delivered by the seller or portfolio manager to the Bank, which has agreed to serve as the custodian for the Partnership's coins. The coins so received will then be placed in the Partnership's safe deposit box at the custodian bank and a description and other pertinent information about each will be recorded on a form, a copy of which will be kept for each coin in the safe deposit box. An independent appraiser engaged by the Partnership to appraise any new coins purchased during any Partnership quarter will appraise each coin's fair market value while held in the safe deposit box and will indicate his appraised value on the form kept by the bank for each coin. Access to the safe deposit box for examination of a coin will require the signatures and presence of either the general partner or the Agent and a representative of the custodian bank. The Agent and the general partner will at all times be bonded against theft up to the fair market value of the portfolio, as adjusted from time to time, at the expense of the Partnership. The signatures and presence of either the General Agent or the Agent will be required for the removal of any coin from the bank.

The general partner expects that the Partnership's net proceeds available for coin investments from time to time will be invested within 6 to 8 months from the date of receipt thereof by the Partnership. The Partnership, if not terminated sooner, will continue for 20 years, at which time its assets will be liquidated in the manner the general partner believes will achieve the most favorable result to the limited partners.

THE OFFERING

The offer is made to eligible investors to become limited partners in a limited partnership called Rare Coins for Qualified Plans. The United subscription price to a limited partner is $10.00 per Unit purchased, with a minimum investment required of 1,000 Units.

Other than the minimum purchase of 1,000 Units per investor, there is no established minimum number of Units offered hereunder which must be sold before any sales are effective. Since this offering is on a "best efforts" basis, there can be no assurances that all, or a significant amount of the Units offered hereunder will be sold. Proceeds from any sales of Units hereunder will not be escrowed pending any future sales, but will, upon receipt by the Partnership, become the property of the Partnership, subject to the limited partners right to request a redemption of some or all of their Units.

Eligible Investors

The Units are offered only to IRA's, Keogh Plans, pension and profit sharing trusts and other tax exempt entities.

USE OF PROCEEDS

The Partnership intends to use the gross proceeds from the sale of Units offered hereunder as set forth below:

	If all Units Offered Hereunder are Sold
Broker's commissions and finder's fees	$ 100,000
Rare European coins	$ 500,000
Pre-1933 rare U.S. copper and silver coins	$1,000,000
Post-1933 rare U.S. copper and silver coins	$ 325,000
Rare U.S. gold coins	$ 450,000
Liquid Investment Reserves	$ 100,000
Expenses (legal, accounting & printing costs)	$ 25,000
	$2,500,000

In the event that less than the maximum number of Units are sold hereunder, the Partnership intends to invest in the same relative proportions of types of coins as set forth in the table above.

REMUNERATION OF GENERAL PARTNER AND AGENT

The general partner will be allocated 1% of the Partnership's income, profits, gains, losses, deductions and credits from Partnership operations. The general partner will also be entitled to receive certain cash and other distributions by virtue of his interest in such. 4% of the value of the Partnership's gross assets, based on a determination by a qualified appraiser, as of the end of each quarter, will be paid to the general partner as a management fee. The fee will be paid in quarterly installments of 1% of the value of the gross assets as determined on the last day of each quarter of the Partnership's tax year. The Partnership's agent who will manage the Partnership's portfolio will be paid a yearly fee of 2% of the fair market value of the Partnership's gross assets in quarterly installments of 1/2% of the gross asset's value. The compensation of the Partnership's agent will be paid by the general partner out of his management fee. The agent will be reimbursed by the Partnership for his expenses while on Partnership business.

APPRAISALS

All coins purchased during any Partnership quarter will be graded and appraised as to current fair market value by a qualified independent appraiser before the end of that quarter. Except as hereinafter provided, coins in the Partnership's portfolio will only be appraised once by an independent appraiser. Thereafter, the following appraisal method will be used and will determine a coins "fair market value" for all purposes under the Agreement, including valuation for the purpose of determining the 8% management fee for the general partner, the computation of net asset value for determination of the price to Investors of Units offered hereunder after the initial three-month offering period and the value of a Partners interest at the time his Units are redeemed:

The fair market value attached to a particular United States coin by the independent appraiser will, on the date of the appraiser's determination, be compared to the average of the bid and ask prices for the coin appearing in the nearest monthly issues of The Coin Dealers Newsletter, Inc. (the "Gray Sheet") prorated to the date of valuation, and a mathematical constant for that particular coin will be determined for use in all future valuations (e.g. 20% higher than the average of the bid and ask prices). All subsequent valuations of a United States coin will then be computed using this multiple and either the latest or the two nearest monthly issues of the Gray Sheet. The valuation of the portfolio for the purposes of determining the quarterly management fee to the general partner will be made on the last day of the Partnership's quarter using the latest monthly issue of the Gray Sheet which quotes bid and ask prices compiled up to the last day of the month. The fair market value of a United States coin on any given day in a month will be determined by using the monthly Gray Sheet and prorating the differences in the average between the bid and ask prices in the two issues nearest to the date the appraisal is to be made.

The fair market value of British coins will be similarly computed using the bid and ask prices appearing in the International Green Sheet (the "Green Sheet") a publication listing the bid and prices for rare British coins among coin dealers.

In the event the appraisal method described above is unable to be performed in the opinion of the general partner, the fair market value of the coins in the Partnership's portfolio will be determined for all purposes under the Agreement by an independent qualified appraiser selected by the general partner.

The Coin Dealers Newsletter, Inc., P.O. Box 2308, Hollywood, California 90028 is a guide to United States coin prices for coin dealers and is published both weekly and in a monthly summary. The weekly issue is not as complete a listing of United States coin prices as is found in the monthly summary. The monthly summary compiles a current bid and ask price for almost every date and type of U.S. coin by monitoring all sale transactions between coin and dealers over the national teletype system linking hundreds of coin shops throughout the United States. The quotes for those coins not individually appearing in the Gray Sheet can be determined from the average bid and ask prices for coins of the same type. The Gray Sheet makes the following representation on its second page of both its weekly issue and monthly summary:

> "The Coin Dealer Newsletter reports the national coin market on a weekly basis. Under the present system, it is impossible to monitor all transactions of offers to buy and sell, but the broad information resources of the Newsletter make it a very accurate reflection of the market.

INVESTORS NOTE: The prices in the Newsletter are from dealer-to-dealer transactions. As an investor, you may place your buy and sell orders through a dealer for a fee, as you would buy stock through a broker."

REDEMPTION RIGHTS

Limited partners may by a written notice to the general partner, request redemption of some or all of their Units at any time at their fair market value on the date the redemption price is paid as determined under the Agreement. However, the Partnership, will not redeem any Units until all liabilities of the Partnership, except liabilities owed to General Partners and to Limited Partners on account of their capital contributions, have been paid or their remains, after the redemption, Partnership property sufficient in value to pay them. The value of the Units upon redemption may be more or less than their cost to the Partner, depending upon the current fair market value of the Partnership's investments. The general partner, in his discretion, may impose a redemption charge to Partners requesting redemption of 5% of the appraised value of the redeemed Units computed as of the date the redemption price is paid during the first three years of the Partnership commencing with the date of its organization, 2% of such appraised value during the 4th through 8th years, but no redemption charge thereafter. Redemption requests that are received at a time when redemption is not permitted under the provisions of the Agreement shall be held without effectiveness until redemption would be permitted under the Agreement, at which time they shall be granted in the order in which received, unless previously withdrawn by a written notice to the general partner.

Mail and in-person requests for the redemption of Units will be made at the fair market value on the business day on which a request in *good order* is received by the general partner. *Good order* means that the request to redeem Units must include the following documentation:

(a) a letter of instruction specifying the number of Units to be redeemed signed by all registered owners of the Units in the exact names in which they are registered with the Partnership;

(b) a guarantee of the signature of each registered owner by any bank, trust company or member of a recognized stock exchange; and

(c) other supporting legal documents, if required, in the case of estates, trusts, guardianships, custodianships, corporations and pension and profit sharing plans.

Any Partner uncertain of requirements for redemption of his Units should consult with the general partner. The proceeds of redemption will be paid in cash within 90 days of receipt of the general partner of the redemption request, provided that such 90-day period shall not run during one or more periods when any such redemption is not permitted under the Agreement, after which the 90-day period shall recommence. The obligation of the Partnership to redeem its Units when called upon to do so by a Partner is mandatory. Limited partners have no right to demand payment of the redemption price for their Units through the use of coins or other property in kind from the Partnership's portfolio.

BENEFITS OF RARE COINS FOR A QUALIFIED PLANS PROGRAM

The Partnership's objective is to provide for capital appreciation.

RISKS OF A RARE COINS FOR QUALIFIED PLANS PROGRAM

Risks Inherent in Rare Coin Investments. Theoretically, at least, the collector demand for coins acquired by the Partnership could diminish or disappear and, therefore, the value of the coins in the portfolio could decrease substantially. Even if the coin market does not decline, there is a major risk that there will be no substantial appreciation therein for protracted periods, in which case a limited partner-investor would realize no significant return on its investment in Units. The Partnership's ability to earn profits and avoid losses, as well as its ability to liquidate its portfolio, is governed by supply and demand criteria beyond its control. There is some risk involved in the grading of coins, both on purchase and sale. Overgrading on purchase may cause too high a price to be paid by the Partnership and undergrading on sale may cause the Partnership to receive too low a price. In addition, the price of the base metal of some rare coins is subject to volatile and unpredictable fluctuations. There is some risk of counterfeits or erroneous classifications in the marketplace. Coins will be examined and evaluated by the Partnership's experienced numismatist prior to purchase, which, in the normal circumstance, will eliminate counterfeits. If the numismatist employed by the Partnership has doubts about the authenticity of a coin it can be sent to the American Numismatic Association Authentication Service in Colorado to obtain a registered certificate of authenticity for the coin. The charges for the American Numismatic Association are modest and will be borne by the Partnership. The registered certificate of authenticity thus obtained would then be maintained with the coin in the Partnership's safe deposit box and should add to the marketability of such coin at the time of its eventual sale. Reputable dealers generally guarantee a refund for erroneously classified or counterfeit coins and the Partnership intends to purchase many, but not necessarily all of its coins, from such dealers.

Grading and Appraisal of Rare Coins. The grading of rare coins is open to dispute among experienced numismatists. Variance in the grade of coins, particularly among the highest graded coins, can cause extraordinary differences in value. The standard system of grading United States coins uses a numbered continuum. The MS-70 grade coin, the theoretical perfect specimen of its type, has no scratches, hairlines or blemishes and may be brilliant or have original toning. MS-65 coins are choice, fully struck specimens without detracting marks and may be brilliant or have original toning. MS-60 coins are average uncirculated pieces that may have bag marks or handling marks, but no wear, and may not have the full luster of coins in the higher grades. Proof coins are made especially for collectors from highly polished dies and are a different category of coins. The "proof" designation is not a grading description. The general partner will instruct the Partnership's coin buyer generally to purchase United States coins of MS-65 grade or better. The grading of European coins does not utilize a grading system as sophisticated as that used for grading United States coins. The general partner will instruct the Partnership's coin buyer generally to purchase the highest grade European coins available. The variance in the grade attached to a coin is a product, in large part, of the appraisers subjective judgment of the condition of the coin and there can be no assurance that the coin buyer employed by the Partnership or the independent appraiser who will grade each coin in the Partnership's portfolio will properly grade and thereby correctly gauge the market value of the Partnership's coins.

Competition. The buying, selling and trading of rare coins is highly competitive. There are no central clearing houses for such activities and the market is composed of thousands of private collectors and full and part-time dealers who are seeking to buy and sell coins at all times. Also, other coin investment partnerships are in existence with substantial capital which are seeking to acquire the same type of coins the Partnership hopes to purchase. Competition may be great in connection with the Partnership's attempts to acquire high quality rare coins, as such coins rarely come onto the marketplace and are much sought after. The demand and consequent prices for certain types of such coins may be so great as to preclude their acquisition by the Partnership.

Sale of Coins from the Partnership's Portfolio. Traditionally, coin dealers buy at wholesale and sell at retail. The repurchase price offered by the coin dealer represents his profit margin. Coin dealers regularly charge buyers from 5% to 30% over the price they paid to acquire a coin. This correspondingly results in coin dealers offering to buy a coin from a seller at a price lower than they would sell a coin once it is in their inventory in order to increase their profit and still offer a competitive price to buyers. This situation has a direct impact on the liquidation proceeds of a coin if it has not appreciated in value from the date of its purchase. A coin bought from a dealer can not generally be sold at the same price paid for the coin when resold to the same or other dealers, barring any appreciation. The dealer purchase and sale price differential does not generally exist with respect to sales between private collectors who do not actively engage in coin sales. Time pressure, (especially if sales are necessary to meet 90-day redemption demands hereunder), availability, and collectors willingness to purchase make it unlikely that the Partnership could sell a large part of its portfolio to collectors.

Tax Exempt Organizations and Unrelated Business Taxable Income. Trusts formed as part of a pension, profit sharing or self-employed persons' retirement plan which are qualified under Section 401 (a) of the Internal Revenue Code (the "Code") and individual retirement accounts qualified under Section 408 of the Code are subject to tax upon their "unrelated business taxable income" which exceeds $1,000 during any fiscal year, even though they are otherwise exempt from payment of any federal income tax. It is possible that if such an entity becomes a limited partner in the Partnership by the purchase of Units hereunder, the income allocated to it under the Agreement will be unrelated business taxable income and, thus, subject to tax at applicable rates. All such entities should consult with their own tax adviser concerning this issue and the Partnership makes no guarantees or assurances in this regard.

Qualification Under the Standards for Fiduciaries Set Forth in Section 404 of the Pension Reform Act of 1974. Neither the Partnership nor its counsel make any guarantees, representations or assurances that purchase of the Units hereunder will qualify under the standards set forth for fiduciaries of qualified retirement plans under Section 404 of the Pension Reform Act of 1974, as amended ("ERISA") with regard to whether an investment in the Partnership satisfies the diversification requirements of Section 404(a)(1)(c) of ERISA or whether the investment is prudent, or any applicable state or local law dealing with the conduct of fiduciaries. Prospective investors are strongly urged to consult with their own tax advisers with regard to this issue and whether an investment in this Partnership meets such requirements.

Potential Dilution of Interests During Any Partnership Quarter. The Units offered hereunder will be sold for a purchase price of $10 per Unit during the first six months of the offering ending December 31, Year One. Thereafter, and for all subsequent sales the price at which a Unit will be sold will be determined by the net asset value of the Partnership's assets per Unit computed as of the date of sale. Because some of the capital contributed to the Partnership in any three-month period may be used to purchase rare coins that in turn may appreciate or depreciate in value and will not be appraised prior to the end of the three-month period, the interests of the holders of Units during any three-month period may be subject to favorable or unfavorable dilution if subsequent Units are sold prior to the next appraisal, because the price at which the subsequent Units are sold in any three-month period will not currently reflect the appreciation or depreciation of coins purchased during the period.

TAX ASPECTS OF A RARE COINS FOR QUALIFIED PLANS PROGRAM

Neither the Partnership nor its Counsel make any guarantees, representations or assurances that purchase of the Units offered hereunder will satisfy any of the fiduciary standards set forth in Section 404 of the Pension Reform Act of 1974, as amended, including whether this investment is "prudent" or whether it will satisfy diversification requirements, or any state or local law or that the income from the Partnership, if any, will not be deemed "unrelated business taxable income" under Sections 511-514 of the Code, and therefore taxable to an otherwise tax exempt entity.

96th Congress 2d Session } COMMITTEE PRINT { CP 96–25

Employee Stock Ownership Plans

An Employer Handbook

Prepared by the Staff of the

COMMITTEE ON FINANCE
UNITED STATES SENATE

RUSSELL B. LONG, *Chairman*

APRIL 1980

Printed for the use of the Committee on Finance

U.S. GOVERNMENT PRINTING OFFICE
48-217 O WASHINGTON : 1980

For sale by the Superintendent of Documents, U.S. Government Printing Office
Washington, D.C. 20402

COMMITTEE ON FINANCE

RUSSELL B. LONG, Louisiana, *Chairman*

HERMAN E. TALMADGE, Georgia
ABRAHAM RIBICOFF, Connecticut
HARRY F. BYRD, JR., Virginia
GAYLORD NELSON, Wisconsin
MIKE GRAVEL, Alaska
LLOYD BENTSEN, Texas
SPARK M. MATSUNAGA, Hawaii
DANIEL PATRICK MOYNIHAN, New York
MAX BAUCUS, Montana
DAVID L. BOREN, Oklahoma
BILL BRADLEY, New Jersey

ROBERT DOLE, Kansas
BOB PACKWOOD, Oregon
WILLIAM V. ROTH, JR., Delaware
JOHN C. DANFORTH, Missouri
JOHN H. CHAFEE, Rhode Island
JOHN HEINZ, Pennsylvania
MALCOLM WALLOP, Wyoming
DAVID DURENBERGER, Minnesota

MICHAEL STERN, *Staff Director*
ROBERT E. LIGHTHIZER, *Chief Minority Counsel*
JOHN E. CURTIS, Jr., *Counsel*

CONTENTS

EMPLOYEE STOCK OWNERSHIP PLANS

An Employer Handbook

(V)

I. INTRODUCTION

This committee publication is intended to serve as a general explanation of employee stock ownership plans for employers, their financial advisors and their attorneys. The term employee stock ownership plan would include both an "ESOP," the employee stock ownership plan described in section 4975(e)(7) of the Internal Revenue Code, and a Tax Credit Employee Stock Ownership Plan (generally referred to as a TRASOP) described in section 409A of the Internal Revenue Code.

An ESOP is an employee benefit plan which also provides indirect benefits for employers and their shareholders. Employees are able to acquire a stock ownership in their employer without the need to invest their own money. In addition, because the ESOP is also a method of corporate finance, the employer is able to generate additional capital through the ESOP for expansion, repaying any indebtedness incurred thereby with tax deductible dollars. Finally, shareholders of closely-held corporations may be provided with a limited market for their stock.

A. What Is An ESOP?

An ESOP is an employee benefit plan which is "qualified" under the Internal Revenue Code. That is, it has been designed to operate in such a way that it satisfies the requirements of the Internal Revenue Code and the income tax regulations. This is important in that employer contributions to a qualified employee benefit plan, such as an ESOP, are tax-deductible to the employer within the limits established by the Internal Revenue Code.

The ESOP is designed to invest primarily in employer stock, and may borrow the funds necessary to purchase employer stock from the employer or its shareholders. Stock purchased by the ESOP is held in trust for employees of the employer, and is distributed to them after their employment with the employer ends and they cease to participate in the ESOP. This means that assets acquired by the ESOP can never be returned to the employer.

B. What Is A TRASOP?

A TRASOP is a form of employee stock ownership plan which was initially created by the Tax Reduction Act of 1975 and the Tax Reform Act of 1976. This is why it was initially referred to as a "TRASOP." In the Revenue Act of 1978, the name was changed to "ESOP." However, this created a great deal of confusion in that the traditional employee stock ownership plan has been referred to as an ESOP. Accordingly, in the Technical Corrections Act of 1979, the name was changed to a "tax credit employee stock ownership plan." However, the Committee recognizes that this type of plan will continue to be known as a TRASOP. An employer adopting a TRASOP receives an additional investment tax credit for contributions to the plan. The purpose of a TRASOP, building stock ownership into employees, is the same as an ESOP. A TRASOP is subject to the same restrictions and requirements imposed by the Internal Revenue Code on ESOPs and other qualified plans. In addition, the TRASOP is required to satisfy the requirements initially set forth in the Tax Reduction Act of 1975, revised in the Tax Reform Act of 1976, and incorporated into section 409A of the Internal Revenue Code by the Revenue Act of 1978.

C. How Does An ESOP Work?

The ESOP is designed to acquire stock of an employer for the benefit of employees. To do so, the ESOP often borrows money from a bank or other lender (including the employer). The stock is purchased directly from the employer or from shareholders. When the ESOP borrows money, the employer generally guarantees to the lender that the ESOP will repay the loan and that the employer will make annual payments to the ESOP sufficient in amount to permit the ESOP to make its annual payments on the indebtedness.

Because the ESOP is qualified, these annual contributions by the employer are generally tax-deductible. The employer is also permitted to make additional contributions of cash or stock to the ESOP each year, as determined by its board of directors. These contributions would also be tax-deductible, provided they do not exceed the limitations imposed by section 404 of the Code. The ESOP uses the proceeds of the loan to purchase stock of the employer.

D. How Does A TRASOP Work?

A TRASOP is also designed to provide stock ownership for employees; however, it is not designed to borrow money to purchase employer stock. To encourage an employer to transfer its stock to the plan, the Congress has provided an additional 1½ percent investment tax credit for employers which do so, beyond the normal 10 percent investment tax credit for which each employer is eligible. Since the employer receives a tax credit for its TRASOP contributions, they are not also tax-deductible.

E. What Do Employees Receive From An ESOP Or A TRASOP?

All cash and employer stock contributed to the ESOP or TRASOP, and employer stock purchased with cash borrowed by the ESOP or contributed by the employer, is allocated each year to the accounts of all employees who are participating in the ESOP or TRASOP. This allocation is done on the basis of an allocation formula to be explained in this handbook under *Allocation to Employees' ESOP and TRASOP Accounts.* All amounts allocated are held for employees in a trust under the plan. The trust is established under a written trust agreement, and is administered by a trustee who is responsible for protecting the interests of employees (and their beneficiaries).

An ESOP, like most employee benefit plans, is designed to benefit employees who remain with the employer the longest and contribute most to the employer's success. Therefore, an employee's ownership interest in cash and employer stock held in the ESOP is usually based on his number of years of employment with the employer. The employee's ownership interest in the ESOP is called his "vested benefit," and the provisions in the ESOP which determine his vested benefit are called the "vesting schedule." Although there are many vesting schedules which may be used by an ESOP, most vesting schedules are set up so that the longer an employee stays with the employer, the greater his vested benefit becomes. On the other hand, each employee who participates in a TRASOP is automatically 100 percent vested in all amounts held in the plan for his benefit.

If an employee terminates employment with the employer for any reason other than his retirement, or in some cases his death, his vested benefit under the ESOP will be determined by referring to the vesting schedule and determined by how many years he has worked for the employer. All cash and employer stock in which the employee does not have a vested benefit because he has not worked for the employer for enough years will be treated as a "forfeiture." Forfeitures are usually allocated among the ESOP accounts of the remaining employees on the same basis as employer contribution to the ESOP are allocated. This allocation method is explained later in this handbook under *Allocation to Employees' ESOP and TRASOP Accounts.*

If an employee retires, or in some cases if he dies, his vested benefit in cash and employer stock held for him in the ESOP will be determined without reference to the vesting schedule. Instead, he will have a 100 percent vested benefit in all ESOP assets held for him.

Even though employer stock and cash are usually put into the ESOP or TRASOP for an employee each year, and held in a special account under his name, he will normally not be able to actually receive a distribution of employer stock and cash from the plan until after his employment with the employer terminates and he ceases to be a participant in the plan.

After an employee's participation in the ESOP or TRASOP ends, he (or his beneficiary) will be eligible to receive a distribution of his vested benefit. There are many permissible times and methods for making the distribution to him. For example, an ESOP or TRASOP may provide that distribution will be made as soon as possible after an employee's termination of employment. On the other hand, the plan may require that any distribution be deferred until some later time, such as the normal retirement date set forth in the plan or the employee's death. However, distribution of a former employee's vested benefit under the ESOP or TRASOP must start soon after his death or attainment of age 65. Payment may be made to a former employee (or his beneficiary) in a lump sum, or it may be made in installments.

Distribution of an employee's vested benefit from an ESOP or TRASOP must normally be made in cash or shares of employer stock as determined by the administrator of the plan, subject to the distributee's right to demand a distribution of his or her benefit in stock. This is explained later in this handbook under *Distribution of ESOP and TRASOP Benefits and Stock Repurchases.*

Once a former employee (or his beneficiary) receives a distribution of his shares of employer stock from the plan, they are his property and he can do what he wants with them. He can vote the shares of employer stock at shareholders' meetings, receive any dividends paid on the stock by the employer, and he may keep the stock as long as he wishes.

However, if the stock is closely-held and he wishes to sell or otherwise transfer ownership of the stock to a third party, he *may* be required by the terms of the plan to first offer to sell the stock to the employer and the ESOP or TRASOP. This requirement is called a "right of first refusal." The employer and the ESOP (or TRASOP) can exercise this right and purchase the employer stock at its fair market value before the participant (or his beneficiary) may sell it to a third party. Generally, the price offered by the prospective buyer would establish the fair market value for the stock. The purpose of this right of first refusal is to protect a closely-held employer by preventing the stock from being acquired by outside parties who have no continuing interest in the employer or the ESOP or TRASOP and to protect the employer from violating any Federal law as a result of having its stock sold when it does not satisfy certain government rules. (These rules are explained later in this handbook under *ESOP and TRASOP Problem Areas*).

In addition, at the time the former employee (or his beneficiary) receives closely-held employer stock from the ESOP or TRASOP, he generally must be given a "put" option, the right to demand that the employer buy his shares of employer stock at their fair market value. In such a case, the provisions in the ESOP or TRASOP may provide that the plan may substitute for the employer and exercise a right to buy the employer stock. However, the plan may not be required by its terms to buy the stock under the put option. The purpose for requiring a put option for employer stock in the ESOP or TRASOP is to assure that each former employee (or his beneficiary) will have some available market for his shares of closely-held employer stock if he wishes to sell.

F. How Does An ESOP Or A TRASOP Benefit Shareholders?

Shareholders of closely-held corporations may not have a market for their stock if they wish to sell. This would also be true for the estate of a deceased shareholder. If the shareholder wishes to sell his stock, or if his estate needs to sell his stock to pay estate taxes, the only market for the stock (assuming that the employer had not adopted an ESOP or TRASOP) would be the employer, other shareholders, or some outside party. The problem for the estate could become critical as the time for paying estate taxes approaches. If the other shareholders lack the necessary cash to purchase the stock, the shareholder or his estate would have to sell the stock to the employer. However, a sale of less than all the stock to the employer could create serious problems for the seller unless the "stock redemption" rules of the Internal Revenue Code are satisfied. This is because the proceeds of the sale could be taxed as a dividend (that is, at ordinary income rates) if the stock redemption rules are not met. In addition, the employer might not have the necessary cash to purchase the stock. A repurchase of stock by the employer would have to be made with after-tax dollars and could seriously impede its operations. In such a situation, the stock might have to be sold to an outside party whose interests and objectives might not be consistent with those of the other shareholders and the employees of the company.

The ESOP or TRASOP may resolve these problems. The plan may act as a purchaser for this stock and the ESOP may borrow money to acquire it. Because the ESOP or TRASOP is a legal entity which is separate from the employer, sales of employer stock to the plan may be made without concern about the Internal Revenue Code's stock redemption rules, provided that the sale is properly structured. This means that the proceeds of the sale in excess of the seller's basis in this stock would be taxed to the seller at capital gains rates rather than as ordinary income. However, it must be pointed out that the selling shareholder or his estate would only be able to sell stock to the ESOP or TRASOP at its "fair market value"; this value is usually determined by an independent evaluation, and might not be as high as the shareholder or his estate think it is. (To sell stock to an ESOP or TRASOP at a price in excess of its fair market value may be treated as a "prohibited transaction" under the Code and the Employee Retirement Income Security Act of 1974, giving rise to excise tax penalties on the proceeds of the sale. It could also result in a determination that the plan is not being operated for the "exclusive benefit" of participants; this could potentially lead to disqualification of the plan under the Internal Revenue Code.) However, within the above limitations, the ESOP or TRASOP does provide a viable market for stock of a closely-held corporation, and in many cases it is the only market for such stock.

G. How Does an ESOP or a TRASOP Benefit Employers?

As a method of corporate finance, the ESOP provides extensive benefits for employers. Its existence as a market for stock in a closely-held corporation could enable the corporation to attract investors who might otherwise not purchase the stock because they normally would encounter difficulty in reselling it. However, it is important to note that the plan may not be obligated in advance to purchase employer stock. In addition, the employer might find that the ESOP or TRASOP serve as strong motivational tools for employees who recognize that they are acquiring an ownership interest in the company. Also, as explained more fully in this handbook under *The* TRASOP. Congress has provided an additional investment tax credit for employers who adopt certain forms of TRASOPs and contribute cash or stock to them. Finally, an ESOP permits the employer to raise capital in a way which carries with it beneficial tax treatment for the principal portion of any debt repayments.

Although it has not been effectively measured, many employers who have adopted an ESOP or TRASOP, and people who have been interested in these plans' motivational effects, feel that the realization by an employee that he has acquired an ownership interest in the company gives him a greater incentive toward his employer. Eventually, data will be developed to measure this phenomenon, but at this time the question of the ESOP's or the TRASOP's motivational value is mostly speculative. However, it has been somewhat documented in recent studies published by the U.S. Department of Commerce and the Department of Labor.

II. THE MECHANICS OF ESOP

A. Qualification Under the Internal Revenue Code

Like all other "qualified" plans, an ESOP must satisfy the requirements of the Internal Revenue Code and the income tax regulations.

That is, the ESOP must be operated under rules regarding eligibility, vesting, and other aspects of the plan which comply with the provisions of the Internal Revenue Code and the requirements of ERISA. In adopting an ESOP, an employer should consult with a professional who is experienced in establishing qualified plans so that the qualification of the ESOP will be assured.

B. Employer and Employee Contributions

1. Employer Contributions

Generally, an employer contribution to an ESOP is entirely within the sole discretion of its Board of Directors. That is, the employer's board of directors must determine the amount of its contribution (by dollar amount, formula or other means) and must notify participants of the amount of the contribution. In addition, the contribution to the plan must be made by the due date for the filing of the employer's Federal income tax return. The contribution may be in cash, company stock, or a combination of both.

However, in the event that the ESOP has borrowed money from a lender and the employer has guaranteed repayment of the loan to the ESOP, the employer's annual contribution to the ESOP generally should not be less than the ESOP's annual debt amortization of the loan (after taking into account dividends on employer stock in the ESOP). Annual dividends on company stock held by the ESOP may be used to pay a portion of the debt, thereby permitting a reduced annual contribution; however, because there can be no assurance as to the amount of the dividend, or even that a dividend will be declared each year, in considering the adoption of an ESOP an employer would be best advised to project an annual contribution to the ESOP in an amount at least equal to the annual ESOP debt payment.

Employer contributions to qualified employee benefit plans, including an ESOP, are tax deductible to the employer within the limitations imposed by section 404 of the Internal Revenue Code, as amended by ERISA.

Section 404(a)(3)(A) of the Internal Revenue Code provides that an employer may contribute to a stock bonus plan ESOP, and claim as a tax deduction, an amount equal to 15 percent of the compensation of participants under the plan for that plan year. In addition, if for any year the employer makes a contribution in an amount less than 15 percent of the compensation of participants under the ESOP, the Code permits the unused deductible amount to be carried forward to succeeding taxable years and to be added to the tax-deductible contribution for those succeeding years so that the employer may contribute, and deduct, an amount not in excess of 25 percent of the compensation of ESOP participants for that taxable year. This carryforward of unused tax-deductible contributions may be done until the unused amount is exhausted.

If the employer maintains an ESOP which consists of a stock bonus plan and a money purchase plan, or if the employer maintains a stock bonus plan ESOP and a separate pension plan, the employer is permitted by Code section 404(a)(7) to contribute, and deduct, up to 25 percent of the covered compensation under the ESOP and pension plan. However, these limitations apply only with regard to employer deductions, and have nothing to do with the limitations on annual allocations to participants' accounts also imposed by the Internal Revenue Code.

Since the ESOP is a qualified defined contribution plan, the employer maintaining the ESOP is subject to the limitations imposed by the Code on the amount which may be allocated to participants' accounts in any year. As stated above, the deduction limitations set forth in the Code may have the effect of imposing an indirect limitation on an employer's annual contribution by establishing a ceiling on the amount of the contribution which may be deducted each year for such a contribution.

The enactment of section 415 of the Code by ERISA imposed a major restriction on the amount of the annual contributions which an employer may make to a qualified plan or plans in any year. The Code now provides that the "annual addition" which may be allocated to the account of a plan participant each year may not exceed the lesser of 25 percent of his covered compensation or $25,000 (adjusted annually for cost-of-living increases). It is important to note that in determining the "annual addition" allocations to a participant's account for a year, the following items must be included: (1) employer contributions to all defined contribution plans in which the employee is a participant, (2) forfeitures and (3) the lesser of (a) one-half of the employee's contributions to the plan or (b) all of the employee's contributions to the plan in excess of 6 percent of his compensation. For example, if an employee earning $100,000 contributed $6,000 to the plan for the year, none of his contributions would be included in the "annual addition." However, if he contributed $10,000 to the plan for the year, $4,000 would be included in the "annual addition" since $4,000 is the lesser of (a) one-half of his contribution ($10,000 divided by 2=$5,000) and (b) his contributions in excess of 6 percent of his compensation ($4,000).

If the employer simultaneously maintains a defined benefit pension plan and a defined contribution plan (including an ESOP or a TRASOP), the section 415(c) limitation still applies. To determine whether the annual allocation to a participant's account is acceptable, section 415(e) applies a formula which adds a defined benefit fraction to a defined contribution (ESOP) fraction, the sum of which cannot exceed 1.4. The defined benefit fraction is: The participant's projected benefit at year end divided by the maximum benefit permitted by ERISA at year end.

This fraction assumes that the participant's compensation for all future years will remain constant. For example, if a participant's projected benefit at year end is $75,000 and the maximum benefit permitted for that employee is $75,000, the defined benefit fraction would be 1.0.

The defined contribution fraction is: The total annual additions to a participant's account through year end divided by the maximum annual additions which could have been made under ERISA.

The defined benefit fraction and defined contribution fraction are added together, and if their total exceeds 1.4, one or more of the employer's plans will be disqualified. It is critical to note that in applying these limitations, all defined contribution plans maintained by an employer are aggregated together, as are all defined benefit plans.

The limiting effect of section 415 of the Code must be recognized. Even though the provisions relating to deductability of employer contributions have the effect of limiting the amount of employer contributions, this is done indirectly. Section 404 only imposes a maximum on the amount of the contribution which may be taken as a tax deduction by the employer in any year; the employer would be free to contribute any additional amounts to the plan which it desired, provided it was not concerned with deducting these additional contributions from its corporate income tax.

In spite of the "chilling effect" the provisions of section 404 would have on the making of additional, nondeductible contributions, the ability to make these contributions continues to exist. However, the section 415 limitations on annual additions specifically preclude the allocation of any employer contributions to a participant's account which, when combined with reallocated forfeitures and in some cases a certain portion of employee contributions in any year, would exceed the maximum limitations established by the Code. This is, of course, extremely important to an employer which is using the ESOP as a financing vehicle and which wishes to borrow the maximum possible amount. If the loan amortization requires an annual ESOP contribution equal to 25 percent of the total covered compensation of all participants (which would be deductible under section 404), the employer might find that, as a result of unexpected forfeitures in a particular year, its contribution might have to be reduced to remain within the limitations on annual additions imposed by the Internal Revenue Code. This might result in an inability of the ESOP to make its full loan amortization in that year. For this reason, when an ESOP is being used as a financing vehicle, the employer might be well advised to project a maximum loan amortization rate, and annual contribution, of no more than 20 percent 22 percent of covered payroll, with the rest of the annual allocation among participants being made up of reallocated forfeitures. In this way, a default in the loan provisions would be unlikely to occur as a result of section 415.

It is important to note that Code section 415(c)(6) permits higher allocation to participants' accounts in ESOPs and TRASOPs, provided that certain requirements imposed by that section are satisfied by the plan.

2. Employee Contributions

In general, the maximum permissible employee contribution to a qualified defined contribution plan under IRS guidelines, including an ESOP, is 6 percent (mandatory) and 10 percent (voluntary) of that employee's covered compensation. However, the use of employee contributions to acquire company stock in an ESOP raises significant securities law issues which an employer adopting an ESOP should consider in deciding whether to require or permit employee contributions thereto. These are explained more fully in this handbook under *ESOP and TRASOP Problem Areas.* It should also be recognized that employee contributions to ESOPs or TRASOPs are not tax-deductible to the employee.

C. Allocations to Employees' ESOP and TRASOP Accounts

Although a stock bonus plan ESOP is not required to set forth a definite employer contribution formula, it must contain a definite formula for the allocation of employer contributions and forfeitures to participants in the plan. Forfeitures result when a participant terminates service without having a 100 percent nonforfeitable interest in all amounts allocated to his account. An employer has the option of adopting different formulae for the allocation of these amounts, provided that there is no discrimination in favor of officers, shareholders or highly compensated employees (the "prohibited group").

The most prevalent allocation formula, and the one required for TRASOPs, is based upon the relative compensation of each participant for the year. That is, if a participant's compensation is $10,000 and the total compensation of all participating employees is $1,000,000, his account would be credited with 1 percent of all employer contributions (plus forfeitures).

For example, his proportionate allocation of a $100,000 annual employer contribution and a forfeiture reallocation of $50,000 would be $1,000 and $500 respectively. Clearly, this formula results in greater dollar allocations for the more highly compensated participants. However, since it is applied equally to each participant, giving equal credit for each dollar of each individual's annual compensation, this formula is deemed not to be discriminatory. Although other factors may be involved which will produce a discriminatory situation, Code section 401(a)(5) specifically states that "Neither shall a plan be discriminatory . . . merely because the contributions or benefits of or on behalf of the employees under the plan bear a uniform relationship to the total compensation, or basic or regular rate of compensation, of such employees . . . ."

An alternative formula for allocating employer contributions and forfeitures, and the most basic, would be to provide an equal amount for each participant. However, this would not recognize that employee benefit programs, like salaries, are intended to reward the more productive employees.

A major problem arises, however, when the annual addition of contributions and forfeitures to the account of a particular participant in a year exceeds the limitations imposed by section 415 of the Code. In such a case, the allocations to this participant's account must be reduced to the extent necessary to conform to the Code restrictions, with the excess being reallocated among the accounts of the remaining participants pursuant to the allocation formula. If the total allocation of contributions and forfeitures is so large that each participant's proportionate share exceeds the Code limitations, ESOP allocations for that year must be reduced or the ESOP may be disqualified. It is also possible for forfeitures to be held in a suspense account for as long as one year to avoid exceeding these limitations.

As stated above, the allocation of TRASOP contributions is based upon each participating employee's relative compensation. However, compensation of an employee in excess of $100,000 may not be taken into account for purposes of determining the allocation of employer contributions.

D. Distribution of ESOP and TRASOP Benefits and Stock Repurchases

A participant's rights as to the timing of his distribution will be set forth in the ESOP or TRASOP. For example, the employer may feel it desirable to distribute a participant's benefits as quickly as possible after his termination of service. Generally, this distribution would be delayed until the close of the plan year in which the employee terminated service.

On the other hand, the employer may wish to defer any such distribution. Deferral of distributions is limited by the Code, which requires that, unless the participant elects otherwise, a plan must pay vested benefits to a participant commencing not later than the 60th day after the latest of the close of the plan year (a) in which the participant attains the earlier of age 65 or the plan's specified normal retirement age, (b) of the 10th anniversary of the year in which the participant commenced participation in the plan, or (c) in which the participant terminates service with the employer.

Even though an employer may defer the distribution of benefits to a terminated participant until the latest of the above dates, the employer may well wish to make distribution at the earliest date. This is because the plan administrator will be required to maintain a constant record of the location of a terminated participant and comply with ERISA reporting and disclosure requirements in order to make distribution of the participant's vested interest at the deferred date. It is no longer permissible for a participant's vested interest to be deemed forfeited merely because he cannot be located. For this reason, the employer may decide to avoid the time and expense required on the part of the plan administrator to maintain these records. In determining when to permit distribution of benefits after a participant terminates service with his employer, the employer must balance a desire to reduce these recordkeeping requirements with a desire to prevent having an employee leave in order to receive a distribution of his benefits.

In addition, an employer may be required to provide a market for any closely held stock distributed to a participant; it may also be desired that the plan actually make the repurchase. However, if all employer contributions are currently being used by the plan to amortize any indebtedness incurred to acquire employer stock, there may not be sufficient cash flow for the employer or the plan to repurchase distributed stock. Accordingly, it may be desirable to defer distributions from the plan.

The way in which a participant's vested benefit may be distributed to him from an ESOP depends upon the form of ESOP which the employer has adopted. If the plan has been designated as an ESOP and meets the requirements of the Treasury regulations, or if the

ESOP has been leveraged, or if the employer maintains a TRASOP, the participant's benefit may be distributed to him (or his beneficiary) in cash or employer stock, as determined by the terms of the plan. However, this is subject to the right of the distributee to demand that the distribution be in shares of employer stock. This right to demand a distribution of employer stock instead of cash must be communicated in writing to the participant (or his beneficiary) before the plan may elect to distribute cash. If the ESOP which the employer has adopted merely consists of a stock bonus plan, which is not intended to be leveraged and which is not an ESOP within the meaning of the Treasury regulations, the participant's benefit distribution may be subject to the rules which have traditionally been applicable to stock bonus plans. That is, the benefit must be distributable in as many whole shares of employer stock as possible, with the value of any fractional shares being distributable in cash.

Any distributee of a benefit consisting of closely-held employer stock from an ESOP or a TRASOP generally must be given a "put option" on the shares of employer stock distributed to him. That is, he must have the right to demand that these shares of employer stock be repurchased from him. The Treasury regulations on leveraged ESOPs and TRASOPs require that if the employer is precluded by law from repurchasing its own shares of stock (for example, a bank), the put option must be to a third party. The Senate Committee on Finance Report on the Revenue Act of 1978 specifically established the following terms which are applicable to any such put option:

1. Upon receipt of the employer stock, the distributee must have up to six months to require that the employer repurchase this stock, at its then fair market value. Although the obligation to repurchase stock under the put option would apply to the employer, not the ESOP or the TRASOP, it is permissible for the ESOP or TRASOP to actually make the purchase in lieu of the employer. If the distributee does not exercise the put option within the six-month period, the option will temporarily lapse.

2. After the close of the employer's taxable year in which the temporary lapse of a distributee's put option occurs, and following a determination of the value of the employer stock (determined in accordance with Treasury regulations) as of the end of that taxable year, the employer will notify each distributee who did not exercise the initial put option in the preceding year of the value of the employer stock. Each such distributee will then have up to three months to require that the employer repurchase his or her shares of employer stock. If the distributee does not exercise this put option, then the employer stock will not be subject to a put option in the future.

3. At the option of the party repurchasing employer stock under the put option, such stock may be repurchased on an installment basis over a period of five years. If the distributee agrees, the repurchase period may be extended to a period of ten years. As security for the installment repurchase, the seller must at least be given a promissory note, the full payment of which could be required by the seller if the repurchaser defaults in the payments of a scheduled installment payment. In addition, if the term of the installment obligation exceeds five years, the employee must be given adequate security for the outstanding amount of the note.

48-217 O - 80 - 3

4. Because a distributee might wish to transfer the ESOP or TRASOP distribution to an IRA in a "tax-free" rollover and because the rollover would have to be made before the expiration of the first six-month put option period, the IRA trustee must be able to exercise the same put option as the actual distributee.

A participant may receive his ESOP or TRASOP benefit in a lump-sum distribution during a single taxable year or in several annual installments. In addition, the TRASOP is subject to an additional restriction in that except in the case of death, retirement, or termination of service, no participant may receive a distribution of any amounts earlier than 84 months following the date it was contributed to the plan. An additional exception to the 84-month limitation would be for dividends paid on employer stock in the TRASOP; these dividends may be distributed to participants in the year they are received by the TRASOP. The major effect of these distribution methods will be discussed later in this handbook under *Taxation of ESOP and TRASOP Benefits.*

E. Voting Rights on ESOPs and TRASOPs

Prior to the enactment of the Revenue Act of 1978, only a TRASOP was required to provide voting rights for employees on employer stock held by the plan. However, the 1978 Act greatly modified this situation.

The Act continued the rule that, for all publicly-traded employer stock acquired by a TRASOP, employees must be entitled to direct the trustee as to the voting of this employer stock on all corporate issues. In addition, the Revenue Act (as revised by the Technical Corrections Act of 1979) specified that this rule would be applicable for publicly-traded employer stock acquired by a leveraged ESOP for taxable years beginning after December 31, 1979.

It was with regard to voting rights on closely-held employer stock held by qualified plans, however, that the Revenue Act of 1978 made its most significant changes. For all closely-held employer stock acquired after December 31, 1979 by a qualified defined contribution plan (ESOP, stock bonus plan, money purchase pension plan, profit sharing plan) which invests more than 10 percent of its assets in such stock, employees must be entitled to direct the trustee as to the voting of such stock on all corporate issues on which State law (or corporate charter) requires *more* than a majority vote.

These same rules are applicable for closely-held employer stock acquired by a TRASOP for taxable years beginning after December 31, 1978.

In the Committee on Finance report on the Revenue Act of 1978, it was mandated that the Treasury Department, working with the Department of Labor, congressional staffs and representatives of private business, conduct a study on voting rights and financial disclosure on employer stock and report to the Congress. Until the study is completed and reviewed by Congress, it is likely that the entire issue of voting rights will be in transition.

F. Use of Dividends On Employer Stock

If an employer which adopts an ESOP or TRASOP pays dividends on its stock, then the shares of stock held in the plan must likewise receive dividends. Rather than being a burden, however, this may prove a strong motivational effect to employees; the receipt by participants of dividends each year on the employer stock in the ESOP or TRASOP provides an annual reminder of their ownership in the employer. For this reason, an employer which has not paid dividends on its stock in the past may decide to do so in the future. Clearly, the ESOP or TRASOP will best benefit the employer and employee if they recognize their commonality of purpose.

Dividends paid on ESOP or TRASOP stock may be used in several ways. These amounts may be allocated to each participant's account, based on the number of shares held in the account. On the other hand, dividends on stock acquired with indebtedness may be used by the ESOP as additional amounts to amortize that indebtedness. Of course, since a TRASOP may not borrow funds to acquire employer stock, dividends on stock held in such a plan would not be used to repay any indebtedness; rather, they would be distributed to participants or allocated to their accounts. Finally, as provided in the Tax Reform Act of 1976, dividends paid on employer stock to an ESOP or TRASOP may be "passed through" the plan and paid to participants, based upon the number of shares of employer stock held in their accounts.

If the dividends are allocated to each participant's account in the ESOP or TRASOP and retained there, the participant will have no current tax liability. The amounts will simply be held and distributed to him along with his other ESOP or TRASOP benefits; at that time the participant will incur an income tax liability as explained later in this handbook under *Taxation of ESOP and TRASOP benefits.*

If dividends are used to amortize ESOP indebtedness, a proportionate amount of employer stock will be allocated to each participant's account, again based upon the number of shares in his account. The tax effect for the participant of the use of dividends in this way will be the same as if the dividends were retained in the ESOP and allocated to participants' accounts.

A participant will be taxed currently at ordinary income rates on any dividends which are "passed through" the ESOP or TRASOP and paid directly to him. In effect, these amounts will constitute extra remuneration to him each year; theoretically, these should make the participant more aware of his ownership in the employer and in the success of the company, since the size of the dividend will be a direct reflection of the employer's profitability.

G. Taxation of ESOP And TRASOP Benefits

When a terminated participant, or his beneficiary, receives a distribution of ESOP or TRASOP benefits, various Federal income tax results may occur. Section 402(a)(1) of the Code provides that, with certain exceptions, a distributee from a qualified employee benefit plan is taxable on the total distribution to him in the year when it is made. However, it is important to recognize that a participant will not be taxed on any distributed amounts which constitute his contributions to the plan. In addition, Code sections 402(a)(2), 402(e), and 2039(f) create certain exceptions for lump-sum distributions from qualified plans.

The actual determination of a participant's tax liability as a result of his distribution from an ESOP, TRASOP, or other qualified plan, is done as a series of factual and mathematical determinations, the first of which is to determine whether it qualifies as a lump-sum distribution and to determine which portion of the distribution is taxable. Pursuant to section 402(e) of the Internal Revenue Code, as amended by ERISA, if a terminated participant receives a distribution of his total ESOP or TRASOP benefits in a single taxable year, as a result of his death, disability, termination of service or attainment of age 59½, it will generally be treated as a lump-sum distribution; his Federal income tax liability on the shares of employer stock distributed to him by the ESOP or TRASOP will be based upon the original cost of the shares to the plan (or their market value at the time of distribution, if lower). That is, the amount of the distribution which is subject to Federal income tax will not include any increase in the value of employer stock while held by the plan. In addition, it will not include the value of any employee contributions to the ESOP or TRASOP.

The balance of the distribution will be taxable to the terminated participant (or his beneficiary). However, a portion of that distribution may be taxable at capital gains rates. This is determined by multiplying the amount of the taxable distribution by a fraction, the numerator of which is the participant's total number of calendar years of participation in the ESOP (or a plan which was amended into the ESOP) prior to 1974 and the denominator of which is his total years of plan participation. This portion will be taxable to the participant as long term capital gain. However, the participant may elect to treat the entire distribution as if it represented post-1973 employer contributions.

Although the remainder of the taxable distribution will be treated as ordinary income, the participant may be eligible for a special ten-year averaging method on this income. This averaging is permitted only for a lump-sum distribution following death or after the individual has been an ESOP or TRASOP participant (including participation in a plan which was amended into the ESOP) for at least five years prior to the distribution year. The election for the special ten-year averaging method is made by filing IRS Form 4972 with the participant's federal income tax return, for the year in which the distribution is made.

If the participant receives his ESOP or TRASOP distribution in more than a single taxable year or if it otherwise fails to qualify as a lump-sum distribution under section 402(e) of the Internal Revenue Code, the entire distribution will be taxed entirely at ordinary income rates, based upon the market value of the shares of employer stock at the time of distribution, and will not be eligible for the special ten-year averaging method.

The participant whose distribution qualifies for lump-sum treatment under section 402(e) will not recognize any taxable gain on the unrealized appreciation in value of his shares of employer stock until he sells the shares, either to the ESOP or TRASOP or the company pursuant to their "right of first refusal" or his "put" option, or to a third party. At that time, all appreciation in the value of the shares while in the ESOP or TRASOP will be taxable to him at long-term capital gain rates. Any appreciation in the value of the shares while they are in his possession will be taxable to him at capital gain rates, but the issue of whether the gain will be long or short term is based solely upon whether he holds the shares for a long enough period following distribution.

If a participant dies and his ESOP or TRASOP benefits are distributed to his designated beneficiary or his estate, $5,000 of the distribution may be excluded from the recipient's gross income, pursuant to section 101(b) of the Internal Revenue Code. In addition, if the entire distribution is paid to a participant's beneficiary in a single year and the distributee agrees in writing not to treat the distribution as a lump-sum distribution, the amount of the distribution will be excluded from the participant's taxable estate under section 2039(c) of the Internal Revenue Code. Finally, the participant may elect to roll over a part or all of his ESOP or TRASOP benefit to an individual retirement account (IRA), thereby deferring any taxability on the amount rolled over to the IRA until it is ultimately distributed to the participant (or beneficiary).

III. THE TRASOP

In the Tax Reduction Act of 1975, Congress created a new form of employee stock ownership plan, the "TRASOP." The Act provided that an employer which adopted a TRASOP and contributed to it an equivalent amount of stock, or cash used to acquire stock, would be eligible for an additional investment tax credit equal to 1 percent of its qualified capital investment each year. In the Tax Reform Act of 1976, Congress increased this additional investment tax credit to 1½ percent and extended its life through 1980, provided that the employer makes a TRASOP contribution equal to the additional ½ percent credit amount and provided that the employees contribute an additional amount equal to the ½ percent credit. By adopting and fully funding a TRASOP, an employer would be eligible for an 11½ percent investment tax credit instead of 10 percent. In the Revenue Act of 1978, the provision for the 1½ percent additional investment tax credit was made a part of the Internal Revenue Code (formerly it was only contained in the Tax Reduction Act of 1975, as amended by the Tax Reform Act of 1976) and its life was extended through 1983. Also, in the Revenue Act of 1978, the Congress also provided that this additional investment tax credit is not subject to any minimum tax. In addition, as explained earlier in this handbook, the Revenue Act of 1978 changed the name of the TRASOP, causing a great deal of confusion. The Technical Corrections Act of 1979 changed the name, hopefully for the last time, to "Tax Credit Employee Stock Ownership Plan."

As a result of the changes made by the Revenue Act of 1978, a TRASOP is required to be a "qualified" plan; this means that it must satisfy the Internal Revenue Code requirements which are applicable to all qualified plans. In addition, it must meet other tests which were set forth in the Tax Reduction Act of 1975, the Tax Reform Act of 1976, and the Revenue Act of 1978 (which are now contained in sections 409A and 48 of the Internal Revenue Code). Some of these additional requirements, such as employee voting rights on employer stock, have been explained elsewhere in this handbook. However, for ease of reference, they will be discussed in this section as well.

As stated above, the Revenue Act of 1978 mandated that the TRASOP be a qualified plan. However, because of the unique relationship between the plan and the investment tax credit, these plans are exempted from the traditional requirement that they be established by the last day of the employer's taxable year to be qualified for that first year. Because an employer may not know the actual amount of its investment tax credit for as long as eight and one-half months following the close of its taxable year, Congress felt that it would be a hardship to require that the plan be established for such a long period prior to its funding date. Accordingly, section 409A of the Internal Revenue Code specifically states that a TRASOP will be qualified for its initial year provided that it is established by the due date (including extensions) for the filing of the employer's Federal income tax return for that year.

Unlike other qualified plans, which may adopt various vesting schedules to determine when a participant has a 100 percent nonforfeitable interest in all amounts held in the plan for him, the TRASOP must provide each participant with an immediate, 100 percent nonforfeitable interest in his account. For employer stock acquired by a TRASOP for taxable years prior to December 31, 1978, this vested benefit may be reduced if the employer recaptures any portion of its investment tax credit. However, the Revenue Act of 1978 provided that for employer stock acquired for future taxable years, no withdrawal of prior contributions is permitted; this means that each employee will always be 100 percent vested in his account in the plan. As in the past, an employer will be able to take a tax deduction for any recaptured investment tax credit (for which no withdrawal from the plan is permitted) or reduce future plan contributions by the amount of the recapture.

Prior to the passage of the Revenue Act of 1978, each employee participating in the TRASOP was required to receive an allocation of the employer's contribution each year, irrespective of whether the employee was employed on the last day of the plan year. Congress recognized that this created an administrative problem for the employer since many employees would leave during the year and still be eligible for a share of the employer's contribution. Accordingly, by making these plans qualified, Congress deleted this problem, allowing these plans to establish the same participation requirements as other qualified plans, such as the requirement that a participant actually be an employee as of the last day of the plan year in order to receive an allocation of the employer's contribution. Any such allocations would be based upon the employee's compensation while he was actually employed, rather than while he was actually participating in the TRASOP, in any year. Of course, like other qualified plans, the TRASOP must satisfy the eligibility, nondiscrimination and coverage tests set forth in the Internal Revenue Code.

The Revenue Act of 1978 expanded the availability of TRASOPs to subsidiary corporations. Prior to its passage, a parent had to own 80 percent of a subsidiary before the subsidiary's employee could be covered under the parent's plan and receive an allocation of the parent's stock. The Revenue Act reduced this ownership requirement to 50 percent for first tier subsidiaries (it remains 80 percent for second tier and lower tier subsidiaries). In addition, the Act guaranteed that a subsidiary (including a 50 percent first tier subsidiary) will not recognize gain from the contribution of its parent corporation's stock to the plan for its employees. It is important to note, however, that the 80 percent standard will continue to be applied for all other purposes of determining the plan's qualified status or possible discrimination.

All TRASOP participants are required to be able to direct the trustee to certain degrees regarding the voting of employer stock held for them in the plan. As explained in this handbook under *Voting Rights On ESOP and TRASOP Stock*, if an employer sponsoring the TRASOP is publicly-traded, participants must be permitted to vote stock held in the plan on all corporate issues. However, if the employer stock is closely-held, the participants must be entitled to vote employer stock acquired for taxable years after December 31, 1979 (December 31, 1978 in the case of a *TRASOP*), on all corporate issues which, by State law or corporate charter, require the affirmative vote of more than a majority of outstanding shares. Traditionally, these would be issues such as corporate mergers, acquisitions, or disposal of substantially all of the employer's assets. As yet, the mechanics for the pass-through of this vote have not been determined.

A major problem area for TRASOPs has been the lack of guidelines regarding the timing of employer and employee contributions for the additional ½ percent investment tax credit. (Employer contributions for the 1 percent additional investment tax credit were required to be made by the filing date for the employer's Federal income tax return for a particular year.) This lack of guidance has presented a major impediment to the use of the additional ½ percent investment tax credit by employers.

The Revenue Act of 1978, as amended by the Technical Corrections Act of 1979, resolved that problem by providing that employees may have up to two years following the close of an employer's taxable year to make their ½ percent tax credit amount contributions to the plan and that the employer's matching contributions will be made as the employees make theirs. In this way, the problem which resulted when employees failed to make the full ½ percent contribution and the employer had to withdraw an already-contributed one-half percent amount (or portion thereof) from the plan because the additional tax credit was deemed to be recaptured is resolved. This change was also necessary because Congress removed the ability of the employer to withdraw prior contributions from the plan if a portion of the investment tax credit is recaptured.

Unlike most qualified plans, a TRASOP may not be integrated with Social Security. This means that participants' benefits may not be reduced by the amount of any Social Security taxes paid by the employer.

A TRASOP is subject to the same rules as an ESOP regarding distribution of benefits to participants (or beneficiaries), with the single difference that, except in the case of dividends or a participant's death, retirement or termination of service, no distribution of benefits may be made by the *TRASOP* prior to 84 months following the date of contribution by the employer. These rules are explained earlier in this handbook under *Distribution of ESOP and TRASOP Benefits and Stock Repurchases*. Like an ESOP, a TRASOP may at times distribute a participant's interest in cash instead of employer stock and, if the employer stock is closely-held, it will be subject to a "put option" by the participant (or beneficiary) and may be subject to a right of first refusal on the part of the plan or the employer. Publicly-traded employer stock, however, is not subject to a "put option" or right of first refusal. Finally, the tax results of a TRASOP distribution for the participant (or beneficiary) are the same as an ESOP distribution, as explained earlier in this handbook under *Taxation of ESOP and TRASOP Benefits.*

IV. ESOP AS A FINANCING TECHNIQUE

A. Basic ESOP Financing Model

Congress has clearly recognized ESOP as a corporate financing vehicle, in addition to its status as an employee benefit plan. Also, in ERISA Congress provided that an ESOP is the only qualified employee plan which may debt finance its acquisitions of employer stock through an extension of credit by a party in interest. The primary purpose for defining ESOP, under ERISA section 407(d)(6) and Code section 4975(e) (7), was to provide ESOPs with the special debt financing exemption from the general prohibited transaction rules under ERISA section 406 and Code section 4975.

Under the Trade Act of 1974 and the Tax Reduction Act of 1975, the Senate Finance Committee specifically defined ESOP as a technique of corporate finance, utilizing a stock bonus plan (which may be combined with a money purchase pension plan) qualified under Code section 401(a), designed to invest primarily in qualifying employer securities, and further designed: (i) to meet general financing requirements of the corporation, including capital growth and transfers in the ownership of corporate stock; (ii) to build into employees beneficial ownership of stock of their employer or its affiliated corporations, substantially in proportion to their relative incomes, without requiring any cash outlay, any reduction in pay or other employee benefits, or the surrender of any other rights on the part of such employees; and (iii) to receive loans or other forms of credit to acquire stock of the employer corporation or its affiliated corporations, with such loans and credit secured primarily by a legally binding commitment from the employer to make future payments to the trust in amounts sufficient to enable such loans to be repaid.

As a technique of corporate finance, an ESOP may utilize the credit of the employer corporation for the purpose of debt financing its acquisitions of employer stock, thereby allowing the employer to finance its capital growth and transfers in the ownership of its stock with pre-tax corporate dollars, while building ownership interests into its employees. The use of ESOP financing of new capital generally involves a loan from an outside lender to finance corporate expansion. The typical transaction is often structured as illustrated in the following diagrams:

In this situation, the ESOP borrows the money from a bank, and signs a promissory note for the money:

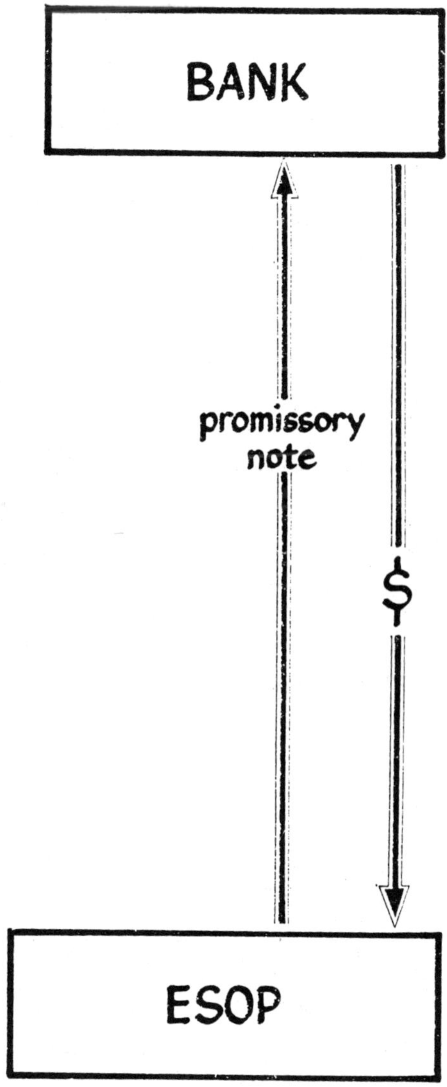

As part of the ESOP loan, the employer gives a written guarantee to the bank, promising that the ESOP will repay the loan and that each year the employer will pay to the ESOP enough money to permit the ESOP to make its annual repayment of the loan:

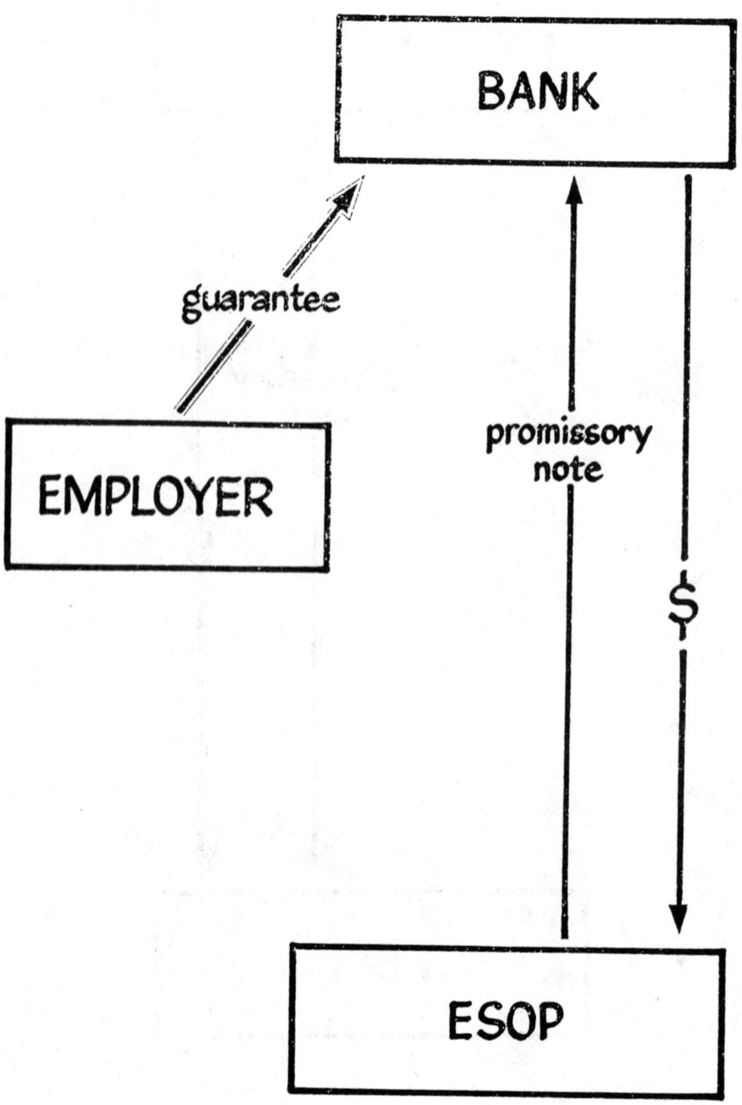

The ESOP then uses the money from the loan to buy stock from the employer:

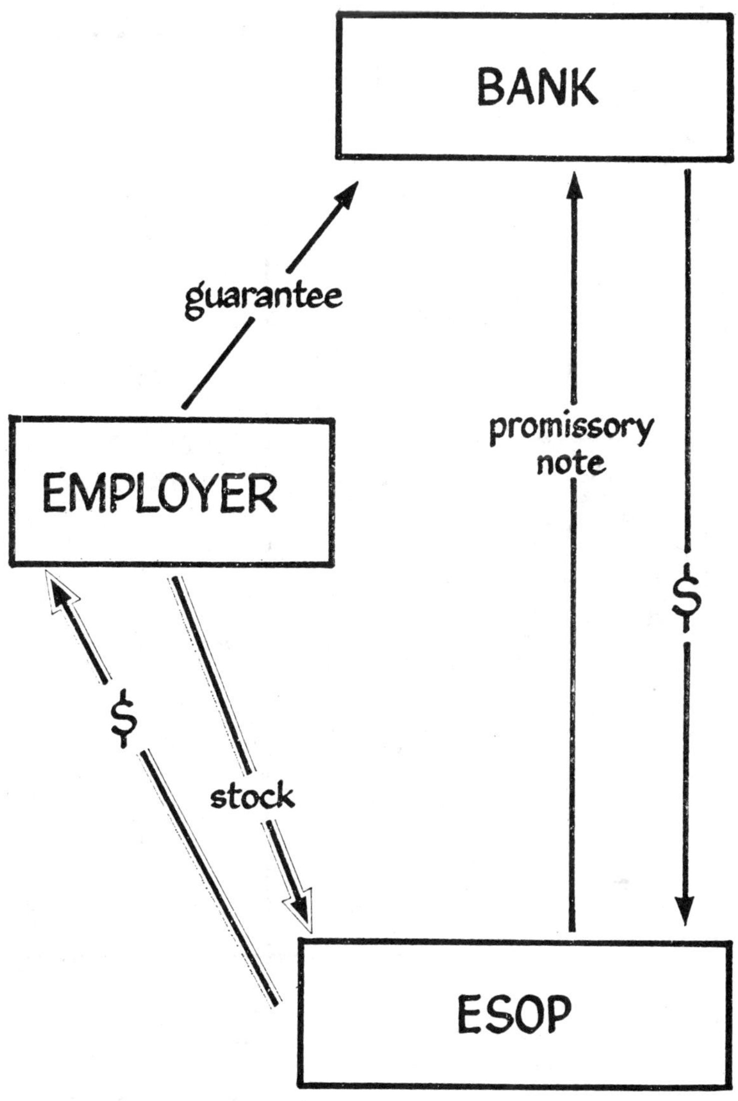

Each year, the employer makes a tax-deductible payment to the ESOP, sufficient to let the ESOP make its annual debt repayment to the bank:

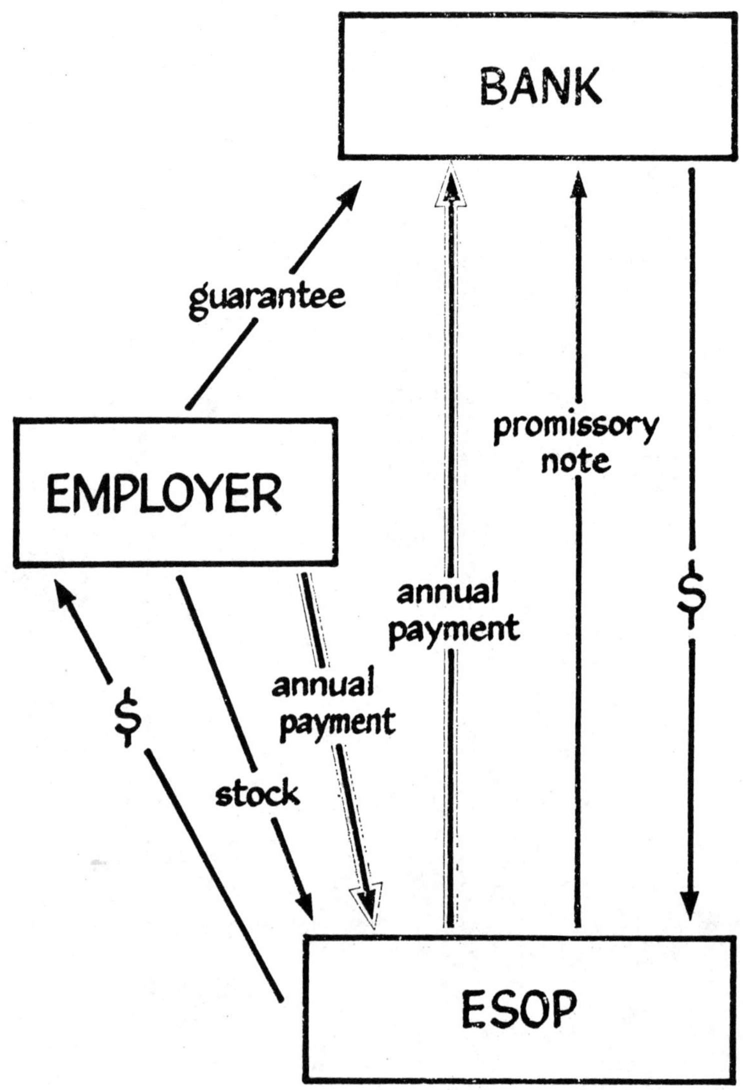

Through this technique of ESOP financing, non-recourse corporate credit has been extended to acquire employer stock for the benefit of employees, while enabling the corporation to finance its capital requirements with pre-tax dollars. In economic terms, it is the earnings generated by the underlying capital which are used to repay the acquisition indebtedness (of the ESOP) incurred for financing new capital. ESOP financing builds beneficial ownership of employer stock into employees, on a tax-deferred basis, without any personal financial risk by the employees and without requiring any reduction in their take-home pay.

B. Other Applications of ESOP Financing

The use of ESOP financing applies not only to the financing of new corporate capital for expansion purposes. With the consent of the lender, existing corporate debt may be refinanced through the ESOP, so that it is repayable (both principal and interest) with pre-tax corporate dollars. An existing corporate debt may be assumed by the ESOP, with the debt repayment guaranteed by the employer corporation. In such a case, the corporation will issue new shares of its stock to the ESOP equal in value to the principal amount of debt transferred to the ESOP. In addition, the new shares may be pledged as collateral to the lender, or specific corporate assets may be pledged as additional security for the loan. As the ESOP loan is repaid to the lender through annual employer contributions (or dividends on employer stock) received by the ESOP, shares of stock are allocated to accounts of participating employees. From the lender's standpoint, the debt should be more secure since repayments are made with pre-tax corporate dollars.

ESOP financing may also be used to finance acquisitions of other corporations. Loans may be secured from outside lenders to raise cash for financing the acquisition. The employees of the acquired corporation may be included as participants in the ESOP to provide a larger payroll base on which to make tax-deductible contributions to the ESOP to repay the debt. In addition, the pre-tax earnings of the acquired corporation are available for debt repayment.

ESOP financing provides an alternative for raising capital to closely-held corporations which are unable or unwilling to raise capital through a public offering of stock. The costs of a public underwriting (including SEC registration) and the expenses of operating as a publicly-traded company may be avoided through the alternative of ESOP financing. In addition, it may be preferable to existing owners and management to build ownership interests into employees of the corporation, rather than to create ownership by outsiders. For corporations which are already publicly-traded, the ESOP provides an alternative to the costs (and underwriting discounts) of a secondary offering of securities.

C. ESOP Financing of Transfers of Ownership

ESOP financing may also be used for the acquisition of employer stock from existing shareholders. Purchases of stock from existing shareholders may be financed through loans from outside lenders to the

ESOP or through loans to the ESOP directly from the employer corporation. Alternatively, the sale of employer stock to an ESOP by an existing shareholder may be effected through a cash (non-financed) transaction, or on an installment basis.

From the corporation's standpoint, a sale of stock to an ESOP by a shareholder enables pre-tax corporate dollars to finance the transaction, as compared to the use of after-tax dollars being used to finance a stock redemption by the corporation. More significant, however, may be the fact that a sale of stock to an ESOP would be treated as a sale to a third party other than the employer and may allow the selling shareholder to treat any gain on the sale as a capital gain, without being subject to the restrictions on corporate redemptions under Code section 302. That is, a sale of stock to an ESOP will not generally be treated as a sale to the corporation which may result in dividend treatment to the shareholder. However, an individual who is considering the sale of employer stock to an ESOP may wish to secure an advance ruling from the Internal Revenue Service so as to ensure capital gains treatment on the proceeds of the sale. In such a case, it would be necessary to satisfy the requirements of Revenue Procedure 77–30, Revenue Procedure 78–18 and Revenue Procedure 78–23.

The use of an ESOP for financing transfers of ownership of corporate stock has broad applications in corporate tax and financial planning, as well as in estate planning for major shareholders of corporations. The ESOP creates an "in-house" market for corporate stock, which may be available to acquire stock offered for sale by existing shareholders during their lifetime, upon their retirement from the business, or in the event of death.

A typical situation may involve a corporation which desires to establish an ESOP for building employee ownership, while at the same time allowing shareholders of non-publicly-traded stock to diversify their personal investments by selling a portion of their stock to the ESOP. An existing shareholder may generally treat any gain on the sale of stock to an ESOP as capital gain, whether he sells all or a part of his stock interest. A lifetime redemption through a sale of stock to the corporation directly will generally be treated as an exchange (rather than as a dividend distribution) only if the redemption is not essentially equivalent to a dividend, or is substantially disproportionate, or results in a termination of a shareholder's interest, under the provisions of Code section 302(b). Many private rulings from the Internal Revenue Service have concluded that a properly structured sale of employer stock by a shareholder to an ESOP (or to any qualified employees' plan) is not a redemption of the stock by the corporation, and therefore produces capital gain tax treatment on the sale proceeds.

Also, upon the death of a major shareholder, the ESOP may acquire all, or a portion, of his stock in the corporation from his estate, without being subject to the redemption limitations under Code sections 302 and 303. This use of an ESOP should permit the estate (and heirs) of the deceased shareholder to retain an ownership interest in the corporation, without the attribution rules of section 318 restricting the degree to which they may achieve diversification of investments.

In addition, an ESOP which has been in operation for several years will generally have had annual evaluations of the fair market value of its stock for purposes of sales of stock to the plan and annual reporting. This would also provide a basis for determining the value of the stock in a closely-held corporation for estate tax purposes, thereby providing greater certainty in estate planning for the major shareholders of the corporation.

An ESOP also provides an effective vehicle for financing the transfer of ownership from a retiring major shareholder to the employees of the corporation. It may be that the employees as a group are the logical successors in ownership, and it may prove difficult for the remaining employees (or the management group) to finance the purchase with personal after-tax dollars. An ESOP allows all employees to acquire ownership interests, with the purchase financed with future pre-tax earnings of the corporation, where employee interests are provided on a tax-deferred basis. In order to finance the acquisition, the ESOP may receive loans from an outside lender, from the corporation, or a portion of the purchase price may be paid to the selling shareholder on an installment basis by the ESOP.

ESOP financing may likewise be used in the divestiture of a corporate division or subsidiary to its employees. The stock of a subsidiary, or the stock of a new corporation established to acquire the business and assets of the division or subsidiary, may be sold to an ESOP. The ESOP may finance the purchase price with third-party loans or through an installment purchase. Any debt financing may be guaranteed, if necessary, by the transferor corporation as well as by the transferee corporation.

ESOP financing is also available to a publicly-traded company which desires to acquire stock for the benefit of its employees and to restrict (or even eliminate) public trading of its stock. However, the entire "going private" issue is extremely complex and an employer should consult experts in the securities law field before attempting to utilize an ESOP for this purpose. In such a case, the ESOP could make a tender offer for all or a portion of the employer's outstanding shares, financing the purchase price through loans from outside lenders or directly from the corporation. The objective of building employee ownership through an ESOP may well provide a valid business purpose for the use of corporate funds for "going private." Again, it is future pre-tax earnings of the corporation which will be available to finance the acquisition of its stock for the benefit of its employees.

D. Non-Financed Acquisitions of Employer Stock

In addition to the use of debt financing for the acquisition of employer stock, an ESOP may be utilized to provide employee ownership on a non-leveraged basis. In such a situation, it would function as a traditional stock bonus plan. Cash contributions to the plan or other eligible individual account plan may be used to acquire employer stock from existing shareholders by cash purchases on an annual basis. In addition, the ESOP may function as a conventional stock bonus plan which annually receives direct contributions of employer stock from the employer corporation. Direct stock contributions by the employer will result in tax deductions under Code section 404(a) (without any cash outlay) equal to the fair market value of the stock as of the date of the contribution.

V. FIDUCIARY RESPONSIBILITY

A. General Requirements Under The Employee Retirement Income Security Act of 1974

Like all qualified plans, an ESOP is subject to the fiduciary responsibility provisions of ERISA and the "exclusive benefit of employees" requirement under the Code. Specifically, the ESOP must satisfy the requirements of ERISA section 404(a)(1), which imposes upon fiduciaries the standard of discharging their duties under the plan ". . . solely in the interest of the participants . . . and for the exclusive purpose of providing benefits to participants. . . ." In addition, the "prudent man" standard of ERISA section 404(a)(1)(B) is applicable to ESOP fiduciaries, and the ESOP loan and stock purchase exemptions from the prohibited transaction provisions of ERISA section 406 must be met when the ESOP acquires employer stock.

In applying these fiduciary standards to an ESOP, it is important to understand the purposes of an ESOP as an employee benefit plan and the basis on which it is recognized for tax-qualified status. In the Revenue Act of 1921, stock bonus plans (the basic element of an ESOP) were first granted (along with profit sharing plans) tax-exempt status. It was not until the Revenue Act of 1926 that such status was extended to pension plans. The purpose for which stock bonus plans were granted tax-exemption was to encourage corporations to provide stock ownership interests to their employees. Providing retirement benefits for employees has always been a secondary purpose for the establishment of a stock bonus plan. In Revenue Ruling 69–65, the Internal Revenue Service stated that the purpose of a stock bonus plan is ". . . to give the employee-participants an interest in the ownership and growth of the employer's business . . ." The existing regulations under Code section 401(a), in defining the three categories of qualified plans, specify retirement benefits as a feature of pension plans, but not as a feature of profit sharing plans and stock bonus plan (except that benefits may be deferred until retirement). There appears to be no requirement under code section 401(a) that a stock bonus plan be a "retirement plan."

It may be argued that ERISA, in stating the objective of protecting retirement security of employees, has now imposed the standard of providing retirement benefits as the objective of all qualified employee benefit plans. However, there are specific references under ERISA to a different standard being applicable to different types of plans.

The definition of "pension plan" in section 3(a) of ERISA recognizes that a "pension plan" is one which "provides retirement income to employees *or* results in a deferral of income by employees for periods extending to the termination of covered employment or beyond." Section 402(b)(1) of ERISA requires " . . a procedure for establishing and carrying out a funding policy and method consistent with the objectives of the plan . . ." (not the objective of retirement security). Section 404(a)(1)(B) of ERISA sets out the prudent man standard as one applicable to ". . . the conduct of an enterprise of a like character and with like aims." The legislative history of ERISA recognizes

". . . the special nature and purpose of employee benefit plans . . ." and ". . . the special purpose . . ." of certain individual account plans which are designed to invest in employer securities. In addition, the definitions under ERISA Section 407(d)(6) and Code section 4975(e)(7) specify that an ESOP is ". . . designed to invest primarily in qualifying employer securities. . . ." The recognition of an ESOP as an employee benefit plan which may borrow to acquire employer stock further demonstrates Congressional intent that an ESOP is not primarily a retirement plan, but rather has as its primary objective the providing of stock ownership interests for employees.

This recognition by Congress of the special purposes of an ESOP does not exempt the ESOP from the general fiduciary standards of ERISA, but rather requires that the interpretation of these standards must be based upon the ESOP objective of providing stock ownership for employees. Retirement benefits may be provided to employees through their stock ownership acquired under an ESOP, but the fiduciaries are primarily directed to provide stock ownership (rather than retirement benefits) for employees in a manner consistent with the fiduciary duties under Title I of ERISA.

Accordingly, it would appear that a prudent ESOP fiduciary, subject to fiduciary duties under ERISA section 404(a)(1), is one which prudently acquires and holds, and in some cases distributes, employer stock for the benefit of participants (and their beneficiaries), prudently using debt financing where appropriate, in a manner consistent with the plan documents and the provisions of title I of ERISA. In order to avoid having ESOP acquisitions of employer stock be prohibited transactions under ERISA section 406 and Code section 4975, the special exemptions under ERISA section 408 must also be complied with by the ESOP fiduciaries.

B. Exclusive Benefit Requirement

ESOP purchases of employer stock must comply with the "exclusive benefit of employees" requirement under Code section 401(a), as well as the "exclusive purpose" and the "solely in the interest of the participants" requirements of ERISA section 404(a)(1)(A). In Revenue Ruling 69–494, the Internal Revenue Service outlined various investment requisites under the exclusive benefit rule which should be satisfied when a qualified employees' trust invests funds in employer securities. That ruling recognized that the exclusive benefit requirement with respect to investments does not prevent others from also deriving some benefit from a transaction with the trust, as a seller would make employer stock available to the trust only if there was a benefit to him by so selling. Accordingly, before ERISA, the Internal Revenue Service established the following "safe harbor" investment test which must be met for a purchase of employer stock to comply with the exclusive benefit requirements:

(1) the cost must not exceed fair market value at the time of purchase;

(2) a fair return commensurate with the prevailing rate must be provided;

(3) sufficient liquidity must be maintained to permit distributions in accordance with the terms of the plan; and

(4) the safeguards and diversity that a prudent investor would adhere to must be present.

With respect to an ESOP, it appears that only the "fair market value" and "prudent investor" requirements are applicable. Revenue Ruling 69–65 specifically exempts stock bonus plans (and presumably any ESOP) from the requirement for a fair return on employer stock. The ESOP is likewise exempt from the diversification of investments requirement under ERISA Section 404(a)(2), as an "eligible individual account plan" to the extent of investments in employer securities.

Therefore, an ESOP's acquisition of employer stock from the employer corporation, or from an existing shareholder, would satisfy the exclusive benefit requirement of ERISA and Code section 401(a), so long as the investment is one that is prudent for an ESOP fiduciary and the purchase price does not exceed fair market value. Section 408(e) of ERISA, which provides for an exemption from the prohibited transaction rules for the acquisition of employer stock from a party in interest, appears to require a purchase price equivalent to the fair market value of the stock.

C. Diversification Exemption

Section 404(a)(2) of ERISA specifically provides that an eligible individual account plan is not subject to the general diversification requirement of section 404(a)(1)(C), nor any diversification requirement under the prudent man standard, to the extent that it acquires and holds qualifying employer securities. ERISA section 407(b)(1) specifically exempts eligible individual account plans from the 10 percent limitation on investments in employer securities. An ESOP is included in the definition of eligible individual account plan under section 407(d)(3) if the ESOP explicitly provides for the acquisition and holding of employer stock. As long as the acquisition and holding of employer stock satisfy the general prudence and exclusive benefit requirements, it would appear that up to 100 percent of the assets under the ESOP may be invested and held in employer stock without violating the fiduciary duties of ERISA section 404(a).

The degree to which an ESOP *must* be invested in employer stock, in order to satisfy the ". . . designed to invest primarily . . ." requirement of ERISA section 407(d)(6)(A) and Code section 4975(e)(7)(A), is not specifically set forth in the Internal Revenue Code or the income tax regulations. This requirement was intended by Congress to be of a qualitative nature (based upon the purposes of an ESOP and its design), rather than a quantitative test to be satisfied at all times.

D. Prohibited Transaction Exemptions

Without the special exemptions provided in ERISA section 408 and Code section 4975(d), ESOP financing transactions might be prohibited transactions under ERISA section 406(a) and Code section 4975(c). Congress, however, recognizing the special purposes and objectives of an ESOP, as both an employee benefit plan and a technique of corporate finance, included exemptions for certain transactions from the general prohibited transactions rules.

1. Acquisitions of Employer Stock

Section 406(a)(1)(A) of ERISA and section 4975(c)(1)(A) of the Internal Revenue Code include as a prohibited transaction a ". . . sale or exchange . . . of any property between a plan and a party in interest (or a disqualified person). . . ." Without an exemption, an ESOP (or any other eligible individual account plan) would be prohibited from acquiring employer stock from the employer corporation or from any shareholder who is a party in interest. This would generally limit acquisitions of employer stock to purchases from shareholders who own (directly or indirectly) less than 10 percent of the employer's stock and are not otherwise "insiders." However, ERISA section 408(e) and Code section 4975(d)(3) provide exemptions that permit the acquisition of employer stock by an ESOP from a party in interest (or a disqualified person) so long as the purchase price constitutes "adequate consideration" and no commission is charged with respect to the transaction.

"Adequate consideration" is defined in ERISA section 3(18) in a manner which generally restates the requirement for "fair market value" set forth in Revenue Ruling 69-494. Where there is a generally recognized market for employer stock, adequate consideration is the price prevailing on a national securities exchange (if applicable), or the offering price established by current bid and asked prices quoted by independent parties. Where there is no generally recognized market for employer stock, adequate consideration is fair market value, as determinated in good faith and in accordance with generally accepted methods of valuing closely-held stock and in accordance with regulations to be promulgated by the Secretary of Labor.

In the event that the purchase price paid for employer stock by an ESOP to a party in interest exceeds adequate consideration, a prohibited transaction results. If the party in interest is a disqualified person as defined in Code section 4975(e)(2), the excise tax and correction requirements of that section are applicable. An initial 5 percent per year excise tax is imposed on the disqualified person, based upon the "amount involved." If the transaction is not "corrected" within the allowable correction period, the additional excise tax of 100 percent of the amount involved is imposed. Any excise tax imposed is paid by the seller, and is not tax deductible.

It is important to note that the Internal Revenue Service, in the self-dealing regulations for private foundations states that a good faith effort to determine fair market value is ordinarily shown where (a) the person making the valuation is not a disqualified person and is both competent to make the valuation and is not in a position to derive an economic benefit from the value utilized, and (b) the method utilized in the valuation is a generally accepted method for valuing for purposes of arm's length business transactions where valuation is a significant factor.

Therefore, the valuation of employer stock is the most significant aspect of ESOP transactions when there is no generally recognized market for employer stock and a valuation by an independent appraiser, experienced in valuing closely-held corporations, is essential for alleviating the potential liabilities for prohibited transaction excise taxes. Presumably, traditional IRS guidelines for valuation in estate tax matters, as set out in Revenue Ruling 59–60, will be the basis for Department of Labor regulations defining fair market value under ERISA.

2. Debt-Financing Transactions

Section 406(a)(1)(B) of ERISA and Code section 4975(c)(1)(B) include as a prohibited transaction any ". . . direct or indirect . . . lending of money or other extension of credit between a plan and a party in interest (or disqualified person). . . ." Without an exemption, this provision would prohibit any debt financing for the acquisition of employer stock by an ESOP, where a party in interest extends credit through a direct loan, a loan guarantee or an installment sale.

However, ERISA section 408(b)(3) and Code section 4975(d)(3) provide an exemption from the prohibited transaction rules, available only to an ESOP and not to other eligible individual account plans, which permits an ESOP to borrow money involving an extension of credit from a party in interest to effect its acquisitions of employer stock. It is this exemption that distinguishes an ESOP from other plans which invest in employer stock and characterizes an ESOP as a technique of corporate finance.

The following conditions are imposed by ERISA for the ESOP loan exemption:

(*a*) the ESOP must satisfy the statutory definition of ERISA section 407(d)(6), Code section 4975(e)(7) and IRS regulations;

(*b*) the loan must be primarily for the benefit of participants;

(*c*) the interest rate must be reasonable; and

(*d*) any collateral given by the ESOP to a party in interest must be limited to qualifying employer securities.

In addition, further guidelines have been established in regulations promulgated by the Internal Revenue Service (and the Department of Labor) through an interpretation of the term ". . . primarily for the benefit of participants. . . ." Certain of the additional conditions for the ESOP loan exemption are clear from legislative history relating to the ESOP financing concept (both before and after ERISA) and from the regulations issued by the Department of Labor. The following additional requirements are included in the regulations and must be satisfied in order to exempt an ESOP debt financing transaction from the general prohibited transaction rules.

(1) The loan (or other extension of credit) must be for the purpose of acquiring employer stock or repaying a prior exempt loan and must be based on equitable and prudent financing terms. The interest rate must not be so high that plan assets might be drained off, and the terms of the loan must be as favorable to the ESOP as the terms resulting from arm's length negotiations between independent parties.

(2) Any collateral pledged by the ESOP (whether or not pledged to a party in interest) must be limited to the shares of employer stock acquired with the proceeds of that loan or freed from prior encumbrance by the proceeds.

(3) In general, any shares of employer stock given as collateral by the ESOP must be released from pledge on a pro-rata basis as loan principal is repaid.

(4) The liability of the ESOP for repayment of the loan must be limited to contributions received from the employer corporation (other than contributions of employer stock) and to earnings on trust assets, including dividends on employer stock.

(5) The lender must have no recourse to assets held in the ESOP other than employer stock remaining pledged as collateral.

If an ESOP debt financing transaction fails to satisfy the conditions for the exemption, a prohibited transaction may result under Code section 4975. In that event, the initial 5 percent per year excise tax would be imposed on any disqualified person extending credit to the ESOP, with the additional 100 percent tax being imposed if the transaction is not corrected. For purposes of the excise tax, the entire loan principal may be the amount involved, or the amount involved may be limited to that portion of the loan (or interest thereon) which causes the prohibited transaction to occur. Correction may require adjustment in the terms of the ESOP loan or, in some situations, rescission of the transaction. The regulations promulgated by the Internal Revenue Service and the Department of Labor deal with this issue on a more in-depth basis.

VI. ESOP AND TRASOP PROBLEM AREAS

A. Conversion of Existing Plans Into ESOP

Many employers maintaining a qualified plan may wish to replace that plan with an ESOP. This can be accomplished by amending the plan (such as a defined contribution plan like a profit sharing plan or money purchase plan) into an ESOP or terminating the plan (such as a defined benefit pension plan) and replacing it with an ESOP. Each such transaction carries with it certain additional responsibilities or potential problem areas which must be considered when conversion to an ESOP is contemplated.

The clearest example of additional responsibilities and potential problem areas which arise occurs when an ESOP replaces an existing defined benefit pension plan. Under the Internal Revenue Code, the replacement of a defined benefit plan by a defined contribution plan (such as an ESOP) constitutes a termination of that plan. Each participant in the defined benefit plan is deemed by the Code to be 100 percent vested in his benefits under the plan to the extent that they have been funded; this overrides any vesting schedule established under the pension plan. In addition, each participant's pension benefit may become subject to the plan termination insurance provisions of ERISA. These pension benefits may be guaranteed up to certain limitations by the Pension Benefit Guaranty Corporation (PBGC). If the employer has failed to sufficiently fund the retirement benefits of its employees under the plan, the PBGC will make up the difference between the guaranteed benefits and the funded amount. This becomes critically important to the employer which considers terminating its pension plan, because the employer may be liable to the PBGC for all or a portion of this amount. This potential liability must be carefully considered.

In addition, the PBGC has established certain procedures which might prove troublesome if the employer wishes to use the assets in the defined benefit pension plan to acquire employer stock under an ESOP. The PBGC requires that each employee be given an opportunity to elect, in writing, to have his pension plan assets converted to employer stock; this brings the closely-held employer into a direct confrontation with the securities laws, as explained more fully later in this handbook under *Securities Laws*, because this is considered an investment decision on the part of the employee and, absent some specific exception from registration, the employer would be compelled to register its securities with the Securities and Exchange Commission (SEC). SEC registration is very expensive. This potential liability must also be carefully considered.

Even if the employer determines that the potential PBGC and SEC obstacles are not insurmountable, a final problem remains. Absent a plan provision which gives employees the investment discretion on plan assets, the conversion of assets which are invested in a diversified portfolio to a single investment (employer stock) could create "prudence" liabilities for the plan trustees, especially if the value of the employer stock decreases in value or fails to increase in value at the same rate as that previously attained by the diversified assets.

It is critical to note that problems relating to asset valuation, prudence and exclusive benefit also exist if an existing profit-sharing plan or money purchase plan is amended into an ESOP and diversified assets are converted to employer securities, although the PBGC and SEC obstacles are not present.

However, this is not to state that conversion of an existing plan to an ESOP should not be undertaken. For example, assuming that existing plan assets are left in a diversified investment portfolio, revision of a profit-sharing plan or money purchase pension plan into an ESOP and investment of future employer contributions in employer stock should present no problem nor should the conversion of a defined benefit pension plan (provided that the plan termination results for the defined benefit plan are not deemed to be too serious). The employer should analyze the objectives in converting the plan to an ESOP and decide whether any potential obstacles present too severe a problem.

B. Securities Laws

As explained earlier in this handbook under *Conversion of Existing Plans into ESOP*, certain aspects of an ESOP may require compliance with the rules and regulations of the SEC. For publicly-traded employers, this should create no problem, since such an employer is already satisfying the reporting requirements of the SEC. However, the filing of an S–8 registration with the SEC may still be necessary. For the closely-held employer, however, the resulting costs of SEC compliance might be too expensive and troublesome. For this reason, the closely-held employer should administer its ESOP in a way which will not subject its stock, or the ESOP, to SEC registration requirements.

Historically, the SEC has not required the registration of the securities of an employer adopting a non-contributory ESOP or TRASOP or of the participants' interests in the ESOP or TRASOP. Initially, as reflected in numerous SEC "no action" letters, this was based upon the determination that there was "no sale" of employer securities to ESOP participants. In later "no action" letters, the SEC based its decision upon a determination that its policies did not warrant the expensive reporting and disclosure which would accompany the sale of these securities.

However, certain aspects of ESOP operation may result in a requirement by the SEC that registration of these securities be made. If employees are required or permitted to make ESOP contributions for the acquisition of employer securities, or, if the employee TRASOP contributions are used to acquire employer securities other than on the public market, this would clearly constitute the sale of these securities to the employees and require SEC registration unless another exemption is available. This would also be true if the ESOP were to give each employee any discretion as to whether or not plan assets were to be used to acquire employer stock. This discretion, like the election required by the PBGC, would be treated as an investment decision and require SEC registration.

With the exception of these limited situations, however, no SEC registration problem should arise for the closely-held employer. However, stock distributed to participants would generally be restricted stock under applicable securities laws.

C. Liquidity Problems

An employer which adopts an ESOP or TRASOP and whose stock is not publicly traded must be sure that the plan is sufficiently funded to permit a distribution of benefits to each participant. This is true whether the participant's benefit is distributed in cash or closely-held employer securities which are resold to the plan or the employer in exchange for cash.

As described earlier in this handbook under *Distribution of ESOP And TRASOP Benefits And Stock Repurchases*, subject to the right of the ESOP or TRASOP participant (or beneficiary) to demand that benefits be distributed in shares of employer stock, the plan may elect to distribute these benefits in cash. In such a case, it is important that the plan have sufficient cash available to make cash distributions to each eligible distributee.

If the distributee elects to demand a distribution of employer stock, and this stock is closely-held, there must be sufficient cash available to permit the employer or the plan to acquire that stock if the distributee exercises his "put" option on these securities and the plan wants to acquire the stock in lieu of the employer, or to permit the plan to exercise its "right of first refusal" in the event the distributee desires to sell this stock to an unrelated third party.

Finally, if the distributee desires to resell this stock at a time when the "put option" has expired, or if the distributee of publicly-traded employer stock desires to resell this stock, the plan may need sufficient cash if it wishes to repurchase this stock.

For this reason, the employer should maintain the plan so as to provide sufficient liquidity from its inception. Reference would be made to the turnover history of plan participants, each participant's annual compensation, and the financial history and future projections of the employer. If an employer encounters difficulties in making these determinations, an analysis should be performed by someone experienced in making such determinations.

VII. EMPLOYEE COMMUNICATIONS

For an ESOP or TRASOP to have its best effects on increased employee motivation and productivity, the committee believes that the plan concepts must be adequately communicated to employees. Clearly, an employee will be most concerned about the economic future of his or her employer if that employee recognizes that he or she has an ownership interest in the company. However, most employers have been unable to develop adequate communications materials to deal with concepts as sophisticated and technical as employee stock ownership plans. Accordingly, the committee has included in this handbook samples of several alternative employee communications materials. These materials are included herein merely as examples, since they are copyrighted by the companies which created them; the committee appreciates the willingness of these companies to have the communications materials included in this handbook.

Chapter Fourteen

GOVERNMENT POSITIONS ON TAX SHELTERS

Because of the large tax shelters offered by some programs and the lack of economic viability of others, it is essential for the I.R.S. to patrol the tax shelters in the market place to prevent tax abuse. The following material issued by the government helps investors to avoid poor quality tax shelters and minimize I.R.S. audits.

EXAMINATION TAX SHELTERS HANDBOOK

Manual Transmittal

Department of the Treasury — Internal Revenue Service

4236–8

January 12, 1981

Purpose

This transmits revised text for Chapter 700, Commodity Option and Futures, for IRM 4236 Examination Tax Shelters Handbook.

Nature of Changes

Section 750, Examination Techniques, has been revised to require the use of Form 6578, Option Straddle Worksheet, to document straddle transactions.

Supply of Forms

An automatic, initial distribution of Form 6578 will be made to all districts without requisition. Additional quantities of the Form can be ordered on Form 16 through regular supply channels.

/s/ John L. Wedick, Jr.
Director,
Examination Division

Filing Instructions

Remove:	*Insert:*
4236–125 through 4236–127	4236–125 through 4236–127

List of Current Pages

Current Manual Supplements

Table of Contents

Table of Contents

(Next page is 5236-2.1)

Table of Contents

Introduction

110 *(3-2-79)* 4236
Purpose of Handbook

(1) This Handbook has been prepared to assist examiners in the examination of tax shelter returns.

(2) This Handbook will enable examiners to shorten the time needed to acquire the skill essential to this specialty. However, nothing contained herein should discourage examiners from improving upon these techniques or from exercising their own initiative and ingenuity when the requirements of a particular taxpayer situation dictates that such action be taken.

120 *(3-2-79)* 4236
Contents and Distribution of this Handbook

121 *(3-2-79)* 4236
Contents

(1) This Handbook is a compilation of the examination techniques used by some of our most experienced revenue agents. They are presented in a manner intended to illustrate the problems frequently encountered in examining cases in the tax shelter area.

(2) The cases are subject to factual development and substantiation from the legal documents connected with each transaction. These techniques are interspersed with discussions of the legal aspects of the particular transaction(s) being considered.

(3) References to the IRC, court decisions, revenue rulings, etc., will be general and brief in nature and should not be relied upon for providing a thorough understanding of this particular subject matter. Rather, these guidelines should be supplemented by further researching a particular tax issue.

(4) These examination methods and techniques are not all-inclusive and are not intended to be mandatory procedures and instructions for field personnel. Examiners should adapt these procedures to the particular case that they have under consideration.

(5) This Handbook does not alter existing technical or procedural instructions contained in the IR Manual. Procedural statements are for emphasis and clarity and are not to be taken as authority for administrative action.

122 *(3-2-79)* 4236
Distribution

Distribution of this Handbook is being made to all revenue agents, full working level tax auditors, appropriate Examination, supervisory and management personnel in all district offices, and to all offices of the Assistant Regional Commissioner (Examination). In addition, distribution is being made to all Appeals Officers and regional Appeals managers.

(Next page is 4236-7)

210 *(3-2-79)* 4236
The Tax Reform Act of 1976

The Tax Reform Act of 1976 enacted several laws which are applicable to motion picture tax shelters. These provisions preclude much of the abuse previously associated with movie shelters. Consideration of the following code sections may eliminate the necessity for much of the detailed audit activity discussed later in this Chapter.

211 *(3-2-79)* 4236
IRC 280—Production Service Motion Pictures

IRC 280 provides that amounts attributable to the production of a film, sound recording, or book, other than costs which are capitalized, are deductible only for those taxable years ending during the period in which the taxpayer reasonably may be expected to receive substantially all of the income he/she will receive from the property. Proration of the production costs is required using the same ratio as the income received for the year bears to the total anticipated income during the period. This provision is effective for amounts paid or incurred after December 31, 1975, for production beginning after December 31, 1975, and applies to all taxpayers except regular corporations.

212 *(3-2-79)* 4236
IRC 465—Limitation of Losses to Amount at Risk

IRC Section 465, which is generally effective for tax years beginning after 1975, prevents taxpayers from deducting losses in excess of the amount actually at risk in film or video tape activities as well as certain other activities. These provisions apply to losses sustained by noncorporate taxpayers (including partners), Subchapter S corporations, and personal holding companies.

220 *(3-2-79)* 4236
Basic Types of Movie Tax Shelter Cases

(1) The first type of movie shelter is the completed film purchase or negative pick-up tax shelter.

(a) In the negative pick-up motion picture tax shelter, a limited partnership is the most commonly chosen entity through which to maximize tax benefits. A syndicate of investors usually forms a limited partnership which purchases a completed film for a cash down payment plus a nonrecourse note given to the seller (the note does not generally become due for a period of 7 to 10 years). The nonrecourse note probably represents at least 75 to 80 percent of the purchase price. (Usually, the leverage factor in this type of transaction is 3 or 4, or more, to 1.) Many of these film transactions involve foreign-produced films.

(b) The partnership usually turns over the function of distributing the picture to a distributor (which may be the same person (or a person related by stock ownership to the person) who sold the film to the partnership), who makes prints, arranges showings and handles advertising and promotion in return for a percentage of the gross receipts.

(c) The nonrecourse note is usually secured by the film rights, and payments on the note prior to the due date are only required to the extent of a percentage of the net proceeds from distribution of the motion picture. No liability exists for the balance of the note except to the extent the taxpayer receives net distributions from the motion picture.

(d) The limited partners are usually high income individuals who have no knowledge of the motion picture film industry.

(e) High income individuals also purchase completed movies, short features, and documentaries for a cash down payment plus a nonrecourse note. These individuals report income and deductions on Schedule C of their individual income tax return. The audit techniques applicable to this type of tax shelter entity are found in sections 250 and 260 of this Handbook.

(2) The second type of movie shelter is the Production Company or Service Company Shelter.

(a) Three parties may be involved in the arrangement: the "owner" of the rights to a screenplay, the production service company, and the distributor of the picture when it is completed. For example, the film rights may be "owned" by a separate entity formed by promoters of the tax shelter solely for that purpose. The completed film may be distributed by a major studio under a separate distribution contract with the "owner." (The film rights may even have been originally acquired by the major studio and assigned to the "owner.") However, the arrangement could involve only two parties. For example, ownership of the film rights could be retained by a major studio that would also distribute the picture.

(b) The owner's requirements for the production of the film are spelled out in considerable detail in the production agreement, and the owner will generally retain some rights of quality control, for example, the right to request added scenes and retakes.

(c) Production services are managed by the general partner or an individual producer who is preselected by the owner.

(d) The production cost of the film comes from capital contributions made by the limited partners and a substantial nonrecourse loan, which may be made by a bank, but is guaranteed by the owner or the distributor of the film.

(e) The limited partnership does not have any ownership interest in the film and it deducts production costs on the cash method of accounting. Because there is no income during the production period, a large loss is generated. The limited partners claim their share of the loss to the extent of their capital contributions and their share of the nonrecourse loan.

(f) After the film is completed, it is delivered to the distributor who makes prints of the negatives and has the film exhibited publicly. The distributor receives a percentage of the gross receipts generated by the film exhibition.

(g) By agreement, the distributor, directly or indirectly through the owner, makes payments to the partnership to cover the production costs plus a profit. Also by agreement, the partnership has no claim to these payments until the nonrecourse loan is repaid.

230 *(3-2-79)* 4236

Features Applicable to Negative Pick-up and Film Production Partnerships

231 *(3-2-79)* 4236

Organizational Entities

The organizational entity used in most motion picture shelters is the limited partnership. The limited partners may be individuals, corporations, 1120-S corporations, trusts, estates, or other partnerships or joint ventures. A limited partner may be another limited partnership. This is called "tiering." See Exhibit 200-2 for an example of partnership tiering.

232 *(3-2-79)* 4236

Letter Rulings

During tax shelter limited partnership examinations, it should be determined if the partnership has received letter rulings. If a partnership has a letter ruling, you should determine if you have the first taxable year of the ruling. A determination should be made as to whether the facts of the consummated transaction agree with the facts set forth in the letter ruling.

233 *(3-2-79)* 4236

Payments to General Partner for Organizing the Limited Partnership

Payments to a general partner or other persons for organizing a limited partnership and for selling the partnership interests constitute payments for capital expenditures within the meaning of IRC 263. Therefore, even though the payment to the general partner for services rendered in organizing the limited partnership are payments within IRC 707, they are not deductible by the partnership under IRC 162, since they are capital expenditures (*Rev. Rul. 75-214,* 1975-1 C.B. 185). Also see IRC 709 for treatment of organization and syndication fees incurred by partnerships in taxable years after December 31, 1975.

234 *(3-2-79)* 4236

Limited Partners who leave the Partnership with Negative Capital Balances

(1) If a limited partner with a negative partnership capital account sells or otherwise disposes of his/her partnership interest, the facts surrounding this transaction must be developed to determine the taxability of the disposition.

(2) If a limited partner sells or otherwise disposes of his/her partnership interest at a time when there is a negative balance in his/her capital account, a determination should be made as to whether that partnership has a valuable contract right to receive a share of the proceeds in a movie film. If the partnership has such a contract right, then IRC 751 (concerning unrealized receivables) should be considered in determining whether this negative balance in the account generates ordinary income on a sale or other disposition of the partnership interest. The value of the contract right, if any, must be established. In any event, the transferor partner's share of partnership liabilities is an amount realized by him/her on the disposition. See IRC 752(d). This is true whether the disposition is a sale or gift. See I.T. Regs. 1.1001-1(e) and *Rev. Rul. 75-194,* 1975-1 C.B. 80.

240 *(3-2-79)* 4236
Accounting Records and Agreements—Completed Film Purchase (Negative Pick-up) Tax Shelters

241 *(3-2-79)* 4236
Accounting Records

The accounting records for the limited partnership are normally maintained by the general partner or an accounting firm. These records are generally maintained on an accrual basis for operating income and expenses. The income forecast method is usually used to compute the depreciation on movie films *(Rev. Rul. 60-358,* 1960-2 C.B. 68; *Rev. Rul. 64-273,* 1964-2 C.B. 62). This method is used because, unlike most other depreciable assets, the useful life of a motion picture is difficult to ascertain. See 282 of this Handbook for computing depreciation by using this method.

242 *(3-2-79)* 4236
Agreements

(1) The following documents should be examined in detail:

(a) The limited partnership agreement and any amendments thereto.

(b) Film purchase agreements.

(c) Loan and financing agreements including terms of nonrecourse note.

(d) Distribution agreements.

(e) Appraisal.

(f) Prospectus. The prospectus covering negative pick-up partnerships may contain the following documents:

1 Tax opinion
2 Partnership agreement
3 Proposed distribution agreement
4 Escrow agreement
5 Subscription agreement
6 Short term notes
7 Acquisition agreement

(g) Distributor's earnings reports

(h) Tax opinion by outside firm

(i) Any other documents deemed pertinent by the examiner in determining the correct tax liability of the transactions.

250 *(3-2-79)* 4236
Investment Credit

(1) Proposed I.T. Reg. 1.48-8 contains tax law changes made by Section 804 of the Tax Reform Act of 1976 relating to the investment credit for movie and television films and tapes. For taxable years beginning after December 31, 1974, taxpayers are entitled to investment credit for qualified films or tapes using an amount equal to 100% of the qualified United States production costs and an applicable percentage of 66⅔% in determining the qualified investment. The credit is allowable only to owners of new property to the extent that they provide risk capital. No credit is allowed for used films or tapes.

(2) An election may be made to determine the credit under the 90% rule rather than the 66⅔% rule. See proposed I.T. Reg 1.48-8 for definitions and further details. Examiners should ensure that duplicate credits have not been claimed by producers, distributors, lenders, or guarantors.

260 *(3-2-79)* 4236
Special Features of Completed Film Purchase (Negative Pick-up) Tax Shelters

261 *(3-2-79)* 4236
General

(1) The purchase price is normally inflated and the cash down payment either equals or exceeds the true value of the movie film. The balance is represented by a nonrecourse interest bearing note.

(2) Prior to 1976, the nonrecourse note is included in both the limited partners' and general partners' bases for their partnership interests in the same ratio in which they share profits. However, if the nonrecourse note is only a contingent obligation, the note is not included in the basis of the movie film or in the partners' bases for their partnership interests. In determining whether an obligation is contingent, the courts look to the objective intent of the parties as reflected in the facts and circumstances of each case.

(3) After 1975, partners' losses are limited to their amounts at risk in the partnership. Therefore, nonrecourse loans are not included in the bases of their partnership interests in computing the allowable loss. See IRC 465.

(4) Factors to be considered in determining if payment of liabilities (nonrecourse loans) is contingent:

(a) The purchase price exceeds fair market value.

1 IRC 752(c) provides that a liability to which property is subject shall, to the extent of the fair market value of such property, be considered as a liability of the owner. Also see *Rev. Rul. 77–110,* 1977–1 C.B. 58.

2 The partnership's appraisal of the film should be reviewed to determine how the film was valued—gross earnings or net earnings. Gross earnings are box office receipts; net earnings are box office receipts less the distributor's share (up to 50 percent or higher) of distribution costs and obligated payments to third parties.

3 If the film appraisal is based on gross receipts or a value that is inflated, then the excess over market value should not be included either in the partnership's basis for the film or in the partner's basis for his/her partnership interest. The related interest deduction also should not be allowed *(Rev. Rul. 77–110,* supra).

(b) The purchase price exceeds film's total anticipated income.

(c) The maturity date of the note is beyond the useful life of the film.

(d) Payments extend over a period of time which exceeds the film's productive life.

(e) No effort is made to promote and distribute the film aggressively.

(f) There is actual default on some payments.

(g) Consider the previous purchase price for the film paid by the seller.

(h) There is no liability for damages in the event default occurs.

(i) Consider the manner in which the sale of the film was handled on the seller's books.

(5) The likelihood that the film will not generate sufficient proceeds (a percentage of which are to be applied to payments on the note) to satisfy the obligation evidenced by the note, is the contingency which excludes the debt from the owner's basis in the film. (See *Marcus v. Commissioner* 30 T.C.M. 1263 (1971) aff'd in unpublished opinion (CA–3, 1974), and *Estate of Franklin v. Commissioner,* 64 T.C. 752 (1975) 544 F2d 1045 (9th cir 1976). In *Franklin,* the taxpayer failed to show that the purported sales price of certain real estate had any relationship to its actual market value. For this reason, the circuit court stated that payment on the principal of the note would yield no equity so long as the unpaid balance exceeded the then fair market value.

(6) Interest on nonrecourse loans is not deductible where the liability is contingent. I.T. Regs. 1.461–1(a)(2) provides for disallowance of interest deductions when it has been determined that a liability is contingent. A liability is contingent when all events have not occurred that determine the fact of a liability. No indebtedness exists within the meaning of IRC 163 when payment is so speculative as to render the obligation practically nonexistent. (Also see *Rev. Rul. 77–110,* supra.)

(7) A determination will have to be made as to whether the partnership activities are engaged in for profit. This is determined by reference to objective standards. Although a reasonable expectation of profit is not required, the facts and circumstances must indicate the taxpayer entered into or continued the activity with the objective of making a profit. The subjective intent of a partner to make a profit cannot neutralize the facts and circumstances. IRC 183(b)(1) permits a deduction for otherwise allowable items without regard to a profit motive such as interest (IRC 163) and taxes (IRC 164).

(a) All other deductions to be taken pursuant to IRC 162 and 212 are allowable only to the extent gross income from the "not for profit activity" exceeds the deductions defined in IRC 183(b)(1). If the film purchaser is a partnership, it is the partnership level, as opposed to the partner level, on which the examiner's attention should be focused.

(b) IRC 183(e)(1) provides that a taxpayer may elect to defer until the close of the fourth taxable year, a determination of whether the presumption provided by IRC 183, that an activity is engaged in for profit, applies.

262 *(3–2–79)* 4236
Requesting Appraisals of Motion Pictures

(1) Valuing films in the movie industry becomes very important when you have a negative pick-up arrangement. Fair market value will generally be the basis for depreciation and investment credit. The following factors should be considered for valuation purposes:

(a) Previous purchase price for film paid by the seller.

(b) Potential for audience acceptance (e.g. known story or star, favorable review of negatives).

(c) Restrictions placed on distributor.

(d) Were the above factors considered in making appraisal and was appraiser qualified and independent?

(2) Once a movie film has been appraised, if the fair market value is less than the cash payment, the examiner should attempt to allocate the difference to a specific item or service. If the difference cannot be allocated, it should be disallowed.

(3) The Service has used outside appraisers contracted through the Southeast Region to determine the FMV of the films. IRM 4216 discusses the procedure for requesting these services from other regions. Form 5202 (Request for Engineering Services) must be used when requesting these services.

263 *(3-2-79)* 4236
Examination Checklist for Negative Pick-up Cases

(1) The following documents should be reviewed when examining negative pick-up motion picture tax shelter partnership cases:

(a) Partnership agreement

(b) Prospectus

(c) Contract of sale

(d) Distribution agreement

(e) Nonrecourse note

(f) Appraisal of film

(g) Loan agreement

(h) Subscription agreement

(i) Syndication sheet

(j) Tax opinion

(k) List of limited partners and identifying information

(l) List of tier partners, if available

(m) List of general partners and identifying information

(n) Distributor's earnings reports

(2) The above documents may have slightly different titles but are, in general, the basic documents necessary to examine movie partnerships. Complete familiarity with these documents will enable you to identify potential tax areas and minimize the time you need to complete the audit.

270 *(3-2-79)* 4236
Accounting Records and Agreements—Production Service Company Tax Shelter

271 *(3-2-79)* 4236
Accounting Records

The accounting records are normally maintained by the general partner or an accounting firm. These records are generally maintained on a cash basis. Verification of income and deductions should be made to the extent deemed necessary.

272 *(3-2-79)* 4236
Agreements Related to Production Service Companies

(1) The following agreements should be examined in detail:

(a) Articles of Limited Partnership—the basic contractual agreement between the general and limited partners. The agreement normally conforms to the Uniform Limited Partnership Act of the state where the partnership is domiciled. Any amendments to the original agreement should also be reviewed. Some of the areas covered by the agreement are:

1 Distribution of profits and losses

2 Liability of limited partners

3 Responsibility of recordkeeping

4 Dissolution of partnership

(b) Production Agreement—a contract between the owner of motion picture rights and screenplay of a particular novel or story and the film production company. This agreement employs the production company to perform all necessary services to deliver to the owners a negative of the picture suitable for use in distribution, exhibition, sale, repeat, or other exploitation of the motion picture commercially. It will usually specify:

1 contract price for the above services;

2 work procedures;

3 default clause;

4 indemnity provisions;

5 liens;

6 insurance; and

7 often a completion bond clause to give film owner guaranty of completion.

(c) Credit Agreement (sometimes referred to as a loan agreement)—a document setting forth conditions for the financing of the production of the movie between the lending institution and the production company. Specifics of liability, collateral, security, repayment, prepayment, default, etc., may be incorporated in this agreement. The provision which holds the film production partnership not liable on the production loan (nonrecourse) is also found in this agreement. Inducement to the lender to provide this loan is the guarantee of repayment by either the film owner or distributor. The assets of these entities, primarily the distributor and not the film production partnership, are the ultimate consideration for release of production funds by the lender. This guarantee may be incorporated in the credit agreement or set out separately in a guarantee-type agreement (sometimes referred to as a letter agreement).

(d) Distribution Agreement (between the film owner and a movie distribution company)—a document generally providing for distribution of the film and any related properties either worldwide or in a limited geographical area. The agreement grants distribution rights usually in all media such as theatrical, nontheatrical, and television (either free or cable). An important provision of this agreement is the distribution of gross receipts from the picture(s). Receipts are usually distributed in the following manner (however, agreements may vary):

1 payment of distributor fees to distributor;

2 reimbursement of distributor advances for film;

3 deferred compensation or contractual commitments due outside parties; and

4 distributions for repayment of nonrecourse loan. (These receipts are usually timed to coincide with the schedule of payments on the nonrecourse debt.)

(e) Security Agreement (between the film owner, the production company, and the lender of the nonrecourse loan)—this agreement assigns to the lender the respective rights, title, and interests, both tangible and intangible, held by the production company and film owner in the film. These include:

1 rights to screenplay and other literary material upon which the picture is based;

2 rights to musical score, lyrics, soundtrack, etc., in relation to the film owned by either film owner or production company;

3 all copyrights and licenses;

4 negatives, dupes, and prints connected with the film regardless of completion stage;

5 rights for the use of personal services or property in connection with the production of the picture;

6 radio and television rights;

7 all rights owned by the film owner and production company in the production and distribution agreements including gross receipts; and

8 all insurance contracts.

(f) Completion guarantee—To further induce the lender to provide funds for production, a completion guarantee is given to the lender by a third party, usually the distributor, agreeing to furnish all funds over the production loan amounts which may be required to complete the picture.

(g) Facilities agreements—Since the film production company is a group of investors who do not physically produce the contracted picture, the actual production and filming is done at an existing film studio or on site locations by studio crews of larger film distribution companies. The facilities agreement is the contract between the film production partnership and the film studio for use of their studios, sets, cameras, crews, etc., in the picture-making process.

(h) Other agreements—The previously defined agreements will be those frequently encountered during the course of the examination of a film production partnership and, perhaps, the most critical in determining income tax ramifications. However, the examiner should also inquire as to the existence of supplemental agreements and amendments, which take the form of letters, exhibits, etc., that alter the original agreements. The examiner should also inquire as to the existence of other agreements, such as:

1 laboratory-pledge holder agreements (agreements between the partnership, film owner, and the laboratory assigning the negative and/or other rights as payment for the services of developing the negative and soundtrack),

2 budget documents,

3 employment contracts,

4 insurance policies, and

5 financial statements and reports.

(i) Refer to Exhibit 200-1 for a flow chart useful in analyzing documents related to Production Service Companies.

280 *(3-2-79)* 4236

Special Features of Production Service Movie Tax Shelters

281 *(3–2–79)* 4236

Nonrecourse Loans

The production costs of the film are financed partly by the capital contributions made by the limited partners and partly by a nonrecourse loan. The nonrecourse loan is generally made by a bank, but is usually guaranteed by the distributor. The bank normally relies on the distributor's guarantee as opposed to the production service company's financial status. The loans are normally repaid out of the distribution proceeds. Some distribution agreements provide that the distributor who guarantees the loan will make payment in a manner that will enable the production service company to meet its schedule of payments to the bank. The service company has no personal liability for repayment of the loan. The technical "guarantor" may be the true borrower. If the service company is not the true borrower, it is not entitled to tax benefits attributable to the loan proceeds. *Rev. Rul. 77–125,* 1977–1 C.B. 130, and *Carnegie Production v. Commissioner* 59 T.C. 642 (1973).

282 *(3–2–79)* 4236

Film Production Costs

(1) Since motion pictures produce no income until completed and released for distribution, income is not clearly reflected by the service company's practice of currently deducting all production expenses. By using the cash basis of accounting, the service company claims large tax losses during the year or years of production when expenditures are high and income is minimal or nonexistent. For years beginning after 1975, see the discussion of IRC 280 at 211 of this Handbook.

(2) For years prior to 1976, the Service takes the position that a distortion of income results where expenditures are deducted in years other than the year in which income attributable to these expenditures is realized (*Rev. Rul. 60–358,* supra). The current deduction of production costs before the receipt of income does not clearly reflect the income of the production service partnership (*Rev. Rul. 77–125,* 1977–1 C.B. 130). A change in the treatment of a material item where absolute adherence to a cash method would otherwise result in a distortion of income may be required (IRC 446(b)).

(3) The production service company's delivery of the film to the distributor or to whomever the contract designates, results in the creation of a partnership asset in the form of a contract right to receive a share of the proceeds. This right to receive proceeds extends beyond the taxable year or years in which the expenditures were made.

(4) *Rev. Rul. 60–358,* supra, provides that because of the uneven flow of income derived from leased or rented motion picture film and because the usefulness of such assets is best measured by the flow of income rather than the passage of time, the income forecast method of depreciation is an acceptable method for computing a reasonable allowance for depreciation of the cost of such films under IRC 167(a). The production service company owns a contract right to compensation for services rather than a depreciable interest in the film. However, recovery of the cost of the contract right is directly related to the uneven flow of income from the film, and the diminution of the economic value of such right is best measured by that flow of income rather than the passage of time. Therefore, the income forecast method is the best method for amortizing the cost of the contract right. The computation of the annual amortization expense follows:

Current year's income
Estimated total income × Cost of film
= Allowable deduction for taxable year.

(5) *Rev. Rul. 78–28,* IRB 1978–4, page 6, provides that in the computation above, the amount of income in the numerator must reflect the same gross income used to compute taxable income from the film for the period. In addition, the denominator may not be less than the amount of the nonrecourse loans secured by the film. If the denominator does not exceed the cost of the film, this may indicate that an inflated purchase price was paid for the film.

283 *(3–2–79)* 4236

Film Production Company, Film Owner, and Film Distributor Relationship

(1) In determining whether a production service company partnership is an independent contractor as opposed to joint venturer with the distributor, and/or film owner, the following questions should be used as guidelines:

(a) Is there a joint venture agreement between the parties?

(b) What business was conducted in the joint names of the parties?

(c) Did the parties file partnership returns or represent themselves as partners?

(d) Are separate books and records kept for the business?

(e) Did the service company make capital contributions to the business, thus indicating assumption of risk in the business? Capital contributions alone would not necessarily mean the service company is a joint venturer. An employer or independent contractor may contribute funds to ensure the success of the business, but only a joint venturer has a proprietary right in the assets of the venture upon withdrawal or upon termination (I.T. Reg. 1.704-1(e)(1)(iv)).

(f) Does the service company have a proprietary right to share the business net profits and an obligation to share the losses?

(g) Do the parties have control over income and capital of the business and does each have the right to make withdrawals?

(h) Do the parties exercise mutual control of and assume mutual responsibility for the business?

284 *(3-2-79)* 4236

Grantor Trusts as Limited Partners

(1) Many limited partners want to secure the benefit of large expenditures during the production phase of a motion picture and transfer the incidence of taxation on ordinary income from the film production partnership to another entity in the delivery year of the completed film. To accomplish this, a limited partner places his/her partnership interest in a grantor trust. See IRC 671-679. The partner makes gifts of cash to a trust and files an appropriate gift tax return. The trust then acquires the partnership interest and the losses from the film production partnership flow through to the grantor. When the limited partnership is about to realize income, the grantor trust is "perfected" into a non-grantor trust, and one of the trust's assets is the limited partnership interest. The audit guidelines as used for limited partners are applicable (see 234 of this Handbook). In addition, the areas listed below should be considered:

(a) Perfection of the trust constitutes an impermissible assignment of income.

(b) Has the taxpayer disposed of his/her interest in the grantor trust?

(c) The assignment of the limited partner's interest in the service production company is a disposition of the partnership interest. (The release of the limited partner from his/her proportionate share of the nonrecourse loan is taxable income to the limited partner.)

(d) If you encounter any of the above issues, you may want to consider a request for Technical Advice.

285 *(3-2-79)* 4236

Examination Checklist for Film Production Cases

(1) The following documents should be reviewed when examining film production motion picture tax shelter partnership cases. The documents may have slightly varying titles but are, in general, the basic documents necessary for the examination. Familiarity with these documents will enable you to identify potential tax adjustments.

(a) ARTICLES OF LIMITED PARTNERSHIP

(b) PRODUCTION AGREEMENT
- (a) entities involved
- (b) films to be produced
- (c) contract price and budget
- (d) schedule of payments
- (e) control of work procedure

(c) CREDIT OR LOAN AGREEMENT
- (a) lender and borrower
- (b) loan amount
- (c) collateral
- (d) security
- (e) guarantor of loan
- (f) loan repayment schedule
- (g) security and assignment agreement

(d) DISTRIBUTION AGREEMENT
- (a) distributor
- (b) film owner
- (c) schedule of distribution of gross receipts
- (d) distribution territory

(e) COMPLETION GUARANTEE
- (a) guarantor
- (b) amount of budget overrun guarantee

(f) FACILITIES AGREEMENT
- (a) entities involved
- (b) location of facilities
- (c) work provided by studio
- (d) disposition of props, sets, etc.

286 *(3-2-79)* 4236
Foreign Entities and Individuals

(1) During the course of the examination, the examiner may encounter foreign entities in the transaction of the film production shelters. These include but are not limited to:

(a) film owners

(b) distributors

(c) lenders

(d) partners (individuals, trusts, corporations, etc.)

(2) If any facts develop during the examination which indicate potential adjustments or tax abuses, a collateral request for assistance should be made to the Office of International Operations.

(Next page is 4236-19)

Exhibit 200-1

Flow Chart of Production Service Company Agreements

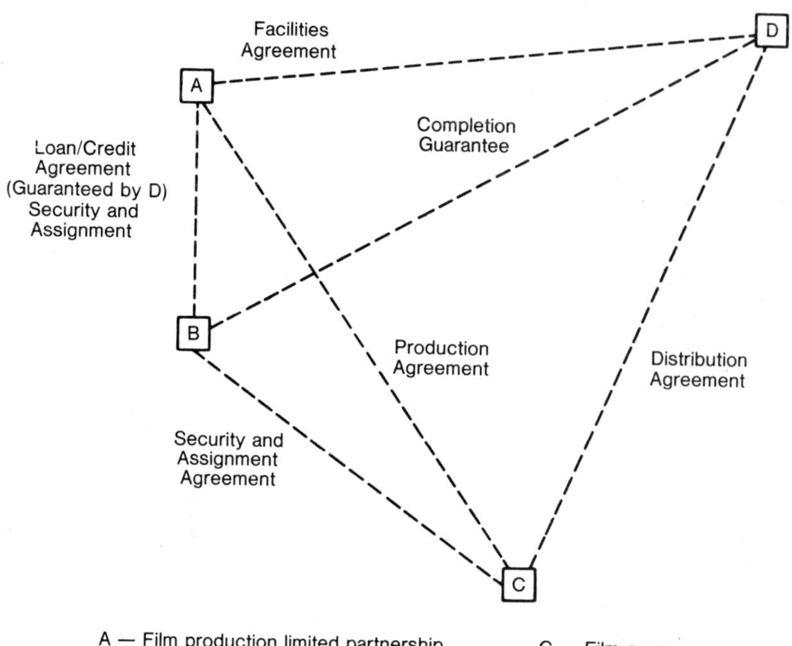

A — Film production limited partnership

B — Lender of nonrecourse production loan

C — Film owner

D — Distributor

Exhibit 200-2

Example of Partnership Tiering

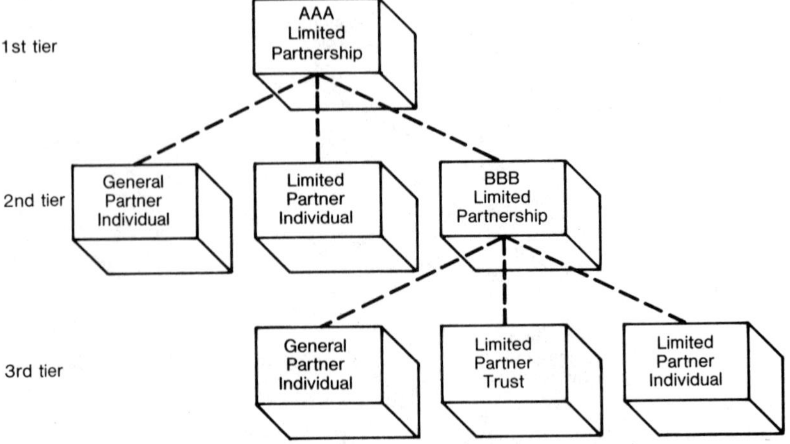

(Next page is 4236-25)

Real Estate Tax Shelters

310 *(11-6-79)* 4236
Background

(1) This Chapter has been prepared to assist revenue agents in the examination of cases in the real estate tax shelter area.

(2) Through the use of this Chapter, examiners will be able to reduce the time needed to acquire the examining skills essential to this speciality. However, nothing contained herein should discourage examiners from improving upon these techniques or exercising their own initiative and ingenuity.

320 *(11-6-79)* 4236
Contents

(1) This Chapter is a compilation of the auditing techniques used by some of our most experienced revenue agents. They are presented in a manner intended to illustrate the problems frequently encountered in examining cases in the real estate tax shelter area.

(2) Real estate tax shelter cases are subject to factual development and substantiation using the legal documents connected with each transaction. These examination techniques are interspersed with discussions of the legal aspects of the particular transaction(s) being considered.

(3) References to the IRC, court decisions, revenue rulings, etc., will be general and brief in nature and should not be relied upon to provide a thorough understanding of the subject matter. Rather, these guidelines should be supplemented by further research on particular tax issues.

(4) These examination methods and techniques are permissive and are not intended to be mandatory procedures and instructions for field personnel. Examiners should adapt these procedures to the particular case under consideration.

(5) This Chapter does not alter existing technical or procedural instructions contained in the IR Manual. In the event of any inconsistencies between these guidelines and the basic text of the IR Manual, the Manual will prevail. Procedural statements in the issuance are for emphasis and clarity and are not to be taken as authority for administrative action.

330 *(11-6-79)* 4236
Introduction

(1) The real estate industry requires the commitment of huge sums of capital over long periods of time for construction of apartment buildings, shopping centers, office buildings, etc. A number of investment vehicles are available to bring about a pooling of financial resources and reaping of financial benefits by the participants. Various legal forms are used for this purpose—the joint venture, the trust, the corporation, and most often the partnership (both general and limited). These various forms differ with respect to type of control, participation in management, personal liability, etc.

(2) Because of the myriad of variations that are available for structuring financial arrangements and the broad choice of vehicles through which the arrangements can operate, the examiner must always remember that the facts and circumstances will dictate into which category a particular case falls, i.e., a Class I, Class II, or Class III shelter, discussed later in this Chapter.

(3) Participation in these shelters is established in a number of ways. An entrepreneur may represent the owner of property, or may acquire property for subsequent resale to investors in the form of partnership interests. Another approach is the actual formation of partnership "shells," which are sold ("syndicated") to other dealers who, in turn, secure limited partners. Additionally, the entrepreneur may syndicate separate parts of the underlying assets to the individual investors in their separate capacities, or as co-owners with other investors, in an attempt to avoid the partnership entity.

(4) In general, the real estate tax shelter is a structure in which a significant portion of the investor's return is derived from "pass-through" deductions which can be used to offset unrelated income, thus creating significant tax benefits. These shelters encourage investments by taxpayers in high tax brackets because of the progressive tax structure. Hence, benefits increase as the tax bracket increases. In effect, the tax shelter allows the taxpayer to postpone the payment of tax or, under some circumstances, even avoid payment of tax. The deferral of tax payment is the equivalent of an

interest-free loan, the economic benefits of which can be significant.

(5) The limited partnership has been the most commonly used vehicle in the structuring of real estate tax shelters, although trusts and other entities are also used. This vehicle enables participants to secure pass-through deductions in excess of risk capital (while limiting personal liability through nonrecourse financing) which can be used to offset other income.

(6) For purposes of clarification, a distinction is made between two types of benefits: economic benefits and tax benefits. Normally, in a soundly structured real estate tax shelter, the economic benefits are predominant and the tax benefits are only a secondary consideration. However, an increasing number of shelters are being formed to reap tax benefits, to the point that many lack economic viability or reality and are structured primarily for tax avoidance purposes. It is these types of shelters, which lack true economic benefits, that the Service will challenge.

340 *(11-6-79)* 4236
The Covenant not to Compete

(1) A recent trend has evolved in which syndicators of real property are structuring into their tax shelters "Covenants Not To Compete." A valid covenant not to compete against an established going business may be proper. However, characterizing a portion of a land sale as a covenant not to compete (e.g., proposing not to build on adjacent property for a year or two) might be considered a "sham" if the facts surrounding the transaction indicate no true basis for the covenant.

(2) Such characterization on the part of a seller (dealer) who has to report any gain as ordinary income, is of no consequence except that it creates a purchasing inducement to a buyer. Such characterization, if determined to be correct, would induce the buyer to deduct part of the purchase price which would otherwise be treated as a nondepreciable cost of the land. See *Rev. Rul. 77-403,* 1977-2, C.B. 302. The examiner should keep in mind that it is the taxpayer's burden to prove the existence of a valid covenant. In many situations, it may be necessary to submit requests for technical advice.

350 *(11-6-79)* 4236
Acquisition of Tax Losses—The "Abusive Tax Shelters"

351 *(11-6-79)* 4236
General

(1) In recent years, many tax shelters have been formed primarily for their tax advantages. High bracketed taxpayers are participants in "transactions structured for a loss," with little or no profit motivation other than the gain realized through tax avoidance.

(2) It should always be kept in mind that the Code allows losses arising from transactions *entered into for profit.* Losses are not allowed from transactions *entered into for loss* (losses for tax avoidance).

(3) A common feature of real estate tax shelters is a turnaround or crossover point at which, after generating tax losses for several years, a partnership begins to generate taxable income. While losses often occur during the formative years of a business, a profit-seeking activity must have as its goal the realization of a profit on the entire operation, which presupposes not only future net earnings but also sufficient net earnings to recoup the losses sustained in earlier years. *Francis X. Benz v. Commissioner,* 63 T.C. 375 (1973).

(4) *Inflated sales prices* are at the base of the majority of the "structured loss" transactions in real estate. Upon initial examination, the sales prices appear to be for fair market value. Often, however, upon detailed analysis of all interrelated factors, this proves to be erroneous. Inflated prices reflected in the current basis of depreciable property give an excessive current depreciation deduction.

(5) Inflated prices (payable well into the future) are accepted by the investors, not because of the value of the underlying property, but because of the current tax effect that can be obtained from them. The arrangement is structured to make the value *appear* to be in the property, but the real value is in the tax advantages that flow from the transaction.

(6) Sophistication in the structuring of abusive shelters is often extensive, requiring broad analysis of intricate interrelationships. From an examination point of view, the basic question appears to be what criteria will be used in determining if a real estate shelter was structured primarily for tax avoidance; i.e., lacks economic reality.

(7) From an economic standpoint, an abusive tax shelter, in substance, is one in which the present value of all future income is less than the present value of all the investment and associated costs of the shelter. In these shelters, the "primary" gain is from the tax advantage. However, a loss return, in and of itself, is not indicative of tax shelter abuse.

(8) The following classification of loss returns should aid in placing the tax shelter "ABUSE" problem in its proper perspective:

(a) CLASS I—*GOOD SHELTERS*—Loss returns that are perfectly legitimate in all respects: Economic viability, form, substance, etc.

(b) CLASS II—*ABUSES WITHIN THE SHELTER*—Loss returns that may contain "elements" or items which are incorrectly handled; i.e.; capitalizable items claimed as current deductions, etc., but in other respects are economically viable.

(c) CLASS III—*ABUSES OF THE SHELTER ITSELF*—Loss returns that lack economic reality or viability in varying degrees. Any transaction that fails to produce a return relative to the risk involved is suspect. Many factors must be considered in making this determination.

352 *(11-6-79)* 4236
Illustrations of the Three Classes of Tax Shelters

An in-depth analysis of returns that appear to be Class I (Good Shelters) or Class II (Abuses Within the Shelter) often reveals them to be, in fact, Class III (Abuses of the Shelter Itself). Illustrations of the three classes are contained in Exhibit 300-1.

360 *(11-6-79)* 4236
How to recognize a Class III Abusive Tax Shelter.

361 *(11-6-79)* 4236
General

(1) It is a well established rule that the substance of a transaction, rather than its form, shall control tax liability. "Form" is the pattern, method, or scheme that appears on the face of the transaction. Substance underlies all outward manifestations. The latitude in this area is as broad as the ingenuity of man. It is suggested that examiners not hesitate to take each bare element of the transaction, strip it of the title given by the taxpayer, and retitle it after evaluation. Often a completely different picture appears. As an example, a so-called "deed" transferring title to property with a provision for retransfer in a few years may very well not be a deed in the common sense, but may represent an option, lease, or mere security device.

(2) A Class III Shelter is one that lacks economic reality or viability when viewed in its entirety. To prove lack of economic reality or viability, an in-depth financial analysis is required. In a sale-leaseback, for example, present valuing of the income stream and residual at each of the lease payment dates over the life of the transaction would be a desirable method. Examiners should ensure that all related variables (leases, leasebacks, carved out economic interests of any nature, etc.) are considered in the engineering valuations. *The key queston is: Was the transaction entered into "primarily for tax avoidance"?* To help answer this question, the examiner must first gain an understanding of the transaction *in its entirety*. The following approach should be utilized:

(a) In *extreme* cases where economic viability is lacking (ofter referred to as lack of beneficial ownership—contrasted to bare legal ownership), the issue often is relatively easy to pinpoint. However, the entire tax shelter area is one of continuing variation and, therefore, the degree of variation can affect the economic viability or lack thereof. In any transaction, the examiner should ascertain the answer to the following questions:

1 Does the price, together with all its related elements, bear a relationship to fair market value?

2 Does the transaction provide any true equity buildup, thus creating a value to forfeit upon possible termination?

3 Does the transaction transfer the *burdens* and *benefits* of ownership?

(b) Inquiry should be made as to whether, based on all the facts and circumstances, the parties intended that ownership of the property pass at the time of the alleged sale. The absence of such intent, however, is not established merely by the use of nonrecourse financing, even though the buyer can "walk away" from a transaction without personal liability. See *Manual D. Mayerson v. Commissioner*, 47 T.C. 340 (1966), acq., 1969-1 C.B. 21; *Rev. Rul. 69-77*, 1969-1 C.B. 59. On the other hand, the fact that a sales price is to be partially amortized should not automatically establish that purported buyers are building equity they stand to forfeit if they fail to complete the transaction. If the sales price is unrelated to the fair market value of the property, such equity may be a mere bookkeeping entry. See *Franklin v. Commissioner,* 544 F2d 1045 (CA-9, 1976) aff'g 64 TC 752. Conceivably, the equity could also represent part of the price paid for an option.

362 *(11-6-79)* 4236
Pertinent Documents to be Examined

(1) To help determine the presence or absence of an "abusive" tax shelter, the examiner should inspect, and when necessary, secure copies of all pertinent documents regarding the transaction.

(2) *Examples:*

(a) Copy of partnership agreement and any amendments.

(b) Copy of recorded certificate of partnership agreement and amendments.

(c) Prospectus, if available.

(d) Projections presented to the limited partners.

(e) Sales circulars, advertisements, brochures of general partner-syndicator, or any other representations made as inducements to enter into the transaction.

(f) Appraisals, valuation reports, options, etc.

(g) Property tax bill and assessments (real and personal).

(h) Escrow documents or abstract documents.

1 Instructions
2 Amendments
3 Closing statements
4 Agreements
5 Commission agreements
6 Other
7 Abstract of title
8 Title policies

(i) Purchase agreements, contracts, liens of any nature, etc.

1 All trust deeds and notes (existing and new)

2 All inclusive deeds of trust ("wrap-around mortgages") and notes

3 Land contracts

4 Other

(j) Subordination agreements of any nature.

(k) Documentation of insurance coverage relative to claimed value.

(l) Construction documents, including building permits.

(m) Lease agreements/sublease agreements.

1 Date lease commences
2 Terms
3 Existence of balloon payments

(n) Side agreements

(o) Options (to extend lease, to repurchase, etc.)

(p) All documentation pertaining to the last arm's-length sale or sales prior to syndication. In this context, "arm's-length" means true third-party participation. The examiner must be alert to situations wherein the parties appear to be at "arm's-length" but actually have side agreements or "understandings" between them.

363 *(11-6-79)* 4236
Additional Examination Procedures

(1) After obtaining the documents described in 362 above and any others that may be relevant, the examiner should utilize the following additional procedures:

(a) Trace all intervening transactions from the last arm's-length sale to the subject syndication sale, keeping in mind the relationship of all parties in the transactions.

(b) Check file with applicable governmental agencies (e.g., State Corporation Commissioner, State Department of Real Estate, Securities and Exchange Commission (SEC)). The Private Placement Memorandum on file with the SEC may contain many of the adverse tax consequences.

(c) Verify payments (by date) made by limited partners to the partnership. Verify *partnership formation date,* watching for *back-dating.*

(d) Ascertain (usually from the partnership agreement) whether *guarantees* were made by the general partner. Some examples are:

1 Guaranteed profits to limited partners.

2 Indemnification of limited partners from loss.

3 Guaranteed return on cash investment.

(e) Determine percentage of ownership by general partner. Some examples are:

1 Capital ownership.
2 Profit participation.
3 Loss participation.
4 Liquidation participation.

(f) Determine methods of payments, and by whom paid and/or owed. Consider the following:

1 Property liens—1st trust deed, 2nd trust deed, etc.

2 All-inclusive trust deed (wrap-around) notes.

3 Payments by cash.

4 Payments by cross credits (i.e., lease payments applied to mortgage payments).

(2) For methods of funding of limited partner contributions to partnership, refer to *Rev. Rul. 72–135,* 1972–1 C.B. 200 and *Rev. Rul. 72–350,* 1972–2 C.B. 394. Consider relationship between general partner and lender.

364 *(11-6-79)* 4236

Additional Questions to be Considered

(1) Additional questions that the examiner should consider in determining whether the transaction "makes sense" from an economic standpoint are:

(a) What is the cash return on the investment relative to the risk? Does this return compare favorably with the "going rate"? If necessary, the examiner should contact mortgage investment brokers, brokerage firms, insurance companies, and bank trust departments to ascertain the "going rate" on various types of investments.

(b) If leased land, what happens at the end of the lease? Does the building revert to the lessor, leaving a partnership with no assets?

(c) What are the provisions in the partnership agreement regarding subsequent "balloon payments"? Is it reasonable to expect the investors on nonrecourse financing to pay off a large balance which is far in excess of the asset's value at that time? Has the partnership provided funds for this purpose?

(d) Is the partnership insuring the asset for less than its "purchase price"?

(e) Are the lease payments to the partnership unrealistially low when compared to the purchase price? Are the lease payments similar or equal to the mortgage payments, so that little or no money flows?

(f) Does the seller-lessee have complete control over the property, thus being, in effect, the beneficial owner (as contrasted to the purchaser, who obtains bare legal ownership)?

365 *(11-6-79)* 4236

Economic Assistance

If, after examining the necessary documents and answering the above questions, the examiner feels that the transaction lacks economic viability, consideration should be given to requesting assistance from an economist in the Economic Advisory Group (see IRM 42(12)4). An economist will analyze the present value of the lease income stream, considering payment dates together with all other related data. If the final analysis reveals a transaction lacking in economic substance, examiners should consider disallowance of all deductions on the basis that the taxpayer has no equity investment in the property and, at best, is only contingently liable for the debts. Alternatively, depending upon the facts, it may be determined that the taxpayer-investor has purchased an *option* which can be written off at expiration. If the taxpayer has entered into the transaction primarily for tax avoidance, the out-of-pocket expenses would not be allowable as a deduction should the partnership "fold." See *Rev. Rul. 70–333,* 1970–1 C.B. 38, re: theft losses.

366 *(11-6-79)* 4236

Valuation

(1) Valuation is the prime consideration in separating Class I (Good Shelters) from Class III (Abusive Shelters). All elements of a transaction have value, whether tangible or intangible. The crux of a good tax shelter audit rests with the proper evaluation of each of those elements when placed in their respective positions, and the ability to arrive at the sum of the values relative to the open market (the true economic market).

(2) Seldom in today's market are major transactions consummated without extensive consideration being given to their tax effect. Therefore, the Service is not merely concerned that there are extensive tax benefits flowing from the transactions, but rather that those benefits have their roots in true economic substance. If that economic substance is lacking, or so thin that the primary purpose is the evasion or avoidance of federal taxes, then such transactions will not be recognized for federal tax purposes. The following may be used as references: *Rev. Rul. 77–110* 1977–1 C.B. 58. *Franklin v. Commissioner,* supra. *Marcus v. Commissioner,* 30 TCM 1263 (1971) aff'd per

curiam in unpublished opinion (CA-3, 1974). *Frank Lyon Co. v. U.S.* 435 U.S. 561 (1978), 1978-1, C.B. 46, revg. 536 F2d 746 (8th Cir. 1976) 76-1.

370 *(11-6-79)* 4236
Business vs. Investment

(1) Examiners should be vigilant as to the nature of the entity under examination; i.e., is it a trade or business as contrasted to a passive investment? The net loss from a partnership *trade or business* is reported on the partner's tax return to arrive at adjusted gross income, per IRC 62. The partnership loss from *investment* assets, *if otherwise deductible,* is included on the partner's return as an itemized deduction, per IRC 63.

(2) In many cases the point might be academic where the partner's return, after claiming partnership losses, still shows a positive taxable income. However, if the partner's return shows a negative taxable income, the use of itemized deductions in computing a net operating loss would be limited to nonbusiness income, per IRC 172.

(3) Additionally, under the Tax Reform Act of 1976, "adjusted itemized deductions" are considered to be a *tax preference item* (IRC 57(b)(1)). Therefore, it is now even more important to recognize the business v. investment characteristics of partnership distributions.

(4) Whether or not an entity is in a "trade or business" may not be an easy determination. The transition point must be defined and most likely will have to be factually determined by the examiner. For example, an entity with a shopping center under construction would not be considered to be engaged in the shopping center business, but when the facilities are finished and operating, it would be engaged in the shopping center business. With the exception of costs relating to IRC 163 (interest), 164 (taxes), and 165 (losses), all costs incurred by the partnership before the transition point should be capitalized, per IRC 263 (see *Richmond Television Corp. v. U.S.,* supra, regarding preopening expenses). The IRC 163, 164, and 165 expenses would have to be taken into account separately, per Section 1.702-1(a)(8)(ii) of the Regulations, and would be allowed only as itemized deductions. (However, in years affected by the Tax Reform Act of 1976, see IRC 189.)

380 *(11-6-79)* 4236
IRC 266

(1) Section 1.266-1(c)(3) of the Regulations provides, in part, that if the taxpayer (partnership) elects to capitalize an item or items under IRC 266, such election shall be exercised by filing a statement indicating the item or items (whether with respect to the same project or to different projects) that the taxpayer (partnership) elects to treat as chargeable to the capital account with the *original* return for the taxable year for which the election is made. The following situation may occur: A taxpayer (partnership) claims certain "trade or business" deductions on its return. The resultant loss on a partner's Schedule E creates a net operating loss for that partner. These expenses could have been capitalized and amortized if the partnership had made a timely election on its original return. Later, IRS establishes that these were pre-trade or business deductions which should have been itemized on Schedule A and denies the net operating loss deduction to the partner. Since no timely election was made, these expenses would also be denied capitalization treatment. For example, a taxpayer claimed a partnership loss on a 1975 return (Schedule E) in the amount of $500,000. After considering other income and deduction items, the taxpayer had a negative taxable income for the year of $750,000. After making the appropriate modifications required by IRC 172, the taxpayer computed a net operating loss and filed a claim for refund of 1972 taxes. Upon examination of the 1975 partnership return, the examiner determined that the entire partnership loss represents amounts paid prior to the partnership's entering into a trade or business. The partnership did not make an election to capitalize the interest expense. The characterization of this partner's loss was determined to be:

(a) Interest	$200,000
(b) Accounting fees	20,000
(c) Legal fees	30,000
(d) Salaries	250,000
	$500,000

(2) The accounting, legal, and salary expenses would have to be capitalized by the partnership per IRC 263 and could not be deducted by the partner.

(3) The interest would be a nonbusiness itemized deduction per IRC 163 and, therefore, could not be used in computing the net operating loss (assuming no nonbusiness income). Since the taxpayer (partnership) had not elected at the time of filing to capitalize the interest under IRC 266, no election is now allowable. The examiner would make applicable adjustments to the NOL carryback.

(4) After the effective date of IRC 189, only the amount of construction period interest that is otherwise amortizable (the current year's deduction) would be subject to election under IRC 266. The balance of the interest would be capitalized under the new law.

390 *(11–6–79)* 4236
Characterization of Specific Items—Class II or Class III

391 *(11–6–79)* 4236
Management Fees and Other Front End Expenses

Partnerships often attempt to deduct large payments in the year of organization that are paid either to the general partner or to "outsiders," but are actually capital in nature. The name given to the payment is often misleading, thus requiring a strict analysis of the substance. Since each payment may require different tax treatment, *Revenue Ruling 75–214* and IRC 709 should be consulted for guidance in this area. See *Richmond Television Corp. v. U.S.,* supra.

392 *(11–6–79)* 4236
Interest Expense

(1) Various types of nondeductible payments may be couched under the term "interest." When the transaction under scrutiny calls for a nominal down payment, examiners should consider, if the facts warrant, disallowing all or part of the "interest expense" under the theory that it is, in reality, either a down payment on principal or a deposit. See *Kenneth D. LaCroix v. Commissioner,* 61 TC 471 (1974).

(2) Additionally, when "interest" is paid to a related entity, care should be taken to ensure that a valid indebtedness exists and that funds have actually been advanced by the lender.

(3) The "material distortion of income" approach, discussed in *Rev. Ruling 68–643,* should be considered when examining prepaid interest transactions by cash-basis taxpayers. Also, the "distortion" test is applied at the partnership level, rather than at the individual partner level *(Resnik v. Commissioner,* 555 F2d 634 (CA–7,1977) aff'd per curiam 66 TC 74). Generally, IRC 461(g) requires prepayments of interest by cash basis taxpayers after January 1, 1976 to be deducted over the period to which it is allocable.

393 *(11–6–79)* 4236
Contingent Liability

As previously discussed relative to Class III Abusive Shelters, interest paid on a contingent liability is not true interest "for the use or forbearance of money." If it appears unlikely that the balance of the loan will ever be paid off, consideration should be given to disallowance of the deduction. See *Marcus v. Commissioner,* supra.

394 *(11–6–79)* 4236
Owner vs. Nominee

(1) In general, tax deductions for a property are allowable only to the party with the "burdens and benefits" of ownership. Thus, in *Franklin v. Commissioner,* supra, the legal owner was denied the deductions because, based on the facts, he did not have the "burdens and benefits" of the property.

(2) In some cases, tax deductions are claimed by a partnership or individual even though the property is legally owned by a related corporation (one reason for such an arrangement is that corporations are not subject to state usury laws). The taxpayer would argue that the corporation is a mere "nominee." However, there are cases to support the proposition that taxpayers cannot disregard their controlled corporations. *(Moline Properties, Inc. v. Commissioner,* 319 U.S. 436 (1943); *National Carbide Corp. v. Commissioner* 336 U.S. 422 (1949); see exception in *Rev. Rul. 75–31,* 1975–1, C.B. 10.)

395 *(11–6–79)* 4236
Retroactive Allocations of Partnership Losses

(1) Examiners should be aware of the prohibition against allocating losses to a new partner, based on transactions occurring before the new partner's entry into the partnership.

(2) Although new amendments to IRC 704, 706(c), and 761 prohibit these retroactive allocations for partnership taxable years beginning after 1975, the Service's position prohibits these allocations for tax purposes in years preceding 1976.

(3) Relying on *Rodman v. Commissioner,* 542 f2d 845 (2d Cir. 1976), and the "assignment of income" doctrine of *Helvering v. Horst,* 311 U.S. 112, 1940-2 C.B. 206, *Rev. Rul. 77-119,* 1977-1 C.B. 177, states that the new partner's distributive share of the partnership's items of income, gain, loss, deduction, or credit may not include any part of such items realized or sustained prior to entry into the partnership.

396 *(11-6-79)* 4236
Sol Diamond Type Cases

(1) In many instances, some of the partners contribute cash and/or other assets, while others (often the general partner) receive a partnership interest for services rendered. The interest may be equal in nature to that of the cash partners, or may be limited in some respect (e.g., interests in losses only, or in profits upon sale of the underlying assets only after a percentage distribution to the limited partners).

(2) The case of *Diamond v. Commissioner,* 56 TC 530 (1971), aff'd 492 F2d 286 (7th Cir. 1974), involved the following facts: A, who had a contract right to purchase a building for $1.1 million, offered to enter into a joint venture with B if B could obtain 100% financing. B obtained such financing, then sold his joint venture interest for $40,000. The question at issue was whether the $40,000 was capital gain or ordinary income. This in turn would depend on whether B's interest, obtained by performing personal services, was a "capital" or a "profit-sharing" interest in the venture. If it was a "capital" interest, the $40,000 would be ordinary income. See Regulation 1.721-1(b). Without discussing the distinction between the two interest, the Court held that the $40,000 was ordinary income. This issue can come up in a different factual setting. For example, A and B agree to form a partnership to which A would contribute property and B would contribute services. It would be necessary to determine from their agreement whether B would have an interest in the partnership property or only an interest in future partnership profits. Since the scope of the Diamond case has not been finally resolved, technical advice should be requested on this issue.

(3) Examiners should analyze the capital accounts for inconsistent contributions by the partners. Some partners may have zero contributions, while others will have contributed the total reflected capital in cash and/or other assets. It has been observed that, in some instances, the fair market value of partner's services has been credited to the partner's capital account and not reported by the partner as income.

3(10)0 *(11-6-79)* 4236
"Self-Destructing Shelters"

Instances have been observed where syndicator-promoters have been marketing "conversion" (ordinary income to capital gains). With the help of nonrecourse financing, the syndicator will acquire assets from entities on the verge of bankruptcy or foreclosure, with the idea of securing for the participants large, short-term, ordinary losses and subsequent capital gains upon termination. The structured transaction is geared to "self destruct" by virtue of the probability (or inevitability) of foreclosure or bankruptcy and accordingly should be challenged on the basis that the transaction was not entered into "for profit," but was a transaction structured for tax avoidance. Additionally, examiners should not overlook the possibility of tax evasion in this area.

3(11)0 *(11-6-79)* 4236
Tax Haven Shelters

(1) Examiners should be alert to situations where international elements are introduced into the tax shelter. Cases have been observed where syndicators have purchased property in the U.S. for fair market value, then transferred it to a foreign "entity" for fair market value. That "entity" then sells the property back to U.S. investors for an amount greatly in excess of the actual value. When international examiners traced the flow of transactions, they found nothing more than a post office box in the foreign country. The examiner should be alert to this type of transaction, or any of a multitude of variations. If international issues are apparent, assistance of the Office of International Operations (OIO) should be requested.

(2) Class III abusive shelters are prevalent in this area, so it is vitally important to ascertain the true fair market value of the underlying assets. The examiner must always remember that even an apparent "arm's-length" transaction may not give the true fair market value unless analyzed in conjunction with the terms of any lease, option, security agreement, or myriad of other documents.

(3) Since the "tax haven shelter" is generally more sophisticated, examiners should be alert to intentional acts which give rise to an evasion of taxes, and, when appropriate, refer cases to the Criminal Investigation Division.

3(12)0 *(11-6-79)* 4236

Basis

(1) It is necessary to differentiate between *basis* and *capital,* since losses are limited to the extent of partner's basis and not necessarily to the extent of the capital account.

(2) If no partner in a limited partnership is personally liable for a partnership debt (nonrecourse financing), each partner will be treated as sharing the liability in the same ratio as his or her ratio for sharing partnership profits. To the extent of each partner's proportionate share of that liability, it becomes an addition to that partner's basis.

(3) However, when a general partner is personally liable for a partnership debt, and the limited partners have no liability for the debt, only the general partner is accorded basis with respect to the liability. Therefore, the basis of the limited partner would be limited to their capital contributions. Outstanding liabilities are deemed to be shared by all of the partners only in situations when neither the general partner nor the limited partners have personal liability. In such cases, basis additions are created for each partner to the extent of the partner's proportionate share of the liability.

(4) Examiners should also be familiar with *Rev. Ruling 72-135,* which holds that a "nonrecourse" loan made by a general partner to the partnership (or a limited partners) was a capital contribution to be added to the basis of the general partner, rather than a loan to be added to the limited partners' basis.

(5) IRC 752(c) limits the extent to which a partner may utilize liabilities to increase basis. The liabilities cannot be used to the extent that they exceed the fair market value of the underlying asset. Therefore, it is important for the examiner to verify whether or not the purchase price is inflated (an inflated purchase price could also result in classification of the shelter as a "Class III-Abusive Tax Shelter"). The important thing to remember, however, is that fair market value must be analyzed within the context of the transaction as structured. As an extreme example, a newly-constructed building (exclusive of land) with an actual construction cost of $1,000,000 was sold for $1,000,000 to the partnership. If this was all that was involved in the transaction, there would be no question that the fair market value would be $1,000,000. However, if this building were to be leased back to the seller for 100 years at a yearly rental of $1 on a triple net lease, the building would be virtually worthless. Why? The owner has nothing more than an income stream of $1 per year, present valued at each time of receipt, plus the present value of the building to be received 100 years in the future. Even if the unlikely assumption is made that the building will be worth $1,000,000 at that time using an interest factor of 9%, the present value of the building today is only $200!

3(13)0 *(11-6-79)* 4236

Special Allocation of Income and Expense Items

3(13)1 *(11-6-79)* 4236

Depreciation

(1) In some instances, the partnership agreement will allocate most or all of the depreciation deduction to a specific partner or partners. Section 1.704-1(b)(2) of the Regulations lists several criteria to be considered in determining the tax credibility of a special allocation of an item of partnership income, gain, loss, deduction, or credit. Two of these criteria are:

(a) Whether the partnership or partner has a *business purpose* for the allocation.

(b) Whether the allocation has *"substantial economic effect."*

(2) These two criteria, as well as several others listed in the Regulations, were substantially explored in *Orrisch v. Commissioner,* 55 TC 395, aff'd CA-9, 1974, in an unpublished opinion in which the Court concluded that there was no business purpose for the transaction. This could also be applicable to other items; e.g., gains, losses, interest, etc.

3(13)2 *(11-6-79)* 4236

Gain or Loss—in General

(1) Examiners should be aware of *Revenue Ruling 75-458,* 1975-2 C.B. 258, which states that partnership allocations will not be recognized where some partners report gains greater than those actually realized by the partnership, while others report losses that were never sustained.

(2) *Example:*
(a) Gain on sale of partnership asset $3,000
(b) Allocation to partners:

A	B	C
$2,000	$2,000	($1,000)

(3) Partners A and B may have excess losses from other sources; therefore, this gain would have no tax effect. Examiners should inspect the Form 1065, Schedules K-1 to determine whether partners are reflecting gains when the net amount on the Form 1065 is a loss, or vice-versa.

3(14)0 *(11-6-79)* 4236
Abandonment or Forfeiture of a Partnership Interest

(1) In the event of foreclosure, when a partner's share of partnership liabilities exceeds the basis in the partnership interest, the partner will be required to recognize gain to the extent of such excess (even if no cash was received from the foreclosure sale). the same result would be true for abandonment; i.e., the decrease in the partner's share of partnership liabilities is treated as a cash distribution, per IRC 752(b). The character of the gain would depend upon the existence of any IRC 751 property in the partnership (i.e., unrealized receivable and substantially appreciated inventory items). For this purpose, IRC 751(c) defines potential IRC 1245 and 1250 depreciation recapture as an "unrealized receivable."

(2) However, even though the partnership may not be holding any IRC 751 assets (thus allowing capital gains upon foreclosure or abandonment), it is entirely possible that a partner may not be allowed any of the partnership's distributable loss in the year of foreclosure or abandonment. See *Revenue Ruling 66-94,* 1966-1 C.B. 166, which states that distributions are taken into consideration *before* losses in computing a partner's adjusted basis for the partnership interest under IRC 705(a). See example in Exhibit 300-3.

3(15)0 *(11-6-79)* 4236
Termination of the Partnership

3(15)1 *(11-6-79)* 4236
General

In the event of termination of a partnership, a limited partner will realize taxable gain to the extent that money distributed to the partner exceeds the adjusted basis of the partnership interest. For this purpose, reduction of liabilities is deemed to be a distribution of money. See IRC 752(b).

3(15)2 *(11-6-79)* 4236
Termination Caused by Sale of Partnership Interest

IRC 708(b)(1)(B) provides for termination of a partnership if, "within a 12-month period there is a sale or exchange of 50 percent or more of the total interest in partnership capital and profits." In years before the effective date of the new Code sections dealing with retroactive allocation of losses, it was a common practice to admit new partners into the partnership at year-end to "buy losses." (See previous discussion at 395 on "Retroactive Allocations of Partnership Losses.") Examiners should scrutinize these types of transactions for possible application of IRC 708(b), paying particular attention to transfers of capital, as well as profits (losses). If IRC 708(b) is applicable, all termination factors apply to the selling partnership, and the "new" partnership has acquired "used" property and accordingly would be limited in its allowable depreciation methods. Additionally, depending upon the particular facts, there may be issues with respect to the recapture provisions of IRC 47, 1245, etc. Also see *Rev. Rul. 75-423,* 1975-2 C.B. 260, concerning contributions of property in exchange for partnership interests. Examiners should also look for deductions of expenses of sale by the partnership incurred on final disposition of partnership assets. Such expenses are an offset against the computation of gain or loss on the sale, which is usually "capital" gain or loss.

3(15)3 *(11-6-79)* 4236
Bankruptcy

The Service position is that in a bankruptcy proceeding the partnership is terminated where its assets and liabilities are transferred to a court-appointed receiver or trustee. *Rev. Rul. 68-48,* 1968-1, C.B. 301. Thus, under the receiver or trustee a new entity is created and any loss of the new entity would not inure to the old partners. Case law is to the contrary in a situation where the assets are transferred to the receiver, (as distinguished from the trustee), on the basis that a new entity is not created, relying on Reg. 1. 641-(b)-2(b). *Kanna v. United States,* 35 AFTR 2d 75-1482 (D. Oregon 1975); *Lister v. United States,* 4 AFTR 2d 5716 (E.D. Va. 1959); *CHM Co. v. Commissioner,* 68 T.C. 31 (1977).

3(16)0 *(11-6-79)* 4236
Attempted Methods of Terminating a Partnership Interest Without Tax Consequences

3(16)1 *(11-6-79)* 4236
General

In many instances, the "day of reckoning" (crossover point) arrives when the partnership starts producing ordinary income to the individual partners. Therefore, partners may want to "extricate" themselves from the partnership as painlessly as possible. An outright "sale" of either the partnership assets or individual partnership interests may result in extensive gains (capital and/or ordinary). Some of the following methods have been attempted to accomplish the necessary extrication while circumventing the harsh effects of an outright sale.

3(16)2 *(11-6-79)* 4236
Tax Free Exchange of Partnership Interests

The Service has nonacquiesced to the decision in *Estate of Meyer v. Commissioner,* 58 TC 311 (1972), aff'd per curiam 503 F2d 556 (CA-9, 1974). The Meyer case holds that IRC 1031, dealing with nonrecognition of gain on like property, applies to the exchange of general partnership interests. The Service's position is that IRC 1031 does not apply, becuase a partnership interest is an "evidence of interest" within the meaning of IRC 1031(a). See *Rev. Rul. 78-135,* 1978-15 I.R.B., page 12.

3(16)3 *(11-6-79)* 4236
Tax Free Transfer to Controlled Corporation

A tax free transfer is allowable, so long as the taxpayer recognizes gain on the transfer to the extent that liabilities transferred exceed adjusted basis ("boot"). See IRC 357(c). The partners may attempt to offset this gain by transferring additional assets to the corporation until the adjusted basis of the assets transferred equals or exceeds the transferred liabilities. However, *Rev. Rul. 70-239,* 1970-1 C.B. 74, holds that, regardless of the form of transfer from the partnership to the corporation, the partnership itself is deemed to be the transferor. Therefore, the transfer of additional assets by the partners to offset excess liabilities of a partnership would not avoid recognition of gain by the partnership. Also, see *Rev. Rul. 66-142,* 1966-1 C.B. 66. It should be noted that the National Office is reconsidering *Rev. Rul. 70-239.*

3(16)4 *(11-6-79)* 4236
Gift Subject to Indebtedness

In the case of a partnership that has liabilities, a gift of a partnership interest will be considered a sale to the extent that the donor partner's allocable share of partnership liabilities exceeds the *adjusted basis* of the partnership interest transferred. Examiners should refer to *Rev. Rul. 60-352,* 1960-2 C.B. 208, *Rev. Rul. 70-626,* 1970-2 C.B. 158, and *Rev. Rul. 75-194,* 1975-1 C.B. 80, for guidance in this area.

3(16)5 *(11-6-79)* 4236
Deferred Sales Trusts

(1) Occasionally attempts are made to make the sale appear to be a tax-free exchange. Often in today's real estate market suitable property cannot be immediately located to consummate a tax-free exchange. In an attempt to qualify the transaction as tax-free, the property is sold outright, and the proceeds are left in an escrow or placed in a trust (usually informal) until suitable replacement property is located. Escrow or trust funds are used to purchase the new property. Taxpayers then claim nonrecognition on the sale, declaring it to be a deferred gain. This type of transaction is a taxable sale and repurchase, not a nontaxable exchange.

(2) The mere fact that property is placed into a trust or other vehicle as a step in consummating an exchange of like-kind property does not preclude a valid tax-free exchange under IRC Section 1031. However, examiners should be alert in all instances where the taxpayer is claiming the benefits of IRC Section 1031 (particularly where a trust or simultaneous escrow was utilized in the transaction) to ensure that the taxpayer received like-kind property. If the taxpayer received cash or other nonqualifying property, either directly or indirectly, the "exchange" should be considered a sale, either in whole or in part. Examiners should utilize any or all of the following information and documents in making their determination: agreements, memorandums of understanding, notes, escrow instructions, assignments, date sequences, credits, cross credits, property encumbrances and payments, property occupancy dates, powers of attorney, agency agreements, etc.

(3) These cases have been observed to be typical "substance versus form" cases, and examiners should not hesitate to make fraud referrals where factual findings warrant. See *Hubert Rutland v. Commissioner,* TC memo 1977-8 (1-17-77). *Starker v. U.S.,* 75-1 USTC 9943 and 77-2 USTC 9512 (D.C. Ore; 1977).

3(17)0 *(11-6-79)* 4236
Accounting Methods—Partner and Partnership

3(17)1 *(11-6-79)* 4236
Accrued Interest

It is not uncommon to find an accrual-basis partnership deducting interest on a bona fide note to a cash-basis partner without actually paying the interest. Examiners should be aware that the individual partner will have ordinary interest income if and when a credit is transferred to the partner's capital account. Additionally, upon termination of the partnership, any property received in satisfaction of the accrued interest liability must be reported as ordinary income. Partners may erroneously consider that their basis consists of their capital account, their loan, and the unpaid interest on the loan (accrued but never reported).

3(17)2 *(11-6-79)* 4236
Accrued Salaries

In some instances partnerships using the accrual method of accounting have deducted (but not paid) salaries, commissions, etc., owed to their cash-basis partners. Although IRC 267 (pertaining to related taxpayers) does not apply to partnerships, examiners should closely scrutinize these types of transactions. If it appears that the liability is so contingent that payment is unlikely, or that the partnership income is not properly reflected (IRC 446(b)), the deduction should not be allowed. Also, an IRC 707(c) payment accrued (but not paid) to a cash-basis partner by an accrual-basis partnership must be reported by the partner in the year accrued by the partnership. I.T. Reg. 1.706-1(a).

3(18)0 *(11-6-79)* 4236
Nonrecourse Financing

(1) Nonrecourse financing is a method of financing whereby the lender accepts a promissory note or other evidence of indebtedness on which the maker is not personally liable. In case of default, the lender can lay claim only to the underlying property which secures the obligation.

(2) *To the extent of the fair market value of the property,* liabilities on that property (recouse or nonrecourse) may be used to increase a partner's adjusted basis in a partnership (IRC 752(c)). Additionally, when none of the partners have any personal liability with respect to a partnership liability, then all partners, *including the limited partners,* are entitled to share in such liability, thereby increasing their individual partnership bases. (Treasury Reg. 1.752-1(e).) Thus, nonrecourse financing is a convenient vehicle for avoiding personal liability, while at the same time allowing maximum tax benefits. (See previous discussion on Basis at 3(12)0.) When a partnership acquires property using nonrecourse financing, however, IRC 752(c) limits the partnership's indebtedness and its basis for depreciation with respect to such financing to an amount not in excess of the *fair market value* of the property. Each partner's share of this liability (and accompanying basis increase) would be correspondingly limited (see *John F. and Mary Tufts v. Commissioner,* 70 TC 73 (8-23-78).) It is essential to obtain a reliable valuation of the underlying property. If the amount of the nonrecourse loan is greatly in excess of the value of the property, the borrower is not likely to pay the loan in order to get an equity in the property. Thus, the entire amount of the loan is contingent and not includible in the basis of the property. On the other hand, if the loan is not contingent, a part of the loan equal to the value of the property would be includible in the basis of the property. Treas. Reg. 1.752-1(e).

(3) If the partnership balance sheet reflects liabilities closely approximating the total assets, a strong possibility exists that nonrecourse financing is being utilized. In most transactions it is unlikely that a lender will advance money secured solely by the underlying asset. Usually equity is required on behalf of the borrower. Such situations raise further questions as to the true value of the underlying asset.

3(19)0 *(11-6-79)* 4236
Financing with a "Wrap-Around" Mortgage (All-Inclusive Deed of Trust)

(1) In this type of transaction, the borrower (purchaser) gives a note, usually nonrecourse, to the lender (seller) for an amount equal to the entire purchase price of the property, less any down payment. The seller usually promises to continue making the payments on any prior encumbrances still existing on the property, which often contain provisions for lower interest rates, prepayment penalties, etc. Thus, the prior encumbrances remain undisturbed and senior to the new obligation.

(2) The "wrap" (all-inclusive deed of trust) is found in a large number of sales of real property to limited partnerships formed for tax shelter purposes. The use of the "wrap-around" mortgage is conducive to tax sheltering by its very nature, allowing for maximum leveraging of a transaction. Maximizing the leverage on a transaction is accomplished by achieving the greatest ratio possible of debt financing to equity capital, usually without personal liability (nonrecourse). See discussion on "Leverage" at 3(21)0.

(3) In most cases, "wraps" are legitimate. However, they are sometimes used to inflate the purchase price of property to an amount in excess of its true value. Additionally, they may be used to facilitate large prepaid interest deductions, as shown in the following example: assume that a piece of property with a fair market value of $1,000,000 is purchased subject to a 1st mortgage of $600,000. If the purchasing partnership gives the seller a note for the $400,000 equity, taken *"subject to"* the underlying encumbrance, the maximum deduction as prepaid interest in a state having a maximum interest rate under the usury law of 10% would be $40,000. However, if the mortgage given by the purchaser is "wrapped around" the existing mortgage, the total obligation of the purchaser becomes $1,000,000, raising the maximum allowable prepayment of interest from $40,000 to $100,000. IRC 461(g) requires that prepaid interest paid after December 31, 1975, be amortized in taxable years ending after December 31, 1975.

3(20)0 *(11-6-79)* 4236
Financing Arrangements

(1) It is not unusual to observe a transaction couched in the form of a sale and leaseback which is merely a financing arrangement. There is a transfer of bare legal title for purposes of security only. Many arrangements are often "thin," and do not pass equitable title for depreciation or other tax purposes. Examiners should look for arrangements where the end result is as if no transfer were made (i.e., a loan).

(2) *Example 1*—A sale of rental property is made for $1 million ($200,000 down, $800,000 nonrecourse note) to a partnership. The property is leased back to the seller on terms that will return the $200,000 cash to the partners over the period of the lease. However, any gain on the property's resale by the partnership is restricted to 5% of the investor's initial cash investment, with the balance reserved to the original seller. The only real gain to the so-called "buyers" is the tax effect. In true ownership the full burdens and benefits exist, and the owner would be entitled to a full share of the profits, without restriction. This is merely a transfer of title for purposes of security, in reality a financing arrangement.

(3) *Example 2*—Rental property with an actual value of $1,000,000 is sold for $700,000 cash. The sales agreement is coupled with an option to reacquire the property four years later for $1,000,000. The so-called "buyer" could be a lender attempting to secure capital gain on what would otherwise be interest income, and the "seller" (borrower) would have four years financing.

3(21)0 *(11-6-79)* 4236
Leverage

(1) Leverage is defined as the ratio of debt financing to equity capital. An excellent leveraging situation would be an instance where a party enters into a transaction for no cash contribution whatsoever, buying the property completely on credit. An even better situation would be where there is no personal liability on the note, with the creditors looking only to the underlying property for relief. See discussion on "Nonrecourse Financing."

(2) In the context of a real estate tax shelter partnership, the partner who entered with no cash contribution would have a capital account of zero but could use the allocable share of partnership liabilities to increase basis, against which partnership losses could be claimed. Example, assuming $1,000,000 purchase:

(a) All cash, no credit. Leverage -0-
(b) $500,000 cash, $500,000 credit. Leverage 1 to 1
(c) $1 cash, $999,999 credit. Leverage 999,999 to 1

3(22)0 *(11-6-79)* 4236
"Tier" Partnerships Using Different Methods of Accounting

(1) Examiners may discover situations in which a partnership is a partner in another partnership, and where each entity is using a different method of accounting. Consideration should be given to distortion of income per IRC 446(b) and IRC 461 (general rule for taxable year of deduction).

(2) Additionally, it has been observed that partnerships sometimes use different accounting methods for the same partnership (e.g., accrual methods for capital accounts, cash method for balance of accounts). The above-mentioned Code sections would also be appropriate in these instances. However, in any examination it should be noted that IRC 446(b) permits a hybrid method of accounting as long as the use of such method clearly reflects the taxpayer's income. Also, it should be remembered that the election of "method of accounting" is vested with the partnership entity.

3(23)0 *(11-6-79)* 4236
Association vs. Limited Partnership

A limited partnership may be considered an association (taxable as a corporation) if it has more corporate than noncorporate characteristics. Whether or not an entity has corporate characteristics is a factual determination in each case. For guidance in this area, examiners should review the case of *Philip G. Larson v. Commissioner,* 66 TC 159 (1976), acq. 1979-19 I.R.B. 6. See also *Rev. Rul.* 79-106, 1979 I.R.B. 21. The examiner should consider *Larson* and *Zuckman v. United States,* 524 F2d 729 (Ct. Cls. 1975), and if faced with a similar fact situation, co-ordinate the case with District Counsel.

3(24)0 *(11-6-79)* 4236
Summonses

(1) During the course of a tax shelter examination, the examiner is often confronted with a reluctance on the part of a taxpayer to furnish documentation necessary to make a proper determination of the correct tax liability. Since all applicable facts should be gathered at the examination level, the examiner should not hesitate to consider the use of a summons when necessary. The examiner should be familiar with IRM Section 4022.

(2) It should be remembered that a partner in a partnership cannot use the Fifth Amendment to resist a summons with regard to partnership records. A partnership is an independent entity. See *U.S. v. Kuta,* 518 F 2d 947 (CA-7, 1975).

3(25)0 *(11-6-79)* 4236
Depreciation

The component method of computing depreciation on real estate tax shelters has become prevalent, particularly since legislation was enacted increasing the ordinary income recapture provisions of IRC 1250. Examiners should be aware that the component method of depreciation should, if properly computed, reflect approximately the same overall useful life for the asset as if it had been depreciated using the composite method. Some taxpayers are using the component method to depreciate buildings over 15 to 20 years when the buildings have actual estimated lives of 40 to 60 years. This is accomplished by allocating improper amounts to the various components having short lives, and by depreciating the "shell" over 25 to 30 years. In appropriate cases, examiners should consider requesting engineering assistance, keeping in mind that this issue only pertains to Class II Shelters. If the shelter lacks economic viability (Class III-Abusive), all losses should be disallowed. See *Rev. Rul. 66-111,* 66-1 C.B. 46, as modified by *Rev. Rul. 73-410,* 73-2 C.B. 53.

3(26)0 *(11-6-79)* 4236
Idaho Power Case

(1) In examinations involving construction of assets, examiners should be familiar with *Idaho Power Co. v. Commissioner,* supra, in which the Supreme Court held that depreciation of assets used to construct other assets must be capitalized under IRC 263 and depreciated over the life of the new asset (i.e., 40-year building).

(2) Examiners should read this case in its entirety, taking special note of the broad rationale used by the Court in arriving at its decision. IRC 263 was deemed to override the specific Code sections which would have otherwise allowed certain deductions.

3(27)0 *(11-6-79)* 4236
Construction Period Expenses: Federal Housing Administration (FHA) Housing Costs

3(27)1 *(11-6-79)* 4236
General

(1) FHA housing projects are typically financed by a 40-year FHA insured mortgage and capital contributed by the limited partners. The insured mortgage note represents a nonrecourse loan; therefore, each partner's basis in his or her partnership interest is increased by a pro rata share of this liability. This basis increase, together with accelerated depreciation and subsidy programs for interest and/or rental income, makes these projects attractive tax shelters. See also "Business vs. Investment" previously discussed at 370.

(2) The housing projects generally begin with a promoter or building contractor becoming a general partner, and with the syndicator also becoming a general partner in some of the partnerships. A brochure or prospectus prepared by the syndicator for marketing the limited partnership interests often contains descriptions of the applicable FHA Program and the specific housing project.

(3) In addition to the normal costs associated with the construction of the building, FHA allows the proceeds of the insured loan to be used to cover:

(a) The loan costs,

(b) The construction period interest expense,

(c) The Federal National Mortgage Association (FNMA), Government National Mortgage Association (GNMA) fees,

(d) The builder's risk insurance,

(e) The builder's bond premium,

(f) The 1st year mortgage insurance premium,

(g) The partnership's legal and organizational costs (not including syndication fee), and

(h) When approved by FHA, additional discounted interest expense, referred to as "interim discount," "construction loan discount," "construction loan fee," or "interest differential."

3(27)2 *(11-6-79)* 4236
Typical Issues

(1) *Administrative Management Fee* ("Packaging Fee," "Syndication Fee," etc.). This fee is usually paid to the general partner or the syndicator for services rendered in organizing and managing the limited partnership throughout its formation period. It generally includes legal and accounting costs for preparing documents. The purpose of this management fee can be found in:

(a) The partnership agreement.

(b) The sales agreement between the syndicator and the general partner.

(c) The brochure or prospectus used in marketing the limited partnership interest. Refer to the previous discussion on "Management Fees" at 391 for proper treatment of this item.

(2) *Developer's Fee.*

(a) In addition to the payments to the syndicator, other payments to partners are often deducted. These payments are usually made to the general partners who are the promoters and who often construct the apartment buildings. Some partnership agreements provide that partners receive compensation for constructing the building, for a rent-up management fee, and/or an "additional developer's fee." The payments are often made and deducted near the time the construction is started and are, in reality, either for working capital or for supervising the building construction.

(b) FHA 221(d) projects involve rehabilitating old buildings into low income rental housing. The promoter's (or developer's) fee in these projects should be capitalized into the rehabilitation costs account (and may qualify for subsequent amortization under IRC 167(k)) to the extent they are allocable to services such as working with architects and contractors.

(c) If the examiner finds that one of the partners has paid a separate fee for investment advice to the syndicator or others regarding the acquisition of his or her partnership interest, the cost should be capitalized. See *Vestal et al v. U.S.*, 498 F2d 487 (CA-8, 1974), rev'g DC.

(3) *Loan Costs.* These costs are usually deducted as current expenses under a "two-loan" theory. In actuality, there is only one FHA insured loan from which construction period draws are made. These loan costs should be capitalized and recovered ratably through amortization over the entire period of the loan. The capitalization is provided for by *Rev. Rul. 70-360*, 1970-2 C.B. 103. Also see *Rev. Rul. 74-395. The loan costs include:*

(a) A 2% finance fee for service of the mortgage,

(b) An FHA examination fee,

(c) An FHA inspection fee,
(d) Title and recording costs, and
(e) Survey costs, if any.

(4) *Interest.* Interest expense appears in four categories. Each category and its related allocation problem is described separately below.

(a) *Interest During Construction.* FHA permits this interest to be withheld from the proceeds of the loan.

1 *Accrual-Basis Entity.* Since this expense relates only to the construction period, it is not deductible. It may be amortized in accordance with IRC 189 or capitalized in accordance with IRC 266. Prior to the Tax Reform Act of 1976, interest was deductible over the construction period.

2 *Cash-Basis Entity.* Since this charge is withheld from the loan proceeds, it is discounted interest which has not been paid by a cash-basis entity. This charge may be deducted ratably over the 40-year period of the loan. See:

a *Burton Foster v. Commissioner,* 32 TCM 243 (1973),

b *Rev. Rul. 75–12,* 1975–1 C.B. 62, and

c *Rev. Rul. 69–188,* 1969–1 C.B. 54, as amplified by *Rev. Rul. 69–582,* 1969–2 C.B. 29.

(b) *The Commitment Fee and Purchase-Marketing Fee.* FHA charges the mortgagee a commitment fee and a purchase-marketing fee and permits them to be withheld from the proceeds of the loan. Since these fees, which are "passed through" to the mortgagor, are not for services rendered to the mortgagor, they constitute interest. See *Rev. Rul. 74–395,* supra, and *Parks v. U.S.,* 434 F supp. 206 (DC, 1977).

1 *Accrual-Basis Entity. Rev. Rul. 74–395* provides that since the loan instrument is silent as to what portion of each payment is discounted interest, the deduction accrues ratably over the 40-year period of the loan.

2 *Cash-Basis Entity.* Since these fees are withheld from the loan proceeds, they constitute discounted interest. Consequently, they may be deducted ratably over the 40-year period of the loan. See citations in (a)2 above.

(c) *Interim Discount, Construction Loan Discount, Construction Loan Fee, or Interest Differential.*

1 FHA sometimes permits the mortgagee to make an additional charge to compensate for the fluctuating interest rate in the money market. This discounted interest pertains to the period before the note and mortgage are sold to FNMA and is usually equivalent to the construction period. Since there are no services involved, this charge also constitutes interest. The discount is generally withheld from the loan proceeds and should be treated the same as "interest during construction" referred to in (a) above.

2 In some cases, the discount will be paid with a separate 40-year promissory note to the mortgagee. There are numerous decisions regarding cash-basis taxpayers who have given notes to cover liabilities. The giving of notes does not satisfy the statutory requirement of payment and does not permit a deduction. See *Hart v. Commissioner,* 54 F2d 848, (CA–1, 1932); *Goodstein et al v. Commissioner,* 267 F2d 127 (CA–1, 1959), aff'g 30 TC 1178; *Nat Harrison Associates Inc. v. Commissioner,* 42 TC 601 (1964).

3 If this charge is paid with separate funds, a cash-basis entity would have prepaid interest that may be deductible under *Rev. Rul. 68–643.* An accrual-basis entity could deduct the charge ratably over the construction period. However, refer to IRC 189 for statutory changes pertaining to construction period interest and prepaid interest under the Tax Reform Act of 1976.

(d) *Installment Payments on FHA Insured Loans.* The interest included in these payments should present no particular problem since it does not begin until after the construction is completed. The FHA 236 program provides for an interest subsidy under which the mortgagor pays somewhat over 1% interest.

(5) *Legal and Organizational Expenses.* FHA permits the mortgagor to use a portion of the loan proceeds for organizing the entity. The examiner may use *Abe Wolkowitz v. Commissioner,* 8 TCM 754 (1949), which holds that organizational expenses of a partnership must be capitalized. (See IRC 709 for treatment of organizational expenses under the Tax Reform Act of 1976.) Additionally, a portion of the funds might be paid to the promoter for services rendered in consulting with architects, contractors, Housing and Urban Development (HUD) officials, local government officials (rezoning and building codes), and the lender. Such costs should be capitalized into the building or loan cost account.

(6) *Builder's Risk Insurance.* This pertains to property and casualty insurance during construction and should be capitalized into the building account. See: *Herbert Shainberg v. Commissioner,* 33 TC 241 (1960); *The Columbia Theatre Co.,* 3 BTA 622, (1926); *Rev. Rul. 66–373,* 1966–2 C.B. 103.

(7) *Bond Premium.* The cost of the builder's performance bond should be capitalized into the building account. See *Estate of George B. Leonard Holding Corp. v. Commissioner,* 26 BTA 46.

(8) *Selling Expenses.* These are commissions for underwriting and directing the sale of the limited partnership interests, which should be capitalized as a syndication expense. Amortization of the expenses is not permitted; only organization fees are amortizable under IRC 709(b).

(9) *Cost Certification (accounting services prior to final closing).* Accounting services in connection with verifying construction costs for a building are an integral part of the total cost of a new building. See *Herber Shainberg v. Commissioner,* supra.

(10) *Amortization*

(a) The loan costs may be amortized over the 40-year loan period starting with the first installment payment. See 3(27)2:(3) above.

(b) The discounted interest is deductible ratably over the 40 year loan period starting with the first installment payment. See 3(27)2:(4) above.

(c) Rehabilitation costs in FHA 221(d) projects may qualify for 60-month amortization under IRC Sec. 167(k).

3(27)3 *(11-6-79)* 4236
Method of Accounting

Ordinarily, rental operations such as FHA low-income housing projects use the cash receipts and disbursements method of accounting for income tax purposes. FHA requires these entities to use the accrual method for FHA subsidy program purposes. Since, prior to the enactment of IRC 189, it was to the partnership's benefit to be on the accrual method of accounting for "interest during construction" and "interim discount" deductions, agents should be alert to the validity of any claim that the accrual method is being used for tax purposes when it is not apparent from the return. After the rental operation has begun, an accrual basis entity would have rental income receivables and accrued expenses payable.

3(27)4 *(11-6-79)* 4236
Documents

(1) Documents generally available for review are listed below.

(a) Partnership agreement.

(b) Sales agreement between promoter and/or contractor and the syndicator.

(c) Brochures used to sell the limited partnership interest.

(d) Commitment for insurance advances (FHA Form No. 2432).

(e) Building loan agreement (FHA Form 2441).

(f) Construction contract—cost plus (FHA Form 2442).

(g) Mortgagee's certificate (FHA Form 2432).

(h) Initial closing statement.

(i) Application for insurance on advances of mortgage proceeds (FHA Form 2403). (There is a separate form for each advance.)

(j) Financial requirements for closing (FHA Form 2883).

(k) Mortgagor's certificate of actual cost (FHA Form 2330).

(l) Final closing statement.

(m) Other Construction Documents:

1 Building permits,

2 Completion notices,

3 Mechanic's lien releases, and

4 Occupancy approvals.

3(28)0 *(11-6-79)* 4236
Defective Trusts

(1) It has been observed in some instances that taxpayers are attempting to use the trust as a vehicle to provide losses for the grantor during the early years of a tax shelter while avoiding the "phantom gain" of Treasury Reg. 1.752-1(d) at the time of termination of the partnership interest. Frequently, a partnership interest will be terminated at the "crossover point," i.e., where the net taxable income exceeds cash flow.

(2) Typically, the technique works in the following manner:

(a) The taxpayer (settlor) forms an irrevocable trust, transferring a sum of money as corpus and designating various relatives as beneficiaries.

(b) The taxpayer files a gift tax return to help establish a completed gift.

(c) The taxpayer purposely drafts the trust instrument in such a "defective" manner that the trust will be treated as a grantor trust and the income and/or losses will be taxed to the settlor. The various defects which will cause this result are covered by IRC 671 through 679.

(d) The trust invests in a tax shelter, which passes losses through to the trust and subsequently to the settlor by reason of the "defect."

(e) A few years later, at the "crossover point", the settlor "cures" the defect, thus causing the trust income to be spread out among the various trust beneficiaries.

(3) Examiners should be alert to these types of trusts and should assert that the settlor suffers a taxable event when the defect is "cured." Since the taxpayer has disposed of his/her interest in the grantor trust, previously claimed depreciation and investment credit, if any, must be recaptured. To the extent he/she is released from his/her share of the nonrecourse loan, he/she now has income. See *Rev. Rul. 77–402,* 1977–2, C.B. 222.

3(29)0 *(11–6–79)* 4236
Governmental Registration Requirements of Limited Partnership Offerings

3(29)1 *(11–6–79)* 4236
Securities and Exchange Commission

(1) Many limited partnership interests are exempted from registering with the SEC by various statutory exemptions. The most commonly utilized exemption is the "private transaction exemption" granted by Section 4(2) of the Securities Act of 1933, as clarified by SEC Rule 146. Rule 146 sets forth various conditions which, if met, create a presumptive private transaction exemption. Some of the conditions required in Rule 146 are as follows:

(a) Limited partnership interests may be sold to no more than 35 investors, with the spouse and other relatives living at home counted as one investor.

(b) Prior to purchase, each offeree must be furnished "the information that would be required to be included in a registration statement filed under the 1933 Act. . ."

(c) Purchasers must be sufficiently sophisticated to "fend for themselves," and they must be given access to the necessary information for this purpose.

(d) The issuer must not use any form of public advertisement as a means of effecting the sale of limited partnership interests.

(2) If the examiner finds that the particular partnership under audit has met the foregoing requirements (as well as the other requirements of Rule 146) and thus qualifies for the "private transaction exemption" from SEC registration, inquiry should be made of the partnership or its representative as to the document used in informing the prospective purchasers of the applicable facts required in (1) (b) and (c) above.

(3) At a minimum, the disclosure document given to the proposed offerees should contain the following information:

(a) A general description of the limited partnership interests being offered, and the capitalization of the limited partners.

(b) A description of how the proceeds of the offering will be used.

(c) A statement of the risks to the investor, including tax risks, competitive risks, risks involved in the lack of liquidity and difficulty of transfer of the limited partnership interests, and any special risks inherent in the business to be conducted by the limited partnership.

(d) General information about the general partner, the directors and officers if it is a corporation, and specific information with respect to the general partner's experience in the business area of the investment.

(e) A summary of every transaction in which the limited partnership intends to engage which may involve a conflict of interest between the investors and the issuer, underwriter, and their affiliates.

(f) A discussion and presentation of the Federal and state tax issues that concern the limited partners. This discussion must be detailed, going beyond the Code and Regulations, as necessary, to discuss all potential issues.

(g) Information relative to the investment policies of the limited partnership, any applicable underwriting arrangements, and any special investment suitability standards. In addition, although they are generally not required in an exempt offering memorandum, it is also desirable to include financial statements and exhibits relative thereto.

(4) The above information, which is nearly as detailed as the information required in a fully registered prospectus, should be of assistance to the examiner and should be one of the first documents requested in the audit.

3(29)2 *(11–6–79)* 4236
State Requirements

Exemption from registration under the 1933 Securities Act does not automatically exempt limited partnership offerings from the qualification requirements of state law. Usually, each set of laws requires separate compliance. Examiners should inquire of their own state agencies as to the specific registration requirements of limited partnership offerings, including the existence of any files that may be available for inspection. In some instances, more than one agency will be involved.

3(30)0 *(11-6-79)* 4236
Conclusion

(1) In *Gordon MacRae v. Commissioner,* 34 TC 20 (1960), the Court stated: "The steps taken, each in itself a legitimate commercial operation, were here each mirror images, and add up to zero. The various purchases and sales, each real *without the other,* neutralize one another and fairly shout to the world the essential nullity of what was done. The choice of the more complicated and involved method of doing nothing had no purpose, save the erection of the facade upon which petitioners now seek to rely."

(2) Examiners must realize that the entire "Tax Shelter" area is continually changing, and their examination techniques must be sufficiently flexible to meet the challenge. They should remember that to aid in determining all relevant facts, the Service has working agreements with most governmental agencies, and channels of communication with these agencies are open.

3(31)0 *(11-6-79)* 4236
Glossary of Terms

The glossary of terms is provided in Exhibit 300-2.

Exhibit 300-1

Illustrations of the Three Classes of Tax Shelters

(1) CLASS I - Economically and substantively viable.

Formation date: 1-1-74 (Operating Entity)

Purchase price	$500,000;	FMV $500,00
Lease - rent (yr.)	60,000;	FMV 60,00
*Investment return	15%;	**Risk rate 15%

Claimed deduction (first year):
- Real estate tax paid
- Interest paid first year
- Management fees (actual services)

*Represents return on investor's out-of-pocket cash investment.
**Or prevailing rate relative to risk involved.

(2) CLASS II - Frequently deduction vs. capitalization: Capital items claimed as ordinary deductions or mishandling or mischaracterization of other specific elements.

Formation Date 06-30-74 (Operational in 1975)
- First year -

Purchase price	$550,000	FMV $500,000
Lease - rent (yr.)	60,000	FMV 60,000
Investment return	15%	Risk Rate 15% (a)

Claimed deductions: (first year)
- Interest prepaid (b)
- Interest on wrap-around mortages (c)
- Real estate taxes
- Payments to general partners (d)
- Management fees (disguised commissions)
- Commissions
- Organization fees
- Loan fees
- Appraisal fees (e)
- Commitment fees (f)
- Construction loan items (g)
- Points (h)
- Preopening expenses (i)(j)
- Timing factor of loans

Exhibit 300–1 Cont. (1)

Illustrations of the Three Classes of Tax Shelters

Notes:

(a) or prevailing rate relative to risk involved.
(b) See IRC 461 (g).
(c) Rev. Rul. 75-99, 1975-1 C.B. 197. Also see IRC 461(g).
(d) Rev. Rul. 75-214, 1975-1 C.B. 185 (organization expense).
(e) Rev. Rul. 74-104, 1974-1 C.B. 70.
(f) Rev. Rul. 75-172, 1975-1 C.B. 145.
(g) Rev. Rul. 74-395, 1974-2 C.B. 45 (one-loan concept). Also Rev. Rul. 68-643, 1968-2 C.B. 76 (distortion).
(h) See IRC 461(g).
(i) Richmond Television Corp. v. U.S., 345 F2d 901 (CA-4 1965).
(j) Idaho Power Co. v. Commissioner, 418 U.S.-1, 1974-2 C.B. 85.

(3) CLASS III - Lacking economic reality or viability.

(a) Example 1

Formation Date - 12-28-75 (operational entity)

Sales price	$1,000,000(1)	FMV $500,000
Lease - rent (yr.)	60,000	FMV 120,000
Return on investment	3%	Risk rate 15%

Claimed deductions: (first year)

Interest prepaid (2)
Interest on wrap-around mortgages (3)
Real estate taxes
Payments to general partners (4)
Management fees (disguised commissions)
Commissions
Organization fees
Loan fees
Appraisal fees
Commitment fees (5)
Construction loan items (6)
Points
Preopening expenses
Timing factor of loans

(1) Apparent excessive price, standing alone, does not establish "abuse"; other factors must be considered.
(2) See IRC 461(g).
(3) Rev. Rul. 75-99. Also see IRC 461(g).
(4) Rev. Rul. 75-214. (Organization expense).
(5) Rev. Rul. 75-172.
(6) Rev. Rul. 74-395. (One-loan concept). Also Rev. Rul 68-643. (Distortion).

Exhibit 300-1 Cont. (2)

Illustrations of the Three Classes of Tax Shelters

(b) Example 2

Syndicator Purchases Property for: $600,000(FMV)
(1st Mortgage Only - No Down Payment)

Payment by Syndicator on 1st Mortgage:

Interest - $600,000 X 6% =	$36,000
Principal	4,000
	$40,000

Syndicator Sells Property (Building Only)
to a Partnership for $1,800,000
(Wrap-around Financing Subject to 1st Mortgage.)

Gross Profit: 66 2/3% reported on
Installment Basis 1,200,000

Terms: Partnership pays $140,000 per year including interest @ 7%. Balloon payment on mortgage at end of lease.

Leaseback from Partnership to Syndicator:
10 year lease @ $140,000 per year.

Partnership loss for 1st year:

Rental income from Syndicator		$140,000
Less Depreciation (20 yr. s/l)	1,800,000 x 5%	(90,000)
Interest	1,800,000 x 7%	126,000)
Net loss for year		$ 76,000

Net effect:

Syndicator:	W/Shelter	W/O Shelter
Interest Income (7% X 1,800,000)	126,000	-0-
Gain on Sale (140,000 Installment pay less 126,000 int. X 66 2/3%	9,332	-0-
	135,332	-0-
Depre. Expense @ 5% S/L (600,000 X 5%)	-0-	30,000
Rent Expense	140,000	-0-
Interest Expense (600,000 X 6%)	36,000	36,000
Net loss for year	(40,668)	(66,000)

Exhibit 300-1 Cont. (3)

Illustrations of the Three Classes of Tax Shelters

Gain on sale and interest income are sheltered by rent expense and interest on first trust.

Partners' Basis:

Assume A and B are equal partners and made no capital contributions during the year

	Partner A	Partner B
Capital Contributions	-0-	-0-
Partners share of liabilities under Regs. 1.752-1(c) (1,800,000 - 14,000 principal payment during year divided by 2)	893,000	893,000
Partnership loss for year	(38,000)	(38,000)
Basis at end of first year	855,000	855,000

Incentive of Parties:

A purchaser would pay a substantial front-end fee to secure a shelter as shown in this example. The incentive: to reduce the tax on other unrelated income. To avoid complicating the example, the fee was deleted. It would usually be reflected by taxpayers as a "wash" (additional deduction to purchaser; additional income to seller). Other interacting factors such as expenses, appreciation, actual economic depreciation, inflation, etc., have been deleted for simplicity.

Exhibit 300-2

Glossary of Terms

◊

(1) *Blind Pool*—A tax sheltered partnership that does not have specific projects or properties to which the proceeds will be committed at the time sale of subscription begins.

(2) *Front-End Load*—A slang term for the total of organizational and offering expenses plus management fees; i.e., the total deduction from the offering amount to arrive at the proceeds of a tax sheltered partnership.

(3) *Joint Venture*—A form of business organization in which the manager and the investors share jointly in the ownership, management, authority, and liability. (Contrast with limited partnership.)

(4) *Limited Partnership*—A form of business organization in which some of the partners exchange their right to participate in management for a limitation on their liability for partnership debts. Commonly, limited partners have liability only to the extent of their investment in the business, plus their share of any undistributed profits. To establish limited liability, there must be at least one general partner who is fully liable for all claims against the business. Limited partnerships are a popular organizational form for tax sheltered investments because of the ease with which tax benefits flow through the partnership to the individual partners. (Contrast with joint venture.) For basis purposes, see Treasury Regulation 1.752-1(e).

(5) *Management Fee*—An amount paid, usually to the general partner of a tax sheltered partnership, to cover organization and offering expenses and/or to repay costs of operating and administering the partnership, frequently expressed as a percentage of the total offering (capitalizable). When paid for services relative to the operation of a going business, the expense is deductible.

(6) *Noncash Charges*—Deductions for items such as depreciation and depletion, which are not actually paid but are subtracted from taxable income (or distributable net income) before calculating tax due.

(7) *"Nonrecourse Loan"*—Any borrowing by an entity structured in such a way that lenders can look only to specific assets pledged in the event of default and not to the individual assets of the mortgagor(s). For partnerships, in the event of a foreclosure, if partnership cash and assets aren't sufficient to repay the loan balance, the partners may be left with a substantial tax bill because of "forgiveness of debt." However, in many cases of foreclosure, various attempts are made to defer the tax consequences through IRC 108 and IRC 1017. See discussion in 3(14)0 of this Handbook regarding abandonment or forfeiture of a partnership interest.

(8) *Promoter*—An individual or business entity that actively secures funds by locating interested investors. Often the promoter is the general partner in the limited partnership.

(9) *Real Estate Syndication*—A legal form of business, such as a corporation, partnership, joint venture, etc., which allows the pooling of financial resources to acquire real property.

(10) *Tax Losses*—A situation that occurs when the deductions generated by a tax shelter exceed revenues. Thus, the investor's taxable income is lower, resulting in a tax saving. Ideally, a tax shelter will generate enough tax losses the first year or first few years to permit the investors to recover their total investment from "tax savings." However, recapture may ultimately limit these benefits.

(11) *Tax Savings*—See: (10) above, Tax Losses.

(12) *Tax Sheltered Cash Flow*—The situation that arises when noncash charges added to other deductions exceed gross income from a tax shelter, resulting in cash available for distribution to investors that may not be currently taxed, or is taxed at a lower rate. Real estate and equipment leasing programs employing accelerated depreciation and high leverage are common sources of tax sheltered cash flow.

(13) *Tax Sheltered Investment*—An investment with a flow-through of tax benefits, generally having some or all of the following characteristics:

(a) Deferral of taxes.

(b) Conversion of ordinary deductions to future capital gains.

(c) Leverage.

The flow-through of tax benefits is a material factor, whether the entity is organized as a limited partnership, joint venture, trust, or Subchapter S Corporation, and whether it is offered to investors as a private program or a public program.

Exhibit 300-2 Cont. (1)

Glossary of Terms

◊

(14) *Conversion*—Applying deductions against ordinary income, while turning future revenues into income taxable at more favorable capital gains rates or lower tax rates.

(15) *Deferral*—The timing of an investment so that deductions take place during the early years and income is realized in later years, or at a time when the tax will be at a more beneficial rate.

(16) *Leverage*—A method of increasing the effectiveness of a shelter by the ratio of risk capital to borrowings. The investor (in certain circumstances) is permitted deductions for interest, management fees, depreciation, etc., on the amount invested, in addition to a pro rata share of the amount the partnership borrows (even on a nonrecourse basis). Any loans, therefore, serve to increase basis. It should be noted that IRC 752(c) limits to fair market value the amount to be considered as a liability of the owner of property.

(17) *Tax Sheltered Partnership*—A tax sheltered investment, usually organized as a limited partnership and created to mutually benefit the various partners (usually a general partner and a group of limited partners). It may be organized as a private program or public program.

(18) *Private Program*—A tax sheltered partnership that is offered and sold pursuant to the private offering exemption available under the Federal Securities Act of 1933 and/or some registration exemption granted by state securities authorities; i.e., a program that is not registered with the Securities and Exchange Commission. (Contrast with Public Program.)

(19) *Public Program*—A tax sheltered partnership that is registered with the Securities and Exchange Commission and distributed in a public offering by broker-dealers and/or employees of the general partner. The principal difference between a public program and a private program is the number of investors, which may be several hundred in a public program, but is limited to 35 in a private program.

In addition to the SEC laws, the various states often have their own statutes and regulations defining the types of partnerships requiring registration with state administrative bodies.

(20) *Triple Net Lease* (also referred to as net net net lease)—a lease under the terms of which the lessee pays all expenses (taxes, utilities, and upkeep) except mortgage payments (principal and interest).

Exhibit 300-3

Example of Loss Computation in Year of Foreclosure

Year 1

Partner's cash contribution	$20,000
Partner's share of partnership liabilities	60,000
Partner's share of loss	(40,000)
Adjusted basis at year-end (including liabilities)	$40,000

Year 2 - (foreclosure at year-end)

Partner's share of liabilities deemed distributed (IRC 752(b))	$60,000
Adjusted basis (without considering Year 2's operating loss)	40,000
Capital gains upon foreclosure (assume no potential IRC 1250 recapture or other IRC 751 assets)	$20,000
Amount of loss which can be utilized by the partner in Year 2	-0-

The basis of the partner's interest is zero after the IRC 752(b) distribution of $60,000, precluding a deduction for any partnership losses in year 2.

Farm Operations Tax Shelters

410 *(3-2-79)* 4236
Background

(1) The examination techniques in this Chapter relate primarily to partnerships, agency syndicators (usually corporations), and agency investors, all of whom are involved in livestock transactions, both breeding and feeding.

(2) Some of the income tax issues on the returns of investors and syndicators, such as the prepayment of fees, interest, and deduction of organizational costs, are encountered in other types of tax shelters, such as oil and gas and real estate.

(3) This chapter concentrates on issues and schemes that are unique to farm operation tax shelters. Examples of these are as follows:

(a) Prepaid feed differs from other prepayments because partnerships, Subchapter S corporations, and individual investors use the cash method of accounting available to farmers, even though inventory is a material income producing item. However, this method of accounting, granted to simplify accounting for farmers, was not intended to permit manipulative abuse of accounting practices.

(b) Also, the purchase of heifers, bulls, milk cows, mink, and other breeding stock at inflated costs when compared to the value of the animals in what is ostensibly an arms-length transaction, is a situation usually not encountered in normal business transactions.

(4) Promoters of the various tax shelter schemes continue to offer different, often constrained, ways for the investor to benefit from the tax laws that apply generally only to farmers. Most of the livestock tax shelters are designed to give the investor large tax deductions, usually late in December, based on acceptable accounting methods employed by and reserved for farmers. Generally, few shelters have economic reality when considered separate from the tax benefits.

(5) A common problem is the recognition of the various forms of livestock tax shelters, especially when viewing only the return of the investor. The discussion of each type of shelter will include some of the reporting characteristics of the investor.

(6) As in other shelter areas, the limited partnership form is often used to maximize tax benefits. Many farm tax shelter syndicators, however, have chosen an agency relationship with individual, trust, and partnership investors.

(7) This Chapter contains schemes, issues and techniques used in farm shelters involving animals. As new schemes are identified in other farm shelters, such as timber, orchard growing, and fish farming, this chapter will be revised to include the issues and techniques unique to them.

420 *(3-2-79)* 4236
Organizational Structure

(1) The organizational structure of the animal tax shelters which file prospectuses with the Securities and Exchange Commission are summarized below.

(a) Agency syndications:
1 Feeder cattle agency agreement
2 Purebred managed cattle herd
3 Commercial managed cattle herd

(b) Limited partnerships:
1 Feeder—Most of the publicly syndicated limited partnerships are feeder operations
2 Breeder
3 Feeder-breeder combination

(c) Subchapter S syndications:
1 Feeder
2 Dairy herd

(2) Many agency syndicators offer programs through prospectuses not registered with the Securities and Exchange Commission. Their offerings are described in prospectuses that are called, for example, "Confidential Investment Memorandum" or "Offering Circular".

(3) Other syndicators offer assorted programs that on the surface appear different, but when analyzed, have similar tax shelter attributes. Some of these programs are:

(a) Managed sow, heifer, and mink programs.

(b) Managed dairy herd programs involving purchased mature cows leased to dairy farmers.

(c) Managed dairy herd programs involving purchased calves raised to maturity or leased to dairy farmers.

430 *(3-2-79)* 4236
Basic Types of Animal Tax Shelters

(1) Shelters involving animals are of two basic types.

(a) Breeder—In this type of transaction a partnership or individual investor buys a commercial or purebred herd, usually cattle, in a program designed to operate for a specific term, commonly 5 to 7 years. These herds are customarily purchased from the promoter or an entity related to the promoter, who continue to manage and care for the primary herd and the progeny.

1 The objective of this type of investment is to gain front-end deductions for depreciation, investment credit, and other expenses, sometimes in excess of the cash investment in the original herd, while creating the potential for long-term capital gain income on the raised progeny which will have no basis.

2 Determination of the fair market value of livestock at the time of purchase and the economic reality of the overall investor program are essential in the development of cases involving breeding livestock and fur bearing animals.

3 There are variations of these shelters that involve, for example, the sale of mature and immature dairy cows to investors for subsequent lease to farmers in a program managed throughout by the syndicator.

4 Two items usually identify investors in set-price herds:

a The cows all have the same cost even though they may have different remaining lives.

b There are no farm expenses other than depreciation and, in some instances, maintenance fees.

(b) Feeder—This type of shelter is formed specifically to obtain a year-end deduction of prepaid feed and other expenses.

1 Most of these shelters, whether limited partnerships or agency arrangements, are formed at year-end for the purpose of entering into an agreement to purchase feed in a leveraged transaction. This often occurs well before the livestock is purchased.

2 Some syndicators offer feeder programs that continue for a term of years, but for many the objective is a one-year deferral of income; that is, a deduction for feed in the initial year leveraged with a nonrecourse loan, and the reporting of the cattle sales and their cost in the subsequent year. The effect is that the shelter investor can "roll-over" or postpone recovery of the initial deduction.

(2) IRC 464 greatly limits deductions for certain farming syndicates for taxable years beginning after December 31, 1975. Similarly, IRC 447 requires certain farming corporations and partnerships to use the accrual method of accounting and to capitalize their preproduction expenses beginning after December 31, 1976. However, the guidelines in this Chapter will continue to be effective for many syndicates and some corporations not covered under the provisions of IRC 447 and 464.

(3) In some instances, syndicators have formed animal shelters which conduct "integrated" feeding and breeding operations.

440 *(3-2-79)* 4236
Features Applicable to Breeder Tax Shelters

441 *(3-2-79)* 4236
Breeder (Managed Herd) Agency Syndications

(1) The breeder herd syndications involve sales of herds by a promoter-operator corporation to investors under an agency agreement. The investors may be individuals, partnerships, trusts, subchapter S corporations, or regular corporations.

(2) Through offering memoranda or prospectuses, breeding herds, usually consisting of units (herds) of ten female animals, are offered for sale to the public. The investor is offered the opportunity or is required to enter into a maintenance contract, whereby for a fee the promoter-operator will feed, care for, and breed the animals and their progeny. The fee usually consists of cash, a percentage of the offspring, or a combination of cash and offspring.

(3) The animals are usually purchased by the promoter-operator at the prevailing market rate and then sold to the investor at an inflated price. The more abusive programs usually have a highly inflated stated purchase price for the animals, require little down payment, and offer a deferred nonrecourse liability for the balance of the purchase price. The nonrecourse note will be paid only out of the proceeds of the sale of the progeny. Other plans may contain a less inflated stated sales price and may require cash payment of the total price over a period of time.

(4) Tax deductions and credits well in excess of the investor's equity are the benefits obtained by taxpayers in the first year of these programs.

442 *(3-2-79)* 4236
The Examination of an Investor in a Breeder Agency Syndication

(1) The examination of the investor's return, whether or not the syndicator's return is examined, is the point at which tax shelter abuses are encountered. The examination may be initiated as a result of normal classification procedures, or it may be the result of an information item or Form 918A (Notice of Examination of Fiduciary, Partnership or Small Business Corporation Return) originating from the examination of the syndicator.

(2) Although an information item or Form 918A may provide useful data upon which to initiate the examination, examiners should never hesitate to make full inquiry into the nature and circumstances of the losses generated by these agency agreements.

(3) The development, documentation, and careful review of the operation and practices of each specific situation are necessary to determine if artificial pricing exists and how the results of artificial pricing of breeder animals can best be characterized. Potential issues vary depending on the stage of the investor's program during the years under examination.

(4) The first years of the inflated herd investor's program are the years when tax abuses are the most obvious. This is the period when the investment credit and first year additional and accelerated depreciation, based on the inflated price, are offsetting other unrelated income in amounts far in excess of the investor's out-of-pocket or economic investment in these programs.

(5) In some instances, the case development should be made with a view toward proposing alternative positions. For example, alternative positions might be: no reasonable expectation of profit, the investor does not have the burdens of ownership, or the depreciation is excessive because it is based on an amount in excess of fair market value. The appropriateness of these various positions will depend on the factual situation, i.e., the contractual relationship and the actual practices of the shelter/promoter and the investor.

(6) The issues in subsequent years may be limited to such items as the nature of the gain on the sale of the progeny and recapture of depreciation. Activities engaged in for the purpose of reducing taxes, rather than earning economic profits, are not the kind of profit-seeking activities contemplated by IRC 162, 212, and 167.

(7) The following documents and records should be obtained during the examination of the investor. Although some syndicators may not have supplied all of this information to the investor, these records must be made available to substantiate such items as basis, asset life, holding period, ownership, and investment credit.

(a) Prospectus or offering memorandum

(b) Sales agreement regarding the herd purchase

(c) Note and installment purchase contract

(d) Security agreements

(e) Maintenance or management agreement

(f) Guarantee or guarantee side letter

(g) Records of payment for herd purchase and other costs

(h) Detailed depreciation schedules

(i) Invoices for maintenance, feed, and other expenses

(j) Periodic and year-end herd status reports to include:

1 Location of herd

2 Registration numbers or other identification of all herd animals

3 Date of birth of each animal

4 Purchase price of each animal

5 Sales reports including the specific animal's identity, age, sex, date sold, price, as well as the identity of the buyer.

443 *(3-2-79)* 4236
Examination of the Syndicator of Managed Breeding Herds

(1) Examination of the syndicator will have two purposes: to determine the accuracy of the return and to determine the correct reporting of the result of the agency agreement at the investor level.

(2) Examiners should examine the investor relationship outlined in the prospectus and the examination potential of the investors' returns with a view toward disseminating or referring the information to the district in which the investors reside.

(a) Identification of the investors should be as specific as can be determined from the syndicator's records. Cancelled checks and other original documents may provide more specific information about the identity of the investors.

(b) The referral should include an overall description of the program and the issues.

(c) Specific investor information, such as payments, financing documents, and reports to the investor, should also be included in the referral when practical.

(3) Determine what the promoter-operator does with the proceeds received from the investors. Is the money used primarily in the herd operations, loaned to related entities, or used for purposes unrelated to the breeding program?

(a) Unrelated use of a substantial amount of the proceeds is supportive of the view that the investor's program lacks economic reality.

(b) The proceeds of these sales are income to the syndicator. Promoter-operator companies may defer the reporting of receipts by creating large reserves for contingencies. Reductions of income to create contingency reserves are not allowable. Deferral of income is the common issue.

1 The titles of these reserves range from accounts payable and inter-company liability to customer deposits and due to herd raisers.

2 The entries to create these accounts may appear complex and often are as creative as the "convincing reasons" given for their existence.

(4) Ascertain the value of the animals sold to investors. This is a critical factor since it is necessary to determine if an inflated price was paid for them.

(a) When syndicators purchase the animals that are soon sold to investors, the examiner's consideration of valuation factors may be limited to the cost of the animals and the cost of maintaining them until sold.

(b) Syndicators who file prospectuses with the Securities and Exchange Commission may be required to state their cost or the fair market value in the prospectus. It is not uncommon for these prospectuses to state value or cost at 30% or less of selling price, some at less than 10%.

(c) The value of raised animals presents a greater valuation problem. Industry averages for a breed are an indication of value. In situations where the syndicator has operated for a few years, the sales of his/her animals to non-investors and the sales price of the individual investor's animals will provide support for valuation computations.

(d) Determine whether the animals were purchased from an individual or entity related to the promoter-operator and, if so, whether they have been purchased on the installment basis. A purchase from a related entity suggests that the price to the promoter-operator company may be inflated. Such a transaction reported on the installment method supports the suggestion. Trace the animal purchased from the related entities to their third party source.

(e) The value of the investor herd is the central factor in the determination that the investor's purchase was not made with a reasonable expectation of profit. An inflated price precludes the possibility of profit in the reasonably forseeable future. See *Arnold L. Ginsberg v. Commissioner,* 35 TCM 860.

(f) When the value of the property is less than the amount of the nonrecourse loan balance, the investor does not have the economic incentive to treat the obligation as if it is a personal obligation. *See Rev. Rul. 77–110,* 77–1 C.B. 58, regarding the purchase of film rights by a limited partnership and the *Estate of Franklin v. Commissioner,* 544 F2d 1045 (CA–9 1976), 76–2 USTC 9773, affg 64 T.C. 752.

(5) Ascertain if the syndicator has guaranteed such items as herd replacement and number of progeny.

(a) Syndicator guarantees may be stated in prospectuses or agreements; some are not stated. Contingency reserves created to defer income of the syndicator are an indication that unstated guarantees exist.

(b) Guarantees are an important factor supporting the position that the investor, as in *Herbert D. Wiener v. Commissioner,* 494 F2d 691 (CA–9 1974), 74–1 USTC 9403, affg per curiam 58 T.C. 81, has not acquired the burdens of ownership. The syndicator, by virtue of these guarantees, may assume significant burdens and risks of ownership of the original herd and/or progeny.

(6) Determine the nature of the loan granted to allow the investors to purchase herds on the installment method. For example, is the loan granted directly by the promoter-operator? If so, is the paper discounted to a bank or other financial institution? If the loan is arranged directly with a bank, determine how it is secured and if the promoter-operator guarantees the note.

(a) The determination of the specific terms of the financing, coupled with the determination that the price of the herd is inflated, can be important for a number of reasons. One is to determine if the transaction has substance. Another is to determine if the liability to repay is so contingent as to preclude consideration of the investor as having the burdens of ownership. See *Estate of Franklin v. Commissioner,* supra, and *Carnegie Productions Inc. v. Commissioner,* 59 T.C. 642.

(b) There are instances in which the installment contract of purchase is no more than a vehicle to inflate the front-end price. For example, an investor might pay $10,000 or less down and have a contractual obligation to pay $40,000 in installments. The same contract can have a provision that allows the investor to sell a specific number of progeny at a specific price on specific dates to the contract holder (the promoter-operator). The guaranteed price for this specific number of animals equals the initial contract balance. The only payments that are real are the down payment and the annual interest. This is graphically illustrated when actual sales show that the animals are worth much less than the amount allowed as credit on the contract.

(c) The financing of the investor's herds may be directly related to the syndicator's method of reporting gross income; that is, contracts between the syndicator and investor might be reported on the installment basis by the syndicator, whereas notes discounted by the syndicator would be considered gross receipts to the syndicator.

(d) The importance of an indepth examination of all the factors of the financing agreement cannot be overemphasized. Some bank loans have little or no substance. Consider a situation in which the syndicator arranges a bank loan for the investor. The proceeds are paid to the syndicator who within a few days pays the same amount to the bank in redemption of the note. The bank charges no interest to either party for the accommodation. The investor's liability to pay this "loan" is limited to a specified price for a certain number of progeny.

(7) Review the manner in which each investor's herd animals are identified. Are the purebred animals registered in the operator's name or the name of the investor? If the herd is not registered, in what manner are the specific animals identified with the investor? There have been instances, in bankruptcies for example, where many of the animals were found not to exist.

(a) Herd identification is an important factor in establishing whether the investor has the burdens of ownership. Some of the syndicators are very careful to identify the original herd; others are not.

(b) Some syndicators do not specifically identify the progeny. All the investor's progeny may, for example, become part of a common pool of animals until selected for sale or placement in the investor's breeding or dairy herd. This is often true in programs that guarantee a specific price for a certain number of progeny.

(c) The lack of identification by itself, or coupled with the uniform prices for progeny, supports the position that the investor does not acquire the burdens of ownership of the herd and progeny until the animals are sold. Thus, the investor's holding period of the progeny begins at the time such animals are sold. This position disclaims the argument that the progeny qualify as IRC 1231 assets.

(8) Inspect and/or examine the individual returns of the principals of the promoter-operator company. These individuals often reduce large salaries with deductions created by investing in the shelter they are promoting.

444 *(3–2–79)* 4236

Issues to Consider in the Initial Years of the Breeding Program

(1) A detailed examination of the documents and records and consideration of all the factors related to herd value, identification, financing and guarantees, and economic feasibility, can result in a number of logical conclusions not often encountered in the examination of taxpayers actively engaged in the business of farming. These conclusions might be that the investor:

(a) Contracted to pay much more than the actual value of the herd;

(b) Has received or was credited with far more than the progeny are worth;

(c) Will not recover his/her investment or does not have a reasonable expectation of profit within the reasonably foreseeable future;

(d) Has fewer burdens of ownership, due to guarantees, than is reasonably expected for a herd-owner; or

(e) Has few, if any, benefits of ownership because substantial maintenance fees and a high percentage of progeny have been given up to herd maintenance.

(2) The Tax Reform Act of 1976 provides in IRC 465 that, for taxable years beginning after 1975, all taxpayers (including partners) other than regular corporations engaged in farming will be allowed losses from farming only to the

extent of the amount that the taxpayer has at risk in that activity. Deductions claimed in excess of the amount at risk should be disallowed. The loss may be deductible in a subsequent year if the amount at risk is later increased.

(3) Deductions should be disallowed if the farming activity is not engaged in for profit. The "not for profit" position should focus primarily on IRC 162, 167 and 212 as opposed to IRC 183.

(a) When an activity is not engaged in for profit, deductions should be disallowed except to the extent allowable by IRC 183.

(b) Pursuant to IRC 183(b), deductions with respect to an activity not engaged in for profit are allowed as follows:

1 If deductions are otherwise allowable without regard to profit motive (i.e., IRC 163 interest and IRC 164 taxes), IRC 183(b)(1) permits deductions for the full amount.

2 All other deductions to be taken pursuant to IRC 162 and 212(1) are allowable only to the extent gross income from the "not for profit activity" exceeds the deductions defined in IRC 183(b)(1). The authority for disallowance of deductions in excess of gross income is found in IRC 162 and 212(1). Regulations under IRC 162, and 212 are then cross-referenced to the nine factors set forth in I.T. Regs. 1.183–2(b).

(c) Factors to be considered when determining whether a transaction is entered into for profit are listed in I.T. Regs. 1.183–2(b). The following should be particularly considered:

1 Activities entered into for purposes of reducing taxes rather than earning economic profits are not profit-seeking activities of the kind contemplated by IRC 162 and 212, as well as IRC 167;

2 The profit expectations must be bona fide. Although a reasonable expectation of profit is not required, the facts and circumstances must indicate that the taxpayer entered into the activity, or continued the activity, with the objective of making a profit. See *Arnold L. Ginsberg v. Commissioner,* 35 TCM 860;

3 A profit must be anticipated in the reasonably foreseeable future. A bona fide profit objective cannot be established simply by a general showing that the return from the investment could exceed the apparently inflated purchase price because of increased herd size and inflation; and

4 An expectation of early losses is consistent with a profit motive only if subsequent net earnings are sufficient to recoup such losses. A delayed cross-over point of profitability, attributable to excessive purchase price, strongly suggests that the taxpayer is investing in the package to reduce taxes rather than to return an economic profit.

(4) Often the purchase price of the animals will be in excess of fair market value. Another issue to be considered is that depreciable basis for the herds in excess of fair market value has not been established. The case of *Bernuth v. Commissioner* 470 F2d 710 (CA–2 1973), 73–1 USTC 9132, affg. 57 T.C. 225, may apply.

(a) There is a large incentive to inflate the purchase price of breeding animals, so examiners should determine the correct amount of the purchase price. Reasonable fair market value should be determined by independent appraisers, when appropriate.

(b) Excess cost as suggested in *Bernuth v. Commissioner,* supra, may represent a premium to the promoter for arranging the breeder package. If so, the premium is a capital expenditure to be recovered upon termination of the taxpayer's investment and not by means of amortization.

(5) Consideration should also be given to proposing that the investor is not the owner of the animals, both original herd and progeny, until termination of the maintenance contract.

(a) To be entitled to deductions under IRC 162, 212, 167, and 163, the taxpayer must have acquired the burdens and benefits of ownership.

(b) Where the investor receives guarantees relating to the replacement of animals or relating to the specific number, sex, or quality of the progeny to be received, see *Herbert D. Weiner v. Commissioner,* supra.

445 *(3-2-79)* 4236

Issues to Consider After the Initial Years of the Investor's Breeding Program

(1) If the statute of limitations has expired on the returns for the early years of an investor's breeding herd program, the issues to be considered may be limited to the nature and amount of income to be reported. The background of each investor's program should be reviewed to determine the operation and effect of the program. Loss limitations under IRC 465 should be computed to determine if the amount at risk has been exceeded.

(a) Examiners should remember that one of the primary objectives of breeding tax shelters is the conversion of ordinary income to long-term capital gain. Prices paid for the original herd and, in some instances, the specified prices to be received for the progeny and original herd have been tailored to maximize tax benefits.

(b) Many programs operate so that the original herd, after write-off, is sold for a nominal price thus avoiding or nearly avoiding recapture. Most of the investor's income is reported as IRC 1231 income from the sale of a specified number of progeny retained until two years of age.

(2) Qualification as IRC 1231 Property—A determination that the investor in a breeding program is not the owner until termination of the maintenance agreement, as discussed in text at 444:(4), precludes IRC 1231 classification for the animals. A full development of the facts should precede all proposals.

(a) Many herd owners hold heifers for little more than two years with no intent to retain them in the herd, apparently relying primarily on age and holding period as being determinative of IRC 1231 qualification. Actual use is the best indication of intent. Culls, those unfit for the breeding herd, would be identified as not being part of the breeding herd in operations well before the animals reach two years. Breeding an animal before sale to another for use in the buyer's herd is not herd use by the seller.

(b) When the taxpayer claims IRC 1231 classification for heifers sold at age two, the animals are not old enough to have been used in the herd and may merely be culls retained until the 24-month Holding period requirement is met. Note that many of the cases on the holding period of cattle and the breeding herd, such as *James M. McDonald v. Commissioner*, 23 T.C. 1091, deal with taxable years when 12 months was the minimum IRC 1231 holding period for cattle and horses.

(c) Price can be an indication of intent to include animals in the herd. A price significantly higher than ordinarily received for culls is an indication that it is a quality animal. The failure to use it in the herd then indicates that it was held primarily for sale, not use.

(d) Many syndicated programs stipulate that the male progeny be retained by the syndicator as payment for herd maintenance, while other herd owners have claimed herd status for large numbers of male calves, more than could or would be used in any normal breeding operation. Others have reported bull sales in the same manner when the operator utilized artificial insemination and required a minimum number of bulls.

(e) The determination of intent requires a full development of the facts. (I.T. Regs. 1.1231-2.)

(3) Recapture of Depreciation—Livestock depreciation after 1969 is subject to recapture. Determination of the recapture should present little problem when the animals are specifically identified in the purchase and sale transaction. Because IRC 1245 applies only to gains, it is important that losses be eliminated from transactions in which gains and losses are netted. IRC 1245 gains are includable in ordinary income.

(4) Investment Credit Recapture—The position that the investor is not the owner, or that the purchase of the animals is subject to IRC 183 in earlier years of the program, would eliminate the investment credit. Identification of each animal throughout the investor's program is necessary to determine that recaptures are properly reported.

(5) Charitable Contribution of Herd Animals—Some syndicators arrange contributions of investor herd progeny to charitable organizations. Usually the syndicator will also arrange an appraisal of the contributed animals. These transactions have examination potential at the investor level. The valuation and qualification as IRC 1231 assets should be scrutinized.

(a) Apart from the valuation considerations, animals not included in the herd, those held for ultimate sale, are subject to the restrictions of IRC 170(e).

(b) Where the animals do qualify as IRC 1231 assets, the recapture provisions of IRC 1245 as well as the IRC 170(e) requirements for use by the donee must be considered.

(6) Transfer of an Investor's Interest in Herd—There are instances in which an investor sells a purebred herd back to the promoter-operator and at the same time purchases a commercial herd from the syndicator.

(a) These transactions have examination potential at the investor level on issues such as investment credit recapture on assets which are not substantially identical, and the determination of IRC 1245 gains.

(b) In such a transaction the investor agrees to sell, and the promoter-operator agrees to buy, all of the young progeny from the first herd at the time they each become two years old. Herd status reports can indicate that the young animals were transferred at the same time as the bulk of the herd and that the purchaser (who issued the reports) had the incidence of ownership in all of the animals well before some of them were two years old. Termination of the investor's incidence of ownership would be shown, for example, by discontinuance of the maintenance charge for these progeny. The investor would look to the age of the young animals at the later date of sale to support IRC 1231 status.

446 *(3-2-79)* 4236
Limited Breeder Partnerships

(1) As indicated earlier, many of the farm operations tax shelters are limited partnerships. Some limited partnerships have been formed to conduct cattle or other animal breeding programs.

(2) Many of the issues involving breeding operations are the same regardless of the organizational form of the shelter program.

(3) The operations of these limited partnerships are similar to the agency syndications. Most are promoted by a corporate general partner.

447 *(3-2-79)* 4236
Examination of Breeder Limited Partnerships

(1) The accounting records for some of the farm operation tax shelters are deceptively simple. Factual development and substantiation from the legal documents connected with each transaction are critical elements of case development. Arguments and documents may be lengthy, technical, and complicated by interaction with other documents.

(2) The items discussed in 441 should be reviewed in the same manner as suggested for the agency syndications.

(3) In addition to verification of deductions, disbursements should be reviewed for items such as:

(a) Payments to partners for all or part of their interest.

(b) Payments to partners for guarantees against losses.

(c) Commissions to accountants, attorneys and/or others for selling partnership interests. These costs may be deducted as professional fees.

(d) Payments to the general partner and others for organizing and promoting the partnership. These are capital expenditures (*Rev. Rul. 75-214,* 75-1 C.B. 185.)

(e) Money diverted for purposes other than those set out in the prospectus, such as loans to the general partner or the purchase of assets unrelated to partnership business.

(4) Verify cash receipts from investors. Review all cash receipts to determine their nature.

(5) Verify that losses claimed by partners for partnership taxable years beginning after 1975 did not exceed the amount at risk in the partnership under IRC 465.

(6) The following documents specifically related to partnerships should also be reviewed. These documents must be considered in determining whether the entity should be treated as a partnership or as an association taxable as a corporation.

(a) prospectus

(b) partnership agreement and certificate of limited partnership.

448 *(3-2-79)* 4236
Issues to Be Considered in a Breeder Limited Partnership

(1) As stated previously, many of the issues involved in a breeding operation are the same regardless of the organizational form. Some of the issues discussed here will be applicable only to partnerships. However, during the examination of a breeder partnership, examiners should also consider those issues discussed in 444 and 445.

(2) Partnership vs. Association Taxable as a Corporation—The partnership organization and operation should be reviewed to determine whether the limited partnership should be treated as a corporation. In some cases, the general partner has a minute interest in profits and losses. In other cases, the general partner has a minimal net worth lending weight to the possibility of taxing the entity as a corporation.

(3) Nonrecourse Loans—Nonrecourse loans for which none of the partners are liable increase the basis of each partner. See IRC Section 752 and I.T. Regs. 1.752-1(e). These loans should be analyzed very carefully to determine that they are, in fact, nonrecourse as to all the partners. Loans from a general partner to a limited partner, or to the limited partnership, may be considered capital contributions by the general partner. See and compare *Rev. Rul. 72-350,* 72-2 C.B. 394 and *Rev. Rul. 72-135,* 72-1 C.B. 200. Consider all aspects of cattle loans. Also, see IRC Sections 465 and 704(d). For tax years beginning after December 31, 1975, nonrecourse loans do not increase the partners basis for the purpose of computing allowable losses. See IRC 465.

(4) Material Distortion of Income—Prepayment of management fees, interest, and other expenses may distort income to the extent that the method of accounting does not clearly reflect income. For deduction of prepaid interest after December 31, 1975, see IRC 461(g). The cash basis tax shelters often prepay expenses for no apparent reason other than the immediate tax deduction. All material prepayments should be challenged by the Service. *Resnick v. Commissioner,* 555 F2d 634 (CA-7 1977), 77-1 USTC 9451, affg. per curiam 66 T.C. 74.)

(5) Organizational Expenditures—Payments to partners and others for the cost of organizing limited partnerships and for selling interests in limited partnerships are capital expenditures. (IRC Section 709; *Rev. Rul. 75-214,* 75-1 C.B. 185; *Cagle v. Commissioner,* 539 F2d 409 (CA-5 1976), 76-2 USTC 9672, affg. 63 T.C. 86.)

(6) Income From Discharge of Indebtedness—Partnership nonrecourse loans usually are secured only by partnership assets, such as cattle. The discharge of a liability is treated as a distribution of money to the partners and may result in income to the partner regardless of the amount of income or loss actually distributed to the partners for the year. A negotiated discharge of indebtedness is also considered to be a distribution to the partners. (*Rev. Rul. 72-205,* 72-1 C.B. 37.)

(a) *Rev. Rul. 76-111,* 76-1 C.B. 214, describes the realization of income in a situation where cattle subject to a nonrecourse loan are exchanged in return for cancellation of the debt.

(b) Inspect investor's returns for years subsequent to large partnership loss deductions. Many taxpayers report no income or a loss in the year their investment is terminated, even though they realize income because of the termination of the partnership's nonrecourse loans.

(c) Some partnerships have entered into questionable transactions to postpone this recovery of income. Some taxpayers have contributed their debit balance capital accounts to newly-formed limited partnerships. The only "asset" offsetting this debit balance capital account in both the old and new partnerships is a credit in the same amount as the "capital". This credit "asset" is the amount of nonrecourse liabilities released by the earlier sale of the partnership feed and cattle; but the partnership's assets were insufficient to pay. Surely, the bank or other creditor has not delayed its bad debt write-off by continuing to carry the "loan" on its balance sheet.

1 Ordinarily, the nonrecourse loan will terminate when the value of cattle on hand and other partnership assets become insufficient to satisfy the loan.

2 Some old cattle shelters rearrange their balance sheets in an attempt to prolong their lives. Others, when insolvent, attempt to effect a termination by failing to file a return in the final year, or

3 Some burned out partnerships merely change service centers by using another business address of the general partner or the address of an affiliate.

(7) Changes in Partnership Interests—All changes in partnership interests should be reviewed for issues such as contributions. (*Rev. Rul. 75-194,* 75-1 C.B. 80.)

(8) Termination or Sale of Partnership Interest—The sale or termination of a partner's interest at a time when his/her capital account has a debit balance (distributable losses have exceeded capital contributions) may indicate a substantial gain to the partner due to the release of his/her share of the liabilities. Often these transactions are not correctly reported by the partner, in part because Schedule K-1, Form 1065, for years prior to 1976, does not show or reflect the termination or transfer of an interest. The sale, transfer or termination of a partnership interest will result in ordinary income in instances where IRC 751 is applicable.

450 *(3-2-79)* 4236
Features Applicable to Feeder Tax Shelters

451 *(3-2-79)* 4236
Feeder Cattle Agency Agreements

(1) Cattle service contracts are agency agreements pursuant to which the syndicator purchases cattle and feed on behalf of the investors. The cattle are fed in commercial feedlots and sold for the account of the investor.

(2) The large syndicators are required to file prospectuses with the Securities and Exchange Commission. The agency agreements may vary but usually are sold in units of from $5,000 to $150,000 initial cash investment. These purchases are usually leveraged and may be for one feeding cycle or for a term of years.

(3) The operations of the promoters of agency agreements may differ a great deal; the tax effects of the agency agreement at the investor level are usually similar to each other. Some of the syndicators either operate, or are affiliated with, feedlot operations that provide services for at least part of their client's cattle. Others contract for feed and services. The prospectus will state, in general terms, the methods of operation.

(4) Customarily, an investor purchases units in December. The syndicator will usually arrange financing and issue a feed invoice in December to support a prepaid feed deduction of two to ten times the investor's initial cash investment. Investor reports are issued monthly or at least for each feeding cycle. In the initial year of the program, the investor will file a Form 1040, Schedule F, showing a prepaid feed deduction and perhaps deductions for prepaid interest and prepaid management fees.

(5) The agency programs are stated in a number of ways. Some highly leveraged programs operate in the following manner:

(a) The agency syndicators designate a portion of the cash investment as management fees and the balance as equity in feeder cattle. Thus, in effect, feed is purchased with borrowed capital.

(b) Management fees are stated as a specific amount per unit or a percentage of the cost of cattle purchased. Either method usually will result in a charge of approximately $5 to $10 per feeder animal purchased.

(c) An equity in cattle is purchased for the investor. This equity may be about 10% of the cost of the feeder cattle. The financing for the balance of the cattle cost might be arranged by the seller of the cattle or the feedlot operator, or the syndicator might negotiate financing with a lending institution. Usually, the cattle financing is nonrecourse as to the investor in the agency agreements.

(d) The investor's feed purchase will ordinarily be financed by loans negotiated by the syndicator. These are nonrecourse loans as to the investor.

(6) Most of the cattle agency syndicators provide a limit on the investor's losses. They may be stated in terms of a percentage of the initial investment or as a percentage of the feed purchased. In most of the cases encountered, the initial cash investment is the maximum amount at risk.

(7) Thus, in the examination of an agency syndicator or investor, the examiner may encounter a program where an individual investor pays $10,000 for a unit or units and signs a nonrecourse feed note for $20,000 or more. Prior to the enactment of IRC 465, the investor would be able to claim a loss in excess of the $10,000 cash invested. The syndicator receives a fee of $1,000 to $2,000 and arranges for the purchase of an equity in up to 200 head of feeder cattle. Generally, the investor's actual losses are limited to the initial investment or a portion of it. Other agency agreements may specify that the investor pays for the feed which is used as collateral for the cattle purchase.

452 *(3-2-79)* 4236
Examination of Returns Involved in Feeder Cattle Agency Agreements

(1) The examination of these cases can be approached from the investor or syndicator level just as syndicated breeding herds can. Refer to 442 and 443 of this Handbook.

(2) This presentation will concentrate on those aspects of a feeder agency agreement which differ from a breeding agency agreement.

(3) Some of the documents to be inspected and their significance are:

(a) Prospectus—The syndications covered by the Federal securities laws are required to disclose the details of the offering and the possible tax consequences. These prospectuses describe the agreements to be signed and often include copies of them. Actual notes and agreements entered into by the investor may vary from the prototype in the prospectus, or they may be modified by other agreements and documents. Smaller syndicators usually provide the investor with a "confidential memorandum", disclosure statement, or prospectus somewhat like those filed with the Securities and Exchange Commission.

(b) Cattle services contract, feeder cattle agency agreement, or management agreement—These agreements state the manner in which the agency arrangement is to be conducted and usually provide the syndicator with a limited power of attorney. Generally, these agreements state the fees to be paid, reports to be issued, and rate of profit and loss sharing.

(c) Feed invoice or commodity purchase agreement—The advance contract for feed is usually made late in the year, often before the investor's cattle are purchased. The syndicator may arrange for the investor to receive a copy of the feed invoice or purchase agreement to support the year-end prepaid feed deduction. This feed invoice may be issued by the syndicator, an affiliate, or by a third party.

1 Often the invoice specifies one commodity such as corn. In actual practice the cattle or other animals are fed a feed mixture. The actual quantity and price of the feed used is reported to the investor in monthly or feeding cycle reports. The investor is then credited with the feed prepayment in the closing statement.

2 Examiners have found, through collateral requests, that delivery was never made on certain invoices for huge quantities of feed. Others have found that the feed purchase contract was assigned to the financial institution that made the feed loan or is related to the institution making the investor's feed loan.

(d) Notes—In some instances, notes have been issued in payment for feed. The notes may be issued by the investor or the syndicator on behalf of the investor. These notes, of course, are not payment by a cash basis taxpayer. (*Philip D. Foley v. Commissioner,* 35 TCM 263.)

1 The note supporting the prepaid feed deduction may be payable to the syndicator or an affiliate finance company that has a working relationship with the syndicator or, in unusual situations, with the investor's bank. The notes are often entwined in the feed purchase agreement, and both must be carefully considered together with other documents.

2 There are reported instances in which the feed supplier advanced the funds to the finance company for the feed loan to the investor, who then "purchased" feed from the supplier through the syndicator. (*James A. Smith v. Commissioner,* 35 TCM 1246).

3 When the investor is not personally liable on the financial portion of the feed debt and the syndicator has guaranteed the debt, the syndicator emerges as the true borrower and the investor as only a nominee.

4 The financing of livestock purchases is usually arranged directly between the syndicator and a bank. The investor then pays interest to the syndicator which represents the cost of financing the feeder cattle.

(e) Security Agreements—These agreements will supplement the feed note. Ordinarily they provide that the borrower's liability does not extend beyond the feed or the feed and the cattle.

(f) Profit and Loss Distribution—These agreements may be a part of the program description, summary, or maintenance agreement, or they may be a separate document. These arrangements often limit losses to a percentage of the initial cash investment. One syndicator, for example, shares profits 50/50 and shares losses of up to 30% of the investor's cash investment 50/50 and assumes 100% of the balance of the losses. In other words, the investor can lose only 15% of the cash invested.

(g) Hedging Transactions and Commodity Futures Contracts—A hedge has been defined as the practice of buying or selling futures to counter-balance an existing position in the trade market and, thus, avoiding the risks of unforeseen major movements in price. A farmer or feeder may hedge on his/her actual position in cattle, feed, grain, or other commodities.

1 Some syndicators offer investors the opportunity to hedge their feed and cattle transactions. Careful anlysis may be necessary to determine whether these future transactions are hedges as opposed to speculative transactions. Speculative futures transactions result in capital gains and losses.

2 The purchase of a commodity future in grain does not qualify as a feed purchase.

(h) Cattle Invoices—The actual purchase date of cattle may indicate distortion of income, especially when the cattle are purchased after the year-end feed purchase, as is sometimes the case.

(i) Closing Statements or Closing Out Summaries—These statements are usually issued at the conclusion of the venture. Together with the feed purchase documentation, monthly reports, investor's payments, and related documents, the statements show the investor's economic gain or loss as well as the tax consequences. In some instances, investors fail to report the recovery of previously deducted items at the termination of their agency agreement.

(j) Letters and Correspondence—Communications with the security salesman, the syndicator, accountants, and attorneys about the shelter investments are important in that they often show how and why the investor's program is conducted.

(k) Cancelled Checks—In addition to verifying the amount paid by the investor, note the endorsements and cancellations on these checks. Apart from substantiating the timeliness of entry into the feeder program, the disposition of these checks can become an important part of a quality collateral request or information report. The source of funds, of course, may become a concern in an examination of an individual.

(4) Early in the examination, determine the scope of the syndicator's operation and relationships with the feed supplier. Examination of agreements with the suppliers along with the books, records, and documents will help clarify these relationships.

(5) The syndicator, as agent, purchases prepaid feed on behalf of the investors. These purchases should be traced through to the delivery and consumption of the feed. Review invoices and purchase agreements in order to verify the payment. Also, verify the disposition of these checks as shown by endorsements and cancellations.

(6) Feed and cattle transactions made by the syndicator, though properly reflected on the syndicator's return, can provide additional support for the disallowance of the investor's deductions. Examiners may encounter the following situations:

(a) The investor's prepaid feed purchase was cancelled shortly after the beginning of the year.

(b) A large portion of the investor's prepaid feed was "sold" back to the supplier in the subsequent year. This "sale" may offset actual purchases and be reported in a net cost of feed figure on the subsequent year return.

(c) The feed supplier, which is affiliated with the syndicator, deposited the prepayment in an escrow account that was drawn on as the cattle were fed.

(d) The money loaned to purchase the investor's feed never leaves the bank through the use of check exchange arrangements similar to those in *James A. Smith,* supra. In these situations, the cash position of everyone remains the same.

(7) The investor documentation disseminated to other districts should include the following as well as the documents referred to in 443.

(a) A local market price for feed at the time of the investor's feed purchase.

(b) Investor's feed invoice.

(c) Reports made to the investor, such as feeding cycle reports.

453 *(3-2-79)* 4236
Issues to Be Considered in Feeder Cattle Agency Agreements

(1) Prepaid Feed—All substantial feed prepayments should be carefully scrutinized.

(a) Examiners have found, through collateral requests, that delivery was never made on certain invoices for large quantities of feed. Others have found that the feed purchase contract was assigned to the financial institution that made the feed loan or is related to the institution making the investor's feed loan. The failure to deliver and the assignment of the purchase contract are strong indications that a check exchange scheme exists.

(b) The cash basis tax shelters often prepay expenses for no apparent reason other than the immediate tax deduction. Other material prepayments are also being challenged by the Service.

1 Prepayments of management fees, interest, and other expenses may materially distort income to the extent that the method of accounting does not clearly reflect income.

2 In a recent case, *Burck v. Commissioner,* 533 F2d 768 (CA-2 1976), 76-1 USTC 9283, affg. 63 T.C. 556, the cash basis taxpayer was allowed only 3/365 of the year's interest paid on December 29. Also, see *Resnick v. Commissioner,* supra, disallowing four years of interest prepaid on the last day of December. Generally, IRC 461(g) requires a pro rata deduction of prepaid interest over the period benefited for the amounts paid after December 31, 1975.

(c) For years subsequent to 1975, deductions by farming syndicates for prepaid feed and supplies are not allowable prior to the taxable year in which they are consumed or used. See IRC 464.

(d) For years prior to 1976, the prepaid feed deduction must meet all three criteria of *Rev. Rul. 75-152,* 75-1 C.B. 144. These tests—deposit, business purpose, and material distortion—are explained in detail in the Revenue Ruling which cites the court cases related to each test. The facts related to each test must be fully developed.

1 The facts related to one test may be supportive of another. For example, lack of business purpose may also support disallowance as distortion of income. The year-end purchase of feed that maximizes the mismatching of expenses and income by an investor who is a new entrant into the farming business is, of itself, an indication of an intent to avoid taxes by materially distorting income.

2 The significance of pricing, delivery, cancellability, availability of feed, and other factors related to the business purpose of the advance purchases are stated in recent Court cases and in *Rev. Rul. 75-152.* Note that few of these cases contemplate prepaid feed deductions by an organized tax shelter. When examining the circumstances of the prepaid feed purchase, examiners should consider that the investor is generally one or two steps removed from the actual feeding operation and has no investment in land, equipment, and feedlot facilities to consider when making a prepaid purchase. Many investors have not yet purchased the cattle; others contract to do so at the time feed is purchased.

3 *Rev. Rul. 75-152* envisions that the taxpayer has acquired or has the reasonable expectation of some business benefit as a result of the prepayment. The Ruling also requires consideration of whether prepayment was a condition imposed by the seller and whether the condition was meaningful. Prepayment in a prearranged program designed to be sold to investors may well lack some of these considerations. Viable alternatives to prepayment, such as hedging and forward contracting, would fix the price without turning the use of interest free capital over to the feeder who may be the only one benefiting from the transaction.

4 Examiners should explore any factors indicating that tax benefits rather than business purpose motivated the transaction. For example, the local market prices for the commodities purchased should be compared with the price paid to the syndicator. Also, consider whether the investor can reasonably contemplate a profit involving a year-end feed purchase when competing with other cattle feeders who purchase feed during the fall harvest season when prices are traditionally lowest.

5 Consider the following questions when developing the business purpose test:

a Did the feedlot operator sell both the feed and the cattle to the taxpayer? If so, what was their relationship to each other? Is there a bona fide sales contract?

b How did the feedlot operator finance and acquire the cattle and feed?

c Were hedges used by the feedlot operator? Was 100% cash purchase necessary?

d What types of feed (corn, milo, etc.) were involved? Were futures available?

e Was the taxpayer's prepaid feed segregated and identified by the feedlot operator at purchase? Did the feedlot operator periodically acquire the taxpayer's feed as required during the year?

f Did the taxpayer secure a discount on purchased feed from current market or the feedlot operator's cost?

g Was the cost of feed, cattle, or other services structured so that the normal profit associated with fattening cattle still accrued to the feedlot operator?

h Was there a reasonable expectation that the taxpayer would recover anything other than his/her capital?

i Was there a stop-loss agreement between the feedlot operator and the taxpayer?

j Did the feedlot operator guarantee any nonrecourse lending from a bank to the taxpayer? Who was the bank really looking to for repayment?

6 Distortion of income and the other factors in *Rev. Rul 75-152* are not in any way

diminished by the absence of leveraging. Consideration should always be given to each of the distortion factors listed in Rev. Rul. 75-152. However, examiners should not limit their consideration of distortion to the four factors in *Rev. Rul. 75-152* which are business practice, amount in relation to past purchases, time of year, and materiality.

(2) Throughout the examination of the cattle service contract investor, keep in mind that the tax deduction may have been the primary objective of the investor and the promoter who designed the program. High bracket taxpayers often enter this and similar programs in a year in which their income is unusually large; thus, the investor is concerned about reducing tax brackets as well as postponement of tax.

454 *(3-2-79)* 4236
Feeder Limited Partnerships

(1) The operations of these limited partnerships are similar to the feeder cattle agency agreements. Most are promoted by a corporate general partner who is directly or indirectly involved in cattle feeding operations.

(2) Many syndicators form a new group of partnerships at the end of each year. The first year return often will report no income and report a deduction for prepaid feed that is 100% to 200% of the partners' contributed capital.

(3) Some cattle may be purchased in the initial year. However, most or all of the feeder cattle are usually purchased during the first full year of operation. The partnerships may then terminate at the end of a feeding cycle or they may continue to operate in subsequent years. Those that continue to operate often prepay feed at the end of each year.

455 *(3-2-79)* 4236
Issues to Be Considered in a Feeder Limited Partnership

(1) Prepaid feed—The prepaid feed issue as it relates to an agency relationship is discussed at 453. The same criteria apply to the partnership deductions. The partnership issues discussed at 448 should also be considered.

(2) Substantially Appreciated Inventory—Feeder shelters in their second year have a zero basis in the feed inventory that was paid for and deducted in the prior year. Thus, the fair market value of the remaining feed will be in excess of the statutory 120% of adjusted basis.

(a) Feeder cattle that consume the prepaid feed also will substantially appreciate as they consume the zero basis feed. Cattle and feed are inventory for the purposes of IRC 751 even though the taxpayer is on the cash basis. (I.T. Regs. 1.751-1(d)(2)(ii).)

(b) IRC 751 applies to receipts from exchanges or distributions in exchange for all or part of a partnership interest that is attributable to unrealized receivables or inventory items which have substantially appreciated.

(c) See text at 448:(8) for a discussion of the sale or termination of a partnership interest.

(3) Other Expenses—Some limited partnerships have erroneously deducted purchases of feed that the cattle consumed before the partnership was formed. In these cases the feed consumed is part of the cost or basis of the cattle and is not deductible by the partnership until the cattle are sold.

(4) Other Considerations

(a) Balance Sheet—The entire balance sheet, including the capital account, should be reviewed for unusual items. The cash basis partnership, of course, does not state feed inventory as an asset even though none of the feed has been consumed.

1 A prepaid feed deduction usually results in a low credit balance or debit balance capital account. A low credit balance or debit balance in the initial year of a partnership is one of the identifying features of the syndicated partnerships seeking a year-end roll-over deduction.

2 Though it does not, by itself, have examination potential, a review of the balance sheet of the syndicated partnerships will show that some of these partnerships, although on a cash basis, have stated the balance sheet according to the accrual method of accounting.

3 Carefully review the balance sheets of the initial and all subsequent returns. Compare ending and beginning balances and analyze all capital account additions and reductions.

460 *(3-2-79)* 4236
Breeder Feeder Operations

461 *(3-2-79)* 4236
General

Some syndicators have formed limited partnerships which conduct "integrated" feeding and breeding operations. Often these programs are not nearly as integrated as the terminology indicates. An examiner might find, for example, that the general partner or an affiliate has sold a breeding herd to the partnership, perhaps for an inflated price, and also arranged financing, feed prepayment, and a feeder contract with an independent feed yard.

462 *(3-2-79)* 4236
Issues to Be Considered

(1) The issues to be considered include those previously discussed in this Chapter, such as prepaid feed and the purchase of animals at an inflated price. Other issues and alternatives should also be considered at the partnership level.

(2) Not for Profit—Disallowance of deductions where an activity is not engaged in for profit should be considered at the partnership level (*Rev. Rul. 77–320,* 1977–2 C.B. 78). See text 444:(3) for a discussion of the "not for profit" position.

(3) Installment Sales—Examiners have encountered cases in which general partner affiliates have sold breeding herds to partnerships and reported the sale on the installment method. Breeder agency investors may report sales of animals in the same manner. The sale of inventory (stock in trade) does not qualify for the installment method of reporting. Animals, unless they qualify as IRC 1231 livestock in the hands of the seller, are stock in trade even though they may be raised livestock and despite the fact that the seller used the cash method for reporting income. (IRC 453(b).) Also, the sale of services does not qualify for the installment method of reporting. (*Town and Country Food Company, Inc.,* 51 T.C. 1049.)

(Next page is 4236–79)

Oil and Gas Tax Shelters

510 *(6–20–79)* 4236
Background

(1) Many oil and gas drilling programs are organized and operated in compliance with existing provisions of the IRC. Taxpayers have the opportunity to "shelter" part of their income by investing in drilling of oil and gas wells as provided by the IRC. Many shelters operate in this manner and are perfectly legitimate. Other programs, however, have resulted in abusive tax shelters; and these are the subject of this Chapter.

(2) Most oil and gas drilling tax shelters are organized as limited partnerships consisting of a general partner and one or more limited partners. The "promoter" or organizer of the program often forms a wholly owned corporation to be the general partner of the partnership with the investors as limited partners. The organizational set-up is often even more complex. The limited partnership formed by the investors and the general partner may become a limited partner in a second partnership (this is what is known as "tiering"). The same corporation is the general partner in each partnership.

(3) The principal characteristics of the oil and gas tax shelters include:

(a) the use of a limited partnership to pass through the deduction for intangible drilling costs (hereafter referred to as IDC);

(b) prior to the Tax Reform Act of 1976, the use of leverage through *nonrecourse loans* (where none of the limited partners were liable for partnership debt) so that limited partners were able to deduct partnership losses in excess of their actual cash; and,

(c) conversion of ordinary income into capital gains.

(4) Tax abuses are more likely to occur during the initial year of the partnership. The greater portion of these guidelines are directed to the examination of the initial partnership return.

(5) The oil and gas tax shelter cases involve the examination of legal documents (prospectuses, drilling contracts, lease assignments, financial arrangements) and the development of the facts relating to the transactions. You will find these examination techniques interspersed with discussions of the legal aspects of the particular transactions involved.

(6) The Tax Reform Act of 1976 enacted specific laws applicable to oil and gas tax shelters. The examiner should make sure that the proper Code sections are applied during the examination. See I.T. Reg. 26CFR 404.6103(k)(6)–1, concerning investigative disclosure and MS 12G–178, C.R. 40G–126, dated April 27, 1977, Investigative Disclosures Under Section 6103(k)(6) of the Internal Revenue Code.

520 *(6–20–79)* 4236
Identification of Returns

(1) The investor's limited partner share of gain or loss is usually reported on Form 1040, Schedule E. However, some partnerships "elect-out" of Form 1065 filing requirements (see IRC 761) so that investors report income and deductions on Schedule C or elsewhere as "coventurers." Examiners of individual returns are often the first Internal Revenue Service employees to encounter tax shelter deductions because the partnership return may not be selected for examination prior to the partner's examination. Examiners should be aware that an "election out" under IRC 761 prevents the partnership from using a special allocation of the intangible drilling cost deduction under IRC 704(b). Deductibility would then be determined under I.T. Reg. 1.612–4.

(2) It should be noted that it is seldom possible to determine that a partnership loss on an individual's return is from an abusive tax shelter without an examination of the partnership return. The following steps should be taken by revenue agents.

(a) Verify the date and amount of the investment. Investments made late in the taxable year, or backdated from the beginning of the next year, indicate the possibility of prepaid drilling expense. The amount and date of the investment should be verified to make sure that the taxpayer is entitled to a loss.

(b) Inspect information shown on the taxpayer's copy of the Schedule K–1 from the partnership and trace to the return.

(c) Compare the loss shown on the partner's return with the amount of his/her investment. If the loss deducted exceeds the partner's investment, it indicates the possibility of a nonrecourse loan.

(d) Specifically, question the investors on the extent of their dealings with the general partner of the fund. Ascertain if the investor has received any loans or agreements to purchase his/her partnership interest in succeeding years. These arrangements can be made with affiliates or business associates, such as the driller or the promoter.

(e) Read the Limited Partnership Agreement and Prospectus or Offering Letter. The limited partner should have a copy of the Offering Letter.

(f) Consider requesting a collateral examination of the partnership return if any of the items in (a) through (e) or other irregularities are discovered. This is especially true for larger losses. For example, a $5,000 individual loss could be part of a partnership loss of $2,000,000, and when scrutinized could result in the identification of other returns that would otherwise escape examination.

530 *(6-20-79)* 4236
Taxable Entity

531 *(6-20-79)* 4236
General

(1) Many oil and gas tax shelters are organized as limited partnerships. Partnerships have requested and received advance rulings from IRS that, based on representations of fact, they meet the requirements for classification as limited partnerships. Other limited partnerships rely on the advice of their counsel that they qualify as limited partnerships.

(2) This classification as a partnership is vital to the operation. If it should be determined that the organization is not a limited partnership but an association taxable as a corporation, the limited partners would lose their allowable deduction for partnership losses.

532 *(6-20-79)* 4236
Examination Procedures for Determining Partnership Classification

(1) Inspect prospectus.

(2) Review ruling letter if one has been received.

(a) Verify that the facts as represented in the ruling request conform with the actual facts of the consummated transaction.

(b) Verify that the operations conform to the facts represented in the ruling request.

(3) Determine that classification as a partnership is correct. Consider:

(a) Transferability of interests.

(b) Personal liability of limited partners.

(c) Centralized management.

(d) Continuity of business.

(e) In order *not* to be classified as an association taxable as a corporation, the funds must *not* have a preponderance of the characteristics listed in (a) through (d) above.

(f) While it is not a requirement, it should be remembered that a limited partnership is not viable until necessary registration documents have been filed with state authorities.

540 *(6-20-79)* 4236
Accounting Methods

(1) Many limited partnerships have elected to compute their distributable income or loss on a cash basis. However, an examiner may encounter a partnership which has adopted the accrual basis of accounting. In *Levin et al v. Commissioner,* 219 F. 2d 588 (CA-3, 1955), the court held that, in the case of an accrual basis taxpayer, the liability to pay an expense does not become fixed until all the events have occurred which obligate the payor to make the payments. Examiners should ascertain that the transactions meet the "all events" test to qualify an item for deduction by an accrual basis taxpayer.

(2) I.T. Regs. 1.461-1(a)(1) provides, in part, that, under the cash receipts and disbursements method of accounting, amounts representing allowable deductions shall, as a general rule, be taken into account for the taxable year in which paid. IRC 446(b) provides, in part, that, if the method of accounting used by the taxpayer does not clearly reflect income, the computation of taxable income shall be made under such method as clearly reflects income. I.T. Regs. 1.461-1(a)(1) provides, in part, that, if an expenditure results in the creation of an asset having a useful life which extends substantially beyond the close of the taxable year, such an expenditure may not be deductible, or may be deductible only in part, for the taxable year in which made. I.T. Regs. 1.461-1(a)(3) does not permit the current deduction of overlapping items if such deduction would materially distort income.

(3) The Commissioner has been successful in requiring taxpayers to change their method of accounting to prevent a material distortion of income. In *Burck v. Commissioner,* 533 F2d 768 (CA-2, 1976), the taxpayer was permitted to deduct only 3/365 of interest paid which would otherwise have been deductible. Also see *Resnik v. Commissioner,* 555 F2d 634 (CA-7, 1977).

(4) Examiners should scrutinize year-end drilling contracts and determine the following:

(a) How much work was done at the end of the year as compared to total depth of the well or wells?

(b) When was well or wells completed? Some programs may never drill wells.

(c) Does the payment represent a deposit?

(d) Is there any provision for substitute wells?

(e) Is the payment to the party who will drill the wells or is it to a party who must secure an actual driller?

(f) Does the payment meet a business purpose? Are dealings at arm's-length between the parties?

(g) If drilling is extended for more than a 12-month period, consider proposing IRC 446(b) as an issue and using I.T. Regs. 1.461–1(a)(1) to prorate the deduction.

(h) The examiner should consider accounting methods in conjunction with prepaid drilling costs. If the conditions mentioned above indicate that little or no drilling has been completed, disallowance of prepaid drilling costs should be considered, and a change in accounting method to clearly reflect income should be proposed as an alternative issue.

550 *(6-20-79)* 4236
Verification of Cash Receipts

(1) The examiner should verify cash receipts to the extent necessary to determine that all subscriptions of the limited partners have been paid. If payments were made by note, the investor's district should be notified so that the validity of the partner's basis for losses may be verified. If the payments were made by contribution of property, determine the validity of the payment.

(2) The examination of cash receipts will disclose any loans made to the partnership. The source of borrowed funds may be important in determining the existence of nonrecourse loans.

560 *(6-20-79)* 4236
Relationship Between Partnership and Drilling Contractor

(1) This is an area that must be carefully explored since this relationship can lead to abuse in IDC and nonrecourse financing. In many cases, the general partner is a wholly-owned subsidiary of a parent company. This subsidiary may have been formed solely to be the general partner in one or more partnerships. The general partner arranges with a drilling contractor (which may be the parent or another subsidiary) for the drilling of wells for the partnership. The limited partners can have no voice in management decisions of the partnership.

(2) An example of this relationship is shown in Exhibit 500–2.

570 *(6-20-79)* 4236
Management Fees

571 *(6-20-79)* 4236
General

(1) This issue arises from payments made by the limited partnership to the general partner. In most instances, this is a flat percentage ranging from 5 to 15 percent of the investor's subscription and is usually paid immediately after the subscription price is paid to the partnership.

(2) The partnership often contends that this is a guaranteed payment to the general partner and is deductible under IRC 707(a) or 707(c). IRC 707(a) provides that, if a partner engages in a transaction with a partnership other than in the capacity of a member of such partnership, the transactions shall be considered as occurring between the partnership and one who is not a partner. IRC 707(c) provides that, to the extent determined without regard to the income of the partnership, payment to a partner for services or the use of capital shall be considered as made to one who is not a member of the partnership, but only for purposes of IRC 61(a) (relating to gross income) and IRC 162(a) (relating to trade or business expenses).

(3) *These expenses must first meet the requirements of IRC 162 as ordinary and necessary business expenses to be deductible.* Any part of the expenditure that is attributable to the organization of the partnership, selling units of participation, acquiring capital assets, or payment for services to be performed after the close of the partnership's current taxable year, does not qualify as a current deduction.

(4) Payment for organization expenses, registration fees, commissions, and future services may not be stated on the partnership return but may be disguised as other expense. This may occur by inflating the general partner's charge for supervision of drilling or operation of leases.

(5) After the publication of *Rev. Rul. 75-214*, 1975-1 C.B. 185, and the decision in *Cagle v. Commissioner*, 539 F2d 409 (CA-5, 1976), some general partners have arranged to have their partnerships assign the general partner all of the first oil and/or gas produced by the partnership until an agreed upon amount is received. *This should be examined closely to determine if this represents an assignment of income by the limited partners.*

572 *(6-20-79)* 4236

Examination Procedures

(1) Determine if management fees have been deducted or capitalized as required by IRC 263 and *Rev. Rul. 75-214*.

(2) Analyze accounts. Ensure that all proper items have been capitalized.

(3) If management fees are not separately stated ascertain the following:

(a) Who paid for organization, registration, and selling commissions.

(b) If they were reimbursed, and how.

(c) If payments are disguised as drilling supervision, well charges, or other general and administrative costs. If so, a reasonable allocation between current expense and capitalizable costs should be made. (You may need to discuss reasonableness of drilling supervision and well charges with an engineering specialist.)

(d) The length of time the partnership existed during the taxable year and the amount of business activity. This will be helpful in determining the reasonableness of management fees charged in the current year.

(4) Example:

Investment by each limited partner	$ 10,000
Number of limited partners	×100
Total subscription price	$1,000,000
Management fee at 15%	×.15
Total paid to general partner	$ 150,000
Disbursement by general partner:	
Legal fees (organizational matters, etc.)	$ 50,000
Selling expenses for units of participation	35,000
Future services (to be performed after close of current tax year)	50,000
Current services	15,000
Total disbursements	$ 150,000

(a) In this example, $135,000 of the "management fee" would not be deductible in the current taxable year. Legal fees and selling expenses represent capital expenditures and are not deductible. See IRC 263. (Also see IRC 709 for proper treatment for taxable years beginning after December 31, 1976.)

580 *(6-20-79)* 4236

Intangible Drilling and Development Costs (IDC)

581 *(6-20-79)* 4236

General

(1) Most oil and gas tax shelters are formed to drill and develop oil and gas properties. While each fund may be somewhat different, the bulk of the IDC for productive and nonproductive wells is allocated to the limited partners, and the general partner bears the capital costs for productive wells. These shelters are attractive to higher-bracket taxpayers because of the current deduction for IDC.

(2) Examiners should be fully cognizant of the techniques discussed in IRM 4232.8, Techniques Handbook for Specialized Industries—Oil and Gas. It is not expected that examiners will encounter all of the problems considered in IRM 4232.8. IRM 4232.8 will serve as an excellent working tool and is incorporated herein by reference.

582 *(6-20-79)* 4236

Option to Deduct Intangible Drilling and Development Costs

(1) IRC 263(c), as implemented by I.T. Regs. 1.612-4, provides an option to charge to capital or expense the intangible drilling and development costs incurred in the development of oil and gas properties. This option is available only to an operator who is defined as one who holds a working or operating interest in any tract or parcel of land either as a fee owner, or under a lease, or any other form or contract granting working or operating rights.

(2) I.T. Regs. 1.612-4(d) provides, in part, that the option granted in paragraph (a) of the section to charge intangible drilling and development costs to expense may be exercised by claiming intangible drilling and development costs as a deduction on the taxpayer's return for the first taxable year in which the taxpayer pays or incurs such costs.

(3) Most partnerships will elect to charge intangible drilling and development costs to expense. The examiner should verify that the partnership qualifies to exercise the option to expense IDC and that the election is properly made.

583 *(6-20-79)* 4236
Definition of Intangible Drilling and Development Costs

The examiner should review 432 and 433 of IRM 4232.8, Techniques Handbook for Specialized Industries—Oil and Gas, for a definition of exploration costs, IDC, and capital expenditures. It should be remembered that the general partner has absolute control over arranging for drilling and will be very liberal in classifying IDC.

584 *(6-20-79)* 4236
Verifying IDC

(1) The examiner should:

(a) Determine if the amount of IDC requires a mandatory referral for engineering assistance under IRM 4216.12. If it does not, consider discussing the IDC issue with the key district engineering group manager or designee. An engineering specialist can provide valuable assistance to an examiner.

(b) Secure a copy of the drilling contract.

1 If the contract is dated near the end of the year, see 590 of this Handbook for prepaid drilling costs.

2 Verify description of well or wells to be drilled.

3 Verify date drilling commenced and was completed.

4 Does contract specify date of payment? Is payment due when drilling is commenced or completed?

(c) Verify reasonableness of drilling costs.

1 The drilling costs may vary for a number of reasons but principally due to availability of drilling rigs and the relationship between the general partner and the drilling contractor. (See 560 of this Handbook.)

2 If drilling costs appear to be excessive, consult with the appropriate engineering specialist to determine the "going rate" for drilling in the area of the partnership's well. If the case will be unagreed, engineering assistance should be requested.

3 Review *Rev. Rul. 73-211,* 1973-1 C.B. 303, and *Bernuth v. Commissioner,* 470 F2d 710 (2nd. Cir. 1972) aff'g. 57 T.C. 225, for possible allocation of excessive IDC to Leasehold Costs.

4 If IDC includes nonrecourse financing, as discussed later, drilling costs may be inflated. In these cases, the examiner should ascertain the actual drilling costs and limit the IDC to actual cash costs expanded for drilling the well.

(d) Be aware that the Tax Reform Act of 1976 designates IDC incurred after December 31, 1975, as a tax preference item.

585 *(6-20-79)* 4236
Effect of Tax Reform Act of 1976

(1) IRC 1254, enacted under the Tax Reform Act of 1976, requires amounts deducted for intangible drilling costs (IDC) on productive wells to be recaptured on disposition of oil or gas property. If a partner sells or exchanges his/her interest in a partnership holding an interest in such property, his/her share of the IDC which is subject to recapture would be treated as an unrealized receivable under IRC 751.

(2) Regarding IRC 1254 the following should be noted:

(a) The new code section works similarly to the old IRC 1254.

(b) The amount subject to ordinary income recapture on disposition of oil and gas property is the total amount of IDC (which is allowable as an expense under IRC 263(c) and I.T. Regs. 1.612-4) less the amount which would have been deductible had the IDC been capitalized and recovered through cost depletion.

(c) The amount recaptured cannot exceed the gain realized.

(d) Once a disposition is determined to exist, recapture is to be recognized regardless of any Code section calling for nonrecognition (however, dispositions by gift, transfers at death, like exchanges, etc., are exempted).

(e) Recapture rules apply to all taxpayers.

590 *(6-20-79)* 4236
Prepaid and/or Inflated Drilling Costs

(1) Many oil and gas funds form separate partnerships when subscriptions of a predetermined amount, maybe 1 or 2 million dollars, are received. Some funds will form a partnership each quarter and often a year-end fund. Typical fund names might be ABC Drilling Program—I, II, III, IV, and V or Drilling Program—A, B, C, D, and E. Obviously, if the partnerships are formed early in the year, all drilling may have been completed or nearly completed before the end of the year. Partnerships formed near the end of the taxable year often deduct prepaid drilling costs that are paid although drilling has not yet occurred. *Rev. Rul. 71-252,* 1971-1 C.B. 146, permits the deduction of IDC in advance of the actual drilling. It should be noted that there are several requirements that must be met before the deduction is allowable If the circumstances in the partnership under examination differ substantially from the requirements stated in *Rev. Rul. 71-252,* strong consideration should be given to disallowing the deduction.

(2) Some of the more abusive tax shelters often inflate IDC by less than arm's-length drill-

ing deals. The general partner may approach a drilling contractor with a drilling package. This package may require the drilling contractor to make a nonrecourse loan to the partnership to be repaid out of a portion of the proceeds of oil and gas produced from the well. The contractor generally does not have the financial resources to make loans.

(a) The use of the nonrecourse loan is illustrated by the following example:

1 C—contractor, makes nonrecourse loan of $500,000 to P—partnership.

2 P has received $500,000 from limited partners.

3 P writes C a check for $925,000 ($500,000 from C's nonrecourse loan plus $425,000, amount received from investors less 15 percent management fee) for drilling costs. These transactions occur before C's check for $500,000 is presented for payment. The $425,000 payment is sufficient money to pay for drilling costs plus a reasonable profit for the driller.

(b) In this case, the partnership's IDC would be limited to the actual amount of money it took to drill the well. No deduction should be allowed for the nonrecourse portion of the transaction since it has no economic reality. Also IRC 704 prohibits the deduction in excess of the amount "at risk." Its only purpose was to inflate IDC and secure a larger deduction for the limited partners. A similar result can be achieved by use of a "friendly" banker. The banker may make a recourse or nonrecourse loan to P. When C receives the money from P for drilling costs, C will either repay the bank or purchase a certificate of deposit which guarantees the loan. These transactions often happen simultaneously and are nothing more than a checkswapping arrangement with no economic substance.

(3) A production payment can also be used as a method of inflating deductions in somewhat the same manner as a nonrecourse loan.

(a) Assume the following:

1 The general partner or a related party to a drilling partnership places $1,000,000 in a financial institution in the form of a certificate of deposit. The general partner may guarantee payment of an expected production payment rather than purchase a certificate of deposit. The bank then purchases a production payment from the partnership for $1,000,000 to be repaid solely from oil and/or gas produced by partnership properties. The document will specify the properties and the percentage of production that will be reserved for retirement of the production payment.

2 The partnership transmits the proceeds of the production payment along with cash contributed by the limited partners to the drilling contractor, who is the general partner or a related party, for drilling wells. As in other cases, the cash raised from the limited partners is sufficient to cover drilling costs.

(b) If this or a similar situation is encountered, the party buying the production payment should be questioned specifically about any securities pledged, directly or indirectly, to secure repayment of the production payment. If such agreements are discovered, consider treating the entire transaction as a sham, thereby reducing the IDC deduction for the partnership.

(4) The examiner should:

(a) Realize that he/she may discover inflated drilling costs and/or prepaid drilling costs.

(b) Determine the date that the partnership commenced business. The later in the tax year the partnership began business the more likelihood of prepaid drilling costs.

(c) Review *Rev. Rul. 71-252* and be familiar with the conditions that must be met before a deduction for prepaid drilling costs can be allowed. Special attention should be directed to the business purpose of prepayment, who proposed payment, how strictly was the contract enforced, were other wells drilled during the year, and when was payment made?

(d) Determine if drilling costs are inflated. If drilling costs are both inflated and prepaid, it is preferable to propose two adjustments:

1 Prepaid drilling costs—portion paid in cash

2 Prepaid drilling costs—portion paid by nonrecourse loan.

(e) Interview all parties to nonrecourse loans. If a bank is involved, the loan officer should be specifically questioned about collateral for the loan in the form of certificates of deposit or other accounts. The examiner should determine the sequence of events and the time elapsed between making the loan and receiving the collateral. In some cases the money never left the bank.

(f) If the nonrecourse loan was made by the drilling contractor, some pertinent questions might be:

1 Have you made loans of this nature before?

2 How did this loan originate? Who suggested it?

3 How much did you expect the drilling costs to be for the well? How much were they?

4 Have you received any repayment on the loan? Do you expect repayment?

5 How did you treat the amount received from the partnership on your records? (Some contractors have reported this as drilling revenue when it did not affect their income tax because of net operating losses and carry backs.)

6 If you did not report it, why not? (He/she may have considered it worthless or of very little value.)

7 Why did you make this deal? (Probably to get the business.)

8 How much money did you have in the bank when you made the loan? What was your working capital at the date of the loan?

9 Did you make your normal profit from drilling aside from the nonrecourse note?

10 What disposition did you make of the payment for drilling?

(g) Determine the partnership's share of the working interest in the lease. If it is less than 100%, find out if other owners were required to enter into drilling contracts and to prepay costs. If not, there was no business purpose for prepaying IDC.

5(10)0 *(6-20-79)* 4236
Nonrecourse Financing

5(10)1 *(6-20-79)* 4236
General

Prior to 1976 nonrecourse financing was used in abusive oil and gas tax shelters to inflate the deduction for IDC so that the deduction was larger than the cash investment. A nonrecourse loan is a loan for which no individual partner or entity is personally liable. The lender has no recourse against any person or entity, but only against the collateralized property, However, with the Tax Reform Act of 1976, investors other than regular corporations are no longer allowed to include nonrecourse loans in their adjusted bases for purposes of computing losses. IRC 465, which is generally effective for tax years beginning after 1975, prevents taxpayers from deducting losses in excess of the amount actually at risk in oil and gas exploration and exploitation activities as well as certain other activities. The new provisions apply to losses sustained by noncorporate taxpayers (including partners), Subchapter S corporations, and personal holding companies. For years prior to 1976, however, IDC may be inflated using nonrecourse loans to artificially increase losses.

5(10)2 *(6-20-79)* 4236
Recognizing the Existence of Nonrecourse Financing

(1) Before the examiner can deal with the issue of nonrecourse financing, he/she must be able to recognize its existence. The nonrecourse financing can be carried out either overtly or covertly. If done overtly, it can be detected on the return; but if done covertly, there is no indication of it on the return. In cases where such financing has been openly used by the partnership in the *initial* year of operation, it can be easily recognized from the return by looking at:

(a) *The Balance Sheet*—Check to see if a substantial liability arises at year-end coupled with an equally substantial deficit in the partners' capital accounts.

(b) *Schedule M*—Check to see if the partnership loss substantially exceeds the capital contributed during the year.

(2) Where there is a *covert* use of such "financing," the face of the partnership return gives no indication of the existence of "nonrecourse financing." For example, a promoter (general partner) may secure from an investor (limited partner) a $2,000 cash subscription. On behalf of the partnership, the promoter will then enter into a $2,000 drilling contract with an operator by the end of the partnership's tax year. The investor, through the partnership, takes a $2,000 IDC deduction. The operator who, as mentioned previously, does not actually do the drilling then subcontracts the drilling to another "drilling" entity for the $2,000. The drilling entity then "lends" $1,000 to the operator or the promoter who, in turn, "lends" this $1,000 to the investor. The $1,000 "loan" is payable solely from production. The obvious net effect of this "deal" is that the investor obtains a $2,000 deduction for only a $1,000 investment without disclosing on the partnership tax return the existence of such "financing."

(3) In most cases, only through in-depth "third-party" questioning will the examiner ever discover the existence of such concealed financing. Along these lines the following steps can be taken:

(a) Read the prospectus or offering statement thoroughly for indications of such "financing."

(b) Question investors as to whether they have received any "money" connected with their investment in the fund, what entity provided this money, and what was the reason for payment.

(c) Question *all* parties to the contract (the operators, drillers, general partners) as to whether any money was directly or indirectly paid to the investors and what was the reason for payment, if any.

5(10)3 *(6-20-79)* 4236
Developing "Nonrecourse Loan" Issues for Years Prior to 1976

(1) Once it is determined that nonrecourse financing exists, the examiner must direct his/her examination toward the development of the following issues regarding such loans:

(a) *The "loan" could be considered a "sham."* The *deduction* and *tax basis* attributable to the loan would therefore be totally disallowed. In order to be able to advocate this position, the examiner should take the following steps in order to show that the true contract was simply the cash portion of such contract and nothing more.

1 An attempt should be made to show that the "financed" portion of the contract was fabricated. This can be done by showing less than arm's-length relationships between the contracting parties or a scratching-the-back relationship of supposed arm's-length entities. For instance, in a less than arm's-length contract between a related general partner and the so-called operator, the contracts could simply be marked up 200% to 300% of what they should be.

2 However, in a contract between a general partner and an operator, where no previous financial relationships can be shown, the operator, in order to get enough cash to cover drilling expenses and procure a right to potential production, will mark up the contracts in the same manner knowing that the general partner knowingly and tacitly will approve the mark up.

3 The lender may lack the financial strength to lend "money." The examiner should check the liquidity and equity position of the lender. In summary, regarding the "sham" agreement, the examiner should be able to prove that the entire "deal" could have been consummated without the intrusion of the so-called "loan."

(b) *The "loan" could be considered a contribution of capital by the lender.* This would have the effect of denying tax basis, to the extent of the "loan," to the partners. Therefore, even though according to the partnership agreement the partners are allocated all deductibles including those "arising from borrowed money," they could deduct these drilling costs only to the extent of their cash contributed (plus any debt for which they may be personally liable). See *Rev. Rul. 72-135,* 1972-1 C.B. 200, and *Rev. Rul. 72-350,* 1972-2 C.B. 394, for examples of situations where the above issue could be proposed.

(c) *The lender could be allocated the intangibles.* Although *Rev. Rul. 68-139,* 1968-1 C.B. 311, sanctions an arrangement whereby the parties to a particular deal can designate who gets the "intangibles" (deductibles), IRC 704(b)(2) clearly provides that the principal purpose of such a sharing arrangement must not be for the purpose of tax avoidance. The examiner could propose that the deductibles be allocated to the parties in accordance with their assumption of actual economic risk. Here we are assuming that the loan is a true loan and not a contribution of capital by the lender; but, due to the risky nature of oil and gas drilling where all parties suffer monetarily if reserves are not discovered, the deductible should be allocated to the lender, not the partnership. This position could be taken where the lender actually lends *money* which is *used* for drilling.

(d) *The loan portion of the contract does not constitute "prepayment" of intangible drilling costs.* This issue could be advocated where, in essence, the loan actually represented an open extension of credit by the lender to the partnership. Here all "prepaid IDC" attributable to the "loan" could be disallowed until such time as "loaned money" was actually turned over to and spent by the entity responsible for drilling.

(e) *The partners' tax bases can be increased by the loan but only to the extent of the fair market value of the underlying collateral.* This seems to be one of the stronger positions examiners can advocate regarding nonrecourse lending. This position would allow partnership deductibles to remain intact but would limit partners' tax bases, for flow-through purposes, to their cash contribution plus the fair market value of the loan collateral. In order to sustain this issue, an engineer's evaluation of the collateral is needed at the time the contract was concluded.

(f) *The "nonrecourse" loan was, in reality, a "recourse loan."* This situation arises where the contracts appear fair and money is loaned for drilling, etc. However, the examiner must read *all* loan and other agreements for indications of loan guarantees. If, for instance, a particular entity "guaranteed" the loan to the partnership, it would, in essence, be the liability of that entity. Under these conditions the partners' tax bases could not be increased by the loan and all deductibles in excess of their cash contributions would be denied.

(g) A *Bernuth*-type position could be advocated. Here the examiner would deny the partnership current deductibility of all drilling deductions in excess of what would be considered a "fair drilling contract." The difference would be capitalized as lease costs. Note that the *Bernuth*-type position is backed by authority only when there is a blended lease acquisition, i.e., a drilling arrangement in which the taxpayer does not have the right to separately bargain for the cost of the drilling. (See *Bernuth vs. Comm.*, supra.)

(h) An example of inflated drilling costs through the use of nonrecourse financing is shown in Exhibit 500-1.

5(11)0 *(6-20-79)* 4236

Disposition of Partnership Interest

5(11)1 *(6-20-79)* 4236

General

(1) Disposition of a partner's interest may be discovered by examination of the partnership return or by examination of an individual return. If an examiner has an individual partner's return, he/she should make appropriate inquiry about any later disposition of the partnership interest.

(2) Schedule K-1 of Form 1065 for 1976 includes questions that will be helpful in identifying partners who many have disposed of their interests during the year. These questions include:

(a) Is the partner a limited partner?

(b) Did his/her partnership interest decrease or terminate during the year?

(c) When did the partner join partnership?

(d) What is the adjusted basis of the partner's interest in the partnership at the end of the taxable year (as determined under IRC 705)?

(e) For each "at-risk" activity, what is the partner's share of partnership liabilities at the end of the taxable year for which the partner is personally liable?

(3) The examiner may want to compare Schedules K-1 for the current year with those for the preceding year to determine disposition of limited partners' interests in the current year.

5(11)2 *(6-20-79)* 4236

Examination Procedures

(1) Once it has been determined that a disposition of a limited partner's interest has been made, the examiner should ascertain the following:

(a) The selling price of the interest or, in the case of a complete liquidation, the cash distribution.

(b) The amount of nonrecourse liabilities from which the limited partner was relieved on the date of the disposition or liquidation.

(c) The limited partner's adjusted basis on the date of sale, liquidation, or distribution.

(2) The issues involved in the limited partner's disposition of his/her interest in an oil and gas partnership are basically similar to any other partnership disposition. The examiner should review the partnership provisions of the IRC and regulations dealing with the sale of a partnership interest.

(3) What is the amount realized?

(a) Sale of a partner's interest—The amount realized is the cash plus the fair market value of other property received. In addition, the limited partner must include in income the amount realized on his/her full share of any liabilities, recourse or nonrecourse, that he/she is considered to have been relieved from upon disposition. (I.T. Regs. 1.752-1(d))

(b) It should be noted that a disposition by gift will result in a taxable event since the amount of the partner's share of liabilities relieved of is considered an amount realized. (I.T. Regs. 1.1001-1(c) and *Rev. Rul. 75-194,* 1975-1 C.B. 80).

(c) The amount realized from a complete liquidation, in most instances, would be identical to (a) above.

(4) What is the adjusted basis of the partner's interest?

(a) The partner's basis must be determined in accordance with IRC 705. IRC 752 permits a partner to increase his/her basis by his/her share of partnership liabilities.

(b) The partner's basis in a complete liquidation would be computed in the same manner.

(5) To what extent does recognizable gain exist?

(a) Sale of a partner's interest—Recognizable gain exists to the extent of the difference between the amount realized and determined in (3) above, and the adjusted basis determined in (4) above.

(b) Complete liquidation of a partner's interest—In the case of complete liquidation where partnership liabilities are involved, IRC 752(b) states that, in essence, the assumption by the partnership of the liquidating partner's share of the partnership liabilities results in a "constructive" distribution of "money" to the partner. IRC 731(a) states that a distribution of money will not be recognized except to the extent it exceeds the adjusted basis of the partner's interest in the partnership immediately before the distribution.

(6) What is the character of the recognized gain?

(a) I.T. Reg. 1.752-1(d) states that, in the case of the sale of a partnership interest, liabilities will be treated in the same manner as liabilities in connection with the sale or exchange of property not associated with a partnership.

(b) IRC 741 states, in part, that in the case of a sale of a partnership interest, gain shall be considered gain from the sale of a capital asset except as otherwise provided in IRC 751 (relating to unrealized receivables and inventory items which have appreciated substantially in value).

(c) IRC 731 sets forth the procedure to be followed in determining gain or loss from partnership distributions to a partner.

(d) IRC 1254 is effective for IDC paid or incurred after December 31, 1975, on dispositions of oil or gas property after December 31, 1975.

5(12)0 *(6-20-79)* 4236
Contribution of Partnership Interest

5(12)1 *(6-20-79)* 4236
General

Examiners may discover instances where taxpayers have contributed their partnership interest to a qualified charitable organization at a greatly inflated value.

5(12)2 *(6-20-79)* 4236
Examination Procedures

(1) The examiner should:

(a) Ask the investor if he/she still has his/her partnership interest on the current date. If the interest has been disposed of, follow appropriate sections of this chapter to determine tax effect from disposition.

(b) Ascertain the value claimed if the interest has been contributed to charity.

(c) Request engineering assistance, if necessary, to determine the fair market value (FMV) of the interest at the date of contribution. Do not rely on the FMV furnished by the charitable organization. The organizations seldom have knowledge of the underlying assets and merely "rubber stamp" the value suggested by the partner and/or the partnership.

(d) Determine if the investor was released from any indebtedness, recourse or nonrecourse, by the gift. Taxable gain could result from the gift.

(2) For example, prior to the Tax Reform Act of 1976, Investor C purchases a partnership interest for $10,000 cash in Partnership P. P arranges for a nonrecourse loan, $10,000 of which is allocable to C. (The partnership return was not examined.) C deducts a partnership loss of $20,000. In the following year, C contributes his/her partnership interest to a charitable organization and claims a contribution of $20,000.

(a) Assume that the partnership interest is worthless. The contribution would be denied and C would realize a gain of $10,000 (release of share of partnership liabilities) from disposition of his/her partnership interest. This gain would be a long-term capital gain under existing law and regulations.

(b) Assume that the FMV of the partnership interest is $5,000. C would be allowed a deduction of $5,000 and would also realize income from the disposition of a partnership interest as discussed above.

5(13)0 *(6-20-79)* 4236
Cancellation of Indebtedness

(1) The following discussion outlines some possible courses of action and possible applications of the partnership provisions of the IRC. These positions have not necessarily been tested by the courts nor are they the result of technical advice requests. They should be applied in this light.

(2) In situations where the substance of the nonrecourse loan has not been attacked by the Service in the initial year of fund operation, the examiner should be aware that the oil and gas limited partnership using such financing arrangements will usually be faced with debt-cancellation income in future years of operation.

(3) Since nonrecourse loans are to be repaid solely from production and are usually collateralized only by the lease upon which a prospective well is to be drilled, there is a strong likelihood that the "notes" will never be fully satisfied. In fact, it is more likely that *no portion* of such loans will ever be repaid due to the fact that very few so-called "wild-cat" wells ever produce liquid hydrocarbons in commercial quantities.

(4) Therefore, once the subsurface structures of the lease have been tested through the drilling of a well and such well is "dry," the collateral (lease) for the note is, in essence, worthless. The examiner is then faced with two issues:

(a) In what year does debt-cancellation occur?

(b) What is the character of the discharge?

(5) Experience has shown that usually general partners will attempt to forestall debt-cancellation income (after leases have been drilled and proven unproductive) by paying "delay rentals" (usually nominal payments made to the owner of the land being leased for purposes of retaining to drill) and/or entering into a contract with the nonrecourse lender calling for a *foreclosure date not before a fixed date* in the future. In these cases the examiner should ascertain the year in which such debt is constructively forgiven. Regardless of the general partner-created contractual complexities, the examiner should look to the underlying facts in order to determine the tax year in which such debt becomes economically worthless.

(6) One fact indicating worthlessness would be the drilling of a dry hole which has been tested for all worthwhile potential oil and has producing "sands." The services of an engineering specialist would be required here. Another supportive fact indicating the year of worthlessness would be a lease abandonment deduction taken on the lease in question. This is a common occurrence due to the general partner's eagerness to obtain optimum deductions for the limited partners and often places the partners in a "whipsaw" position—the examiner will either have a disallowance of a lease abandonment deduction or forgiveness of indebtedness income.

(7) Once the examiner has fixed the year of worthlessness, he/she must concern himself/herself with the character of such "debt-cancellation" income. The general partner will probably claim capital gains treatment. He/she may submit any one or more of the following arguments:

(a) that contractual foreclosure provisions mandate the transaction as a "sale or exchange."

(b) that IRC 752(b) in conjunction with IRC 731(a) creates a partnership distribution which, if it exceeds the partners' adjusted bases for their interests, results in capital gain to the extent of the excess.

(8) The general partner's foreclosure argument can usually be soundly refuted by pointing out that if the lease is worthless, there is nothing of substance upon which to foreclose. The illusion of foreclosure obviously does not create a "sale or exchange" and, hence, capital gain treatment.

(9) An IRC 752(b)/731(a) argument presents more of a problem since it appears to mandate capital gains treatment on gains recognized from discharge of indebtedness. However, it should be remembered that most nonrecourse loans were borrowed for drilling—they are part of a contract calling for *drilling services* to be rendered rather than for the purpose of purchasing a capital asset. The character of the underlying property, then, is obviously not a capital asset though repayment is to be generated, in essence, from a capital asset (lease). It follows that partners should not be permitted capital gains treatment upon complete forgiveness of loans not connected with the purchase of a capital asset. The examiner, in this instance, should advocate that no sale or exchange has taken place and that IRC 61(a)12 prevails, thereby creating *ordinary* income. (See *Parker vs. Delaney,* 186 F2d 455 (CA–1, 1951)) Such ordinary income, created at the *partnership* level, will be passed through the partnership to the limited partners. IRC 752(b) and 731(a) now become relevant. The debt-cancellation income increases the partners' tax bases under IRC 705(a)(1)(B) by an amount equivalent to the tax basis reduction called for under IRC 731(a). Thus, the "transaction" results in a "wash" as far as the partners' tax bases are concerned. The IRC 752(b)/731(a)

(argument does not "create" capital gains treatment.

5(14)0 *(6–20–79)* 4236
Income Funds

5(14)1 *(6–20–79)* 4236
General

(1) Although not as popular as exploration funds, the examiner may occasionally encounter income funds organized as limited partnerships. The initial deductions are much smaller for the income funds and, therefore, are not as attractive to investors.

(2) The income fund or program is formed for the purpose of buying and operating oil/gas properties. A number of producing properties will be purchased and the profits will be returned to the investors throughout the life of the properties. These funds provide less risk to the investor and generally appeal to a smaller group of investors than the exploration or drilling funds.

(3) Tax abuses are more likely to occur in the initial year and usually involve one or more accounts such as management fees, allocation of costs between leasehold costs and lease equipment, depreciation and/or depletion, and investment credit.

5(14)2 *(6–20–79)* 4236
Examination Procedures

(1) The examiner should:

(a) Determine if the case is a mandatory referral for engineering assistance.

(b) Secure a copy of purchase contracts for oil and/or gas properties. Be alert for evidence of self-dealing between the general partner, and/or related companies, and the fund.

(c) Determine the proper allocation of purchase price between leasehold costs and lease equipment. It may be necessary to contact the seller of the properties to determine the book value of these assets on his/her records.

(d) Determine the proper amount of depreciation and depletion.

(e) See 570 of this Handbook for a discussion of management fees. Management fees may be disguised through excessive charges for general and administrative expenses.

(f) Determine the reasonableness of charges made for supervision, generally a fixed monthly charge per well.

(g) Determine the proper amount of investment credit for lease equipment.

5(15)0 *(6–20–79)* 4236
Drilling for Interest

Rev. Rul. 77–176, 1977–1 C.B. 77, deals with a situation where a driller, in consideration for drilling a well at a designated location on a leased tract of land, receives from the lessee of the land an assignment of the entire working interest (subject to an overriding royalty interest reserved by the lessee) in the drill site and a fractional working interest in the remainder of the tract. The ruling holds that the driller can elect to expense the intangible drilling costs and must include in income the value of the fractional interest in the tract exclusive of the drilling site; and the lessee is deemed to have sold such interest at fair market value resulting in a gain or loss. Such value would increase his/her basis in the overriding royalty interest reserved in the drill site. The fair market value of the interest received is determined as of the date of transfer. If the driller receives cash or an interest in another property in return for drilling, the cash or fair market value of such other property is includible in the driller's income.

Exhibit 500-1

Example of Inflated Drilling Costs:

◊

Subscriptions secured from investors	$1,000,000
Less: corporation management fee (9% × total estimated contracts) + other fees	200,000
Cash investment available for drilling contracts	800,000
Multiple used to add 60% loan	× 2.5
Total amount of negotiated contracts	$2,000,000
Capital lease costs (assume 20% of contracts)	(400,000)
Intangible Drilling Costs ("IDC")	1,600,000
Management fee paid by fund (from subscriptions) to corporation	200,000
Capital lease cost abandonment by year-end	200,000
Investor write-off in initial year (partnership loss)	$2,000,000

*Proof**

Let × = total amount of contracts drawn up

Given: Operator's "loan" of 60% of contract

Therefore, funds "cash" share of contract is 40%

Fund invests—$800,000

Then: 2/5 × = 800,000

× = 800,000 × 5/2

× = $2,000,000

Exhibit 500-2

Example of Relationship Between Partnership and Drilling Contractor.

Corporation A

(Parent)

Corp. B General Partner	Corp. C. Drilling Contractor

(a) In this example, Corporation A owns 100 percent of Corporations B and C. B is the general partner of an oil and gas drilling partnership and contracts with C to drill a number of wells for the partnership. C may or may not own drilling rigs. For this example, assume that C does not own any rigs. It follows that C will have to contract with a driller who owns rigs to actually drill the wells. It can be seen that B and C do not necessarily deal at arm's-length, and the amount paid to C may greatly exceed the cost that C must incur to secure drilling. It is not uncommon for the amounts paid by B to be twice the amount that C pays to the ultimate driller when the well has been drilled.

(b) When this situation is encountered, it may be necessary to interview the driller to verify the actual drilling costs. Appropriate adjustments should be made to drilling expenses claimed by the partnership. The deduction for IDC should not exceed the actual costs incurred in drilling.

Exhibit 500-2 Cont.

Example of Relationship Between Partnership and Drilling Contractor.

(c) This situation may also raise the question of the timing of the payment of the IDC, particularly if B pays C at the end of the taxable year, but C does not contract or pay for the drilling of wells until the next taxable year.

(d) The common parent may also own a company that has drilling rigs. The amount and time of payment are at the sole discretion of the general partner. In this instance, the examiner should consult with an engineering specialist to determine the reasonableness of the IDC claimed. Excessive charges may be allocated to leasehold costs. (Bernuth v. Commissioner, 470 F2d 710 CA-2, 1973, and Rev. Rul. 73-211, 1973-1 C.B. 303).

(Next page is 4236-103)

Coal Tax Shelters

610 *(9-20-79)* 4236
Introduction

(1) Most coal tax shelters are organized as limited partnership consisting of a general partner and one or more limited partners. The "promoter" or organizer of the program often forms a wholly-owned corporation to be the general partner of the partnership. The limited partners are the investors, and there may be any number of limited partners in one partnership. The principal characteristics of the coal shelter include:

(a) the use of a limited partnership to pass through the deduction for net operating losses.

(b) the use of leverage through *nonrecourse loans* (where none of the limited partners are liable for partnership debt) so that limited partners are able to deduct partnership losses in excess of their actual cash with respect to liabilities incurred before January 1, 1977. (See IRC 465.)

(c) the conversion of ordinary income into capital gains through application of IRC 631(c).

(d) the use of multiple entities to form a shelter.

(2) The Revenue Act of 1978, effective for years beginning after December 31, 1978, eliminated the deductibility of losses through the use of nonrecourse loans for individuals, Subchapter S corporations, and closely held corporations as well as partnerships. This was done by expanding the provisions of IRC 465 to include all activities except real estate and by incorporating the loss limitation provisions of IRC 704(d) for partnerships into IRC 465.

(3) Tax abuses are more likely to occur during the initial year. The greater portion of these guidelines are directed to the examination of the initial required return.

(4) Coal tax shelter cases involve the examination of legal documents (prospectuses, mining contracts, lease assignments, financial arrangements, sale contracts), and the development of the facts relating to the transactions. You will find these examination techniques interspersed with discussions of the legal aspects of the particular transactions involved.

620 *(9-20-79)* 4236
Relationship Between Lessor and Sublessor

(1) This is an area that must be carefully explored since this relationship can lead to abuse of advance payment and nonrecourse financing. In many cases the general partner is a wholly-owned entity of the promoter. This entity may have been formed solely to be the general partner in one or more partnership. The general partner has full management authority for the partnership. The limited partners have no voice in management decisions of the partnership.

(2) The following is an example of a typical coal tax shelter.

(a) A corporation secures a coal lease from the mineral owner. The corporation, generally owned by the syndicator or promoter, pays a relatively nominal amount to the mineral owner (generally from $10,000 ro $25,000). The promoter then forms a partnership consisting of himself/herself or his/her corporation as general partner and one or two limited partners. The partnership then acquires the subject coal lease from the corporation. The form of payment is usually $100,000 to $500,000 cash.

(b) Subsequently, the promoter syndicates a second partnership. The second partnership initially consists of a general partner (either the promoter or an entity related to or controlled by the promoter) and one limited partner. This partnership executes binding contracts with the first partnership for the purchase of coal in place. It also executes contracts for the extraction and sale of the coal and/or for management services. The mining contract, sales agreement, and management contract generally are entered into with entities related to or controlled by the promoter. When all necessary contracts have been executed, the promoter arranges for a broker to find investors for the venture. After a sufficient number of investors have been found, the original partnership agreement is amended to substitute the new investors (limited partners) for the original limited partner. The capital contribution made by the original limited partner is returned to him/her by the partnership.

(c) The second partnership is formed for the stated purpose of extracting and selling coal and generally consists of 30 or more limited partners who contribute 4 to 5 million dollars to partnership capital. These contributions consist of up to 1 million dollars in cash and 3 to 4 million dollars in nonrecourse notes executed by the partners in favor of the partnership. The partnership uses the contributed capital to pay incidental partnership formation expenses and an advanced royalty to the first partnership. It claims a deduction for advance royalty payments and distributes it to the investors (partners), who deduct the partnership loss on their tax returns. Investors usually pay approximately $20,000 cash each for their partnership interests which returns them a deduction of approximately $100,000.

(d) A schematic representation of this shelter is found at Exhibit 600-2.

630 *(9-20-79)* 4236
Characteristics of Coal Shelter Entities

631 *(9-20-79)* 4236
Tier I

This entity is generally a corporation which obtains a primary lease from the mineral owner and subleases to the tier II entity. Since it is practically impossible to identify a tier I entity solely from inspection of the return, it is anticipated that the examiner will have to identify this entity through inspection of the lease contracts, prospectus, sales agreements, etc.

632 *(9-20-79)* 4236
Tier II Return

(1) A typical tier II coal tax shelter return may disclose either taxable income or a net operating loss. It is not uncommon to find that a tier II structure of a coal tax shelter entity has invested in its related tier III structures or an unrelated tier III structure in order to shelter its own income derived from the advance payments received. The common denominators of a tier II structure are a large note receivable and a large deferred income item. The deferred receivable (executed by the tier III partnership in favor of the tier II partnership for the noncash portion of the advance royalty) usually equals the total of the nonrecourse notes delivered to the tier III partnership as part of the payment by the partners for their partnership interests.

(2) The tier II structure may be a partnership, Subchapter S corporation, an 1120 corporation, or a trust.

633 *(9-20-79)* 4236
Partnership (Tier III) Return

(1) Most tier III returns are identifiable by the following characteristics:

(a) few line items appearing on the return,

(b) large advanced royalty or Mine Opening and Land Development (MOLD) costs,

(c) little or no operating income,

(d) large numbers of partners (usually 30 or more).

(e) large net operating losses.

634 *(9-20-79)* 4236
Investor's Return

(1) The investor's partnership share of gain or loss is usually reported on Form 1040, Schedule E. However, some partnerships "elect-out" of Form 1065 filing requirements (see IRC 761) so that investors report income and deductions on Schedule C or elsewhere as "co-venturers."

(2) It should be noted that it is seldom possible to determine that a partnership loss on an individual's return is from an abusive tax shelter without an examination of the partnership return. The following steps should be taken by the examiner.

(a) Verify the date and amount of the investment to ensure that the taxpayer is entitled to a loss.

(b) Inspect information shown on the taxpayer's copy of the Schedule K-1 from the partnership, and trace it to the return.

(c) Compare the loss shown on the partner's return with the amount of his/her investment. If the loss deducted exceeds the partner's investment, it indicates the possibility of a nonrecourse loan.

(d) Specifically question the investor on the extent of his or her dealings with the general partner of the fund. Ascertain if the investor has received any actual loans or agreements to repurchase his/her partnership interest in succeeding years. These arrangements can be made with affiliates or business associates, such as the lessor or the promoter.

(e) Read the limited partnership agreement and prospectus or offering letter. The limited partner should have a copy of the offering letter.

(f) For procedures relating to the examination of individuals reporting partnership income or loss, tax auditors should see IRM 4222.1:(14) and revenue agents IRM 4222.1:(15).

(g) Consider possibility of investor's check being back dated. Is check number out of date sequence when compared to prior and subsequent checks written?

640 *(9-20-79)* 4236
Taxable Entity

641 *(9-20-79)* 4236
General

(1) Most coal tax shelters have been organized as limited partnerships. The limited partnerships generally rely on the advice of their counsel that they qualify as limited partnerships.

(2) This qualification as a partnership is vital to the operation. If it should be determined that the organization is not a limited partnership, but actually an association taxable as a corporation, the limited partners would lose their allowable deduction for partnership losses.

642 *(9-20-79)* 4236
Examination Procedures for Determining Qualification as a Partnership

(1) Inspect prospectus. A complete prospectus should contain the following:

(a) Geologic report

(b) Financial feasibility study

(c) Copy of nonrecourse note

(d) Copy of lease

(e) In addition, there may be an agreement with the contract miner.

(2) Review ruling letter if one has been received.

(a) Verify that the facts are correctly stated in the ruling request.

(b) Verify that the operations conform to the facts stated in the ruling request.

(3) Determine that qualification as a partnership is correct.

In order *not* to be considered as an association taxable as a corporation, the entity must *not* have a preponderance of the characteristics listed in (a) through (d) below. See I.T. Reg. 301.7701-2.

(a) transferability of interests;

(b) personal liability of limited partners;

(c) centralized management; and

(d) continuity of business.

(4) While it is not a requirement, it should be remembered that in most states a limited partnership is not viable until necessary registration documents have been filed with state authorities.

643 *(9-20-79)* 4236
Election Under IRC 761(a)

(1) Entities which attempt to defeat the application of IRC 704(d) by filing or inferring that an IRC 761(a) election applies, must be those type entities specified under IRC 761(a) and I.T. Reg. 1.761-2.

(2) Under the regulations at I.T. Reg. 1.761-2, there are two types of associations which may elect not to be treated as a partnership for tax purposes. The first type is an investing partnership which does not carry on a trade or business, but the participants own the property as coowners, and receive the right to separately take or dispose of their share of any property acquired or retained (I.T. Reg. 1.761-2(a)(2)). The most common example is a neighborhood investment club. The second type of entity which may elect not to be treated as a partnership for tax purposes is an association formed under a joint operating agreement. The essential characteristics of a joint operating agreement association are (a) the co-ownership of property either in fee or under lease or other form of contract granting exclusive operating rights; (b) the right to take in kind or dispose of their shares of any property produced, extracted, or used; and (c) the participants do not jointly sell services or property produced or extracted (I.T. Regs. 1.761-2(a)(3)).

(3) Therefore, a coal partnership, organized as a partnership, would generally not qualify to elect-out under IRC 761. The examiner, if in doubt as to the applicability of the election, should request technical advice.

650 *(9-20-79)* 4236
Examination Techniques

651 *(9-20-79)* 4236
General

(1) Most limited partnerships have elected to compute their distributable income or loss on the accrual basis. In *Levin v. Commissioner,* 219 F. 2d 588 (CA-3, 1955), the court held that in the case of an accrual basis taxpayer, the liability to pay an expense does not become fixed until all the events have occurred which obligate the payor to make the payments. Examiners should ascertain that the transactions meet the "all events" test to qualify for deduction by an accrual basis taxpayer (see I.T. Reg. 1.446-1(c)(1)(ii)).

(2) I.T. Regs. 1.461-1(a)(1) provides, in part, that under the cash receipts and disbursements method of accounting, amounts representing allowable deductions shall, as a general rule, be taken into account for the taxable year in which paid. IRC 446(b) provides, in part, that if the method of accounting used by the taxpayer does not clearly reflect income, the computation of taxable income shall be made under such method as, in the opinion of the Secretary, clearly reflects income. I.T. Regs. 1.461-1(a)(1) provides, in part, that if an expenditure results in the creation of an asset having a useful life which extends substantially beyond the close of the taxable year, such an expenditure may not be deductible, or may be deductible only in part, for the taxable year in which made. I.T. Regs. 1.461-1(a)(3) does not permit the current deduction of overlapping items if such deduction would materially distort income.

(3) The Commissioner has been successful in requiring taxpayers to change their method of accounting to prevent material distortion. In *Burck v. Commissioner,* 533 F2d 768 (CA-2, 1976), the taxpayer was permitted to deduct only 3/365 of interest paid which would otherwise have been deductible. Also see *Resnik v. Commissioner,* 555 F2d 634 (CA-7, 1977).

652 *(9-20-79)* 4236

Areas of Consideration

(1) Examiners should scrutinize mining records and mining contracts and determine the following:

(a) How much work was completed at the end of the year toward development of the mine?

(b) At the time of the examination, is the property in production or in development?

(c) When was production commenced?

(d) Does the cash advance royalty payment represent a deposit or bonus?

(e) Are either advance royalty or earned royalty payments considerably higher than similar royalties payable under arm's-length leases?

(f) Is the cash advance payment from the party who will mine the property or is it from a party who must secure a contract miner?

(g) Does the promissary note meet a business purpose? Did the cash payment get to the mine site in the form of equipment, etc.?

(h) If production is delayed for more than a 12-month period, is there a possible adjustment under IRC 446(b)?

(i) If a sublease is involved, what is the source of the sublessor's rights.

653 *(9-20-79)* 4236

Verification of Cash Receipts

(1) The examiner should verify cash receipts of the partnership to the extent necessary to determine that all subscriptions of the limited partners have been paid. If payments were made by note, the investor's district should be notified so that the validity of the partner's basis for losses may be verified. If the payments were made by a contribution of property, determine the validity of the payment and the value assigned to the property.

(2) The examination of cash receipts will disclose any loans made to the partnership. The source of borrowed funds may be important in determining the existence of nonrecourse loans.

(3) Trace invested cash. How was it spent? To whom was it paid? Was a related entity involved? Who was the ultimate recipient?

(4) This information may uncover unreported income issues. Additionally, if the money did not go to the mine site in the form of equipment, supplies, etc., it is an indication that no intent to actively extract the mineral exists.

654 *(9-20-79)* 4236

Management Fees

(1) This issue arises from payments made by the limited partnership to the general partner. In most instances, it is a flat percentage ranging from five to fifteen percent of the investor's subscription and is usually paid immediately after the subscription price is paid to the partnership.

(2) The partnership often contends that this is a guaranteed payment to the general partner and is deductible under IRC 707(a) or 707(c). IRC 707(a) provides that if a partner engages in a transaction with a partnership other than in the capacity of a member of such partnership, the transactions shall be considered as occurring between the partnership and one who is not a partner. IRC 707(c) provides that to the extent determined without regard to the income of the partnership, payment to a partner for services or the use of capital shall be considered as made to one who is not a member of the partnership, but only for purposes of IRC 61(a) (relating to gross income) and IRC 162(a) (relating to trade or business expenses).

(3) These expenses must first meet the requirements of IRC 162 as ordinary and necessary business expenses to be deductible. Any part of the expenditure that is attributable to the organization of the partnership, selling units of participation, acquiring capital assets, or payment for services to be performed after the close of the partnership's current year, does not qualify as a current deduction.

(4) Payment for organization expenses, registration fees, commissions, future services, and other expenses which may not be deductible, may not be stated separately on the partnership return but may be disguised as other expense. One means of concealing the true nature of the expense is to inflate the general partner's fee for management.

655 *(9-20-79)* 4236
Examination Procedures for Management Fees

(1) Determine if management fees have been deducted or capitalized as required by IRC 263 and *Rev. Rul. 75-214*, 1975-1 C.B. 185.

(2) Analyze accounts. If capitalized, ensure that all proper items have been capitalized.

(3) If management fees are not separately stated, ascertain the following:

(a) Who paid for organization, registration, and selling commissions?

(b) How were they reimbursed?

(c) Who negotiated the leases?

(d) How long did the partnership exist during the taxable year, and how much business activity was there? (This will be helpful in determining the reasonableness of management fees charged in the current year.)

(4) In the following example, $135,000 of the "management fee" would not be deductible in the current year. Legal fees and selling expenses represent capital expenditures and are not deductible per IRC 263. Example:

Investment by each limited partner	$ 10,000
Number of limited partners	× 100
Total subscription price	$1,000,000
Management fee at 15%	× .15
Total paid to general partner	$ 150,000
Disbursement by general partner:	
Legal fees (organizational matters, etc.)	$ 50,000
Selling expenses for units of participation	35,000
Future services (to be performed after close of current tax year)	50,000
Current services	15,000
Total disbursements	$150,000

656 *(9-20-79)* 4236
Organization Cost and Syndication Fees

(1) Before the Tax Reform Act of 1976, partnerships frequently deducted these costs on the basis that they were guaranteed payments to a partner. IRC 709 was added to deal specifically with this situation. It provides that for taxable years beginning after December 31, 1975, no current deduction is allowable for either organization or syndication expenses for a partnership or for any of its partners. IRC 709 does allow partnerships to amortize organization costs under these conditions:

(a) over no less than 60 months;

(b) beginning with the month the partnership begins business;

(c) if elected to do so on their first return; and

(d) for taxable years beginning after December 31, 1976.

(2) There is no provision for allowing deductions or amortization of syndication expenses.

(3) The only definition of organization costs given by IRC 709 are those which "are incident to the creation of the partnership." It would appear that organization costs would be nominal in comparison to syndication costs as they would only include such costs as salary, legal fees, and accounting fees incident to preparing partnership agreements, tax advice, and the cost of setting up an accounting system. The major portion of expenses, such as the cost of preparing a prospectus, registering with the Securities and Exchange Commission and various state regulatory agencies, sales salary and commission, travel and entertainment, and advertising would fall into the category of syndication cost.

(4) Due to recent revenue rulings, court cases, and IRC 709, organization and syndication expenses of partnerships may be more likely to be concealed in some way in the future. Possible areas to consider are:

(a) Did the limited partners claim as an itemized deduction a legal fee, tax advice fee, surety fee, etc., incurred in connection with the partnership? IRC 709 specifically refers to partners as well as partnerships.

(b) Is there a first year management fee or a guarantee of a specified profit for the organizing partner in the early years of the partnership which is designed to compensate him/her for organization or syndication costs?

(c) If no organization or syndication costs are apparent from the records of the partnership, it may be necessary to examine the general partner or other entity that established the partnership to determine what costs were incurred by them. Since IRC 709 specifically provides that such costs are not deductible by a partner, and you may not be able to establish any reimbursements to the organizing partner, any such expenses he or she may have incurred and deducted on his or her tax return may be disallowed as capital expenditures under IRC 709.

(d) Syndication fees may be labeled organization costs and amortized. This, too, will require a detailed examination of the organizing partner's records to prove. Also, keep in mind that there is no provision for any amortization for taxable years beginning prior to January 1, 1977.

657 *(9–20–79)* 4236
Royalties

(1) An advance royalty paid on and after October 29, 1976, is not deductible unless paid pursuant to a binding contract entered into prior to October 29, 1976 (see *Rev. Rul. 77–489,* 1977–2 C.B. 177).

(2) The minimum portion of an advance royalty is deductible (See Reg. 1.612–3(b)(3)). The examiner should determine if the advance payment covers a period beyond one taxable year. If so, see 651:(1) of this Handbook.

(3) The examiner should attempt to obtain copies of engineering reports and laboratory test analyses of the coal. Can coal under the lease be extracted profitably? Are partnership transactions economically compatible with stated objectives of the lease and partnership agreement? Engineering assistance should be requested if necessary. If engineering analysis shows that coal reserves are inadequate or that the coal can not be mined profitably, the rationale under *Franklin v. Commissioner,* 544 F2d. 1045 (CA–9, 1976) affg. 64 TC 752, and *Rev. Rul. 77–110,* 1977–1 C.B. 58, should be considered. If advance royalties cover substantially all of the reserves, the transaction may be considered a purchase of the coal in place.

658 *(9–20–79)* 4236
Exploration & Development Expenses

658.1 *(9–20–79)* 4236
General

Many coal tax shelters are formed for the purpose of financing the exploration of coal leases and/or the development of coal leases. Under IRC 617 each investor may elect to deduct his/her allocable portion of the exploration expenses; and under IRC 616, his/her allocable portion of the development expense. In order to avoid the recapture provisions of IRC 617, exploration expenses may often be classified by the investor and/or partnership as development expenses. Development expenses may also include the expenses of mining which may be properly deductible only as a cost of coal sold. Since tax shelters are usually designed to allow the investor to maximize the deduction of his/her investment in the initial year, examiners will often find that the improper deductions of exploration and development expenses may be the vehicle for these deductions.

658.2 *(9–20–79)* 4236
Exploration Expenses

Regulation 1.617–1(a) defines exploration expenses as those paid or incurred for ascertaining the existance, location, extent, or quality of any deposit of ore or other mineral for which a deduction for depletion is allowable under Section 613. Exploration expenses do not include the acquisition of depreciable assets. However, the depreciation of these assets may be an exploration cost. Geological surveys, core drillings, geochemical surveys, metalurgical work on mineral samples, mining, processing, and marketing feasibility studies, and cost of obtaining easement rights are all examples of exploration expenses. Once a commercially marketable quantity of coal is found, determined by actions of the taxpayer, the expenditures thereafter are either development expenses deductible under IRC 616, or operating costs inventoriable as a cost of coal sold. It is important to determine that the taxpayer has properly defined exploration expenses in the year they are paid or accrued in order that they may be properly recaptured, if applicable, at a later date.

658.3 *(9–20–79)* 4236
Development Expenses

As previously mentioned, development expenses, also referred to as MOLD (Mine Opening and Land Development) expenses, are expenses incurred by the taxpayer to gain access to a mineral deposit for commercial production. These expenses include construction of nondepreciable roads, sinking shafts, boring tunnels, and in general, making the deposits accessible to the mining operation. Expenditures that are depreciable are not development expenses, but the amount of depreciation may be. In order to increase the size of the investor's deduction, mining costs may be improperly included in development expenses. For example, the removal of overburden (soil that is removed to expose the coal) in surface mining, which is a cost of goods sold under I.T. Reg. 1.61–3, may be included in the development costs. Depreciable items such as rail spurs and tracks leading into mine shafts may be improperly deducted rather than capitalized. In addition, the taxpayer may include his/her exploration expenses in the development costs which would preclude recapture at a later date.

658.4 *(9-20-79)* 4236
Examination Techniques

(1) The examiner should take the following steps:

(a) Review the engineering referral guidelines in IRM 4216 to determine whether engineering assistance is required. Requests for engineering assistance should be made as early as possible to preclude delays in closing.

(b) Determine the source of funds used to pay the expenditures.

(c) Determine how much of the expenses were paid and how much were accrued.

(d) If the expenses were accrued, consider the provisions of IRC 461 and 466 and their possible application as to whether the accrual clearly reflects income.

(e) Review the lease/sublease to determine whether a valid economic interest in the lease exists. If it is a sublease, determine whether valid leases underly the sublease and whether the sublessor has the power to sublease.

(f) Determine the extent and use of nonrecourse financing.

(g) Determine whether the amounts paid are reasonable. Engineering assistance should be considered in making this determination.

(h) Obtain geological and geophysical data including core sample results, core drilling maps, drilling programs, etc. An engineer is usually required to interpret this data.

(i) Interview the taxpayers' geologists and independent geologists, and obtain and review their reports.

(j) Obtain and review budgets and programs to determine the phases and current status of the deposit.

(k) If little or none of the above data is available from the taxpayer under examination, look for other tiers that may be the source of the required data.

659 *(9-20-79)* 4236
Nonrecourse Financing

659.1 *(9-20-79)* 4236
General

(1) Prior to 1976, nonrecourse financing was used in many abusive tax shelters to inflate the deductions so that they were larger than the cash investment. A nonrecourse loan is a loan for which no individual partner or entity is personally liable. The lender has no recourse against any person or entity, but only against the collateralized property. However, with the Tax Reform Act of 1976, partners are no longer allowed to include nonrecourse loans in their adjusted bases for purposes of computing losses. IRC 704(d), which is generally effective for tax years beginning after 1976, prevents partners from deducting losses in excess of the amount actually at risk in partnership activities. For years beginning after December 31, 1978, the Revenue Act of 1978 repealed the special partnership at risk rule under IRC 704(d). It substituted the provisions of IRC 465, which was expanded to include *all* activities that are part of a trade or business engaged in for the production of income.

(2) Examiners should be aware that partnerships may have elected to have the partners report their portion of the tax shelter's income and expenses separately on their individual, corporate, or trust returns. This "electing out" under IRC 761 is an attempt to overcome the limitations of IRC 704(d) by ignoring the possible existence of a partnership.

659.2 *(9-20-79)* 4236
Recognizing the Existence of Nonrecourse Financing

(1) Before the examiner can deal with the issue of nonrecourse financing, he/she must be able to recognize its existence. The nonrecourse financing can be carried out either overtly or covertly. If done overtly, it can be detected on the return, but if done covertly, there will be no indication of it on the return. In cases where such financing has been openly used by the partnership in the initial year of operation, it can be recognized from the return by inspecting:

(a) *The Balance Sheet*—Check to see if a substantial liability arises at year-end, coupled with an equally substantial deficit in the partners' capital accounts.

(b) *Schedule M*—Check to see if the partnership loss substantially exceeds the capital contributed during the year.

(2) Where there is a *covert* use of such "financing," the face of the partnership return gives no indication of the existence of nonrecourse financing.

(3) In most cases, only through in-depth "third-party" questioning will the examiner ever discover the existence of such concealed financing. The following steps may aid in identifying nonrecourse financing.

(a) Read the prospectus or offering statement thoroughly for indications of such financing.

(b) Question investors as to whether they've received any "money" connected with their investment in the fund, what entity provided this money, and what the reason was for payment.

(c) Question *all* parties to the contract as to whether any money was paid directly or indirectly to the investors and what the reason was for payment, if any.

659.3 *(9-20-79)* 4236

Developing Nonrecourse Loan Issues for Years Prior to 1976

(1) Once it is determined that nonrecourse financing exists, the examiner must direct his/her examination toward the development of the following issues regarding such loans:

(a) *The "loan" could be considered a "sham."* The *deduction* and *tax basis* attributable to the loan could therefore be totally disallowed. In order to be able to advocate this position, the examiner should consider the following in order to show that the true contract was simply the cash portion of such contract and nothing more:

1 Develop the position that the financed portion of the contract was fabricated. This can be done by showing less than arm's-length relationships or transactions between the contracting parties. For instance, in a less than arm's-length contract between a related general partner and the so-called sublessor, the contracts could simply be marked up 200% or 300% of what they otherwise would be.

2 However, in a contract between a general partner and a sublessor, where no previous financial relationship can be shown, the sublessor, in order to get enough cash to cover mining expenses and procure a right to potential production, will mark up the contracts in the same manner, knowing that the general partner knowingly and tacitly will approve the markup.

3 The lender may lack the financial strength to lend "money." The examiner should check the liquidity and equity position of the lender. In summary, regarding the "sham" agreement, the examiner should be able to prove that the entire "deal" could have been consummated without the intrusion of the so-called "loan."

(b) *The "loan" could be considered a contribution of capital by the lender.* This would have the effect of denying tax basis, to the extent of the "loan," to the partners. Therefore, even though according to the partnership agreement the partners are allocated all deductibles including those "arising from borrowed money," they could deduct these mining costs only to the extent of their cash or bases in other property contributed plus any other debts which qualify. See *Rev. Rul. 72-135,* 1972-1 C.B. 200, and *Rev. Rul. 72-350,* 1972-2 C.B. 394, for examples of situations where the above issue could be proposed.

(c) *The partners' tax bases can be increased by the loan but only to the extent of the fair market value of the underlying collateral* IRC 752(c). This seems to be one of the stronger positions examiners can advocate regarding nonrecourse lending. This position would allow partnership deductibles to remain intact but would limit partners' tax bases, for flow-through purposes, to their cash contribution plus the fair market value of the loan collateral. In order to sustain this issue, an engineer's evaluation of the collateral is needed at the time the contract is concluded.

(d) *The "nonrecourse" loan was, in reality, a "recourse loan."* The examiner must read *all* loan and other agreements for indications of loan guarantees. If, for instance, a particular entity "guaranteed" the loan to the partnership, the loan would be, in essence, the liability of that entity. Under these conditions the partners' tax bases could not be increased by the loan, and all deductibles in excess of their cash contributions and/or bases in property contributed would be denied.

659.4 *(9-20-79)* 4236

Cancellation of Indebtedness

(1) The following discussion outlines some possible courses of action and possible applications of the partnership provisions of the IRC which should be considered by the examiner.

(2) In situations where the substance of the nonrecourse loan has not been attacked by the Service in the initial year of fund operation, the examiner should be aware that the tax shelter limited partnership using such financing arrangements will usually be faced with debt-cancellation income in future years of operation.

(3) Experience has shown that usually general partners will attempt to forestall debt-cancellation income by paying "minimum royalties" (usually nominal payments made to the owner of the land being leased for purposes of retaining to mine) and/or entering into a contract with the nonrecourse lender calling for a *foreclosure date not before a fixed date* in the future. In these cases the examiner should ascertain the year in which such debt is constructively forgiven. Regardless of the general partner-created contractual complexities, the examiner should look to the underlying facts in order to determine the tax year in which the debt is forgiven or cancelled.

(4) The constructive termination of the partnership may also be an indication of forgiveness of indebtedness. The following items indicate that an issue involving the constructive termination of the partnership should be considered:

(a) Laboratory reports on core samples indicating a mineral with no present market.

(b) Failure by the entity to file tax returns.

(c) Repossession of mining equipment.

(d) Failure to initiate any mining activity.

(e) Failure to meet the terms of debt instruments (i.e., nonrecourse notes).

(f) Inadequate capital for the development of a mining operation combined with reluctance of investors to invest additional capital.

660 *(9–20–79)* 4236

Development of Fraud Aspects

(1) If indications of the following are found, the examiner should refer the case to Criminal Investigation function under appropriate regional guidelines.

(a) CONSPIRACY: Are two or more general partners or promoters involved? Is there any indication that they made false or misleading statements to investors or regulatory agencies?

(b) AIDING & ABETTING: Applicability to return preparer? If the lease is worthless or nonexistent, was this known by the preparer? What records did the general partner furnish the return preparer?

(c) EVASION: Did the general partner, promoter, or syndicator report fees, guaranteed payments, etc.? Who is the ultimate receiver of investor funds?

670 *(9–20–79)* 4236

Sources of Information

671 *(9–20–79)* 4236

Federal Government

(1) Bureau of Land Management (BLM)

(a) The Bureau of Land Management has sufficient data to establish whether the subject property is under an existing lease, if there is current activity on the lease, and the identity of the lessee. Additionally, all subleases of Federal lands must be approved by BLM. Therefore, an examiner can obtain the identity of all subsequent sublessors. The BLM determines the royalty rate on all minerals extracted from Federal lands. The examiner should contact the regional BLM office serving his or her geographic area.

(b) The Bureau of Land Management has jurisdiction over the original public domain. This automatically excludes Connecticut, Delaware, Georgia, Kentucky, Maine, Maryland, Massachusetts, New Hampshire, New Jersey, New York, North Carolina, Pennsylvania, Rhode Island, South Carolina, Tennessee, Texas, Vermont, Virginia, and West Virginia.

(c) No vacant public lands remain in Illinois, Indiana, Iowa, Missouri, or Ohio.

(d) Bureau field offices and areas served are shown in Exhibit 600–3.

(2) Environmental Protection Agency (EPA)—Generally, the EPA requires that an Environmental Impact Statement be filed prior to any mining activity. This statement includes historical data of the proposed mining area, the extent and volume of the proposed mining activity, and the intended reclamation steps to be taken by the extractor. The examiner should contact the EPA office located in the state of the leased property.

(3) Securities and Exchange Commission (SEC)—The SEC, in many cases, will have copies of the prospectus, offering announcements, and financial statements of the limited partnership. Although most limited partnerships operating as coal tax shelters claim exemption from registration under the Securities Act of 1933 by virtue of claimed compliance with Rule 146 of the Securities Act, nevertheless, the SEC may have compiled a file on such partnership. Usually, each IRS district has a designated laison with SEC. The examiner should work through the established liaison. Since all SEC information requests are routed through National Office, the examiner should first determine if nec-

essary information is available from his/her state's SEC office.

672 *(9-20-79)* 4236
State Government

(1) Secretary of State—The Secretary of State will usually have copies of the partnership prospectus, copies of the offering letters, and corporate information. The corporate information includes the corporate charter and the identification of the incorporators.

(2) Department of Mines—Normally, a state department of mines will have available geological surveys showing the extent of various minerals throughout the state; mining permit applications and mining permits issued; and mine production reports. The examiner should find such information useful in determining the economic feasibility of the project under consideration.

(3) State Securities Commission

(a) Basically, the state Securities Commission will have the same information available as the Federal SEC.

(b) Although the aforementioned captioned state agencies may vary nominally from state to state, the information should be available in any state which has coal mining activity.

673 *(9-20-79)* 4236
Local Government

(1) County Recorder/County Court/Clerk of Courts—Leases of private property are normally recorded in the county of the geographic property location. Any subsequent subleases are also recorded. Such records are public information, and the examiner merely has to scrutinize the indices to locate the subject transactions. However, it should be noted that most promoters of coal tax shelters are in the business of selling tax shelters, and not necessarily interested in mining coal. Therefore, the subject lease transactions may not have been recorded. Those states which have adopted the "Uniform Principal and Partnership Act" also require that a copy of the partnership agreement be filed in the county where the partnership has a business location.

680 *(9-20-79)* 4236
Glossary of Terms

A glossary of terms is provided in Exhibit 600-1. The glossary is not intended to include all terms used in the text.

Exhibit 600-1

Glossary of Terms

◊

Advance Royalty—An amount prepaid by the lessee to the lessor pursuant to a lease contract. This amount is recoupable against future production. The prepaid period is greater than one year, usually for the entire term of lease.

Amount at-risk—For purposes of the at-risk loss limitation rule, the amount at-risk in any one activity is:

(1) the amount of money and the adjusted basis of property contributed to the activity, and

(2) any amounts borrowed for use in the activity where the taxpayer is personally liable for repayment of the loan or has pledged property other than that used in the activity as security (but only to the extent of the net fair market value of his or her interest in the property).

Certain borrowed amounts are excluded from consideration as being at-risk if:

(1) borrowed from someone who:

(a) has an interest (other than as a creditor) in the activity, or

(b) is related to the taxpayer as defined in IRC 267(b).

(2) the taxpayer is protected against loss through nonrecourse financing, guarantees, stop-loss agreements, or other similar arrangements.

Association—Two or more individuals, corporations, partnerships, trusts, etc., that participate in an organization which has the characteristics of a corporation (I.T. Reg. 301.7701-2).

Development Expense—Those expenses which are incurred after a commercially marketable quantity of coal has been determined (IRC 616). Does not include any amount deductible under IRC 162 or any amount includable in cost of goods sold (Reg. 1.61-3).

Economic Feasibility—From an economic standpoint, an abusive tax shelter is one in which the present value of all future income is less than the present value of all the investments and associated costs in the shelter: that is, the investment is for noneconomic purposes. In abusive tax shelters the "primary" gain is from the tax advantage.

Exploration Expenses—Those expenses paid or incurred for ascertaining the existence, location, extent, or quality of any deposit of ore or other mineral for which a deduction for depletion is allowable under IRC 613. Reg. 1.617-1.

General Partner—A member of the organization who, except as provided in Reg. Section 301.7701-2(d)(2) is personally liable for the obligations of the partnership.

Investor—As used in the guidelines, an investor is one who invests in a limited partnership; used interchangeably with limited partner.

Investor Contract—Legal document signed by the investor obligating investor to subscribe for a specified number of units of the limited partnership shares. May also include a power of attorney in favor of general partner to enable general partner to exercise all authority granted limited partners by the partnership agreement.

Joint Operation—The collective participation in an underlying lease by two or more co-owner associations.

Lease—The assignment of operating rights in a mineral property by the owner to another person for no immediate consideration or for cash or its equivalent, but retaining a nonoperating interest in the mining production.

Lease Bonus—An amount paid in advance to the lessor by the lessee to procure operating rights. This amount is not recoverable from production payments. Such payment must be capitalized and depleted over the life of the property by the lessee (Reg. 1.162-11).

Leverage—The use of borrowed funds to finance a business venture.

Limited Partner—One who may not be held responsible for partnership debts, and whose potential personal liability is confined to the amount of money or other property that the partner contributed or is required to contribute to the partnership.

Minimum Royalty—An amount payable regardless of production. Payment must be recoverable by payor from future production. Payor may elect to deduct payment as current expense (Reg. 1.612-3(b)).

Nonrecourse Loan—In this context, any borrowing by a tax-sheltered partnership or other entity structured in such a way that lenders can look *only* to specific assets pledged for repayment, and *not* to the individual assets of the various participants.

Offering Letter—A written document tendered to a potential investor by the promoter. The

Exhibit 600–1 Cont.

Glossary of Terms

◊

offering letter sets forth the location, purpose, and number of available units in the program. Additionally, it informs the investor of the amount and terms of payment for purchase of the units.

Organization Costs—Those costs which are incident to the creation of the partnership (IRC 709). Such costs include salary, legal fees, and accounting costs incident to preparing partnership agreements, tax advice, and setting up the accounting system.

Private Program—A tax-sheltered partnership which is offered and sold pursuant to the private offering exemption available under the Securities Act of 1933 or some registration exemption granted by the securities authorities of one or more states; that is, a program which is not registered with the Securities and Exchange Commission.

Promoter—An individual or business entity that actively secures funds by locating interested investors. Quite often the promoter is the general partner in the limited partnership.

Prospectus—A written document furnished to the investor by the promoter. This document sets forth, among other things, the program in general, the description of the mineral property, the lease and sublease, the nature and extent of all satellite agreements, the risk factors, the possible tax consequences, and the partnership agreement.

Public Program—A tax-sheltered partnership which is registered with the Securities and Exchange Commission and distributed in a public offering by broker-dealers or employees of the general partner. The principal difference between a public program and a private program is the number of investors, which may be several hundred in a public program, but must be limited to 35 or less in a private program (see Rule 146, Securities Act 1933).

Reserves—Minerals mineable at a profit.

Syndication Fee—Includes the cost of preparing the prospectus, registering with the SEC and various state regulatory agencies, sales salary and commissions, travel and entertainment, and advertising.

Tiering—Coal tax shelters are generally formed by the use of multiple entities through which the lease transactions flow, resulting in a pyramidal structure, i.e., the initial lease transaction is consumated by a tier I entity. The tier II then subdivides the underlying lease in fragments and subleases each fragment to a tier III entity.

Exhibit 600-2

Schematic Representation of Coal Tax Shelter discussed at 620:(2).

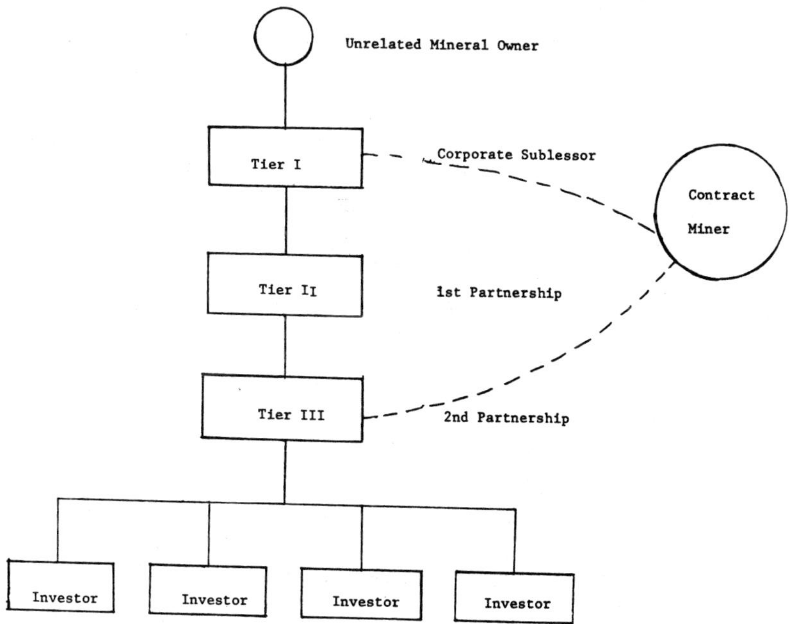

Exhibit 600-3

Bureau of Land Management Field Offices and Areas Served

ALASKA	555 Cordova Street Anchorage, Alaska 99501 (907-277-1561)
ARIZONA	2400 Valley Bank Center Phoenix, Arizona 85073 (602-261-3831)
CALIFORNIA	Room 2841, Federal Building 2800 Cottage Way Sacramento, California 95825 (916-484-4217)
COLORADO	Room 700, Colorado State Bank Building 1600 Broadway Denver, Colorado 80202 (303-837-4481)
IDAHO	Room 398, Federal Building 550 West Fort Street P. O. Box 042 Boise, Idaho 83724 (208-342-2711)
MONTANA NORTH DAKOTA SOUTH DAKOTA MINNESOTA (Except Minerals)	Granite Tower Building P. O. Box 30157 Billings, Montana 59101 (406-245-6711)
NEVADA	3008 Federal Building 300 Booth Street Reno, Nevada 89502 (702-784-5459)
NEW MEXICO OKLAHOMA TEXAS	U.S. Post Office & Federal Building P. O. Box 1449 South Federal Place Santa Fe, New Mexico 87501 (505-988-6243)
OREGON WASHINGTON	729 Northeast Oregon Street P. O. Box 2965 Portland, Oregon 97208 (503-234-3361 & 4024)
UTAH	University Club Building 136 East South Temp Salt Lake City, Utah 84111 (801-524-5311)

Exhibit 600-3 Cont.

Bureau of Land Management Field Offices and Areas Served

WYOMING KANSAS NEBRASKA	Joseph C. O'Mahoney Federal Center 2120 Capitol Avenue P. O. Box 1828 Cheyenne, Wyoming 82001 (307-778-2220, ext. 2384)
ARKANSAS IOWA LOUISIANA MINNESOTA (Minerals only) and all states east of the Mississippi River	Eastern States Land Office 7981 Eastern Avenue Silver Spring, Maryland 20910

Commodity Options and Futures

710 *(5-30-80)* 4236
Background

(1) Commodity options (options) and future delivery contracts (futures) tax shelter arrangements have been marketed, with increasing success, to high income taxpayers. The distinction between options contracts and futures contracts has been of importance from a tax standpoint because options contracts are covered by IRC 1234, while futures contracts are not. These tax shelters frequently use silver as the principal commodity, but the techniques are equally applicable to other commodities; e.g., tax shelters involving the use of interest rate futures (in Treasury Bills and GNMA Certificates) are being seen with increasing frequency.

(2) Each of these shelter arrangements involve buy/sell transactions which are balanced because, as the underlying commodity market price moves up or down, one part of the transaction (leg) becomes more valuable, while the remaining part (the other leg) becomes less valuable in approximately the same proportion.

(3) These tax shelters generally have little or no expectation of profit or loss, although they do entail actual market purchases and sales. Instead they are designed to artificially reduce and/or defer a tax liability by producing tax gains or losses that do not reflect economic realities. An example of their use is to convert short-term capital gain or ordinary income in one year into long term capital gain in another.

(4) The following basic tax shelter arrangements have been employed by taxpayers.

(a) The simultaneous buying and selling of futures contracts in silver, Treasury Bills or GNMA Certificates, or other commodities (often called "spreads", "straddles" or "tax straddles").

(b) The simultaneous purchase of spot commodities by use of highly leveraged (usually nonrecourse) financing and sale of a futures contract for the same commodity in a like amount (usually referred to as a "cash and carry" transaction).

(c) The use of option contracts to buy and sell silver, or other commodities (often called an option "straddle" or "spread").

(d) The purchase of a commodity (using conventional financing) and a related sale of a futures contract in the same commodity for a like amount (hedging). (Note: Although hedging transactions are sometimes used as components of tax shelters they are also frequently used by commodity users as a form of price insurance. *See* Rev. Rul. 72-179, 1972-1 C.B.57).

(5) A glossary of terms used in commodity transactions is included in Exhibit 700-1.

720 *(5-30-80)* 4236
Commodity Transactions

(1) Some straddles are entered into with an anticipation of making a profit. These straddles involve a degree of market risk which can result in a loss. Usually, this type of straddle will consist of two contracts, a buy and a sell with different delivery months, which are simultaneously entered into and closed. The price differential between the buy and sell is known as the spread from which profit or loss is determined.

(2) Tax straddles are more complicated than profit-motivated straddles and involve several straddles which are clustered and usually extend beyond one tax year. The employment of several straddles provides protection against changes in the price of the commodity or the spread, the price differential between delivery dates.

721 *(5-30-80)* 4236
Futures Straddle Tax Shelters

(1) One form of a straddle shelter (butterfly spread) is described in Rev. Rul. 77-185, 1977-1 C.B. 48. Frequently, more than one account is used in completing the entire series of transactions. On larger schemes, several dealers may be involved for the purpose of disguising the balanced nature of the transactions. One account will have the loss futures, another the gain futures, or one dealer will have the buy futures, another dealer the sell futures in the same quantity that comprises the other half of the balanced transactions.

(2) A balanced transaction in futures will be initiated some time before the end of the tax year. The losing portion of the straddle will be closed out in order to claim a loss, with the simultaneous re-establishment of an identical buy or sell with a different contract month. In the following tax year, the balanced transaction will be closed out after the six-month holding period resulting in a net capital gain (See IRC 1222(11). Section 1402 of the Tax Reform Act of 1976

retained the 6 month holding period for futures transactions) Note that it is the Service's position that as there is no "closed and completed transaction" until all transactions are closed out, the loss of the first "leg" of the straddle would not be allowed in the first year, but rather would be carried over and netted against the gain resulting from the second "leg" of the straddle in a subsequent year.

722 *(5–30–80)* 4236
Options Tax Shelters

(1) Paired straddle arrangements in options were used either to convert capital loss to ordinary loss in one tax year or to convert ordinary income into short-term capital gain in a subsequent year (which then could be converted into long-term capital gain by use of a "commodities spread," as described in Rev. Rul. 77–185). For example, if a taxpayer had a significant capital loss, or loss carryover, from an unrelated transaction, the paired straddle arrangement was used to convert the loss to ordinary loss by grouping the transactions in one tax year. Alternatively, the paired straddle could be used to convert ordinary income from other sources into capital gain by spreading the transactions over two tax years. It should be noted, however, that these shelters are of little effect after the effective date of the Tax Reform Act of 1976 which amended section 1234(b)(1) of the Code. Prior to September 1, 1976, granted options could give rise to ordinary loss under certain circumstances; options granted after that date can give rise only to short-term capital gain or loss. Thus, the tax shelter described in paragraph 2 is effective only if the loss "leg" is based on an option granted prior to September 1, 1976 (although the option can be closed out at a later date).

(2) This arrangement was used by U.S. taxpayers who had American commodity dealers as intermediaries between themselves and London commodity dealers.

(a) The arrangement was initiated with a payment to the American dealer who used the monies to establish a "discretionary margin account" with the London dealer. The discretionary margin account agreement ususally provided for the London dealer to have complete control and discretion over trading done in the account.

1 Under the rules of the London Metal Exchange, the holder of an option can exercise the option only on a given date referred to as the "expiration date." This is unlike the typical American option that can be exercised at any time. This factor is important because it prevents the holder of the option from exercising it before the grantor has accomplished the grantor's tax purposes.

(b) The "paired straddle arrangement" scheme consisted of several transactions involving the granting and purchasing of options of like quantity. For example, the taxpayer entered into four transactions on January 2, 1976, when *y* ounces of silver sold for 7.5*x* dollars. The premium paid or received for each transaction was 3*x* dollars. The four transactions were as follows:

1 *Transaction 1*—granting a call option with a prompt date of October 1, 1976, to sell *y* ounces of silver for 5*x* dollars.

2 *Transaction 2*—purchasing a call option with a prompt date of November 1, 1976 to buy *y* ounces of silver for 5*x* dollars.

3 *Transaction 3*—granting a put option with a prompt date of October 1, 1976, to buy *y* ounces of silver for 10*x* dollars.

4 *Transaction 4*—purchasing a put option with a prompt date of November 1, 1976, to sell *y* ounces of silver for 10*x* dollars.

(c) On September 30, 1976, when *y* ounces of silver sold for 9*x* dollars, the taxpayer closed out *Transaction 1* for 4*x* dollars (difference between 9*x* fair market value and 5*x* call price), sold the call option in *Transaction 2* for 4*x* dollars, and sold the put option in *Transaction 4* for 1*x* dollar (difference between the 10*x* put price and 9*x* fair market value). On October 1, 1976, the holder of the put option in *Transaction 3,* sold the silver to the taxpayer for 10*x* dollars who immediately sold it for 9*x* dollars, its fair market value on that date.

(d) The respective results of these four transactions are summarized as follows:

1 *Transaction 1*—1*x* dollars ordinary loss (difference between 4*x* dollars paid to close out the call and 3*x* dollars premium received to grant the call). See Rev. Rul. 78-181, 1978-1 C.B. 261.

2 In *Transaction 2*—1*x* dollars long-term capital gain (4*x* dollars selling price minus 3*x* dollars premium paid for the call option). See IRC 1234(a).

3 *Transaction 3*—2*x* dollars short-term capital gain on the silver sold (9*x* dollars amount realized minus basis of 7*x* dollars (10*x* dollars exercise price minus premium received of 3*x* dollars)).

4 *Transaction 4*—the taxpayer claimed 2*x* dollars long-term capital loss (3*x* dollars premium paid for the option minus 1*x* dollars received on its sale).

5 The net results of all four transactions are 1*x* dollars ordinary loss and 1*x* dollars short-term capital gain.

723 *(5-30-80)* 4236
Variations of the Basic Tax Shelters

(1) The basic component of the London Options tax shelters was the fact that the loss "leg" produced ordinary loss. Although section 1234 has been amended to preclude the use of options transactions to produce ordinary loss, such results may be achieved through the use of interest rate futures transactions. Under IRC 1221(5), transactions in Treasury Bills produce ordinary income or loss. Although it is current Service position that Treasury Bills futures are capital assets, transactions are currently being structured so that the loss "leg" is closed out by taking delivery and subsequently selling the actual Treasury Bill. This transaction, combined with trades in GNMA futures on the gain "leg" (as both Treasury Bills futures and GNMA futures are ultimately based on the same interest factors, a transaction in one type or contract can be used to "hedge" the other) achieves the result of producing ordinary loss balanced by a capital gain at little or no economic cost to the taxpayer.

(2) A variation of the basic option scheme involves transactions conducted through a Bermuda company. The scheme differs in the following manner:

(a) The options, *i.e.*, a granted put balanced by a taken put or a granted call by a taken call, are "hedged" by futures.

(b) The opening futures straddle is not closed out or "switched" as described in Rev. Rul. 77-185.

(3) A simple variant of the type of "straddle" described in Rev. Rul. 77-185 involves the purchase with borrowed funds (usually on a nonrecourse basis) of "spot" silver combined with a six to twelve month's futures contract to deliver an equal quantity. This scheme is sometimes referred to as the "cash and carry" silver shelter.

(a) The futures contract "hedges" the transaction and reduces the risk.

(b) Since the purchase and loan arrangement probably preclude actual delivery of the spot silver until the loan is paid, or the futures contract closed against the delivery obligation of the seller, the purchase of the spot silver and payment of interest appear to be part of a package arrangement undertaken solely or primarily to convert ordinary income into capital gain by claiming an interest deduction in the initial year and an offsetting capital gain in the subsequent year.

730 *(5-30-80)* 4236
Issue Identification

(1) Tax shelter transactions involving commodity straddles can be found on all types of income tax returns, divided between various returns, or scattered throughout different parts of the same return. They may involve different investment houses or different commodities. Therefore, care should be taken to examine all the commodity transactions of a taxpayer and then match them. It is not uncommon to find part of a tax avoidance scheme reported on a partnership return and part on the income tax return of each partner.

(2) Examples of how these transactions may be reflected on tax returns:

(a) An ordinary loss may be reported on Form 4797 (Supplemental Schedule of Gains and Losses), as "miscellaneous income," or on Schedule C (Profit or (Loss) from Business or Professions), or as other income on Form 1040.

(b) Capital gains and losses may be reported on Schedule D (Capital Gains and Losses).

(3) Schedule D indicators of possible tax shelter commodity schemes are:

(a) Transactions reported with a commodity or option as "kind of property and description."

(b) Transactions with no description given (particularly *short-term* gains or losses).

(c) Transactions with an ambiguous description and the date sold is *prior* to the date acquired.

(d) Ordinary losses from options with almost equal offsetting capital gains.

(4) Since gains and losses may be reported in different years, inspection of prior and subse-

quent year tax returns is essential in determining the extent of possible shelter schemes when commodity transactions are indicated during an examination.

740 *(5-30-80)* 4236

Examination Considerations

(1) Economic Reality of Commodity Transactions

(a) To be entitled to the loss deduction provided by IRC 165(c)(2), an individual investor, not in the commodity trade or business, has the burden of demonstrating that the options and futures transactions were entered into for profit. Evidence to establish the taxpayer's profit expectations can be broken down into at least two major areas of consideration:

1 Evidence that the taxpayer truly intended to profit from the transactions.

2 Evidence that the taxpayer had the potential for a profit from the transactions.

(b) I.T. Regs. 1.165-1(b) provides that the substance of *transactions* (not necessarily one transaction) will be determinative over mere form in the deductibility of losses. When one part of a straddle is closed out and simultaneously reopened (differing only in the commodity delivery date), the taxpayer's economic position has not changed sufficiently to establish that the transaction is for profit, rather than to obtain a tax loss, or that there is a closed and completed transaction for tax purposes.

(2) Deductions for Out-of-Pocket Expenses for Commodity Transactions

(a) In accordance with Rev. Rul. 77-185, when a determination is made that the taxpayer's dominant motive was not profit from the commodity arrangement but only to reduce income tax liability, no deduction for out-of-pocket expenses will be allowed under the provisions of IRC 165(c)(2).

(3) Ordinary Loss Deduction From Commodity Transactions

(a) Rev. Rul. 78-181 provides, in part, that ordinary gain or loss will be recognized when a taxpayer repurchases an option granted prior to September 2, 1976 from the option holder before the option life expires. September 2, 1976, is the effective date of IRC 1234(b) which provides that with respect to the grantor of an option all commodity option closing transactions will be treated as gain or loss from the sale or exchange of a short-term capital asset. A closing transaction is defined as any termination of the taxpayer's obligation under the commodity option other than through the exercise or lapse of the option. Commodity dealers are specifically exempted from the provision of IRC 1234(b).

750 *(1-12-81)* 4236

Examination Techniques

(1) Examiners should be aware that only part of a series of interrelated commodity transactions may be reflected on the return. Examination of the entire commodity account, or related accounts, covering a period of at least two tax years, may be necessary to determine if a tax shelter scheme is present.

(2) Examiners should secure documentation which includes the following:

(a) All contractual agreements between the taxpayer and the dealer.

(b) Records of all funds paid to and received from the dealer.

(c) All transaction confirmation documents issued for all commodity accounts.

(d) All transaction summary documents issued by the dealer.

(e) All monthly statements of account for all commodity accounts.

(f) Any correspondence between the taxpayer and the dealer which relates to the commodity accounts.

(3) Arrange the transaction confirmation documents in chronological transaction date order. Pair up the transactions in like quantity buy/sell or sell/buy order to facilitate understanding the sequence of transactions. Forms 6578 and 6578-A, Option Straddle Worksheet should be used to schedule and summarize the transactions for London Metal Exchange cases.

(4) Each balanced transaction pair can be compared to commodity market price quotations. The quotations include opening prices, high, low, and closing prices for each contract month traded. Compute the spread for all four quotations for the contract months involved to determine the range of the spread. If the spread for the contract month on the dealer confimation slips is outside the range of the quotation spread computed, the presumption would be that the dealer determines the gain or loss from transactions and not the market. If this is the case, arguments presented by the taxpayer about profit and risk potential would have little or no merit for purposes of IRC 165(c)(2).

(5) The London Exchange

(a) The London dealers buy and sell only to themselves, on behalf of the taxpayer, in various commodity transactions. This is accomplished by the U.S. taxpayer establishing a "discretionary margin account" with a London commodity dealer. Due to the lack of arm's-length trading, it is important to determine whether a prudent investor would engage in option and futures transactions and reach the same economic and income tax result.

(b) Examiners should consider the following when reviewing the discretionary margin account agreement:

1 Determine whether the investors payment is a margin deposit or a commission.

2 Determine whether this type of agreement is used in bona fide trades (spot, future, and option) or is used solely for tax shelters.

3 Determine whether the London dealer has complete discretion as to price and time for trading.

(c) Examination of the trading account itself is recommended. It is possible for one taxpayer to have several commodity accounts. It is also possible for one commodity account to be shared by numerous taxpayers. Concentrating on the examination of the trading account should reduce confusion.

(d) A debit/credit analysis of the option and futures transactions trading account can be made on a transaction day-by-day basis. Option granting premiums received, futures sold, and any taxpayer investments are credits. Options taken, futures purchased, and commissions charged are debits. On any day that a net debit balance results in this analysis, the inference is that the London dealer is advancing funds to the taxpayer's trading account. If so, this is a situation where the London dealer is at risk rather than the taxpayer.

(e) Determine exactly what the margin requirements are. It may be possible that there is *no* margin requirement imposed on the taxpayer by the London dealer. However, inquiry should be made as to why a margin call by the London dealer was not made when the debit balance occurred.

(6) Examiners should, at a minimum, obtain information from the taxpayer with respect to the following areas.

(a) Establishment of the commodity account—Analyze information provided by the taxpayer on why specific commodity transactions were selected for investment. Consideration should be given to the taxpayer's knowledge and prior experience with commodities.

(b) Management of the commodity account—Determine whether the account is managed in total by the taxpayer's agent. Determine the type of input the taxpayer has with respect to decisions to be made.

(c) Cost—Determine the costs for the commodity account. Determine the type of payment required, i.e. commission, margin, or other fees. Determine whether there are any stipulations that the taxpayer will absorb additional fees or risk in any transactions and whether guarantees are offered by the agent.

760 *(5-30-80)* 4236

Information Sources

(1) *Metals Week Price Handbook* is issued each year with daily price quotations for the entire year on most metal commodities traded in the world.

(2) The *London Times* reports price quotations and market activity for all London commodities on a daily basis.

(3) The *Journal of Commerce* reports price quotations and market activity for all commodity transactions on a daily basis.

(4) The *Wall Street Journal* reports limited price quotations for London commodities and extensive U.S. commodity market prices on a daily basis. Silver prices are reported only from the London Silver Market.

(5) Additional information is available on the London Metal Exchange and London commodities in *The London Metal Exchange—A Commodity Market,* by Robert Gibson-Jarvie, published by Woodhead-Faulkner Ltd., in 1976, and *Getting Started in London Commodities,* second edition by the editor C.W.J. Granger, published by Investor Publications, Inc., in 1975 and revised in 1977.

Exhibit 700–1

Glossary

Account Sale—A statement by a broker to a commodity customer when a futures transaction is closed out. Sometimes referred to as a P & S (Purchase and Sale Statement) it shows the net profit or loss on the transaction with commission and other proper changes set forth and taken into account.

Backwardation—A London term used when an earlier delivery date of a particular commodity is priced higher than a later delivery date of the same commodity. This is the opposite of a contango.

Balanced Transaction—Any form of simultaneous commodity transactions that have one like quantity transaction becoming more valuable while the other like quantity transaction becomes less valuable as the underlying commodity market price is increasing or decreasing. This term includes any futures spread or option straddle transactions.

Basis—The difference between the spot or cash price of a commodity and the futures price of the same or related commodity, usually computed to the near future.

Bear Straddle—A commodity transaction where the "sell" month of the straddle comes before the "buy" month.

Bucketing—Directly or indirectly taking the opposite side of a customer's order into the handling broker's own account into an account in which the broker has an interest, without execution on an exchange.

Bull Straddle—A commodity transaction where the "buy" month of the straddle comes before the "sell" month.

Butterfly Spread—A special form of a futures spread involving double balanced transactions, rather than single, which are practically mirror images of each other. For example: Buy 21 March; sell 21 July; and buy 21 December; sell 21 July. The purpose is to minimize the possibility of gains or losses from changes in the futures transactions spread.

Call—An option contract giving the buyer the right to *buy* a commodity for a specific price within a specific time. Call options tend to become more valuable as the market price of the underlying commodity *increases.*

Commodity Option—A right, usually purchased, to buy or sell a commodity at a specific price within a specific time, ragardless of the market price of the underlying commodity. Commodity options are created, and sold, by the grantor. Purchasers are referred to as holders or takers. See also Call, Put, and Option Writing.

Contango—A term used when the later delivery date of a particular commodity is priced higher than an earlier delivery date of the same commodity. The difference in price represents a prepayment of interest and commodity handling charges. The opposite of backwardation.

Declaration Date—The last date on which the holder has the right to exercise the option. If the buyer fails to declare by such date, the option automatically expires. The declaration date is on the contract. Also called the *expiration* date.

Delivery Month—The month when delivery of the underlying commodity is contemplated by the parties to a future.

Discretionary Account—Term used to describe a special account in which the holder of the account gives written power of attorney to someone else, often his broker, to buy and sell without prior approval of the holder; often referred to as the "managed account" or Controlled Account.

Exercise Price—The contract price for which a future will be bought or sold if and when an option is exercised by an option holder. Also called the "striking price."

Expiration Date—The date on which an option contract expires; the last day on which an option can be exercised.

Financial Instruments—Currency, securities, and indices of their value. Examples include shares, mortgages, commercial paper and Treasury bills and bonds.

Futures—Any bilateral contract which specifies a delivery of the commodity at any date in the future after the transaction date. Normally, it specifies a minimum of 3 months to a maximum of 15 months. Sometimes termed a futures contract.

G.N.M.A.—Pass through mortgage-backed certificates guaranteed by the Government National Mortgage Association (GNMA or Ginnie Mae). The certificates are backed by pools of FHA insured and/or VA guaranteed residential mortgages, with the mortgage and note held in safekeeping by a custodial financial institution.

Exhibit 700-1 Cont.

Glossary

Grantor—The creator or seller of an option. Also referred to as an option writer.

Hedging—Taking a position in a futures market opposite to a position held in the cash market to minimize the risk of financial loss from an adverse price change; a purchase or sale of futures as a temporary substitute for a cash transaction that will occur later.

Interest Rate Futures—Futures contracts traded on commodities such as GNMA's, issuances of the U.S. Treasury, or commercial paper, the value of which is determined by yield. Currency is excluded from this category, even though interest rates are a factor in currency values.

Leg—One side of a balanced transaction. Also see Long Position and Short Position.

Long Position—The portion of a balanced transaction in futures that is initiated by the purchase of a future. A long position is terminated by an offsetting sale or by taking delivery of the underlying commodity.

Lot—The unit of measure in which a commodity is traded on a commodity market. This can vary from market to market for the same commodity. For instance, one lot of London silver is 10,000 troy ozs., whereas one lot of New York silver is 5,000 troy ozs.

Option—A right on the part of one party, based on contract, to buy (call) or sell (put) something.

Option Writing—A phrase used by the Chicago Board of Options Exchange to describe the creation of a stock option in that exchange.

P & S (Purchase and Sale) Statement—A statement sent by a commission house to a customer when any part of a futures position is offset, showing the number of contracts involved, the prices at which the contracts were bought or sold, the gross profit or loss, the commission charges, the net profit or loss on the transactions, and the balance.

Parity—The term used to describe the intrinsic value of a call option when the market price of the commodity underlying the call option is *less* than the exercise price, but the market price plus the premium equals or exceeds the exercise price. Also, the term is used to describe the intrinsic value of a put option when the market price of the commodity underlying the put option is *more* than the exercise price, but the exercise price plus the premium equals or exceeds the market price.

Position—A term used to indicate the existence of an option or future. An option or future is initiated by opening a position and terminated by closing a position.

Prompt Date—Term for delivery date.

Put—An option to *sell* a commodity for a specific price within a specific time. Put options tend to become more valuable as the market price of the underlying commodity *decreases.*

Short Position—The portion of a balanced transaction in futures that is initiated by the sale of a future. A short position is terminated by an offsetting purchase or by making delivery of the underlying commodity.

Spot—The term for the actual commodity being delivered on the transaction date at the present price rather than a future delivery price.

Spread—The difference in the prices of futures contracts of the same commodity with different delivery dates.

Straddle—A term used for any form of offsetting commodity transactions such as:

(1) Like commodity futures in two different market places.

(2) Commodity options with different delivery dates.

Striking Price—See Exercise Price.

Taker—The purchaser or holder of an option contract.

Tax Straddle—A special form of balanced transactions in futures that includes a purported or claimed "closing out" of the loss leg in the current tax year to create short-term capital loss coupled with the reestablishment of a nearly identical leg and the simultaneous closing out of the balanced transactions positions in a subsequent tax year.

Treasury Bills—Short term U.S. government obligations. Treasury bills generally are issued with 13, 26 or 52 week maturities. They are sold at a discount from the face value at maturity. For example, a one-year Treasury bill worth $10,000 at maturity may sell for $9,600. The $400 difference is the discount; 4 percent ($400 divided by $9,600) is the yield.

Treasury Bonds—Medium or long term obligations of the U.S. government. If not callable, these bonds pay interest semi-annually until they are mature, at which time the principal and the final interest payment is paid to the investor. If they are callable, the Treasury can call the bond back in advance of maturity, paying accrued interest to the investor at that time. Until such time as the bond is called, the semi-annual interest is paid.

(Next page is 4236-143)

Equipment Leasing Tax Shelters

810 *(8–7–79)* 4236
Background

(1) The equipment leasing industry has grown spectacularly within the last decade as an alternative to the more conventional procedure of borrowing money to finance the acquisition of capital equipment and facilities that require high investments over long periods of time. Many taxpayers are now using leasing as a vehicle to acquire costly assets such as airplanes, computers, railway cars, oil tankers, etc.

(2) Traditional incentives for the lessee include the immediate deduction of rental costs and the avoidance of high outlays of working capital to acquire the property.

(3) A major incentive to the lessor is the use of equipment leasing as a sales aid when prospective buyers are unable to finance the purchase of their equipment.

(4) In many instances, equipment leasing ventures are being turned into abusive tax shelters. The cost of equipment is being inflated by the use of nonrecourse loans that would permit the lessor to claim an artificially high depreciation deduction and investment tax credit.

(5) In an abusive tax shelter, the true investor or owner of the property may be obscured among the complexities of the transactions, so that the wrong party claim the benefits of ownership and, therefore, the tax benefits of accelerated depreciation and investment credit. In this situation, the true owner might actually be the lessee who is not in need of the accelerated depreciation deduction and investment credit. The tax benefits would incorrectly accrue to the lessor, who may be in a high tax bracket and in need of a tax shelter.

(6) The Tax Reform Act of 1976 introduced IRC 465 to prevent taxpayers from deducting losses in excess of the amount at risk in equipment leasing activities for tax years beginning after 1975. Taxpayers are at risk in an activity to the extent of the money and the adjusted basis of property they contribute to the activity. Taxpayers are also at risk for loans for which they have personal liability or have pleged personal assets as security which are used to finance the activity. The "at risk" provisions of the Tax Reform Act of 1976 were applied to losses sustained by noncorporate taxpayers, electing small business corporations, and personal holding companies. Regular corporations were not affected.

(7) The Revenue Act of 1978, which is effective for tax years beginning after 1978, applies the provisions of IRC 465 to noncorporate taxpayers and all corporations in which five or fewer individuals own more than 50% of the stock, except for closely held corporations in which at least 50% of the gross receipts are attributable to equipment leasing.

820 *(8–7–79)* 4236
Equipment Leasing Entities

821 *(8–7–79)* 4236
Corporate Entities

(1) Examiners can expect to see the corporate entity used most frequently in equipment leasing shelters. Although the Revenue Act of 1978 applied the provisions of IRC 465 to closely held corporations for the first time, corporations that are not closely held continue to be excluded. Through nonrecourse financing, these corporations are still permitted to deduct losses in excess of their at risk contributions.

(2) Occasionally a corporate lessor will utilize a grantor trust as a vehicle to claim equipment leasing losses. In this situation, the corporate lessor (grantor) will create a trust and name itself the beneficiary. All income, expenses, and credits of the trust are funneled back to the grantor in the same manner as a partnership would work. A grantor trust arrangement is generally used for off balance sheet financing purposes or for other business reasons. Keep in mind that the lessor should receive the same tax benefits whether or not a grantor trust exists.

822 *(8–7–79)* 4236
Noncorporate Entities

Examiners will not encounter many equipment leasing tax shelters where noncorporate lessors are involved, since IRC 48(d) of the 1971 Tax Reform Act substantially restricted the use of investment tax credits, and the Tax Reform Act of 1976 limited loss deductions to amounts at risk.

830 *(8–7–79)* 4236
Economic Reality in Equipment Leases

831 *(8-7-79)* 4236
General

(1) A primary purpose of any business venture should be to generate a profit. Every venture will not make a profit; however, the potential for profit realization should always exist.

(2) In a recent case, *Arnold L. Ginsburg, v. Comm.*, 35 TCM 860, 1976, the central points were whether the taxpayer could anticipate a profit, whether the amount of profit was predetermined, and if the taxpayer was covered by stop loss agreements. (In a stop loss agreement, the promoter of the venture agrees to reimburse the investor's losses in excess of a certain amount.) It was the taxpayer's burden to show that there was a reasonable expectation of a profit.

(3) A critical time in a tax shelter venture is the turnaround or crossover point when, after generating tax losses for several years, the taxpayer begins to generate taxable income. While losses are usually sustained in the formative years of the venture, a profit seeking activity must have as its goal the realization of a profit on the overall operation. The venture should eventually be expected to generate sufficient income to overcome losses in earlier years.

832 *(8-7-79)* 4236
Determining Whether a Venture is Structured for Profit

(1) In examining equipment leasing shelters, one of the major considerations is whether the transaction was structured for profit or primarily for tax avoidance. Does it lack economic reality?

(2) There are several tests for determining the economic viability of a shelter, e.g. present value of future income, rate of return, and burdens and benefits of ownership. These and other tests are discussed further in text at 852 and 872 through 874.

840 *(8-7-79)* 4236
Sale and Leaseback

841 *(8-7-79)* 4236
General Information

(1) Normally, tax considerations are a primary reason for sale and leaseback transactions.

(2) In the typical sale and leaseback arrangement, a corporate taxpayer sells its property outright to a second party and immediately leases the property back from the new owner. The lease is generally for a term of 20 to 30 years with additional renewal periods. There may also be a repurchase option. The seller-lessee usually agrees to a net lease in which the lessee assumes the majority of the risks and burdens or ownership such as taxes, insurance, maintenance, and other expenses. Ordinarily, the rent paid allows a nominal rate of return in addition to the lessor's principal and interest payments.

842 *(8-7-79)* 4236
Advantages of Sales and Leasebacks

(1) One favorable tax advantage is that the seller-lessee is entitled to a rent deduction that could be greater than the sum of the depreciation and interest expense that would have been deductible if the property had not been sold. This is true particularly if the property has been fully depreciated, or if it is being leased over a shorter term than its expected useful life.

(2) A seller-lessee may be in a tax position where he/she has no need for the interest and depreciation deductions and investment credit that are associated with the leased property. In this situation, he/she may sell the asset to a buyer who is in need of a tax shelter. An arrangement might be made whereby the seller would immediately lease the property back from the buyer at a rental fee favorable to the lessee. The rental fee would be sufficient for the buyer-lessor to make principal and interest payments on the newly acquired property and permit a nominal rate of return on the investment. Rental income received by the lessor would be offset by interest and depreciation deductions associated with the leased property.

843 *(8-7-79)* 4236
Substance vs. Form

(1) Sale and leaseback transactions should be scrutinized to determine whether a legitimate business purpose exists, or if the transaction was structured only as a tax avoidance scheme. To do this, the examiner should consider what benefits, if any, the lessor is deriving from the sale and leaseback transaction other than a favorable tax write-off.

(2) If the examiner suspects that a sale and leaseback transaction is a tax avoidance scheme, reference should be made to text at 870 for suggested audit techniques that might be used.

844 *(8-7-79)* 4236

Sale vs. Financing Arrangement

(1) Some tax avoidance schemes may take the form of a sale and leaseback, when in substance the arrangement is actually a loan between the "lessor" and "lessee." By using this approach, the depreciation, interest expense, and investment credit, if any, would be disallowed to the lessor and allowed to the lessee. Keep in mind that the lessee may likely be in a tax situation where he/she cannot use these additional deductions and credits. The Service's position would be that rental payments received by the lessor are in reality prinicpal and interest payments from the lessee since a sale never took place. The lessee still owns the property for tax purposes and the lessor is acting as a conduit to make interest and principal payments on the leased property for the lessee. The downpayment made by the lessor to purchase the property would be considered a loan to the lessee. In effect, the instrument by which the seller-lessee purports to convey legal ownership to the buyer-lessor is in reality no more than security for a loan on the property.

(2) See *Helvering v. F. & R. Lazarus and Co.*, 308 U.S. 252, (1939), 1939-2 CB 208; *John Shillito Co. v. U.S.*, 39 F.2d 830 (6th Cir., 1942); and *John Shillito Co. v. Connor,* 42-2 USTC 9769 (D.C. Ohio, 1942). In these cases, the taxpayers' actions indicated that sales and not loans had been transacted. The courts ruled, however, that the transactions were not sales but actually loans secured by the properties in question.

(3) Recently, the Government unsuccessfully used an approach similar to the *Lazarus* case noted above in *Frank Lyon Company v. U.S.*, 98 SCt 1291, rev'g 536 F.2d,746 (8th Cir., 1976). On April 18, 1978, the Supreme Court ruled that the transaction was a genuine sale and leaseback and not a mere financing arrangement. The Government placed great reliance on *Lazarus,* claiming that it was a precedent that should be controlling in the *Lyon* case. The Supreme Court, however, made a distinction between *Lazarus* and *Lyon.* In *Lazarus* the sale and leaseback transaction involved only two parties, and the Court acknowledged that the conclusion reached in that case was correct. In *Lyon* there were three parties involved (lessee, lessor, and an independent mortgagee) rather than a simpler two party arrangement. It was the opinion of the Court that the presence of a third party, an independent mortgagee, "significantly distinguished this case from *Lazarus.*"

(4) Numerous factors were involved on both sides of the question regarding the reality of the arrangement, but of major importance appears to be the fact that *Lyon* was exclusively liable on the notes held by the independent mortgagee. A reasonable possibility exists that, if the notes were partially or fully guaranteed by the seller-lessee, the Supreme Court may have decided against *Lyon* and in favor of the Government. A favorable implication derived from the unfavorable *Lyon* decision is that the Court noted "the nonfamily and nonprivate nature of the entire transaction." The Court also emphasized that the transaction was shaped by features other than tax avoidance—the diversification in the case of *Lyon* and the legal requirements of the lessee to sell and leaseback the property.

(5) Also noteworthy is the Court's mention of the fact that the Government would receive the same amount of revenue no matter how the transaction was viewed. This will not be true in many instances, especially in family trust arrangements, which are discussed in text at 860.

(6) Another consideration regarding the *Lyon* case is that even though an independent trustee (such as a family lawyer) could conceivably be regarded as the third party that was so vital to the *Lyon* decision, he/she may not be in as independent a position as the financial company in the present case. The trustee will generally have less independence and a smaller role in packaging the leaseback transaction than an unrelated financial institution.

(7) It is suggested that if an issue similar to the *Lyon* case is being considered, the examiner should consider requesting technical advice from the National Office.

845 *(8-7-79)* 4236

Fair Market Value of Leased Property

(1) Consideration should be given to whether or not the lessor utilized nonrecourse financing to purchase the leased property.

(2) If nonrecourse financing is present and exceeds the fair market value of the property purchased, the leasing transaction should not be recognized for tax purposes since the taxpayer has no equity in the property as long as the unpaid balance of the purchase price exceeds the existing fair market value. By aban-

doning the transaction, the buyer-lessor can lose no more than a mere chance to acquire an equity in the future, should the value of the acquired property increase to an amount greater than the nonrecourse financing. It is not reasonable to expect investors to pay off a nonrecourse loan when the note exceeds the fair market value of the property. See *Franklin v. Commissioner,* 554 F.2d 1045 (CA 9, 1976), aff'g 64 TC 752; *Decon Corporation v. Comm.,* 65 TC 829 (1976); *Bolger v. Comm.,* 59 TC 760 (1973); *Edna Morris v. Comm.,* 59 TC 21 (1972).

(3) If the purchase price of the property exceeds its fair market value, and nonrecourse financing is *not* involved, the examiner should determine the cause of the discrepancy. Consideration should be given to reducing the basis of the property by the excess purchase price over the fair market value. This, of course, will result in smaller interest and depreciation deductions to the lessor. Be particularly alert for this type of situation if related parties are involved.

(4) If the fair market value of the property is materially less than the purchase price, mention of this fact should be recorded in the prospectus and/or footnotes to the certified financial statements. Comments to this effect may also be found in financial statements given to lending institutions if additional financing is needed. Comments in the minutes may disclose material facts, and there is also the possibility that an appraisal was made prior to the purchase which shows that the fair market value is less than the purchase price. Insurance policies may insure the property for an amount substantially below its purchase price. Personal property tax returns may report the smaller fair market value figure in lieu of the purchase price in order to take advantage of a lower personal property tax rate. The purchase price of the last arm's-length sale might also help in determining the current fair market value.

850 *(8-7-79)* 4236
Leveraged Leasing

851 *(8-7-79)* 4236
Introduction

(1) Equipment leases generally fall into two categories, leveraged leases or unleveraged leases, depending on the degree to which each is financed.

(2) A leveraged lease transaction generally involves three parties and includes:

(a) A lessor who commits a small percentage of his/her own funds (usually 20% to 30%) for the purchase of the property, borrows the remainder of the purchase price in a nonrecourse loan, then leases the property to another party on a net lease basis. (In a net lease arrangement, the lessee agrees to keep the property in good repair and is responsible for all property expenses, including taxes and insurance, during the term of the lease.)

(b) A lender who finances a substantial portion of the purchase price on a nonrecourse basis, relying solely on the leased property and the lease contract itself as security for the loan.

(c) A lessee who is obligated to make lease payments that will normally return the lessor the full purchase price of the property and perhaps a nominal profit. The lessee generally agrees to a net lease arrangement, discussed in (a) above.

(3) Unleveraged leasing requires the lessor to use his/her own funds to purchase the property. These leases are rarely found in tax shelters due to the lack of extraordinary tax benefits that would result and the substantial cost of the assets.

852 *(8-7-79)* 4236
Criteria for Determining Whether a Transaction is a Leasing Arrangement or a Mere Financing Arrangement

(1) The lessee's right to the leased asset is derived from the lease agreement. The agreement, although cast in the form of a lease, may in substance be a conditional sales contract. This determination is made based on the intent of the parties in light of the facts existing at the time of the execution of the agreement.

(2) No one factor is controlling in determining the intent when the agreement is executed. However, if one or more of the following circumstances exists, the examiner should consider characterizing the transaction as a sale rather than a lease:

(a) Lessee acquires equity in the property through his/her "lease" payments. For example, after 50% of the lease payments have been made, the lessee may acquire a 25% ownership interest in the asset.

(b) Lessee acquires title to the asset after a required number of lease payments.

(c) Lessee's total lease payments are due in a relatively short period of time and substantially cover the total amount required to acquire the asset.

(d) Lease payments substantially exceed the fair rental value of the property. This may indicate that the asset is actually being purchased and that the financing is for a period less then the useful life of the asset.

(e) Provision may be made for the property to be acquired by the lessee at the end of the lease term for a nominal sum.

(f) Lessee participates in the investment with the lessor by providing loan guarantees or stop loss agreements to the lessor.

(g) Lessor has little or no at risk investment in the leased asset. Note one of the requirements relating to leveraged leasing under *Rev. Proc. 75–21,* 1975–1 C.B. 715, modified by *Rev. Proc 76–30,* 1976–2 C.B. 647, is that at all times during the lease term the lessor should have a minimum "at risk" investment of 20 percent.

(3) Consider the following example: A lessor and lessee enter into an agreement whereby the lessee agrees to lease a computer for $31,000 per year that has an annual fair rental value of $15,000. The lease will run for 84 months (7 years) at which time the lessee will acquire title to the computer for $8,000. The lessor generally sells this type of computer for $155,000, which is equal to the present value of the seven lease payments at a 10% rate of return ($150,900) plus the present value of the $8,000 payment to the lessor at the conclusion of the lease. The life of the computer is 14 years. The lessee agrees to insure the equipment and keep it in good repair.

(a) In this example it would appear that a sale and not a lease has taken place. The lessee is paying almost double the monthly fair rental value and will take title to the computer in a relatively short period of time. The total rental payments are equal to the cost of the computer plus a 10% annual return on the unpaid balance of the cost. The lessee is accepting the burdens of ownership by insuring the property and agreeing to keep it in good repair.

(b) By handling this transaction as a lease rather than a sale, the lessee is able to deduct the rental payments, which approximate the cost of the computer, over 7 years rather than depreciating the asset over 14 years if the transaction was properly treated as a sale. If the computer is acquired and sold in a subsequent year by the lessee, any gain would not be subject to IRC 1245 recapture, since depreciation was not claimed. In this type of arrangement the lessor also generally passes the investment credit on to the lessee pursuant to IRC 48(d). It is clearly to the benefit of the "lessee" to treat this arrangement as a lease rather than a purchase.

(4) Examiners should look to the substance of the transaction rather than the form to determine if an abusive tax shelter exists.

(a) A determination should be made as to who has the burdens and benefits of ownership.

(b) The substance of a transaction, rather than its legal form, is controlling for Federal income tax purposes. If the burdens and benefits of ownership still inure to the lessee after a sale and leaseback transaction, it is indicative that the seller is still the owner of the property. Calling a transaction a sale and leaseback does not make it one, if in fact it is something else.

(c) By using this approach the lessor would not be entitled to deductions related to the leased property since the lessee still retains ownership for Federal income tax purposes. See *Rev. Rul. 68–590,* 1968–2 C.B. 66, amplified by *Rev. Rul. 73–134,* 1973–1 C.B. 60; *Rev. Rul. 72–543,* 1972–2 C.B. 87; *Rev. Rul. 74–290,* 1974–1 C.B. 41.

860 *(8-7-79)* 4236
Family Trust—Leaseback

861 *(8-7-79)* 4236
General Information

(1) The family trust-leaseback offers a taxpayer the opportunity for substantial tax savings over a period of years, provided he/she is able to deduct the rent payments which he/she makes to the trust.

(2) The advantage to the taxpayer of such an arrangement is to shift income to a family member by setting up a trust and conveying income producing property to the trust. If the trust requirements of IRC 671 through 678 are met, trust income will be taxed to the beneficiary rather than the grantor.

(3) When the taxpayer transfers property which is used in his/her trade business to a family trust, an arrangement will be made for the grantor to lease the property back. With this type of provision, grantors have been able to shift income to lower bracket taxpayers and also to deduct the rent paid to the trust as a business expense. In a leaseback arrangement the grantor usually ends up with a rent deduction greater than the depreciation he/she would have been entitled to on the income-pro-

ducing property had he/she not transferred it to a trust.

862 *(8-7-79)* 4236
Example of a Family Trust-Leaseback Arrangement

(1) A typical example of a trust-leaseback arrangement involves an individual in a high tax bracket who owns equipment that is used in his/her business. Assume the equipment has a cost of $4,000 and is being depreciated over a 10-year life. By using the straight line depreciation method, the annual depreciation deduction is $400.

(2) If the equipment has a fair rental value of $800 per year, the taxpayer can get a larger deduction by transferring the equipment to a family trust, then leasing it back from the trust for $800 per year. The taxpayer now has an $800 yearly rental deduction, rather than an annual depreciation deduction of $400.

(3) Also assume that the $800 rental income paid by the taxpayer to the trust is divided equally between the trust and the taxpayer's son. The trust will put aside $400 each year as a depreciation reserve and the balance will be paid to the son. What has happened is that the father, who is in a high tax bracket, effectively transfers $400 of his income to his son who is in a lower tax bracket. The purpose of this trust-leaseback arrangement would be tax avoidance and the transaction should be challenged as a sham. The examiner should consider disallowing the rental expense and treating the payment to the trust as a gift.

863 *(8-7-79)* 4236
Validity of Rental Deductions

(1) The courts consider the circumstances of each case in determining the validity of rental deductions. Three areas have been regularly explored by the courts in making this determination.

(a) Lack of equity interest—IRC 162(a)(3) specifically provides that a rental deduction is available only where the taxpayer does not hold title or have any equitable interest in the property in question. Following this concept, rent expense has not been allowed by the courts where the taxpayer retained a reversionary interest in the property.

1 *Furman v. Comm.*, 45 TC 360 (1966), aff'd per curiam 381 F.2d 22 (5th Cir., 1967).

2 *Van Zandt v. Comm.*, 341 F.2d 440 (5th Cir., 1965).

3 *Hall v. U.S.*, 208 FSupp. 584 (D.C. N.Y., 1962).

(b) Business purpose—economic reality. A business purpose must be served or economic viability must exist. Several courts have denied deductions where the transaction served no business purpose and was arranged solely to permit a division of the taxpayer's income.

1 *Van Zandt v. Comm.*, supra.

2 *Perry v. U.S.*, 520 F.2d 235 (4th Cir., 1975), rev'g DC 376 FSupp 15 (1974).

3 *Mathews v. Comm.*, 520 F.2d 323 (5th Cir., 1975); Cert. denied, 96 SCt 1463.

4 *Penn v. Comm.*, 51 TC 144 (1968).

5 *Failor v. U.S.*, DC, Washington (1966), 66-2 USTC 9766, and 18 AFTR 2d, 6030.

(c) Independent Trustee. The independence of the trustee has been a major factor in determining if rent expense could be deducted. The courts have usually denied deductions where control has effectively remained in the hands of the grantor.

1 *Sidney W. Penn*, supra.

2 *Irvine K. Furman*, supra.

3 *Oakes v. Comm.*, 44 TC 524, 1966.

870 *(8-7-79)* 4236
Examination Techniques

The techniques cited below provide guidance in developing equipment leasing issues.

871 *(8-7-79)* 4236
General Techniques

(1) The following techniques apply to a broad range of equipment leasing transactions.

(2) The examiner should obtain and analyze the following documents:

(a) Sales contracts,

(b) Closing documents,

(c) Deeds or titles,

(d) Loan agreements,

(e) Leases,

(f) Guarantees of lease payments, and

(g) Loan guarantees.

(3) The examiner should be alert for stop loss agreements, loans of the lessor that are guaranteed by the lessee, inflated purchase prices, transfer of title from the lessor to the lessee at the conclusion of the lease, and inflated lease payments. These may indicate a sale rather than a lease.

(4) The transaction should be traced to the last arm's-length sale, if possible, to aid in determining if there is an inflated purchase price.

(5) The examiner should determine if the transaction reflects economic reality. See text at 852, 872, 873, and 874 for details of the burdens and benefits test, the present value test, and the rate of return test.

(6) Determine if the transaction utilizes nonrecourse financing, stop loss agreements, or other agreements that would limit the purchaser-lessor's potential liability. If the transaction does contain nonrecourse or other financing that limits risk, see IRC 465. The examiner should also determine whether the nonrecourse financing exceeds the fair market value of the leased asset. If so, disallowance of the deductions related to the leased asset should be considered since the taxpayer has no equity in it. See *Franklin v. Comm.*, supra; *Decon Corporation*, supra; *David F. Bolger*, supra; *Edna Morris*, supra.

(7) Determine if the form of the transaction reflects the substance of the transaction. The relationship between the various parties and the terms of the agreements must be carefully scrutinized to determine the true intent of the lease arrangement. The burdens and benefits test, discussed in text at 852, may also be helpful in this analysis.

872 *(8-7-79)* 4236
Present Value Test

(1) The fair market value of a leased asset may be measured using the present value of the future income stream (rents) plus the present value of the salvage. If the present value of the future income stream does not exceed the present value of the total investment in the asset, then the examiner should question the lessor's motives for entering into the transaction.

(2) The present value of future rents at a given rate of return should approximate the fair market value of the leased asset. The examiner can use this test to help determine if the asset was acquired by the purchaser-lessor at an inflated price.

(3) The following example demonstrates the present value computation.

(a) Facts:

Purchase price of leased property	$2,500
Salvage value	$1,000
Annual rental income	$350
Annual expenses attributable to leased property	$150
Net annual income from leased property	$200
Length of lease	10 years

(b) Based on these facts, it appears that he taxpayer will have a total net profit on his/her investment of $500 since annual net income of $200 for a 10-year period plus salvage value of $1,000 equals $3,000, and the purchase price was $2,500. However, if the present value concept is applied to these same facts, the results will show that the taxpayer incurred a loss on the investment.

(c) Exhibit 800-1 shows the present value of the future income stream and the salvage at the end of 10 years assuming a 6% interest rate (the higher the assumed interest rate, the lower the present value).

(d) The $2,030 present value was obtained by multiplying the annual net income and the salvage value by the applicable factor for each period associated with the 6% rate of return. See present value table at Exhibit 800-2.

(e) The present value of the future income stream and salvage in the above example is $2,030. The investor would therefore lose $470 on his/her $2,500 investment which would indicate the transaction was not entered into for a profit.

(4) Keep in mind that the true fair market value of a leased asset can generally be measured by the present value of the future income stream.

(5) Depending on other factors involved in this type of issue, it could be argued that the taxpayer's basis should be reduced to an amount equal to the present value of the future income stream. This is especially true if a sophisticated taxpayer, such as a lending institution or insurance company is involved, since many of their investment decisions are based on the present value concept.

(6) Another approach would be to disallow the entire transaction as a sham if the cost of the property is artificially inflated. This approach should be considered if other key factors are present such as the guarantee of all or part of the purchaser-lessor's loan by the seller-lessee, failure to show legitimate business purpose for the inflated purchase price, and/or the involvement of related parties.

873 *(8-7-79)* 4236
Rate of Return Test

(1) Another method of determining the economic viability of an equipment leasing arrangement is to compare its market rate of return (or at least the risk free rate of return) to those for other similar investments. If the transaction was entered into for a profit, then the rate of return should at least equal the risk free rate of return.

In cases where the tax shelter's rate of return is less than the risk free return, then the investor's motives for investing should be carefully studied.

(2) Inflated prices for assets are at the base of tax shelter transactions "structured for a loss." On the surface the transaction may appear to have been based on fair market value; however, upon analysis, a different conclusion may be reached. Inflated costs included in the depreciable basis of the property gives inflated depreciation deductions and inflated investment tax credits.

(3) Another indication of potential tax shelter abuse is insufficient rents. The rents charged may be less than the fair rental value, or they may appear insufficient due to the inflated price paid for the property. One may question why someone would enter into one of these transactions. The answer is not for economic gain but for tax losses. Tax losses plus investment credits are a "tax free return" that gives the participant a profit from his/her losses.

(4) The following is an example of the effect of an inflated sales price on rate of return.

(a)	FMV	Transaction
(b) Cost	$300,000	$1,200,000
(c) Rent	30,000	30,000
(d) Return	10%	2.5

Here is can be seen that the return on the transaction is 2.5% per year, while the ordinary return on this type asset should be 10%. The low rate of return in this case reflects the inflated purchase price of the asset rather than insufficient rents.

(5) The following examination techniques can be used in conjunction with the rate of return test:

(a) Determine the going rate of return for various investments in this area by contacting bank trust departments, mortgage investment brokers, insurance companies, etc.

(b) Determine the prime lending rate by either contacting banks or obtaining publications which reflect market fluctuations in the rate.

874 *(8–7–79)* 4236
Guarantee of Note by Seller-Lessee

The examiner should determine whether the seller-lessee is guaranteeing the note of the buyer-lessor. If this situation exists, the lessor would not be entitled to the deductions associated with the loan proceeds guaranteed by the lessee. See *Rev. Rul. 77–125,* 1977–1 C.B. 130 and *Rev. Rul. 78–30,* 1978–1 C.B. 133.

875 *(8–7–79)* 4236
Loss Limitations Based on the Amount at Risk

The provisions of IRC 465 should be considered whenever equipment leasing transactions are examined and financing is used which involves no risk to the investor(s). See 810 of this chapter for a discussion of IRC 465.

880 *(8–7–79)* 4236
Depreciation

881 *(8–7–79)* 4236
Reasonable Salvage Value

(1) Generally, lessors of equipment select an accelerated method of depreciation. Examiners should determine whether the accumulated depreciation has reduced the lessor's basis in the asset below the salvage value. I.T. Reg. 1.167(a)(1)(a) provides that an asset may not be depreciated below salvage.

(2) In some cases it may be necessary to obtain engineering assistance to determine the valuations. In other cases the examiner may be able to contact equipment brokers, read industry publications, or examine taxpayer records to determine reasonable salvage value.

882 *(8–7–79)* 4236
Example of Depreciation Adjustment Based on Reasonable Salvage Value

(1) An asset to be leased was purchased for $7,500,000. The lessor computes depreciation using double declining balance and a 12-year useful life. The lessor has recorded salvage value at $850,000. The taxpayer's prior asset history indicates that the salvage value at the end of 12 years should be $2,250,000.

(2) Projected depreciation over the 12-year life is shown in Exhibit 800–3.

(3) In the seventh year the lessor should only claim depreciation of $11,685, which would bring the book value to $2,500,000. No depreciation is allowable after the seventh year.

883 *(8–7–79)* 4236
Date Placed in Service

Depreciation of an asset does not begin until an asset has been placed in service. See I.T. Regulations 1.167–(a)(10)(b). An asset is not considered placed in service until it has been installed and is operational. In leased asset situations there may be a great physical distance between the leased property and the lessor. Confirmation as to when the equipment was operational should be obtained.

884 *(8–7–79)* 4236
Example of Adjustment Based on Date Placed in Service

The lessor, a calendar year taxpayer, purchases a computer and leases it on November 20, 1977. The lessee takes delivery of the computer December 15, 1977; however, due to the holidays, the electrical connections and software installation were not completed until January 1978. The lessor cannot claim depreciation in 1977 since the asset was not operational or placed in service before the end of the year.

885 *(8–7–79)* 4236
Examination Techniques for Determining Date Placed in Service

(1) Contact lessor to establish when the asset was installed and when the asset was operational.

(2) Local regulations may require certain permits or zoning applications. These may indicate when approval was given for installation of the asset and when installation was completed.

(3) Read lease carefully. In some instances, the lessee does not begin paying rent until thirty days after the asset is accepted as installed.

890 *(8–7–79)* 4236
Investment Tax Credit

891 *(8–7–79)* 4236
Limitations on Certain Noncorporate Lessors

(1) I.T. Reg. 1.46–4(d) provides certain narrow criteria under which a noncorporate lessor may claim investment tax credit. These criteria are:

(a) Lessor must have manufactured or produced the leased equipment, or

(b) The lease term plus renewal options must be less than 50% of the useful life of the property, and

(c) During the first 12 months of the lease the sum of the deductions allowed to the lessor under IRC 162 must exceed fifteen percent of rental income produced by the property.

(2) Care should be taken to ensure that noncorporate lessors have not included expenses of unrelated properties in the 15% test in order to meet the requirements of I.T. Reg. 1.46–4(d)(3).

892 *(2–27–80)* 4236
Pass Through of Investment Credit to Lessee

(1) The lessor can make an election pursuant to IRC 48(d) to pass the investment tax credit through to the lessee. I.T. Reg. 1.48–4 contains specific requirements for the manner and timing of the election. The Code and Regulations impose the following conditions:

(a) The property must be new IRC 38 property in the hands of the lessor.

(b) The lessee must be the original user of the property.

(c) A lessor must provide a statement to the lessee that identifies the lessee and lessor, described the leased property, and gives the estimated useful life of the property, the date the property was transferred, and the basis of the leased property in the hands of the lessee.

(d) The lessor may not be an institution or organization described in IRC 593, IRC 851 through 858, or IRC 1381(a).

(2) If the foregoing conditions are met, the lessee, rather than the lessor, is treated as the actual owner of the property for purposes of the credit. Moreover, if the property is disposed of or if it otherwise ceases to be IRC 38 property in the hands of the lessee, the property is subject to investment credit recapture. The term of the lease is used to determine the applicable percentage limitation for computing the investment tax credit.

(3) Example—Taxpayer B leases a new storage tank to Taxpayer C with a useful life of 10 years. The lease agreement is for a term of 6 years, and the fair market value of the leased asset is $300,000. B has elected under IRC 48(d) to pass the investment credit through to C. C is allowed to claim the credit on a qualified investment of $300,000 ($300,000 × 100%). I.T. Regs. 1.48–4(d) provides criteria under which the estimated useful life of leased property shall be determined. In this instance, the

useful life for computation of the qualified investment is the useful life in B's hands, 10 years.

(4) Examiners should verify that the requirements of I.T. Reg. 1.48–4 have been met. To determine whether leased equipment is new or used, obtain serial numbers and/or model numbers of the equipment. Manufacturers or equipment brokers can usually determine from these numbers the date that the equipment was manufactured.

8(10)0 *(8–7–79)* 4236
Tax Preference Items

(1) For leased IRC 1245 property, accelerated depreciation that is in excess of what would be allowed under the straight line method is considered a tax preference item. See IRC 57(a)(3). The Tax Reform Act of 1976 has substantially reduced the exclusions and increased the rate in computing the minimum tax.

(2) Example—An asset costing $50,000 with a useful life of 10 years is depreciated using the double declining balance method. For the first year depreciation per the return is $10,000. The amount allowable under the straight line method would be $5,000. The excess $5,000 is a tax preference item.

(3) Whenever a lessor is claiming accelerated depreciation on leased equipment, examiners should verify that the excess over straight line depreciation is being reported as a tax preference item. The tax preference item could be a substantial amount when the leased assets are such items as airplanes, oil tankers, or computers.

8(11)0 *(8–7–79)* 4236
Lease Acquisition Costs

(1) The costs of obtaining the lease, i.e. syndicators fees, travel, legal fees, filing costs, etc. should be capitalized. These costs are amortizable over the life of the lease via the straight line method and do not qualify as IRC 38 property for investment tax credit purposes.

(2) In the initial year of the lease, it is important to verify that acquisition costs are not included as part of the asset cost, and that they are not being currently deducted. The examiner may need to analyze accounts that are likely to contain these expenses; e.g., legal and professional fees, miscellaneous expenses.

(Next page is 4236–157)

Exhibit 800-1

Computation of Present Value of $200 per year at 6% Rate of Return From Example at 872(3)

Year	Annual Net Income	Present Value Rate	Present Value of $200
1	$200	6%	$188
2	200	6%	178
3	200	6%	168
4	200	6%	158
5	200	6%	150
6	200	6%	140
7	200	6%	134
8	200	6%	126
9	200	6%	118
10	200	6%	112
Salvage Value	1,000	6%	558
	3,000		2,030

Exhibit 800–2

Present Value Table

PRESENT VALUE OF $1

$(1 + i)^{-n}$

n \ i	½%	1%	1¼%	1½%	2%	2½%
1	0.9950 2488	0.9900 9901	0.9876 5432	0.9852 2167	0.9803 9216	0.9756 0976
2	0.9900 7450	0.9802 9605	0.9754 6106	0.9706 6175	0.9611 6878	0.9518 1440
3	0.9851 4876	0.9705 9015	0.9634 1833	0.9563 1699	0.9423 2233	0.9285 9941
4	0.9802 4752	0.9609 8034	0.9515 2428	0.9421 8423	0.9238 4543	0.9059 5064
5	0.9753 7067	0.9514 6569	0.9397 7706	0.9282 6033	0.9057 3081	0.8838 5429
6	0.9705 1808	0.9420 4524	0.9281 7488	0.9145 4219	0.8879 7138	0.8622 9687
7	0.9656 8963	0.9327 1805	0.9167 1593	0.9010 2679	0.8705 6018	0.8412 6524
8	0.9608 8520	0.9234 8322	0.9053 9845	0.8877 1112	0.8534 9037	0.8207 4657
9	0.9561 0468	0.9143 3982	0.8942 2069	0.8745 9224	0.8367 5527	0.8007 2836
10	0.9513 4794	0.9052 8695	0.8831 8093	0.8616 6723	0.8203 4830	0.7811 9840
11	0.9466 1489	0.8963 2372	0.8722 7746	0.8489 3323	0.8042 6304	0.7621 4478
12	0.9419 0534	0.8874 4923	0.8615 0860	0.8363 8742	0.7884 9318	0.7435 5589
13	0.9372 1924	0.8786 6260	0.8508 7269	0.8240 2702	0.7730 3253	0.7254 2038
14	0.9325 5646	0.8699 6297	0.8403 6809	0.8118 4928	0.7578 7502	0.7077 2720
15	0.9279 1688	0.8613 4947	0.8299 9318	0.7998 5150	0.7430 1473	0.6904 6556
16	0.9233 0037	0.8528 2126	0.8197 4635	0.7880 3104	0.7284 4581	0.6736 2493
17	0.9187 0684	0.8443 7749	0.8096 2602	0.7763 8526	0.7141 6256	0.6571 9506
18	0.9141 3616	0.8360 1731	0.7996 3064	0.7649 1159	0.7001 5937	0.6411 6591
19	0.9095 8822	0.8277 3992	0.7897 5866	0.7536 0747	0.6864 3076	0.6255 2772
20	0.9050 6290	0.8195 4447	0.7800 0855	0.7424 7042	0.6729 7133	0.6102 7094
21	0.9005 6010	0.8114 3017	0.7703 7881	0.7314 9795	0.6597 7582	0.5953 8629
22	0.8960 7971	0.8033 9621	0.7608 6796	0.7206 8763	0.6468 3904	0.5808 6467
23	0.8916 2160	0.7954 4179	0.7514 7453	0.7100 3708	0.6341 5592	0.5666 9724
24	0.8871 8567	0.7875 6613	0.7421 9707	0.6995 4392	0.6217 2149	0.5528 7535
25	0.8827 7181	0.7797 6844	0.7330 3414	0.6892 0583	0.6095 3087	0.5393 9059
26	0.8783 7991	0.7720 4796	0.7239 8434	0.6790 2052	0.5975 7928	0.5262 3472
27	0.8740 0986	0.7644 0392	0.7150 4626	0.6689 8574	0.5858 6204	0.5133 9973
28	0.8696 6155	0.7568 3557	0.7062 1853	0.6590 9925	0.5743 7455	0.5008 7778
29	0.8653 3488	0.7493 4215	0.6974 9978	0.6493 5887	0.5631 1231	0.4886 6125
30	0.8610 2973	0.7419 2292	0.6888 8867	0.6397 6243	0.5520 7089	0.4767 4269
31	0.8567 4600	0.7345 7715	0.6803 8387	0.6303 0781	0.5412 4597	0.4651 1481
32	0.8524 8358	0.7273 0411	0.6719 8407	0.6209 9292	0.5306 3330	0.4537 7055
33	0.8482 4237	0.7201 0307	0.6636 8797	0.6118 1568	0.5202 2873	0.4427 0298
34	0.8440 2226	0.7129 7334	0.6554 9429	0.6027 7407	0.5100 2817	0.4319 0534
35	0.8398 2314	0.7059 1420	0.6474 0177	0.5938 6608	0.5000 2761	0.4213 7107
36	0.8356 4492	0.6989 2495	0.6394 0916	0.5850 8974	0.4902 2315	0.4110 9372
37	0.8314 8748	0.6920 0490	0.6315 1522	0.5764 4309	0.4806 1093	0.4010 6705
38	0.8273 5073	0.6851 5337	0.6237 1873	0.5679 2423	0.4711 8719	0.3912 8492
39	0.8232 3455	0.6783 6967	0.6160 1850	0.5595 3126	0.4619 4822	0.3817 4139
40	0.8191 3886	0.6716 5314	0.6084 1334	0.5512 6232	0.4528 9042	0.3724 3062
41	0.8150 6354	0.6650 0311	0.6009 0206	0.5431 1559	0.4440 1021	0.3633 4695
42	0.8110 0850	0.6584 1892	0.5934 8352	0.5350 8925	0.4353 0413	0.3544 8483
43	0.8069 7363	0.6518 9992	0.5861 5656	0.5271 8153	0.4267 6875	0.3458 3886
44	0.8029 5884	0.6454 4546	0.5789 2006	0.5193 9067	0.4184 0074	0.3374 0376
45	0.7989 6402	0.6390 5492	0.5717 7290	0.5117 1494	0.4101 9680	0.3291 7440
46	0.7949 8907	0.6327 2764	0.5647 1397	0.5041 5265	0.4021 5373	0.3211 4576
47	0.7910 3390	0.6264 6301	0.5577 4219	0.4967 0212	0.3942 6836	0.3133 1294
48	0.7870 9841	0.6202 6041	0.5508 5649	0.4893 6170	0.3865 3761	0.3056 7116
49	0.7831 8250	0.6141 1921	0.5440 5579	0.4821 2975	0.3789 5844	0.2982 1576
50	0.7792 8607	0.6080 3882	0.5373 3905	0.4750 0468	0.3715 2788	0.2909 4221

Exhibit 800-2 Cont. (1)

Present Value Table

PRESENT VALUE OF $1 (CONTINUED)

$(1 + i)^{-n}$

n \ i	3%	3½%	4%	5%	6%	7%
1	0.9708 7379	0.9661 8357	0.9615 3846	0.9523 8095	0.9433 9623	0.9345 7944
2	0.9425 9591	0.9335 1070	0.9245 5621	0.9070 2948	0.8899 9644	0.8734 3873
3	0.9151 4166	0.9019 4271	0.8889 9636	0.8638 3760	0.8396 1928	0.8162 9788
4	0.8884 8705	0.8714 4223	0.8548 0419	0.8227 0247	0.7920 9366	0.7628 9521
5	0.8626 0878	0.8419 7317	0.8219 2711	0.7835 2617	0.7472 5817	0.7129 8618
6	0.8374 8426	0.8135 0064	0.7903 1453	0.7462 1540	0.7049 6054	0.6663 4222
7	0.8130 9151	0.7859 9096	0.7599 1781	0.7106 8133	0.6650 5711	0.6227 4974
8	0.7894 0923	0.7594 1156	0.7306 9021	0.6768 3936	0.6274 1237	0.5820 0910
9	0.7664 1673	0.7337 3097	0.7025 8674	0.6446 0892	0.5918 9846	0.5439 3374
10	0.7440 9391	0.7089 1881	0.6755 6417	0.6139 1325	0.5583 9478	0.5083 4929
11	0.7224 2128	0.6849 4571	0.6495 8093	0.5846 7929	0.5267 8753	0.4750 9280
12	0.7013 7988	0.6617 8330	0.6245 9705	0.5568 3742	0.4969 6936	0.4440 1196
13	0.6809 5134	0.6394 0415	0.6005 7409	0.5303 2135	0.4688 3902	0.4149 6445
14	0.6611 1781	0.6177 8179	0.5774 7508	0.5050 6795	0.4423 0096	0.3878 1724
15	0.6418 6195	0.5968 9062	0.5552 6450	0.4810 1710	0.4172 6506	0.3624 4602
16	0.6231 6694	0.5767 0591	0.5339 0818	0.4581 1152	0.3936 4628	0.3387 3460
17	0.6050 1645	0.5572 0378	0.5133 7325	0.4362 9669	0.3713 6442	0.3165 7439
18	0.5873 9461	0.5383 6114	0.4936 2812	0.4155 2065	0.3503 4379	0.2958 6392
19	0.5702 8603	0.5201 5569	0.4746 4242	0.3957 3396	0.3305 1301	0.2765 0832
20	0.5536 7575	0.5025 6588	0.4563 8695	0.3768 8948	0.3118 0473	0.2584 1900
21	0.5375 4928	0.4855 7090	0.4388 3360	0.3589 4236	0.2941 5540	0.2415 1309
22	0.5218 9250	0.4691 5063	0.4219 5539	0.3418 4987	0.2775 0510	0.2257 1317
23	0.5066 9175	0.4532 8563	0.4057 2633	0.3255 7131	0.2617 9726	0.2109 4688
24	0.4919 3374	0.4379 5713	0.3901 2147	0.3100 6791	0.2469 7855	0.1971 4662
25	0.4776 0557	0.4231 4699	0.3751 1680	0.2953 0277	0.2329 9863	0.1842 4918
26	0.4636 9473	0.4088 3767	0.3606 8923	0.2812 4073	0.2198 1003	0.1721 9549
27	0.4501 8906	0.3950 1224	0.3468 1657	0.2678 4832	0.2073 6795	0.1609 3037
28	0.4370 7675	0.3816 5434	0.3334 7747	0.2550 9364	0.1956 3014	0.1504 0221
29	0.4243 4636	0.3687 4815	0.3206 5141	0.2429 4632	0.1845 5674	0.1405 6282
30	0.4119 8676	0.3562 7841	0.3083 1867	0.2313 7745	0.1741 1013	0.1313 6712
31	0.3999 8715	0.3442 3035	0.2964 6026	0.2203 5947	0.1642 5484	0.1227 7301
32	0.3883 3703	0.3325 8971	0.2850 5794	0.2098 6617	0.1549 5740	0.1147 4113
33	0.3770 2625	0.3213 4271	0.2740 9417	0.1998 7254	0.1461 8622	0.1072 3470
34	0.3660 4490	0.3104 7605	0.2635 5209	0.1903 5480	0.1379 1153	0.1002 1934
35	0.3553 8340	0.2999 7686	0.2534 1547	0.1812 9029	0.1301 0522	0.0936 6294
36	0.3450 3243	0.2898 3272	0.2436 6872	0.1726 5741	0.1227 4077	0.0875 3546
37	0.3349 8294	0.2800 3161	0.2342 9685	0.1644 3563	0.1157 9318	0.0818 0884
38	0.3252 2615	0.2705 6194	0.2252 8543	0.1566 0536	0.1092 3885	0.0764 5686
39	0.3157 5355	0.2614 1250	0.2166 2061	0.1491 4797	0.1030 5552	0.0714 5501
40	0.3065 5684	0.2525 7247	0.2082 8904	0.1420 4568	0.0972 2219	0.0667 8038
41	0.2976 2800	0.2440 3137	0.2002 7793	0.1352 8160	0.0917 1905	0.0624 1157
42	0.2889 5922	0.2357 7910	0.1925 7493	0.1288 3962	0.0865 2740	0.0583 2857
43	0.2805 4294	0.2278 0590	0.1851 6820	0.1227 0440	0.0816 2962	0.0545 1268
44	0.2723 7178	0.2201 0231	0.1780 4635	0.1168 6133	0.0770 0908	0.0509 4643
45	0.2644 3862	0.2126 5924	0.1711 9841	0.1112 9651	0.0726 5007	0.0476 1349
46	0.2567 3653	0.2054 6787	0.1646 1386	0.1059 9668	0.0685 3781	0.0444 9859
47	0.2492 5876	0.1985 1968	0.1582 8256	0.1009 4921	0.0646 5831	0.0415 8747
48	0.2419 9880	0.1918 0645	0.1521 9476	0.0961 4211	0.0609 9840	0.0388 6679
49	0.2349 5029	0.1853 2024	0.1463 4112	0.0915 6391	0.0575 4566	0.0363 2410
50	0.2281 0708	0.1790 5337	0.1407 1262	0.0872 0373	0.0542 8836	0.0339 4776

Exhibit 800-2 Cont. (2)

Present Value Table

PRESENT VALUE OF $1 (CONCLUDED)

$(1 + i)^{-n}$

n \ i	8%	9%	10%	11%	12%	13%	14%	15%
1	0.925926	0.917431	0.909091	0.900901	0.892857	0.884956	0.877193	0.869565
2	0.857339	0.841680	0.826446	0.811622	0.797194	0.783147	0.769468	0.756144
3	0.793832	0.772183	0.751315	0.731191	0.711780	0.693050	0.674972	0.657516
4	0.735030	0.708425	0.683013	0.658731	0.635518	0.613319	0.592080	0.571753
5	0.680583	0.649931	0.620921	0.593451	0.567427	0.542760	0.519369	0.497177
6	0.630170	0.596267	0.564474	0.534641	0.506631	0.480319	0.455587	0.432328
7	0.583490	0.547034	0.513158	0.481658	0.452349	0.425061	0.399637	0.375937
8	0.540269	0.501866	0.466507	0.433926	0.403883	0.376160	0.350559	0.326902
9	0.500249	0.460428	0.424098	0.390925	0.360610	0.332885	0.307508	0.284262
10	0.463193	0.422411	0.385543	0.352184	0.321973	0.294588	0.269744	0.247185
11	0.428883	0.387533	0.350494	0.317283	0.287476	0.260698	0.236617	0.214943
12	0.397114	0.355535	0.318631	0.285841	0.256675	0.230706	0.207559	0.186907
13	0.367698	0.326179	0.289664	0.257514	0.229174	0.204165	0.182069	0.162528
14	0.340461	0.299246	0.263331	0.231995	0.204620	0.180677	0.159710	0.141329
15	0.315242	0.274538	0.239392	0.209004	0.182696	0.159891	0.140096	0.122894
16	0.291890	0.251870	0.217629	0.188292	0.163122	0.141496	0.122892	0.106865
17	0.270269	0.231073	0.197845	0.169633	0.145644	0.125218	0.107800	0.092926
18	0.250249	0.211994	0.179859	0.152822	0.130040	0.110812	0.094561	0.080805
19	0.231712	0.194490	0.163508	0.137678	0.116107	0.098064	0.082948	0.070265
20	0.214548	0.178431	0.148644	0.124034	0.103667	0.086782	0.072762	0.061100
21	0.198656	0.163698	0.135131	0.111742	0.092560	0.076798	0.063826	0.053131
22	0.183941	0.150182	0.122846	0.100669	0.082643	0.067963	0.055988	0.046201
23	0.170315	0.137781	0.111678	0.090693	0.073788	0.060144	0.049112	0.040174
24	0.157699	0.126405	0.101526	0.081705	0.065882	0.053225	0.043081	0.034934
25	0.146018	0.115968	0.092296	0.073608	0.058823	0.047102	0.037790	0.030378
26	0.135202	0.106393	0.083905	0.066314	0.052521	0.041683	0.033149	0.026415
27	0.125187	0.097608	0.076278	0.059742	0.046894	0.036888	0.029078	0.022970
28	0.115914	0.089548	0.069343	0.053822	0.041869	0.032644	0.025507	0.019974
29	0.107328	0.082155	0.063039	0.048488	0.037383	0.028889	0.022375	0.017369
30	0.099377	0.075371	0.057309	0.043683	0.033378	0.025565	0.019627	0.015103
31	0.092016	0.069148	0.052099	0.039354	0.029802	0.022624	0.017217	0.013133
32	0.085200	0.063438	0.047362	0.035454	0.026609	0.020021	0.015102	0.011420
33	0.078889	0.058200	0.043057	0.031940	0.023758	0.017718	0.013248	0.009931
34	0.073045	0.053395	0.039143	0.028775	0.021212	0.015680	0.011621	0.008635
35	0.067635	0.048986	0.035584	0.025924	0.018940	0.013876	0.010194	0.007509
36	0.062625	0.044941	0.032349	0.023355	0.016910	0.012279	0.008942	0.006529
37	0.057986	0.041231	0.029408	0.021040	0.015098	0.010867	0.007844	0.005678
38	0.053690	0.037826	0.026735	0.018955	0.013481	0.009617	0.006880	0.004937
39	0.049713	0.034703	0.024304	0.017077	0.012036	0.008510	0.006035	0.004293
40	0.046031	0.031838	0.022095	0.015384	0.010747	0.007531	0.005294	0.003733
41	0.042621	0.029209	0.020086	0.013860	0.009595	0.006665	0.004644	0.003246
42	0.039464	0.026797	0.018260	0.012486	0.008567	0.005898	0.004074	0.002823
43	0.036541	0.024584	0.016600	0.011249	0.007649	0.005219	0.003573	0.002455
44	0.033834	0.022555	0.015091	0.010134	0.006830	0.004619	0.003135	0.002134
45	0.031328	0.020692	0.013719	0.009130	0.006098	0.004088	0.002750	0.001856
46	0.029007	0.018984	0.012472	0.008225	0.005445	0.003617	0.002412	0.001614
47	0.026859	0.017416	0.011338	0.007410	0.004861	0.003201	0.002116	0.001403
48	0.024869	0.015978	0.010307	0.006676	0.004340	0.002833	0.001856	0.001220
49	0.023027	0.014659	0.009370	0.006014	0.003875	0.002507	0.001628	0.001061
50	0.021321	0.013449	0.008519	0.005418	0.003460	0.002219	0.001428	0.000923

Exhibit 800–3

Projecting Depreciation of Assets Purchased for $7,500,000 using Double Declining Balance Method.

From Example at 882.

Year	Depreciation Claimed	Book Value At Year End
1	$1,250,000	$6,250,000
2	1,041,688	5,208,312
3	868,069	4,340,243
4	723,388	3,616,855
5	602,821	3,014,034
6	502,349	2,511,685
7	418,623	2,093,062
8	348,851	1,744,211
9	290,708	1,453,503
10	242,255	1,211,248
11	201,879	1,009,369
12	168,232	841,137

DEFERRED VARIABLE ANNUITY

Internal Revenue News Release IR-2164, September 21, 1979

[Code Sec. 1014. Also, Code Sec. 72]

Annuities: Basis of property acquired from a decedent: Deferred variable annuity contract.—The IRS has announced a ruling on a beneficiary's acquisition of a deferred variable annuity contract upon the death of the owner of the contract before the first annuity payment is made under the contract. Rev. Rul. 70-143, 1970-1 CB 167, is revoked.

The Internal Revenue Service announced a new ruling dealing with a beneficiary's acquisition of a deferred variable annuity contract upon the death of the owner of the contract before the first annuity payment is made under the contract.

The ruling holds that, if the beneficiary elects to receive a lump-sum payment under the contract, the excess of the amount received over the amount the decedent paid for the contract is, as in the case of a straight deferred annuity, includible in the beneficiary's gross income.

The new ruling revokes Revenue Ruling 70-143, which appears in Cumulative Bulletin 1970-1 at page 167.

The new ruling does not apply to deferred variable annuity contracts purchased prior to Oct. 21, 1979, including any contributions applied to such contracts pursuant to a binding commitment entered into before that date. The new ruling applies to all other amounts contributed to deferred variable annuity contracts on or after Oct. 21, 1979.

Revenue Ruling 79-335 is attached and will also appear in Internal Revenue Bulletin No. 1979-43, dated Oct. 22, 1979. Rev. Rul. 79-335.

Issue

The Internal Revenue Service has reconsidered its position in Rev. Rul. 70-143, 1970-1 C.B. 167, regarding a beneficiary's basis in the right to the accumulated value under a deferred variable annuity contract.

Facts

An individual purchased from an insurance company a contract that provides for a variable annuity. The contract was a customary deferred variable annuity contract, which permitted the contract owner to elect for the designated annuitant one of several typical variable annuity installment options, including a simple variable life annuity, a variable life annuity with a specified number of guaranteed installments, and a joint and survivor variable life annuity.

The owner is credited at the date of purchase of the variable annuity contract with accumulation units that represent the owner's proportionate interest in an accumulation fund on the basis of the value of accumulation units as of the valuation date applicable to the owner's payment. The accumulation units fluctuate in value as the accumulation fund fluctuates in value.

The accumulation fund, which is managed by the insurance company, consists of assets purchased by the insurance company and held for the exclusive benefit of the owners (and their beneficiaries) of variable annuity contracts Securities and Exchange Commission as a diversified open-end investment company.

Under the terms of the annuity contract, upon surrender of the contract, a cash redemption value is payable to an owner-annuitant upon proper application at any time prior to the annuity starting date. The cash redemption value payable is determined by multiplying the number of accumulation units held to the credit of the contract by the current value of each accumulation unit at the time of redemption.

In the event of the contract owner's death prior to the first annuity payment under the contract, the named beneficiary (or the owner's estate if the beneficiary predeceases the owner) has the right to surrender the contract for the then value of the owner's interest in the insurance company's accumulation fund (in a lump-sum), unless one of the beneficiary settlement options has been selected by the owner-annuitant in accordance with the terms of the contract. If no such beneficiary settlement option has been selected the beneficiary may elect, in lieu of that one lump-sum payment, to receive the accumulated value of the contract either in the form of a simple variable life annuity or a variable life annuity with a specified number of guaranteed payments.

Law and Analysis

Section 1014(a) of the Internal Revenue Code provides that the basis of property in the hands of a person acquiring the property from a decedent is the fair market value of the property at the date of the decedent's death or, if the decedent's executor so elects, at the alternate valuation date prescribed in section 2032.

Section 1014(b)(9) of the Code provides, in the case of persons dying after December 31, 1953, that property acquired from the decedent by reason of death, form of ownership, or other conditions (if by reason thereof the property is required to be included in determining the value of the decedent's gross estate) shall, for purposes of section 1014(a), be considered to have been acquired from or to have passed from the decedent. However, section 1014(b)(9)(A) provides that the foregoing provision shall not apply to annuities described in section 72.

In general, section 72 of the Code deals with the tax treatment of annuities. Section 72(e) determines the amounts or portions of amounts to be included in gross income when such amounts are not paid as an annuity, but are nevertheless received under or in discharge of a contract involving amounts payable as annuities.

Section 1.72-1(a) of the Income Tax Regulations provides that section 72 of the Code prescribes a rules relating to the inclusion in gross income of amounts received under a life insurance, endowment, or annuity contract unless such amounts are specifically excluded from gross income under other provisions of chapter 1 of the Code. In general, these rules provide that amounts subject to the provisions of section 72 are includible in the gross income of the recipient except to the extent that they are considered to represent a reduction or return of premiums or other consideration paid.

Section 1.72-1(b) of the regulations provides that, for the purpose of determining the extent to which amounts received represent a reduction or return of premiums or other consideration paid, the provisions of section 72 of the Code distinguish between "amounts received as an annuity" and "amounts not received as an annuity." In general, "amounts received as an annuity" are amounts that are payable at regular intervals over a period of more than one full year from the date on which they are deemed to begin, provided the total of the amount so payable or the period for which they are to be paid can be determined as of that date. See section 1.72-2(b)(2) and (3). Any other amounts to which the provisions of section 72 apply are considered to be "amounts not received as an annuity." See section 1.72-11.

Section 1.72-2(a)(1) of the regulations provides that the contracts under which amounts paid will be subject to the provisions of section 72 of the Code include contracts that are considered to be life insurance, endowment, and annuity contracts in accordance with the customary practice of life insurance companies. For purposes of section 72, however, it is immaterial whether such contracts are entered into with an insurance company.

Section 1.72-2(b)(1)(i) of the regulations provides that, in general, the amounts to which section 72 of the Code applies are any amounts received under the contracts described in section 1.72-2(a)(1). However, if such amounts are specifically excluded from gross income under other provisions of chapter 1 of the Code, section 72 shall not apply for the purpose of including such amounts in gross income. For example, section 72 does not apply to amounts received under a life insurance contract if such amounts are paid by reason of the death of the insured and are excludable from gross income under section 101(a). See also sections 101(d), relating to proceeds of life insurance paid at a date later than death, and 104(a)(4), relating to compensation for injuries or sickness.

Since the contract in question is considered to be an annuity contract in accordance with the customary practice of life insurance companies, any amount received under any of the available options in the contract (and not specifically excluded from gross income under other provisions of chapter 1 of the Code) is an amount to which section 72 of the Code applies.

Rev. Rul. 70-143 holds, under similar facts, that the right to the accumulated value under the annuity contract is not an annuity described in section 72 of the Code, because it would not be received on or after the annuity starting date.

This conclusion was reached on the basis of section 1.72-2 (b)(2) of the regulations, which provides, in part, that amounts subject to section 72 of the Code are considered to be amounts received as an annuity only in the event they are received on or after the "annuity starting date." However, section 72 also applies to amounts not received as an annuity. See section 72(e) and section 1.72-11.

Rev. Rul. 55-313, 1955-1 C.B. 219, concerns a deferred annuity contract that provides that, upon the death of the contract owner prior to the date of the first annuity payment, the issuing insurance company will pay to the beneficiary an amount equal to the consideration paid for the contract or the cash surrender value of the contract upon the death of the owner, whichever is greater. The revenue ruling holds that the excess of the amount of the payment to the beneficiary over the amount of the consideration paid for the contract is includible in the gross income of the beneficiary.

The basis rule prescribed in section 1014(b)(9) of the Code, fair market value at death, pertains to property acquired from the decedent.

In the instant case, the property that will be acquired by the beneficiary is an interest in the benefits provided under the annuity contract. Those benefits accord to the contract owner, or in the event of the owner's death, the named beneficiary, the right to surrender the contract at any time before the annuity starting date and to receive in return an amount equal to the accumulated value under the contract. This right is an option. Upon the death of the owner, several other options under the contract, such as the right to select a variable life annuity, also pass to the beneficiary. The fact that the beneficiary may, after the death of the contract owner, elect to receive a lump-sum payment in return for the accumulated value does not render the property acquired from the decedent an interest in something other than an annuity contract. In general, section 72 of the Code provides extensive rules for determining the extent, if any, to which payments under the various settlement options provided by variable annuity contracts are includible in gross income. Since this variable annuity contract is subject to the provisions of section 72, the exclusion of section 1014(b)(9)(A) applies.

Holdings

For purposes of section 1014 of the Code, the deferred variable annuity contract is an annuity described in section 72.

If the beneficiary of the variable annuity contract in this case elects to receive the lump-sum payment under the contract, the excess of the amount received over the amount of the consideration paid for the contract is, as in the case of a straight deferred annuity, includible in the gross income of the beneficiary. See section 72(e) of the Code; and Rev. Rul. 55-313.

Effect on Other Revenue Rulings

Rev. Rul. 70-143 is revoked.

Prospective Application

Under the authority contained in section 7805(b) of the Code, the conclusion in this revenue ruling will be applied to deferred variable annuity contracts purchased prior to Oct. 21, 1979, including any contributions applied to such contracts pursuant to a binding commitment entered into before that date. This revenue ruling will apply to all other amounts contributed to deferred variable annuity contracts on or after Oct. 21, 1979.

TAX SHELTER REVENUE RULINGS

Part I. Rulings and Decisions Under the Internal Revenue Code of 1954

Section 167.—Depreciation

26 CFR 1.167(h)-1: Life tenants and beneficiaries of trusts and estates.

Whether income beneficiaries of a trust arrangement may deduct depreciation. See Rev. Rul. 80-75, page 26.

Section 170.—Charitable, Etc., Contributions and Gifts

26 CFR 1.170A-1: Charitable, etc., contributions and gifts; allowance of deduction.

Charitable contributions; fair market value; gems. A taxpayer purchased an assortment of gems from a promoter who asserted that the price was "wholesale" and who claimed that, if the taxpayer held the gems for over one year and then contributed them to charity, the taxpayer would be entitled to deduct three times the price paid. The deduction allowable is the fair market value of the gems at the time of the contribution, not an artificially calculated estimate of value. The best evidence of the maximum fair market value is the price at which the promoter sold the gems to the taxpayer.

Rev. Rul. 80-69

ISSUE

How is the fair market value of property contributed to charity determined for federal income tax purposes under the circumstances described below?

FACTS

During 1978, an individual taxpayer who was not a dealer in gems purchased an assortment of gems for 500*x* dollars from a promoter who asserted that the price was "wholesale", even though the promoter and various other dealers engaged in numerous similar sales at similar prices with individuals who were not dealers in gems. The promoter represented that if the taxpayer held the gems for over one year and then contributed them to charity the taxpayer would be entitled to a deduction of 1500*x* dollars at the time of contribution. The promoter contended that the value at the time of contribution would be at least three times as much as the price paid by the taxpayer. The taxpayer contributed the gems to a public museum 13 months after purchase, claiming a charitable contributions deduction of 1500*x* dollars. The museum is an organization described in section 170(c) of the Internal Revenue Code, contributions to which are deductible under section 170(a)(1). The museum will use the gems in a manner related to its exempt purposes.

LAW AND ANALYSIS

Section 170(a)(1) of the Code allows as a deduction any charitable contribution (as defined in section 170(c)) payment of which is made within the taxable year.

Section 1.170A-1(c)(1) of the Income Tax Regulations provides that if a charitable contribution is made in property other than money, the amount of the contribution is the fair market value of the property at the time of contribution, reduced as provided in section 170(e)(1) of the Code.

Section 1.170A-1(c)(2) of the regulations provides that the fair market value is the price at which the property would change hands between a willing buyer and a willing seller, neither being under any compulsion to buy or sell and both having a reasonable knowledge of relevant facts.

The definition of fair market value depends upon a knowledgeable willing buyer and a knowledgeable willing seller. To determine fair market value, reference is made to the most active marketplace at the time of the donor's contribution. The best evidence of fair market value depends on actual transactions and not on some artificially calculated estimate of value contrary to the prices at which the very gems at issue changed hands in the marketplace. The 500*x* dollars at which the promoter sold the gems to the taxpayer and others, rather than a mere speculative claim of what the gems would be worth, is the best evidence of the maximum fair market value of the gems.

HOLDING

For federal income tax purposes the fair market value of the gems was no greater than 500*x* dollars.

Section 263.—Capital Expenditures

26 CFR 1.263(c)-1: Intangible drilling and development costs in the case of oil and gas wells.

Whether a cash basis taxpayer may, under the circumstances described, deduct the prepayment of intangible drilling and development costs in the taxable year the prepayment is made or must deduct the prepayment rateably as the costs are actually incurred. See Rev. Rul. 80-71, page 7.

Section 461.—General Rule for Taxable Year of Deduction

26 CFR 1.461-1: General rule for taxable year of deduction.
(Also Section 612; 1.612-3.)

Advanced mineral royalties paid or incurred under minimum royalty provisions. An advanced mineral royalty resulting from a minimum royalty provision and covering a 12-month period extending beyond the taxable year when paid or incurred is not fully deductible in the year when paid or incurred. Only the portion properly attributable to the current taxable year is deductible in the current taxable year. The cost of minerals extracted in subsequent years must be reduced by the advanced royalties deducted to date. Rev. Rul. 77-489 amplified.

Rev. Rul. 80-70

ISSUE

Is an advanced mineral royalty resulting from a minimum royalty provision and covering a 12 month period extending beyond the taxable year when the liability is paid or incurred deductible in full in the year when paid or incurred by a taxpayer using either the cash receipts and disbursements method or the accrual method of accounting?

FACTS

Situation 1

X uses the cash receipts and disbursements method of accounting and files its federal income tax returns on a calendar year basis. On December 1,

1977, *X* and *Y* entered into a lease agreement under which *X* obtained the operating mineral interest in a mineral property from *Y*. The agreement requires *X* to pay *Y* a production royalty of 5 percent of the proceeds received from the sale of minerals extracted during each lease year over the 10 year lease term. Regardless of production, *X* is required to make a nonrefundable payment to *Y* of 60*x* dollars on the first day (December 1) of each annual leasing period. Production royalties otherwise due each lease year are to be reduced by the 60*x* dollars paid on December 1 of each year. In any year in which the minimum royalty exceeds the production royalties, the excess is to be applied to reduce the production royalties due for any subsequent year.

The mineral reserves committed to the lease are substantially in excess of those sufficient for complete pay-out of the total minimum royalty and it is practical to extract a quantity of the mineral over the term of the agreement in excess of that necessary for complete payout of the total minimum royalty.

On December 1, 1977, *X* paid 60*x* dollars to *Y* for the lease period December 1, 1977, through November 30, 1978. *X* extracted no minerals from the leased property during December 1977. In accordance with section 1.612-3(b)(3) of the Income Tax Regulations, *X* elected to treat the advanced royalties as deductions from gross income for the year in which the advanced royalties are paid or accrued.

Situation 2

The facts are the same as in *Situation 1* except that *X* uses the accrual method of accounting and executes a negotiable promissory note on December 1 of each lease year payable on demand to *Y* as payment for the 60*x* dollars.

LAW AND ANALYSIS

Section 461(a) of the Internal Revenue Code provides that the amount of any deduction shall be taken for the taxable year that is the proper taxable year under the method of accounting used in computing taxable income.

Section 1.461-1(a)(1) of the regulations provides that, under the cash receipts and disbursements method of accounting, amounts representing allowable deductions shall, as a general rule, be taken into account for the taxable year in which paid.

Section 1.461-1(a)(2) of the regulations provides that, under the accrual method of accounting, an expense is deductible for the taxable year in which all the events have occurred that determine the fact of the liability and the amount thereof can be determined with reasonable accuracy.

Section 1.612-3(b)(3) of the regulations provides that the payor shall treat the advanced royalties paid or accrued in connection with mineral property as deductions from gross income for the year the mineral product, in respect of which the advanced royalties were paid or accrued, is sold. However, in the case of advanced mineral royalties paid or accrued in connection with mineral property as a result of a minimum royalty provision, the payor, at its option, may instead treat the advanced royalties as deductions from gross income for the year in which the advanced royalties are paid or accrued. This subparagraph further provides that no deduction is allowed under this provision that is disallowed under other provisions of the Code such as section 461.

Rev. Rul. 77-489, 1977-2 C.B. 177, addresses the deductibility of cumulative advanced minimum royalties due over the term of a ten year lease. Rev. Rul. 77-489 provides two situations in which a taxpayer using the cash receipts and disbursements method of accounting and a taxpayer using the accrual method of accounting attempt to accelerate the deduction for the payment of the cumulative advanced minimum royalties either by paying the full amount of these royalties due over the ten year lease term in cash or by executing a negotiable promissory note payable on demand for these royalties. In both situations in Rev. Rul. 77-489, payment of the cumulative advanced minimum royalties due over the ten year lease was made on the first day of the taxable year. Rev. Rul. 77-489 concludes that, for both the taxpayers, only that portion of the advanced minimum royalties that is properly attributable to the initial year of the lease is deductible in that year. The present situation differs from Rev. Rul. 77-489 in that it involves only a 12 month portion of the cumulative advanced minimum royalty due over the ten year lease and the period used for fixing liability under the lease is not coextensive with the taxable year of payment or accrual.

In *Zaninovich v. Commissioner,* 69 T.C. 605 (1978), a taxpayer deducted in the year of payment a full 12 months' rent that was attributable to 2 taxable years. In disallowing the deduction, the court stated the general rule for rental deductions as provided in *University Properties, Inc. v. Commissioner,* 45 T.C. 416, 421 (1966), *aff'd,* 378 F.2d 83 (9th Cir. 1967):

> Rentals may be deducted as such only for the year or years to which they are applied. If they are paid for the continued use of the property beyond the years in which paid they are not deductible in full in the year paid but must be deducted ratably over the years during which the property is so used.

In both situations 1 and 2, *X* has elected pursuant to section 1.612-3(b)(3) of the regulations to treat the advanced royalties as deductions from gross income for the year in which the advanced royalties are paid or accrued. This election is in lieu of deducting the advanced royalties in the year the mineral product in respect of which the advanced royalties were paid or accrued is sold.

In *Burnet v. Hutchinson Coal Co.,* 64 F.2d 275 (4th Cir. 1933), and *Commissioner v. Jamison Coal and Coke Co.,* 67 F.2d 342 (3rd Cir. 1933), the courts indicated that minimum royalty payments are like rent. In accordance with *Zaninovich,* the portion of the payment made by cash or negotiable promissory note for the advanced royalties applicable to the months in the lease period occurring in 1978 is not deductible in 1977. This result is the same for both the taxpayer using the cash receipts and disbursements method of accounting and the taxpayer using the accrual method of accounting. See *Smith v. Commissioner,* 51 T.C. 429 (1968).

In both *Situation 1* and *Situation 2,* *X* may deduct only 5*x* dollars of the advanced royalty resulting for the minimum royalty provision for the taxable year 1977. For subsequent taxable years remaining on the lease *X* may deduct 60*x* dollars of advanced royalties, consisting of 55*x* dollars from the lease year beginning in the prior taxable year and 5*x* dollars from the lease year beginning in the current taxable year. However, if production occurs in subsequent taxable years, the taxpayer must reduce the cost of minerals extracted by the amount of the advanced royalties that have been deducted to date.

HOLDING

An advanced mineral royalty resulting from a minimum royalty provision and covering a 12 month period extending beyond the taxable year when paid or the liability is incurred is not deductible in full in the year when paid or the liability is incurred by either a taxpayer using the cash method of accounting or a taxpayer using the accrual method of accounting. Only that portion of an advanced minimum royalty paid or incurred that is properly attributable to the current taxable year is deductible by either of these taxpayers. Furthermore, if production occurs in subsequent taxable years, the taxpayer must reduce the cost of minerals extracted by the amount of the advanced royalties that have been deducted to date.

EFFECT ON OTHER RULINGS

Rev. Rul. 77-489 is amplified.

---

26 CFR 1.461-1: General rule for taxable year of deduction.
(Also Sections 263, 612; 1.263(c)-1, 1.612-4.)

Intangible drilling costs; limited partnership; year of deduction. An oil and gas limited partnership made advance payments, at a fixed rate per well, for the costs of drilling oil and gas wells to the parent of its corporate general partner. The parent owned no drilling equipment and subcontracted the actual drilling of the wells to independent drilling contractors, who were paid on a footage and day work basis upon completion of the contracts. These prepayments are not deductible until paid to the independent contractors. Rev. Rul. 71-252 distinguished.

Rev. Rul. 80-71

ISSUE

Whether under the circumstances described below a limited partnership that uses the cash receipts and disbursements method of accounting is entitled to deduct in the tax year amounts that are paid within the tax year as "intangible drilling and development costs," and optionally expensed under the provisions of section 1.612-4 of the Income Tax Regulations.

FACTS

A limited partnership (*LP*) was organized in 1975 for the exploration and development of oil and gas lands. *LP* was formed by 100*x* limited partners who each contributed $1,000*x* to the limited partnership. The general partner of *LP* is corporation *X* whose parent, corporation *Y*, is the general contractor that will arrange for the drilling, completion, and equipping of the oil and gas wells. The partnership reports its income on a calendar year basis.

The partnership agreement provides that corporation *X* will transfer to *LP*, as its contribution to capital, certain oil and gas leases, mineral rights, equipment, and a specified amount of cash. The limited partners are allocated the deduction for intangible drilling and development costs.

As general partner, corporation *X* has control over the operations of the partnership, including the authority to make any expenditures and incur any obligation that it deems necessary, as well as to make the determination of which wells will be drilled. Corporation *Y*, as general contractor, will conduct the drilling, testing, and completion, or if nonproductive, the abandonment of each well in which *LP* participates. *Y* will charge a fixed fee for such services.

In October 1975, corporation *X*, acting on behalf of *LP*, entered into an agreement with corporation *Y* for the drilling of wells on tracts covered by leasehold interests previously contributed to *LP* by *X*. For certain of the proposed drill sites the entire working or operating interests were held by *LP*. For other proposed drill sites, *LP* owned only an undivided fraction of the working interest, and drilling was to be a joint undertaking between *LP* and other co-owners.

The agreement set forth a fixed price ($10,000*x*) for the intangible costs of drilling and completion of each well and a separate fixed price ($8,000*x*) for the drilling and abandonment without attempted completion of any that was abandoned after drilling commenced. For all wells to be drilled for *LP*, the agreement required that the designated fixed prices for drilling and completion be remitted to *Y* on or before December 31, 1975. In the event that any well was drilled and abandoned without completion, the difference between the price advanced on or before December 31 and the fixed price for drilling without completion was to be credited toward the cost of drilling anothe well or wells at locations to be designated in the future. The agreement did not specify any date for commencement of drilling operations by corporation *Y*.

In accordance with the terms of the agreement, on December 31, 1975, *LP* advanced to *Y* sums representing *LP*'s portion of the fixed prices for well drilling to be performed on or after January 1, 1976. Having previously elected to expense intangible drilling and development costs, *LP* deducted the advance payments in its Form 1065 partnership return for the year 1975, a year in which *LP* had no income or other expense.

Y owned no drilling equipment, and the actual drilling of the wells was subcontracted to independent drilling contractors. The contracts were of the conventional footage and day work variety and did not require any payments to be made by *Y* to the drillers prior to completion of performance by the drillers.

LAW AND ANALYSIS

Section 263(c) of the Internal Revenue Code provides that, notwithstanding section 263(a), regulations shall be prescribed by the Secretary granting taxpayers an election to deduct, as expenses, intangible drilling and development costs in the case of oil and gas wells. In accordance with section 263(c), section 1.612-4(a) of the regulations provides that intangible drilling and development costs incurred by an operator in the development of oil and gas properties may at the taxpayer's option be chargeable to capital or to expense.

Section 446(a) of the Code provides that taxable income shall be computed under the method of accounting the taxpayer employs to regularly compute its income in keeping its books. Section 446(c) provides that certain methods are permissible subject to the requirement of section 446(b). Section 446(b) provides that if the method used by the taxpayer does not clearly reflect income, the computation of taxable income shall be made under such method as, in the opinion of the Secretary, does clearly reflect income.

Section 461 of the Code provides that the amount of any deduction allowed by subtitle A shall be taken for the taxable year that is the proper taxable year under the method of accounting used in computing taxable income.

Section 1.446-1(a)(1) of the regulations provides that the term, "method of accounting", includes not only the overall method of accounting of a taxpayer but also the accounting treatment of any item of income or deduction.

Section 1.461-1(a) of the regulations provides that if an expenditure results in the creation of an asset having a useful life that extends substantially beyond the close of the taxable year, such expenditure may not be deductible or may be deductible only in part, for the taxable year in which made.

Therefore, if the method adopted by the taxpayer for a particular item or transaction does not clearly reflect income, section 446(b) specifically empowers the Commissioner to compute taxable income under such method as, in the opinion of the Commissioner, does clearly reflect income.

In Rev. Rul. 71-252, 1971-1 C.B. 146, a taxpayer using the cash receipts and disbursements method of accounting deducted in the year paid intangible drilling and development costs. In that revenue ruling the taxpayer began in 1969 investigating the oil and gas producing potential of a certain tract of land. After receiving a favorable report thereon the taxpayer acquired, in October 1969, a lease of the oil and gas operating interest in the tract. On December 31, 1969, the taxpayer executed a written drilling contract with a drilling contractor. On the same day, as required by the terms of the contract, the taxpayer paid 100*x* dollars to the contractor. In March 1970, the well was completed successfully for the production of oil and gas. After discussing ***Pauley v. United States,*** (S.D. Cal., 1963), Rev. Rul. 71-252 holds that the 100*x* dollars intangible drilling and development costs were deductible by the taxpayer in 1969, the year they were paid.

The prepayment in ***Pauley*** was occasioned by the drillers' concern with Pauley's willingness and ability to pay when the driller needed operating funds. The driller had no earlier business dealings with Pauley, but knew that he was involved in many other business activities. The court found that the driller required prepayment of the drilling expenses for sufficient business reasons. The drilling permit was not issued until December 30, 1947, and other "complicated and diverse" negotiations were being carried out late in 1947 by Pauley. Drilling activities commenced immediately after December 31, 1947, and proceeded without any substantial delay until completion on March 12, 1948.

These findings evidenced a bona fide, arm's length transaction entered into for a valid business purpose, and provided the basis for the court's holding that the prepayment was an allowable expense in the year payment was made and deductible in that year. Further, the prepayment was exhausted within two and one-half months of payment.

Intangible drilling and development costs are capital in nature. However, section 263(c) of the Code, as implemented by section 1.612-4(a) of the regulations, provides taxpayers an election to expense intangible drilling and development expenditures that otherwise would be capitalized under section 263(a). Merely because a taxpayer has elected to charge intangible drilling and developments costs to expense, it does not follow that all amounts paid are deductible in the year of payment when such payment is made in advance of the rendering of services by the drilling contractor. Prepaid intangible drilling and development costs are subject to the same standards applicable to other prepaid expense items. Section 263(c) does not permit a taxpayer unlimited control of the timing of the deduction for drilling and development costs. Instead, the timing of a deduction must meet the specific limitations of section 1.461-1(a) of the regulations in order to meet the clear reflection of income requirement contained in section 446(b).

Here, at the time the prepayments were made neither the date for commencing nor completing drilling of the wells was specified. Furthermore, the prepayments for the intangible drilling costs were made by *LP* (the investor group partnership) to *Y*, the general contractor (and the parent of *X*, the general partner), who in turn was to contract with the actual drilling contractor for the drilling of the well. The prepayments could also be applied to later, not as yet contracted for, wells to the extent of unsuccessful completions. All of this indicates that the prepayments by *LP* to *Y* were not made in accordance with customary business practice.

The prepayments themselves were assets having useful lives that extended substantially beyond the close of *LP*'s 1975 tax year. Since *LP* had no income for the year of the deduction, the facts indicate the expenditures here were prompted by the federal income tax advantages that resulted from the deduction.

Considering the facts and circumstances in the present case in the light of the above analysis, *LP*'s deduction for the prepaid intangible drilling and development costs results in a substantial distortion of *LP*'s income for the year of payments.

HOLDING

LP's prepayments are not deductible in 1975. However, the payments are deductible in the tax year or years *Y* pays the independent drilling contractors under their conventional footage and day work contracts with *Y*, if the clear reflection of income requirements of section 446(b) of the Code are satisfied.

EFFECT ON OTHER REVENUE RULINGS

Rev. Rul. 71-252 is distinguished.

Section 465.—Deductions Limited to Amount at Risk in Case of Certain Activities

Foreign gold mine; amount at risk. A taxpayer invested a specified amount in a tax shelter arrangement whereby the taxpayer leased a foreign mining company's interest in a gold reserve. The taxpayer authorized the promoter of the arrangement to sell an option on the gold to be extracted and stipulated that the proceeds from the sale of the option and the original investment were to be used for development of the gold reserve. The option can only be exercised after the gold has been extracted, and the holder of the option cannot compel the extraction. The taxpayer is not at risk, within the meaning of section 465 of the Code, with respect to the proceeds from the sale of the option.

Rev. Rul. 80-72

ISSUE

Do the "at risk" provisions of section 465 of the Internal Revenue Code apply under the circumstances described below?

FACTS

In 1979, *M*, a consortium of private foreign corporations, marketed a tax shelter arrangement purporting to give investors a tax write-off equal to four times the cash invested. *A*, an individual, invested 100*x* dollars in the arrangement.

In connection with this investment, *A* executed the following documents:

1. A "mineral claim lease" whereby *A* leases from *P*, a foreign mining company, the mineral rights to a gold reserve located in *X*, a foreign country. Under the lease, *A* is entitled to explore, develop and extract all recovered gold on the premises until 1986, the date of expiration of the lease. *A* must pay *P* a certain royalty per gram for all the recovered gold after first deducting all the tax due to *X*, extraction costs and the development costs. *A* also agreed to expend 400*x* dollars for the development to ready the claim for extraction no later than December 31, 1979. However, *A* is not obligated to extract the gold. Whether and when the gold is actually extracted is within the control of *A*.

2. An authorization agreement under which *A* authorizes *M* to sell for 300*x* dollars a gold option, described below, on the total minerals to be extracted under the terms of the mineral claim lease. The authorization further specifies that the proceeds from the sale of the gold option shall be used with the 100*x* dollars remitted by *A* to pay for development of the claim by a contractor that *M* retains on *A*'s behalf.

3. A gold option by which for a 300*x* dollar premium, *A* grants to *C*, a party obtained by *M*, the option to purchase all the gold contained in the mineral claim lease subject to the tax due to *X*, lessor royalty, development costs, and extraction cost. After payment of the above costs, the exercise price for the remaining gold shall be approximately one-third the current fair market value of gold. *C* as option holder agrees that the option can only be exercised after the gold has been extracted. Further, *C* cannot compel the extraction of gold. If necessary arrangements are not made for extracting the gold prior to the expiration date of the option in 1986, *A* acknowledges and agrees that the option holder has the first right of refusal for entering into a new lease for the mineral claim with *P*. In the gold option, *M* represents that gold in commercially marketable quantities has been shown to exist in the mineral claim.

After receipt of the above, *M* sent *A* copies of the executed documents in addition to invoices and cancelled checks for development of the mining claim in the amount of 400*x* dollars. These were dated on or before December 31, 1979. On *A*'s 1979 tax return, *A* claimed a 400*x* dollars deduction for development expenditures under section 616(a) of the Code.

LAW AND ANALYSIS

Section 616(a) of the Code provides that except where the taxpayer elects otherwise as provided in section 616 (b), there shall be allowed as a deduction in computing taxable income all expenditures paid or incurred during the taxable year for the development of a mine or other natural deposit (other than an oil or gas well) if paid or incurred after the existence of ores or minerals in commercially marketable quantities has been disclosed.

Section 465 of the Code provides that in the case of an individual engaged in an activity to which this section applies, any loss from such activity for the taxable year shall be allowed only to the extent of the aggregate amount with respect to which the taxpayer is at risk (within the meaning of subsection (b)) for such activity at the close of the taxable year.

For taxable years beginning after December 31, 1978, section 465(c)(3)(A) of the Code provides that section 465 applies to each activity engaged in by the taxpayer in carrying on a trade or business or for the production of income.

Section 465(b)(1) of the Code provides that a taxpayer shall be considered at risk for an activity with respect to amounts, including the amount of money and the adjusted basis of other property, contributed by the taxpayer to the activity, and amounts borrowed with respect to such activity (as determined under paragraph (2)).

Section 465(b)(2) of the Code provides that a taxpayer shall be considered at risk with respect to amounts borrowed for use in an activity to the extent that the taxpayer is personally liable for the repayment of such amounts or has pledged property, other than property used in such activity, as security for such borrowed amount.

Section 465(b)(4) of the Code provides that notwithstanding any other provision of this section, a taxpayer shall not be considered at risk with respect to amounts protected against loss through nonrecourse financing, guarantees, stop loss agreements, or other similar arrangements.

See the Senate Committee on Finance Report on the Tax Reform Act of 1976, S. Rep. No. 94-938, 94th Cong., 2d Sess. 1 (1976), 1976-3 C.B. (Vol. 3) 57, at 87.

The legislative history indicates that Congress intended the at risk provisions to cover arrangements the effect of which is to insulate taxpayers from "economic loss."

In this case, *A* has obtained 300*x* dollars by selling an option that can be exercised only if gold is found and extracted by or on behalf of *A*. If no gold is found, or if *A* fails to extract any gold found, *A* will have no obligation to the option holder, *C*. Moreover, as part of the same arrangement, *A* will expend the 300*x* dollars (plus the 100*x* dollars remitted by *A*) to pay for development of the claim. Thus, *A*'s at risk position in relation to the 300*x* dollars is substantially the same as if the 300*x* dollars had been borrowed from *C* on a nonrecourse basis repayable only from *A*'s interest in the activity. Under these facts the selling of the option is an "other similar arrangement" to nonrecourse financing as provided in section 465(b)(4), whereby *A* is effectively protected from any true economic risk.

HOLDING

A is not at risk within the meaning of section 465 of the Code with respect to the 300*x* dollars premium received on the sale of the option. Further the 100*x* deduction attributable to *A*'s actual cash investment is deductible on *A*'s 1979 tax return only to the extent that *A* can prove that it was expended during the taxable year for the development of a mine and that the existence of ores in commercially marketable quantities had previously been disclosed in that mine.

Section 612.—Basis for Cost Depletion

26 CFR 1.612-3: Depletion; treatment of bonus and advanced royalty.

Advanced royalties; cash and nonrecourse notes. Under section 1.612-3(b) of the regulations, neither a cash nor an accrual basis taxpayer may deduct as advanced mineral royalties the amount of nonrecourse notes that are payable only to the extent of the proceeds received from the sale of the minerals. Cash paid as advanced royalties is a deferred expense to be taken into account when the minerals are sold.

Rev. Rul. 80-73

ISSUE

In what year and to what extent may a taxpayer using the cash receipts and disbursements method of accounting deduct cash and notes given as advanced royalties; and similarly, in what year and to what extent may a taxpayer using the accrual method of accounting deduct notes given as advance royalties?

FACTS

On January 1, 1977, *A*, an individual, and *Y* entered into a lease agreement under which *A* obtained an operating mineral interest in mineral property owned by *Y*. The agreement provides that a minimum advanced royalty is due *Y* each lease year over the 10-year lease term in the amount of 600*x* dollars, payable at the beginning of each lease year. The lease further provides that, for the first year, payment of the royalty is to be made in cash and a promissory note, and for all subsequent years payments may be made entirely with notes. The amount of the minimum annual royalty reasonably reflects the value of the leasehold interest. *A* is a cash method, calendar year taxpayer.

On January 1, 1977, *B*, an individual, also entered into the same type of agreement with *Y* except that the advanced mineral royalties payable at the beginning of each lease year may be made entirely with promissory notes. *B* is an accrual method, calendar year taxpayer.

In both cases the notes are unsecured, nonrecourse, non-interest bearing, have no maturity date, and are payable only to the extent of the proceeds received from the sale of the minerals.

On January 1, 1977, *A* gave *Y* 150*x* dollars in cash and a note for 450*x* dollars. *B* gave *Y* a note for 600*x* dollars.

LAW AND ANALYSIS

Section 1.612-3(b)(1) of the Income Tax Regulations provides that advanced royalties exist when the owner of an operating interest in a mineral deposit or standing timber is required to pay royalties on a specified number of units of such mineral or timber annually whether or not extracted or cut within the year, and the owner may apply any amounts paid on account of units not extracted or cut within the year against the royalty on the mineral or timber thereafter extracted or cut.

Section 1.612-3(b)(3) of the regulations provides that the payor shall treat the advanced royalties paid or accrued in connection with mineral property as deductions from gross income for the year the mineral product, in respect of which the advanced royalties were paid or accrued, is sold. However, if advanced mineral royalties are paid or accrued in connection with mineral property as a result of a minimum royalty provision, the payor, at its option, may instead treat the royalties as deductions from gross income for the years in which the advanced royalties are paid or accrued. A minimum royalty provision requires that a substantially uniform amount of royalties be paid at least annually either over the life of the lease or for a period of 20 years.

Under section 1.612-3(b) of the regulations advanced royalties may only be deducted when payment is not contingent upon the extraction of the mineral. Here, payments of the notes are contingent upon extraction and sale of the minerals. Consequently, except for the cash payment, all royalties both as to *A* and *B* are not advanced royalties paid or accrued within the meaning of section 1.612-3(b) of the regulations because there is no fixed liability to pay any royalty until the minerals are produced and sold. The cash payment is an advanced royalty, but does not result from a minimum royalty provision because substantially uniform royalties are not required to be paid each year over the life of the lease.

Moreover, the giving of the note by *A* does not constitute payment. For a payment to be deductible by a cash method taxpayer there must be a depletion of assets and, therefore, the payment must be in cash or its equivalent. If the note is never paid, the cash method maker has not parted with anything other than a promise to pay. A promise to pay is not cash or its equivalent. *See Eckert v. Burnet,* 283 U.S. 140 (1931), X-1 C.B. 241; *Page v. Rhode Island Hospital Trust Co. Executor,* 88 F.2d 192 (1st Cir. 1937).

HOLDING

A deduction is not allowable to *A* or *B* for the amount of the notes because under section 1.612-3(b) of the regulations an advanced royalty must be payable whether or not the minerals are extracted and sold. Here the notes are payable only out of the proceeds received from the sale of the minerals. While the 150*x* dollars actually paid in cash by *A* is an advanced royalty under section 1.612-3(b), it is deductible only for the year the mineral product, in respect of which the advance royalties were paid, is sold because it does not result from a minimum royalty provision.

For years after December 31, 1978, see also section 465 as amended by the Revenue Act of 1978.

---

26 CFR 1.612-3: Depletion; treatment of bonus and advanced royalty.

Whether an advanced mineral royalty resulting from a minimum royalty provision and covering a 12 month period extending beyond the taxable year when the liability is paid or incurred is deductible in full in the year when paid or incurred by a taxpayer using either the cash receipts and disbursements method or the accrual method of accounting. See Rev. Rul. 80-70, page 5.

---

26 CFR 1.612-4: Charges to capital and to expense in case of oil and gas wells.

Whether a cash basis taxpayer may, under the circumstances described, deduct the prepayment of intangible drilling and development costs in the taxable year the prepayment is made or must deduct the prepayment rateably as the costs are actually incurred. See Rev. Rul. 80-71, page 7.

---

26 CFR 5a.612-1: Changes to capital and to expense in case of geothermal wells.

T.D. 7669

TITLE 26.—INTERNAL REVENUE.—CHAPTER I, SUBCHAPTER A, PART 5a.—TEMPORARY INCOME TAX REGULATIONS UNDER THE ENERGY TAX ACT OF 1978

Option to Capitalize or Deduct Intangible Drilling and Development Costs in the Case of Wells Drilled for any Geothermal Deposit

AGENCY: Internal Revenue Service, Treasury.

ACTION: Temporary regulations.

SUMMARY: This document provides Temporary Income Tax Regulations relating to the option to capitalize or deduct intangible drilling and development costs in the case of wells drilled for any geothermal deposit. Changes to the applicable tax law were made by the Energy Tax Act of 1978 [Pub. L. 95-618, 1978-3 C.B. (Vol. 2) 1]. In addition, the rules contained in the temporary regulations set forth in this document also serve as a notice of proposed rulemaking by which the rules contained therein are proposed to be prescribed as final regulations.

DATES: These temporary regulations are effective for taxable years ending on or after October 1, 1978, with respect to geothermal wells commenced on or after that date. Written comments and requests for a public hearing must be delivered or mailed by March 31, 1980.

ADDRESS: Send comments and requests for a public hearing to: Commissioner of Internal Revenue, Attention: CC:LR:T (LR-202-78), Washington, D.C. 20224.

FOR FURTHER INFORMATION CONTACT: David B. Cubeta of the Legislation and Regulations Division, Office of the Chief Counsel, Internal Revenue Service, 1111 Constitution Avenue, N.W., Washington, D.C. 20224 (Attention: CC:LR:T) (202-566-3926).

SUPPLEMENTARY INFORMATION:

BACKGROUND

This document contains temporary regulations under section 612 of the Internal Revenue Code of 1954. The temporary regulations are required to implement section 402(a) and (e) of the Energy Tax Act of 1978 (92 Stat. 3174).

The regulations promulgated in this document are also proposed to be prescribed as final Income Tax Regulations (26 CFR Part 1) under section 612 of the Internal Revenue Code of 1954.

WAIVER OF PROCEDURAL REQUIREMENTS OF TREASURY DIRECTIVE

The expeditious adoption of the provisions contained in this document is necessary because of the need for immediate guidance to taxpayers eligible for the option to deduct as expenses intangible drilling and development costs in the case of wells drilled for any geothermal deposit. For this reason, Jerome Kurtz, Commissioner of Internal Revenue, has determined that the provisions of paragraphs 8 through 14 of the Treasury Department directive implementing Executive Order 12044 must be waived.

COMMENTS AND REQUESTS FOR A PUBLIC HEARING

Before adoption of the final regulations proposed in this document, consideration will be given to any written comments that are submitted (preferably six copies) to the Commissioner of Internal Revenue. All comments will be available for public inspection and copying. A public hearing will be held upon written request to the Commissioner by any person who has submitted written comments. If a public hearing, is held, notice of the time and place will be published in the Federal Register.

DRAFTING INFORMATION

The principal author of these regulations is David B. Cubeta of the Legislation and Regulations Division of the Office of Chief Counsel, Internal Revenue Service. However, personnel from other offices of the Internal Revenue Service and Treasury Department participated in developing the regulation, both on matters of substance and style.

Adoption of amendments to the regulations

Accordingly, a new Part 5a, Temporary Income Tax Regulations under the Energy Tax Act of 1978, is added to Title 26 of the Code of Federal Regulations and the following temporary regulations are adopted:

§ 5a.612-1 Charges to capital and to expense in case of geothermal wells.

(a) *Option with respect to intangible drilling and development costs.* In accordance with the provisions of section 263(c), intangible drilling and development costs incurred by an operator (one who holds a working or operating interest in any tract or parcel of land either as a fee owner or under a lease or any other form of contract granting working or operating rights) in the development of a geothermal deposit (as defined in section 613(e)(3) and the regulations thereunder) may at the operator's option be chargeable to capital or to expense. This option applies to all expenditures made by an operator for wages, fuel, repairs, hauling, supplies, etc., incident to and necessary for the drilling of wells and the preparation of wells for the production of geothermal steam or hot water. Such expenditures have for convenience been termed intangible drilling and development costs. They include the cost to operators of any drilling or development work (excluding amounts payable only out of production or gross or net proceeds from production, if such amounts are depletable income to the recipient, and amounts properly allocable to cost of depreciable property) done for them by contractors under any form of contract, including turnkey contracts. Examples of items to which this option applies are all amounts paid for labor, fuel, repairs, hauling, and supplies, or any of them, which are used—

(1) In the drilling, shooting, and cleaning of wells,

(2) In such clearing of ground, draining, road making, surveying, and geological work as are necessary in preparation for the drilling of wells, and

(3) In the construction of such derricks, tanks, pipelines, and other physical structures as are necessary for the drilling of wells and the preparation of wells for the production of geothermal steam or hot water.

In general, this option applies only to expenditures for those drilling and developing items which in themselves do not have a salvage value. For the purpose of this option, labor, fuel, repairs, hauling, supplies, etc. are not considered as having a salvage value, even though used in connection with the installation of physical property which has a salvage value. Included in this option are all costs of drilling and development undertaken (directly or through a contract) by an operator of a geothermal property whether incurred by the operator prior or subsequent to the formal grant or assignment of operating rights (a leasehold interest, or other form of operating rights, or working interest); except that in any case where any drilling or development project is undertaken for the grant or assignment of a fraction of the operating rights, only that part of the costs thereof which is attributable to such fractional interest is within this option. In the excepted cases, costs of the project undertaken, including depreciable equipment furnished, to the extent allocable to fractions of the operating rights held by others, must be capitalized as the depletable capital cost of the fractional interest thus acquired.

(b) *Recovery of optional items, if capitalized.* (1) Items recoverable through depletion: If the taxpayer charges such expenditures as fall within the option to capital account, the amounts so capitalized and not deducted as a loss are recoverable through depletion insofar as they are not represented by physical property. For the purposes of this section the expenditures for clearing ground, draining, road making, surveying, geological work, excavation, grading, and the drilling, shooting, and cleaning of wells, are considered not to be represented by physical property, and when charged to capital account are recoverable through depletion.

(2) Items recoverable through depreciation: If the taxpayer charges such expenditures as fall within the option to capital account, the amounts so capitalized and not deducted as a loss are recoverable through depreciation insofar as they are represented by physical property. Such expenditures are amounts paid for wages, fuel, repairs, hauling, supplies, etc. used in the installation of casing and equipment and in the construction on the property of derricks and other physical structures.

(3) In the case of capitalized intangible drilling and development costs incurred under a contract, such costs shall be allocated between the foregoing classes of items specified in subparagraphs (1) and (2) for the purpose of determining the depletion and depreciation allowances.

(4) Option with respect to cost of nonproductive wells: If the operator has elected to capitalize intangible drilling and development costs, then an additional option is accorded with respect to intangible drilling and development costs incurred in drilling a nonproductive well. Such costs incurred in drilling a nonproductive well may be deducted by the taxpayer as an ordinary loss provided a proper election is made in the taxpayer's original or amended return for the first taxable year ending on or after October 1, 1978, in which such a nonproductive well is completed. The taxpayer must make a clear statement of election under this option in the return or amended return. The election may be revoked by the filing of an amended return that does not contain such a statement. The absence of a clear indication in such return of an election to deduct as ordinary losses intangible drilling and development

costs of nonproductive wells shall be deemed to be an election to recover such costs through depletion to the extent that they are not represented by physical property, and through depreciation to the extent that they are represented by physical property. Upon the expiration of the time for filing a claim for credit or refund of any overpayment of tax imposed by chapter 1 of the Code with respect to the first taxable year ending on or after October 1, 1978 in which a nonproductive well is completed, the taxpayer is bound for all subsequent years by his exercise of the option to deduct intangible drilling and development costs of nonproductive wells as an ordinary loss or his deemed election to recover such costs through depletion or depreciation.

(c) *Nonoptional items distinguished.* (1) Capital items: The option with respect to intangible drilling and development costs does not apply to expenditures by which the taxpayer acquires tangible property ordinarily considered as having a salvage value. Examples of such items are the costs of the actual materials in those structures which are constructed in the wells and on the property, and the cost of drilling tools, pipe, casing, tubing, tanks, engines, boilers, machines, etc. The option does not apply to any expenditure for wages, fuel, repairs, hauling, supplies, etc., in connection with equipment, facilities, or structures, not incident to or necessary for the drilling of wells, such as structures for treating geothermal steam or hot water. These are capital items and are recoverable through depreciation.

(2) Expense items: Expenditures which must be charged off as expense, regardless of the option provided by this section, are those for labor, fuel, repairs, hauling, supplies, etc., in connection with the operation of the wells and of other facilities on the property for the production of geothermal steam or hot water.

(d) *Manner of making election.* The option granted in paragraph (a) of this section to charge intangible drilling and development costs to expense may be exercised by claiming intangible drilling and development costs as a deduction on the taxpayer's original or amended return for the first taxable year ending on or after October 1, 1978, in which the taxpayer pays or incurs such costs with respect to a geothermal well commenced on or after that date. No formal statement is necessary. The exercise of the option may be revoked by the filing of an amended return that does not claim such a deduction. If the taxpayer fails to deduct such costs as expenses in any such return, he shall be deemed to have elected to recover such costs through depletion to the extent that they are not represented by physical property, and through depreciation to the extent that they are represented by physical property. Upon the expiration of the time for filing a claim for credit or refund of any overpayment of tax imposed by chapter 1 of the Code with respect to the first taxable year ending on or after October 1, 1978, in which the taxpayer pays or incurs intangible drilling and development costs with respect to a geothermal well commenced on or after that date, the taxpayer is bound by his exercise of the option to charge such costs to expense or his deemed election to recover such costs through depletion or depreciation for that year and for all subsequent years.

(e) *Effective date.* The option granted by paragraph (a) of this section is available only for taxable years ending on or after October 1, 1978, with respect to geothermal wells commenced on or after that date.

There is need for the immediate guidance provided by the provisions contained in this Treasury decision. For this reason, it is found impracticable to issue this Treasury decision with notice and public procedure under subsection (b) of section 553 of Title 5 of the United States Code or subject to the effective date limitation of subsection (d) of that section.

This Treasury decision is issued under the authority contained in sections 263 and 7805 of the Internal Revenue Code of 1954 (92 Stat. 3201; 26 U.S.C. 263; 68A Stat. 917; 26 U.S.C. 7805).

JEROME KURTZ,
Commissioner of Internal Revenue.

Approved January 16, 1980.

DONALD C. LUBICK,
Assistant Secretary of the Treasury.

(Filed by the Office of the Federal Register on January 29, 1980, 8:45 a.m., and published in the issue of the Federal Register for January 30, 1980, 45 F.R. 6778)

Section 671.—Trust Income, Deductions, and Credits Attributable to Grantors and Others as Substantial Owners

26 CFR 1.671-1. Grantors and others treated as substantial owners; scope.

"Foreign tax haven double trust"; income for benefit of grantor. An example is set forth of a "foreign tax haven double trust" in which an agent in a foreign country, who is named as the "creator", created a trust in that country, naming the taxpayer as trustee. The trust received certain income-producing property from the taxpayer. The "creator" then created a second trust in the same country naming the first trust as trustee. The creation of both trusts will be considered a sham, and the substance of the transaction will control.

Rev. Rul. 80-74

ISSUE

What are the federal income tax consequences of the scheme to create trusts in a foreign country in the circumstances described below?

FACTS

The taxpayer is a U.S. citizen. In 1979, the taxpayer attended a meeting arranged by a promoter of the "foreign tax haven double trust." The promoter represented that the "double trust" would radically reduce or eliminate the United States income tax liabilities of the taxpayer. According to the promoter, the "double trust" would also provide various other benefits such as avoidance of probate, elimination of federal estate and gift tax liability, and avoidance of various state and local taxes. Also, according to the promoter, the "double trust" is a contractual arrangement known as a "pure trust" and the taxpayer has a constitutional right to create such trusts without fear of interference by federal or state authority.

Under the promoter's direction, the taxpayer agreed to the creation of a "double trust" arrangement. Pursuant to this agreement, the promoter directed an agent in a foreign country to create a trust in that country, referred to as "Trust 1," for the taxpayer. The foreign agent, referred to as the "creator," named the taxpayer as trustee and the taxpayer transferred to Trust 1 certain income-producing real estate and corporate securities, and the assets of the taxpayer's sole proprietorship. The foreign "creator" of Trust 1 then created a second trust (Trust 2) in the same foreign country, naming Trust 1 as trustee of Trust 2.

Except for the names of the trustees, Trust 1 and Trust 2 are identical. Each trust instrument provides that the original trustee may select a second trustee and that the two trustees may name a third trustee. The trusts each provided for broad powers of the trustees to deal with trust property, in their sole discretion, in any fashion that they choose. The instruments also contain the statement that a resolution by the trustees to take an action shall itself be evidence that such action is within their authority. The trustees are empowered to distribute trust property, as they see fit, to whomever they choose.

The term of each trust is stated to be 25 years, but the trustees are explicitly empowered to extend or shorten the term. Each trust instrument also contains a statement that nothing in its terms shall be construed as intended to evade or contravene any law.

The taxpayer, in accordance with the promoter's advice, distributed income received by Trust 1 to Trust 2, as soon as it was received by Trust 1. Trust 2 retains the income amounts, and, from time to time, makes distributions to the taxpayer and to other members of the taxpayer's family as directed by the taxpayer as trustee of Trust 1.

The business assets and operations transferred to Trust 1 continue to be managed by the taxpayer in essentially the same fashion as before the taxpayer entered into the "double trust" arrangement.

LAW AND ANALYSIS

Section 61 of the Internal Revenue Code provides that the term gross income means all income "from whatever source" derived, including, among other things, income from an interest in an estate or trust.

The substance, rather than the form, of a transaction in which a taxpayer is involved govern the tax consequences of the transaction. See, for example, *Commission v. Court Holding Company,* 324 U.S. 331 (1945), Ct. D. 1636, 1945 C.B. 58; *Helvering v. Clifford,* 309 U.S. 331 (1940), Ct. D. 1444, 1940-1 C.B. 105; *Gregory v. Helvering,* 293 U.S. 465, Ct. D. 911, XIV-1 C.B. 193 (1935).

Subpart E of subchapter J of the Code (sections 671-679) deals with grantor trusts. Under section 671, if the grantor is treated as the owner of a trust as a result of application of the rules in subpart E, then those items of income, deductions, and credits that are attributable to the trust are includible, in computing the grantor's taxable income, to the extent that such items would be taken into account in determining the tax liability of an individual.

Section 7701(a)(31) of the Code defines "foreign trust" to mean a trust, the income of which, from sources without the United States which is not effectively connected with the conduct of a trade or business within the United States, is not includible in gross income under subtitle A.

Under Subpart E of the Code income of a trust over which the grantor has retained substantial dominion or control is taxable to the grantor rather than to the trust which received the income or to the beneficiary to whom the income may be distributed. In the present case, the taxpayer, while purporting to, did not give up ownership and control of the assets. The use of a "creator" in the foreign country is irrelevant as the taxpayer is the grantor of both trusts for federal tax purposes. The taxpayer's transfer of property to Trust 1 is a contribution by the taxpayer as the grantor. The taxpayer is also the grantor of Trust 2, because of the taxpayer's control over Trust 1. See sections 674, 675, 676, and 677 of the Code.

HOLDINGS

The purported creation of Trust 1 and Trust 2 is a sham and the form of the transaction will be given no tax effect. Since the taxpayer effectively continues to own and control the assets, the arrangements between the trusts will be given no effect for tax purposes. See Rev. Rul. 75-257, 1975-2 C.B. 251, dealing with the income tax treatment of transfers of an individual's property and "lifetime services" to a "family estate" trust, and the case of *Wesenberg v. Commissioner,* 69 T.C. 1005 (1978), where a similar transaction was described by the court as a "flagrant tax avoidance scheme."

Moreover, Subpart E of the Code (sections 671-679) requires the taxpayer, as the grantor of the trusts, to include all items of income, deductions, or credits against tax attributable to either Trust 1 or Trust 2 in computing the taxpayer's taxable income.

See also section 679 (treating the grantor of a foreign trust as owner) and section 1491 (imposing an excise tax on transfers to foreign trusts).

No deduction is allowable under section 212 of the Code for the taxpayer's expenses with respect to the "double trusts." *See* Rev. Rul. 79-324, 1979-42 I.R.B. 12.

Section 7701.—Definitions

26 CFR 301.7701-2: Associations.
(Also Section 167; 1.167(h)-1.)

Trust treated as association; income beneficiaries' deductions. An example is provided of a business arrangement that is a trust under local law, but is classified as an association taxable as a corporation for federal tax purposes. The income beneficiaries of such an arrangement may not deduct any depreciation or amortization on any property held by the association.

Rev. Rul. 80-75

ISSUE

How will the trust arrangement described below be classified for federal tax purposes?

FACTS

A promoter established a trust that was funded by contributions from various individuals designated as income beneficiaries. Each individual contributed 100x dollars for an income interest in the trust, with the remainder interest passing to other persons designated by them. The trust agreement provides that the income of the trust is distributable to the income beneficiaries for a period of 12 years, at which time it will terminate and its remaining assets will be distributed to the remaindermen. No beneficiary has a power under local law to terminate the trust, nor will the death, insanity, bankruptcy, retirement, resignation or expulsion of any beneficiary cause the trust to be dissolved. The trustee has, in addition to other powers, the power to engage in business, and has continuing exclusive authority to make the management decisions necessary for the conduct of the trust business. The agreement further provides that the beneficiaries may not transfer, pledge or assign their beneficial interests in the trust. Under local law the beneficiaries are not personally liable for the debts of the trust.

The trustee used the contributed funds as a downpayment to purchase from the inventor a patent for exploitation by the trust in a business activity described in section 465(c) of the Internal Revenue Code. The balance of the stated purchase price for the patent was financed by giving a full-recourse note to the inventor, with the properties as security. The promoter and the trustee selected by the promoter represent that the trust qualifies as an ordinary trust under the provisions of subparts A, B, C, and D, (section 641 and following), part I, subchapter J, chapter 1 of the Code, and that the income beneficiaries are entitled to deduct, under section 167(h), any depreciation or amortization of the trust as if they were absolute owners of the properties held by the trust. The promoter further represents that the beneficiaries are not subject to the loss limiting rules of section 465 with respect to such depreciation.

LAW AND ANALYSIS

Section 7701(a)(3) of the Internal Revenue Code provides that the term "corporation" includes associations, joint-stock companies, and insurance companies.

In general, the term "trust" as used in the Internal Revenue Code refers to an arrangement created by a will or an inter vivos declaration whereby trustees take title to property for the purpose of protecting or conserving it for the beneficiaries under the ordinary rules applied in chancery or probate courts. See section 301.7701-4(a) of the Procedure and Administration Regulations.

There are other arrangements which while trusts under local law are not classified as trusts under the Internal Revenue Code because they are not arrangements to protect and conserve property for the beneficiaries. Rather, these trusts, which are often known as business or commercial trusts, are created by the beneficiaries as a device to carry on a profit-making business.

Section 301.7701-2(a)(1) of the regulations provides that an "association" is an organization whose characteristics require it to be classified for purposes of taxation as a corporation rather than as another type of organization such as a partnership or trust. An organization will be treated as an association if its corporate characteristics are such that the organization more nearly resembles a corporation than a partnership or trust. The regulations refer to six characteristics ordinarily found in a pure corporation that, taken together, distinguish it from other organizations. These are: (1) associates, (2) an objective to carry on business and divide the gains therefrom, (3) continuity of life, (4) centralization of management, (5) liability for corporate debts limited to corporate property, and (6) free transferability of interests. Section 301.7701-2(a)(3) provides that an unincorporated organization will not be classified as an association unless such organization has more corporate characteristics than noncorporate characteristics. However, in determining whether an organization has more corporate characteristics than noncorporate characteristics, all characteristics common to both types of organizations shall not be considered.

Because centralization of management, continuity of life, free transferability of interests, and limited liability are generally common to trusts and corporations, the determination of whether a trust that has such characteristics is to be treated for tax purposes as a trust or as an association depends on whether there are associates and an objective to carry on business and divide the gains therefrom. This trust arrangement has associates and an objective to carry on business and divide the gains therefrom. Thus, under the regulations, it will be classified as an association for federal tax purposes. However, it should be noted that if, under the regulations, the arrangement could have been classified as a trust, it would have been a grantor trust pursuant to Rev. Rul. 78-175, 1978-1 C.B. 144, each grantor would have been treated as engaged in the section 465 activity of the trust and therefore subject to the loss limitations of that section.

HOLDING

The arrangement is classified as an association taxable as a corporation for federal tax purposes. Therefore, the income beneficiaries may not deduct any depreciation or amortization on any property held by the association.

INDEX

The following index cites broad concepts for the most part, but includes more specific references to concepts in the Introduction and Glossaries. More precise indexing throughout the text of such terms as "accelerated depreciation," "minimum tax," etc., has not been undertaken since entries such as these are introduced in each chapter, example and discussion of benefits, risks and taxes as applicable, and are to be approached in the content of the chapter or example in which they are included.

The Economic Recovery Tax Act of 1981

To Our Clients:

On August 4, 1981, Congress passed the most comprehensive revision of the Internal Revenue Code since it was amended in 1954. This booklet will provide you with a general awareness of the new tax rules.

The purpose of the Economic Recovery Tax Act of 1981 (the Act) is to reduce the federal income tax burdens on individuals and businesses, thereby putting more dollars into the private sector in the hope that capital will be reinvested in business enterprises and the American economy revitalized. For individuals, the Act provides across-the-board income tax rate reductions phased-in over the next four years. After 1984, the individual tax schedules will be adjusted annually for inflation. Also, the maximum tax rate on all income is reduced to 50 percent, the top rate on long-term capital gains is reduced to 20 percent, and the estate and gift tax burdens are substantially reduced. For employees and self-employed persons, the Act offers substantial savings incentives. Not only have Individual Retirement Accounts (IRAs) been expanded, but provisions have also been enacted encouraging the use of Employee Stock Ownership Plans (ESOPs) and incentive stock options.

For businesses the present system of tax depreciation is eliminated and a completely new simplified system is adopted. In general, businesses will write-off their depreciable assets at a much faster rate than under prior law. Numerous provisions in the Act will aid small business. Such provisions include an increase in the used property limitation on the investment tax credit, a slight decrease in the corporate income tax rates, and liberalization of the rules governing the election of the LIFO method of inventory valuation.

In addition, specific incentives will aid financial institutions and high technology industries. For the former, interest received on certain savings certificates will be tax-exempt thereby encouraging deposits. For the latter, a special tax credit will encourage research and experimentation.

The vast scope of the changes to the tax law incorporated in the Act will undoubtedly result in a rethinking of traditional tax planning ideas. However, because of the Act's complexity and its large number of provisions, we only summarize the major provisions of the Act in this booklet and make some tax planning suggestions. Accordingly, we urge you to contact us if you have any questions concerning the impact of the Act on you or your business.

Peat, Marwick, Mitchell & Co.
August 5, 1981

2402000124

Contents

I. Provisions Affecting Individuals

The Act provides tax relief to all individuals to offset the increased tax burden resulting from inflation by granting across-the-board rate cuts, a one-step reduction in the maximum individual tax rate from 70 to 50 percent, some relief from the so-called "marriage penalty" and eventually the indexation of taxes for inflation. These and other provisions are highlighted below.

Individual Tax Rate Changes

Prior to the Act, tax rates for individuals ranged from 14 to 70 percent with the maximum rate on earned income being 50 percent. Although the Act's rate cuts have been widely publicized as "5-10-10" — 5 percent in 1981, 10 percent in 1982, and an additional 10 percent in 1983 — the *actual* rate reductions from 1980 rates will be 1.25 percent for 1981, 10 percent for 1982, 19 percent for 1983, and 23 percent for 1984.

Reduction in Top Tax Rate

The top individual tax rate will be reduced from 70 to 50 percent as of January 1, 1982. However, since the present maximum tax on personal service income is 50 percent and the Act did not change this rate, individuals whose income consists primarily of salary or professional fees will benefit less under the Act than individuals with significant amounts of interest and dividend income.

The table set forth below illustrates the projected annual tax savings for a taxpayer with all personal service income who files a joint return for the years 1981 through 1984, as compared with 1980.

Projected Annual Tax Savings
Personal Service Taxable Income (Joint Return)

Year	$20,000	$60,000	$100,000	$200,000
1981	$ 40	$ 246	$ 496	$ 1,121
1982	332	1,973	2,229	2,229
1983	619	3,664	5,488	5,676
1984	764	4,510	7,278	8,278

Impact on Capital Gains

The Act will reduce the top tax rate on long-term capital gains for individuals from 28 to 20 percent. (The Act does not change either the one-year holding period requirement for long-term capital gain or loss treatment or the corporate capital gains rate.) So that investors will not be discouraged from realizing gains in 1981, the Act contains a special rule under which the 20 percent top tax rate applies to capital gains on sales or exchanges occurring after June 9, 1981. However, the special rule does not apply to proceeds received during 1981 relating to sales or exchanges that occurred before June 10, 1981.

Tax Planning Considerations

The reduction of the tax rates suggests several tax planning opportunities.

Defer Recognition of Income Until 1982

Since the major impact of the tax rate reductions is not effective until 1982, cash basis taxpayers should consider deferring the receipt of income until 1982. Also, many individuals have invested in tax shelters which, if disposed of, would generate substantial income taxable at ordinary income rates. They should consider deferring disposition of these investments until 1982.

It is not necessary for investors to wait until 1982 to sell capital assets since the Act contains a special provision that will apply the 20 percent top capital gains tax rate on sales or exchanges occurring after June 9, 1981. Alternatively, they should consider deferring a portion of the gain on the sale of their property until 1982, or later, by selling on the installment basis.

Accelerate Deductions to 1981

Taxpayers in current tax brackets in excess of 50 percent should consider taking deductions in 1981 since these deductions may be worth more in 1981 than in subsequent years. Some of the opportunities to accelerate deductions include the following.

- State income taxes that will be due in 1982 may be prepaid in 1981 in order to generate a deduction.
- The purchase of a boat, airplane, mobile home, car, or truck may be accelerated to 1981 in order to use the sales tax deduction in 1981.
- Charitable contributions may be made in 1981.
- Taxpayers should consider investing in tax shelters that will generate tax losses in 1981 and will not generate income until later years. Caution: a tax-oriented investment must not be made solely on the basis of the purported tax write-off. The investment should make sound economic sense without regard to the tax benefits.

Adjustment to Alternative Minimum Tax

The Act conforms the alternative minimum tax to the maximum capital gains tax by reducing the top alternative minimum tax rate from 25 to 20 percent effective for taxable years beginning after 1981. A special rule is provided for 1981 to ensure that capital gain on sales or exchanges after June 9, 1981 will not be subject to an alternative minimum tax rate greater than 20 percent.

Indexation

To mitigate any future increase in tax burden caused by continuing inflation, the Act contains a provision to adjust individual income taxes for inflation after 1984.

"Marriage Penalty" Relief

Under prior law, a higher income tax was imposed on the income of a two-earner married couple than would have been imposed if each spouse were taxed as a single person. Generally, the so-called "marriage penalty" increased as a couple's income rose and also as the difference between the amounts earned by each spouse narrowed.

To reduce (but not completely eliminate) the discrimination against two-earner married couples, the Act permits these couples to deduct on their joint returns 10 percent of the first $30,000 of earnings of the lower earning spouse. This deduction will be phased in over two years. A 5 percent deduction, or a maximum of $1,500, will be allowed for taxable years beginning in 1982 and the full 10 percent, or a maximum of $3,000, for subsequent taxable years. An important feature of the provision is that the deduction will be available regardless of whether a couple itemizes their deductions.

Deductions for Charitable Contributions

The Act allows taxpayers who do not itemize their deductions to deduct a portion of their charitable contributions in computing their taxable income. For 1982 and 1983 the maximum amount of the deduction is limited to $25 (for a $100 contribution).

Sale of a Principal Residence

The Act modifies and liberalizes prior law for sales of a principal residence after July 20, 1981, and for certain earlier sales, by providing the following.

- The exclusion from income for taxpayers age 55 or older is increased from $100,000 to $125,000.
- The period for replacing a principal residence to qualify for deferral of tax on the gain from the sale of the former residence is increased from 18 months to two years.

Child Care Credit

For 1982 and subsequent years, the Act increases the amount of the child care credit and converts it to a sliding scale percentage credit. The following table illustrates the maximum allowable child care credit under the Act.

Maximum Amount of Child Care Credit

Adjusted Gross Income	One Dependent	Two or More Dependents
$10,000	$720	$1,440
20,000	600	1,200
30,000 or more	480	960

Adoption Expense Deduction

For 1981 and subsequent years, the Act provides a maximum $1,500 deduction for certain expenses incurred in connection with the adoption of handicapped children or children who are members of a minority.

State Legislators' Expenses

The Act generally permits a state legislator to deduct a certain amount of living expenses while the state legislature is in session. The provision generally applies to taxable years beginning after 1975.

Tax Shelter Provisions

Tax Straddles

An increasingly popular tax oriented investment employed in recent years involves investment in balanced positions (commonly referred to as tax straddles) in various commodity and financial futures instruments. These investments are structured to generate ordinary loss in the current year, while deferring the gain side of the transaction until later years. In certain circumstances it is also possible to convert ordinary income or short-term capital gain to long-term capital gain. Because of the leveraged nature of these investments, a relatively small investment can generate a large tax loss. The Act's provisions, however, go far beyond any tax shelter problem and affect dealers and traders who would not normally be thought of as passive tax shelter investors.

To clarify the tax rules in this area, the Act provides the following.

- In general, losses from straddle transactions are deferred to the extent the taxpayer has unrealized gains in offsetting straddle positions. Any straddle losses disallowed in the current year are carried forward and allowed in the first subsequent year in which there is no unrealized appreciation in an offsetting position acquired before the disposition of the loss position.

  A tax straddle composed entirely of futures contracts is not subject to this loss deferral rule; instead, such straddles are subject to the mark-to-market system discussed below. Also, a special rule applies to certain "identified straddles" under which a loss is recognized no earlier than the day on which the taxpayer disposes of all the positions which comprise the straddle.

  Property subject to these limitations includes any personal property or interest in personal property, such as a futures contract, a forward contract, or an option which is actively traded. The limitations do not apply, however, to corporate stock, short-term stock options, and real estate.

- All regulated futures contracts must be marked-to-market at the end of each year which means that unrealized gains and losses are taxed as if 60 percent were long-term and 40 percent were short-term. Any net losses can be carried back for three years and offset mark-to-market gains; however, losses may be carried back to taxable years no earlier than taxable years ending in 1981.

Special transitional rules are provided to allow a five-year spread for 1981 gains.

- Interest and other carrying charges, such as storage, insurance, and transportation costs, incurred to purchase or carry an interest in a tax straddle must be capitalized and added to the basis of the property which is part of the straddle. Thus, these costs are reflected in the gain or loss upon the disposition of the property.

- Hedging transactions conducted in the normal course of a trade or business are exempt from these provisions.

- Treasury bills are treated as capital assets. However, acquisition discount on Treasury bills continues to be taxed as ordinary income.

- A dealer in securities must identify a security as one held for investment on the day of acquisition. In the absence of specific identification, the security will be treated as held by the dealer in his trade or business. Floor specialists are allowed seven business days to make the necessary identification. A special transition rule is provided for the remainder of 1981.

- Gain or loss from the cancellation, lapse, or termination of a right or obligation with respect to personal property (other than stock) that is, or would be, a capital asset in the hands of the taxpayer will be treated as gains or losses from the sale or exchange of a capital asset. The Act makes clear that the cancellation of forward contracts in commodity and financial instruments will generate capital gain or loss. This provision is clearly aimed at recently promoted investment devices that sought to generate ordinary loss by the cancellation, as opposed to the sale or exchange, of forward contracts.

These provisions are generally effective for property acquired and positions established after June 23, 1981. The new rules do not apply to tax straddles established before this date.

Construction Period Interest and Tax Limitation

The Tax Reform Act of 1976 limited the immediate deduction of interest and taxes paid or accrued during the construction of a building. The Act excludes low-income housing from this limitation.

Low-Income Housing Rehabilitation Expenses

The Act raises the amount of low-income housing rehabilitation expenditures paid or incurred after 1980 which are eligible for 60-month amortization from $20,000 to $40,000 per unit in certain situations provided the units are for sale to tenants.

Savings Incentives for Individuals

In addition to general individual tax relief, the Act contains specific provisions to encourage individual savings.

All-Savers Certificate

The "All-Savers Certificate" permits an individual to exclude up to $1,000 of interest income ($2,000 in the case of individuals filing a joint tax return) from one-year certificates issued by qualifying financial institutions after September 30, 1981, and before January 1, 1983. While the certificate issuance period is only 15 months, the interest exclusion is effectively available to taxpayers for over two years. This is due to the fact that interest earned on a certificate issued on December 31, 1982, will not be taxable until December 1983.

The interest rates on the certificates must equal a rate at the date of issue that will permit the yield to equal 70 percent of the yield on 52 week Treasury bills. Thus, if the most recent issue of 52-week Treasury bills were discounted to yield 15 percent, the yield on a qualifying certificate would be 10.5 percent. Once established, the yield on the certificate will remain unchanged during its entire one-year term. To discourage the early withdrawal from a certificate, the Act provides that all the interest earned on a prematurely withdrawn certificate will be fully taxable.

The following points should be considered before investing in All-Savers Certificates.

- An individual should consider investing in a certificate only if the individual's marginal tax rate is more than 30 percent. Otherwise, the yield on these certificates would not compare favorably to the after-tax yield on other fully taxable money market instruments.

- The amount of the investment must be carefully considered to ensure that the earnings on these certificates do not exceed the maximum interest exclusions mentioned above since any such interest would not be exempt from tax.

In light of this new provision, the Act repeals beginning in 1982, the exclusion from income of up to $200 ($400 in the case of a joint return) of dividends and interest. For taxable years beginning after December 31, 1981, $100 of qualifying dividend income per individual may be excluded from income.

Exclusion for Certain Interest Income

For taxable years beginning after December 31, 1984, an individual who itemizes deductions can exclude up to 15 percent of $3,000 ($6,000 in the case of a joint return) of interest income or net interest income, whichever is less. Thus, the maximum exclusion will be $450 ($900 on a joint return). The amount subject to the exclusion is reduced by any forfeiture penalties incurred upon the early withdrawal of a certificate of deposit from a financial institution.

Certain interest income, such as interest on indebtedness issued by an individual, interest on indebtedness issued by a partnership, estate, or certain trusts, and interest on indebtedness issued by most corporations, is excluded from this provision. Also, to determine net interest income, all interest expense, other than interest on property used as a dwelling unit by the taxpayer (including a vacation home) and interest on trade or business indebtedness, is subtracted from the interest income. Thus, interest expense on margin accounts, automobile loans, personal loans, insurance loans, etc., is netted against interest income in determining the proper interest exclusion.

Special Interest Disallowance Rule

The tax law has long contained provisions that disallow a deduction for interest expense on indebtedness incurred to purchase or carry obligations earning tax-exempt interest income. The Act expands this interest expense disallowance provision further to apply to any indebtedness incurred to purchase or hold a tax-exempt "All-Savers Certificate" or an investment earning interest subject to the interest exclusion rule that will be effective in 1985. Thus, care must be exercised to ensure that this interest disallowance provision does not cause some of the individual's interest expense to be nondeductible upon investment of funds in these newly created savings incentives.

Dividend Reinvestment Plan of Public Utilities

Present law provides that shareholders electing to receive stock in lieu of cash dividends must report the value of the stock dividends as taxable income. However, the Act provides that with respect to stock dividends after December 31, 1981, and before January 1, 1986, a shareholder of a qualified public utility may elect to exclude from income up to $750 ($1,500 in the case of a joint return). The value of the stock in excess of the excluded amount will be treated as taxable income. Individuals, other than nonresident aliens, are eligible for the exclusion. However, individuals owning more than 5 percent of the voting power or value of the stock in the utility are not eligible.

The Act sets forth rules defining a "qualified public utility" and the type and amount of stock that may be issued. There are also special rules to prevent the immediate sale of the stock without the recognition of income. Under these rules, if this stock, or stock owned on the dividend record date, is sold within one year after the dividend distribution date, any gain will be treated as ordinary income.

Retirement Savings Provisions

New Dollar Limitations

In an attempt to encourage and to provide incentives for retirement savings, the Act expands and, in many instances, greatly liberalizes the rules relating to individual retirement accounts (IRAs) generally effective for taxable years beginning after December 31, 1981.

The $1,500 maximum annual deductible contribution limit has been increased to $2,000. The manner in which the contribution is computed has also been liberalized. The Act permits a deductible contribution without any percentage limitation. Thus, earnings of only $2,000 will permit the maximum contribution.

Deduction of Voluntary Employee Contributions
Perhaps the most far-reaching of the individual retirement plan changes is the one that permits a deductible contribution by a person already covered by a qualified employer or government plan. If the employer permits, the deductible employee contribution may be made directly to the employer's plan, including simplified employee pension plans. Individuals will also be entitled to establish their own IRA.

Taxation of Employee Contributions Upon Distribution
No change is made in the taxation of distributions from IRAs. Distributions of deductible employee contributions to employer plans, including increments from qualified employer or government plans are fully taxable as ordinary income. Unlike lump-sum distributions from qualified plans, they do not qualify for favorable income tax treatment. However, favorable gift and estate tax treatment is available. Tax-free rollovers of deductible employee contributions will be allowed under rules similar to those allowing rollovers from IRAs. Deductible employee contributions retain their character after a rollover.

The Act does not permit the distribution of deductible employee contributions from a qualified plan before age 59½ unless made on account of death or disability. The penalty for a premature distribution is a 10 percent nondeductible tax. In contrast to IRA rules which require distributions commencing no later than the year in which the individual attains age 70½, deductible employee contributions made to a qualified employer or government plan may be retained subsequent to such date. If, however, such amounts are rolled over to an IRA, the normal rules pertaining to the timing and distribution of such amounts would apply.

Contributions by Nonworking Former Spouse
The Act provides relief for a nonworking divorced individual whose former spouse had contributed to a spousal IRA during three of the five preceding taxable years (prior to the divorce). Where such requirements are met, the individual will be allowed to contribute and deduct annually up to $1,125 to an IRA even if he or she remarries. This measure is intended to afford nonworking divorced individuals the same opportunities to continue an IRA as other workers.

Spousal IRAs
The Act retains the benefit of permitting an additional contribution to an IRA where an individual and a nonworking spouse file a joint return. Consistent

with the overall increase in IRA limits, the Act increases the annual maximum limit to $2,250 from $1,750. Unlike prior law which required equal amounts contributed to each spouse's account, the Act requires only the additional contribution to be contributed to the non working spouse's IRA. The working spouse, however, may contribute further amounts up to the maximum to the nonworking spouse's IRA.

Retirement Plans for Self-Employed Individuals

Increased Contribution Limits

In an attempt to make self-employed retirement plans ("H.R. 10" or "Keogh") more attractive, the Act increases the maximum deductible amount from $7,500 to $15,000 for defined contribution plans with comparable amendments for defined benefit Keogh plans. Conforming amendments are made for Subchapter S corporations and simplified employee pensions (SEPs). The 15 percent limitation upon which contributions are based is unchanged. Since the primary impetus for the recent surge in incorporation of partnerships (especially professional service partnerships) has been to take advantage of larger retirement plan deductions, it is anticipated that the increase to $15,000 will result in fewer incorporations.

In determining the amount of compensation to which the 15 percent limitation is applied, the Act increases the dollar amount upon which contributions are based from $100,000 to $200,000 (for Keogh plans, Subchapter S plans, and SEPs). However, if contributions are based on compensation in excess of $100,000, then the rate of employer contributions for any plan participant cannot be less than 7½ percent of that participant's compensation (before taking into account integration of the plan with Social Security).

Example

For purposes of the XYZ Keogh Plan, X, a self-employed individual, earns $150,000 and A, his employee, earns $20,000. Both are participants in the plan. If the plan contribution on behalf of X takes into account his compensation in excess of $100,000, the contribution on behalf of A must be at least $1,500 (7.5% x $20,000).

Loans to Partners

The Act extends to all partners (formerly applicable only to greater than 10 percent partners) the rule that a loan from, or the use of an interest in a Keogh plan as security for a loan, will be treated as a distribution. Accordingly, loans to all partners under age 59½, except disabled partners, result in the imposition of a 10 percent penalty tax in addition to the income tax on the distribution.

The provisions relating to Keogh plans are generally effective for taxable years beginning after December 31, 1981. However, a loan outstanding on December 31, 1981, to a partner who is not an owner-employee will not be treated as one subject to the penalty provisions unless renegotiated, extended, renewed, or revised after that date.

Removal of Ban on Contributions Upon Plan Termination

Generally, a Keogh plan benefitting at least one greater than 10 percent owner is required, as a condition of qualification, to provide for the discontinuance of contributions on behalf of such individuals for a period of five years after the individual receives a distribution from the plan prior to attaining age 59½. The Act makes an exception to this rule for taxable years beginning after December 31, 1980, where the premature distribution is made on account of the plan's termination.

Return of Excess Contributions

To discourage the accumulation of tax-free income caused by contributions to Keogh plans in excess of deductible limitations, previous legislation imposed a nondeductible 6 percent penalty tax on the excess. Although the law permits the correction of excess contributions for subsequent years, no relief was provided for the taxable year for which the excess contribution was made. For years beginning after December 31, 1981, if the excess and any income attributable to it is returned by the filing date of the individual's tax return, the Act provides that no penalty tax will be imposed.

Incentive Stock Options

The Act creates a "new" type of stock option known as an "Incentive Stock Option" under which favorable tax treatment will be afforded to the option holder if certain conditions are met.

Under current law, employer stock options are not entitled to preferential treatment. Individuals who receive their options in consideration for services recognize ordinary income, at the date of exercise, equal to the difference between the option price and the then fair market value of the stock. The employer is allowed a deduction for compensation at the same time and in the same amount as the income recognized by the employee.

In most cases, the option holder would need cash to both exercise the option and pay the income tax liability due because of the exercise. In many cases, individuals affected by SEC rules would be prohibited by law from disposing of the stock currently to meet the costs of exercise. Further, if the stock value were to decrease by the time the stock could be sold without penalty, the employee would have a capital loss equal to the decline in value between exercise date and date of sale.

Provisions of the Act

The Act incorporates some of the features of the restricted stock option plan popular before 1964 and the qualified stock option plan, which was phased out between 1976 and May 21, 1981.

Options granted according to an incentive stock option plan provide for no tax consequences at either the date of grant or date of exercise. The employee receives favorable long-term capital gain treatment upon sale if the following requirements are met.

- The stock is not disposed of within two years after the option is granted and one year after the date of exercise.
- The option holder is employed by the company granting the option (or an affiliate) continuously from the time of grant until three months before exercise (12 months if disabled).

If the holding period requirements are not satisfied, the employee will recognize, at the time of sale, ordinary income equal to either (1) the gain realized upon sale or (2) the difference between the option price and the fair market value of the stock on the date of exercise, whichever is less. Any additional gain would be long-term or short-term capital gain, depending on how long the stock was held. If the employment requirements are not met, ordinary income will be recognized at the time of exercise. Deductions are not allowed to the employer, unless the employee recognizes ordinary income.

Terms of the Option

The option must meet various requirements to be classified as an incentive stock option.

- Shareholder approval must be obtained within 12 months of adoption of a plan that specifies the number of shares to be issued and the employees or classes of employees eligible to receive options.
- The option must be granted within 10 years after the adoption of the plan (or the date approved by the shareholders, if earlier).
- The option must be exercised within 10 years of the date of the grant, but if it is granted to a more than 10 percent employee-shareholder, then the exercise period is reduced to five years.
- The option cannot be transferred except by death and can only be exercised (during the employee's lifetime) by the employee. If the option is transferred by death, the holding period requirements do not apply to the beneficiary.
- A good-faith effort must be made to determine that the option price is at least equal to the fair market value of the stock on the date of the grant. In the case of a more than 10 percent employee-stockholder, the option price must be at least 110 percent of the fair market value of the stock on the date of the grant.
- The option cannot be exercised while any previously granted incentive stock option is outstanding. An option will be considered outstanding for this

purpose until it is exercised or lapses, even if it has been cancelled.

- Only options to purchase up to $100,000 of stock may be granted under the plan in any calendar year after 1980. To the extent not granted, one-half of the unused limitation amount may be carried over for three years.

Other Significant Provisions
The Act includes several other significant provisions.

- The spread between the option price and the fair market value of the stock is not considered an item of tax preference for minimum tax purposes.

- Payment with previously acquired employer stock is allowed.

- An employer may make an additional payment in cash or property at the time of exercise.

Effective Date
Generally, the new rules apply to options granted after 1975 and exercised after 1980 or outstanding at that time. However, for options granted before 1981, a corporation may elect to have the option treated as an incentive stock option. These options, however, are limited to annual grants of $50,000 per employee and a $200,000 maximum. Presumably, this provision allows the corporation to benefit from the tax deduction that otherwise would have been lost.

From the date of enactment, the corporation has one year to modify existing plans to conform to the incentive stock option rules for options granted after 1975.

Observations
The incentive stock option will have a significant effect on compensation planning for all companies, and these rules may be applicable to options already exercised in 1981. Incentive stock option plans will probably become the cornerstone of executive compensation plans involving capital accumulation.

It is possible to take advantage of these rules for some existing options and corporations should immediately review their plans to determine if it is desirable to amend the plans to conform to the new rules.

Since the rules require incentive stock options to be exercised chronologically, a corporation may elect to treat some previously granted options as being other than incentive stock options, thus removing them from the exercise order.

Fringe Benefit Moratorium

The Act extends, until December 31, 1983, the temporary freeze on the issuance of rules or regulations that would change the tax treatment of certain fringe benefits. Unlike the freeze enacted in the 1978 legislation, however, the new freeze order does not prohibit the issuance of regulations regarding commuting expenses.

II. Provisions Affecting Expatriates

Foreign Earned Income Exclusion

Because the present tax provisions governing Americans working overseas were heavily criticized for their complexity and adverse impact on the employment of Americans abroad and the promotion of U.S. exports, Congress significantly simplified the foreign earned income provisions. The Act repeals the array of special deductions available to expatriates since 1978 for cost of living, schooling, home leave travel, and hardship area employment.

For taxable years beginning after 1981, the Act contains the following significant provisions.

- Individuals whose tax home is in a foreign country and who are either (1) U.S. citizens establishing bona fide residence in a foreign country or (2) U.S. citizens or residents present outside the United States for a period of 330 days in a consecutive 12-month period, may now elect to exclude earned income attributable to services performed overseas from their gross income. The maximum annual exclusion for 1982 is set at $75,000, pro-rated daily and increasing $5,000 per year until 1986, when the maximum exclusion will be $95,000.

- Non-excluded income is to be taxed as if it were the first income earned, that is, at the lower marginal rate brackets. The exclusion of earned income can thus serve to reduce the rate of tax on nonexcludable investment income.

- Qualifying expatriates may also separately elect an exclusion for reasonable housing costs (excluding otherwise deductible interest and taxes) attributable to employer-provided amounts in excess of 16 percent of the salary paid to a U.S. government employee at the GS-14, Step 1 level. This exclusion is in addition to the maximum foreign earned income exclusion. Special rules apply where adverse conditions prevent an individual's family from residing with the individual and where excess housing costs are not attributable to employer-provided amounts.

- Credits for foreign taxes and deductions allocable to excluded income, including those for moving expenses, are not allowed.

- Both the exclusion of foreign earned income and the exclusion based on excess housing costs are elective. These elections apply until revoked, although a revocation precludes a new election for five years after the year of revocation, except with the consent of the Secretary of the Treasury.

Meals or Lodging

Under the Act, lodging or meals furnished in a camp located in a foreign country continue to be considered furnished on the business premises of the employer and are thus excludable from gross income. However, unlike prior law, this provision applies for taxable years beginning after 1981 regardless of whether an individual elects to exclude foreign earned income.

III. Provisions Affecting Estate and Gift Taxation

The changes in the Act that could have the most drastic effect on tax planning are those made by provisions involving estate and gift taxes. These amendments fall into three broad categories:

- Increase in unified credit;
- Reduction in top-bracket rates; and
- Unlimited marital deduction.

In addition, other estate tax provisions favorably modify rules involved with special-use valuation for farms and other closely held businesses and change the rules for transfers made in contemplation of death. The most significant change in gift taxes is the increase in the annual gift tax exclusion from $3,000 to $10,000. Other miscellaneous provisions are also made to the estate and gift tax rules.

Increase in Unified Credit

The gift tax is generally computed by applying the rate schedule to cumulative taxable transfers made during the donor's lifetime and subtracting any gift taxes payable on previous gifts. The tax is then further reduced by a unified credit to the extent still available. The estate tax is an extension of the gift tax and is computed similarly.

Under prior law, the unified credit was $47,000 for transfers made after 1980. Thus, there was no estate or gift tax liability on taxable transfers up to $175,625. The Act increases the credit from $47,000 to $192,800, phased in over a six-year period and based on the following schedule:

Transfers Made and Decedents Dying in	Unified Credit	Amount of Transfers Not Taxed	Lowest Tax Bracket Rate
1982	$ 62,800	$225,000	32%
1983	79,300	275,000	34
1984	96,300	325,000	34
1985	121,800	400,000	34
1986	155,800	500,000	37
1987 and later	192,800	600,000	37

As illustrated in the table, gift and estate tax transfers up to $600,000 will be free of tax starting in 1987. The filing requirements were amended to conform to the increase in the credit. It is estimated that after the increase in the credit becomes fully implemented, only a small percentage of all estates will be taxable.

Reduction in Top-Bracket Rates

The Act phases in a reduction of the top brackets from the current rate of 70 percent down to a maximum rate of 50 percent over a four-year period based on the following schedule:

Transfers Made and Decedents Dying in	Top-Bracket Rate	Top-Bracket Amount in Excess of
1982	65%	$4,000,000
1983	60	3,500,000
1984	55	3,000,000
1985 and later	50	2,500,000

Thus when fully implemented, transfers will be taxable at progressive marginal rates ranging between 37 percent and 50 percent.

Unlimited Marital Deduction and Related Issues

The principal purpose behind the original marital deduction legislation was to allow one spouse to transfer one half of his or her estate to the other spouse without incurring a gift or estate tax liability. This would place individuals living in separate property states in a similar position to those residing in community property states.

Changes in Marital Deductions

The Act eliminates all of the quantitative limitations on the gift and estate tax marital deductions. All qualifying transfers between spouses (including community property) will be allowed to pass free of gift and estate taxes. The primary purpose behind the change appears to be Congress' feeling that a husband and wife represent one economic unit for estate and gift taxes as they do for income taxes.

Interplay Between Marital Deduction and Step-up in Basis

The basis of property acquired from the decedent is equal to the amount at which it was included in the decedent's gross estate. This is generally the fair market value at date of death or the alternate valuation date if elected. Thus in the case of appreciated property, the beneficiary will receive a "step-up" in basis and the appreciation will generally escape income taxes. This provision will be applicable to property eligible for the unlimited marital deduction.

The Act curbs a potential abuse whereby a donor could transfer low basis property to a decedent just before death, in the hope of reacquiring it with a step-up in basis, and avoiding income taxes on the appreciation. With an unlimited marital deduction, the step-up could be tax free in the case of a deathbed transfer to a spouse.

Therefore, the Act provides a special carryover basis rule for appreciated property received by the decedent by way of gift within one year of the decedent's death, where the property passes back to the original donor or donor's spouse. This provision, however, also covers gifts outside the interspousal situation. The new provision will apply to property acquired by the decedent after December 31, 1981.

Terminable Interest Rule

Under prior law, so-called "terminable interests" did not qualify for the marital deduction. For example, the gift of an income interest to a spouse with the remainder interest to a third party would not qualify for the marital deduction.

If certain conditions are met, the Act will allow life estates transferred to the spouse to qualify for the unlimited marital deduction. Generally, at the election of the executor (or donor) where a spouse receives certain life estates, the entire property will be deemed to pass to the spouse without tax. However, the spouse or spouse's estate will be subject to transfer taxes at either the time of disposal or upon death, whichever is earlier.

The decedent (donor) may maintain greater control of the disposition of the property without tax consequences. However, this control will eliminate the flexibility of the spouse to minimize his or her estate tax.

Planning

While interspousal gifts will generally not cause estate or gift taxation, planning and maintenance of records is still important because, at a minimum, the step-up in basis rules will apply notwithstanding the size of the estate.

Joint Interests Between Spouses

The tax treatment of jointly held property between spouses becomes important only (1) in determining the basis of the property in the hands of the survivor and (2) in determining if certain other provisions apply such as deferred payments of estate taxes and redemptions to pay estate taxes. It is no longer important in determining how much is to be included in the gross estate.

The Act provides that each spouse is to be treated as one-half owner of jointly held property regardless of which spouse paid for the property. Thus upon the death of the decedent, only one half would be included in the gross estate; the other one half would not. Accordingly, only one half of such property will receive a step-up in basis under the rules providing for amounts received from the decedent. This change eliminates the often complex determinations of the taxability of jointly owned property.

Gift Tax Filing Requirements

The unlimited marital deduction has the effect of eliminating the need for the filing of gift tax returns for all qualifying interspousal transfers.

Effective Date

The unlimited marital deduction provisions apply generally to gifts made and decedents dying after 1981. There is, however, a transitional rule to protect those individuals who may have used a so-called "formula" marital deduction provision in previously executed wills and trusts.

Under such clauses the amount passing to the surviving spouse is determined by the amount of the maximum marital deduction. Applying the formula to the new provisions may cause more property to pass to the surviving spouse than was anticipated when the document was executed. Accordingly, the new unlimited marital deduction will not apply to transfers under wills executed or trusts created up to 30 days after enactment where the document contains a maximum marital deduction formula clause. However, if the new provisions are desired, the testator or grantor will have to amend the document to refer specifically to the unlimited marital deduction. If, however, state law is amended to construe the formula clause as referring to the increased amount, no amendment to the documents would be necessary. On the other hand, if such a state law is passed and the testator wants the prior rules to apply, it appears an amendment to the will would be required.

Transfers Made in Contemplation of Death

Under prior law, where gifts are made within three years of a decedent's death, the value of the property is included in the gross estate as if it had never been gifted. The estate, however, receives a credit against the tax for any gift tax paid. The effect of this rule is to include in the gross estate only the appreciation in the property between the date of gift and the date of death. A narrow exception to this rule applies (except for gifts of life insurance) where no gift tax return was required to be filed.

The Act eliminates the gift-in-contemplation-of-death rules on most transfers by decedents dying after 1981. Accordingly, gifts made within three years of death will be excluded from the decedent's gross estate. The recipient, however, will be denied a step-up in basis. The prior gift-in-contemplation-of-death rules still apply for transfers of life insurance and other interests that would have been included in the gross estate under other rules had the decedent kept the interest transferred.

Further, these rules continue to apply for the purpose of determining whether the estate qualifies for certain special relief provisions (for example, favorable redemption, valuation, and deferral of payment rules). They also apply in certain other limited circumstances involving the unlimited marital deduction.

This provision is effective for decedents dying after 1981 and may have some effect on prior transfers.

Current Use Valuation of Certain Property

For estate tax purposes, real property must ordinarily be valued at its highest and best use. If certain requirements were met, however, pre-Act provisions allowed certain family farms and other real estate used in closely held businesses to be valued at current use rather than highest and best use. The pre-Act provisions limited the discount to $500,000. There were many other provisions designed to help keep the property in the family. One of the provisions was a recapture of the tax benefit if such property was either disposed of to nonfamily members or ceased to be held for the qualified use within 15 years.

The Act makes numerous technical changes in the current use valuation provisions altering most of the major requirements of the law. Some of the significant items include:

- Phase-in of discount limitation from $500,000 to $750,000 over a three-year period ($600,000 in 1981, $700,000 in 1982, $750,000 thereafter);
- Liberalization of active management requirement; and
- Reduction in recapture period from 15 to 10 years.

Except as noted above, the effective date is generally for decedents dying after 1981. Certain other clarifying provisions are given retroactive treatment for decedents dying after 1976.

Gift Taxes

Increase in Annual Exclusion

Donors are allowed to transfer a specific amount to each donee per year without incurring a gift tax liability. In addition, where gifts are made by a spouse to a third party, such gifts may be treated (with the consent of the other spouse) as being made one half by each. Thus, where a married couple agrees, the annual exclusion is doubled. The amount of exclusion has been $3,000 since 1942 and was intended to reduce the administrative burden for record keeping of small gifts. Because of the increase in price levels since 1942, Congress felt it was necessary to increase the annual exclusion to $10,000.

The increase applies generally to gifts after 1981. However, because many trust documents may have been drafted with a reference to the maximum amount of exclusion allowed by law, Congress provides a transitional rule to protect the grantors of such trusts. Accordingly, rules similar to those discussed under the marital deduction section are provided such trusts.

Annual gift giving is a technique used for both income and estate tax planning purposes. The significant change in the exclusion increases the tax planning opportunities in many situations.

Transfers for Educational and Medical Expenses

Under prior law, certain payments for educational or medical expenses, for which the donor did not have a legal obligation to provide, could be classified as gifts subject to tax. Most of these cases involved payments of tuition for children who were no longer minors or medical payments for elderly relatives.

The new law provides an unlimited annual exclusion for qualifying payments made directly to the institution or person furnishing the educational or medical service. It is important to recognize that although there is no requirement that the person receiving the benefit be related to the donor, the payments must not be reimbursements to the donee, but rather payments made directly to the service provider.

Other Estate and Gift Tax Provisions

In addition to the provisions described above, generally for years after 1981, the Act:

- Simplifies and liberalizes rules for extension of time to pay estate taxes attributable to closely held businesses;
- Allows an estate and gift tax charitable deduction for donations of works of art that are subject to copyright even though the copyright is not transferred;
- Allows for valid disclaimers even if not recognized under local law;
- Repeals the provision allowing testamentary tax-free transfers to certain minor children;
- Extends the transitional rule one year for generation-skipping transfers to include persons dying before 1983 where the trust or will was not amended; and
- Starting with 1982 transfers, gift tax returns are to be filed and taxes paid annually — generally on April 15 following the calendar year in which the gift was made.

General Observations

The changes made by the Act will effectively eliminate estate and gift taxes for the vast majority of individuals. Although this may reduce the need for estate tax planning, there is an increased need for other planning for the orderly transfer of property between family members. In addition, there may be a tendency to take advantage of the full marital deduction to avoid estate and gift taxes. This may increase the estate tax of the surviving spouse. This increase in tax may be minimized or eliminated through proper estate planning for the family unit.

With the changes made by the Act, all wills and trusts should be reviewed along with the long-term liquidity needs of the estate.

IV. Provisions Affecting Businesses

Accelerated Cost Recovery System (Depreciation)

The Act responds to concerns that the economy is faltering because of reduced capital investment by business. By offering a more rapid capital cost recovery system - the "accelerated cost recovery system" (ACRS) - there are greater incentives for increased capital investments. It is expected that these outlays will result in a higher national productivity and a lower inflation rate. ACRS also attempts to simplify prior law by greatly reducing controversies between taxpayers and the Internal Revenue Service over depreciation matters.

Instead of depreciation deductions, businesses are entitled to "recovery deductions" under ACRS as the means of recouping their capital outlays made after 1980. The concept of ACRS eliminates the need to determine each asset's useful life. Also unnecessary is the selection of a depreciation method and a salvage value or the election to use the Class Life Asset Depreciation Range System (commonly known as ADR). In a move toward simplification, ACRS provides a five class system of cost recovery. The taxpayer determines the recovery deduction for an asset by applying a statutory percentage to the unadjusted basis of the property. The appropriate percentage is dependent on the property's class. Generally, equipment falls into a 3-year or a 5-year class, and buildings fall into a 15-year class. A 10-year and a 15-year class are reserved for certain limited equipment and buildings. Since more rapid recovery deductions apply to low income rental housing, the Act essentially treats such property as a separate class. Public utility property does not qualify for ACRS if normalization of the tax benefits is not used by the taxpayer for ratemaking purposes.

Three-year property includes automobiles, light duty trucks, machinery and equipment used for research and development, and other short-lived tangible personal property. Five-year property generally includes all other tangible personal property not included in the other personal property recovery classes, including most machinery and equipment. Included in the 10-year class is certain public utility personal property, theme and amusement park property, railroad tank cars, manufactured homes, and qualified coal utilization property. The 15-year public utility class covers longer-lived public utility tangible personal property.

The following chart illustrates the flow of many recovery assets to the various classes.

Tangible Personal Property

For years 1981 through 1984, the four classes for personal property contain statutory percentages that are designed to provide benefits approximating the 150 percent declining balance method for the early years and the straight-line method in the later years. The "half-year convention" is used for the year of acquisition. After 1984, the recovery deductions are accelerated in two steps to eventually approximate the benefits of using a 200 percent declining balance method with a switch to the sum-of-the-years-digits method.

Determination of Appropriate Recovery Class

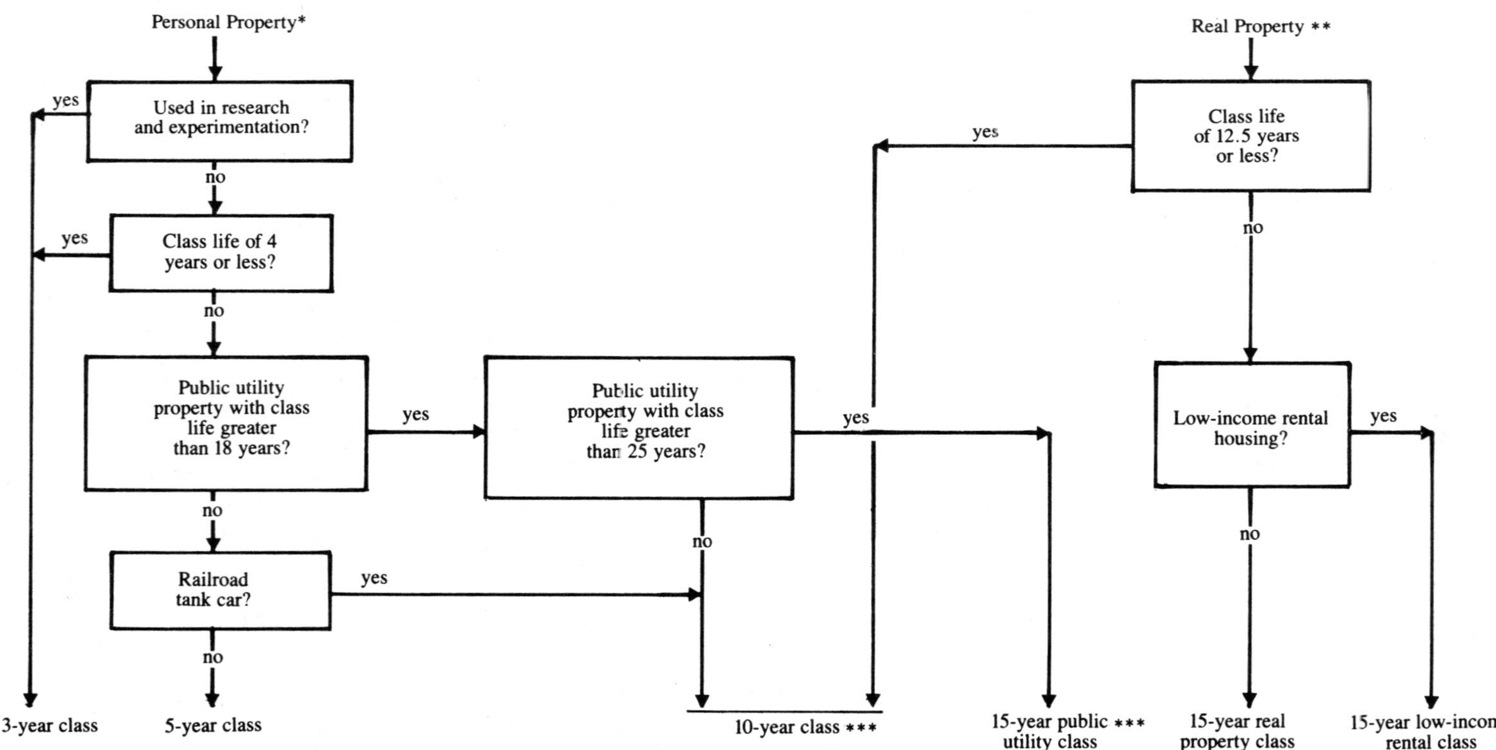

* Generally personal property, but also includes other tangible property (other than buildings) used as an integral part of certain qualified activities (manufacturing, etc.). Also includes research facilities, facilities used for bulk storage of fungible commodities, single-purpose agricultural or horticultural structures, and storage facilities for petroleum or its primary products.

**Any real property subject to depreciation other than property described in the footnote above. Includes elevators and escalators.

***Certain coal utilization burners and boilers and related conversion equipment are included in the ten year class if such equipment replaces or converts oil or gas utilization burners and boilers.

Note: Certain property subject to amortization (pollution control facilities, certain expenditures for child care facilities, etc.) are not defined as property subject to the recovery deduction of $168.

In lieu of the accelerated cost recovery deductions, taxpayers are given the option to use a method of recovery based on the straight-line depreciation method, which is applicable to all property in a class placed in service that year. Taxpayers also have a choice of recovery periods in using this alternative method. The available periods are:

- 3, 5, or 12 years for 3-year property;
- 5, 12, or 25 years for 5-year property;
- 10, 25, or 35 years for 10-year property; and
- 15, 35, or 45 years for 15-year public utility property.

Gains or losses generally are recognized upon disposition of recovery property. As under prior law, the portion of gain on the disposition of personal property that represents recapture of recovery deductions is treated as ordinary income.

Real Property

For real property other than low-income rental housing, recovery deductions approximate the benefits of using the 175 percent declining balance method for the early years and the straight-line method in the later years. The recovery deductions in the years of acquisition and disposition will take into account the number of months the property was held as opposed to the use of a convention as is used for personal property. Low-income rental housing is permitted recovery deductions based on the 200 percent declining balance method with a switch to straight line.

An option to use a straight-line recovery system is also permitted for real property. Unlike personal property rules, this election is allowed on a property-by-property basis. The recovery periods that are available in using this method are 15, 35, or 45 years. This alternative may be attractive to businesses wishing to limit deductions.

Nonresidential property is subject to full recovery deduction recapture upon disposition. Therefore, only gain in excess of all recovery deductions taken is treated as capital gain. If, however, the optional straight-line recovery system is used, then all gain is capital gain. For all residential property, gain upon disposition is treated as ordinary income only to the extent that the recovery deductions allowed under ACRS exceed those permitted under a straight-line allowance over a 15-year period. Thus, if the optional straight-line recovery system is used, all gain is capital gain.

The new rules do not permit the use of component depreciation; therefore, the recovery deductions for an entire building must be computed using one recovery method and period. An exception is provided for a substantial improvement to the building which will be treated as a separate building.

Anti-Churning Rules
Generally, the provisions affecting capital cost recovery apply to property placed in service after 1980. The Act, however, contains strict rules to prevent the churning of assets after 1980 for the purpose of bringing assets within the new ACRS rules. Therefore, recovery property acquired in certain post-1980 transactions will continue to be subject to old depreciation rules. These anti-churning provisions are complex and include such transactions as sale-leaseback arrangements.

Investment Tax Credit
In tandem with ACRS, the Act allows, in effect, a 6 percent investment tax credit for qualifying property in the 3-year class and a 10 percent credit for qualifying property in other classes. This ensures that virtually all property will generate as much or more credit than under prior law.

Similar to prior law, a recapture tax is imposed upon early disposition of investment credit property. The percentage of the original credit claimed that must be recaptured is shown below for property that is not held at least:

	1 year	2 years	3 years	4 years	5 years
3-year property	100%	66%	33%	—	—
All other property	100	80	60	40%	20%

Other principal changes are as follows.

- The Act extends the investment credit to storage facilities for petroleum and its primary products and to certain leased railroad rolling stock used both within and without the United States.
- The qualified progress expenditure rules have been modified to eliminate the 7-year useful life requirement.
- For noncorporate lessors, who have to meet certain tests in order to claim investment credit, the Act permits the useful life of any recovery property to be the present class life for such property under prior law. This provision applies to leases entered into after June 25, 1981.

The following table illustrates the effects of the new law. The Federal income tax effects of depreciation or recovery deductions and investment credit under the old and new laws are compared for investments made prior to 1985 of $1,000 in business assets having various useful lives. An investment in

Tax Benefits Compared for $1,000 Investment Made Prior to 1985 Under New and Prior Law

	New Law			Prior Law			
Type of Asset*	Depreciation	ITC**	Total	Depreciation	ITC**	Total	Increased Tax Benefit
Automobile (3 yr)	$360	$ 60	$420	$370	$ 30	$400	$ 20
Equipment (5 yr)	330	100	430	340	70	410	20
Equipment (7 yr)	330	100	430	320	100	420	10
Machinery (10 yr)	330	100	430	290	100	390	40
Machinery (20 yr)	330	100	430	220	100	320	110
Public Utility Equipment (20 yr)	270	100	370	220	100	320	50
Public Utility Equipment (30 yr)	220	100	320	170	100	270	50
Building (35 yr)	230	—	230	120	—	120	110

* The years in parentheses indicate depreciable life under prior law.
** ITC—investment tax credit

NOTE: The above figures are the tax-effected present value of deductions and credits for a $1,000 investment in various business assets. Depreciation under prior law was calculated using the half-year convention and the maximum benefits available. A 12 percent discount factor and a 46 percent tax rate were assumed.

personal property made after 1984 would receive stepped up rates of recovery under the new law, and result in an even greater tax benefit than shown in the table. The table is for illustrative purposes only and is intended to provide a starting point for evaluating the Act's impact on business assets. Consequently, the figures are rounded to the nearest ten's digit for ease in use. This may result in some distortion. It should be noted that variations in the discount rate used to calculate the present value of depreciation and recovery deductions will affect the margin of benefit provided by the Act. A higher discount rate increases the comparative benefits of the Act. A lower discount rate has the opposite effect. Investment tax credit is neutral to the discount rate.

Limited Expensing

The Act permits limited expensing of costs of recovery property that qualifies for the investment tax credit. Upon election, a taxpayer may deduct up to $5,000 of cost in 1982 and 1983, up to $7,500 in 1984 and 1985, and up to $10,000 in 1986 and thereafter. Expense amounts will be excluded from basis in calculating recovery deductions and the investment tax credit. The former "additional first year depreciation" rules were repealed for property placed in service after December 31, 1980. It should be noted that neither the old nor the new expensing provisions apply to property placed in service in 1981.

Minimum Tax

As under prior law, accelerated recovery deductions on leased personal property are an item of tax preference subject to the minimum tax for noncorporate taxpayers. The preference amount is the excess of the recovery deduction over a straight-line allowance using a 5-, 8-, 15-, or 22-year life for 3-year, 5-year, 10-year, and 15-year public utility property, respectively.

Similarly, the preference for accelerated depreciation on 15-year real property applies under the Act, as under prior law. The preference amount is the excess of the recovery deduction over a straight-line allowance using a 15-year life. Unlike under prior law, this is a preference item for only noncorporate taxpayers. The legislative committee reports, however, state that this accelerated deduction on real estate is a tax preference item for all taxpayers.

Foreign Assets

Unlike depreciation under prior law, recovery deductions for assets used predominantly outside the United States are specifically addressed under the Act. For personal property, recovery deductions are based on the 200 percent declining balance with a switch to straight-line over the class life under prior law. For real property, the recovery period is 35 years, and the recovery deductions approximate the benefits of using the 150 percent declining balance method with a switch to straight-line.

Some flexibility is provided by permitting a straight-line method over certain optional lives instead of accelerated recovery. For personal property, however,

the optional life period elected may not be shorter than the class life under prior law. For real property, the lives permitted are 35 or 45 years.
We expect that the present regulations keying the reduction in earnings and profits of controlled foreign corporations to depreciation allowable under prior law will be changed to reflect the new rules for recovery deductions.

Earnings and Profits

To maintain consistency with prior law, the Act provides that for purposes of computing earnings and profits, the straight-line recovery method is to be used. The recovery periods to be used are 5, 12, 25, 35, and 35 years for 3-year, 5-year, 10-year, 15-year real property, and 15-year public utility property, respectively. If a longer recovery period is elected, that period must be used in computing earnings and profits. A special 5-year rule is provided for costs deducted under the first year limited expensing rule.

As under prior law, most foreign corporations are exempt from this straight-line requirement and may continue to reduce earnings and profits by all allowable depreciation and recovery deductions. For foreign tax credit purposes, the new recovery deduction rates provide some degree of flexibility, which should continue to permit a matching of effective foreign tax rates with the incidence of current U.S. taxation.

Special Rule for Leases

The Act recognizes that certain corporations may not be in the tax position to absorb the additional tax benefits associated with ACRS. To encourage full utilization of ACRS, the Act makes significant changes to the tax rules to encourage leasing transactions. The effect of these special rules is to replace present tax rules on leasing with liberalized rules pursuant to which the parties can shift the tax benefits to the lessor. Congress hopes that a portion of these tax benefits will be shared with the lessees through the form of lower rental payments.

The Act provides an election under which the parties can choose to have the transaction treated as a lease if three requirements are met:

- The lessor is a "regular" corporation (i.e., a corporation other than a Subchapter S corporation or a personal holding company);
- The lessor's minimum investment in the leased property is at all times not less than 10 percent of the adjusted basis of the property; and
- The term of the lease (including extensions) does not exceed 90 percent of the useful life of the property for depreciation purposes or 150 percent of the present class life of the property.

If all of these requirements are satisfied, the transaction will be treated as a lease regardless of any other factors contained in the lease agreements.

Partnerships, all the partners of which are regular corporations, and grantor trusts, all the direct or indirect beneficiaries of which are regular corporations, will be treated as corporate lessors.

Extended Carryover Period for Losses and Credits

To aid economically distressed industries, the Act extends the carryover period for net operating losses and certain credits. For most businesses, net operating losses incurred in taxable years ending after 1975 can now be carried over for 15 years, thereby giving taxpayers a 15 year period in which to absorb their tax losses against future income.

With respect to credits, the carryover periods for unused investment credit and certain other credits were extended to 15 years. Depending on the type of credit, the effective dates of the new provisions vary.

Used Property Investment Credit Limitation

Under prior law, the amount of used property eligible for the investment tax credit is limited to $100,000. To encourage investment in used property, the Act increases the limitation on used property to $125,000 for taxable years beginning in 1981 through 1984 and to $150,000 for subsequent years.

At-Risk Rules and the Investment Tax Credit

The Tax Reform Act of 1976 severely limited the deductibility of tax shelter losses through enactment of the at-risk rules. Under the at-risk provisions, tax losses from all activities other than real estate are limited to the investor's actual economic investment in the activity. These rules apply to all taxpayers except for regular business corporations that are not closely held corporations.

The Act extends the at-risk rules to the investment tax credit. These rules limit the investment tax credit on both new and used property and apply to all activities other than real estate. The new provision requires a separate at-risk computation and has its own special rules which distinguish it from the at-risk rules applicable to tax losses. The following rules apply:

- The taxpayer's basis in the property will be limited to the taxpayer's amount at risk as of the close of the taxable year. For example, if a computer costing $1 million is purchased by an individual in 1982 with $200,000 in cash and an $800,000 nonrecourse note, the taxpayer's qualified investment credit basis would generally be limited to the $200,000 at risk so that on the taxpayer's 1982 tax return the investment tax credit would be $20,000 (10 percent of $200,000).

- Unlike the present at-risk limitation, there will be an exception for certain nonrecourse financing (which is generally not considered to be an amount at risk) where the borrowing is from certain unrelated lenders, such as financial institutions, insurance companies, and pension trusts. To take advantage of this exception a taxpayer must at all times be at risk with respect to at least 20 percent of the basis of the property. Thus, in certain instances, the at-risk rules may limit tax losses, but not the investment tax credit even though the financing is on a nonrecourse basis. In the example stated above, if the nonrecourse financing is from an unrelated insurance company, the individual's investment tax credit would be $100,000 (10 percent of $1,000,000). However, the deduction for tax losses would be limited to $200,000 in 1982 since the at-risk limitation applicable to tax losses would treat the nonrecourse indebtedness as an amount that is not at risk.

- Subsequent increases or decreases in a taxpayer's at-risk amount could result in additional credit or the recapture of previously claimed credit.

- The at-risk limitation does not apply to certain energy tax credits if a taxpayer has a minimum at-risk investment of 25 percent.

- The at-risk limitation does not apply to corporations that are not Subchapter S or closely held corporations.

- The investment credit at-risk limitation has its own special effective date. It applies only to property placed in service by the taxpayer after February 18, 1981. However, it will not apply to property placed in service after February 18, 1981, if the property was acquired by the taxpayer according to a binding contract entered before February 19, 1981.

Rehabilitation Credit

As a general rule, buildings do not qualify for the regular 10 percent investment tax credit. The Revenue Act of 1978, however, extended the investment tax credit to certain qualified rehabilitation expenditures made in connection with existing nonresidential buildings in use for at least 20 years. At least 20 years must have elapsed between qualifying rehabilitations and at least 75 percent of the existing exterior walls must remain in place after the rehabilitation. The Act completely revises this tax credit for rehabilitation expenditures and repeals the special 60-month amortization provision relating to certified historic structure rehabilitation expenditures.

The Act creates three levels of investment tax credit for certain rehabilitation expenditures based on the age of the building. These levels and other considerations are enumerated below.

- The investment tax credit percentage is 15 percent for structures at least 30 years old, 20 percent for structures at least 40 years old, and 25 percent for certified historic structures.

- Unlike prior law, the tax basis of the building must be reduced by the amount of the tax credit (unless the credit is for a certified historic rehabilitation), thereby reducing the amount of cost recovery deductions allowed with respect to the building.

- These provisions generally apply to expenditures incurred after December 31, 1981, in taxable years ending after that date. The special amortization provision is repealed for rehabilitations beginning after 1981.

- Special transitional rules are provided for rehabilitation expenditures qualifying under prior law but not under the Act (e.g., modernizing a building more than 20, but less than 30, years old) as well as for rehabilitation of certified historic structures commenced before the Act.

- These provisions apply to residential structures if the rehabilitation is a certified historic rehabilitation.

- To correct a clerical error in a bill enacted last year, the Act provides an exception to the present rule denying the rehabilitation credit for property used by a tax-exempt organization or a governmental unit. This provision is effective retroactively to July 30, 1980.

Tax Planning Ideas and Observations

Taxpayers unable to fully use the tax benefits related to the accelerated cost recovery deductions and the investment tax credits should consider the following.

- Leasing either personal property or real property instead of purchasing such assets. Through careful negotiation of lease agreements, a portion of the tax benefits available to the lessor can be passed through to the lessee in the form of lower rental payments.

- Computing recovery deductions based on the straight-line depreciation method over the minimum or a longer recovery period. This optional recovery method is available on a property-by-property basis for real property and a recovery-class by recovery-class basis for tangible personal property.

- The present value of a current deduction that cannot be fully utilized until future years is substantially diminished. Thus, the increased net operating loss carryover provisions should not be relied upon to provide a significant benefit in planning for the future.

- Highly profitable taxpayers may want to begin or increase leasing activities. By leasing property to others, the accelerated deductions and credits can effectively shelter other current income while maintaining the desired after-tax yield from the leasing activities.

- If property is acquired by using, in part, nonrecourse debt, such financing should be obtained from certain qualified lenders to avoid the investment credit at-risk rules.

- Stock savings and loan associations should consider minimizing their cost recovery deductions in order to maximize their earnings and profits. In this manner, the potential penalty tax on distributions to stockholders in excess of accumulated earnings and profits may be avoided.

- If a rehabilitation of an older building is planned, consideration should be given to postponing the rehabilitation if only a few years remain until the building is in the next higher "age" class.

- Due to the various effective dates for extended net operating loss and tax credit carryovers, it is possible that some carryovers might not be subject to the new rules.

- Although the rule prohibiting component depreciation with respect to real property applies generally to property not eligible for investment tax credit, it may still be beneficial to segregate costs that may qualify for investment tax credit at the time a building is constructed or acquired. It appears these segregated costs may qualify for the 5-year class for recovery deductions and a 10 percent investment tax credit.

Research and Experimentation Credit

A taxpayer who incurs research and experimentation expenses may generally elect to deduct or amortize such expenditures for tax purposes. Under prior law no specific tax credit was provided for these expenditures.

To stimulate research activity in the United States, the Act provides a nonrefundable income tax credit of 25 percent for certain qualifying expenses incurred by a taxpayer after June 30, 1981, and before January 1, 1986.

The credit applies whether or not a taxpayer has made an election to deduct or capitalize such expenditures. The credit is limited to 25 percent of the "incremental" research amount. Generally, the incremental research amount is the excess of the current year's research expenditures over the average research expenditures during a specified base period. When fully implemented, the base period will be the three preceding taxable years although special base year transitional rules are provided for the first two taxable years in which a taxpayer claims the credit.

The Act essentially uses the same definition of research expenditures as used under present law, however, it is important to note that the expenditures must be incurred in carrying on a trade or business, not merely in connection with a trade or business. Thus, there remains the subjective question of whether a taxpayer is carrying on a trade or business.

Allocation of Research and Development Expense

Expenses for research and development under prior law were generally allocated to all items of gross income reasonably connected with certain broadly defined product categories to which the research was directed. Apportionment of allocated expenses between United States and foreign source gross income was made in part on the basis of where the research was performed and in part on the basis of sales income from U.S. and foreign sources.

Under the Act, all research and experimentation expenditures paid or incurred for research conducted in the United States are to be allocated and apportioned to United States source income for a two-year period. This change should relieve pressures on research-oriented corporations experiencing foreign tax credit limitation problems due to the necessity under prior law to apportion part of their research expenditures against foreign source income. This provision is effective for the first taxable years beginning after date of enactment.

Contributions of Research Property

Generally taxpayers who donate inventory items can only deduct their cost basis in (rather than the fair market value of) the donated property. In 1976, Congress enacted an exception to this general rule for corporations contributing inventory to be used by certain targeted groups.

The Act allows corporations an increased deduction for contributions of certain research or experimentation property to educational institutions. The deduction for qualified contributions is limited to the basis of the property plus 50 percent of the property's unrealized appreciation. The contribution is limited, however, to twice the basis of the property. This provision is effective for contributions made after the date of enactment.

The Jobs Tax Credit

The Revenue Act of 1978 changed the jobs tax credit by providing that the credit would only apply to certain wages paid to members of a targeted group. The targeted jobs tax credit was scheduled to expire on December 31, 1981. The Act both extends and modifies this credit. The extension provides that wages paid or incurred to members of targeted groups hired before 1983 will continue to qualify for the credit.

Corporate Charitable Contributions

For taxable years beginning after December 31, 1981, the Act provides that a corporation will be able to deduct amounts of contributions up to 10 percent of its taxable income. The limit is currently 5 percent.

Deduction for Gifts and Awards

The Act increases the amount that employers can deduct for the cost of awards of tangible personal property made to employees in recognition of length of service or for safety achievement. Effective for taxable years ending on or after the date of enactment, the old $100 per item limit is increased to $400.

Employee Stock Ownership Plans

Payroll-Based Tax Credit ESOP

Congress has encouraged the establishment of employee stock ownership plans (ESOPs) since 1974. However, due to the nature of the ESOP rules, labor-intensive industries have not had the same impetus as others to adopt these plans. Consistent with Congress' support of the ESOP concept, the Act provides for a temporary (through 1987) income tax credit for contributions to a tax credit ESOP based on compensation. The payroll-based credit (0.5 percent for 1983 and 1984; 0.75 percent for 1985, 1986, and 1987) is allowed only where not more than one third of the employer's contributions are allocated to officers, 10-percent shareholders, or highly compensated individuals. The rules relating to investment tax credit ESOPs, scheduled to expire after 1983, will now terminate one year sooner.

Limitations on Credit

The amount of the income tax credit is limited to either (1) the employer's tax liability or (2) $25,000, plus 90 percent of the excess over $25,000, whichever is less. Where the employer is a member of a controlled group of corporations, the $25,000 amount will be apportioned among the group. Any excess may be carried back three years and then forward 10 years. If there is still an unused credit, it may then be deducted in full.

To be eligible for the tax credit, the plan must meet the requirements of qualified plans and the new tax credit ESOP. Further, the employer must transfer employer securities to the plan in an amount at least equal to the credit not later than 30 days after the due date, including extensions, of the tax return in which the tax credit is earned. Cash may be contributed if the plan purchases employer securities within 30 days after receipt.

Contributions to Leveraged ESOPs

For taxable years beginning after 1981, the Act significantly liberalizes the deduction rules for contributions to leveraged ESOPs with respect to payment of principal and interest on loans.

Timing of Distributions from ESOPs

Employer securities allocated to a participant's account under a tax credit ESOP cannot be distributed before 84 months after the securities are allocated. Exceptions are provided in the case of separation from service, death, or disability. An additional exception is now created when a participant becomes employed by another corporation that purchases a subsidiary of the selling corporation. This change appears to be a clarifying amendment and applies to distributions made after March 29, 1975.

Cash Distributions from ESOPs

The Act liberalizes the distribution rules so as to allow closely held corporations desiring to restrict the ownership of their stock to adopt ESOPs for taxable years beginning after 1981. A similar rule is provided in the case of an ESOP established by a bank prohibited by law from purchasing its own securities, and by professional associations whose stock ownership is legally restricted.

Changes to Other Stock Plans

The Act provides as follows:

- Profit-sharing plans holding nonpublicly traded securities of the employer are no longer required to pass through voting rights to participants.

- Participants receiving nonpublicly traded securities from a stock bonus plan after 1981 must be given the right to sell that stock to the employer.

Motor Carrier Operating Rights

Prior to July 1980, one of the most valuable assets of the motor carrier business was its motor carrier operating rights. Substantial amounts were paid for these rights reflecting the protection against competition afforded such owners under Interstate Commerce Commission rules. On July 1, 1980, legislation was enacted which substantially eased entry into the interstate motor carrier business and, thus, severely diminished the value of motor carrier operating rights. Shortly after this legislation, the Financial Accounting Standards Board issued an opinion requiring a one year write off for investment in these operating rights.

To reduce the economic loss suffered by interstate motor carriers because of the deregulation of their business, the Act provides that the cost of motor carrier operating rights can be amortized over a 60-month period. The 60-month period begins July 1, 1980 (or, subject to the taxpayer's election, the first month of the taxpayer's first taxable year beginning after July 1, 1980). Where the motor carrier operating rights were held in a subsidiary, special rules are provided for the deduction.

V. Provisions Primarily Affecting Small Business

Corporate Tax Rate Reductions

The Act reduces corporate tax rates over a two-year period but only in the lower corporate tax brackets. The following table compares the regular corporate tax rates under the Act with the regular corporate tax rates in effect for taxable years beginning before January 1, 1982.

Corporate Tax Rate Table

Taxable Income	1981	1982	1983
$0 to $25,000	17%	16%	15%
$25,000 to $50,000	20	19	18
$50,000 to $75,000	30	30	30
$75,000 to $100,000	40	40	40
Over $100,000	46	46	46

Subchapter S Corporations

The tax law has long provided an election whereby certain small business corporations (Subchapter S corporations) can be treated in a manner similar to partnerships. The Act liberalizes the Subchapter S provisions for taxable years beginning after December 31, 1981. The Act increases the maximum number of shareholders permitted for a Subchapter S corporation from 15 to 25 and also allows certain trusts to be Subchapter S shareholders.

Accumulated Earnings Tax

The Act increases the amount of accumulated earnings which a corporation may accumulate without justification from $150,000 to $250,000 effective for taxable years beginning after December 31, 1981. This increase generally does not apply to service corporations.

LIFO Inventory Method Provisions

The LIFO inventory method treats the last goods manufactured or purchased as the first goods sold. In an inflationary period, the LIFO method offers significant tax benefits because the taxpayer is able to deduct its most recently incurred higher costs while previously incurred lower costs remain in inventory. By using LIFO, a taxpayer avoids currently paying taxes on the inflationary profits that are in the inventory. Despite the benefits offered by the LIFO method, many taxpayers, particularly small businesses, have not elected to use it because of its complexity. While the Act specifically deals with only two provisions intended to make the use of LIFO more accessible to businesses, it addresses some of the more complex LIFO issues by authorizing the issuance of regulations permitting the use of government price indexes.

LIFO Election

When LIFO is elected, the inventory for the first year preceding the year of the LIFO election must be stated at cost. The restatement of the preceding year's inventory to cost typically requires an income-increasing adjustment that is included in income through an amended return for the year preceding the year of the LIFO election.

The Act partially eliminates the immediate income impact and permits the income-increasing adjustment to be included in income ratably over a three-year period commencing with the year of the LIFO election. The Act thus eliminates the need for the filing of an amended return upon electing LIFO as well as the resultant interest expense on the additional tax due for the prior year. The three-year allocation of the adjustment is effective for taxable years beginning after December 31, 1981.

LIFO Pooling

There are two general approaches to the LIFO method: the specific goods method and the more commonly used dollar-value method. The specific goods method accounts for inventory on a unit basis while the dollar-value method accounts for inventory on the basis of a pool or pools of dollar investment. Selecting an appropriate number of dollar-value LIFO pools is a difficult task and is subject to review by the Internal Revenue Service.

The Act eliminates the doubt for certain small businesses in selecting an appropriate number of pools. Small businesses are permitted by the Act to use a dollar-value LIFO pool to compute their inventory value. A small business eligible for the one-pool method is one whose average annual gross receipts for a three-year period do not exceed $2,000,000. To ensure that only small businesses qualify for the one-pool method, the Act treats a controlled group as one taxpayer in making the average annual gross receipts test. A person is considered a member of a controlled group if such person would be treated as a single employer pursuant to the rules for determining the jobs tax credit for members of a controlled group.

The election to use a dollar-value LIFO pool may be made without the consent of the Internal Revenue Service, and the year of the election is treated as the new base year. The election of the one-pool method is effective for taxable years beginning after December 31, 1981.

The three-year $2,000,000 average annual gross receipts test must be satisfied each year, including years subsequent to the initial one-pool election. However, one potential problem posed by the Act is that it is silent as to what a taxpayer must do if it fails to meet the test for a particular year.

VI. Provisions Affecting Financial Institutions

Many financial institutions have been experiencing severe economic problems in the recent past. Several factors have led to these problems. First, many depositors have shifted their funds to new higher-yielding certificates or to money market funds. This shifting of funds has caused a great deal of disintermediation. Second, many financial institutions heavily involved in residential mortgage lending have made long-term, low-interest rate loans in the past. Thus, the interest paid on customer deposits exceeds the amount of interest received on the outstanding loans. Third, the high interest rates charged on the new loans, particularly mortgage loans, have discouraged many potential borrowers and fewer loans are being made.

To alleviate some of these problems and to assist financial institutions with the most severe economic problems, the Act makes several changes. One change deals with the new "All-Savers Certificate." Other changes add new or technical provisions to existing law involving reorganizations and bad-debt reserves.

All-Savers Certificate

The All-Savers Certificate provisions will permit financial institutions to issue a one-year certificate that will contain a yield equal to 70 percent of the yield on the most recent auction of 52-week Treasury bills. The interest earned by the depositor on qualifying certificates will be tax-exempt to the depositor (subject to certain limitations), yet fully deductible by the financial institution. The provision will apply to qualifying certificates issued after September 30, 1981, and before January 1, 1983.

The Act requires that financial institutions issuing such certificates use a portion of the funds received to provide qualified residential financing. For most financial institutions, the amount of qualified residential financing required in any calendar quarter during the term of this provision must be at least 75 percent of either (1) the face amount of the All-Savers Certificates issued during the calendar quarter or (2) the qualified net savings for the quarter, whichever is less. The term "qualified net savings" is defined as the excess of deposits paid into savings and certificate accounts (excluding jumbo certificates) over amounts withdrawn from such accounts.

The term "qualified residential financing" is defined to include single and multifamily residential and construction loans, certain securities evidencing an interest in such loans, mobile home loans, and agricultural loans.

A financial institution that does not satisfy the qualified residential financing requirement for any calendar quarter cannot issue such certificates until the requirements are satisfied.

Reorganizations

The provisions affecting reorganizations of financial institutions apply primarily to savings and loan associations and are effective as of January 1, 1981. These provisions can be broken down into three parts: (1) tax-free reorganizations, (2) Federal Savings and Loan Insurance Corporation (FSLIC) assistance, and (3) distributions by a savings and loan association to FSLIC.

Tax-Free Reorganizations

The tax-free reorganization provisions modify the recently enacted Bankruptcy Tax Act with respect to both stock and mutual savings and loan associations. Prior to these modifications, there were concerns that the necessary element of the exchange of equity in the merged corporation for equity in the acquiring corporation, inherent in all tax-free reorganizations, would not be met in the merger of a troubled mutual association into a stock association if no stock were issued to the former depositors in the mutual association. The Act treats the deposits in the stock association and in the mutual association as equity interests. Thus, provided the depositors of the troubled mutual association become depositors in the acquiring stock association, the exchange of equity requirement will be satisfied.

To obtain tax-free reorganization treatment, three tests must be satisfied: (1) the acquiring association must acquire substantially all the assets of the merged association, (2) substantially all of the liabilities of the merged association must become liabilities of the acquiring association, and (3) the appropriate regulatory authority must certify that the merged association is, or will be, insolvent, facing substantial dissipation of assets or earnings, or in an unsafe or unsound condition to transact business.

The Act also liberalizes the rules for the limitation on net operating loss carryovers in a tax-free reorganization. Thus, a large amount of any net operating loss carryover attributable to the merged association should be available to the acquiring association in subsequent years. However, the expanded net operating loss carryover period available to most corporate taxpayers under the Act is not available to financial institutions.

FSLIC Assistance

The Act makes it clear that FSLIC assistance payments received after December 31, 1980, are not income and do not require the reduction in the basis of assets of the recipient association.

Distributions to FSLIC

Under prior law, distributions by a savings and loan association to shareholders in excess of the amount of earnings and profits accumulated after 1951 were treated as distributed out of the bad-debt reserves. Such an excess distribution triggered a substantial penalty tax. With some limitations, the Act provides that any such excess distributions made to the FSLIC with respect to an interest acquired by the FSLIC because of a financial assistance agreement are not subject to these penalty tax provisions.

Bad-Debt Reserves

The Act makes one change to the percentage of eligible loans bad-debt reserve addition rules affecting financial institutions. It provides that for taxable years beginning in 1982 the allowable percentage will be 1.0 percent. For taxable years beginning after 1982, the rate will be 0.6 percent as under present law. Correlative adjustments are also made to the base year provisions affecting the percentage of eligible loans bad-debt deduction computations.

VII. Windfall Profit Tax

The Crude Oil Windfall Profit Tax Act of 1980 imposes an excise tax on the production of domestic crude oil. Differing tax schemes apply to oil depending on the classification of the crude oil. Independent producers qualify for lower tax rates on specified types and quantities of crude oil. Royalty owners are not eligible for the rate reductions applicable to independent producers. However, prior law did provide qualified royalty owners with a credit of up to $1,000 against the windfall profit tax (WPT) imposed during 1980.

The Act contains four changes to the computation of WPT.

- A $2,500 royalty owner credit is provided for 1981. For 1982 through 1984, royalty owners will be exempt from WPT on two barrels per day increasing to three barrels per day for 1985 and subsequent years. Oil removed after December 31, 1980, qualifies under these provisions. The Act also contains administrative provisions that allow royalty owners to realize this credit through certain reduced withholding procedures.

- A WPT exemption is provided for stripper oil (generally oil from properties producing 10 barrels or less of crude oil a day per well) extracted by independent producers. Oil removed in 1983 and thereafter qualifies under this provision.

- The tax rate on "newly discovered" oil is decreased from 30 percent to 15 percent over five years, as reflected below:

Year	Rate
1982	27.5%
1983	25.0
1984	22.5
1985	20.0
1986 and later	15.0

  Oil removed after December 31, 1981, qualifies under this provision.

- Certain oil interests of residential child care agencies are exempted from the WPT. This provision is effective for taxable years beginning after 1980.

Although the House bill contained a provision stabilizing the percentage depletion rate for oil and gas at 22 percent, this provision was deleted in conference. Thus, the rate for oil and gas percentage depletion will dip to 20 percent in 1981, 18 percent in 1982, 16 percent in 1983, and 15 percent in 1984 and thereafter.

VIII. Administrative and Miscellaneous Provisions

The Act contains various administrative changes designed to aid the Internal Revenue Service and to encourage compliance by taxpayers with the tax rules. Also, the Act contains a large number of miscellaneous provisions designed to impact a limited number of taxpayers. This section highlights the Act's administrative and miscellaneous provisions which may be of interest.

Interest and Penalty Provisions

The Act changes the provisions in the tax law for interest on amounts owed to the Internal Revenue Service by taxpayers, or vice versa, to more closely align them with commercial reality. The Act also stiffens certain penalty provisions. These new interest and penalty provisions include the following.

- The interest rate on refunds and deficiencies will be established annually at 100 percent (rather than 90 percent) of the average prime rate.

- The civil and criminal penalties for filing false withholding information (false W-4's) are raised to $500 and $1,000, respectively, from the present penalties of $50 and $500.

- A penalty is made applicable for overstatements to the value or basis of a taxpayer's property. The amount of the penalty can vary from a 10 to a 30 percent addition to tax depending upon the amount of the overstatement.

- An addition to tax will be assessed equal to 50 percent of the interest on "negligent" underpayments.

- A penalty equal to $10 per information return will be assessed against taxpayers who fail to file certain information returns. The maximum penalty will be $25,000.

- A penalty is added when persons file returns claiming fictitious deposits of tax.

Estimated Taxes for Corporations

Generally, a corporation must make estimated tax payments during a year equal to 80 percent of its current year tax liability. In certain circumstances under prior law, a corporation whose taxable income exceeded $1,000,000 in any of the three preceding years could satisfy the estimated tax requirements by paying in only 60 percent of its current tax liability.

The Act phases in an 80 percent requirement for taxable years beginning after December 31, 1981. In 1982 and 1983 the estimated tax payments of these corporations must equal at least 65 and 75 percent, respectively, of its current year tax liability. For 1984 and subsequent years, the 80 percent requirement will apply.

Disclosure of Audit Information

To preclude efforts by certain taxpayers to force the Internal Revenue Service to disclose data used in establishing its audit techniques, the Act makes it clear that the Internal Revenue Service cannot be required to disclose the information it uses in developing audit standards.

Tax-Exempt Obligations

Interest on bonds issued by a state or political subdivision and certain industrial development bonds are exempt from federal income tax. The Act liberalizes the existing provisions of the law for certain volunteer fire department obligations and for bonds used to finance certain mass commuting vehicles leased to publicly owned mass transit systems.

Foreign Investment Companies

For sales or exchanges of stock of a foreign investment company (typically a foreign corporation either registered under the Investment Company Act of 1940, or engaged in certain investment activities under this Act and controlled by United States persons) made after the date of enactment, the Act modifies the amount of gain taxable to shareholders at ordinary income rates.

Foreign Investment in U.S. Real Property

Present law attempts to put real estate investment in the United States owned by nonresident aliens and foreign corporations on a par with the U.S. tax treatment of domestic investors. The Act contains several clarifying technical corrections to these rules designed to close potential loopholes and correct certain inequities. These corrections are effective for dispositions after June 18, 1980.

Property Transferred for the Performance of Service

The present rule is that an individual who receives property for the performance of services must report that income in the taxable year when received. The amount to be reported is the value of the property received. If, however, at the time of transfer the interest in the property is subject to a substantial risk of forfeiture and is not transferable, the employee will report income in an amount equal to the fair market value of the property when the property becomes transferable or is no longer subject to the substantial risk of forfeiture.

SEC and Pooling of Interest Restrictions

Some courts have held that the rules imposed by section 16(b) of the Securities Exchange Act of 1934 are not a restriction that prohibits transferability. The Act treats stock subject to section 16(b) as being subject to a substantial risk of forfeiture.

Also, under certain Accounting Series Releases, pooling of interest accounting will be applicable if no affiliate of either company in a business combination sells or reduces the risk on any common stock received in the business combination until such time as financial results covering at least 30 days of post-merger combined operations have been published. To comply with this requirement, certain shares of stock may be subject to restrictions on transfer.

Since the Act treats both types of restrictions as substantial risks of forfeiture, employees who receive such stock for the performance of services will have the opportunity to elect to be taxed on the value of the stock upon receipt or when the restrictions lapse.

Observations

- There are limitations imposed by registration requirements of state and federal securities laws upon the sale or other disposition of stock in addition to the ones addressed by the Act. Apparently, stock transferred subject to such restrictions will not receive the benefit of the changes made by the Act.

- These relief provisions apply to taxable years beginning after 1981.

Imputed Interest Rates

When property is sold on the installment basis, present law requires that a minimum portion of the installment payment be treated as interest. The sales contract should provide for a minimum interest rate of 9 percent. Otherwise, a 10 percent rate is imposed.

The Act reduces the 10 percent interest rate to 7 percent in the case of installment sales of land of less than $500,000 to certain family members. The provision applies to transactions occurring after June 30, 1981.

Qualified Group Legal Services Plans

The exclusion from an employee's income of certain employer contributions to qualified group legal services plans was due to expire on December 31, 1981. The Act extends the income exclusion until December 31, 1984.